MICHELIN

Road Atlas

USA CANADA MEXICO

NORTH AMERICA

Legend .... **Cover flap**

Key to Map Pages .... **Inside front cover**

How to Use this Atlas **2**

Listing of State and City Maps **3**

United States Interstate Map **4–5**

Canada Highway Map **6–7**

Michelin Scenic Drives **8–11, 301–302**

Maps **12–187**

- United States 12–155

BONUS MAPS! *Washington DC to Boston*

- Large-Scale Northeast Corridor Maps 144–151
- Canada 156–183
- Mexico 184–187

Index with City and Local Maps **188–283**

- United States 188–276
- Canada 277–282
- Mexico 283

City to City Distance Chart **284–285**

Distances and Driving Times across North America **286–287**

Tourism and Border Crossing Information **288**

Parks Index with GPS Coordinates **289–300**

- United States 289–297
- Canada 298–300

ROAD MAPS are organized geographically. *United States, Canada, and Mexico road maps are organized in a grid layout, starting in the northwest of each country. To find your way, use either the* ***Key to Map Pages*** *inside the front cover, the* ***Listing of State and City Maps*** *on page 3, or the* ***index*** *in the back of the atlas.*

COUNTRY COLORS
Colors represent countries throughout the atlas.
Red → Canada
Green → Mexico
Blue → United States
Purple → United States (Northeast Corridor)

MAP SCALES
Scale bars are shown at a constant length throughout the atlas for quick and easy scale comparison between regions.

DRIVING DISTANCES
Use this chart to check driving distances between major cities within each map. Refer to distance and driving time information at the back of the atlas for travel over greater distances.

LOCATOR MAPS
A quick glance at this miniature map lets you check which states and/or provinces are shown on each page.

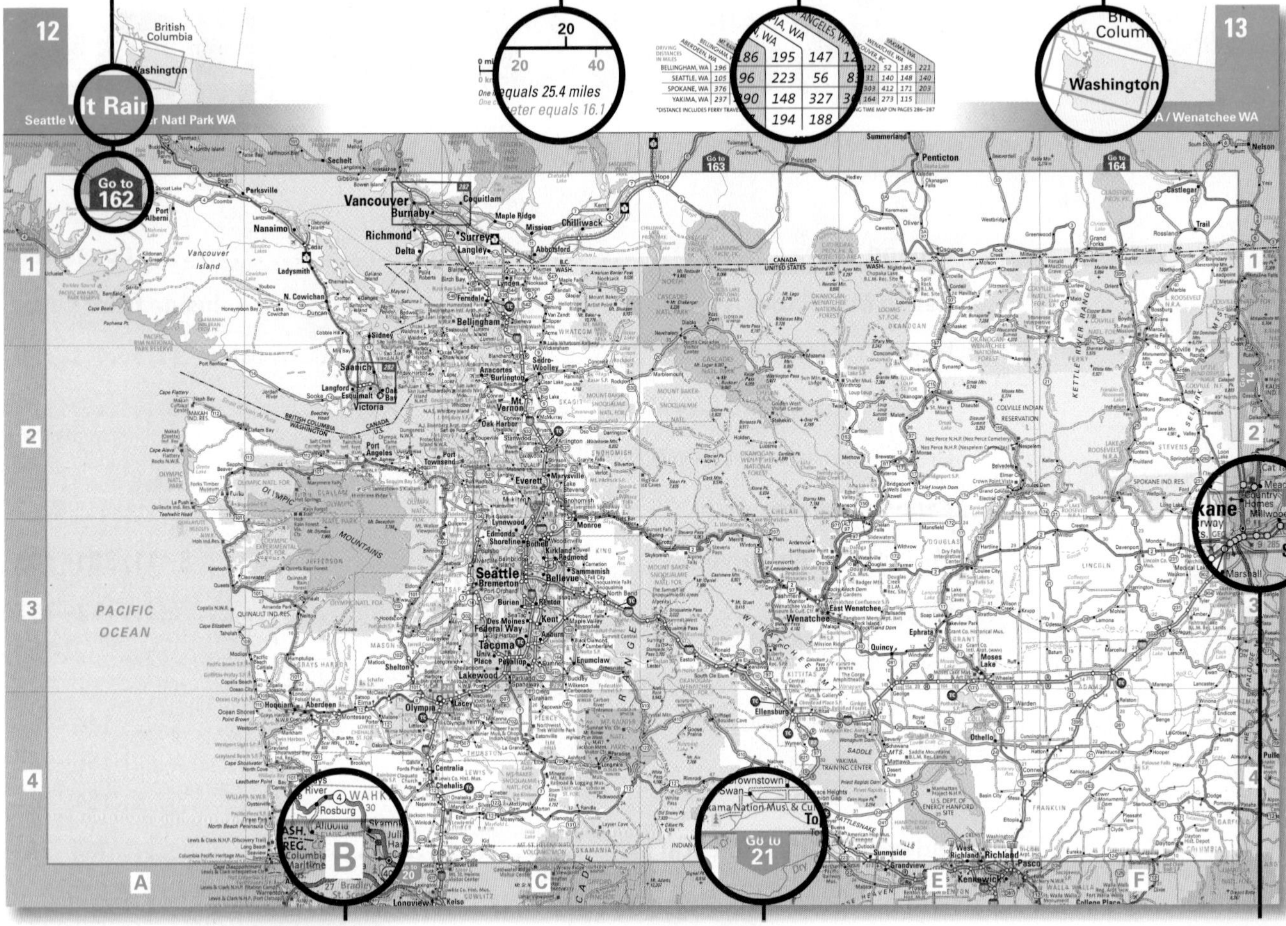

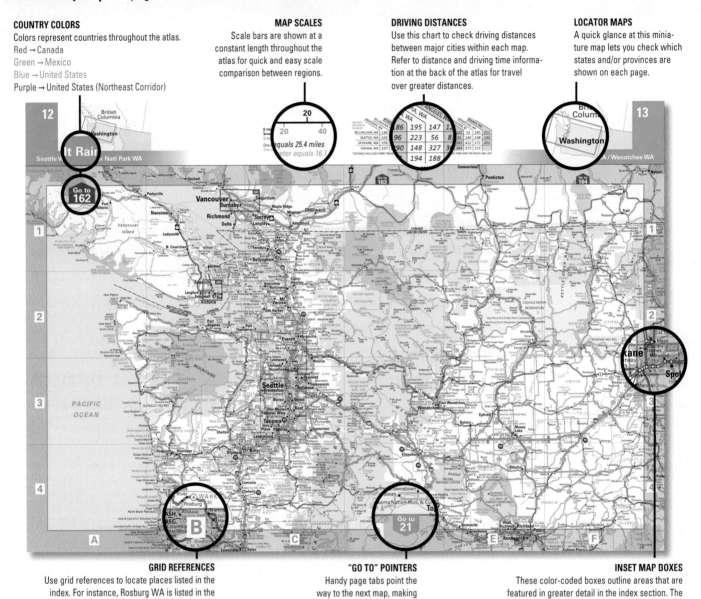

GRID REFERENCES
Use grid references to locate places listed in the index. For instance, Rosburg WA is listed in the index with "12" and "B4", indicating that the town may be found on page 12 in grid square B4.

"GO TO" POINTERS
Handy page tabs point the way to the next map, making navigation a breeze.

INSET MAP BOXES
These color-coded boxes outline areas that are featured in greater detail in the index section. The tab with "263" (above) indicates that a detailed map of Spokane may be found on page 263 (below).

HOW THE INDEX WORKS
Cities and towns are listed alphabetically, with separate indexes for the United States, Canada, and Mexico. Figures after entries indicate page number and grid reference. Entries in bold color indicate cities with detailed inset maps. The U.S. index also includes counties and parishes, which are shown in bold black type.

INSET MAP INDEXES
Many inset maps have their own indexes. Metro area inset map indexes list cities and towns; downtown inset map indexes list points of interest.

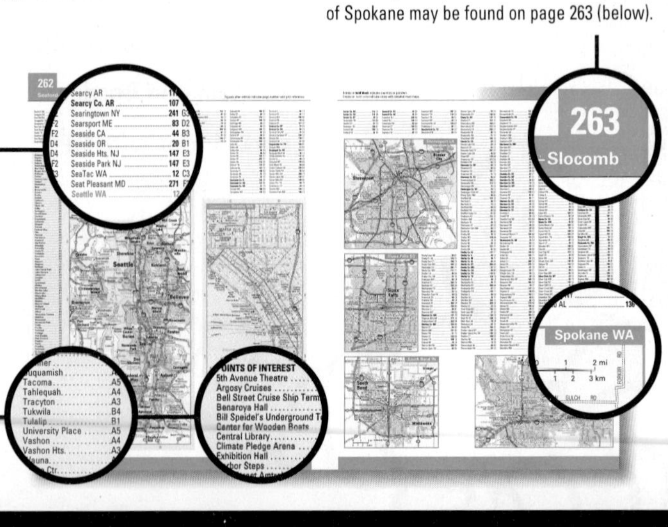

Listing of State and City Maps

UNITED STATES pages 12–155

ALABAMA (AL) 119–120, 127–128, 135–137
Birmingham 195
Huntsville 221
Mobile 236
Montgomery 236
ALASKA (AK) 154–155
Anchorage 189
Juneau 223
ARIZONA (AZ) 46–48, 53–55
Flagstaff 213
Phoenix 249
Phoenix Downtown 249
Tucson 268
Yuma 276
ARKANSAS (AR) 106–108, 116–118, 124–126
Fayetteville 212
Hot Springs 219
Little Rock 227
CALIFORNIA (CA) 28–29, 36–37, 44–46, 52–54
Bakersfield 192
Fresno 214
Los Angeles 228
Los Angeles Downtown 230
Monterey Bay 236
Oxnard/Ventura 247
Palm Springs 247
Sacramento 255
San Diego 258
San Diego Downtown 258
San Francisco Bay Area 259
San Francisco Downtown 260
Santa Barbara 260
Stockton 265
COLORADO (CO) 32–34, 40–42, 48–50
Colorado Springs 205
Denver 209
Denver Downtown 209
Fort Collins 213
Pueblo 252
CONNECTICUT (CT) 94–95, **148–150**
Hartford 218
New Haven/Bridgeport 238
Stamford 264
Waterbury 273
DELAWARE (DE) 103–104, 114, **145–146**
Dover 211
Wilmington 274
DISTRICT OF COLUMBIA (DC) ... 103–104, 114, **144**
Washington 270
Washington Downtown 272
FLORIDA (FL) 135–143
Daytona Beach 208
Fort Myers 214
Jacksonville 222
Key West 224
Melbourne/Titusville 232
Miami/Fort Lauderdale 233
Miami Downtown 233
Orlando 246
Panama City 247
Pensacola 247
Tallahassee 265
Tampa/St. Petersburg 266
GEORGIA (GA) 120–121, 128–130, 137–139
Atlanta 190
Atlanta Downtown 191
Augusta 191
Columbus 205
Macon 231
Savannah 261
HAWAII (HI) 152–153
Honolulu 219
IDAHO (ID) 14–15, 22–24, 30–31
Boise 196
Idaho Falls 221
Pocatello 250
ILLINOIS (IL) 73–75, 87–89, 97–99, 108–109
Chicago 203
Chicago Downtown 202
Peoria 247
Quad Cities (Davenport IA) 208
Rockford 255
Springfield 264
INDIANA (IN) 89–90, 99–100, 109
Evansville 212
Fort Wayne 214
Indianapolis 221
Indianapolis Downtown 222
South Bend 263
IOWA (IA) 27, 35, 72–74, 86–88
Cedar Rapids 200
Davenport/Quad Cities 208
Des Moines 210
KANSAS (KS) 42–43, 50–51, 96, 106
Kansas City 224
Topeka 267
Wichita 273
KENTUCKY (KY) 99–101, 108–111
Frankfort 214
Lexington 227
Louisville 230
LOUISIANA (LA) 124–126, 132–135
Baton Rouge 194
Lafayette 225
New Orleans 239
New Orleans Downtown 239
Shreveport 263
MAINE (ME) 81–85
Augusta 191
Portland 251
MARYLAND (MD) 102–104, 114, **144–146**
Annapolis 189
Baltimore 193
Baltimore Downtown 194
Washington DC 270
MASSACHUSETTS (MA) 94–95, **150–151**
Boston 197
Boston Downtown 197
New Bedford/Fall River 238
Springfield 264
Worcester 275
MICHIGAN (MI) 65, 68–71, 75–77, 89–90
Ann Arbor 190
Detroit 210
Detroit Downtown 210
Flint 213
Grand Rapids 215
Kalamazoo 223
Lansing 225
MINNESOTA (MN) 19, 27, 64–67, 72–73
Duluth 211
Minneapolis/St. Paul 235
Minneapolis Downtown 236
MISSISSIPPI (MS) 118–119, 125–127, 133–135
Biloxi/Gulfport 195
Jackson 222
Vicksburg 269
MISSOURI (MO) 86–87, 96–98, 106–108
Branson 198
Jefferson City 223
Kansas City 224
St. Louis 256
St. Louis Downtown 256
Springfield 264
MONTANA (MT) 14–17, 22–25
Billings 194
Great Falls 215
Helena 218
Missoula 236
NEBRASKA (NE) 33–35, 42–43, 86, 96
Lincoln 227
Omaha 245
NEVADA (NV) 29–31, 37–38, 45–46, 53
Carson City 199
Las Vegas 226
Las Vegas Strip 226
Reno 253
NEW HAMPSHIRE (NH) 81–82, 84, 94–95
Concord 206
Manchester 231
NEW JERSEY (NJ) 93–94, 104–105, **145–148**
Atlantic City 191
Newark (New York NY) 240
Trenton 268
NEW MEXICO (NM) 48–49, 55–57
Albuquerque 189
Las Cruces 226
Santa Fe 260
NEW YORK (NY) 78–81, 92–95, 105, **147–149**
Albany/Schenectady/Troy 188
Buffalo/Niagara Falls 198
New York 240
Manhattan/New York 242
Rochester 254
Syracuse 265
NORTH CAROLINA (NC) 111–113, 115, 120–123
Asheville 190
Charlotte 201
Fayetteville 213
Greensboro/Winston-Salem 216
Raleigh/Durham/Chapel Hill 253
Wilmington 275
NORTH DAKOTA (ND) 17–19, 25–27
Bismarck 196
Fargo 212
OHIO (OH) 90–91, 100–102
Akron 188
Canton 199
Cincinnati 204
Cleveland 204
Cleveland Downtown 205
Columbus 206
Dayton 208
Toledo 267
Youngstown/Warren 276
OKLAHOMA (OK) 49–51, 59, 106, 116
Oklahoma City 244
Tulsa 269
OREGON (OR) 20–22, 28–30
Eugene 212
Portland 251
Salem 257
PENNSYLVANIA (PA) 91–94, 102–104, **146–147**
Allentown/Bethlehem 189
Erie 212
Harrisburg 218
Lancaster 225
Philadelphia 248
Philadelphia Downtown 248
Pittsburgh 250
Pittsburgh Downtown 250
Scranton/Wilkes-Barre 261
York 275
RHODE ISLAND (RI) 95, **149–151**
Newport 239
Providence 251
SOUTH CAROLINA (SC) 121–123, 130–131
Charleston 200
Columbia 205
Greenville/Spartanburg 217
Myrtle Beach 237
SOUTH DAKOTA (SD) 25–27, 33–35
Pierre 249
Rapid City 253
Sioux Falls 263
TENNESSEE (TN) 108–111, 118–121
Chattanooga 201
Knoxville 225
Memphis 232
Nashville 237
TEXAS (TX) 49–51, 56–63, 116, 124, 132–133
Amarillo 189
Austin 192
Corpus Christi 206
Dallas/Fort Worth 207
Dallas Downtown 207
El Paso 211
Houston 220
Houston Downtown 220
Lubbock 231
McAllen 232
San Antonio 257
San Antonio Downtown 257
Waco 269
UTAH (UT) 31–32, 38–40, 46–48
Ogden 244
Provo 252
Salt Lake City 257
VERMONT (VT) 81–82, 94
Burlington 199
Montpelier 237
VIRGINIA (VA) 102–104, 110–115, **144**
Charlottesville 201
Norfolk/Hampton Roads 243
Richmond 254
Roanoke 254
Washington DC 270
Williamsburg 274
WASHINGTON (WA) 12–14, 20–22
Olympia 245
Seattle/Tacoma 262
Seattle Downtown 262
Spokane 263
Yakima 275
WEST VIRGINIA (WV) ... 91, 101–103, 111–112, **144**
Charleston 200
Huntington 221
WISCONSIN (WI) 64–65, 67–69, 73–75
Green Bay 216
Madison 231
Milwaukee 234
Milwaukee Downtown 234
Racine/Kenosha 252
WYOMING (WY) 23–25, 31–33
Casper 199
Cheyenne 202
PUERTO RICO (PR) 187
San Juan 276

CANADA pages 155–183

ALBERTA (AB) 155, 157–160, 164–165
Calgary 277
Edmonton 277
BRITISH COLUMBIA (BC) 155–158, 162–164
Vancouver 282
Victoria 282
MANITOBA (MB) 161, 166–168
Winnipeg 282
NEW BRUNSWICK (NB) 177–181
Fredericton 277
Saint John 280
NEWFOUNDLAND & LABRADOR (NL) 182–183
St. John's 280
NORTHWEST TERRITORIES (NT) 155
NOVA SCOTIA (NS) 180–182
Halifax 277
NUNAVUT (NU) 6–7
ONTARIO (ON) 167–174
Hamilton 278
London 278
Niagara Falls (Buffalo NY) 198
Ottawa 279
Sudbury 281
Toronto 281
Toronto Downtown 281
Windsor (Detroit MI) 210
PRINCE EDWARD ISLAND (PE) 179–182
Charlottetown 277
QUÉBEC (QC) 171, 174–179, 182–183
Gatineau (Ottawa ON) 279
Montréal 279
Québec 280
Sherbrooke 281
SASKATCHEWAN (SK) 159–161, 165–166
Regina 280
Saskatoon 280
YUKON (YT) 155

MEXICO pages 184–187

Cancún 283
Guadalajara 283
México 283
Monterrey 283

0 mi 125 250 375
0 km 125 250 375 500
One inch equals 217 miles
One centimeter equals 138 kilometers

United States Interstate Map

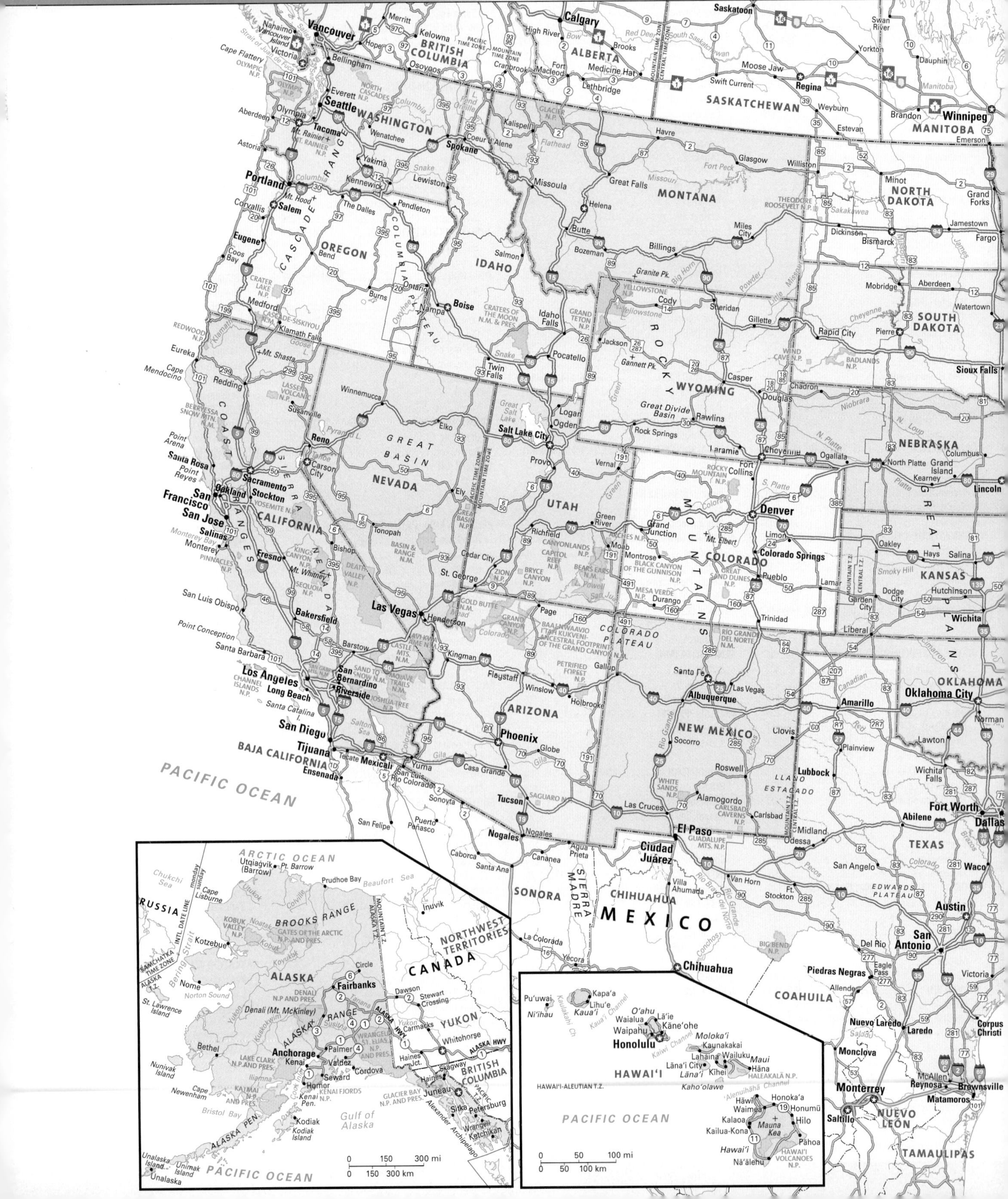

CANADA
ONTARIO
QUÉBEC
NEW BRUNSWICK
MINNESOTA
WISCONSIN
MICHIGAN
IOWA
ILLINOIS
INDIANA
OHIO
PA.
NEW YORK
VT.
N.H.
MAINE
MASS.
R.I.
CT.
N.J.
DEL.
MD.
WEST VIRGINIA
VIRGINIA
KENTUCKY
TENNESSEE
NORTH CAROLINA
SOUTH CAROLINA
GEORGIA
FLORIDA
ALABAMA
MISSISSIPPI
LOUISIANA
ARKANSAS
MISSOURI
OZARK PLATEAU
APPALACHIAN MOUNTAINS
ATLANTIC OCEAN
GULF OF MEXICO
BAHAMAS
CUBA
Lake Superior
Lake Michigan
Lake Huron
Lake Erie
Lake Ontario
EASTERN TIME ZONE
CENTRAL TIME ZONE
Kenora
Dryden
Fort Frances
International Falls
Thunder Bay
Nipigon
Geraldton
Hearst
Kapuskasing
Timmins
Kirkland Lake
Rouyn-Noranda
Val-d'Or
Matagami
Chibougamau
Wawa
Marathon
Sault Ste. Marie
Sudbury
North Bay
Pembroke
Ottawa
Montreal
Québec
Trois-Rivières
Drummondville
Sherbrooke
Saguenay
Alma
St-Félicien
Baie-Comeau
Rimouski
Matane
Mont-Joli
Rivière-du-Loup
Edmundston
Campbellton
Bathurst
Miramichi
Woodstock
Fredericton
Saint John
Presque Isle
Houlton
Bangor
Augusta
Portland
Bar Harbor
Toronto
Hamilton
Kitchener
London
Barrie
Orillia
Peterborough
Kingston
Oshawa
Brampton
St.Catharines
Niagara Falls
Sarnia
Windsor
Duluth
Superior
Bemidji
St. Cloud
Minneapolis
St. Paul
Rochester
Winona
La Crosse
Eau Claire
Wausau
Green Bay
Appleton
Sheboygan
Madison
Milwaukee
Racine
Chicago
Rockford
Joliet
Gary
South Bend
Fort Wayne
Kalamazoo
Grand Rapids
Lansing
Flint
Saginaw
Detroit
Ann Arbor
Toledo
Cleveland
Akron
Youngstown
Pittsburgh
Erie
Buffalo
Rochester
Syracuse
Utica
Albany
Binghamton
Scranton
Williamsport
State College
Altoona
Harrisburg
Allentown
Newark
New York
Trenton
Philadelphia
Wilmington
Baltimore
Dover
Annapolis
Washington
Atlantic City
Burlington
Montpelier
Concord
Manchester
Boston
Worcester
Springfield
Hartford
New Haven
Bridgeport
Providence
New Bedford
Cape Cod
Nantucket Island
Martha's Vineyard
Sioux City
Fort Dodge
Mason City
Waterloo
Dubuque
Cedar Rapids
Des Moines
Davenport
Rock Island
Council Bluffs
Omaha
Ottumwa
Peoria
Bloomington
Champaign
Springfield
Decatur
Quincy
Hannibal
Indianapolis
Lafayette
Terre Haute
Dayton
Columbus
Cincinnati
Mansfield
Lima
Wheeling
Morgantown
Parkersburg
Cumberland
Huntington
Charleston
Lexington
Frankfort
Louisville
Evansville
Owensboro
Paducah
Bowling Green
Pikeville
Bristol
Kansas City
Topeka
St. Joseph
Lawrence
Emporia
Columbia
Jefferson City
St. Louis
Rolla
Cape Girardeau
Springfield
Joplin
Poplar Bluff
Cairo
Clarksville
Nashville
Knoxville
Johnson City
Chattanooga
Memphis
Jackson
Tulsa
Muskogee
McAlester
Fayetteville
Ft. Smith
Little Rock
Pine Bluff
Jonesboro
Texarkana
El Dorado
Durant
Paris
Longview
Shreveport
Monroe
Nacogdoches
Alexandria
Natchez
Lake Charles
Beaumont
Houston
Galveston
Huntsville
Lafayette
Baton Rouge
New Orleans
Houma
Hattiesburg
Jackson
Meridian
Tupelo
Columbus
Greenville
Tuscaloosa
Birmingham
Gadsden
Huntsville
Decatur
Montgomery
Selma
Dothan
Mobile
Biloxi
Pensacola
Panama City
Tallahassee
Atlanta
Marietta
Macon
Columbus
Albany
Valdosta
Augusta
Savannah
Brunswick
Jacksonville
St. Augustine
Lake City
Gainesville
Ocala
Daytona Beach
Orlando
Cape Canaveral
Melbourne
Tampa
St. Petersburg
Sarasota
Ft. Pierce
West Palm Beach
Fort Myers
Naples
Fort Lauderdale
Miami
Key West
Florida Keys
Roanoke
Danville
Petersburg
Richmond
Charlottesville
Newport News
Hampton
Norfolk
Virginia Beach
Salisbury
Winston-Salem
Greensboro
Durham
Raleigh
Fayetteville
Jacksonville
Wilmington
Cape Fear
Cape Hatteras
Charlotte
Asheville
Mt. Mitchell
Greenville
Spartanburg
Columbia
Myrtle Beach
Charleston
Grand Bahama
Freeport
Abaco Island
Eleuthera
Nassau
New Providence
Andros Island
Cat Island
San Salvador
Great Guana Cay
Rum Cay
Havana
Straits of Florida
Cape May
Delaware Bay
Gulf of Maine
Bay of Fundy

Canada Highway Map

0 mi 200 400
0 km 200 400 600

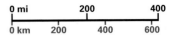

One inch equals 250 miles/Un pouce équivaut à 250 milles
One cm equals 159 km/Un cm équivaut à 159 km

Devon Island
Lancaster Sound
SIRMILIK NATL. PARK
Bylot Island
BAFFIN BAY
GREENLAND (KALAALLIT NUNAAT)
(Denmark)
Prince Regent Inlet
Arctic Bay
Borden Peninsula
Brodeur Peninsula
Pond Inlet
Clyde River
BAFFIN ISLAND
Davis Strait
Qikiqtarjuaq
Gulf of Boothia
Igloolik
AUYUITTUQ NATL. PARK
Cumberland Peninsula
Nettilling Lake
Kugaaruk
MELVILLE PENINSULA
Prince Charles Island
Foxe Basin
Pangnirtung
Cumberland Sound
Amadjuak Lake
Repulse Bay
NUNAVUT
UKKUSIKSALIK NATL. PARK
Hall Peninsula
Iqaluit
EASTERN TIME ZONE
LABRADOR SEA
Foxe Peninsula
Cape Dorset
Foxe Channel
Southampton Island
Coral Harbour
Salisbury Island
Kimmirut
Meta Incognita Peninsula
Resolution Island
Détroit d'Hudson / Hudson Strait
Nottingham Island
Evans Str.
Chesterfield Inlet
Rankin Inlet
Whale Cove
Coats Island
Ivujivik
Salluit
Kangiqsujuaq
Akpatok Island
Cape Chidley
TORNGAT MOUNTAINS NATL. PARK
Mt. Caubvik / Mont d'Iberville 1,652 m
CENTRAL TIME ZONE
EASTERN TIME ZONE
Mansel Island
PÉNINSULE D'UNGAVA
Kangirsuk
Baie d'Ungava / Ungava Bay
TORNGAT MOUNTAINS
Ottawa Islands
Puvirnituq
Kuujjuaq
Nain
Natuashish
Hopedale
BAIE D'HUDSON / HUDSON BAY
NEWFOUNDLAND AND LABRADOR
LABRADOR
Cartwright
Red Bay
St. Anthony
NEWFOUNDLAND TIME ZONE
Umiujaq
Lac à l'Eau Claire
Schefferville
Happy Valley-Goose Bay
Churchill Falls
Smallwood Res.
Blanc-Sablon
St. Barbe
TERRA NOVA NATL. PARK
Bonavista
Gander
St. John's
Belcher Islands
Sanikiluaq
Lac Bienville
Caniapiscau
NEWFOUNDLAND TIME ZONE
HEURE DE L'ATLANTIQUE / ATLANTIC TIME ZONE
HEURE DE L'EST / EASTERN TIME ZONE
Grand Falls-Windsor
NEWFOUNDLAND ISLAND
Argentia
Fort Severn
Kuujjuarapik
Labrador City
Fermont
Wabush
Atikonak Lake
Natashquan
GROS MORNE NATL. PARK
Corner Brook
Stephenville
Grand Bank
Peawanuck
Lac Burton
Rés. de la Grande-Deux
Rés. de la Grande-Trois
Rés. de Caniapiscau
Havre-St-Pierre
RÉS. DE PARC NAT. DE L'ARCHIPEL-DE-MINGAN
Channel-Port aux Basques
St-Pierre
ST-PIERRE AND MIQUELON (France)
Baie James / James Bay
Chisasibi
Radisson
Lac Sakami
QUÉBEC
Réservoir Manicouagan
Sept-Îles
Port-Menier
Île d'Anticosti
Akimiski I.
Wemindji
Webequie
Attawapiskat
Big Trout Lake
Kashechewan
Mt. Jacques-Cartier 1,268 m
PARC NAT. DE FORILLON
Gaspé
Golfe du St-Laurent / Gulf of St. Lawrence
Îles-de-la-Madeleine
Cap-aux-Meules
CAPE BRETON HIGHLANDS NATL. PARK
Sandy Lake
Lac Manouane
Lac Mistassini
Waskaganish
Baie-Comeau
Matane
Sydney
ONTARIO
Central Patricia
Moosonee
Moose Factory
Chibougamau
Réservoir Pipmuacan
Rimouski
Campbellton
Bathurst
KOUCHIBOUGUAC N.P.
PRINCE EDWARD I.
Charlottetown
P.E.I.
Souris
Lake St. Joseph
Chapais
Matagami
Lac St-Jean
Saguenay
Sioux Lookout
Savant Lake
Armstrong
Hearst
Kapuskasing
Lake Abitibi
Réservoir Gouin
St-Félicien
Jonquière
Edmundston
Grand Falls
Miramichi
NEW BRUNSWICK
Summerside
Moncton
Truro
SABLE I. NATL. PARK RES.
Sable I. (Nova Scotia)
Lac Seul
Dryden
Silver Dollar
Rainy L.
Lake Nipigon
Rouyn-Noranda
Val-d'Or
Québec
MAINE
Fredericton
FUNDY N.P.
Saint John
Calais
Dartmouth
Halifax
Lunenburg
NOVA SCOTIA
Marathon
Timmins
Kirkland Lake
PARC NAT. DE LA MAURICIE
Trois-Rivières
Drummondville
Sherbrooke
Bangor
Digby
KEJIMKUJIK NATL. PARK
Yarmouth
Fort Frances
International Falls
Thunder Bay
PUKASKWA N.P.
Lake Superior
Sault Ste. Marie
Elliot Lake
Sudbury
North Bay
Pembroke
Ottawa
Gatineau
Montréal
Cornwall
Burlington
Montpelier
Augusta
Portland
Duluth
Sault Ste. Marie
Espanola
BRUCE PENINSULA N.P.
GEORGIAN BAY ISLANDS N.P.
Parry Sound
Huntsville
Midland
Orillia
Peterborough
Kingston
Lake Champlain
N.H.
Concord
MICHIGAN
Escanaba
Alpena
Lake Huron
Owen Sound
Barrie
Oshawa
Watertown
VT.
MASS.
Boston
WISCONSIN
Minneapolis
St. Paul
Eau Claire
Green Bay
Toronto
Lake Ontario
Kitchener
Hamilton
Rochester
Syracuse
Albany
Springfield
Providence
R.I.
CT.
ATLANTIC OCEAN
Rochester
La Crosse
Mississippi
Sarnia
London
Brantford
Niagara Falls
Buffalo
NEW YORK
Hartford
New Haven
Milwaukee
Madison
Lake Michigan
Lansing
Detroit
Windsor
Lake Erie
Erie
Scranton
New York
NEW JERSEY
PENNSYLVANIA
Waterloo
Dubuque
Chicago
POINT PELEE N.P.
Cleveland
Allentown
Trenton
Philadelphia
NOTE: Legislated standard time zone boundaries shown; observed time may differ locally.

Experience the thrill of the open roads of North America with these great Scenic Drives from Michelin. The famous star ratings highlight natural and cultural attractions along the way.

★★★ **Worth a special journey**
★★ **Worth a detour**
★ **Worth a visit**

Michelin Scenic Drives are indicated by a green and yellow dashed line (▬▬▬) on corresponding atlas maps for easy reference. The following 16 drives are also plotted for your use.

North Coast/Mendocino★★ .... Maps 259, 36
Napa Valley/Sonoma★★ .... Map 36
Willamette Valley★ .... Maps 251, 20, 257, 212
Florida Panhandle★ .... Maps 265, 137, 136, 247
Coastal Carolinas★★ .... Maps 115, 123, 275, 237, 131, 200, 261
San Juan Country★★ .... Map 40
Snake River Valley★ .... Maps 221, 23, 22, 196, 30
Hill Country★★ .... Maps 192, 61, 60, 257
Southern New Mexico★ .... Maps 211, 56, 226, 48, 49, 57
New Jersey Pine Barrens★ .... Maps 191, 147, (105, 104)
Litchfield Hills★★ .... Maps 148, 94
Hudson River Valley★★★ .... Maps 240, 148, 94
Thompson Canyon★ .... Maps 282, 163
Alberta Badlands★★★ .... Maps 277, 164, 165
Saint John River Valley★★ .... Maps 277, 180, 178
Annapolis Valley/Atlantic Shore★★ .... Maps 180, 181, 277
Blue Heron Drive★★ .... Maps 277, 181

ABBREVIATIONS

N	North	**NL**	National Lakeshore
E	East	**NM**	National Memorial/ National Monument
S	South	**NMP**	National Military Park
W	West	**NP**	National Park
NE	Northeast	**NPR**	National Park Reserve
NW	Northwest	**NRA**	National Recreation Area
SE	Southeast	**NWR**	National Wildlife Refuge
SW	Southwest	**PP**	Provincial Park
Hwy.	Highway	**SHP**	State Historical Park
Pkwy.	Parkway	**SHS**	State Historic Site
Rte.	Route	**SP**	State Park
Mi	Miles	**SR**	State Reserve
Km	Kilometers	**VC**	Visitor Center
Sq Ft	Square Feet		
NHS	National Historic Site		

For detailed coverage of the attractions, and for where to dine and stay overnight, see Michelin's North America **Regional Atlas Series**, designed for the way you drive, and Michelin's **Green Guide** and **Short Stays** collections, the ultimate guidebooks for the independent traveler.

NORTHWEST

Anchorage/Fairbanks/Denali★★★

892 miles/1,436 kilometers
Maps 189, 154, 155

From **Anchorage★**, Alaska's largest city, take Rte. 1 (Glenn Hwy. and Tok Cutoff) N and then E through the broad Matanuska Valley to the small town of **Tok**. The route passes agricultural communities, the **Matanuska Glacier** and the Wrangell Mountains before heading up the Copper River Basin. From Tok, take the Alaska Hwy. (Rte. 2) NW to **Fairbanks★**, a friendly town with a frontier feel. The road passes the **Trans-Alaska Pipeline** and **Big Delta SHP** then parallels the Tanana River. From Fairbanks, opt for Rte. 3 W which crosses the river at Nenana, then veers S to **Denali NP★★★**, home of spruce forests, grassy tundra, grizzlies, moose and North America's highest peak, **Mount McKinley** (20,320ft). Return S to Anchorage via Rtes. 3 and 1.

Mount McKinley, Denali NP
© zzvision/Getty Images Plus

Badlands★★★

164 miles/264 kilometers Maps 253, 26

From **Rapid City★**, South Dakota, drive SE on Rte. 44 through Farmingdale and Scenic, then east to Interior to enter **Badlands NP★★★**. Take Rte. 377 NE 2mi to Cedar Pass and stop at the park's Ben Reifel VC. From there, Cliff **Shelf Nature Trail★★** (.5mi) is popular for its shady junper trees; **Castle Trail★★★** (4.5mi) is spectacular in early morning when the moonscape valley and pointed spires get first light. Turn left onto Rte. 240, **Badlands Loop Road★★★**, along the northern rim, where prairie grasslands give way to buttes and hoodoos. **Pinnacles Overlook★★** is a sweeping viewpoint to the south.
Drive N to I-90, and cross the Interstate N to Wall. On Main St. visit **Wall Drug★**, a "drug store in name only" with over 20 shops filled with historical photos, 6,000 pairs of cowboy boots, wildlife exhibits and Western art displayed in five dining rooms. In the backyard a roaring, 80ft **Tyrannosaurus** sends toddlers running. Leave Wall on I-90, driving W. Take Exit 67 to Ellsworth Air Force Base, where the **South Dakota Air and Space Museum** displays stealth bombers and other aircraft. Continue W on I-90 back to Rapid City to conclude the tour.

Badlands NP
© kwiktor/Getty Images Plus

Black Hills★★

244 miles/393 kilometers Maps 253, 26, 25

From **Rapid City★**, drive S on US-16 then US-16A S past Keystone. Take Rte. 244 W to **Mount Rushmore NM★★★**. Continue W on Rte 244 to the junction of US-16/385. Enroute S to Custer, **Crazy Horse Memorial★** honors the famous Sioux chief. From Custer, head S on US-385 through Pringle to the junction of Rte. 87. Take Rte. 87 N through **Wind Cave NP★★** and into **Custer SP★★★**. Follow **Wildlife Loop Road★★** (access S of Blue Bell, across from Rte. 342 junction) E and N to US-16A. Then travel W to join scenic **Needles Highway★★** (Rte. 87) NW to US-16/385 N. Where US-16 separates, continue N on US-385 to **Deadwood★★**, a former gold camp. Turn left onto US-14A, driving SW through **Lead★**, site of the former **Homestake Gold Mine★★**, to Cheyenne Crossing. Drive N on US-14A to I-90, turning SE back to Rapid City.

Mount Rushmore NM

Columbia River Gorge★★

83 miles/134 kilometers Maps 251, 20, 21

From **Portland★★**, Oregon's largest city, take I-84 E to Exit 17 in Troutdale. There, head E on the winding **Historic Columbia River Highway★★** (US-30), which skirts the steep cliffs above the river. For great **views★★**, stop at **Vista House at Crown Point**. You'll pass the 620ft **Multnomah Falls★★** and moss-draped **Oneonta Gorge**. At Ainsworth State Park (Exit 35), rejoin I-84 and travel E to Mosier (Exit 69), where US-30, with its hairpin turns, begins again. Continue E on US-30, stopping at **Rowena Crest Viewpoint★★** for grand vistas—and wildflowers. Just past the Western-style town called The Dalles, take US-197 N to conclude the tour at **The Dalles Lock** and **Dam VC★★**.

Grand Tetons/Yellowstone★★★

224 miles/361 kilometers Map 24

Note: parts of this tour are closed in winter.

From **Jackson★★**, drive N on US-26/191/89 to Moose. Turn left onto Teton Park Rd. to access **Grand Teton NP★★★** and **Jenny Lake Scenic Drive★★★**. From Teton Park Rd., drive N to the junction of US-89/191/287 (**John D. Rockefeller Jr. Memorial Pkwy.**) and follow the parkway N into **Yellowstone NP★★★** to **West Thumb**. Take Grand Loop Rd. W to **Old Faithful★★★**, the world's most famous geyser. Continue N on the Grand Loop Rd., passing **Norris Geyser Basin★★** en route to **Mammoth Hot Springs★★★**. Turn E on Grand Loop Rd. to Tower Junction, then S into **Grand Canyon of the Yellowstone★★★**. Continue S from Canyon Village through **Hayden Valley★★** to Yellowstone Lake. Head SW, back to West Thumb, to conclude the tour.

Mount Moran, Grand Teton NP

Pacific Coast/Olympic Peninsula★★★

419 miles/675 kilometers Maps 245, 12

From the state capital of **Olympia**, drive N on US-101 to Discovery Bay. Detour on Rte. 20 NE to **Port Townsend★★**, a well-preserved Victorian seaport. From Discovery Bay, head W on US-101 through **Port Angeles** to the **Heart O' the Hills** park entrance for **Olympic NP★★★** to see **Hurricane Ridge★★★**. Back on US-101, head E then S to the park entrance that leads to **Hoh Rain Forest★★★**. Follow US-101 S, then E after Queets to **Lake Quinaulte**, home to bald eagles, trumpeter swans and loons. Continue S on US-101 to Aberdeen, taking Rte. 105 to the coast. At Raymond, return to US-101 heading S to **Long Beach**. Follow Rte. 103 N past the former cannery town of **Oysterville** to **Leadbetter Point★** on Willapa Bay, where oysters are still harvested. Return S to **Ilwaco** and drive E and S on US-101 to Astoria, Oregon, to end the tour.

The Oregon Coast★★★

368 miles/592 kilometers Maps 20, 28

Leave **Astoria★**, Oregon's first settlement, via US-101, heading SW. **Fort Clatsop National Memorial★★** recalls Lewis and Clark's historic stay. **Cannon Beach★** boasts a sandy beach and tall coastal rock. At the farming community of **Tillamook★**, go west on 3rd

Cannon Beach, Oregon Coast

St. to **Cape Meares** to begin **Three Capes Scenic Drive★★**. Continue S, rejoining US-101 just beyond Pacific City. Drive S on US-101 through **Newport★**, then **Yachats★**, which neighbors **Cape Perpetua Scenic Area★★**. From **Florence** to **Coos Bay★** stretches **Oregon Dunes National Recreation Area★★**. At Coos Bay, take Cape Arago Hwy. W to tour the gardens of **Shore Acres State Park★**. Drive S on the highway to rejoin US-101. Pass **Bandon★**, known for its cheese factory, and Port Orford, with its fishing fleet. Farther S, **Boardman State Park★** shelters Sitka spruce, Douglas fir and **Natural Bridge Cove**. End the tour at **Brookings**.

SOUTHWEST

Big Bend Area★★

581 miles/935 kilometers
Maps 211, 56, 57, 62, 60

Head S from **El Paso★** via I-10, then E to Kent. Take Rte. 118 S to Alpine, passing **McDonald Observatory★** (telescope tours) and **Fort Davis NHS★★**. Continue S to Study Butte to enter **Big Bend NP★★★**, edged by the Rio Grande River and spanning 1,252sq mi of spectacular canyons, lush bottomlands, sprawling desert and mountain woodlands. The park has more species of migratory and resident birds than any other national park. Travel E to the main VC at Panther Junction in the heart of the park (US-385 and Rio Grande Village Dr.). Then take US-385 N to Marathon. Turn E on US-90 to Langtry, site of **Judge Roy Bean VC★**. Continue E to **Seminole Canyon SP★★**, with its 4,000-year-old pictographs. Farther E, **Amistad NRA★** is popular for water sports. Continue on US-90 to conclude the tour in Del Rio.

Canyonlands of Utah★★★

481 miles/774 kilometers Maps, 39, 40

From **St. George★**, drive NE on I-15 to Exit 16. Take Rte. 9 E to Springdale, gateway to **Zion NP★★★**, with its sandstone canyon, waterfalls and hanging gardens. Continue E on Rte. 9 to Mt. Carmel Junction, turn left onto US-89 and head N to the junction with Rte. 12. Take Rte. 12 SE to **Bryce Canyon NP★★★**, with its colored rock formations. Continue SE on Rte. 12 to Cannonville, then S to **Kodachrome Basin SP★★**, where sandstone chimneys rise from the desert floor. Return to Cannonville, and drive NE on Rte. 12 through Boulder to Torrey. Take Rte. 24 E through **Capitol Reef NP★★**—with its unpaved driving roads and trails—then N to I-70. Travel E on I-70 to Exit 182, then S on US-191 to Rte. 313 into **Canyonlands NP★★★** to **Grand View Point Overlook**. Return to US-191, turning S to access **Arches NP★★★**—the greatest concentration of natural stone arches in the country. Continue S on US-191 to **Moab★** to end the tour.

Canyonlands NP

Central Coast/Big Sur★★★

118 miles/190 kilometers Maps 236, 44

From **Cannery Row★** in **Monterey★★**, take Prescott Ave. to Rte. 68. Turn right and continue to Pacific Grove Gate (on your left) to begin scenic **17-Mile Drive★★**, a private toll road. Exit at Carmel Gate to reach the upscale beach town of **Carmel★★**, site of Carmel **mission★★★**. The town's Scenic Road winds S along the beachfront. Leave Carmel by Hwy. 1 S. Short, easy trails at **Point Lobos SR★★** line the shore. Enjoy the wild beauty of the **Big Sur★★★** coastline en route to San Simeon, where **Hearst Castle★★★**, the magnificent estate of a former newspaper magnate, overlooks the Pacific Ocean. Continue S on Hwy. 1 to **Morro Bay**, where the tour ends.

Bixby Creek Bridge, Big Sur

Colorado Rockies★★★

499 miles/803 kilometers
Maps 209, 41, 33, 40

Note: Rte. 82 S of Leadville to Aspen is closed mid-Oct to Memorial Day due to snow.

From **Golden★★**, **W of Denver★★**, drive W on US-6 along Clear Creek to Rte. 119, heading N on the *Peak to* **Peak Highway★★** to **Nederland★**. Continue N on Rte. 72, then follow Rte. 7 N to the town of **Estes Park★★**. Take US-36 W to enter **Rocky Mountain NP★★★**. Drive **Trail Ridge Road★★★** (US-34)

Colorado Rockies
© Danny35/Getty Images Plus

S to the town of **Grand Lake★**. Continue S to Granby, turn left on US-40 to I-70 at Empire. Head W on I-70 past **Georgetown★** and through **Eisenhower Tunnel**. You'll pass ski areas Arapahoe Basin, **Keystone Resort★** and **Breckenridge★★**. At Exit 195 for **Copper Mountain Resort★**, take Rte. 91 S to **Leadville★★**, Colorado's former silver capital. Then travel S on US-24 to Rte. 82 W over **Independence Pass★★** to **Aspen★★★**. Head NW to I-70, passing **Glenwood Springs★★** with its **Hot Springs Pool★★**. Drive E on I-70 along **Glenwood Canyon★★** and the Colorado River to **Vail★★**. Continue E on I-70 to the old mining town of **Idaho Springs** to return to Golden via Rte. 119.

Lake Tahoe Loop★★

71 miles/114 kilometers Map 37

Begin in **Tahoe City** at the intersection of Rtes. 89 and 28. Drive S on Rte. 89. **Ed Z'berg-Sugar Pine Point State Park★** encompasses a promontory topped by **Ehrman Mansion★** and other historic buildings. Farther S, **Emerald Bay State Park★★** surrounds beautiful **Emerald Bay★★**. At the bay's tip stands **Vikingsholm★★**, a mansion that resembles an ancient Nordic castle. At **Tallac Historic Site★★**, preserved summer estates recall Tahoe's turn-of-the-19C opulence. From Tahoe Valley, take Rte. 50 NE. **South Lake Tahoe**, the lake's largest town, offers lodging, dining and shopping. High-rise hotel-casinos characterize neighboring **Stateline** in Nevada. Continue N to Spooner Junction. Then follow Nevada Rte. 28 N to **Sand Harbor** (7mi), where picnic tables and a sandy beach fringe a sheltered cove. Continue through Kings Beach to end the tour at Tahoe City.

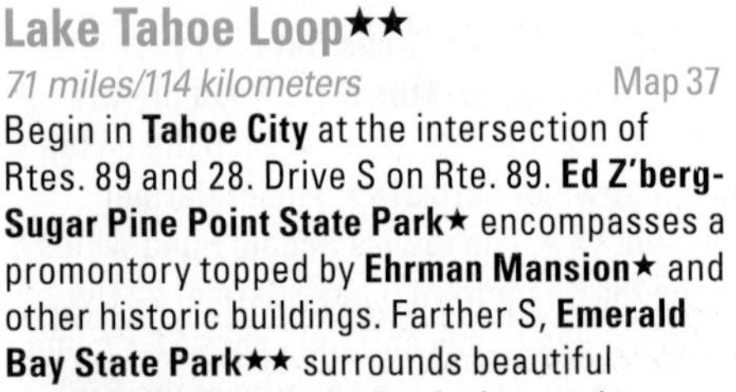
Emerald Bay, Lake Tahoe
© Donyanedomam/Getty Images Plus

Maui's Hana Highway★★

108 miles/174 kilometers Map 153

Leave **Kahului** on Rte. 36 E toward **Paia**, an old sugar-plantation town. Continue E on Rte. 36, which becomes Rte. 360, the **Hana Highway★★**. The road passes **Ho'okipa Beach Park**, famous for windsurfing, and **Puohokamoa Falls**, a good picnic stop, before arriving in **Hana**, a little village on an attractive bay. If adventurous, continue S on the Pulaui Highway to **Ohe'o Gulch★★** in **Haleakala NP★★★**, where small waterfalls tumble from the SE flank of the dormant volcano Haleakala. Past the gulch the grave of aviator **Charles Lindbergh** can be found in the churchyard at Palapala Hoomau Hawaiian Church. End the tour at Kipahulu.

Haleakala volcano crater, Maui
© MNStudio/Getty Images Plus

Redwood Empire★★

182 miles/293 kilometers Maps 36, 28

In **Leggett**, S of the junction of Hwy. 1 and US-101, go N on US-101 to pass through a massive redwood trunk at **Chandelier Drive-Thru Tree Park**. To the N, see breathtaking groves along 31mi **Avenue of the Giants★★★**. **Humboldt Redwoods SP★★** contains **Rockefeller Forest★★**, the world's largest virgin redwood forest. From US-101, detour 4mi to **Ferndale★**, a quaint Victorian village. N. along US-101, **Eureka★** preserves a logging camp cookhouse and other historic sites. The sleepy fishing town of **Trinidad★** is home to a marine research lab. **Patrick's Point SP★★** offers dense forests, agate-strewn beaches and clifftop **view★★**. At **Orick**, enter the **Redwood National and State Parks★★★**, which protect a 379ft-high, 750-year-old **tree★**. The tour ends in Crescent City.

Avenue of the Giants, Redwood Empire
© GaryRBenson/Getty Images Plus

Santa Fe Area★★★

267 miles/430 kilometers
Maps 189, 48, 260, 49

From **Albuquerque★**, drive E on I-40 to Exit 175 and take Rte. 14, the **Turquoise Trail★★**, N to **Santa Fe★★★**. This 52mi back road runs along the scenic Sandia Mountains and passes dry washes, arroyos and a series of revived "ghost towns." Continue N on US-84/285, turning NE onto Rte. 76, the **High Road to Taos★★**. East of Vadito, take Rte. 518 N to Rte. 68 N into the rustic Spanish colonial town

Taos Pueblo, Santa Fe Area
© miroslav_1/Getty Images Plus

of **Taos★★**, a center for the arts. Head N on US-64 to the junction of Rte. 522. Continue W on US-64 for an 18mi round-trip detour to see the 1,200ft-long, three-span **Rio Grande Gorge Bridge** over the river. Return to Rte. 522 and take this route, part of the **Enchanted Circle★★** Scenic Byway, N to **Questa**, starting point for white-water trips on the Rio Grande. Turn onto Rte. 38, heading E to the old mining town of **Eagle Nest**. There, detour 23mi E on US-64 to **Cimarron**, a Wild West haunt. Back at Eagle Nest, travel SW on US-64, detouring on Rte. 434 S to tiny **Angel Fire**. Return to Taos on US-64 W to end the tour.

Sedona/Grand Canyon NP★★★

482 miles/776 kilometers
Maps 249, 54, 47, 213

Drive N from **Phoenix★** on I-17 to Exit 298 and take Rte. 179 N toward **Sedona★★** in the heart of **Red Rock Country★★★**. The red-rock formations are best accessed by four-wheel-drive vehicle via 12mi **Schnebly Hill Road★** (off Rte. 179, across Oak Creek bridge from US-89A "Y" junction), which offers splendid **views★★★**. Then head N on Rte. 89A through Sedona to begin 14mi drive of **Oak Creek Canyon★★**. Continue N on Rte. 89A and I-17 to **Flagstaff★★**, commercial hub for the region. Take US-180 NW to Rte. 64, which leads N to the **South Rim★★★** of **Grand Canyon NP★★★**. Take the shuttle (or drive, if permitted) along **West Rim Drive★★** to **Hermits Rest★**. Then travel **East Rim Drive★★★** (Rte. 64 E) to **Desert View Watchtower★** for **views★★★** of the canyon. Continue to the junction with US-89 at Cameron. Return S to Flagstaff, then S to Phoenix via I-17.

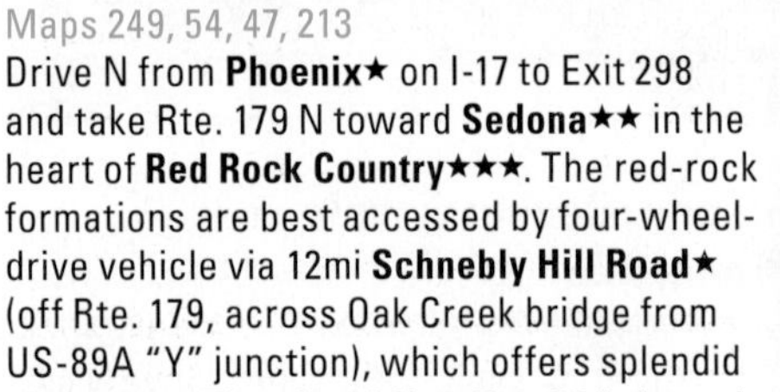
Grand Canyon NP

NORTHEAST

The Berkshires Loop★★★

57 miles/92 kilometers Map 94

From **Great Barrington**, take US-23 E to Monterey, turning left onto Tyringham Rd., which becomes Monterey Rd., to experience scenic **Tyringham Valley★**. Continue N on Main Rd. to Tyringham Rd., which leads to **Lee**, famous for its marble. Then go NW on US-20 to **Lenox★**, with its inviting inns and restaurants. Detour on Rte. 183 W to **Tanglewood★**, site of a popular summer music festival. Return to Lenox and drive N on US-7 to **Pittsfield**, the commercial capital of the region. Head W on US-20 to enjoy **Hancock Shaker Village★★★**, a museum village that relates the history of a Shaker community established here in 1790. Rte. 41 S passes West Stockbridge, then opt for Rte. 102 SE to **Stockbridge★★** and its picturesque **Main Street★**. Follow US-7 S to the junction with Rte. 23, passing **Monument Mountain★** en route. Return to Great Barrington.

Cape Cod★★★

164 miles/264 kilometers Maps 151, 95

At US-6 and Rte. 3, cross **Cape Cod Canal** via Sagamore Bridge and turn onto Rte. 6A to tour the Cape's **North Shore★★**. Bear right onto Rte. 130 to reach **Sandwich★**, famous for glass manufacturing. Continue on Rte. 6A E to Orleans. Take US-6 N along **Cape Cod National Seashore★★★**, with its wooded and marshland trails, to reach **Provincetown★★**, a seaside town and longtime LGBTQ retreat offering **dune tours★★** and summer theater. Return to Orleans and take Rte. 28 S through **Chatham★**, then W to Hyannis, where ferries depart for **Nantucket★★★**. Continue to quaint **Falmouth★**. Take Surf Dr., which becomes Oyster Pond Rd. to nearby **Woods Hole**, a world center for marine research and departure point for ferries to **Martha's Vineyard★★**. Take Woods Hole Rd., N to Rte. 28. Cross the canal via Bourne Bridge and head E on US-6 to end the tour at Rte. 3.

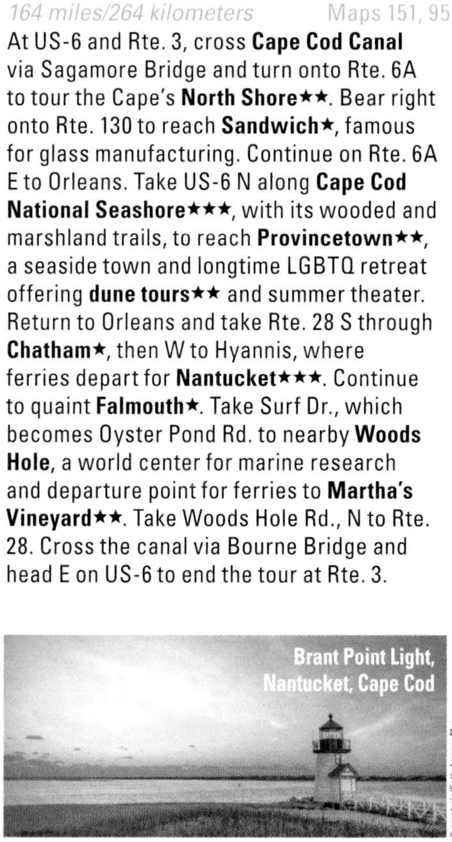

Brant Point Light, Nantucket, Cape Cod

© grantreig/Getty Images Plus

Maine Coast★★

238 miles/383 kilometers

Maps 82, 251, 83

From **Kittery**, drive N on US-1 to **York★**, then along US-1A to see the 18C buildings of **Colonial York★★**. Continue N on coastal US-1A to **Ogunquit★**. Rejoin US-1 and head N to Rte. 9, turn right, and drive to **Kennebunkport**, with its colorful shops. Take Rte. 9A/35 to **Kennebunk**. Then travel N on US-1 to **Portland★★**, Maine's largest city, where the **Old Port★★** brims with galleries and boutiques. Take US-1 N through the outlet town of **Freeport**, then on to **Brunswick**, home of **Bowdoin College**. Turn NE through **Bath★**, **Wiscasset**, **Rockland**, **Camden★★**, **Searsport** and **Bucksport**. At Ellsworth, take Rt. 3 S to enter **Acadia NP★★★** on **Mount Desert Island★★★**, where **Park Loop Road★★★** (closed in winter) parallels open coast. From the top of **Cadillac Mountain★★★**, the **views★★★** are breathtaking. The tour ends at **Bar Harbor★**, a popular charming town just outside Acadia NP.

Acadia NP, Maine Coast

© Douglas Rissing/Getty Images Plus

Mohawk Valley★

114 miles/184 kilometers

Maps 188, 94, 80

From the state capital of **Albany★**, take I-90 NW to Exit 25 for I-890 into **Schenectady**, founded by Dutch settlers in 1661. Follow Rte. 5 W along the Mohawk River. In Fort Hunter, **Schoharie Crossing SHS★** stretches along a canal towpath. Near Little Falls, **Herkimer Home SHS** (Rte. 169 at Thruway Exit 29A) interprets colonial farm life. Rte. 5 continues W along the Erie Canal to Utica. From Utica, drive W on Rte. 49 to Rome, where the river turns N and peters out. The tour ends in Rome, site of **Fort Stanwix NM★**.

South Shore Lake Superior★

530 miles/853 kilometers

Maps 211, 64, 65, 69

From **Duluth★**, drive SE on I-535/US-53 to the junction of Rte. 13 at Parkland. Follow Rte. 13 E to quaint Bayfield, gateway to **Apostle Islands NL★★**, accessible by boat. Head S to the junction of US-2, and E through Ashland, Ironwood and Wakefield. There, turn left onto Rte. 28, heading NE to Bergland, and turning left onto Rte. 64. Drive N to Silver City and take Rte. M-107 W into **Porcupine Mountains Wilderness SP★**. Return to Rte. 64 and go E to Ontonagon. Take Rte. 38 SE to Greenland, then follow Rte. 26 NE to Houghton. Cross to Hancock on US-41 and continue NE to Phoenix. Turn left onto Rte. 26 to Eagle River and on to Copper Harbor via **Brockway Mountain Drive★★**. Return S to Houghton via US-41, then travel S and E past Marquette, turning left onto Rte. 28. Head E to Munising, then take County Road H-58 E and N through **Pictured Rocks NL★**. End the tour at Grand Marais.

Villages of Southern Vermont★★

118 miles/190 kilometers Map 81

Head N from the resort town of **Manchester★** by Rte. 7A. At Manchester Center, take Rte. 11 E past **Bromley Mountain**, a popular ski area, to Peru. Turn left on the backroad to **Weston★**, a favorite tourist stop along Rte. 100. Continue to **Chester**, turning right onto Rte. 35 S to reach **Grafton★**, with its **Old Tavern**. Farther S, Rte. 30 S from Townshend leads to **Newfane** and its lovely **village green★**. Return to Townshend, then travel W, following Rte. 30 through West Townshend, passing **Stratton Mountain** en route to Manchester. S of Manchester by Rte. 7A, the crest of Mt. Equinox is accessible via **Equinox Skyline Drive** (fee). Then continue S on Rte. 7A to end the tour at **Arlington**, known for its trout fishing.

The White Mountains Loop★★★

127 miles/204 kilometers Map 81

From the all-season resort of Conway, drive N on Rte. 16 to **North Conway★**, abundant with tourist facilities. Continue N on US-302/Rte. 16 through **Glen**, passing **Glen Ellis Falls★** and **Pinkham Notch★★** en route to Glen House. There, drive the Auto Road to the top of **Mount Washington★★★** (or take guided van tour). Head N on Rte. 16 to Gorham, near the Androscoggin River, then W on US-2 to Jefferson Highlands. Travel SW on Rte. 115 to Carroll, then S on US-3 to Twin Mountain. Go SW on US-3 to join I-93. Head S on I-93/Rte.3, passing scenic **Franconia Notch★★★** and **Profile Lake★★**. Bear E on Rte. 3 where it separates from the interstate to visit **The Flume★★**, a natural gorge 90ft deep. Rejoin I-93 S to the intersection with Rte. 112. Head E on Rte. 112 through Lincoln on the **Kancamagus Highway★★★** until it joins Rte. 16 back to Conway.

White Mountain National Forest

© DenisTangneyJr/Getty Images Plus

Michelin Scenic Drives - continues on page 301

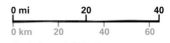

0 mi 20 40
0 km 20 40 60
One inch equals 25.4 miles
One centimeter equals 16.1 kilometers

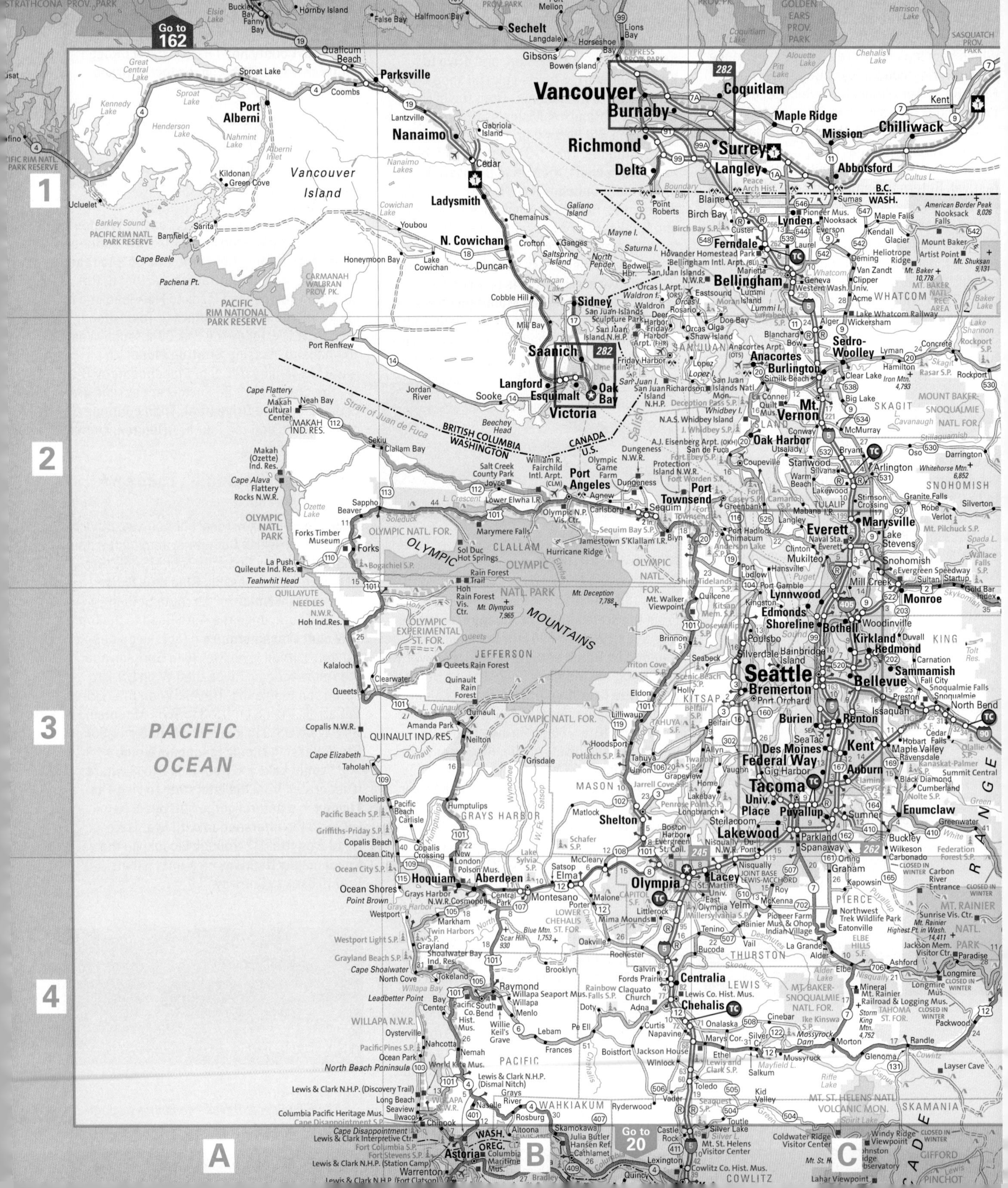

DRIVING DISTANCES IN MILES

	ABERDEEN, WA	BELLINGHAM, WA	MT. RAINIER NP, WA	OKANOGAN, WA	OLYMPIA, WA	PORT ANGELES, WA	SEATTLE, WA	SPOKANE, WA	TACOMA, WA	VANCOUVER, BC	WENATCHEE, WA	YAKIMA, WA
BELLINGHAM, WA	196		186	195	147	127*	88	360	122	52	185	221
SEATTLE, WA	105	88	96	223	56	83*		278	31	140	148	140
SPOKANE, WA	376	360	290	148	327	362*	278		303	412	171	203
YAKIMA, WA	237	221	87	194	188	223*	140	203	164	273	115	

*DISTANCE INCLUDES FERRY TRAVEL

SEE ALSO DISTANCE AND DRIVING TIME MAP ON PAGES 286–287

British Columbia
Washington

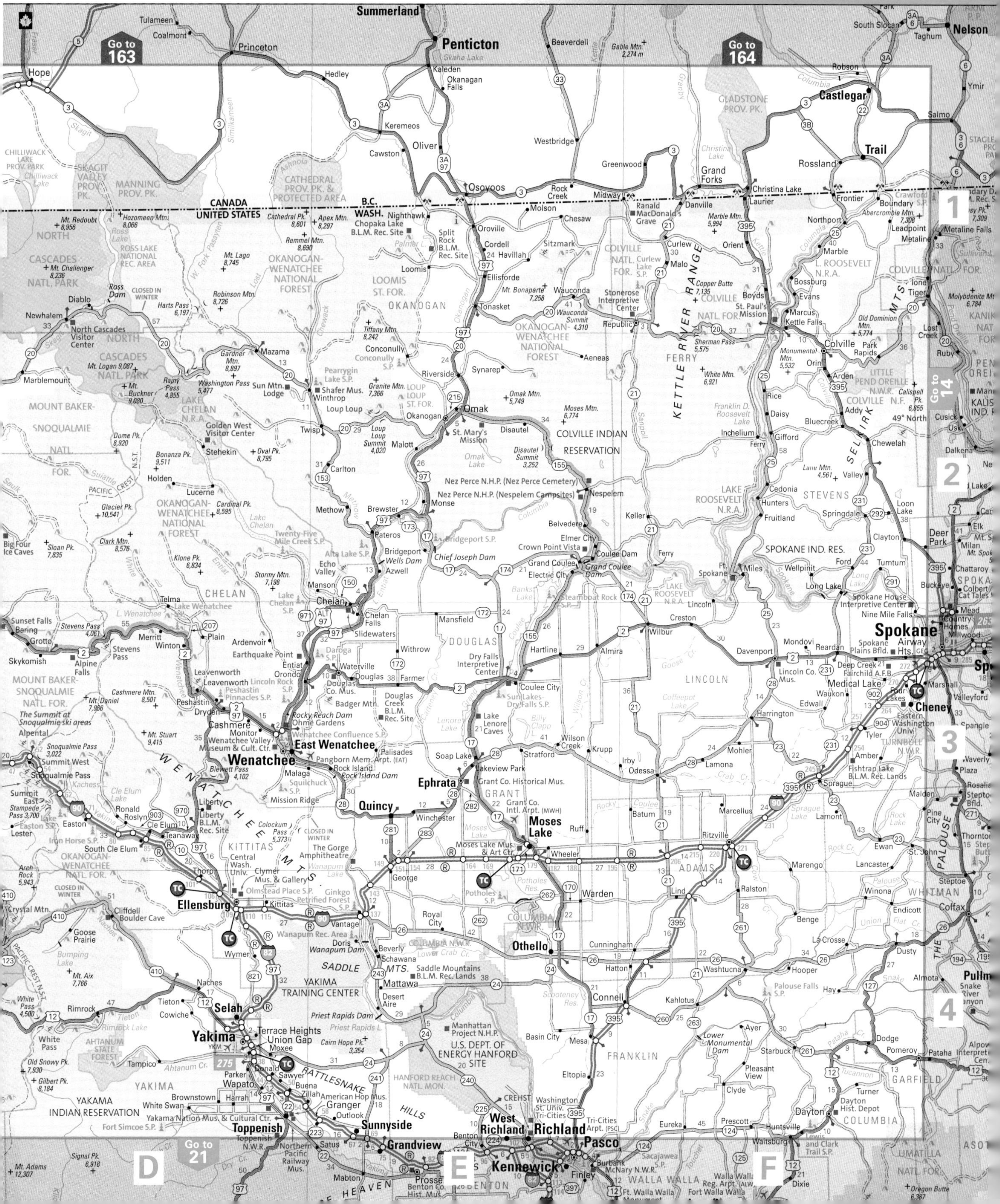
Go to 163
Go to 164
Go to 14
Go to 21
CANADA
UNITED STATES
B.C.
WASH.
Penticton
Summerland
Princeton
Hope
Osoyoos
Oliver
Castlegar
Trail
Nelson
Omak
Okanogan
Wenatchee
East Wenatchee
Chelan
Ephrata
Quincy
Moses Lake
Othello
Ellensburg
Yakima
Selah
Toppenish
Sunnyside
Grandview
Richland
West Richland
Kennewick
Pasco
Spokane
Cheney
Colville
Republic
Connell
Ritzville
COLVILLE INDIAN RESERVATION
YAKAMA INDIAN RESERVATION
SPOKANE IND. RES.
NORTH CASCADES NATL. PARK
OKANOGAN-WENATCHEE NATIONAL FOREST
COLVILLE NATL. FOR.
LAKE ROOSEVELT N.R.A.
KETTLE RIVER RANGE
SELKIRK MTS
WENATCHEE MTS
SADDLE MTS.
RATTLESNAKE HILLS
YAKIMA TRAINING CENTER
U.S. DEPT. OF ENERGY HANFORD SITE
DOUGLAS
GRANT
LINCOLN
ADAMS
FRANKLIN
KITTITAS
CHELAN
OKANOGAN
STEVENS
WHITMAN
COLUMBIA
GARFIELD
THE PALOUSE
1
2
3
4
D
E
F

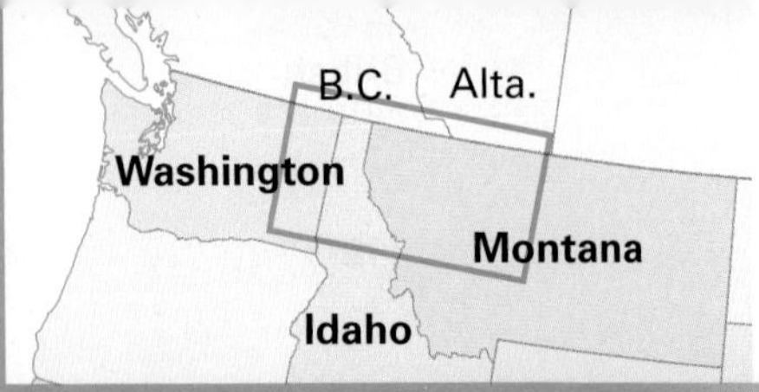
B.C.
Alta.
Washington
Montana
Idaho

Spokane WA / Coeur d'Alene ID

0 mi 20 40
0 km 20 40 60
One inch equals 25.4 miles
One centimeter equals 16.1 kilometers

Go to 164
Go to 13
Go to 22
Cranbrook
Fernie
Nelson
Castlegar
Trail
Rossland
Grand Forks
Greenwood
Salmo
Creston
Kingsgate
Roosville
BRITISH COLUMBIA
MONTANA
CANADA
U.S.
IDAHO
MONT.
WASHINGTON
IDAHO
PACIFIC TIME ZONE
MOUNTAIN TIME ZONE
Colville
Kettle Falls
Republic
Chewelah
Newport
Bonners Ferry
Sandpoint
Libby
Troy
Eureka
Spokane
Spokane Valley
Cheney
Medical Lake
Deer Park
Post Falls
Hayden
Coeur d'Alene
Rathdrum
Kellogg
Wallace
St. Maries
Plummer
Tekoa
Colfax
Pullman
Moscow
Clarkston
Lewiston
Orofino
Dayton
Walla Walla
Ritzville
Davenport
Sprague
Superior
St. Regis
Thompson Falls
Plains
Hot Springs
KETTLE RIVER RANGE
SELKIRK MTS.
PURCELL MTS.
SALISH MTS.
CABINET MOUNTAINS
COEUR D'ALENE MOUNTAINS
ST. JOE MTS.
BITTERROOT RANGE
ROCKY MTS.
COLVILLE NATL. FOR.
KANIKSU NATL. FOR.
KOOTENAI NATIONAL FOREST
LOLO NATL. FOR.
ST. JOE NATL. FOREST
CLEARWATER NATIONAL FOREST
NEZ PERCE-CLEARWATER NATIONAL FOREST
COLVILLE INDIAN RESERVATION
SPOKANE IND. RES.
COEUR D'ALENE IND. RES.
NEZ PERCE IND. RES.
STEVENS
PEND OREILLE
BONNER
BOUNDARY
KOOTENAI
LINCOLN
SPOKANE
WHITMAN
LATAH
BENEWAH
SHOSHONE
MINERAL
SANDERS
GARFIELD
COLUMBIA
ASOTIN
LEWIS
FERRY
A
B
C
1
2
3
4

DRIVING DISTANCES IN MILES

	BONNERS FERRY, ID	BROWNING, MT	COEUR D'ALENE, ID	COLVILLE, WA	GREAT FALLS, MT	HELENA, MT	KALISPELL, MT	LEWISTON, ID	MISSOULA, MT	SHELBY, MT	SPOKANE, WA	WEST GLACIER, MT
GREAT FALLS, MT	369	124	364	471		85	222	420	199	82	398	192
LEWISTON, ID	196	413	118	176	420	334	315		221	448	103	348
MISSOULA, MT	244	201	167	274	199	114	116	221		227	201	136
SPOKANE, WA	110	336	34	73	398	313	238	103	201	426		271

SEE ALSO DISTANCE AND DRIVING TIME MAP ON PAGES 286–287

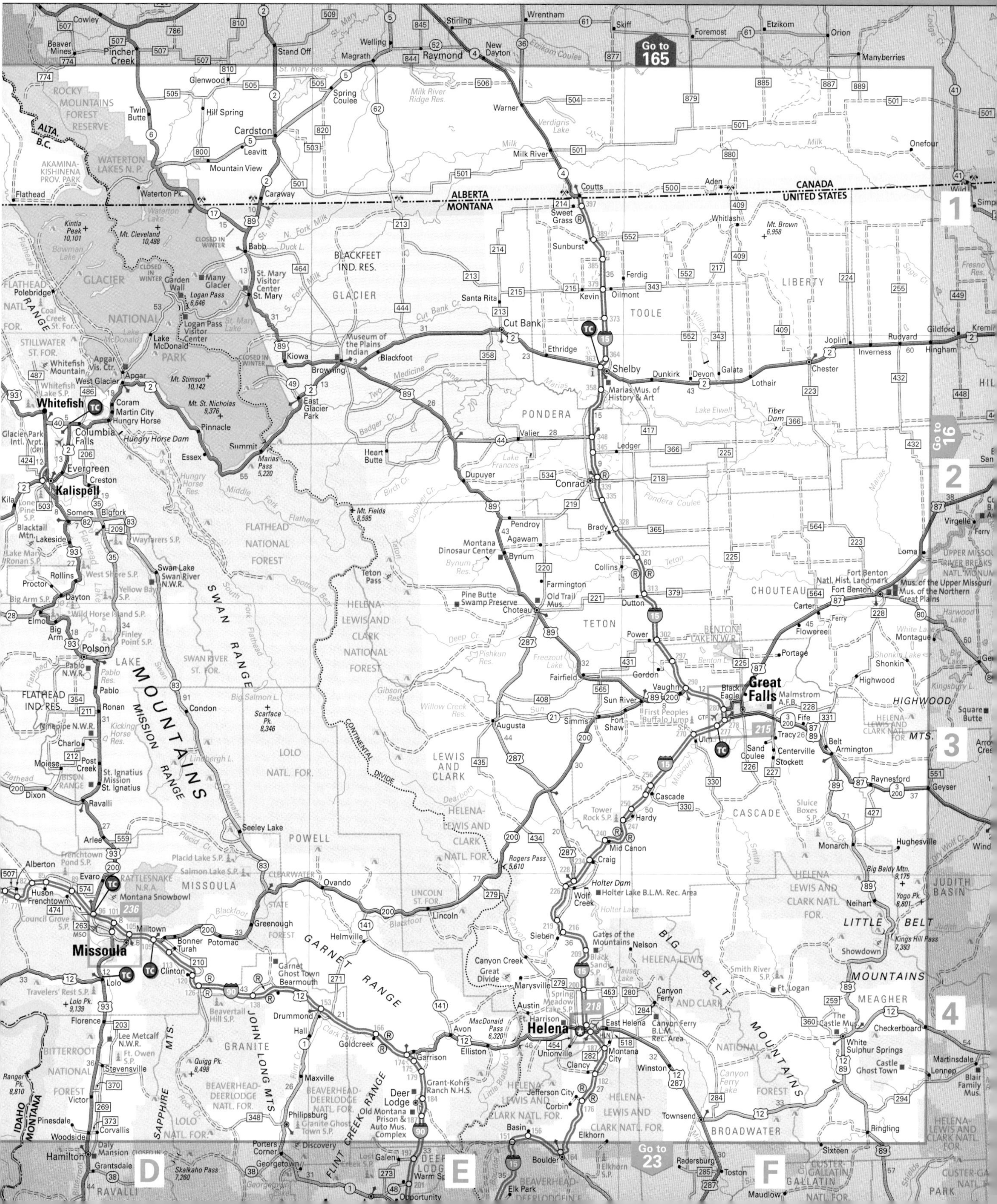

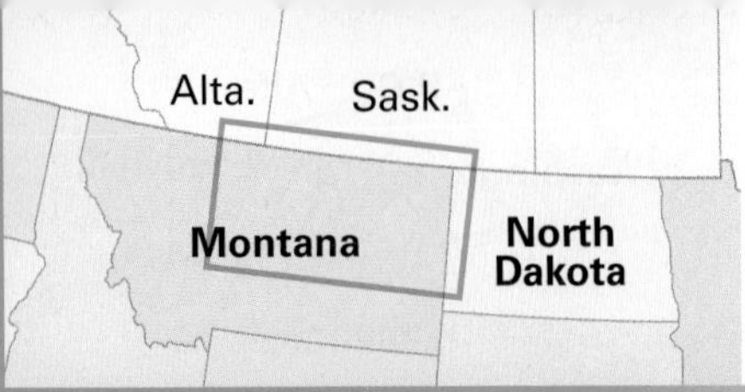

0 mi 20 40
0 km 20 40 60

One inch equals 25.4 miles
One centimeter equals 16.1 kilometers

Great Falls MT / Havre MT

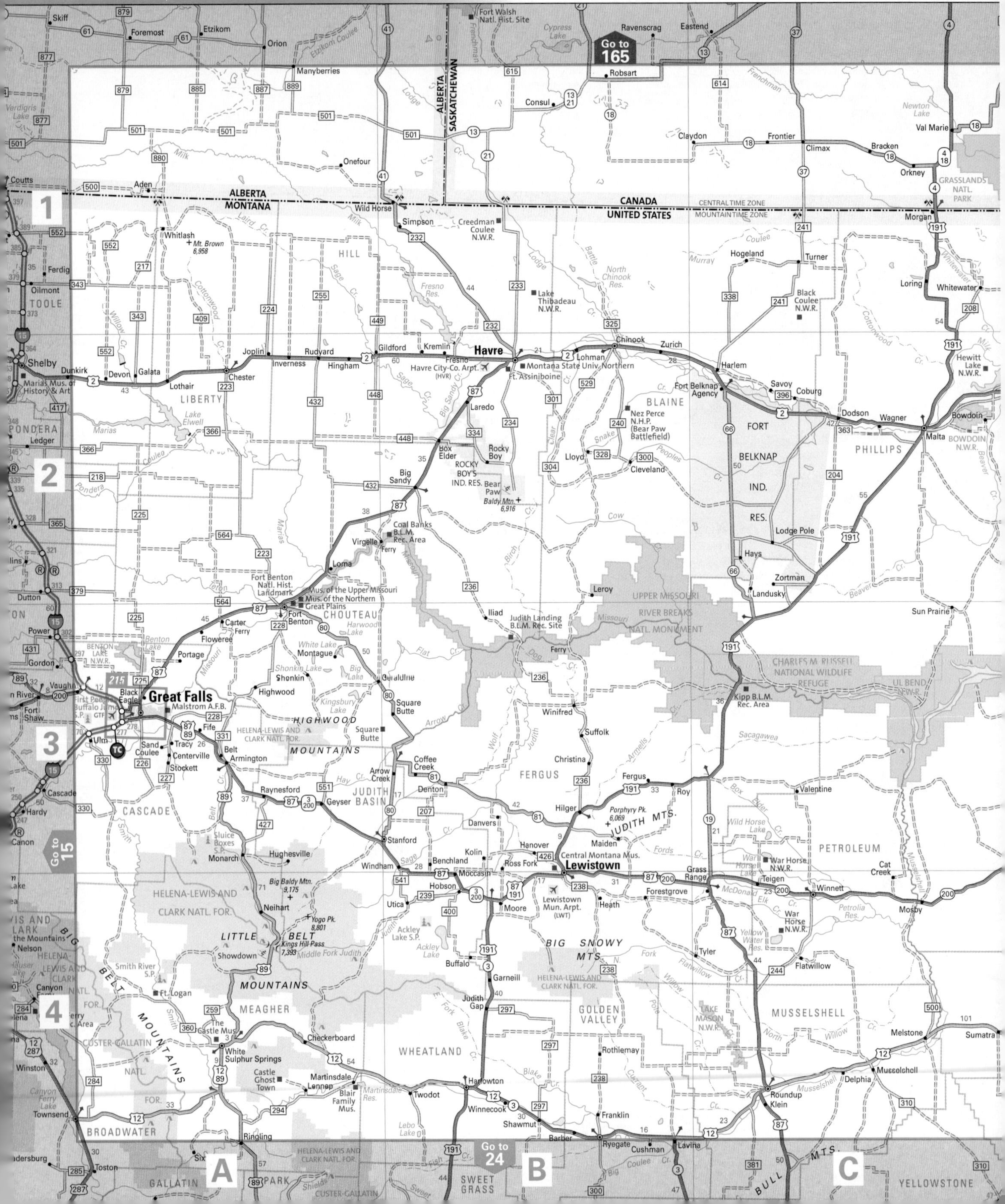

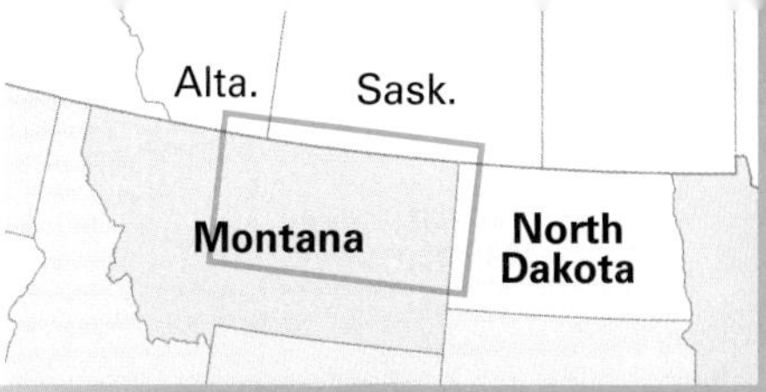

DRIVING DISTANCES IN MILES

	GLASGOW, MT	GLENDIVE, MT	GREAT FALLS, MT	HARLOWTON, MT	HAVRE, MT	LEWISTOWN, MT	MALTA, MT	MILES CITY, MT	ROUNDUP, MT	SHELBY, MT	WILLISTON, ND	WOLF POINT, MT
GLENDIVE, MT	147		351	309	306	242	217	74	219	408	106	98
GREAT FALLS, MT	277	351		133	118	109	207	329	183	82	422	326
HAVRE, MT	159	306	118	210		175	89	345	198	102	304	208
WILLISTON, ND	145	106	422	415	304	324	215	180	325	406		96

SEE ALSO DISTANCE AND DRIVING TIME MAP ON PAGES 286–287

0 mi 20 40
0 km 20 40 60

One inch equals 25.4 miles
One centimeter equals 16.1 kilometers

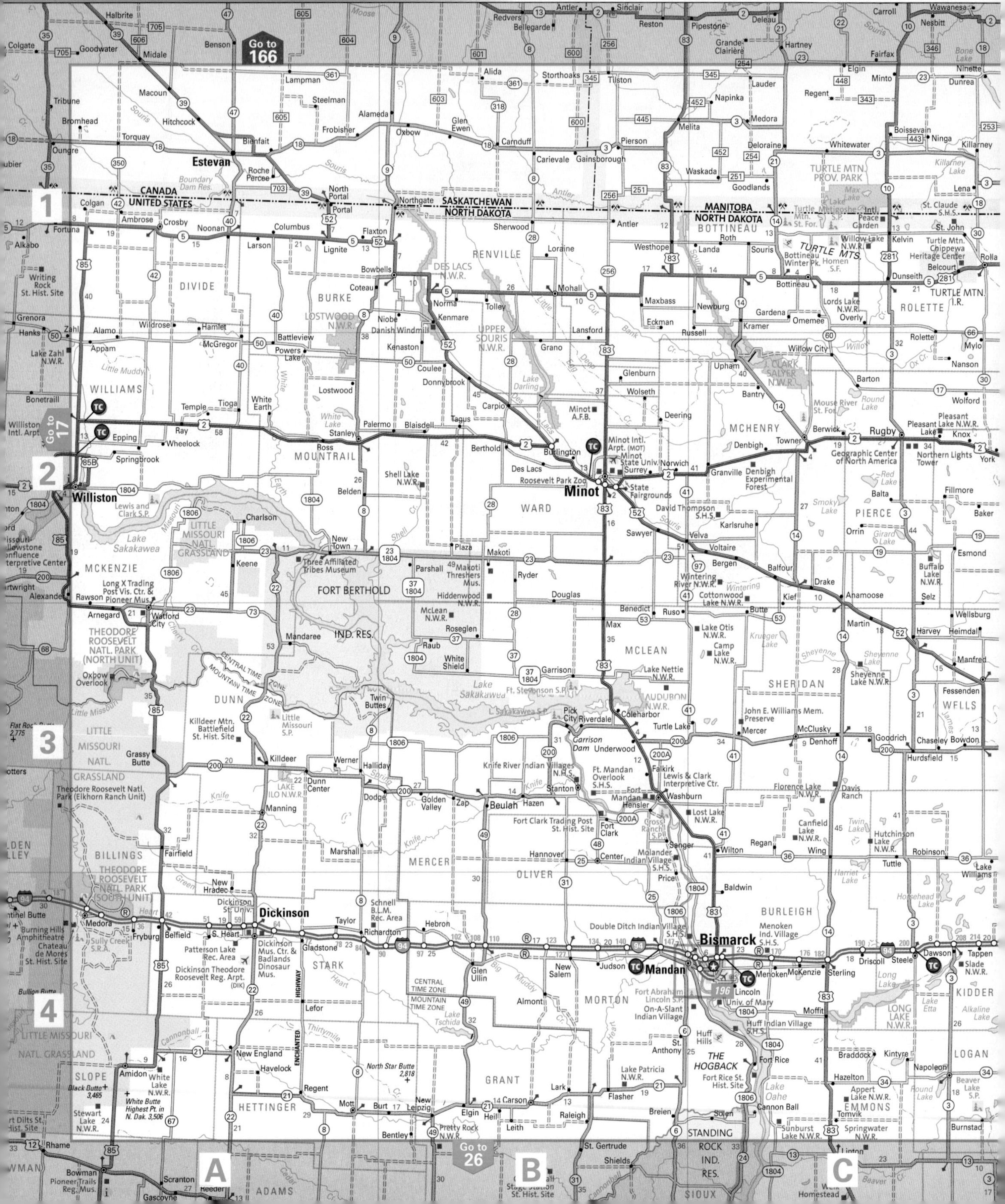

DRIVING DISTANCES IN MILES

	BISMARCK, ND	BOTTINEAU, ND	DETROIT LAKES, MN	DICKINSON, ND	FARGO, ND	GRAND FORKS, ND	JAMESTOWN, ND	MINOT, ND	PEMBINA, ND	RUGBY, ND	THIEF RIVER FALLS, MN	WILLISTON, ND
BISMARCK, ND		189	244	97	199	274	105	116	347	153	319	229
FARGO, ND	199	271	45	291		79	97	268	152	221	113	424
GRAND FORKS, ND	274	198	125	367	79		173	212	77	148	61	340
MINOT, ND	116	76	313	178	268	212	171		238	64	276	128

SEE ALSO DISTANCE AND DRIVING TIME MAP ON PAGES 286–287

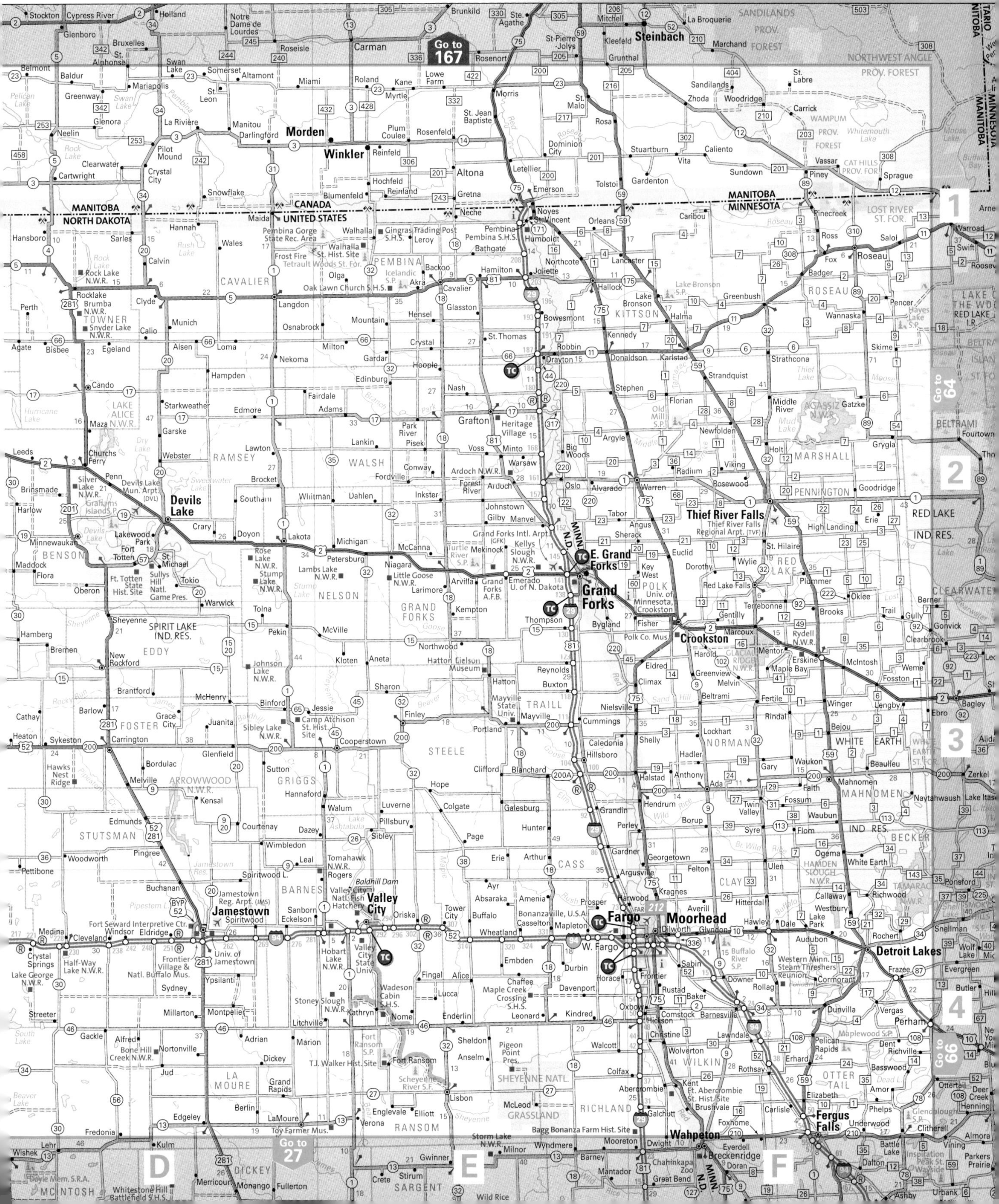

Portland OR / Eugene OR

0 mi 20 40
0 km 20 40 60

One inch equals 25.4 miles
One centimeter equals 16.1 kilometers

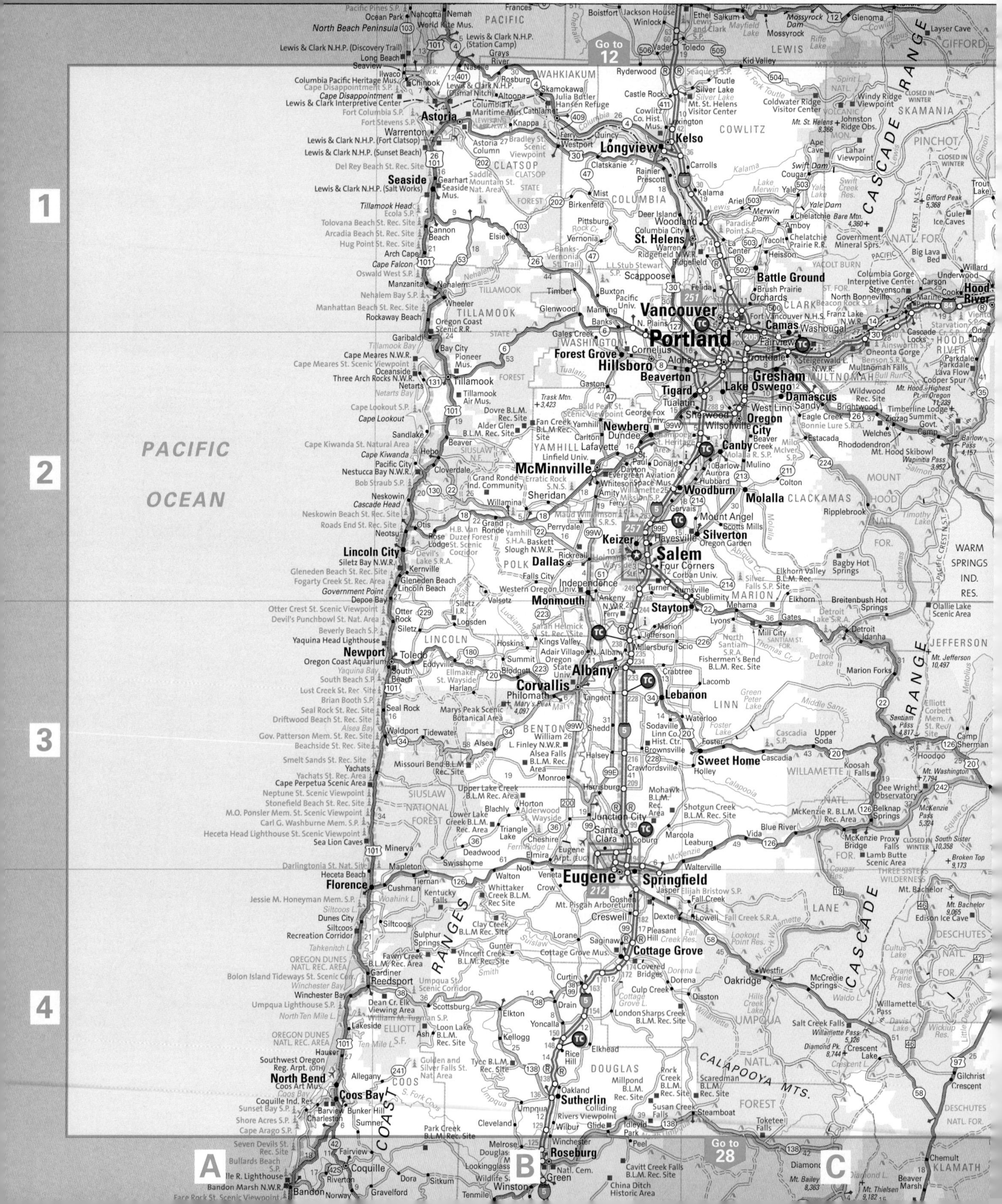

DRIVING DISTANCES IN MILES

	ASTORIA, OR	BEND, OR	BURNS, OR	COOS BAY, OR	EUGENE, OR	KENNEWICK, WA	LA GRANDE, OR	NEWPORT, OR	PORTLAND, OR	SALEM, OR	THE DALLES, OR	WALLA WALLA, WA
BEND, OR	252		142	227	115	245	295	183	158	134	137	276
EUGENE, OR	216	115	257	105		328	377	101	112	65	198	359
KENNEWICK, WA	306	245	256	440	328		111	328	212	264	131	49
PORTLAND, OR	97	158	299	224	112	212	261	116		48	82	243

SEE ALSO DISTANCE AND DRIVING TIME MAP ON PAGES 286–287

Washington
Montana
Oregon
Idaho
Wyoming

0 mi 20 40
0 km 20 40 60

One inch equals 25.4 miles
One centimeter equals 16.1 kilometers

Boise ID / La Grande OR

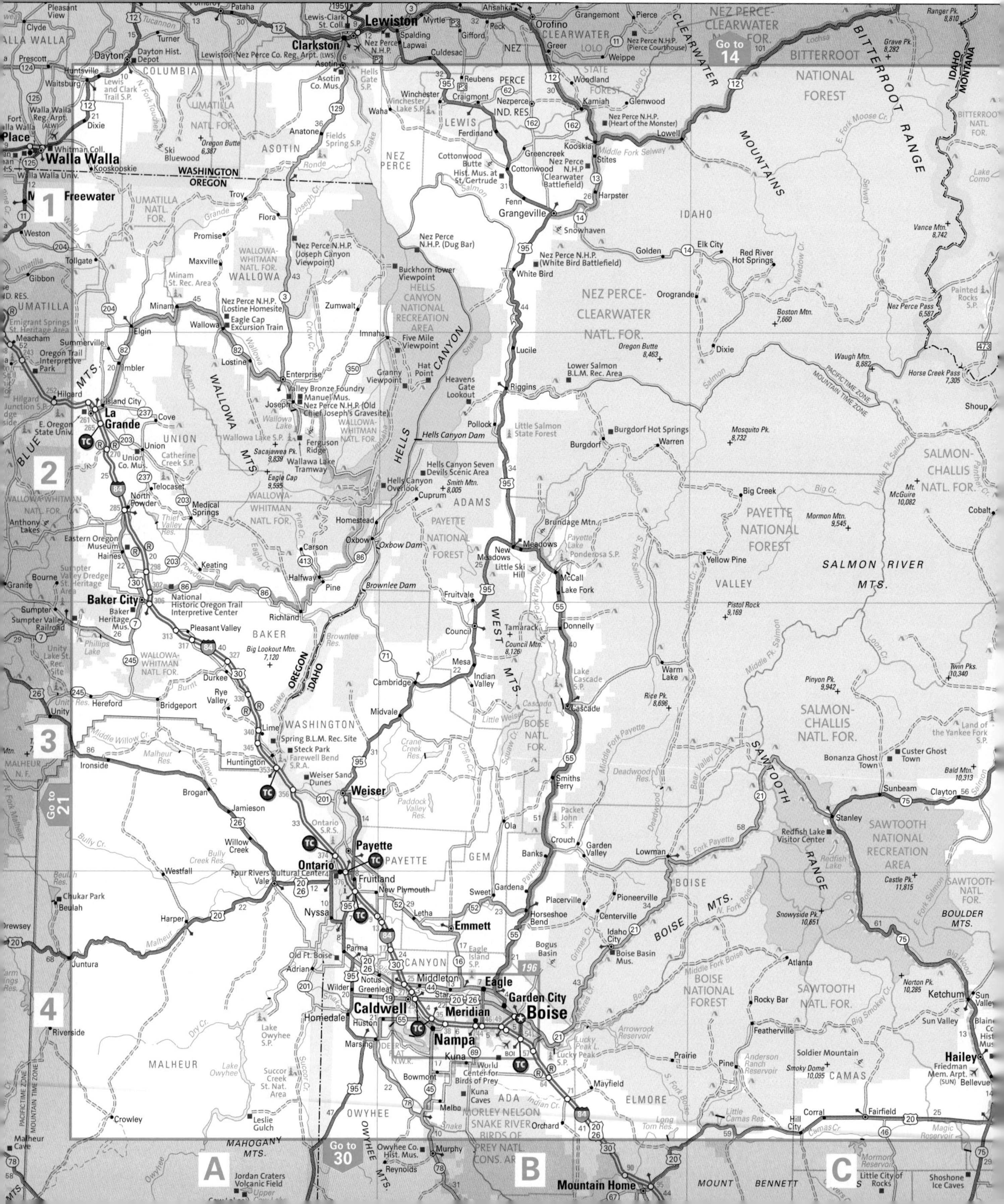
Lewiston
Clarkston
Walla Walla
Freewater
La Grande
Baker City
Enterprise
Joseph
Wallowa
Elgin
Union
Halfway
Grangeville
White Bird
Riggins
New Meadows
McCall
Donnelly
Cascade
Council
Cambridge
Weiser
Payette
Ontario
Fruitland
Vale
Nyssa
Emmett
Caldwell
Nampa
Meridian
Eagle
Garden City
Boise
Kuna
Mountain Home
Stanley
Ketchum
Hailey
Fairfield
Idaho City
Orofino
Kamiah
Kooskia
HELLS CANYON NATIONAL RECREATION AREA
NEZ PERCE-CLEARWATER NATL. FOR.
BITTERROOT NATIONAL FOREST
PAYETTE NATIONAL FOREST
SALMON-CHALLIS NATL. FOR.
BOISE NATIONAL FOREST
SAWTOOTH NATIONAL RECREATION AREA
SAWTOOTH NATL. FOR.
WALLOWA-WHITMAN NATL. FOR.
UMATILLA NATL. FOR.
WALLOWA MTS.
BLUE MTS.
SALMON RIVER MTS.
BOISE MTS.
SAWTOOTH RANGE
BITTERROOT RANGE
WEST MTS.
MORLEY NELSON SNAKE RIVER BIRDS OF PREY NATL. CONS. AREA
Go to 14
Go to 21
Go to 30
1
2
3
4
A
B
C

DRIVING DISTANCES IN MILES

	BOISE, ID	BOZEMAN, MT	BUTTE, MT	GRANGEVILLE, ID	HAMILTON, MT	IDAHO FALLS, ID	JACKSON, WY	LA GRANDE, OR	ONTARIO, OR	SALMON, ID	SUN VALLEY, ID	W. YELLOWSTONE, MT
BOISE, ID		485	486	202	339	288	378	170	58	247	163	395
BUTTE, MT	486	81		290	103	203	275	566	541	150	312	162
IDAHO FALLS, ID	288	199	203	483	272		92	455	342	168	153	109
W. YELLOWSTONE, MT	395	90	162	451	264	109	128	562	449	244	252	

SEE ALSO DISTANCE AND DRIVING TIME MAP ON PAGES 286–287

Washington
Montana
Oregon
Idaho
Wyoming

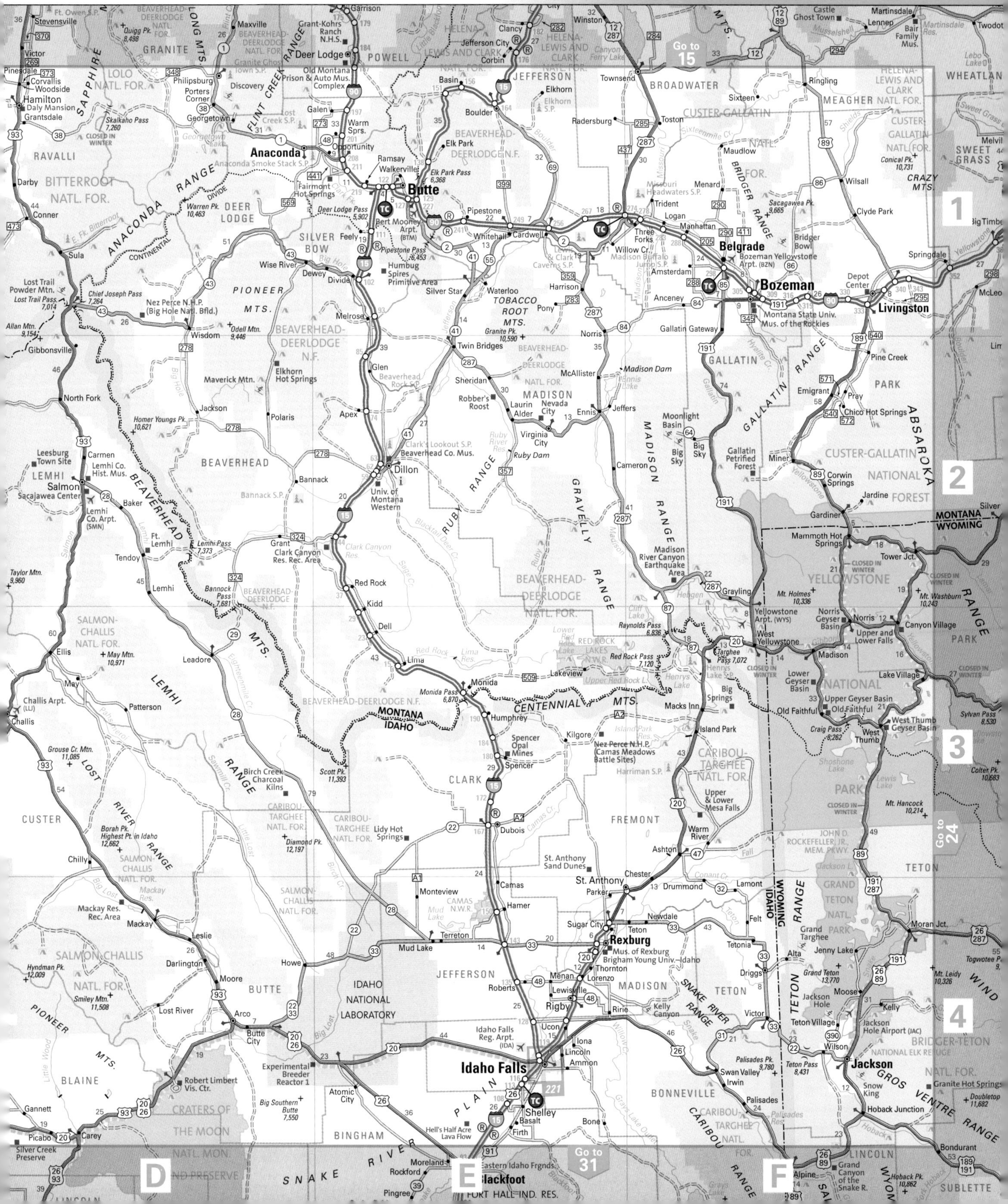
Butte
Anaconda
Deer Lodge
Bozeman
Belgrade
Livingston
Dillon
Salmon
Hamilton
Idaho Falls
Rexburg
Jackson
West Yellowstone
Blackfoot
Arco
Challis
BEAVERHEAD-DEERLODGE N.F.
CUSTER-GALLATIN NATL. FOR.
SALMON-CHALLIS NATL. FOR.
CARIBOU-TARGHEE NATL. FOR.
BITTERROOT NATL. FOR.
YELLOWSTONE NATIONAL PARK
GRAND TETON NATL. PARK
IDAHO NATIONAL LABORATORY
CRATERS OF THE MOON NATL. MON. AND PRESERVE
SNAKE RIVER PLAIN
MONTANA
IDAHO
WYOMING
Go to 15
Go to 24
Go to 31
1
2
3
4
D
E
F

0 mi 20 40
0 km 20 40 60
One inch equals 25.4 miles
One centimeter equals 16.1 kilometers

DRIVING DISTANCES IN MILES

	BILLINGS, MT	BOZEMAN, MT	BUFFALO, WY	CODY, WY	GILLETTE, WY	JACKSON, WY	MILES CITY, MT	RAPID CITY, SD	SHERIDAN, WY	SPEARFISH, SD	W. YELLOWSTONE, MT	WORLAND, WY
BILLINGS, MT		141	165	111	233	287	144	379	131	333	232	161
BUFFALO, WY	165	306		180	70	342	237	216	34	170	396	91
SPEARFISH, SD	333	474	170	350	100	512	186	53	202		564	261
W. YELLOWSTONE, MT	232	90	396	147	464	128	376	610	363	564		236

SEE ALSO DISTANCE AND DRIVING TIME MAP ON PAGES 286–287

0 mi 20 40
0 km 20 40 60
One inch equals 25.4 miles
One centimeter equals 16.1 kilometers

DRIVING DISTANCES IN MILES

	ABERDEEN, SD	BROOKINGS, SD	HOT SPRINGS, SD	HURON, SD	MITCHELL, SD	MOBRIDGE, SD	PIERRE, SD	RAPID CITY, SD	SIOUX FALLS, SD	WAHPETON, ND	WALL, SD	WATERTOWN, SD
ABERDEEN, SD		150	412	90	146	99	160	357	204	154	303	98
PIERRE, SD	160	188	247	115	155	107		193	226	301	138	189
RAPID CITY, SD	357	390	56	313	275	243	193		346	543	55	436
SIOUX FALLS, SD	204	57	401	127	73	303	226	346		210	292	103

SEE ALSO DISTANCE AND DRIVING TIME MAP ON PAGES 286–287

0 mi 20 40
0 km 20 40 60
One inch equals 25.4 miles
One centimeter equals 16.1 kilometers

Medford OR / Redding CA

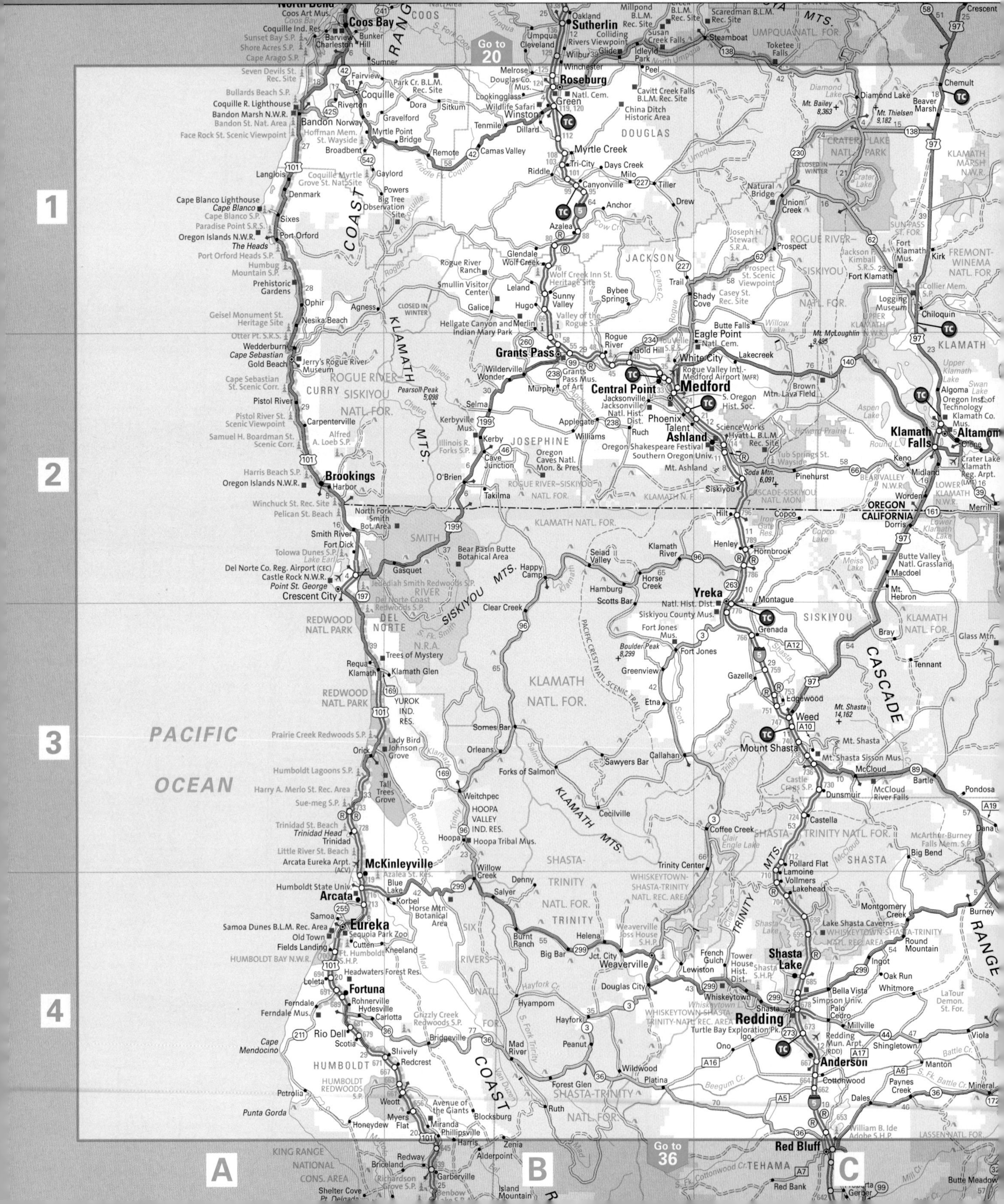

DRIVING DISTANCES IN MILES

	ALTURAS, CA	CRATER LAKE NP, OR	CRESCENT CITY, CA	EUREKA, CA	KLAMATH FALLS, OR	LAKEVIEW, OR	LASSEN VOLCANIC NP, CA	MEDFORD, OR	REDDING, CA	ROSEBURG, OR	SUSANVILLE, CA	WINNEMUCCA, NV
LAKEVIEW, OR	56	153	282	332	98		192	171	199	265	161	212
MEDFORD, OR	176	80	111	192	76	171	208		148	94	221	383
REDDING, CA	143	198	189	133	141	199	63	148		242	114	364
SUSANVILLE, CA	105	226	303	247	170	161	74	221	114	315		250

SEE ALSO DISTANCE AND DRIVING TIME MAP ON PAGES 286–287

0 mi 20 40
0 km 20 40 60
One inch equals 25.4 miles
One centimeter equals 16.1 kilometers

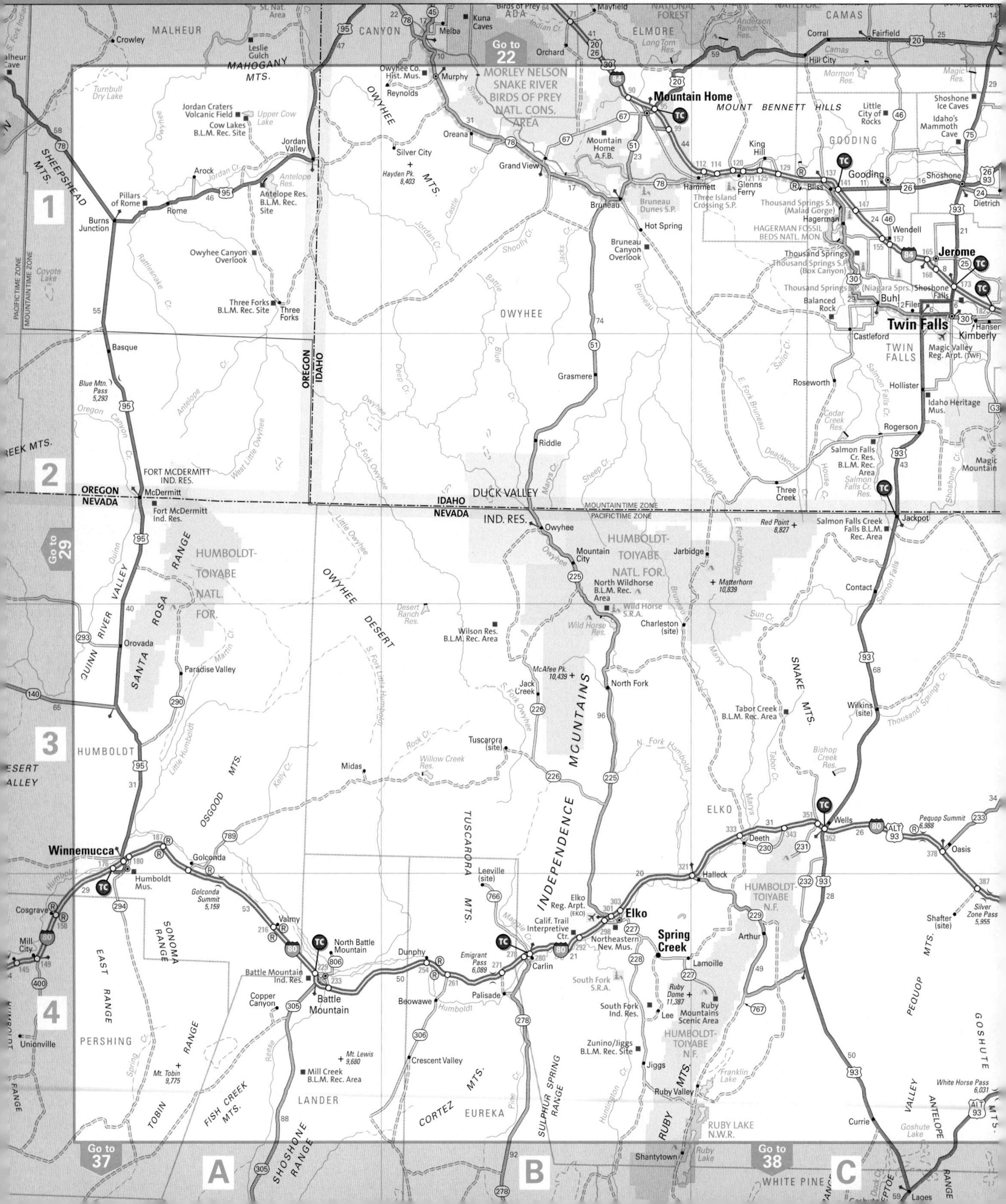

DRIVING DISTANCES IN MILES

	BRIGHAM CITY, UT	ELKO, NV	EVANSTON, WY	MONTPELIER, ID	MOUNTAIN HOME, ID	OGDEN, UT	POCATELLO, ID	PROVO, UT	SALT LAKE CITY, UT	TWIN FALLS, ID	WELLS, NV	WINNEMUCCA, NV
ELKO, NV	286		314	375	194	267	283	279	232	167	50	127
POCATELLO, ID	107	283	200	87	193	127		205	159	116	233	410
SALT LAKE CITY, UT	56	232	82	145	295	37	159	47		217	182	359
TWIN FALLS, ID	165	167	259	204	86	185	116	264	217		117	294

SEE ALSO DISTANCE AND DRIVING TIME MAP ON PAGES 286–287

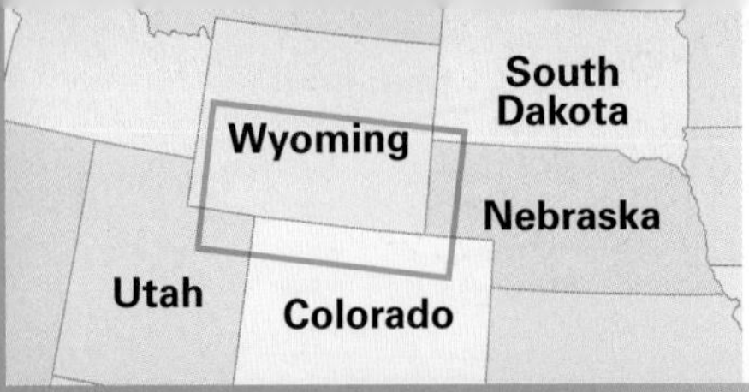

0 mi 20 40
0 km 20 40 60
One inch equals 25.4 miles
One centimeter equals 16.1 kilometers

Rock Springs WY / Craig CO

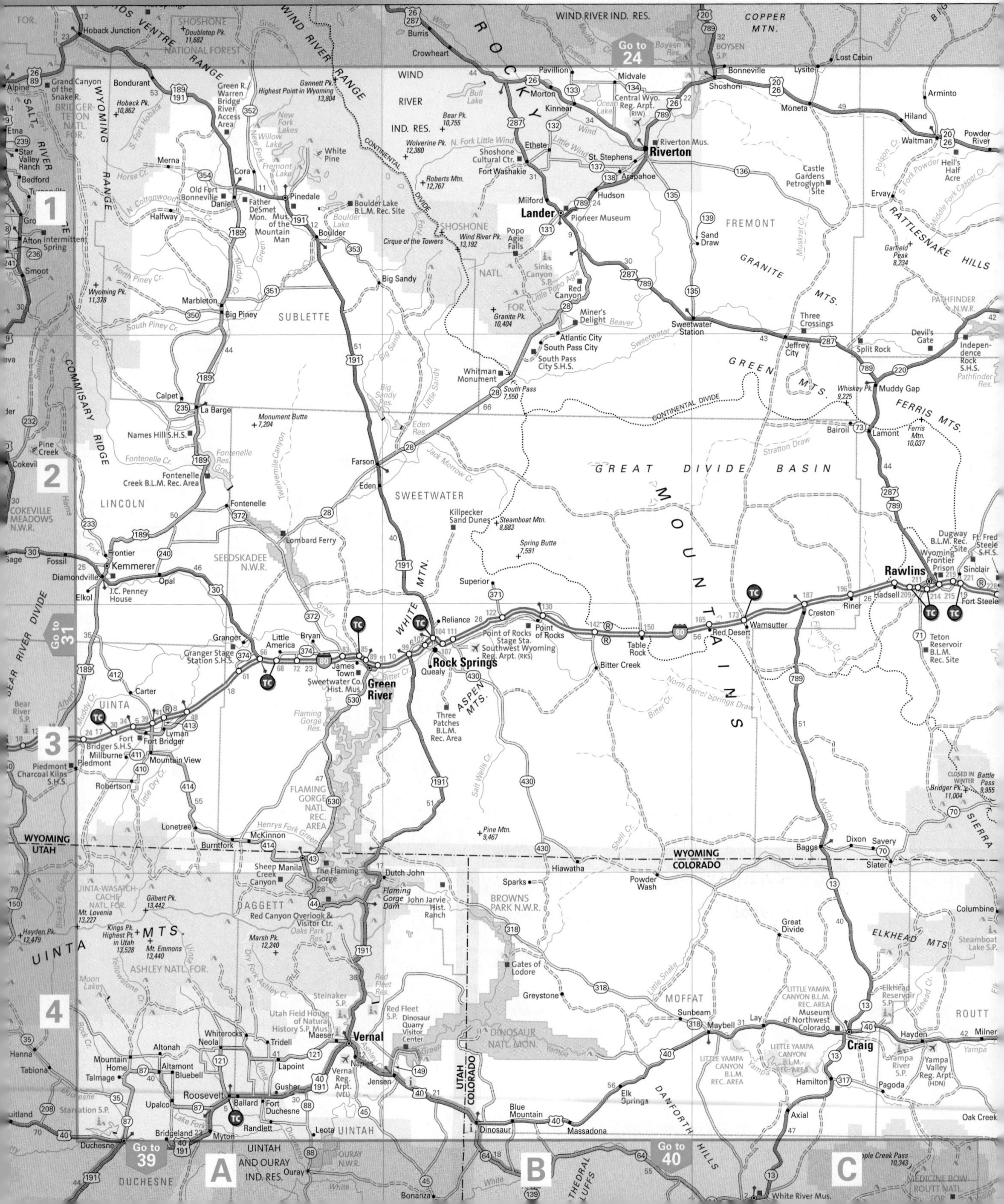

DRIVING DISTANCES IN MILES

	CASPER, WY	CHEYENNE, WY	CRAIG, CO	FORT COLLINS, CO	KEMMERER, WY	LANDER, WY	LARAMIE, WY	PINEDALE, WY	RAWLINS, WY	ROCK SPRINGS, WY	SCOTTSBLUFF, NE	VERNAL, UT
CASPER, WY		175	234	217	297	144	148	271	117	214	173	322
CHEYENNE, WY	175		221	44	342	276	52	355	151	260	111	367
CRAIG, CO	234	221		194	257	221	171	269	117	149	331	123
ROCK SPRINGS, WY	214	260	149	273	86	118	210	98	110		370	111

SEE ALSO DISTANCE AND DRIVING TIME MAP ON PAGES 286–287

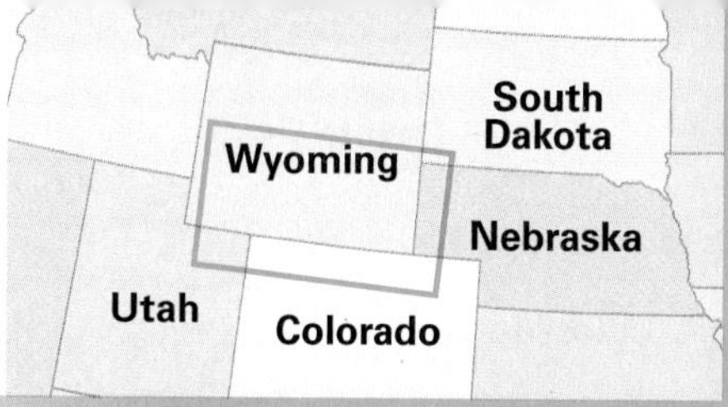

0 mi 20 40
0 km 20 40 60
One inch equals 25.4 miles
One centimeter equals 16.1 kilometers

North Platte NE / Chadron NE

DRIVING DISTANCES IN MILES

	CHADRON, NE	GRAND ISLAND, NE	LINCOLN, NE	MCCOOK, NE	NORFOLK, NE	NORTH PLATTE, NE	OGALLALA, NE	OMAHA, NE	SCOTTSBLUFF, NE	SIOUX CITY, IA	STERLING, CO	YANKTON, SD
GRAND ISLAND, NE	373		95	147	105	143	196	150	318	180	281	167
LINCOLN, NE	453	95		226	119	223	275	58	397	153	361	218
NORTH PLATTE, NE	230	143	223	67	248		53	278	175	373	138	310
OMAHA, NE	508	150	58	281	115	278	330		452	99	416	163

SEE ALSO DISTANCE AND DRIVING TIME MAP ON PAGES 286–287

0 mi 20 40
0 km 20 40 60

One inch equals 25.4 miles

One centimeter equals 16.1 kilometers

San Francisco CA / Sacramento CA

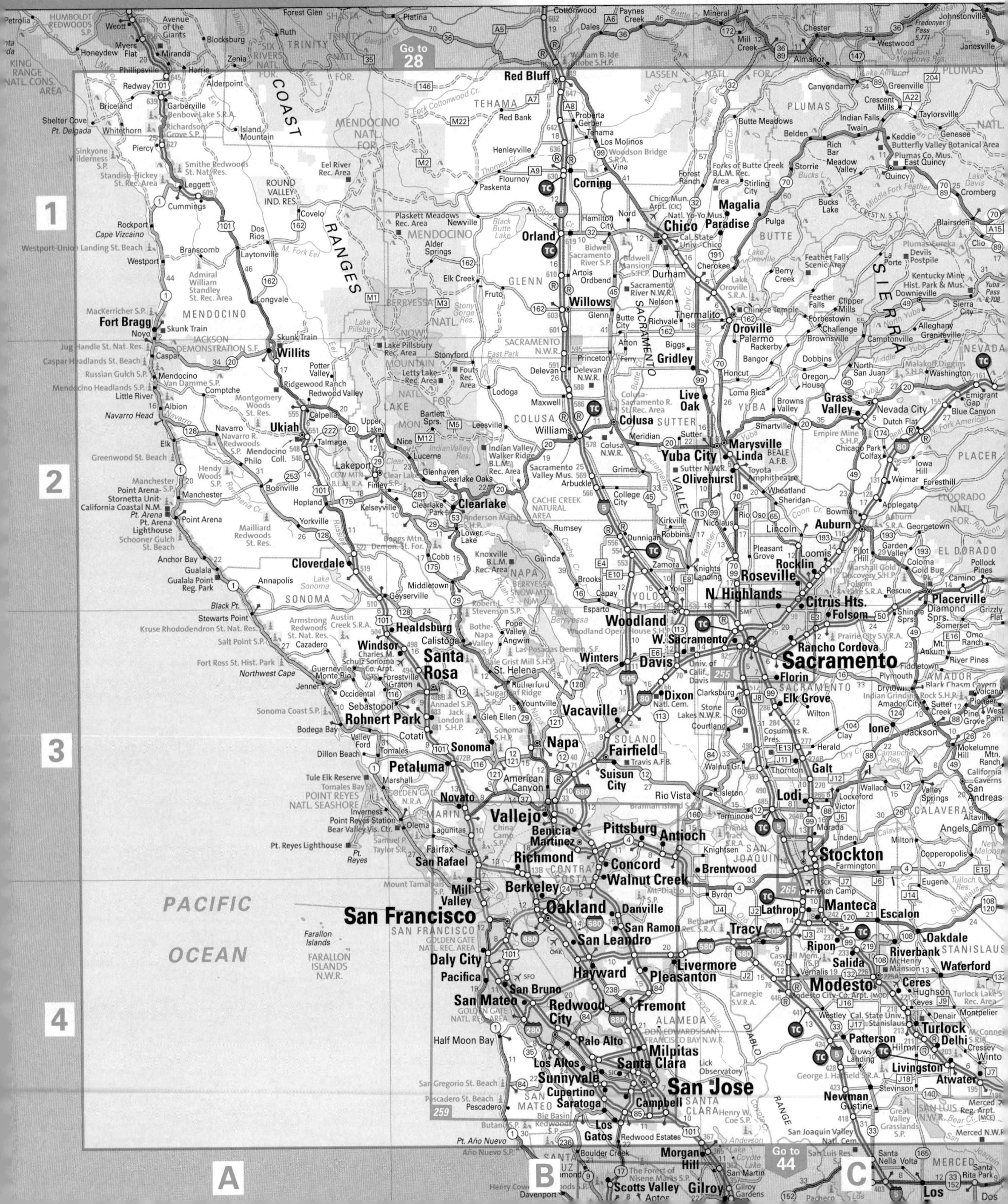

DRIVING DISTANCES IN MILES

	AUSTIN, NV	CHICO, CA	MERCED, CA	RENO, NV	SACRAMENTO, CA	SAN FRANCISCO, CA	SAN JOSE, CA	S. LAKE TAHOE, CA	STOCKTON, CA	TONOPAH, NV	UKIAH, CA	YOSEMITE VIL., CA
RENO, NV	171	164	243		132	217	245	59	177	237	261	199
SACRAMENTO, CA	302	88	118	132		87	115	100	48	329	153	170
SAN FRANCISCO, CA	387	182	131	217	87		43	185	82	352	116	183
YOSEMITE VIL., CA	280	257	79	199	170	183	168	180	123	199	289	

SEE ALSO DISTANCE AND DRIVING TIME MAP ON PAGES 286–287

California
Nevada

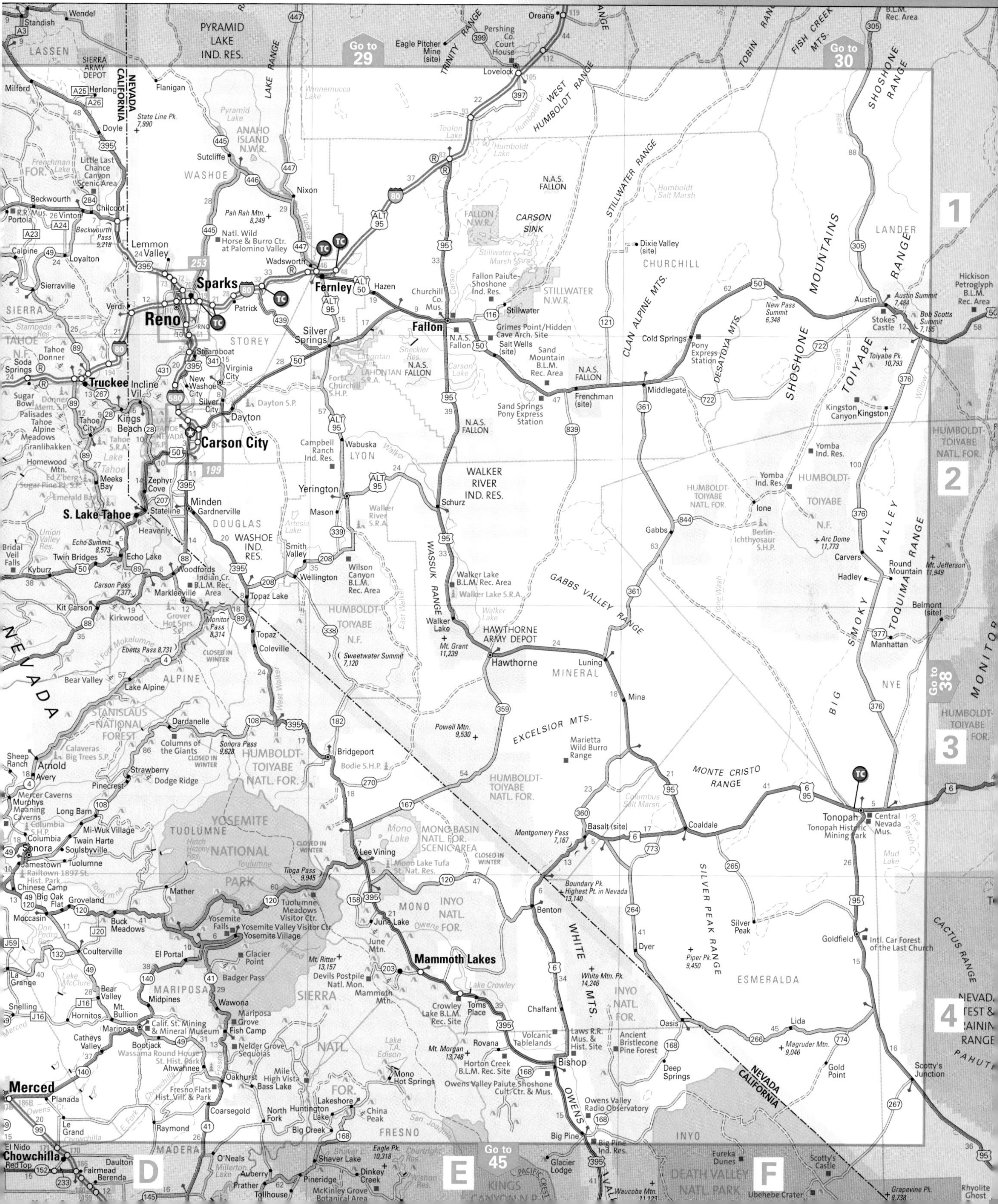
PYRAMID LAKE IND. RES.
Go to 29
Go to 30
Go to 38
Go to 45
Lovelock
Fernley
Fallon
Sparks
Reno
Carson City
Truckee
S. Lake Tahoe
Minden
Gardnerville
Yerington
Hawthorne
Tonopah
Austin
Bridgeport
Lee Vining
Mammoth Lakes
Bishop
Big Pine
Merced
Chowchilla
Sonora
Mariposa
Oakhurst
Goldfield
STOREY
LYON
DOUGLAS
WASHOE
CHURCHILL
MINERAL
ESMERALDA
NYE
ALPINE
MARIPOSA
MADERA
FRESNO
MONO
INYO
WALKER RIVER IND. RES.
HAWTHORNE ARMY DEPOT
YOSEMITE NATIONAL PARK
STANISLAUS NATIONAL FOREST
HUMBOLDT-TOIYABE NATL. FOR.
INYO NATL. FOR.
SIERRA NATL. FOR.
MONO BASIN NATL. FOR. SCENIC AREA
DEATH VALLEY NATL. PARK
STILLWATER N.W.R.
SHOSHONE MOUNTAINS
TOIYABE RANGE
TOQUIMA RANGE
BIG SMOKY VALLEY
WHITE MTS.
SILVER PEAK RANGE
MONTE CRISTO RANGE
EXCELSIOR MTS.
GABBS VALLEY RANGE
WASSUK RANGE
CLAN ALPINE MTS.
STILLWATER RANGE
WEST HUMBOLDT RANGE
CARSON SINK
NEVADA
CALIFORNIA
1
2
3
4
D
E
F

Nevada
Utah

0 mi 20 40
0 km 20 40 60
One inch equals 25.4 miles
One centimeter equals 16.1 kilometers

Ely NV / Great Basin Natl Park NV

Go to 30
Go to 37
Go to 45
Go to 46
A
B
C
1
2
3
4
SHOSHONE RANGE
TOIYABE RANGE
SMOKY VALLEY
TOQUIMA RANGE
MONITOR RANGE
HOT CREEK RANGE
FISH CREEK RANGE
SULPHUR SPRING RANGE
DIAMOND MTS.
RUBY
BUTTE MOUNTAINS
CHERRY CREEK RANGE
EGAN RANGE
STEPTOE
SCHELL CR. RANGE
ANTELOPE RANGE
SNAKE RANGE
DEEP CREEK RANGE
CONFUSION RANGE
PANCAKE RANGE
RAILROAD VALLEY
GRANT RANGE
SEAMAN RANGE
KAWICH RANGE
REVEILLE RANGE
CACTUS RANGE
BELTED RANGE
GROOM RANGE
PAHRANAGAT RANGE
PAHUTE MESA
DELAMAR MTS.
CLOVER MTS.
WILSON CREEK RANGE
LAKE VALLEY
INDIAN PEAK RANGE
LANDER
EUREKA
ELKO
WHITE PINE
NYE
LINCOLN
NEVADA
UTAH
PACIFIC TIME ZONE
MOUNTAIN TIME ZONE
Ruby Valley
HUMBOLDT-TOIYABE NATL. FOR.
RUBY LAKE N.W.R.
Shantytown
Ruby Lake
Currie
White Horse Pass 6,031
Dutch Mtn. 7,794
Gold Hill Ghost Town
Goshute Lake
Lages
Goshute Canyon and Cave
Cherry Creek
Ibapah
GOSHUTE IND. RES.
Goshute
Callao
Tippett
Ibapah Pk. 12,087
Newark Lake
Blue Mass Scenic Area
Trout Creek
Austin
Austin Summit 7,484
Stokes Castle
Bob Scotts Summit 7,195
Hickison Petroglyph B.L.M. Rec. Area
Tonkin Spring B.L.M. Rec. Area
Eureka
Eureka Sentinel Mus.
Eureka Opera House
Diamond Pk. 10,614
Summit Mtn. 10,461
Toiyabe Pk. 10,793
Little Antelope Summit 7,438
Robinson Summit 7,539
Illipah Res. B.L.M. Rec. Area
Mt. Hamilton 10,745
Steptoe (site)
McGill
Ely Arpt. (ELY)
Garnet Hill
Ruth
Ely
Lane
E. Ely
Nev. Northern Railway Mus.
Ward Mtn. B.L.M. Rec. Area
North Schell Pk. 11,883
Cleve Creek B.L.M. Rec. Site
Cave Lake S.P.
Connors Pass 7,733
Salt Marsh Lake
Gandy
Mt. Moriah 12,050
Sacramento Pass 7,136
Eskdale
Kingston Canyon
Kingston
Potts (site)
Ward Charcoal Ovens S.H.P.
Majors Place
Baker
Garrison
Wheeler Pk. 13,063
Lehman Caves
GREAT BASIN NATL. PARK
Shoshone
Pruess Lake
Duckwater
Duckwater Ind. Res.
Currant Mtn. 11,513
Currant Summit 6,999
Preston
Lund
Minerva (site)
DESERT EXPERIMENTAL RANGE
Carvers
Round Mountain
Mt. Jefferson 11,949
Hadley
Belmont (site)
Manhattan
Currant
Adams-McGill Res.
Sunnyside
Lunar Crater Volcanic Field Natl. Natural Landmark
Troy Pk. 11,298
Nyala (site)
Mt. Wilson 9,296
Warm Springs Summit 6,293
Warm Springs (site)
Tonopah
Central Nev. Mus.
Tonopah Hist. Mining Park
Michael Heizer's City
BASIN & RANGE NATIONAL MONUMENT
Spring Valley S.P.
Meadow Valley B.L.M. Rec. Site
Ursine
Hamlin Valley
Zane
Beryl
Pioche
Caselton
Echo Canyon S.P.
Cathedral Gorge S.P.
Modena
Panaca
Uvada
Mud Lake
TONOPAH TEST RANGE
Goldfield
Intl. Car Forest of the Last Church
EXTRATERRESTRIAL HIGHWAY
Queen City Summit 5,935
Tempiute (site)
Rachel
Hiko
Caliente
Caliente Railroad Depot
Kershaw-Ryan S.P.
Rainbow Canyon
Newcastle
DIXIE NATL. FOR.
Enterprise
Mountain Meadows Monument
Pinto
WASHINGTON
Lost Pk. 7,514
Beaver Dam S.P.
Central
Baker Dam B.L.M. Rec. Site
Pine Valley
NEVADA TEST & TRAINING RANGE
Ash Springs
Alamo
Delamar Lake
Elgin
Elgin Schoolhouse S.H.S.
Scotty's Junction
Groom Lake
PAHRANAGAT N.W.R.
Gunlock
Gunlock S.P.
Veyo
Snow Canyon S.P.
PAIUTE IND. RES.
Shivwits
Dixie State Univ.
Ivins
Santa Clara
Jacob Hamblin Home
St. George
Joshua Tree Natural Area
DESERT NATL. WILDLIFE REFUGE
NEVADA NATIONAL SECURITY SITE
Grapevine Pk. 8,738
Carp
MORMON MTS.
MEADOW VALLEY MTS.

DRIVING DISTANCES IN MILES	AUSTIN, NV	BAKER, NV	CEDAR CITY, UT	DELTA, UT	ELY, NV	GREEN RIVER, UT	PROVO, UT	ST. GEORGE, UT	SALINA, UT	SPRINGDALE, UT	TONOPAH, NV	TORREY, UT
ELY, NV	147	68	198	156		332	243	216	224	261	167	307
PROVO, UT	426	193	204	88	243	137		256	94	266	410	172
SALINA, UT	371	187	128	68	224	108	94	180		190	411	78
SPRINGDALE (ZION), UT	408	193	64	205	261	297	266	45	190		339	191

SEE ALSO DISTANCE AND DRIVING TIME MAP ON PAGES 286–287

Nevada
Utah

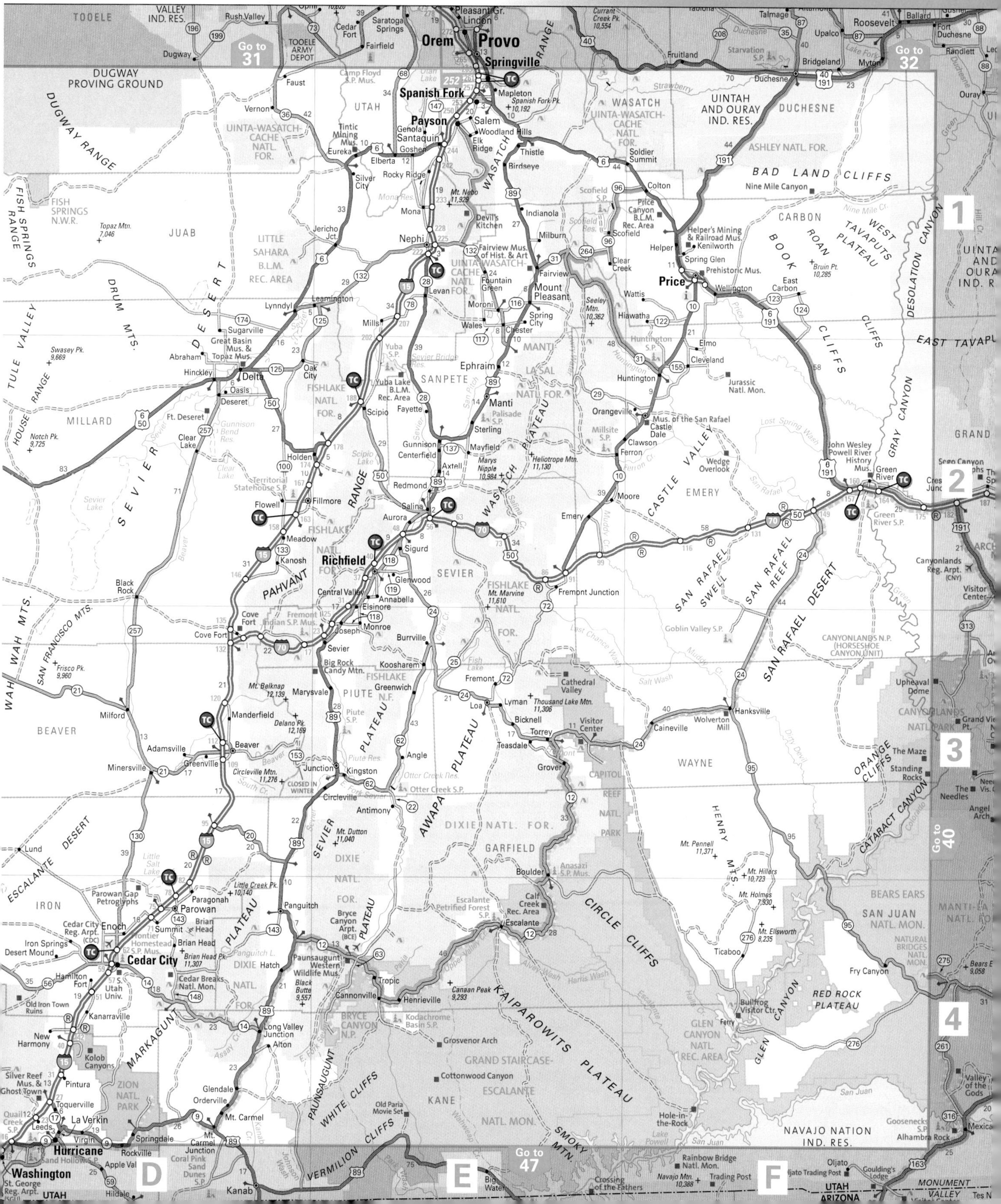
Go to 31
Go to 32
Go to 40
Go to 47
Provo
Orem
Springville
Spanish Fork
Payson
Nephi
Price
Richfield
Salina
Fillmore
Delta
Beaver
Cedar City
Parowan
Hurricane
Washington
Kanab
Green River
Hanksville
Manti
Ephraim
Panguitch
Escalante
Torrey
DUGWAY PROVING GROUND
SEVIER DESERT
ESCALANTE DESERT
WASATCH PLATEAU
SAN RAFAEL SWELL
SAN RAFAEL DESERT
KAIPAROWITS PLATEAU
CIRCLE CLIFFS
BOOK CLIFFS
ROAN CLIFFS
HENRY MTS.
GLEN CANYON NATL. REC. AREA
GRAND STAIRCASE-ESCALANTE NATL. MON.
ZION NATL. PARK
BRYCE CANYON N.P.
CAPITOL REEF NATL. PARK
CANYONLANDS NATL. PARK
DIXIE NATL. FOR.
FISHLAKE NATL. FOR.
MANTI-LA SAL NATL. FOR.
UINTAH AND OURAY IND. RES.
NAVAJO NATION IND. RES.
JUAB
MILLARD
SANPETE
SEVIER
EMERY
WAYNE
GARFIELD
BEAVER
IRON
KANE
CARBON
DUCHESNE
UTAH
1
2
3
4
D
E
F

Utah
Colorado

0 mi 20 40
0 km 20 40 60
One inch equals 25.4 miles
One centimeter equals 16.1 kilometers

Grand Junction CO / Durango CO

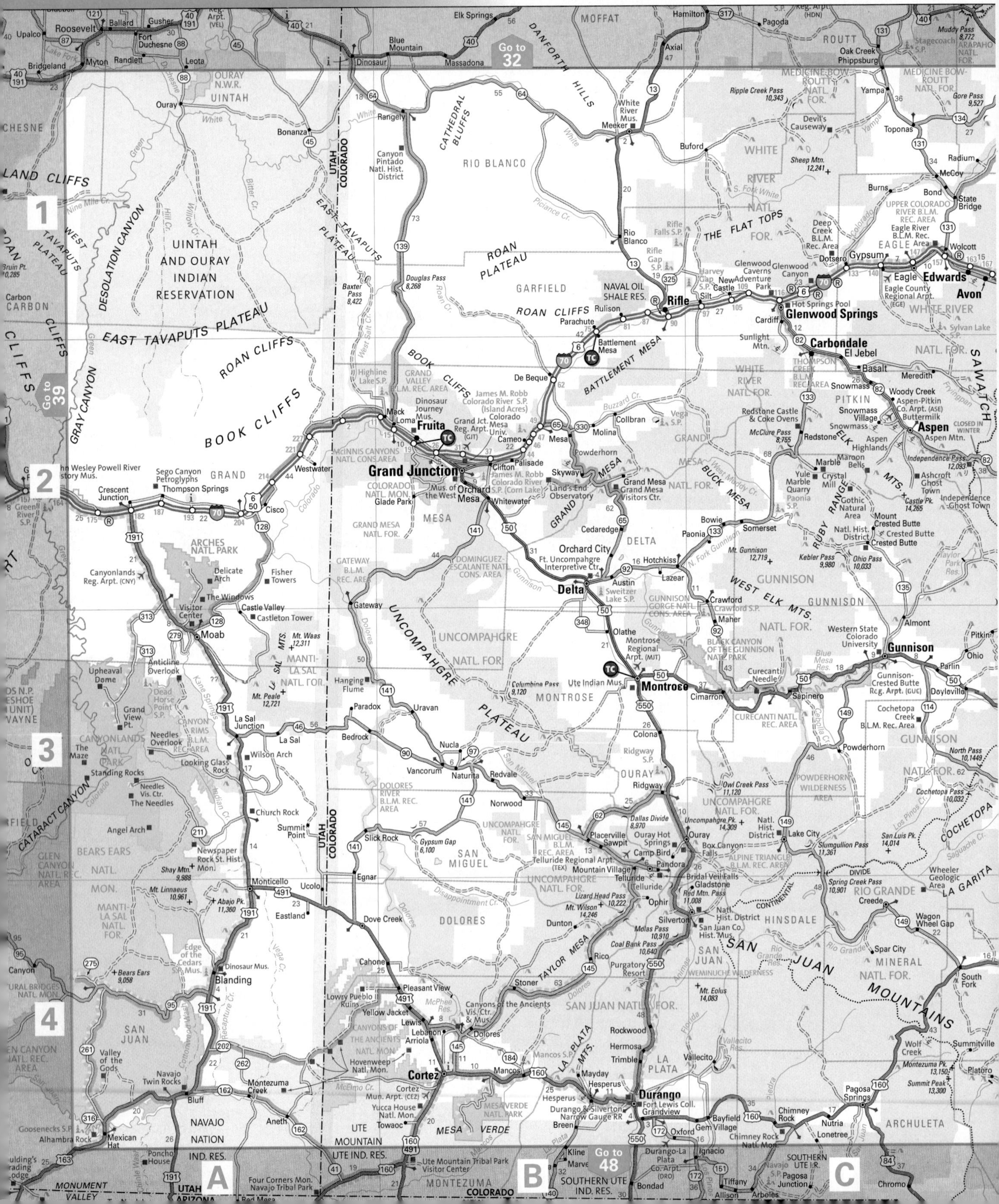
1
2
3
4
A
B
C
Go to 32
Go to 39
Go to 48
UTAH
COLORADO
MOFFAT
ROUTT
RIO BLANCO
GARFIELD
MESA
DELTA
MONTROSE
OURAY
SAN MIGUEL
DOLORES
HINSDALE
SAN JUAN
LA PLATA
MONTEZUMA
ARCHULETA
MINERAL
GUNNISON
PITKIN
EAGLE
GRAND
UINTAH
UINTAH AND OURAY INDIAN RESERVATION
NAVAJO NATION
UTE MOUNTAIN UTE IND. RES.
SOUTHERN UTE IND. RES.
BOOK CLIFFS
ROAN CLIFFS
ROAN PLATEAU
EAST TAVAPUTS PLATEAU
WEST TAVAPUTS PLATEAU
DESOLATION CANYON
GRAY CANYON
CATHEDRAL BLUFFS
DANFORTH HILLS
THE FLAT TOPS
BATTLEMENT MESA
GRAND MESA
UNCOMPAHGRE PLATEAU
WEST ELK MTS.
RUBY RANGE
SAN JUAN MOUNTAINS
LA PLATA MTS.
TAYLOR MESA
MESA VERDE
COCHETOPA
LA GARITA
SAWATCH
CATARACT CANYON
ARCHES NATL. PARK
CANYONLANDS NATL. PARK
MESA VERDE NATL. PARK
BLACK CANYON OF THE GUNNISON NATL. PARK
COLORADO NATL. MON.
CANYONS OF THE ANCIENTS NATL. MON.
BEARS EARS NATL. MON.
MANTI-LA SAL NATL. FOR.
WHITE RIVER NATL. FOR.
GRAND MESA NATL. FOR.
GUNNISON NATL. FOR.
UNCOMPAHGRE NATL. FOR.
SAN JUAN NATL. FOR.
RIO GRANDE NATL. FOR.
CURECANTI NATL. REC. AREA
Grand Junction
Fruita
Delta
Montrose
Gunnison
Glenwood Springs
Rifle
Aspen
Carbondale
Eagle
Edwards
Avon
Meeker
Rangely
Dinosaur
Vernal
Roosevelt
Moab
Monticello
Blanding
Bluff
Cortez
Durango
Pagosa Springs
Telluride
Ouray
Silverton
Ridgway
Paonia
Hotchkiss
Cedaredge
Palisade
Clifton
Orchard Mesa
Nucla
Naturita
Dove Creek
Dolores
Mancos
Bayfield
Ignacio
Creede
Lake City
Crescent Junction
Green River
Thompson Springs
Cisco
La Sal
Parachute
De Beque
Silt
New Castle
Basalt
Snowmass Village
Crested Butte
Ouray N.W.R.
Douglas Pass 8,268
Baxter Pass 8,422
McClure Pass 8,755
Independence Pass 12,093
Red Mtn. Pass 11,008
Molas Pass 10,910
Coal Bank Pass 10,640
Lizard Head Pass 10,222
Dallas Divide 8,970
Mt. Peale 12,721
Mt. Waas 12,311
Mt. Wilson 14,246
Uncompahgre Pk. 14,309
Mt. Eolus 14,083
Continental Divide
MONUMENT VALLEY
UTAH ARIZONA

DRIVING DISTANCES IN MILES

	ALAMOSA, CO	ASPEN, CO	COLORADO SPRS., CO	CORTEZ, CO	DENVER, CO	DURANGO, CO	GRAND JUNCTION, CO	GREEN RIVER, UT	MOAB, UT	MONTROSE, CO	PUEBLO, CO	TRINIDAD, CO
COLORADO SPRS., CO	162	157		359	70	314	318	418	404	236	43	127
DENVER, CO	230	164	70	452		337	250	350	337	277	111	196
DURANGO, CO	152	244	314	45	337		169	214	160	107	271	260
GRAND JUNCTION, CO	261	135	318	203	250	169		102	88	62	360	444

SEE ALSO DISTANCE AND DRIVING TIME MAP ON PAGES 286–287

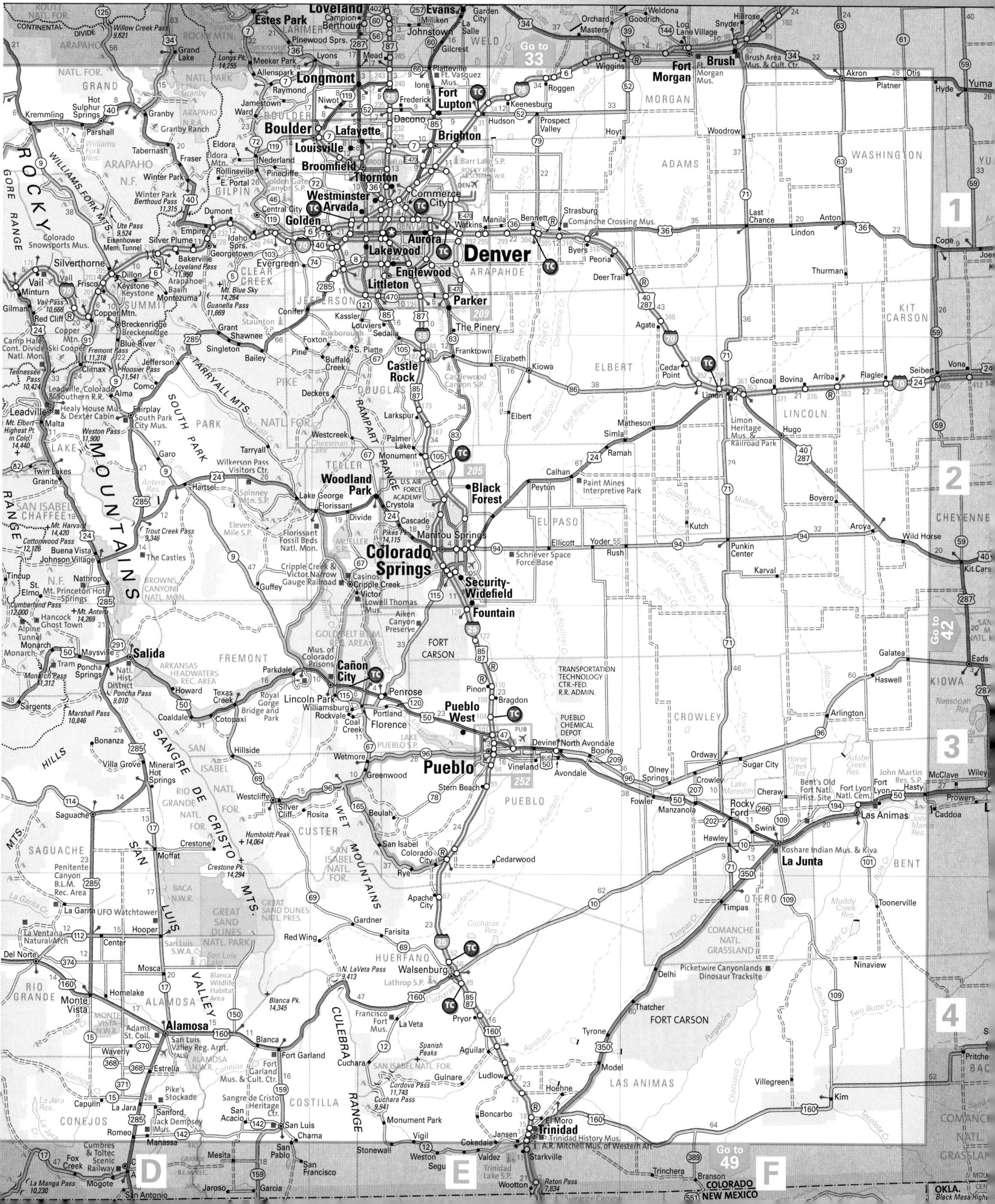

0 mi 20 40
0 km 20 40 60
One inch equals 25.4 miles
One centimeter equals 16.1 kilometers

Garden City KS / Dodge City KS

DRIVING DISTANCES IN MILES

	BURLINGTON, CO	DODGE CITY, KS	EMPORIA, KS	GARDEN CITY, KS	HAYS, KS	LAMAR, CO	MANHATTAN, KS	McCOOK, NE	OAKLEY, KS	SALINA, KS	TOPEKA, KS	WICHITA, KS
GARDEN CITY, KS	167	52	290		139	98	272	167	79	204	311	205
OAKLEY, KS	88	136	293	79	87	156	247	88		179	286	268
SALINA, KS	266	164	118	204	93	335	72	240	179		111	92
WICHITA, KS	354	153	85	205	181	303	131	329	268	92	137	

SEE ALSO DISTANCE AND DRIVING TIME MAP ON PAGES 286–287

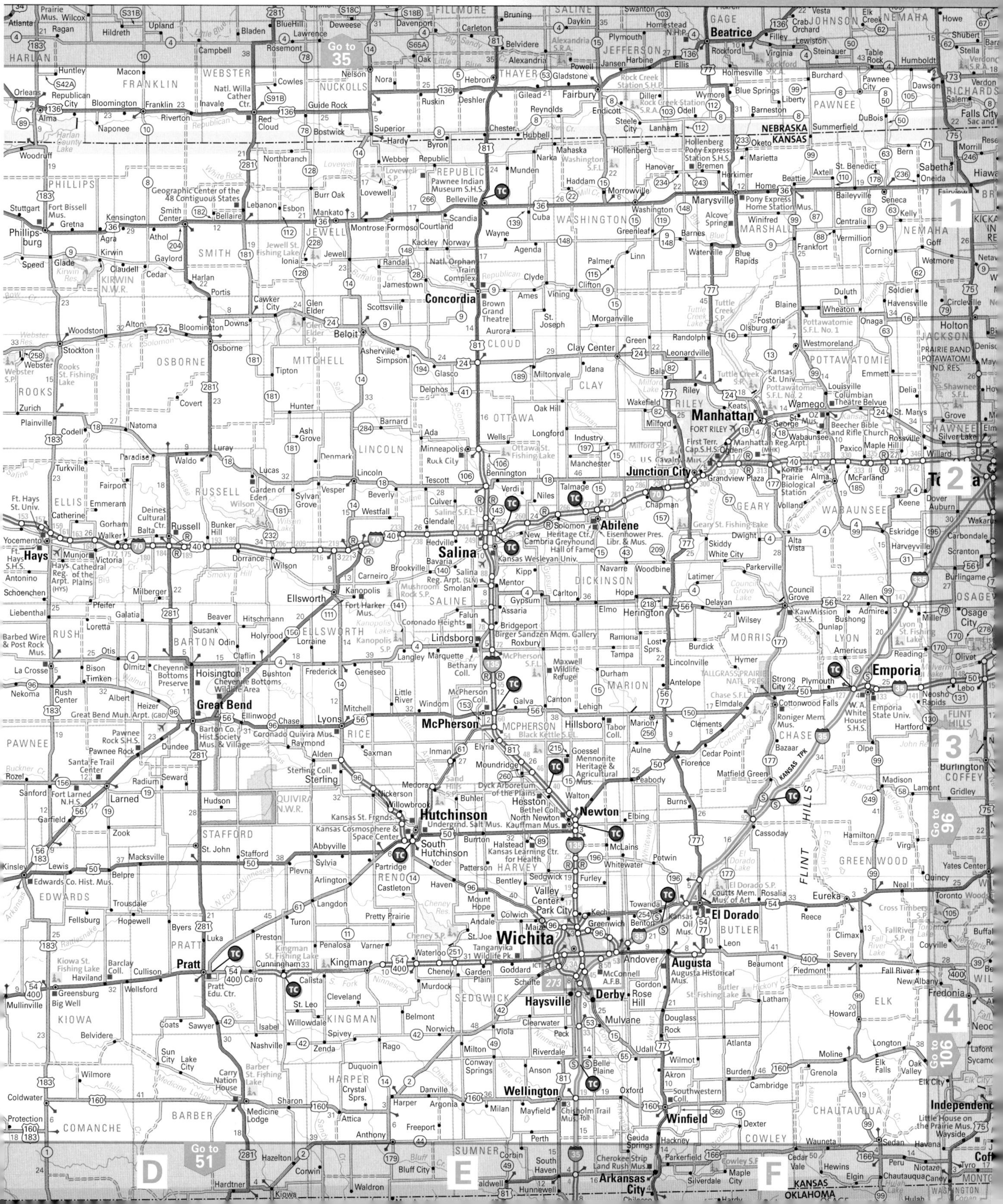

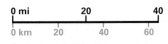

0 mi 20 40
0 km 20 40 60
One inch equals 25.4 miles
One centimeter equals 16.1 kilometers

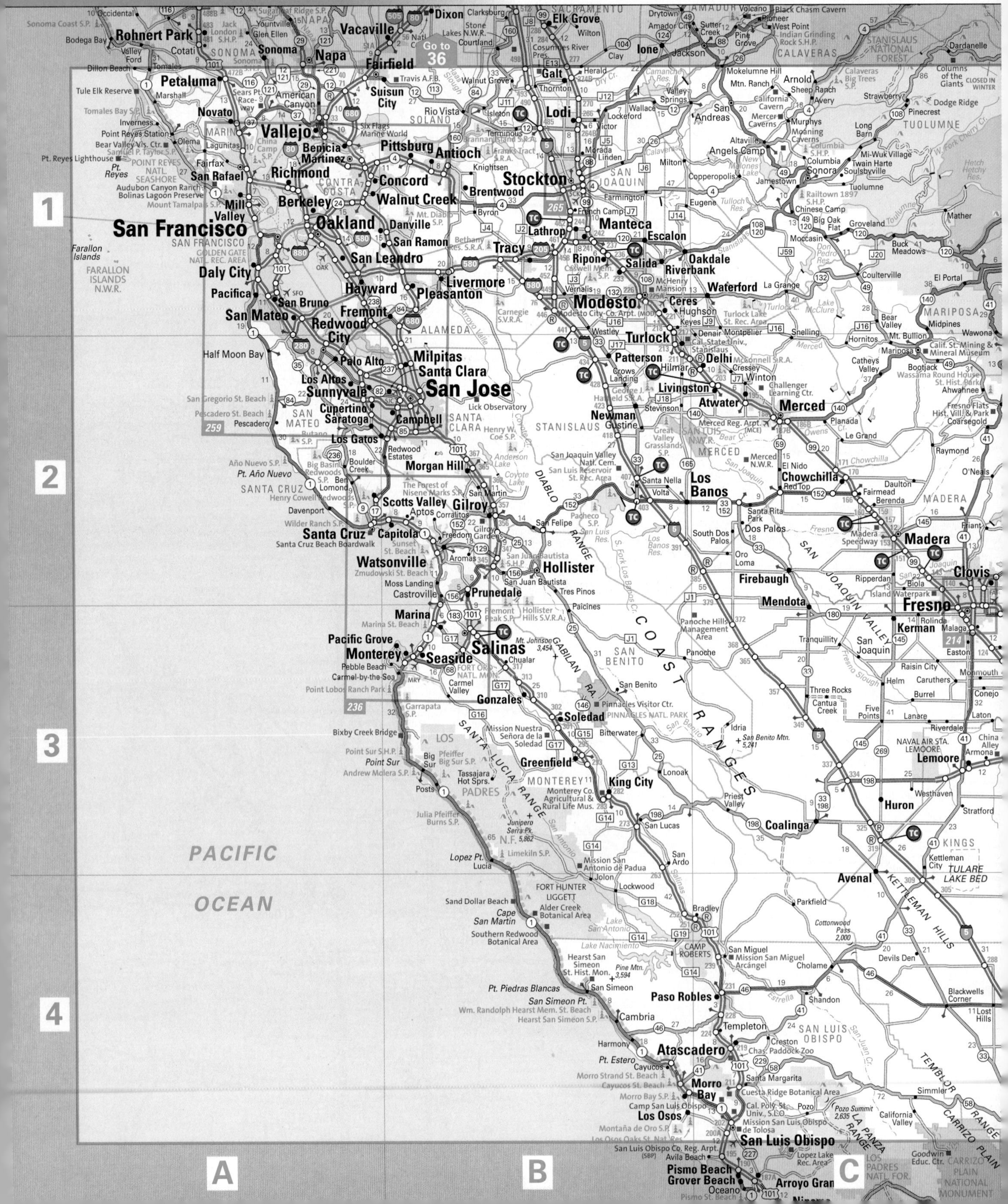

DRIVING DISTANCES IN MILES

	BAKERSFIELD, CA	BISHOP, CA	DEATH VALLEY, CA	FRESNO, CA	RIDGECREST, CA	SALINAS, CA	SAN FRANCISCO, CA	SAN JOSE, CA	SAN LUIS OBISPO, CA	STOCKTON, CA	TONOPAH, NV	YOSEMITE VIL., CA
BAKERSFIELD, CA		215	236	111	99	209	287	245	119	243	318	200
BISHOP, CA	215		169	219	141	302	283	269	333	223	119	130
FRESNO, CA	111	219	333		196	145	190	153	134	130	288	90
SAN JOSE, CA	245	269	437	153	344	61	43		191	68	338	168

SEE ALSO DISTANCE AND DRIVING TIME MAP ON PAGES 286–287

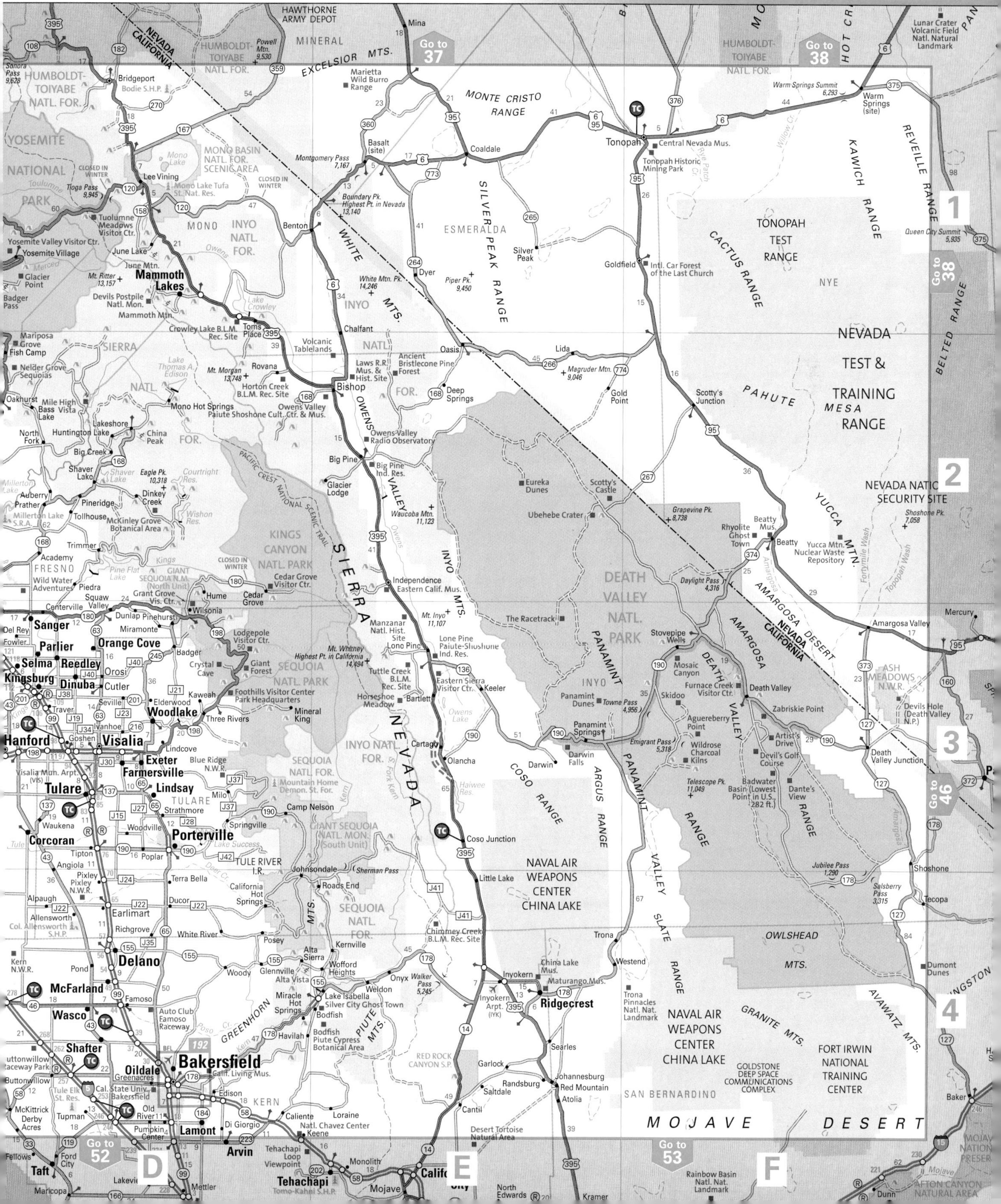

Nevada
Utah
California
Arizona

0 mi 20 40
0 km 20 40 60
One inch equals 25.4 miles
One centimeter equals 16.1 kilometers

Las Vegas NV / St George UT

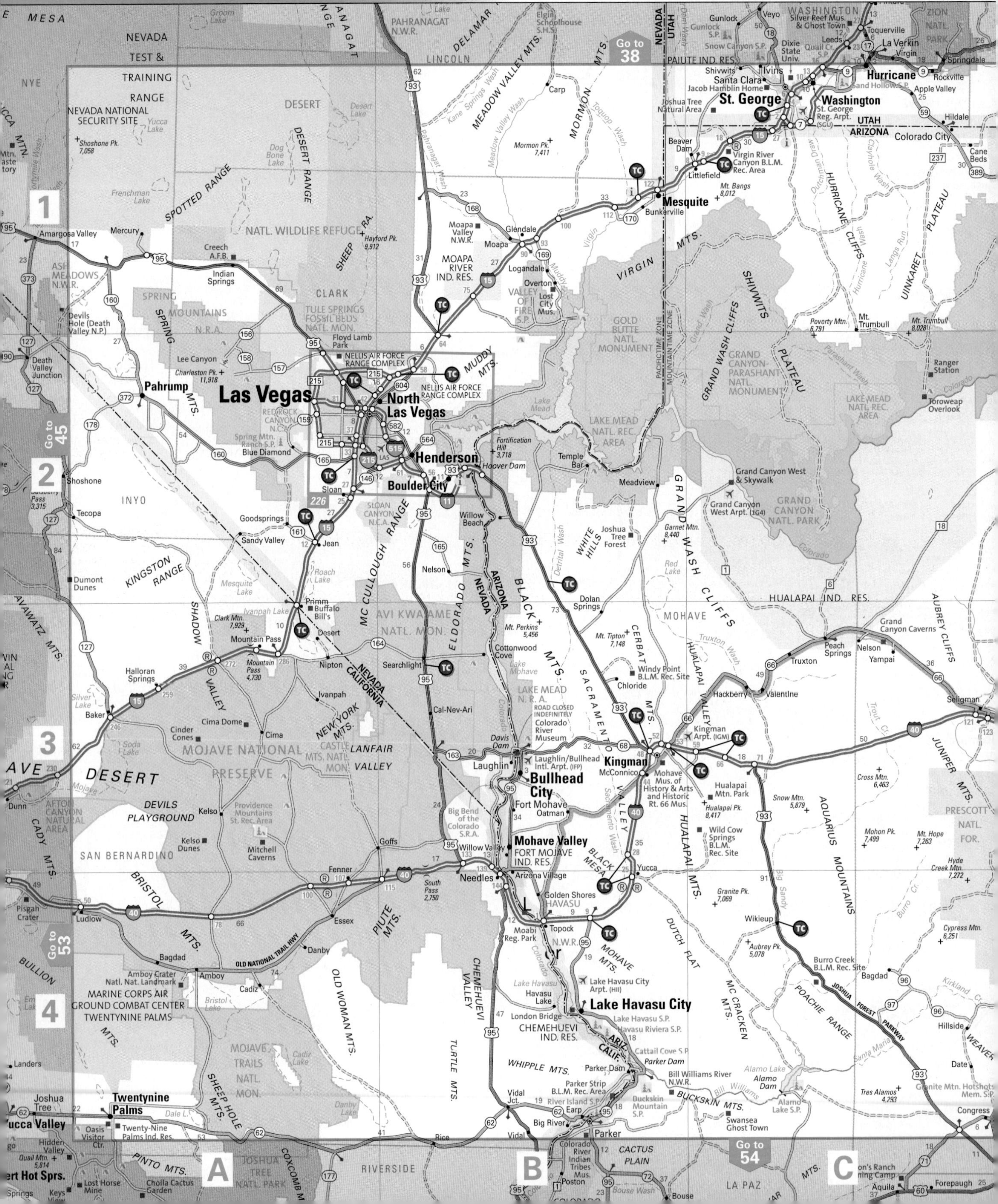
Las Vegas
North Las Vegas
Henderson
Boulder City
St. George
Washington
Hurricane
Mesquite
Kingman
Bullhead City
Laughlin
Needles
Mohave Valley
Lake Havasu City
Parker
Pahrump
Twentynine Palms
Yucca Valley
NEVADA TEST & TRAINING RANGE
NEVADA NATIONAL SECURITY SITE
NATL. WILDLIFE REFUGE
SPRING MOUNTAINS N.R.A.
LAKE MEAD NATL. REC. AREA
GRAND CANYON-PARASHANT NATL. MONUMENT
GOLD BUTTE NATL. MONUMENT
GRAND CANYON NATL. PARK
HUALAPAI IND. RES.
MOJAVE NATIONAL PRESERVE
MOJAVE TRAILS NATL. MON.
MARINE CORPS AIR GROUND COMBAT CENTER TWENTYNINE PALMS
AVI KWA AME NATL. MON.
SLOAN CANYON N.C.A.
RED ROCK CANYON N.C.A.
CHEMEHUEVI IND. RES.
FORT MOJAVE IND. RES.
NELLIS AIR FORCE RANGE COMPLEX
Hoover Dam
Davis Dam
Parker Dam
Grand Canyon West & Skywalk
Go to 38
Go to 45
Go to 53
Go to 54
1
2
3
4
A
B
C
NEVADA
UTAH
ARIZONA
CALIFORNIA
PACIFIC TIME ZONE
MOUNTAIN TIME ZONE

DRIVING DISTANCES IN MILES

	CHINLE, AZ	FLAGSTAFF, AZ	GRAND CANYON, AZ	HOLBROOK, AZ	KAYENTA, AZ	KINGMAN, AZ	LAKE HAVASU CITY, AZ	LAS VEGAS, NV	LAUGHLIN, NV	PAGE, AZ	PRESCOTT, AZ	ST. GEORGE, UT
FLAGSTAFF, AZ	216		89	93	152	148	209	249	182	135	89	271
GRAND CANYON, AZ	232	89		182	153	175	236	276	209	136	131	272
LAS VEGAS, NV	465	249	276	341	374	103	154		94	277	251	118
ST. GEORGE, UT	358	271	272	353	255	221	272	118	212	159	369	

SEE ALSO DISTANCE AND DRIVING TIME MAP ON PAGES 286–287

Utah
Colorado
Arizona
New Mexico
Okla.
Texas

0 mi 20 40
0 km 20 40 60
One inch equals 25.4 miles
One centimeter equals 16.1 kilometers

Albuquerque NM / Farmington NM

Durango
Farmington
Aztec
Bloomfield
Shiprock
Gallup
Grants
Albuquerque
Rio Rancho
Los Alamos
Española
Los Lunas
Belen
Socorro
Cuba
Chama
Dulce
Pagosa Springs
Chinle
St. Johns
Springerville
Eagar
Quemado
Magdalena
Bernalillo
Corrales
Milan
UTAH
ARIZONA
COLORADO
NEW MEXICO
ARIZONA NEW MEXICO
SAN JUAN
MONTEZUMA
LA PLATA
ARCHULETA
CONEJOS
RIO ARRIBA
SANDOVAL
MCKINLEY
CIBOLA
BERNALILLO
VALENCIA
SOCORRO
CATRON
APACHE
NAVAJO NATION INDIAN RES.
UTE MOUNTAIN UTE IND. RES.
SOUTHERN UTE IND. RES.
JICARILLA APACHE IND. RES.
ZUNI IND. RES.
NAVAJO (RAMAH) IND. RES.
ACOMA PUEBLO
LAGUNA PUEBLO
ISLETA PUEBLO
CHACO CULTURE N.H.P.
CHUSKA MTS.
ZUNI MTS.
JEMEZ MTS.
DATIL MTS.
GALLINAS MTS.
BEAR MTS.
NORTH PLAINS
CHACO MESA
SAN JUAN BASIN
Go to 40
Go to 47
Go to 56
1
2
3
4
A
B
C

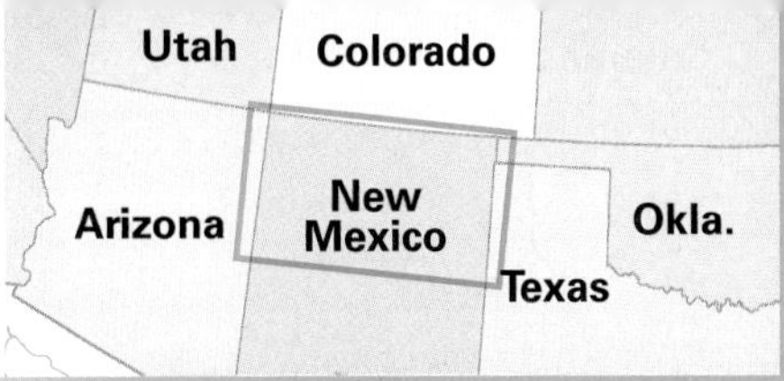

DRIVING DISTANCES IN MILES

	ALBUQUERQUE, NM	CLAYTON, NM	CLOVIS, NM	DURANGO, CO	FARMINGTON, NM	GALLUP, NM	SANTA FE, NM	SOCORRO, NM	TAOS, NM	TRINIDAD, CO	TUCUMCARI, NM	VAUGHN, NM
ALBUQUERQUE, NM		266	220	212	181	141	55	77	123	242	174	104
FARMINGTON, NM	181	368	401	50		120	205	263	211	300	355	284
SANTA FE, NM	55	216	213	207	205	197		132	68	192	167	96
TUCUMCARI, NM	174	111	82	386	355	316	167	251	195	198		98

SEE ALSO DISTANCE AND DRIVING TIME MAP ON PAGES 286–287

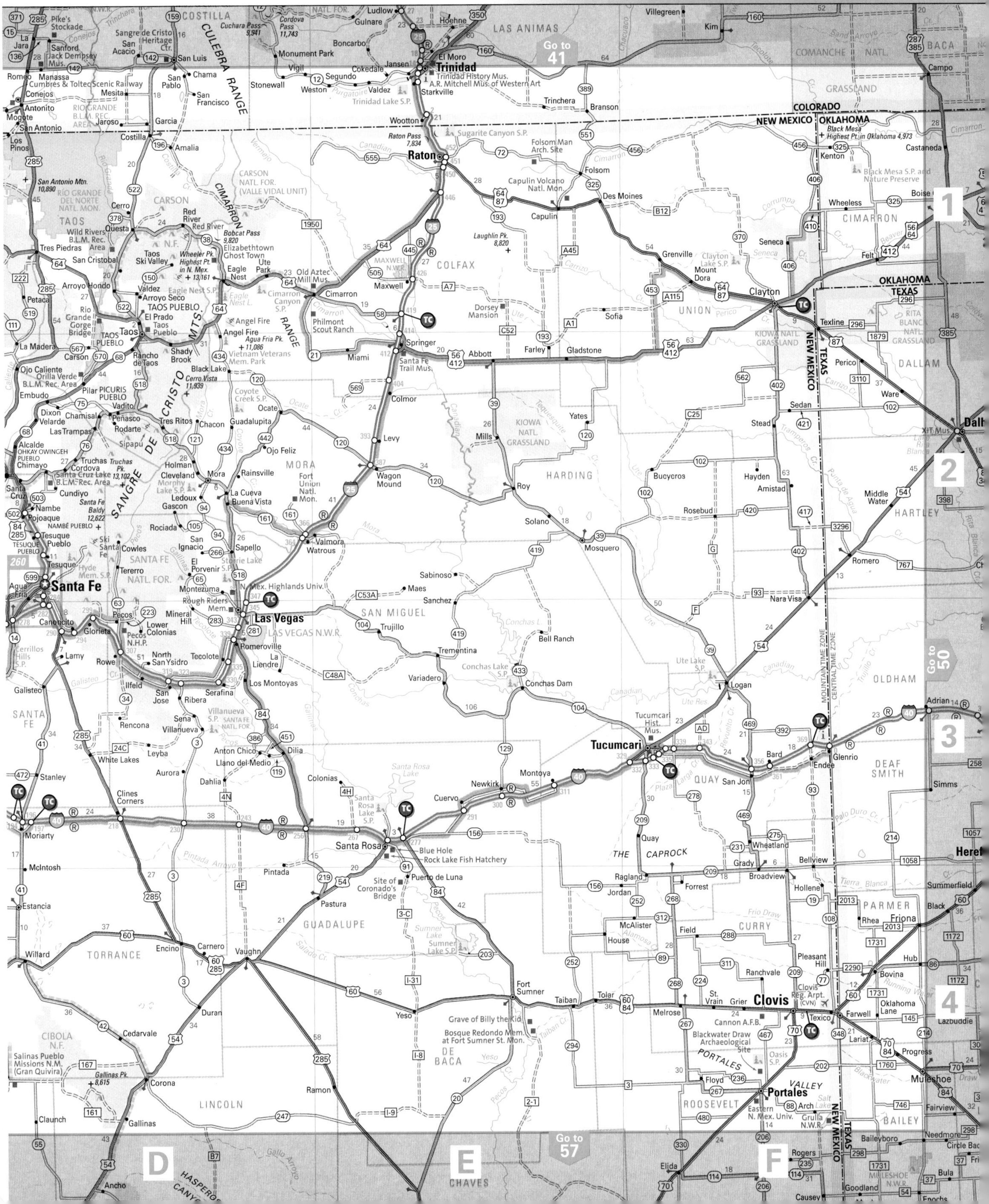

0 mi 20 40
0 km 20 40 60
One inch equals 25.4 miles
One centimeter equals 16.1 kilometers

Amarillo TX / Liberal KS

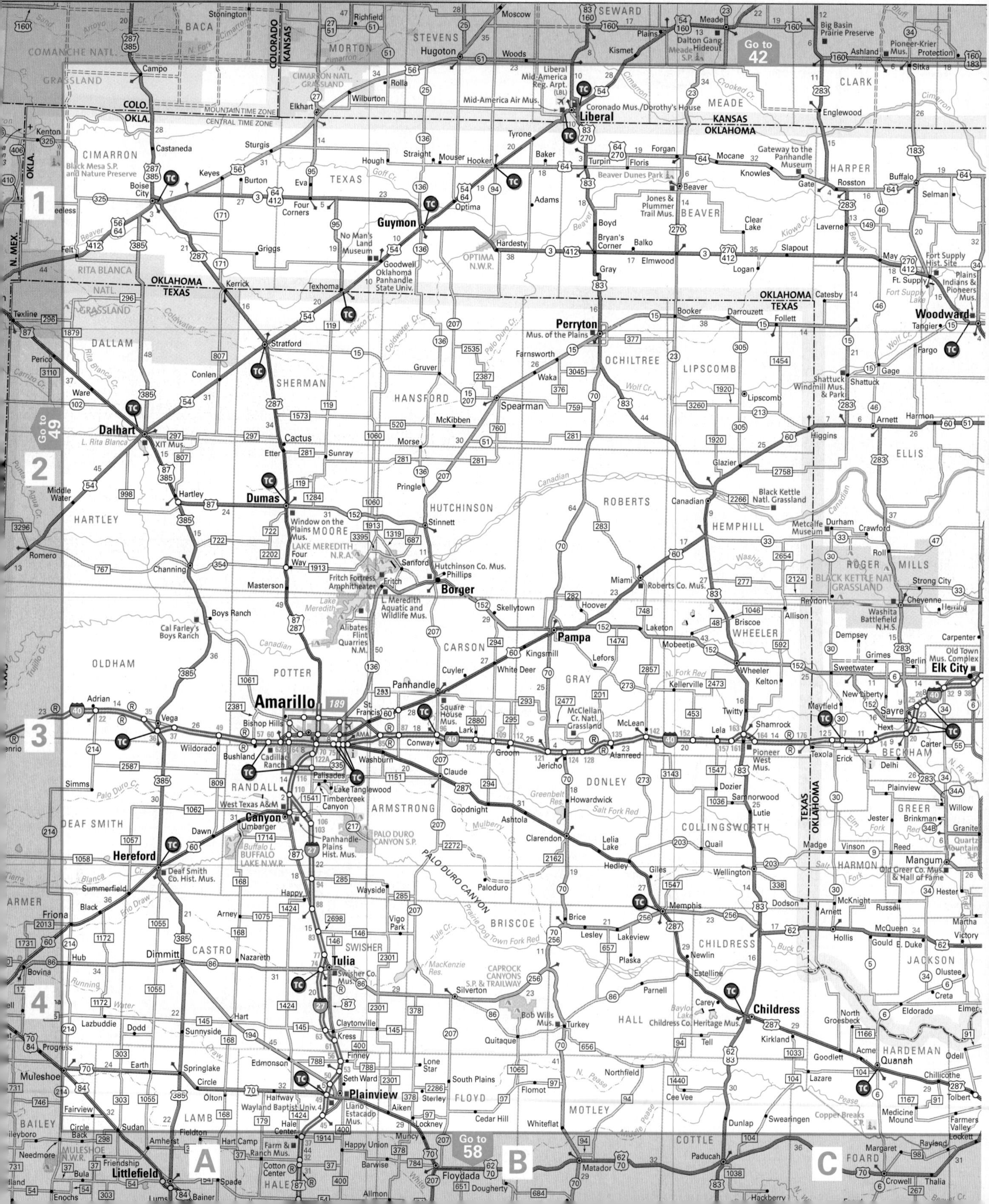

Go to 42
Go to 49
Go to 58

DRIVING DISTANCES IN MILES

	AMARILLO, TX	ARDMORE, OK	BARTLESVILLE, OK	CHILDRESS, TX	CLINTON, OK	ENID, OK	LAWTON, OK	LIBERAL, KS	OKLAHOMA CITY, OK	STILLWATER, OK	TULSA, OK	WOODWARD, OK
AMARILLO, TX		361	419	118	177	298	240	165	262	329	371	177
LAWTON, OK	240	103	243	124	98	142		287	85	152	194	175
OKLAHOMA CITY, OK	262	99	157	225	85	84	85	259		67	109	143
TULSA, OK	371	206	48	334	194	117	194	321	109	71		205

SEE ALSO DISTANCE AND DRIVING TIME MAP ON PAGES 286–287

0 mi 20 40
0 km 20 40 60
One inch equals 25.4 miles
One centimeter equals 16.1 kilometers

Los Angeles CA / Santa Barbara CA

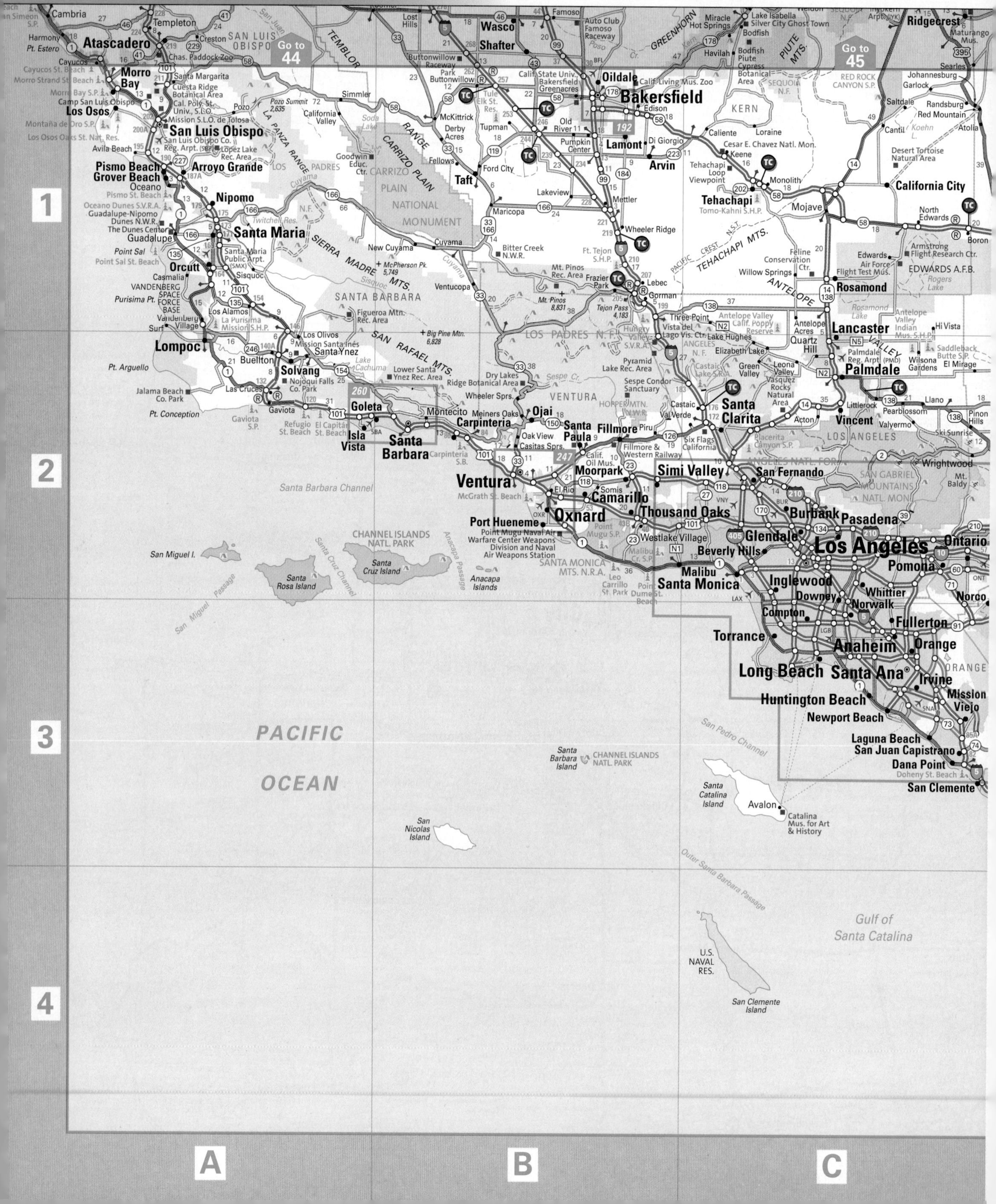

DRIVING DISTANCES IN MILES	BAKERSFIELD, CA	BARSTOW, CA	BLYTHE, CA	EL CENTRO, CA	LOS ANGELES, CA	NEEDLES, CA	PALM SPRINGS, CA	SAN BERNARDINO, CA	SAN DIEGO, CA	SAN LUIS OBISPO, CA	SANTA BARBARA, CA	YUMA, AZ
LOS ANGELES, CA	111	118	230	234		263	110	62	124	190	97	294
SAN DIEGO, CA	234	181	211	117	124	326	143	111		314	221	177
SANTA BARBARA, CA	150	213	325	330	97	358	205	157	221	93		391
YUMA, AZ	403	294	103	65	294	187	171	225	177	483	391	

SEE ALSO DISTANCE AND DRIVING TIME MAP ON PAGES 286–287

Phoenix AZ / Yuma AZ

0 mi 20 40
0 km 20 40 60
One inch equals 25.4 miles
One centimeter equals 16.1 kilometers

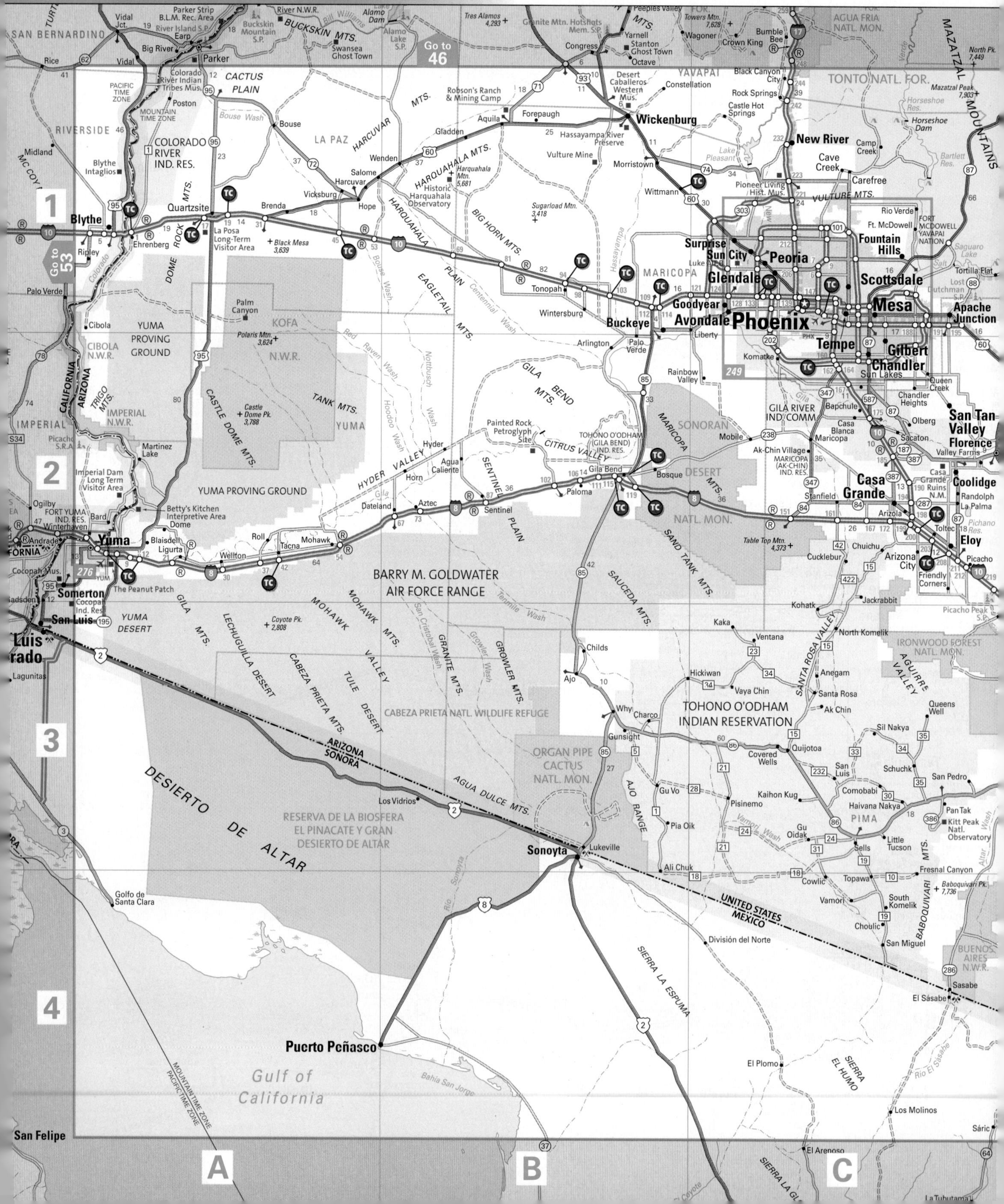

DRIVING DISTANCES IN MILES

	BLYTHE, CA	CASA GRANDE, AZ	DOUGLAS, AZ	EAGAR, AZ	GLOBE, AZ	LORDSBURG, NM	NOGALES, AZ	PHOENIX, AZ	SAFFORD, AZ	SILVER CITY, NM	TUCSON, AZ	YUMA, AZ
LORDSBURG, NM	417	228	101	184	155		185	278	77	45	161	401
PHOENIX, AZ	140	50	237	227	92	278	181		169	322	118	183
TUCSON, AZ	258	68	120	242	106	161	65	118	128	205		241
YUMA, AZ	103	179	360	401	265	401	304	183	368	446	241	

SEE ALSO DISTANCE AND DRIVING TIME MAP ON PAGES 286–287

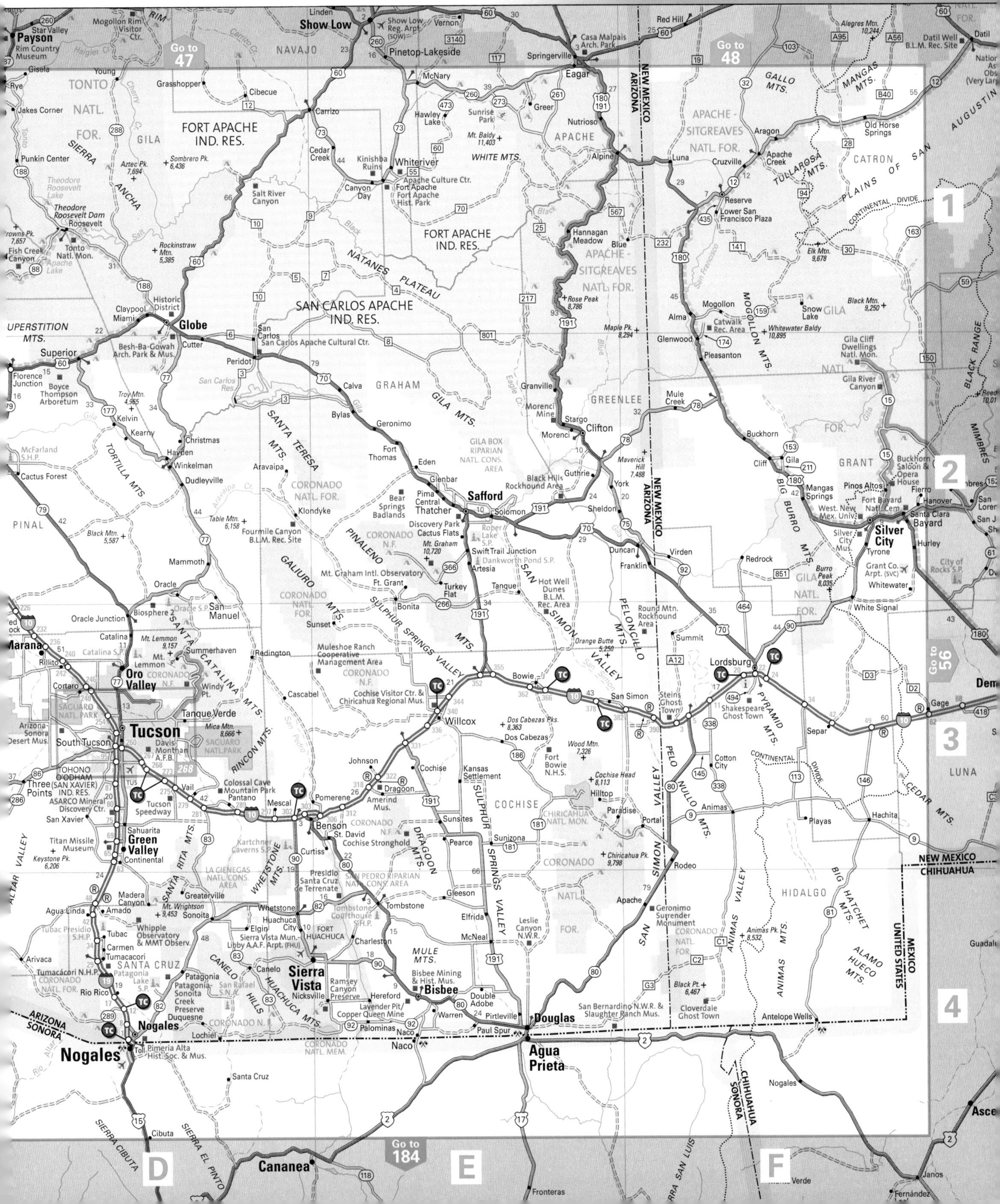

El Paso TX / Las Cruces NM

0 mi 20 40
0 km 20 40 60
One inch equals 25.4 miles
One centimeter equals 16.1 kilometers

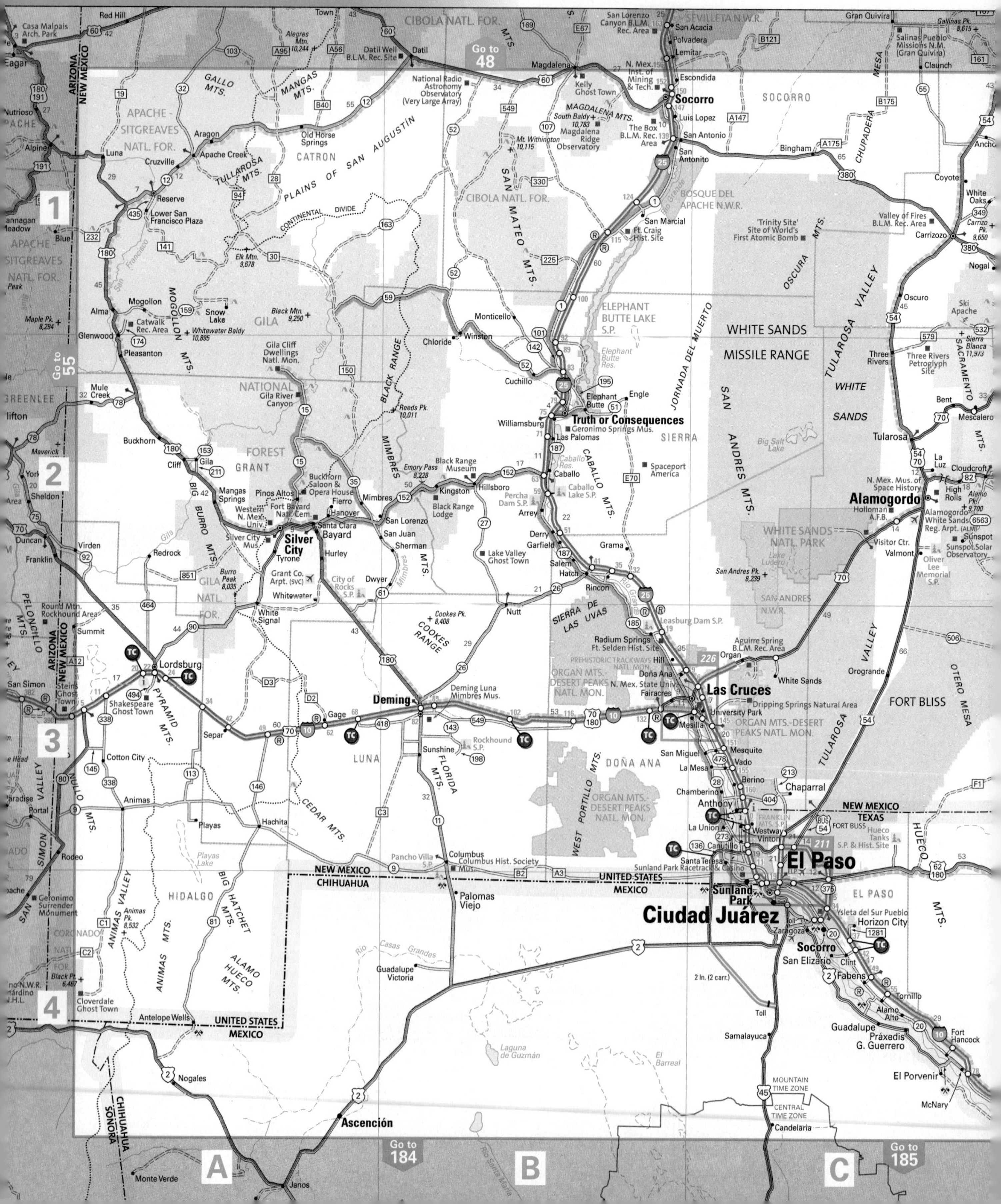

DRIVING DISTANCES IN MILES

	ALAMOGORDO, NM	CARLSBAD, NM	EL PASO, TX	HOBBS, NM	LAS CRUCES, NM	LORDSBURG, NM	ODESSA, TX	PECOS, TX	PORTALES, NM	ROSWELL, NM	SILVER CITY, NM	SOCORRO, NM
CARLSBAD, NM	144		162	70	203	321	137	87	168	76	311	241
EL PASO, TX	86	162		232	42	160	285	209	295	203	150	190
LAS CRUCES, NM	65	203	42	250		122	325	250	274	182	111	146
ROSWELL, NM	117	76	203	117	182	304	201	163	92		293	164

SEE ALSO DISTANCE AND DRIVING TIME MAP ON PAGES 286–287

0 mi 20 40
0 km 20 40 60
One inch equals 25.4 miles
One centimeter equals 16.1 kilometers

Lubbock TX / Abilene TX

ING ANCES ILES

	ABILENE, TX	BIG SPRING, TX	BROWNWOOD, TX	DALLAS, TX	FORT WORTH, TX	LUBBOCK, TX	ODESSA, TX	SAN ANGELO, TX	SHERMAN, TX	TEMPLE, TX	WACO, TX	WICHITA FALLS, TX
ABILENE, TX		110	78	191	153	166	176	91	249	194	235	144
DALLAS, TX	191	298	190		32	354	364	265	64	130	94	141
LUBBOCK, TX	166	106	247	354	317		142	185	322	358	399	207
WACO, TX	235	343	124	94	87	399	409	219	159	40		201

SEE ALSO DISTANCE AND DRIVING TIME MAP ON PAGES 286–287

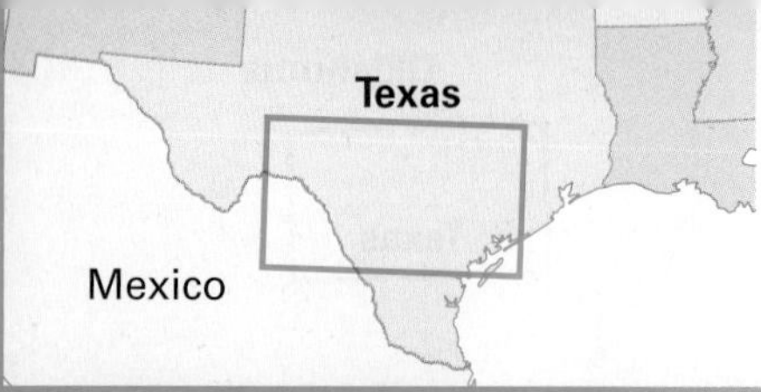
Texas
Mexico

0 mi 20 40
0 km 20 40 60
One inch equals 25.4 miles
One centimeter equals 16.1 kilometers

Del Rio TX / Eagle Pass TX

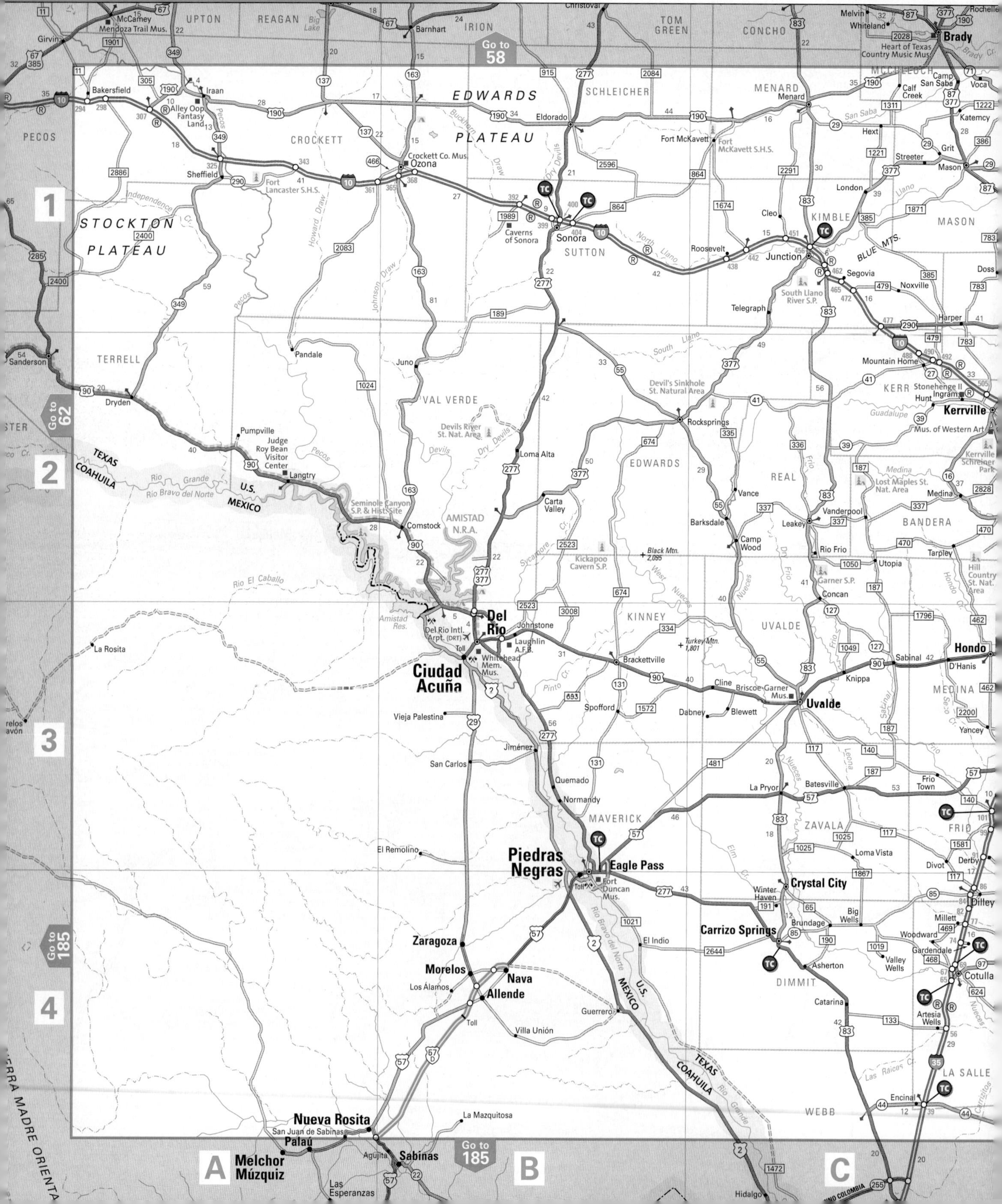
Go to 58
Go to 62
Go to 185
1
2
3
4
A
B
C
EDWARDS PLATEAU
STOCKTON PLATEAU
UPTON
REAGAN
IRION
TOM GREEN
CONCHO
PECOS
CROCKETT
SCHLEICHER
MENARD
McCULLOCH
MASON
KIMBLE
SUTTON
TERRELL
VAL VERDE
EDWARDS
REAL
KERR
BANDERA
KINNEY
UVALDE
MEDINA
MAVERICK
ZAVALA
FRIO
DIMMIT
LA SALLE
WEBB
TEXAS
COAHUILA
U.S.
MEXICO
McCamey
Mendoza Trail Mus.
Barnhart
Girvin
Bakersfield
Iraan
Alley Oop Fantasy Land
Sheffield
Fort Lancaster S.H.S.
Ozona
Crockett Co. Mus.
Eldorado
Fort McKavett
Fort McKavett S.H.S.
Menard
Melvin
Whiteland
Heart of Texas Country Music Mus.
Brady
Camp San Saba
Calf Creek
Voca
Katemcy
Hext
Grit
Streeter
Mason
London
Cleo
Sonora
Caverns of Sonora
Roosevelt
Junction
Segovia
Noxville
South Llano River S.P.
Telegraph
Harper
Mountain Home
Stonehenge II
Hunt
Ingram
Kerrville
Mus. of Western Art
Kerrville Schreiner Park
Doss
Sanderson
Dryden
Pandale
Juno
Devils River St. Nat. Area
Pumpville
Judge Roy Bean Visitor Center
Langtry
Seminole Canyon S.P. & Hist. Site
Comstock
AMISTAD N.R.A.
Amistad Res.
Loma Alta
Carta Valley
Rocksprings
Devil's Sinkhole St. Natural Area
Vance
Barksdale
Camp Wood
Leakey
Vanderpool
Lost Maples St. Nat. Area
Medina
Tarpley
Hill Country St. Nat. Area
Rio Frio
Utopia
Garner S.P.
Concan
Kickapoo Cavern S.P.
Black Mtn. 2,095
Turkey Mtn. 1,801
Del Rio
Del Rio Intl. Arpt. (DRT)
Johnstone
Laughlin A.F.B.
Whitehead Mem. Mus.
Ciudad Acuña
Brackettville
Spofford
Cline
Briscoe-Garner Mus.
Uvalde
Dabney
Blewett
Knippa
Sabinal
Hondo
D'Hanis
Yancey
La Rosita
Vieja Palestina
Jiménez
San Carlos
Quemado
Normandy
La Pryor
Batesville
Frio Town
El Remolino
Piedras Negras
Eagle Pass
Fort Duncan Mus.
Loma Vista
Crystal City
Winter Haven
Big Wells
Brundage
Carrizo Springs
Divot
Derby
Dilley
Millett
Woodward
Gardendale
Cotulla
Asherton
Valley Wells
Catarina
Artesia Wells
Encinal
El Indio
Zaragoza
Morelos
Nava
Allende
Los Álamos
Guerrero
Villa Unión
La Mazquitosa
Nueva Rosita
San Juan de Sabinas
Palaú
Agujita
Sabinas
Melchor Múzquiz
Las Esperanzas
Hidalgo
Rio Grande
Rio Bravo del Norte
Rio El Caballo
Pecos
Devils
Dry Devils
Nueces
West Nueces
Frio
Sabinal
Medina
Guadalupe
Llano
North Llano
South Llano
Independence Cr.
Howard Draw
Johnson Draw
Sycamore Cr.
Pinto Cr.
Elm Cr.
Leona
Las Raices Cr.
BLUE MTS.
Toll
Go to 185

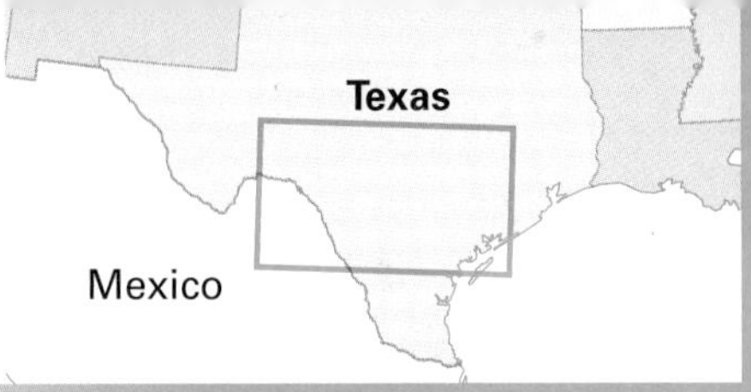

DRIVING DISTANCES IN MILES

	AUSTIN, TX	BEEVILLE, TX	COLLEGE STATION, TX	COLUMBUS, TX	DEL RIO, TX	EAGLE PASS, TX	FREDERICKSBURG, TX	SAN ANTONIO, TX	SONORA, TX	TEMPLE, TX	UVALDE, TX	VICTORIA, TX
AUSTIN, TX		136	108	92	229	226	78	78	244	67	159	123
DEL RIO, TX	229	235	322	277		55	178	152	89	295	70	268
SAN ANTONIO, TX	78	110	171	128	152	145	67		172	144	82	118
VICTORIA, TX	123	56	160	87	268	254	186	118	292	187	198	

SEE ALSO DISTANCE AND DRIVING TIME MAP ON PAGES 286–287

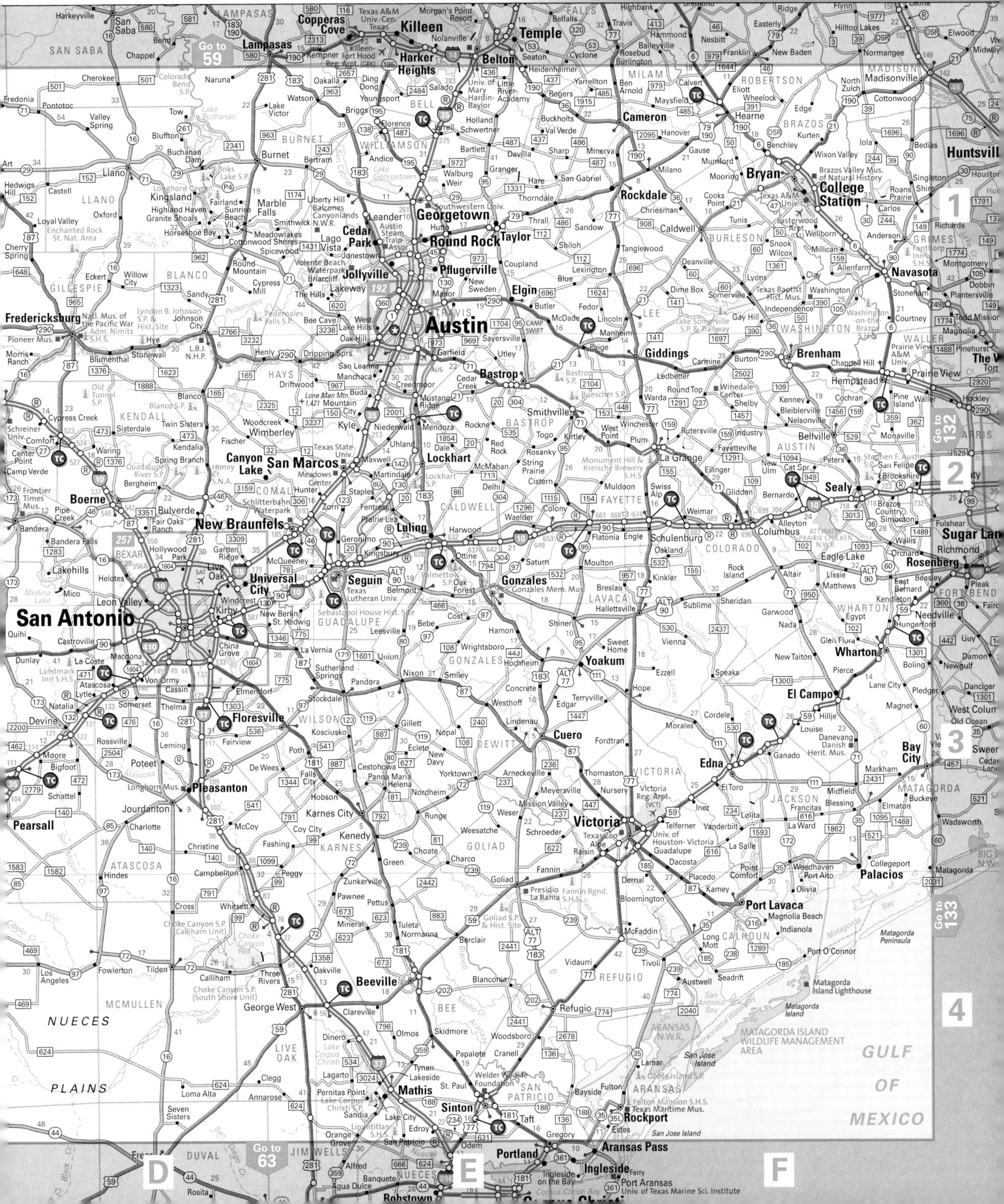

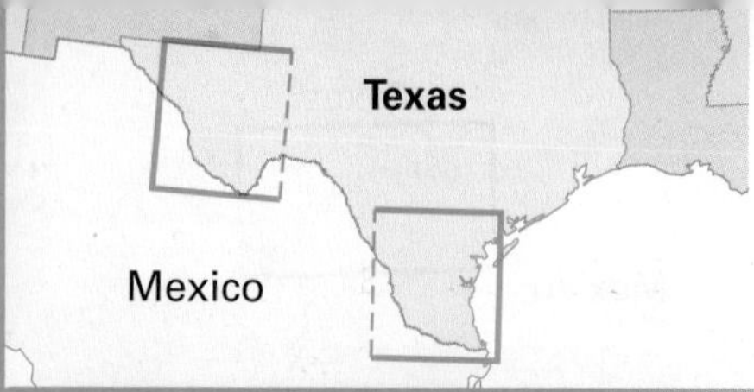

DRIVING DISTANCES IN MILES	ALPINE, TX	BIG BEND NP, TX	FORT STOCKTON, TX	ODESSA, TX	PECOS, TX	VAN HORN, TX
ALPINE, TX		97	65	151	96	110
FORT STOCKTON, TX	65	123		86	58	119
ODESSA, TX	151	209	86		76	163
VAN HORN, TX	110	207	119	163	87	

SEE ALSO DISTANCE AND DRIVING TIME MAP ON PAGES 286–287

0 mi 10 20 30
0 km 20 40
One inch equals 25.4 miles
One centimeter equals 16.1 kilometers

Odessa TX / Big Bend Natl Park TX

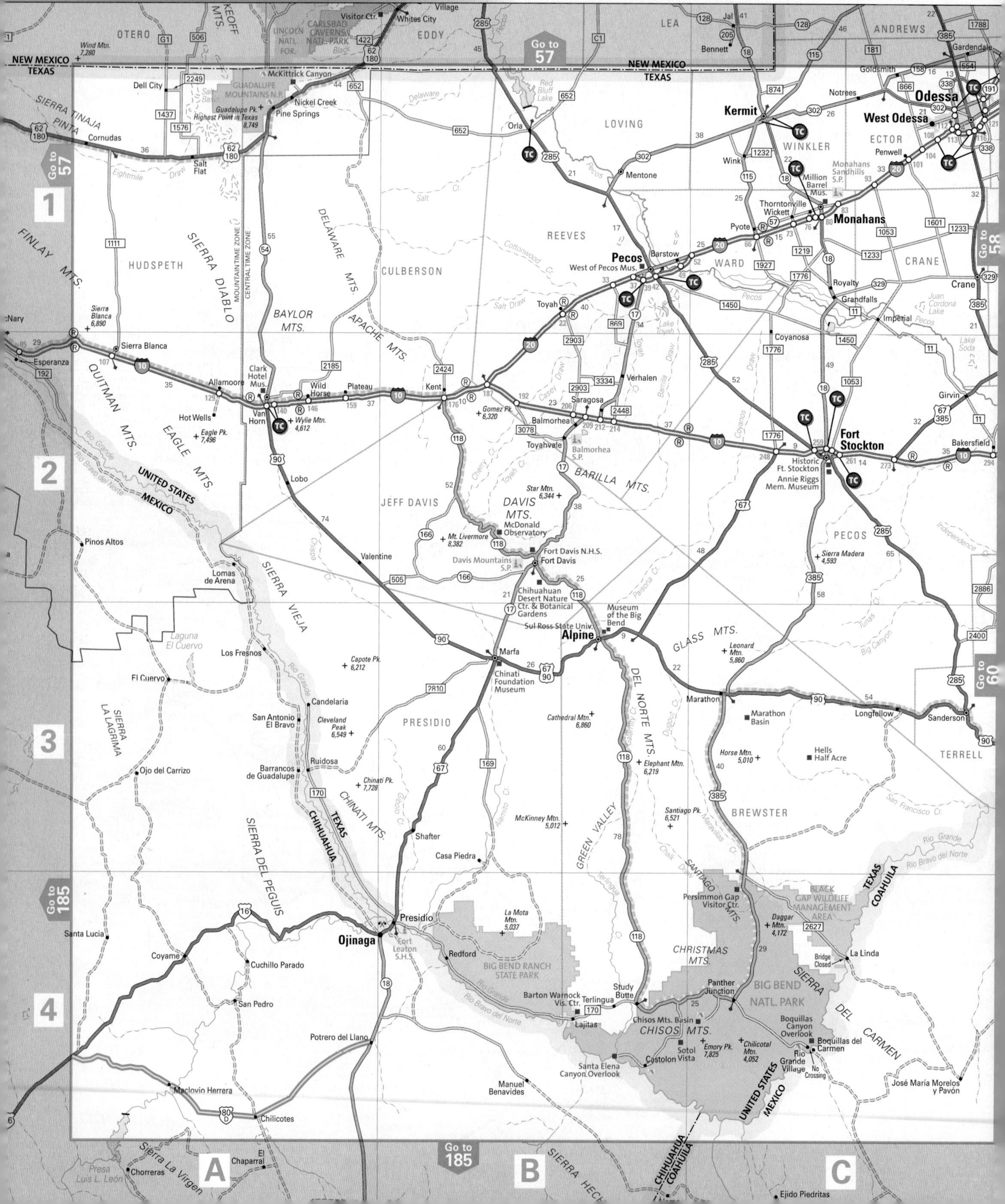

DRIVING DISTANCES IN MILES

	BEEVILLE, TX	BROWNSVILLE, TX	CARRIZO SPRS., TX	CORPUS CHRISTI, TX	HARLINGEN, TX	KINGSVILLE, TX	LAREDO, TX	MCALLEN, TX	VICTORIA, TX
BROWNSVILLE, TX	192		282	157	27	119	202	61	226
CORPUS CHRISTI, TX	59	157	199		131	38	141	152	94
LAREDO, TX	130	202	79	141	176	124		144	186
MCALLEN, TX	168	61	223	152	35	114	144		221

SEE ALSO DISTANCE AND DRIVING TIME MAP ON PAGES 286–287

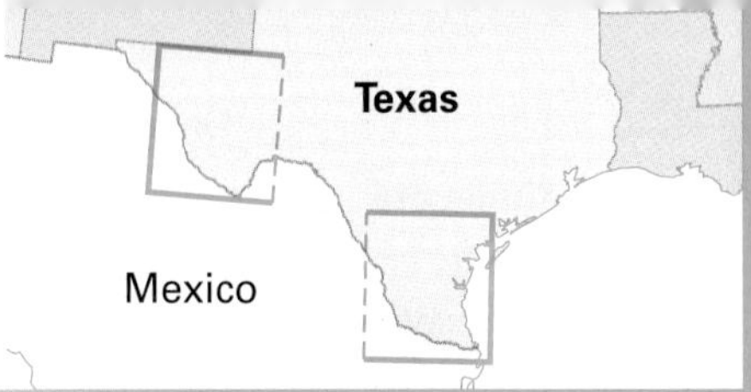

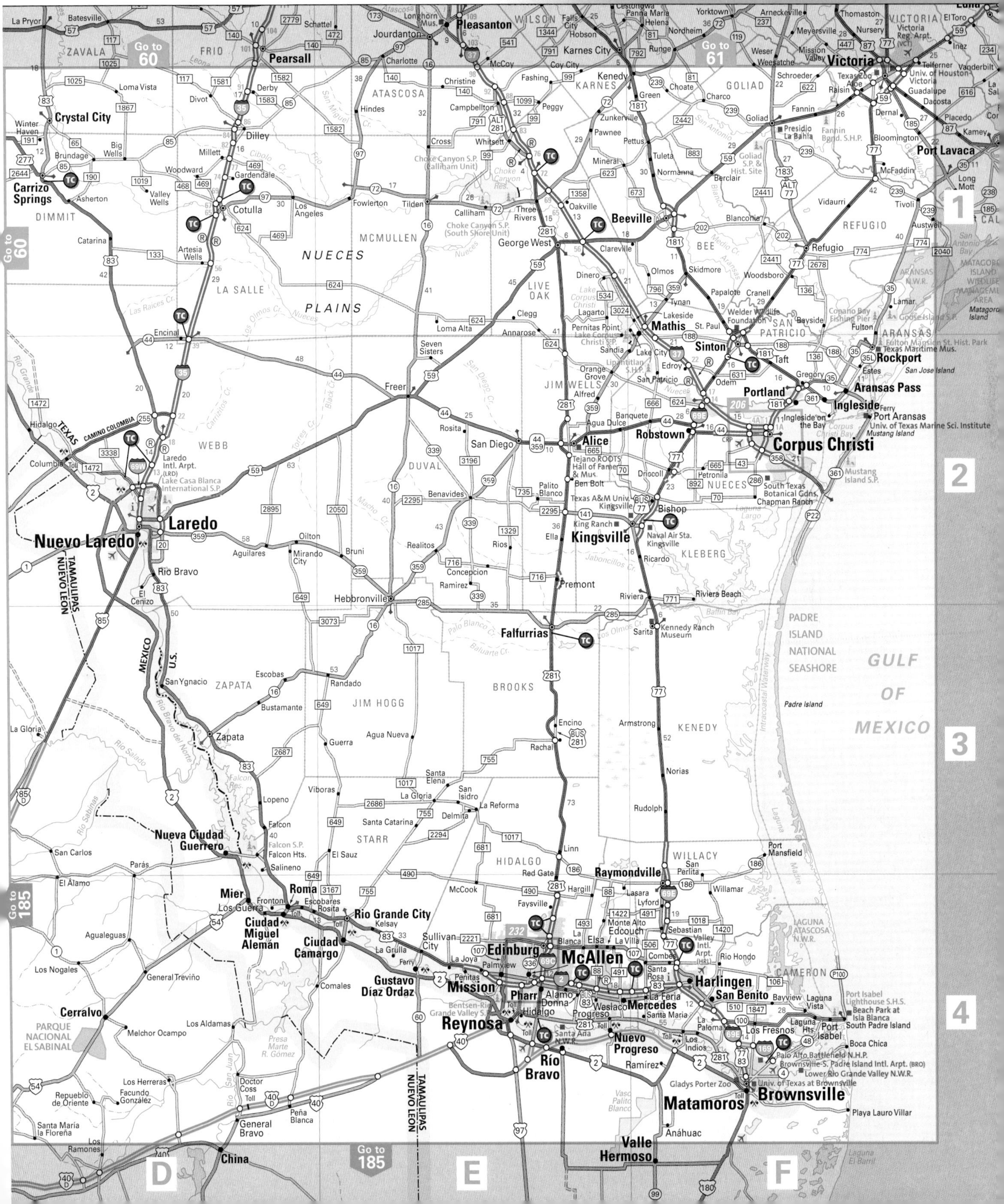

0 mi 20 40
0 km 20 40 60
One inch equals 25.4 miles
One centimeter equals 16.1 kilometers

Duluth MN / International Falls MN

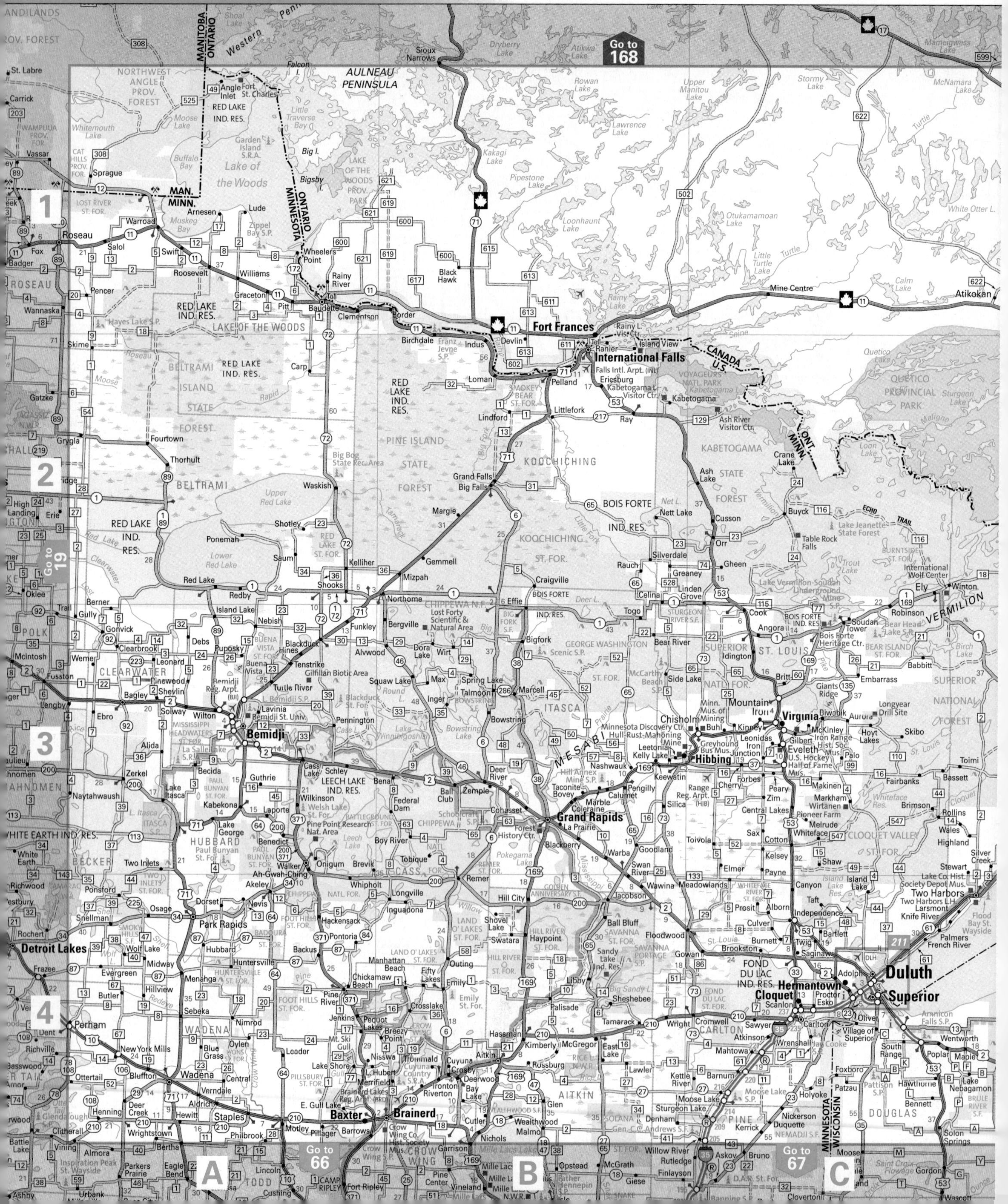

DRIVING DISTANCES IN MILES

	ASHLAND, WI	BEMIDJI, MN	BRAINERD, MN	DETROIT LAKES, MN	DULUTH, MN	GRAND PORTAGE, MN	HOUGHTON, MI	INTERNAT'L FALLS, MN	IRONWOOD, MI	ISHPEMING, MI	THUNDER BAY, ON	VIRGINIA, MN
BEMIDJI, MN	239		96	91	153	295	362	109	254	384	314	124
DULUTH, MN	92	153	116	202		143	215	157	107	238	183	61
HOUGHTON, MI	132	362	325	412	215	358		370	108	87	654	274
INTERNAT'L FALLS, MN	247	109	190	200	157	245	370		262	393	205	97

SEE ALSO DISTANCE AND DRIVING TIME MAP ON PAGES 286–287

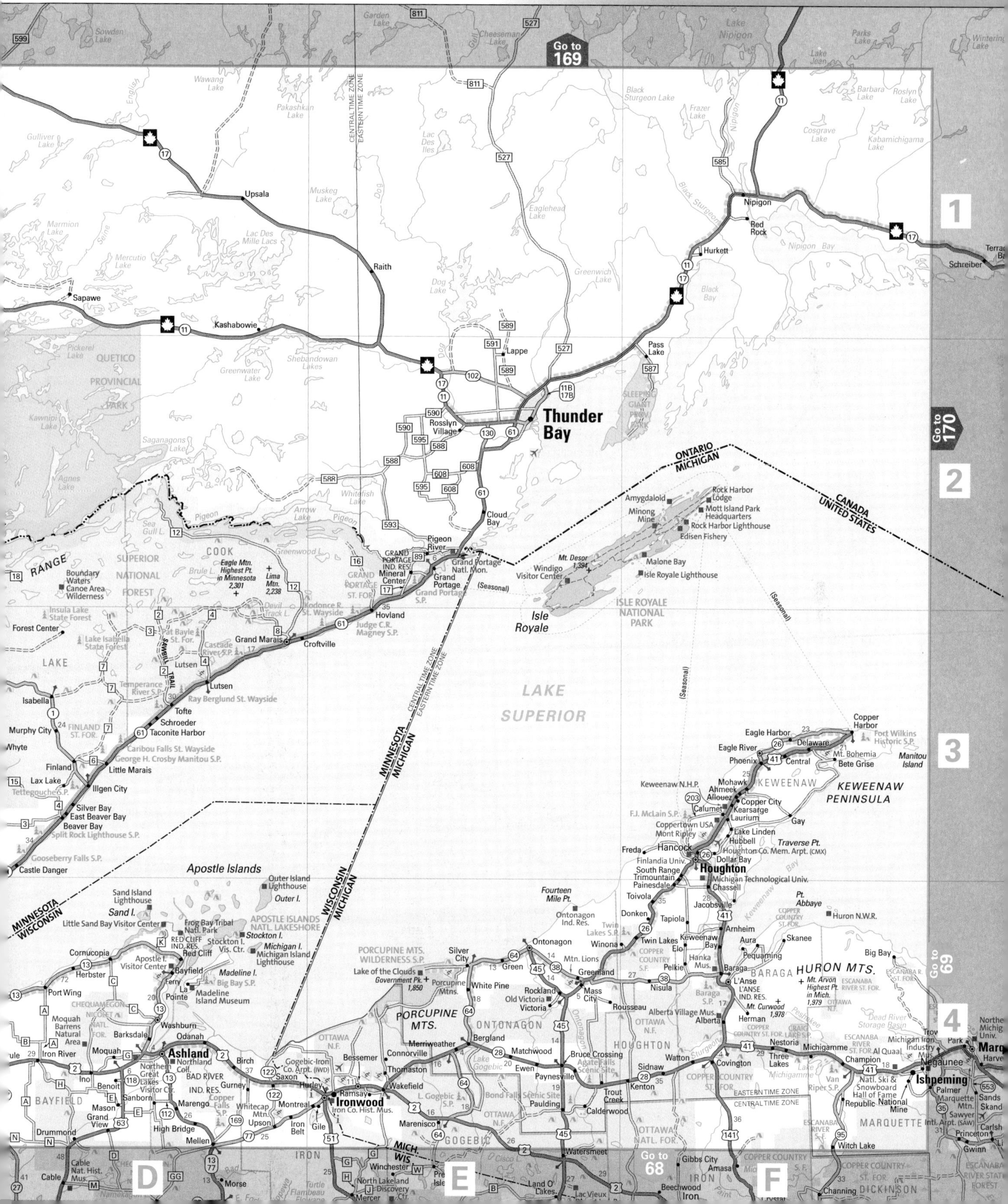

0 mi 10 20 30 40
0 km 10 20 30 40 50 60

One inch equals 18.4 miles
One centimeter equals 11.7 kilometers

DRIVING DISTANCES IN MILES

	ASHLAND, WI	BRAINERD, MN	DULUTH, MN	EAU CLAIRE, WI	FERGUS FALLS, MN	MARSHALL, MN	MINNEAPOLIS, MN	MORRIS, MN	RICE LAKE, WI	ST. CLOUD, MN	ST. PAUL, MN	WILLMAR, MN
EAU CLAIRE, WI	167	220	155		267	236	93	247	57	156	83	193
MINNEAPOLIS, MN	196	129	158	93	176	148		156	103	64	10	92
ST. CLOUD, MN	205	62	149	156	117	131	64	98	155		73	63
WILLMAR, MN	263	112	206	193	113	68	92	57	196	63	102	

SEE ALSO DISTANCE AND DRIVING TIME MAP ON PAGES 286–287

0 mi 10 20 30 40
0 km 10 20 30 40 50 60
One inch equals 18.4 miles
One centimeter equals 11.7 kilometers

DRIVING DISTANCES IN MILES	ESCANABA, MI	GREEN BAY, WI	IRON MOUNTAIN, MI	IRONWOOD, MI	L'ANSE, MI	MANISTIQUE, MI	MARINETTE, WI	MARQUETTE, MI	RHINELANDER, WI	STEVENS POINT, WI	TRAVERSE CITY, MI	WAUSAU, WI
ESCANABA, MI		111	52	178	134	54	57	65	132	185	252	171
GREEN BAY, WI	111		96	202	178	165	54	175	124	87	363	93
MARQUETTE, MI	65	175	79	145	70	86	122		147	238	269	204
WAUSAU, WI	171	93	133	121	176	225	112	204	58	35	423	

SEE ALSO DISTANCE AND DRIVING TIME MAP ON PAGES 286–287

0 mi 10 20 30 40
0 km 10 20 30 40 50 60

One inch equals 18.4 miles
One centimeter equals 11.7 kilometers

Sault Ste Marie MI / Traverse City MI

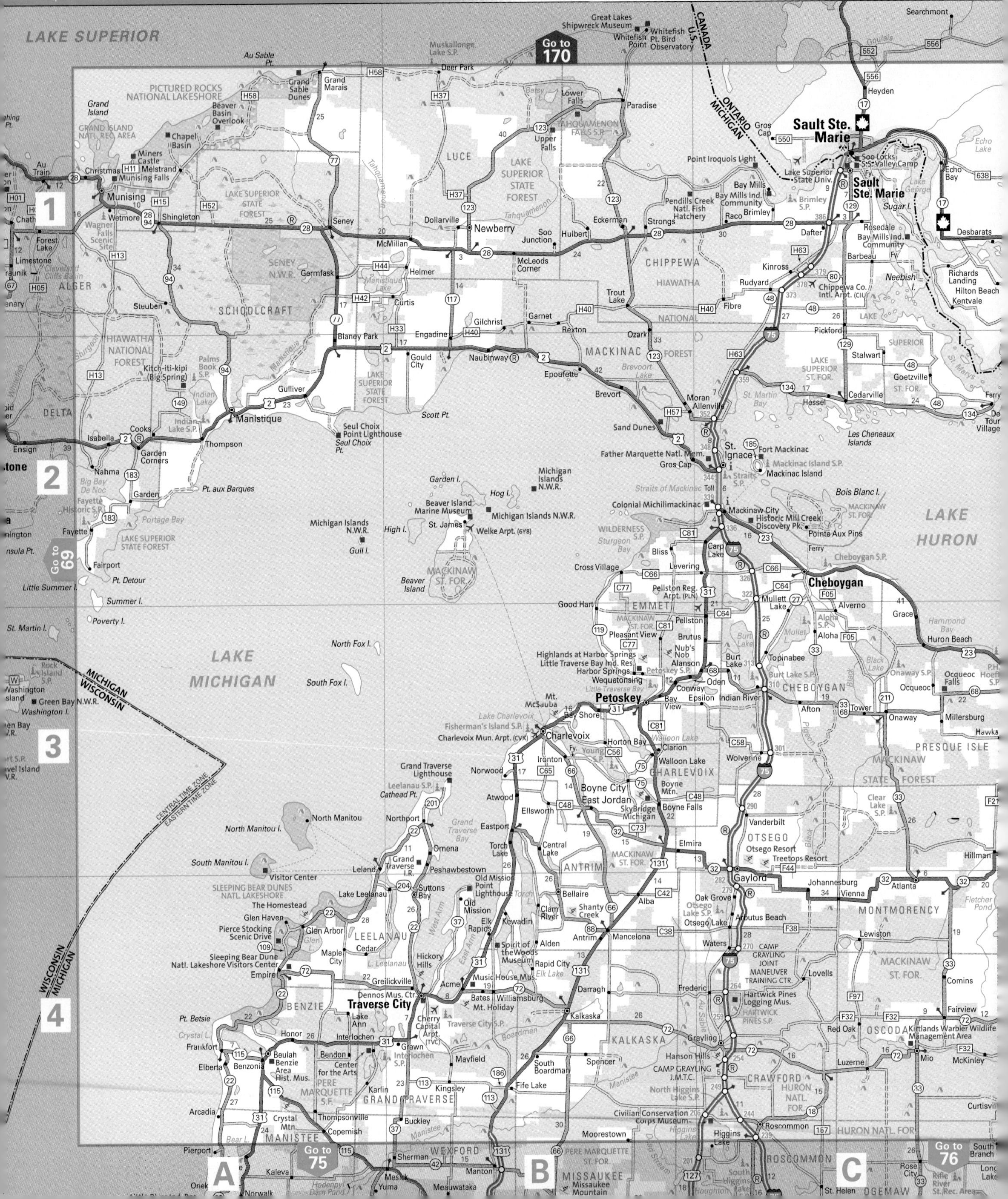

DRIVING DISTANCES IN MILES	ALPENA, MI	CHEBOYGAN, MI	GAYLORD, MI	GRAYLING, MI	MACKINAW CITY, MI	MANISTIQUE, MI	MUNISING, MI	PETOSKEY, MI	ROGERS CITY, MI	SAULT STE. MARIE, MI	SUDBURY, ON	TRAVERSE CITY, MI
ALPENA, MI		78	76	95	94	187	215	101	38	148	334	141
MACKINAW CITY, MI	94	16	60	87		95	123	38	58	57	242	106
SAULT STE. MARIE, MI	148	71	114	142	57	120	120	93	112		186	160
TRAVERSE CITY, MI	141	115	65	52	106	198	226	67	135	160	346	

SEE ALSO DISTANCE AND DRIVING TIME MAP ON PAGES 286–287

0 mi 10 20 30 40
0 km 10 20 30 40 50 60

One inch equals 18.4 miles
One centimeter equals 11.7 kilometers

Mankato MN / Fort Dodge IA

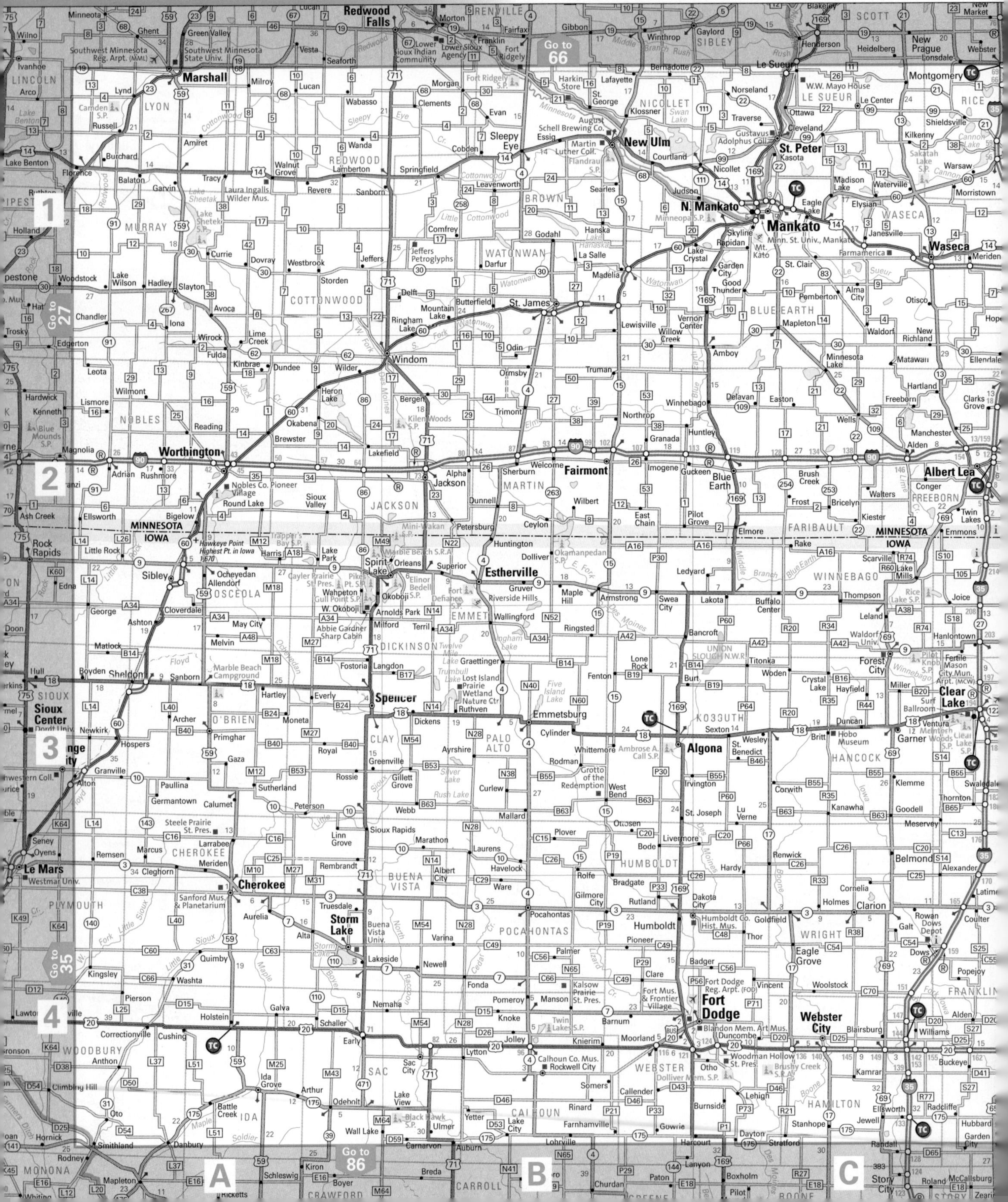

DRIVING DISTANCES IN MILES

	ALBERT LEA, MN	DECORAH, IA	DUBUQUE, IA	FORT DODGE, IA	LA CROSSE, WI	MANKATO, MN	MASON CITY, IA	ROCHESTER, MN	SPENCER, IA	WATERLOO, IA	WINONA, MN	WORTHINGTON, MN
FORT DODGE, IA	124	186	200		245	138	97	183	95	108	225	148
MANKATO, MN	56	151	253	138	149		100	80	123	186	128	108
ROCHESTER, MN	62	68	170	183	71	80	103		189	116	51	174
WATERLOO, IA	130	79	93	108	138	186	79	116	189		144	244

SEE ALSO DISTANCE AND DRIVING TIME MAP ON PAGES 286–287

0 mi 10 20 30 40
0 km 10 20 30 40 50 60

One inch equals 18.4 miles
One centimeter equals 11.7 kilometers

Milwaukee WI / Madison WI

DRIVING DISTANCES IN MILES

	CADILLAC, MI	DUBUQUE, IA	GRAND RAPIDS, MI	GREEN BAY, WI	KALAMAZOO, MI	MADISON, WI	MILWAUKEE, WI	MUSKEGON, MI	OSHKOSH, WI	ROCKFORD, IL	SHEBOYGAN, WI	TOMAH, WI
GRAND RAPIDS, MI	99	364		393	53	335	277	40	363	271	332	424
GREEN BAY, WI	492	229	393		362	135	115	400	50	211	61	162
MADISON, WI	434	93	335	135	304		78	341	86	78	132	98
MILWAUKEE, WI	377	167	277	115	247	78		285	87	95	54	168

SEE ALSO DISTANCE AND DRIVING TIME MAP ON PAGES 286–287

0 mi 10 20 30 40
0 km 10 20 30 40 50 60

One inch equals 18.4 miles
One centimeter equals 11.7 kilometers

Detroit MI / Lansing MI

DRIVING DISTANCES IN MILES

	ANN ARBOR, MI	BAD AXE, MI	BATTLE CREEK, MI	CADILLAC, MI	DETROIT, MI	FLINT, MI	HAMILTON, ON	LANSING, MI	LONDON, ON	MT. PLEASANT, MI	PORT HURON, MI	SAGINAW, MI
DETROIT, MI	42	107	116	209		62	203	86	128	149	58	97
LANSING, MI	63	140	56	131	86	53	270		191	67	117	86
PORT HURON, MI	101	81	175	211	58	64	154	117	75	155		100
SAGINAW, MI	87	64	142	116	97	36	253	86	174	60	100	

SEE ALSO DISTANCE AND DRIVING TIME MAP ON PAGES 286–287

0 mi 10 20 30 40
0 km 10 20 30 40 50 60

One inch equals 18.4 miles
One centimeter equals 11.7 kilometers

Buffalo NY / Rochester NY

DRIVING DISTANCES IN MILES

	BATH, NY	BUFFALO, NY	ITHACA, NY	NIAGARA FALLS, NY	ONEONTA, NY	OSWEGO, NY	ROCHESTER, NY	SYRACUSE, NY	TORONTO, ON	TUPPER LAKE, NY	UTICA, NY	WATERTOWN, NY
BUFFALO, NY	113		153	20	263	158	74	152	106	321	199	210
ROCHESTER, NY	78	74	89	88	200	73		88	181	257	135	146
SYRACUSE, NY	105	152	59	166	118	38	88		260	176	53	65
UTICA, NY	152	199	108	213	65	81	135	53	307	131		86

SEE ALSO DISTANCE AND DRIVING TIME MAP ON PAGES 286–287

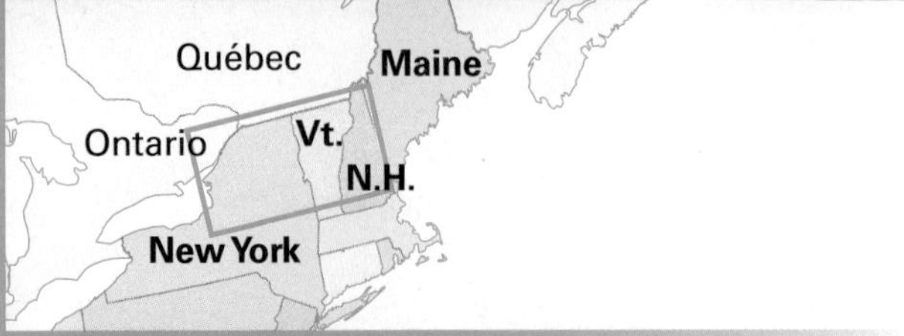

0 mi 10 20 30 40
0 km 10 20 30 40 50 60

One inch equals 18.4 miles
One centimeter equals 11.7 kilometers

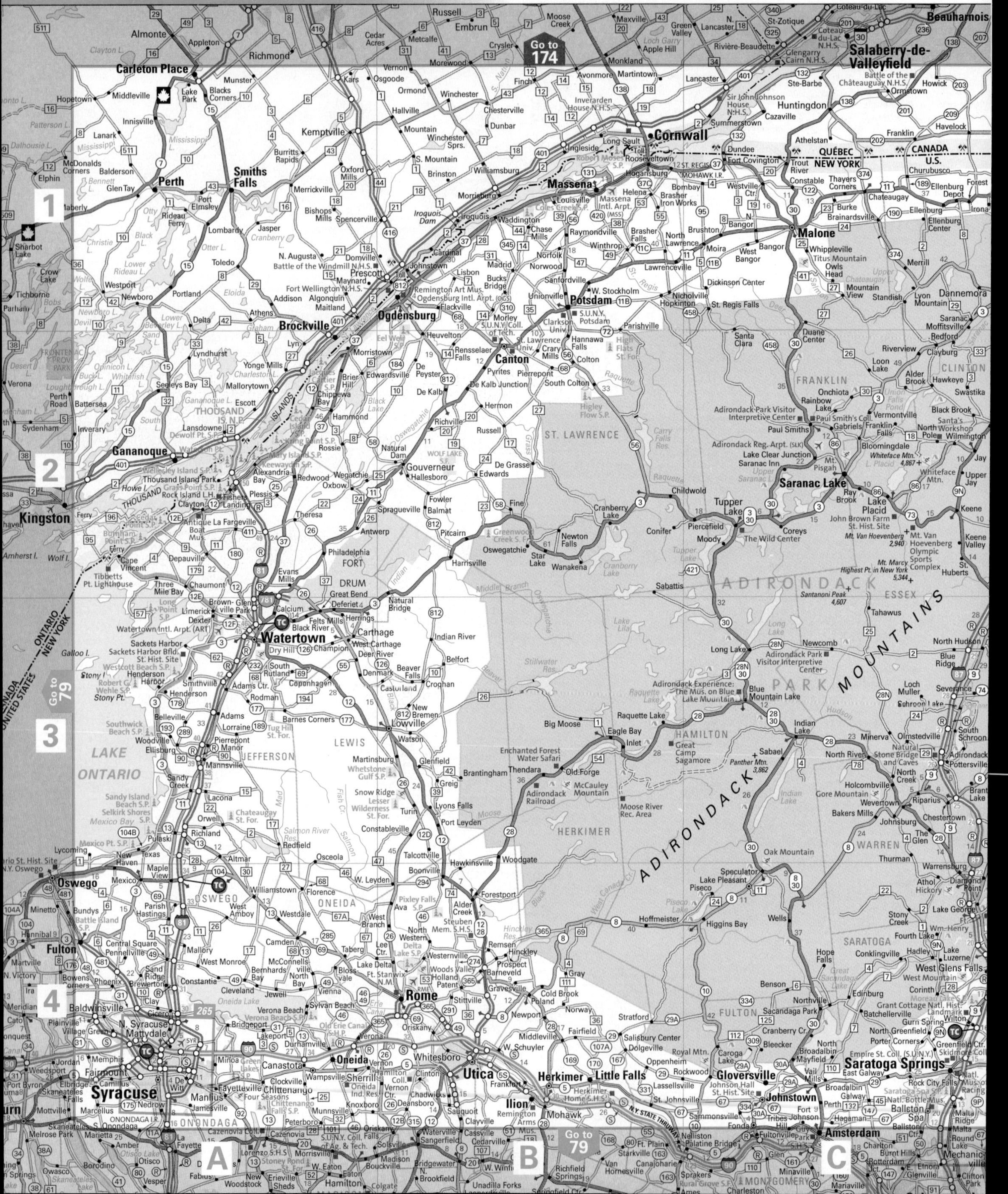

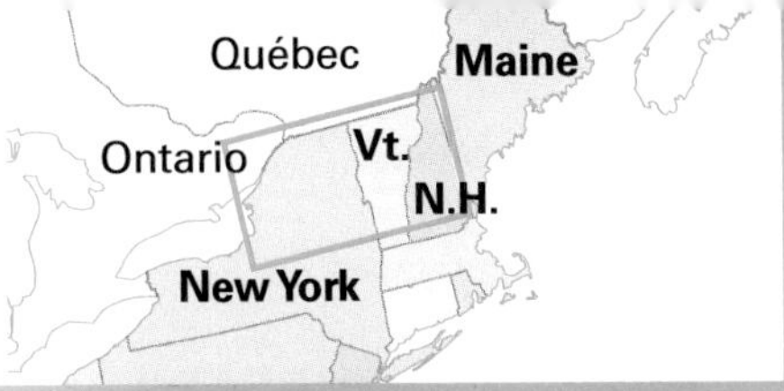

DRIVING DISTANCES IN MILES

	BURLINGTON, VT	CONCORD, NH	LAKE PLACID, NY	OGDENSBURG, NY	PLATTSBURGH, NY	RUTLAND, VT	ST. JOHNSBURY, VT	SARATOGA SPRS., NY	SYRACUSE, NY	UTICA, NY	WATERTOWN, NY	WHITE RIVER JCT., VT
BURLINGTON, VT		150	68	208	51	69	76	115	230	183	195	91
CONCORD, NH	150		215	357	198	104	104	173	280	228	312	59
LAKE PLACID, NY	68	215		96	49	133	141	106	192	148	126	156
WATERTOWN, NY	195	312	126	68	167	244	319	179	65	86		289

SEE ALSO DISTANCE AND DRIVING TIME MAP ON PAGES 286–287

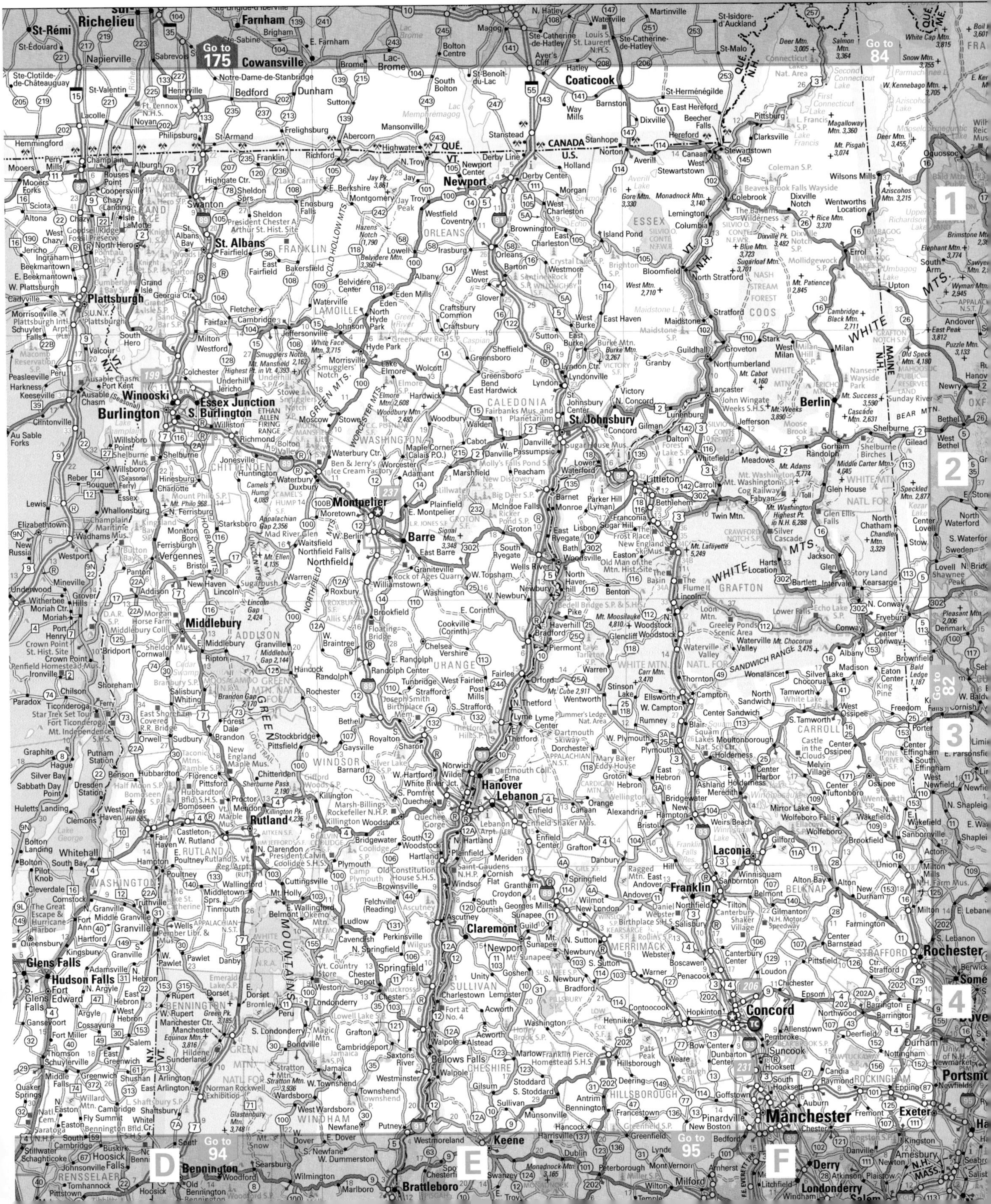

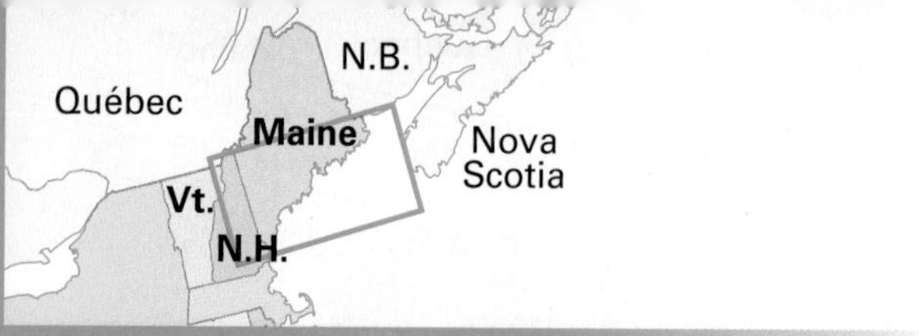

0 mi 10 20 30 40
0 km 10 20 30 40 50 60

One inch equals 18.4 miles
One centimeter equals 11.7 kilometers

Portland ME / Augusta ME

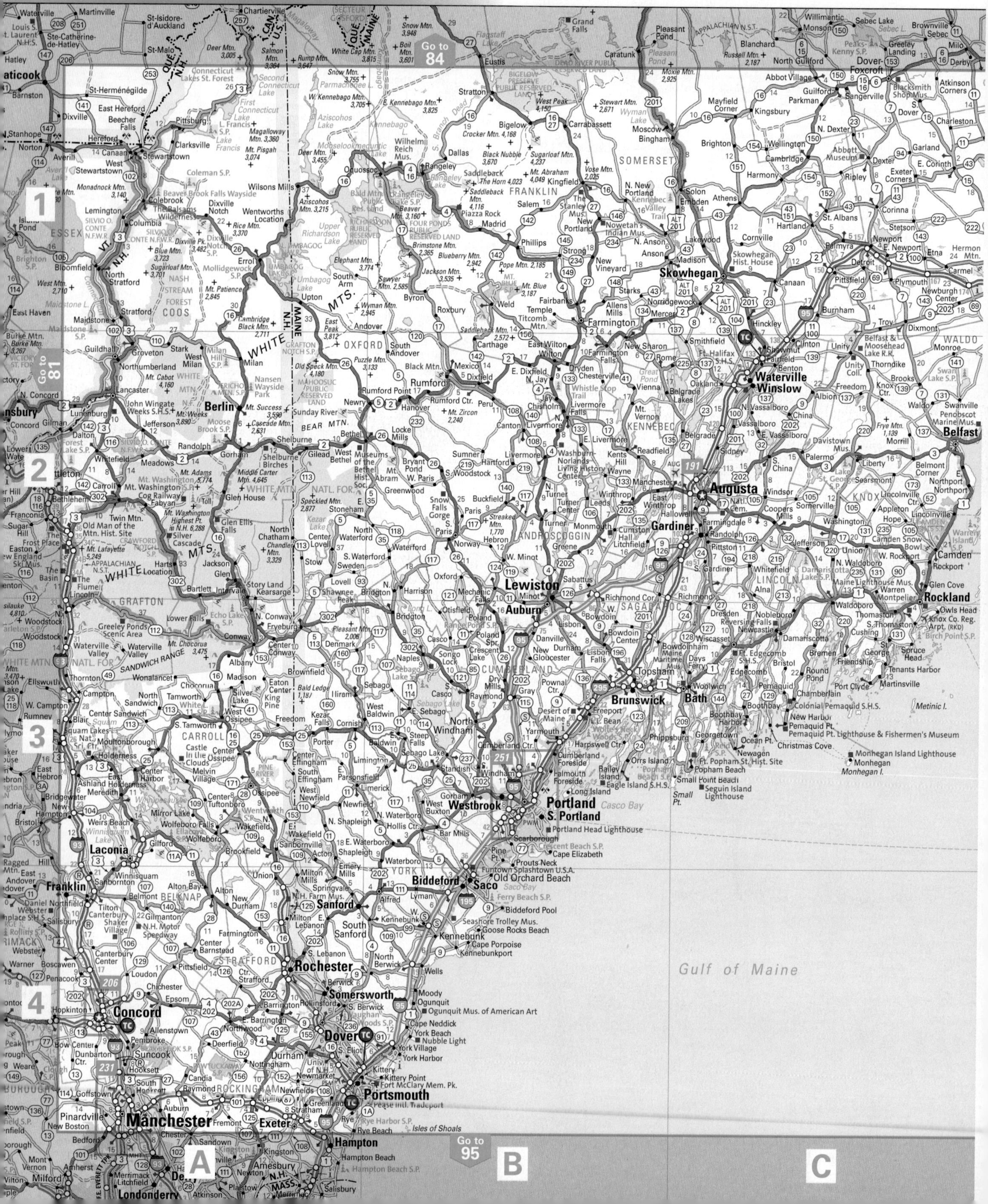

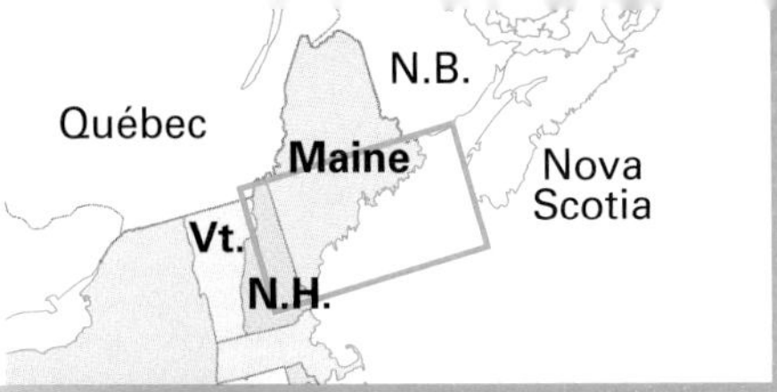

DRIVING DISTANCES IN MILES

	AUGUSTA, ME	BANGOR, ME	BAR HARBOR, ME	BERLIN, NH	CALAIS, ME	CONCORD, NH	CONWAY, NH	LEWISTON, ME	MACHIAS, ME	PORTLAND, ME	PORTSMOUTH, NH	WATERVILLE, ME
AUGUSTA, ME		77	120	110	173	141	97	35	158	58	110	20
BANGOR, ME	77		45	160	97	214	170	108	83	131	184	56
BAR HARBOR, ME	120	45		204	112	257	214	151	71	175	227	100
PORTLAND, ME	58	131	175	93	228	83	62	36	213		53	84

SEE ALSO DISTANCE AND DRIVING TIME MAP ON PAGES 286–287

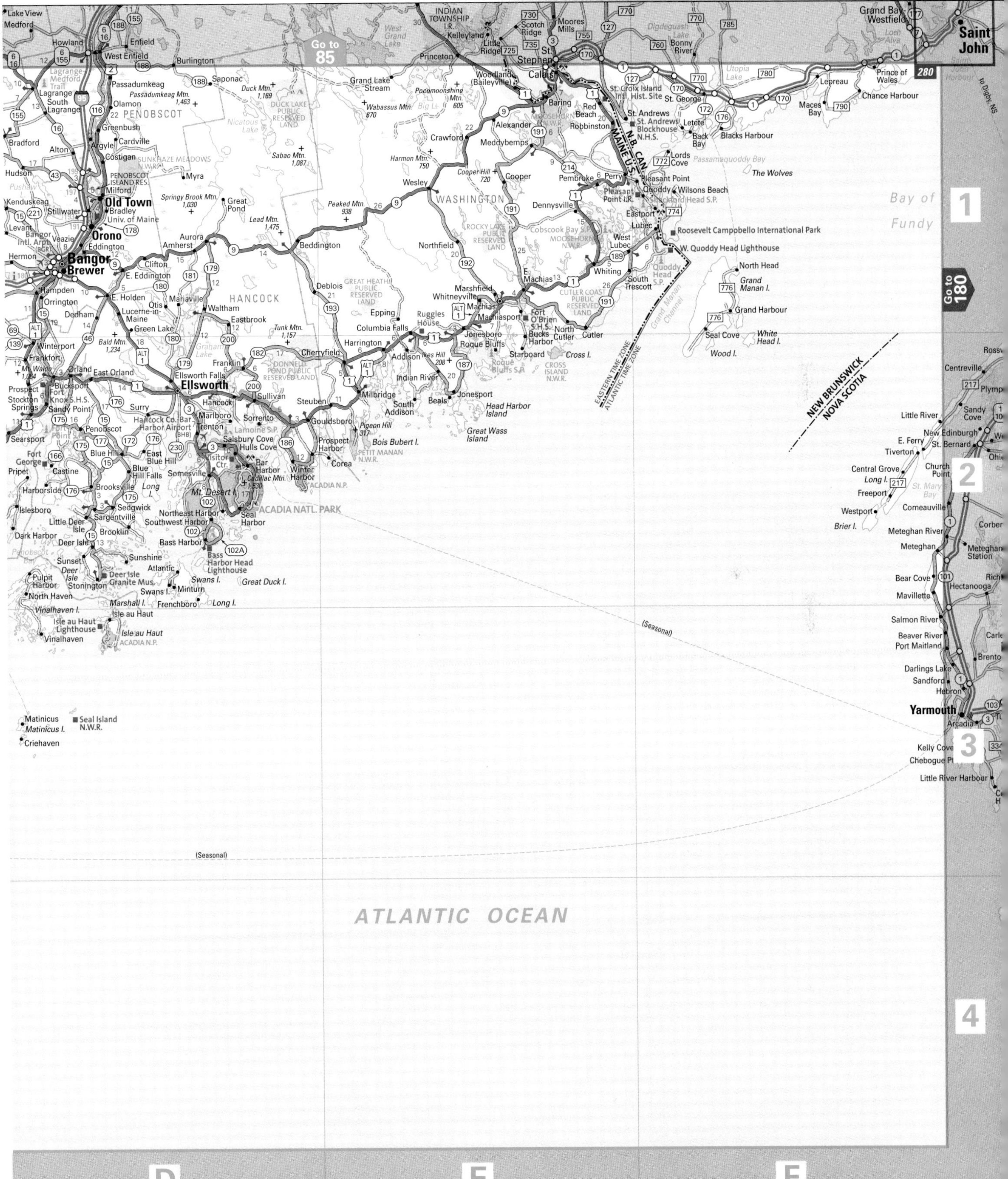

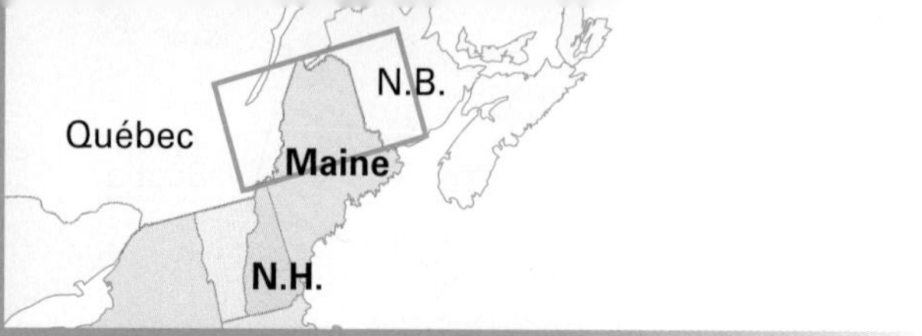
Québec
N.B.
Maine
N.H.

0 mi 10 20 30 40
0 km 10 20 30 40 50 60
One inch equals 18.4 miles
One centimeter equals 11.7 kilometers

Greenville ME / Allagash ME

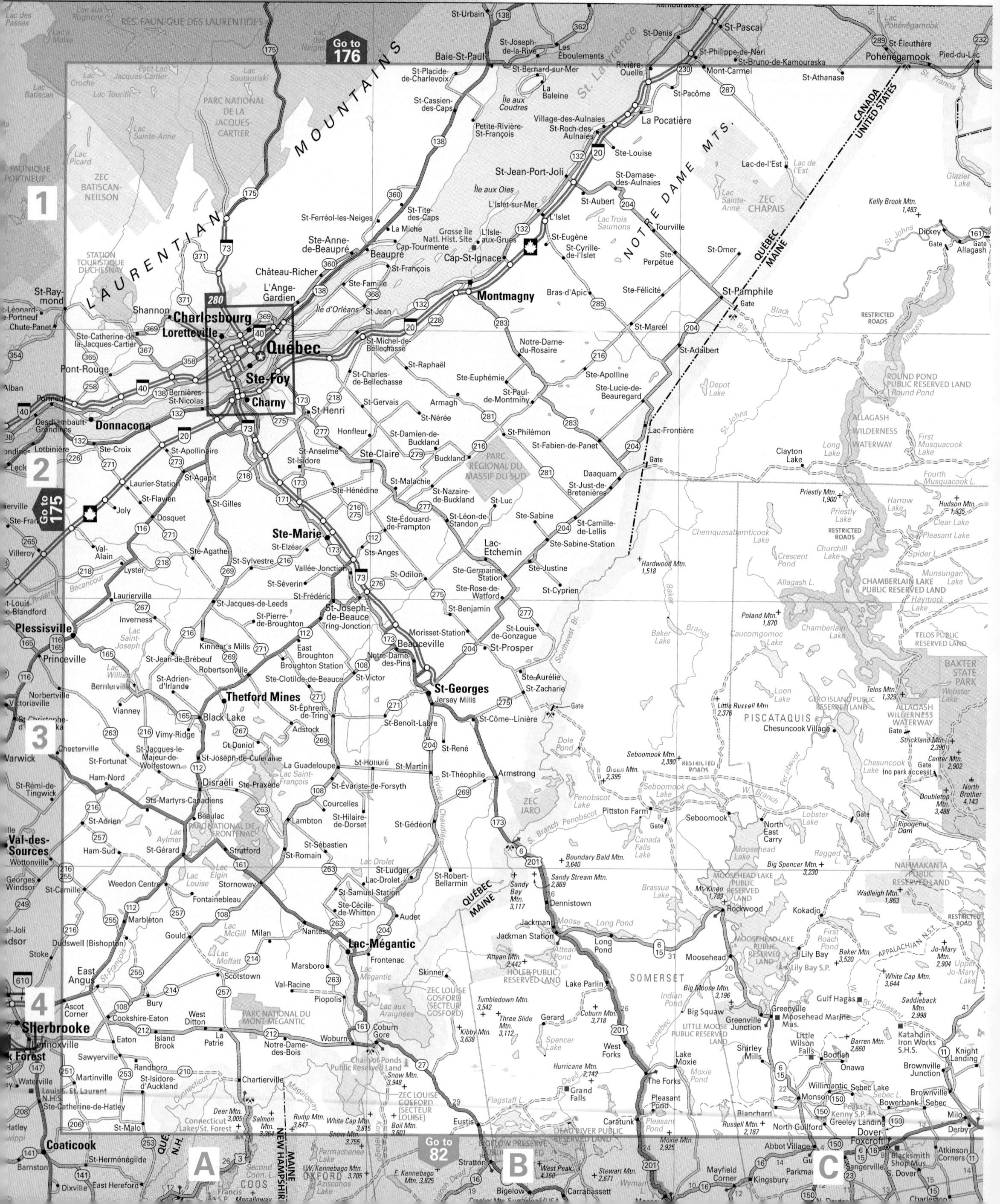
RÉS. FAUNIQUE DES LAURENTIDES
LAURENTIAN MOUNTAINS
NOTRE DAME MTS.
PARC NATIONAL DE LA JACQUES-CARTIER
ZEC BATISCAN-NEILSON
STATION TOURISTIQUE DUCHESNAY
Go to 176
Go to 175
Go to 82
St-Urbain
Baie-St-Paul
St-Joseph-de-la-Rive
Les Éboulements
St-Bernard-sur-Mer
Île aux Coudres
La Baleine
St. Lawrence
Rivière-Ouelle
St-Denis
St-Pascal
St-Philippe-de-Néri
St-Bruno-de-Kamouraska
Mont-Carmel
St-Pacôme
La Pocatière
Village-des-Aulnaies
St-Roch-des-Aulnaies
Ste-Louise
St-Jean-Port-Joli
St-Damase-des-Aulnaies
St-Aubert
L'Islet-sur-Mer
L'Islet
Tourville
St-Eugène
St-Cyrille-de-l'Islet
Ste-Perpétue
St-Omer
Lac-de-l'Est
ZEC CHAPAIS
CANADA
UNITED STATES
QUÉBEC
MAINE
Pohénégamook
St-Éleuthère
Pied-du-Lac
St-Athanase
St-Placide-de-Charlevoix
St-Cassien-des-Caps
Petite-Rivière-St-François
St-Tite-des-Caps
St-Ferréol-les-Neiges
La Miche
Grosse Île Natl. Hist. Site
L'Isle-aux-Grues
Cap-Tourmente
Ste-Anne-de-Beaupré
Beaupré
Cap-St-Ignace
St-François
Château-Richer
L'Ange-Gardien
Ste-Famille
Île d'Orléans
St-Jean
Montmagny
Bras-d'Apic
Ste-Félicité
St-Pamphile
St-Marcel
Notre-Dame-du-Rosaire
St-Adalbert
Charlesbourg
Loretteville
Québec
Ste-Foy
Charny
St-Michel-de-Bellechasse
St-Raphaël
Ste-Euphémie
St-Paul-de-Montminy
Ste-Apolline
Ste-Lucie-de-Beauregard
Shannon
St-Raymond
Ste-Catherine-de-la-Jacques-Cartier
Pont-Rouge
Bernières-St-Nicolas
Donnacona
Deschambault-Grondines
Lotbinière
Ste-Croix
St-Henri
St-Charles-de-Bellechasse
St-Gervais
Armagh
St-Nérée
Honfleur
St-Damien-de-Buckland
Buckland
St-Philémon
St-Fabien-de-Panet
Lac-Frontière
PARC RÉGIONAL DU MASSIF DU SUD
St-Apollinaire
St-Agapit
Ste-Claire
St-Anselme
St-Isidore
St-Malachie
St-Nazaire-de-Buckland
Daaquam
St-Just-de-Bretenières
Laurier-Station
St-Flavien
Joly
Dosquet
St-Gilles
Ste-Hénédine
Ste-Édouard-de-Frampton
St-Léon-de-Standon
St-Luc
Ste-Sabine
St-Camille-de-Lellis
Ste-Sabine-Station
Val-Alain
Lyster
Ste-Agathe
Ste-Marie
St-Elzéar
St-Sylvestre
Vallée-Jonction
Sts-Anges
St-Odilon
Lac-Etchemin
Ste-Germaine-Station
Ste-Justine
Ste-Rose-de-Watford
St-Cyprien
St-Séverin
St-Frédéric
Plessisville
Laurierville
Inverness
St-Jacques-de-Leeds
St-Pierre-de-Broughton
St-Joseph-de-Beauce
Tring-Jonction
St-Benjamin
Morisset-Station
St-Louis-de-Gonzague
St-Prosper
Princeville
Kinnear's Mills
East Broughton
Broughton Station
Notre-Dame-des-Pins
Beauceville
St-Jean-de-Brébeuf
Robertsonville
St-Adrien-d'Irlande
Ste-Clotilde-de-Beauce
St-Victor
St-Georges
Jersey Mills
Ste-Aurélie
St-Zacharie
Thetford Mines
Black Lake
St-Éphrem-de-Tring
St-Benoît-Labre
St-Côme--Linière
Vianney
Vimy-Ridge
Adstock
St-René
St-Fortunat
St-Jacques-le-Majeur-de-Wolfestown
St-Joseph-de-Coleraine
La Guadeloupe
St-Honoré
St-Martin
St-Théophile
Armstrong
Ham-Nord
Disraëli
Ste-Praxède
St-Évariste-de-Forsyth
Courcelles
St-Hilaire-de-Dorset
Lambton
St-Gédéon
ZEC JARO
Sts-Martyrs-Canadiens
Beaulac
PARC NATIONAL DE FRONTENAC
St-Sébastien
St-Romain
Stratford
St-Gérard
Ham-Sud
Val-des-Sources
Wottonville
Weedon Centre
Stornoway
Lac Drolet
St-Ludger
Lac-Drolet
St-Samuel-Station
Ste-Cécile-de-Whitton
Audet
St-Robert-Bellarmin
Fontainebleau
Marbleton
Gould
Milan
Nantes
Lac-Mégantic
Frontenac
Dudswell (Bishopton)
Stoke
East Angus
Scotstown
Marsboro
Val-Racine
Piopolis
Sherbrooke
Ascot Corner
Bury
Cookshire-Eaton
West Ditton
La Patrie
Notre-Dame-des-Bois
Woburn
Coburn Gore
Lennoxville
Eaton
Island Brook
Sawyerville
Randboro
Martinville
St-Isidore-d'Auckland
Chartierville
Waterville
Ste-Catherine-de-Hatley
St-Malo
Coaticook
St-Herménégilde
Barnston
Dixville
East Hereford
PARC NATIONAL DU MONT-MÉGANTIC
ZEC LOUISE GOSFORD (SECTEUR GOSFORD)
ZEC LOUISE GOSFORD (SECTEUR LOUISE)
Chain of Ponds Public Reserved Land
Skinner
Jackman
Jackman Station
Dennistown
Long Pond
Moosehead
Lake Parlin
HOLEB PUBLIC RESERVED LAND
Gerard
West Forks
Lake Moxie
The Forks
Pleasant Pond
Caratunk
Grand Falls
Eustis
Stratton
Bigelow
Carrabassett
DEAD RIVER PUBLIC RESERVED LAND
BIGELOW PRESERVE
SOMERSET
PISCATAQUIS
OXFORD
COOS
MAINE
NEW HAMPSHIRE
Dickey
Allagash
RESTRICTED ROADS
ROUND POND PUBLIC RESERVED LAND
ALLAGASH WILDERNESS WATERWAY
Clayton Lake
CHAMBERLAIN LAKE PUBLIC RESERVED LAND
TELOS PUBLIC RESERVED LAND
BAXTER STATE PARK
GERO ISLAND PUBLIC RESERVED LAND
Chesuncook Village
Pittston Farm
Seboomook
North East Carry
MOOSEHEAD LAKE PUBLIC RESERVED LAND
Rockwood
Kokadjo
NAHMAKANTA PUBLIC RESERVED LAND
Lily Bay
Lily Bay S.P.
Greenville
Greenville Junction
Big Squaw
Moosehead Marine Mus.
LITTLE MOOSE PUBLIC RESERVED LAND
Gulf Hagas
Katahdin Iron Works S.H.S.
Shirley Mills
Little Wilson Falls
Bodfish
Onawa
Willimantic
Monson
Sebec Lake
Brownville
Brownville Junction
Knight Landing
Bowerbank
Sebec
Milo
Derby
Kenny S.P.
Greeley Landing
Blanchard
North Guilford
Dover-Foxcroft
Abbot Village
Guilford
Sangerville
Parkman
Blacksmith Shop Mus.
S. Dover
Atkinson Corners
Mayfield Corner
Kingsbury
Kelly Brook Mtn. 1,483
Priestly Mtn. 1,900
Hudson Mtn. 1,935
Hardwood Mtn. 1,518
Poland Mtn. 1,870
Telos Mtn. 1,329
Little Russell Mtn. 2,376
Strickland Mtn. 2,390
Center Mtn. 2,902
North Brother 4,143
Doubletop Mtn. 3,488
Seboomook Mtn. 2,390
Green Mtn. 2,395
Boundary Bald Mtn. 3,640
Sandy Stream Mtn. 2,869
Sandy Bay Mtn. 3,117
Big Spencer Mtn. 3,230
Wadleigh Mtn. 1,863
Attean Mtn. 2,442
Baker Mtn. 3,520
Jo-Mary Mtn. 2,904
White Cap Mtn. 3,644
Saddleback Mtn. 2,998
Big Moose Mtn. 3,196
Tumbledown Mtn. 3,542
Three Slide Mtn. 3,112
Kibby Mtn. 3,638
Coburn Mtn. 3,718
Barren Mtn. 2,660
Hurricane Mtn. 2,142
Snow Mtn. 3,948
Deer Mtn. 3,005
Salmon Mtn. 3,364
Rump Mtn. 3,647
White Cap Mtn. 3,815
Boil Mtn. 3,601
Snow Mtn. 3,755
W. Kennebago Mtn. 3,705
E. Kennebago Mtn. 3,825
West Peak 4,150
Stewart Mtn. 2,671
Russell Mtn. 2,187
Moxie Mtn. 2,925
Ripogenus Dam
A
B
C
1
2
3
4

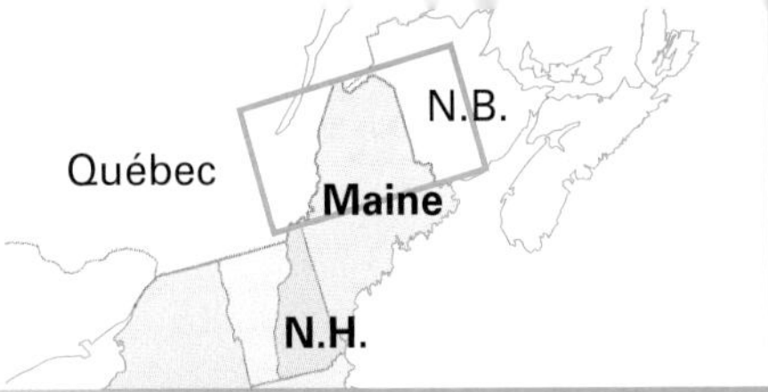

DRIVING DISTANCES IN MILES

	BANGOR, ME	CALAIS, ME	CARIBOU, ME	FREDERICTON, NB	GREENVILLE, ME	HOULTON, ME	JACKMAN, ME	LINCOLN, ME	MADAWASKA, ME	MILLINOCKET, ME	PRESQUE ISLE, ME	QUÉBEC, QC
HOULTON, ME	122	91	55	73	155		204	83	102	73	42	286
LINCOLN, ME	51	77	135	114	83	83	132		174	35	122	231
MADAWASKA, ME	214	207	50	167	212	102	269	174		164	62	182
PRESQUE ISLE, ME	162	133	13	113	166	42	215	122	62	113		246

SEE ALSO DISTANCE AND DRIVING TIME MAP ON PAGES 286–287

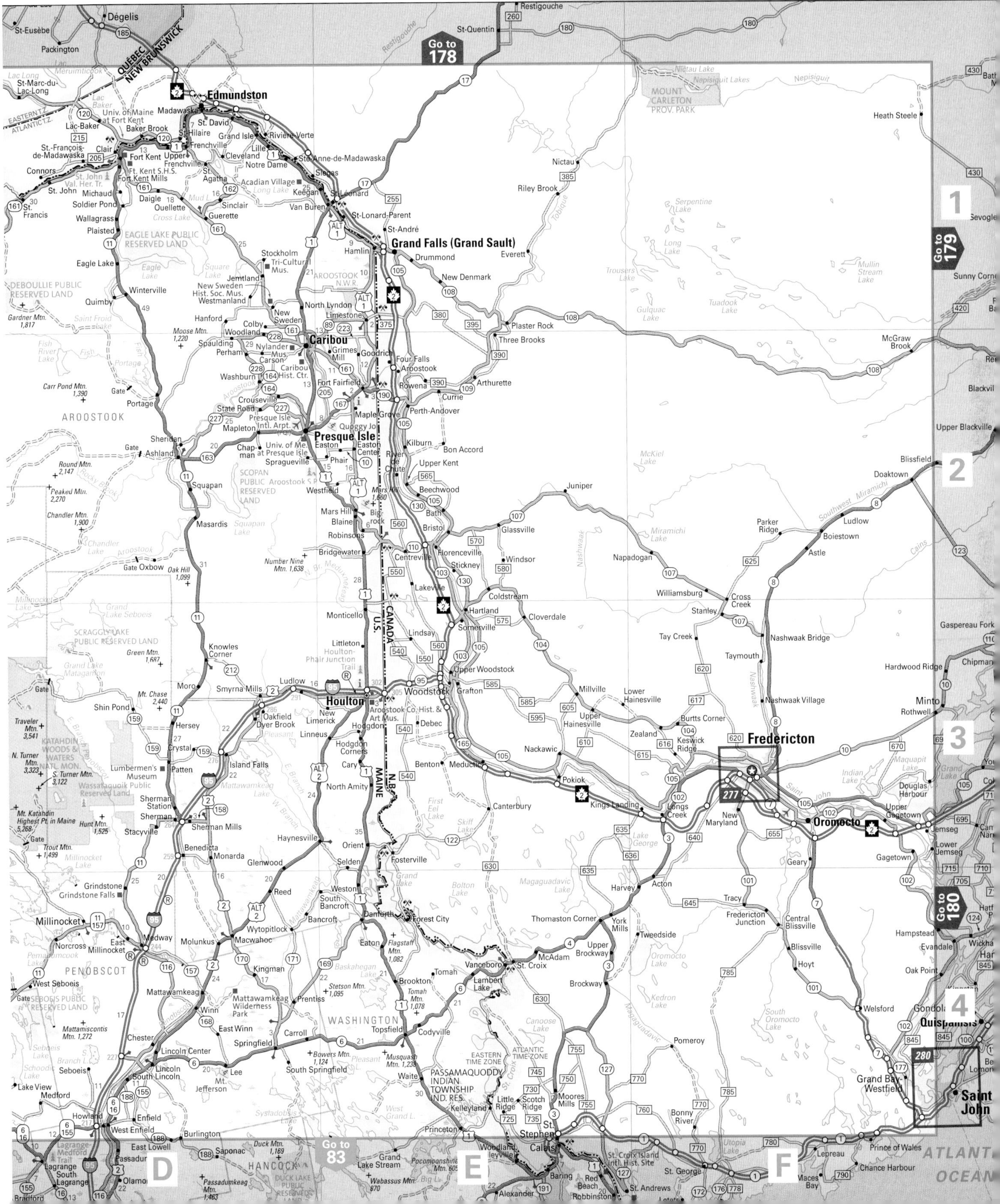

0 mi 10 20 30 40
0 km 10 20 30 40 50 60

One inch equals 18.4 miles
One centimeter equals 11.7 kilometers

Des Moines IA / Omaha NE

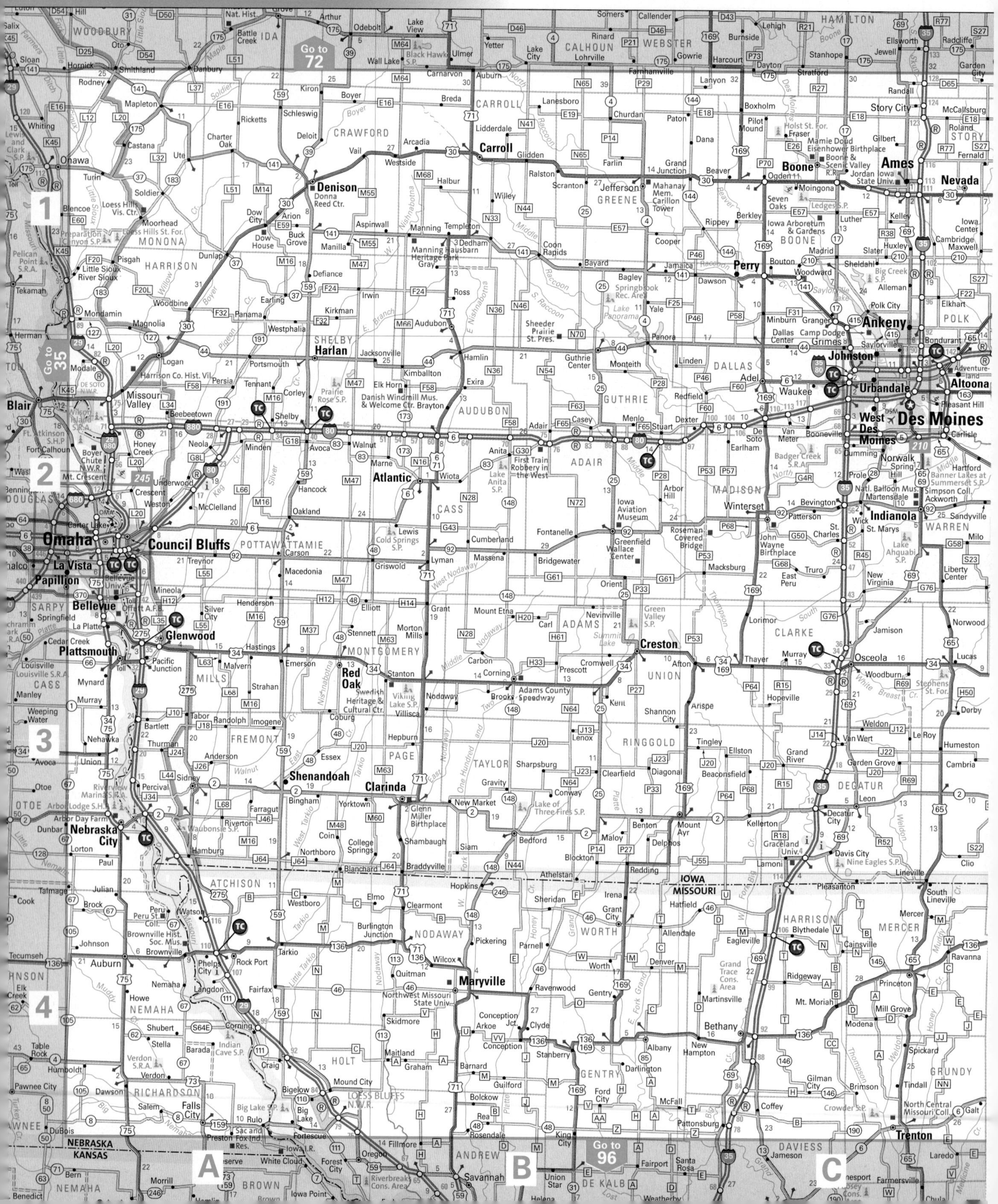

DRIVING DISTANCES IN MILES

	AMES, IA	BURLINGTON, IA	CARROLL, IA	CEDAR RAPIDS, IA	CRESTON, IA	DAVENPORT, IA	DES MOINES, IA	IOWA CITY, IA	KIRKSVILLE, MO	MARYVILLE, MO	OMAHA, NE	OTTUMWA, IA
CEDAR RAPIDS, IA	108	106	173		211	87	129	28	170	276	266	111
DES MOINES, IA	34	157	90	129	81	171		113	145	146	136	86
IOWA CITY, IA	136	82	195	28	195	59	113		143	260	250	83
OMAHA, NE	171	328	97	266	98	308	136	250	275	112		221

SEE ALSO DISTANCE AND DRIVING TIME MAP ON PAGES 286–287

0 mi 10 20 30 40
0 km 10 20 30 40 50 60
One inch equals 18.4 miles
One centimeter equals 11.7 kilometers

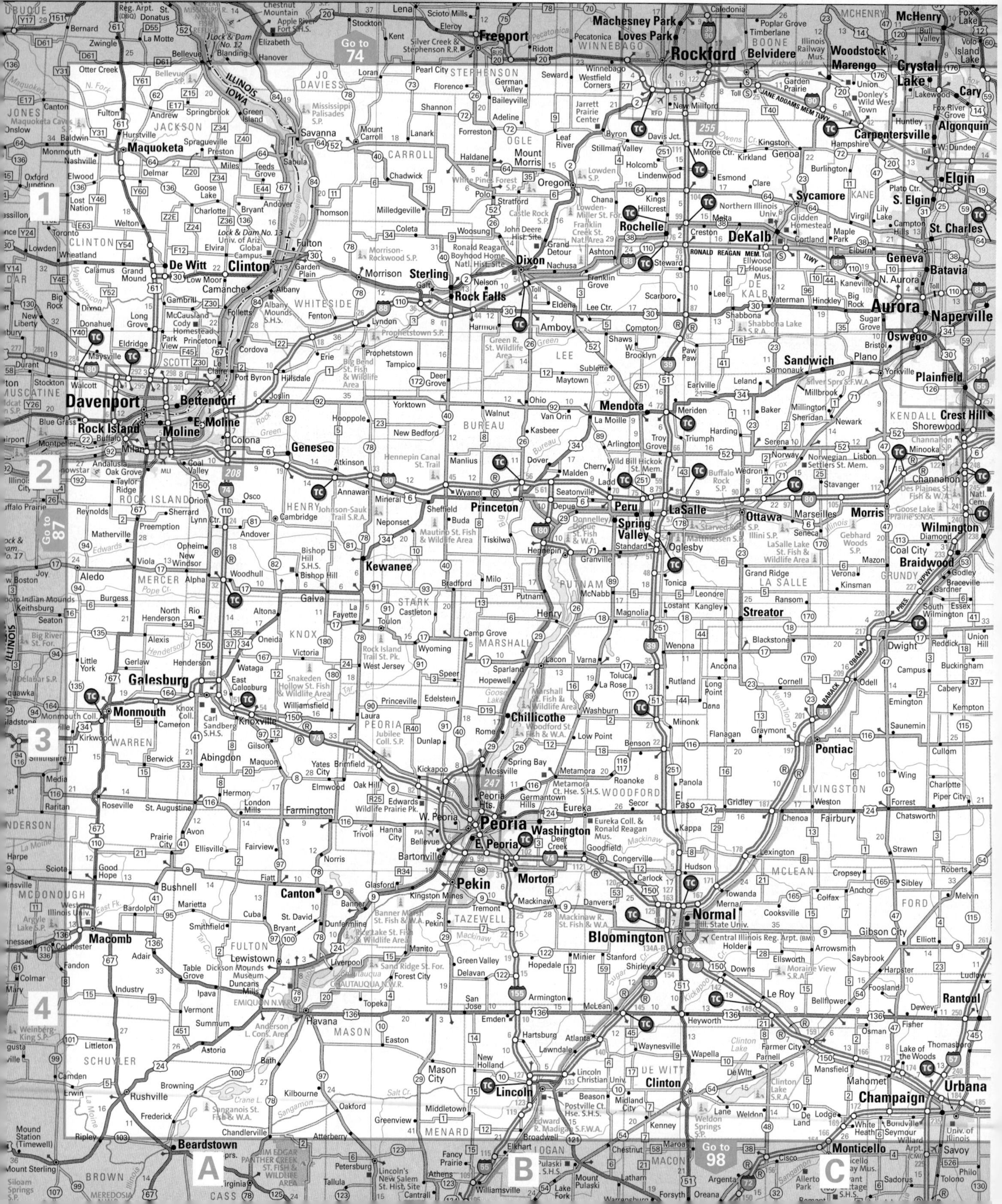

DRIVING DISTANCES IN MILES

	BLOOMINGTON, IL	CHAMPAIGN, IL	CHICAGO, IL	DAVENPORT, IA	JOLIET, IL	KALAMAZOO, MI	KOKOMO, IN	LAFAYETTE, IN	LA SALLE, IL	PEORIA, IL	ROCKFORD, IL	SOUTH BEND, IN
CHAMPAIGN, IL	54		141	192	115	255	145	94	117	94	189	198
CHICAGO, IL	135	141		170	40	150	158	121	98	168	86	93
PEORIA, IL	41	94	168	99	132	291	235	184	63		135	234
SOUTH BEND, IN	201	198	93	248	105	76	86	104	164	234	183	

SEE ALSO DISTANCE AND DRIVING TIME MAP ON PAGES 286–287

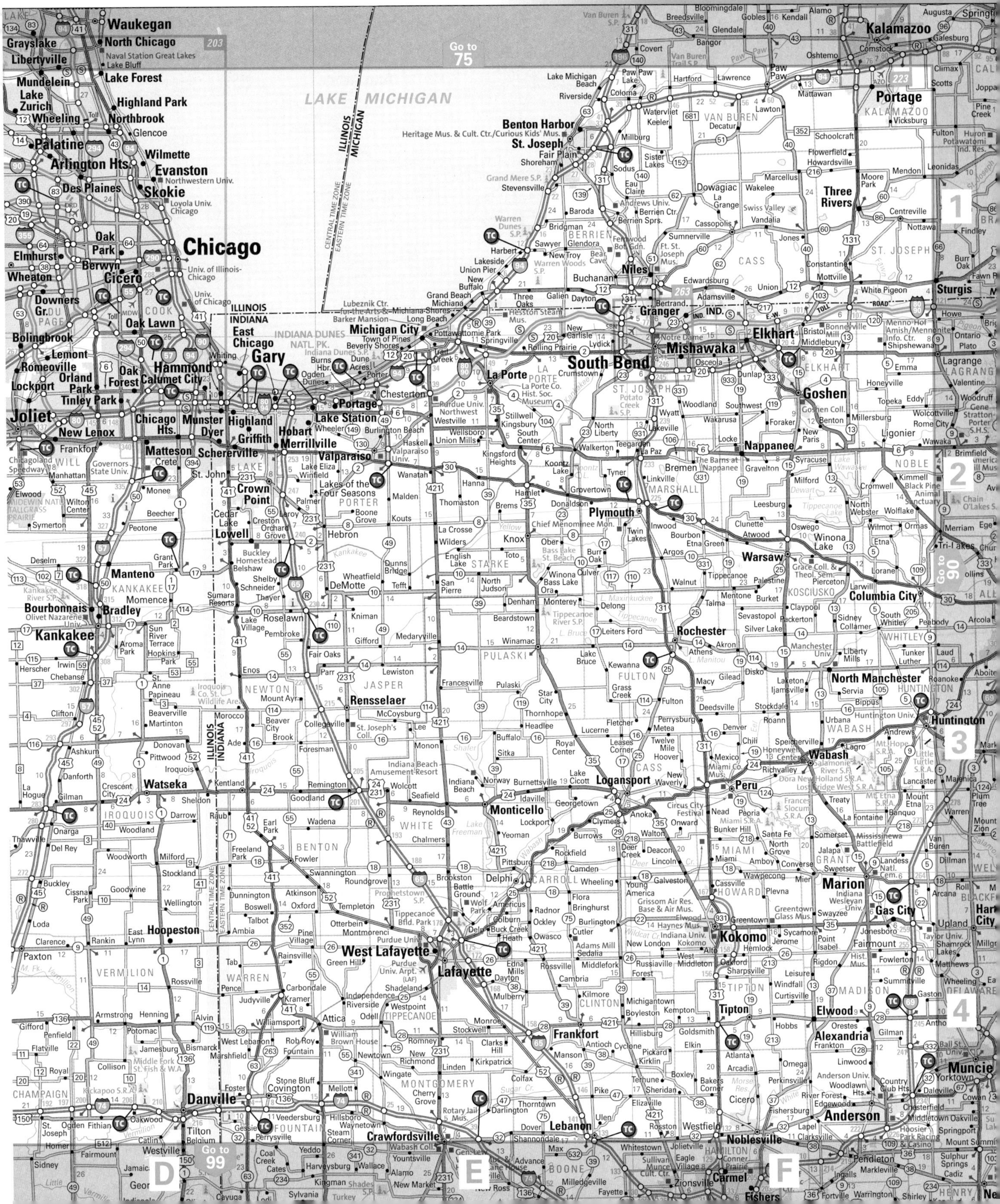

0 mi 10 20 30 40
0 km 10 20 30 40 50 60

One inch equals 18.4 miles

One centimeter equals 11.7 kilometers

Fort Wayne IN / Toledo OH

DRIVING DISTANCES IN MILES

	AKRON, OH	CLEVELAND, OH	COLUMBUS, OH	DETROIT, MI	ERIE, PA	FORT WAYNE, IN	LIMA, OH	MANSFIELD, OH	MUNCIE, IN	TOLEDO, OH	WHEELING, WV	YOUNGSTOWN, OH
CLEVELAND, OH	38		144	171	106	214	163	81	287	119	162	75
FORT WAYNE, IN	237	214	186	170	322		66	151	75	109	290	274
MANSFIELD, OH	66	81	67	156	179	151	93		209	105	141	112
TOLEDO, OH	142	119	148	60	227	109	83	105	180		261	179

SEE ALSO DISTANCE AND DRIVING TIME MAP ON PAGES 286–287

0 mi 10 20 30 40
0 km 10 20 30 40 50 60

One inch equals 18.4 miles
One centimeter equals 11.7 kilometers

Pittsburgh PA / Erie PA

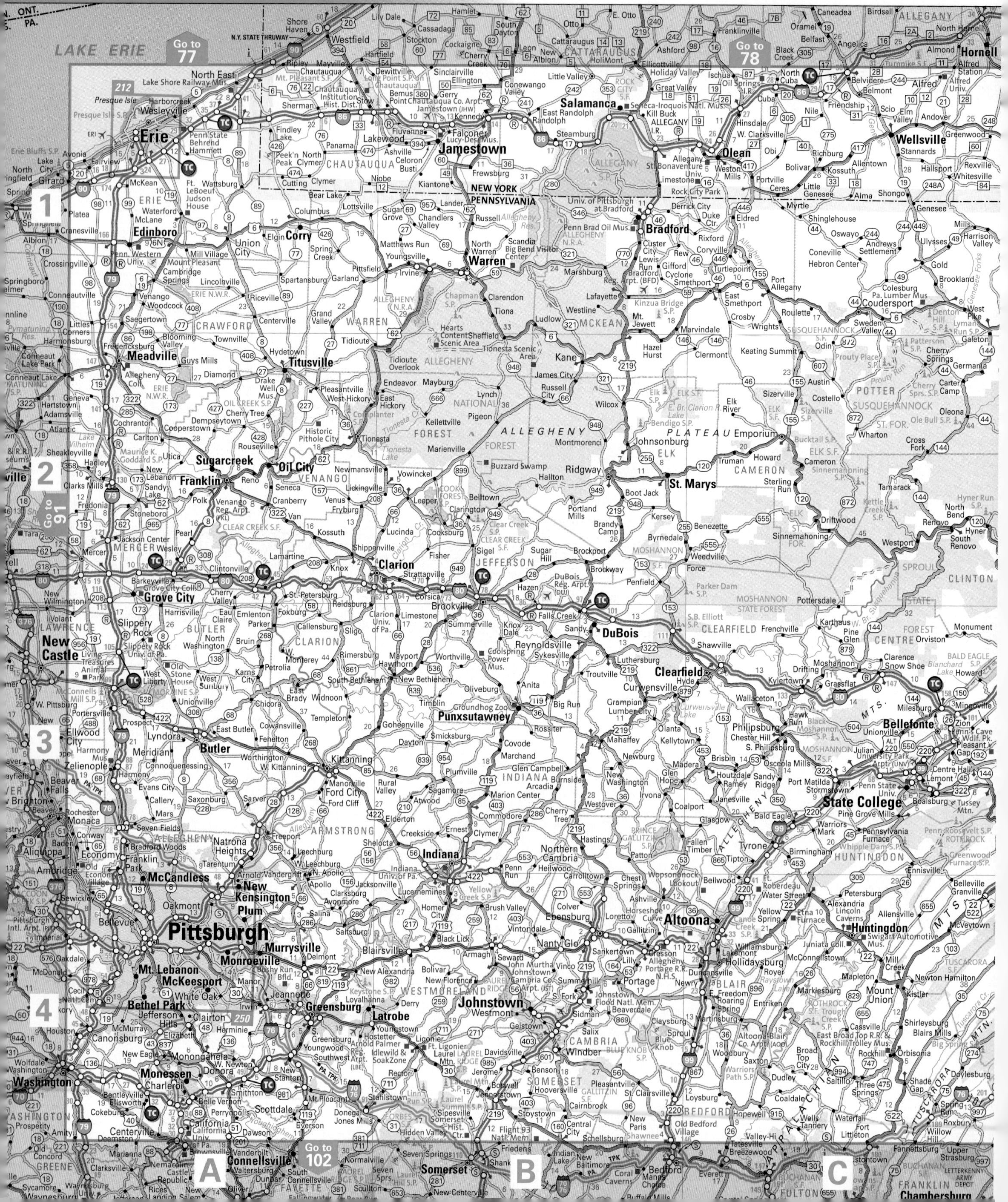

DRIVING DISTANCES IN MILES

	ALLENTOWN, PA	ALTOONA, PA	BINGHAMTON, NY	ELMIRA, NY	ERIE, PA	HARRISBURG, PA	JOHNSTOWN, PA	PITTSBURGH, PA	READING, PA	SCRANTON, PA	STATE COLLEGE, PA	WILLIAMSPORT, PA
ALLENTOWN, PA		218	132	188	361	82	217	284	37	76	165	116
HARRISBURG, PA	82	140	181	157	298		138	205	65	119	88	83
PITTSBURGH, PA	284	99	363	284	126	205	73		262	301	139	215
SCRANTON, PA	76	185	61	117	317	119	233	301	103		149	83

SEE ALSO DISTANCE AND DRIVING TIME MAP ON PAGES 286–287

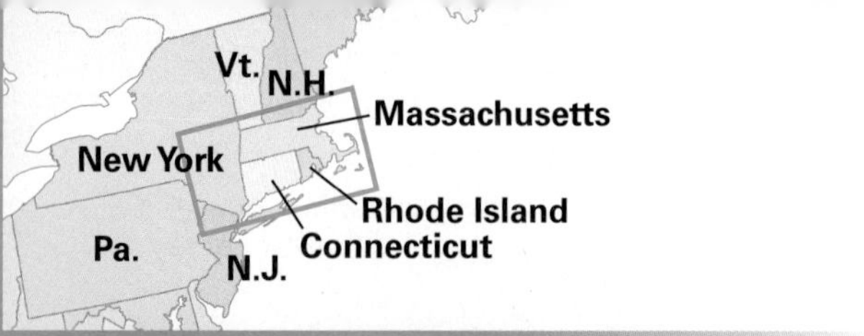

0 mi 10 20 30 40
0 km 10 20 30 40 50 60

One inch equals 18.4 miles

One centimeter equals 11.7 kilometers

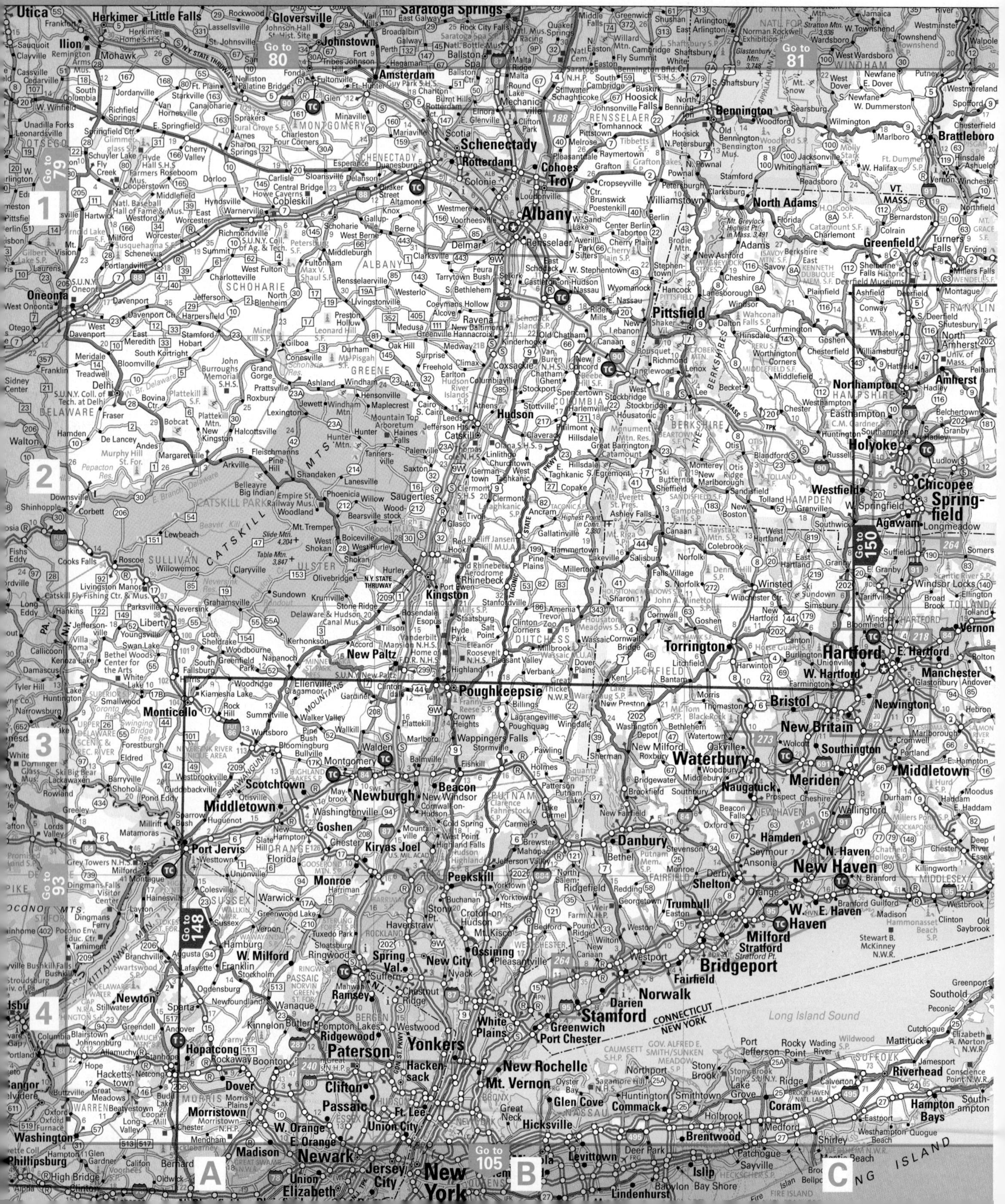

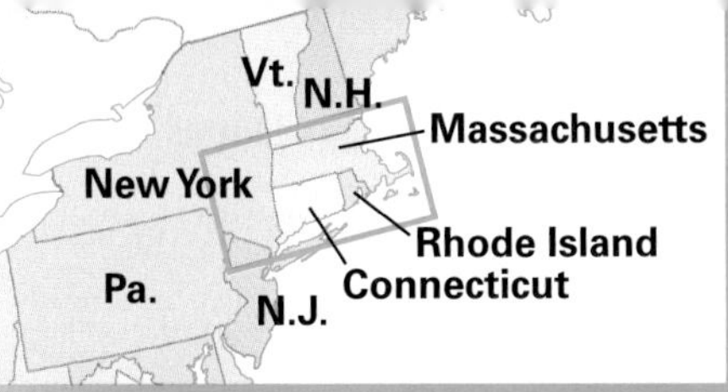

DRIVING DISTANCES IN MILES

	ALBANY, NY	BOSTON, MA	HARTFORD, CT	MANCHESTER, NH	NEWBURGH, NY	NEW HAVEN, CT	NEW YORK, NY	ONEONTA, NY	PROVIDENCE, RI	PROVINCETOWN, MA	SPRINGFIELD, MA	WORCESTER, MA
ALBANY, NY		172	111	145	89	150	151	81	170	271	86	133
BOSTON, MA	172		102	54	201	139	215	251	52	117	95	46
HARTFORD, CT	111	102		131	99	39	115	190	73	200	25	62
NEW YORK, NY	151	215	115	245	56	78		193	177	292	141	176

SEE ALSO DISTANCE AND DRIVING TIME MAP ON PAGES 286–287

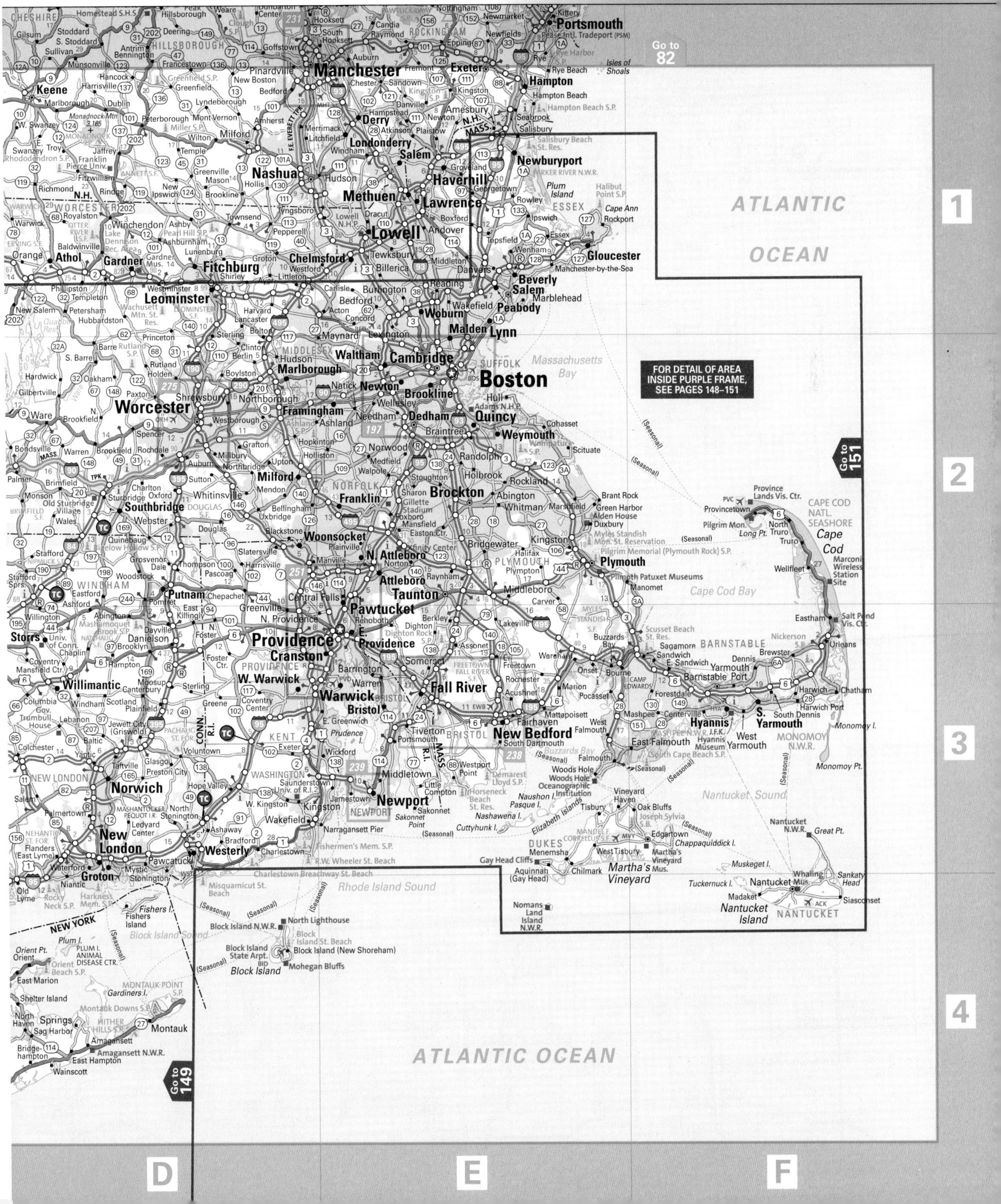

0 mi 10 20 30 40

0 km 10 20 30 40 50 60

One inch equals 18.4 miles

One centimeter equals 11.7 kilometers

Kansas City MO / Topeka KS

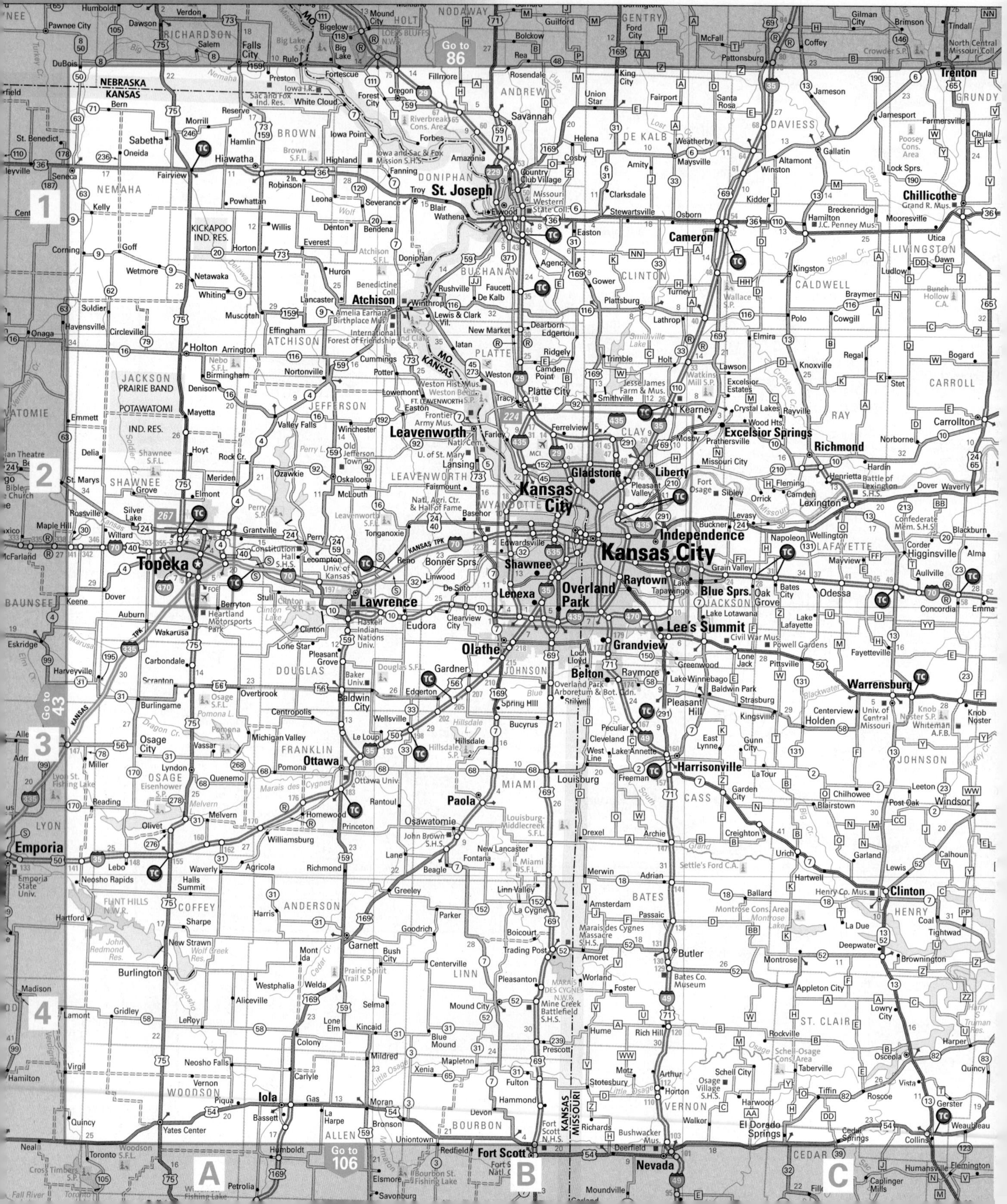

DRIVING DISTANCES IN MILES	COLUMBIA, MO	IOLA, KS	JEFFERSON CITY, MO	KANSAS CITY, MO	LAWRENCE, KS	MACON, MO	OSAGE BEACH, MO	QUINCY, IL	ROLLA, MO	ST. JOSEPH, MO	SEDALIA, MO	TOPEKA, KS
JEFFERSON CITY, MO	32	263		161	198	88	44	131	65	217	64	225
KANSAS CITY, MO	129	106	161		37	148	173	251	226	56	97	63
ST. JOSEPH, MO	185	154	217	56	76	131	229	210	282		153	71
TOPEKA, KS	193	100	225	63	26	209	236	314	289	71	161	

SEE ALSO DISTANCE AND DRIVING TIME MAP ON PAGES 286–287

0 mi 10 20 30 40
0 km 10 20 30 40 50 60

One inch equals 18.4 miles
One centimeter equals 11.7 kilometers

St Louis MO / Springfield IL

DRIVING DISTANCES IN MILES

	BLOOMINGTON, IN	CHAMPAIGN, IL	DECATUR, IL	EFFINGHAM, IL	EVANSVILLE, IN	INDIANAPOLIS, IN	LOUISVILLE, KY	MT. VERNON, IL	ST. LOUIS, MO	SPRINGFIELD, IL	TERRE HAUTE, IN	VINCENNES, IN
EVANSVILLE, IN	117	192	184	117		166	114	90	170	247	107	51
INDIANAPOLIS, IN	47	123	177	137	166		112	205	239	212	77	123
ST. LOUIS, MO	223	179	116	103	170	239	264	81		97	169	185
SPRINGFIELD, IL	209	87	40	89	247	212	326	158	97		155	169

SEE ALSO DISTANCE AND DRIVING TIME MAP ON PAGES 286–287

0 mi 10 20 30 40
0 km 10 20 30 40 50 60
One inch equals 18.4 miles
One centimeter equals 11.7 kilometers

Cincinnati OH / Louisville KY

DRIVING DISTANCES IN MILES

	CHARLESTON, WV	CHILLICOTHE, OH	CINCINNATI, OH	COLUMBUS, OH	DAYTON, OH	HUNTINGTON, WV	LEXINGTON, KY	LOUISVILLE, KY	MAYSVILLE, KY	PARKERSBURG, WV	WHEELING, WV	ZANESVILLE, OH
CHARLESTON, WV		121	202	168	198	52	176	251	155	73	176	155
CINCINNATI, OH	202	108		109	52	150	85	100	63	191	235	164
COLUMBUS, OH	168	47	109		70	135	193	207	114	108	130	58
LEXINGTON, KY	176	191	85	193	135	126		80	67	249	319	247

SEE ALSO DISTANCE AND DRIVING TIME MAP ON PAGES 286–287

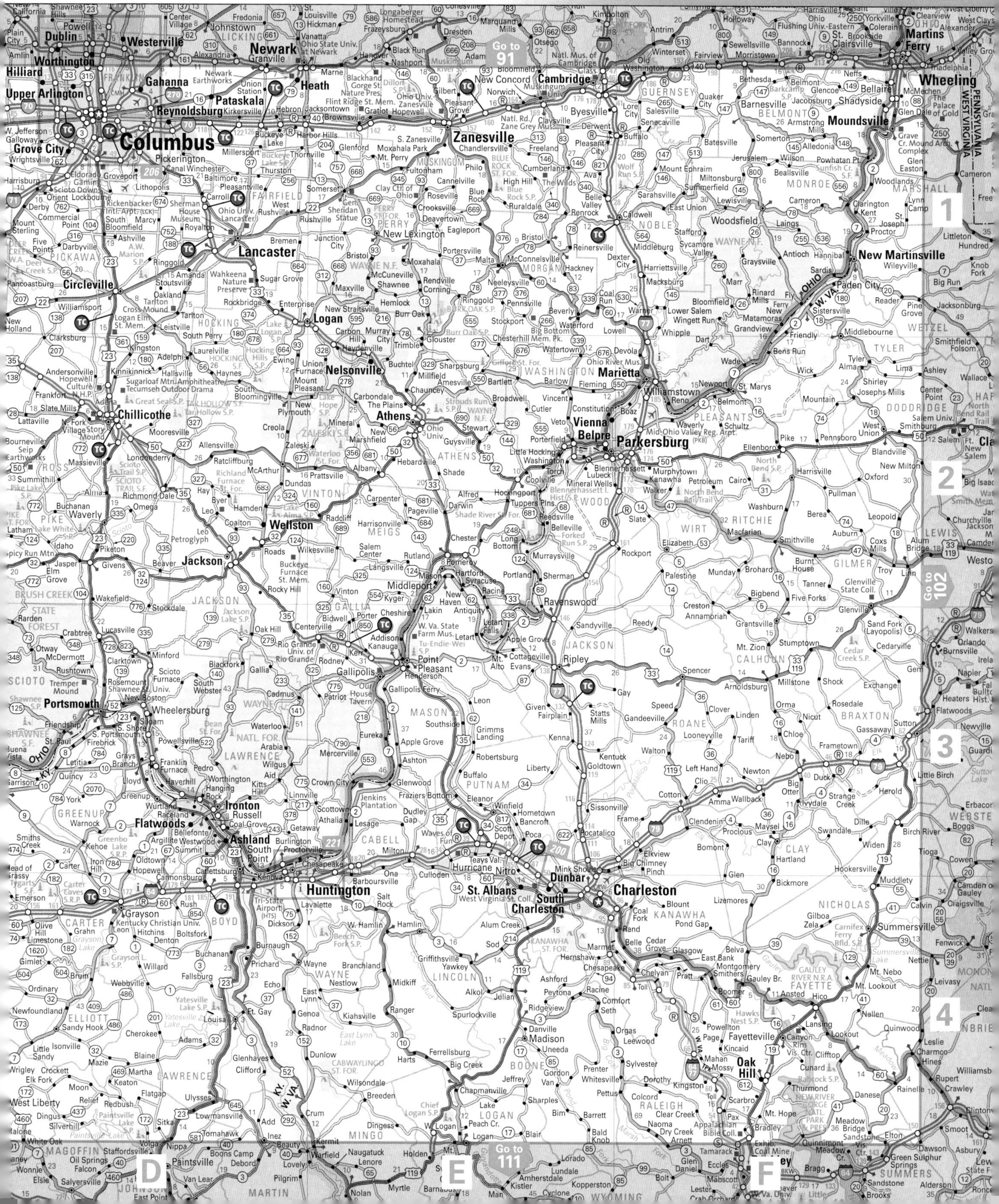

0 mi 10 20 30 40
0 km 10 20 30 40 50 60

One inch equals 18.4 miles
One centimeter equals 11.7 kilometers

Charlottesville VA / Morgantown WV

DRIVING DISTANCES IN MILES

	BALTIMORE, MD	CHARLOTTESVILLE, VA	CUMBERLAND, MD	ELKINS, WV	FREDERICKSBURG, VA	FRONT ROYAL, VA	GETTYSBURG, PA	HAGERSTOWN, MD	MORGANTOWN, WV	SALISBURY, MD	WASHINGTON, DC	WHEELING, WV
BALTIMORE, MD		161	140	229	98	110	62	76	211	106	38	290
CHARLOTTESVILLE, VA	161		163	142	70	74	190	141	204	235	118	279
MORGANTOWN, WV	211	204	71	62	252	161	181	138		317	205	76
WASHINGTON, DC	38	118	134	192	54	73	80	70	205	115		284

SEE ALSO DISTANCE AND DRIVING TIME MAP ON PAGES 286–287

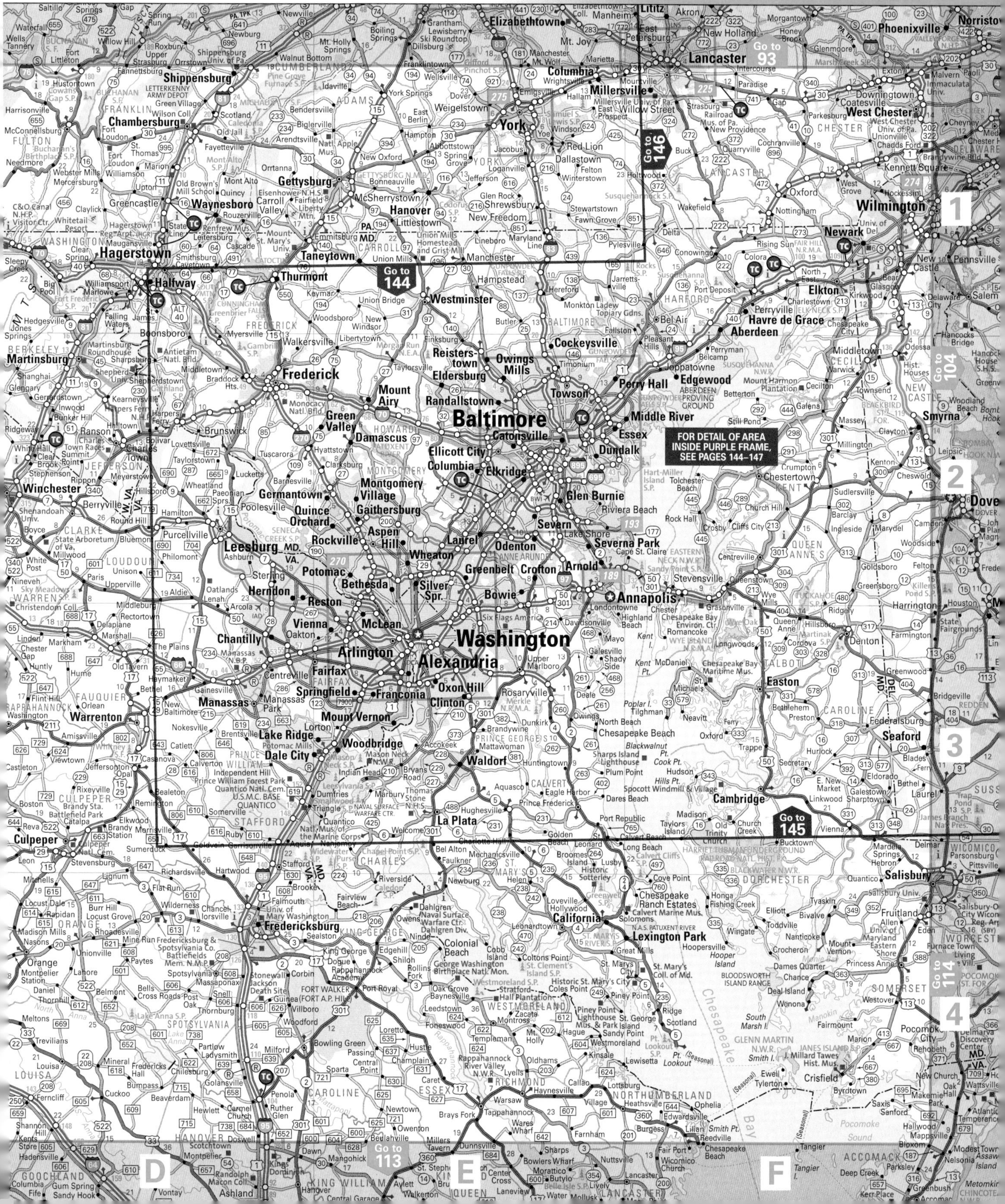

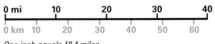

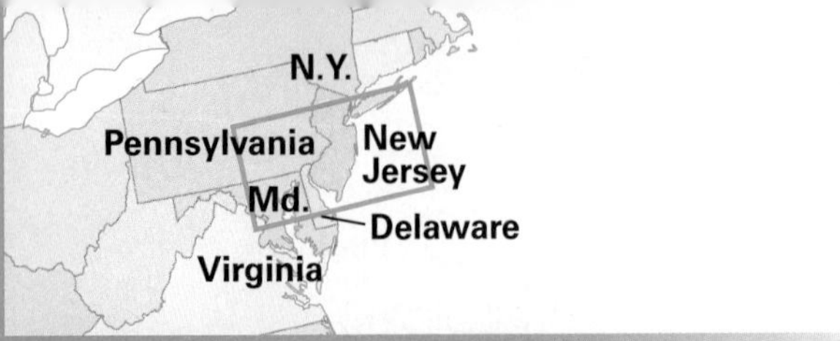

0 mi 10 20 30 40
0 km 10 20 30 40 50 60

One inch equals 18.4 miles
One centimeter equals 11.7 kilometers

DRIVING DISTANCES IN MILES

	ALLENTOWN, PA	ATLANTIC CITY, NJ	BALTIMORE, MD	DOVER, DE	HARRISBURG, PA	LANCASTER, PA	NEWARK, NJ	NEW YORK, NY	PHILADELPHIA, PA	TRENTON, NJ	WASHINGTON, DC	WILMINGTON, DE
HARRISBURG, PA	82	171	83	126		44	154	165	109	135	123	102
NEW YORK, NY	84	125	192	160	165	165	11		91	55	228	120
PHILADELPHIA, PA	63	62	104	74	109	79	80	91		34	140	30
WASHINGTON, DC	188	186	38	94	123	123	218	228	140	179		110

SEE ALSO DISTANCE AND DRIVING TIME MAP ON PAGES 286–287

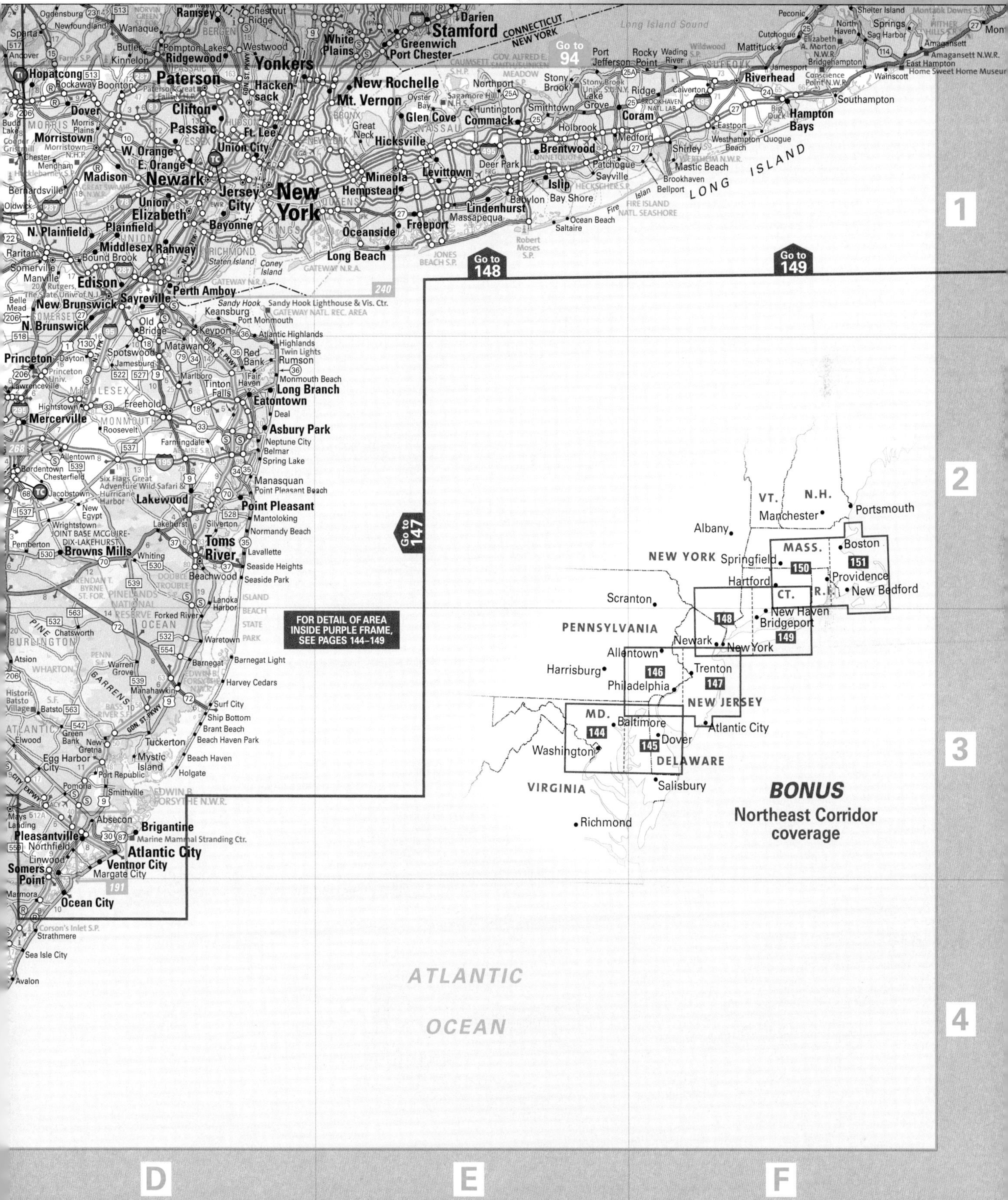

0 mi 10 20 30 40
0 km 10 20 30 40 50 60

One inch equals 18.4 miles
One centimeter equals 11.7 kilometers

Tulsa OK / Fayetteville AR

DRIVING DISTANCES IN MILES

	BARTLESVILLE, OK	BRANSON, MO	FAYETTEVILLE, AR	INDEPENDENCE, KS	JOPLIN, MO	MOUNTAIN HOME, AR	MUSKOGEE, OK	NEWPORT, AR	ROLLA, MO	SPRINGFIELD, MO	TULSA, OK	WEST PLAINS, MO
BRANSON, MO	213		95	188	111	84	181	178	147	41	225	109
FAYETTEVILLE, AR	154	95		165	88	127	86	241	227	121	113	182
SPRINGFIELD, MO	177	41	121	153	70	112	193	219	110		189	109
TULSA, OK	48	225	113	86	116	237	52	344	295	189		293

SEE ALSO DISTANCE AND DRIVING TIME MAP ON PAGES 286–287

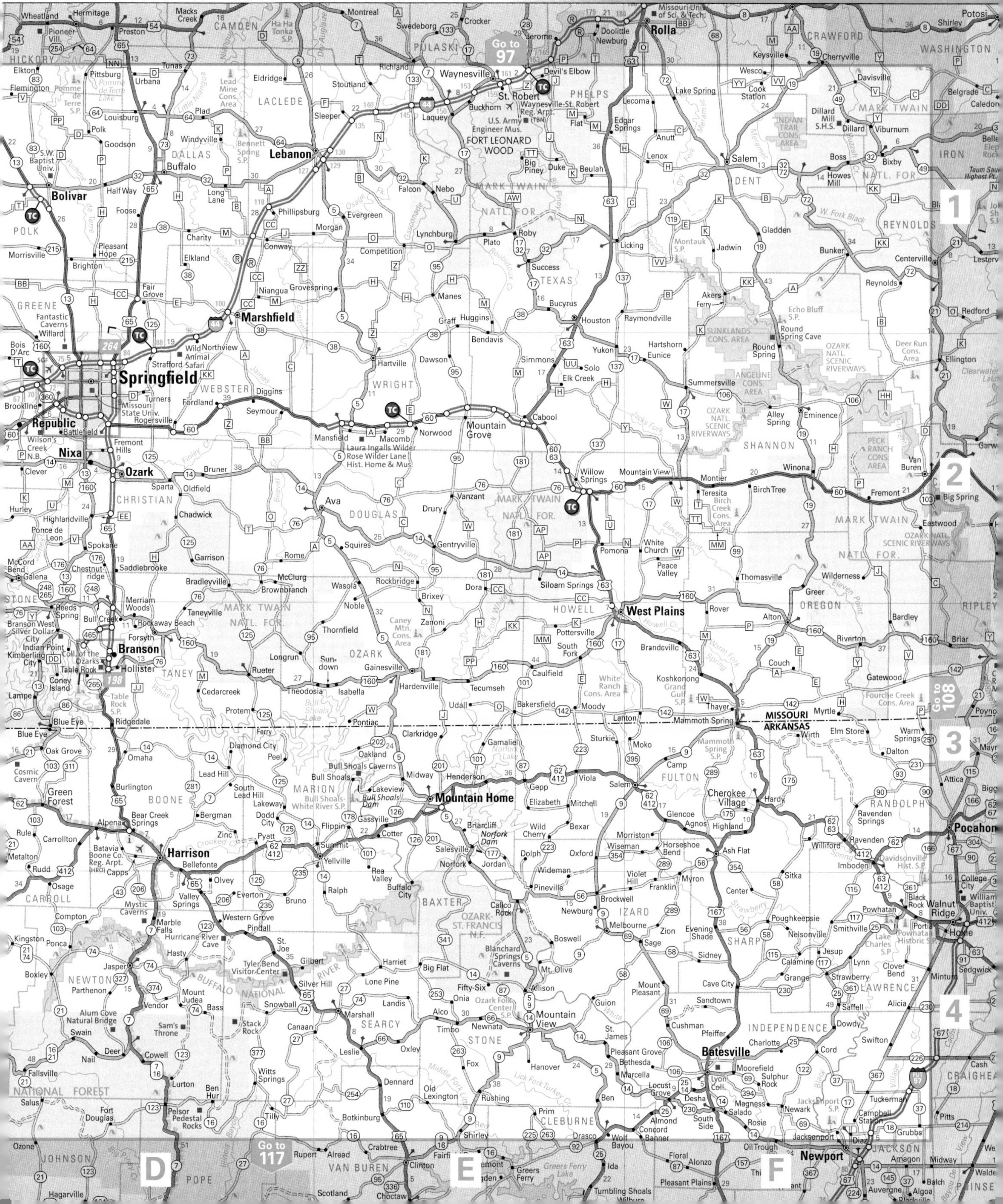

0 mi 10 20 30 40
0 km 10 20 30 40 50 60

One inch equals 18.4 miles
One centimeter equals 11.7 kilometers

Jonesboro AR / Cape Girardeau MO

DRIVING DISTANCES IN MILES

	BOWLING GREEN, KY	CAPE GIRARDEAU, MO	CARBONDALE, IL	CLARKSVILLE, TN	DYERSBURG, TN	HOPKINSVILLE, KY	JACKSON, TN	JONESBORO, AR	NASHVILLE, TN	OWENSBORO, KY	PADUCAH, KY	POPLAR BLUFF, MO
BOWLING GREEN, KY		199	206	63	217	63	196	349	68	76	135	239
CAPE GIRARDEAU, MO	199		46	155	112	136	161	155	197	168	67	75
JONESBORO, AR	349	155	199	268	101	249	160		285	304	178	81
NASHVILLE, TN	68	197	204	46	178	68	132	285		141	133	237

SEE ALSO DISTANCE AND DRIVING TIME MAP ON PAGES 286–287

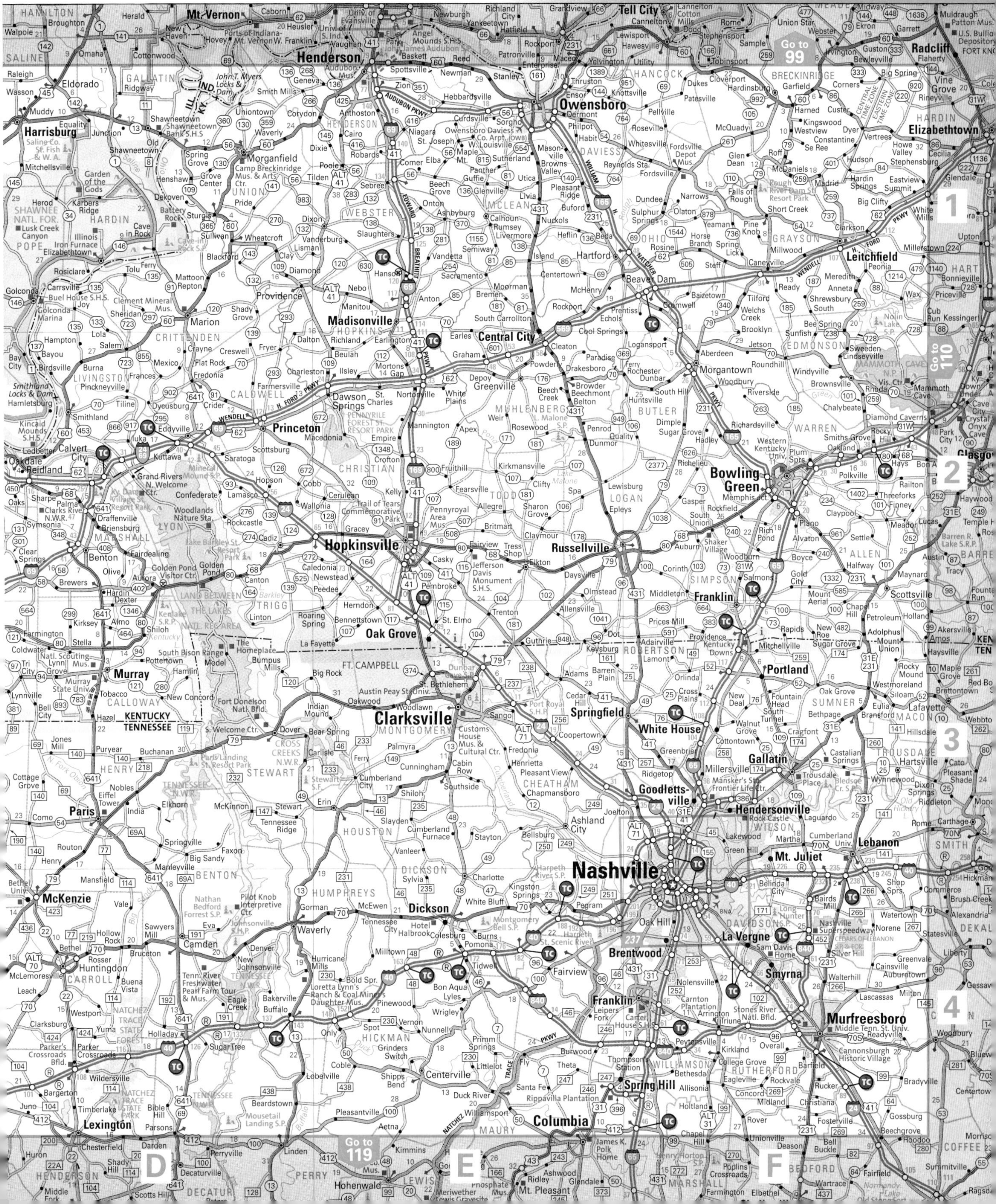

0 mi 10 20 30 40
0 km 10 20 30 40 50 60

One inch equals 18.4 miles
One centimeter equals 11.7 kilometers

Knoxville TN / Richmond KY

DRIVING DISTANCES IN MILES

	ASHEVILLE, NC	BECKLEY, WV	BRISTOL, TN/VA	COOKEVILLE, TN	GATLINBURG, TN	HICKORY, NC	JOHNSON CITY, TN	KNOXVILLE, TN	LONDON, KY	MAMMOTH CAVE NP, KY	PIKEVILLE, KY	RICHMOND, KY
BRISTOL, TN/VA	83	140		224	118	98	24	117	213	348	116	265
HICKORY, NC	78	196	98	291	147		98	185	280	415	214	332
KNOXVILLE, TN	109	256	117	107	40	185	107		100	234	202	151
LONDON, KY	205	287	213	129	136	280	203	100		136	121	53

SEE ALSO DISTANCE AND DRIVING TIME MAP ON PAGES 286–287

0 mi 10 20 30 40
0 km 10 20 30 40 50 60

One inch equals 18.4 miles

One centimeter equals 11.7 kilometers

Greensboro NC / Roanoke VA

DRIVING DISTANCES IN MILES

	DANVILLE, VA	GREENSBORO, NC	LYNCHBURG, VA	NORFOLK, VA	RALEIGH, NC	RICHMOND, VA	ROANOKE, VA	ROANOKE RAPIDS, NC	ROCKY MOUNT, NC	WILLIAMSBURG, VA	WINSTON-SALEM, NC	WYTHEVILLE, VA
GREENSBORO, NC	46		106	230	69	200	101	132	124	237	30	120
RALEIGH, NC	89	69	140	179		157	156	84	54	204	96	186
RICHMOND, VA	160	200	114	91	157		192	91	127	49	228	256
ROANOKE, VA	83	101	55	285	156	192		190	211	243	107	78

SEE ALSO DISTANCE AND DRIVING TIME MAP ON PAGES 286–287

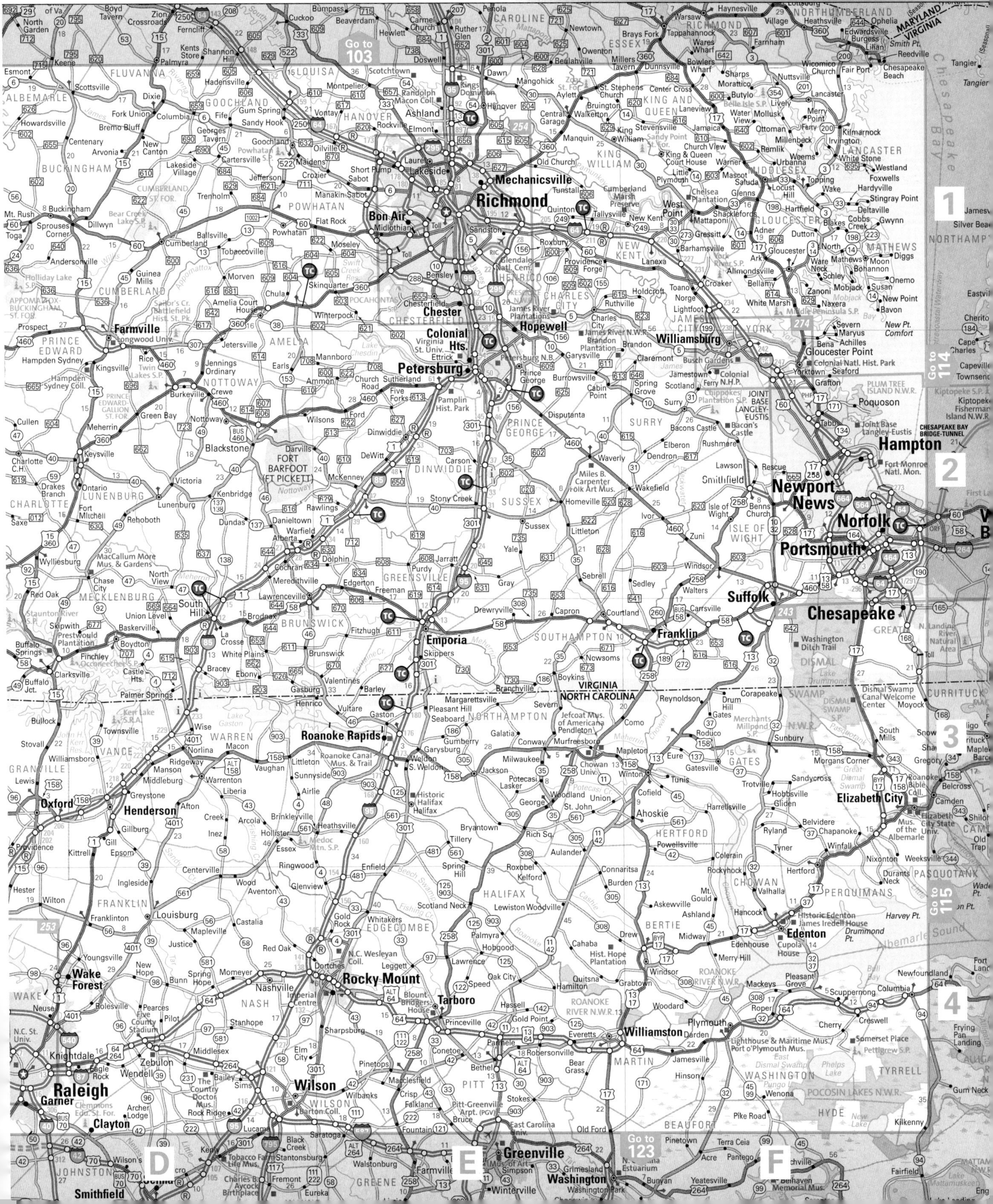

Md.
Delaware
Virginia
North Carolina

Norfolk VA / Ocean City MD

0 mi 10 20 30 40
0 km 10 20 30 40 50 60

One inch equals 18.4 miles

One centimeter equals 11.7 kilometers

Washington
Arlington
Alexandria
Annapolis
Richmond
Fredericksburg
Williamsburg
Hampton
Newport News
Norfolk
Portsmouth
Virginia Beach
Chesapeake
Suffolk
Petersburg
Salisbury
Ocean City
Easton
Cambridge
Seaford
Milford
Lewes
Chincoteague
Crisfield
Chesapeake Bay
ATLANTIC
OCEAN
FOR DETAIL OF AREA INSIDE PURPLE FRAME, SEE PAGES 144–145
Go to 104
Go to 103
Go to 144
Go to 145
Go to 113
Go to 115
MARYLAND
VIRGINIA
NORTH CAROLINA
1
2
3
4
A
B
C

DRIVING DISTANCES IN MILES

	ELIZABETH CITY, NC	GREENVILLE, NC	MOREHEAD CITY, NC	NAGS HEAD, NC	NEW BERN, NC	NORFOLK, VA	OCEAN CITY, MD	RICHMOND, VA	SALISBURY, MD	VIRGINIA BEACH, VA	WASHINGTON, DC	WILLIAMSBURG, VA
MOREHEAD CITY, NC	150	82		184	35	185	326	241	321	206	352	221
NAGS HEAD, NC	59	135	184		149	82	214	179	209	94	284	131
NORFOLK, VA	50	130	185	82	151		138	91	133	18	196	43
WASHINGTON, DC	243	270	352	284	317	196	139	108	115	212		153

SEE ALSO DISTANCE AND DRIVING TIME MAP ON PAGES 286–287

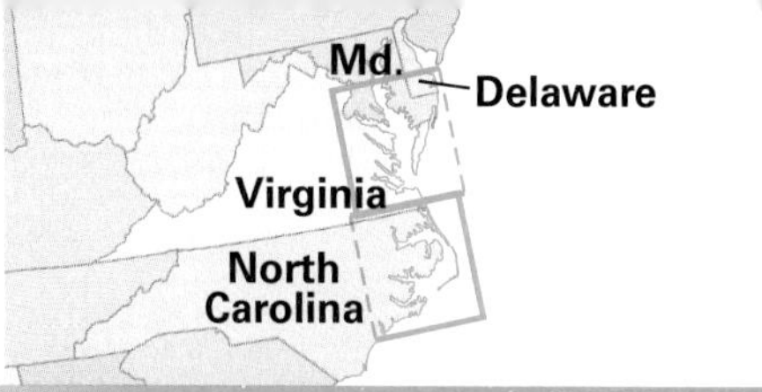

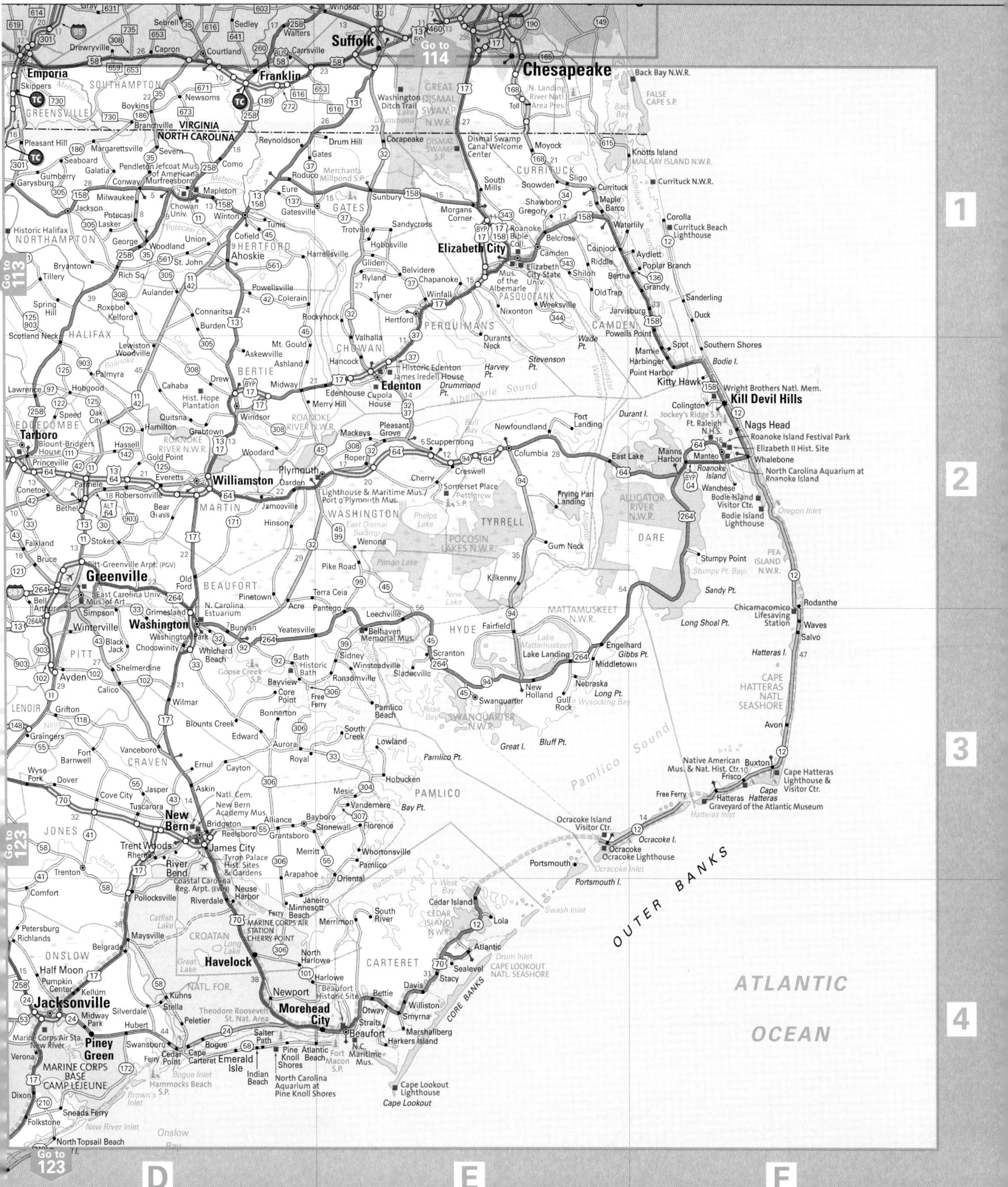

Oklahoma
Arkansas
Texas

0 mi 10 20 30 40
0 km 10 20 30 40 50 60

One inch equals 18.4 miles
One centimeter equals 11.7 kilometers

Muskogee
Okmulgee
Henryetta
Checotah
Eufaula
McAlester
Sallisaw
Van Buren
Fort Smith
Alma
Ozark
Stigler
Poteau
Greenwood
Booneville
Paris
Waldron
Heavener
Wilburton
Mena
Atoka
Antlers
Hugo
Idabel
De Queen
Broken Bow
Nashville
Paris
Clarksville
New Boston
Texarkana
BOSTON MTS.
SANS BOIS MTS.
KIAMICHI MTS.
OUACHITA
OUACHITA NATL. FOR.
MTS.
Go to 106
Go to 51
Go to 59
Go to 124
1
2
3
4
A
B
C
OKLAHOMA TEXAS
ARKANSAS OKLAHOMA
ARK. TEXAS

DRIVING DISTANCES IN MILES

	ARKADELPHIA, AR	FORT SMITH, AR	HENRYETTA, OK	HOT SPRINGS, AR	LITTLE ROCK, AR	MCALESTER, OK	MENA, AR	NEWPORT, AR	PARIS, TX	PINE BLUFF, AR	RUSSELLVILLE, AR	TEXARKANA, AR/TX
FORT SMITH, AR	152		100	126	165	114	81	220	214	210	87	180
HOT SPRINGS, AR	37	126	224		65	193	75	154	207	76	67	117
LITTLE ROCK, AR	72	165	263	65		278	141	89	242	45	81	153
TEXARKANA, AR/TX	83	180	227	117	153	188	99	241	92	163	180	

SEE ALSO DISTANCE AND DRIVING TIME MAP ON PAGES 286–287

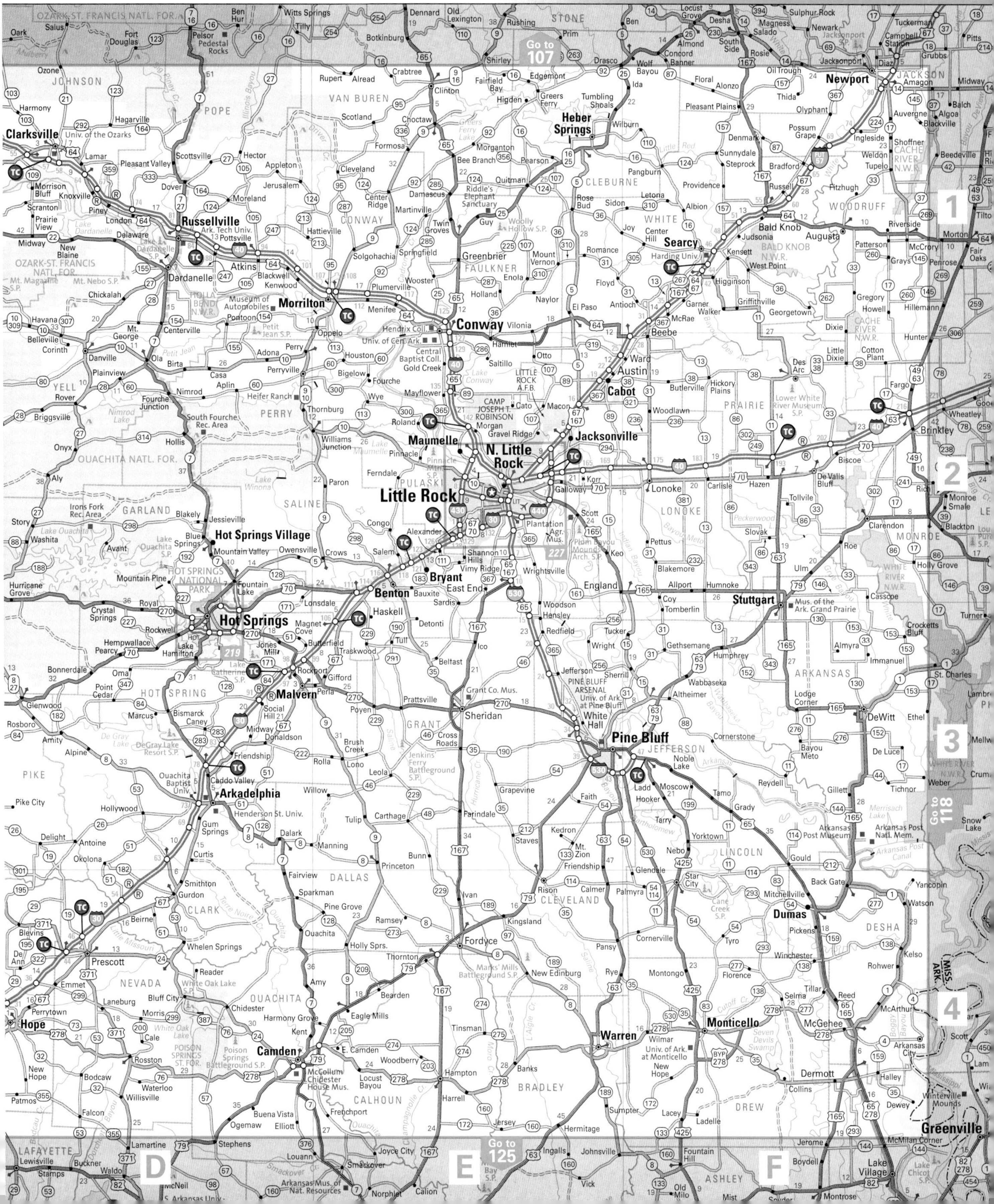

0 mi 10 20 30 40
0 km 10 20 30 40 50 60

One inch equals 18.4 miles
One centimeter equals 11.7 kilometers

Memphis TN / Oxford MS

DRIVING DISTANCES IN MILES

	BIRMINGHAM, AL	CLARKSDALE, MS	COLUMBIA, TN	COLUMBUS, MS	DECATUR, AL	FLORENCE, AL	GREENVILLE, MS	HUNTSVILLE, AL	JACKSON, TN	MEMPHIS, TN	OXFORD, MS	TUPELO, MS
BIRMINGHAM, AL		248	161	122	83	121	286	101	223	241	185	136
HUNTSVILLE, AL	101	260	79	163	25	65	318		205	216	196	148
MEMPHIS, TN	241	76	210	175	191	156	148	216	91		85	109
TUPELO, MS	136	113	159	66	123	92	172	148	107	109	50	

SEE ALSO DISTANCE AND DRIVING TIME MAP ON PAGES 286–287

Atlanta GA / Chattanooga TN

0 mi 10 20 30 40
0 km 10 20 30 40 50 60

One inch equals 18.4 miles
One centimeter equals 11.7 kilometers

DRIVING DISTANCES IN MILES

	ANNISTON, AL	ASHEVILLE, NC	ATHENS, GA	ATLANTA, GA	AUGUSTA, GA	CHATTANOOGA, TN	GADSDEN, AL	GATLINBURG, TN	GREENVILLE, SC	HUNTSVILLE, AL	MANCHESTER, TN	SPARTANBURG, SC
ATLANTA, GA	91	207	70		149	113	117	187	146	191	180	173
AUGUSTA, GA	240	179	97	149		266	266	240	110	334	333	118
CHATTANOOGA, TN	120	225	170	113	266		94	156	245	109	69	272
GREENVILLE, SC	238	64	104	146	110	245	264	125		313	311	30

SEE ALSO DISTANCE AND DRIVING TIME MAP ON PAGES 286–287

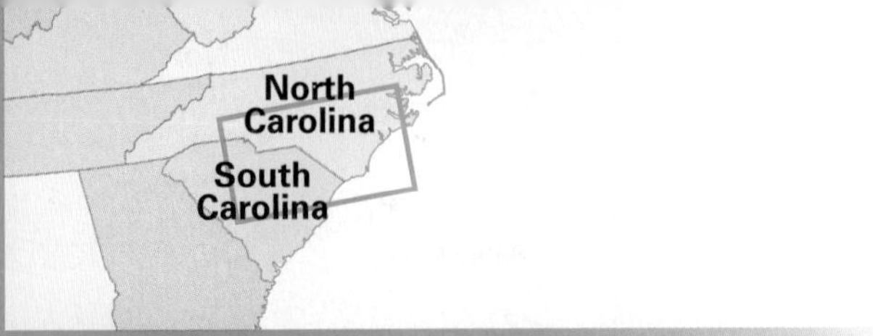
North Carolina
South Carolina

0 mi 10 20 30 40
0 km 10 20 30 40 50 60
One inch equals 18.4 miles
One centimeter equals 11.7 kilometers

Charlotte NC / Columbia SC

Hickory
Conover
Newton
Salisbury
Kannapolis
Mooresville
Concord
Asheboro
Siler City
Sanford
Lincolnton
Shelby
Gastonia
Charlotte
Mint Hill
Matthews
Albemarle
Troy
Gaffney
York
Rock Hill
Monroe
Wadesboro
Rockingham
Hamlet
Southern Pines
Pinehurst
Laurinburg
Lancaster
Chester
Union
Cheraw
Bennettsville
Hartsville
Darlington
Florence
Dillon
Marion
Mullins
Newberry
Winnsboro
Camden
Columbia
Lexington
Irmo
Cayce
Batesburg-Leesville
Sumter
Manning
Lake City
Kingstree
Aiken
Orangeburg
Andrews
Georgetown
Go to 111
Go to 112
Go to 121
Go to 130
Go to 131
1
2
3
4
A
B
C
N. CAROLINA
S. CAROLINA

DRIVING DISTANCES IN MILES

	CHARLOTTE, NC	COLUMBIA, SC	FAYETTEVILLE, NC	FLORENCE, SC	GOLDSBORO, NC	HICKORY, NC	LUMBERTON, NC	MOREHEAD CITY, NC	MYRTLE BEACH, SC	ROCK HILL, SC	SUMTER, SC	WILMINGTON, NC
CHARLOTTE, NC		91	139	107	208	47	128	298	173	26	115	205
COLUMBIA, SC	91		170	80	240	139	139	289	146	70	45	199
MYRTLE BEACH, SC	173	146	116	66	170	220	83	165		181	93	71
WILMINGTON, NC	205	199	92	120	100	292	77	95	71	220	158	

SEE ALSO DISTANCE AND DRIVING TIME MAP ON PAGES 286–287

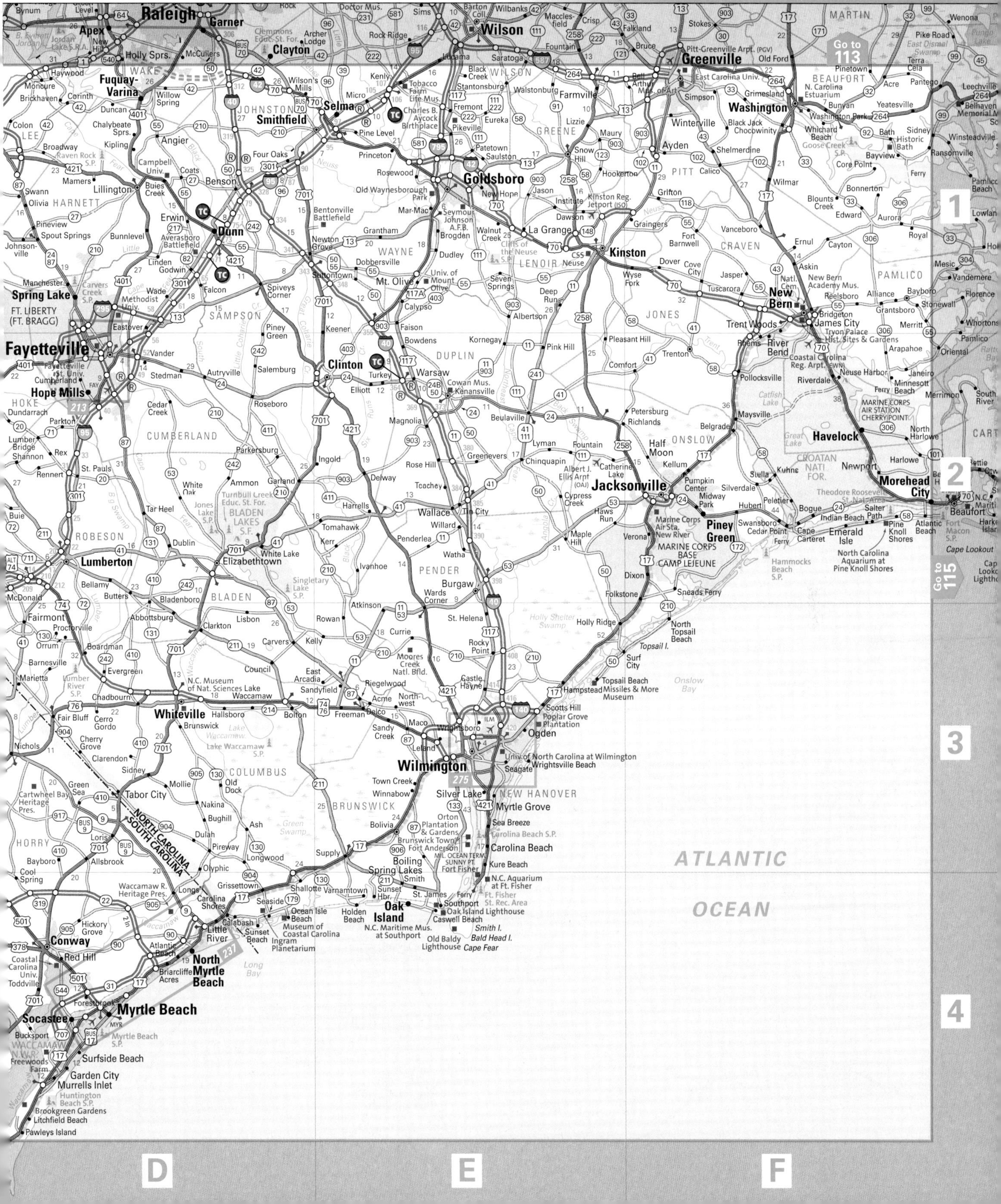

0 mi 10 20 30 40
0 km 10 20 30 40 50 60

One inch equals 18.4 miles
One centimeter equals 11.7 kilometers

Shreveport LA / Tyler TX

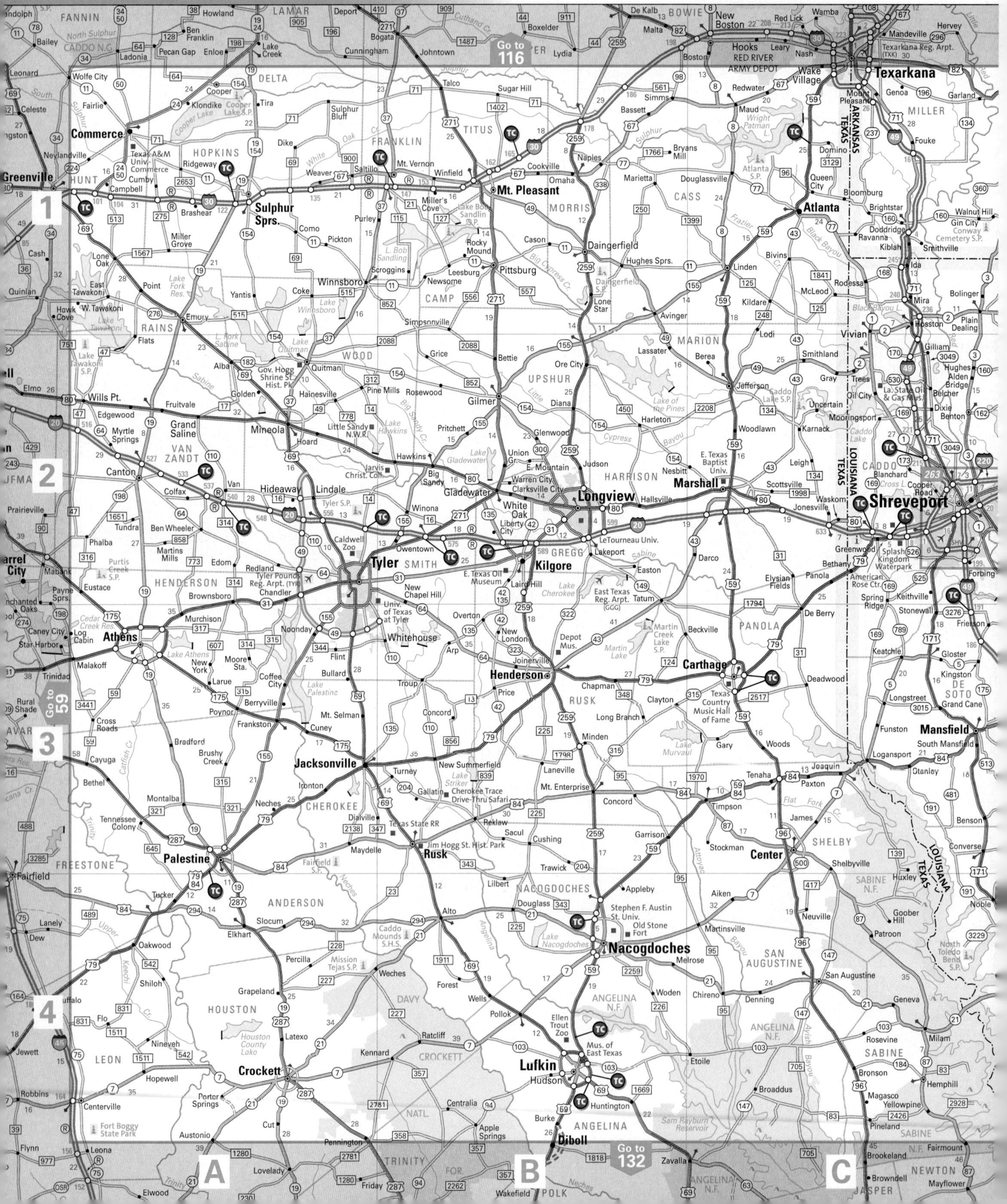

DRIVING DISTANCES IN MILES

	ALEXANDRIA, LA	EL DORADO, AR	GREENVILLE, TX	LONGVIEW, TX	LUFKIN, TX	MONROE, LA	NACOGDOCHES, TX	NATCHEZ, MS	NATCHITOCHES, LA	SHREVEPORT, LA	TEXARKANA, AR/TX	TYLER, TX
ALEXANDRIA, LA		147	276	179	160	96	167	76	55	121	190	213
MONROE, LA	96	86	267	170	223		203	95	100	103	172	204
SHREVEPORT, LA	121	96	165	68	121	103	101	198	73		69	102
TYLER, TX	213	196	77	42	82	204	76	288	164	102	118	

SEE ALSO DISTANCE AND DRIVING TIME MAP ON PAGES 286–287

0 mi 10 20 30 40
0 km 10 20 30 40 50 60

One inch equals 18.4 miles
One centimeter equals 11.7 kilometers

Jackson MS / Hattiesburg MS

DRIVING DISTANCES IN MILES

	BIRMINGHAM, AL	EVERGREEN, AL	GREENVILLE, MS	HATTIESBURG, MS	JACKSON, MS	MCCOMB, MS	MERIDIAN, MS	NATCHEZ, MS	SELMA, AL	TUSCALOOSA, AL	VICKSBURG, MS	WINONA, MS
HATTIESBURG, MS	239	184	215		90	75	89	142	193	183	132	180
JACKSON, MS	241	243	125	90		76	91	102	195	185	42	94
MERIDIAN, MS	149	152	216	89	91	167		194	104	94	133	113
TUSCALOOSA, AL	61	211	225	183	185	261	94	287	82		227	144

SEE ALSO DISTANCE AND DRIVING TIME MAP ON PAGES 286–287

0 mi 10 20 30 40
0 km 10 20 30 40 50 60
One inch equals 18.4 miles
One centimeter equals 11.7 kilometers

Montgomery AL / Columbus GA

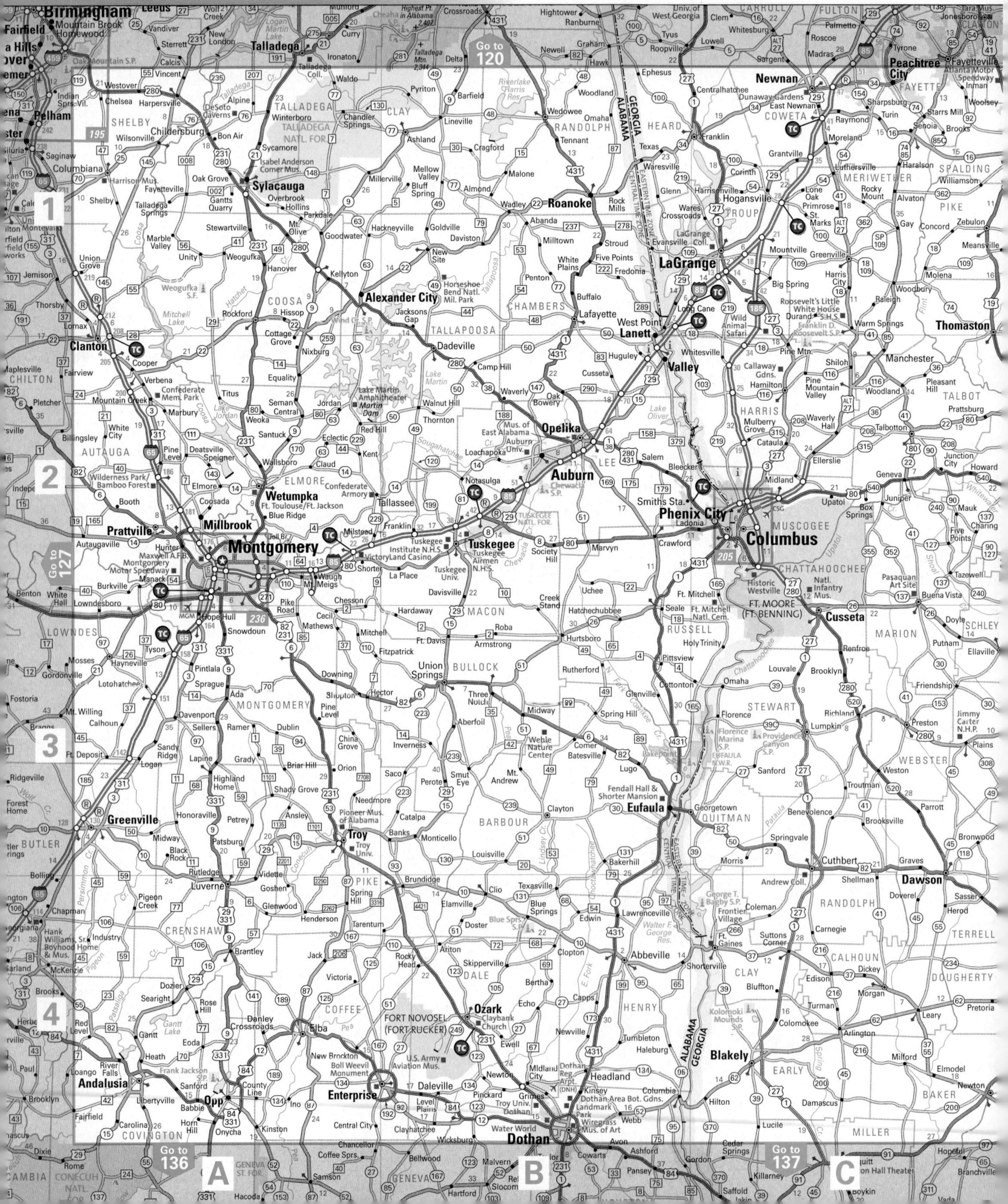

DRIVING DISTANCES IN MILES

	ALBANY, GA	ATLANTA, GA	AUBURN, AL	AUGUSTA, GA	BIRMINGHAM, AL	COLUMBUS, GA	DOTHAN, AL	LA GRANGE, GA	MACON, GA	MONTGOMERY, AL	TIFTON, GA	WAYCROSS, GA
ALBANY, GA		180	121	226	253	86	83	129	102	165	43	116
COLUMBUS, GA	86	106	34	249	167		97	46	95	79	135	208
MACON, GA	102	84	151	123	234	95	186	114		203	102	159
MONTGOMERY, AL	165	158	54	301	88	79	103	95	203		214	287

SEE ALSO DISTANCE AND DRIVING TIME MAP ON PAGES 286–287

Alabama
Georgia

McDonough
Griffin
Jackson
Barnesville
Forsyth
Macon
Milledgeville
Eatonton
Sandersville
Louisville
Waynesboro
Augusta
Thomson
Millen
Dublin
Swainsboro
Statesboro
Metter
Fort Valley
Warner Robins
Perry
Cochran
Hawkinsville
Eastman
Vidalia
Americus
Cordele
Hazlehurst
Baxley
Jesup
Fitzgerald
Ocilla
Albany
Sylvester
Tifton
Douglas
Alma
Waycross
Camilla
Moultrie
Adel
Nashville
Go to 121
Go to 130
Go to 138
1
2
3
4
D
E
F

South Carolina
Georgia

0 mi 10 20 30 40
0 km 10 20 30 40 50 60

One inch equals 18.4 miles
One centimeter equals 11.7 kilometers

Savannah GA / Hilton Head Island SC

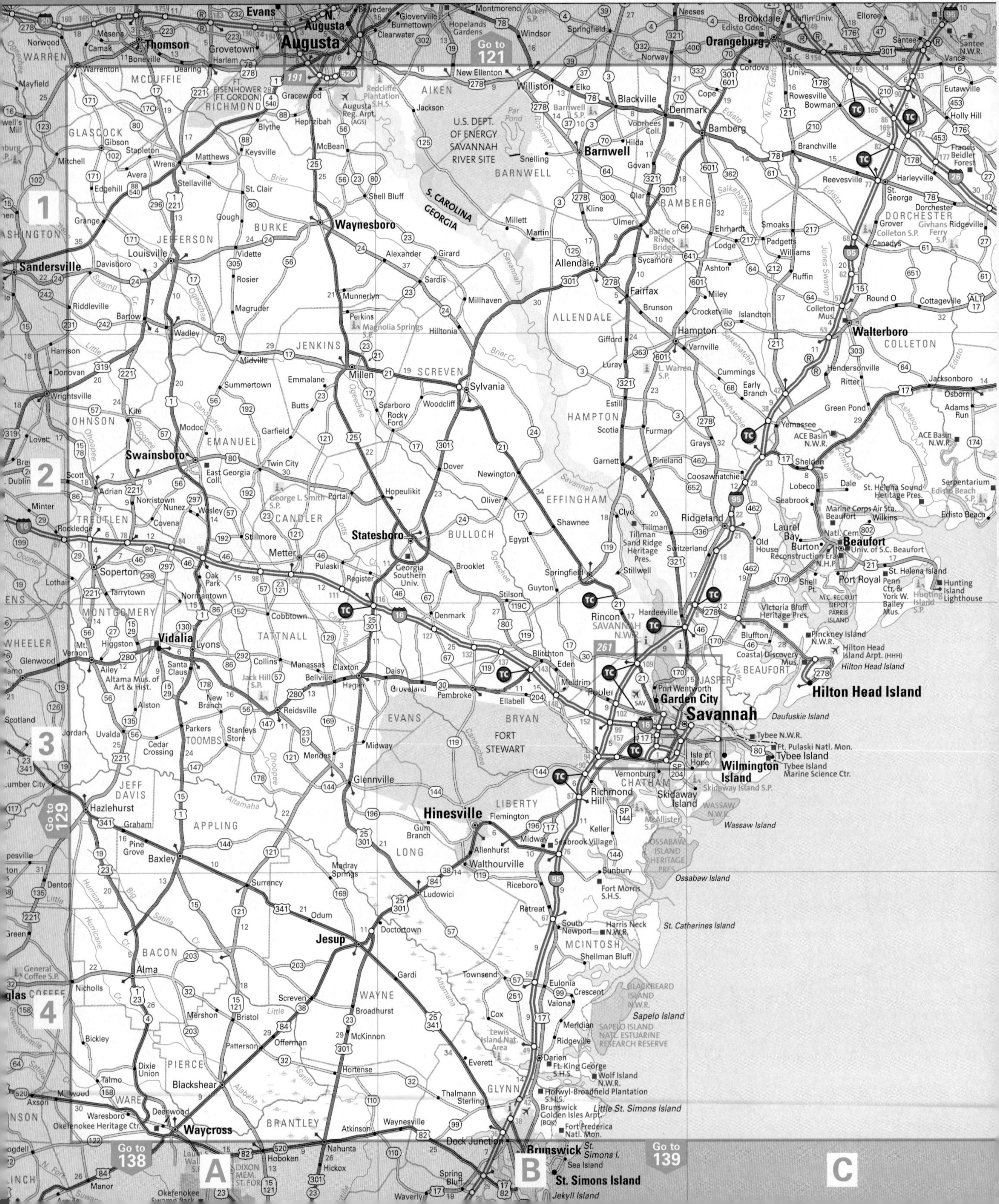
Augusta
Evans
N. Augusta
Thomson
Orangeburg
Go to 121
Barnwell
Bamberg
Denmark
Williston
Blackville
Waynesboro
Louisville
Sandersville
Millen
Sylvania
Allendale
Hampton
Walterboro
Swainsboro
Statesboro
Metter
Vidalia
Lyons
Ridgeland
Beaufort
Port Royal
Hilton Head Island
Savannah
Garden City
Pooler
Wilmington Island
Skidaway Island
Richmond Hill
Hinesville
Jesup
Baxley
Hazlehurst
Alma
Blackshear
Waycross
Brunswick
St. Simons Island
Jekyll Island
Sapelo Island
St. Catherines Island
Ossabaw Island
Wassaw Island
Daufuskie Island
Go to 129
Go to 138
Go to 139
U.S. DEPT. OF ENERGY SAVANNAH RIVER SITE
FORT STEWART
S. CAROLINA
GEORGIA
1
2
3
4
A
B
C

DRIVING DISTANCES IN MILES

	AUGUSTA, GA	BEAUFORT, SC	BRUNSWICK, GA	CHARLESTON, SC	GEORGETOWN, SC	HILTON HEAD I., SC	HINESVILLE, GA	ORANGEBURG, SC	SAVANNAH, GA	STATESBORO, GA	WALTERBORO, SC	WAYCROSS, GA
AUGUSTA, GA		126	194	142	181	127	157	74	135	81	111	184
CHARLESTON, SC	142	66	175		58	95	138	73	107	150	51	203
HILTON HEAD I., SC	127	32	113	95	157		75	116	35	88	64	141
SAVANNAH, GA	135	42	78	107	163	35	41	123		53	71	106

SEE ALSO DISTANCE AND DRIVING TIME MAP ON PAGES 286–287

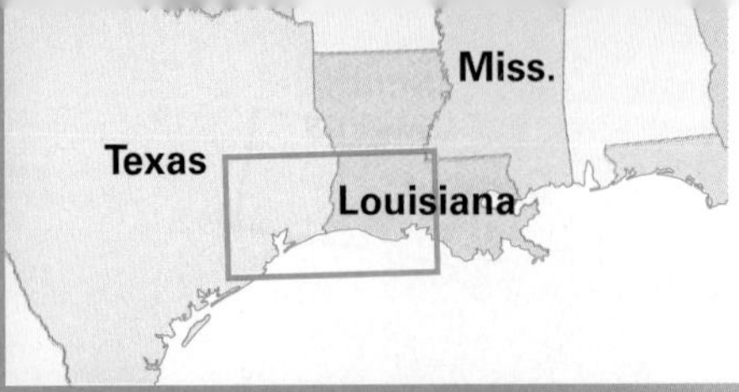

0 mi 10 20 30 40
0 km 10 20 30 40 50 60

One inch equals 18.4 miles
One centimeter equals 11.7 kilometers

Houston TX / Beaumont TX

DRIVING DISTANCES IN MILES

	ALEXANDRIA, LA	BEAUMONT, TX	DE RIDDER, LA	FREEPORT, TX	GALVESTON, TX	HOUSTON, TX	HUNTSVILLE, TX	LAFAYETTE, LA	LAKE CHARLES, LA	LUFKIN, TX	OPELOUSAS, LA	PORT ARTHUR, TX
BEAUMONT, TX	157		82	143	75	84	157	133	57	112	144	18
HOUSTON, TX	241	84	166	61	53		75	217	141	121	228	93
LAFAYETTE, LA	87	133	119	276	208	217	290		76	216	27	130
LAKE CHARLES, LA	100	57	49	200	132	141	214	76		140	87	54

SEE ALSO DISTANCE AND DRIVING TIME MAP ON PAGES 286–287

0 mi 10 20 30 40
0 km 10 20 30 40 50 60
One inch equals 18.4 miles
One centimeter equals 11.7 kilometers

New Orleans LA / Baton Rouge LA

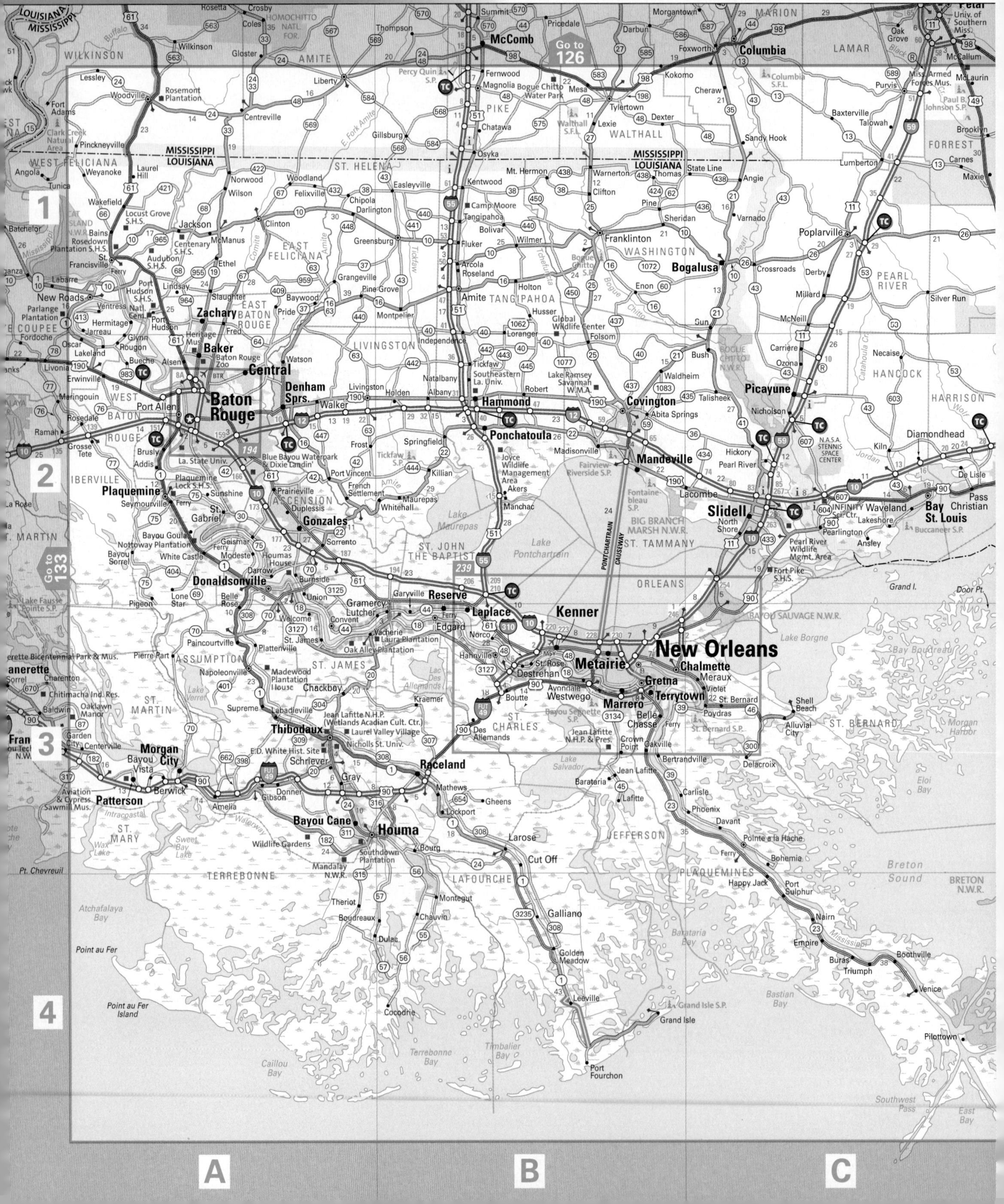

DRIVING DISTANCES IN MILES

	BATON ROUGE, LA	BILOXI, MS	GULFPORT, MS	GULF SHORES, AL	HAMMOND, LA	HATTIESBURG, MS	HOUMA, LA	MCCOMB, MS	MOBILE, AL	NEW ORLEANS, LA	PASCAGOULA, MS	PENSACOLA, FL
BATON ROUGE, LA		151	140	254	51	174	101	102	205	91	170	264
BILOXI, MS	151		12	110	106	82	148	161	61	93	20	120
MOBILE, AL	205	61	75	48	159	97	201	215		146	41	58
NEW ORLEANS, LA	91	93	81	195	57	115	57	111	146		112	205

SEE ALSO DISTANCE AND DRIVING TIME MAP ON PAGES 286–287

0 mi 10 20 30 40
0 km 10 20 30 40 50 60
One inch equals 18.4 miles
One centimeter equals 11.7 kilometers

Pensacola FL / Panama City FL

1
2
3
4
A B C

DRIVING DISTANCES IN MILES

	BREWTON, AL	DE FUNIAK SPRS, FL	DOTHAN, AL	FT. WALTON BEACH, FL	MARIANNA, FL	MOBILE, AL	PANAMA CITY, FL	PENSACOLA, FL	PERRY, FL	TALLAHASSEE, FL	THOMASVILLE, GA	VALDOSTA, GA
PANAMA CITY, FL	143	65	82	64	61	160		102	160	104	134	186
PENSACOLA, FL	57	82	152	39	138	58	102		256	200	230	282
TALLAHASSEE, FL	201	123	110	166	68	247	104	200	52		35	85
VALDOSTA, GA	283	204	133	247	149	329	186	282	66	85	42	

SEE ALSO DISTANCE AND DRIVING TIME MAP ON PAGES 286–287

0 mi 10 20 30 40
0 km 10 20 30 40 50 60
One inch equals 18.4 miles
One centimeter equals 11.7 kilometers

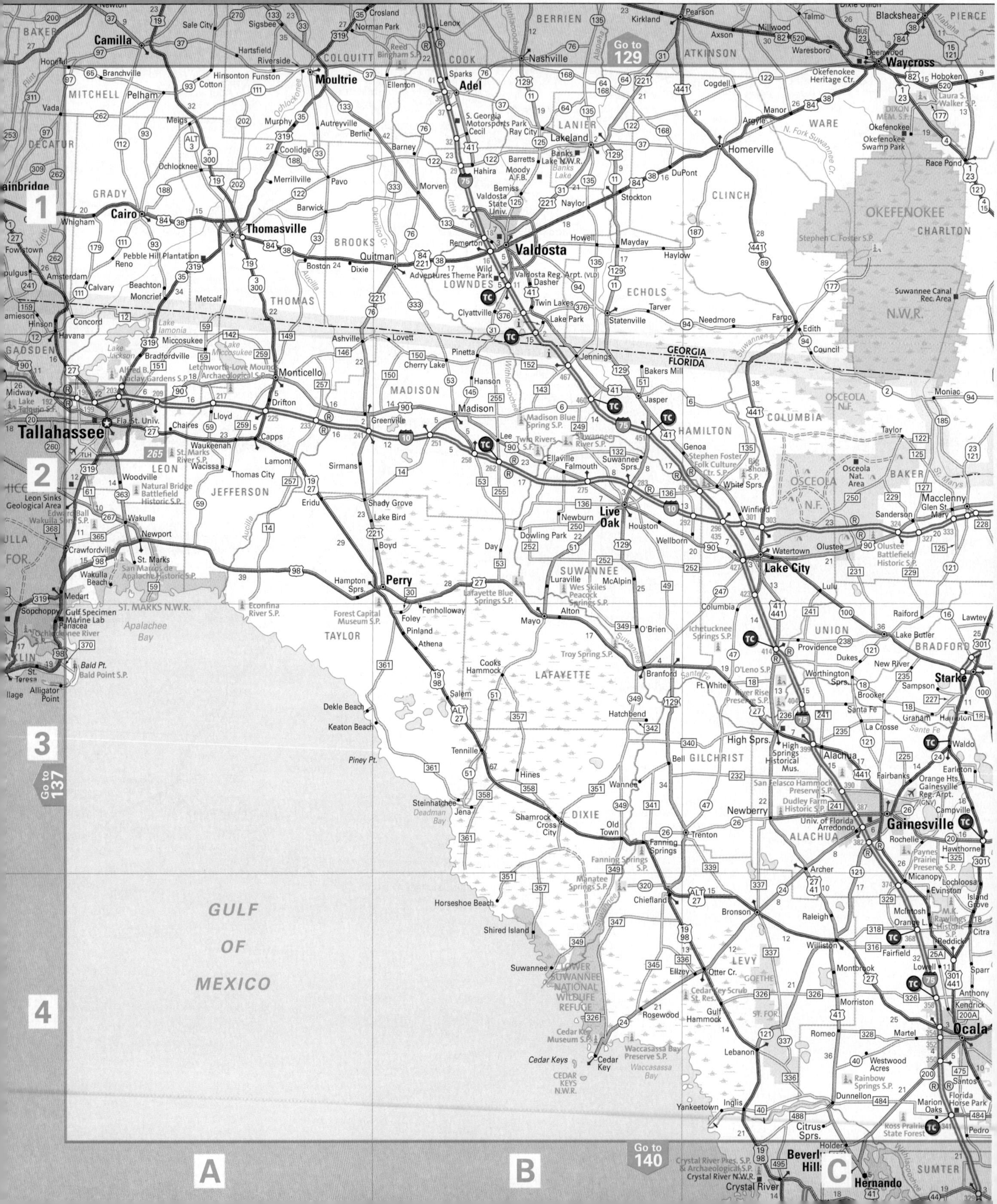

DRIVING DISTANCES IN MILES

	BRUNSWICK, GA	DAYTONA BEACH, FL	GAINESVILLE, FL	JACKSONVILLE, FL	LAKE CITY, FL	OCALA, FL	PERRY, FL	ST. AUGUSTINE, FL	STARKE, FL	TALLAHASSEE, FL	VALDOSTA, GA	WAYCROSS, GA
DAYTONA BEACH, FL	160		99	91	154	77	225	53	92	258	209	173
JACKSONVILLE, FL	69	91	70		62	101	133	41	45	166	117	78
OCALA, FL	171	77	40	101	80		120	81	57	186	137	170
TALLAHASSEE, FL	235	258	152	166	109	186	52	207	145		85	146

SEE ALSO DISTANCE AND DRIVING TIME MAP ON PAGES 286–287

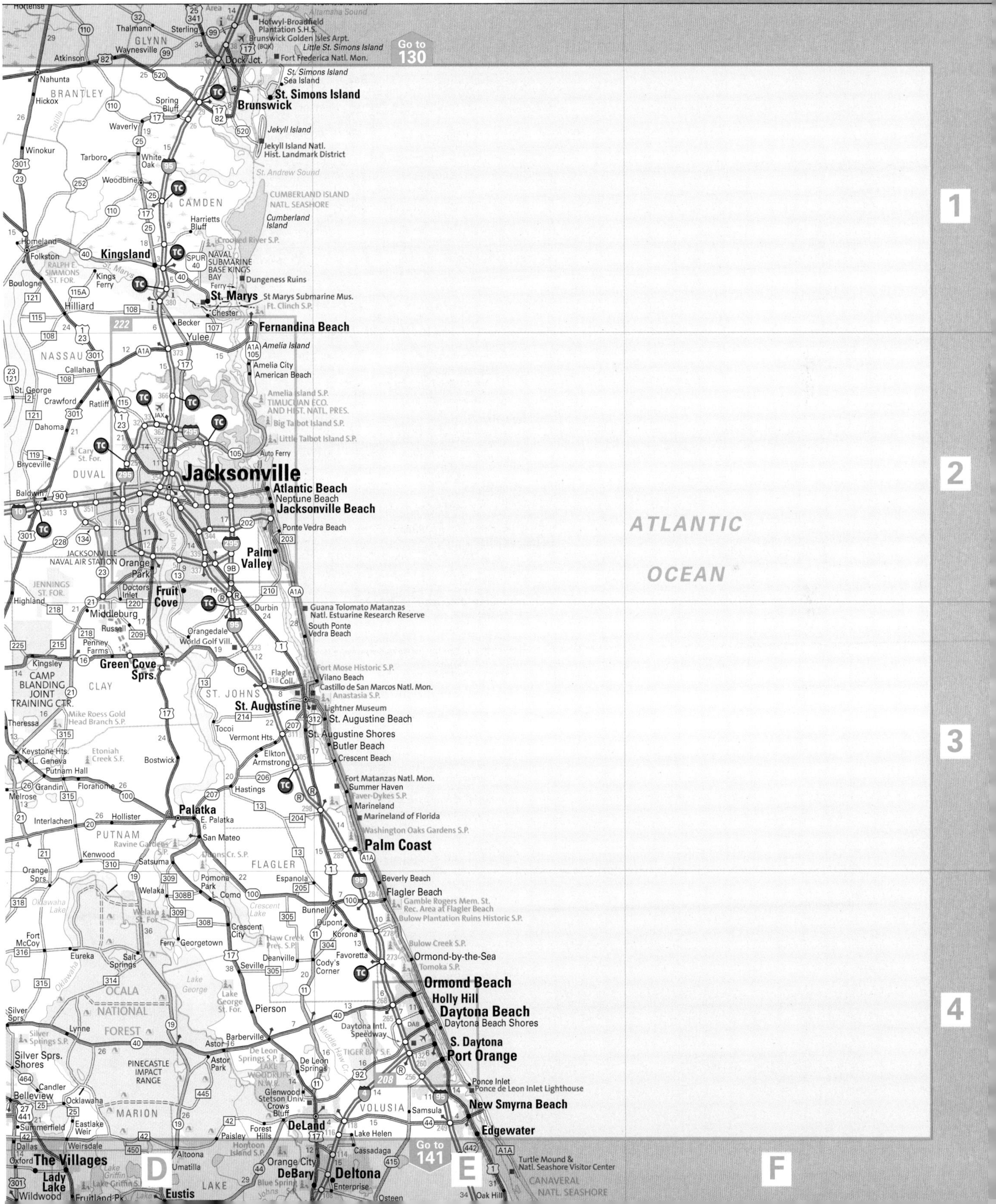

Florida

0 mi 10 20 30 40
0 km 10 20 30 40 50 60

One inch equals 18.4 miles
One centimeter equals 11.7 kilometers

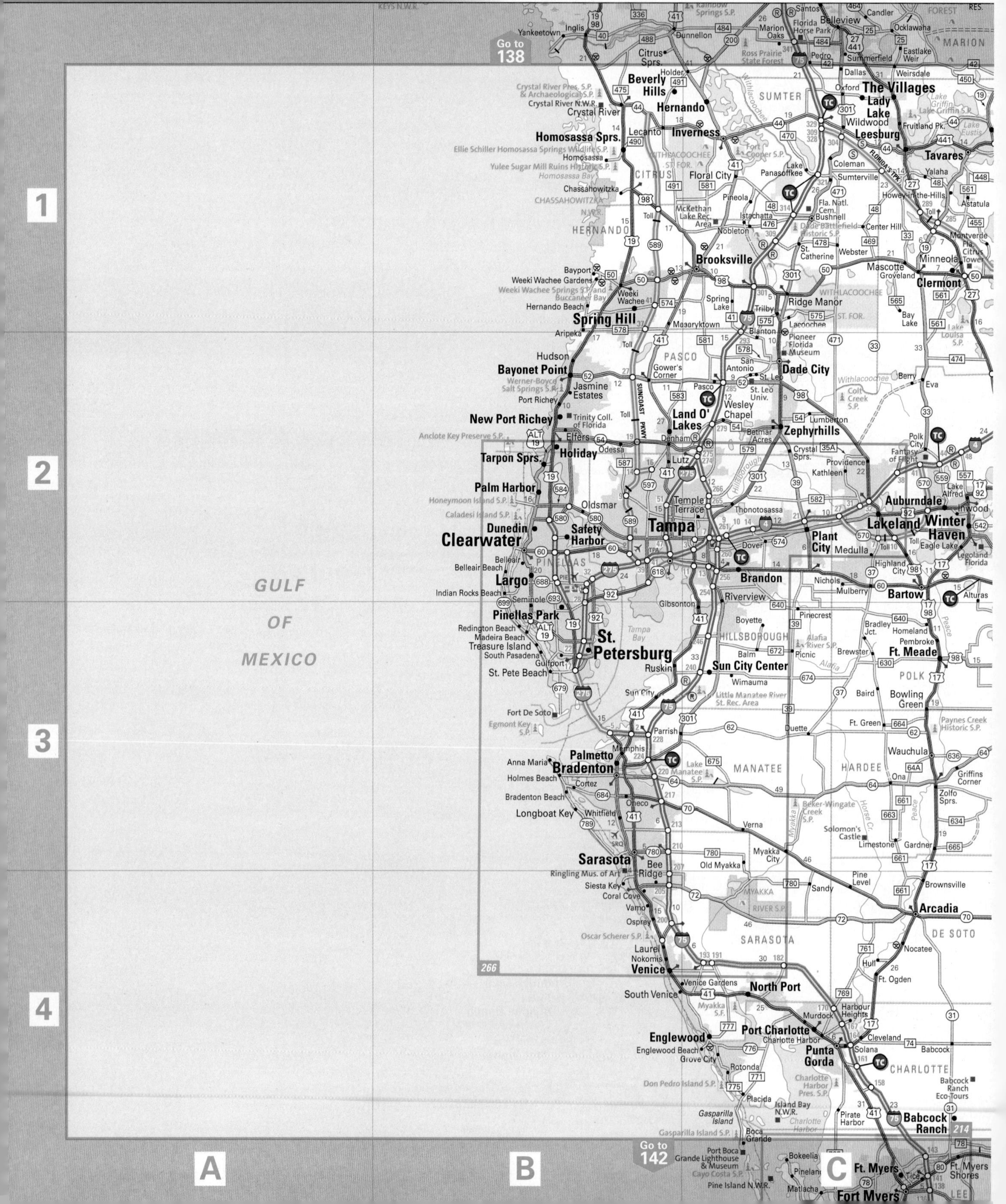
Go to 138
Go to 142
1
2
3
4
A
B
C
GULF
OF
MEXICO
266
214
Yankeetown
Inglis
Dunnellon
Citrus Springs
Rainbow Springs S.P.
Marion Oaks
Florida Horse Park
Santos
Belleview
Candler
Ocklawaha
MARION
Ross Prairie State Forest
Pedro
Summerfield
Eastlake Weir
Crystal River Pres. S.P. & Archaeological S.P.
Crystal River N.W.R.
Crystal River
Beverly Hills
Holder
Hernando
Inverness
Lecanto
Homosassa Sprs.
Ellie Schiller Homosassa Springs Wildlife S.P.
Homosassa
Yulee Sugar Mill Ruins Historic S.P.
Homosassa Bay
Chassahowitzka
CHASSAHOWITZKA N.W.R.
HERNANDO
CITRUS
SUMTER
Dallas
Oxford
The Villages
Lady Lake
Wildwood
Leesburg
Fruitland Pk.
Tavares
Coleman
Sumterville
Lake Panasoffkee
Floral City
Fort Cooper S.P.
WITHLACOOCHEE ST. FOR.
McKethan Lake Rec. Area
Pineola
Istachatta
Nobleton
Fla. Natl. Cem.
Bushnell
Dade Battlefield Historic S.P.
Center Hill
Howey-in-the-Hills
Yalaha
Astatula
Montverde
Minneola
Clermont
Mascotte
Groveland
Webster
St. Catherine
Brooksville
Bayport
Weeki Wachee Gardens
Weeki Wachee Springs S.P. and Buccaneer Bay
Weeki Wachee
Hernando Beach
Spring Hill
Aripeka
Masaryktown
Spring Lake
Ridge Manor
Trilby
Lacoochee
Blanton
Pioneer Florida Museum
Dade City
Bay Lake
Lake Louisa S.P.
Hudson
Bayonet Point
Werner-Boyce Salt Springs S.P.
Jasmine Estates
Port Richey
PASCO
Gower's Corner
San Antonio
St. Leo
St. Leo Univ.
Pasco
Land O' Lakes
Wesley Chapel
Zephyrhills
Lumberton
Colt Creek S.P.
Berry
Eva
New Port Richey
Trinity Coll. of Florida
Anclote Key Preserve S.P.
Elfers
Holiday
Tarpon Sprs.
Odessa
Denham
Lutz
Betmar Acres
Crystal Sprs.
Providence
Kathleen
Polk City
Fantasy of Flight
Palm Harbor
Honeymoon Island S.P.
Caladesi Island S.P.
Oldsmar
Temple Terrace
Thonotosassa
Auburndale
Lake Alfred
Inwood
Dunedin
Clearwater
Safety Harbor
Tampa
Plant City
Lakeland
Winter Haven
Dover
Medulla
Eagle Lake
Legoland Florida
Belleair
Belleair Beach
PINELLAS
Largo
Brandon
Highland City
Nichols
Mulberry
Bartow
Alturas
Indian Rocks Beach
Seminole
Riverview
Pinellas Park
Gibsonton
Pinecrest
Bradley Jct.
Homeland
Pembroke
Redington Beach
Madeira Beach
Treasure Island
South Pasadena
Gulfport
St. Pete Beach
St. Petersburg
Tampa Bay
HILLSBOROUGH
Alafia River S.P.
Balm
Picnic
Brewster
Ft. Meade
Ruskin
Sun City Center
Wimauma
Little Manatee River St. Rec. Area
Sun City
POLK
Baird
Bowling Green
Fort De Soto
Egmont Key S.P.
Parrish
Duette
Ft. Green
Paynes Creek Historic S.P.
Memphis
Palmetto
Anna Maria
Bradenton
Holmes Beach
Cortez
Bradenton Beach
Lake Manatee S.P.
MANATEE
HARDEE
Wauchula
Ona
Griffins Corner
Zolfo Sprs.
Oneco
Longboat Key
Whitfield
Beker-Wingate Creek S.P.
Verna
Solomon's Castle
Limestone
Gardner
Sarasota
Bee Ridge
Ringling Mus. of Art
Old Myakka
Myakka City
Siesta Key
Coral Cove
Vamo
Osprey
MYAKKA RIVER S.P.
Sandy
Pine Level
Brownsville
Arcadia
Oscar Scherer S.P.
SARASOTA
DE SOTO
Laurel
Nokomis
Venice
Nocatee
Hull
Ft. Ogden
Venice Gardens
South Venice
North Port
Myakka S.F.
Murdock
Harbour Heights
Port Charlotte
Charlotte Harbor
Cleveland
Babcock
Englewood
Englewood Beach
Grove City
Rotonda
Punta Gorda
Solana
CHARLOTTE
Don Pedro Island S.P.
Charlotte Harbor Pres. S.P.
Babcock Ranch Eco-Tours
Placida
Island Bay N.W.R.
Gasparilla Island
Gasparilla Island S.P.
Boca Grande
Pirate Harbor
Babcock Ranch
Port Boca Grande Lighthouse & Museum
Cayo Costa S.P.
Pine Island N.W.R.
Bokeelia
Pineland
Matlacha
Ft. Myers
Tice
Ft. Myers Shores
Fort Myers
LEE

DRIVING DISTANCES IN MILES

	FORT MYERS, FL	FORT PIERCE, FL	LAKELAND, FL	MELBOURNE, FL	OKEECHOBEE, FL	ORLANDO, FL	PUNTA GORDA, FL	ST. PETERSBURG, FL	SARASOTA, FL	TAMPA, FL	TITUSVILLE, FL	W. PALM BEACH, FL
FORT PIERCE, FL	126		122	57	36	120	127	197	150	172	95	57
ORLANDO, FL	155	120	56	72	108		131	107	130	82	40	169
SARASOTA, FL	74	150	85	190	114	130	50	35		60	170	184
TAMPA, FL	123	172	37	142	162	82	99	25	60		121	223

SEE ALSO DISTANCE AND DRIVING TIME MAP ON PAGES 286–287

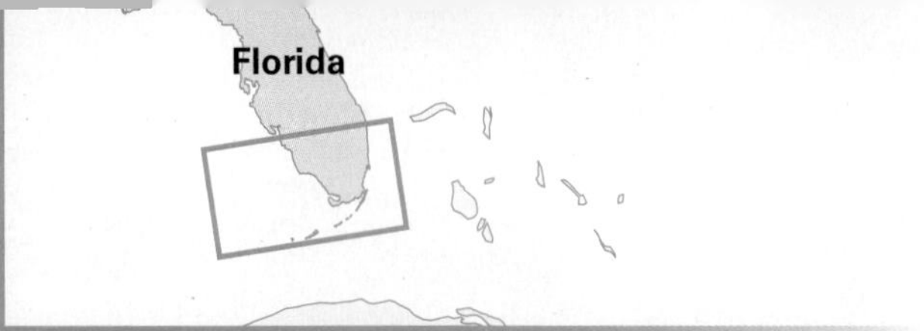
Florida

0 mi 10 20 30 40
0 km 10 20 30 40 50 60
One inch equals 18.4 miles
One centimeter equals 11.7 kilometers

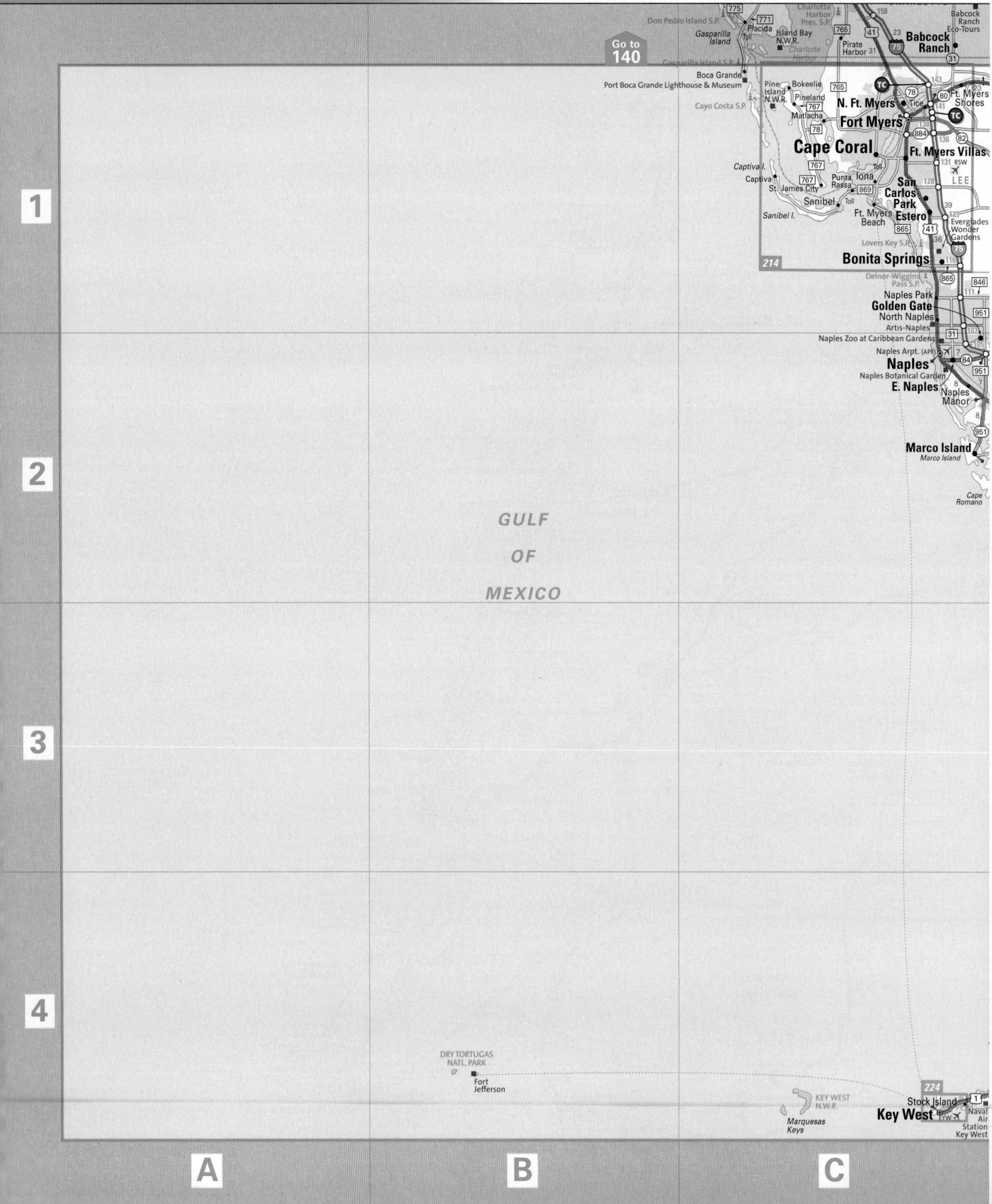
Go to 140
GULF
OF
MEXICO
Don Pedro Island S.P.
Gasparilla Island
Placida
Charlotte Harbor Pres. S.P.
Island Bay N.W.R.
Pirate Harbor
Babcock Ranch Eco-Tours
Babcock Ranch
Gasparilla Island S.P.
Boca Grande
Port Boca Grande Lighthouse & Museum
Cayo Costa S.P.
Pine Island N.W.R.
Bokeelia
Pineland
Matlacha
N. Ft. Myers
Tice
Ft. Myers Shores
Fort Myers
Cape Coral
Ft. Myers Villas
Captiva I.
Captiva
St. James City
Punta Rassa
Iona
Sanibel
Sanibel I.
San Carlos Park
Ft. Myers Beach
Estero
Everglades Wonder Gardens
LEE
Lovers Key S.P.
Bonita Springs
214
Delnor-Wiggins Pass S.P.
Naples Park
Golden Gate
North Naples
Artis-Naples
Naples Zoo at Caribbean Gardens
Naples Arpt. (APF)
Naples
Naples Botanical Garden
E. Naples
Naples Manor
Marco Island
Cape Romano
DRY TORTUGAS NATL. PARK
Fort Jefferson
KEY WEST N.W.R.
Marquesas Keys
224
Stock Island
Key West
Naval Air Station Key West
1
2
3
4
A
B
C

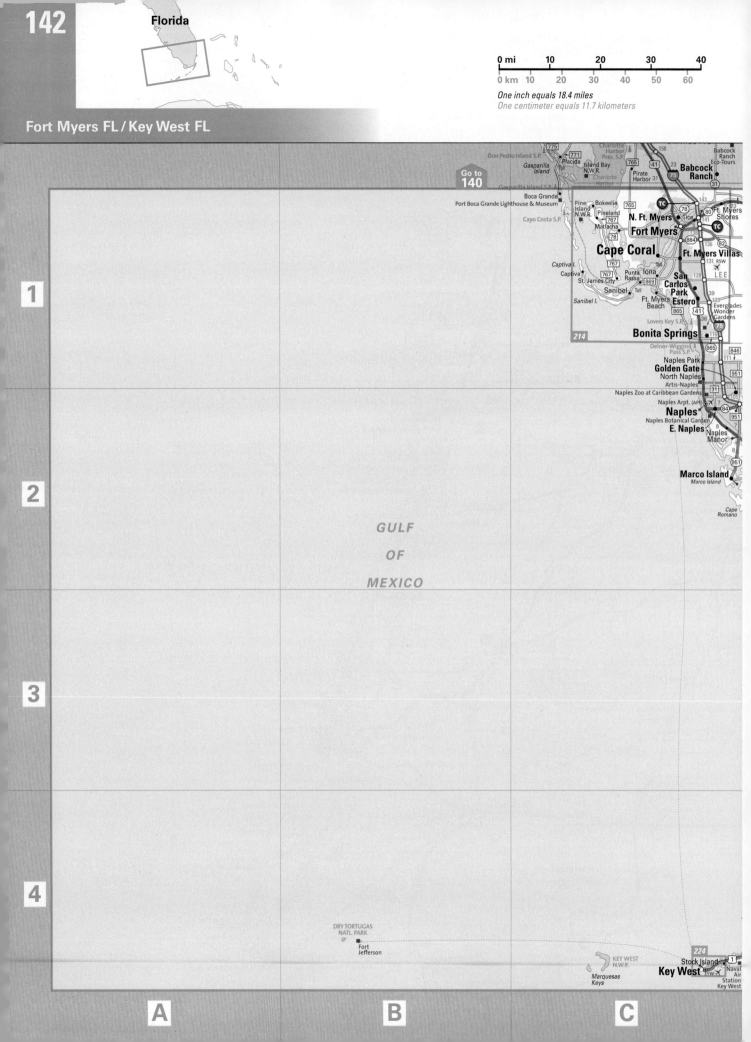

DRIVING DISTANCES IN MILES

	BELLE GLADE, FL	BOCA RATON, FL	FLAMINGO, FL	FORT LAUDERDALE, FL	FORT MYERS, FL	HOMESTEAD, FL	KEY LARGO, FL	KEY WEST, FL	MARATHON, FL	MIAMI, FL	NAPLES, FL	W. PALM BEACH, FL
FORT MYERS, FL	84	155	227	139		174	195	308	260	155	36	125
KEY WEST, FL	235	211	181	190	308	133	113		48	168	273	234
MIAMI, FL	83	44	87	23	155	34	55	168	120		121	67
W. PALM BEACH, FL	41	28	153	48	125	100	121	234	186	67	144	

SEE ALSO DISTANCE AND DRIVING TIME MAP ON PAGES 286–287

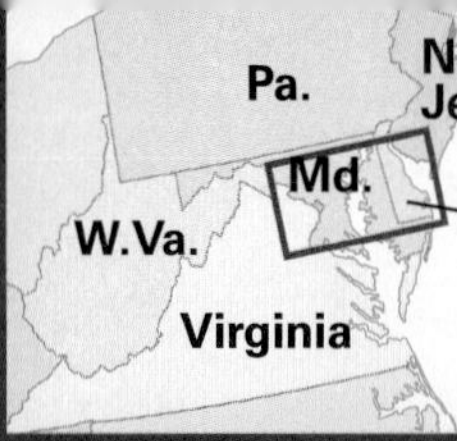

BONUS MAPS!

0 mi 5 10 15 20
0 km 5 10 15 20 25 30

One inch equals 9.85 miles
One centimeter equals 6.25 kilometers

Northeast Corridor / Washington DC

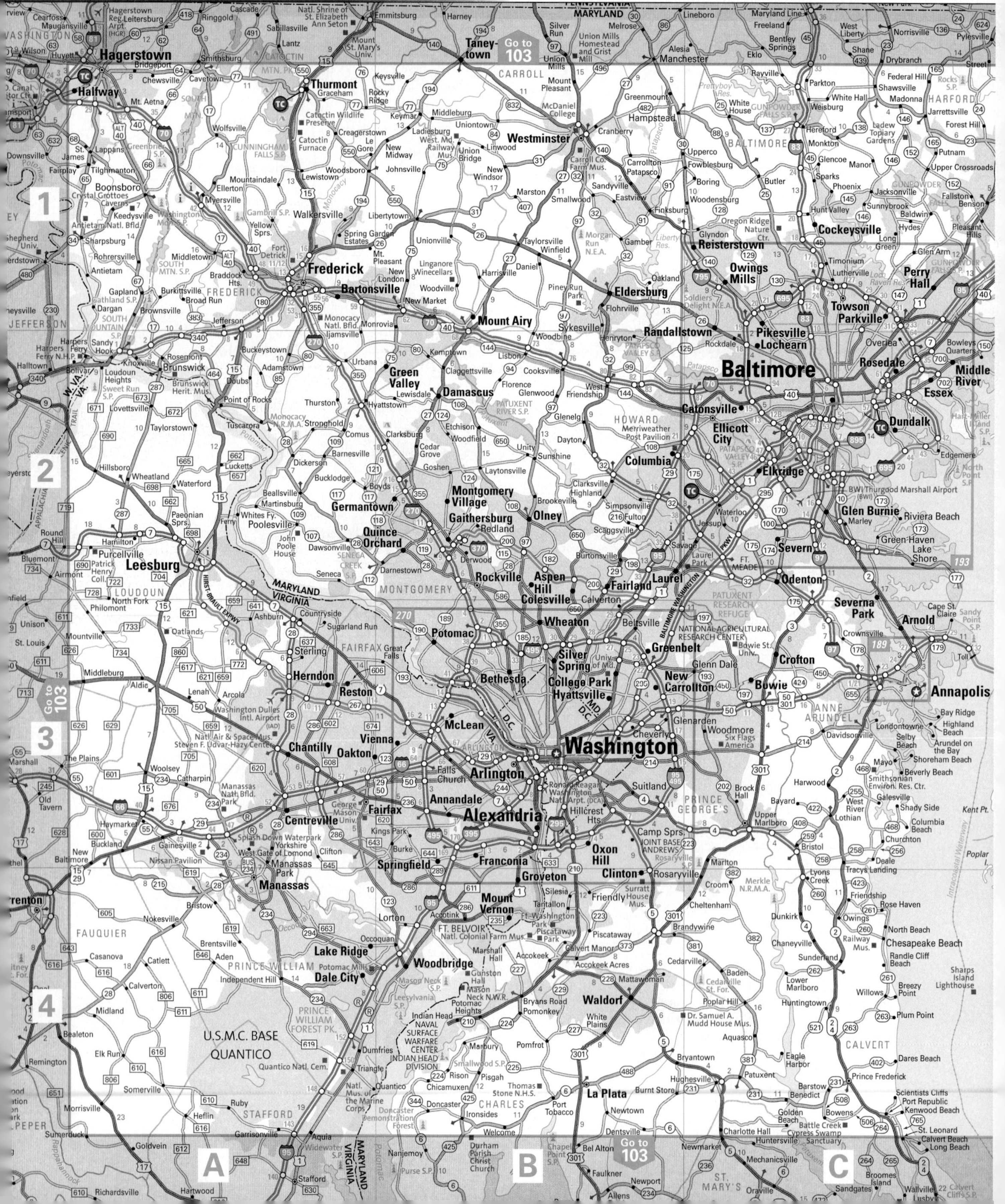

DRIVING DISTANCES IN MILES	ANNAPOLIS, MD	BALTIMORE, MD	CAMBRIDGE, MD	DOVER, DE	ELKTON, MD	FREDERICK, MD	HAGERSTOWN, MD	LEESBURG, VA	MANASSAS, VA	REHOBOTH BEACH, DE	VINELAND, NJ	WASHINGTON, DC
BALTIMORE, MD	25		78	98	58	51	76	71	67	111	109	38
DOVER, DE	62	98	64		40	135	160	135	131	43	77	94
FREDERICK, MD	73	51	128	135	106		28	25	61	161	158	44
WASHINGTON, DC	31	38	87	94	94	44	70	38	31	120	145	

SEE ALSO DISTANCE AND DRIVING TIME MAP ON PAGES 286–287

BONUS MAPS!

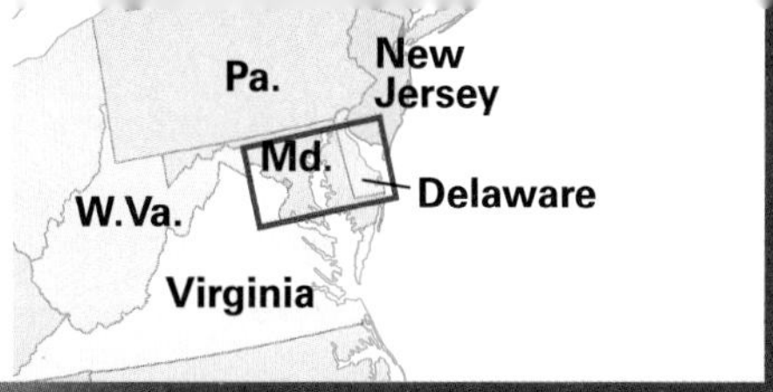

Pa.
New Jersey
Md.
Delaware
W.Va.
Virginia

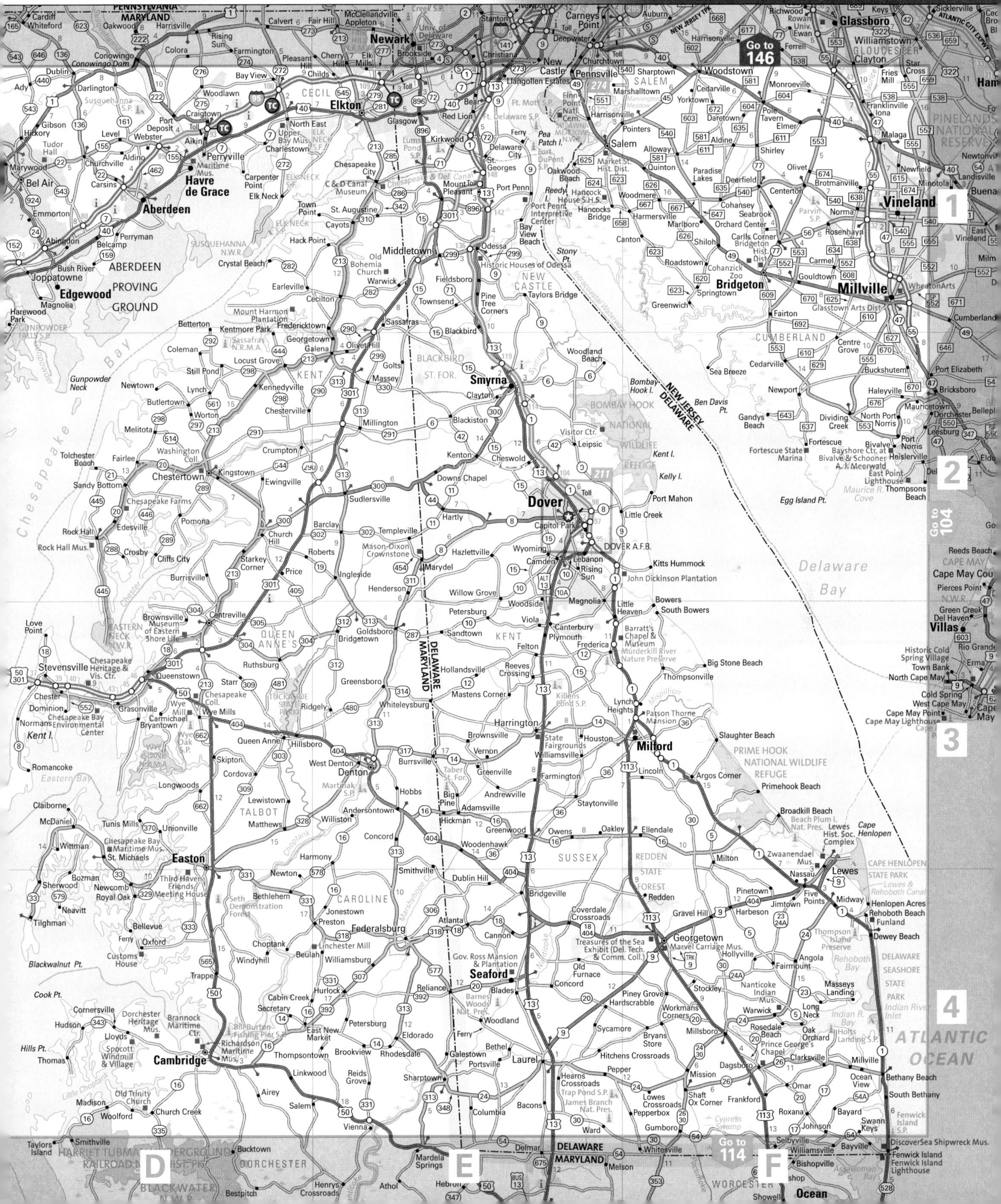

PENNSYLVANIA
MARYLAND
Newark
Elkton
Glassboro
Go to 146
Havre de Grace
Aberdeen
Edgewood
ABERDEEN PROVING GROUND
Salem
Vineland
Bridgeton
Millville
Middletown
Smyrna
Odessa
Chestertown
Dover
DOVER A.F.B.
BOMBAY HOOK NATIONAL WILDLIFE REFUGE
NEW JERSEY
DELAWARE
Delaware Bay
Villas
Cape May
Go to 104
Stevensville
Centreville
Easton
Denton
Harrington
Milford
PRIME HOOK NATIONAL WILDLIFE REFUGE
Lewes
Cape Henlopen
Georgetown
Seaford
Cambridge
Laurel
Federalsburg
Rehoboth Beach
Dewey Beach
Bethany Beach
South Bethany
Fenwick Island
ATLANTIC OCEAN
DELAWARE
MARYLAND
Go to 114
Ocean
Chesapeake Bay
CECIL
KENT
QUEEN ANNE'S
TALBOT
CAROLINE
SUSSEX
DORCHESTER
SALEM
CUMBERLAND
NEW CASTLE
1
2
3
4
D
E
F

New York
Penn.
New Jersey
Md.
Delaware

BONUS MAPS!

0 mi 5 10 15 20
0 km 5 10 15 20 25 30
One inch equals 9.85 miles
One centimeter equals 6.25 kilometers

Northeast Corridor / Philadelphia PA

Go to 104
Go to 145
Pottsville
Schuylkill Haven
Hamburg
Kutztown
Allentown
Bethlehem
Easton
Phillipsburg
Northampton
Whitehall
Emmaus
Quakertown
Perkasie
Sellersville
Souderton
Telford
Doylestown
Lansdale
Montgomeryville
Hatboro
Horsham
Ambler
Willow Grove
Norristown
King of Prussia
Conshohocken
Collegeville
Phoenixville
Pottstown
Reading
Wyomissing
Shillington
Laureldale
Lebanon
Lititz
Ephrata
Akron
Lancaster
Millersville
Downingtown
Coatesville
Exton
West Chester
Philadelphia
Ardmore
Drexel Hill
Lansdowne
Springfield
Yeadon
Darby
Collingswood
Cherry Hill
Camden
Pennsauken
Chester
Kennett Sq.
Oxford
Wilmington
Elsmere
Newark
Elkton
New Castle
Havre de Grace
Aberdeen
Edgewood
Perry Hall
Middletown
Glassboro
Lindenwold
Vineland
Salem
Bridgeton
Woodstown
Pennsville
SCHUYLKILL
LEBANON
BERKS
LEHIGH
NORTHAMPTON
BUCKS
MONTGOMERY
CHESTER
LANCASTER
DELAWARE
PHILADELPHIA
YORK
HARFORD
CECIL
NEW CASTLE
SALEM
GLOUCESTER
PENNSYLVANIA
MARYLAND
A
B
C
1
2
3
4

DRIVING DISTANCES IN MILES	ALLENTOWN, PA	ATLANTIC CITY, NJ	ELKTON, MD	LANCASTER, PA	LONG BRANCH, NJ	NEW BRUNSWICK, NJ	NEW YORK, NY	PHILADELPHIA, PA	READING, PA	TOMS RIVER, NJ	TRENTON, NJ	WILMINGTON, DE
NEW YORK, NY	84	125	137	165	55	34		91	118	75	55	120
PHILADELPHIA, PA	63	62	50	79	77	55	91		63	58	34	30
TRENTON, NJ	66	77	88	105	53	22	55	34	89	48		68
WILMINGTON, DE	77	86	20	53	106	90	120	30	56	85	68	

SEE ALSO DISTANCE AND DRIVING TIME MAP ON PAGES 286–287

BONUS MAPS!

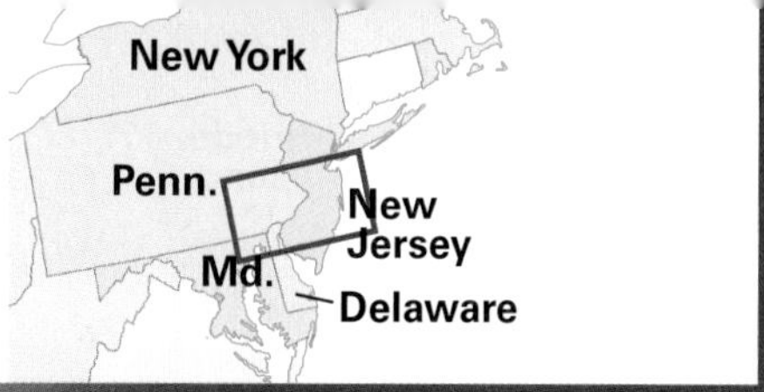
New York
Penn.
New Jersey
Md.
Delaware

New York
Elizabeth
Edison
New Brunswick
Princeton
Trenton
Toms River
Lakewood
Asbury Park
Long Branch
Point Pleasant
Atlantic City
ATLANTIC OCEAN
PINELANDS NATIONAL RESERVE
JOINT BASE MCGUIRE-DIX-LAKEHURST
Go to 148
Go to 105
FOR CONTINUATION SEE INSET AT RIGHT

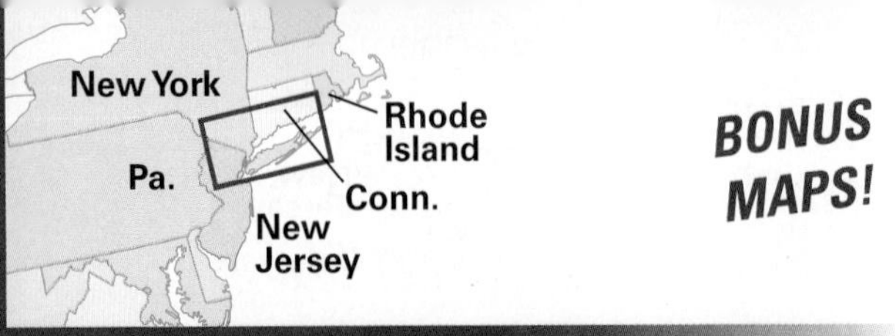
New York
Rhode Island
Pa.
Conn.
New Jersey

BONUS MAPS!

0 mi 5 10 15 20
0 km 5 10 15 20 25 30
One inch equals 9.85 miles
One centimeter equals 6.25 kilometers

Go to 94
Go to 147
New Paltz
Poughkeepsie
Arlington
Monticello
Middletown
Newburgh
Beacon
Goshen
Port Jervis
Kiryas Joel
Monroe
Peekskill
Danbury
Ossining
Spring Valley
New City
West Milford
Newton
Hopatcong
Paterson
Yonkers
Mt. Vernon
New Rochelle
White Plains
Stamford
Greenwich
Port Chester
Norwalk
Westport
Darien
Clifton
Passaic
Morristown
Newark
Jersey City
New York
Hempstead
Mineola
Elizabeth
Edison
New Brunswick
Perth Amboy
Huntington Station
Long Beach
Massapequa Park
Babylon
CONNECTICUT
NEW YORK
NEW JERSEY
1
2
3
4
A
B
C

DRIVING DISTANCES IN MILES

	BRIDGEPORT, CT	DANBURY, CT	HARTFORD, CT	NEWARK, NJ	NEWBURGH, NY	NEW HAVEN, CT	NEW LONDON, CT	NEW YORK, NY	PATERSON, NJ	RIVERHEAD, NY	STAMFORD, CT	WATERBURY, CT
BRIDGEPORT, CT		31	56	69	73	19	64	60	71	115	21	33
NEWARK, NJ	69	79	125		66	88	134	11	18	88	48	108
NEW HAVEN, CT	19	35	39	88	78		46	78	89	133	40	30
NEW YORK, NY	60	69	115	11	56	78	124		16	78	38	99

SEE ALSO DISTANCE AND DRIVING TIME MAP ON PAGES 286–287

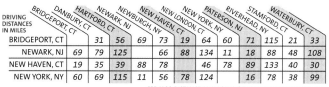

BONUS MAPS!

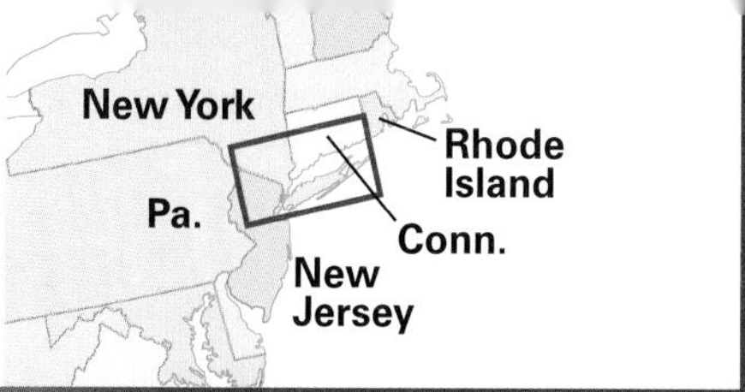
New York
Rhode Island
Pa.
Conn.
New Jersey

Northeast Corridor / New Haven CT

Hartford
New Britain
Bristol
Waterbury
Middletown
Meriden
Wallingford
Naugatuck
Hamden
New Haven
West Haven
Milford
Bridgeport
Norwich
New London
Groton
Westerly
Willimantic
Long Island Sound
Block Island Sound
CONNECTICUT
NEW YORK
RHODE ISLAND
LONG ISLAND
Riverhead
Southampton
Hampton Bays
Montauk
Orient Pt.
ATLANTIC OCEAN
Go to 150
1
2
3
4
D
E
F

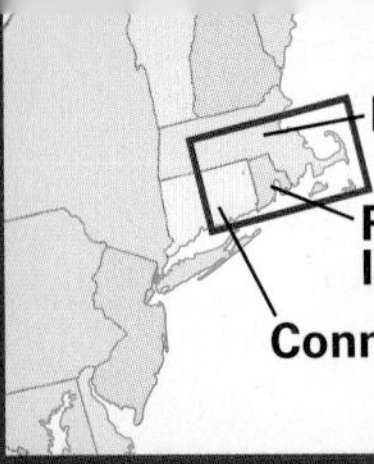

BONUS MAPS!

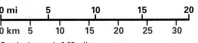

0 mi 5 10 15 20
0 km 5 10 15 20 25 30
One inch equals 9.85 miles
One centimeter equals 6.25 kilometers

Northeast Corridor / Hartford CT

DRIVING DISTANCES IN MILES

	BOSTON, MA	GLOUCESTER, MA	HARTFORD, CT	HYANNIS, MA	NEW BEDFORD, MA	NEW LONDON, CT	NEWPORT, RI	PLYMOUTH, MA	PROVIDENCE, RI	PROVINCETOWN, MA	SPRINGFIELD, MA	WORCESTER, MA
BOSTON, MA		35	102	72	60	109	73	41	52	117	95	46
HARTFORD, CT	102	136		155	104	46	85	127	73	200	25	62
PROVIDENCE, RI	52	92	73	71	33	58	33	41		117	75	43
SPRINGFIELD, MA	95	129	25	148	127	71	111	120	75	193		55

SEE ALSO DISTANCE AND DRIVING TIME MAP ON PAGES 286–287

BONUS MAPS!

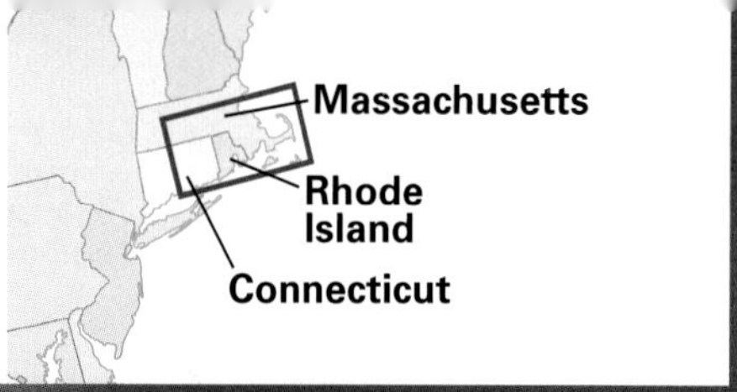

CANADA
UNITED STATES
MEXICO
HAWAII

0 mi 10 20 30 40
0 km 10 20 30 40 50 60
One inch equals 18.4 miles
One centimeter equals 11.7 kilometers

Honolulu HI / Lihue HI

1

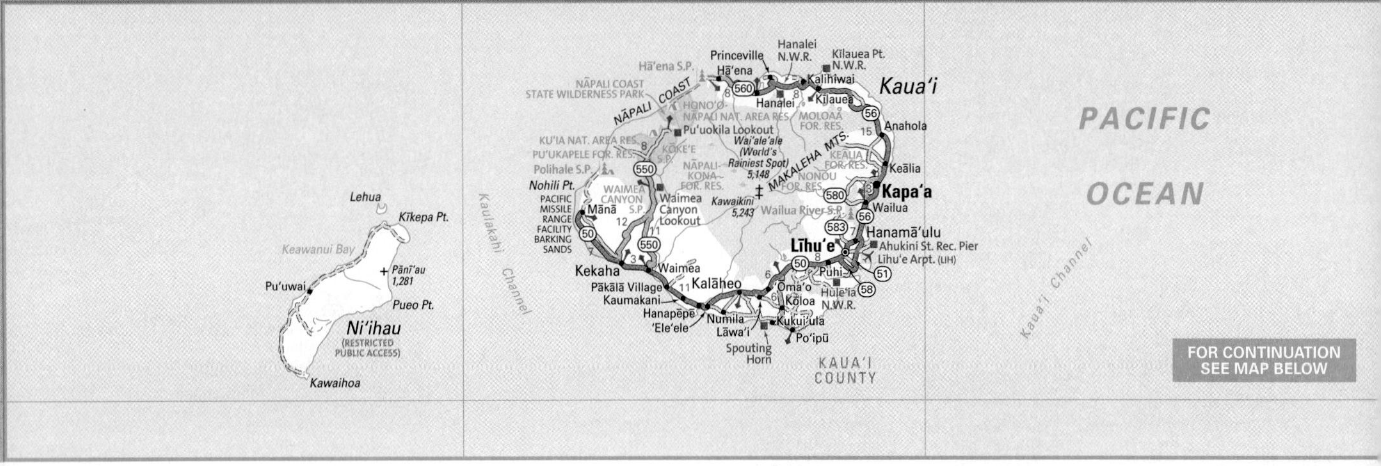
PACIFIC OCEAN
Kaua'i
Princeville
Hanalei N.W.R.
Kīlauea Pt. N.W.R.
Hā'ena S.P.
Hā'ena
Hanalei
Kalihiwai
Kīlauea
NĀPALI COAST STATE WILDERNESS PARK
NĀPALI COAST
Anahola
Pu'uokila Lookout
Wai'ale'ale (World's Rainiest Spot) 5,148
MAKALEHA MTS.
Kealia
Polihale S.P.
Nohili Pt.
PACIFIC MISSILE RANGE FACILITY BARKING SANDS
Mānā
Waimea Canyon Lookout
Kawaikini 5,243
Kapa'a
Wailua
Wailua River S.P.
Hanamā'ulu
Līhu'e
Ahukini St. Rec. Pier
Lihu'e Arpt. (LIH)
Kekaha
Waimea
Pākālā Village
Kaumakani
Hanapēpē
'Ele'ele
Kalāheo
Numila
Lāwa'i
'Oma'o
Kōloa
Hulē'ia N.W.R.
Puhi
Kukui'ula
Po'ipū
Spouting Horn
KAUA'I COUNTY
Kaulakahi Channel
Kaua'i Channel
Lehua
Kīkepa Pt.
Keawanui Bay
Pānī'au 1,281
Pu'uwai
Pueo Pt.
Ni'ihau
(RESTRICTED PUBLIC ACCESS)
Kawaihoa
FOR CONTINUATION SEE MAP BELOW

2

3

4

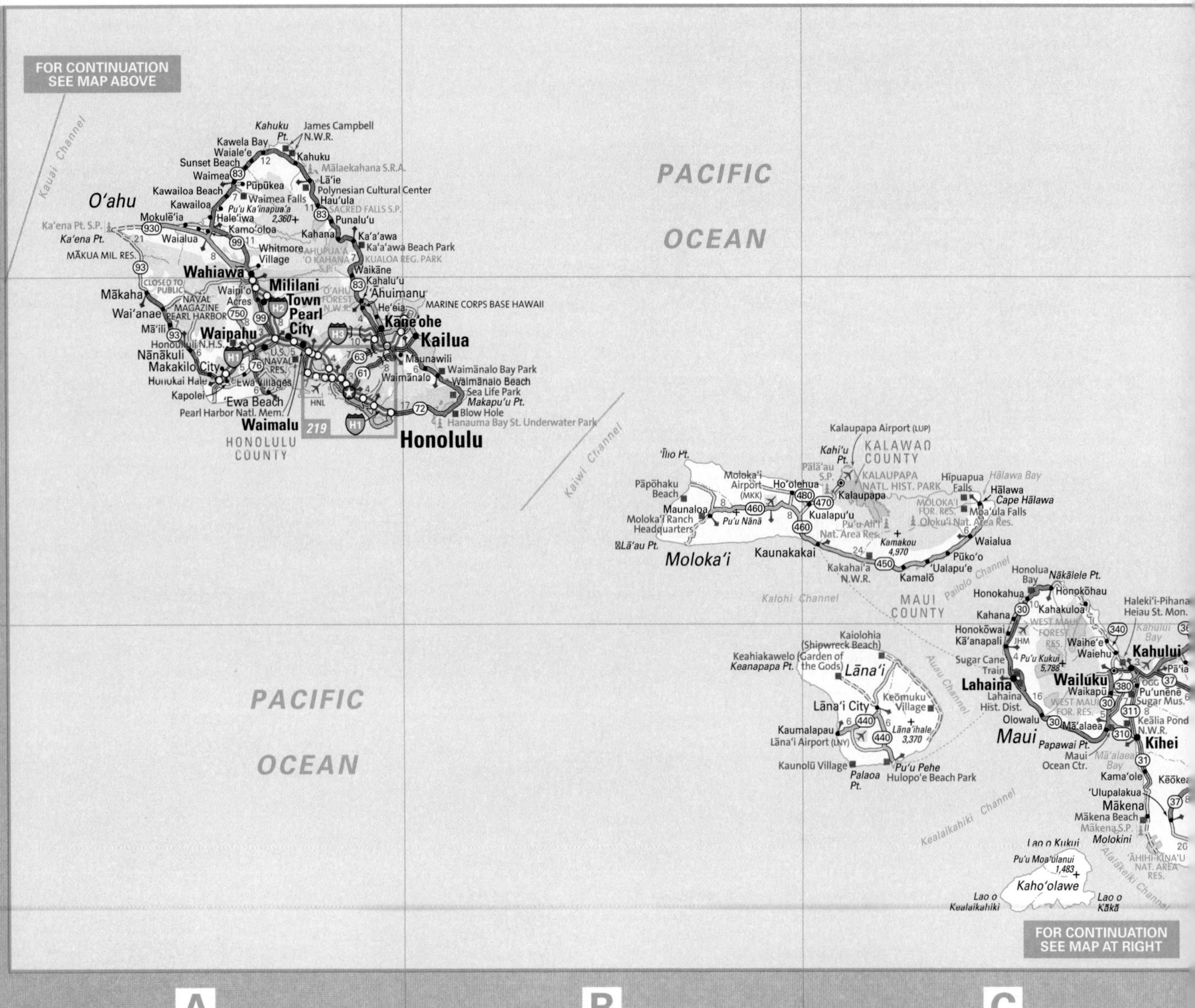
FOR CONTINUATION SEE MAP ABOVE
Kauai Channel
O'ahu
PACIFIC OCEAN
Kahuku Pt.
James Campbell N.W.R.
Kawela Bay
Waiale'e
Kahuku
Sunset Beach
Waimea
Pūpūkea
Waimea Falls
Kawailoa Beach
Kawailoa
Hale'iwa
Mokulē'ia
Waialua
Kamo'oloa
Pu'u Ka'inapua'a 2,360
Mālaekahana S.R.A.
Lā'ie
Polynesian Cultural Center
Hau'ula
SACRED FALLS S.P.
Punalu'u
Kahana
Ka'a'awa
Ka'a'awa Beach Park
KUALOA REG. PARK
Waikāne
Kahalu'u
'Āhuimanu
He'eia
MARINE CORPS BASE HAWAII
Kāne'ohe
Kailua
Maunawili
Waimānalo
Waimānalo Bay Park
Waimānalo Beach
Sea Life Park
Makapu'u Pt.
Blow Hole
Hanauma Bay St. Underwater Park
Ka'ena Pt. S.P.
Ka'ena Pt.
MĀKUA MIL. RES.
Whitmore Village
Wahiawā
Mililani Town
Pearl City
Waipahu
Mākaha
Wai'anae
Mā'ili
Nānākuli
Makakilo City
Honokai Hale
Kapolei
'Ewa Beach
'Ewa Villages
Pearl Harbor Natl. Mem.
Waimalu
HNL
Honolulu
HONOLULU COUNTY
Kaiwi Channel
Kalaupapa Airport (LUP)
Kahi'u Pt.
KALAWAO COUNTY
KALAUPAPA NATL. HIST. PARK
Kalaupapa
'Īlio Pt.
Pāpōhaku Beach
Moloka'i Airport (MKK)
Ho'olehua
Maunaloa
Moloka'i Ranch Headquarters
Pu'u Nānā
Kualapu'u
Hīpuapua Falls
Hālawa Bay
Hālawa
Cape Hālawa
Mo'a'ula Falls
Lā'au Pt.
Moloka'i
Kaunakakai
Kamakou 4,970
Waialua
Pūko'o
'Ualapu'e
Kamalō
Kakahai'a N.W.R.
Kalohi Channel
MAUI COUNTY
Pailolo Channel
Kaiolohia (Shipwreck Beach)
Keahiakawelo (Garden of the Gods)
Keanapapa Pt.
Lāna'i
Lāna'i City
Keōmuku Village
Kaumalapau
Lāna'i Airport (LNY)
Lāna'ihale 3,370
Kaunolū Village
Palaoa Pt.
Pu'u Pehe
Hulopo'e Beach Park
'Au'au Channel
Honolua Bay
Nākālele Pt.
Honokahua
Honokōhau
Kahakuloa
Kahana
Honokōwai
Kā'anapali
Sugar Cane Train
Lahaina
Lahaina Hist. Dist.
Olowalu
Pu'u Kukui 5,788
Waihe'e
Waiehu
Kahului
Wailuku
Waikapū
Pu'unēnē Sugar Mus.
Mā'alaea
Kealia Pond N.W.R.
Maui
Papawai Pt.
Maui Ocean Ctr.
Mā'alaea Bay
Kihei
Kama'ole
'Ulupalakua
Mākena
Mākena Beach
Mākena S.P.
Molokini
Kealaikahiki Channel
Lae o Kukui
Pu'u Mo'aulanui 1,483
Kaho'olawe
Lae o Kealaikahiki
Lae o Kākā
FOR CONTINUATION SEE MAP AT RIGHT

A B C

CANADA
UNITED STATES
MEXICO
HAWAII

DRIVING DISTANCES IN MILES	HĀNA	HILO	HONOLULU	HO'OLEHUA	KAHULUI	KAILUA	KAILUA-KONA	LAHAINA	LANAI CITY	LIHUE	WAHIAWĀ	WAIMEA
HILO	149*		217*	169*	121*	235*	88	142*	155*	319*	234*	54
HONOLULU	129*	217*		54*	101*	14	185*	92*	74*	102*	23	172*
KAHULUI	42	121*	101*	76*		119*	109*	23	57*	202*	118*	79*
LIHUE	230*	319*	102*	156*	202*	120*	285*	225*	176*		119*	174*

*DISTANCE INCLUDES AIR TRAVEL

SEE ALSO DISTANCE AND DRIVING TIME MAP ON PAGES 286–287

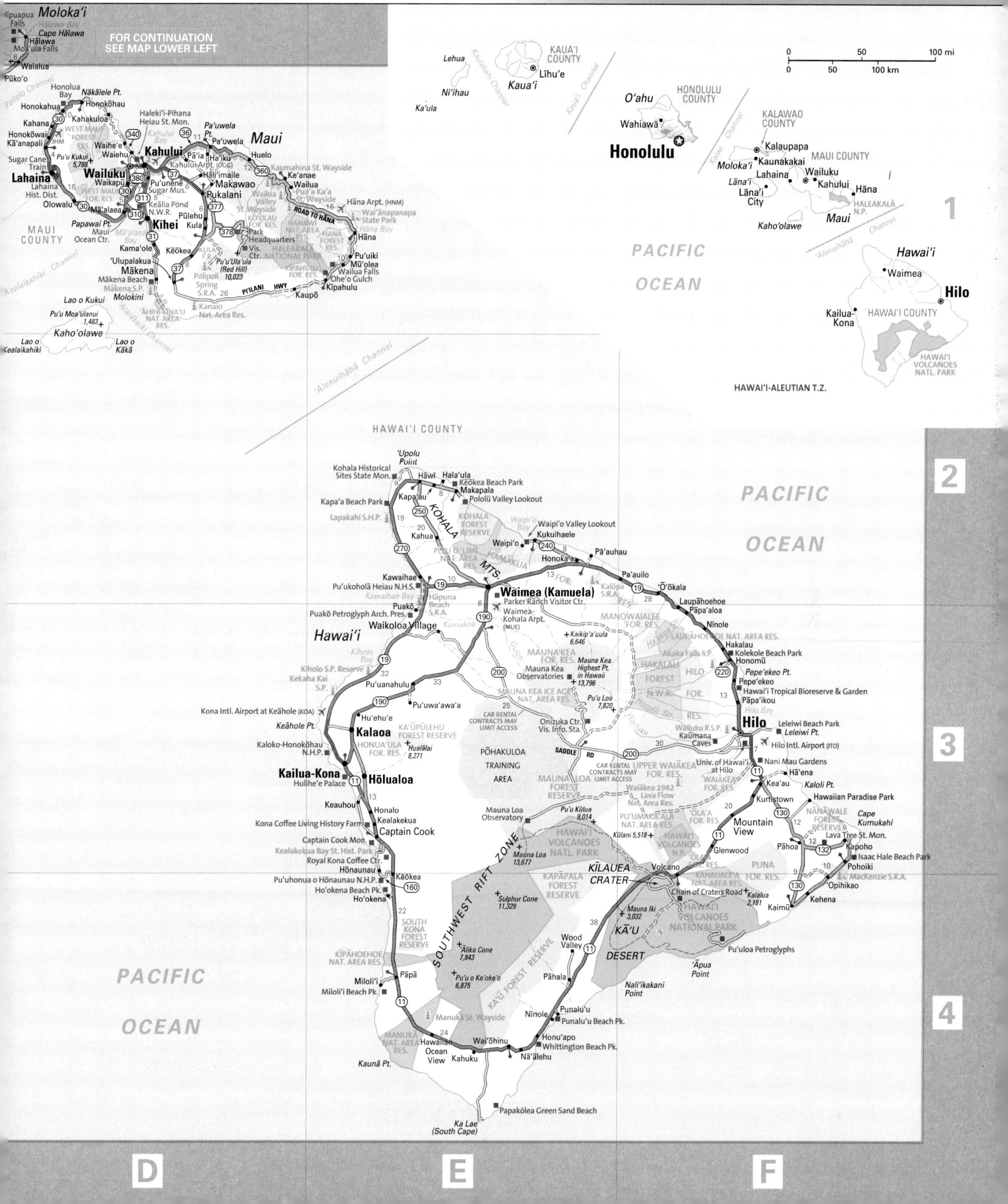
Moloka'i
FOR CONTINUATION SEE MAP LOWER LEFT
Maui
Lahaina
Wailuku
Kahului
Kīhei
Mākena
Makawao
Pukalani
Hāna
MAUI COUNTY
Kaho'olawe
Kaua'i
KAUA'I COUNTY
Līhu'e
Ni'ihau
O'ahu
HONOLULU COUNTY
Honolulu
Wahiawā
KALAWAO COUNTY
MAUI COUNTY
Lāna'i City
Hawai'i
Waimea
Hilo
Kailua-Kona
HAWAI'I COUNTY
HAWAI'I VOLCANOES NATL. PARK
PACIFIC OCEAN
HAWAI'I-ALEUTIAN T.Z.
0 50 100 mi
0 50 100 km
HAWAI'I COUNTY
Hawai'i
Waimea (Kamuela)
Kailua-Kona
Hōlualoa
Kalaoa
Captain Cook
Hilo
Volcano
KĪLAUEA CRATER
Mountain View
Pāhoa
Kea'au
Nā'ālehu
Pāhala
KA'Ū DESERT
SOUTHWEST RIFT ZONE
HAWAI'I VOLCANOES NATL. PARK
Mauna Kea Highest Pt. in Hawaii 13,796
Mauna Loa 13,677
Ka Lae (South Cape)
PACIFIC OCEAN
1
2
3
4
D
E
F

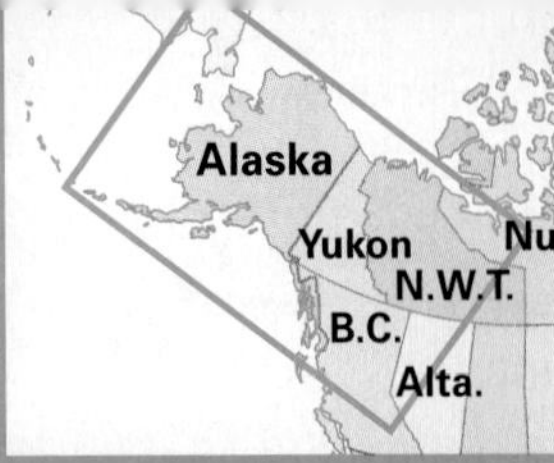
Alaska
Yukon
Nunavut
N.W.T.
B.C.
Alta.

0 mi 100 200
0 km 100 200 300
One inch equals 142 miles
One centimeter equals 90 kilometers

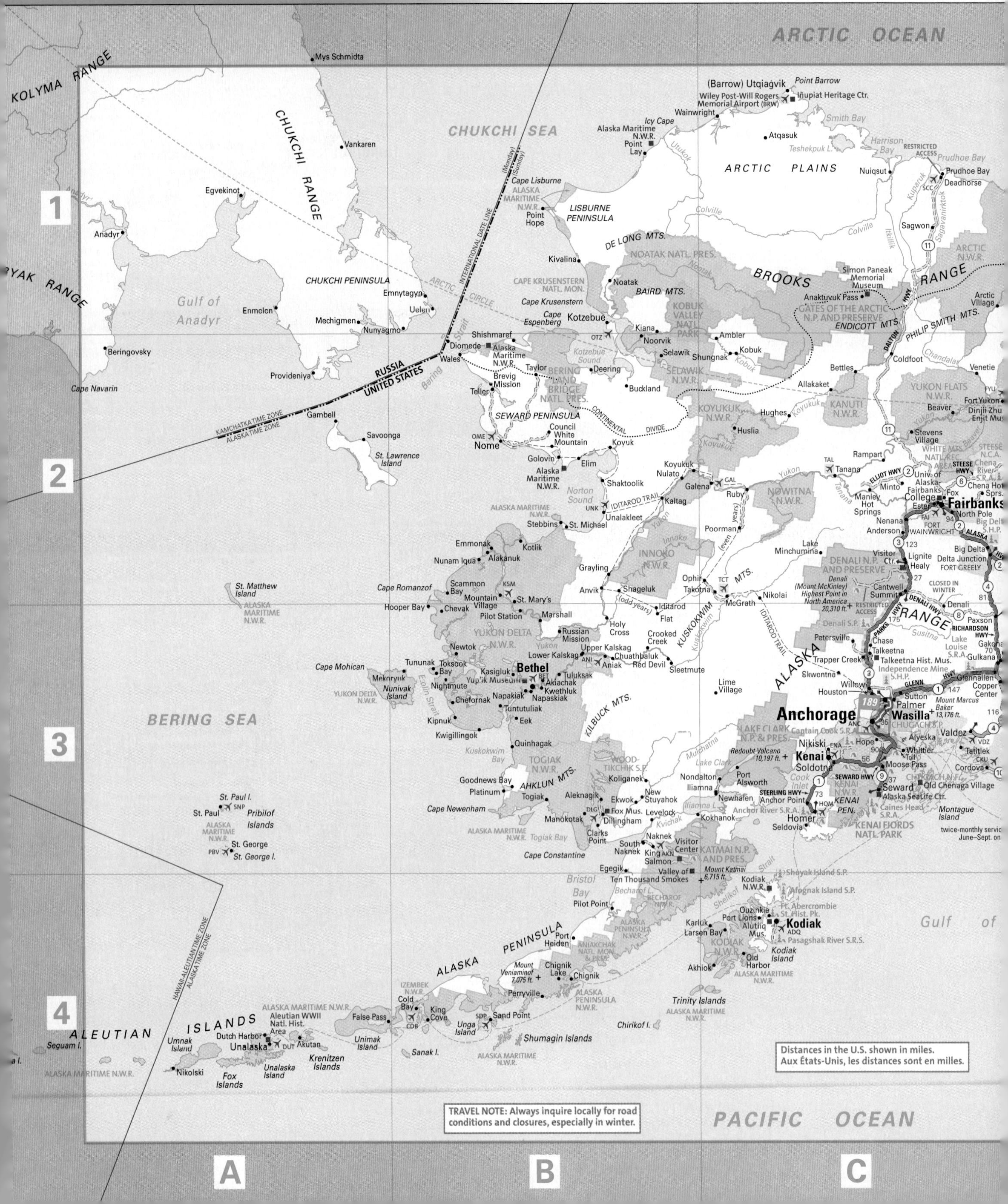
ARCTIC OCEAN
CHUKCHI SEA
BERING SEA
PACIFIC OCEAN
Gulf of
KOLYMA RANGE
CHUKCHI RANGE
RYAK RANGE
CHUKCHI PENINSULA
Gulf of Anadyr
Mys Schmidta
Vankaren
Egvekinot
Anadyr
Enmelen
Emnytagyn
Uelen
Mechigmen
Nunyagmo
Beringovsky
Provideniya
Cape Navarin
Gambell
Savoonga
St. Lawrence Island
RUSSIA
UNITED STATES
INTERNATIONAL DATE LINE
(Monday)
(Sunday)
KAMCHATKA TIME ZONE
ALASKA TIME ZONE
ARCTIC CIRCLE
Bering Strait
(Barrow) Utqiaġvik
Point Barrow
Wiley Post-Will Rogers Memorial Airport (BRW)
Iñupiat Heritage Ctr.
Wainwright
Icy Cape
Alaska Maritime N.W.R.
Point Lay
Atqasuk
Smith Bay
Teshekpuk L.
Harrison Bay
RESTRICTED ACCESS
Prudhoe Bay
Deadhorse
ARCTIC PLAINS
Nuiqsut
Cape Lisburne
ALASKA MARITIME N.W.R.
Point Hope
LISBURNE PENINSULA
DE LONG MTS.
NOATAK NATL. PRES.
Colville
Sagwon
ARCTIC N.W.R.
Kivalina
Noatak
BAIRD MTS.
BROOKS RANGE
Simon Paneak Memorial Museum
Anaktuvuk Pass
GATES OF THE ARCTIC N.P. AND PRESERVE
ENDICOTT MTS.
PHILIP SMITH MTS.
Arctic Village
CAPE KRUSENSTERN NATL. MON.
Cape Krusenstern
KOBUK VALLEY NATL. PARK
Cape Espenberg
Kotzebue
Kiana
Noorvik
Ambler
Shungnak
Kobuk
Selawik
SELAWIK N.W.R.
Shishmaref
Diomede
Alaska Maritime N.W.R.
Wales
Kotzebue Sound
Deering
Taylor
BERING LAND BRIDGE NATL. PRES.
Brevig Mission
Teller
Buckland
SEWARD PENINSULA
CONTINENTAL DIVIDE
Council
White Mountain
Nome
Golovin
Elim
Koyuk
Alaska Maritime N.W.R.
Coldfoot
Bettles
Allakaket
Chandalar
Venetie
YUKON FLATS N.W.R.
Fort Yukon
Beaver
Dinjii Zhu Enjit Mu
Hughes
KANUTI N.W.R.
KOYUKUK N.W.R.
Huslia
Stevens Village
Rampart
Tanana
ELLIOT HWY
Minto
Manley Hot Springs
Univ. of Alaska-Fairbanks
College
Ester
Fairbanks
Fox
Chena Hot Spr.
STEESE N.C.A.
North Pole
Big Delta S.H.P.
FORT WAINWRIGHT
Nenana
Anderson
Koyukuk
Nulato
Galena
Ruby
NOWITNA N.W.R.
Shaktoolik
Norton Sound
IDITAROD TRAIL
Kaltag
Unalakleet
ALASKA MARITIME N.W.R.
Stebbins
St. Michael
Poorman
Lake Minchumina
Emmonak
Kotlik
Nunam Iqua
Alakanuk
INNOKO N.W.R.
Grayling
Anvik
Shageluk
Ophir
Takotna
McGrath
Nikolai
Iditarod
Flat
Holy Cross
Scammon Bay
Cape Romanzof
Mountain Village
St. Mary's
Pilot Station
Hooper Bay
Chevak
Marshall
YUKON DELTA N.W.R.
Russian Mission
Upper Kalskag
Lower Kalskag
Chuathbaluk
Aniak
Red Devil
Crooked Creek
KUSKOKWIM MTS.
Sleetmute
St. Matthew Island
ALASKA MARITIME N.W.R.
Newtok
Tununak
Toksook Bay
Nightmute
Cape Mohican
Mekoryuk
Nunivak Island
YUKON DELTA N.W.R.
Chefornak
Kasigluk
Yup'ik Museum
Bethel
Akiachak
Kwethluk
Tuluksak
Napakiak
Napaskiak
Tuntutuliak
Eek
Kipnuk
Kwigillingok
Kuskokwim Bay
Quinhagak
KILBUCK MTS.
TOGIAK N.W.R.
AHKLUN MTS.
WOOD-TIKCHIK S.P.
Goodnews Bay
Platinum
Togiak
Cape Newenham
Koliganek
Aleknagik
Ekwok
New Stuyahok
Fox Mus.
Dillingham
Manokotak
Levelock
Clarks Point
Togiak Bay
Cape Constantine
South Naknek
Naknek
King Salmon
Visitor Center
KATMAI N.P. AND PRES.
Egegik
Valley of Ten Thousand Smokes
Mount Katmai 6,715 ft.
Bristol Bay
Becharof L.
BECHAROF N.W.R.
Pilot Point
Kokhanok
Iliamna L.
Iliamna
Nondalton
Newhalen
Port Alsworth
Lake Clark
LAKE CLARK N.P. & PRES.
Redoubt Volcano 10,197 ft.
Lime Village
DENALI N.P. AND PRESERVE
Denali (Mount McKinley) Highest Point in North America 20,310 ft.
RESTRICTED ACCESS
Denali S.P.
Visitor Ctr.
Lignite
Healy
Cantwell
Summit
CLOSED IN WINTER
Denali
ALASKA RANGE
DENALI HWY
PARKS HWY
RICHARDSON HWY
Big Delta
Delta Junction
FORT GREELY
Paxson
Sustina
Lake Louise S.R.A.
Gakona
Gulkana
Glennallen
Copper Center
Petersville
Chase
Talkeetna
Talkeetna Hist. Mus.
Independence Mine S.H.P.
Trapper Creek
Skwentna
Willow
Houston
Sutton
Palmer
Wasilla
Mount Marcus Baker 13,176 ft.
Anchorage
Captain Cook S.P.
CHUGACH S.P.
Nikiski
Kenai
Soldotna
Hope
Alyeska
Whittier
Moose Pass
Valdez
Tatitlek
Cordova
Seward
SEWARD HWY
STERLING HWY
Old Chenega Village
Alaska SeaLife Ctr.
Anchor Point
Anchor River S.R.A.
Homer
Seldovia
KENAI PEN.
KENAI N.W.R.
Caines Head S.R.A.
KENAI FJORDS NATL. PARK
Montague Island
twice-monthly service June–Sept. only
Cook Inlet
Shuyak Island S.P.
Afognak Island S.P.
Kodiak N.W.R.
Shelikof Strait
Ouzinkie
Ft. Abercrombie St. Hist. Pk.
Port Lions
Alutiiq Mus.
Kodiak
Pasagshak River S.R.S.
Karluk
Larsen Bay
KODIAK N.W.R.
Old Harbor
Kodiak Island
Akhiok
ALASKA MARITIME N.W.R.
Trinity Islands
ALASKA MARITIME N.W.R.
Chirikof I.
St. Paul I.
St. Paul
Pribilof Islands
ALASKA MARITIME N.W.R.
St. George
St. George I.
ALASKA PENINSULA
Port Heiden
ANIAKCHAK NATL. MON. & PRES.
ALASKA PENINSULA N.W.R.
Mount Veniaminof 7,075 ft.
Chignik Lake
Chignik
Perryville
IZEMBEK N.W.R.
Cold Bay
King Cove
False Pass
Unga Island
Sand Point
Shumagin Islands
Unimak Island
Sanak I.
ALASKA MARITIME N.W.R.
ALEUTIAN ISLANDS
Aleutian WWII Natl. Hist. Area
Dutch Harbor
Unalaska
Akutan
Krenitzen Islands
Umnak Island
Unalaska Island
Nikolski
Fox Islands
Seguam I.
ALASKA MARITIME N.W.R.
HAWAII-ALEUTIAN TIME ZONE
ALASKA TIME ZONE
Distances in the U.S. shown in miles.
Aux États-Unis, les distances sont en milles.
TRAVEL NOTE: Always inquire locally for road conditions and closures, especially in winter.
1
2
3
4
A
B
C

DRIVING DISTANCES IN MILES

	ANCHORAGE, AK	DAWSON CREEK, BC	DENALI NP, AK	FAIRBANKS, AK	HOMER, AK	JUNEAU, AK	PRINCE GEORGE, BC	PRINCE RUPERT, BC	SKAGWAY, AK	TOK, AK	WHITEHORSE, YT	YELLOWKNIFE, NT
ANCHORAGE, AK		1516	275	378	225	841*	1679	1514	807	323	697	1844
DAWSON CREEK, BC	1516		1503	1400	1740	963*	224	625	862	1193	819	741
FAIRBANKS, AK	378	1400	103		603	726*	1564	1398	691	207	581	1729
WHITEHORSE, YT	697	819	684	581	921	211*	982	817	110	374		1147

*DISTANCE INCLUDES FERRY TRAVEL

SEE ALSO DISTANCE AND DRIVING TIME MAP ON PAGES 286–287

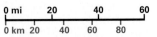

0 mi 20 40 60
0 km 20 40 60 80
One inch equals 40.3 miles/Un pouce équivaut à 40.3 milles
One centimeter equals 25.4 km/Un cm équivaut à 25.4 km

Prince Rupert BC / Terrace BC

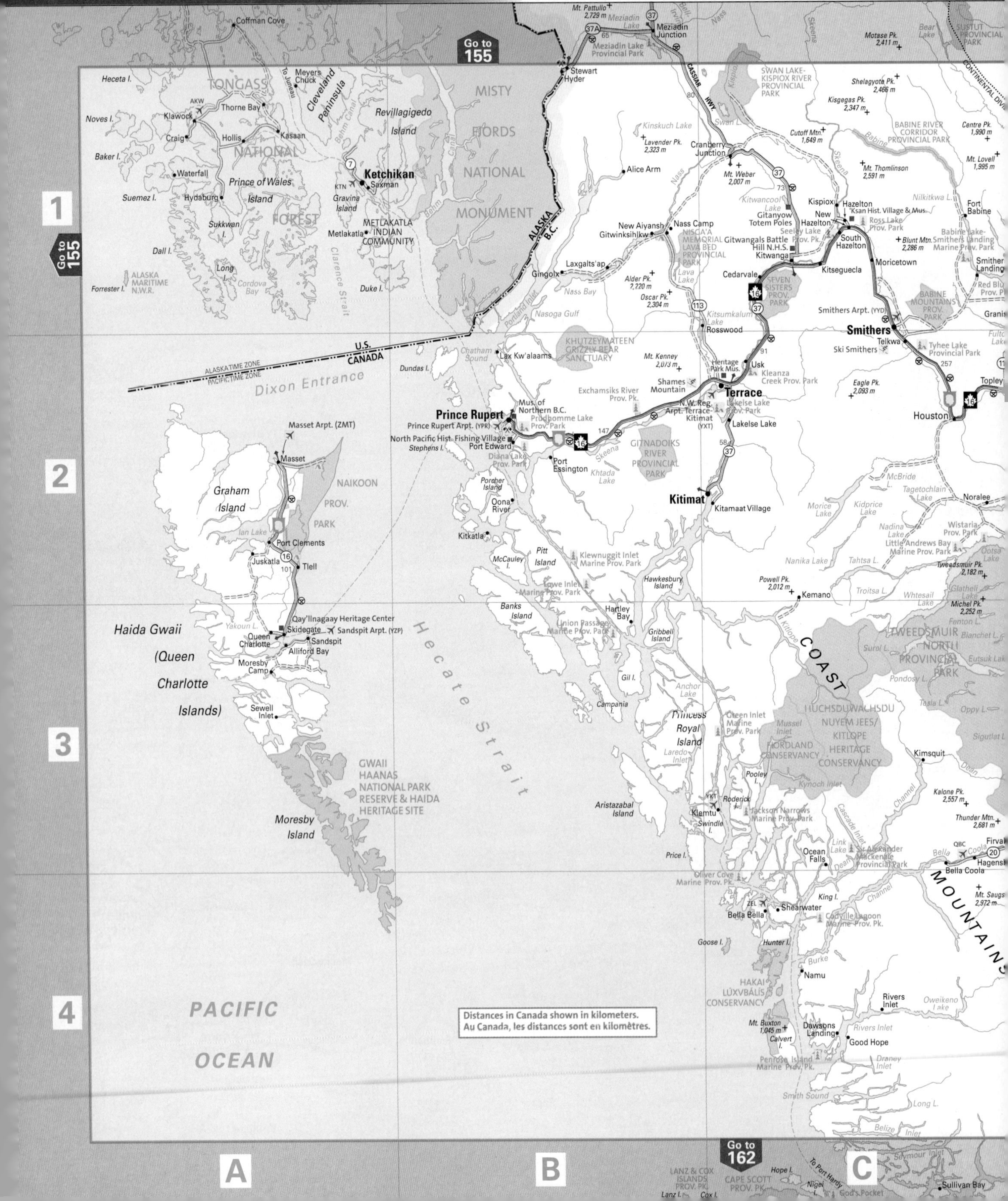

DRIVING DISTANCES IN KM / DISTANCES ROUTIÈRES EN KM

	DAWSON CREEK, BC	GRANDE PRAIRIE, AB	KAMLOOPS, BC	KITIMAT, BC	100 MILE HOUSE, BC	PRINCE GEORGE, BC	PRINCE RUPERT, BC	SMITHERS, BC	STEWART, BC	TERRACE, BC	VALEMOUNT, BC	WILLIAMS LAKE, BC
DAWSON CREEK, BC		124	931	1041	734	406	1130	777	1109	983	642	644
PRINCE GEORGE, BC	406	530	525	635	328		724	371	703	577	295	238
PRINCE RUPERT, BC	1130	1254	1249	205	1052	724		353	463	147	1019	962
WILLIAMS LAKE, BC	644	768	287	873	90	238	962	609	941	815	332	

SEE ALSO DISTANCE AND DRIVING TIME MAP ON PAGES 286–287 / VOIR AUSSI CARTE DES DISTANCES ET DES TEMPS DE PARCOURS PAGES 286–287

0 mi 20 40 60
0 km 20 40 60 80
One inch equals 40.3 miles/Un pouce équivaut à 40.3 milles
One centimeter equals 25.4 km/Un cm équivaut à 25.4 km

Grande Prairie AB / Jasper AB

DRIVING DISTANCES IN KM / DISTANCES ROUTIÈRES EN KM	DAWSON CREEK, BC	EDMONTON, AB	FORT MCMURRAY, AB	GRANDE PRAIRIE, AB	JASPER, AB	LLOYDMINSTER, AB/SK	MEADOW LAKE, SK	N. BATTLEFORD, SK	PEACE RIVER, AB	SLAVE LAKE, AB	VALEMOUNT, BC	WHITECOURT, AB
EDMONTON, AB	597		439	462	367	238	415	375	484	251	488	177
GRANDE PRAIRIE, AB	124	462	756		397	700	824	837	197	318	518	279
JASPER, AB	521	367	796	397		605	782	742	578	464	121	271
N. BATTLEFORD, SK	972	375	814	837	742	137	158		866	633	863	559

SEE ALSO DISTANCE AND DRIVING TIME MAP ON PAGES 286–287 / VOIR AUSSI CARTE DES DISTANCES ET DES TEMPS DE PARCOURS PAGES 286–287

0 mi 20 40 60
0 km 20 40 60 80
One inch equals 40.3 miles/Un pouce équivaut à 40.3 milles
One centimeter equals 25.4 km/Un cm équivaut à 25.4 km

Prince Albert SK / La Ronge SK

DRIVING DISTANCES IN KM / DISTANCES ROUTIÈRES EN KM

	FLIN FLON, MB	GILLAM, MB	GRAND RAPIDS, MB	LA LOCHE, SK	LA RONGE, SK	LYNN LAKE, MB	MEADOW LAKE, SK	NIPAWIN, SK	N. BATTLEFORD, SK	PRINCE ALBERT, SK	THE PAS, MB	THOMPSON, MB
FLIN FLON, MB		676	402	889	613	703	633	388	571	375	141	380
MEADOW LAKE, SK	633	1309	867	305	496	1336		399	158	258	569	1013
PRINCE ALBERT, SK	375	1051	609	514	238	1078	258	141	196		311	781
THOMPSON, MB	380	296	328	1269	697	323	1013	640	977	781	470	

SEE ALSO DISTANCE AND DRIVING TIME MAP ON PAGES 286–287 / VOIR AUSSI CARTE DES DISTANCES ET DES TEMPS DE PARCOURS PAGES 286–287

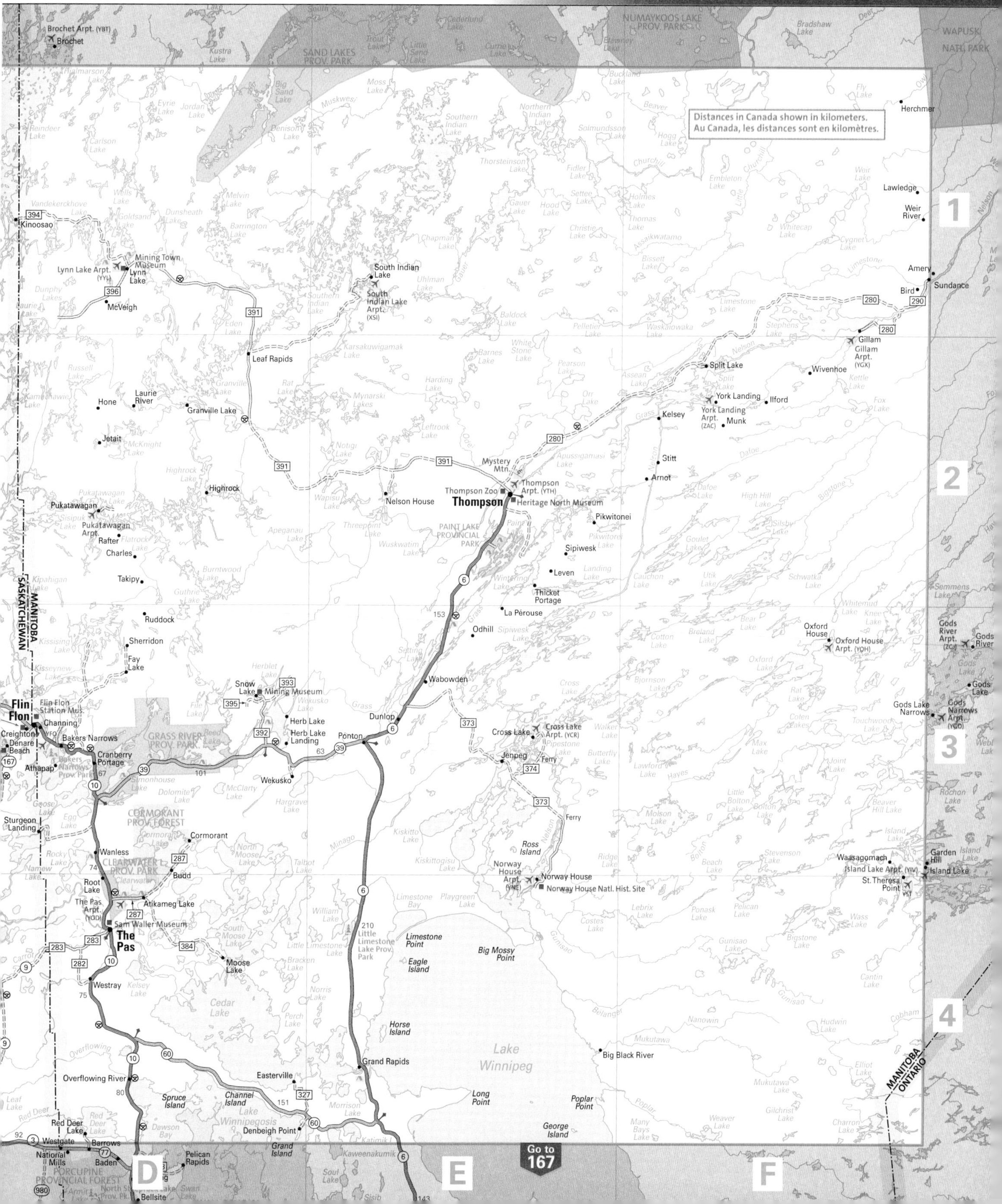

Nanaimo BC / Campbell River BC

0 mi 20 40
0 km 20 40 60

One inch equals 25.4 miles/Un pouce équivaut à 25.4 milles
One cm equals 16.1 km/Un cm équivaut à 16.1 km

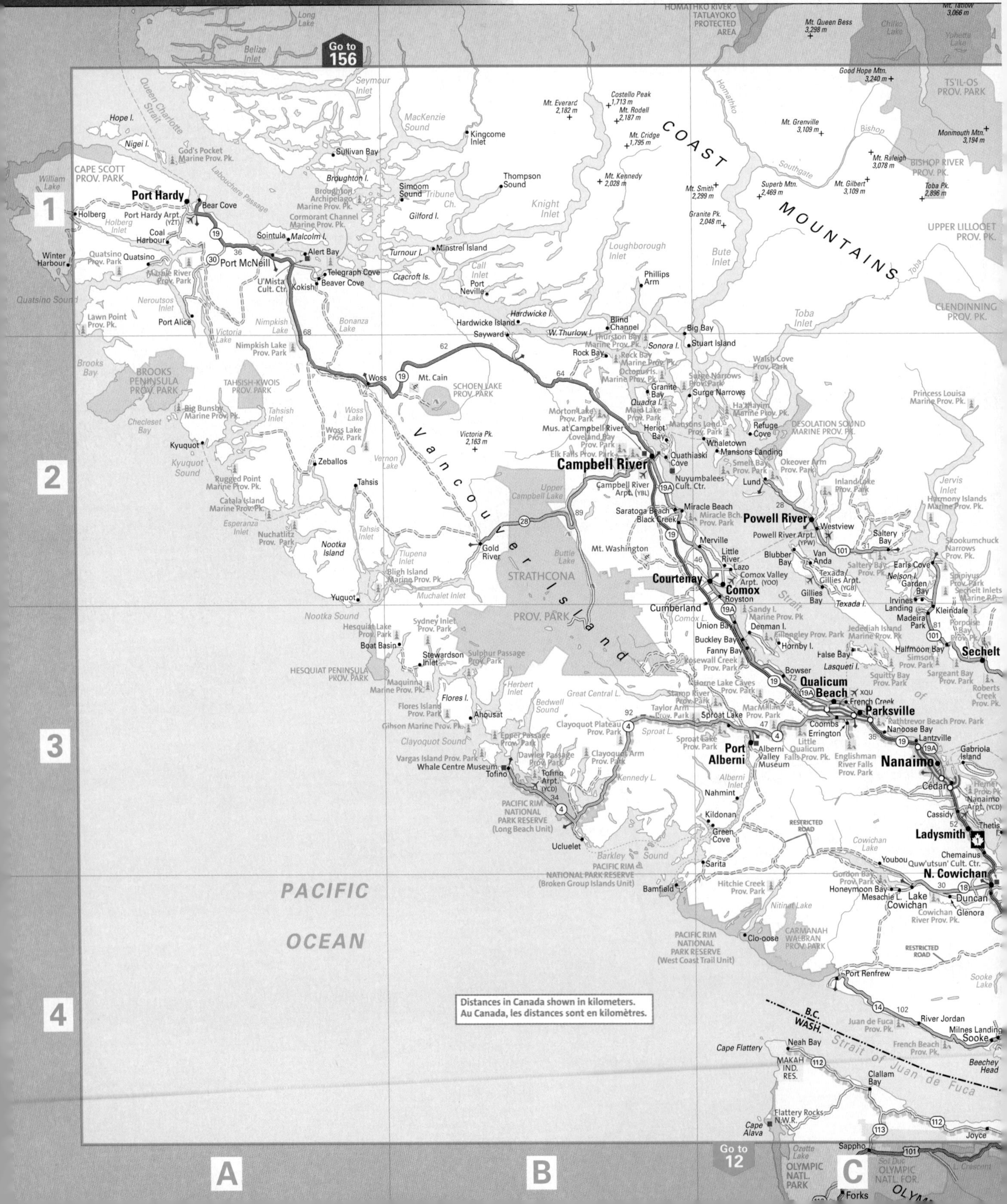

DRIVING DISTANCES IN KM / DISTANCES ROUTIÈRES EN KM

	CAMPBELL RIVER, BC	KAMLOOPS, BC	KELOWNA, BC	MERRITT, BC	NANAIMO, BC	OSOYOOS, BC	PORT ALBERNI, BC	PORT HARDY, BC	SALMON ARM, BC	VANCOUVER, BC	VICTORIA, BC	WHISTLER, BC
KAMLOOPS, BC	512		163	87	363	231	441	750	108	355	393	475
NANAIMO, BC	153	363	403	279		404	82	391	471	23	113	104
VANCOUVER, BC	172	355	395	271	23	396	101	410	463		69	123
VICTORIA, BC	266	393	433	309	113	434	195	504	501	69		192

SEE ALSO DISTANCE AND DRIVING TIME MAP ON PAGES 286–287 / VOIR AUSSI CARTE DES DISTANCES ET DES TEMPS DE PARCOURS PAGES 286–287

0 mi 20 40 60
0 km 20 40 60 80

One inch equals 40.3 miles/Un pouce équivaut à 40.3 milles
One centimeter equals 25.4 km/Un cm équivaut à 25.4 km

Calgary AB / Banff AB

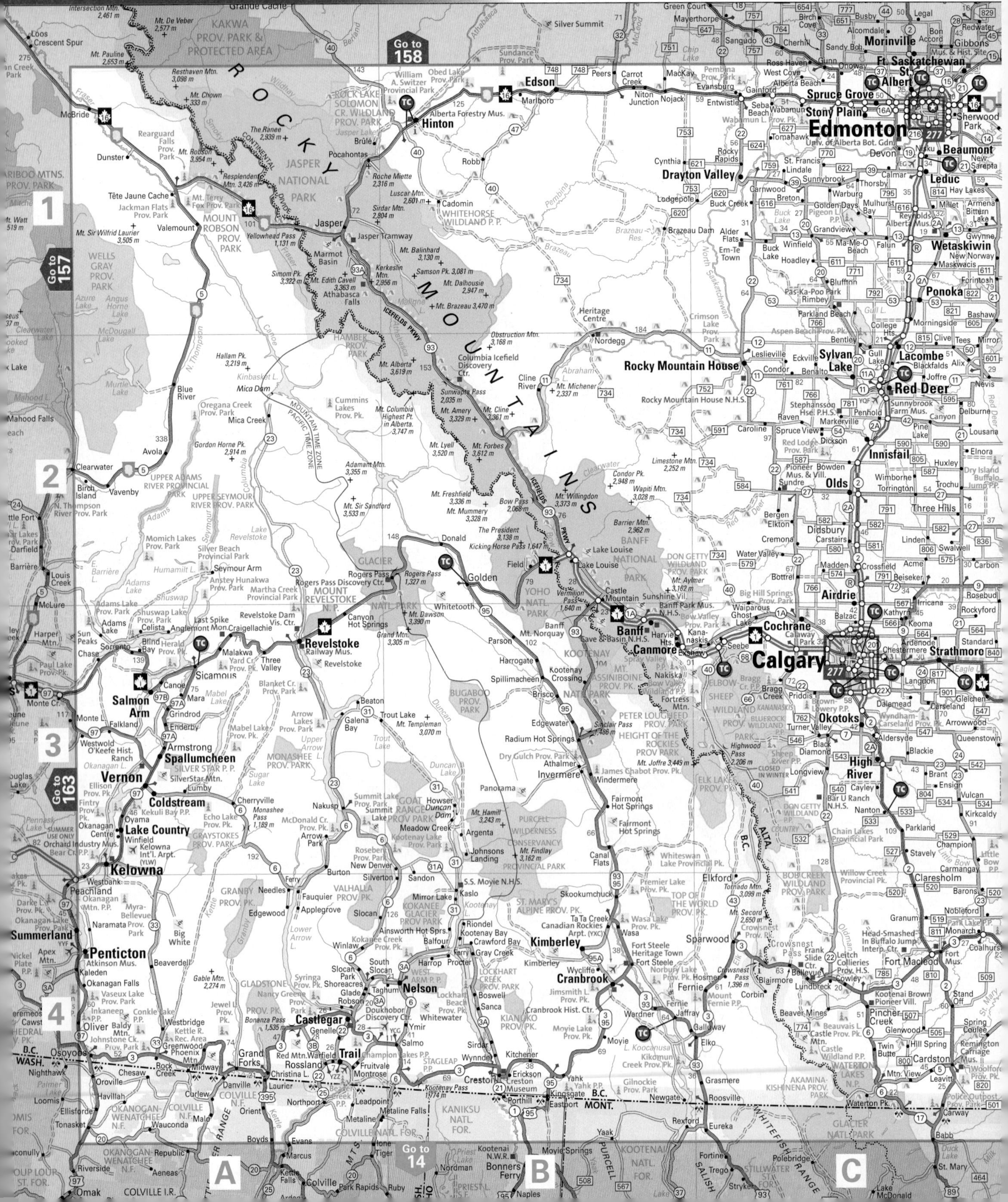

DRIVING DISTANCES IN KM / DISTANCES ROUTIÈRES EN KM

	BANFF, AB	CALGARY, AB	CRANBROOK, BC	EDMONTON, AB	JASPER, AB	KELOWNA, BC	LETHBRIDGE, AB	LLOYDMINSTER, AB/SK	MEDICINE HAT, AB	RED DEER, AB	SASKATOON, SK	SWIFT CURRENT, SK
CALGARY, AB	128		383	296	396	638	216	534	285	145	620	503
EDMONTON, AB	412	296	679		367	934	512	238	579	150	513	676
LETHBRIDGE, AB	344	216	306	512	612	809		605	164	360	650	382
SASKATOON, SK	748	620	969	513	880	1255	650	275	486	639		267

SEE ALSO DISTANCE AND DRIVING TIME MAP ON PAGES 286–287 / VOIR AUSSI CARTE DES DISTANCES ET DES TEMPS DE PARCOURS PAGES 286–287

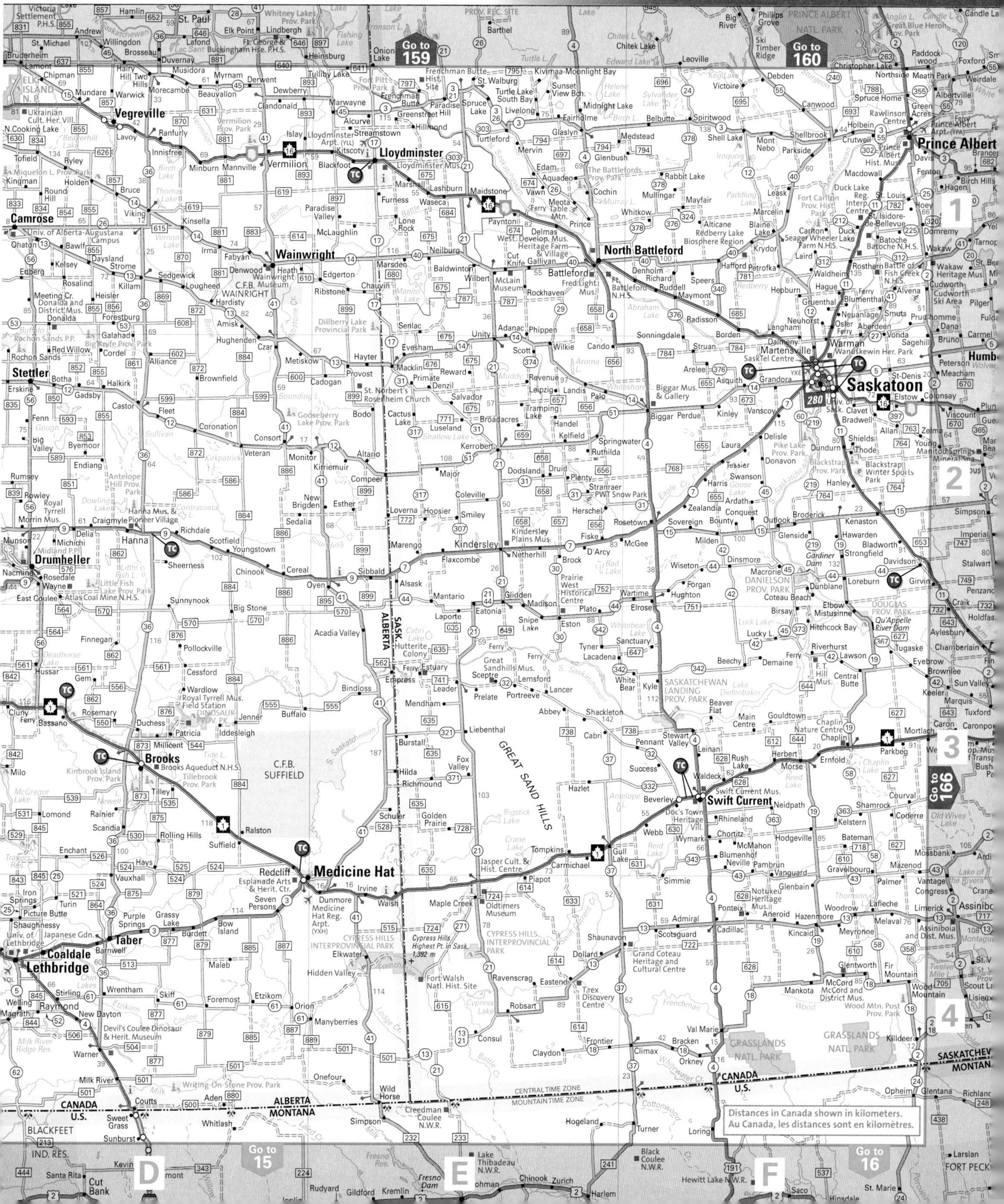

0 mi 20 40 60
0 km 20 40 60 80

One inch equals 40.3 miles/Un pouce équivaut à 40.3 milles
One centimeter equals 25.4 km/Un cm équivaut à 25.4 km

Saskatoon SK / Regina SK

DRIVING DISTANCES IN KM / DISTANCES ROUTIÈRES EN KM

	BRANDON, MB	DAUPHIN, MB	GRAND RAPIDS, MB	MOOSE JAW, SK	PORTAGE LA PRAIRIE, MB	PRINCE ALBERT, SK	REGINA, SK	SASKATOON, SK	SWIFT CURRENT, SK	THE PAS, MB	WINNIPEG, MB	YORKTON, SK
BRANDON, MB		166	525	448	134	745	377	639	618	570	216	270
REGINA, SK	377	366	787	68	511	368		261	241	557	593	195
SASKATOON, SK	639	502	689	224	691	141	261		267	578	773	331
WINNIPEG, MB	216	322	430	664	82	819	593	773	834	611		442

SEE ALSO DISTANCE AND DRIVING TIME MAP ON PAGES 286–287 / VOIR AUSSI CARTE DES DISTANCES ET DES TEMPS DE PARCOURS PAGES 286–287

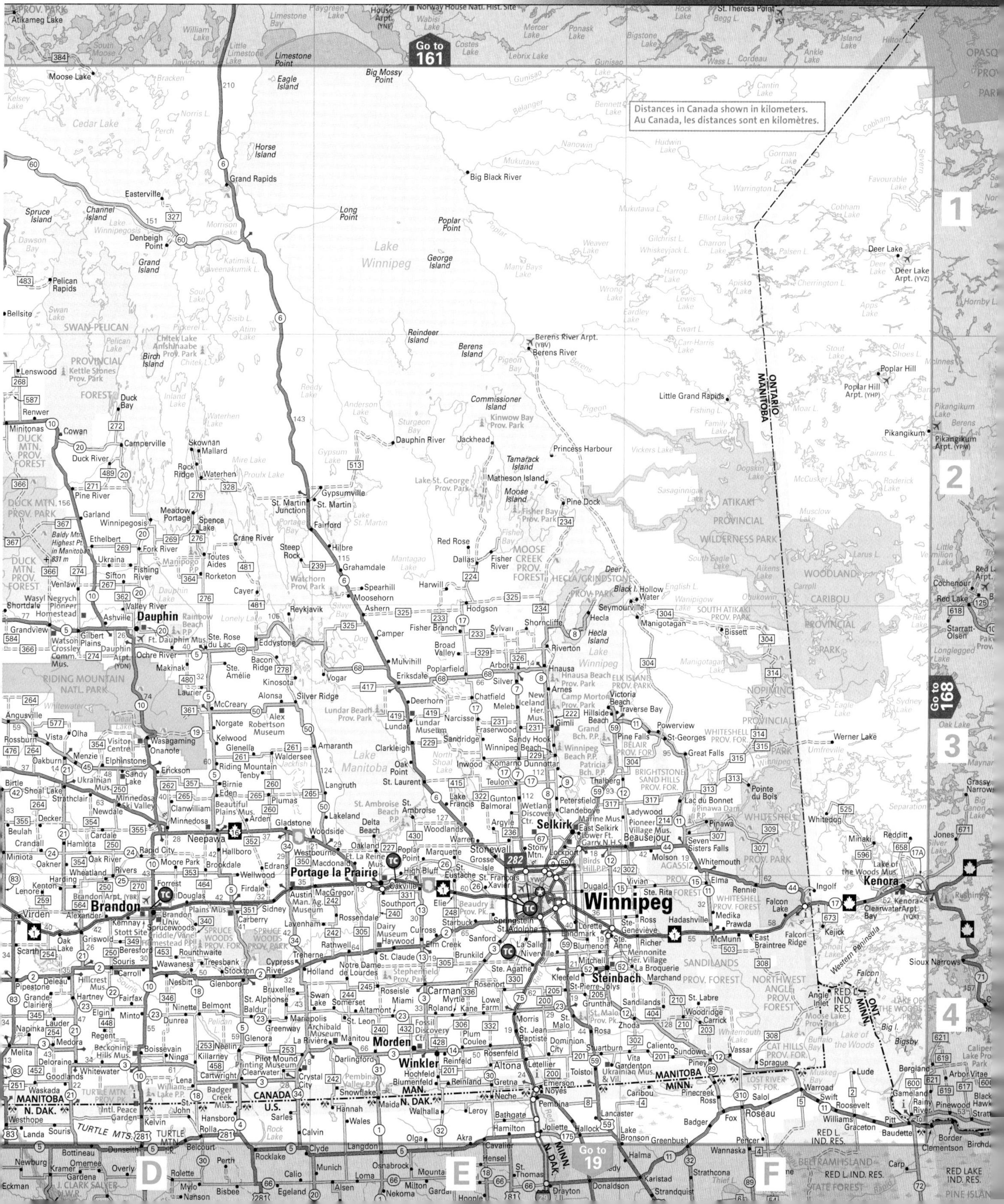

0 mi 20 40 60
0 km 20 40 60 80
One inch equals 40.3 miles/Un pouce équivaut à 40.3 milles
One centimeter equals 25.4 km/Un cm équivaut à 25.4 km

Kenora ON / Fort Frances ON

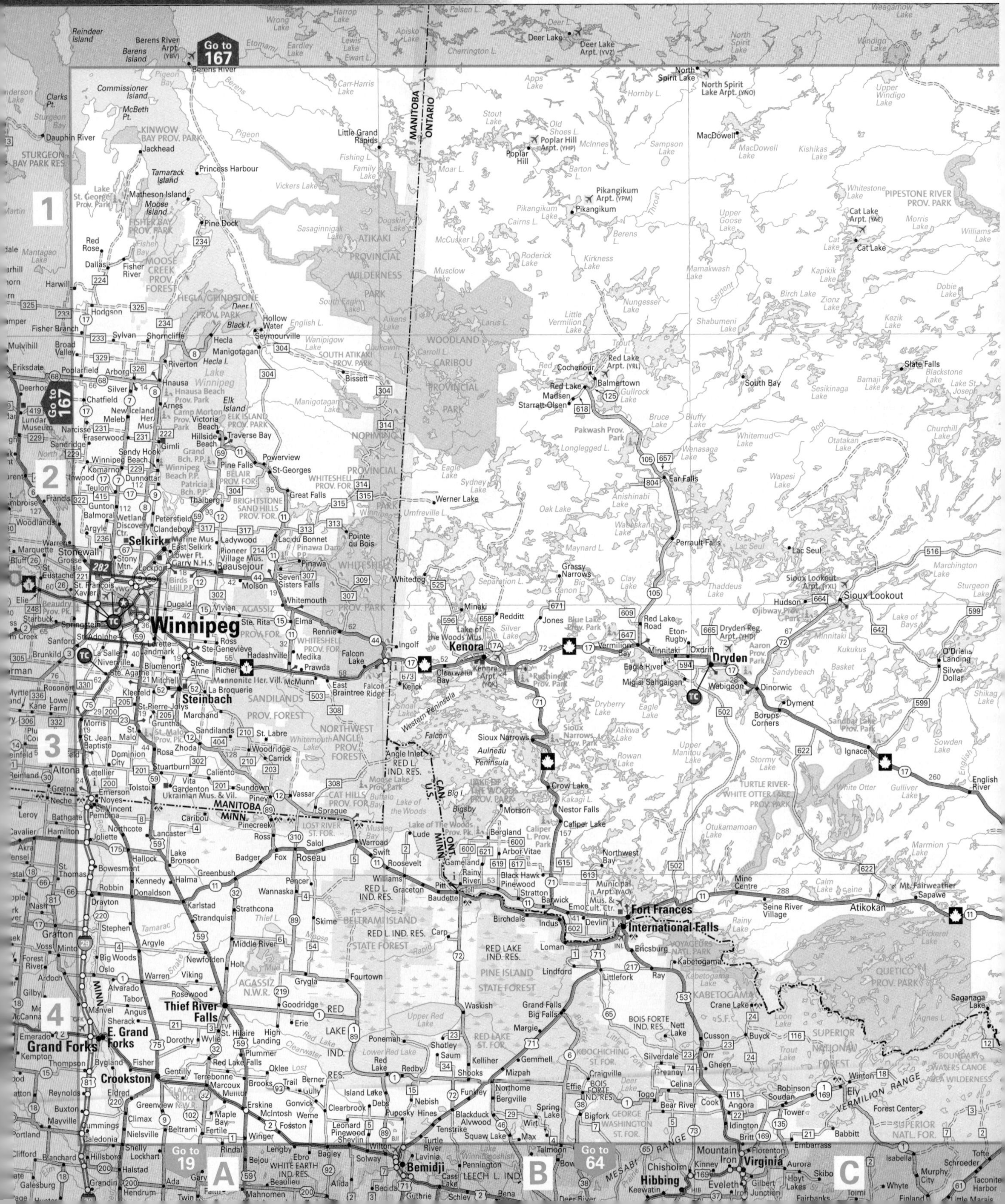

DRIVING DISTANCES IN KM / DISTANCES ROUTIÈRES EN KM	DRYDEN, ON	FORT FRANCES, ON	GERALDTON, ON	GRAND FORKS, ND	HEARST, ON	KENORA, ON	MARATHON, ON	NIPIGON, ON	STEINBACH, MB	THUNDER BAY, ON	WAWA, ON	WINNIPEG, MB
FORT FRANCES, ON	190		627	315	845	215	641	445	310	335	805	420
KENORA, ON	140	215	772	429	990		786	585	184	480	950	205
THUNDER BAY, ON	340	335	292	650	510	480	306	110	664		470	685
WINNIPEG, MB	345	420	977	228	1195	205	991	790	55	685	1155	

SEE ALSO DISTANCE AND DRIVING TIME MAP ON PAGES 286–287 / VOIR AUSSI CARTE DES DISTANCES ET DES TEMPS DE PARCOURS PAGES 286–287

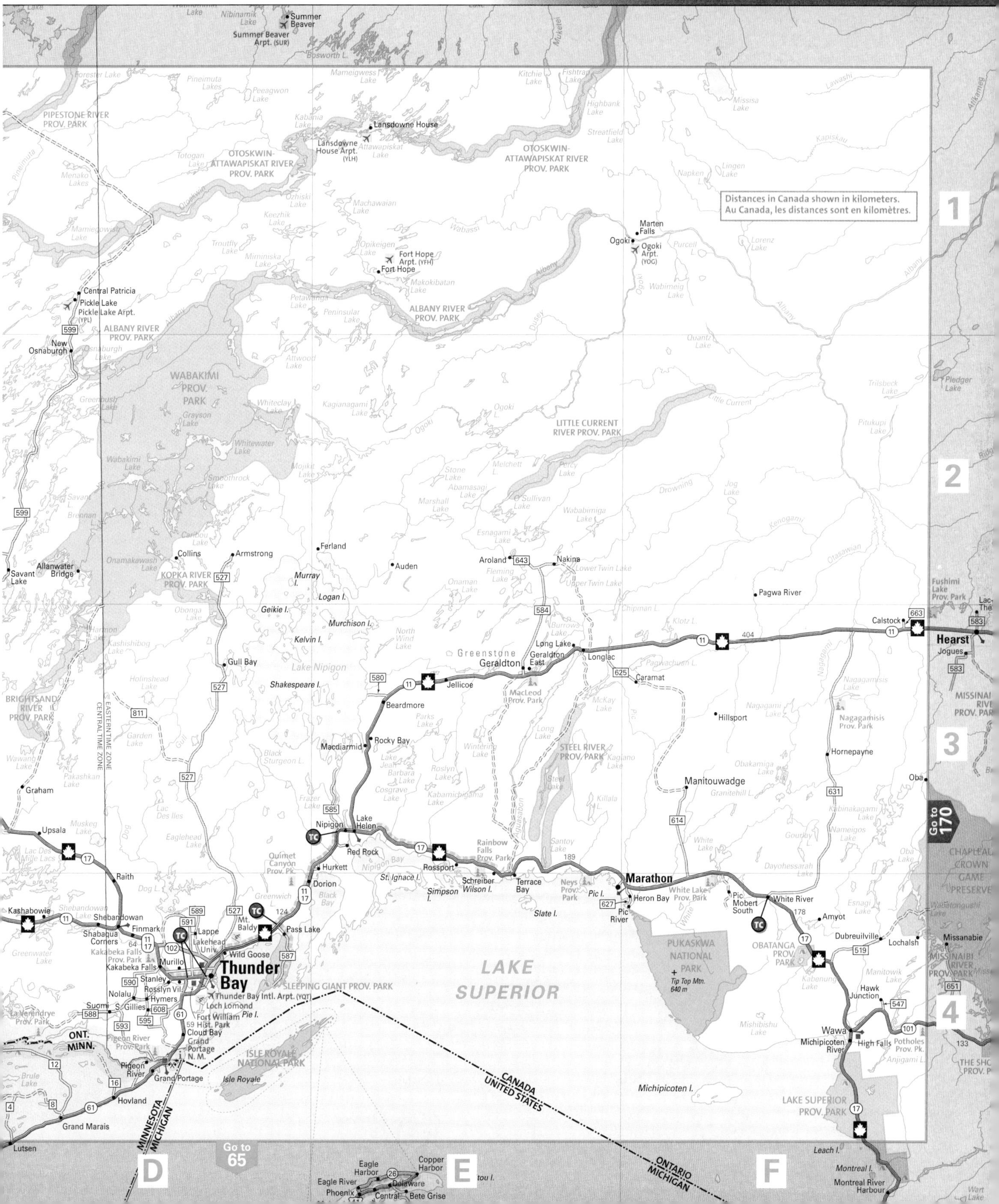

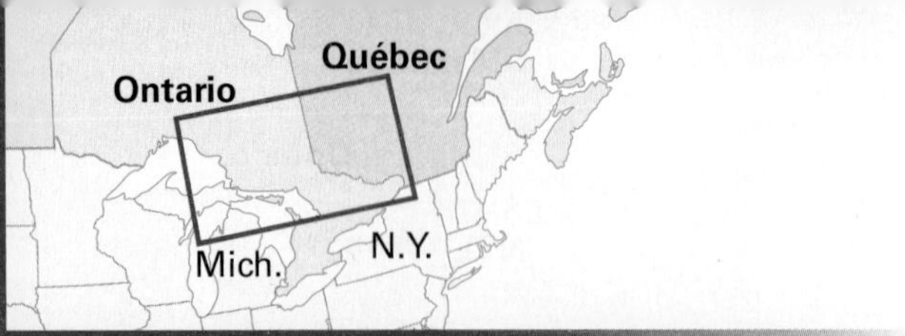

0 mi 20 40 60
0 km 20 40 60 80

One inch equals 40.3 miles/Un pouce équivaut à 40.3 milles
One centimeter equals 25.4 km/Un cm équivaut à 25.4 km

Sudbury ON / Sault Ste Marie ON

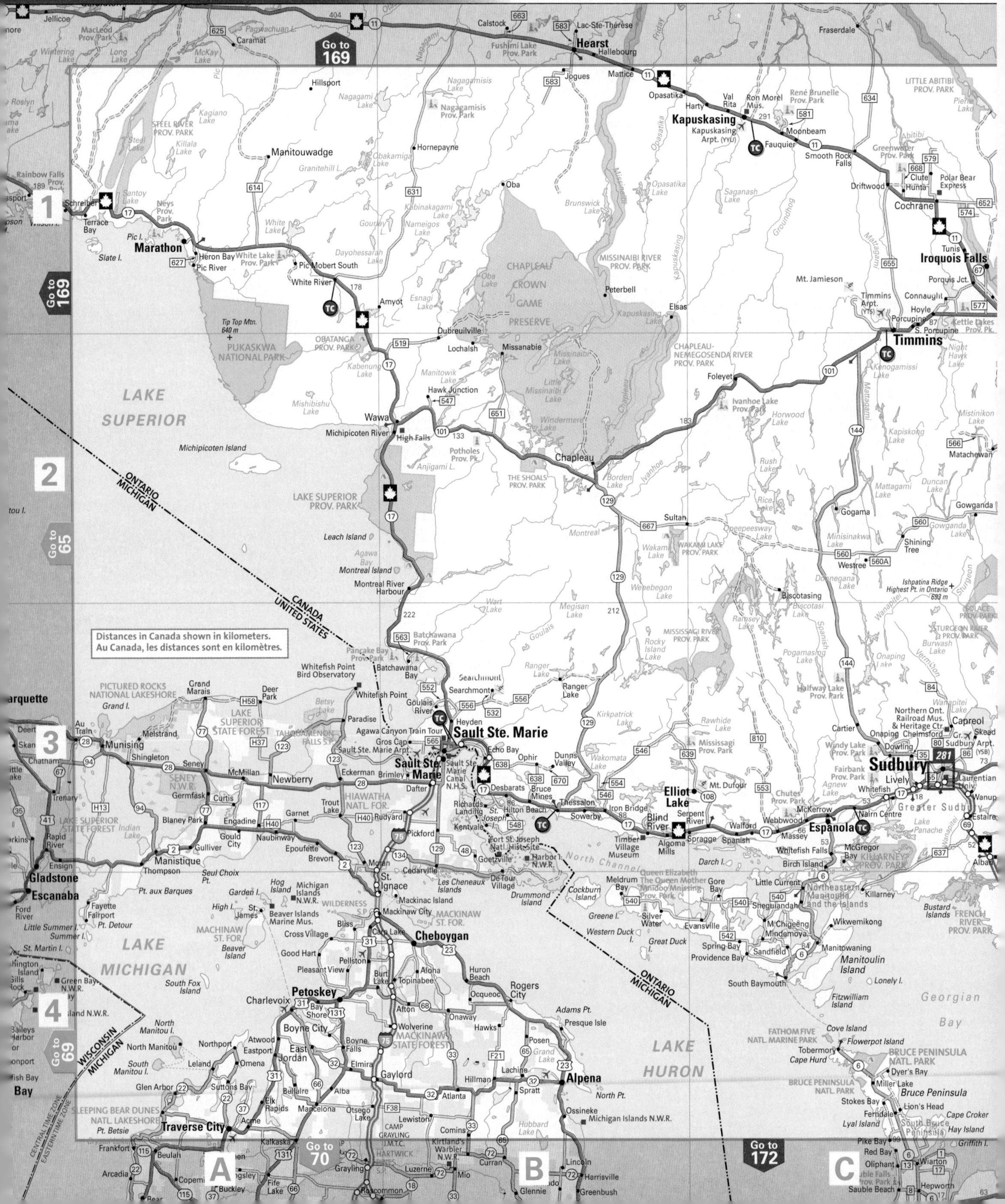

Go to 169

DRIVING DISTANCES IN KM / DISTANCES ROUTIÈRES EN KM	HEARST, ON	HUNTSVILLE, ON	KIRKLAND LAKE, ON	MONT-LAURIER, QC	NORTH BAY, ON	ORILLIA, ON	OTTAWA, ON	ROUYN-NORANDA, QC	SAULT STE. MARIE, ON	SUDBURY, ON	TIMMINS, ON	WAWA, ON
KIRKLAND LAKE, ON	370	370		505	250	578	610	154	580	315	140	475
OTTAWA, ON	955	350	610	209	364	415		456	787	488	730	1015
SAULT STE. MARIE, ON	545	560	580	1004	430	562	787	734		305	440	225
SUDBURY, ON	550	250	315	699	124	263	488	469	305		290	530

SEE ALSO DISTANCE AND DRIVING TIME MAP ON PAGES 286–287 / VOIR AUSSI CARTE DES DISTANCES ET DES TEMPS DE PARCOURS PAGES 286–287

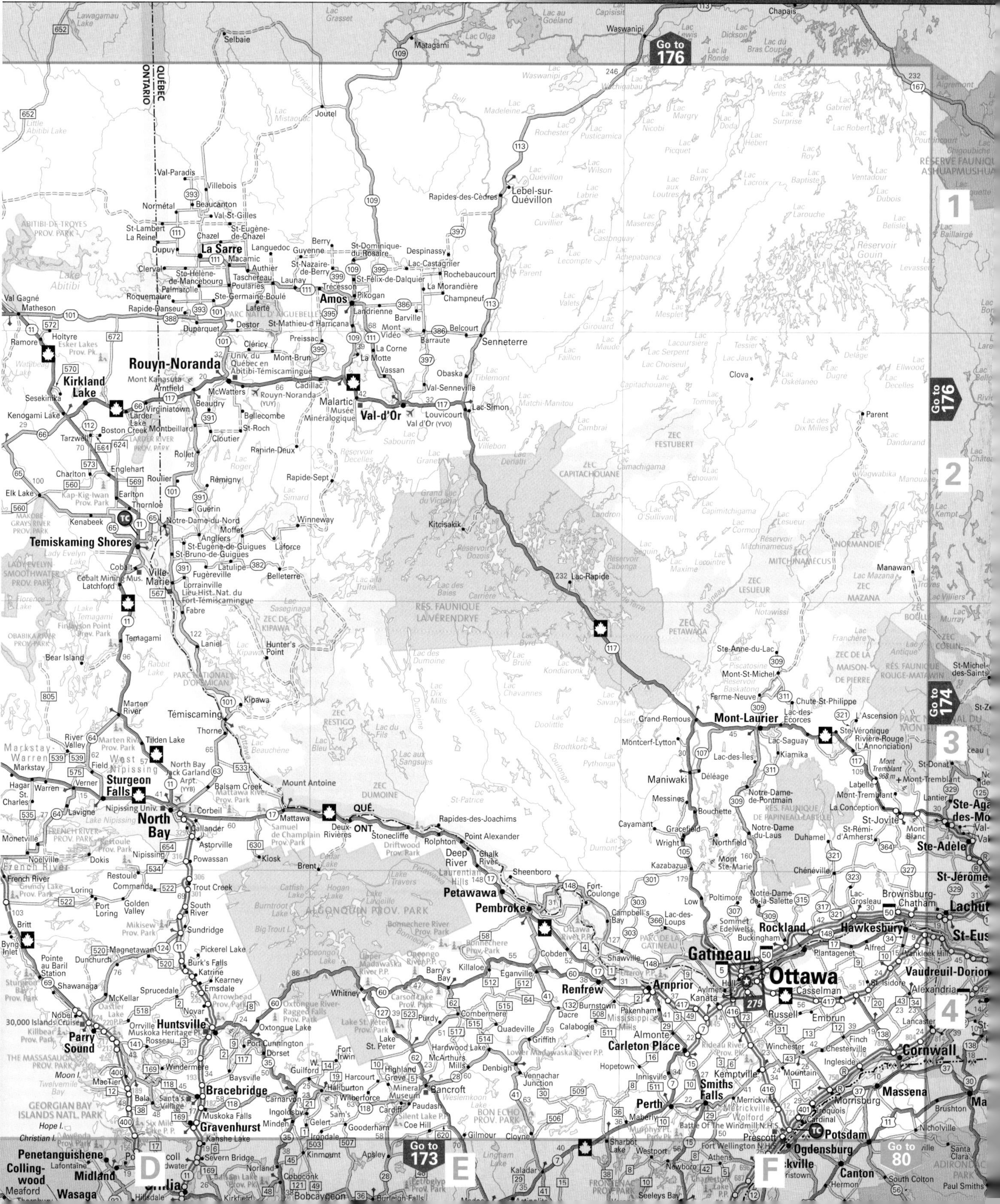

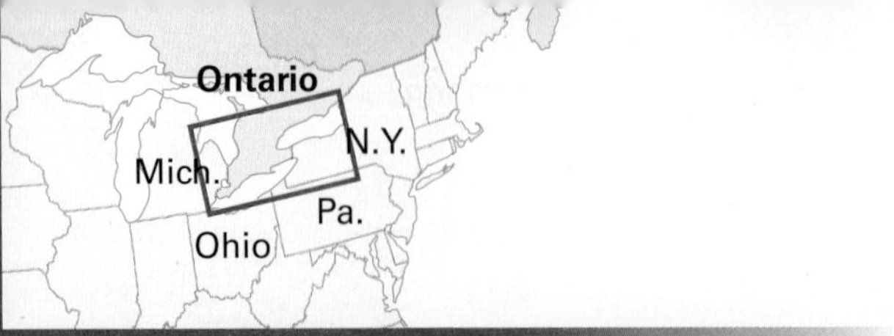

0 mi 20 40
0 km 20 40 60
One inch equals 25.4 miles/Un pouce équivaut à 25.4 milles
One cm equals 16.1 km/Un cm équivaut à 16.1 km

London ON / Windsor ON

DRIVING DISTANCES IN KM / DISTANCES ROUTIÈRES EN KM	BARRIE, ON	HAMILTON, ON	KINGSTON, ON	KITCHENER, ON	LONDON, ON	NIAGARA FALLS, ON	ORILLIA, ON	OWEN SOUND, ON	PETERBOROUGH, ON	SARNIA, ON	TORONTO, ON	WINDSOR, ON
KINGSTON, ON	350	330		430	430	390	317	430	180	530	260	620
NIAGARA FALLS, ON	200	68	390	130	190		237	260	260	290	130	380
TORONTO, ON	90	70	260	105	185	130	127	190	135	280		370
WINDSOR, ON	430	310	620	285	190	380	467	390	490	160	370	

SEE ALSO DISTANCE AND DRIVING TIME MAP ON PAGES 286–287 / VOIR AUSSI CARTE DES DISTANCES ET DES TEMPS DE PARCOURS PAGES 286–287

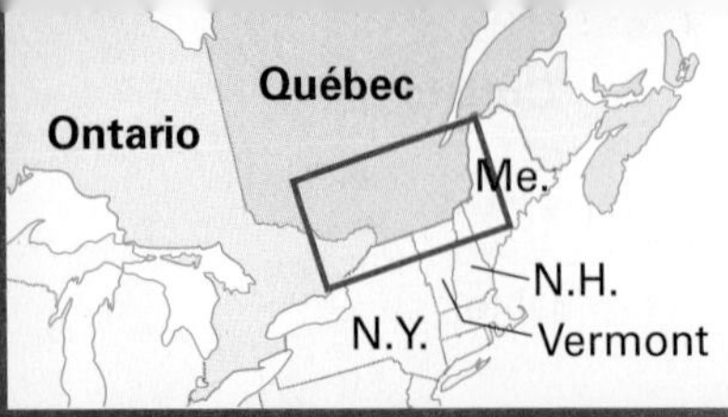

0 mi 20 40
0 km 20 40 60

One inch equals 25.4 miles/Un pouce équivaut à 25.4 milles
One cm equals 16.1 km/Un cm équivaut à 16.1 km

Ottawa ON / Montréal QC

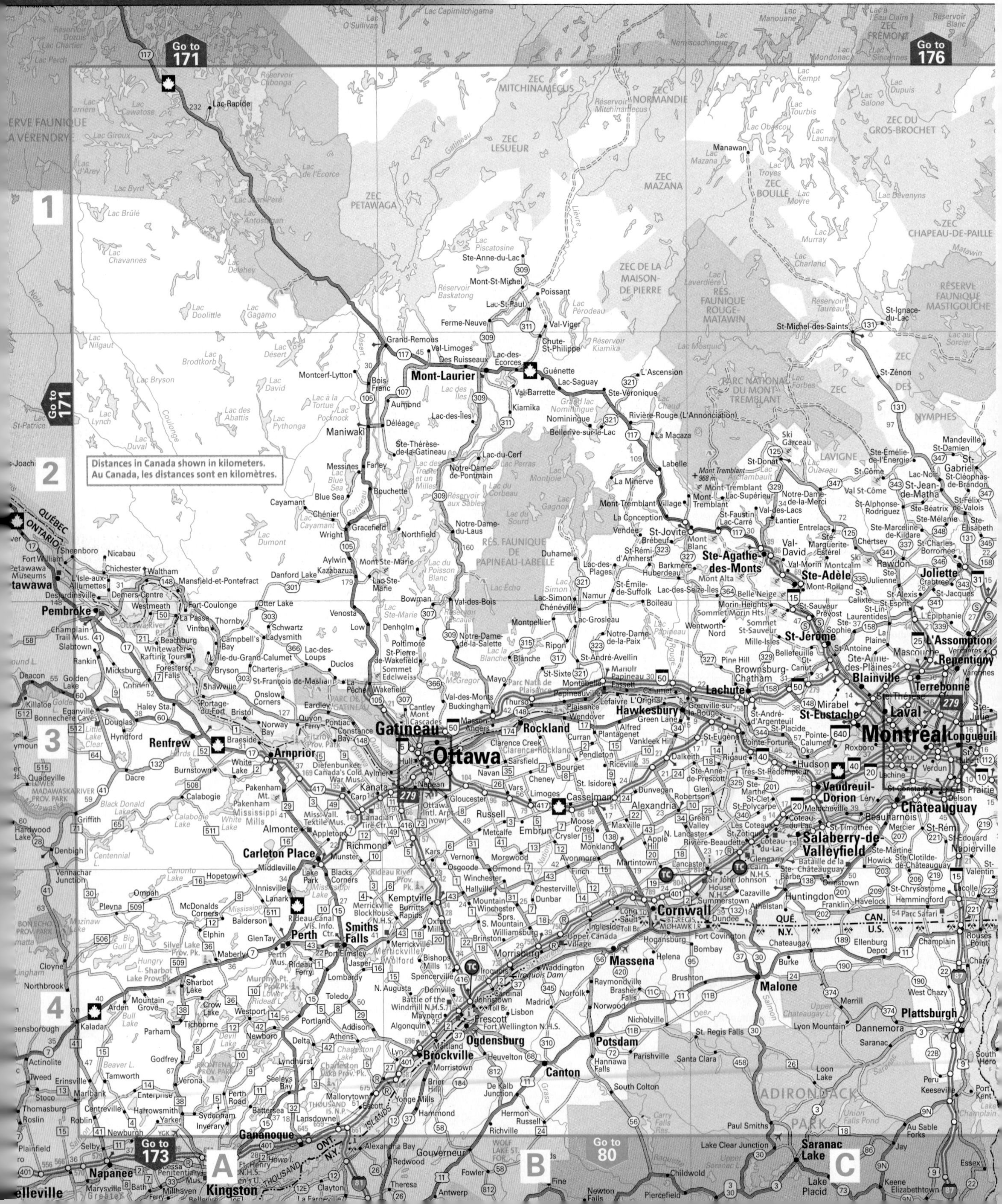

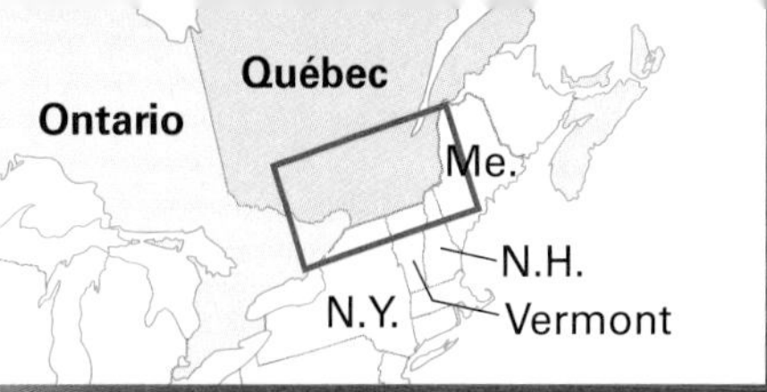

DRIVING DISTANCES IN KM / DISTANCES ROUTIÈRES EN KM	BURLINGTON, VT	CORNWALL, ON	DRUMMONDVILLE, QC	KINGSTON, ON	MONT-LAURIER, QC	MONTRÉAL, QC	MONT-TREMBLANT, QC	OTTAWA, ON	QUÉBEC, QC	ST-GEORGES, QC	SHERBROOKE, QC	TROIS-RIVIÈRES, QC
MONTRÉAL, QC	153	103	116	283	230		126	194	250	325	143	146
OTTAWA, ON	360	97	310	175	209	194	208		444	485	337	340
QUÉBEC, QC	394	353	151	533	445	250	298	444		102	233	135
SHERBROOKE, QC	174	246	82	426	402	143	269	337	233	148		158

SEE ALSO DISTANCE AND DRIVING TIME MAP ON PAGES 286–287 / VOIR AUSSI CARTE DES DISTANCES ET DES TEMPS DE PARCOURS PAGES 286–287

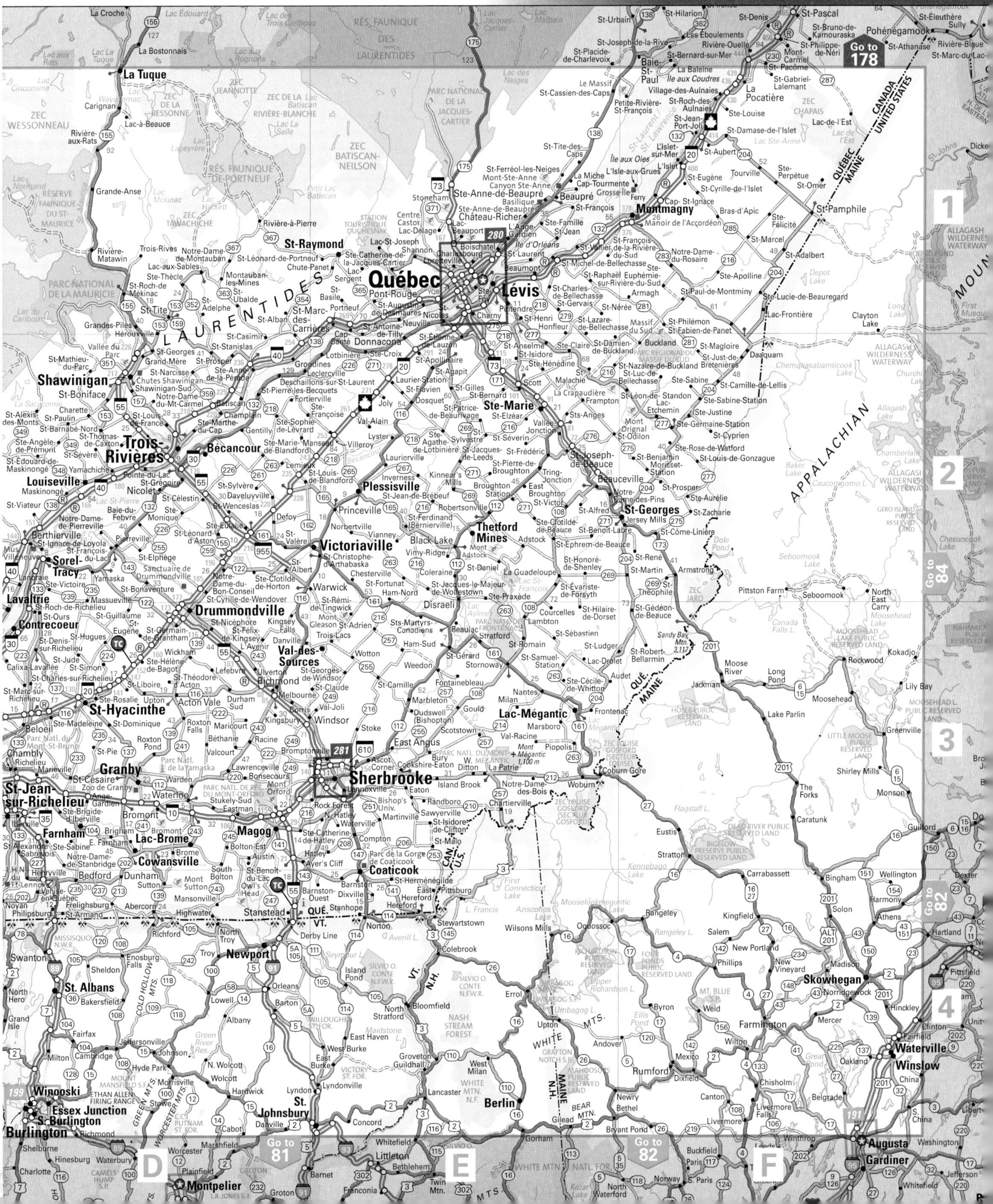

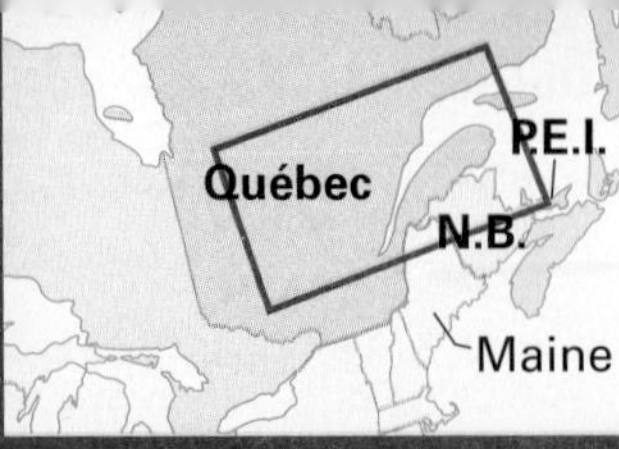
Québec
P.E.I.
N.B.
Maine

0 mi 20 40 60
0 km 20 40 60 80
One inch equals 40.3 miles/Un pouce équivaut à 40.3 milles
One centimeter equals 25.4 km/Un cm équivaut à 25.4 km

Chicoutimi QC / Chibougamau QC

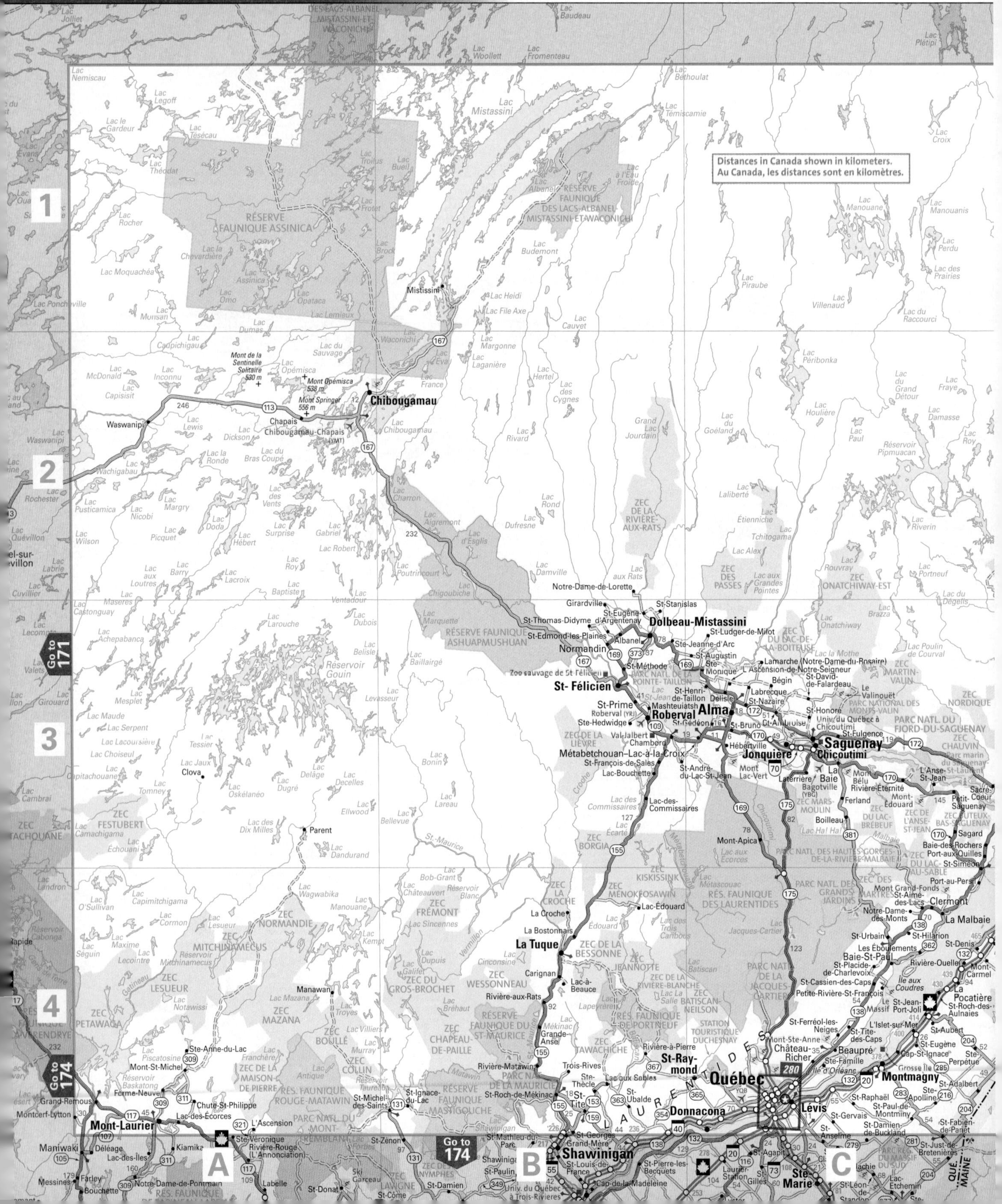
Distances in Canada shown in kilometers.
Au Canada, les distances sont en kilomètres.
1
2
3
4
A
B
C
Go to 171
Go to 174
Go to 174
Lac Mistassini
RÉSERVE FAUNIQUE ASSINICA
RÉSERVE FAUNIQUE DES LACS-ALBANEL-MISTASSINI-ET-WACONICHI
Mistissini
Chibougamau
Chapais
Chibougamau-Chapais (YMT)
Waswanipi
Mont Opémisca 538 m
Mont Springer 556 m
Mont de la Sentinelle Solitaire 530 m
RÉSERVE FAUNIQUE ASHUAPMUSHUAN
Réservoir Gouin
Réservoir Pipmuacan
Lac Péribonka
Dolbeau-Mistassini
Normandin
St-Félicien
Roberval
Alma
Saguenay
Chicoutimi
Jonquière
Métabetchouan–Lac-à-la-Croix
La Baie
Bagotville (YBG)
PARC NATL. DU FIORD-DU-SAGUENAY
RÉS. FAUNIQUE DES LAURENTIDES
PARC NATL. DES GRANDS JARDINS
PARC NATL. DE LA JACQUES-CARTIER
La Tuque
Parent
Clova
Manawan
Mont-Laurier
Maniwaki
Shawinigan
Grand-Mère
Trois-Rivières
Donnacona
St-Raymond
Québec
Lévis
Ste-Marie
Montmagny
Baie-St-Paul
La Malbaie
Clermont
La Pocatière
St-Jean-Port-Joli
Beaupré
Château-Richer
L'Islet-sur-Mer
RÉSERVE FAUNIQUE DU ST-MAURICE
RÉSERVE FAUNIQUE ROUGE-MATAWIN
RÉSERVE FAUNIQUE MASTIGOUCHE
PARC NATL. DU MONT-TREMBLANT
PARC NATL. DE LA MAURICIE
ZEC FESTUBERT
ZEC MITCHINAMECUS
ZEC LESUEUR
ZEC PETAWAGA
ZEC MAZANA
ZEC BOULLÉ
ZEC COLLIN
ZEC NORMANDIE
ZEC FRÉMONT
ZEC CHAPEAU-DE-PAILLE
ZEC WESSONNEAU
ZEC DU GROS-BROCHET
ZEC TAWACHICHE
ZEC DE LA BESSONNE
ZEC BORGIA
ZEC KISKISSINK
ZEC DE LA RIVIÈRE-AUX-RATS
ZEC DES PASSES
ZEC ONATCHIWAY-EST
ZEC MARTIN-VALIN
ZEC DE LA LIÈVRE
L A U R E N T I D E S
QUÉ. MAINE

DRIVING DISTANCES IN KM / DISTANCES ROUTIÈRES EN KM	BAIE-COMEAU, QC	CAMPBELLTON, NB	CHIBOUGAMAU, QC	CHICOUTIMI, QC	EDMUNDSTON, NB	GASPÉ, QC	HAVRE-ST-PIERRE, QC	MATANE, QC	MIRAMICHI, NB	QUÉBEC, QC	RIMOUSKI, QC	SEPT-ÎLES, QC
CHICOUTIMI, QC	435	444	359		269	771	884	348	622	211	253	667
EDMUNDSTON, NB	368	188	628	269		534	817	249	268	317	180	600
GASPÉ, QC	287	340	1130	771	534		743	294	518	706	389	526
QUÉBEC, QC	408	508	570	211	317	706	857	412	582		507	640

SEE ALSO DISTANCE AND DRIVING TIME MAP ON PAGES 286–287 / VOIR AUSSI CARTE DES DISTANCES ET DES TEMPS DE PARCOURS PAGES 286–287

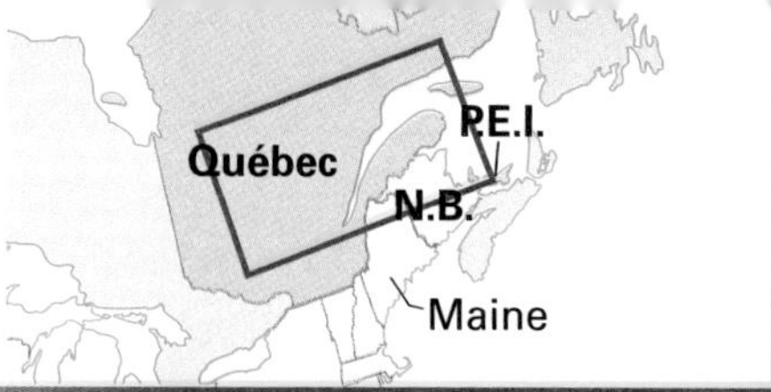
Québec
P.E.I.
N.B.
Maine

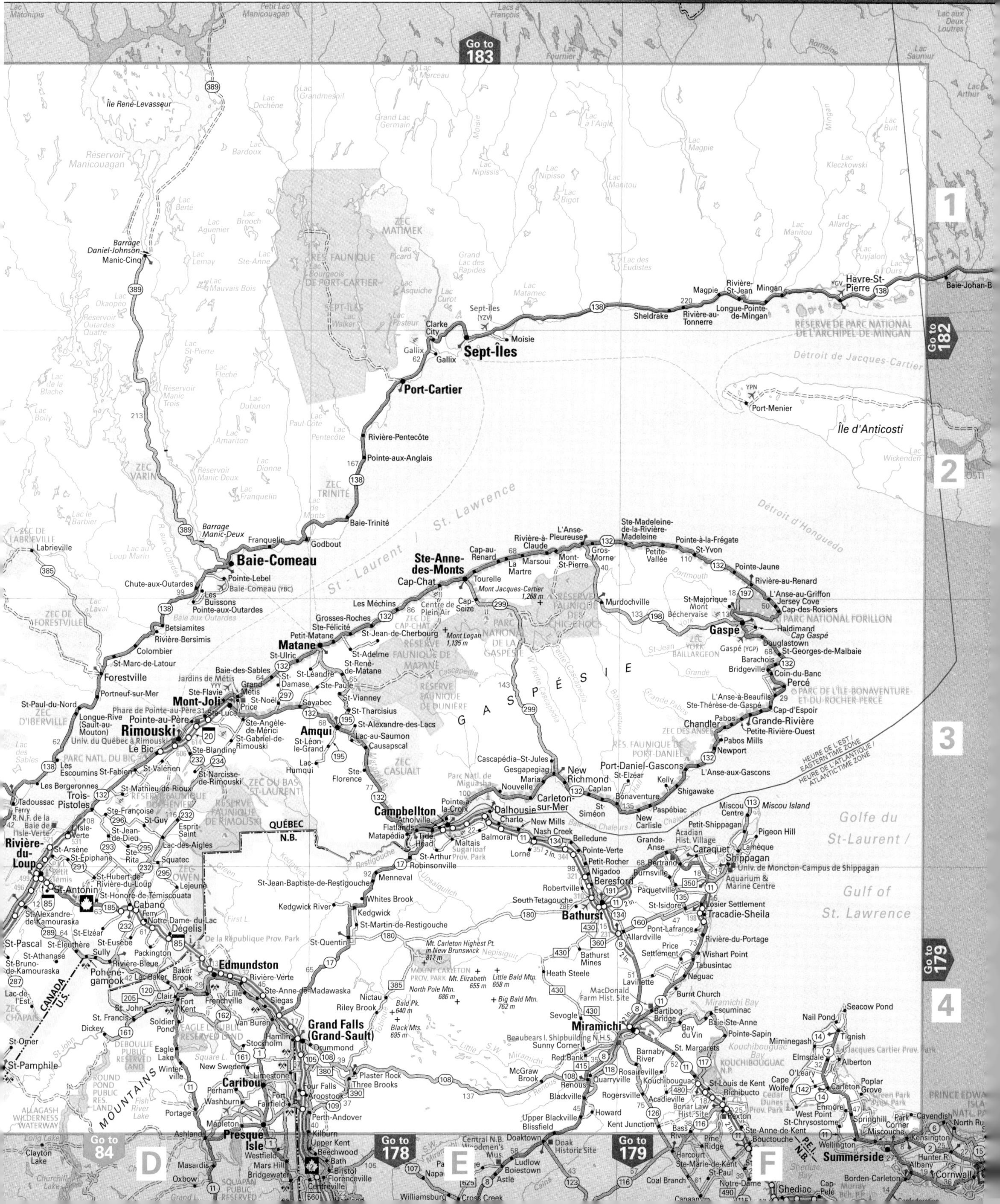
Go to 183
Go to 182
Go to 179
Go to 84
Go to 178
Go to 179
1
2
3
4
D
E
F
Réservoir Manicouagan
Île René-Levasseur
Barrage Daniel-Johnson
Manic-Cinq
Sept-Îles
Port-Cartier
Clarke City
Gallix
Moisie
Sheldrake
Rivière-au-Tonnerre
Magpie
Rivière-St-Jean
Longue-Pointe-de-Mingan
Mingan
Havre-St-Pierre
Baie-Johan-B
RÉSERVE DE PARC NATIONAL DE L'ARCHIPEL-DE-MINGAN
Détroit de Jacques-Cartier
Port-Menier
Île d'Anticosti
Détroit d'Honguedo
Rivière-Pentecôte
Pointe-aux-Anglais
Baie-Trinité
Godbout
Franquelin
Barrage Manic-Deux
Baie-Comeau
Pointe-Lebel
Chute-aux-Outardes
Pointe-aux-Outardes
Betsiamites
Rivière-Bersimis
Colombier
St-Marc-de-Latour
Forestville
Portneuf-sur-Mer
St-Paul-du-Nord
Longue-Rive
Les Escoumins
Les Bergeronnes
Tadoussac
St. Lawrence
St-Laurent
Ste-Anne-des-Monts
Cap-Chat
Les Méchins
Grosses-Roches
Ste-Félicité
Petit-Matane
Matane
St-Ulric
Baie-des-Sables
Mont-Joli
Pointe-au-Père
Rimouski
Le Bic
Trois-Pistoles
Rivière-du-Loup
Amqui
Sayabec
Lac-au-Saumon
Causapscal
Mont Jacques-Cartier 1,268 m
Mont Logan 1,135 m
PARC NATIONAL DE LA GASPÉSIE
G A S P É S I E
Murdochville
Gaspé
PARC NATIONAL FORILLON
Cap Gaspé
Douglastown
Percé
Chandler
Grande-Rivière
Port-Daniel-Gascons
New Carlisle
Paspébiac
Bonaventure
New Richmond
Carleton-sur-Mer
Campbellton
Dalhousie
Matapédia
Pointe-à-la-Croix
QUÉBEC
N.B.
Bathurst
Beresford
Caraquet
Shippagan
Miscou Island
Tracadie-Sheila
Miramichi
Golfe du St-Laurent /
Gulf of St. Lawrence
Edmundston
Dégelis
Grand Falls (Grand-Sault)
Perth-Andover
Presque Isle
Caribou
Richibucto
Bouctouche
Summerside
Kensington
Mt. Carleton Highest Pt. in New Brunswick 817 m
CANADA
U.S.
NOTRE DAME MOUNTAINS
HEURE DE L'EST / EASTERN TIME ZONE
HEURE DE L'ATLANTIQUE / ATLANTIC TIME ZONE

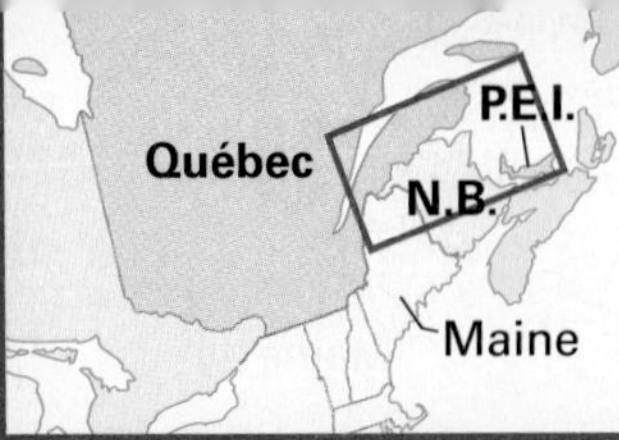
Québec
P.E.I.
N.B.
Maine

0 mi 20 40
0 km 20 40 60
One inch equals 25.4 miles/Un pouce équivaut à 25.4 milles
One cm equals 16.1 km/Un cm équivaut à 16.1 km

Rimouski QC / Edmundston NB

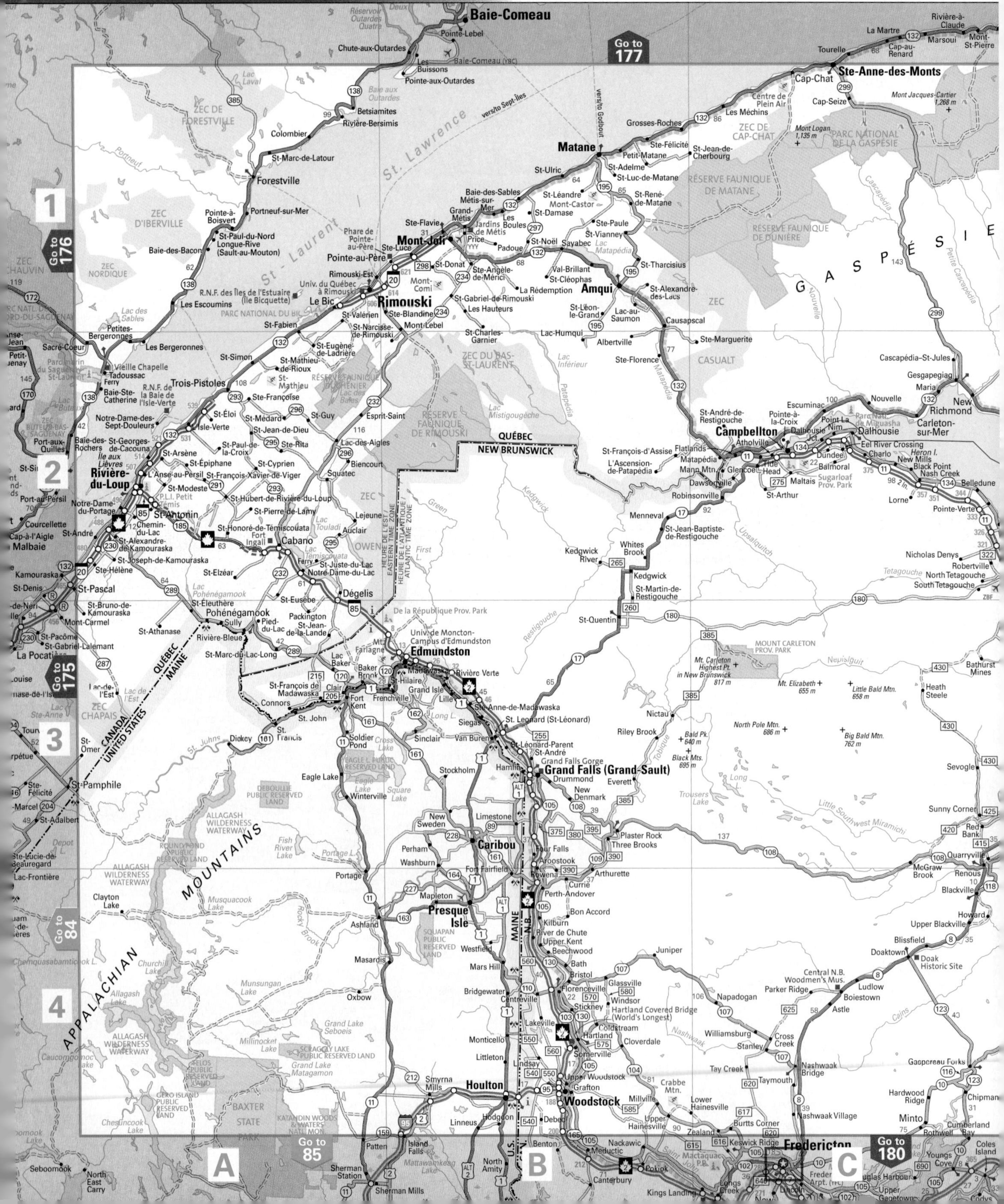
Baie-Comeau
Pointe-Lebel
Chute-aux-Outardes
Go to 177
Buissons
Pointe-aux-Outardes
Baie-Comeau (YBC)
Réservoir Outardes Quatre
Lac Laval
ZEC DE FORESTVILLE
Betsiamites
Rivière-Bersimis
Colombier
St-Marc-de-Latour
Forestville
Portneuf-sur-Mer
Pointe-à-Boisvert
St-Paul-du-Nord
Longue-Rive (Sault-au-Mouton)
Baie-des-Bacon
ZEC D'IBERVILLE
ZEC NORDIQUE
ZEC CHAUVIN
Go to 176
Les Escoumins
R.N.F. des Îles de l'Estuaire (Île Bicquette)
Lac des Sables
Petites-Bergeronnes
Les Bergeronnes
Sacré-Coeur
Tadoussac
Vieille Chapelle
Baie-Ste-Catherine
Notre-Dame-des-Sept-Douleurs
Port-aux-Quilles
Baie-des-Rochers
St-Georges-de-Cacouna
Île aux Lièvres
Rivière-du-Loup
Trois-Pistoles
St-Simon
R.N.F. de la Baie de l'Isle-Verte
Isle-Verte
St-Éloi
St-Arsène
St-Épiphane
L'Anse-au-Persil
St-Modeste
Port-au-Persil
Notre-Dame-du-Portage
St-Antonin
St-André
St-Alexandre-de-Kamouraska
St-Joseph-de-Kamouraska
St-Hélène
Kamouraska
St-Denis
St-Pascal
St-Bruno-de-Kamouraska
Mont-Carmel
St-Pacôme
St-Gabriel-Lalemant
La Pocatière
Go to 175
St-Athanase
Pohénégamook
St-Éleuthère
Sully
Rivière-Bleue
St-Marc-du-Lac-Long
Lac-de-l'Est
ZEC CHAPAIS
St-Omer
St-Pamphile
Ste-Félicité
St-Adalbert
Ste-Lucie-de-Beauregard
Lac-Frontière
Clayton Lake
Go to 84
Go to 85
QUÉBEC
MAINE
CANADA
UNITED STATES
St. Lawrence
St-Laurent
Matane
Petit-Matane
Ste-Félicité
St-Jean-de-Cherbourg
Grosses-Roches
Les Méchins
Cap-Chat
Ste-Anne-des-Monts
Tourelle
La Martre
Marsoui
Rivière-à-Claude
Mont-St-Pierre
Cap-au-Renard
Cap-Seize
Centre de Plein Air
ZEC DE CAP-CHAT
Mont Logan 1,135 m
Mont Jacques-Cartier 1,268 m
PARC NATIONAL DE LA GASPÉSIE
RÉSERVE FAUNIQUE DE MATANE
RÉSERVE FAUNIQUE DE DUNIÈRE
GASPÉSIE
St-Ulric
St-Adelme
St-Luc-de-Matane
St-Léandre
Mont-Castor
St-René-de-Matane
St-Damase
Ste-Paule
St-Vianney
Baie-des-Sables
Métis-sur-Mer
Grand-Métis
Les Boules
Jardins de Métis
Ste-Flavie
Mont-Joli
Price
Padoue
St-Noël
Sayabec
Lac Matapédia
Val-Brillant
St-Cléophas
St-Tharcisius
Amqui
St-Alexandre-des-Lacs
Lac-au-Saumon
St-Léon-le-Grand
Causapscal
Albertville
Lac-Humqui
Ste-Marguerite
Ste-Florence
ZEC CASUALT
Phare de Pointe-au-Père
Pointe-au-Père
Ste-Luce
St-Donat
Ste-Angèle-de-Mérici
La Rédemption
Mont-Comi
Rimouski-Est
Univ. du Québec à Rimouski
Le Bic
Rimouski
PARC NATIONAL DU BIC
St-Fabien
St-Valérien
St-Narcisse-de-Rimouski
Ste-Blandine
Mont-Lebel
St-Gabriel-de-Rimouski
Les Hauteurs
St-Charles-Garnier
ZEC DU BAS-ST-LAURENT
St-Eugène-de-Ladrière
St-Mathieu-de-Rioux
Lac St-Mathieu
RÉSERVE FAUNIQUE DU CHENIER
Ste-Françoise
St-Médard
St-Jean-de-Dieu
St-Guy
Esprit-Saint
RÉSERVE FAUNIQUE DE RIMOUSKI
Lac Mistigougèche
St-Paul-de-la-Croix
Ste-Rita
Lac-des-Aigles
Biencourt
St-Cyprien
St-François-Xavier-de-Viger
Squatec
St-Hubert-de-Rivière-du-Loup
St-Pierre-de-Lamy
Lejeune
Auclair
St-Honoré-de-Témiscouata
Lac Touladi
Cabano
Fort Ingall
Lac Témiscouata
St-Juste-du-Lac
Notre-Dame-du-Lac
St-Elzéar
St-Eusèbe
Dégelis
Packington
St-Jean-de-la-Lande
Pied-du-Lac
Lac Pohénégamook
ZEC OWEN
HEURE DE L'EST EASTERN TIME ZONE
HEURE DE L'ATLANTIQUE ATLANTIC TIME ZONE
De la République Prov. Park
Univ. de Moncton-Campus d'Edmundston
Edmundston
Mt. Farlagne
Lac Baker
Baker Brook
Madawaska
Rivière Verte
St-Hilaire
Grand Isle
Lille
Ste-Anne-de-Madawaska
St-François de Madawaska
Clair
Fort Kent
Frenchville
Connors
St. John
St. Francis
Dickey
Siegas
St. Leonard (St-Léonard)
Van Buren
Sinclair
Long L.
Soldier Pond
Cross Lake
EAGLE L. PUBLIC RESERVED LAND
Eagle Lake
Square Lake
Winterville
Stockholm
St-Léonard-Parent
St-André
Hamlin
Grand Falls Gorge
Grand Falls (Grand-Sault)
Drummond
New Denmark
Everett
DEBOULLIE PUBLIC RESERVED LAND
ALLAGASH WILDERNESS WATERWAY
ROUND POND PUBLIC RESERVED LAND
Fish River Lake
Portage L.
Portage
New Sweden
Limestone
Perham
Washburn
Caribou
Four Falls
Aroostook
Fort Fairfield
Rowena
Arthurette
Currie
Perth-Andover
Bon Accord
Mapleton
Presque Isle
Ashland
SQUAPAN PUBLIC RESERVED LAND
Westfield
Kilburn
River de Chute
Upper Kent
Beechwood
Bath
Bristol
Mars Hill
Masardis
Florenceville
Glassville
Windsor
Centreville
Bridgewater
Stickney
Hartland Covered Bridge (World's Longest)
Coldstream
Hartland
Lakeville
Monticello
Cloverdale
Somerville
Littleton
Upper Woodstock
Lindsay
Woodstock
Grafton
Houlton
Smyrna Mills
Debec
Linneus
Hodgdon
Benton
Meductic
Canterbury
Nackawic
Pokiok
Mactaquac P.P.
Millville
Crabbe Mtn.
Lower Hainesville
Upper Hainesville
Zealand
Burtts Corner
Keswick Ridge
Fredericton
Go to 180
Fredericton Arpt. (YFC)
Kings Landing
Upper Gagetown
Douglas Harbour
Youngs Cove
Coles Island
Oxbow
Patten
Island Falls
Mattawamkeag Lake
North Amity
Sherman Station
Sherman Mills
Seboomook
North East Carry
Chesuncook Lake
BAXTER STATE PARK
KATAHDIN WOODS & WATERS NATL MON.
GERO ISLAND PUBLIC RESERVED LAND
FELOS PUBLIC RESERVED LAND
SCRAGGLY LAKE PUBLIC RESERVED LAND
Grand Lake Matagamon
Grand Lake Seboeis
Millinocket Lake
Munsungan Lake
Musquacook Lake
Churchill Lake
Allagash Lake
Caucomgomoc Lake
APPALACHIAN MOUNTAINS
QUÉBEC
NEW BRUNSWICK
MAINE
N.B.
U.S.
St-André-de-Restigouche
Pointe-à-la-Croix
Escuminac
Nouvelle
Parc Natl. de Miguasha
Carleton-sur-Mer
New Richmond
Maria
Gesgapegiag
Cascapédia–St-Jules
Campbellton
Atholville
Dalhousie Jct.
Point La Nim
Dalhousie
Eel River Crossing
Heron I.
Charlo
New Mills
Black Point
Nash Creek
Belledune
Dundee
Balmoral
Tide Head
Maltais
Sugarloaf Prov. Park
St-Arthur
Flatlands
Matapédia
Mann Mtn.
Glencoe
Dawsonville
Robinsonville
St-François-d'Assise
L'Ascension-de-Patapédia
Menneval
St-Jean-Baptiste-de-Restigouche
Whites Brook
Kedgwick River
Kedgwick
St-Martin-de-Restigouche
St-Quentin
Lorne
Pointe-Verte
Nicholas Denys
Robertville
North Tetagouche
South Tetagouche
MOUNT CARLETON PROV. PARK
Mt. Carleton Highest Pt. in New Brunswick 817 m
Mt. Elizabeth 655 m
Little Bald Mtn. 658 m
Bathurst Mines
Heath Steele
Nictau
Riley Brook
North Pole Mtn. 686 m
Big Bald Mtn. 762 m
Bald Pk. 640 m
Black Mts. 695 m
Sevogle
Sunny Corner
Red Bank
Plaster Rock
Three Brooks
Quarryville
McGraw Brook
Renous
Blackville
Howard
Upper Blackville
Blissfield
Doaktown
Doak Historic Site
Central N.B. Woodmen's Mus.
Parker Ridge
Ludlow
Boiestown
Astle
Juniper
Napadogan
Williamsburg
Stanley
Cross Creek
Tay Creek
Taymouth
Nashwaak Bridge
Nashwaak Village
Gaspereau Forks
Hardwood Ridge
Minto
Chipman
Rothwell
Cumberland Bay
Matapédia
Restigouche
Kedgwick
Upsalquitch
Tobique
Nepisiguit
Little Southwest Miramichi
Trousers Lake
Long L.
Nashwaak
Cains
Saint John

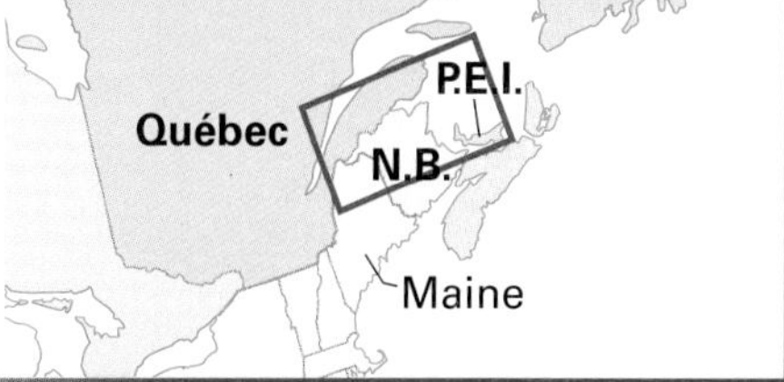
Québec
P.E.I.
N.B.
Maine

DRIVING DISTANCES IN KM / DISTANCES ROUTIÈRES EN KM

	BATHURST, NB	BORDEN-CARLETON, PE	CAMPBELLTON, NB	CHARLOTTETOWN, PE	EDMUNDSTON, NB	FREDERICTON, NB	GASPÉ, QC	GRAND FALLS, NB	MATANE, QC	MIRAMICHI, NB	MONCTON, NB	RIMOUSKI, QC
CHARLOTTETOWN, PE	338	56	438		629	362	791	581	562	273	164	596
EDMUNDSTON, NB	189	428	188	638		279	534	57	249	268	447	180
MATANE, QC	262	506	168	562	249	553	294	331		346	487	95
MONCTON, NB	206	108	306	164	447	170	659	390	487	141		502

SEE ALSO DISTANCE AND DRIVING TIME MAP ON PAGES 286–287 / VOIR AUSSI CARTE DES DISTANCES ET DES TEMPS DE PARCOURS PAGES 286–287

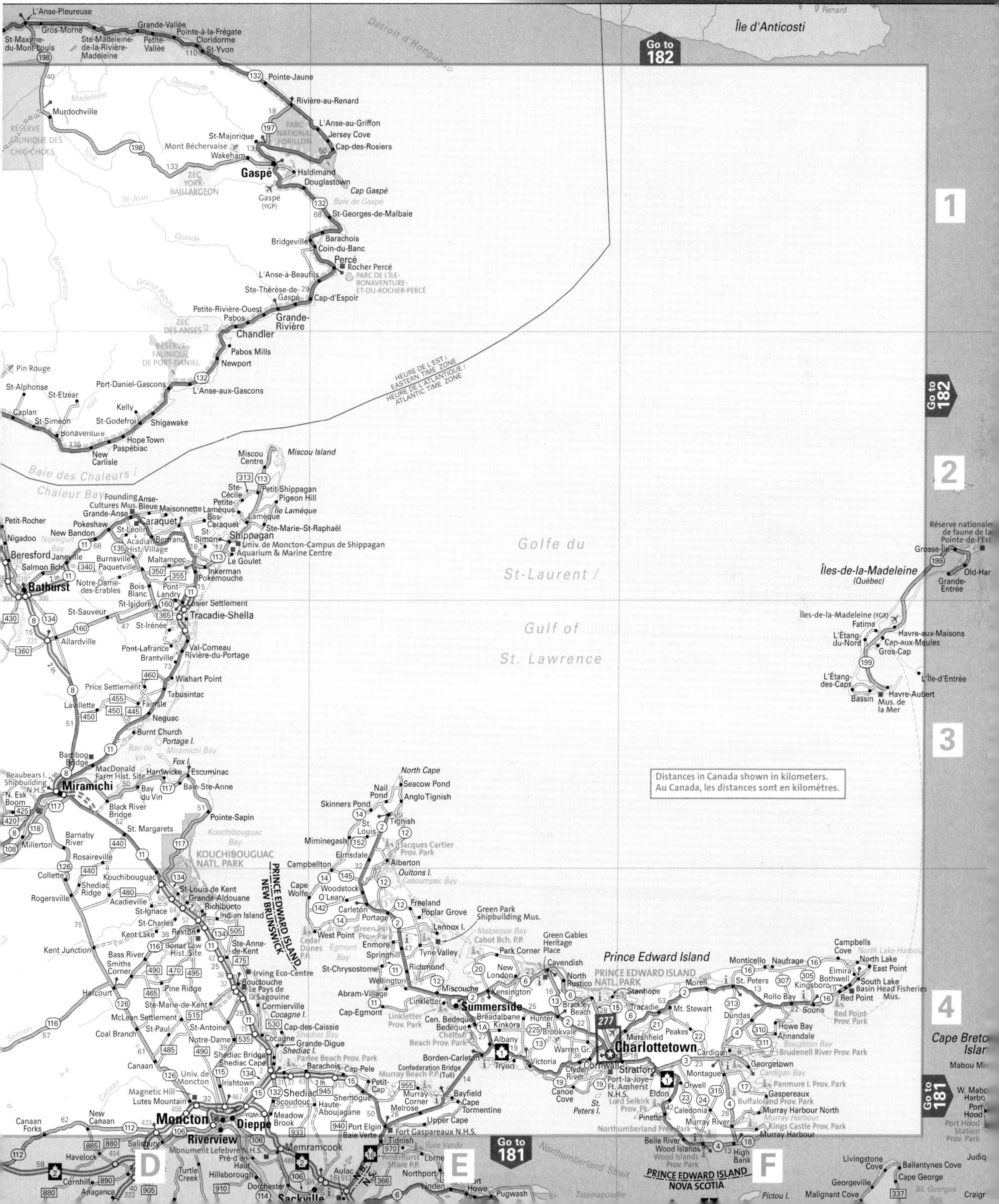
Go to 182
Go to 181
Île d'Anticosti
Détroit d'Honguedo
Gaspé
Percé
Rocher Percé
PARC DE L'ÎLE-BONAVENTURE-ET-DU-ROCHER-PERCÉ
PARC NATIONAL FORILLON
Cap Gaspé
Chandler
Murdochville
RÉSERVE FAUNIQUE DES CHIC-CHOCS
ZEC YORK-BAILLARGEON
HEURE DE L'EST / EASTERN TIME ZONE
HEURE DE L'ATLANTIQUE / ATLANTIC TIME ZONE
Baie des Chaleurs / Chaleur Bay
Miscou Island
Caraquet
Shippagan
Bathurst
Tracadie-Sheila
Miramichi
KOUCHIBOUGUAC NATL. PARK
Golfe du St-Laurent / Gulf of St. Lawrence
Îles-de-la-Madeleine (Québec)
Distances in Canada shown in kilometers.
Au Canada, les distances sont en kilomètres.
PRINCE EDWARD ISLAND / NEW BRUNSWICK
Prince Edward Island
PRINCE EDWARD ISLAND NATL. PARK
Summerside
Charlottetown
Moncton
Dieppe
Riverview
Confederation Bridge (Toll)
Northumberland Strait
PRINCE EDWARD ISLAND / NOVA SCOTIA
Cape Breton Island
1
2
3
4
D
E
F

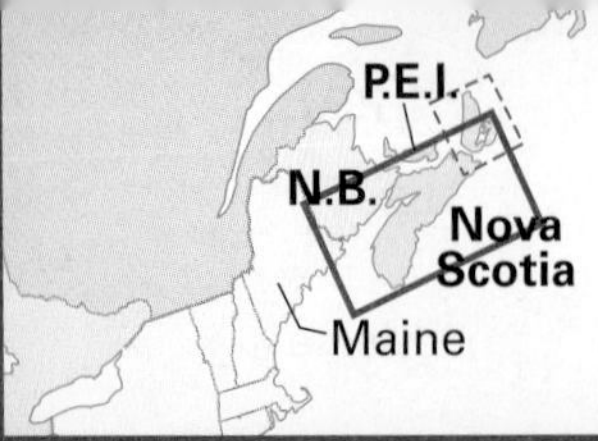

0 mi 20 40
0 km 20 40 60

One inch equals 25.4 miles/Un pouce équivaut à 25.4 milles
One cm equals 16.1 km/Un cm équivaut à 16.1 km

Saint John NB / Yarmouth NS

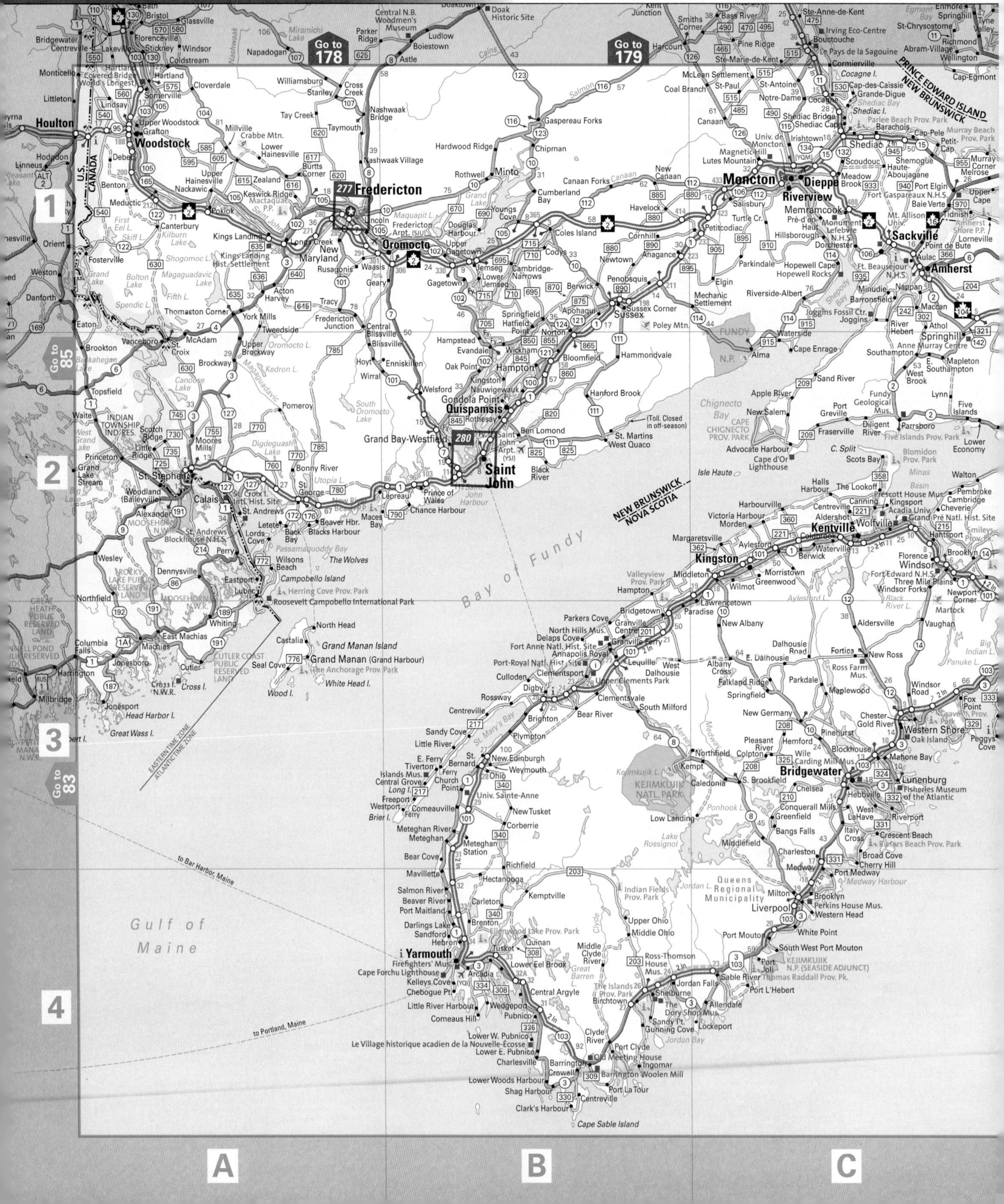

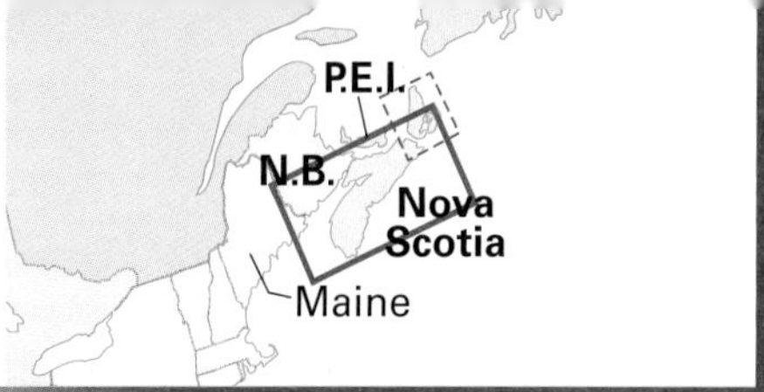

DRIVING DISTANCES IN KM / DISTANCES ROUTIÈRES EN KM

	CHARLOTTETOWN, PE	CHÉTICAMP, NS	DIGBY, NS	FREDERICTON, NB	HALIFAX, NS	MONCTON, NB	PORT HAWKESBURY, NS	SAINT JOHN, NB	ST. STEPHEN, NB	SYDNEY, NS	TRURO, NS	YARMOUTH, NS
HALIFAX, NS	322	425	235	462		260	265	410	515	415	89	339
MONCTON, NB	164	481	231	170	260		374	150	278	497	182	599
SAINT JOHN, NB	350	640	72	114	410	150	497		119	647	321	176
SYDNEY, NS	374	173	623	689	415	497	123	647	766		326	727

SEE ALSO DISTANCE AND DRIVING TIME MAP ON PAGES 286–287 / VOIR AUSSI CARTE DES DISTANCES ET DES TEMPS DE PARCOURS PAGES 286–287

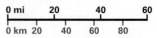

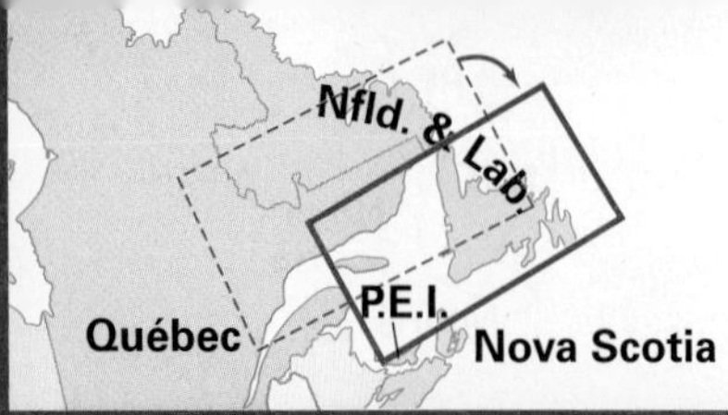

0 mi 20 40 60
0 km 20 40 60 80

One inch equals 40.3 miles/Un pouce équivaut à 40.3 milles
One centimeter equals 25.4 km/Un cm équivaut à 25.4 km

Corner Brook NL / Channel-Port aux Basques NL

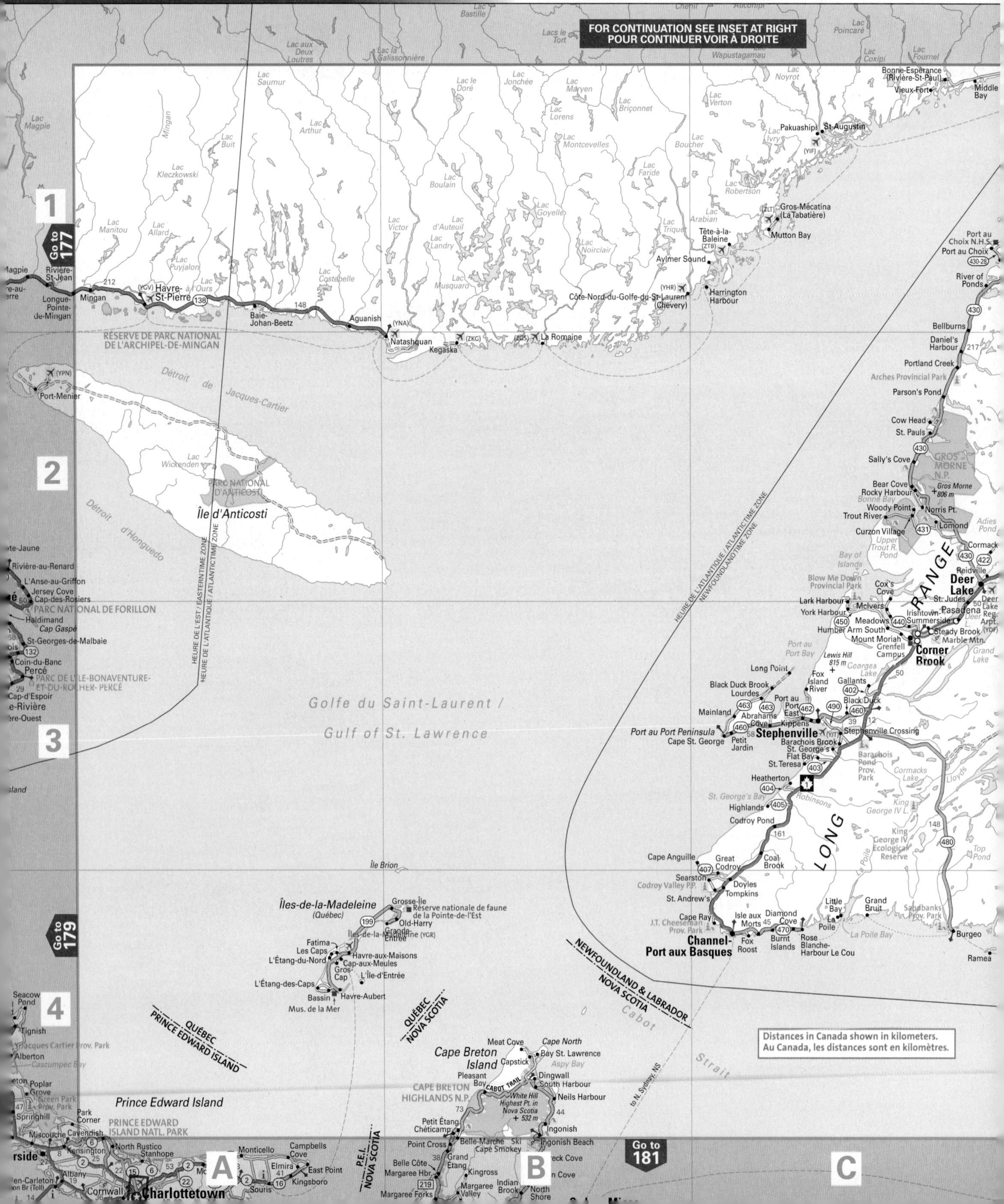

Distances in Canada shown in kilometers.
Au Canada, les distances sont en kilomètres.

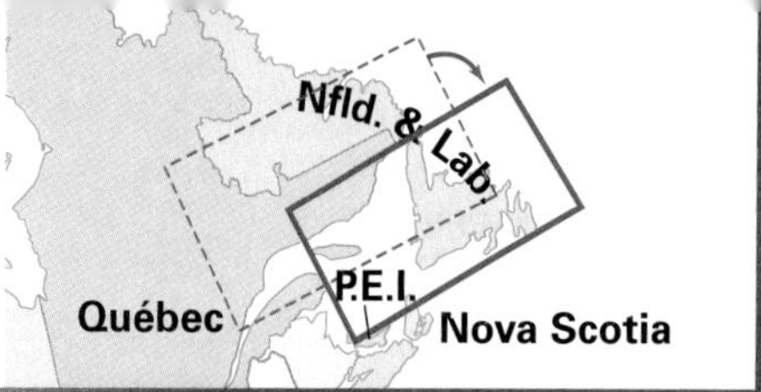

DRIVING DISTANCES IN KM / DISTANCES ROUTIÈRES EN KM

	ARGENTIA, NL	BISHOP'S FALLS, NL	BONAVISTA, NL	CHAN.-PT. AUX BASQUES, NL	CORNER BROOK, NL	DEER LAKE, NL	GANDER, NL	GRAND FALLS-WINDSOR, NL	MARYSTOWN, NL	ST. ANTHONY, NL	ST. JOHN'S, NL	STEPHENVILLE, NL
BISHOP'S FALLS, NL	363		307	482	280	225	72	18	384	628	393	339
CHAN.-PT. AUX BASQUES, NL	845	482	789		202	257	554	464	866	660	875	151
CORNER BROOK, NL	643	280	587	202		55	352	262	664	458	673	59
ST. JOHN'S, NL	134	393	296	875	673	618	321	411	293	1021		732

SEE ALSO DISTANCE AND DRIVING TIME MAP ON PAGES 286–287 / VOIR AUSSI CARTE DES DISTANCES ET DES TEMPS DE PARCOURS PAGES 286–287

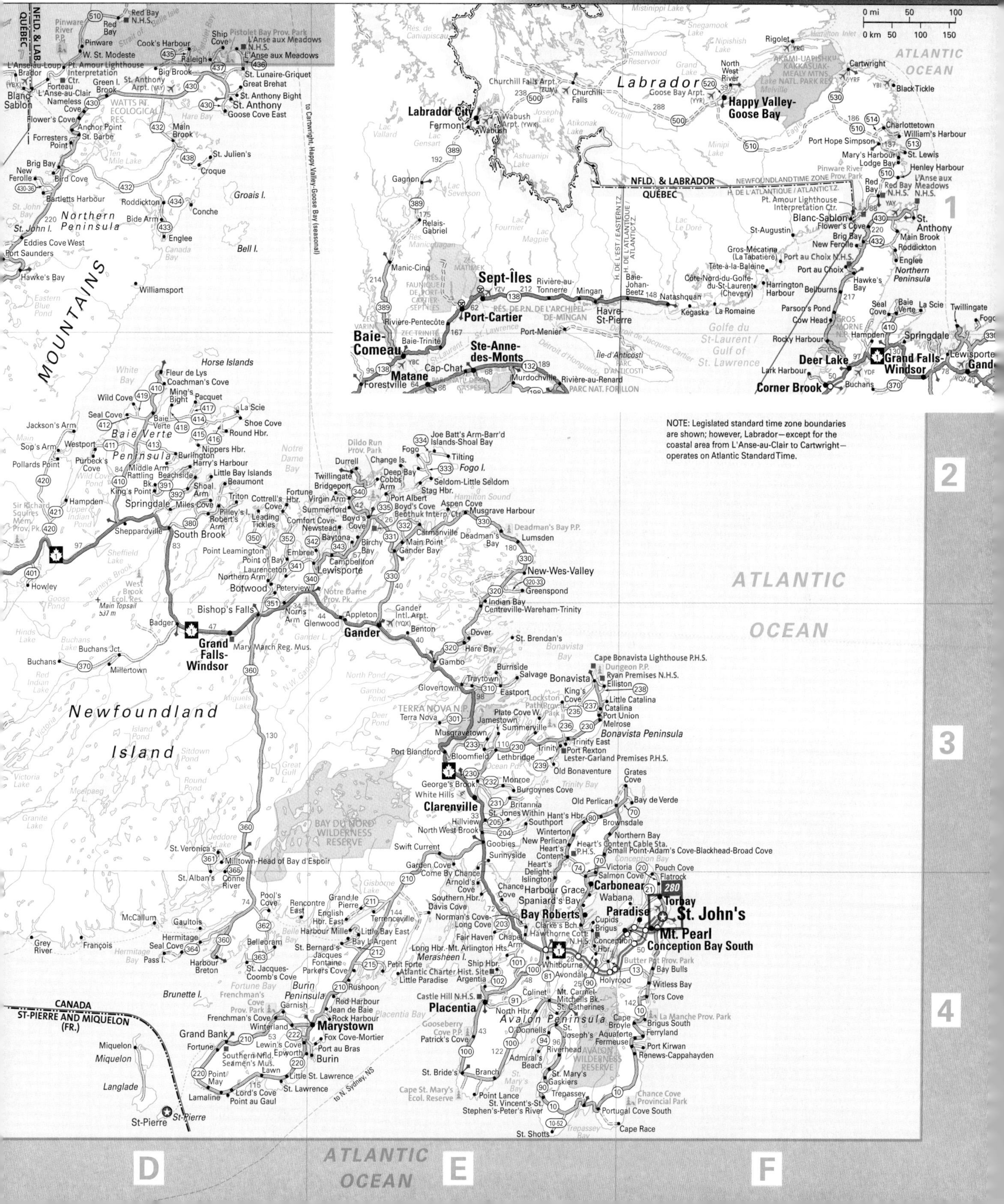

0 mi 50 100 150
0 km 50 100 150 200

One inch equals 83.75 miles/Una pulgada igual a 83.75 millas
One centimeter equals 53 km/Un centímetro igual a 53 km

Mexicali MEX / Culiacán MEX

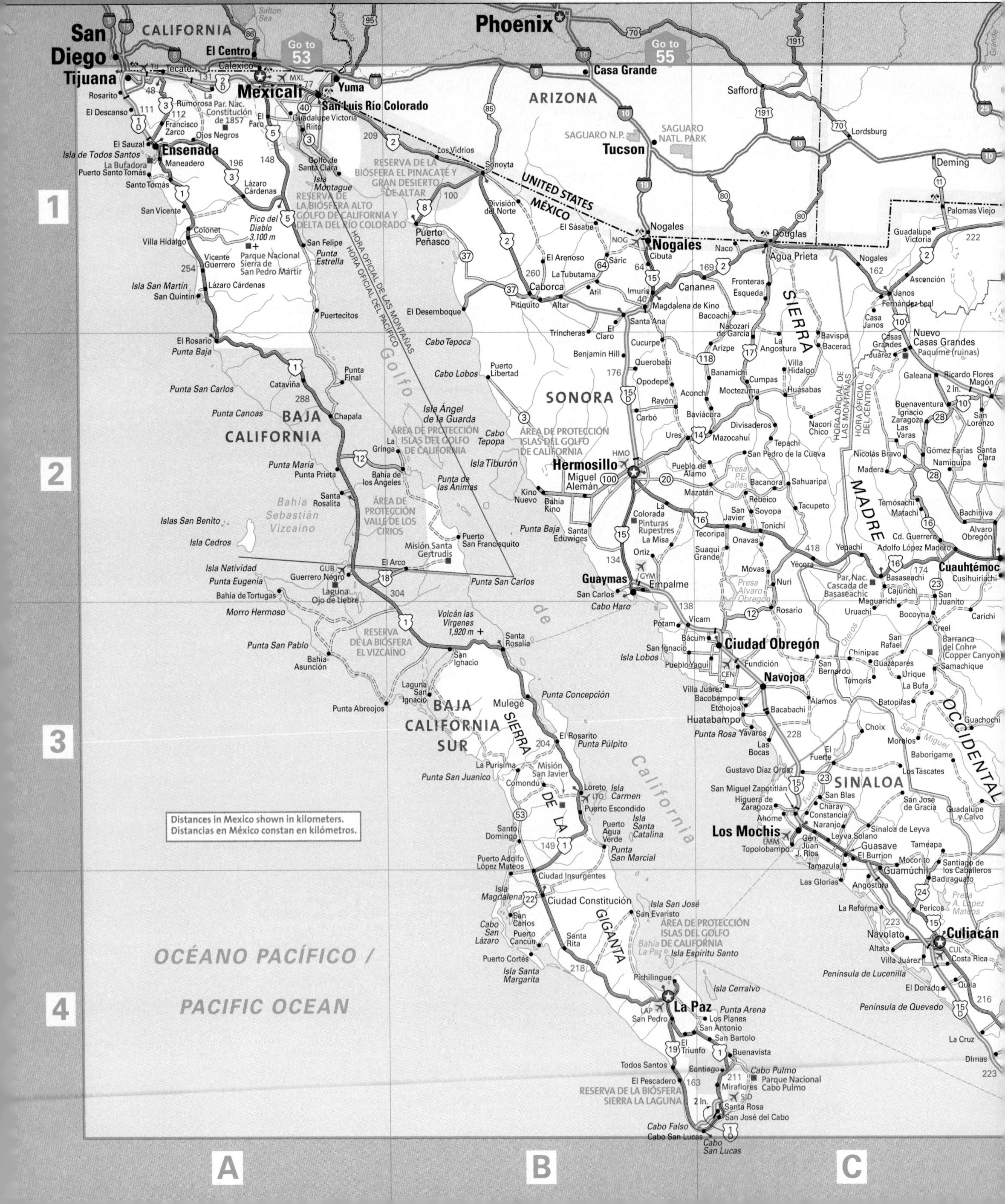

DRIVING DISTANCES IN KM / DISTANCIAS DE MANEJO EN KM

	CHIHUAHUA	CIUDAD JUÁREZ	CIUDAD VICTORIA	CULIACÁN	DURANGO	HERMOSILLO	MAZATLÁN	MÉXICO	MONTERREY	SAN LUIS POTOSÍ	TIJUANA	TORREÓN
CHIHUAHUA		385	1086	919	686	579	1209	1538	808	1155	1456	449
HERMOSILLO	579	795	1666	706	941		729	1810	1387	1416	884	1028
MONTERREY	808	1236	288	924	689	1387	901	892		509	2362	359
TORREÓN	449	834	637	914	266	1028	892	1089	359	706	1905	

SEE ALSO DISTANCE AND DRIVING TIME MAP ON PAGES 286–287 / CONSULTE, PARA DISTANCIAS Y TIEMPO DE MANEJO, EN LAS PÁGINAS 286-287

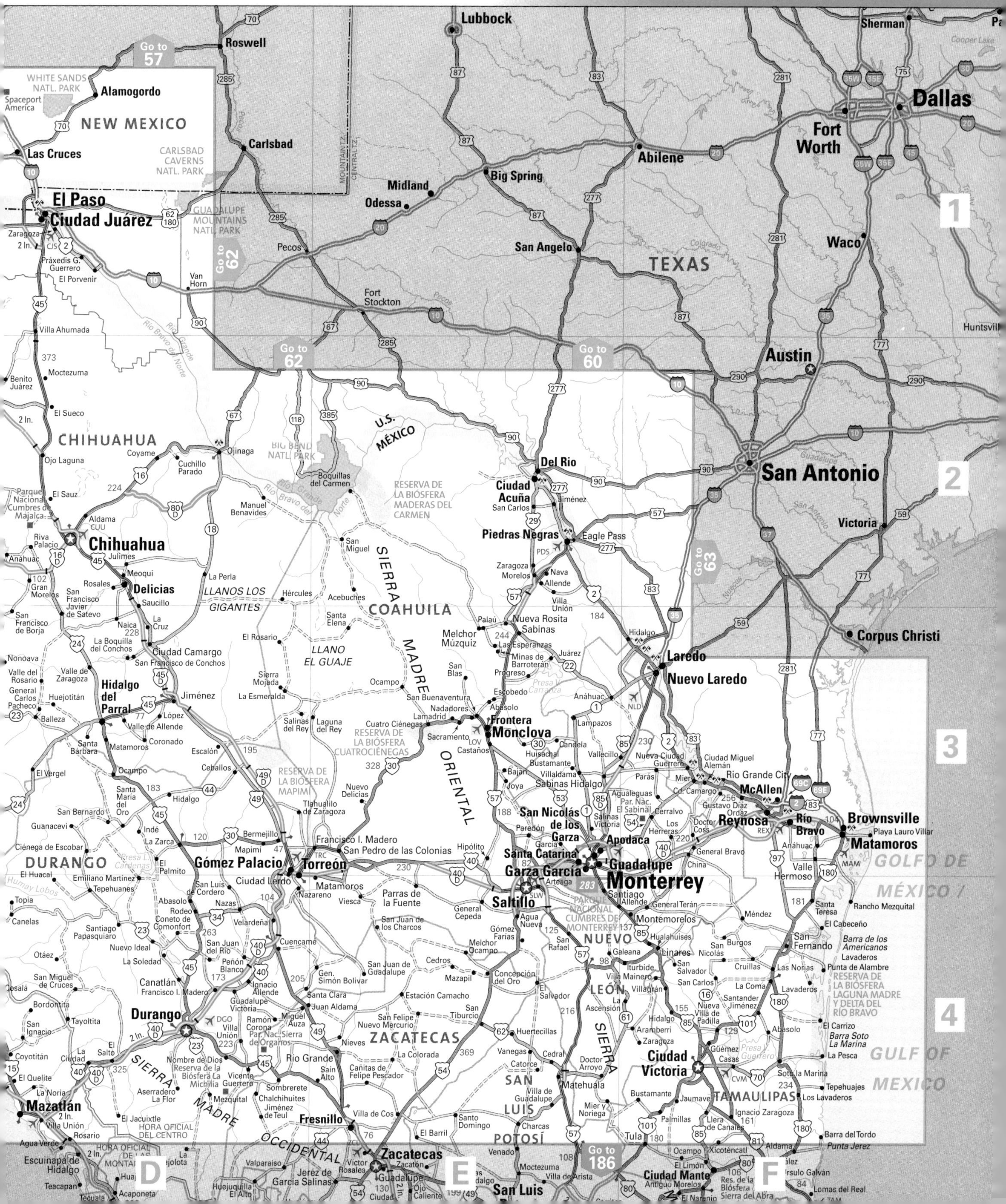

0 mi 50 100 150
0 km 50 100 150 200

One inch equals 83.75 miles/Una pulgada igual a 83.75 millas
One centimeter equals 53 km/Un centímetro igual a 53 km

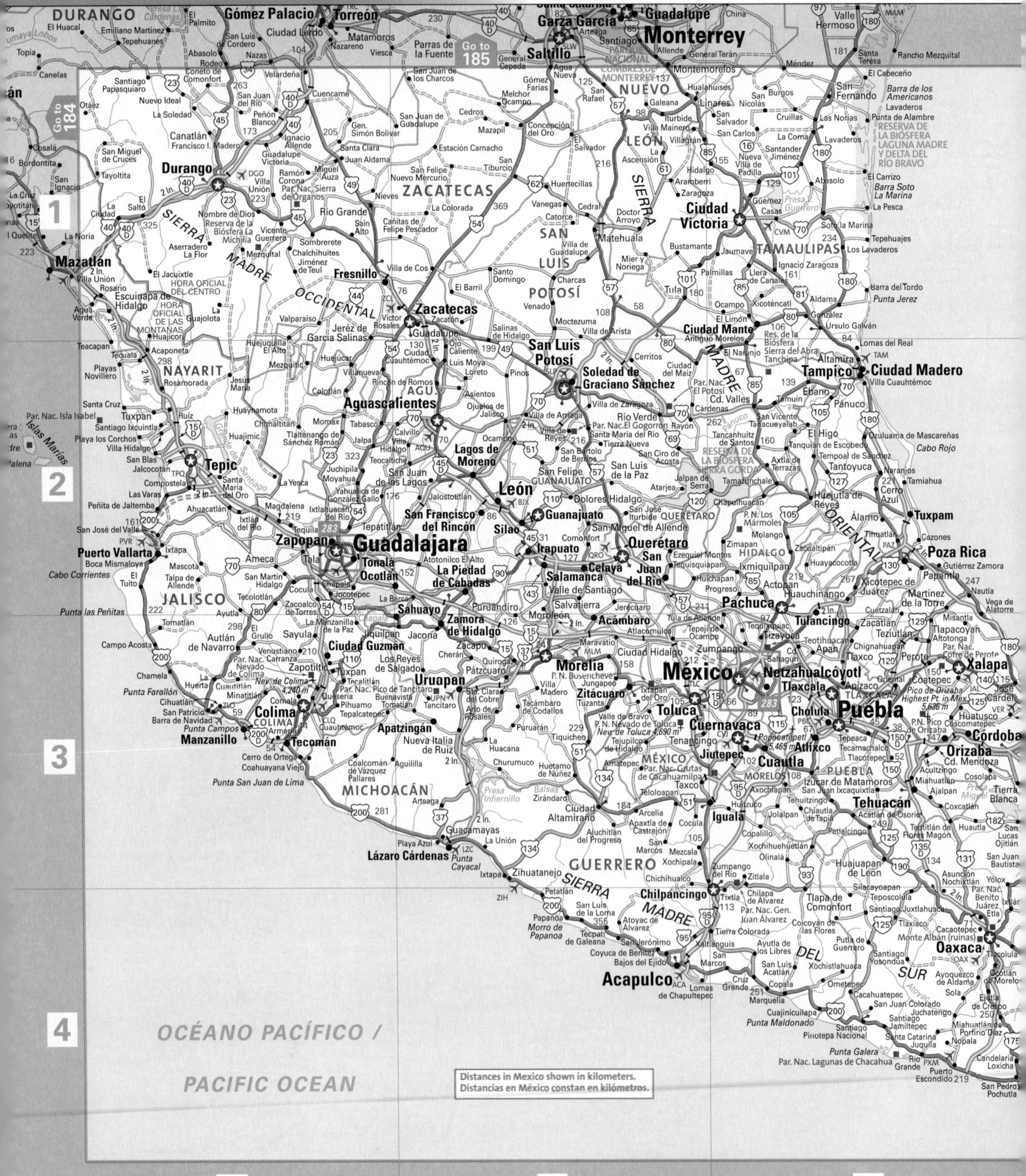

DRIVING DISTANCES IN KM / DISTANCIAS DE MANEJO EN KM

	ACAPULCO	CANCÚN	CIUDAD VICTORIA	DURANGO	GUADALAJARA	MAZATLÁN	MÉRIDA	MÉXICO	PUEBLA	SAN LUIS POTOSÍ	TUXTLA GUTIÉRREZ	VERACRUZ
GUADALAJARA	897	2275	774	599		523	1904	578	691	336	1510	943
MÉRIDA	1777	321	1725	2182	1904	2408		1326	1282	1707	786	995
MÉXICO	422	1736	682	856	578	1081	1326		133	381	932	365
SAN LUIS POTOSÍ	834	2161	438	475	336	687	1707	381	496		1313	747

SEE ALSO DISTANCE AND DRIVING TIME MAP ON PAGES 286–287 / CONSULTE, PARA DISTANCIAS Y TIEMPO DE MANEJO, EN LAS PÁGINAS 286-287

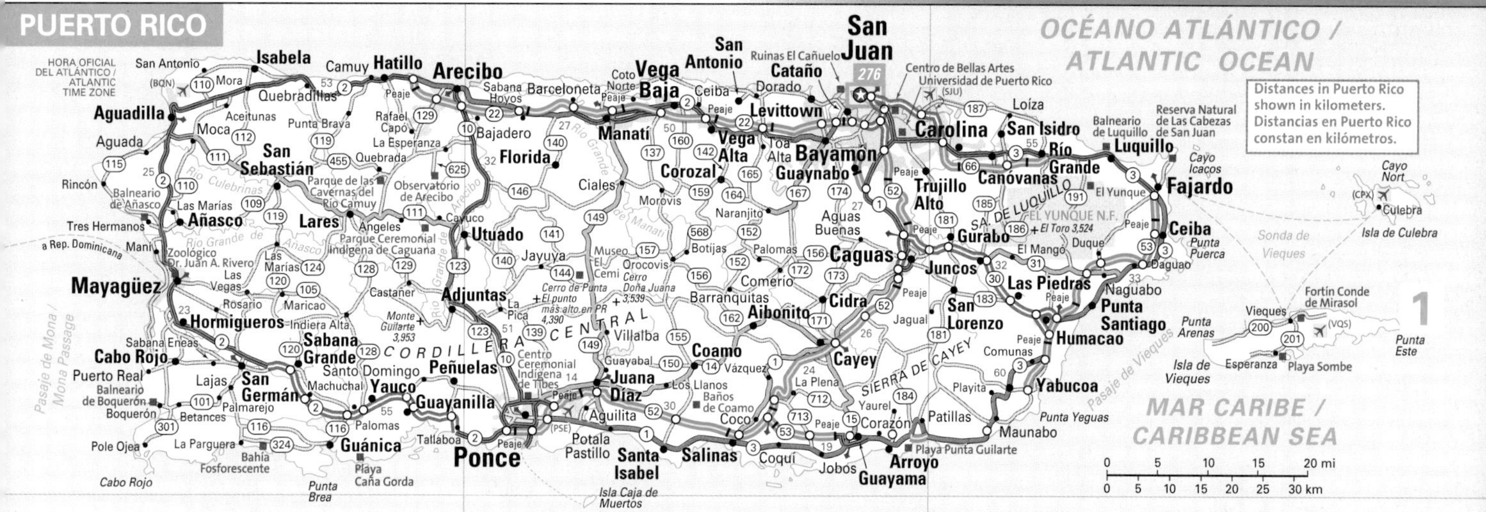

Figures after entries indicate page number and grid reference.

UNITED STATES

A

Abbeville AL 128 B4
Abbeville GA 129 E3
Abbeville LA 133 F3
Abbeville MS 118 C3
Abbeville SC 121 E3
Abbeville Co. SC 121 E3
Abbotsford WI 68 A4
Abbottstown PA 103 E1
Abercrombie ND 19 F4
Aberdeen ID 31 E1
Aberdeen MD 145 D1
Aberdeen MS 119 D4
Aberdeen NC 122 C1
Aberdeen OH 100 C3
Aberdeen SD 27 E2
Aberdeen WA 12 B4
Abernathy TX 58 A1
Abilene KS 43 E2
Abilene TX 58 C3
Abingdon IL 88 A3
Abingdon MD 145 D1
Abingdon VA 111 E3
Abington MA 151 D2
Abita Sprs. LA 134 B2
Absarokee MT 24 B2
Absecon NJ 147 F4
Acadia Par. LA 133 E2
Accokeek MD 144 B4
Accokeek Acres MD 144 B4
Accomac VA 114 C3
Accomack Co. VA 114 C3
Accord MA 151 D2
Accord NY 94 A3
Achille OK 59 F1
Achilles VA 113 F2
Ackerman MS 126 C1
Ackley IA 73 D4
Acme MI 69 F4
Acomita Lake NM 48 B3
Acton CA 52 C2
Acton MA 150 C1
Acushnet MA 151 D3
Acworth GA 120 C3
Ada MN 19 F3
Ada OH 90 B3
Ada OK 51 F4
Ada Co. ID 22 B4
Adair IA 86 B2
Adair OK 106 A3
Adair Co. IA 86 B2
Adair Co. KY 110 B2
Adair Co. MO 87 D4
Adair Co. OK 106 B4
Adairsville GA 120 B3
Adair Vil. OR 20 B3
Adairville KY 109 F3
Adams MA 94 C1
Adams MN 73 D2
Adams NE 35 F4
Adams NY 79 E2
Adams OR 21 F1
Adams TN 109 E3
Adams WI 74 A1
Adams Ctr. NY 79 E2
Adams Co. CO 41 F1
Adams Co. ID 22 B2
Adams Co. IL 87 F4
Adams Co. IN 90 A3
Adams Co. IA 86 B3
Adams Co. MS 126 A4
Adams Co. NE 35 D4
Adams Co. ND 26 A1
Adams Co. OH 100 C3
Adams Co. PA 103 E1
Adams Co. WA 13 F4
Adams Co. WI 74 A2
Adamston NJ 147 E3
Adamstown MD 144 A2
Adamstown PA 146 A2
Adamsville AL 119 F4
Adamsville RI 151 D4
Adamsville TN 119 D1
Addis LA 134 A2
Addison AL 119 E3
Addison IL 203 C4
Addison ME 83 E2
Addison MI 90 B1
Addison NY 93 D1
Addison TX 207 D1
Addison Co. VT 81 D3
Adel GA 137 F1
Adel IA 86 C2
Adelanto CA 53 D2
Adelphi MD 270 E1
Adelphia NJ 147 E2
Adena OH 91 F4
Adrian GA 129 F2
Adrian MI 90 B1
Adrian MN 72 A2
Adrian MO 96 B4
Advance IN 99 E1
Advance MO 108 D2
Adwolf VA 111 F2
Affton MO 256 B3
Afton IA 86 C3
Afton NY 93 F1
Afton OK 106 B3
Afton WY 31 F1
Agawam MA 150 A2
Agency IA 87 E3
Agency MO 96 B1
Agoura Hills CA 228 A2
Agua Dulce TX 63 E2
Agua Fria NM 49 D2
Aguilar CO 41 E4
Ahoskie NC 113 F3
Ahsahka ID 14 B4
Ahuimanu HI 152 A3
Aiken SC 121 F4
Aiken Co. SC 122 A4
Ainsworth IA 87 F2
Ainsworth NE 34 C1
Airmont NY 148 B3
Airport Drive MO 106 B2
Airway Hts. WA 13 F3
Aitkin MN 64 B4
Aitkin Co. MN 64 B4
Ajo AZ 54 B3
Ak-Chin Vil. AZ 54 C2
Akiachak AK 154 B3
Akins OK 116 B1
Akron AL 127 E1
Akron CO 41 F1
Akron IN 89 F3
Akron IA 35 F1
Akron MI 76 B2
Akron NY 78 B3
Akron OH 91 E3
Akron PA 146 A2
Akutan AK 154 A4
Alabaster AL 127 F1
Alachua FL 138 C3

Albany / Schenectady / Troy NY
Schenectady
Scotia
Rotterdam
Niskayuna
Colonie
Latham
Cohoes
Troy
Watervliet
Loudonville
Roessleville
Westmere
Albany
Rensselaer
Delmar
Voorheesville

Albany D3	E. Greenbush E3	Maywood D2	Scotia C1
Alplaus C1	Elsmere D3	McCormack Corners C2	Sherwood Park E3
Best E3	Ft. Hunter C2	McKownville D3	Slingerlands D3
Bethlehem Ctr. D3	Glenmont D3	Meadowdale C3	Snyders Corners E3
Boght Corners E1	Glenridge C1	Menands E3	Speigletown E1
Calico Colony D1	Grant Hollow E1	Mohawk View D2	Sycaway E2
Clifton Gardens D1	Green Island E2	New Salem C3	Troy E2
Clifton Park D1	Grooms Corners D1	New Scotland C3	Unionville D3
Clifton Park Ctr. D1	Guilderland C2	Newtonville E2	Verdoy D2
Clinton Park E3	Guilderland Ctr. C2	Niskayuna D2	Vischer Ferry D1
Cohoes E2	Halfmoon E1	Normanville D3	Voorheesville C3
Colonie D2	Hartmans Corners C2	N. Bethlehem D3	Waterford E1
Crescent E1	Hawthorne Hill D1	Rensselaer E3	Watervliet E2
Defreestville E3	Latham E2	Rexford D1	W. Hill C1
Delmar D3	Loudonville E2	Roessleville D2	Westmere D2
Dunnsville C2	Luther E3	Rotterdam C1	Wynantskill E2
Dunsbach Ferry E1	Maple Wood E2	Schenectady C1	

Alachua Co. FL 138 C3
Alakanuk AK 154 B2
Alamance Co. NC 112 C4
Alameda CA 259 C3
Alameda NM 48 C3
Alameda Co. CA 36 B4
Alamo CA 259 D2
Alamo GA 129 E3
Alamo NM 48 B4
Alamo TN 108 C4
Alamo TX 63 E4
Alamogordo NM 56 C2
Alamo Hts. TX 257 E2
Alamosa CO 41 D4
Alamosa Co. CO 41 D4
Alanson MI 70 C3
Alapaha GA 129 E4
Alba MO 106 B2
Albany CA 259 C2
Albany GA 129 D4
Albany IL 88 A1
Albany IN 90 A4
Albany KY 110 B3
Albany LA 134 B2
Albany MN 66 B2
Albany MO 86 B4
Albany NY 94 B1
Albany OH 101 E2
Albany OR 20 B3
Albany TX 58 C2
Albany WI 74 B4
Albany Co. NY 94 B1
Albany Co. WY 33 E2
Albemarle NC 122 B1
Albemarle Co. VA 102 C4
Albers IL 98 B3
Albert City IA 72 B4
Albert Lea MN 72 C2
Alberton MT 15 D4
Albertville AL 120 A3
Albertville MN 66 C3
Albia IA 87 D3
Albin VA 102 C2
Albion ID 31 D2
Albion IL 99 D4
Albion IN 90 A2
Albion IA 87 D1
Albion MI 76 A4
Albion NE 35 E3
Albion NY 78 B3
Albion PA 91 F1
Albion WA 14 A4
Albuquerque NM 48 C3
Alburg VT 81 D1
Alburnett IA 87 E1
Alburtis PA 146 B1
Alcalde NM 49 D2
Alcester SD 35 F1
Alcoa TN 110 C4
Alcona Co. MI 71 D4
Alcorn MS 126 A3
Alcorn Co. MS 119 D2
Alda NE 35 D4
Aldan PA 248 B4
Alden IA 72 C4
Alden MN 72 C2
Alden NY 78 B3
Alderson WV 112 A1
Alderwood Manor WA 262 B2
Aldine TX 220 C1
Aledo IL 87 F2
Aledo TX 59 F2
Alex OK 51 E3
Alexander AR 117 E2
Alexander ND 17 F2
Alexander City AL 128 A1
Alexander Co. IL 108 C2
Alexander Co. NC 112 A4
Alexandria AL 120 A4
Alexandria IN 89 F4
Alexandria KY 100 B3
Alexandria LA 125 E4
Alexandria MN 66 B2
Alexandria SD 27 E4
Alexandria TN 110 A4
Alexandria VA 144 B3
Alexandria Bay NY 79 E1
Alexis IL 88 A3
Alfalfa Co. OK 51 D1
Alford FL 136 C1
Alfred ME 82 B4
Alfred NY 92 C1
Alger OH 90 B3
Alger Co. MI 69 E1
Algoa TX 132 B4
Algodones NM 48 C3
Algoma MS 118 C3
Algoma WI 69 D4
Algona IA 72 B3
Algona WA 262 B5
Algonac MI 76 C4
Algonquin IL 88 C1
Algood TN 110 A3
Alhambra CA 228 D2
Alhambra IL 98 B3
Alice TX 63 E2
Aliceville AL 127 E1
Ali Chuk AZ 54 B3
Aliquippa PA 91 F3
Aliso Viejo CA 229 G6
Allamakee Co. IA 73 F3
Allamuchy NJ 94 A4
Allardt TN 110 B3
Allegan MI 75 F4
Allegan Co. MI 75 F4
Allegany NY 92 C1
Allegany Co. MD 102 C1
Allegany Co. NY 78 C4
Alleghany Co. NC 111 F3
Alleghany Co. VA 102 A4
Allegheny Co. PA 92 A4
Allen NE 35 F2
Allen OK 51 F3
Allen SD 26 B4
Allen TX 59 F2
Allen Co. IN 90 A3
Allen Co. KS 96 A4
Allen Co. KY 109 F2
Allen Co. OH 90 B3
Allendale MI 75 F3
Allendale NJ 148 B3
Allendale SC 130 B1
Allendale Co. SC 130 B1
Allenhurst GA 130 B3
Allenhurst NJ 147 F2
Allen Par. LA 133 E1
Allen Park MI 210 B4
Allenspark CO 41 D1
Allenton RI 150 C4
Allenton WI 74 C2
Allentown NJ 147 D2
Allentown PA 146 B1
Allenwood NJ 147 E2
Allerton IA 87 D3

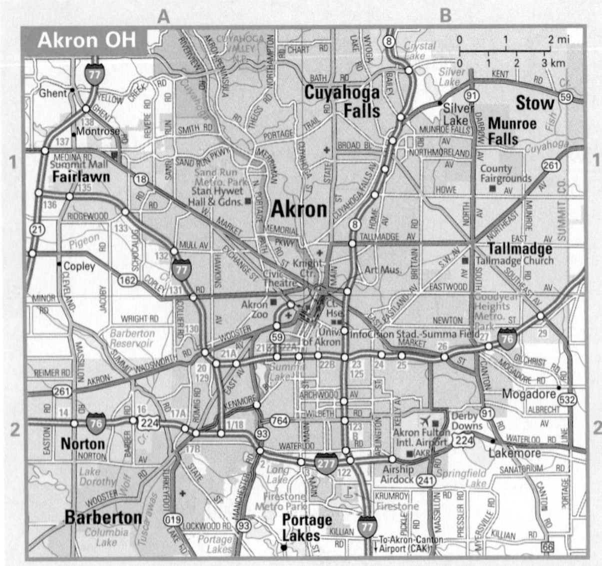
Akron OH
Akron
Cuyahoga Falls
Stow
Munroe Falls
Fairlawn
Tallmadge
Norton
Barberton
Portage Lakes
Mogadore
Lakemore

Akron A1	Fairlawn A1	Montrose A1	Silver Lake B1
Barberton A2	Ghent A1	Munroe Falls B1	Stow B1
Copley A1	Lakemore B2	Norton A2	Tallmadge B1
Cuyahoga Falls B1	Mogadore B2	Portage Lakes A2	

Entries in **bold black** indicate counties or parishes.
Entries in bold color indicate cities with detailed inset maps.

Allgood AL	119	F4
Alliance NE	34	A2
Alliance NC	115	D3
Alliance OH	91	E3
Allison IA	73	D4
Allison Gap VA	111	F2
Alloway NJ	145	F1
Alpine CA	53	D4
Alpine NJ	148	B3
Alpine TX	62	B3
Alpine UT	31	F4
Alpine WY	31	F1
Alpine Co. CA	37	D3
Alsen LA	134	A2
Alton MO	107	F3
Alton NH	81	F4
Altona IL	88	A3
Altona NY	81	D1
Alton Bay NH	81	F4
Altoona AL	120	A3
Altoona IA	86	C2
Amber OK	51	E3
Amberley OH	204	B2
Ambler PA	146	C2
Amboy IL	88	B1
Amboy MN	72	C2
Amboy WA	20	C1
Ambridge PA	92	A3
Amidon ND	18	A4
Amissville VA	103	D3
Amite LA	134	B1
Amite Co. MS	126	A4
Amity AR	117	D3
Amity OR	20	B2
Amityville NY	148	C4
Anahuac TX	132	B3
Anamoose ND	18	C2
Anamosa IA	87	F1
Anchorage AK	154	C3
Anchorage KY	230	F1
Anchor Pt. AK	154	C3
Anchorville MI	76	C4
Anderson Co. TN	110	C4
Anderson Co. TX	124	A4
Andersonville OH	101	D2
Andover CT	150	A3
Andover IL	88	A2
Andover KS	43	F4
Andover MA	95	E1
Andover MN	67	D3
Andover NJ	94	A4
Andover NY	92	C1
Andover OH	91	F2
Andrew Co. MO	96	B1
Andrews IN	89	F3
Andrews NC	121	D1
Andrews SC	122	C4
Andrews TX	57	F3
Andrews Co. TX	57	F3
Androscoggin Co. ME	82	B2
Aneta ND	19	E3
Aneth UT	40	A4
Angel Fire NM	49	D2
Angelica NY	78	B4
Angelina Co. TX	124	B4
Angels Camp CA	36	C3
Angier NC	123	D1
Angleton TX	132	A4
Angola IN	90	A2
Angola NY	78	A4
Angola on the Lake NY	78	A4
Angoon AK	155	E4
Anguilla MS	126	A1
Angwin CA	36	B3
Aniak AK	154	B3
Anita IA	86	B2
Ankeny IA	86	C1
Anmoore WV	102	A2
Anna IL	108	C1
Anna OH	90	B4
Anna TX	59	F1
Annabella UT	39	E2
Anna Maria FL	140	B3
Annandale MN	66	C3
Annandale NJ	147	D1
Annandale VA	144	B3
Annapolis MD	144	C3
Ann Arbor MI	76	B4
Annawan IL	88	A2
Anne Arundel Co. MD	144	C3
Annetta TX	59	E2
Anniston AL	120	A4
Annsville NY	148	B2
Annville KY	110	C1
Annville PA	93	E4
Anoka MN	67	D3

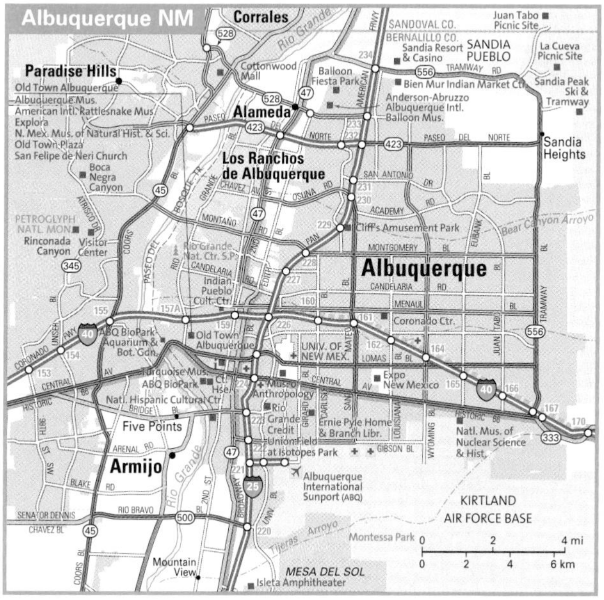
Albuquerque NM
Corrales
Paradise Hills
Alameda
Los Ranchos de Albuquerque
Albuquerque
Sandia Heights
SANDIA PUEBLO
Armijo
Five Points
KIRTLAND AIR FORCE BASE
MESA DEL SOL
Albuquerque International Sunport (ABQ)
Isleta Amphitheater
0 2 4 mi
0 2 4 6 km

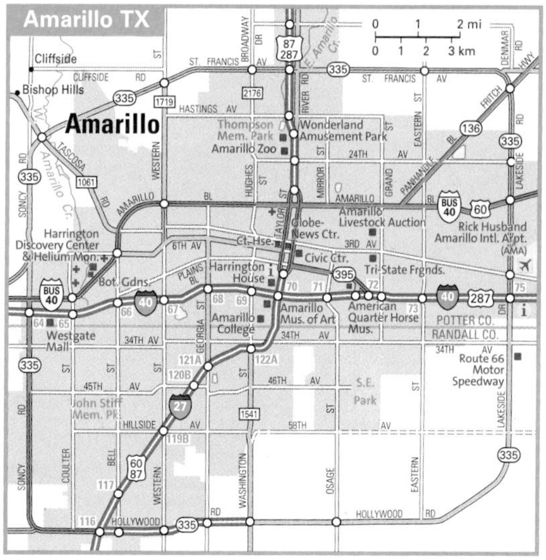
Amarillo TX
Amarillo
Cliffside
Bishop Hills
Wonderland Amusement Park
Amarillo Zoo
Rick Husband Amarillo Intl. Arpt. (AMA)
POTTER CO.
RANDALL CO.
0 1 2 mi
0 1 2 3 km

Amelia LA	134	A3
Amelia OH	100	B2
Amelia City FL	139	D2
Amelia Co. VA	113	D2
Amelia C.H. VA	113	D1
Amenia NY	94	B3
American Beach FL	139	D2
American Canyon CA	36	B3
American Falls ID	31	E1
American Fork UT	31	F4
Americus GA	129	D3
Americus KS	43	F3
Amery WI	67	E3
Ames IA	86	C1
Ames TX	132	B3
Amesbury MA	95	E1
Amherst MA	150	A1
Amherst NH	95	D1
Amherst NY	78	B3
Amherst OH	91	D2
Amherst TX	57	F1
Amherst VA	112	C1
Amherst WI	74	B1
Amherst Co. VA	112	C1
Amherstdale WV	111	F1
Ammon ID	23	E4
Amory MS	119	D4
Amsterdam MT	23	F1
Amsterdam NY	94	A1
Amsterdam OH	91	F4
Anacoco LA	125	D4
Anaconda MT	23	D1
Anacortes WA	12	C2
Anadarko OK	51	D3
Anaheim CA	52	C3
Anahola HI	152	B1
Andale KS	43	E4
Andalusia AL	128	A4
Andalusia IL	87	F2
Anderson CA	28	C4
Anderson IN	89	F4
Anderson MO	106	B3
Anderson SC	121	E3
Anderson TX	61	F1
Anderson Co. KS	96	A4
Anderson Co. KY	100	A4
Anderson Co. SC	121	E2
Allyn WA	12	C3
Alma AR	116	C1
Alma GA	129	F4
Alma KS	43	F2
Alma MI	76	A2
Alma NE	43	D1
Alma WI	73	E1
Almena KS	42	C1
Almena WI	67	E3
Almon GA	121	D4
Almont MI	76	C3
Aloe TX	61	E3
Aloha OR	20	B2
Alorton IL	256	C3
Alpaugh CA	45	D4
Alpena MI	71	D3
Alpena SD	27	E3
Alpena Co. MI	71	D4
Alpha IL	88	A2
Alpha NJ	146	C1
Alpharetta GA	120	C3
Alsip IL	203	D6
Alta IA	72	A4
Alta UT	31	F4
Alta WY	23	F4
Altadena CA	228	D1
Altamahaw NC	112	B4
Altamont IL	98	C2
Altamont KS	106	A2
Altamont NY	94	B1
Altamont OR	28	C2
Altamont TN	120	A1
Altamonte Sprs. FL	141	D1
Alta Vista KS	43	F2
Altavista VA	112	C2
Altha FL	137	D2
Altheimer AR	117	F3
Alto GA	121	D3
Alto TX	124	B4
Alton IL	98	A3
Alton IA	35	F1
Alton KY	100	B4
Altoona KS	106	A1
Altoona PA	92	C4
Altoona WI	67	F4
Alturas CA	29	D3
Altus AR	116	C1
Altus OK	51	D4
Alum Creek WV	101	E4
Alva FL	143	D1
Alva OK	51	D1
Alvarado TX	59	E3
Alvin TX	132	B4
Alvord TX	59	E1
Ama LA	239	B2
Amado AZ	55	D4
Amador Co. CA	36	C3
Amagansett NY	149	F3
Amalga UT	31	E2
Amana IA	87	E1
Amanda OH	101	D1
Amarillo TX	50	A3
Amawalk NY	148	B2

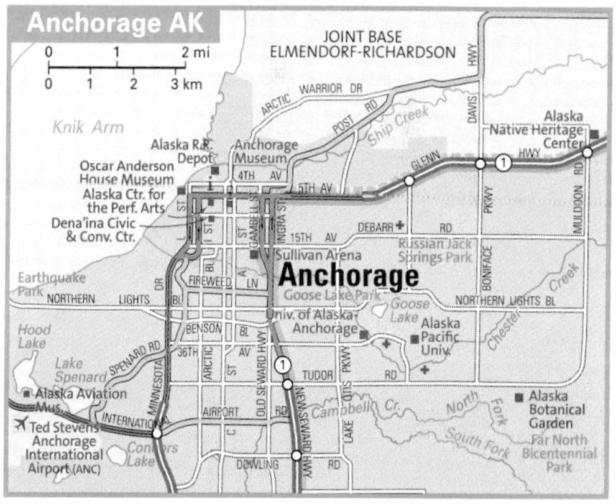
Anchorage AK
Anchorage
JOINT BASE ELMENDORF-RICHARDSON
Knik Arm
Alaska Native Heritage Center
Ted Stevens Anchorage International Airport (ANC)
Alaska Botanical Garden
Far North Bicentennial Park
0 1 2 mi
0 1 2 3 km

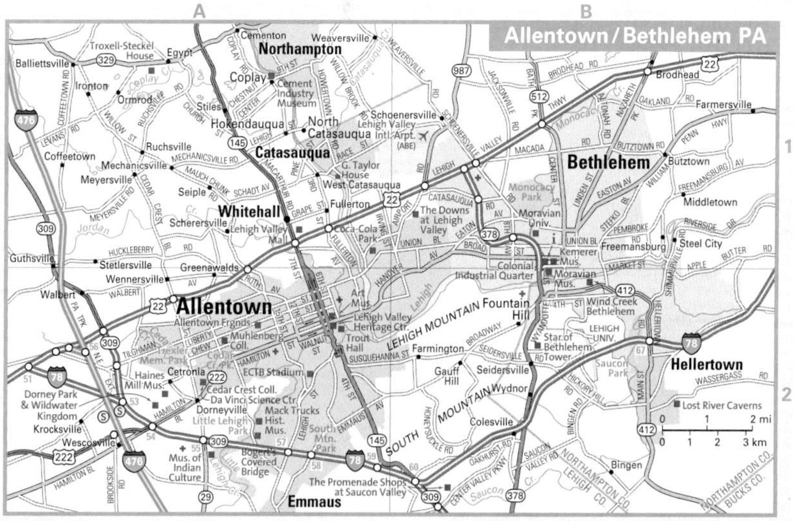
Allentown / Bethlehem PA
Allentown
Bethlehem
Northampton
Catasauqua
Whitehall
Coplay
Hellertown
Emmaus
Fountain Hill
Freemansburg
0 1 2 mi
0 1 2 3 km

Allentown	A2	
Balliettsville	A1	
Bethlehem	B1	
Bingen	B2	
Brodhead	B1	
Butztown	B1	
Catasauqua	A1	
Cementon	A1	
Cetronia	A2	
Coffeetown	A1	
Colesville	B2	
Coplay	A1	
Dorneyville	A2	
Egypt	A1	
Emmaus	A2	
Farmersville	B1	
Farmington	B2	
Fountain Hill	B2	
Freemansburg	B1	
Fullerton	A1	
Gauff Hill	B2	
Greenawalds	A2	
Guthsville	A2	
Hellertown	B2	
Hokendauqua	A1	
Ironton	A1	
Krocksville	A2	
Mechanicsville	A1	
Meyersville	A1	
Middletown	B1	
Northampton	A1	
N. Catasauqua	A1	
Ormrod	A1	
Ruchsville	A1	
Schoenersville	B1	
Scherersville	A1	
Seidersville	B2	
Seiple	A1	
Steel City	B1	
Stetlersville	A1	
Stiles	A1	
Walbert	A2	
Weaversville	A1	
Wennersville	A2	
Wescosville	A2	
W. Catasauqua	A1	
Whitehall	A1	
Wydnor	B2	

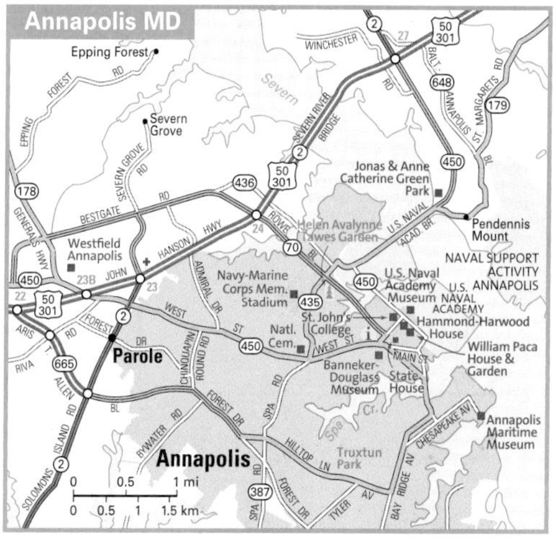
Annapolis MD
Annapolis
Parole
Epping Forest
Severn Grove
Westfield Annapolis
NAVAL SUPPORT ACTIVITY ANNAPOLIS
U.S. Naval Academy Museum
0 0.5 1 mi
0 0.5 1 1.5 km

Figures after entries indicate page number and grid reference.

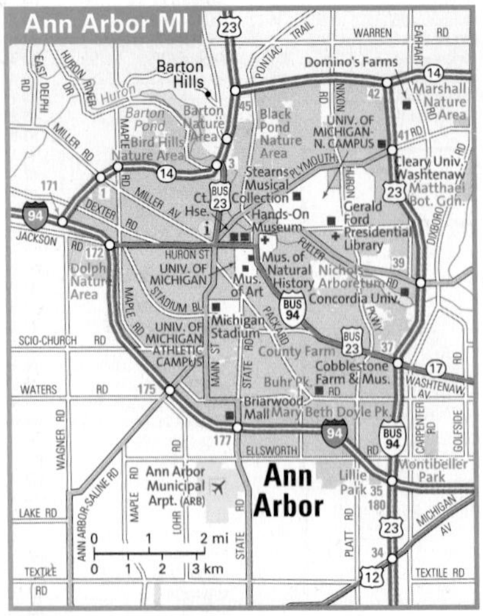

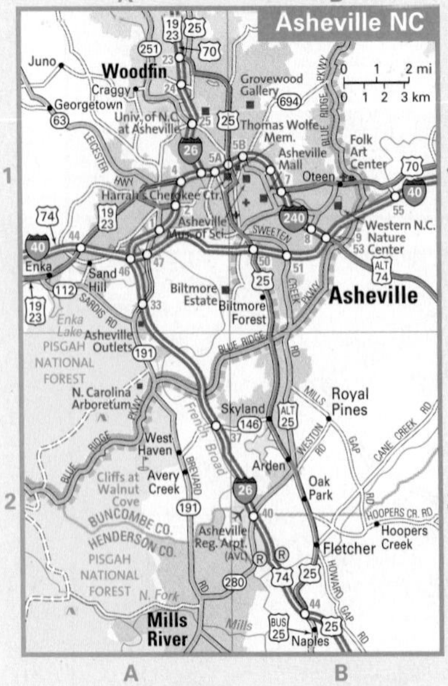

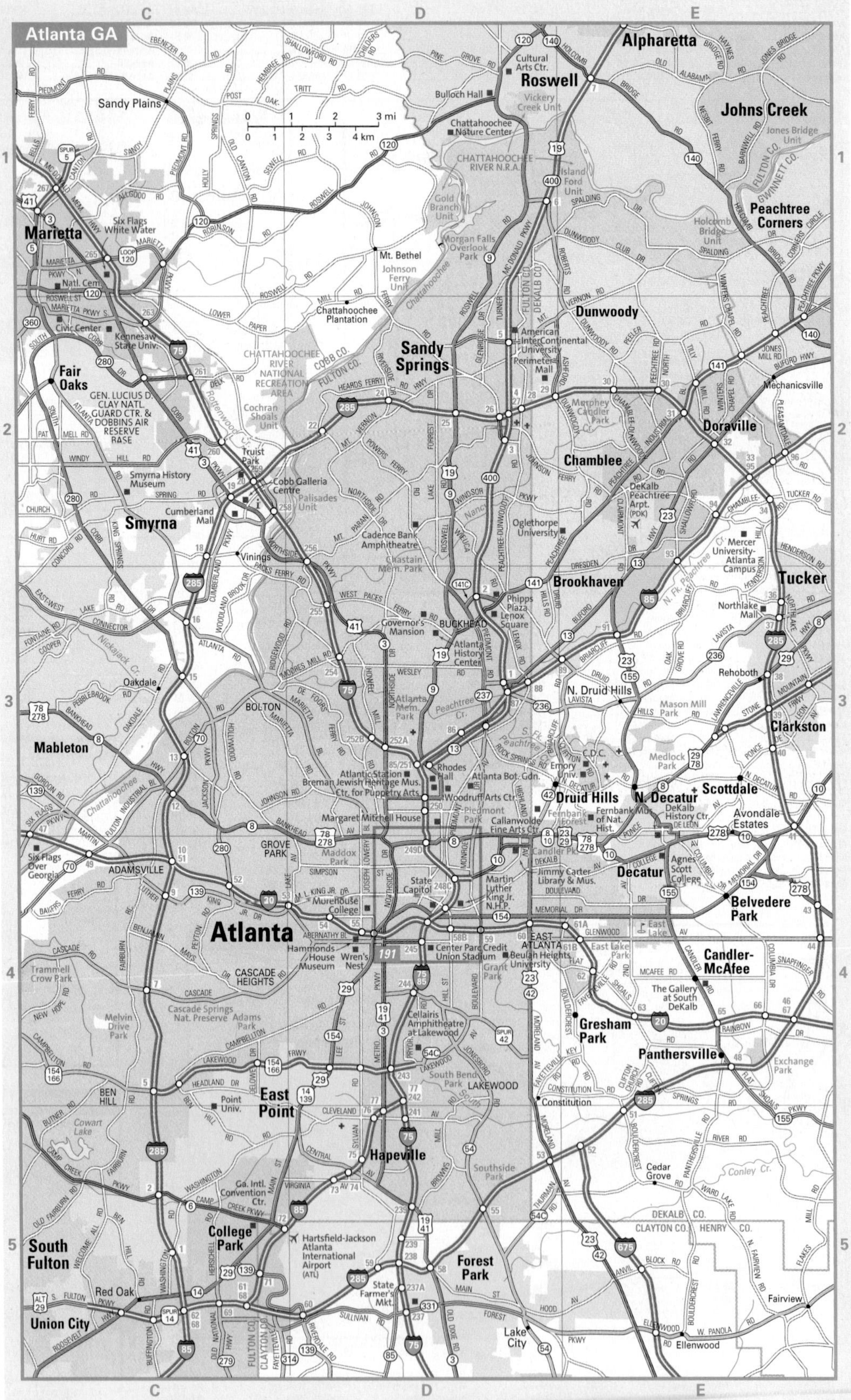

Entries in **bold black** indicate counties or parishes.
Entries in bold color indicate cities with detailed inset maps.

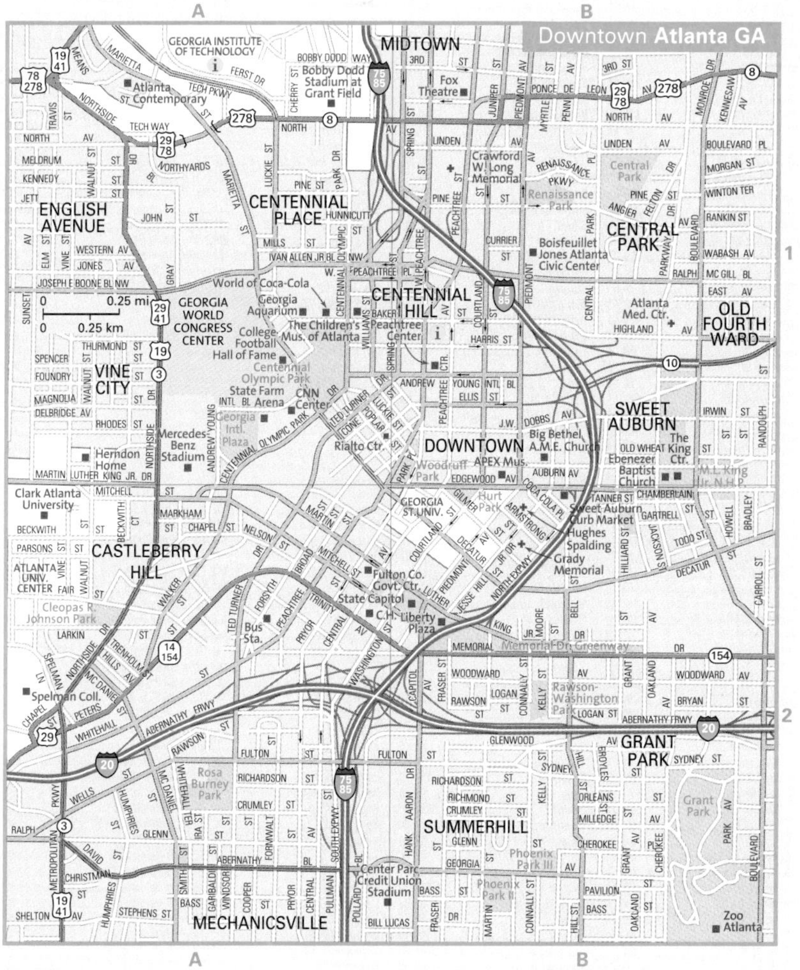
Downtown Atlanta GA
MIDTOWN
GEORGIA INSTITUTE OF TECHNOLOGY
ENGLISH AVENUE
CENTENNIAL PLACE
CENTRAL PARK
CENTENNIAL HILL
OLD FOURTH WARD
VINE CITY
SWEET AUBURN
DOWNTOWN
CASTLEBERRY HILL
GRANT PARK
SUMMERHILL
MECHANICSVILLE

POINTS OF INTEREST

APEX Museum . . . B1
Atlanta Contemporary . . . A1
Atlanta University Center . . . A2
Big Bethel African Meth. Episcopal Church . B1
Bobby Dodd Stadium at Grant Field . . . A1
Boisfeuillet Jones Atlanta Civic Center . . . B1
Bus Station . . . A2
Center Parc Credit Union Stadium . . . A2
City Hall . . . A2
Clark Atlanta University . . . A2
CNN Center . . . A1
Ebenezer Baptist Church . . . B1
Fox Theatre . . . B1
Fulton County Government Center . . . A2
Georgia Aquarium . . . A1
Georgia Institute of Technology . . . A1
Georgia State University . . . B2
Georgia World Congress Center . . . A1
Herndon Home . . . A1
The King Center . . . B1
Liberty Plaza . . . B2
Martin Luther King, Jr. Natl. Hist. Park . . . B1
Mercedes-Benz Stadium . . . A1
Peachtree Center . . . B1
Rialto Center . . . A1
Spelman College . . . A2
State Capitol . . . B2
State Farm Arena . . . A1
Sweet Auburn Curb Market . . . B2
The Children's Mus. of Atlanta . . . A1
World of Coca-Cola . . . A1
Zoo Atlanta . . . B2

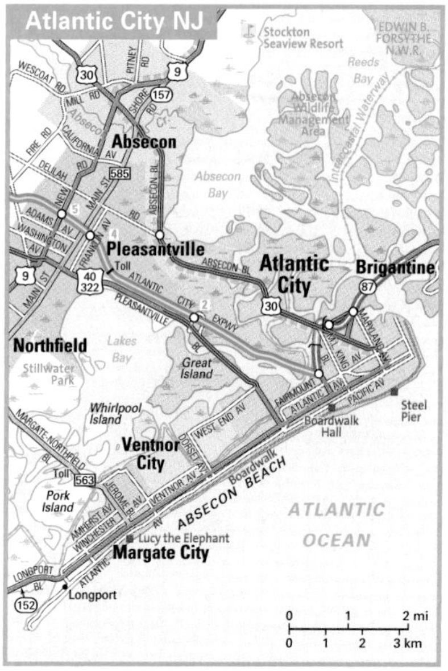
Atlantic City NJ
Absecon
Pleasantville
Atlantic City
Brigantine
Northfield
Ventnor City
Margate City
Longport
ATLANTIC OCEAN

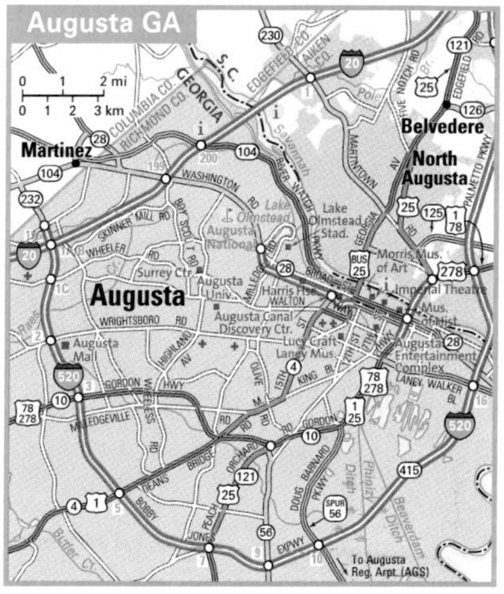
Augusta GA
Martinez
North Augusta
Belvedere
Augusta

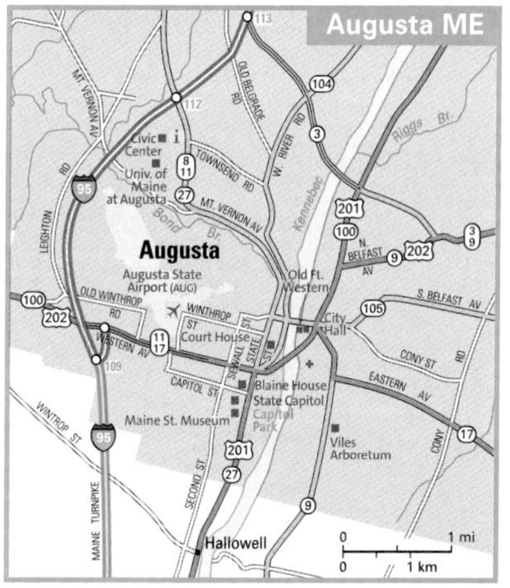
Augusta ME
Augusta
Hallowell

Arcade GA 121 D3
Arcade NY 78 B4
Arcadia CA 228 E2
Arcadia FL 140 C4
Arcadia IN 89 F4
Arcadia KS 106 B1
Arcadia LA 125 D2
Arcadia MO 108 A1
Arcadia OH 90 C3
Arcadia WI 73 E1
Arcadia Lakes SC 205 F1
Arcanum OH 100 B1
Arcata CA 28 A4
Archbald PA 93 F2
Archbold OH 90 B2
Archdale NC 112 B4
Archer FL 138 C3
Archer City TX 59 D1
Archer Co. TX 59 D1
Archie MO 96 B3
Archuleta Co. CO 40 C4
Arco ID 23 D4
Arcola IL 99 D1
Arcola MS 126 A1
Arcola TX 132 A4
Arden CA 255 B2
Arden DE 146 B3
Ardencroft DE 274 E1
Arden Hills MN 235 C1
Ardentown DE 274 E1
Ardmore AL 119 F2
Ardmore OK 51 F4
Ardmore PA 146 C3
Ardmore TN 119 F2
Ardonia NY 148 B1
Arena WI 74 A3
Arenac Co. MI 76 B1
Arendtsville PA 103 E1
Argenta IL 98 C1
Argentine MI 76 B4
Argo AL 119 F4
Argonia KS 43 E4
Argos IN 89 F2
Argos Corner DE 145 F3
Argyle MN 19 F2
Argyle TX 59 E2
Argyle WI 74 A4
Arimo ID 31 E1
Aripeka FL 140 B1
Ariton AL 128 B4
Arizola AZ 54 C2
Arizona City AZ 54 C2
Arkadelphia AR 117 D3
Arkansas City AR 117 F4
Arkansas City KS 51 E1
Arkansas Co. AR 117 F3
Arkoma OK 116 B1
Arkport NY 78 C4
Arlee MT 15 D3
Arlington GA 128 C4
Arlington IA 73 E4
Arlington KS 43 E4
Arlington KY 108 C2
Arlington MA 151 D1
Arlington MN 66 C4
Arlington NE 35 F3
Arlington NY 148 B1
Arlington OH 90 C3
Arlington OR 21 E1
Arlington SD 27 F3
Arlington TN 118 B1
Arlington TX 59 E2
Arlington VT 81 D4
Arlington VA 144 B3
Arlington WA 12 C2
Arlington Co. VA 144 B3
Arlington Hts. IL 89 D1
Arlington Hts. OH 204 B2
Arma KS 106 B1
Armada MI 76 C3
Armijo NM 48 C3
Armona CA 44 C3
Armonk NY 148 C2
Armour SD 27 E4
Armstrong IA 72 B2
Armstrong Co. PA 92 A3
Armstrong Co. TX 50 B3
Arnaudville LA 133 F2
Arnett OK 50 C2
Arnold CA 37 D3
Arnold MD 144 C3
Arnold MN 64 C4
Arnold MO 98 A3
Arnold NE 34 C3
Arnold PA 92 A4
Arnolds Park IA 72 A3
Aroma Park IL 89 D3
Aromas CA 44 B2
Aroostook Co. ME 85 D2
Arp TX 124 B3
Arredondo FL 138 C3
Arroyo Grande CA 52 A1
Arroyo Hondo NM 49 D1
Arroyo Seco NM 49 D1
Artesia CA 228 E4
Artesia MS 127 D1
Artesia NM 57 E2
Arthur IL 98 C1
Arthur NE 34 B3
Arthur ND 19 E3
Arthur TN 110 C3
Arthur Co. NE 34 B3
Arthurdale WV 102 B2
Arundel on the Bay MD 144 C3
Arundel Vil. MD 193 C4
Arvada CO 41 E1
Arvin CA 52 B1
Asbury IA 73 F4
Asbury Park NJ 147 F2
Ascension Par. LA 134 A2
Ascutney VT 81 E4
Asharoken NY 148 C3
Ashaway RI 150 C4
Ashburn GA 129 D4
Ashburn VA 144 A3
Ashburnham MA 95 D1
Ashdown AR 116 C4
Asheboro NC 112 B4
Ashe Co. NC 111 F3
Asherton TX 60 C4
Asheville NC 121 E1
Ashfield MA 94 C1
Ash Flat AR 107 F3
Ashford AL 137 D1
Ash Fork AZ 47 D3
Ash Grove MO 106 C1
Ashkum IL 89 D3
Ashland AL 128 B1
Ashland CA 259 D3
Ashland IL 98 B1
Ashland KS 42 C4
Ashland KY 101 D3
Ashland ME 85 D2
Ashland MA 150 C1
Ashland MS 118 C2
Ashland MO 97 E3
Ashland MT 25 D1
Ashland NE 35 F3
Ashland NH 81 F3
Ashland OH 91 D3
Ashland OR 28 C2
Ashland PA 93 E3
Ashland VA 113 E1
Ashland WI 65 D4
Ashland City TN 109 E3
Ashland Co. OH 91 D3
Ashland Co. WI 67 F1
Ashley IL 98 C4
Ashley IN 90 A2
Ashley MI 76 A3
Ashley ND 27 D1
Ashley PA 261 A2
Ashley Co. AR 125 F1
Ashmore IL 99 D1
Ashtabula OH 91 F1
Ashtabula Co. OH 91 F1
Ashton ID 23 F3
Ashton IL 88 B1
Ashton RI 150 C3
Ashuelot NH 94 C1
Ashville AL 120 A4
Ashville OH 101 D1
Ashwaubenon WI 68 C4
Asotin WA 14 B4
Asotin Co. WA 22 A1
Aspen CO 40 C2
Aspen Hill MD 144 B2
Aspen Park CO 209 A4
Aspermont TX 58 C2
Aspinwall PA 250 C1
Assaria KS 43 E3
Assinippi MA 151 E2
Assonet MA 151 D3
Assumption IL 98 C1
Assumption Par. LA 134 A3
Astatula FL 140 C1
Astor FL 139 D4
Astoria IL 88 A4
Astoria OR 20 B1
Atascadero CA 44 C4
Atascosa Co. TX 61 D3
Atchison KS 96 B1
Atchison Co. KS 96 A2
Atchison Co. MO 86 A4
Atco NJ 147 D4
Atglen PA 146 A3
Athena OR 21 F1
Athens AL 119 F2
Athens GA 121 D4
Athens IL 98 B1
Athens ME 82 C1
Athens MI 90 A1
Athens NY 94 B2
Athens OH 101 E2
Athens PA 93 E1
Athens TN 120 C1
Athens TX 124 A3
Athens WV 112 A1
Athens WI 68 A3
Athens Co. OH 101 E2
Atherton CA 259 C5
Athol ID 14 B2
Athol MA 95 D1
Atkins AR 117 D1
Atkins IA 87 E1
Atkins VA 111 F2
Atkinson IL 88 A2
Atkinson NE 35 D1
Atkinson NH 95 E1
Atkinson Co. GA 129 E4
Atlanta GA 120 C4
Atlanta IL 88 B4
Atlanta IN 89 F4
Atlanta MI 70 C4
Atlanta NY 78 C4
Atlanta TX 124 C1
Atlantic IA 86 B2
Atlantic Beach FL 139 D2
Atlantic Beach NY 147 F1
Atlantic Beach NC 115 D4
Atlantic City NJ 147 F4
Atlantic Co. NJ 147 D4
Atlantic Highlands NJ 147 E1
Atlantis FL 143 F1
Atmore AL 135 F1
Atoka OK 51 F4
Atoka TN 118 B1
Atoka Co. OK 51 F4
Attala Co. MS 126 C1
Attalla AL 120 A3
Attapulgus GA 137 E1
Attawaugan CT 150 B3
Attica IN 89 D4
Attica KS 43 E4
Attica MI 76 C3
Attica NY 78 B3
Attica OH 90 C3
Attleboro MA 151 D2
Atwater CA 36 C4
Atwater MN 66 B3
Atwater OH 91 E3
Atwood IL 98 C1
Atwood KS 42 B1
Atwood TN 108 C4
Auberry CA 45 D2
Aubrey TX 59 F2
Auburn AL 128 B2
Auburn CA 36 C2
Auburn GA 121 D3
Auburn IL 98 B1
Auburn IN 90 A2
Auburn KS 96 A3
Auburn KY 109 F2
Auburn ME 82 B3
Auburn MA 150 B2
Auburn MI 76 B2
Auburn NE 86 A4
Auburn NY 79 D3
Auburn PA 146 A1
Auburn WA 12 C3
Auburn WY 31 F1
Auburndale FL 140 C2
Auburndale WI 68 A4
Auburn Hills MI 210 B1
Audrain Co. MO 97 E2
Audubon IA 86 B1
Audubon NJ 248 D4
Audubon PA 248 A1
Audubon Co. IA 86 B2
Audubon Park KY 230 D2
Audubon Park NJ 248 D4
Auglaize Co. OH 90 B4
Au Gres MI 76 B1
Augusta AR 117 F1
Augusta GA 121 F4
Augusta IL 87 F4
Augusta KS 43 F4
Augusta KY 100 C3
Augusta ME 82 C2
Augusta MI 75 F4
Augusta MT 15 E3
Augusta WI 67 F4
Augusta Co. VA 102 B4

Figures after entries indicate page number and grid reference.

Aulander NC 113 E3
Ault CO 33 E4
Aumsville OR 20 B2
Aurelia IA 72 A4
Aurora CO 41 E1
Aurora IL 88 C1
Aurora IN 100 B2
Aurora MN 64 C3
Aurora MO 106 C2
Aurora NE 35 E4
Aurora NY 79 D4
Aurora NC 115 D3
Aurora OH 91 E2
Aurora OR 20 C2
Aurora SD 27 F3
Aurora TX 59 E2
Aurora UT 39 E2
Aurora Co. SD 27 D4
Au Sable MI 76 C1
Autaugaville AL 127 F2
Auxvasse MO 97 E2
Ava IL 98 B4
Ava MO 107 E2
Avalon CA 52 C3
Avalon NJ 105 D4
Avalon PA 250 A1
Avawam KY 111 D2
Avella PA 91 F4
Avenal CA 44 C3
Avenel NJ 147 E1
Aventura FL 143 F2
Averill Park NY 94 B1
Avery CA 37 D3
Avery Co. NC 111 F4
Avery Creek NC 121 E1
Avilla IN 90 A2
Avis PA 93 D2
Aviston IL 98 B3
Avon MN 66 C2
Avon NY 78 C3
Avon NC 115 F3
Avon OH 91 D2
Avon PA 146 A2
Avon SD 35 E1
Avon-by-the-Sea NJ 147 F2
Avondale AZ 54 C1
Avondale CO 41 E3
Avondale LA 134 B3
Avondale MO 224 C2
Avondale PA 146 B3
Avondale RI 149 F2
Avondale Estates GA 190 E3
Avonia PA 91 F1
Avon Lake OH 91 D2
Avonmore PA 92 A4
Avon Park FL 141 D3
Avoyelles Par. LA 125 F4

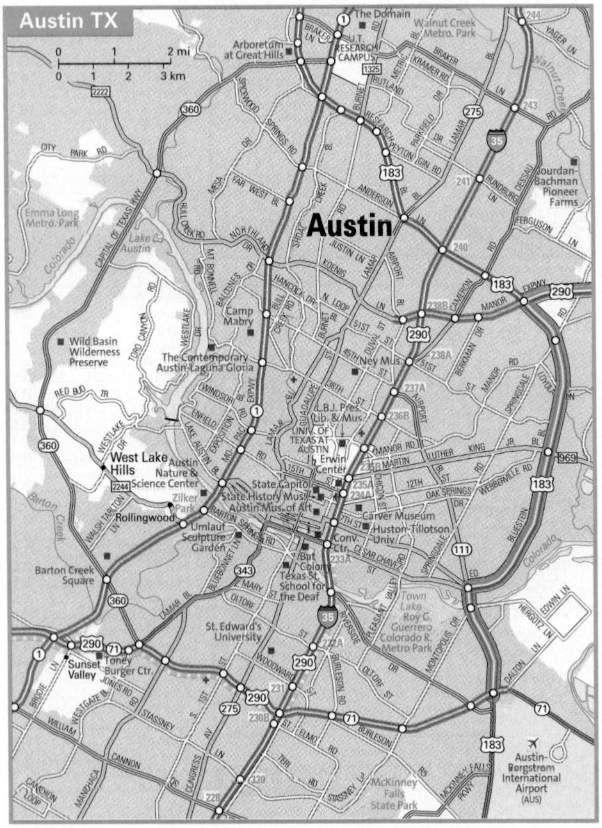

Au Sable Forks NY 81 D2
Austin AR 117 E2
Austin IN 99 F3
Austin MN 73 D2
Austin NV 37 F1
Austin PA 92 C2
Austin TX 61 E1
Austin Co. TX 61 F2
Austintown OH 91 F3
Autauga Co. AL 127 F2
Avoca AR 106 C3
Avoca IA 86 A2
Avoca NY 78 C4
Avoca PA 261 C2
Avoca WI 74 A3
Avon AL 137 D1
Avon CO 40 C1
Avon CT 94 C3
Avon IL 88 A3
Avon IN 99 F1
Awendaw SC 131 D1
Axtell KS 43 F1
Axtell NE 35 D4
Ayden NC 115 D3
Ayer MA 95 D1
Aynor SC 122 C3
Azalea Park FL 246 D2
Azle TX 59 E2
Aztec NM 48 B1
Azusa CA 228 E2

B

Babbie AL 128 A4
Babbitt MN 64 C3
Babcock Ranch FL 140 C4
Babylon NY 148 C4
Baca Co. CO 42 A4
Bacon Co. GA 129 F4
Baconton GA 129 D4
Bad Axe MI 76 C2
Baden PA 92 A3
Badger IA 72 C4
Badin NC 122 B1
Bagdad AZ 46 C4
Bagdad FL 135 F2
Baggs WY 32 C3
Bagley MN 64 A3
Bahama NC 112 C4
Bailey NC 113 D4
Bailey Co. TX 49 F4
Bailey Island ME 82 B3
Bailey's Crossroads VA 270 B4
Bailey's Prairie TX 132 A4
Baileyton AL 119 F3
Baileyton TN 111 D3
Bainbridge GA 137 D1
Bainbridge IN 99 E1
Bainbridge NY 79 E4
Bainbridge OH 101 D2
Bainbridge Island WA 12 C3
Baird TX 58 C3
Baiting Hollow NY 149 E3
Baker LA 134 A2
Baker MT 17 F4
Baker City OR 21 F2
Baker Co. FL 138 C2
Baker Co. GA 128 C4
Baker Co. OR 21 F3
Bakersfield CA 45 D4
Bakersville NC 111 E4
Bala-Cynwyd PA 146 C3
Balaton MN 72 A1
Balch Sprs. TX 207 E3
Balcones Hts. TX 257 E2
Bald Knob AR 117 F1
Baldwin FL 139 D2
Baldwin GA 121 D3
Baldwin IL 98 B4
Baldwin LA 133 F3
Baldwin MD 144 C1
Baldwin MI 75 F2
Baldwin PA 250 C3
Baldwin WI 67 E4
Baldwin City KS 96 A3
Baldwin Co. AL 135 E1
Baldwin Co. GA 129 E1
Baldwin Harbor NY 147 F1
Baldwin Park CA 228 E2
Baldwinsville NY 79 D3
Baldwinville MA 95 D1
Baldwyn MS 119 D3
Balfour NC 121 E1
Bal Harbour FL 233 B3
Ball LA 125 E4
Ballantine MT 24 C1
Ballard UT 32 A4
Ballard Co. KY 108 C2
Ballentine SC 122 A3
Ball Ground GA 120 C3
Ballinger TX 58 C4
Ballouville CT 150 B3
Ballston Spa NY 80 C4
Ballville OH 90 C2
Ballwin MO 98 A3
Bally PA 146 B1
Balmorhea TX 62 B2
Balmville NY 148 B1
Balsam Lake WI 67 E3
Baltic CT 149 F1
Baltic OH 91 E4
Baltic SD 27 F4
Baltimore MD 144 C2
Baltimore OH 101 D1
Baltimore Co. MD 144 C1
Baltimore Highlands MD 193 C4
Bamberg SC 130 C1
Bamberg Co. SC 130 B1
Bancroft ID 31 E1
Bancroft IA 72 B3
Bancroft KY 230 F1
Bancroft MI 76 B3
Bancroft NE 35 F2
Bancroft WV 101 E3
Bandera TX 61 D2
Bandera Co. TX 60 C2
Bandon OR 28 A1
Bangor ME 83 D1
Bangor MI 75 E4
Bangor PA 93 F3
Bangor WI 73 F2
Bangs TX 59 D4
Banks OR 20 B1
Banks Co. GA 121 D3
Banner Co. NE 33 F3
Banner Elk NC 111 F4
Banner Hill TN 111 E4
Bannertown NC 112 A3
Banning CA 53 D2
Bannockburn IL 203 C2
Bannock Co. ID 31 E1
Banquete TX 63 F2
Bantam CT 94 C3
Baraboo WI 74 A2
Baraga MI 65 F4
Baraga Co. MI 65 F4
Barataria LA 134 B3
Barber Co. KS 43 D4
Barberton OH 91 E3
Barbour Co. AL 128 B3
Barbour Co. WV 102 A2
Barbourmeade KY 230 F1
Barboursville WV 101 E4
Barbourville KY 110 C2
Bardstown KY 110 A1
Bardwell KY 108 C2
Bardwell TX 59 F3
Bareville PA 146 A2
Bargersville IN 99 F1
Bar Harbor ME 83 D2
Barker NY 78 B3
Barling AR 116 C1
Barlow KY 108 C2
Bar Mills ME 82 B3
Barnegat NJ 147 E4
Barnegat Light NJ 147 E4
Barnegat Pines NJ 147 E3
Barnes Co. ND 19 D4
Barnesville GA 129 D1
Barnesville MN 19 F4
Barnesville OH 101 F1
Barneveld WI 74 A3
Barnhart MO 98 A4
Barnsboro NJ 146 C4
Barnsdall OK 51 F1
Barnstable MA 151 F3
Barnstable Co. MA 151 E4
Barnum MN 64 C4
Bar Nunn WY 33 D1
Barnwell SC 130 B1
Barnwell Co. SC 130 B1
Baroda MI 89 E1
Barrackville WV 102 A1
Barre MA 150 B1
Barre VT 81 E2
Barren Co. KY 110 A2
Barre Plains MA 150 B1
Barrett TX 132 B3
Barrington IL 203 B2
Barrington NH 81 F4
Barrington NJ 248 D4
Barrington RI 151 D3
Barrington Hills IL 203 A2
Barron WI 67 E3
Barron Co. WI 67 E3
Barrow AK 154 C1
Barrow Co. GA 121 D3
Barry IL 97 F1
Barry Co. MI 75 F4
Barry Co. MO 106 C2
Barstow CA 53 D1
Barstow MD 144 C4
Bartelso IL 98 B3
Bartholomew Co. IN 99 F2
Bartlesville OK 51 F1
Bartlett IL 203 A3
Bartlett NE 35 D2
Bartlett NH 81 F2
Bartlett TN 118 B1
Bartlett TX 61 E1
Barton MD 102 C1
Barton VT 81 E1
Barton Co. KS 43 D3
Barton Co. MO 106 B1
Bartonsville MD 144 A1
Bartonville IL 88 B3
Bartow FL 140 C2
Bartow Co. GA 120 B3
Barview OR 20 A4
Basalt CO 40 C2
Basalt ID 23 E4
Basehor KS 96 B2
Basile LA 133 E2
Basin MT 15 E4
Basin WY 24 C3
Basin City WA 13 E4
Baskett KY 99 E4
Basking Ridge NJ 148 A4
Bassett NE 35 D1
Bassett VA 112 B2
Bass Harbor ME 83 D2
Bass Lake IN 89 E2
Bastrop LA 125 F2
Bastrop TX 61 E2
Bastrop Co. TX 61 E2
Basye VA 102 C3
Batavia IL 88 C1
Batavia IA 87 E3
Batavia NY 78 B3
Batavia OH 100 B2
Batesburg-Leesville SC 122 A4
Bates Co. MO 96 B4
Batesville AR 107 F4
Batesville IN 100 A2
Batesville MS 118 B3
Batesville TX 60 C3
Bath ME 82 C3
Bath MI 76 A3
Bath NY 78 C4
Bath PA 93 F3
Bath Co. KY 100 C4
Bath Co. VA 102 B4
Baton Rouge LA 134 A2
Battle Creek IA 72 A4
Battle Creek MI 75 F4
Battle Creek NE 35 E2
Battlefield MO 107 D2
Battle Ground IN 89 E4
Battle Ground WA 20 C1
Battle Lake MN 19 F4
Battlement Mesa CO 40 B2
Baudette MN 64 A1
Baumstown PA 146 B2
Bauxite AR 117 E2
Bawcomville LA 125 E2
Baxley GA 129 F3
Baxter IA 87 D1
Baxter MN 64 A4
Baxter TN 110 A4
Baxter Co. AR 107 E4
Baxter Estates NY 241 G2
Baxter Sprs. KS 106 B2
Bay AR 108 A4
Bayard IA 86 B1
Bayard NE 33 F2
Bayard NM 55 F2
Bayboro NC 115 D3
Bay City MI 76 B2
Bay City OR 20 B2
Bay City TX 61 F3
Bay Co. FL 136 C2
Bay Co. MI 76 B2
Bayfield CO 40 C4
Bayfield WI 65 D4
Bayfield Co. WI 65 D4
Bay Harbor Islands FL 233 C4
Bay Head NJ 147 E3
Bay Hill FL 246 B3
Baylor Co. TX 59 D1
Bay Minette AL 135 E1
Bayonet Pt. FL 140 B2
Bayonne NJ 148 B4
Bayou Cane LA 134 A3
Bayou George FL 136 C2
Bayou Goula LA 134 A2
Bayou La Batre AL 135 E2
Bayou Vista LA 134 A3
Bayou Vista TX 132 B4
Bay Park NY 241 G5
Bay Pines FL 266 A3
Bay Pt. CA 259 D1
Bayport MN 67 D4
Bayport NY 149 D4
Bay Ridge MD 144 C3
Bay St. Louis MS 134 C2
Bay Shore NY 149 D4
Bayshore Gardens FL 266 B5
Bay Side NJ 147 E4
Bayside WI 234 D1
Bay Sprs. MS 126 C3
Baytown TX 132 B3
Bay View OH 91 D2
Bay Vil. OH 204 D2
Bayville NJ 147 E3
Bayville NY 148 C3
Beach ND 17 F4
Beach City OH 91 E3
Beach City TX 132 B3
Beach Haven NJ 147 E4
Beach Haven Gardens NJ 147 E4
Beach Haven Terrace NJ 147 E4
Beachwood NJ 147 E3
Beachwood OH 204 G2
Beacon IA 87 D2
Beacon NY 148 B1
Beacon Falls CT 149 D1
Beadle Co. SD 27 D3
Bealeton VA 103 D3
Beals ME 83 E2
Bean Sta. TN 111 D3
Bear DE 145 E1
Bear Creek AL 119 E3
Bearden AR 117 E4
Beardstown IL 98 A1
Bear Lake Co. ID 31 F2
Bear River City UT 31 E3
Beasley TX 132 A4
Beatrice AL 127 F4
Beatrice NE 35 F4
Beatty NV 45 F2
Beattyville KY 110 C1
Beatyestown NJ 94 A4
Beaufort NC 115 E4
Beaufort SC 130 C2
Beaufort Co. NC 113 F4
Beaufort Co. SC 130 C3
Beaumont CA 53 D2
Beaumont MS 135 D1
Beaumont TX 132 C3
Beaumont Place TX 220 D2
Beauregard Par. LA 133 D2
Beaver OK 50 C1
Beaver PA 91 F3
Beaver UT 39 D3
Beaver WV 111 F1
Beaver City NE 42 C1
Beaver Co. OK 50 C1
Beaver Co. PA 91 F3
Beaver Co. UT 39 D3
Beavercreek OH 100 C1
Beaver Crossing NE 35 E4
Beaverdale PA 92 B4
Beaver Dam KY 109 E1
Beaver Dam WI 74 B2
Beaver Falls PA 91 F3
Beaverhead Co. MT 23 D2
Beaver Meadows PA 93 E3
Beaver Sprs. PA 93 D3
Beaverton MI 76 A2
Beaverton OR 20 C2
Beavertown PA 93 D3
Bechtelsville PA 146 B1
Beckemeyer IL 98 B3
Becker MN 66 C3
Becker Co. MN 19 F3
Beckett NJ 146 C4
Beckham Co. OK 50 C3
Beckley WV 111 F1
Beckville TX 124 C3
Bedford IN 99 F3
Bedford IA 86 B3
Bedford KY 100 A3
Bedford MA 151 D1
Bedford NH 95 D1
Bedford NY 148 C2
Bedford OH 204 G3
Bedford PA 102 C1
Bedford TX 207 B2
Bedford VA 112 B1
Bedford Co. PA 92 C4
Bedford Co. TN 120 A1
Bedford Co. VA 112 B1
Bedford Hts. OH 204 G3
Bedford Hills NY 148 C2
Bedford Park IL 203 D5
Beebe AR 117 F2
Bee Cave TX 61 E1
Beech Bottom WV 91 F4
Beech Creek PA 93 D3
Beecher IL 89 D2
Beech Grove IN 99 F1
Beechwood Vil. KY 230 E1
Bee Co. TX 61 E4
Beemer NE 35 F2
Bee Ridge FL 140 B4
Beersheba Sprs. TN 120 A1
Beesleys Pt. NJ 147 F4
Beeville TX 61 E4
Beggs OK 51 F2
Bel Air MD 145 D1
Belcamp MD 145 D1
Belchertown MA 150 A1
Belcourt ND 18 C1
Belding MI 75 F3
Belen NM 48 C4
Belfair WA 12 C3
Belfast ME 82 C2
Belfast NY 78 B4
Belfast PA 93 F3
Belfield ND 18 A4
Belford NJ 147 E1
Belfry MT 24 B2
Belgium WI 75 D2
Belgrade MN 66 B3
Belgrade MT 23 F1
Belgrade Lakes ME 82 B2
Belhaven NC 115 E3
Belinda City TN 109 F4
Belington WV 102 A2
Belknap Co. NH 81 F4
Bell CA 228 D3
Bellair FL 222 C4
Bellaire MI 69 F4
Bellaire OH 101 F1
Bellaire TX 132 A3
Bellamy AL 127 E2
Bella Villa MO 256 B3
Bella Vista AR 106 C3
Bella Vista CA 28 C4
Bellbrook OH 100 C1
Bell Buckle TN 119 F1
Bell Co. KY 110 C3
Bell Co. TX 61 E1
Belle MO 97 F4
Belle WV 101 F4
Belleair FL 140 B2
Belleair Beach FL 140 B2
Belleair Bluffs FL 266 A2
Belle Ctr. OH 90 C4
Belle Chasse LA 134 B3
Bellefontaine OH 90 B4
Bellefontaine Neighbors MO 256 C1
Bellefonte AR 107 D3
Bellefonte DE 146 B4
Bellefonte KY 101 D3
Bellefonte PA 92 C3
Belle Fourche SD 25 F3
Belle Glade FL 143 E1
Belle Haven VA 114 B3
Belle Isle FL 141 D1
Bellemeade KY 230 F2
Belle Plaine IA 87 E1
Belle Plaine KS 43 E4
Belle Plaine MN 66 C4
Belle Rose LA 134 A3
Bellerose NY 241 G3
Bellerose Terrace NY 241 G3
Belle Terre NY 149 D3
Belle Vernon PA 92 A4
Belleview FL 139 D4
Belleville IL 98 B3
Belleville KS 43 E1
Belleville MI 90 C1
Belleville NJ 148 B4
Belleville PA 92 C4
Belleville WI 74 B3
Bellevue ID 22 C4
Bellevue IL 88 B3
Bellevue IA 74 A4
Bellevue KY 204 B3
Bellevue MI 76 A4
Bellevue NE 86 A2
Bellevue OH 204 B3
Bellevue PA 92 A4
Bellevue WA 12 C3
Bellevue WI 74 C1
Bellflower CA 228 D3
Bell Gardens CA 228 D3
Bellingham MA 150 C2
Bellingham WA 12 C1
Bellmawr NJ 146 C3
Bellmead TX 59 E4
Bellows Falls VT 81 E4
Bellport NY 149 D4
Bells TN 108 C4
Bells TX 59 F1
Bellview FL 247 A1
Bellville OH 91 D3
Bellville TX 61 F2
Bellwood IL 203 C4
Bellwood NE 35 E3
Bellwood PA 92 C4
Bellwood VA 254 B3
Belmar NJ 147 F2
Belmond IA 72 C3
Belmont CA 259 B5
Belmont MA 151 D1
Belmont MS 119 D3
Belmont NH 81 F4
Belmont NY 92 C1
Belmont NC 122 A1

Entries in **bold black** indicate counties or parishes.
Entries in **bold color** indicate cities with detailed inset maps.

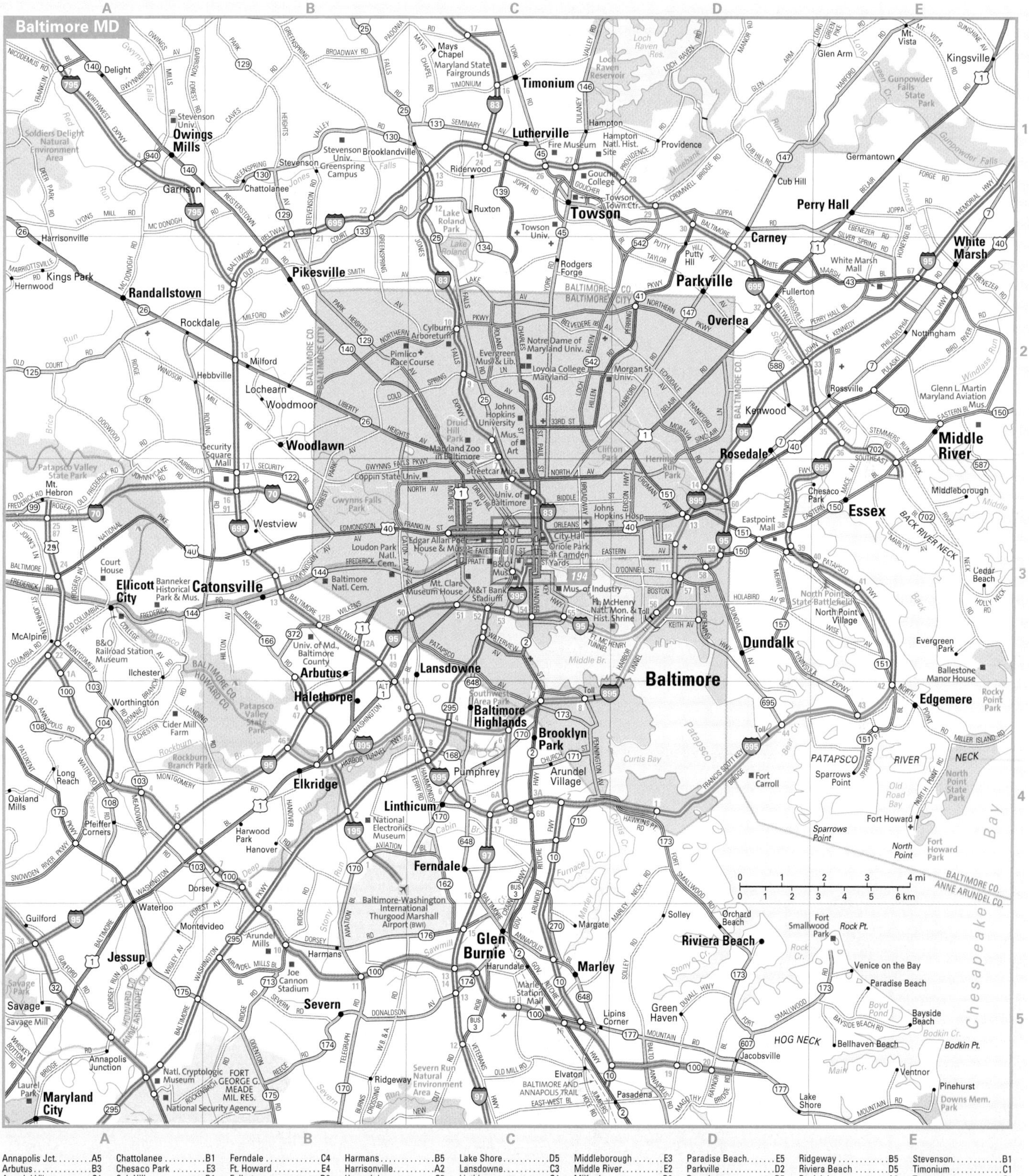
Baltimore MD
Baltimore
Towson
Timonium
Lutherville
Owings Mills
Pikesville
Randallstown
Carney
Parkville
Perry Hall
White Marsh
Overlea
Rosedale
Middle River
Essex
Dundalk
Edgemere
Catonsville
Ellicott City
Woodlawn
Arbutus
Halethorpe
Lansdowne
Baltimore Highlands
Brooklyn Park
Linthicum
Elkridge
Ferndale
Glen Burnie
Marley
Riviera Beach
Jessup
Severn
Maryland City
Baltimore-Washington International Thurgood Marshall Airport (BWI)
National Security Agency
Patapsco Valley State Park
Gunpowder Falls State Park
North Point State Park
Chesapeake Bay
Loch Raven Reservoir
0 1 2 3 4 mi
0 1 2 3 4 5 6 km

Annapolis Jct. A5
Arbutus B3
Arundel Vil. C4
Baltimore D3
Baltimore Highlands ... C4
Bayside Beach E5
Bellhaven Beach E5
Brooklandville C1
Brooklyn Park C4
Carney D1
Catonsville B3
Cedar Beach E3
Chattolanee B1
Chesaco Park E3
Cub Hill D1
Delight A1
Dorsey B4
Dundalk D3
Edgemere E4
Elkridge B4
Ellicott City A3
Elvaton C5
Essex E3
Evergreen Park E3
Ferndale C4
Ft. Howard E4
Fullerton D2
Garrison A1
Germantown E1
Glen Arm E1
Glen Burnie C5
Green Haven D5
Guilford A5
Halethorpe B4
Hampton C1
Hanover B4
Harmans B5
Harrisonville A2
Harundale C5
Harwood Park B4
Hebbville A2
Hernwood A2
Ilchester A3
Jacobsville D5
Jessup A5
Kenwood D2
Kings Park A2
Kingsville E1
Lake Shore D5
Lansdowne C3
Linthicum C4
Lipins Corner C5
Lochearn B2
Long Reach A4
Lutherville C1
Margate C5
Marley C5
Maryland City A5
Mays Chapel C1
McAlpine A3
Middleborough E3
Middle River E2
Milford B2
Montevideo A5
Mt. Hebron A3
Mt. Vista E1
N. Point Vil. E3
Nottingham E2
Oakland Mills A4
Orchard Beach D5
Overlea D2
Owings Mills A1
Paradise Beach E5
Parkville D2
Pasadena D5
Perry Hall E1
Pfeiffer Corners A4
Pikesville B2
Pinehurst E5
Providence D1
Pumphrey C4
Putty Hll D2
Randallstown A2
Riderwood C1
Ridgeway B5
Riviera Beach D5
Rockdale A2
Rodgers Forge C2
Rosedale D2
Rossville E2
Ruxton C1
Savage A5
Severn B5
Solley D5
S. Gate C5
Sparrows Pt. E4
Stevenson B1
Timonium C1
Towson C1
Venice on the Bay E5
Ventnor E5
Waterloo A5
Westview B3
White Marsh E2
Woodlawn B2
Woodmoor B2
Worthington A4

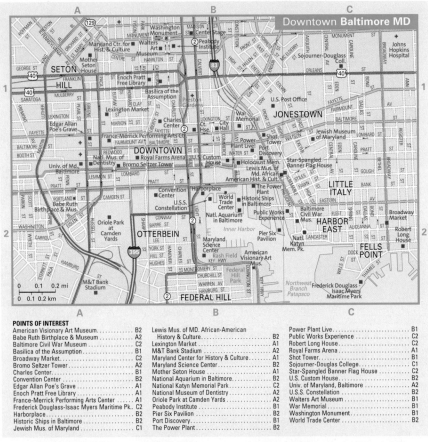

Figures after entries indicate page number and grid reference.

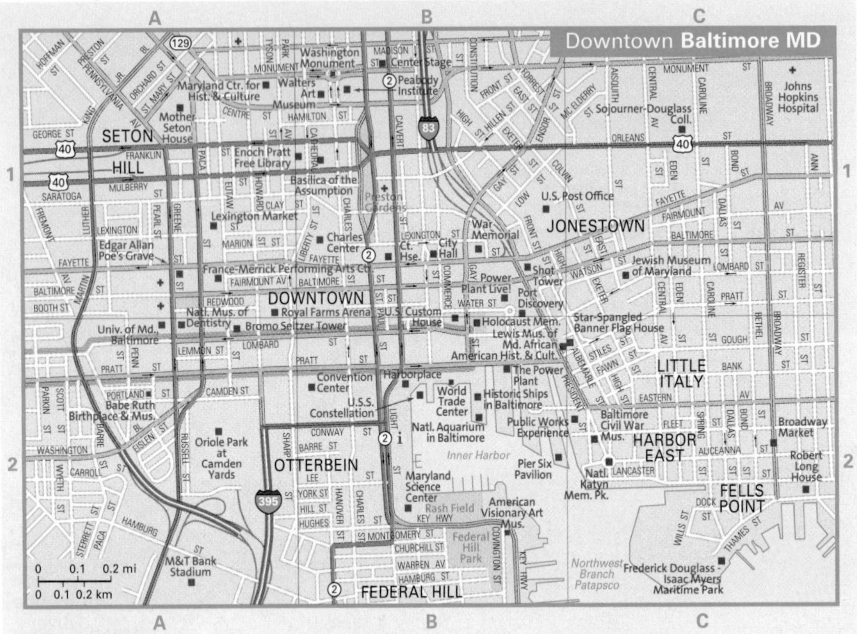

POINTS OF INTEREST

American Visionary Art Museum	B2	Lewis Mus. of MD. African-American History & Culture	B2	Power Plant Live	B1
Babe Ruth Birthplace & Museum	A2	Lexington Market	A1	Public Works Experience	C2
Baltimore Civil War Museum	C2	M&T Bank Stadium	A2	Robert Long House	C2
Basilica of the Assumption	B1	Maryland Center for History & Culture	A1	Royal Farms Arena	A1
Broadway Market	C2	Maryland Science Center	B2	Shot Tower	B1
Bromo Seltzer Tower	A2	Mother Seton House	A1	Sojourner-Douglas College	C1
Charles Center	B1	National Aquarium in Baltimore	B2	Star-Spangled Banner Flag House	C2
Convention Center	B2	National Katyn Memorial Park	C2	U.S. Custom House	B2
Edgar Allan Poe's Grave	A1	National Museum of Dentistry	A2	Univ. of Maryland, Baltimore	A2
Enoch Pratt Free Library	A1	Oriole Park at Camden Yards	A2	U.S.S. Constellation	B2
France-Merrick Performing Arts Center	A1	Peabody Institute	B1	Walters Art Museum	B1
Frederick Douglass-Isaac Myers Maritime Pk.	C2	Pier Six Pavilion	B2	War Memorial	B1
Harborplace	B2	Port Discovery	B1	Washington Monument	B1
Historic Ships in Baltimore	B2	The Power Plant	B2	World Trade Center	B2
Jewish Mus. of Maryland	C1				

Belmont WV 101 F2
Belmont WI 74 A4
Belmont Corner ME 82 C2
Belmont Co. OH 101 F1
Bel-Nor MO 256 B2
Beloit KS 43 E1
Beloit OH 91 F3
Beloit WI 74 B4
Belpre OH 101 E2
Bel-Ridge MO 256 B2
Belt MT 15 F3
Belton KY 109 E2
Belton MO 96 B3
Belton SC 121 C3
Belton TX 59 E4
Beltrami Co. MN 64 A2
Beltsville MD 144 B3
Belvedere CA 259 B2
Belvedere SC 121 F4
Belvedere Park GA 190 E4
Belvidere IL 74 B4
Belvidere NJ 93 F3
Belwood NC 121 F1
Belzoni MS 126 B1
Bement IL 98 C1
Bemidji MN 64 A3
Bemiss GA 137 F1
Benavides TX 63 E2
Ben Avon PA 250 A1
Benbrook TX 207 A3
Bend OR 21 D3
Bendersville PA 103 E1
Benewah Co. ID 14 B3
Benham KY 111 D2
Ben Hill Co. GA 129 E3
Benicia CA 36 B3
Benjamin TX 58 C1
Benkelman NE 42 B1
Benld IL 98 B2
Ben Lomond CA 44 A2
Bennet NE 35 F4
Bennett CO 41 E1
Bennett Co. SD 26 B4
Bennettsville SC 122 C2
Bennington KS 43 E2
Bennington NE 35 F3
Bennington NH 81 E4
Bennington VT 94 C1
Bennington Co. VT 81 D4
Benoit MS 118 A4
Bensenville IL 203 C4
Bensley VA 113 E1
Benson AZ 55 D3
Benson MD 144 C1
Benson MN 66 A3
Benson NC 123 D1
Benson Co. ND 19 D2
Bent Co. CO 41 F3
Bent Creek NC 121 E1
Bentleyville OH 204 G3
Bentleyville PA 92 A4
Benton AR 117 E2
Benton IL 98 C4
Benton KS 43 F4
Benton KY 109 D2
Benton LA 124 C2
Benton ME 82 C2
Benton MO 108 B2
Benton PA 93 E2
Benton TN 120 C1
Benton WI 74 A4
Benton City WA 21 E1
Benton Co. AR 106 B3
Benton Co. IN 89 D3
Benton Co. IA 87 E1
Benton Co. MN 66 C2
Benton Co. MS 118 C2
Benton Co. MO 97 D4
Benton Co. OR 20 B3
Benton Co. TN 109 D4
Benton Co. WA 21 E1
Benton Harbor MI 89 E1
Bentonia MS 126 B2
Bentonville AR 106 C3
Benzie Co. MI 69 F4
Benzonia MI 69 E4
Berea KY 110 C1
Berea OH 91 E2
Berea SC 217 A2
Beresford SD 35 F1
Bergen NY 78 B3
Bergen Co. NJ 148 B3
Bergenfield NJ 148 B3
Bergholz OH 91 F4
Bergman AR 107 D3
Berino NM 56 C3
Berkeley CA 36 B4
Berkeley IL 203 C4
Berkeley MO 256 B1
Berkeley RI 150 C3
Berkeley Co. SC 131 D1
Berkeley Co. WV 103 D2
Berkeley Hts. NJ 148 A4
Berkeley Sprs. WV 102 C1
Berkley MA 151 D3
Berkley MI 210 B2
Berks Co. PA 146 B1
Berkshire CT 149 D2
Berkshire Co. MA 94 C2
Berlin CT 149 E1
Berlin GA 137 F1
Berlin MD 114 C2
Berlin MA 150 C1
Berlin NH 81 F2
Berlin NJ 147 D3
Berlin OH 91 E4
Berlin PA 102 C1
Berlin WI 74 B1
Berlin Hts. OH 91 D2
Bermuda Run NC 112 A4
Bernalillo NM 48 C3
Bernalillo Co. NM 48 C3
Bernardston MA 94 C1
Bernardsville NJ 148 A4
Berne IN 90 A3
Bernice LA 125 E2
Bernice OK 106 B3
Bernie MO 108 B3
Bernstadt KY 110 C2
Bernville PA 146 A1
Berrien Co. GA 129 E4
Berrien Co. MI 89 E1
Berrien Sprs. MI 89 E1
Berry AL 119 E4
Berryville AR 106 C3
Berryville TX 124 A3
Berryville VA 103 D2
Berthold ND 18 B2
Berthoud CO 33 E4
Bertie Co. NC 113 F4
Bertram IA 87 F1
Bertram TX 61 D1
Bertrand MI 89 F1
Bertrand MO 108 B2
Bertrand NE 35 D4
Berwick LA 134 A3
Berwick ME 82 A4
Berwick PA 93 E3
Berwyn IL 89 D1
Berwyn PA 146 B3
Berwyn Hts. MD 270 E2
Bessemer AL 127 F1
Bessemer MI 65 E4
Bessemer PA 91 F3
Bessemer City NC 122 A1
Bethalto IL 98 B3
Bethany CT 149 D1
Bethany IL 98 C1
Bethany MO 86 C4
Bethany OK 51 E3
Bethany WV 91 F4
Bethany Beach DE 145 F4
Bethel AK 154 B3
Bethel CT 148 C2
Bethel DE 145 E4
Bethel ME 82 B2
Bethel NC 113 E4
Bethel OH 100 C2
Bethel VT 81 E3
Bethel VA 103 D3
Bethel Acres OK 51 F3
Bethel Hts. AR 106 C3
Bethel Park PA 92 A4
Bethel Sprs. TN 119 D1
Bethesda MD 144 B3
Bethesda OH 101 F1
Bethlehem CT 149 D1
Bethlehem GA 121 D4
Bethlehem MD 145 D4
Bethlehem NH 81 F2
Bethlehem NC 111 F4
Bethlehem PA 146 C1
Bethlehem Ctr. NY 188 D3
Bethpage NY 148 C4
Betmar Acres FL 140 C2
Bettendorf IA 88 A2
Bettsville OH 90 C2
Beulah CO 41 E3
Beulah MI 69 E4
Beulah MS 118 A4
Beulah ND 18 B3
Beulaville NC 123 E2
Beverly MA 151 F1
Beverly NJ 147 D3
Beverly OH 101 E1
Beverly WV 102 B3
Beverly Beach FL 139 E4
Beverly Beach MD 144 C3
Beverly Hills CA 52 C2
Beverly Hills FL 140 B1
Beverly Hills MI 210 B2
Beverly Hills MO 256 B2
Beverly Shores IN 89 E2
Bevier MO 97 E1
Bevil Oaks TX 132 C2
Bevis OH 204 A1
Bexar Co. TX 61 D2
Bexley OH 206 C2
Bibb Co. AL 127 F1
Bibb Co. GA 129 D2
Bicknell IN 99 E3
Bicknell UT 39 E3
Biddeford ME 82 B4
Bienville Par. LA 125 D2
Big Bear City CA 53 D2
Big Bear Lake CA 53 D2
Big Beaver PA 91 F3
Big Bend WI 74 C3
Big Chimney WV 101 F3
Big Coppitt Key FL 143 D4
Big Delta AK 154 C2
Big Flats NY 93 D1
Bigfork MT 15 D2
Biggs CA 36 B2
Big Horn Co. MT 24 C2
Big Horn Co. WY 24 C3
Big Lake MN 66 C3
Big Lake TX 58 A4
Big Lake WA 12 C2
Biglerville PA 103 E1
Big Oak Flat CA 37 D4
Big Pine CA 37 E4
Big Pine Key FL 143 D4
Big Piney WY 32 A1
Big Rapids MI 75 F2
Big River CA 46 B4
Big Run PA 92 B3
Big Sandy MT 16 B2
Big Sandy TN 109 D3
Big Sandy TX 124 B2
Big Sky MT 23 F2
Big Spr. TX 58 A3
Big Sprs. NE 34 B3
Big Stone City SD 27 F2
Big Stone Co. MN 27 F2
Big Stone Gap VA 111 E2
Big Timber MT 24 A1
Big Water UT 47 D1
Big Wells TX 60 C4
Billerica MA 95 E1
Billings MO 106 C2
Billings MT 24 C1
Billings NY 148 B1
Billings OK 51 E1
Billings Co. ND 18 A3
Billington Hts. NY 78 B4
Biloxi MS 135 D2
Biltmore Forest NC 121 E1
Bingen PA 189 B2
Binger OK 51 D3
Bingham ME 82 B1
Bingham Co. ID 23 E4
Bingham Farms MI 210 B2
Binghamton NY 93 E1
Biola CA 44 C2
Birch Bay WA 12 C1
Birch Run MI 76 B3
Birch Tree MO 107 F2
Birchwood Vil. MN 235 E1
Bird City KS 42 B1
Bird Island MN 66 B4
Birdsboro PA 146 B2
Birmingham AL 119 F4
Birmingham MI 76 C4
Birnamwood WI 68 B4
Biron WI 74 A1
Bisbee AZ 55 E4
Biscayne Park FL 233 B4
Biscoe AR 117 F2
Biscoe NC 122 C1
Bishop CA 37 E4
Bishop TX 63 F2
Bishopville SC 122 B3
Bismarck MO 108 A1
Bismarck ND 18 C4
Bison SD 26 A2
Bithlo FL 141 D1
Bitter Sprs. AZ 47 D1
Biwabik MN 64 C3
Bixby OK 106 A4
Blackbird DE 145 E1
Black Canyon City AZ 47 D4
Black Creek NC 123 E1
Black Creek WI 68 C4
Black Diamond WA 12 C3
Blackduck MN 64 A3
Black Eagle MT 15 F3
Black Earth WI 74 A3
Blackfoot ID 31 E1
Blackford Co. IN 90 A4
Black Forest CO 41 E2
Blackhawk SD 26 A3
Black Hawk Co. IA 73 E4
Black Jack MO 256 B1
Black Lick PA 92 B4
Blacklick Estates OH 206 C3
Black Mtn. NC 121 E1
Black River NY 79 E1
Black River Falls WI 73 F1
Black Rock AR 107 F4
Black Rock NM 48 A3
Blacksburg SC 122 A1
Blacksburg VA 112 A2
Blackshear GA 129 F4
Blackstone MA 150 C2
Blackstone VA 113 D2
Blackville SC 130 B1
Blackwell OK 51 E1
Blackwells GA 120 C3
Blackwood NJ 146 C3
Bladenboro NC 123 D3
Bladen Co. NC 123 D2
Bladensburg MD 270 E3
Blades DE 145 E4
Blaine ME 85 E2
Blaine MN 67 D3
Blaine TN 110 C4
Blaine WA 12 C1
Blaine Co. ID 23 D4
Blaine Co. MT 16 B2
Blaine Co. NE 34 C2
Blaine Co. OK 51 D2
Blair NE 35 F3
Blair OK 51 D4
Blair WI 73 F1
Blair Co. PA 92 C4
Blairs VA 112 C3
Blairstown IA 87 E1
Blairstown NJ 93 F3
Blairsville GA 121 D2

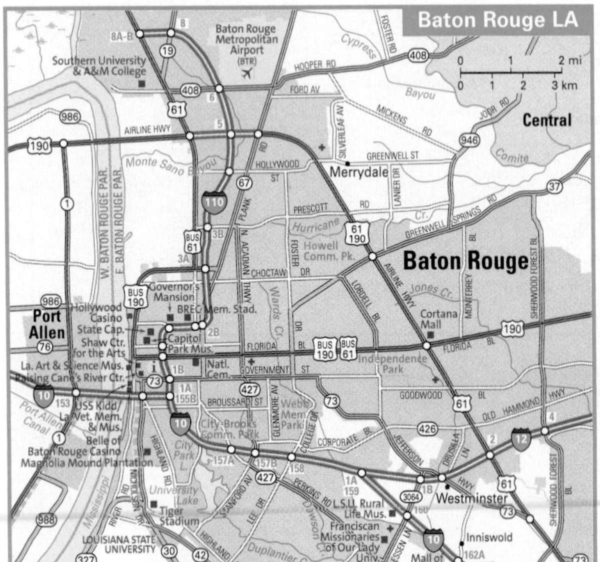

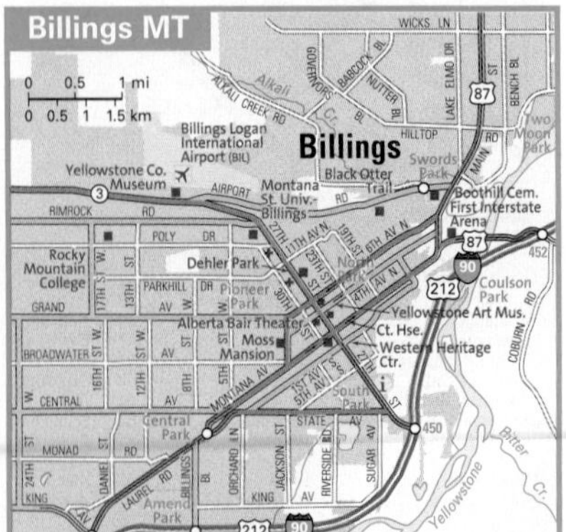

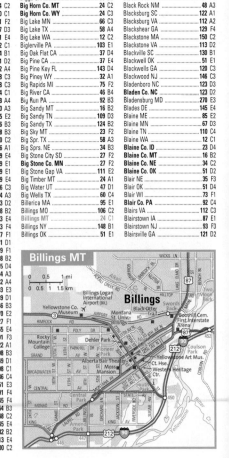

Entries in **bold black** indicate counties or parishes.
Entries in **bold color** indicate cities with detailed inset maps.

Blairsville PA 92 B4
Blakely GA 128 C4
Blakely PA 93 F2
Blakes VA 113 F1
Blanca CO 41 D4
Blanchard LA 124 C2
Blanchard OK 51 E3
Blanchard PA 93 D3
Blanchardville WI 74 A3
Blanchester OH 100 C2
Blanco TX 61 D2
Blanco Co. TX 61 D1
Bland MO 97 F4
Bland VA 112 A2
Bland Co. VA 111 F2
Blanding UT 40 A4
Blandinsville IL 87 F4
Blandon PA 146 B1
Blasdell NY 78 B3
Blauvelt NY 148 B3
Blawenburg NJ 147 D1
Blawnox PA 250 C1
Bleckley Co. GA 129 E2
Bledsoe Co. TN 110 B4
Blennerhassett WV 101 E2
Blessing TX 61 F3
Bliss ID 30 C1
Bliss Corner MA 238 C2
Blissfield MI 90 B1
Blocher IN 100 A3
Bloomdale OH 90 C2
Bloomer WI 67 F3
Bloomfield CT 150 A3
Bloomfield IN 99 E2
Bloomfield IA 87 E3
Bloomfield KY 100 A4
Bloomfield MO 108 B2
Bloomfield NE 35 E1
Bloomfield NJ 148 B4
Bloomfield NM 48 B1
Bloomfield NY 78 C3
Bloomfield WI 74 C4
Bloomfield Hills MI 210 B1
Bloomingburg OH 100 C1
Bloomingdale FL 266 D2
Bloomingdale IL 203 B3
Bloomingdale NJ 148 A3
Bloomingdale TN 111 E3
Blooming Grove NY 148 B1
Blooming Grove TX 59 F3
Blooming Prairie MN 73 D2
Bloomington CA 229 H2
Bloomington ID 31 F2
Bloomington IL 88 C4
Bloomington IN 99 F2
Bloomington MN 67 D4
Bloomington TX 61 F4
Bloomington WI 73 F3
Bloomsburg PA 93 E3
Bloomsbury NJ 146 C1
Bloomville OH 90 C3
Blossburg PA 93 D2
Blossom TX 116 A4
Blount Co. AL 119 F3
Blount Co. TN 110 C4
Blountstown FL 137 D2
Blountsville AL 119 F3
Blountville TN 111 E3
Blowing Rock NC 111 F4
Bloxom VA 114 C2
Blue Anchor NJ 147 D4
Blue Ash OH 100 B2
Blue Bell PA 146 C2
Blue Diamond NV 46 A2
Blue Earth MN 72 C2
Blue Earth Co. MN 72 C1
Bluefield VA 111 F2
Bluefield WV 111 F2
Blue Grass IA 87 F2
Blue Hill ME 83 D2
Blue Hill NE 35 D4
Blue Hills CT 150 A3
Blue Island IL 203 D6
Blue Lake CA 28 B4

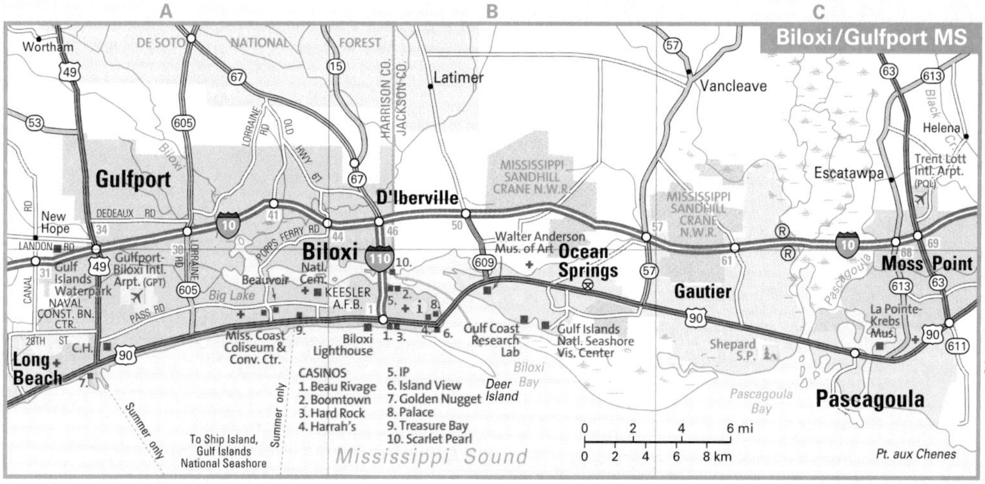

Biloxi A2
D'Iberville B1
Escatawpa C1
Fontainebleau B2
Gautier C2
Gulfport A1
Helena C1
Latimer B1
Long Beach A2
Moss Pt. C2
New Hope A1
Ocean Sprs. B2
Pascagoula C2
Vancleave C1
Wortham A1

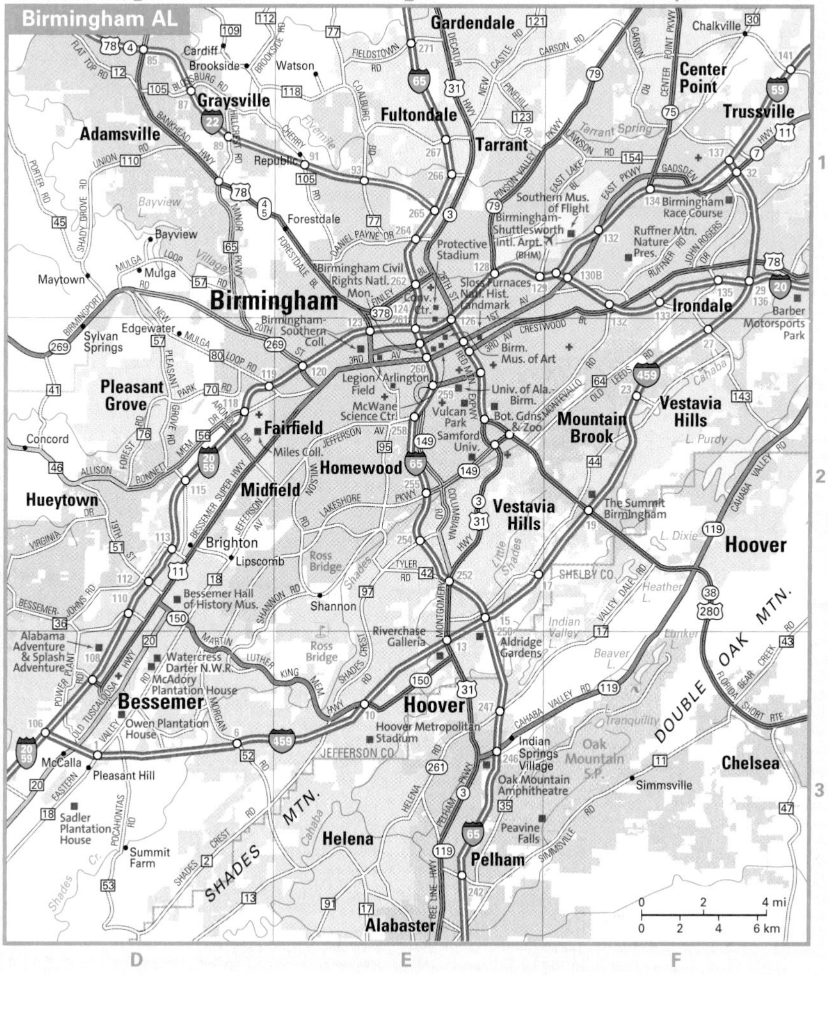

Adamsville D1
Alabaster E3
Bayview D1
Bessemer D3
Birmingham E1
Brighton D2
Brookside D1
Cardiff D1
Center Pt. F1
Chalkville F1
Chelsea F3
Concord D2
Edgewater D2
Fairfield D2
Forestdale E1
Fultondale E1
Gardendale E1
Graysville D1
Helena E3
Homewood E2
Hoover E3
Hueytown D2
Indian Sprs. Vil. E3
Irondale F1
Lipscomb D2
Maytown D1
McCalla D3
Midfield D2
Mtn. Brook F2
Mulga D1
Pelham E3
Pleasant Grove D2
Pleasant Hill D3
Republic E1
Shannon E2
Simmsville F3
Summit Farm D3
Sylvan Sprs. D2
Tarrant City E1
Trussville F1
Vestavia Hills E2
Watson E1

Blue Mound IL 98 C1
Blue Mound TX 207 A2
Blue Mounds WI 74 A3
Blue Mtn. MS 118 C2
Blue Pt. NY 149 D4
Blue Rapids KS 43 F1
Blue Ridge AL 128 A2
Blue Ridge GA 120 C2
Blue Ridge TX 59 F2
Blue Ridge VA 112 B1
Blue Ridge Manor KY 230 F2
Blue River CO 41 D2
Blue Sprs. MO 96 C2
Bluff UT 40 A4
Bluff City TN 111 E3
Bluffdale UT 31 E4
Bluffs IL 98 A1
Bluffton IN 90 A3
Bluffton OH 90 B3
Bluffton SC 130 C3
Bluford IL 98 C4
Blunt SD 26 C3
Blythe CA 53 F3
Blythe GA 129 F1
Blytheville AR 108 B4
Boalsburg PA 92 C3
Boardman OH 91 F3
Boardman OR 21 E1
Boardman Bridge CT 148 C1
Boaz AL 120 A3
Boaz WV 101 F2
Bobtown PA 102 A1
Boca Grande FL 140 C4
Boca Raton FL 143 F1
Bodega Bay CA 36 A3
Bodfish CA 45 E4
Boerne TX 61 D2
Bogalusa LA 134 C1
Bogart GA 121 D4
Bogata TX 116 A4
Boger City NC 122 A1
Bogota NJ 240 D1
Bogue NC 115 D4
Bogue Chitto MS 127 D2
Bohners Lake WI 74 C4
Boiling Spr. Lakes NC 123 E3
Boiling Sprs. NC 121 F1
Boiling Sprs. PA 93 D4
Boiling Sprs. SC 121 F2
Boise ID 22 B4
Boise City OK 50 A1
Boise Co. ID 22 C4
Bokchito OK 59 F1
Bokeelia FL 142 C1
Bokoshe OK 116 B1
Boley OK 51 F3
Boling TX 61 F3
Bolingbrook IL 89 D2
Bolivar MO 107 D1
Bolivar NY 92 C1
Bolivar OH 91 E3
Bolivar TN 118 C1
Bolivar WV 144 A2
Bolivar Co. MS 118 A4
Bolivia NC 123 E3
Bollinger Co. MO 108 B2
Bolton CT 150 A3
Bolton MS 126 B2
Bolton NC 123 D3
Bolton Landing NY 81 D3
Bon Air VA 113 E1
Bonaire GA 129 D2
Bonanza AR 116 C1
Bonanza OR 29 D2
Bonaparte IA 87 E3
Bond Co. IL 98 B3
Bondsville MA 150 A2
Bonduel WI 68 C4
Bondurant IA 86 C2
Bonesteel SD 35 D1
Bonham TX 59 F1
Bon Homme Co. SD 35 E1
Bonifay FL 136 C1
Bonita CA 258 C2
Bonita Sprs. FL 142 C1
Bonneauville PA 103 E1
Bonner MT 15 D4
Bonner Co. ID 14 B2
Bonners Ferry ID 14 B1
Bonner Sprs. KS 96 B2
Bonne Terre MO 98 A4
Bonnet Shores RI 150 C4
Bonneville Co. ID 23 F4
Bonney Lake WA 262 B5
Bonnieville KY 110 A1
Bono AR 108 A4
Bonsall CA 53 D3
Booker TX 50 B1
Boomer WV 101 F4
Boone CO 41 E3
Boone IA 86 C1
Boone NC 111 F3
Boone Co. AR 107 D3
Boone Co. IL 74 B4
Boone Co. IN 99 F1
Boone Co. IA 86 C1
Boone Co. KY 100 B2
Boone Co. MO 97 E2
Boone Co. NE 35 E3
Boone Co. WV 101 E4
Booneville AR 116 C1
Booneville KY 110 C1
Booneville MS 119 D2
Boonsboro MD 144 A1
Boonton NJ 148 A3
Boonville CA 36 A2
Boonville IN 99 E4
Boonville MO 97 D2
Boonville NY 79 E2
Boonville NC 112 A3
Boothbay ME 82 C3
Boothbay Harbor ME 82 C3
Boothville LA 134 C4
Bootjack CA 37 D4
Borden IN 99 F3
Borden Co. TX 58 B2
Bordentown NJ 147 D2
Borger TX 50 B2
Boron CA 52 C1
Borrego Sprs. CA 53 E3
Boscobel WI 73 F3
Bosque Co. TX 59 E3
Bosque Farms NM 48 C4
Bossier City LA 124 C2
Bossier Par. LA 125 D1
Boston GA 137 E1
Boston MA 151 D1
Boswell IN 89 D4
Boswell OK 59 F1
Boswell PA 92 B4
Botetourt Co. VA 112 B1
Bothell WA 12 C3
Botkins OH 90 B4
Botsford CT 149 D2
Bottineau ND 18 C1
Bottineau Co. ND 18 C1
Botto KY 110 C2
Boulder CO 41 E1
Boulder MT 23 E1
Boulder City NV 46 B2
Boulder Co. CO 41 D1
Boulder Creek CA 44 A2
Boundary Co. ID 14 B1
Bound Brook NJ 147 D1
Bountiful UT 31 E4
Bourbon IN 89 F2
Bourbon MO 97 F4
Bourbon Co. KS 96 B4
Bourbon Co. KY 100 B4
Bourbonnais IL 89 D2
Bourne MA 151 E3
Bouse AZ 54 A1
Boutte LA 134 B3
Bovey MN 64 B3
Bovill ID 14 B4
Bovina TX 49 F4
Bowbells ND 18 B1
Bow Ctr. NH 81 F4
Bowdle SD 27 D2
Bowdoin Ctr. ME 82 B3
Bowdoinham ME 82 B3
Bowdon GA 120 B4
Bowen IL 87 F4
Bowers DE 145 F3
Bowie AZ 55 E3

Figures after entries indicate page number and grid reference.

Bowie MD 144 C3
Bowie TX 59 E1
Bowie Co. TX 116 B4
Bowleys Quarters MD 144 C2
Bowling Green FL 140 C3
Bowling Green KY 109 F2
Bowling Green MO 97 F2
Bowling Green OH 90 C2
Bowling Green VA 103 D4
Bowman GA 121 E3
Bowman ND 25 F1
Bowman SC 130 C1
Bowman Co. ND 25 F1
Bow Mar CO 209 B4
Boxborough MA 150 C1
Box Butte Co. NE 34 A2
Box Elder MT 16 B2
Box Elder SD 26 A3
Box Elder Co. UT 31 D3
Boxford MA 151 F1
Boyce LA 125 E4
Boyce VA 103 D2
Boyceville WI 67 E3
Boyd TX 59 E2
Boyd WI 67 F4
Boyd Co. KY 101 D4
Boyd Co. NE 35 D1
Boyden IA 35 F1
Boydton VA 113 D3
Boyertown PA 146 B2
Boyette FL 140 C3
Boykins VA 113 E3
Boyle MS 118 A4
Boyle Co. KY 110 B1
Boyne City MI 70 B3
Boynton Beach FL 143 F1
Boys Town NE 245 A2
Bozeman MT 23 F1
Braceville IL 88 C2
Bracken Co. KY 100 C3
Brackettville TX 60 B3
Bradbury CA 228 E2
Braddock PA 250 C2
Braddock Hts. MD 144 A1
Braddock Hills PA 250 C2
Bradenton FL 140 B3
Bradenton Beach FL 140 B3
Bradford AR 117 F1
Bradford IL 88 B2
Bradford NH 81 E4
Bradford OH 90 B4
Bradford PA 92 B1
Bradford RI 150 C4
Bradford TN 108 C4
Bradford VT 81 E3
Bradford Co. FL 138 C3
Bradford Co. PA 93 E2
Bradfordville FL 137 E2
Bradford Woods PA 92 A3
Bradley AR 125 D1
Bradley IL 89 D3
Bradley ME 83 D1
Bradley WV 101 F4
Bradley Beach NJ 147 F2
Bradley Co. AR 117 E4

Brandywine MD 144 B4
Brandywine Manor PA 146 B3
Branford CT 149 D2
Branford FL 138 B3
Branson MO 107 D3
Brant Beach NJ 147 E4
Brantley AL 128 A4
Brantley Co. GA 129 F4
Brant Rock MA 151 E2
Braselton GA 121 D3
Brasher Falls NY 80 B1
Bratenahl OH 204 F1
Brattleboro VT 94 C1
Brawley CA 53 E4
Braxton Co. WV 101 F3
Bray OK 51 E4
Braymer MO 96 C1
Brazil IN 99 E1
Brazoria TX 132 A4
Brazoria Co. TX 132 A4
Brazos Co. TX 61 F1
Brea CA 229 F3
Breathitt Co. KY 111 D1
Breaux Bridge LA 133 F2
Breckenridge CO 41 D1
Breckenridge MI 76 A2
Breckenridge MN 27 F1
Breckenridge TX 59 D2
Breckenridge Hills MO 256 B2

Brentwood MO 256 B2
Brentwood NY 149 D4
Brentwood PA 250 B3
Brentwood TN 109 F4
Bressler PA 218 C2
Brevard NC 121 E1
Brevard Co. FL 141 E2
Brewer ME 83 D1
Brewerton NY 79 D3
Brewster MA 151 F3
Brewster MN 72 A2
Brewster NE 34 C2
Brewster NY 148 C2
Brewster OH 91 E3
Brewster WA 13 E2
Brewster Co. TX 62 C3
Brewster Hill NY 148 C1
Brewton AL 135 F1
Briar TX 59 E2
Briarcliff TX 61 D1
Briarcliffe Acres SC 123 D4
Briarcliff Manor NY 148 B2
Briar Creek PA 93 E3
Briarwood KY 230 F1
Briceville TN 110 C4
Brickerville PA 146 A2
Bridge City LA 239 B2
Bridge City TX 132 C3
Bridgehampton NY 149 F3

Bridgewater MA 151 D2
Bridgewater NJ 147 D1
Bridgewater NY 79 E3
Bridgewater SD 27 E4
Bridgewater VA 102 C4
Bridgman MI 89 E1
Bridgton ME 82 B3
Brielle NJ 147 E2
Brier WA 262 B2
Brigantine NJ 147 F4
Brigham City UT 31 E3
Bright IN 100 B2
Brighton AL 195 D2
Brighton CO 41 E1
Brighton IL 98 A2
Brighton IA 87 E2
Brighton MI 76 B4
Brighton NY 78 C3
Brighton TN 118 B1
Brightwaters NY 149 D4
Brightwood VA 102 C3
Brilliant AL 119 E3
Brilliant OH 91 F4
Brillion WI 74 C1
Brimfield IL 88 B3
Brinckerhoff NY 148 B1
Brinkley AR 117 F2
Brinnon WA 12 C3
Brisbane CA 259 B3

Brook IN 89 D3
Brookdale SC 122 A4
Brooke VA 103 D4
Brooke Co. WV 91 F4
Brookfield CT 148 C1
Brookfield IL 203 C5
Brookfield MA 150 B2
Brookfield MO 97 D1
Brookfield OH 276 C1
Brookfield WI 234 B2
Brookfield Ctr. CT 148 C1
Brookhaven MS 126 B4
Brookhaven NY 149 D4
Brookhaven PA 248 A4
Brookings OR 28 A2
Brookings SD 27 F3
Brookings Co. SD 27 F3
Brookland AR 108 A4
Brooklandville MD 193 C1
Brooklawn NJ 248 C4
Brooklet GA 130 B2
Brookline MA 151 D1
Brookline NH 95 D1
Brooklyn CT 150 B3
Brooklyn IL 256 C2
Brooklyn IN 99 F1
Brooklyn IA 87 E1
Brooklyn MI 90 B1
Brooklyn OH 204 E2

Browning MT 15 E2
Brownsboro TX 124 A3
Brownsburg IN 99 F1
Brownsdale MN 73 D2
Browns Mills NJ 147 D3
Brownstown IL 98 C2
Brownstown IN 99 F3
Browns Valley MN 27 F1
Brownsville CA 36 C1
Brownsville KY 109 F2
Brownsville MN 73 F2
Brownsville OR 20 B3
Brownsville PA 102 B1
Brownsville TN 118 C1
Brownsville TX 63 F4
Brownsville WI 74 C2
Brownton MN 66 C4
Brownville NY 79 E1
Brownville Jct. ME 84 C4
Brownwood TX 59 D4
Broxton GA 129 E4
Broyhill Park VA 270 B4
Bruce MS 118 C3
Bruce SD 27 F3
Bruce WI 67 F3
Bruceton TN 109 D4
Bruceville-Eddy TX 59 E4
Brule Co. SD 27 D4
Brundidge AL 128 B4

Buckner KY 100 A4
Buckner MO 96 C2
Bucks Co. PA 146 C1
Bucksport ME 83 D2
Bucksport SC 123 D4
Bucoda WA 12 C4
Bucyrus OH 90 C3
Buda IL 88 B2
Buda TX 61 E2
Budd Lake NJ 94 A4
Bude MS 126 A4
Buellton CA 52 A2
Buena NJ 147 D4
Buena WA 13 D4
Buena Park CA 228 E3
Buena Ventura Lakes FL 246 C5
Buena Vista CO 41 D2
Buena Vista GA 128 C2
Buena Vista MI 76 B2
Buena Vista VA 112 C1
Buena Vista Co. IA 72 B4
Buffalo IN 89 E3
Buffalo IA 87 F2
Buffalo KY 110 A1
Buffalo MN 66 C3
Buffalo MO 107 D1
Buffalo NY 78 B3
Buffalo ND 19 E4
Buffalo OK 50 C1

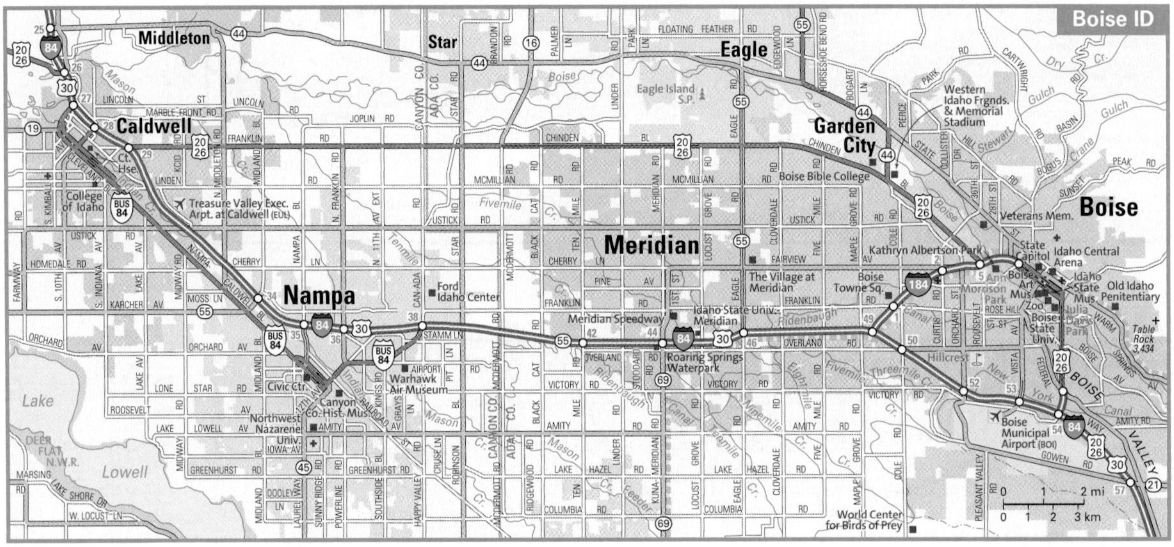

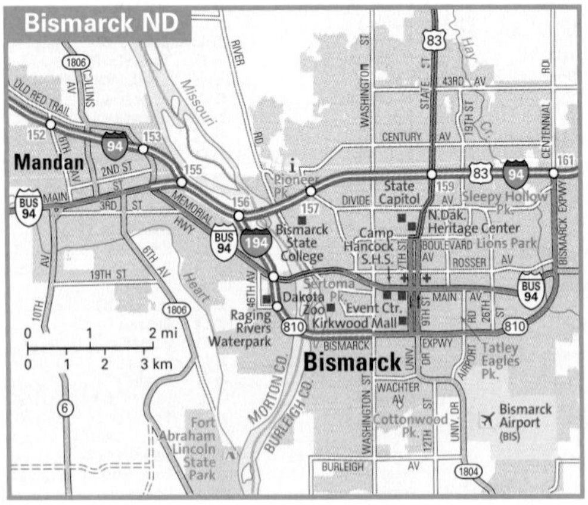

Bradley Co. TN 120 C1
Bradley Jct. FL 140 C3
Bradner OH 90 C2
Brady TX 58 C4
Braham MN 67 D2
Braidwood IL 88 C2
Brainerd MN 64 B4
Braintree MA 151 D2
Bramwell WV 111 F1
Branch Co. MI 90 A1
Branchville AL 119 F4
Branchville NJ 94 A4
Branchville SC 130 C1
Brandenburg KY 99 F4
Brandon FL 140 C2
Brandon MS 126 B3
Brandon SD 27 F4
Brandon VT 81 D3
Brandon WI 74 C2

Breckinridge Co. KY 99 F4
Brecksville OH 204 F3
Breese IL 98 B3
Breezy Pt. MD 144 C4
Breezy Pt. MN 64 B4
Breinigsville PA 146 B1
Bremen GA 120 B4
Bremen IN 89 F2
Bremen KY 109 E1
Bremen OH 101 D1
Bremer Co. IA 73 E3
Bremerton WA 12 C3
Bremond TX 59 F4
Brenham TX 61 F2
Brent AL 127 F1
Brent FL 135 F2
Brentsville VA 144 A4
Brentwood CA 36 B3
Brentwood MD 270 E2

Bridgeport AL 120 A2
Bridgeport CA 37 E3
Bridgeport CT 149 D2
Bridgeport IL 99 D3
Bridgeport MD 144 A1
Bridgeport MI 76 B3
Bridgeport NE 34 A3
Bridgeport NY 79 E3
Bridgeport PA 248 A1
Bridgeport TX 59 E2
Bridgeport WA 13 E2
Bridgeport WV 102 A2
Bridger MT 24 B2
Bridgeton MO 256 B1
Bridgeton NJ 145 F1
Bridgetown OH 204 A2
Bridgeview IL 203 D5
Bridgeville DE 145 E4
Bridgeville PA 250 A3

Briscoe Co. TX 50 B4
Bristol CT 149 D1
Bristol FL 137 D2
Bristol IN 89 F1
Bristol NH 81 F3
Bristol PA 147 D2
Bristol RI 151 D3
Bristol SD 27 E2
Bristol TN 111 E3
Bristol VT 81 D2
Bristol VA 111 E3
Bristol WI 74 C4
Bristol Co. MA 151 D3
Bristol Co. RI 151 D3
Bristow OK 51 F2
Britt IA 72 C3
Brittany Farms PA 146 C2
Britton MI 90 B1
Britton SD 27 E1
Broadalbin NY 80 C4
Broad Brook CT 150 A3
Broadmoor CA 259 B3
Broadus MT 25 E2
Broadview IL 203 C4
Broadview Hts. OH 204 F3
Broadwater Co. MT 15 F4
Broadway NC 123 D1
Broadway VA 102 C3
Brock Hall MD 144 C3
Brockport NY 78 C3
Brockton MA 151 D2
Brockton MT 17 E2
Brockway PA 92 B2
Brocton NY 78 A4
Brodhead KY 110 C1
Brodhead WI 74 B4
Brodheadsville PA 93 F3
Brogden NC 123 E1
Broken Arrow OK 106 A4
Broken Bow NE 35 D3
Broken Bow OK 116 B3
Bromley KY 204 A3
Bronson FL 138 C4
Bronson MI 90 A1
Bronte TX 58 C3
Bronwood GA 128 C3
Bronx Co. NY 148 B4

Brooklyn WI 74 B3
Brooklyn Ctr. MN 235 B1
Brooklyn Hts. OH 204 F2
Brooklyn Park MD 193 C4
Brooklyn Park MN 235 B1
Brookneal VA 112 C2
Brook Park OH 204 E3
Brookport IL 108 C2
Brooks GA 128 C1
Brooks KY 100 A4
Brooks ME 82 C2
Brooks Co. GA 137 F1
Brooks Co. TX 63 E3
Brookshire TX 61 F2
Brookside AL 195 D1
Brookside DE 146 B4
Brookside OH 91 F4
Brookside Vil. TX 220 C4
Brookston IN 89 E3
Brooksville FL 140 C1
Brooksville KY 100 C3
Brooksville MS 127 D1
Brookville IN 100 A2
Brookville NY 148 C4
Brookville OH 100 B1
Brookville PA 92 B2
Brookwood AL 127 F1
Broomall PA 146 C3
Broome Co. NY 93 F1
Broomfield CO 41 E1
Broomfield Co. CO 41 E1
Brooten MN 66 B3
Broussard LA 133 F2
Broward Co. FL 143 E1
Browerville MN 66 B2
Brown City MI 76 C3
Brown Co. IL 87 F4
Brown Co. IN 99 F2
Brown Co. KS 96 A1
Brown Co. MN 72 B1
Brown Co. NE 34 C1
Brown Co. OH 100 C3
Brown Co. SD 27 E1
Brown Co. TX 59 D3
Brown Co. WI 74 C1
Brown Deer WI 234 C1
Brownfield TX 58 A2

Brunson SC 130 B1
Brunswick GA 139 D1
Brunswick ME 82 B3
Brunswick MD 144 A2
Brunswick MO 97 D2
Brunswick OH 91 E2
Brunswick Co. NC 123 E3
Brunswick Co. VA 113 D3
Brush CO 33 F4
Brush Prairie WA 20 C1
Brushy OK 116 B1
Brusly LA 134 A2
Bryan OH 90 B2
Bryan TX 61 F1
Bryan Co. GA 130 B3
Bryan Co. OK 59 F1
Bryans Road MD 144 B4
Bryant AR 117 E2
Bryant SD 27 E3
Bryantville MA 151 E2
Bryn Athyn PA 248 D1
Bryn Mawr PA 146 C3
Bryson TX 59 D2
Bryson City NC 121 D1
Buchanan GA 120 B4
Buchanan MI 89 E1
Buchanan NY 148 B2
Buchanan VA 112 B1
Buchanan Co. IA 73 E4
Buchanan Co. MO 96 B1
Buchanan Co. VA 111 F2
Buchanan Dam TX 61 D1
Buchtel OH 101 E2
Buckeye AZ 54 B1
Buckeye Lake OH 101 D1
Buckfield ME 82 B2
Buckhannon WV 102 A2
Buckhead Ridge FL 141 E4
Buckingham PA 146 C2
Buckingham VA 113 D1
Buckingham Co. VA 113 D1
Buckland AK 154 B2
Buckley IL 89 D4
Buckley MI 69 F4
Buckley WA 12 C3
Bucklin KS 42 C4
Bucklin MO 97 D1

Buffalo SC 121 F2
Buffalo SD 25 F1
Buffalo TX 59 F4
Buffalo WV 101 E3
Buffalo WY 25 D3
Buffalo Ctr. IA 72 C2
Buffalo City WI 73 E1
Buffalo Co. NE 35 D4
Buffalo Co. SD 27 D3
Buffalo Co. WI 67 E4
Buffalo Grove IL 203 C2
Buffalo Lake MN 66 B4
Buford GA 120 C3
Buhl ID 30 C1
Buhl MN 64 C3
Buhler KS 43 E3
Buies Creek NC 123 D1
Bullard TX 124 A3
Bullhead SD 26 C1
Bullhead City AZ 46 B3
Bullitt Co. KY 99 F4
Bulloch Co. GA 130 B2
Bullock Co. AL 128 B3
Bulls Gap TN 111 D3
Bull Shoals AR 107 E3
Bull Valley IL 74 C4
Bulverde TX 61 D2
Buna TX 132 C2
Buncombe Co. NC 111 E4
Bunker Hill IL 98 B2
Bunker Hill IN 89 F3
Bunker Hill OR 20 A4
Bunker Hill WV 103 D2
Bunker Hill Vil. TX 220 B2
Bunkerville NV 46 B1
Bunkie LA 133 E1
Bunnell FL 139 E4
Buras LA 134 C4
Burbank CA 52 C2
Burbank IL 203 D5
Burbank WA 21 E1
Burden KS 43 F4
Bureau Co. IL 88 B2
Burgaw NC 123 E2
Burgettstown PA 91 F4
Burgin KY 110 B1
Burien WA 12 C3

Entries in **bold black** indicate counties or parishes.
Entries in **bold color** indicate cities with detailed inset maps.

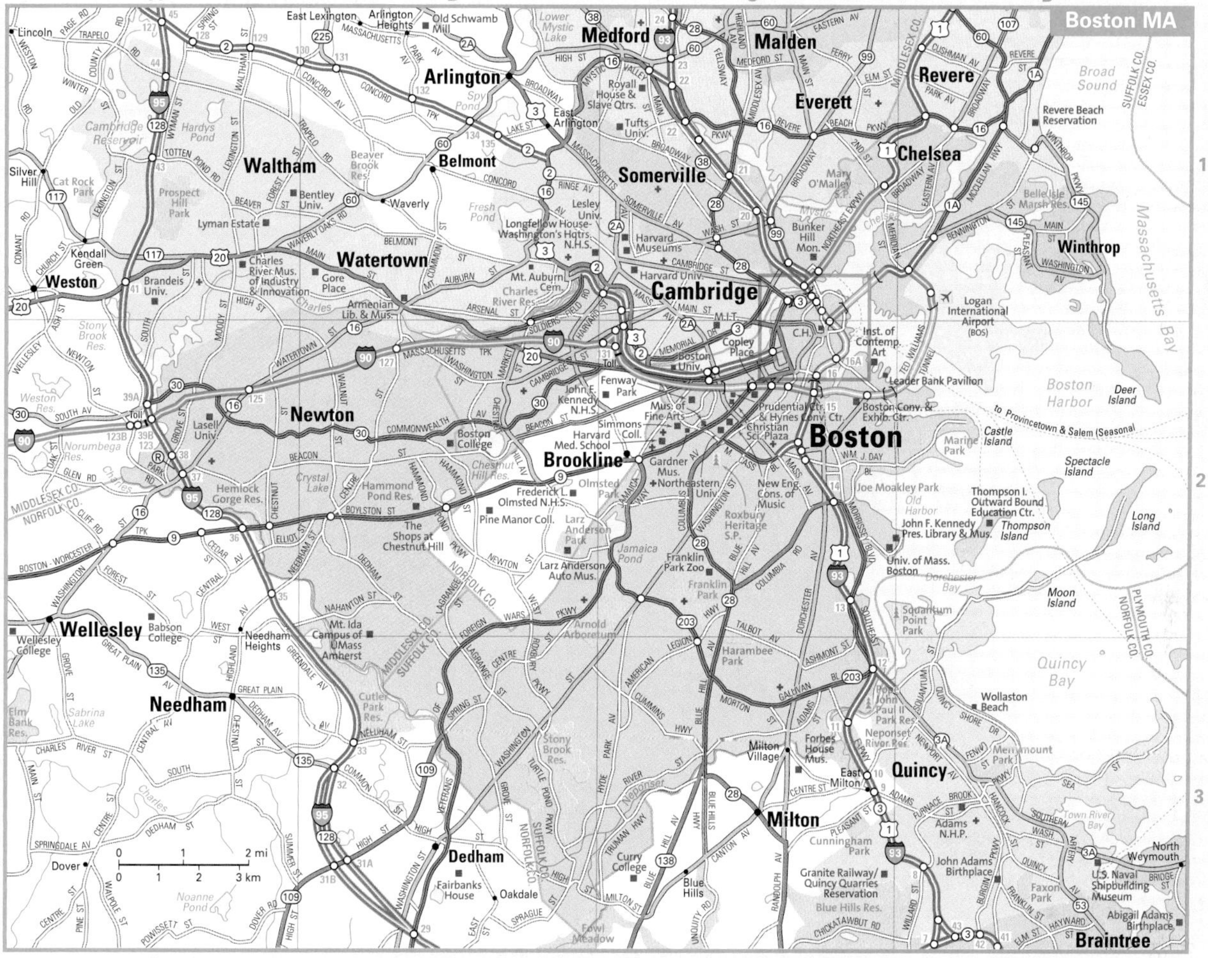

Arlington...........B1
Arlington Hts........B1
Belmont............B1
Blue Hills C3
Boston.............C2
Brookline C2
Cambridge C1
Chelsea.............D1
Dedham.............B3
Dover...............A3
E. Arlington.........B1
E. Lexington B1
E. Milton C3
Everett.............C1
Kendall Green A1
Lincoln.............A1
Malden C1
Medford C1
Milton C3
Milton Vil...........C3
Needham A3
Needham Hts........A2
Newton.............B2
N. Weymouth........D3
Oakdale.............B3
Quincy..............D3
Revere..............D1
Silver Hill A1
Somerville...........C1
Waltham............A1
Watertown..........B1
Waverly.............B1
Wellesley A2
Weston A1
Winthrop............D1

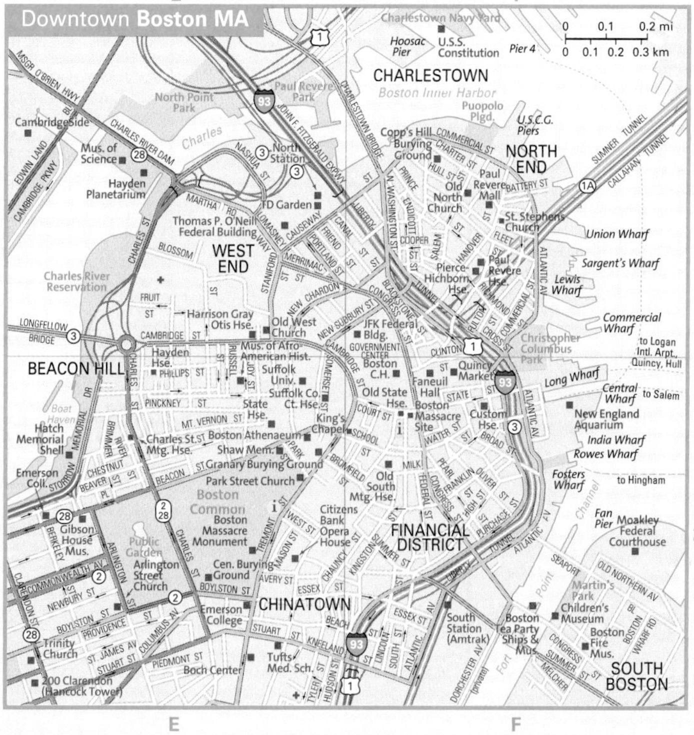

POINTS OF INTEREST
200 Clarendon (Hancock Tower)...........E2
Arlington Street Church..................E2
Boch Center..............................E2
Boston Athenaeum.........................E2
Boston City Hall.........................F2
Boston Fire Museum.......................F2
Boston Massacre Monument.................E2
Boston Massacre Site.....................F2
Boston Tea Party Ships & Museum..........F2
Central Burying Ground...................E2
Charles Street Meeting House.............E2
Children's Museum........................F2
Citizens Bank Opera House................E2
Copp's Hill Burying Ground...............F1
Custom House.............................F2
Emerson College..........................E2
Faneuil Hall.............................F2
Gibson House Museum......................E2
Granary Burying Ground...................E2
Harrison Gray Otis House.................E1
Hatch Memorial Shell.....................E2
Hayden House.............................E2
Hayden Planetarium.......................E1
JFK Federal Building.....................F1
King's Chapel............................E2
Moakley Federal Courthouse...............F2
Museum of Afro-American Hist..............E2
Museum of Science........................E1
New England Aquarium.....................F2
North Station............................E1
Old North Church.........................F1
Old South Meeting House..................F2
Old State House..........................F2
Old West Church..........................E1
Park Street Church.......................E2
Paul Revere House........................F1
Paul Revere Mall.........................F1
Pierce-Hichborn House....................F1
Quincy Market............................F2
St. Stephens Church......................F1
Shaw Memorial............................E2
South Station (Amtrak)...................F2
State House..............................E2
Suffolk County Court House...............E2
Suffolk Univ.............................E2
TD Garden................................E1
Thomas P. O'Neill Federal Building.......E1
Trinity Church...........................E2
Suffolk County Court House...............E2
Tufts Medical School.....................E2
U.S.S. Constitution......................F1

Burkburnett TX **59** D1
Burke SD **35** D1
Burke VA **144** B3
Burke Co. GA **129** F1
Burke Co. NC **111** F4
Burke Co. ND **18** A1
Burkesville KY **110** A2
Burkoville VA **113** D2
Burleigh Co. ND **18** C4
Burleson TX **59** E3
Burleson Co. TX **61** F1
Burley ID **31** D1
Burley WA **262** A4
Burlingame CA **259** B4
Burlingame KS **96** A3
Burlingham NY **148** A1
Burlington CO **42** A2
Burlington CT **94** C3
Burlington IA **87** F3
Burlington KS **96** A4
Burlington KY **100** B2
Burlington MA **151** D1
Burlington NJ **147** D2
Burlington NC **112** C4
Burlington ND **18** B2
Burlington OH **101** D3
Burlington VT 81 D2
Burlington WA **12** C2
Burlington WI **74** C4
Burlington WY **24** C3
Burlington Co. NJ **147** D3
Burlington Jct. MO **86** B4
Burlison TN **118** B1
Burnet TX **61** D1
Burnet Co. TX **61** D1
Burnett Co. WI **67** D2
Burnettown SC **121** F4
Burney CA **28** C4
Burnham IL **203** E6
Burnham PA **93** D3
Burning Sprs. KY **110** C2
Burns OR **21** E4
Burns TN **109** E4
Burns WY **33** F3
Burns Flat OK **51** D3
Burns Harbor IN **89** E2
Burnside KY **110** B2
Burnsville MN **67** D4
Burnsville MS **119** D2
Burnsville NC **111** E4
Burnsville WV **102** A3
Burnt Hills NY **94** B1
Burr Oak MI **90** A1
Burr Ridge IL **203** C5
Burrton KS **43** E3
Burt IA **72** B3
Burt MI **76** B3
Burt Co. NE **35** F2
Burton MI **76** B3
Burton OH **91** E2
Burton SC **130** C2
Burtonsville MD **144** B2
Burwell NE **35** D2
Busby MT **25** D2
Bushnell FL **140** C1
Bushnell IL **88** A4
Bushyhead OK **106** A3
Butler AL **127** D3
Butler GA **129** D2
Butler IN **90** A2
Butler KY **100** B3
Butler MO **96** B4
Butler NJ **148** A3
Butler OH **91** D4
Butler PA **92** A3
Butler WI **234** B1
Butler Beach FL **139** E3
Butler Co. AL **127** F3
Butler Co. IA **73** D4
Butler Co. KS **43** F4
Butler Co. KY **109** F2
Butler Co. MO **108** A2
Butler Co. NE **35** E3
Butler Co. OH **100** B2
Butler Co. PA **92** A3
Butner NC **112** C4
Butte MT **23** E1
Butte NE **35** D1
Butte Co. CA **36** C1
Butte Co. ID **23** D4
Butte Co. SD **25** F2
Butte Falls OR **28** C1
Butterfield MN **72** B1
Buttonwillow CA **45** D4

Figures after entries indicate page number and grid reference.

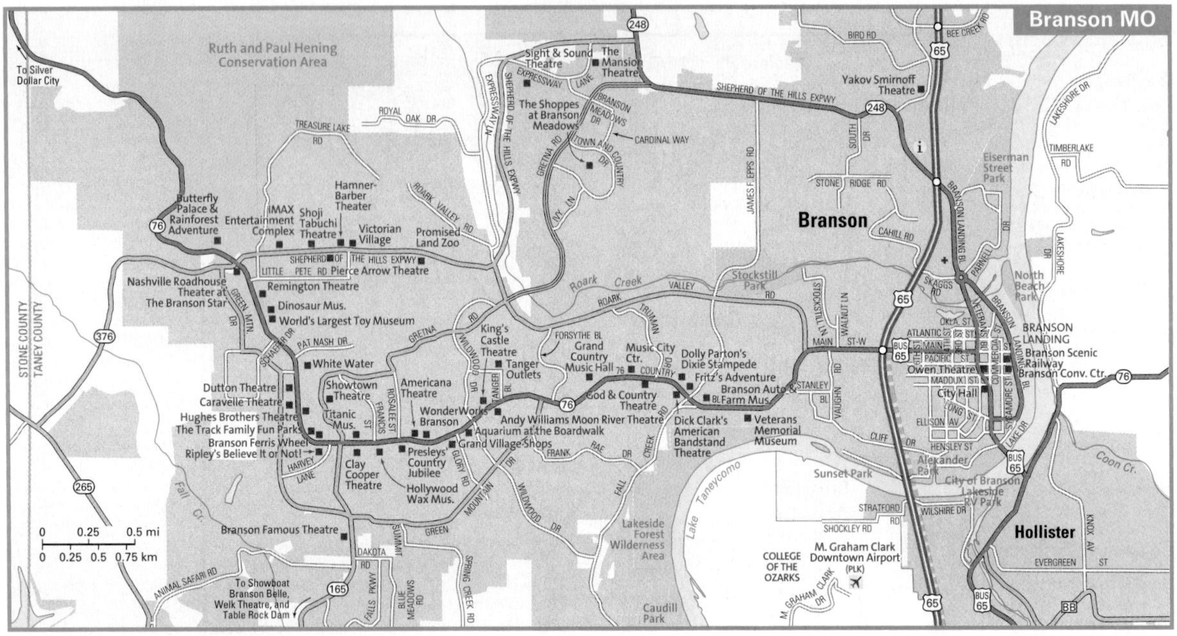
Branson MO
Ruth and Paul Hening Conservation Area
To Silver Dollar City
Branson
Hollister
STONE COUNTY
TANEY COUNTY
Lake Taneycomo
COLLEGE OF THE OZARKS
M. Graham Clark Downtown Airport (PLK)
Branson Landing
Branson Scenic Railway
Branson Conv. Ctr.
Dolly Parton's Dixie Stampede
Andy Williams Moon River Theatre
Shepherd of the Hills Expwy
0 0.25 0.5 mi
0 0.25 0.5 0.75 km

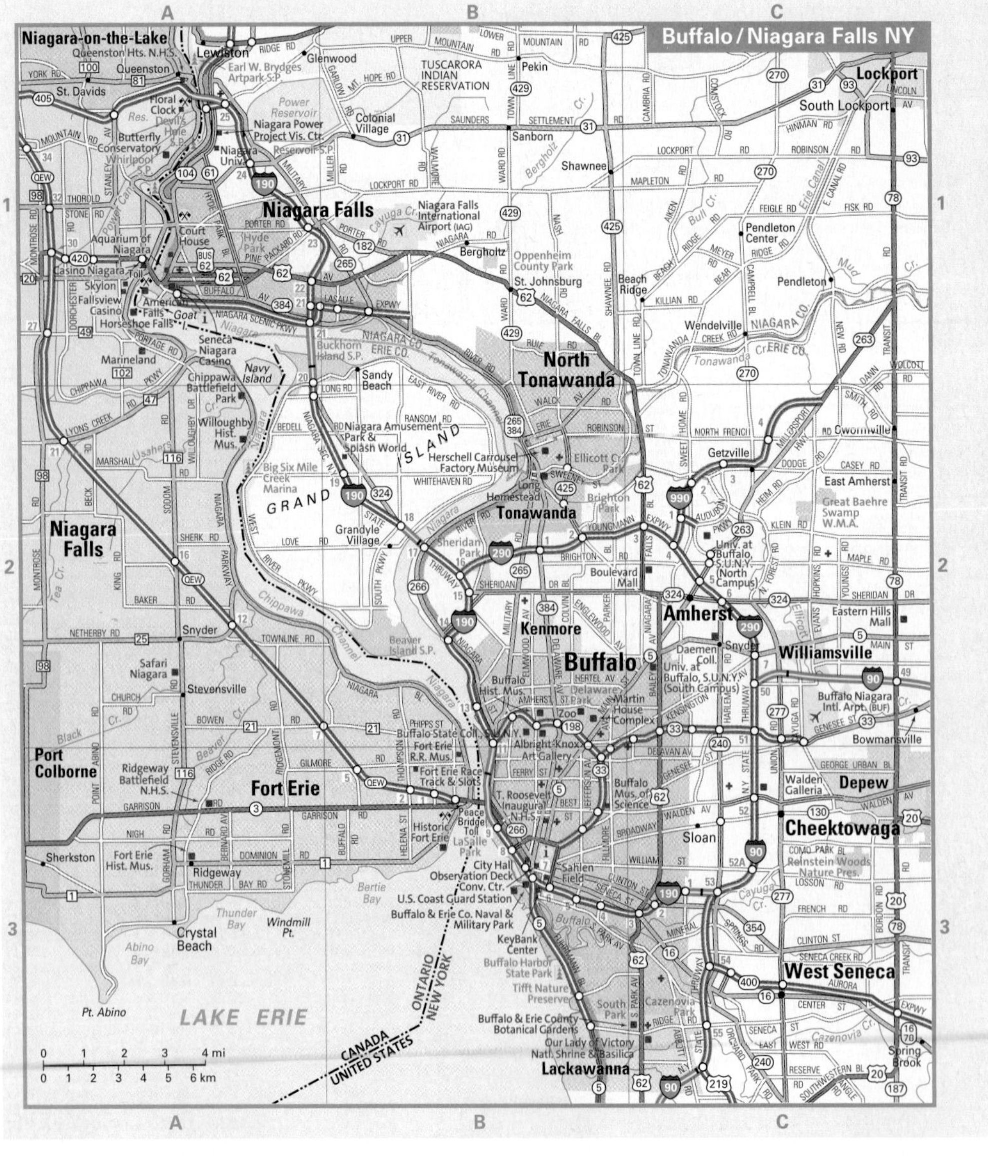
Buffalo / Niagara Falls NY
A
B
C
1
2
3
Niagara-on-the-Lake
Lewiston
Lockport
Niagara Falls
North Tonawanda
Grand Island
Tonawanda
Kenmore
Amherst
Williamsville
Buffalo
Cheektowaga
Depew
West Seneca
Lackawanna
Fort Erie
Port Colborne
Crystal Beach
Lake Erie
CANADA
UNITED STATES
ONTARIO
NEW YORK
0 1 2 3 4 mi
0 1 2 3 4 5 6 km

Amherst C2
Beach Ridge C1
Bergholtz B1
Bowmansville C2
Buffalo. B2
Cheektowaga. C3
Colonial Vil. B1
Crystal Beach A3
Depew. C3
E. Amherst C2
Ft. Erie. A3
Getzville C2
Glenwood A1
Grandyle Vil.. . . . . B2
Kenmore B2
Lackawanna. B3
Lewiston A1
Lockport C1
Niagara Falls, NY A1
Niagara Falls, ON A2
Niagara-on-the-Lake . A1
N. Tonawanda B1
Pekin B1
Pendleton C1
Pendleton Ctr. C1
Port Colborne. A3
Queenston A1
Ridgeway A3
St. Davids A1
St. Johnsburg B1
Sanborn B1
Sandy Beach B1
Shawnee. B1
Sherkston A3
Sloan C3
Snyder, NY C2
Snyder, ON. A2
S. Lockport. C1
Spring Brook C3
Stevensville A2
Swormville C2
Tonawanda B2
Wendelville C1
W. Seneca C3
Williamsville. C2

Butts Co. GA 129 D1
Buttzville NJ 93 F3
Buxton NC 115 F3
Buxton ND 19 E3
Buzzards Bay MA 151 E3
Byers CO 41 E1
Byers TX 59 D1
Byesville OH 101 E1
Byfield MA 151 F1
Byhalia MS 118 B2
Bylas AZ 55 E2
Byng OK 51 F3
Bynum AL 120 A4
Byram MS 126 B3
Byrdstown TN 110 B3
Byrnes Mill MO 98 A3
Byron CA 36 C4
Byron GA 129 D2
Byron IL 88 B1
Byron MI 76 B3
Byron MN 73 D1
Byron WY 24 C3
Byron Ctr. MI 75 F3

C
Cabarrus Co. NC 122 B1
Cabazon CA 53 D3
Cabell Co. WV 101 E3
Cabin John MD 270 B2
Cable WI 67 F1
Cabool MO 107 E2
Cabot AR 117 E2
Cabot VT 81 E2
Cache OK 51 D4
Cache Co. UT 31 F3
Cactus TX 50 A2
Cactus Flats AZ 55 E2
Caddo OK 51 F4
Caddo Co. OK 51 D3
Caddo Mills TX 59 F2
Caddo Par. LA 124 C2
Caddo Valley AR 117 D3
Cade LA 133 F2
Cadillac MI 75 F1
Cadiz KY 109 D2
Cadiz OH 91 F4
Cadott WI 67 F4
Cadyville NY 81 D1
Cahokia IL 98 A3
Cairo GA 137 E1
Cairo IL 108 C2
Cairo NE 35 D3
Cairo NY 94 B2
Cajah's Mtn. NC 111 F4
Calabasas CA 228 A2
Calabash NC 123 D4
Calais ME 83 E1
Calaveras Co. CA 36 C3
Calcasieu Par. LA 133 D2
Calcium NY 79 E1
Calcutta OH 91 F3
Caldwell AR 118 A1
Caldwell ID 22 B4
Caldwell KS 51 E1
Caldwell NJ 240 A2
Caldwell OH 101 F1
Caldwell TX 61 F1
Caldwell Co. KY 109 D2
Caldwell Co. MO 96 C1
Caldwell Co. NC 111 F4
Caldwell Co. TX 61 E2
Caldwell Par. LA 125 E3
Caledonia MI 75 F4
Caledonia MN 73 E2
Caledonia MS 119 D4
Caledonia NY 78 C3
Caledonia OH 90 C3
Caledonia Co. VT 81 E2
Calera AL 127 F1
Calera OK 59 F1
Calexico CA 53 E4
Calhan CO 41 E2
Calhoun GA 120 B3
Calhoun KY 109 E1
Calhoun MO 96 C3
Calhoun TN 120 C1
Calhoun City MS 118 C4
Calhoun Co. AL 120 A4
Calhoun Co. AR 117 E4
Calhoun Co. FL 137 D2
Calhoun Co. GA 128 C4
Calhoun Co. IL 98 A2
Calhoun Co. IA 72 B4
Calhoun Co. MI 90 A1
Calhoun Co. MS 118 C3
Calhoun Co. SC 122 B4
Calhoun Co. TX 61 F4
Calhoun Co. WV 101 F3
Calhoun Falls SC 121 E3
Calico Rock AR 107 E4
Caliente NV 38 C4
Califon NJ 104 C1
California MD 103 E4
California MO 97 E3
California PA 92 A4
California City CA 52 C1
Calimesa CA 229 K3
Calion AR 125 E1
Calipatria CA 53 E4
Calistoga CA 36 B3
Callahan FL 139 D2
Callahan Co. TX 58 C3
Callaway FL 136 C2

Entries in **bold black** indicate counties or parishes.
Entries in bold color indicate cities with detailed inset maps.

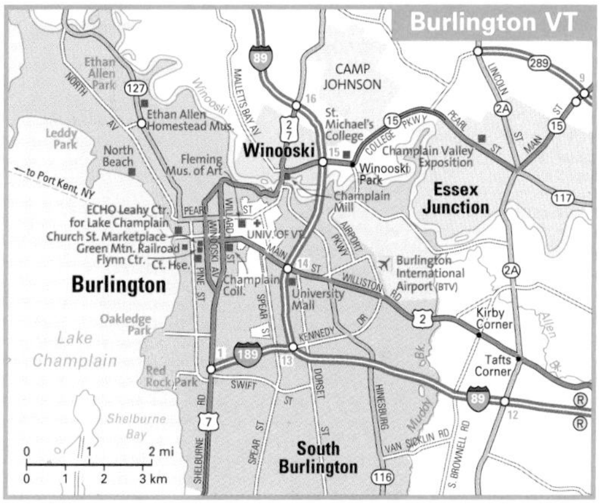
Burlington VT
Burlington
South Burlington
Winooski
Essex Junction
Lake Champlain
Camp Johnson
Burlington International Airport (BTV)
0 1 2 mi
0 1 2 3 km

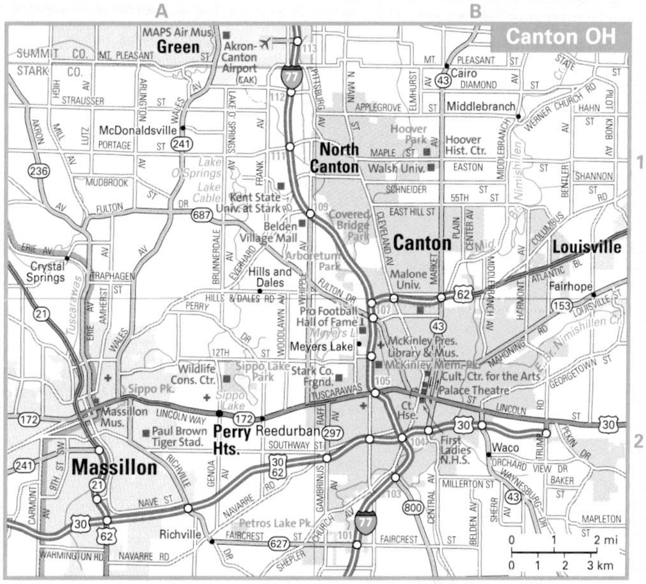
Canton OH
Canton
North Canton
Massillon
Louisville
Green
Perry Hts.
0 1 2 mi
0 1 2 3 km

Cairo B1	Green A1	McDonaldsville A1	Perry Hts. A2
Canton B1	Hills and Dales A1	Meyers Lake B2	Reedurban A2
Crystal Sprs. A1	Louisville B1	Middlebranch B1	Richville A2
Fairhope B1	Massillon A2	N. Canton B1	Waco B2

Carson City NV
Carson City
Douglas Co.
Washoe Co.
0 1 2 mi
0 1 2 3 km

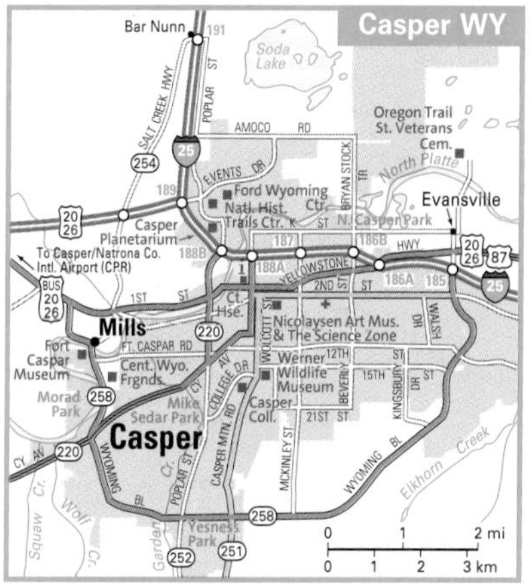
Casper WY
Casper
Mills
Evansville
Bar Nunn
0 1 2 mi
0 1 2 3 km

Callaway NE 34 C3
Callaway Co. MO 97 E3
Calloway Co. KY 109 D3
Calmar IA 73 E3
Cal-Nev-Ari NV 46 B3
Calpella CA 36 A2
Calumet MI 65 F3
Calumet OK 51 E3
Calumet City IL 89 D2
Calumet Co. WI 74 C1
Calumet Park IL 203 E6
Calvert TX 61 F1
Calvert Beach MD 103 E3
Calvert City KY 109 D2
Calvert Co. MD 144 C4
Calvert Manor MD 144 B4
Calverton MD 144 B3
Calverton NY 149 E3
Calverton Park MO 256 B1
Camanche IA 88 A1
Camargo KY 100 C4
Camarillo CA 52 B2
Camas WA 20 C1
Camas Co. ID 22 C4
Cambria CA 44 B4
Cambria IL 108 C1
Cambria WI 74 B2
Cambria Co. PA 92 B4
Cambridge ID 22 B3
Cambridge IL 88 A2
Cambridge IA 86 C1
Cambridge MD 145 D4
Cambridge MA 151 D1
Cambridge MN 67 D3
Cambridge NE 34 C4
Cambridge NY 81 D4
Cambridge OH 101 E1
Cambridge VT 81 D1
Cambridge WI 74 B3
Cambridge City IN 100 A1
Cambridge Sprs. PA 92 A1
Camden AL 127 F3
Camden AR 117 D4
Camden DE 145 E2
Camden IN 89 E3
Camden ME 82 C2
Camden MI 90 A1
Camden NJ 146 C3
Camden NY 79 E3
Camden NC 115 E1
Camden OH 100 B1
Camden SC 122 B3
Camden TN 109 D4
Camden Co. GA 139 D1
Camden Co. MO 97 D4
Camden Co. NJ 147 D4
Camden Co. NC 115 E1
Camden Pt. MO 96 B2
Camdenton MO 97 D4
Cameron AZ 47 E2
Cameron LA 133 D3
Cameron MO 96 C1
Cameron SC 122 B4
Cameron TX 61 E1
Cameron WV 102 A1
Cameron WI 67 E3
Cameron Co. PA 92 C2
Cameron Co. TX 63 F4
Cameron Par. LA 133 D3
Camilla GA 129 D4
Camillus NY 79 D3
Camino CA 36 C2
Campbell CA 36 B4
Campbell FL 141 D2
Campbell MO 108 B3
Campbell OH 91 F3
Campbell TX 59 F2
Campbell Co. KY 100 B3
Campbell Co. SD 26 C1
Campbell Co. TN 110 C3
Campbell Co. VA 112 C2
Campbell Co. WY 25 E3
Campbell Hall NY 148 A1
Campbellsburg IN 99 F3
Campbellsburg KY 100 A3
Campbellsport WI 74 C2
Campbellsville KY 110 A1
Campbellton FL 136 C1
Camp Co. TX 124 B1
Camp Douglas WI 74 A1
Camp Hill AL 128 B2
Camp Hill PA 93 D4
Campion CO 33 E4
Campobello SC 121 F1
Camp Pt. IL 87 F4
Camp Sprs. MD 144 B3
Campti LA 125 D3
Campton KY 111 D1
Campton NH 81 F3
Camp Verde AZ 47 D4
Camp Wood TX 60 C2
Cana VA 112 A3
Canaan CT 94 B2
Canaan ME 82 C1
Canaan NH 81 E3
Canaan VT 81 F1
Canadian TX 50 C2
Canadian Co. OK 51 E3
Canajoharie NY 79 F3
Canal Fulton OH 91 E3
Canal Pt. FL 141 E4
Canal Winchester OH 101 D1
Canandaigua NY 78 C3
Canaseraga NY 78 C4
Canastota NY 79 E3
Canby MN 27 F3
Canby OR 20 C2
Candler Co. GA 129 F2
Cando ND 19 D2
Candor NY 93 E1
Candor NC 122 C1
Caney KS 106 A2
Caneyville KY 109 F1
Canfield OH 91 F3
Canisteo NY 78 C4
Canistota SD 27 E4
Cannelton IN 99 E4
Cannon Ball ND 18 C4
Cannon Beach OR 20 B1
Cannon Co. TN 110 A4
Cannondale CT 148 C2
Cannon Falls MN 67 D4
Cannonsburg KY 101 D4
Canon GA 121 E3
Canon City CO 41 E3
Canonsburg PA 92 A4
Canterbury DE 145 E3
Canton CT 94 C3
Canton GA 120 C3
Canton IL 88 A4
Canton KS 43 E3
Canton MA 151 D2
Canton MS 126 B2
Canton MO 87 F4
Canton NY 80 B2
Canton NC 121 E1
Canton OH 91 E3
Canton OK 51 D2
Canton PA 93 D2
Canton SD 27 F4
Canton TX 124 A2
Cantonment FL 135 F2
Cantua Creek CA 44 C3
Canute OK 51 D3
Canutillo TX 56 C3
Canyon TX 50 A3
Canyon City OR 21 F3
Canyon Co. ID 22 B4
Canyon Day AZ 55 E1
Canyon Lake CA 229 J5
Canyon Lake TX 61 D2
Canyonville OR 28 B1
Capac MI 76 C3
Cape Canaveral FL 141 E2
Cape Carteret NC 115 D4
Cape Charles VA 114 B3
Cape Coral FL 142 C1
Cape Cottage ME 251 B2
Cape Elizabeth ME 82 B3
Cape Girardeau MO 108 B1
Cape Girardeau Co. MO 108 B1
Cape May NJ 104 C4
Cape May Co. NJ 104 C4
Cape May C.H. NJ 104 C4
Cape Neddick ME 82 B4
Cape Porpoise ME 82 B4
Cape St. Claire MD 144 C3
Cape Vincent NY 79 D1
Capitan NM 57 D1
Capitola CA 44 B2
Capitol Hts. MD 270 E3
Capitol Park DE 145 E2
Capron IL 74 C4
Captain Cook HI 153 E3
Caraway AR 108 A4
Carbonado WA 12 C4
Carbon Cliff IL 208 C2
Carbon Co. MT 24 B2
Carbon Co. PA 93 F3
Carbon Co. UT 39 F1
Carbon Co. WY 33 D2
Carbondale CO 40 C2
Carbondale IL 108 C1
Carbondale KS 96 A3
Carbondale PA 93 F2
Carbon Hill AL 119 E4
Cardiff MD 146 A4
Cardiff NJ 147 F4
Cardington OH 90 C4
Cardwell MO 108 A4
Carefree AZ 54 C1
Carencro LA 133 F2
Carey ID 23 D4
Carey OH 90 C3
Caribou ME 85 D2
Caribou Co. ID 31 E1
Carleton MI 90 C1
Carlin NV 30 B4
Carlinville IL 98 B2
Carlisle AR 117 F2
Carlisle IN 99 E3
Carlisle IA 86 C2
Carlisle KY 100 C4
Carlisle MA 150 C1
Carlisle OH 100 B1
Carlisle PA 93 D4
Carlisle SC 122 A2
Carlisle Co. KY 108 C2
Carl Jct. MO 106 B2
Carlls Corner NJ 145 F1
Carlsbad CA 53 D4
Carlsbad NM 57 E3
Carlsborg WA 12 B2
Carlstadt NJ 240 C2
Carlton MN 64 C4
Carlton OR 20 B2
Carlton Co. MN 64 C4
Carlyle IL 98 B3
Carlyss LA 133 D2
Carmel IN 99 F1
Carmel ME 82 C1
Carmel NY 148 C1
Carmel-by-the-Sea CA 44 B3
Carmel Valley CA 44 B3
Carmen AZ 55 D4
Carmi IL 99 D4
Carmichael CA 255 C2
Carnation WA 12 C3
Carnegie OK 51 D3
Carnegie PA 250 A2
Carnesville GA 121 D3
Carney MD 193 D1
Carney OK 51 F2
Carneys Pt. NJ 146 B4
Caro MI 76 B2
Caroleen NC 121 F1
Carolina RI 150 C4
Carolina Beach NC 123 E3
Carolina Shores NC 123 D4
Caroline Co. MD 145 E4
Caroline Co. VA 103 E4
Carol Stream IL 203 B4
Carpendale WV 102 C1
Carpentersville IL 88 C1
Carpinteria CA 52 B2
Carrabelle FL 137 D3
Carrboro NC 112 C4
Carriere MS 134 C2
Carrier Mills IL 108 C1
Carrington ND 19 D3
Carrizo Sprs. TX 60 C4
Carrizozo NM 56 C1
Carroll IA 86 B1
Carroll Co. AR 107 D4
Carroll Co. GA 120 B4
Carroll Co. IL 88 B1
Carroll Co. IN 89 E4
Carroll Co. IA 86 B1
Carroll Co. KY 100 A3
Carroll Co. MD 144 B1
Carroll Co. MS 118 B4
Carroll Co. MO 96 C2
Carroll Co. NH 81 F3
Carroll Co. OH 91 E3
Carroll Co. TN 109 D4
Carroll Co. VA 112 A3
Carrollton AL 127 E1
Carrollton GA 120 B4
Carrollton IL 98 A2
Carrollton KY 100 A3
Carrollton MI 76 B2
Carrollton MS 118 B4
Carrollton MO 96 C2
Carrollton OH 91 F4
Carrollton TX 59 F2
Carrolltown PA 92 B4
Carroll Valley PA 103 D1
Carrollwood FL 266 C1
Carson CA 228 D4
Carson IA 86 A2
Carson ND 18 B4
Carson WA 20 C1
Carson City MI 76 A3
Carson City NV 37 D2
Carson Co. TX 50 B3
Carsonville MI 76 C2
Carter Co. KY 101 D4
Carter Co. MO 108 A2
Carter Co. MT 25 F2
Carter Co. OK 51 E4
Carter Co. TN 111 E3
Carteret NJ 147 E1
Carteret Co. NC 115 E4
Carter Lake IA 86 A2
Cartersville GA 120 B3
Carterville IL 108 C1
Carterville MO 106 B2
Carthage AR 117 E3
Carthage IL 87 F4
Carthage IN 100 A1
Carthage MS 126 C2
Carthage MO 106 C2
Carthage NY 79 E1
Carthage NC 122 C1
Carthage TN 110 A3
Carthage TX 124 C3
Caruthers CA 44 C3
Caruthersville MO 108 B4
Carver MA 151 E3
Carver MN 66 C4
Carver Co. MN 66 C4
Cary IL 88 C1
Cary MS 126 A2
Cary NC 112 C4
Caryville TN 110 C3
Casa Blanca AZ 54 C2
Casa Blanca NM 48 B3
Casa Grande AZ 54 C2
Cascade CO 41 E2
Cascade ID 22 B3
Cascade IA 73 F4
Cascade MD 103 D1
Cascade MT 15 F3
Cascade WI 74 C2
Cascade Co. MT 15 F3
Cascade Locks OR 20 C1
Casco ME 82 B3
Casco WI 69 D4
Caseville MI 76 C1
Casey IL 99 D2
Casey IA 86 B2
Casey Co. KY 110 B1
Caseyville IL 256 D2
Cashion OK 51 E2
Cashmere WA 13 D3
Cashton WI 73 F2
Casitas Sprs. CA 52 B2
Casper WY 33 D1
Caspian MI 68 C2
Cassadaga FL 141 D1
Cassadaga NY 78 A4
Cass City MI 76 C2
Cass Co. IL 98 A1
Cass Co. IN 89 F3
Cass Co. IA 86 B2
Cass Co. MI 89 F1
Cass Co. MN 64 B4
Cass Co. MO 96 C3
Cass Co. NE 35 F3
Cass Co. ND 19 E3
Cass Co. TX 124 C1
Casselberry FL 141 D1
Casselton ND 19 E4
Cassia Co. ID 31 D2
Cass Lake MN 64 A3
Cassopolis MI 89 F1
Cassville MO 106 C3
Cassville NJ 147 E2
Cassville WV 102 A1
Cassville WI 73 F4
Castaic CA 52 C2
Castalia OH 91 D2
Castanea PA 93 D3
Castile NY 78 B4
Castine ME 83 D2
Castleberry AL 127 F4
Castle Dale UT 39 F2
Castleford ID 30 C1
Castle Hayne NC 123 E3
Castle Hills TX 257 E2
Castle Rock CO 41 E2
Castle Rock WA 20 B1
Castle Shannon PA 250 B3
Castleton VT 81 D3
Castleton-on-Hudson NY 94 B1
Castle Valley UT 40 A3
Castlewood SD 27 F3
Castlewood VA 111 E2
Castro Co. TX 50 A4
Castro Valley CA 259 D3
Castroville CA 44 B2
Castroville TX 61 D3
Caswell Co. NC 112 C3
Catahoula Par. LA 125 F3
Catalina AZ 55 D3
Catasauqua PA 146 B1
Catawba NC 112 A4
Catawba SC 122 A2
Catawba Co. NC 122 A1
Catawba Island OH 91 D2
Catawissa PA 93 E3
Catharpin VA 144 A3
Cathcart WA 262 B2
Cathedral City CA 53 E3
Cathlamet WA 20 B1
Catlettsburg KY 101 D3
Catlin IL 89 D4
Cato NY 79 D3
Catonsville MD 144 C2
Catoosa OK 106 A3
Catoosa Co. GA 120 B2
Catron Co. NM 48 A4
Catskill NY 94 B2
Cattaraugus NY 78 A4
Cattaraugus Co. NY 78 A4
Cavalier ND 19 E1
Cavalier Co. ND 19 D1
Cave City AR 107 F4
Cave City KY 110 A2

Figures after entries indicate page number and grid reference.

Cave Creek AZ 54 C1
Cave Jct. OR 28 B2
Cave Spr. GA 120 B3
Cave Spr. VA 112 B2
Cave Sprs. AR 106 C3
Cavetown MD 144 A1
Cawker City KS 43 D1
Cawood KY 111 D2
Cayce SC 122 A3
Cayucos CA 44 B4
Cayuga IN 99 E1
Cayuga NY 79 D3
Cayuga Co. NY 79 D4
Cayuga Hts. NY 79 D4
Cazenovia NY 79 E3
Cecil PA 92 A4
Cecil Co. MD 145 E1
Cecilia KY 110 A1
Cecilia LA 133 F2
Cecilton MD 145 E1
Cedar Bluff AL 120 A3
Cedar Bluff VA 111 F2
Cedar Bluffs NE 35 F3
Cedar Brook NJ 147 D4
Cedarburg WI 74 C3
Cedar City UT 39 D4
Cedar Co. IA 87 F1
Cedar Co. MO 106 C1
Cedar Co. NE 35 E1
Cedar Creek NE 35 F3
Cedar Crest NM 48 C3
Cedaredge CO 40 B2
Cedar Falls IA 73 D4
Cedar Fort UT 31 E4
Cedar Grove FL 136 C2
Cedar Grove MD 144 B2
Cedar Grove NJ 148 A3
Cedar Grove NM 48 C3
Cedar Grove WV 101 F4
Cedar Grove WI 75 D2
Cedar Hill MO 98 A4
Cedar Hill TX 207 C3
Cedar Hills OR 251 C2
Cedarhurst NY 241 G5
Cedar Key FL 138 B4
Cedar Lake IN 89 D2
Cedar Park TX 61 E1
Cedar Pt. NC 115 D4
Cedar Rapids IA 87 E1
Cedar Rapids NE 35 E3
Cedar Sprs. MI 75 F3
Cedartown GA 120 B3
Cedar Vale KS 51 F1
Cedarville AR 116 C1
Cedarville IL 74 B4
Cedarville NJ 145 F2
Cedarville OH 100 C1
Celebration FL 141 D1
Celeste TX 59 F2
Celina OH 90 B4
Celina TN 110 A3
Celina TX 59 F2
Celoron NY 92 B1
Cement OK 51 E3
Cement City MI 90 B1
Centennial CO 209 C4
Center CO 41 D4
Center MO 97 F1
Center NE 35 E1
Center ND 18 B3
Center TX 124 C3
Center Barnstead NH 81 F4
Centerbrook CT 149 E2
Center Brunswick NY 94 B1
Centerburg OH 91 D4
Center City MN 67 D3
Centereach NY 149 D3
Centerfield UT 39 E2
Center Harbor NH 81 F3
Center Hill FL 140 C1
Center Line MI 210 C2
Center Moriches NY 149 D4
Center Ossipee NH 81 F3
Center Pt. AL 119 F4
Center Pt. IA 87 E1
Center Pt. TX 61 D2
Centerport NY 148 C3
Centerton AR 106 C3
Centerton NJ 147 D3
Centertown KY 109 E1
Center Valley PA 146 C1
Centerville GA 129 D2
Centerville IN 100 B1
Centerville IA 87 D3
Centerville LA 133 F3
Centerville MA 151 F3
Centerville MO 108 A1
Centerville OH 100 B1
Centerville PA 92 A4
Centerville SC 121 E3
Centerville SD 35 F1
Centerville TN 109 E4
Centerville TX 124 A4
Centerville UT 31 E4
Central AZ 55 E2
Central SC 121 E2
Central TN 111 E3
Central Bridge NY 79 F4
Central City AR 116 C1
Central City CO 41 D1
Central City IL 98 C3
Central City IA 87 F1
Central City KY 109 E1
Central City NE 35 E3
Central City PA 92 B4
Central Falls RI 150 C3
Central High OK 51 E4
Centralia IL 98 C3
Centralia KS 43 F1
Centralia MO 97 E2
Centralia WA 12 B4
Central Islip NY 149 D4
Central Lake MI 69 F3
Central Park WA 12 B4
Central Pt. OR 28 B2
Central Square NY 79 D3
Central Valley (Woodbury) NY 148 B2
Central Vil. CT 150 B3
Central Vil. MA 151 D4
Centre AL 120 A3
Centre Co. PA 92 C3
Centre Hall PA 92 C3
Centreville AL 127 F1
Centreville IL 98 A3
Centreville MD 145 D3
Centreville MI 89 F1
Centreville MS 134 A1
Centreville VA 144 A3
Centuria WI 67 E3
Century FL 135 F1
Ceres CA 36 C4
Ceresco NE 35 F3
Cerritos CA 228 E4
Cerro Gordo IL 98 C1
Cerro Gordo Co. IA 73 D3
Chackbay LA 134 A3
Chadbourn NC 123 D3
Chadron NE 34 A1
Chaffee MO 108 B2
Chaffee Co. CO 41 D2
Chaffinville MA 150 B1
Chagrin Falls OH 91 E2
Chalco NE 35 F3
Chalfant PA 250 D2
Chalfont PA 146 C2
Chalkville AL 195 F1
Challenge CA 36 C1
Challis ID 23 D3
Chalmers IN 89 E3
Chalmette LA 134 B3
Chama NM 48 C1
Chamberino NM 56 C3
Chamberlain SD 27 D4
Chamberlayne Farms VA 254 B1
Chambersburg PA 103 D1
Chambers Co. AL 128 B1
Chambers Co. TX 132 B3
Chamblee GA 120 C4
Chamisal NM 49 D2
Champaign IL 88 C4
Champaign Co. IL 89 D4
Champaign Co. OH 90 C4
Champion Hts. OH 91 F2
Champlain NY 81 D1
Chancellor SD 27 F4
Chandler AZ 54 C2
Chandler IN 99 E4
Chandler OK 51 F2
Chandler TX 124 A2
Chandler Hts. AZ 54 C2
Chandlerville IL 88 A4
Chanhassen MN 66 C4
Chanahon IL 88 C2
Channel Lake IL 74 C4
Channelview TX 132 B3
Channing TX 50 A2
Chantilly VA 144 A3
Chanute KS 106 A1
Chaparral NM 56 C3
Chapel Hill NC 112 C4
Chapel Hill TN 119 F1
Chapin IL 98 A1
Chapin SC 122 A3
Chaplin KY 100 A4
Chapman KS 43 F2
Chapmanville WV 101 E4
Chappaqua NY 148 B2
Chappell NE 34 A3
Chardon OH 91 E2
Charenton LA 133 F3
Chariton IA 87 D3
Chariton Co. MO 97 D1
Charlack MO 256 B2
Charleroi PA 92 A4
Charles City IA 73 D3
Charles City VA 113 E1
Charles City Co. VA 113 E1
Charles Co. MD 144 B4
Charles Mix Co. SD 27 D4
Charleston AR 116 C1
Charleston IL 99 D2
Charleston ME 82 C1
Charleston MS 118 B3
Charleston MO 108 C2
Charleston SC 131 D2
Charleston TN 120 C1
Charleston UT 31 F4
Charleston WV 101 E4
Charleston Co. SC 131 D2
Charlestown IN 100 A3
Charlestown MD 145 D1
Charlestown NH 81 E4
Charlestown RI 150 C4
Charles Town WV 103 D2
Charlevoix MI 69 F3
Charlevoix Co. MI 70 B3
Charlo MT 15 D3
Charlotte MI 76 A4
Charlotte NC 122 A1
Charlotte TN 109 E4
Charlotte TX 61 D3
Charlotte Co. FL 140 C4
Charlotte Co. VA 113 D2
Charlotte C.H. VA 113 D2
Charlotte Hall MD 144 C4
Charlotte Harbor FL 140 C4
Charlottesville VA 102 C4
Charlton MA 150 B2
Charlton NY 94 B1
Charlton City MA 150 B2
Charlton Co. GA 138 C1
Charlton Depot MA 150 B2
Charter Oak CA 229 F2
Charter Oak IA 86 A1
Chartley MA 151 D2
Chase KS 43 D3
Chase City VA 113 D2
Chase Co. KS 43 F3
Chase Co. NE 34 B4
Chaska MN 66 C4
Chassahowitzka FL 140 B1
Chassell MI 65 F4
Chateaugay NY 80 C1
Chatfield MN 73 E2
Chatham IL 98 B1
Chatham LA 125 E2
Chatham MA 151 F3
Chatham NJ 148 A4
Chatham NY 94 B2
Chatham VA 112 C2
Chatham Co. GA 130 B3
Chatham Co. NC 112 C4
Chatom AL 127 D4
Chatsworth GA 120 C2
Chatsworth IL 88 C3
Chattahoochee FL 137 D1
Chattahoochee Co. GA 128 C2
Chattanooga OK 51 D4
Chattanooga TN 120 B2
Chattaroy WV 111 E1
Chattooga Co. GA 120 B3
Chatwood PA 146 B3
Chaumont NY 79 D1
Chauncey OH 101 E2
Chautauqua Co. KS 43 F4
Chautauqua Co. NY 78 A4
Chauvin LA 134 B4
Chaves Co. NM 57 E2
Chazy NY 81 D1
Cheatham Co. TN 109 E3
Cheat Lake WV 102 B1
Chebanse IL 89 D3
Cheboygan MI 70 C2
Cheboygan Co. MI 70 C3
Checotah OK 116 A1
Cheektowaga NY 78 B3
Chefornak AK 154 B3
Chehalis WA 12 B4
Chelan WA 13 E3
Chelan Co. WA 13 D2
Chelmsford MA 95 E1
Chelsea AL 127 F1
Chelsea MA 151 D1
Chelsea MI 76 B4
Chelsea NY 148 B1
Chelsea OK 106 A3
Chelsea VT 81 E3
Cheltenham MD 144 C4
Cheltenham PA 248 C2
Chelyan WV 101 F4
Chemung Co. NY 93 E1
Chenango Bridge NY 93 E1
Chenango Co. NY 79 E4
Chenequa WI 74 C3
Cheney KS 43 E4
Cheney WA 13 F3
Cheneyville LA 133 E1
Chenoa IL 88 C3
Chenoweth OR 21 D1
Chepachet RI 150 C3
Cheraw SC 122 C2
Cheriton VA 114 B3
Cherokee AL 119 D2
Cherokee IA 72 A4
Cherokee KS 106 B1
Cherokee OK 51 D1
Cherokee Co. AL 120 A3
Cherokee Co. GA 120 C3
Cherokee Co. IA 72 A3
Cherokee Co. KS 106 B2
Cherokee Co. NC 121 D1
Cherokee Co. OK 106 B4
Cherokee Co. SC 121 F2
Cherokee Co. TX 124 A3
Cherokee Forest SC 217 A1
Cherokee Vil. AR 107 F3
Cherry Co. NE 34 B1
Cherry Creek NY 78 A4
Cherryfield ME 83 E2
Cherry Grove OH 204 C3
Cherry Hill NJ 146 C3
Cherry Hills Vil. CO 209 C4
Cherryvale KS 106 A2
Cherryvale SC 122 B4
Cherry Valley AR 118 A1
Cherry Valley NY 79 F4
Cherryville NC 122 A1
Chesaning MI 76 B3
Chesapeake OH 101 D3
Chesapeake VA 113 F3
Chesapeake WV 101 F4
Chesapeake Beach MD 144 C4
Chesapeake City MD 145 E1
Chesapeake Ranch Estates MD 103 F4
Cheshire CT 149 D1
Cheshire MA 94 C1
Cheshire Co. NH 81 E4
Chesilhurst NJ 147 D4
Chesnee SC 121 F2
Chester CA 29 D4
Chester CT 149 E2
Chester IL 98 B4
Chester MD 145 D3
Chester MA 94 C2
Chester MT 15 F2
Chester NH 81 F4
Chester NJ 94 A4
Chester NY 148 A2
Chester PA 146 C3
Chester SC 122 A2
Chester VT 81 E4
Chester VA 113 E1
Chester WV 91 F3
Chester Co. PA 146 B3
Chester Co. SC 122 A2
Chester Co. TN 119 D1
Chester Depot VT 81 E4
Chesterfield IN 89 F4
Chesterfield MO 98 A3
Chesterfield SC 122 B2
Chesterfield VA 113 E1
Chesterfield Co. SC 122 B2
Chesterfield Co. VA 113 E1
Chester Hts. PA 146 B3
Chester Hill PA 92 C3
Chesterland OH 91 E2
Chesterton IN 89 E2
Chestertown MD 145 D2
Chestnut Mtn. GA 121 D3
Chestnut Ridge NY 148 B3
Cheswick PA 250 D1
Cheswold DE 145 E2
Chetek WI 67 E3
Chetopa KS 106 B2
Chevak AK 154 B3
Cheverly MD 144 B3
Cheviot OH 100 B2
Chevy Chase MD 270 C2
Chevy Chase View MD 270 C1
Chewelah WA 13 F2
Cheyenne OK 50 C3
Cheyenne WY 33 E3
Cheyenne Co. CO 42 A2
Cheyenne Co. KS 42 B1
Cheyenne Co. NE 34 A3
Cheyenne Wells CO 42 A2
Cheyney PA 146 B3
Chicago IL 89 D1
Chicago Hts. IL 89 D2
Chicago Ridge IL 203 D5
Chichester NH 81 F4
Chickamauga GA 120 B2
Chickasaw AL 135 E1
Chickasaw Co. IA 73 E3
Chickasaw Co. MS 118 C4
Chickasha OK 51 E3
Chico CA 36 B1
Chico TX 59 E2
Chicopee MA 150 A2
Chicora PA 92 A3
Chicot Co. AR 125 F1
Chiefland FL 138 B4
Chilchinbito AZ 47 F1
Chilcoot CA 37 D1
Childersburg AL 128 A1
Childress TX 50 C4
Childress Co. TX 50 C4
Chilhowie VA 111 F2
Chillicothe IL 88 B3
Chillicothe MO 96 C1
Chillicothe OH 101 D2
Chillicothe TX 50 C4
Chillum MD 270 D2
Chiloquin OR 28 C1
Chilton WI 74 C1
Chilton Co. AL 127 F2
Chimayo NM 49 D2
China TX 132 C3
China Grove NC 122 B1
China Grove TX 61 D3
Chinchilla PA 261 E1
Chincoteague VA 114 C2
Chinle AZ 47 F2
Chino CA 229 G3
Chino Hills CA 229 G3
Chinook MT 16 B2
Chinook WA 20 B1
Chino Valley AZ 47 D4
Chipita Park CO 205 C1
Chipley FL 136 C1
Chippewa Co. MI 70 B1
Chippewa Co. MN 66 A3
Chippewa Co. WI 67 F3
Chippewa Falls WI 67 F4
Chippewa Lake OH 91 E3
Chisago City MN 67 D3
Chisago Co. MN 67 D3
Chisholm ME 82 B2
Chisholm MN 64 C3
Chittenango NY 79 E3
Chittenden VT 81 D3

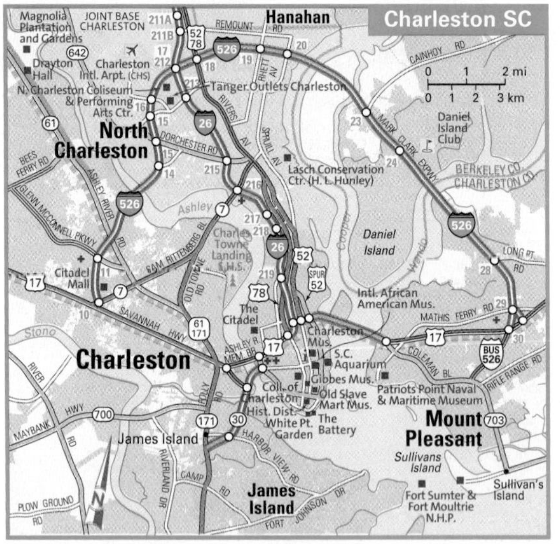

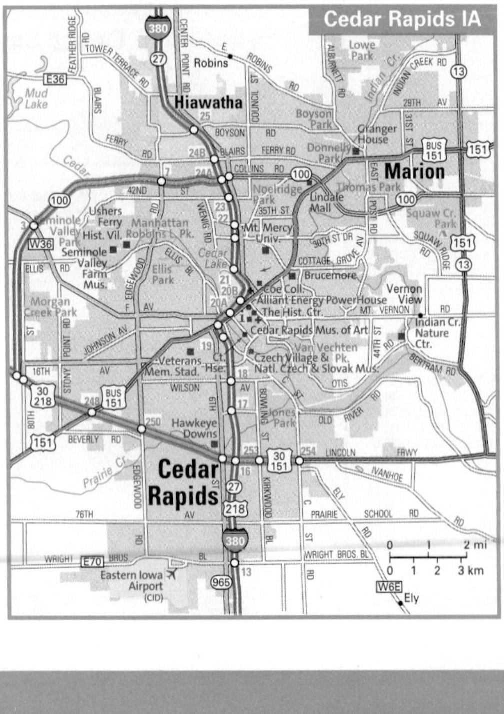

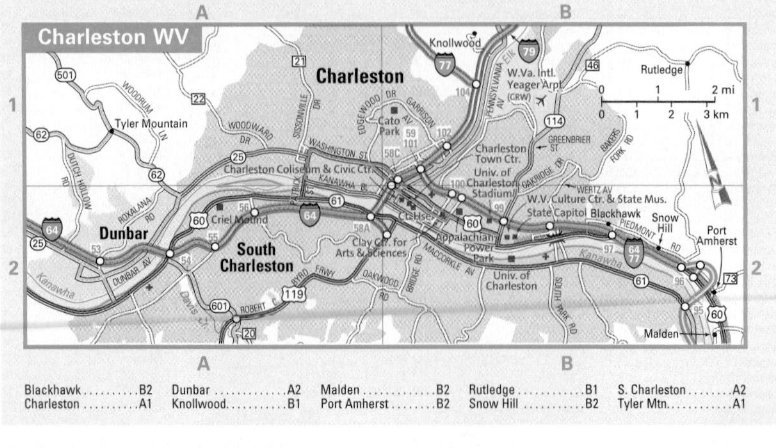

Blackhawk B2	Dunbar A2	Malden B2	Rutledge B1	S. Charleston A2
Charleston A1	Knollwood B1	Port Amherst B2	Snow Hill B2	Tyler Mtn. A1

Entries in **bold black** indicate counties or parishes.
Entries in **bold color** indicate cities with detailed inset maps.

Chittenden Co. VT 81 D2
Chocowinity NC 115 D3
Choctaw OK 51 E3
Choctaw Co. AL 127 E3
Choctaw Co. MS 126 C1
Choctaw Co. OK 116 A3
Choteau MT 15 E3
Choudrant LA 125 E2
Chouteau OK 106 A3
Chouteau Co. MT 15 F2
Chowan Co. NC 113 F4
Chowchilla CA 44 C2
Chrisman IL 99 D1
Chrisney IN 99 E4
Christiana PA 146 A3
Christian Co. IL 98 B1
Christian Co. KY 109 E2
Christian Co. MO 107 D2
Christiansburg OH 90 B4
Christiansburg VA 112 A2
Christmas FL 141 D1
Christopher IL 98 C4
Chualar CA 44 B3
Chubbuck ID 31 E1
Chugwater WY 33 E2
Chuichu AZ 54 C2
Chula Vista CA 53 D4
Chuluota FL 141 D1
Church Hill MD 145 D2
Church Hill TN 111 E3
Churchill OH 276 C2
Churchill PA 250 D2
Churchill Co. NV 37 F1
Church Pt. LA 133 E2
Church Rock NM 48 A3
Churchton MD 144 C3
Churchtown NJ 146 B4
Churchville MD 145 D1
Churchville NY 78 C3
Churubusco IN 90 A2
Cibecue AZ 55 D1
Cibola Co. NM 48 B4
Cibolo TX 257 F1
Cicero IL 89 D1
Cicero IN 89 F4
Cimarron KS 42 C4
Cimarron NM 49 E1
Cimarron Co. OK 50 A1
Cincinnati OH 100 B2
Cinnaminson NJ 146 C3
Circle MT 17 E3
Circle Pines MN 235 C1
Circleville NY 148 A1
Circleville OH 101 D1
Circleville UT 39 E3
Cisco TX 59 D3
Cisne IL 98 C3
Cissna Park IL 89 D4
Citra FL 138 C4
Citronelle AL 135 E1
Citrus Co. FL 140 B1
Citrus Hts. CA 36 C3
Citrus Park FL 266 B1
Citrus Sprs. FL 138 C4
City View SC 217 A2
Clackamas OR 251 D3
Clackamas Co. OR 20 C2
Claflin KS 43 D3
Claiborne Co. MS 126 A3
Claiborne Co. TN 110 C3
Claiborne Par. LA 125 D2
Clairton PA 92 A4
Clallam Bay WA 12 B2
Clallam Co. WA 12 B2
Clancy MT 15 E4
Clanton AL 127 F2
Clara City MN 66 B4
Clare MI 76 A2
Clare Co. MI 76 A1
Claremont CA 229 G2
Claremont MN 73 D1
Claremont NH 81 E4
Claremont NC 112 A4
Claremont VA 113 F2
Claremore OK 106 A3
Clarence IA 87 F1
Clarence LA 125 D3
Clarence MO 97 E1
Clarence PA 92 C3
Clarence Ctr. NY 78 B3
Clarendon AR 117 F2
Clarendon TX 50 B3
Clarendon Co. SC 122 B4
Clarendon Hills IL 203 C5
Clarinda IA 86 B3
Clarion IA 72 C4
Clarion PA 92 B2
Clarion Co. PA 92 A3
Clarissa MN 66 B2
Clark NJ 147 E1
Clark SD 27 E2
Clark Co. AR 117 D4
Clark Co. ID 23 E3
Clark Co. IL 99 D2
Clark Co. IN 100 A3
Clark Co. KS 42 C4
Clark Co. KY 100 B4
Clark Co. MO 87 E4
Clark Co. NV 46 A1
Clark Co. OH 100 C1
Clark Co. SD 27 E2
Clark Co. WA 20 C1
Clark Co. WI 67 F4
Clarkdale AZ 47 D4
Clarke Co. AL 127 E4
Clarke Co. GA 121 D4
Clarke Co. IA 86 C3
Clarke Co. MS 127 D3
Clarke Co. VA 103 D2
Clarkesville GA 121 D2
Clarkfield MN 66 A4
Clark Fork ID 14 B2
Clarks LA 125 E3
Clarksboro NJ 146 C3
Clarksburg MD 144 B2
Clarksburg WV 102 A2
Clarksdale MS 118 A3
Clarks Green PA 261 E1
Clarks Grove MN 72 C2
Clarks Hill IN 89 E4
Clarkson KY 109 F1
Clarkson NE 35 F2
Clarks Summit PA 93 F2
Clarkston GA 190 E3
Clarkston UT 31 E2
Clarkston WA 14 B4
Clarksville AR 117 D1
Clarksville DE 145 F4
Clarksville IN 100 A4
Clarksville IA 73 D4
Clarksville MD 144 B2
Clarksville MO 97 F2
Clarksville TN 109 E3
Clarksville TX 116 B4
Clarksville VA 113 D3
Clarksville City TX 124 B2
Clarkton MO 108 B3
Clarkton NC 123 D3
Claryville KY 100 B3
Clatskanie OR 20 B1
Clatsop Co. OR 20 B1
Claude TX 50 B3
Claverack NY 94 B2
Clawson MI 210 C2
Claxton GA 130 A3
Clay AL 119 F4
Clay KY 109 D1
Clay WV 101 F3
Clay Ctr. KS 43 E2
Clay Ctr. NE 35 E4
Clay City IL 99 D3
Clay City IN 99 E2
Clay City KY 110 C1
Claycomo MO 224 C2
Clay Co. AL 128 B1
Clay Co. AR 108 A3
Clay Co. FL 139 D3
Clay Co. GA 128 C4
Clay Co. IL 98 C3
Clay Co. IN 99 E2
Clay Co. IA 72 B3
Clay Co. KS 43 E2
Clay Co. KY 110 C2
Clay Co. MN 19 F4
Clay Co. MS 118 C4
Clay Co. MO 96 B2
Clay Co. NE 35 E4
Clay Co. NC 121 D1
Clay Co. SD 35 F1
Clay Co. TN 110 A3
Clay Co. TX 59 D1
Clay Co. WV 101 F3
Clayhatchee AL 128 B4
Claymont DE 146 B3
Claypool AZ 55 D1
Claypool Hill VA 111 F2
Claysburg PA 92 C4
Claysville PA 91 F4
Clayton AL 128 B3
Clayton CA 259 E2
Clayton DE 145 E2
Clayton GA 121 D2
Clayton IL 87 F4
Clayton IN 99 F1
Clayton LA 125 F4
Clayton MO 98 A3
Clayton NJ 146 C4
Clayton NM 49 F1
Clayton NY 79 E1
Clayton NC 113 D4
Clayton OH 100 B1
Clayton OK 116 A2
Clayton Co. GA 120 C4
Clayton Co. IA 73 F3
Clearbrook MN 64 A3
Clear Creek IN 99 F2
Clear Creek Co. CO 41 D1
Clearfield PA 92 C3
Clearfield UT 31 E3
Clearfield Co. PA 92 C3
Clearlake CA 36 B2
Clear Lake IA 72 C3
Clear Lake SD 27 F3
Clear Lake WA 12 C2
Clear Lake WI 67 E3
Clearlake Oaks CA 36 B2
Clear Lake Shores TX 132 B3
Clear Spr. MD 103 D1
Clearview WV 91 F4
Clearwater FL 140 B2
Clearwater KS 43 E4
Clearwater MN CC C3
Clearwater SC 121 F4
Clearwater Co. ID 14 C4
Clearwater Co. MN 64 A3
Cleaton KY 109 E2
Cleburne TX 59 E3
Cleburne Co. AL 120 B4
Cleburne Co. AR 107 E4
Cle Elum WA 13 D3
Clementon NJ 146 C3
Clemmons NC 112 A4
Clemson SC 121 E2
Clendenin WV 101 F3
Cleona PA 93 E4
Cleora OK 106 B3
Clermont FL 140 C1
Clermont IN 99 F1
Clermont IA 73 E3
Clermont Co. OH 100 C2
Cleveland AL 119 F3
Cleveland FL 140 C4
Cleveland GA 121 D2
Cleveland MN 72 C1
Cleveland MS 118 A4
Cleveland MO 96 B3
Cleveland NY 79 E3
Cleveland NC 112 A4
Cleveland OH 91 E2
Cleveland OK 51 F2
Cleveland TN 120 B1
Cleveland TX 132 B2
Cleveland UT 39 F2
Cleveland WI 75 D2
Cleveland Co. AR 117 E4
Cleveland Co. NC 121 F1
Cleveland Co. OK 51 E3
Cleveland Hts. OH 91 E2
Clever MO 107 D2
Cleves OH 100 B2
Clewiston FL 141 E4
Cliffside NC 121 F1
Cliffside Park NJ 148 B3
Cliffwood Beach NJ 147 E1
Clifton AZ 55 E2
Clifton CO 40 B2
Clifton ID 31 E2
Clifton IL 89 D3
Clifton KS 43 E1
Clifton NJ 148 B3
Clifton TN 119 D1
Clifton TX 59 E4
Clifton Forge VA 112 B1
Clifton Hts. PA 248 B3
Clifton Park NY 94 B1
Clifton Sprs. NY 78 C3
Climax MI 75 F4
Clinchco VA 111 E2
Clinch Co. GA 138 C1
Clint TX 56 C4
Clinton AR 117 E1
Clinton CT 149 E2
Clinton IL 88 C4
Clinton IN 99 E1

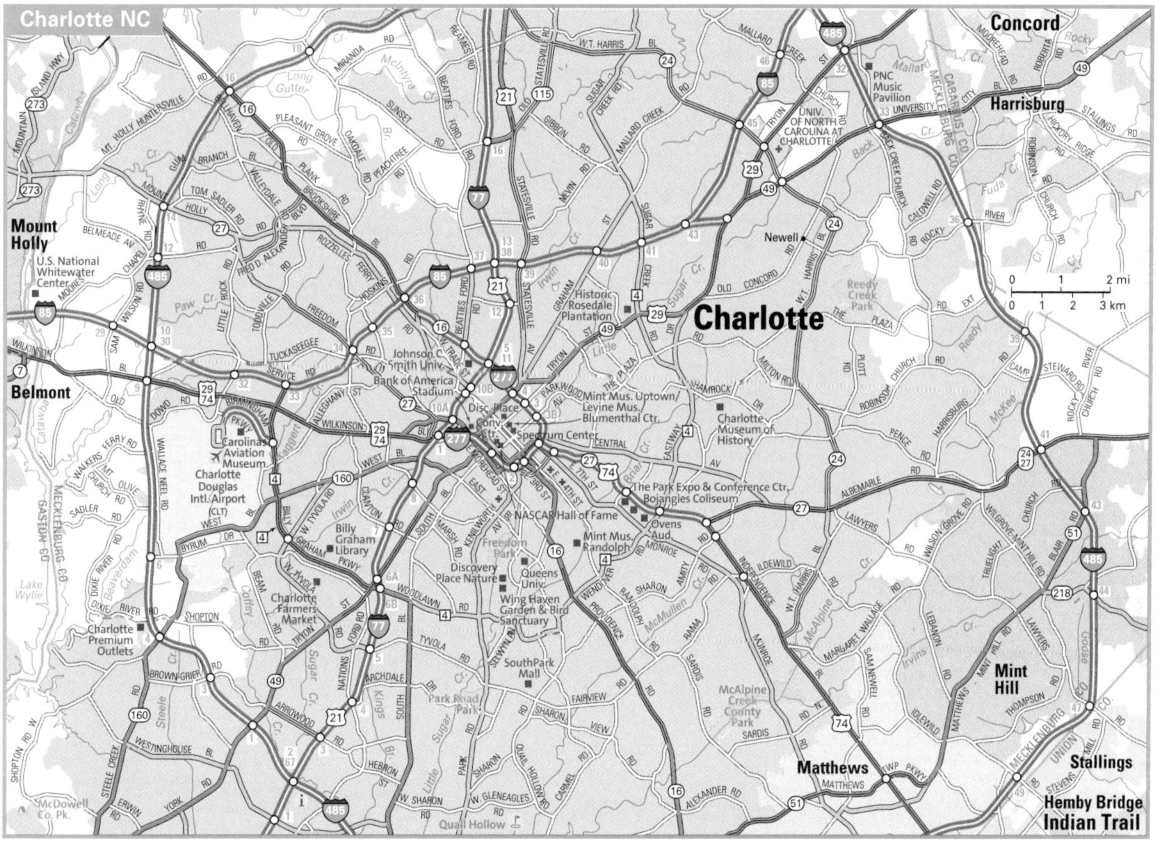

Charlotte NC
Charlotte
Concord
Harrisburg
Mount Holly
Belmont
Newell
Mint Hill
Matthews
Stallings
Hemby Bridge
Indian Trail
U.S. National Whitewater Center
Charlotte Douglas Intl. Airport (CLT)
Carolinas Aviation Museum
Billy Graham Library
Johnson C. Smith Univ.
Bank of America Stadium
Spectrum Center
NASCAR Hall of Fame
Charlotte Museum of History
The Park Expo & Conference Ctr.
Bojangles Coliseum
Ovens Aud.
Mint Mus. Randolph
Queens Univ.
Wing Haven Garden & Bird Sanctuary
Freedom Park
Discovery Place Nature
SouthPark Mall
Park Road Park
Charlotte Farmers Market
Charlotte Premium Outlets
McAlpine Creek County Park
McDowell Co. Pk.
Quail Hollow
Lake Wylie
UNIV. OF NORTH CAROLINA AT CHARLOTTE
PNC Music Pavilion
Reedy Creek Park
Historic Rosedale Plantation
MECKLENBURG CO.
GASTON CO.
CABARRUS CO.
UNION CO.
0 1 2 mi
0 1 2 3 km

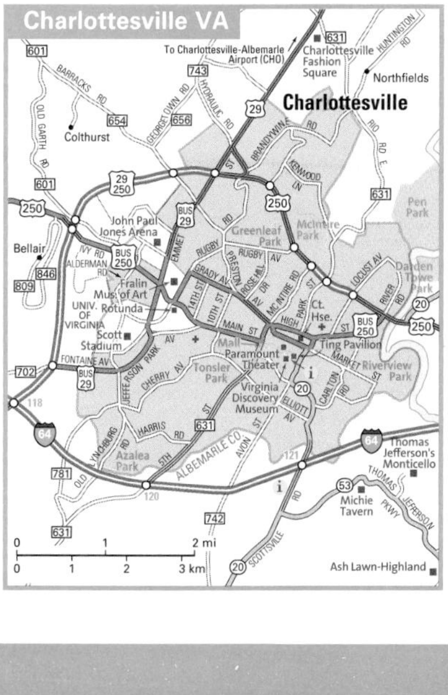

Charlottesville VA
Charlottesville
To Charlottesville-Albemarle Airport (CHO)
Charlottesville Fashion Square
Northfields
Colthurst
Bellair
John Paul Jones Arena
Fralin Mus. of Art
UNIV. OF VIRGINIA
Rotunda
Scott Stadium
McIntire Park
Greenleaf Park
Paramount Theater
Ting Pavilion
Tonsler Park
Virginia Discovery Museum
Riverview Park
Azalea Park
Thomas Jefferson's Monticello
Michie Tavern
Ash Lawn-Highland
Pen Park
Darden Towe Park
0 1 2 mi
0 1 2 3 km

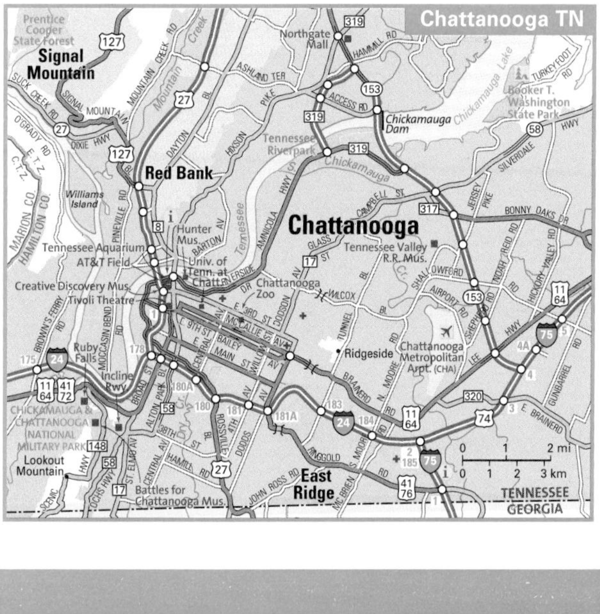

Chattanooga TN
Chattanooga
Signal Mountain
Red Bank
East Ridge
Ridgeside
Prentice Cooper State Forest
Northgate Mall
Booker T. Washington State Park
Chickamauga Dam
Tennessee Riverpark
Williams Island
Tennessee Aquarium
AT&T Field
Hunter Mus.
Univ. of Tenn. at Chatt.
Creative Discovery Mus.
Tivoli Theatre
Chattanooga Zoo
Tennessee Valley R.R. Mus.
Ruby Falls
Incline Rwy.
CHICKAMAUGA & CHATTANOOGA NATIONAL MILITARY PARK
Lookout Mountain
Battles for Chattanooga Mus.
Chattanooga Metropolitan Arpt. (CHA)
MARION CO.
HAMILTON CO.
TENNESSEE
GEORGIA
0 1 2 mi
0 1 2 3 km

Figures after entries indicate page number and grid reference.

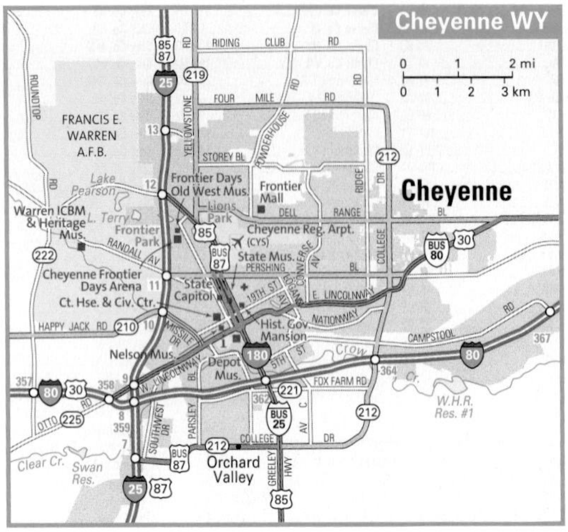
Cheyenne WY
0 1 2 mi
0 1 2 3 km
FRANCIS E. WARREN A.F.B.
Cheyenne
Frontier Days Old West Mus.
Frontier Mall
Warren ICBM & Heritage Mus.
Lake Pearson
L. Terry
Frontier Park
Cheyenne Reg. Arpt. (CYS)
State Mus.
Cheyenne Frontier Days Arena
Ct. Hse. & Civ. Ctr.
State Capitol
Hist. Gov. Mansion
Nelson Mus.
Depot Mus.
W.H.R. Res. #1
Clear Cr.
Swan Res.
Orchard Valley
RIDING CLUB RD
FOUR MILE RD
DELL RANGE BL
LINCOLNWAY
NATIONWAY
CAMPSTOOL RD
FOX FARM RD
COLLEGE DR
HAPPY JACK RD
Crow Cr.

Clinton IA 88 A1
Clinton KY 108 C3
Clinton LA 134 A1
Clinton ME 82 C2
Clinton MD 144 B4
Clinton MA 150 C1
Clinton MI 90 B1
Clinton MS 126 B2
Clinton MO 96 C4
Clinton MT 15 D4
Clinton NJ 147 D1
Clinton NY 79 E3
Clinton NC 123 E2
Clinton OH 91 E3
Clinton OK 51 D3
Clinton SC 121 F3
Clinton TN 110 C4
Clinton UT 244 A2
Clinton WA 12 C2
Clinton WI 74 B4
Clinton Co. IL 98 B3
Clinton Co. IN 89 E4
Clinton Co. IA 88 A1
Clinton Co. KY 110 B2
Clinton Co. MI 76 A3
Clinton Co. MO 96 B1
Clinton Co. NY 80 C2
Clinton Co. OH 100 C2
Clinton Co. PA 92 C2
Clintondale NY 148 B1
Clintonville WI 68 C4
Clintwood VA 111 E2
Clio AL 128 B4
Clio MI 76 B3
Clio SC 122 C2
Cloquet MN 64 C4
Closter NJ 148 B3
Cloud Co. KS 43 E2
Cloudcroft NM 56 C2
Clover SC 122 A1
Cloverdale CA 36 A2
Cloverdale IN 99 E1
Cloverdale VA 112 B1
Cloverleaf TX 220 D2
Cloverport KY 109 F1
Clovis CA 44 C2
Clovis NM 49 F4
Clute TX 132 A4
Clyde CA 259 D1
Clyde KS 43 E1
Clyde NY 79 D3
Clyde NC 121 E1
Clyde OH 90 C2
Clyde TX 58 C3
Clyde Hill WA 262 B3
Clyde Park MT 23 F1
Clymer PA 92 B3
Coachella CA 53 E3
Coahoma TX 58 B3
Coahoma Co. MS 118 A3
Coal City IL 88 C2
Coal City WV 111 F1
Coal Co. OK 51 F4
Coal Creek CO 41 E3
Coaldale PA 93 E3
Coal Fork WV 101 F4
Coalgate OK 51 F4
Coal Grove OH 101 D3
Coal Hill AR 116 C1
Coaling AL 127 F1
Coalinga CA 44 C3
Coalmont TN 120 A1
Coal Mtn. GA 120 C3
Coal Run Vil. KY 111 E1
Coal Valley IL 88 A2
Coalville UT 31 F4
Coatesville IN 99 E1
Coatesville PA 146 B3
Coats NC 123 D1
Cobb CA 36 B2
Cobb Co. GA 120 C4
Cobb Island MD 103 E4
Cobden IL 108 C1
Cobleskill NY 79 F4
Coburg OR 20 B3
Cochise Co. AZ 55 E3
Cochiti NM 48 C3
Cochituate MA 150 C1
Cochran GA 129 E2
Cochran Co. TX 57 F1
Cochranton PA 92 A2
Cochranville PA 146 A3
Cocke Co. TN 111 D4
Cockeysville MD 144 C1
Cockrell Hill TX 207 D2
Cocoa FL 141 E2
Cocoa Beach FL 141 E2
Cocoa West FL 232 A2
Coconino Co. AZ 47 D3
Coconut Creek FL 233 B1
Codington Co. SD 27 E2
Cody WY 24 B3
Coeburn VA 111 E2
Coeur d'Alene ID 14 B3
Coffee Co. AL 128 A4
Coffee Co. GA 129 E4
Coffee Co. TN 120 A1
Coffeen IL 98 B2
Coffeeville MS 118 B4
Coffey Co. KS 96 A4
Coffeyville KS 106 A2
Coggon IA 73 E4
Cohasset MA 151 E1
Cohasset MN 64 B3
Cohocton NY 78 C4
Cohoes NY 94 B1
Cohutta GA 120 B2
Cokato MN 66 C3
Cokeburg PA 92 A4
Coke Co. TX 58 B4
Coker AL 127 E1
Cokeville WY 31 F2
Colbert GA 121 D3
Colbert OK 59 F1
Colbert Co. AL 119 E2
Colby KS 42 B2
Colby WI 68 A4
Colchester CT 149 E1
Colchester IL 87 F4
Colchester VT 81 D2
Colcord OK 106 B3
Colden NY 78 B4
Cold Spr. KY 204 B3
Cold Spr. MN 66 C3
Cold Spr. NY 148 B1
Coldspring TX 132 B2
Coldwater KS 43 D4
Coldwater MI 90 A1
Coldwater MS 118 B2
Coldwater OH 90 B4
Cole OK 51 E3
Colebrook NH 81 F1
Cole Camp MO 97 D3
Cole Co. MO 97 E3
Coleman FL 140 C1
Coleman MI 76 A2
Coleman TX 58 C3
Coleman WI 68 C3
Coleman Co. TX 58 C3
Coleraine MN 64 B3
Coleridge NE 35 E1
Coles Co. IL 99 D1
Colesville MD 144 B2
Colfax CA 36 C2
Colfax IL 88 C4
Colfax IN 89 E4
Colfax IA 87 D2
Colfax LA 125 E4
Colfax WA 14 A4
Colfax WI 67 E4
Colfax Co. NE 35 F3
Colfax Co. NM 49 E1
Collbran CO 40 B2
College AK 154 C2
Collegedale TN 120 B2
College Park GA 120 C4
College Park MD 270 E1
College Place WA 21 F1
College Sta. TX 61 F1
Collegeville IN 89 E3
Collegeville PA 146 B2
Colleton Co. SC 130 C2
Colleyville TX 59 E2
Collier Co. FL 143 D1
Collierville TN 118 B2
Collin Co. TX 59 F2
Collingdale PA 248 B4
Collingswood NJ 146 C3
Collingsworth Co. TX 50 C3
Collins GA 129 F3
Collins IA 87 D1
Collins MS 126 C4
Collins Park DE 274 D3
Collinsville AL 120 A3
Collinsville IL 98 B3
Collinsville MS 127 D2
Collinsville OK 106 A3
Collinsville TX 59 F1
Collinsville VA 112 B3
Collinwood TN 119 E1
Colma CA 259 B3
Colman SD 27 F4
Colmar PA 146 C2
Colmar Manor MD 270 E3
Colmesneil TX 132 C1
Colo IA 87 D1
Cologne MN 66 C4
Cologne NJ 147 D4
Coloma MI 89 F1
Colome SD 34 C1
Colon MI 90 A1
Colona IL 88 A2
Colonia NJ 147 E1
Colonial Beach VA 103 E4
Colonial Hts. TN 111 E3
Colonial Hts. VA 113 E2
Colonial Park PA 218 C1
Colonie NY 94 B1
Colony KS 96 A4
Colorado City AZ 46 C1
Colorado City CO 41 E3
Colorado City TX 58 B3
Colorado Co. TX 61 F2
Colorado Sprs. CO 41 E2
Colquitt GA 137 D1
Colquitt Co. GA 137 F1
Colstrip MT 25 D1
Colton CA 229 J2
Colton SD 27 F4
Columbia AL 128 B4
Columbia CA 37 D3
Columbia CT 149 F1
Columbia FL 138 C3
Columbia IL 98 A3
Columbia KY 110 B2
Columbia LA 125 F3
Columbia MD 144 B2
Columbia MS 126 B4
Columbia MO 97 E3
Columbia NC 113 F4
Columbia PA 103 E1
Columbia SC 122 A3
Columbia TN 119 F1
Columbia Beach MD 144 C3
Columbia City IN 89 F2
Columbia City OR 20 C1
Columbia Co. AR 125 D1
Columbia Co. FL 138 C2

CHICAGO MAP INDEX

Addison C4
Algonquin A2
Alsip D6
Arlington Hts. C2
Aurora A5
Bannockburn C2
Barrington B2
Barrington Hills A2
Bartlett A3
Batavia A4
Bedford Park D5
Bellwood C4
Bensenville C4
Berkeley C4
Berwyn D4
Bloomingdale B3
Blue Island D6
Bolingbrook B6
Bridgeview D5
Broadview C4
Brookfield C5
Buffalo Grove C2
Burbank D5
Burnham E6
Burr Ridge C5
Burtons Bridge A1
Calumet City E6
Calumet Park E6
Carol Stream B4
Carpentersville A2
Cary A2
Chicago E4
Chicago Ridge D5
Cicero D4
Clarendon Hills C5
Countryside C5
Crest Hill B6
Crestwood D6
Crystal Lake A1
Darien C5
Deerfield C2
Deer Park B2
Des Plaines C3
Diamond Lake B1
Dixmoor E6
Dolton E6
Downers Grove B5
E. Dundee A2
Elgin A3
Elk Grove Vil. C3
Elmhurst C4
Elmwood Park D4
Evanston D3
Evergreen Park D5
Forest Lake B1
Forest Park D4
Forest View D5
Fox River Grove A2
Franklin Park C4
Geneva A4
Glencoe D2
Glendale Hts. B4
Glen Ellyn B4
Glenview D2
Golf D3
Grayslake B1
Green Oaks C1
Hanover Park B3
Harvey E6
Harwood Hts. D3
Hawthorn Woods B1
Hazel Crest E6
Hickory Hills D5
Highland Park D2
Highwood D1
Hillside C4
Hinsdale C5
Hodgkins C5
Hoffman Estates B3
Holiday Hills A1
Homer Glen C6
Hometown D5
Indian Creek C1
Indian Head Park C5
Inverness B2
Island Lake A1
Itasca B3
Ivanhoe B1
Justice D5
Kenilworth D2
Kildeer B2
Knollwood C1
La Grange C5
La Grange Park C4
Lake Barrington B1
Lake Bluff C1
Lake Forest C1
Lake in the Hills A2
Lakemoor A1
Lake Zurich B2
Lemont B6
Libertyville C1
Lincolnshire C2
Lincolnwood D3
Lisle B5
Lockport B6
Lombard B4
Long Grove C2
Lyons D5
Markham D6
Maywood C4
McCook D5
McHenry A1
Medinah B3
Melrose Park C4
Merrionette Park D6
Mettawa C1
Midlothian D6
Montgomery A5
Morton Grove D3
Mount Prospect C3
Mundelein B1
Naperville B5
Niles D3
Norridge D3
N. Aurora A5
N. Barrington B2
Northbrook D2
N. Chicago C1
Northfield D2
Northlake C4
N. Riverside D4
Oak Brook C4
Oakbrook Terrace C4
Oak Forest D6
Oak Lawn D5
Oak Park D4
Oakwood Hills A1
Orland Hills C6
Orland Park C6
Oswego A5
Palatine B2
Palos Hts. D6
Palos Hills D5
Palos Park D6
Park Ridge C3
Phoenix E6
Plainfield A6
Port Barrington A1
Posen D6
Prairie Grove A1
Prospect Hts. C2
Riverdale E6
River Forest D4
River Grove D4
Riverside D4
Riverwoods C2
Robbins D6
Rolling Meadows B3
Romeoville B6
Rondout C1
Roselle B3
Rosemont C3
St. Charles A4
Schaumburg B3
Schiller Park C3
Skokie D3
Sleepy Hollow A2
S. Barrington B2
S. Elgin A3
S. Holland E6
Stickney D5
Stone Park C4
Streamwood B3
Summit D5
Tinley Park D6
Tower Lakes B1
Trout Valley A1
Valley View A3
Vernon Hills C1
Villa Park C4
Volo B1
Warrenville A4
Wauconda B1
Wayne A4
Westchester C4
W. Chicago A4
W. Dundee A2
Western Sprs. C5
Westmont C5
Wheaton B4
Wheeling C2
Willowbrook C5
Willow Sprs. C5
Wilmette D3
Winfield B4
Winnetka D2
Wood Dale C3
Woodridge B5
Worth D6

Columbia Co. GA 121 F4
Columbia Co. NY 94 B2
Columbia Co. OR 20 B1
Columbia Co. PA 93 E3
Columbia Co. WA 13 F4
Columbia Co. WI 74 B3
Columbia Falls MT 15 D2
Columbia Hts. MN 235 C2
Columbiana AL 127 F1
Columbiana OH 91 F3
Columbiana Co. OH 91 F3
Columbiaville MI 76 B3
Columbiaville NY 94 B2
Columbine Valley CO 209 B4
Columbus GA 128 C2
Columbus IN 99 F2
Columbus KS 106 B2
Columbus MS 119 D4

POINTS OF INTEREST

875 N. Michigan Av. (John Hancock Ctr.) B1
900 North Michigan Shops B1
Adler Planetarium & Astronomy Museum C3
American Writers Museum B2
Art Institute of Chicago B2
Auditorium Theatre B2
Buckingham Fountain B2
Cadillac Palace Theatre B2
Centennial Fountain & Arc B2
Chicago Architecture Foundation B2
Chicago Board of Trade B2
Chicago Children's Museum C1
Chicago Cultural Center B2
Chicago Fire Marker A3
Chicago Mercantile Exchange A2
Chicago Stock Exchange B2
Chicago Theatre B2
Chicago Yacht Club C2
CIBC Theatre B2
City Hall B2
Civic Opera House A2
Cloud Gate B2
Crown Fountain B2
Daley Plaza B2
Dearborn Station B3
East-West University B3
The Field Museum C3
Goodman Theatre B2
Harris Theater B2
Harold Washington Library Center B2
Huntington Bank Pavilion at Northerly Island C3
James R. Thompson Center B2
Jane Addams Hull-House Mus. A3
Jay Pritzker Pavillion B2
John G. Shedd Aquarium C3
Merchandise Mart A2
Monadnock Building B2
Moody Bible Institute B1
Mus. of Broadcast Communications B2
Mus. of Contemporary Art B1
Mus. of Contemporary Photography B3
Navy Pier C1
Nederlander Theatre B2
Newberry Library B1
New Maxwell Street Market A3
Northwestern Univ. (Chi. Campus) C1
Petrillo Band Shell B2
The Shops at North Bridge B1
Soldier Field C3
Spertus Institute B3
Symphony Center B2
Tribune Tower B1
Trump Intl. Hotel & Tower B2
Union Station A2
Univ. of Illinois at Chicago A3
Water Tower B1
Water Tower Place B1
Willis Tower A2
Wrigley Building B1

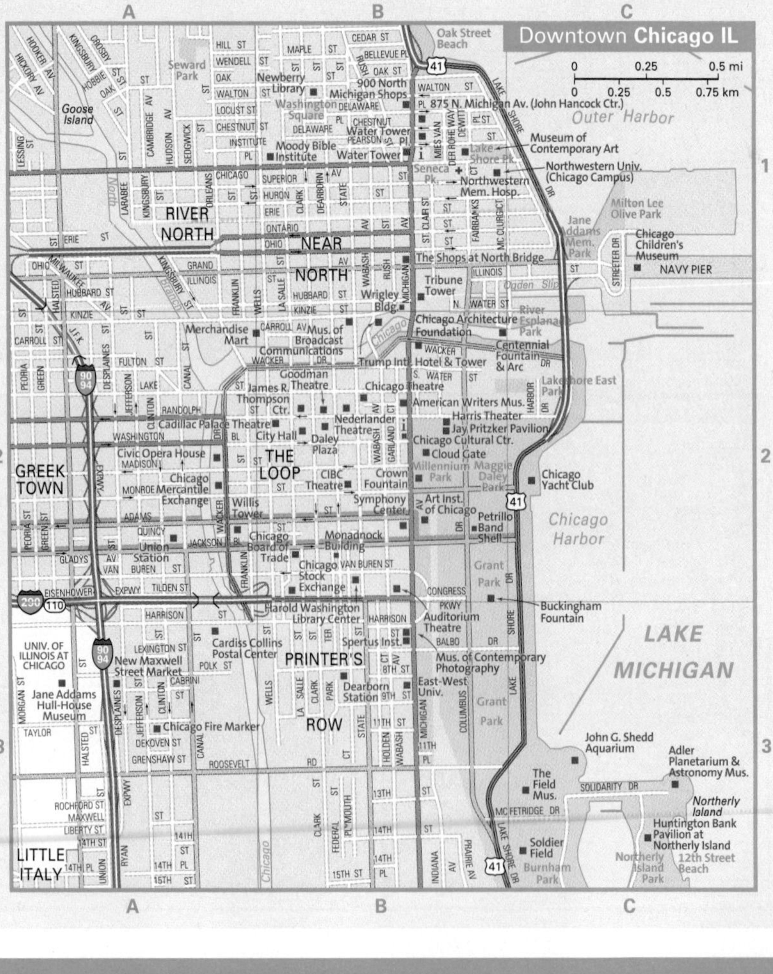
Downtown Chicago IL
0 0.25 0.5 mi
0 0.25 0.5 0.75 km
Outer Harbor
Oak Street Beach
Goose Island
Seward Park
Newberry Library
Washington Square
Moody Bible Institute
Water Tower
Museum of Contemporary Art
Lake Shore Pk.
Northwestern Univ. (Chicago Campus)
Northwestern Mem. Hosp.
Milton Lee Olive Park
Jane Addams Mem. Park
Chicago Children's Museum
NAVY PIER
RIVER NORTH
NEAR NORTH
The Shops at North Bridge
Tribune Tower
Wrigley Bldg.
Merchandise Mart
Mus. of Broadcast Communications
Chicago Architecture Foundation
Centennial Fountain & Arc
Trump Intl. Hotel & Tower
Goodman Theatre
Chicago Theatre
James R. Thompson Ctr.
Nederlander Theatre
Cadillac Palace Theatre
City Hall
Daley Plaza
American Writers Mus.
Harris Theater
Jay Pritzker Pavilion
Chicago Cultural Ctr.
Cloud Gate
Millennium Park
Maggie Daley Park
Lakeshore East Park
Chicago Yacht Club
GREEK TOWN
Civic Opera House
Chicago Mercantile Exchange
THE LOOP
CIBC Theatre
Crown Fountain
Symphony Center
Art Inst. of Chicago
Petrillo Band Shell
Chicago Harbor
Willis Tower
Chicago Board of Trade
Union Station
Monadnock Building
Chicago Stock Exchange
Grant Park
Harold Washington Library Center
Buckingham Fountain
Auditorium Theatre
Spertus Inst.
Cardiss Collins Postal Center
UNIV. OF ILLINOIS AT CHICAGO
New Maxwell Street Market
Jane Addams Hull-House Museum
PRINTER'S ROW
Dearborn Station
Mus. of Contemporary Photography
East-West Univ.
Chicago Fire Marker
LAKE MICHIGAN
John G. Shedd Aquarium
Adler Planetarium & Astronomy Mus.
The Field Mus.
Northerly Island
Huntington Bank Pavilion at Northerly Island
12th Street Beach
Soldier Field
Burnham Park
LITTLE ITALY

Entries in **bold black** indicate counties or parishes.
Entries in **bold color** indicate cities with detailed inset maps.

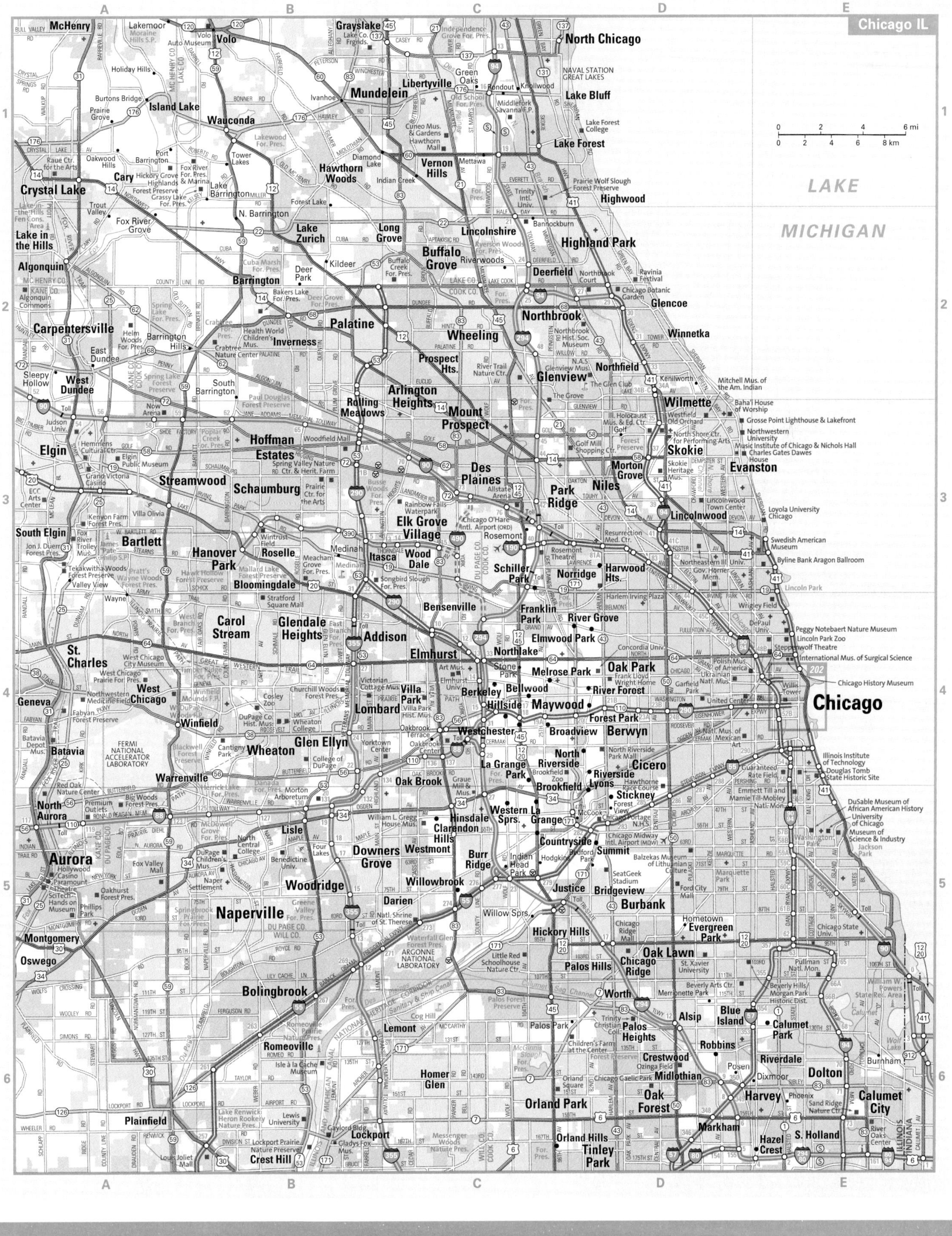

Figures after entries indicate page number and grid reference.

Columbus MT 24 B1
Columbus NE 35 E3
Columbus NJ 147 D2
Columbus NM 56 B3
Columbus NC 121 F1
Columbus OH 101 D1
Columbus TX 61 F2
Columbus WI 74 B3
Columbus Co. NC 123 D3
Columbus Grove OH 90 B3
Columbus Jct. IA 87 F2
Colusa CA 36 B2
Colusa Co. CA 36 B2
Colver PA 92 B4
Colville WA 13 F2
Colwich KS 43 E4
Colwyn PA 248 B4
Comal Co. TX 61 D2
Comanche OK 51 E4
Comanche TX 59 D3
Comanche Co. KS 43 D4
Comanche Co. OK 51 D4
Comanche Co. TX 59 D3
Combes TX 63 F4
Comer GA 121 E3
Comfort TX 61 D2
Commack NY 148 C3
Commerce CA 228 D3
Commerce GA 121 D3
Commerce OK 106 B2
Commerce TX 124 A1
Commerce City CO 41 E1
Commercial Pt. OH 101 D1
Como MS 118 B3
Como TX 124 A1
Como WI 74 C4
Compton CA 52 C3
Comstock MI 75 F4
Comstock NY 81 D4
Comstock Park MI 75 F3
Concho Co. TX 58 C4
Concord AL 195 D2
Concord CA 36 B3
Concord MA 150 C1
Concord MI 90 B1
Concord MO 256 B3

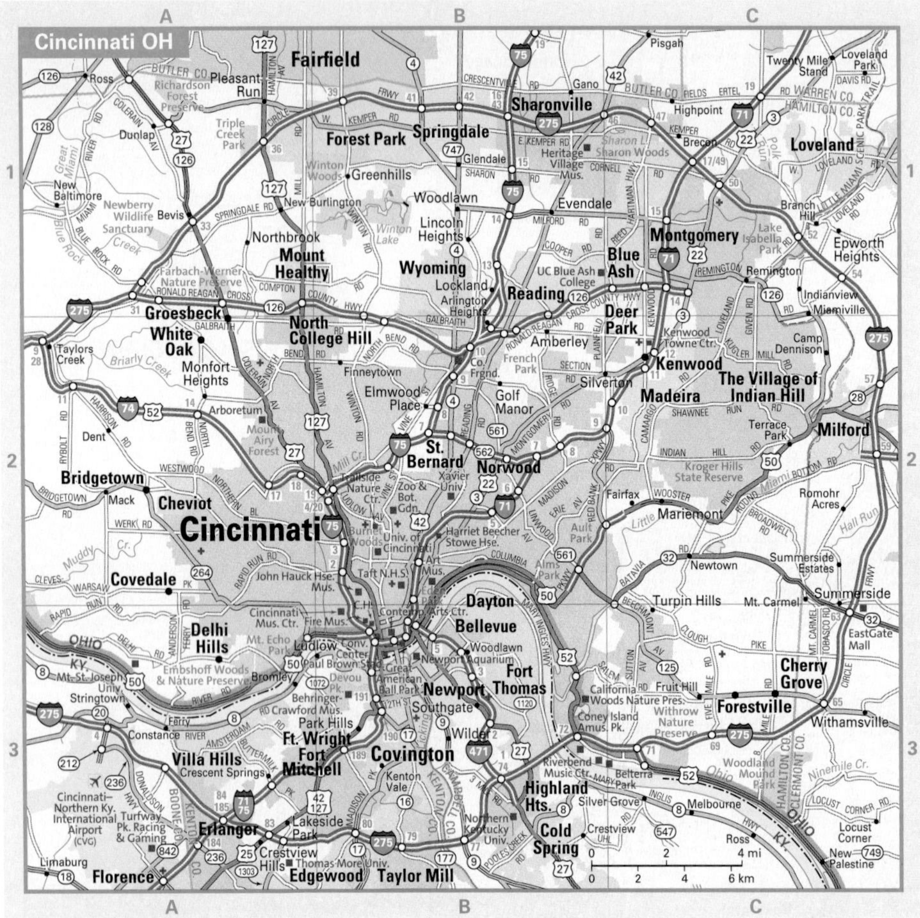
Cincinnati OH
Cincinnati
Fairfield
Sharonville
Springdale
Forest Park
Loveland
Montgomery
Blue Ash
Reading
Norwood
Covington
Newport
Florence

Amberley B2
Arlington Hts. B2
Bellevue B3
Bevis A1
Blue Ash C1
Branch Hill C1
Brecon C1
Bridgetown A2
Bromley A3
Camp Dennison C2
Cherry Grove C3
Cheviot A2
Cincinnati A2
Cold Spr. B3
Constance A3
Covedale A2
Covington B3
Crescent Sprs. A3
Crestview B3
Crestview Hills A3
Dayton B2
Deer Park C2
Delhi Hills A3
Dent A2
Dunlap A1
Edgewood B3
Elmwood Place B2
Epworth Hts. C1
Erlanger A3
Evendale B1
Fairfax C2
Fairfield B1
Finneytown B2
Florence A3
Forest Park B1
Forestville C3
Ft. Mitchell A3
Ft. Thomas B3
Ft. Wright B3
Fruit Hill C3
Gano B1
Glendale B1
Golf Manor B2
Greenhills B1
Groesbeck A2
Highland Hts. B3
Highpoint C1
Indianview C1
Kenton Vale B3
Kenwood C2
Lakeside Park A3
Limaburg A3
Lincoln Hts. B1
Lockland B1
Locust Corner C3
Loveland C1
Loveland Park C1
Ludlow A3
Mack A2
Madeira C2
Mariemont C2
Melbourne C3
Miamiville C1
Milford C2
Monfort Hts. A2
Montgomery C1
Mt. Carmel C2
Mt. Healthy A1
New Baltimore A1
New Burlington A1
New Palestine C3
Newport B3
Newtown C2
Northbrook A1
N. College Hill A2
Norwood B2
Park Hills B3
Pisgah C1
Pleasant Run A1
Reading B1
Remington C1
Romohr Acres C2
Ross, KY C3
Ross, OH A1
St. Bernard B2
Sharonville B1
Silver Grove C3
Silverton B2
Southgate B3
Springdale B1
Stringtown A3
Summerside C2
Summerside Estates C2
Taylor Mill B3
Taylors Creek A2
Terrace Park C2
The Vil. of Indian Hill C2
Turpin Hills C3
Twenty Mile Stand C1
Villa Hills A3
White Oak A2
Wilder B3
Withamsville C3
Woodlawn, KY B3
Woodlawn, OH B1
Wyoming B1

Cleveland OH
LAKE ERIE
Cleveland
Euclid
Lakewood
Parma
Westlake
Strongsville
Solon

Avon D2
Avon Lake D2
Bay Village D2
Beachwood G2
Bedford G3
Bedford Heights G3
Bentleyville G3
Berea D3
Bratenahl F1
Brecksville F3
Broadview Heights F3
Brooklyn E2
Brooklyn Heights F2
Brook Park E3
Cleveland E1
Cleveland Heights F2
Cuyahoga Heights F2
E. Cleveland F1
Euclid G1
Fairview Park D2
Garfield Heights F3
Gates Mills G1
Glenwillow G3
Highland Heights G1
Highland Hills G2
Hunting Valley G2
Independence F3
Lakewood E2
Linndale E2
Lyndhurst G2
Macedonia G3
Maple Heights F3
Mayfield G1
Mayfield Heights G2
Middleburg Heights E3
Moreland Hills G2
Newburgh Heights F2
Northfield G3
N. Olmsted D2
N. Randall G2
N. Ridgeville D3
N. Royalton E3
Oakwood G3
Olmsted Falls D3
Orange G2
Parma E3
Parma Heights E3
Pepper Pike G2
Richmond Heights G1
Rocky River E2
Sagamore Hills F3
Seven Hills F3
Shaker Heights G2
Solon G3
S. Euclid G1
Strongsville E3
Twinsburg G3
University Heights G2
Valley View F3
Walton Hills G3
Warrensville Heights G2
Westlake D2
Wickliffe G1
Willoughby Hills G1
Woodmere G2

Entries in **bold black** indicate counties or parishes.
Entries in **bold color** indicate cities with detailed inset maps.

Concord NH 81 F4
Concord NC 122 B1
Concord TN 110 C4
Concord VA 112 C1
Concordia KS 43 E1
Concordia MO 96 C2
Concordia Par. LA 125 F4
Concrete WA 12 C2
Condon OR 21 E2
Conecuh Co. AL 127 F4
Conehatta MS 126 C2
Conejos CO 49 D1
Conejos Co. CO 41 D4
Conestoga PA 146 A3
Confluence PA 102 B1
Congers NY 148 B2
Congress AZ 46 C4
Conklin NY 93 F1
Conneaut OH 91 F1
Conneaut Lake PA 91 F2
Conneaut Lake Park PA 91 F2
Conneautville PA 91 F1
Connell WA 13 F4
Connellsville PA 102 B1
Connersville IN 100 A1
Conover NC 111 F4
Conovertown NJ 147 F4
Conrad IA 87 D1
Conrad MT 15 E2
Conroe TX 132 A2
Conshohocken PA 146 C2
Constantia NY 79 E3
Constantine MI 89 F1
Continental OH 90 B3
Contoocook NH 81 F4
Contra Costa Co. CA 36 B3
Convent LA 134 A3
Converse IN 89 F3
Converse LA 124 C3
Converse TX 257 F2
Converse Co. WY 33 E1
Convoy OH 90 A3
Conway AR 117 E1
Conway FL 246 C3
Conway MO 107 D1
Conway NH 81 F3
Conway NC 113 E3
Conway PA 91 F3
Conway SC 123 D4
Conway Co. AR 117 E1
Conway Sprs. KS 43 E4
Conyers GA 120 C4
Conyngham PA 93 E3
Cook MN 64 C3
Cook Co. GA 129 E4
Cook Co. IL 89 D1
Cook Co. MN 65 D2
Cooke Co. TX 59 E1
Cookeville TN 110 A4
Cooleemee NC 112 A4
Coolidge AZ 54 C2
Coolidge GA 137 E1
Coolidge TX 59 F4
Cool Valley MO 256 B1
Coon Rapids IA 86 B1
Coon Rapids MN 67 D3
Coon Valley WI 73 F2
Cooper TX 124 A1
Cooper City FL 233 A3
Cooper Co. MO 97 D3
Coopersburg PA 146 C1
Coopers Mills ME 82 C2
Cooperstown NY 79 F4
Cooperstown ND 19 E3
Coopersville MI 75 F3
Coopertown TN 109 E3
Coosa Co. AL 128 A1
Coosada AL 128 A2
Coos Bay OR 20 A4
Coos Co. NH 81 F1
Coos Co. OR 20 B4
Copalis Beach WA 12 B3
Copan OK 51 F1
Copenhagen NY 79 E2
Copiague NY 148 C4
Copiah Co. MS 126 A3
Coplay PA 189 A1
Copley OH 188 A1
Coppell TX 207 C1
Copperas Cove TX 59 E4
Copperhill TN 120 C2
Copperopolis CA 36 C3
Coquille OR 28 A1
Coral Gables FL 143 E2
Coral Hills MD 270 E4
Coral Sprs. FL 143 E1
Coralville IA 87 F2
Coram MT 15 D2
Coram NY 149 D3
Coraopolis PA 250 A1
Corbin KY 110 C2
Corcoran CA 45 D3
Corcoran MN 66 C3
Cordaville MA 150 C1
Cordele GA 129 D3
Cordova AL 119 E4
Cordova AK 154 C3
Cordova IL 88 A2
Cordova MD 145 D3
Cordova NC 122 C2
Cordova TN 118 B1
Corea ME 83 E2
Corfu NY 78 B3
Corinna ME 82 C1
Corinne UT 31 E3
Corinth MS 119 D2
Corinth NY 80 C4
Corinth TX 59 E2
Corn OK 51 D3
Cornelia GA 121 D3
Cornelius NC 122 A1
Cornelius OR 20 B2
Cornell WI 67 F3
Cornersville TN 119 F1
Cornfields AZ 47 F2
Corning AR 108 A3
Corning CA 36 B1
Corning IA 86 B3
Corning NY 93 D1
Corning OH 101 E1
Cornish ME 82 A3
Cornville AZ 47 D4
Cornwall PA 93 E4
Cornwall-on-Hudson NY 148 B1
Corona CA 53 D3
Coronado CA 53 D4
Corpus Christi TX 63 F2
Corrales NM 48 C3
Corralitos CA 44 B2
Correctionville IA 72 A4
Corrigan TX 132 B1
Corry PA 92 A1
Corryton TN 110 C4
Corsica SD 27 E4
Corsicana TX 59 F3

Black Forest D1
Cascade C1
Chipita Park C1
Colorado Sprs. D1
Crystola C1
Fountain D2
Green Mtn. Falls C1
Manitou Sprs. C2
Security-Widefield D2
Stratmoor Hills D2

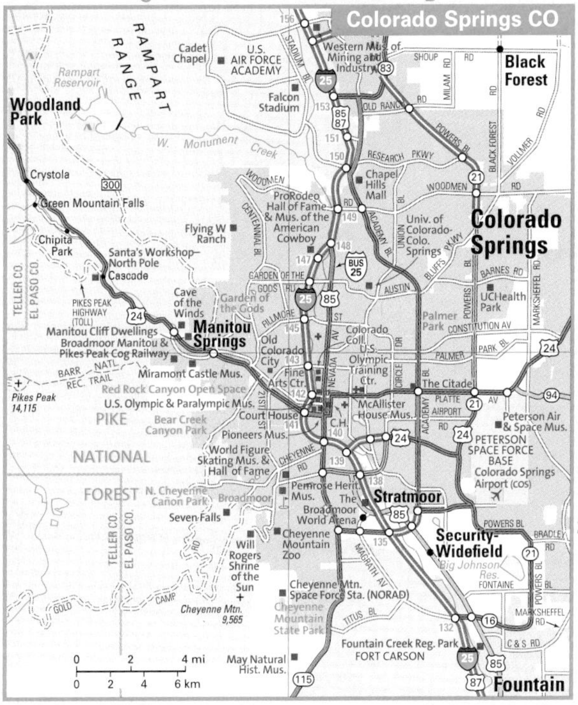
Colorado Springs CO
C
D
RAMPART RANGE
Rampart Reservoir
Woodland Park
Cadet Chapel
U.S. AIR FORCE ACADEMY
Western Mus. of Mining and Industry
Black Forest
Falcon Stadium
W. Monument Creek
Crystola
Green Mountain Falls
Chipita Park
Santa's Workshop-North Pole
Cascade
PIKES PEAK HIGHWAY (TOLL)
Manitou Cliff Dwellings
Broadmoor Manitou & Pikes Peak Cog Railway
Manitou Springs
Flying W Ranch
ProRodeo Hall of Fame & Mus. of the American Cowboy
Chapel Hills Mall
Univ. of Colorado-Colo. Springs
Colorado Springs
Cave of the Winds
Garden of the Gods
Miramont Castle Mus.
Red Rock Canyon Open Space
Pikes Peak 14,115
U.S. Olympic & Paralympic Mus.
Bear Creek Canyon Park
PIKE
NATIONAL
FOREST
Colorado Coll.
U.S. Olympic Training Ctr.
The Citadel
McAllister House Mus.
Court House
Pioneers Mus.
World Figure Skating Mus. & Hall of Fame
Peterson Air & Space Mus.
PETERSON SPACE FORCE BASE
Colorado Springs Airport (COS)
UCHealth Park
Palmer Park
N. Cheyenne Cañon Park
Seven Falls
Will Rogers Shrine of the Sun
Cheyenne Mountain Zoo
Broadmoor World Arena
Stratmoor
Security-Widefield
Big Johnson Res.
Cheyenne Mtn. Space Force Sta. (NORAD)
Cheyenne Mountain State Park
Cheyenne Mtn. 9,565
Fountain Creek Reg. Park
FORT CARSON
May Natural Hist. Mus.
Fountain
0 2 4 mi
0 2 4 6 km

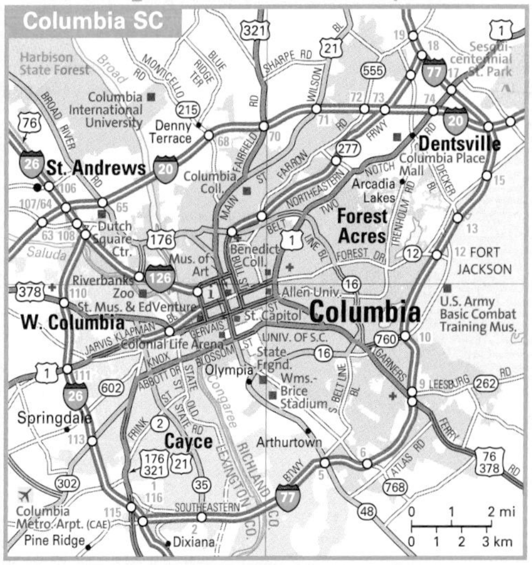
Columbia SC
E
F
Harbison State Forest
Columbia International University
Denny Terrace
St. Andrews
Columbia Coll.
Dentsville
Columbia Place Mall
Arcadia Lakes
Sesqui-centennial St. Park
Dutch Square Ctr.
Forest Acres
12 FORT JACKSON
Benedict Coll.
Mus. of Art
Riverbanks Zoo
S.C. Mus. & EdVenture
Allen Univ.
St. Capitol
W. Columbia
Columbia
U.S. Army Basic Combat Training Mus.
Colonial Life Arena
UNIV. OF S.C.
State Frgnd.
Olympia
Wms.-Brice Stadium
Springdale
Cayce
Arthurtown
Columbia Metro. Arpt. (CAE)
Pine Ridge
Dixiana
0 1 2 mi
0 1 2 3 km

Arcadia Lakes F1
Arthurtown F2
Cayce E2
Columbia F2
Denny Terrace E1
Dentsville F1
Dixiana E2
Forest Acres F1
Olympia E2
Pineridge E2
St. Andrews E1
Springdale E2
W. Columbia E2

Cottondale AL 127 E1
Cottondale FL 136 C1
Cotton Plant AR 117 F2
Cottonport LA 133 F1
Cotton Valley LA 125 D2
Cottonwood AL 137 D1
Cottonwood AZ 47 D4
Cottonwood CA 28 C4
Cottonwood ID 22 B1
Cottonwood MN 66 A4
Cottonwood Co. MN 72 A1
Cottonwood Cove NV 46 B3
Cottonwood Falls KS 43 F3
Cottonwood Hts. UT 257 B3
Cottonwood Shores TX 61 D1
Cotuit MA 151 E4
Cotulla TX 60 C4
Coudersport PA 92 C1
Coulee City WA 13 E3
Coulee Dam WA 13 E2
Coulterville IL 98 B4
Council ID 22 B3
Council Bluffs IA 86 A2
Council Grove KS 43 F2
Country Club Hills MO 256 B1
Country Club Vil. MO 96 B1
Country Homes WA 14 A3
Country Knolls NY 94 B1
Countryside IL 203 C5
Countryside VA 144 A3
Coupeville WA 12 C2
Courtdale PA 261 B1
Courtland AL 119 E2
Courtland MN 72 B1
Courtland MS 118 B3
Courtland VA 113 E3
Courtney TX 61 F1
Coushatta LA 125 D3
Cove OR 21 F2
Covedale OH 204 A2
Covelo CA 36 A1
Coventry CT 150 A3
Coventry Ctr. RI 150 C3
Covert MI 75 E4
Covina CA 229 F2
Covington GA 121 D4
Covington IN 89 D4
Covington KY 100 B2
Covington LA 134 B2
Covington OH 90 B4
Covington OK 51 E2
Covington TN 118 B1
Covington VA 112 B1
Covington WA 262 B4
Covington Co. AL 128 A4
Covington Co. MS 126 C4
Cowan TN 120 A1
Cowan Hts. CA 229 F4
Coward SC 122 C4
Cowarts AL 137 D1
Cowden IL 98 C2
Cowen WV 102 A3
Coweta OK 106 A4
Coweta Co. GA 128 C1
Cowley WY 24 C2
Cowley Co. KS 43 F4
Cowlitz Co. WA 20 C1
Cowpens SC 121 F2
Coxsackie NY 94 B2
Cozad NE 34 C4
Crab Orchard KY 110 B1
Crab Orchard TN 110 B4
Crab Orchard WV 111 F1
Crafton PA 250 A2
Craig AK 155 E4
Craig CO 32 C4
Craig Beach OH 91 F3
Craig Co. OK 106 A2
Craig Co. VA 112 B1
Craighead Co. AR 108 A4
Craigmont ID 22 B1
Craigsville VA 102 B4
Craigsville WV 102 A4
Crainville IL 108 C1
Cramerton NC 122 A1
Cranbury NJ 147 D2
Crandall TX 59 F2
Crandon WI 68 B3
Crane MO 106 C2
Crane TX 58 A4
Crane Co. TX 57 F4
Cranesville PA 91 F1
Cranford NJ 147 E1
Cranston RI 150 C3
Craven Co. NC 115 D3
Crawford CO 40 C2
Crawford GA 121 E4
Crawford MS 127 D1
Crawford NE 33 F1
Crawford TX 59 E4
Crawford Co. AR 116 C1
Crawford Co. GA 129 D2
Crawford Co. IL 99 D2
Crawford Co. IN 99 F4
Crawford Co. IA 86 A1
Crawford Co. KS 106 B1
Crawford Co. MI 70 C4
Crawford Co. MO 97 F4
Crawford Co. OH 90 C3
Crawford Co. PA 91 F1
Crawford Co. WI 73 F3
Crawfordsville AR 118 B1
Crawfordsville IN 89 E4
Crawfordville FL 137 E2
Crawfordville GA 121 E4
Creal Sprs. IL 108 C1
Creede CO 40 C4
Creedmoor NC 112 C4
Creek Co. OK 51 F2
Creekside KY 230 F1
Creighton NE 35 E2
Crenshaw MS 118 B3
Crenshaw Co. AL 128 A4
Creola AL 135 E1
Cresaptown MD 102 C1
Crescent IA 86 A2
Crescent OK 51 E2
Crescent Beach FL 139 E3
Crescent City CA 28 A2
Crescent City FL 139 D4
Crescent City IL 89 D3
Crescent Sprs. KY 204 A3
Cresco IA 73 E2
Cresson PA 92 B4

Downtown Cleveland OH
A
B
LAKE ERIE
0 0.25 0.5 mi
0 0.25 0.5 0.75 km
Voinovich Park
William G. Mather Mus.
Rock and Roll Hall of Fame & Mus.
Intl. Women's Air & Space Mus.
Great Lakes Science Center
Burke Lakefront Airport (BKL)
Cleveland Browns Stadium
USS Cod
Cleveland Police Mus.
Ct. Hse.
C.H.
Convention Ctr.
The Mall
THE FLATS
Jacobs Pavilion at Nautica
Public Sq.
Federal Ct. Hse.
Tower City Center
Cleveland Arcade
Playhouse Square
Lutheran Hosp.
Rocket Mortgage Fieldhouse
Progressive Field
CLEVELAND STATE UNIV.
West Side Mkt.

Corson Co. SD 26 C1
Cortaro AZ 55 D3
Corte Madera CA 259 A2
Cortez CO 40 B4
Cortez FL 140 B3
Cortland IL 88 C1
Cortland NE 35 F4
Cortland NY 79 D4
Cortland OH 91 F2
Cortland Co. NY 79 E4
Corunna MI 76 B3
Corvallis MT 15 D4
Corvallis OR 20 B3
Corydon IN 99 F4
Corydon IA 87 D3
Corydon KY 109 E1
Coryell Co. TX 59 E4
Coshocton OH 91 E4
Coshocton Co. OH 91 E4
Cosmopolis WA 12 B4
Cosmos MN 66 B4
Costa Mesa CA 228 E5
Costilla Co. CO 41 E4
Cotati CA 36 B3
Coto de Caza CA 229 G5
Cottage City MD 270 E3
Cottage Grove MN 67 D4
Cottage Grove OR 20 B4
Cottage Grove WI 74 B3
Cottage Hill FL 135 F1
Cottageville SC 130 C1
Cottageville WV 101 E3
Cotter AR 107 E3
Cottle Co. TX 58 B1
Cotton Co. OK 51 D4

POINTS OF INTEREST

Burke Lakefront Airport B1
Cleveland Arcade A2
Cleveland Browns Stadium A1
Cleveland Police Museum A1
Cleveland State University B2
Convention Center A1
Great Lakes Science Center A1
International Women's Air & Space Museum B1
Jacobs Pavilion at Nautica A1
Playhouse Square B2
Progressive Field A2
Rock and Roll Hall of Fame & Museum A1
Rocket Mortgage Fieldhouse A2
Tower City Center A2
U.S.S. Cod B1
West Side Market A2
William G. Mather Museum A1

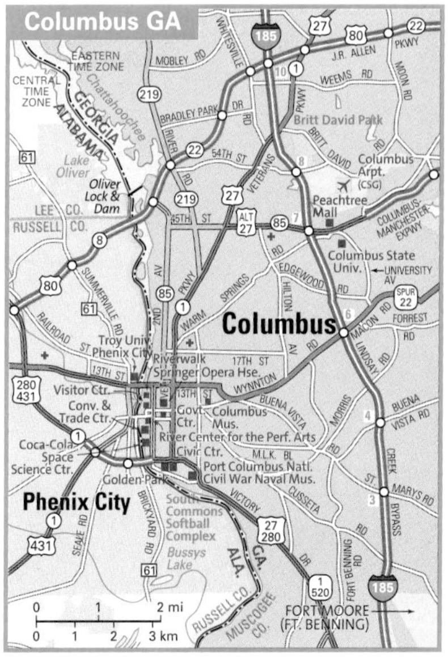
Columbus GA
EASTERN TIME ZONE
CENTRAL TIME ZONE
GEORGIA
ALABAMA
Chattahoochee
Britt David Park
Columbus Arpt. (CSG)
Lake Oliver
Oliver Lock & Dam
Peachtree Mall
LEE CO.
RUSSELL CO.
Columbus State Univ.
Columbus
Troy Univ. Phenix City
Riverwalk
Springer Opera Hse.
Visitor Ctr., Conv. & Trade Ctr.
Govt. Ctr.
Columbus Mus.
River Center for the Perf. Arts
Civic Ctr.
Coca-Cola Space Science Ctr.
Golden Park
Port Columbus Natl. Civil War Naval Mus.
Phenix City
South Commons Softball Complex
Bussys Lake
GA.
ALA.
MUSCOGEE CO.
FORT MOORE (FT. BENNING)
0 1 2 mi
0 1 2 3 km

Figures after entries indicate page number and grid reference.

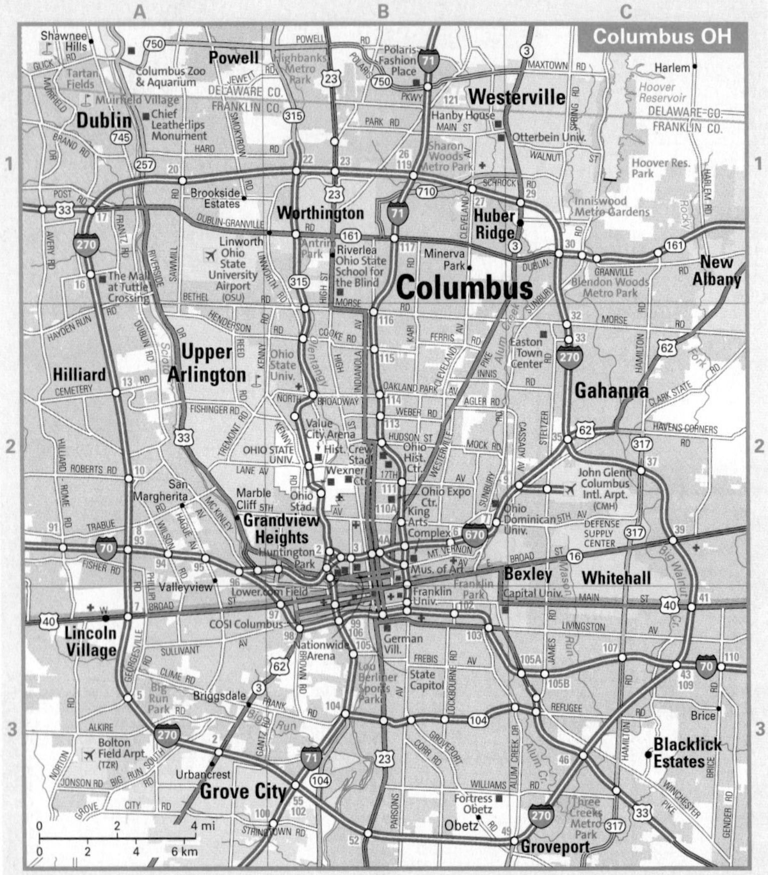
Columbus OH
Powell
Westerville
Dublin
Worthington
Huber Ridge
New Albany
Columbus
Upper Arlington
Hilliard
Gahanna
Grandview Heights
Bexley
Whitehall
Lincoln Village
Blacklick Estates
Grove City
Groveport
Obetz
Briggsdale
Urbancrest
Brice
0 2 4 mi
0 2 4 6 km

Bexley C2
Blacklick Estates C3
Brice C3
Briggsdale A3
Brookside Estates A1
Columbus B1
Dublin A1
Gahanna C2
Grandview Hts. B2
Grove City A3
Groveport C3
Harlem C1
Hilliard A2
Huber Ridge C1
Lincoln Vil. A3
Linworth B1
Marble Cliff A2
Minerva Park B1
New Albany C1
New Rome A3
Obetz B3
Powell A1
Riverlea B1
San Margherita A2
Shawnee Hills A1
Upper Arlington A2
Urbancrest A3
Valleyview A2
Westerville C1
Whitehall C2
Worthington B1

Cressona PA 146 A1
Crested Butte CO 40 C2
Crest Hill IL 89 D2
Crestline CA 53 D2
Crestline OH 91 D3
Creston IA 86 B3
Creston OH 91 E3
Crestview FL 136 B1
Crestview KY 204 B3
Crestview Hills KY 204 A3
Crestwood IL 203 D6
Crestwood KY 100 A4
Crestwood MO 256 B3
Crestwood Vil. NJ 147 E3
Creswell OR 20 B4
Crete IL 89 D2
Crete NE 35 F4
Creve Coeur MO 256 A2
Crewe VA 113 D2
Cricket NC 111 F4
Cridersville OH 90 B3
Crimora VA 102 C4
Cripple Creek CO 41 E2
Crisfield MD 103 F4
Crisp Co. GA 129 D3
Crittenden KY 100 B3
Crittenden Co. AR 110 B1
Crittenden Co. KY 109 D2
Crivitz WI 68 C3
Crocker MO 97 E4
Crockett CA 259 C1
Crockett TX 124 A4
Crockett Co. TN 108 C4
Crockett Co. TX 60 A1
Crofton KY 109 E2
Crofton MD 144 C3
Crofton NE 35 E1
Croghan NY 79 E2
Crompond NY 148 B2
Cromwell CT 149 E1
Crook Co. OR 21 D3
Crook Co. WY 25 F3
Crooked Lake Park FL 141 D3
Crooks SD 27 F4
Crookston MN 19 F3
Crooksville OH 101 E1
Crosby MN 64 B4
Crosby ND 18 A1
Crosby TX 132 B3
Crosby Co. TX 58 A1
Crosbyton TX 58 B1
Cross City FL 137 F3
Cross Co. AR 118 A1
Crossett AR 125 F1
Cross Hill SC 121 F3
Cross Keys NJ 146 C4
Crosslake MN 64 B4
Cross Plains TN 109 F3
Cross Plains TX 59 D3
Cross Plains WI 74 B3
Cross Roads TX 59 F2
Crossville AL 120 A3
Crossville IL 99 D4
Crossville TN 110 B4
Crosswicks NJ 147 D2
Croswell MI 76 C3
Crothersville IN 99 F3
Croton Falls NY 148 C2
Croton-on-Hudson NY 148 B2
Crow Agency MT 24 C1
Crowder MS 118 B3
Crowder OK 116 A1
Crowell TX 58 C1
Crowley LA 133 E2
Crowley TX 59 E2
Crowley Co. CO 41 F3
Crown Hts. NY 148 B1
Crown Pt. IN 89 D2
Crown Pt. LA 134 B3
Crownpoint NM 48 B2
Crown Pt. NY 81 D3
Crownsville MD 144 C3
Crow Wing Co. MN 66 C1
Croydon PA 248 E2
Crozet VA 102 C4
Cruger MS 126 B1
Crump TN 119 D1
Crystal MN 235 B2
Crystal NM 48 A2
Crystal Beach FL 266 A1
Crystal City MO 98 A4
Crystal City TX 60 C4
Crystal Falls MI 68 C2
Crystal Lake CT 150 A3
Crystal Lake IL 88 C1
Crystal Lakes OH 100 C1
Crystal River FL 140 B1
Crystal Sprs. FL 140 C2
Crystal Sprs. MS 126 B3
Cuba IL 88 A4
Cuba MO 97 F4
Cuba NM 48 C2
Cuba NY 92 C1
Cuba City WI 74 A4
Cudahy CA 228 D3
Cudahy WI 75 D3
Cuddebackville NY 148 A1
Cudjoe Key FL 143 D4
Cuero TX 61 E3
Culberson Co. TX 57 E4
Culbertson MT 17 F2
Culbertson NE 34 C4
Culdesac ID 14 B4
Cullen LA 125 D1
Cullman AL 119 F3
Cullman Co. AL 119 F3
Culloden WV 101 E3
Cullowhee NC 121 D1
Culpeper VA 103 D3
Culpeper Co. VA 103 D3
Culver IN 89 E2
Culver OR 21 D3
Culver City CA 228 C3
Cumberland IN 99 F1
Cumberland KY 111 D2
Cumberland MD 102 C1
Cumberland NC 123 D2
Cumberland VA 113 D1
Cumberland WI 67 E3
Cumberland Ctr. ME 82 B3
Cumberland Co. IL 99 D2
Cumberland Co. KY 110 A2
Cumberland Co. ME 82 B3
Cumberland Co. NJ 145 F2
Cumberland Co. NC 123 D2
Cumberland Co. PA 103 D1
Cumberland Co. TN 110 B4
Cumberland Co. VA 113 D1
Cumberland Foreside ME 82 B3
Cumberland Hill RI 150 C2
Cumby TX 124 A1
Cuming Co. NE 35 F2
Cumming GA 120 C3
Cunningham KS 43 D4
Cupertino CA 36 B4
Curlew FL 266 A1
Currituck NC 115 E1
Currituck Co. NC 115 E1
Curry Co. NM 49 F4
Curry Co. OR 28 A2
Curtis NE 34 C4
Curwensville PA 92 B3
Cushing OK 51 F2
Cushing TX 124 B3
Cushman AR 107 F4
Cusseta GA 128 C3
Custer SD 25 F4
Custer Co. CO 41 E3
Custer Co. ID 23 D3
Custer Co. MT 25 E1
Custer Co. NE 34 C3
Custer Co. OK 51 D2
Custer Co. SD 25 F4
Cut and Shoot TX 132 A2
Cut Bank MT 15 E1
Cutchogue NY 149 E3
Cuthbert GA 128 C3
Cutler CA 45 D3
Cutler Bay FL 143 E3
Cutlerville MI 75 F3
Cut Off LA 134 B3
Cutten CA 28 A4
Cuyahoga Co. OH 91 E2
Cuyahoga Falls OH 91 E3
Cuyahoga Hts. OH 204 F2
Cygnet OH 90 C2
Cynthiana IN 99 D4
Cynthiana KY 100 B4
Cypress CA 228 E4
Cypress Quarters FL 141 E4
Cyril OK 51 E3

D

Dacono CO 41 E1
Dacula GA 121 D3
Dade City FL 140 C2
Dade Co. GA 120 B2
Dade Co. MO 106 C1
Dadeville AL 128 B2
Daggett CA 53 D1
Daggett Co. UT 32 A4
Dagsboro DE 145 F4
Dahlgren VA 103 E4
Dahlonega GA 120 C3
Daingerfield TX 124 B1
Daisetta TX 132 B2
Dakota City IA 72 C4
Dakota City NE 35 F2
Dakota Co. MN 67 D4
Dakota Co. NE 35 F2
Dale IN 99 E4
Dale City VA 144 A4
Dale Co. AL 128 B4
Daleville AL 128 B4
Daleville IN 89 F4
Daleville VA 112 B1
Dalhart TX 50 A2
Dallam Co. TX 50 A2
Dallas GA 120 B4
Dallas NC 122 A1
Dallas OR 20 B2
Dallas PA 93 E2
Dallas TX 59 F2
Dallas Ctr. IA 86 C2
Dallas City IL 87 F3
Dallas Co. AL 127 F3
Dallas Co. AR 117 E4
Dallas Co. IA 86 C2
Dallas Co. MO 107 D1
Dallas Co. TX 59 F2
Dallastown PA 103 E1
Dalton GA 120 B2
Dalton MA 94 C1
Dalton OH 91 E3
Dalton PA 93 F2
Dalton City IL 98 C1
Dalton Gardens ID 14 B3
Dalworthington Gardens TX 207 B3
Daly City CA 36 B4
Dalzell SC 122 B3
Damariscotta ME 82 C3
Damascus MD 144 B2
Damascus OR 20 C2
Damascus VA 111 F3
Damon TX 132 A4
Dana IN 99 E1
Dana Pt. CA 52 C3
Danboro PA 146 C2
Danbury CT 148 C2
Danbury NC 112 B3
Danbury TX 132 A4
Dandridge TN 111 D4
Dane WI 74 B3
Dane Co. WI 74 B3
Danforth IL 89 D3
Dania Beach FL 143 F2
Daniel MD 144 B1
Daniels Co. MT 17 E1
Danielson CT 150 B3
Danielsville GA 121 D3
Dannemora NY 80 C1
Dansville NY 78 C4
Dante VA 111 E2
Danube MN 66 B4
Danvers IL 88 B4
Danvers MA 151 F1
Danville AR 117 D2
Danville CA 36 B4
Danville IL 89 D4
Danville IN 99 F1
Danville IA 87 F3
Danville KY 110 B1
Danville NH 95 E1
Danville OH 91 D4
Danville PA 93 E3
Danville VT 81 E2
Danville VA 112 C3
Danville WV 101 E4
Daphne AL 135 E2
Darby MT 23 D1
Darby PA 146 C3
Dardanelle AR 117 D1
Dardenne Prairie MO 98 A3
Dare Co. NC 115 F2
Dares Beach MD 144 C4
Darien CT 148 C3
Darien GA 130 B4
Darien IL 203 C5
Darien WI 74 C4
Darke Co. OH 100 B1
Darlington IN 89 E4
Darlington SC 122 C3
Darlington WI 74 A4
Darlington Co. SC 122 B3
Darmstadt IN 99 D4
Darnestown MD 144 B2
Darrington WA 12 C2
Dasher GA 137 F1
Dassel MN 66 C3
Dauphin PA 93 D4
Dauphin Co. PA 93 D4
Dauphin Island AL 135 E2
Davenport FL 141 D2
Davenport IA 88 A2
Davenport ND 19 E4
Davenport OK 51 F2
Davenport WA 13 F3
David City NE 35 F3
Davidson NC 122 A1
Davidson Co. NC 112 B4
Davidson Co. TN 109 F4
Davidsville PA 92 B4
Davie FL 143 E2
Davie Co. NC 112 A4
Daviess Co. IN 99 E3
Daviess Co. KY 109 E1
Daviess Co. MO 96 C1
Davis CA 36 B3
Davis IL 74 B4
Davis OK 51 F4
Davis WV 102 B2
Davisboro GA 129 F1
Davis Co. IA 87 E3
Davis Co. UT 31 E3
Davison MI 76 B3
Davison Co. SD 27 E4
Davy WV 111 F1
Dawes Co. NE 34 A1
Dawson GA 128 C3
Dawson MN 27 F2
Dawson TX 59 F3
Dawson Co. GA 120 C3
Dawson Co. MT 17 F3
Dawson Co. NE 35 D4
Dawson Co. TX 58 A2
Dawson Sprs. KY 109 E2
Dawsonville GA 120 C3
Day Co. SD 27 E2
Dayton ID 31 E2
Dayton IN 89 E4
Dayton IA 72 C4
Dayton KY 204 B2
Dayton MN 66 C3
Dayton NV 37 D2
Dayton NJ 147 D1
Dayton OH 100 B1
Dayton OR 20 B2
Dayton TN 120 B1
Dayton TX 132 B3
Dayton VA 102 C3
Dayton WA 13 F4
Dayton WY 24 C2
Daytona Beach FL 139 E4
Daytona Beach Shores FL 139 E4
Dayville CT 150 B3
Deadwood SD 25 F3
Deaf Smith Co. TX 49 F3
Deal NJ 147 F2
Deale MD 144 C3
Deal Island MD 103 F4
Dearborn MI 76 C4
Dearborn MO 96 B1
Dearborn Co. IN 100 B2
Dearborn Hts. MI 210 B3
Dearing KS 106 A2
DeArmanville AL 120 A4
Deary ID 14 B4
Deaver WY 24 B2
De Baca Co. NM 49 E4
DeBary FL 141 D1
De Beque CO 40 B2
Decatur AL 119 F2
Decatur AR 106 B3
Decatur GA 120 C4
Decatur IL 98 C1
Decatur IN 90 A3
Decatur MI 89 F1
Decatur MS 126 C2
Decatur NE 35 F2
Decatur TN 120 C1
Decatur TX 59 E2
Decatur Co. GA 137 E1
Decatur Co. IN 100 A2

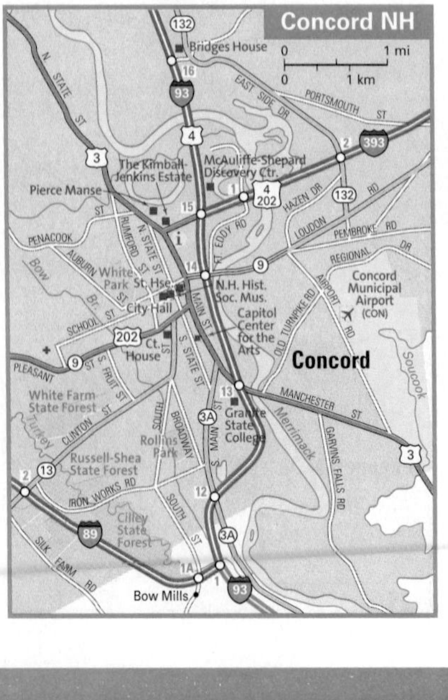
Concord NH
Bridges House
0 1 mi
0 1 km
Concord
Pierce Manse
The Kimball-Jenkins Estate
McAuliffe-Shepard Discovery Ctr.
N.H. Hist. Soc. Mus.
City Hall
Capitol Center for the Arts
Concord Municipal Airport (CON)
White Farm State Forest
Russell-Shea State Forest
Granite State College
Bow Mills

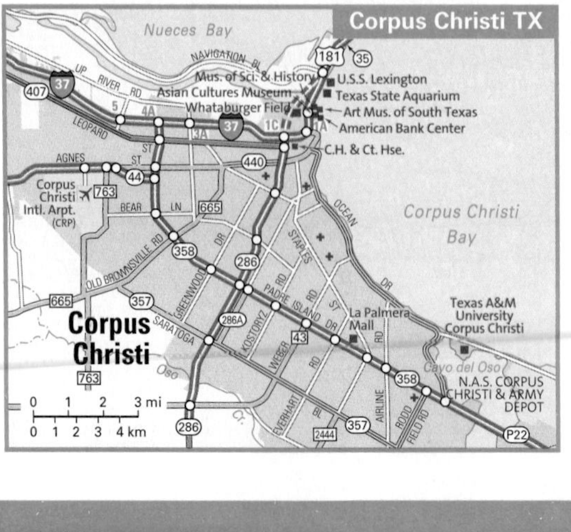
Corpus Christi TX
Nueces Bay
Mus. of Sci. & History
U.S.S. Lexington
Texas State Aquarium
Asian Cultures Museum
Whataburger Field
Art Mus. of South Texas
American Bank Center
C.H. & Ct. Hse.
Corpus Christi Intl. Arpt. (CRP)
Corpus Christi Bay
Corpus Christi
La Palmera Mall
Texas A&M University Corpus Christi
N.A.S. Corpus Christi & Army Depot
0 1 2 3 mi
0 1 2 3 4 km

Entries in **bold black** indicate counties or parishes.
Entries in **bold color** indicate cities with detailed inset maps.

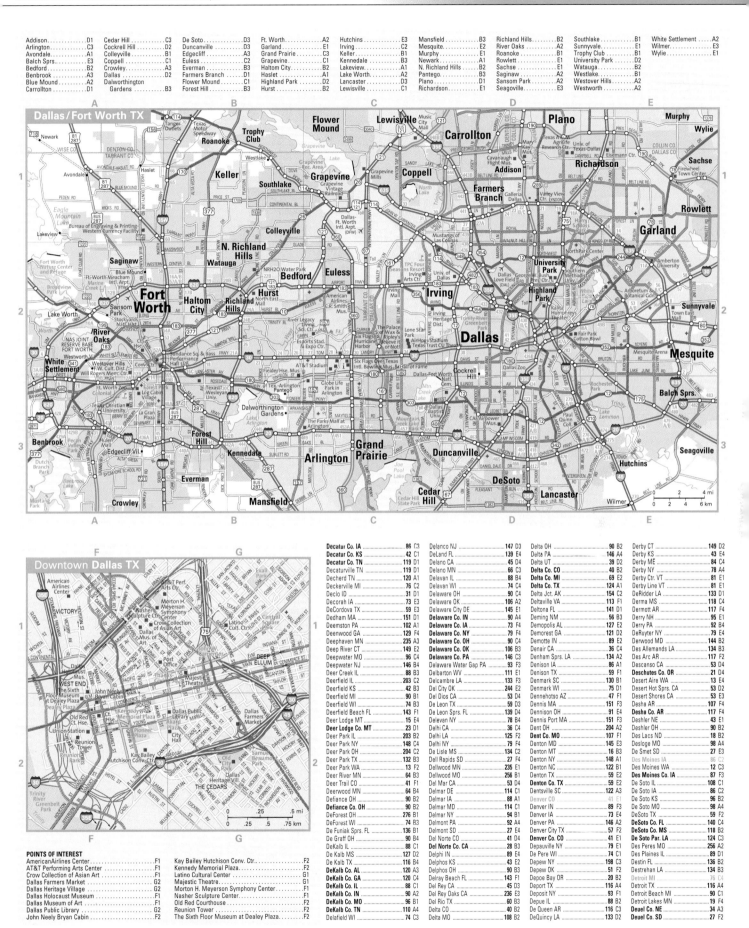

Addison D1
Arlington C3
Avondale A1
Balch Sprs. E3
Bedford B2
Benbrook A3
Blue Mound A2
Carrollton D1
Cedar Hill C3
Cockrell Hill D2
Colleyville B1
Coppell C1
Crowley A3
Dallas D2
Dalworthington Gardens B3
De Soto D3
Duncanville D3
Edgecliff A3
Euless C2
Everman B3
Farmers Branch D1
Flower Mound C1
Forest Hill B3
Ft. Worth A2
Garland E1
Grand Prairie C3
Grapevine C1
Haltom City B2
Haslet A1
Highland Park D2
Hurst B2
Hutchins E3
Irving C2
Keller B1
Kennedale B3
Lakeview A1
Lake Worth A2
Lancaster D3
Lewisville C1
Mansfield B3
Mesquite E2
Murphy E1
Newark A1
N. Richland Hills B2
Pantego B3
Plano D1
Richardson E1
Richland Hills B2
River Oaks A2
Roanoke B1
Rowlett E1
Sachse E1
Saginaw A2
Sansom Park A2
Seagoville E3
Southlake B1
Sunnyvale E1
Trophy Club B1
University Park D2
Watauga B2
Westlake B1
Westover Hills A2
Westworth A2
White Settlement A2
Wilmer E3
Wylie E1

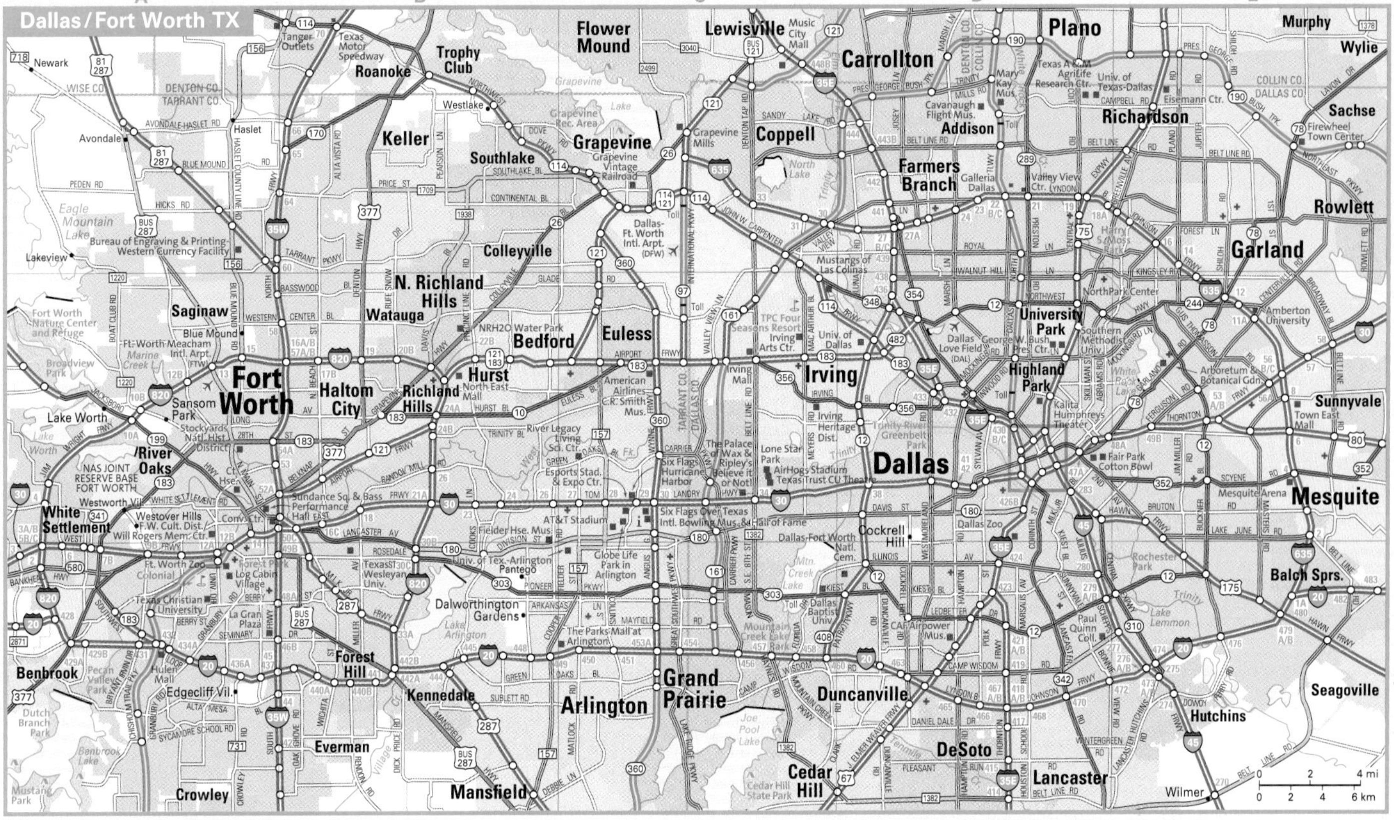
Dallas/Fort Worth TX
A
B
C
D
E
1
2
3
0
2
4 mi
0
2
4
6 km

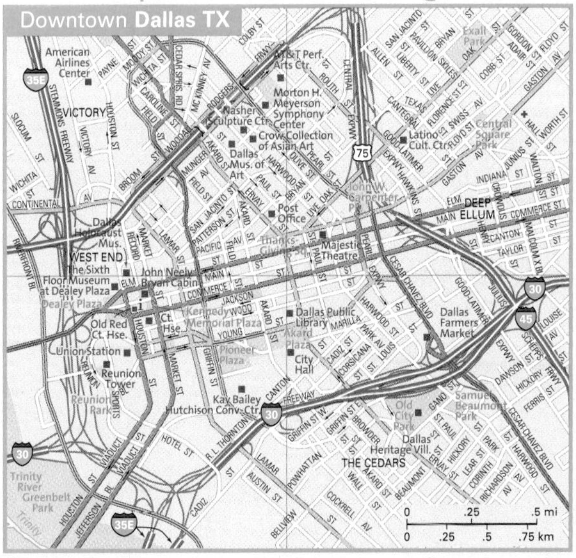
Downtown Dallas TX
F
G
1
2
0
.25
.5 mi
0
.25
.5
.75 km

POINTS OF INTEREST

AmericanAirlines Center F1
AT&T Performing Arts Center F1
Crow Collection of Asian Art F1
Dallas Farmers Market G2
Dallas Heritage Village G2
Dallas Holocaust Museum F1
Dallas Museum of Art F1
Dallas Public Library G2
John Neely Bryan Cabin F2
Kay Bailey Hutchison Conv. Ctr. F2
Kennedy Memorial Plaza F2
Latino Cultural Center G1
Majestic Theatre G1
Morton H. Meyerson Symphony Center F1
Nasher Sculpture Center F1
Old Red Courthouse F2
Reunion Tower F2
The Sixth Floor Museum at Dealey Plaza F2

Decatur Co. IA 86 C3
Decatur Co. KS 42 C1
Decatur Co. TN 119 D1
Decaturville TN 119 D1
Decherd TN 120 A1
Deckerville MI 76 C2
Declo ID 31 D1
Decorah IA 73 E3
DeCordova TX 59 E3
Dedham MA 151 D1
Deemston PA 102 A1
Deenwood GA 129 F4
Deephaven MN 235 A3
Deep River CT 149 E2
Deepwater MO 96 C4
Deepwater NJ 146 B4
Deer Creek IL 88 B3
Deerfield IL 203 C2
Deerfield KS 42 B3
Deerfield MI 90 B1
Deerfield WI 74 B3
Deerfield Beach FL 143 F1
Deer Lodge MT 15 E4
Deer Lodge Co. MT 23 D1
Deer Park IL 203 B2
Deer Park NY 148 C4
Deer Park OH 204 C2
Deer Park TX 132 B3
Deer Park WA 13 F2
Deer River MN 64 B3
Deer Trail CO 41 F1
Deerwood MN 64 B4
Defiance OH 90 B2
Defiance Co. OH 90 B2
DeForest OH 276 B1
DeForest WI 74 B3
De Funiak Sprs. FL 136 B1
De Graff OH 90 B4
DeKalb IL 88 C1
De Kalb MS 127 D2
De Kalb TX 116 B4
DeKalb Co. AL 120 A3
DeKalb Co. GA 120 C4
DeKalb Co. IL 88 C1
DeKalb Co. IN 90 A2
DeKalb Co. MO 96 B1
DeKalb Co. TN 110 A4
Delafield WI 74 C3
Delanco NJ 147 D3
DeLand FL 139 E4
Delano CA 45 D4
Delano MN 66 C3
Delavan IL 88 B4
Delavan WI 74 C4
Delaware OH 90 C4
Delaware OK 106 A2
Delaware City DE 145 E1
Delaware Co. IN 90 A4
Delaware Co. IA 73 F4
Delaware Co. NY 79 F4
Delaware Co. OH 90 C4
Delaware Co. OK 106 B3
Delaware Co. PA 146 C3
Delaware Water Gap PA 93 F3
Delbarton WV 111 E1
Delcambre LA 133 F3
Del City OK 244 E2
Del Dios CA 53 D4
De Leon TX 59 D3
De Leon Sprs. FL 139 D4
Delevan NY 78 B4
Delhi CA 36 C4
Delhi LA 125 F2
Delhi NY 79 F4
De Lisle MS 134 C2
Dell Rapids SD 27 F4
Dellwood MN 235 E1
Dellwood MO 256 B1
Del Mar CA 53 D4
Delmar DE 114 C1
Delmar IA 88 A1
Delmar MD 114 C1
Delmar NY 94 B1
Delmont PA 92 A4
Delmont SD 27 E4
Del Norte CO 41 D4
Del Norte Co. CA 28 B3
Delphi IN 89 E4
Delphos KS 43 E2
Delphos OH 90 B3
Delray Beach FL 143 F1
Del Rey CA 45 D3
Del Rey Oaks CA 236 E3
Del Rio TX 60 B3
Delta CO 40 B2
Delta MO 108 B2
Delta OH 90 B2
Delta PA 146 A4
Delta UT 39 D2
Delta Co. CO 40 B2
Delta Co. MI 69 E2
Delta Co. TX 124 A1
Delta Jct. AK 154 C2
Deltaville VA 113 F1
Deltona FL 141 D1
Deming NM 56 B3
Demopolis AL 127 E2
Demorest GA 121 D2
Demotte IN 89 E2
Denair CA 36 C4
Denham Sprs. LA 134 A2
Denison IA 86 A1
Denison TX 59 F1
Denmark SC 130 B1
Denmark WI 75 D1
Dennehotso AZ 47 F1
Dennis MA 151 F3
Dennison OH 91 E4
Dennis Port MA 151 F3
Dent OH 204 A2
Dent Co. MO 107 F1
Denton MD 145 E3
Denton MT 16 B3
Denton NY 148 A1
Denton NC 122 B1
Denton TX 59 E2
Denton Co. TX 59 E2
Dentsville SC 122 A3
Denver CO 41 E1
Denver IN 89 F3
Denver IA 73 E4
Denver PA 146 A2
Denver City TX 57 F2
Denver Co. CO 41 E1
Depauville NY 79 E1
De Pere WI 74 C1
Depew NY 198 C3
Depew OK 51 F2
Depoe Bay OR 20 B2
Deport TX 116 A4
Deposit NY 93 F1
Depue IL 88 B2
De Queen AR 116 C3
DeQuincy LA 133 D2
Derby CT 149 D2
Derby KS 43 E4
Derby ME 84 C4
Derby NY 78 A4
Derby Ctr. VT 81 E1
Derby Line VT 81 E1
DeRidder LA 133 D1
Derma MS 118 C4
Dermott AR 117 F4
Derry NH 95 E1
Derry PA 92 B4
DeRuyter NY 79 E4
Derwood MD 144 B2
Des Allemands LA 134 B3
Des Arc AR 117 F2
Descanso CA 53 D4
Deschutes Co. OR 21 D4
Desert Aire WA 13 E4
Desert Hot Sprs. CA 53 D2
Desert Shores CA 53 E3
Desha AR 107 F4
Desha Co. AR 117 F4
Deshler NE 43 E1
Deshler OH 90 B2
Des Lacs ND 18 B2
Desloge MO 98 A4
De Smet SD 27 E3
Des Moines IA 86 C2
Des Moines WA 12 C3
Des Moines Co. IA 87 F3
De Soto IL 108 C1
De Soto IA 86 C2
De Soto KS 96 B2
De Soto MO 98 A4
DeSoto TX 59 F2
DeSoto Co. FL 140 C4
DeSoto Co. MS 118 B2
De Soto Par. LA 124 C3
Des Peres MO 256 A2
Des Plaines IL 89 D1
Destin FL 136 B2
Destrehan LA 134 B3
Detroit MI 76 C4
Detroit TX 116 A4
Detroit Beach MI 90 C1
Detroit Lakes MN 19 F4
Deuel Co. NE 34 A3
Deuel Co. SD 27 F2

Figures after entries indicate page number and grid reference.

Barstow C2	Cleveland C2	Davenport A1	Le Claire C1	Panorama Park B1	Riverdale B1
Bettendorf B1	Coal Valley B2	E. Moline B1	Milan B2	Port Byron C1	Rock Island A2
Buffalo A2	Colona C2	Hampton C1	Moline B2	Rapids City C1	Silvis C2
Carbon Cliff C2					

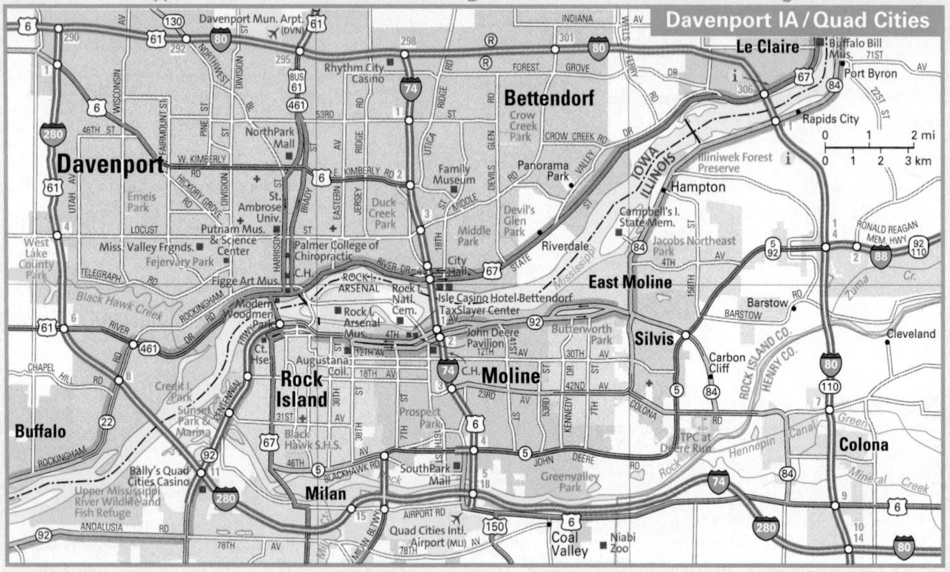

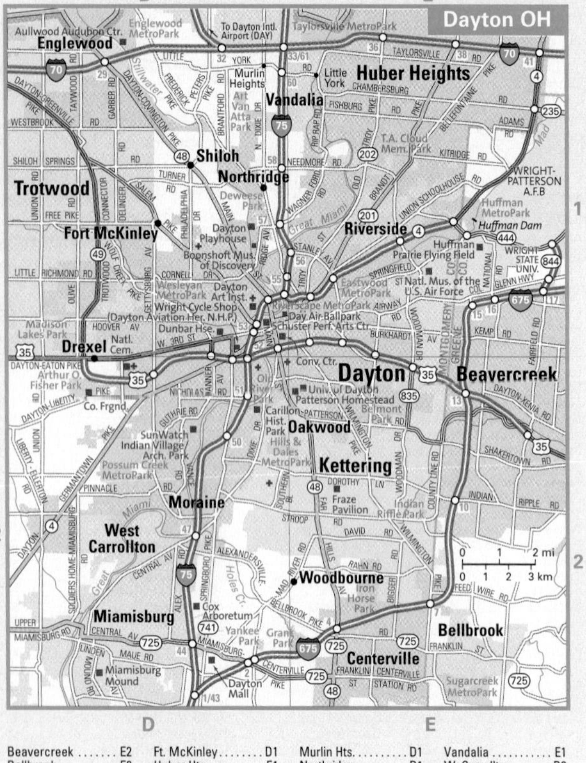

Beavercreek E2	Ft. McKinley D1	Murlin Hts. D1	Vandalia E1
Bellbrook E2	Huber Hts. E1	Northridge D1	W. Carrollton D2
Centerville E2	Kettering E2	Oakwood E2	Woodbourne E2
Dayton E2	Little York E1	Riverside E1	
Drexel D1	Miamisburg D2	Shiloh D1	
Englewood D1	Moraine D2	Trotwood D1	

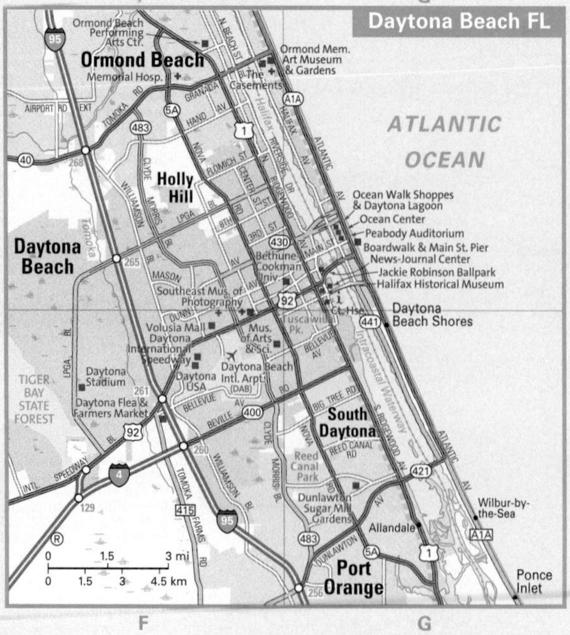

Allandale G2	Holly Hill F1	Port Orange G2
Daytona Beach F1	Ormond Beach F1	S. Daytona G2
Daytona Beach Shores G2	Ponce Inlet G2	Wilbur-by-the-Sea G2

De Valls Bluff AR 117 F2
Deville LA 125 E4
Devils Lake ND 19 D2
Devine TX 61 D3
Devola OH 101 F2
Devon PA 248 A2
Dewar OK 116 A1
Dewey OK 51 F1
Dewey Beach DE 145 F4
Dewey Co. OK 51 D2
Dewey Co. SD 26 C2
Dewey-Humboldt AZ 47 D4
Deweyville TX 132 C2
Deweyville UT 31 E3
DeWitt AR 117 F3
De Witt IA 88 A1
DeWitt MI 76 A3
De Witt NE 35 F4
De Witt NY 79 E3
De Witt Co. IL 88 B4
DeWitt Co. TX 61 E3
Dexter GA 129 E2
Dexter IA 86 C2
Dexter ME 82 C1
Dexter MI 76 B4
Dexter MO 108 B2
Dexter NM 57 E2
Dexter NY 79 E1
Dexter OR 20 C4
Diablo CA 259 D2
Diamond IL 88 C2
Diamond MO 106 C2
Diamond Bar CA 229 F3
Diamond City AR 107 D3
Diamondhead MS 134 C2
Diamond Hill RI 150 C2
Diamond Sprs. CA 36 C2
Diamondville WY 31 F2
Diaz AR 107 F4
D'Iberville MS 135 D2
Diboll TX 132 B1
Dickens TX 58 B1
Dickens Co. TX 58 B1
Dickenson Co. VA 111 E2
Dickey Co. ND 27 D1
Dickeyville WI 73 F4
Dickinson ND 18 A4
Dickinson TX 132 B4
Dickinson Co. IA 72 B3
Dickinson Co. KS 43 E2
Dickinson Co. MI 69 D2
Dickson OK 51 F4
Dickson TN 109 E4
Dickson City PA 93 F2
Dickson Co. TN 109 E4
Dierks AR 116 C3
Dieterich IL 98 C2
Dighton KS 42 C3
Dighton MA 151 D3
Dike IA 73 D4
Dilkon AZ 47 F3
Dill City OK 51 D3
Dilley TX 60 C4
Dillingham AK 154 B3
Dillon CO 41 D1
Dillon MT 23 E2
Dillon SC 122 C3
Dillon Co. SC 122 C3
Dillonvale OH 91 F4
Dillsboro IN 100 A2
Dillsburg PA 93 D4
Dillwyn VA 113 D1
Dilworth MN 19 F4
Dimmit Co. TX 60 C4
Dimmitt TX 50 A4
Dimondale MI 76 A4
Dinosaur CO 32 B4
Dinuba CA 45 D3
Dinwiddie VA 113 E2
Dinwiddie Co. VA 113 E2
District Hts. MD 271 F4
Divernon IL 98 B1
Divide Co. ND 17 F1
Dixfield ME 82 B2
Dixie Co. FL 137 F3
Dixmoor IL 203 E6
Dixon CA 36 B3
Dixon IL 88 B1
Dixon KY 109 E1
Dixon MO 97 E4
Dixon MT 15 D3
Dixon Co. NE 35 F1
D'Lo MS 126 B3
Dobbins Hts. NC 122 C2
Dobbs Ferry NY 148 B3
Dobson NC 112 A3
Dock Jct. GA 139 D1
Doctor Phillips FL 246 B3
Doctors Inlet FL 139 D2
Doddridge Co. WV 102 A2
Dodge NE 35 F2
Dodge Ctr. MN 73 D1
Dodge City AL 119 F3
Dodge City KS 42 C4
Dodge Co. GA 129 E3
Dodge Co. MN 73 D1
Dodge Co. NE 35 F3
Dodge Co. WI 74 C2
Dodgeville WI 74 A3
Doerun GA 129 D4
Doland SD 27 E2
Dolan Sprs. AZ 46 B3
Dolgeville NY 79 F3
Dollar Bay MI 65 F3
Dolores CO 40 B4
Dolores Co. CO 40 B4
Dolton IL 203 E6
Doña Ana NM 56 B3
Dona Ana Co. NM 56 B3
Donald OR 20 B2
Donaldsonville LA 134 A2
Donalsonville GA 137 D1
Dongola IL 108 C1
Doniphan MO 108 A3
Doniphan NE 35 E4
Doniphan Co. KS 96 B1
Donley Co. TX 50 B3
Donna TX 63 E4
Donnellson IA 87 F3
Donora PA 92 A4
Doolittle MO 97 E4
Dooly Co. GA 129 D3
Doon IA 27 F4
Door Co. WI 69 D4
Dora AL 119 F4
Doraville GA 120 C4
Dorchester NE 35 F4
Dorchester WI 68 A4
Dorchester Co. MD 103 F4
Dorchester Co. SC 130 C1
Dormont PA 250 B3
Dorr MI 75 F4
Dorris CA 28 C2
Dorset VT 81 D4
Dorsey MD 193 B4
Dortches NC 113 D4
Dos Palos CA 44 C2
Dothan AL 128 B4
Double Sprs. AL 119 E3
Doubs MD 144 A2
Dougherty Co. GA 128 C4
Douglas AL 120 A3
Douglas AZ 55 E4
Douglas GA 129 E4
Douglas MA 150 C2
Douglas MI 75 E4
Douglas WY 33 E1
Douglas Co. CO 41 E2
Douglas Co. GA 120 C4
Douglas Co. IL 99 D1
Douglas Co. KS 96 A3
Douglas Co. MN 66 B2
Douglas Co. MO 107 E2
Douglas Co. NE 35 F3
Douglas Co. NV 37 D2
Douglas Co. OR 20 B4
Douglas Co. SD 27 E4
Douglas Co. WA 13 E3
Douglas Co. WI 64 C4
Douglass KS 43 F4
Douglass Hills KY 230 F2
Douglassville PA 146 B2
Douglasville GA 120 C4
Dousman WI 74 C3
Dove Creek CO 40 A4
Dover AR 117 D1
Dover DE 145 E2
Dover FL 140 C2
Dover ID 14 B2
Dover MA 151 D1
Dover NH 82 A4
Dover NJ 148 A3
Dover OH 91 E4
Dover PA 103 E1
Dover TN 109 D3
Dover-Foxcroft ME 82 C1
Dover Plains NY 94 B3
Dowagiac MI 89 F1
Dow City IA 86 A1
Dowling Park FL 137 F2
Downers Grove IL 89 D1
Downey CA 52 C2
Downey ID 31 E2
Downieville CA 36 C1
Downingtown PA 146 B3
Downs IL 88 C4
Downs KS 43 D1
Dows IA 72 C4
Doyle TN 110 A4
Doylestown OH 91 E3
Doylestown PA 146 C2
Doyline LA 125 D2
Drain OR 20 B4
Drake ND 18 C2
Drakesboro KY 109 E2
Drakes Branch VA 113 D2
Draper UT 31 E4
Dravosburg PA 250 C3
Drayton ND 19 E2
Dresden OH 91 D4
Dresden TN 108 C3
Dresser WI 67 D3
Drew MS 118 A4
Drew Co. AR 117 F4
Drexel MO 96 B3
Drexel NC 111 F4
Drexel OH 208 D1
Drexel Hill PA 146 C3
Driggs ID 23 F4
Dripping Sprs. TX 61 D2
Driscoll TX 63 F2
Druid Hills GA 190 D3
Drummond MT 15 E4
Drumright OK 51 F2
Dryden ME 82 B2
Dryden MI 76 C3
Dryden NY 79 D4
Dryden VA 111 D2
Dry Mills ME 82 B3
Dry Prong LA 125 E4
Dry Ridge KY 100 B3
Duarte CA 228 E2
Dubach LA 125 E2
Dublin CA 259 E3
Dublin GA 129 E2
Dublin IN 100 A1
Dublin MD 145 D1
Dublin OH 90 C4
Dublin PA 146 C2
Dublin TX 59 D3
Dublin VA 112 A2
Dubois ID 23 E3
DuBois PA 92 B3
Dubois WY 24 B4
Dubois Co. IN 99 E3
Duboistown PA 93 D2
Dubuque IA 73 F4
Dubuque Co. IA 73 F4
Duchesne UT 32 A4
Duchesne Co. UT 39 F1
Duck Hill MS 118 B4
Ducktown TN 120 C2
Ducor CA 45 D4
Dudley MA 150 B2
Dudleyville AZ 55 D2
Duenweg MO 106 B2
Due West SC 121 E3
Dufur OR 21 D2
Dugger IN 99 E2
Dukes Co. MA 151 E4

Entries in **bold black** indicate counties or parishes.
Entries in **bold color** indicate cities with detailed inset maps.

Denver CO
Boulder
Erie
Lafayette
Louisville
Superior
Broomfield
Thornton
Brighton
Westminster
Northglenn
Federal Heights
Arvada
Dupont
Commerce City
Wheat Ridge
Edgewater
Golden
Applewood
Denver
Lakewood
Glendale
Aurora
Englewood
Sheridan
Cherry Hills Village
Greenwood Village
Centennial
Littleton
Highlands Ranch
Lone Tree
Parker
Evergreen

Applewood B3
Arvada B2
Aspen Park A4
Aurora D3
Bergen Park A3
Boulder A1
Bow Mar B4
Brighton D1
Broomfield B1
Centennial C4
Cherry Hills Vil. C4
Columbine Valley B4
Commerce City C2
Denver C3
Dupont C2
Edgewater B3
Eldorado Sprs. A1
El Rancho A3
Englewood C3
Erie B1
Evergreen A4
Federal Hts. B2
Foxfield D4
Glendale C3
Golden A3
Greenwood Vil. C4
Henderson C2
Highlands Ranch C4
Idledale A3
Indian Hills A4
Kittredge A4
Lafayette B1
Lakeside B3
Lakewood B3
Littleton B4
Lochbuie D1
Lone Tree C4
Louisville B1
Morrison A4
Mtn. View B3
Northglenn C2
Parker D4
Pleasant View B3
Sheridan B4
Superior B1
Thornton C1
Watkins D3
Wattenberg C1
Welby C2
Westminster B2
Wheat Ridge B3

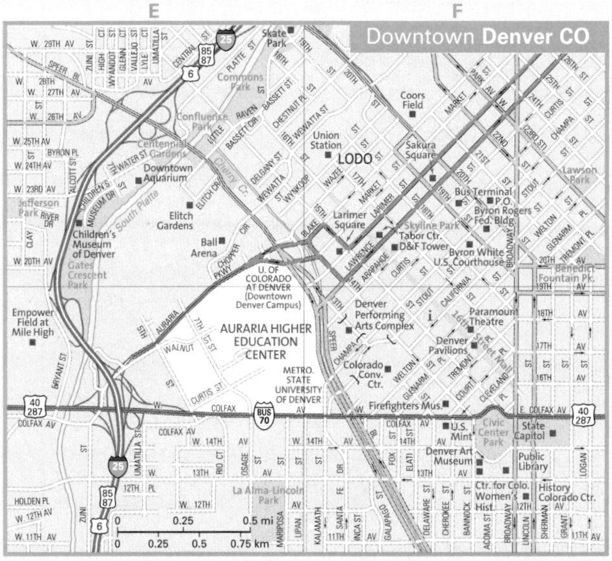
Downtown Denver CO
LODO
Coors Field
Union Station
Auraria Higher Education Center

POINTS OF INTEREST

16th Street Mall F2
Auraria Higher Education Center E2
Ball Arena E1
Bus Terminal F1
Byron Rogers Federal Building F1
Byron White U.S. Courthouse F1
Center for Colorado Women's History F2
Children's Museum of Denver E1
Colorado Convention Center F2
Coors Field F1
D&F Tower F1
Denver Art Museum F2
Denver Pavilions F2
Denver Performing Arts Complex F2
Downtown Aquarium E1
Elitch Gardens E1
Empower Field at Mile High E2
Firefighters Museum F2
History Colorado Center F2
Larimer Square F1
LoDo F1
Metropolitan State Univ. of Denver E2
Paramount Theatre F2
Post Office F1
Public Library F2
Sakura Square F1
Skate Park E1
State Capitol F2
Tabor Center F1
Union Station F1
U.S. Mint F2
Univ. of Colorado at Denver (Downtown Denver Campus) E2

Dulac LA **134** B4
Dulce NM **48** C1
Duluth GA **120** C3
Duluth MN **64** C4
Dumas AR **117** F4
Dumas MS **118** C2
Dumas TX **50** A2
Dumfries VA **144** A4
Dumont CO **41** D1
Dumont IA **73** D4
Dunbar PA **102** B1
Dunbar WV **101** E4
Duncan AZ **55** F2
Duncan MS **118** A3
Duncan OK **51** E4
Duncan SC **121** F2
Duncannon PA **93** D4
Duncansville PA **92** C4
Duncanville TX **59** F2
Dundalk MD **144** C2
Dundas MN **73** D1
Dundee FL **141** D2
Dundee MI **90** C1
Dundee NY **79** D4
Dundee OR **20** B2
Dundy Co. NE **42** B1
Dunean SC **217** A2
Dunedin FL **140** B2
Dunellen NJ **147** E1
Dunes City OR **20** A4
Dunkerton IA **73** E4
Dunkirk IN **90** A4
Dunkirk MD **144** C4
Dunkirk NY **78** A4
Dunkirk OH **90** C3
Dunklin Co. MO **108** B4
Dunlap IL **88** B3
Dunlap IN **89** F2
Dunlap IA **86** A1
Dunlap TN **120** B1
Dunleith DE **274** D2
Dunmore PA **93** F2
Dunn NC **123** D1
Dunn Co. ND **18** A3
Dunn Co. WI **67** E3
Dunnellon FL **138** C4
Dunn Loring VA **270** A3
Dunn's Corners RI **150** C4
Dunnstown PA **93** D3
Dunseith ND **18** C1
Dunsmuir CA **28** C3
Dunwoody GA **190** E2
DuPage Co. IL **89** D1
Duplin Co. NC **115** C4
Dupo IL **98** A3
Dupont CO **209** C2
Dupont PA **261** C2
DuPont WA **12** C3
Dupree SD **26** B2
Duquesne MO **106** B2
Duquesne PA **250** D3
Du Quoin IL **98** B4
Durand IL **74** B4
Durand MI **76** B3
Durand WI **67** E4
Durango CO **40** B4
Durant IA **87** F2
Durant MS **126** B1
Durant OK **59** F1
Durham CA **36** B1
Durham CT **149** E1
Durham NH **82** A4
Durham NC **112** C4
Durham OR **251** C3

Figures after entries indicate page number and grid reference.

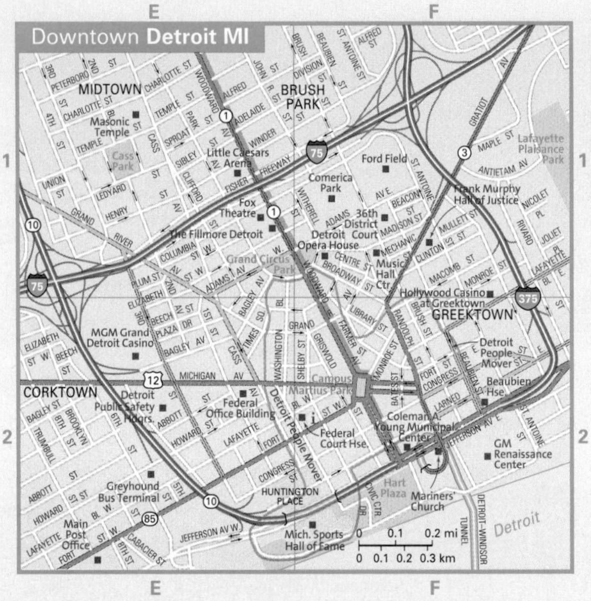

POINTS OF INTEREST

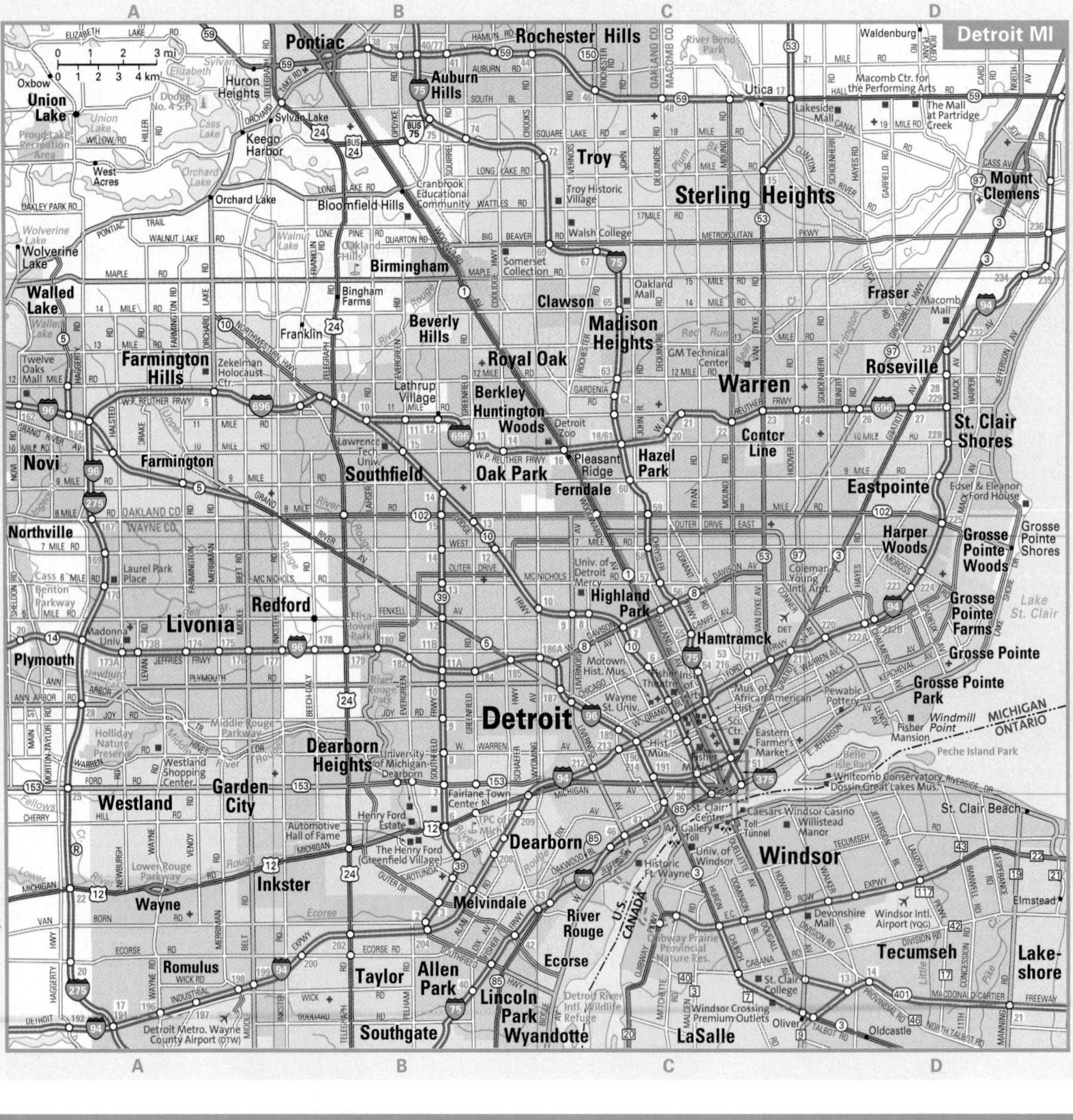

Entries in **bold black** indicate counties or parishes.
Entries in **bold color** indicate cities with detailed inset maps.

Durham Co. NC 112 C4
Duryea PA 93 F2
Dushore PA 93 E2
Duson LA 133 E2
Dustin OK 51 F3
Dutchess Co. NY 148 C1
Dutch Neck NJ 147 D2
Dutton MT 15 F2
Duval Co. FL 139 D2
Duval Co. TX 63 E2
Duvall WA 12 C3
Earlville IL 88 C2
Earlville IA 73 F4
Earlville NY 79 E4
Earlville PA 146 B2
Early IA 72 A4
Early TX 59 D4
Early Co. GA 128 C4
Earlysville VA 102 C4
Earth TX 50 A4
Easley SC 121 E2
E. Alton IL 98 A3

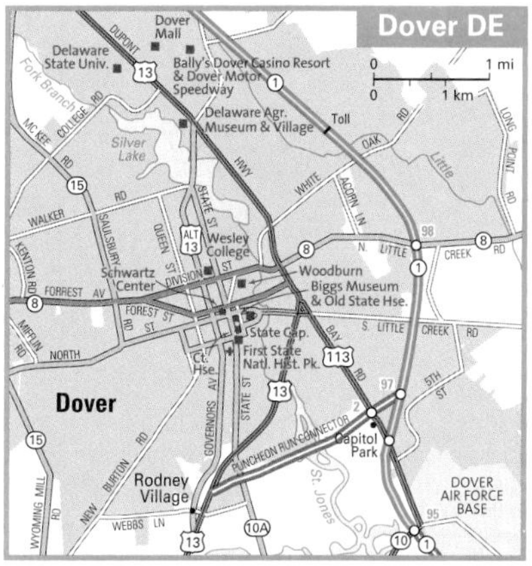

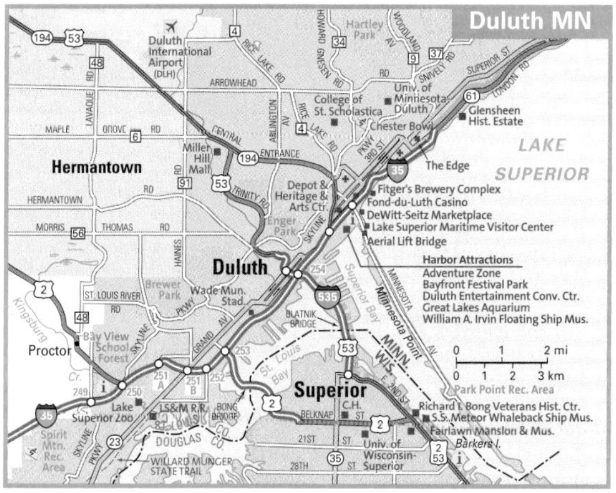

Eastgate WA 262 B3
E. Glacier Park MT 15 D2
E. Glastonbury CT 149 E1
E. Glenville NY 94 B1
E. Grand Forks MN 19 E2
E. Grand Rapids MI 215 B2
E. Greenbush NY 188 E3
E. Greenville PA 146 B1
E. Greenwich RI 150 C3
E. Gull Lake MN 64 A4
E. Haddam CT 149 E1
Eastham MA 151 F3
E. Hampton CT 149 E1
Easthampton MA 150 A1
E. Hampton NY 149 F3
E. Hanover NJ 148 A3
E. Hardwick VT 81 E2
E. Hartford CT 150 A3
E. Harwich MA 151 F3
E. Haven CT 149 D2
E. Helena MT 15 E4
E. Highland Park VA 254 B1
E. Holden ME 83 D1
E. Hope ID 14 B2
E. Ithaca NY 79 D4
E. Jordan MI 69 F3
Eastlake OH 91 E2
Eastland TX 59 D3
Eastland Co. TX 59 D3
E. Lansdowne PA 248 B3
E. Lansing MI 76 A4
E. Lebanon ME 82 A4
E. Liverpool OH 91 F3
E. Longmeadow MA 150 A2
E. Los Angeles CA 228 D3
Eastman GA 129 E3
E. Marion MA 151 E3
E. Marion NY 149 E2
E. McKeesport PA 250 D3
E. Meadow NY 148 C4
E. Middlebury VT 81 D3
E. Middletown NY 148 A1
E. Millcreek UT 257 B2
E. Millinocket ME 85 D4
E. Moline IL 88 A2
E. Montpelier VT 81 E2
E. Moriches NY 149 E4
E. Mtn. TX 124 B2
E. Naples FL 142 C2
E. Nassau NY 94 B1
E. Newark NJ 240 B3
E. Newnan GA 128 C1
E. Northport ME 82 C2
E. Northport NY 148 C3
E. Olympia WA 12 C4
Easton CA 44 C3
Easton CT 148 C2
Easton ME 85 E2
Easton MD 145 D3
Easton PA 93 F3
Easton TX 124 B2
E. Orange NJ 148 A4
E. Orleans MA 151 F3
Eastover NC 123 D1
Eastover SC 122 B4
E. Palatka FL 139 D3
E. Palestine OH 91 F3
E. Palo Alto CA 259 D5
E. Patchogue NY 149 D4
E. Peoria IL 88 B3
E. Petersburg PA 146 A2
E. Pittsburgh PA 250 D2
Eastpoint FL 137 D3
E. Point GA 120 C4
Eastpointe MI 210 D2
Eastport ME 83 F1
Eastport NY 149 E3
E. Poultney VT 81 D3
E. Prairie MO 108 C2
E. Prospect PA 103 E1
E. Providence RI 150 C3
E. Quincy CA 36 C1
E. Quogue NY 149 E3
E. Randolph NY 92 B1
E. Ridge TN 120 B2
E. Rochester NY 254 G2
E. Rockaway NY 147 F1
E. Rockingham NC 122 C2
E. Rutherford NJ 240 C2
E. St. Louis IL 98 A3
E. Sandwich MA 151 E3
E. Setauket NY 149 D3
E. Shoreham NY 149 D3
Eastsound WA 12 C1
E. Spencer NC 112 A4
E. Stroudsburg PA 93 F3
E. Swanzey NH 95 D1
E. Syracuse NY 265 B2
E. Tawakoni TX 59 F2
E. Tawas MI 76 B1
E. Texas PA 146 B1
E. Thermopolis WY 24 C4
E. Troy WI 74 C4
E. Vassalboro ME 82 C2
Eastview MD 144 D1
Eastview TN 119 D2
E. Village CT 149 D2
Eastville VA 114 B3
E. Wareham MA 151 E3
E. Washington PA 92 A4
E. Wenatchee WA 13 D3
E. Wilton ME 82 B2
E. Winthrop ME 82 B2
Eastwood LA 125 D2
E. York PA 275 F1
Eaton CO 33 E4
Eaton IN 90 A4
Eaton OH 100 B1
Eaton Co. MI 76 A4
Eaton Estates OH 91 D2
Eaton Park FL 266 E2
Eaton Rapids MI 76 A4
Eatons Neck NY 148 C3
Eatonton GA 129 E1
Eatontown NJ 147 E2
Eatonville FL 246 C1
Eatonville WA 12 C4
Eau Claire MI 89 F1
Eau Claire WI 67 F4
Eau Claire Co. WI 67 F4
Ebensburg PA 92 B4
Eccles WV 111 F1
Echo OR 21 E1
Echols Co. GA 138 B1
Eclectic AL 128 A2
Economy PA 92 A3
Ecorse MI 210 C4
Ecru MS 118 C3
Ector TX 59 F1
Ector Co. TX 57 F3
Edcouch TX 63 E4
Eddington ME 83 D1
Eddy Co. NM 57 E2
Eddy Co. ND 19 D3
Eddystone PA 248 A4
Eddyville IA 87 D2
Eddyville KY 109 D2
Eden ID 31 D1
Eden MD 103 F4
Eden NY 78 A4
Eden NC 112 B3
Eden TX 58 C4
Eden WI 74 C2
Eden WY 32 A2
Eden Prairie MN 235 A4
Edenton NC 113 F4
Eden Valley MN 66 D3
Edenville NY 148 A2
Edgar NE 35 E4
Edgar WI 68 A4
Edgar Co. IL 99 D1
Edgard LA 134 B3
Edgartown MA 151 E4
Edgecliff Vil. TX 207 A3
Edgecombe Co. NC 113 E4
Edgefield SC 121 F4
Edgefield Co. SC 121 F4
Edgeley ND 19 D4
Edgemere MD 144 C2
Edgemont SD 25 F4
Edgemoor DE 146 B4
Edgerton KS 96 B3
Edgerton MN 27 F4
Edgerton MO 96 B2
Edgerton OH 90 A2
Edgerton WI 74 B3
Edgerton WY 25 D4
Edgewater AL 195 D2
Edgewater CO 209 B3
Edgewater FL 139 E4
Edgewater NJ 240 D2
Edgewater Park NJ 147 D3
Edgewood FL 246 C3
Edgewood IN 89 F4
Edgewood IA 73 F4
Edgewood KY 204 B3
Edgewood MD 145 D1
Edgewood NM 48 C3
Edgewood OH 91 F1
Edgewood PA 250 C2
Edgewood TX 124 A2
Edgewood WA 262 B5
Edina MN 67 D4
Edina MO 87 E4
Edinboro PA 92 A1
Edinburg IL 98 B1
Edinburg NJ 147 D2
Edinburg ND 19 E2
Edinburg TX 63 E4
Edinburg VA 102 C3
Edinburgh IN 99 F2
Edison GA 128 C4
Edison NJ 147 E1
Edisto Beach SC 130 C2
Edmond OK 51 E2
Edmonds WA 12 C3
Edmondson AR 118 B1
Edmonson Co. KY 109 F2
Edmonston MD 270 E2
Edmonton KY 110 A2
Edmore MI 76 A2
Edmore ND 19 D2
Edmunds Co. SD 27 D2
Edmundson MO 256 B1
Edna KS 106 A2
Edna TX 61 F3
Edon OH 90 A2
Edwards CO 40 C1
Edwards MS 126 A2
Edwardsburg MI 89 F1
Edwards Co. IL 99 D4
Edwards Co. KS 43 D4
Edwards Co. TX 60 B2
Edwardsville IL 98 B3
Edwardsville KS 96 B2
Edwardsville PA 261 A1
Effingham IL 98 C2
Effingham KS 96 A1
Effingham Co. GA 130 B2
Effingham Co. IL 98 C2
Effort PA 93 F3
Egan SD 27 F3
Egg Harbor City NJ 147 D4
Egypt PA 189 A1
Ehrenberg AZ 53 F3
Ehrhardt SC 130 C1
Ekalaka MT 25 F1
Elaine AR 118 A3
Elam PA 146 B3
Elba AL 128 A4
Elba NY 78 B3
Elberfeld IN 99 E4
Elberta AL 135 F2
Elberta MI 69 E4
Elberta UT 39 E1
Elbert Co. CO 41 E2
Elbert Co. GA 121 E3
Elberton GA 121 E3
Elbow Lake MN 27 F1
Elbridge NY 79 D3
Elburn IL 88 C1
El Cajon CA 53 D4
El Campo TX 61 F3
El Cenizo TX 63 D2
El Centro CA 53 E4
El Cerrito CA 229 H4
El Cerrito CA 259 B2
Eldersburg MD 144 B1
Eldon IA 87 E3
Eldon MO 97 E4
Eldon OK 106 B4
Eldora IA 73 D4
El Dorado AR 125 E1
Eldorado IL 109 D1
El Dorado KS 43 F4
Eldorado OK 50 C4
Eldorado TX 60 B1
El Dorado Co. CA 36 C2
Eldorado Sprs. CO 209 A1
El Dorado Sprs. MO 96 C4
Eldred PA 92 C1
Eldridge IA 88 A2
Eleanor WV 101 E3
Electra TX 59 D1
Electric City WA 13 E2
Eleele HI 152 B1
Elephant Butte NM 56 B2
Eleva WI 67 F4
Elfers FL 140 B2
Elfrida AZ 55 E4
Elgin AZ 55 D4
Elgin IL 88 C1
Elgin IA 73 E3
Elgin MN 73 E1
Elgin NE 35 E2
Elgin ND 18 B4
Elgin OK 51 D4
Elgin OR 21 F1
Elgin SC 122 A3
Elgin SC 122 B2
Elgin TX 61 E1
El Granada CA 259 B5
Elida OH 90 B3
Elihu KY 110 B2
Elizabeth CO 41 E2
Elizabeth IL 74 A4
Elizabeth LA 133 E1
Elizabeth NJ 148 A4
Elizabeth PA 92 A4
Elizabeth WV 101 F2
Elizabeth City NC 113 F3
Elizabeth Lake CA 52 C2
Elizabethton TN 111 E3
Elizabethtown IL 109 D1
Elizabethtown KY 110 A1
Elizabethtown NY 81 D2
Elizabethtown NC 123 D2
Elizabethtown PA 93 E4
Elizabethville PA 93 D4
El Jebel CO 40 C2
Elkader IA 73 F3
Duxbury MA 151 E2
Duxbury VT 81 E2
Dwaar Kill NY 148 A1
Dwarf KY 111 D1
Dwight IL 88 C3
Dyer AR 116 C1
Dyer IN 89 D2
Dyer TN 108 C4
Dyer Co. TN 108 C4
Dyersburg TN 108 C4
Dyersville IA 73 F4
Dyess AR 118 B1
Dysart IA 87 E1

E

Eads CO 42 A3
Eagan MN 235 D4
Eagar AZ 48 A4
Eagle CO 40 C1
Eagle ID 22 B4
Eagle NE 35 F4
Eagle WI 74 C3
Eagle Bend MN 66 B1
Eagle Butte SD 26 B2
Eagle Co. CO 40 C1
Eagle Grove IA 72 C4
Eagle Lake FL 140 C2
Eagle Lake ME 85 D1
Eagle Lake MN 72 C1
Eagle Lake TX 61 F2
Eagle Mtn. UT 31 E4
Eagle Nest NM 49 D1
Eagle Pass TX 60 B4
Eagle Pt. OR 28 C2
Eagle River MI 65 F3
Eagle River WI 68 B2
Eagleton Vil. TN 110 C4
Eagleville PA 146 C2
Eagleville TN 109 F4
Earle AR 118 A1
Earlham IA 86 C2
Earlimart CA 45 D4
Earlington KY 109 E2
Earlsboro OK 51 F3
E. Arcadia NC 123 E3
E. Arlington VT 81 D4
E. Atlantic Beach NY 241 G5
E. Aurora NY 78 B4
E. Bank WV 101 F4
E. Barre VT 81 E2
E. Barrington NH 81 F4
E. Baton Rouge Par. LA 134 A1
E. Bend NC 112 A3
E. Berlin PA 103 E1
E. Bernard TX 61 F2
E. Bernstadt KY 110 C2
E. Bethel MN 67 D3
E. Blackstone MA 150 C2
E. Brady PA 92 A3
E. Brewster MA 151 F3
E. Brewton AL 135 F1
E. Bridgewater MA 151 D2
E. Brookfield MA 150 B2
E. Brooklyn CT 150 B3
E. Brunswick NJ 147 E1
E. Butler PA 92 A3
E. Camden AR 117 E4
E. Canton OH 91 E3
E. Carbon UT 39 F1
E. Carroll Par. LA 126 A2
Eastchester NY 148 B3
E. Chicago IN 89 D2
E. Cleveland OH 91 E2
E. Dennis MA 151 F3
E. Douglas MA 150 C2
E. Dublin GA 129 E2
E. Dubuque IL 73 F4
E. Duke OK 50 C4
E. Dundee IL 203 A2
E. Ellijay GA 120 C2
E. End AR 117 E2
E. Falmouth MA 151 E4
E. Feliciana Par. LA 134 A1
E. Flat Rock NC 121 E1
E. Freehold NJ 147 E2
E. Freetown MA 151 D3
E. Gaffney SC 121 F1
E. Galesburg IL 88 A3

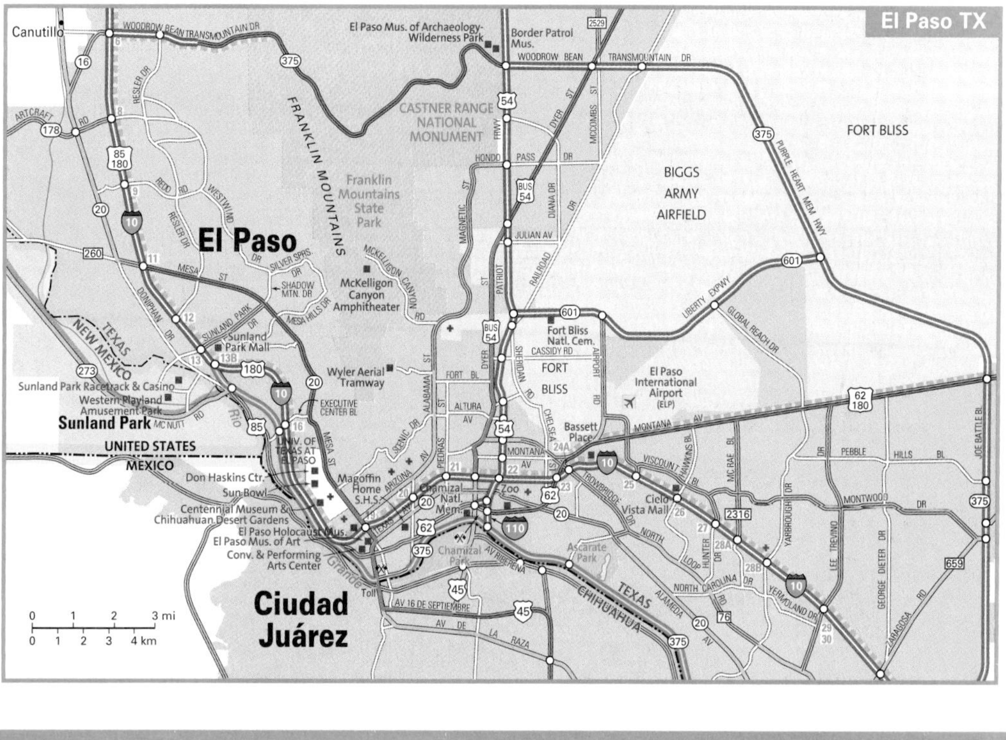

Figures after entries indicate page number and grid reference.

Elk City OK 50 C3
Elk Co. KS 43 F4
Elk Co. PA 92 B2
Elk Grove CA 36 C3
Elk Grove Vil. IL 203 C3
Elkhart IN 89 F2
Elkhart KS 50 A1
Elkhart TX 124 A4
Elkhart Co. IN 89 F2
Elkhart Lake WI 74 C2
Elkhorn CA 236 E2
Elk Horn IA 86 B2
Elkhorn WI 74 C4
Elkhorn City KY 111 E1
Elkin NC 112 A3
Elkins AR 106 C4
Elkins WV 102 A3
Elkland PA 93 D1
Elkmont AL 119 F2
Elk Mound WI 67 E4
Elko NV 30 B4
Elko Co. NV 30 C3
Elko New Market MN 67 D4
Elk Pt. SD 35 F1
Elk Rapids MI 69 F4
Elkridge MD 144 C2
Elk Ridge UT 39 E1
Elk River MN 66 C3
Elk Run Hts. IA 73 E4
Elkton KY 109 E2
Elkton MD 145 E1
Elkton MI 76 C2
Elkton SD 27 F3
Elkton TN 119 F2
Elkton VA 102 C3
Elkview WV 101 F3
Elkville IL 98 B4
El Lago TX 132 B3
Ellaville GA 129 D3
Ellenboro NC 121 F1
Ellenboro WV 101 F2
Ellendale DE 145 F3
Ellendale MN 72 C2
Ellendale ND 27 D1
Ellensburg WA 13 D4
Ellenton FL 266 B4
Ellenville NY 94 A3
Ellerbe NC 122 C2
Ellerslie MD 102 C1
Ellettsville IN 99 F2
Ellicott NY 78 B4
Ellicott City MD 144 C2
Ellijay GA 120 C2
Ellington CT 150 A3
Ellington MO 108 A2
Ellinwood KS 43 D3
Elliott Co. KY 101 D4
Ellis KS 42 C2
Ellis Co. KS 43 D2
Ellis Co. OK 50 C2
Ellis Co. TX 59 F3
Ellisport WA 262 A4
Elliston MT 15 E4
Elliston VA 112 B2
Ellisville MS 126 C4
Ellisville MO 256 A2
Elloree SC 122 B4
Ellsworth IA 72 C4
Ellsworth KS 43 E2
Ellsworth ME 83 D2
Ellsworth MI 69 F3
Ellsworth MN 27 F4
Ellsworth PA 92 A4
Ellsworth WI 67 E4
Ellsworth Co. KS 43 E3
Ellwood City PA 91 F3
Elma IA 73 D3
Elma NY 78 B3
Elma WA 12 B4
Elm City NC 113 D4
Elm Creek NE 35 D4
Elmendorf TX 61 D3
Elmer NJ 145 F1
Elm Grove WI 234 B2
Elmhurst IL 89 D1
Elmira NY 93 D1
El Mirage AZ 249 A1
Elmira Hts. NY 93 D1
Elm Mott TX 59 E4
Elmo UT 39 F2
Elmont NY 148 C4
Elmont VA 113 E1
El Monte CA 228 E2
Elmore MN 72 C2
Elmore OH 90 C2
Elmore City OK 51 E4
Elmore Co. AL 128 A2
Elmore Co. ID 22 B4
Elm Sprs. AR 106 C3
Elmville CT 150 B3
Elmwood IL 88 A3
Elmwood NE 35 F4
Elmwood WI 67 E4
Elmwood Park IL 203 D4
Elmwood Park NJ 240 C1
Elmwood Place OH 204 B2
Elnora IN 99 E3
Elnora NY 94 B1
Elon NC 112 C4
Eloy AZ 54 C2
El Paso IL 88 B3
El Paso TX 56 C4
El Paso Co. CO 41 E2
El Paso Co. TX 56 C4
El Portal FL 233 B4
El Prado NM 49 D1
El Reno OK 51 E3
El Rio CA 52 B2
El Rito NM 48 C1
Elroy WI 74 A2
Elsa TX 63 E4
Elsah IL 98 A2
Elsberry MO 98 A2
El Segundo CA 228 C3
Elsie MI 76 A3
Elsinore UT 39 E3
Elsmere DE 146 B4
Elsmere KY 100 B2
Elsmere NY 188 D3
El Sobrante CA 259 C1
Elton LA 133 E2
Elvaton MD 193 C5
Elverson PA 146 B2
Elwood IL 89 D2
Elwood IN 89 F4
Elwood KS 96 B1
Elwood NE 34 C4
Elwood NJ 147 D4
Elwood UT 31 E3
Ely IA 87 E1
Ely MN 64 C2
Ely NV 38 B2
Elyria OH 91 D2
Elysburg PA 93 E3
Elysian MN 72 C1
Emanuel Co. GA 129 F2
Emerado ND 19 E2
Emerald Isle NC 115 D4
Emerson GA 120 C3
Emerson NE 35 F2
Emerson NJ 148 B3
Emery SD 27 E4
Emery UT 39 E2
Emery Co. UT 39 F2
Emery Mills ME 82 A4
Emeryville CA 259 C2
Emigsville PA 103 E1
Emily MN 64 B4
Eminence KY 100 A4
Eminence MO 107 F2
Emlenton PA 92 A2
Emmaus PA 146 B1
Emmet AR 117 D4
Emmet Co. IA 72 B3
Emmet Co. MI 70 B3
Emmetsburg IA 72 B3
Emmett ID 22 B4
Emmitsburg MD 103 D1
Emmonak AK 154 B2
Emmons Co. ND 18 C4
Emmorton MD 145 D1
Emory TX 124 A1
Emory VA 111 F2
Empire CO 41 D1
Empire LA 134 C4
Empire NV 29 E4
Empire City OK 51 E4
Emporia KS 43 F3
Emporia VA 113 E3
Emporium PA 92 C2
Emsworth PA 250 A1
Encampment WY 33 D3
Encinal TX 60 C4
Encinitas CA 53 D4
Enderlin ND 19 E4
Endicott NY 93 E1
Endicott WA 13 F4
Endwell NY 93 E1
Energy IL 108 C1
Enfield CT 150 A2
Enfield IL 99 D4
Enfield NH 81 E3
Enfield NC 113 E4
Enfield Ctr. NH 81 E3
England AR 117 E3
Englewood CO 41 E1
Englewood FL 140 C4
Englewood NJ 148 B3
Englewood OH 100 B1
Englewood TN 120 C1
Englewood Beach FL 140 C4
Englewood Cliffs NJ 240 D1
English IN 99 F4
Englishtown NJ 147 E2
Enhaut PA 218 C2
Enid OK 51 E1
Enigma GA 129 E4
Enka NC 121 E1
Ennis MT 23 E2
Ennis TX 59 F3
Enoch UT 39 D4
Enochville NC 122 B1
Enola PA 218 A1
Enon OH 100 C1
Enoree SC 121 F2
Enosburg Falls VT 81 D1
Ensley FL 135 F2
Ensor KY 109 E1
Enterprise AL 128 B4
Enterprise KS 43 F2
Enterprise MS 127 D3
Enterprise OR 22 A2
Enterprise UT 38 C4
Enterprise WV 102 A2
Entiat WA 13 D3
Enumclaw WA 12 C3
Ephraim UT 39 E2
Ephrata PA 146 A2
Ephrata WA 13 E3
Epping NH 81 F4
Epps LA 125 F2
Epworth IA 73 F4
Epworth Hts. OH 204 C1
Equality IL 109 D1
Erath LA 133 F3
Erath Co. TX 59 D3
Erda UT 31 E4
Erial NJ 146 C4
Erick OK 50 C3
Erie CO 209 B1
Erie IL 88 A2
Erie KS 106 A1
Erie PA 92 A1
Erie Co. NY 78 B4
Erie Co. OH 91 D2
Erie Co. PA 92 A1
Erin TN 109 E3
Erlanger KY 100 B2
Erwin NC 123 D1
Erwin TN 111 E4
Erwinville LA 134 A2
Escalante UT 39 E4
Escalon CA 36 C4
Escambia Co. AL 136 A1
Escambia Co. FL 135 F1
Escanaba MI 69 D2
Escatawpa MS 195 C1
Escobares TX 63 D4
Escondido CA 53 D4
Esko MN 64 C4
Eskridge KS 43 F2
Esmeralda Co. NV 37 F4
Española NM 49 D2
Espanong NJ 148 A3
Esparto CA 36 B2
Espy PA 93 E3
Essex CT 149 E2
Essex IA 86 A3
Essex MD 144 C2
Essex MA 151 F1
Essex MO 108 B2
Essex Co. MA 151 F1
Essex Co. NJ 148 A3
Essex Co. NY 80 C3
Essex Co. VT 81 F1
Essex Co. VA 103 E4
Essex Fells NJ 240 A2
Essex Jct. VT 81 D2
Essexville MI 76 B2
Estacada OR 20 C2
Estancia NM 49 D4
Estelle LA 239 C2
Estelline SD 27 F3
Estell Manor NJ 104 C3
Ester AK 154 C2
Estero FL 142 C1
Estes Park CO 33 E4
Etherville IA 72 B2
Estherwood LA 133 E2
Estill SC 130 B2
Estill Co. KY 110 C1
Estill Sprs. TN 120 A1
Estral Beach MI 90 C1
Ethan SD 27 E4
Ethel MS 126 C1
Ethete WY 32 B1
Ethridge TN 119 E1
Etna CA 28 B3
Etna PA 250 C1
Etna Green IN 89 F2
Etowah NC 121 E1
Etowah TN 120 C1
Etowah Co. AL 120 A3
Ettrick VA 113 E2
Ettrick WI 73 F1
Eubank KY 110 B2
Euclid OH 91 E2
Eudora AR 126 A1
Eudora KS 96 B3
Eufaula AL 128 B3
Eufaula OK 116 A1
Eugene OR 20 B4
Euharlee GA 120 B3
Euless TX 207 C2
Eunice LA 133 E2
Eunice NM 57 F3
Eupora MS 118 C4
Eureka CA 28 A4
Eureka IL 88 B3
Eureka KS 43 F4
Eureka MO 98 A3
Eureka MT 14 C1
Eureka NV 38 A1
Eureka SD 27 D1
Eureka UT 39 E1
Eureka Co. NV 30 B4
Eureka Mill SC 122 A2
Eureka Sprs. AR 106 C3
Eustace TX 59 F3
Eustis FL 140 C1
Eustis NE 34 C4
Eutaw AL 127 E2
Eva AL 119 F3
Evadale TX 132 C2
Evangeline Par. LA 133 E1
Evans CO 33 E4
Evans GA 121 F4
Evans WV 101 E3
Evans City PA 92 A3
Evans Co. GA 130 B3
Evansdale IA 73 E4
Evans Mills NY 79 E1
Evanston IL 89 D1
Evanston WY 31 F3
Evansville IL 98 B4
Evansville IN 99 D4
Evansville MN 66 A2
Evansville WI 74 B4
Evansville WY 33 D1
Evaro MT 15 D4
Evart MI 75 F1
Evarts KY 111 D2
Eveleth MN 64 C3
Evendale OH 204 B1
Evening Shade AR 107 F4
Everett MA 197 C1
Everett PA 102 C1
Everett WA 12 C2
Everglades City FL 143 D2
Evergreen AL 127 F4
Evergreen CO 41 D1
Evergreen MT 15 D2
Evergreen Park IL 203 D5
Everly IA 72 A3
Everman TX 207 B3
Everson PA 92 A4
Everson WA 12 C1
Evesboro NJ 147 D3
Ewa Beach HI 152 A3
Ewa Villages HI 152 A3
Ewing NE 35 E2
Ewing NJ 147 D2
Ewing VA 111 D3
Excel AL 127 F4
Excelsior Sprs. MO 96 C2
Exeter CA 45 D3
Exeter MO 106 C3
Exeter NE 35 E4

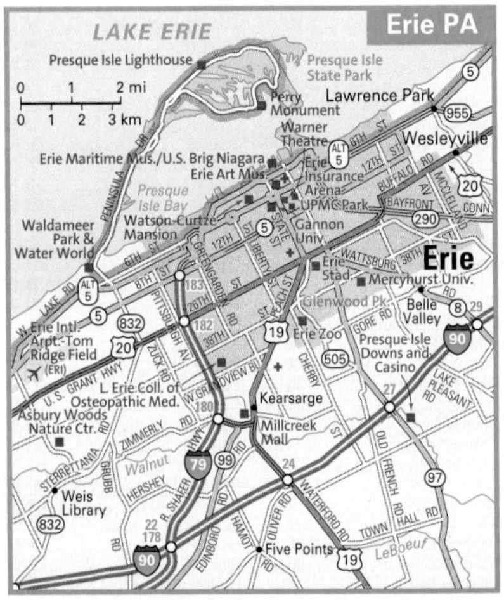

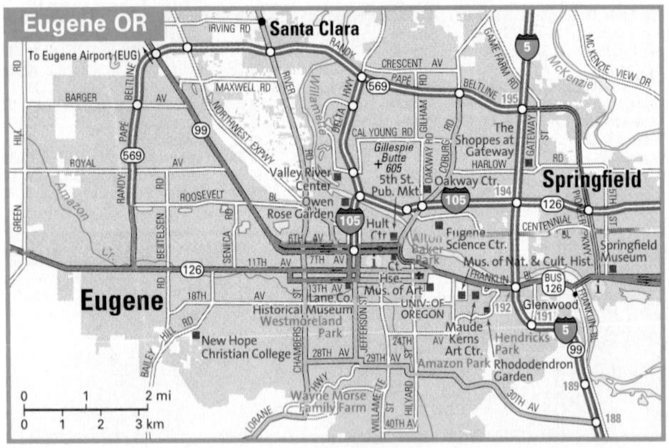

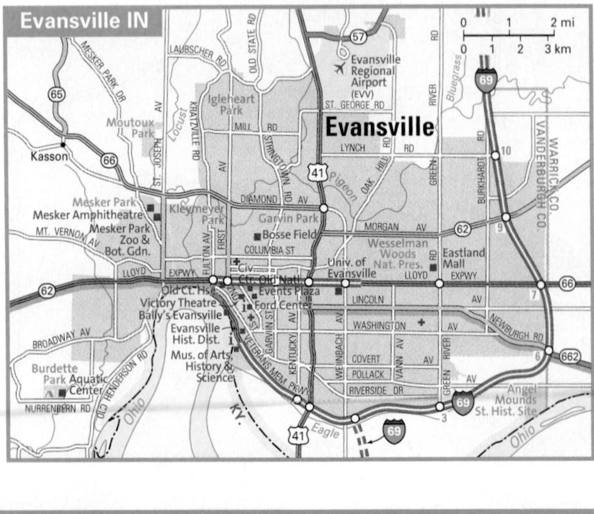

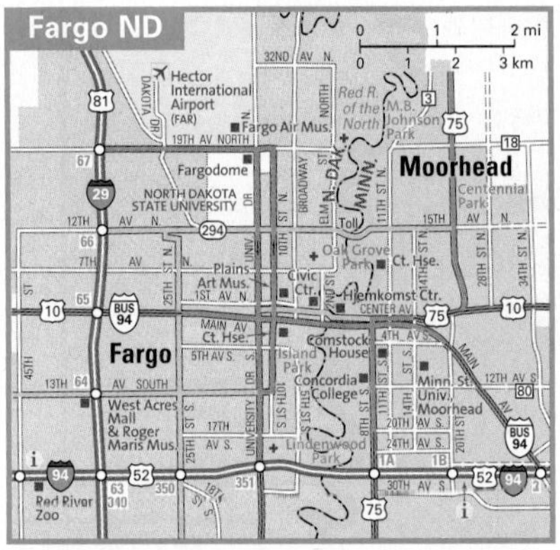

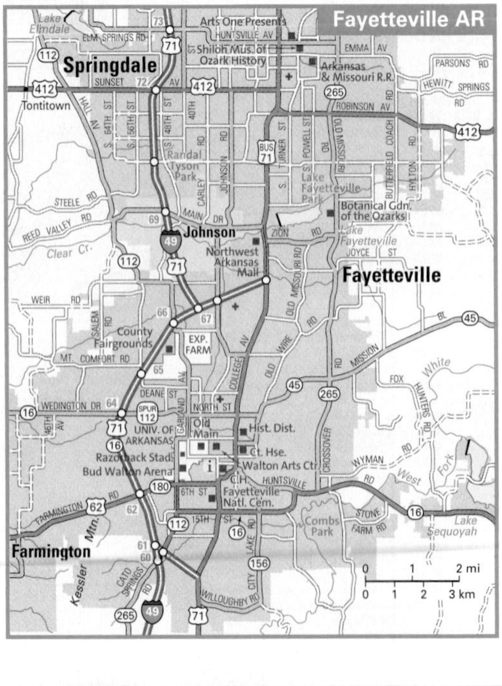

Entries in **bold black** indicate counties or parishes.
Entries in bold color indicate cities with detailed inset maps.

Exeter NH 82 A4
Exeter PA 261 C1
Exeter RI 150 C4
Exira IA 86 B2
Exmore VA 114 B3
Experiment GA 129 D1
Exton PA 146 B3
Eyota MN 73 E1

F
Fabens TX 56 C4
Factoryville PA 93 F2
Fairacres NM 56 B3
Fairbank IA 73 E4
Fairbanks AK 154 C2
Fairbanks FL 138 C3
Fairbanks ME 82 B1
Fair Bluff NC 123 D3
Fairborn OH 100 C1
Fairburn GA 120 C4
Fairbury IL 88 C3
Fairbury NE 43 E1
Fairchance PA 102 B1
Fairchild WI 67 F4
Fairchilds TX 132 A4
Fairfax CA 36 B3
Fairfax DE 274 E1
Fairfax IA 87 E1
Fairfax MN 66 B4
Fairfax MO 86 A4
Fairfax OH 204 C2
Fairfax OK 51 F1
Fairfax SC 130 B1
Fairfax VT 81 D1
Fairfax VA 144 A3
Fairfax Co. VA 144 A3
Fairfield AL 119 F4
Fairfield CA 36 B3
Fairfield CT 149 D2
Fairfield ID 22 C4
Fairfield IL 99 D4
Fairfield IA 87 E3
Fairfield ME 82 C2
Fairfield MT 15 E3
Fairfield NE 35 E4
Fairfield NJ 240 A1
Fairfield OH 100 B2
Fairfield TX 59 F4
Fairfield WA 14 B3
Fairfield Bay AR 117 E1
Fairfield Co. CT 149 D2
Fairfield Co. OH 101 D1
Fairfield Co. SC 122 A3
Fairfield Glade TN 110 B4
Fairgrove MI 76 B2
Fair Grove MO 107 D1
Fairhaven MA 151 D3
Fair Haven MI 76 C4
Fair Haven NJ 147 E2
Fair Haven NY 79 D3
Fair Haven VT 81 D3
Fairhope AL 135 E2
Fairland IN 99 F1
Fairland MD 144 B2
Fairland OK 106 B2
Fair Lawn NJ 148 B3
Fairlawn OH 188 A1
Fairlawn VA 112 A2
Fairlea WV 112 A1
Fairless Hills PA 147 D2
Fairmead CA 44 C2
Fairmont MN 72 B2
Fairmont NE 35 E4
Fairmont NC 123 D3
Fairmont WV 102 A2
Fairmont City IL 256 C2
Fairmount GA 120 C3
Fairmount IL 99 D1
Fairmount IN 89 F4
Fairmount MD 103 F4
Fairmount NY 79 D3
Fairmount ND 27 F1
Fairmount TN 120 B1
Fairmount Hts. MD 270 E3
Fair Oaks CA 255 C1
Fair Oaks GA 120 C4
Fair Oaks Ranch TX 61 D2
Fair Plain MI 89 E1
Fairplains NC 111 F3
Fairplay CO 41 D2
Fairport NY 78 C3
Fairport Harbor OH 91 E1
Fairton NJ 145 F1
Fairview AL 119 F3
Fairview GA 120 B2
Fairview MI 70 C4
Fairview MT 17 F2
Fairview NJ 148 B3
Fairview NC 121 E1
Fairview NC 122 B1
Fairview OK 51 D2
Fairview OR 20 C2
Fairview PA 91 F1
Fairview TN 109 E4
Fairview TX 59 F2
Fairview UT 39 E1
Fairview WV 102 A1
Fairview WY 31 F1
Fairview Hts. IL 98 B3
Fairview Park IN 99 E1
Fairview Park OH 204 D2
Fairview Shores FL 246 C1
Fairway KS 224 B3
Faison NC 123 E1
Faith NC 122 B1
Faith SD 26 B2
Falconer NY 92 B1
Falcon Hts. MN 235 C2
Falfurrias TX 63 E3
Falkville AL 119 F3
Fall Branch TN 111 E3
Fallbrook CA 53 D3
Fall City WA 12 C3
Fall Creek WI 67 F4
Falling Waters WV 103 D1
Fallon NV 37 E1
Fallon Co. MT 17 F4
Fall River MA 151 D3
Fall River WI 74 B2
Fall River Co. SD 33 F1
Fall River Mills CA 29 D3
Falls Church VA 144 B3
Falls City NE 86 A4
Falls City OR 20 B2
Falls City TX 61 E3
Falls Co. TX 59 F4
Falls Creek PA 92 B3
Fallston MD 144 C1
Fallston NC 122 A1
Falmouth KY 100 B3
Falmouth MA 151 E4
Falmouth VA 103 D4
Falmouth Foreside ME 82 B3
Fancy Farm KY 108 C2
Fannett TX 132 C3
Fannin Co. GA 120 C2
Fannin Co. TX 59 F1
Fanning Sprs. FL 138 B3
Fanwood NJ 147 E1
Fargo ND 19 F4
Far Hills NJ 148 A4
Faribault MN 73 D1
Faribault Co. MN 72 C2
Farley IA 73 F4
Farmer City IL 88 C4
Farmers Branch TX 207 D1
Farmersburg IN 99 E2
Farmers Mills NY 148 C1
Farmersville CA 45 D3
Farmersville IL 98 B2
Farmersville OH 100 B1
Farmersville PA 189 B1
Farmersville TX 59 F2
Farmerville LA 125 E2
Farmingdale ME 82 C2
Farmingdale NJ 147 E2
Farmingdale NY 148 C4
Farmington AR 106 C4
Farmington CT 94 C3
Farmington IL 88 A3
Farmington IA 87 E3
Farmington ME 82 B1
Farmington MI 210 A2
Farmington MN 67 D4
Farmington MS 119 D2
Farmington MO 108 A1
Farmington NH 81 F4
Farmington NM 48 B1
Farmington UT 31 E3
Farmington WV 102 A1
Farmington Hills MI 210 A2
Farmingville NY 149 D3
Farmland IN 90 A4
Farmville NC 115 C2
Farmville VA 113 D2
Farragut IA 86 A3
Farragut TN 110 C4
Farrell PA 91 F2
Farr West UT 244 A1
Farson WY 32 A2
Farwell MI 76 A2
Farwell TX 49 F4
Faulk Co. SD 27 D2
Faulkner Co. AR 117 E1
Faulkton SD 27 D2
Fauquier Co. VA 144 A4
Favoretta FL 139 E4
Fayette AL 119 E4
Fayette IA 73 E3
Fayette MS 126 A4
Fayette MO 97 D2
Fayette OH 90 B2
Fayette Co. AL 119 E4
Fayette Co. GA 120 C4
Fayette Co. IL 98 C2
Fayette Co. IN 100 A1
Fayette Co. IA 73 E4
Fayette Co. KY 100 B4
Fayette Co. OH 100 C1
Fayette Co. PA 102 B1
Fayette Co. TN 118 C1
Fayette Co. TX 61 E2
Fayette Co. WV 101 F4
Fayetteville AR 106 C4
Fayetteville GA 120 C4
Fayetteville NY 79 E3
Fayetteville NC 123 D2
Fayetteville PA 103 D1
Fayetteville TN 119 F1
Fayetteville WV 101 F4
Fearrington Vil. NC 112 C4
Feasterville PA 248 D1
Federal Hts. CO 209 B2
Federalsburg MD 145 E4
Federal Way WA 12 C3
Felicity OH 100 C3
Felida WA 20 C1
Fellowship NJ 147 D3
Fellsmere FL 141 E3
Felton CA 236 D1
Felton DE 145 E3
Fennimore WI 73 F3
Fennville MI 75 E4
Fenton MI 76 B4
Fenton MO 256 A3
Fentress Co. TN 110 B3
Fenwick Island DE 114 C1
Ferdinand IN 99 E4
Fergus Co. MT 16 B3
Fergus Falls MN 19 F4
Ferguson KY 110 B2
Ferguson MO 256 B1
Fernandina Beach FL 139 D1
Fernan Lake Vil. ID 14 B3
Ferndale CA 28 A4
Ferndale MD 193 C4
Ferndale MI 210 C2
Ferndale PA 146 C1
Ferndale WA 12 C1
Fernley NV 37 E1
Fern Park FL 246 C1
Ferrell NJ 146 C4
Ferrellsburg WV 101 E4
Ferrelview MO 96 B2
Ferriday LA 125 F4
Ferris TX 59 F3
Ferron UT 39 E2
Ferrum VA 112 B2
Ferry Co. WA 13 F2
Ferry Pass FL 135 F2
Ferrysburg MI 75 E3
Fertile MN 19 F3
Fessenden ND 18 C3
Festus MO 98 A4
Fieldale VA 112 B3
Fielding UT 31 E2
Fieldsboro NJ 147 D2
Fife WA 262 B5
Fife Lake MI 69 F4
Filer ID 30 C1
Fillmore CA 52 B2
Fillmore IN 99 E1
Fillmore UT 39 D2
Fillmore Co. MN 73 E2
Fillmore Co. NE 35 E4
Fincastle KY 230 F1
Fincastle VA 112 B1
Findlay IL 98 C1
Findlay OH 90 C3
Finley ND 19 E3
Finley WA 21 E1
Finney Co. KS 42 B3
Finneytown OH 204 B2
Fircrest WA 262 A5
Firebaugh CA 44 C2
Firth ID 23 E4
Firth NE 35 F4
Firthcliffe NY 148 B1
Fisher IL 88 C4
Fisher Co. TX 58 B2
Fishers IN 99 F1
Fishersville VA 102 C4
Fishkill NY 148 B1
Fishkill Plains NY 148 B1
Fiskdale MA 150 B2
Fitchburg MA 95 D1
Fitchburg WI 74 B3
Fitchville CT 149 F1
Fitzgerald GA 129 E4
Fitzwilliam NH 95 D1
Five Corners MA 151 D2
Flagler CO 41 F2
Flagler Beach FL 139 E4
Flagler Co. FL 139 D3
Flagstaff AZ 47 E3
Flagtown NJ 147 D1
Flanagan IL 88 C3
Flanders NY 149 E3
Flanders (E. Lyme) CT 149 F2
Flandreau SD 27 F3
Flasher ND 18 B4
Flathead Co. MT 14 C2
Flat Lick KY 110 C2
Flatonia TX 61 E2
Flat Rock MI 90 C1
Flat Rock NC 112 A3
Flat Rock NC 121 E1
Flatwoods KY 101 D3
Flatwoods WV 102 A3
Fleetwood PA 146 B1
Fleming CO 34 A4
Fleming Co. KY 100 C4
Fleming-Neon KY 111 E2
Flemingsburg KY 100 C3
Flemington NJ 147 D1
Flemington PA 93 D3
Fletcher NC 121 E1
Fletcher OK 51 D4
Flint MI 76 B3
Flint TX 124 A3
Flippin AR 107 E3
Flohrville MD 144 B1
Flomaton AL 135 F1
Floodwood MN 64 C4
Flora IL 98 C3
Flora IN 89 E4
Flora MS 126 B2
Florala AL 136 B1
Floral City FL 140 C1
Floral Park NY 241 G3
Flora Vista NM 48 B1
Flordell Hills MO 256 C1
Florence AL 119 E2
Florence AZ 54 C2
Florence CA 228 D3
Florence CO 41 E3
Florence KS 43 F3
Florence KY 100 B2
Florence MS 126 B3
Florence MT 15 D4
Florence NJ 147 D2
Florence OR 20 B4
Florence SC 122 C3
Florence SD 27 E2
Florence TX 61 E1
Florence WI 68 C2
Florence Co. SC 122 C3
Florence Co. WI 68 C2
Floresville TX 61 D3
Florham Park NJ 148 A4
Florida NY 148 A2
Florida City FL 143 E3
Florien LA 125 D4
Florin CA 36 C3
Florissant MO 98 A3
Flourtown PA 248 B1
Flovilla GA 129 D1
Flower Hill NY 241 G2
Flower Mound TX 207 C1
Flowery Branch GA 121 D3
Flowood MS 126 B3
Floyd VA 112 B2
Floydada TX 58 B1
Floyd Co. GA 120 B3
Floyd Co. IN 99 F4
Floyd Co. IA 73 D3
Floyd Co. KY 111 E1
Floyd Co. TX 50 B4
Floyd Co. VA 112 A2
Flushing MI 76 B3
Flushing OH 91 F4
Fluvanna Co. VA 113 D1
Flying Hills PA 146 A2
Foard Co. TX 58 C1
Fogelsville PA 146 B1
Folcroft PA 248 B4
Foley AL 135 E2
Foley MN 66 C2
Folkston GA 139 D1
Follansbee WV 91 F4
Folly Beach SC 131 D2
Folsom CA 36 C3
Folsom LA 134 B2
Folsom NJ 147 D4

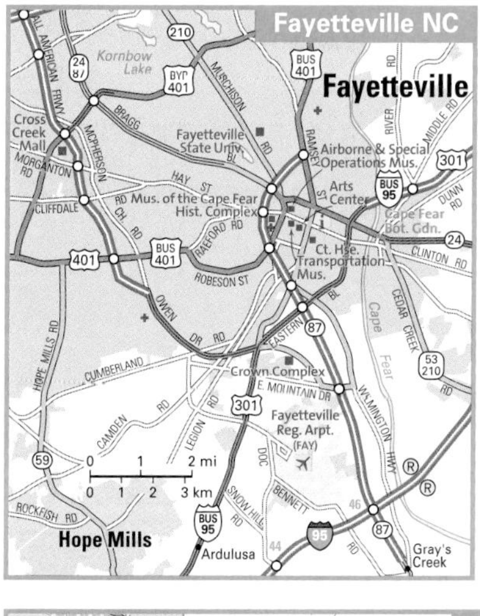

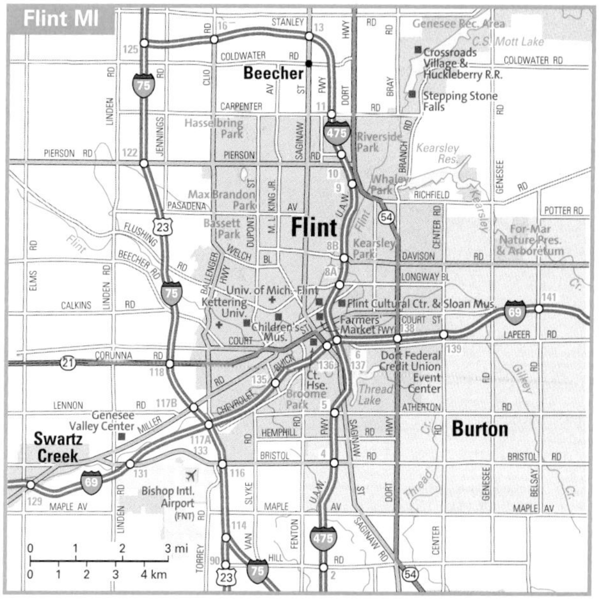

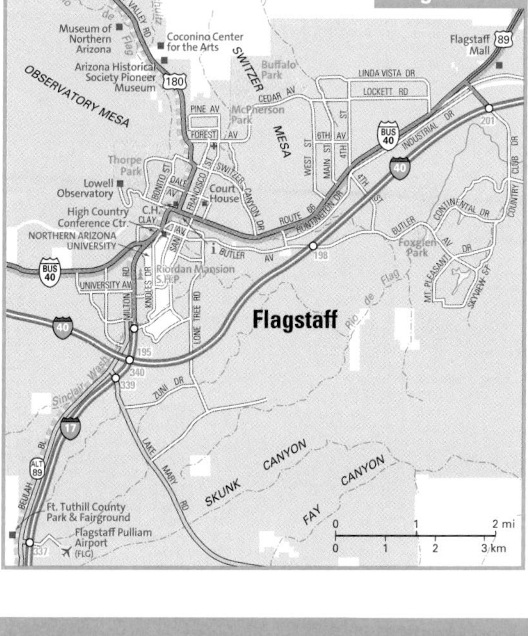

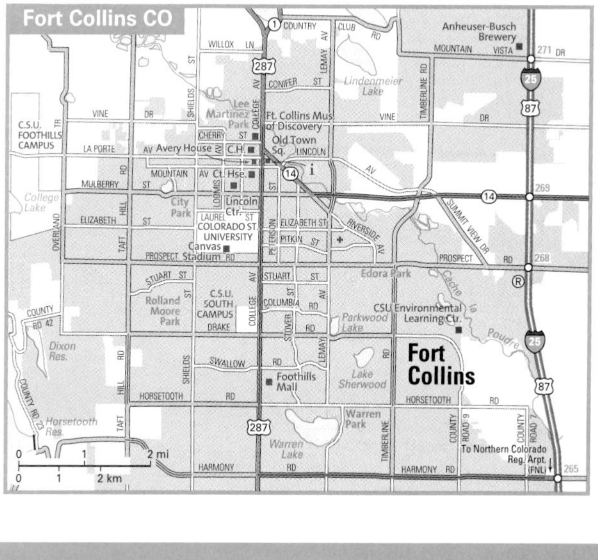

Figures after entries indicate page number and grid reference.

Folsom PA 248 A4
Fonda IA 72 B4
Fonda NY 79 F3
Fond du Lac WI 74 C2
Fond du Lac Co. WI 74 C2
Fontana CA 229 H2
Fontana WI 74 C4
Fontanelle IA 86 B2
Foothill Farms CA 255 C1
Footville WI 74 B4
Ford City CA 52 B1
Ford City PA 92 A3
Ford Co. IL 88 C4
Ford Co. KS 42 C4
Fordland MO 107 D2
Fordoche LA 133 F2
Fords NJ 240 A6
Fords Prairie WA 12 B4
Fordsville KY 109 F1
Fordville ND 19 E2
Fordyce AR 117 E4
Foreman AR 116 C4
Forest MS 126 C2
Forest OH 90 C3
Forest VA 112 C1
Forest Acres SC 205 F1
Forestbrook SC 123 D4
Forest City FL 246 B1
Forest City IA 72 C3
Forest City NC 121 F1
Forest City PA 93 F2
Forest Co. PA 92 B2
Forest Co. WI 68 C2
Forestdale AL 195 E1
Forestdale MA 151 E3
Forest Dale VT 81 D3
Forest Grove OR 20 B2
Forest Grove PA 250 A1
Forest Hts. MD 270 D5
Foresthill CA 36 C2
Forest Hill LA 133 E1
Forest Hill TX 59 E2
Forest Hills FL 139 D4
Forest Hills KY 230 F2
Forest Hills PA 250 C2
Forest Lake IL 203 B1
Forest Lake MN 67 D3
Forest Park GA 190 D5
Forest Park IL 203 D4
Forest Park OH 100 B2
Forest Park OK 244 E2
Forest View IL 203 D5
Forestville CA 36 A3
Forestville MD 271 F4
Forestville NY 78 A4
Forestville OH 100 B2
Forgan OK 50 C1
Forked River NJ 147 E3
Forkland AL 127 E2
Forks WA 12 A2
Forman ND 27 E1
Forney TX 59 F2
Forrest IL 88 C3
Forrest City AR 118 A2
Forrest Co. MS 126 C4
Forreston IL 88 B1
Forsyth GA 129 D1
Forsyth IL 98 C1
Forsyth MO 107 D3
Forsyth MT 25 D1
Forsyth Co. GA 120 C3
Forsyth Co. NC 112 A4
Ft. Ann NY 81 D4
Ft. Ashby WV 102 C2
Ft. Atkinson WI 74 B3
Ft. Belknap Agency MT 16 C2
Ft. Bend Co. TX 132 A4
Ft. Benton MT 15 F2
Ft. Bragg CA 36 A1
Ft. Branch IN 99 D4
Ft. Myers Beach FL 142 C1
Ft. Myers Shores FL 142 C1
Ft. Myers Villas FL 142 C1
Ft. Oglethorpe GA 120 B2
Ft. Payne AL 120 A3
Ft. Peck MT 17 D2
Ft. Pierce FL 141 E3
Ft. Pierre SD 26 C3
Ft. Pillow TN 108 B4
Ft. Plain NY 79 F3
Ft. Recovery OH 90 A4
Ft. Salonga NY 148 C3
Ft. Scott KS 106 B1
Ft. Shaw MT 15 F3
Ft. Shawnee OH 90 B3
Ft. Smith AR 116 C1
Ft. Stockton TX 62 C2
Ft. Sumner NM 49 E4
Ft. Thomas KY 204 B3
Ft. Thompson SD 27 D3
Fountain CO 41 E2
Fountain NC 113 E4
Fountain City IN 100 B1
Fountain City WI 73 E1
Fountain Co. IN 89 D4
Fountain Green UT 39 E1
Fountain Hill PA 146 C1
Fountain Hills AZ 54 C1
Fountain Inn SC 121 F2
Fountain Lake AR 117 D2
Fountain Valley CA 228 E5
Four Corners OR 20 B2
Four Corners TX 220 A3
Four Mile NJ 147 D3
Four Oaks NC 123 D1
Four Seasons MO 97 D4
Fowblesburg MD 144 C1
Fowler CA 44 C3
Fowler CO 41 F3
Fowler IN 89 D3
Frankfort IN 89 E4
Frankfort KS 43 F1
Frankfort KY 100 B4
Frankfort MI 69 E4
Frankfort NY 79 F3
Frankfort OH 101 D2
Franklin GA 128 C1
Franklin ID 31 E2
Franklin IL 98 B1
Franklin IN 99 F2
Franklin KY 109 F3
Franklin LA 133 F3
Franklin ME 83 D2
Franklin MA 150 C2
Franklin MI 210 B2
Franklin MN 66 B4
Franklin NE 43 D1
Franklin NH 81 F4
Franklin NJ 148 A2
Franklin NC 121 D1

Bokeelia	A1	Flamingo Bay	A1	Matlacha	A1	St. James City	A2
Bonita Sprs.	B2	Ft. Myers	B1	N. Ft. Myers	B1	San Carlos Park	B2
Cape Coral	A1	Ft. Myers Beach	B2	Pine Island Ctr.	A1	Sanibel	A2
Captiva	A2	Ft. Myers Shores	B1	Pineland	A1	Tice	B1
Estero	B2	Ft. Myers Villas	B1	Punta Rassa	A2	Truckland	B2

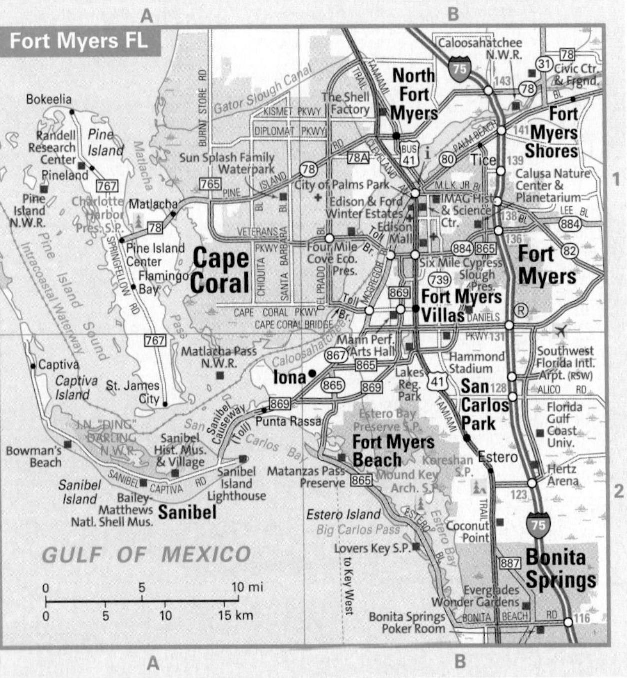

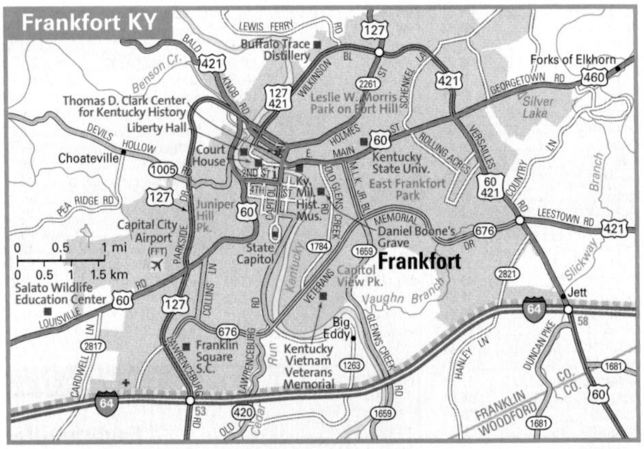

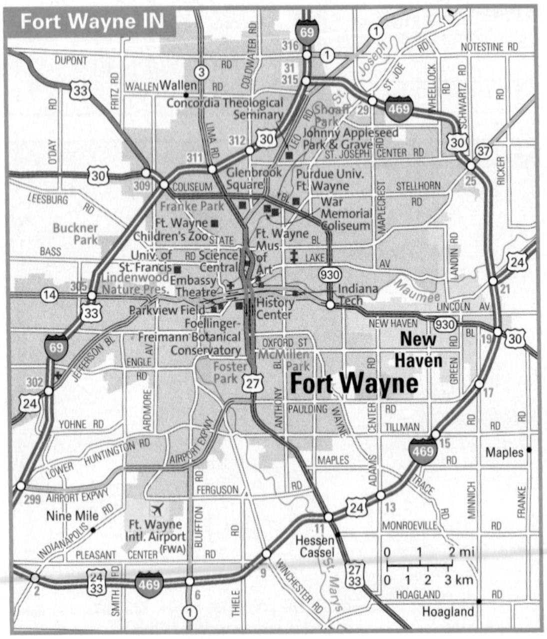

Ft. Bridger WY 32 A3
Ft. Calhoun NE 35 F3
Ft. Chiswell VA 112 A2
Ft. Cobb OK 51 D3
Ft. Collins CO 33 E4
Ft. Covington NY 80 C1
Ft. Davis TX 62 B2
Ft. Defiance AZ 48 A2
Ft. Deposit AL 128 A3
Ft. Dodge IA 72 C4
Ft. Dodge KS 42 C4
Ft. Duchesne UT 32 A4
Ft. Edward NY 81 D4
Ft. Fairfield ME 85 E2
Ft. Gaines GA 128 C4
Ft. Garland CO 41 D4
Ft. Gates TX 59 E4
Ft. Gay WV 101 D4
Ft. Gibson OK 106 A4
Ft. Grant AZ 55 E2
Ft. Hall ID 31 E1
Ft. Hancock TX 56 C4
Ft. Johnson NY 80 C4
Ft. Jones CA 28 B3
Ft. Kent ME 85 D1
Ft. Kent Mills ME 85 D1
Ft. Laramie WY 33 E2
Ft. Lauderdale FL 143 F2
Ft. Lawn SC 122 A2
Ft. Lee NJ 148 B3
Ft. Loramie OH 90 B4
Ft. Lupton CO 41 E1
Ft. Madison IA 87 F3
Ft. McKinley OH 208 D1
Ft. Meade FL 140 C3
Ft. Mill SC 122 A2
Ft. Mitchell KY 204 A3
Ft. Montgomery NY 148 B2
Ft. Morgan CO 33 F4
Ft. Myers FL 142 C1
Ft. Totten ND 19 D2
Ft. Towson OK 116 A3
Fortuna CA 28 A4
Ft. Valley GA 129 D2
Fortville IN 99 F1
Ft. Walton Beach FL 136 B2
Ft. Washakie WY 32 B1
Ft. Washington PA 248 C1
Ft. Wayne IN 90 A3
Ft. Wingate NM 48 A3
Ft. Worth TX 59 E2
Ft. Wright KY 204 B3
Ft. Yates ND 26 C1
Forty Fort PA 261 B1
Ft. Yukon AK 154 C2
Fossil OR 21 E2
Fosston MN 19 F3
Foster Ctr. RI 150 C3
Foster City CA 259 C4
Foster Co. ND 19 D3
Fostoria MI 76 C3
Fostoria OH 90 C3
Fouke AR 124 C1
Fowler KS 42 C4
Fowler MI 76 A3
Fowlerville MI 76 B4
Foxboro MA 151 D2
Fox Chapel PA 250 C1
Fox Chase KY 100 A4
Fox Crossing WI 74 C1
Foxfield CO 209 D4
Fox Island WA 262 A5
Fox Lake IL 74 C4
Fox Lake WI 74 B2
Fox Pt. WI 234 D1
Fox River Grove IL 88 C1
Frackville PA 93 E3
Framingham MA 150 C1
Francesville IN 89 E3
Francis UT 31 F4
Francisco IN 99 E4
Francis Creek WI 75 D1
Franconia VA 144 B3
Frankenmuth MI 76 B3
Frankford DE 145 F4
Frankfort IL 89 D2
Franklin OH 100 B1
Franklin PA 92 A2
Franklin TN 109 F4
Franklin TX 59 F4
Franklin VA 113 F3
Franklin WV 102 B3
Franklin WI 74 C3
Franklin Co. AL 119 E3
Franklin Co. AR 116 C1
Franklin Co. FL 137 D3
Franklin Co. GA 121 D3
Franklin Co. ID 31 F2
Franklin Co. IL 98 C4
Franklin Co. IN 100 A2
Franklin Co. IA 72 C4
Franklin Co. KS 96 A3
Franklin Co. KY 100 B4
Franklin Co. ME 82 B1
Franklin Co. MA 150 A1
Franklin Co. MS 126 A4
Franklin Co. MO 97 F3
Franklin Co. NE 43 D1
Franklin Co. NY 80 C2

Entries in **bold black** indicate counties or parishes.
Entries in **bold color** indicate cities with detailed inset maps.

Franklin Co. NC 113 D4
Franklin Co. OH 101 D1
Franklin Co. PA 103 D1
Franklin Co. TN 120 A1
Franklin Co. TX 124 B1
Franklin Co. VT 81 D1
Franklin Co. VA 112 B2
Franklin Co. WA 13 F4
Franklin Furnace OH 101 D3
Franklin Grove IL 88 B1
Franklin Par. LA 125 F2
Franklin Park IL 203 C4
Franklin Park PA 92 A3
Franklin Sprs. GA 121 E3
Franklin Square NY 241 G4
Franklinton LA 134 B1
Franklinton NC 113 D4
Franklinville NJ 145 F1
Franklinville NY 78 B4
Franklinville NC 112 B4
Frankston TX 124 A3
Frankton IN 89 F4
Frannie WY 24 B2
Fraser CO 41 D1
Fraser MI 210 D2
Frazee MN 19 F4
Frazer MT 17 E2
Frazeysburg OH 91 D4
Frazier Park CA 52 B1
Frederic WI 67 E2
Frederica DE 145 E3
Frederick CO 41 E1
Frederick MD 144 A1
Frederick OK 51 D4
Frederick SD 27 D1
Frederick Co. MD 144 A1
Frederick Co. VA 102 C2
Fredericksburg IA 73 E3
Fredericksburg PA 92 A2
Fredericksburg PA 93 E4
Fredericksburg TX 61 D2
Fredericksburg VA 103 D4
Fredericktown MO 108 A1
Fredericktown OH 91 D4
Fredonia AZ 47 D1
Fredonia KS 106 A1
Fredonia KY 109 D2
Fredonia NY 78 A1
Fredonia PA 91 F2
Fredonia WI 74 C2
Freeborn Co. MN 72 C2
Freeburg IL 98 B3
Freeburg PA 93 D3
Freedom CA 44 B2
Freedom WI 74 C1
Freehold NJ 147 E2
Freeland MI 76 B2
Freeland PA 93 E3
Freeland WA 262 A1
Freeman MO 96 B3
Freeman SD 27 E4
Freemansburg PA 146 C1
Freeport FL 136 B2
Freeport IL 74 B4
Freeport ME 82 B3
Freeport NY 147 F1
Freeport PA 92 A3
Freeport TX 133 E4
Freer TX 63 E2
Freestone Co. TX 59 F4
Freetown IN 99 F2
Freetown NY 149 F3
Freeville NY 79 D4
Freewood Acres NJ 147 E2
Fremont CA 36 B4
Fremont IN 90 A1
Fremont IA 87 E2
Fremont MI 75 F2
Fremont NE 35 F3
Fremont NH 81 F4
Fremont NC 123 E1
Fremont OH 90 C2
Fremont WI 74 B1
Fremont Co. CO 41 D3
Fremont Co. ID 23 F3
Fremont Co. IA 86 A3
Fremont Co. WY 32 C1
Fremont Hills MO 107 D2
Frenchburg KY 100 C4
French Camp CA 36 C4
French Lick IN 99 F3
French Settlement LA 134 A2
Frenchtown MT 15 D4
Frenchtown NJ 146 C1
Frenchville ME 85 D1
Fresno CA 44 C3
Fresno TX 220 B4
Fresno Co. CA 37 E4
Frewsburg NY 92 B1
Friant CA 44 C2
Friars Pt. MS 118 A3
Friday Harbor WA 12 B2
Fridley MN 67 D3
Friedens PA 102 C1
Friedensburg PA 146 A1
Friend NE 35 E4
Friendly MD 144 B4
Friendship ME 82 C3
Friendship NY 92 C1
Friendship TN 108 C4
Friendship WI 74 A1
Friendsville MD 102 B1
Friendsville TN 110 C4
Friendswood TX 132 B4
Fries VA 112 A3
Frio Co. TX 60 C3
Friona TX 49 F4
Frisco CO 41 D1
Frisco TX 59 F2
Frisco City AL 127 F4
Fritch TX 50 B2
Froid MT 17 F2
Fromberg MT 24 B2
Frontenac FL 232 A1
Frontenac KS 106 B1
Frontenac MO 256 B2
Frontier ND 19 F4
Frontier Co. NE 34 C4
Fronton TX 63 D4
Front Royal VA 102 C3
Frost TX 59 F3
Frostburg MD 102 C1
Frostproof FL 141 D3
Fruita CO 40 B2
Fruit Cove FL 139 D2
Fruit Hts. UT 31 E3
Fruit Hill OH 204 C3
Fruitland ID 22 A4
Fruitland IA 87 F2
Fruitland MD 103 F4
Fruitland NM 48 B1
Fruitland Park FL 140 C1
Fruitport MI 75 E3
Fruitville FL 266 C5
Fryeburg ME 81 F3
Fulda MN 72 A2
Fullerton CA 52 C3
Fullerton MD 193 D2
Fullerton NE 35 E3
Fulshear TX 132 A3
Fulton IL 88 A1
Fulton KY 108 C3
Fulton MD 144 B2
Fulton MS 119 D3
Fulton MO 97 E3
Fulton NY 79 D3
Fulton TX 61 E4
Fulton Co. AR 107 F3
Fulton Co. GA 120 C3
Fulton Co. IL 88 A4
Fulton Co. IN 89 F3
Fulton Co. KY 108 C3
Fulton Co. NY 79 F3
Fulton Co. OH 90 B2
Fulton Co. PA 103 D1
Fultondale AL 119 F4
Fultonville NY 79 F3
Fuquay-Varina NC 123 D1
Furnas Co. NE 42 C1
Fyffe AL 120 A3

G

Gabbs NV 37 F2
Gackle ND 19 D4
Gadsden AL 120 A3
Gadsden AZ 53 F4
Gadsden TN 108 C4
Gadsden Co. FL 137 D2
Gaffney SC 121 F2
Gage Co. NE 35 F4
Gahanna OH 101 D1
Gail TX 58 A2
Gainesboro TN 110 A3
Gaines Co. TX 57 F2
Gainesville FL 138 C3
Gainesville GA 121 D3
Gainesville MO 107 E3
Gainesville TX 59 E1
Gainesville VA 144 A3
Gaithersburg MD 144 A2
Galatia IL 108 C1
Galax VA 112 A3
Galena AK 154 C2
Galena IL 74 A4
Galena IN 99 F4
Galena KS 106 B2
Galena MO 107 D2
Galena Park TX 220 C3
Galesburg IL 88 A3
Galesburg MI 75 F4
Gales Ferry CT 149 F1
Galesville WI 73 F1
Galeton PA 92 C1
Galeville NY 265 A1
Galien MI 89 E1
Galilee RI 150 C4
Galion OH 91 D3
Galisteo NM 49 D3
Gallatin MO 96 C1
Gallatin TN 109 F3
Gallatin Co. IL 109 D1
Gallatin Co. KY 100 B3
Gallatin Co. MT 23 F2
Gallatin Gateway MT 23 F1
Gallaway TN 118 B1
Gallia Co. OH 101 E3
Galliano LA 134 B4
Gallipolis OH 101 E3
Gallitzin PA 92 B4
Gallup NM 48 A3
Galt CA 36 C3
Galva IL 88 A2
Galva KS 43 E3
Galveston IN 89 F3
Galveston KY 111 E1
Galveston TX 132 B4
Galveston Co. TX 132 B4
Gamaliel KY 110 A3
Gambell AK 154 A2
Gamber MD 144 B1
Gambier OH 91 D4
Gamewell NC 111 F4
Ganado AZ 47 F2
Ganado TX 61 F3
Gang Mills NY 93 D1
Gann Valley SD 27 D3
Gansevoort NY 81 D4
Gantt SC 217 A2
Gap PA 146 A3
Garber OK 51 E1
Gardena CA 228 C4
Garden City AL 119 F3
Garden City CO 33 E4
Garden City GA 130 B3
Garden City ID 22 B4
Garden City KS 42 B3
Garden City MI 210 A3
Garden City MO 96 C3
Garden City NY 241 G3
Garden City SC 123 D4
Garden City TX 58 A3
Garden City UT 31 F2
Garden City South NY 241 G4
Garden Co. NE 34 A3
Gardendale AL 119 F4
Gardendale MI 76 C3
Gardendale TX 58 A3
Garden Grove CA 228 E4
Garden Home OR 251 C2
Garden Plain KS 43 E4
Garden Ridge TX 61 D2
Garden View PA 93 D2
Gardenville PA 146 C1
Gardiner ME 82 C2
Gardiner MT 23 F2
Gardiner NY 148 B1
Gardner IL 88 C2
Gardner KS 96 B3
Gardner MA 95 D1
Gardnertown NY 148 B1
Gardnerville NV 37 D2
Garfield AR 106 C3
Garfield NJ 148 B3
Garfield TX 61 E2
Garfield WA 14 D4
Garfield Co. CO 40 B1
Garfield Co. MT 17 D3
Garfield Co. NE 35 D2
Garfield Co. OK 51 E1
Garfield Co. UT 39 E3
Garfield Co. WA 14 A4
Garfield Hts. OH 91 E2
Garibaldi OR 20 B2
Garland NC 123 D2
Garland TX 59 F2
Garland UT 31 E2
Garland Co. AR 117 D2
Garnavillo IA 73 F3
Garner IA 72 C3
Garner KY 111 D1
Garner NC 113 D4
Garnett KS 96 A4
Garrard Co. KY 110 C1
Garretson SD 27 F4
Garrett IN 90 A2
Garrett Co. MD 102 B2
Garrett Park MD 270 C1
Garrettsville OH 91 F2
Garrison KY 101 D3
Garrison MD 193 A1
Garrison ND 18 B3
Garrison TX 124 B3
Garrisonville VA 144 A4
Garvin Co. OK 51 E4
Garwin IA 87 D1
Gary IN 89 D2
Gary SD 27 F2
Gary WV 111 F1
Garysburg NC 113 E3
Garyville LA 134 B3
Garza Co. TX 58 B2
Gas KS 96 A4
Gas City IN 89 F4
Gasconade Co. MO 97 F3
Gasport NY 78 B3
Gassaway WV 101 F3
Gassville AR 107 E3
Gaston IN 89 F4
Gaston NC 113 E3
Gaston OR 20 B2
Gaston SC 122 A4
Gaston Co. NC 122 A1
Gastonia NC 122 A1
Gate City VA 111 E3
Gates NY 78 C3
Gates OR 20 C3
Gates TN 108 B4
Gates Co. NC 113 F3
Gates Mills OH 204 G1
Gatesville NC 113 F3
Gatesville TX 59 E4
Gatlinburg TN 111 D4
Gauley Bridge WV 101 F4
Gautier MS 135 D2
Gayle Mill SC 122 A2
Gaylord MI 70 C3
Gaylord MN 66 C4
Gaylordsville CT 148 C1
Gays Mills WI 73 F3
Gayville SD 35 E1
Gearhart OR 20 B1
Geary OK 51 D3
Geary Co. KS 43 F2
Geauga Co. OH 91 E2
Geddes SD 35 D1
Geistown PA 92 B4
Gem Co. ID 22 B3
Genesee ID 14 B4
Genesee MI 76 B3
Genesee Co. MI 76 B3
Genesee Co. NY 78 B3
Geneseo IL 88 A2
Geneseo NY 78 C4
Geneva AL 136 C1
Geneva FL 141 D1
Geneva IL 88 C1
Geneva IN 90 A3
Geneva NE 35 E4
Geneva NY 79 D3
Geneva OH 91 F1
Geneva WA 12 C1
Geneva Co. AL 136 C1
Geneva-on-the-Lake OH 91 F1
Genoa IL 88 C1
Genoa NE 35 E3
Genoa OH 90 C2
Genoa City WI 74 C4
Genola UT 39 E1
Gentry AR 106 B3
Gentry Co. MO 86 B4
George IA 72 A2
George WA 13 E4
George Co. MS 135 D1
Georgetown CA 36 C2
Georgetown CO 41 D1
Georgetown CT 148 C2
Georgetown DE 145 F4
Georgetown GA 128 C3
Georgetown ID 31 F1
Georgetown IL 99 D1
Georgetown IN 99 F4
Germantown WI 74 C3
Germantown Hills IL 88 B3
Geronimo OK 51 D4
Geronimo TX 61 E2
Gerrardstown WV 103 D2
Gervais OR 20 B2
Gettysburg OH 90 B4
Gettysburg PA 103 E1
Gettysburg SD 26 C2
Geyserville CA 36 A2
Ghent KY 100 A3
Ghent NY 94 B2
Ghent OH 188 A1
Gholson TX 59 E4
Giants Neck CT 149 F2
Gibbon MN 66 B4
Gibbon NE 35 D4
Gibbsboro NJ 147 D3
Gibbstown NJ 146 C3
Gibraltar MI 90 C1
Gibsland LA 125 D2
Gibson GA 129 F1
Gibson MD 145 D1
Gibson NC 122 C2
Gibsonburg OH 90 C2
Gibson City IL 88 C4
Gibson Co. IN 99 E4
Gibson Co. TN 108 C4
Gibsonton FL 140 C3
Gibsonville NC 112 B4
Giddings TX 61 F2
Gideon MO 108 B3
Gifford FL 141 E3
Gifford IL 89 D4
Gig Harbor WA 12 C3
Gila Bend AZ 54 B2
Gila Co. AZ 55 D1
Gilbert AZ 54 C2
Gilbert IA 86 C1
Gilbert LA 125 F3
Gilbert MN 64 C3
Gilbert SC 122 A4
Gilmore City IA 72 B4
Gilpin Co. CO 41 D1
Gilroy CA 44 B2
Gilt Edge TN 118 B1
Ginger Blue MO 106 B3
Girard IL 98 B2
Girard KS 106 B1
Girard OH 91 F2
Girard PA 91 F1
Girardville PA 93 E3
Gisela AZ 47 E4
Glacier Co. MT 15 E1
Gladbrook IA 87 D1
Gladden AZ 54 B1
Glades Co. FL 141 D4
Glade Spr. VA 111 F2
Gladewater TX 124 B2
Gladstone MI 69 D2
Gladstone MO 96 B2
Gladstone ND 18 A4
Gladstone OR 251 D3
Gladwin MI 76 A1
Gladwin Co. MI 76 A1
Glandorf OH 90 B3
Glasco KS 43 E2
Glasco NY 94 B2
Glascock Co. GA 129 F1
Glasford IL 88 B4
Glasgow DE 145 E1
Glasgow KY 110 A2
Glasgow MO 97 D2
Glasgow MT 17 D2
Glasgow VA 112 C1
Glasgow WV 101 F4
Glasgow Vil. MO 256 C1
Glassboro NJ 146 C4
Glasscock Co. TX 58 A3
Glassmanor MD 270 D5
Glassport PA 250 C3
Glastonbury CT 150 A3
Gleason TN 108 C3
Glenaire MO 224 C2
Glen Allen AL 119 E4
Glen Allen VA 254 B1
Glen Alpine NC 111 F4
Glenarden MD 144 B3
Glenburn ND 18 B2
Glenburn PA 93 F2
Glen Burnie MD 144 C2
Glen Carbon IL 98 B3
Glencoe AL 120 A4
Glencoe IL 89 D1
Glencoe MN 66 C4
Glencoe OK 51 F2
Glen Cove ME 82 C2
Glen Cove NY 148 C3
Glendale AZ 54 C1
Glendale CA 52 C2
Glendale CO 209 C3
Glendale MO 256 B2
Glendale OH 204 B1
Glendale OR 28 B1
Glendale RI 150 C2
Glendale UT 39 D4
Glen Dale WV 101 F1
Glendale WI 234 C1
Glendale Hts. IL 203 B4
Glendive MT 17 F3
Glendo WY 33 E1
Glendora CA 229 F2
Glendora NJ 146 C3
Glen Elder KS 43 D1
Glen Ellen CA 36 B3
Glen Ellyn IL 203 B4
Glen Gardner NJ 104 C1
Glenham NY 148 B1
Glen Lyon PA 93 E2
Glen Mills MA 151 F1
Glenmoor OH 91 F3
Glenmora LA 133 E1
Glennallen AK 154 C3
Glenn Co. CA 36 B1
Glenn Dale MD 144 C3
Glenn Hts. TX 59 F3

Ada B2
Cascade B2
Comstock Park A1
E. Grand Rapids B2
Grand Rapids B1
Grandville A2
Jenison A2
Kentwood B2
Marne A1
Tallmadge A1
Walker A2
Wyoming A2

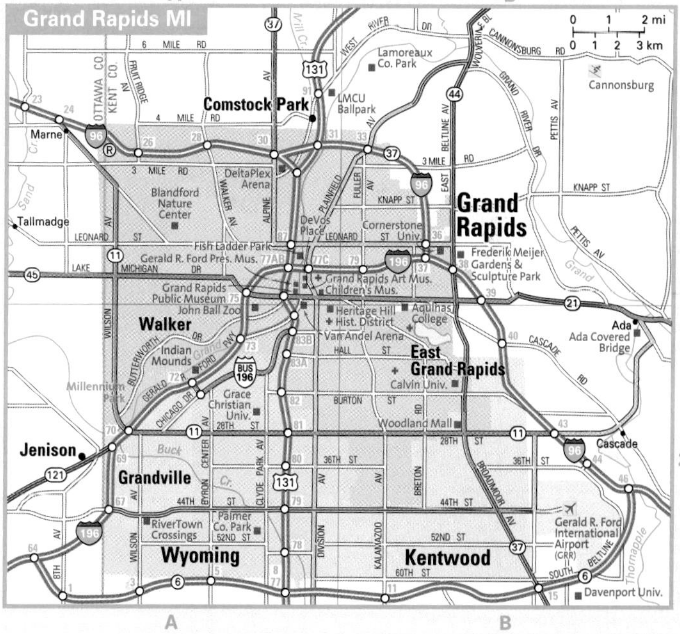

Figures after entries indicate page number and grid reference.

Glenns Ferry ID 30 C1
Glennville GA 130 A3
Glenolden PA 146 C3
Glenpool OK 51 F2
Glen Raven NC 112 C4
Glen Ridge NJ 240 B2
Glen Rock NJ 148 B3
Glen Rock PA 103 E1
Glenrock WY 33 D1
Glen Rose TX 59 E3
Glen St. Mary FL 138 C2
Glens Falls NY 81 D4
Glenside PA 146 C2
Glen Ullin ND 18 B4
Glenview IL 203 D2
Glenview KY 230 E1
Glenview Hills KY 230 E1
Glenville MN 73 D2
Glenville WV 101 F3
Glenwood AR 117 D3
Glenwood GA 129 F3
Glenwood IA 86 A3
Glenwood MD 144 B2
Glenwood MN 66 B2
Glenwood UT 39 E2
Glenwood City WI 67 E3
Glenwood Sprs. CO 40 C1
Glidden IA 86 B1
Glide OR 20 B4
Globe AZ 55 D1
Glorieta NM 49 D3
Gloster MS 126 A4
Gloucester MA 151 F1
Gloucester VA 113 F1
Gloucester City NJ 146 C3
Gloucester Co. NJ 146 C4
Gloucester Co. VA 113 F1
Gloucester Pt. VA 113 F2
Glouster OH 101 E2
Gloversville NY 79 F3
Gloverville SC 121 F4
Glyndon MD 144 C1
Glyndon MN 19 F4
Glynn Co. GA 130 B4
Gnadenhutten OH 91 E4
Gobles MI 75 F4
Goddard KS 43 E4
Godeffroy NY 148 A1
Godfrey IL 98 A2
Godley IL 88 C2
Godley TX 59 E3
Goessel KS 43 E3
Goffstown NH 81 F4
Gogebic Co. MI 65 E4
Golconda IL 109 D1
Golconda NV 30 A3
Gold Bar WA 12 C2
Gold Beach OR 28 A2
Golden CO 41 E1
Golden IL 87 F4
Golden Beach FL 233 C3
Golden Beach MD 144 C4
Golden Bridge NY 148 C2
Golden City MO 106 C1
Goldendale WA 21 D1
Golden Gate FL 142 C1
Golden Meadow LA 134 B4
Goldenrod FL 246 D1
Golden Valley MN 235 B2
Golden Valley Co. MT 16 B4
Golden Valley Co. ND 17 F3
Goldfield IA 72 C4
Goldfield NV 37 F4
Gold Hill OR 28 B2
Goldonna LA 125 D3
Goldsboro NC 123 E1
Goldsboro PA 93 D4
Goldsby OK 51 E3
Goldthwaite TX 59 D4
Goleta CA 52 B2
Golf Manor OH 204 B2
Goliad TX 61 E4
Goliad Co. TX 61 E3
Gonzales CA 44 B3
Gonzales LA 134 A2
Gonzales TX 61 E2
Gonzales Co. TX 61 E3
Gonzalez FL 135 F2
Goochland VA 113 D1
Goochland Co. VA 113 D1
Goodfield IL 88 B3
Good Hope AL 119 F3
Goodhue MN 73 D1
Goodhue Co. MN 73 D1
Gooding ID 30 C1
Gooding Co. ID 30 C1
Goodland IN 89 D3
Goodland KS 42 B2
Goodlettsville TN 109 F3
Goodman MS 126 B1
Goodman MO 106 B3
Goodrich MI 76 B3
Goodsprings NV 46 A2
Good Thunder MN 72 C1
Goodview MN 73 E1
Goodwater AL 128 A1
Goodwell OK 50 B1
Goodyear AZ 54 C1
Goose Creek SC 131 D1
Gordo AL 127 E1
Gordon AL 137 D1
Gordon GA 129 E1
Gordon NE 34 A1
Gordon PA 93 E3
Gordon Co. GA 120 B3
Gordonsville TN 110 A4
Gordonsville VA 102 C4
Gordonville PA 146 A3
Gore OK 116 B1
Goreville IL 108 C1
Gorham ME 82 B3
Gorham NH 81 F2
Gorham NY 78 C4
Gorman NC 112 C4
Gorman TX 59 D3
Goshen AR 106 C4
Goshen CA 45 D3
Goshen IN 89 F2
Goshen KY 100 A3
Goshen MD 144 B2
Goshen NY 148 A2
Goshen OR 20 B4
Goshen UT 39 E1
Goshen VA 102 B4
Goshen Co. WY 33 F2
Gosnell AR 108 B4
Gosper Co. NE 34 C4
Gosport IN 99 E2
Gotha FL 246 A2
Gothenburg NE 34 C4
Gould AR 117 F3
Goulding FL 247 B1
Goulds FL 143 E3
Gouldtown NJ 145 F1
Gouverneur NY 79 E1
Gove KS 42 C2
Gove Co. KS 42 C2
Gowanda NY 78 A4
Gower MO 96 B1
Gowrie IA 72 B4
Grabill IN 90 A2
Grace ID 31 F1
Graceville FL 136 C1
Graceville MN 27 F1
Grady AR 117 F3
Grady Co. GA 137 E1
Grady Co. OK 51 E4
Graettinger IA 72 B3
Graford TX 59 D2
Grafton IL 98 A2
Grafton MA 150 C2
Grafton ND 19 E2
Grafton OH 91 D2
Grafton WV 102 A2
Grafton WI 74 C3
Grafton Co. NH 81 F2
Graham KY 109 E2
Graham NC 112 C4
Graham TX 59 D2
Graham WA 12 C4
Graham Co. AZ 55 E2
Graham Co. KS 42 C2
Graham Co. NC 121 D1
Grainger Co. TN 111 D3
Grain Valley MO 96 C2
Grambling LA 125 E2
Gramercy LA 134 B3
Granada CO 42 A3
Granbury TX 59 E3
Granby CO 41 D1
Granby CT 94 C2
Granby MA 150 A1
Granby MO 106 C2
Grand Bay AL 135 E2
Grand Blanc MI 76 B3
Grand Canyon AZ 47 D2
Grand Coteau LA 133 F2
Grand Coulee WA 13 E2
Grand Co. CO 41 D1
Grand Co. UT 40 A2
Grandfield OK 51 D4
Grand Forks ND 19 E2
Grand Forks Co. ND 19 E3
Grand Haven MI 75 E3
Grandin NJ 147 D1
Grand Island NE 35 E4
Grand Isle LA 134 B4
Grand Isle VT 81 D1
Grand Isle Co. VT 81 D1
Grand Jct. CO 40 B2
Grand Jct. IA 86 C1
Grand Lake CO 33 D4
Grand Ledge MI 76 A4
Grand Marais MN 65 D3
Grand Meadow MN 73 D2
Grand Mound IA 88 A1
Grand Prairie TX 207 C3
Grand Rapids MI 75 F3
Grand Rapids MN 64 B3
Grand Rapids OH 90 B2
Grand Ridge FL 137 D1
Grand Rivers KY 109 D2
Grand Saline TX 124 A2
Grand Terrace CA 229 J3
Grand Tower IL 108 B1
Grand Traverse Co. MI 69 F4
Grandview CO 40 B4
Grand View ID 30 B1
Grandview IN 99 E4
Grandview IA 87 F2
Grandview MO 96 B3
Grandview TX 59 E3
Grandview WA 21 E1
Grandview Hts. OH 206 B2
Grandview Plaza KS 43 F2
Grandville MI 75 F3
Grandy NC 115 F1
Granger IN 89 F1
Granger IA 86 C1
Granger TX 61 E1
Granger WA 13 E4
Grangeville ID 22 B1
Granite OK 50 C3
Granite UT 257 B3
Granite City IL 98 A3
Granite Co. MT 15 D4
Granite Falls MN 66 A4
Granite Falls NC 111 F4
Granite Falls WA 12 C2
Granite Quarry NC 122 B1
Granite Shoals TX 61 D1
Granite Sprs. NY 148 B2
Graniteville SC 121 F4
Graniteville VT 81 E2
Grannis AR 116 C3
Grant AL 120 A2
Grant MI 75 F3
Grant MN 67 D3
Grant NE 34 B4
Grant City MO 86 B4
Grant Co. AR 117 E3
Grant Co. IN 89 F3
Grant Co. KS 42 B4
Grant Co. KY 100 B3
Grant Co. MN 27 F1
Grant Co. NE 34 B2
Grant Co. NM 55 F2
Grant Co. ND 18 B4
Grant Co. OK 51 E1
Grant Co. OR 21 F3
Grant Co. SD 27 F2
Grant Co. WA 13 E3
Grant Co. WV 102 B2
Grant Co. WI 73 F3
Grant Hollow NY 188 E1
Grant Par. LA 125 E4
Grant Park IL 89 D2
Grants NM 48 B3
Grantsburg WI 67 D2
Grantsdale MT 23 D1
Grants Pass OR 28 B2
Grantsville MD 102 B1
Grantsville UT 31 E4
Grantsville WV 101 F3
Grant Town WV 102 A1
Grantville GA 128 C1
Grantville PA 93 E4
Granville IL 88 B2
Granville NY 81 D4
Granville ND 18 C2
Granville OH 91 D4
Granville Co. NC 113 D3
Grapeland TX 124 A4
Grapeview WA 12 C3
Grapevine TX 59 E2
Grasonville MD 145 D3
Grass Lake MI 76 B4
Grass Valley CA 36 C2
Graterford PA 146 B2
Gratiot Co. MI 76 A3
Gratis OH 100 B1
Graton CA 36 A3
Gratz PA 93 E4
Gravel Ridge AR 117 E2
Graves Co. KY 108 C3
Gravette AR 106 B3
Grawn MI 69 F4
Gray GA 129 D1
Gray KY 110 C2
Gray LA 134 A3
Gray ME 82 B3
Gray TN 111 E3
Gray Co. KS 42 C4
Gray Co. TX 50 B3
Gray Court SC 121 F2
Grayland WA 12 B4
Grayling MI 70 C4
Graymoor-Devondale KY 230 E1
Grays Harbor Co. WA 12 B3
Grayslake IL 74 C4
Grayson GA 121 D4
Grayson KY 101 D4
Grayson LA 125 E3
Grayson Co. KY 109 F1
Grayson Co. TX 59 F1
Grayson Co. VA 111 F3
Gray Summit MO 98 A3
Graysville AL 119 F4
Graysville TN 120 B1
Grayville IL 99 D4
Greasewood AZ 47 F3
Great Barrington MA 94 B2
Great Bend KS 43 D3

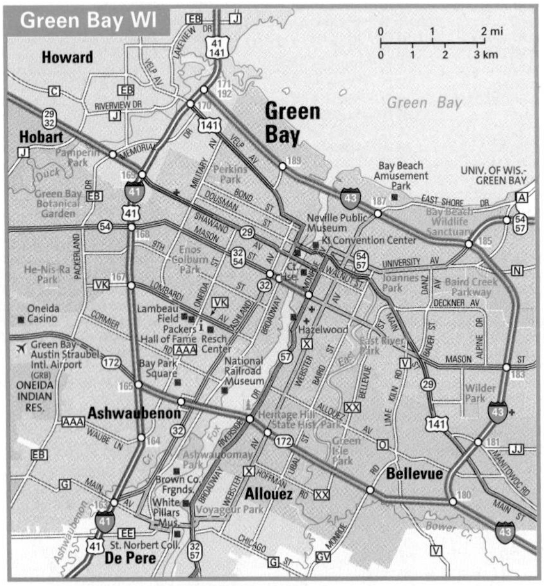

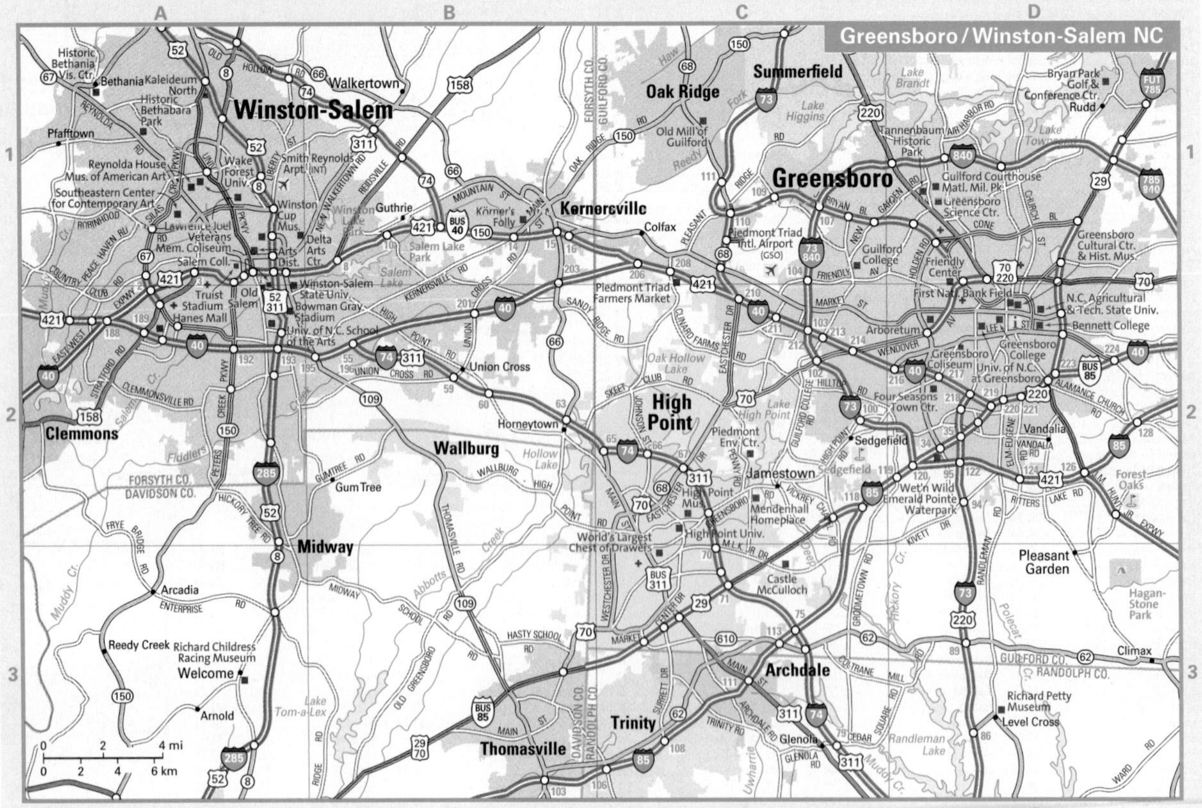

Arcadia	A3	Climax	D3	Guthrie	B1	Level Cross	D3	Reedy Creek	A3	Trinity	C3	Welcome	A3
Archdale	C3	Colfax	C1	High Pt.	C2	Midway	A3	Rudd	D1	Union Cross	B2	Winston-Salem	A1
Arnold	A3	Glenola	C3	Horneytown	B2	Oak Ridge	C1	Sedgefield	C2	Vandalia	D2		
Bethania	A1	Greensboro	C1	Jamestown	C2	Pfafftown	A1	Summerfield	C1	Walkertown	B1		
Clemmons	A2	Gum Tree	B2	Kernersville	B1	Pleasant Garden	D3	Thomasville	B3	Wallburg	B2		

Entries in **bold black** indicate counties or parishes.
Entries in **bold color** indicate cities with detailed inset maps.

Great Bend NY 79 E1
Great Bend PA 93 F1
Great Falls MT 15 F3
Great Falls SC 122 A2
Great Falls VA 144 B3
Great Meadows NJ 94 A4
Great Mills MD 103 E4
Great Neck NY 148 B4
Great Neck Estates NY 241 G3
Great Neck Gardens NY 241 G2
Great Neck Plaza NY 241 G2
Great River NY 149 D4
Greece NY 78 C3
Greeley CO 33 E4
Greeley NE 35 D3
Greeley Co. KS 42 B3
Greeley Co. NE 35 D3
Greeleyville SC 122 B4
Green OH 91 E3
Green OR 28 B1
Greenacres CA 45 D4
Greenacres FL 143 F1
Greenback TN 110 C4
Green Bay WI 68 C4
Greenbelt MD 144 B3
Greenbrier AR 117 E1
Greenbrier TN 109 F3
Greenbrier Co. WV 102 A4
Greenbush MA 151 E2
Greenbush MN 19 F1
Greencastle IN 99 E1
Greencastle PA 103 D1
Green City MO 87 D4
Green Co. KY 110 A1
Green Co. WI 74 B4
Green Cove Sprs. FL 139 D3
Green Creek NJ 104 C4
Greendale IN 100 B2
Greendale MO 256 B2
Greendale WI 234 C3
Greene IA 73 D3
Greene ME 82 B2
Greene NY 79 E4
Greene Co. AL 127 E2
Greene Co. AR 108 A3
Greene Co. GA 121 E4
Greene Co. IL 98 A2
Greene Co. IN 99 E2
Greene Co. IA 86 B1
Greene Co. MS 127 D4
Greene Co. MO 107 D1
Greene Co. NY 94 A2
Greene Co. NC 115 C3
Greene Co. OH 100 C1
Greene Co. PA 102 A1
Greene Co. TN 111 D3
Greene Co. VA 102 C4
Greenevers NC 123 E2
Greeneville TN 111 D4
Greenfield CA 44 B3
Greenfield IL 98 A2
Greenfield IN 99 F1
Greenfield IA 86 B2
Greenfield MA 94 C1
Greenfield MO 106 C1
Greenfield NH 95 D1
Greenfield OH 100 C2
Greenfield TN 108 C4
Greenfield WI 234 C3
Green Forest AR 107 D3
Green Harbor MA 151 E2
Green Haven MD 144 C2
Green Haven NY 148 C1
Green Hill TN 109 F3
Greenhills OH 204 B1
Green Island NY 188 E2
Green Lake WI 74 B2
Green Lake Co. WI 74 B2
Greenland AR 106 C4
Greenland NH 82 A4
Green Lane PA 146 B2
Greenleaf ID 22 A4
Greenlee Co. AZ 55 E2
Greenmount MD 144 B1
Green Mtn. Falls CO 205 C1
Green Oaks IL 203 C1
Green Park MO 256 B3
Green Pond NJ 148 A3
Greenport NY 149 E3
Green River UT 39 F2
Green River WY 32 A3
Greensboro AL 127 E2
Greensboro FL 137 D2
Greensboro GA 121 D4
Greensboro MD 145 E3
Greensboro NC 112 B4
Greensboro Bend VT 81 E2
Greensburg IN 100 A2
Greensburg KS 43 D4
Greensburg KY 110 A2
Greensburg LA 134 B1
Greensburg PA 92 A4
Green Sprs. OH 90 C2
Greensville Co. VA 113 E2
Greentown IN 89 F4
Greentown OH 91 E3
Green Tree PA 250 B2
Greenup IL 99 D2
Greenup KY 101 D3
Greenup Co. KY 101 D3
Green Valley AZ 55 D3
Green Valley CA 52 C2
Green Valley IL 88 B4
Green Valley MD 144 B2
Greenview IL 88 B4
Green Vil. PA 103 D1
Greenville AL 128 A3
Greenville CA 36 C1
Greenville DE 146 B3
Greenville FL 137 F2
Greenville GA 128 C1
Greenville IL 98 B3
Greenville IN 99 F4
Greenville KY 109 E2
Greenville ME 84 C4
Greenville MI 75 F3
Greenville MS 126 A1
Greenville MO 108 A2
Greenville NH 95 D1
Greenville NY 94 B2
Greenville NC 115 D2
Greenville OH 90 A4
Greenville PA 91 F2
Greenville RI 150 C3
Greenville SC 121 E2
Greenville TX 59 F2
Greenville VA 102 B4
Greenville WI 74 C1
Greenville Co. SC 121 E2
Greenville Jct. ME 84 C4
Greenwich CT 148 C3
Greenwich NY 81 D4
Greenwich OH 91 D3
Greenwood AR 116 C1
Greenwood DE 145 E3
Greenwood FL 137 D1
Greenwood IN 99 F1
Greenwood LA 124 C2
Greenwood MS 118 B4
Greenwood MO 96 B3
Greenwood NE 35 F3
Greenwood SC 121 F3
Greenwood WI 68 A4
Greenwood Co. KS 43 F3
Greenwood Co. SC 121 F3
Greenwood Lake NY 148 A2
Greenwood Vil. CO 209 C4
Greer SC 121 F2
Greer Co. OK 50 C3
Greers Ferry AR 117 E1
Gregg Co. TX 124 B2
Gregory SD 35 D1
Gregory TX 63 F2
Gregory Co. SD 35 D1
Greilickville MI 69 F4
Grenada MS 118 B4
Grenada Co. MS 118 B4
Gresham OR 20 C2
Gresham WI 68 C4
Gresham Park GA 190 E4
Gretna FL 137 D2
Gretna LA 134 B3
Gretna NE 35 F3
Gretna VA 112 C2
Greybull WY 24 C3
Gridley CA 36 B2
Gridley IL 88 C3
Gridley KS 96 A4
Griffin GA 129 D1
Griffith IN 89 D2
Grifton NC 115 D3
Griggs Co. ND 19 D3
Griggsville IL 98 A1
Grimes AL 128 B4
Grimes IA 86 C2
Grimes Co. TX 132 A2
Grinnell IA 87 D1
Griswold IA 86 B2
Groesbeck OH 204 A2
Groesbeck TX 59 F4
Groom TX 50 B3
Grosse Pointe MI 210 D3
Grosse Pointe Farms MI 210 D3
Grosse Pointe Park MI 210 D3
Grosse Pointe Shores MI 210 D3
Grosse Pointe Woods MI 76 C4
Grosse Tete LA 133 F2
Grosvenor Dale CT 150 B2
Groton CT 149 F2
Groton MA 95 D1
Groton NY 79 D4
Groton SD 27 E2
Groton VT 81 E2
Groton Long Pt. CT 149 F2
Grottoes VA 102 C4
Grove OK 106 B3
Grove City FL 140 C4
Grove City MN 66 B3
Grove City OH 101 D1
Grove City PA 92 A2
Grove Hill AL 127 E4
Groveland CA 37 D4
Groveland FL 140 C1
Groveland MA 95 E1
Groveport OH 101 D1
Grover NC 122 A1
Grover Beach CA 52 A1
Groves TX 132 C3
Groveton NH 81 F2
Groveton TX 132 B1
Groveton VA 144 B4
Grovetown GA 121 F4
Grubbs AR 107 F4
Gruetli-Laager TN 120 A1
Grundy VA 111 E2
Grundy Ctr. IA 73 D4
Grundy Co. IL 88 C2
Grundy Co. IA 73 D4
Grundy Co. MO 86 C4
Grundy Co. TN 120 A1
Gruver TX 50 B2
Guadalupe AZ 249 C3
Guadalupe CA 52 A1
Guadalupe Co. NM 49 E4
Guadalupe Co. TX 61 E3
Guerneville CA 36 A3
Guernsey WY 33 E2
Guernsey Co. OH 91 E4
Gueydan LA 133 E3
Guilderland NY 188 C2
Guildhall VT 81 F2
Guilford CT 149 E2
Guilford ME 82 C1
Guilford MD 193 A5
Guilford Co. NC 112 B4
Guin AL 119 E4
Gulf Breeze FL 135 F2
Gulf Co. FL 137 D3
Gulfport FL 140 B3
Gulfport MS 135 D2
Gulf Shores AL 135 E2
Gulf Stream FL 143 F1
Gun Barrel City TX 59 F3
Gunnison CO 40 C3
Gunnison MS 118 A4
Gunnison UT 39 E2
Gunnison Co. CO 40 C2
Gunter TX 59 F1
Guntersville AL 120 A3
Guntown MS 119 D3
Gurdon AR 117 D4
Gurley AL 119 F2
Gurn Spr. NY 80 C4
Gustavus AK 155 D4
Gustine CA 36 C4
Guthrie KY 109 E3
Guthrie OK 51 E2
Guthrie TX 58 C1
Guthrie Ctr. IA 86 B2
Guthrie Co. IA 86 B2
Guthriesville PA 146 B3
Guttenberg IA 73 F4
Guttenberg NJ 240 D2
Guymon OK 50 B1
Guys TN 119 D2
Guyton GA 130 B2
Gwinn MI 69 D1
Gwinner ND 27 E1
Gwinnett Co. GA 121 D4
Gwynn VA 113 F1
Gypsum CO 40 C1
Gypsum KS 43 E2

H

Haakon Co. SD 26 B3
Habersham Co. GA 121 D2
Hacienda Hts. CA 228 E3
Hackberry LA 133 D3
Hackensack NJ 148 B3
Hackett AR 116 C1
Hackettstown NJ 94 A4
Hackleburg AL 119 E3
Haddam CT 149 E1
Haddonfield NJ 146 C3
Haddon Hts. NJ 248 D4
Hadley MA 150 A1
Hadley NY 80 C4
Hagaman NY 80 C4
Hagan GA 129 F3
Hagerhill KY 111 D1
Hagerman ID 30 C1
Hagerman NM 57 E2
Hagerstown IN 100 A1
Hagerstown MD 144 A1
Hahira GA 137 F1
Hahnville LA 134 B3
Haiku HI 153 D1
Hailey ID 22 C4
Haileyville OK 116 A2
Haines AK 155 D3
Haines OR 21 F2
Haines City FL 141 D2
Halaula HI 153 E2
Halawa HI 152 C3
Hale Ctr. TX 58 A1
Hale Co. AL 127 E2
Hale Co. TX 58 A1
Haledon NJ 148 B3
Haleiwa HI 152 A2
Hales Corners WI 74 C3
Haleyville AL 119 E3
Halfmoon NY 188 E1
Half Moon NC 115 D4
Half Moon Bay CA 36 B4
Halfway MD 144 A1
Halfway OR 22 A2
Halifax MA 151 D2
Halifax NC 113 E3
Halifax PA 93 D4
Halifax VA 112 C2
Halifax Co. NC 113 E4
Halifax Co. VA 112 C2
Haliimaile HI 153 D1
Hallam PA 103 E1
Hallandale Beach FL 143 F2
Hall Co. GA 121 D3
Hall Co. NE 35 D4
Hall Co. TX 50 B4
Hallettsville TX 61 F3
Halliday ND 18 A3
Hallock MN 19 E1
Hallowell ME 82 C2
Halls TN 108 C4
Hallsburg TX 59 F4
Halls Crossroads TN 110 C4
Halls Gap KY 110 B1
Hallstead PA 93 F1
Hallsville MO 97 E2
Hallsville TX 124 B2
Halsey OR 20 B3
Halstad MN 19 F3
Halstead KS 43 E3
Haltom City TX 207 B2
Hamblen Co. TN 111 D3
Hamburg AR 125 F1
Hamburg IA 86 A3
Hamburg MN 66 C4
Hamburg NJ 148 A2
Hamburg NY 78 B4
Hamburg PA 146 A1
Hamden CT 149 D2
Hamden OH 101 D2
Hamel IL 98 B3
Hamilton AL 119 D3
Hamilton GA 128 C2
Hamilton IL 87 F4
Hamilton IN 90 A2
Hamilton MI 75 F4
Hamilton MO 96 C1
Hamilton MT 23 D1
Hamilton NY 79 E3
Hamilton NC 113 E4
Hamilton OH 100 B2
Hamilton RI 150 C4
Hamilton TX 59 E4
Hamilton VA 144 A2
Hamilton City CA 36 B1
Hamilton Co. FL 138 C2
Hamilton Co. IL 98 C4
Hamilton Co. IN 99 F1
Hamilton Co. IA 72 C4
Hamilton Co. KS 42 A3
Hamilton Co. NE 35 E4
Hamilton Co. NY 79 F2
Hamilton Co. OH 100 B2
Hamilton Co. TN 120 B1
Hamilton Co. TX 59 D4
Hamilton Square NJ 147 D2
Ham Lake MN 67 D3
Hamler OH 90 B2
Hamlet IN 89 E2
Hamlet NC 122 C2
Hamlin TX 58 C2
Hamlin WV 101 E4
Hamlin Co. SD 27 E3
Hammon OK 50 C3
Hammond IL 98 C1
Hammond IN 89 D2
Hammond LA 134 B2
Hammond WI 67 E4
Hammondsport NY 78 C4
Hammondville AL 120 A2
Hammonton NJ 147 D4
Hamorton PA 146 B3
Hampden ME 83 D1
Hampden Co. MA 150 A2
Hampden Sydney VA 113 D2
Hampshire IL 88 C1
Hampshire Co. MA 94 C2
Hampshire Co. WV 102 C2
Hampstead MD 144 B1
Hampstead NH 95 E1
Hampton AR 117 E4
Hampton FL 138 C3
Hampton GA 129 D1
Hampton IL 208 C1
Hampton IA 73 D4
Hampton MD 193 C1
Hampton NE 35 E4
Hampton NH 95 E1
Hampton NJ 104 C1
Hampton PA 103 E1
Hampton SC 130 B2
Hampton TN 111 E3
Hampton VA 113 F2
Hampton Bays NY 149 E3
Hampton Beach NH 95 E1
Hampton Co. SC 130 B2
Hampton Park NY 149 E3
Hamtramck MI 210 C3
Hana HI 153 E1
Hanahan SC 131 D1
Hanamaulu HI 152 B1
Hanapepe HI 152 B1
Hanceville AL 119 F3
Hancock MD 102 C1
Hancock MI 65 F3
Hancock MN 66 A3
Hancock NH 81 E4
Hancock NY 93 F1
Hancock Co. GA 129 E1
Hancock Co. IL 87 F4
Hancock Co. IN 100 A1
Hancock Co. IA 72 C3
Hancock Co. KY 109 F1
Hancock Co. ME 83 D1
Hancock Co. MS 134 C2
Hancock Co. OH 90 B3
Hancock Co. TN 111 D3
Hancock Co. WV 91 F4
Hand Co. SD 27 D3
Hanford CA 45 D3
Hankinson ND 27 F1
Hanley Hills MO 256 B2
Hanna WY 33 D2
Hanna City IL 88 B3
Hannibal MO 97 F1
Hannibal NY 79 D3
Hanover CT 149 F1
Hanover IL 74 A4
Hanover IN 100 A3
Hanover KS 43 F1
Hanover MA 151 E2
Hanover MN 66 C3
Hanover NH 81 E3
Hanover NJ 148 A3
Hanover OH 91 D4
Hanover PA 103 E1
Hanover VA 113 E1
Hanover Co. VA 103 D4
Hanover Park IL 203 B3
Hansen ID 30 C1
Hansford Co. TX 50 B2
Hanson KY 109 E1
Hanson MA 151 D2
Hanson Co. SD 27 E4
Hapeville GA 190 D5
Happy TX 50 A4
Happy Camp CA 28 B2
Happy Valley OR 251 D2
Harahan LA 239 B2
Haralson Co. GA 120 B4
Harbert MI 89 E1
Harbeson DE 145 F4
Harbor OR 28 A2
Harbor Beach MI 76 C2
Harbor Bluffs FL 266 A2
Harbor Hills NY 241 G2
Harbor Hills OH 101 D1
Harbor Sprs. MI 70 B3
Harbour Hts. FL 140 C4
Hardee Co. FL 140 C3
Hardeeville SC 130 B3
Hardeman Co. TN 118 C1
Hardeman Co. TX 50 C4
Hardin IL 98 A2
Hardin KY 109 D2
Hardin MO 96 C2
Hardin MT 24 C1
Hardin TX 132 B2
Hardin Co. IL 109 D1
Hardin Co. IA 73 D4
Hardin Co. KY 110 A1
Hardin Co. OH 90 C3
Hardin Co. TN 119 D1
Hardin Co. TX 132 C2
Harding Co. NM 49 E2
Harding Co. SD 25 F1
Hardinsburg KY 109 F1
Hardwick GA 129 E1
Hardwick VT 81 E2
Hardy AR 107 F3
Hardy Co. WV 102 C2
Harewood Park MD 145 D1
Harford Co. MD 144 C1
Hargill TX 63 E4
Harker Hts. TX 59 E4
Harkers Island NC 115 E4
Harlan IA 86 A2
Harlan KY 111 D2
Harlan Co. KY 111 D2
Harlan Co. NE 35 D4
Harlem FL 141 D4
Harlem GA 129 F1
Harlem MT 16 C2
Harleysville PA 146 C2
Harleyville SC 130 C1
Harlingen TX 63 F4
Harlowton MT 16 B4
Harmon Co. OK 50 C4
Harmony IN 99 E1
Harmony MN 73 E2
Harmony NC 112 A4
Harmony PA 92 A3
Harmony RI 150 C3
Harnett Co. NC 123 D1
Harney Co. OR 21 E4
Harold KY 111 E1
Harper KS 43 E4
Harper TX 60 C1
Harper Co. KS 43 E4
Harper Co. OK 50 C1
Harpersville AL 128 A1
Harper Woods MI 210 D2
Harrah OK 51 E3
Harrah WA 13 D4
Harriman NY 148 B2
Harriman TN 110 B4
Harrington DE 145 E3
Harrington ME 83 E2
Harrington WA 13 F3
Harris MN 67 D3
Harrisburg AR 118 A1
Harrisburg IL 109 D1
Harrisburg NE 33 F3
Harrisburg NC 122 B1
Harrisburg OR 20 B3
Harrisburg PA 93 D4
Harrisburg SD 27 F4
Harris Co. GA 128 C2
Harris Co. TX 132 A3

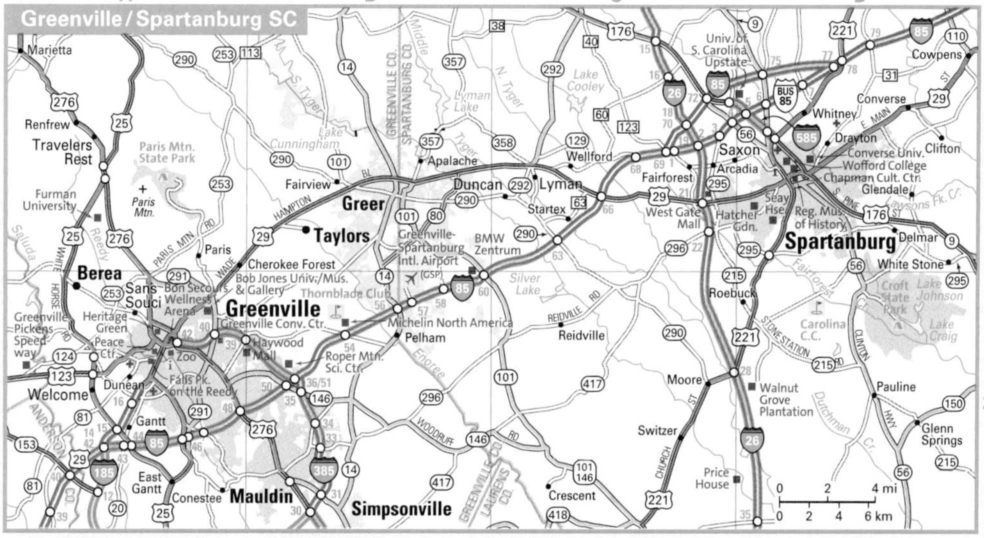
Greenville / Spartanburg SC
A
B
C
D
1
2
Marietta
Renfrew
Travelers Rest
Paris Mtn. State Park
Furman University
Paris Mtn.
Berea
Sans Souci
Paris
Greer
Taylors
Greenville
Cherokee Forest
Bob Jones Univ./Mus. & Gallery
Bon Secours Wellness Arena
Greenville Conv. Ctr.
Haywood Mall
Roper Mtn. Sci. Ctr.
Falls Pk. on the Reedy
Heritage Green
Peace Ctr.
Zoo
Welcome
Dunean
Gantt
East Gantt
Conestee
Mauldin
Simpsonville
Fairview
Thornblade Club
Apalache
Duncan
Lyman
Startex
Wellford
Fairforest
Greenville-Spartanburg Intl. Airport (GSP)
BMW Zentrum
Michelin North America
Pelham
Reidville
Silver Lake
Lake Cunningham
Lyman Lake
Lake Cooley
Univ. of S. Carolina Upstate
Saxon
Arcadia
Whitney
Converse
Cowpens
Drayton
Converse Univ.
Wofford College
Chapman Cult. Ctr.
Clifton
Glendale
West Gate Mall
Hatcher Gdn.
Seay Hse.
Reg. Mus. of History
Spartanburg
Delmar
White Stone
Croft State Park
Lake Johnson
Lake Craig
Carolina C.C.
Roebuck
Moore
Walnut Grove Plantation
Pauline
Glenn Springs
Switzer
Price House
Crescent
0 2 4 mi
0 2 4 6 km

Apalache B1
Arcadia C1
Berea A2
Cherokee Forest A1
Clifton D1
Conestee A2
Converse D1
Cowpens D1
Crescent C2
Delmar D1
Drayton D1
Duncan C1
Dunean A2
E. Gantt A2
Fairforest C1
Fairview B1
Gantt A2
Glendale D1
Glenn Sprs. D2
Greenville A2
Greer B1
Lake Forest A2
Lyman C1
Marietta A1
Mauldin B2
Moore C2
Paris A1
Pauline D2
Pelham B2
Reidville C2
Renfrew A1
Roebuck D2
Sans Souci A2
Saxon C1
Simpsonville B2
Spartanburg D1
Startex C1
Switzer C2
Taylors B1
Travelers Rest A1
Welcome A2
Wellford C1
White Stone D1
Whitney D1

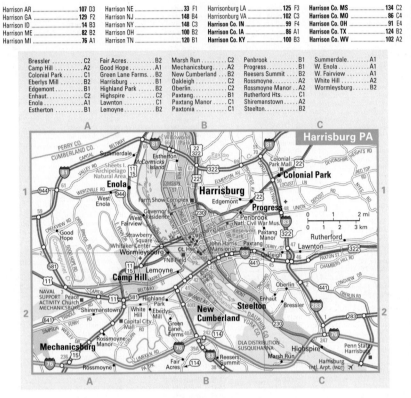

Figures after entries indicate page number and grid reference.

Harrison AR 107 D3
Harrison GA 129 F2
Harrison ID 14 B3
Harrison ME 82 B2
Harrison MI 76 A1
Harrison NE 33 F1
Harrison NJ 148 B4
Harrison NY 148 C3
Harrison OH 100 B2
Harrison TN 120 B1
Harrisonburg LA 125 F3
Harrisonburg VA 102 C3
Harrison Co. IN 99 F4
Harrison Co. IA 86 A1
Harrison Co. KY 100 B3
Harrison Co. MS 134 C2
Harrison Co. MO 86 C4
Harrison Co. OH 91 E4
Harrison Co. TX 124 B2
Harrison Co. WV 102 A2

Bressler C2
Camp Hill A2
Colonial Park C1
Eberlys Mill B2
Edgemont B1
Enhaut C2
Enola A1
Estherton B1
Fair Acres B2
Good Hope A1
Green Lane Farms B2
Harrisburg B1
Highland Park B2
Highspire C2
Lawnton C1
Lemoyne B2
Marsh Run C2
Mechanicsburg A2
New Cumberland B2
Oakleigh C2
Oberlin C2
Paxtang B1
Paxtang Manor C1
Paxtonia C1
Penbrook B1
Progress B1
Reesers Summit B2
Rossmoyne A2
Rossmoyne Manor A2
Rutherford Hts. C1
Shiremanstown A2
Steelton B2
Summerdale A1
W. Enola A1
W. Fairview A1
White Hill A2
Wormleysburg B2

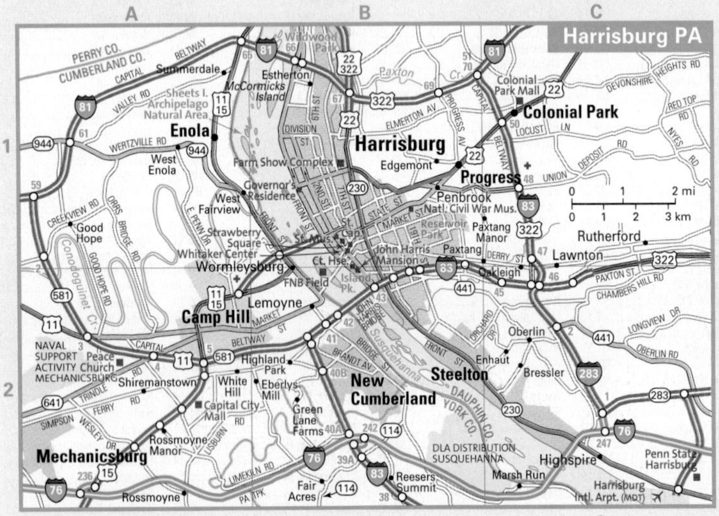
Harrisburg PA
Harrisburg
Enola
Colonial Park
Progress
Camp Hill
Lemoyne
Mechanicsburg
New Cumberland
Steelton
Wormleysburg
Lawnton
Rutherford
Highspire
Penbrook
Paxtang
Oberlin
Enhaut
Bressler
Shiremanstown
Rossmoyne
0 1 2 mi
0 1 2 3 km

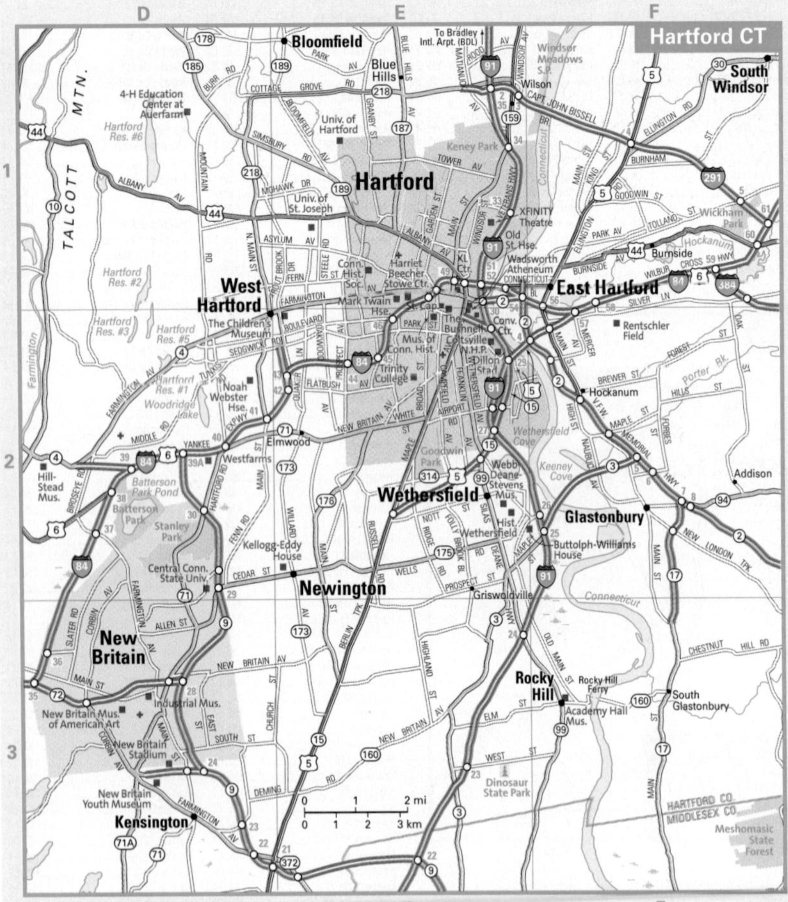
Hartford CT
Hartford
Bloomfield
Blue Hills
South Windsor
West Hartford
East Hartford
Wethersfield
Glastonbury
Newington
New Britain
Rocky Hill
Kensington
Elmwood
Hockanum
Wilson
Addison
0 1 2 mi
0 1 2 3 km

Addison F2
Bloomfield E1
Blue Hills E1
Burnside F1
E. Hartford F1
Elmwood E2
Glastonbury F2
Griswoldville E2
Hartford E1
Hockanum F2
Kensington D3
New Britain D3
Newington E2
Rocky Hill F3
S. Glastonbury F3
S. Windsor F1
W. Hartford D2
Wethersfield E2
Wilson E1

Harrisonville MO 96 B3
Harristown IL 98 C1
Harrisville MD 146 A4
Harrisville MI 71 D4
Harrisville NH 95 D1
Harrisville NY 79 E1
Harrisville PA 92 A3
Harrisville RI 150 C2
Harrisville UT 31 E3
Harrisville WV 101 F2
Harrodsburg KY 110 B1
Harrogate TN 110 C3
Harrold SD 27 D3
Hart MI 75 E2
Hart TX 50 A4
Hart Co. GA 121 E3
Hart Co. KY 110 A2
Hartford AL 136 C1
Hartford AR 116 C2
Hartford CT 150 A3
Hartford IL 98 A3
Hartford IA 86 C2
Hartford KS 43 F3
Hartford KY 109 E1
Hartford MI 89 F1
Hartford SD 27 F4
Hartford WV 101 E2
Hartford WI 74 C3
Hartford City IN 90 A4
Hartford Co. CT 150 A3
Hartington NE 35 E1
Hartland ME 82 C1
Hartland VT 81 E3
Hartland WI 74 C3
Hartley IA 72 A3
Hartley Co. TX 50 A2
Hartly DE 145 E2
Hartman AR 116 C1
Harts WV 101 E4
Hartselle AL 119 F3
Hartshorne OK 116 A2
Hartsville SC 122 B3
Hartsville TN 109 F3
Hartville MO 107 E2
Hartville OH 91 E3
Hartwell GA 121 E3
Harvard IL 74 C4
Harvard MA 150 C1
Harvard NE 35 E4
Harvest AL 119 F2
Harvey IL 203 E6
Harvey LA 239 C2
Harvey MI 69 D1
Harvey ND 18 C3
Harvey Co. KS 43 E3
Harveysburg OH 100 C2
Harveys Lake PA 93 E2
Harwich MA 151 F3
Harwich Port MA 151 F3
Harwinton CT 94 C3
Harwood ND 19 F4
Harwood Hts. IL 203 D3
Hasbrouck Hts. NJ 240 C1
Haskell AR 117 E3
Haskell OK 106 A4
Haskell TX 58 C2
Haskell Co. KS 42 B4
Haskell Co. OK 116 B1
Haskell Co. TX 58 C2
Haskins OH 90 C2
Haslet TX 207 A1
Haslett MI 76 A4
Hastings FL 139 D3
Hastings MI 75 F4
Hastings MN 67 D4
Hastings NE 35 E4
Hastings PA 92 B3
Hatboro PA 146 C2
Hatch NM 56 B2
Hatfield AR 116 C3
Hatfield IN 99 E4
Hatfield MA 150 A1
Hatfield PA 146 C2
Hatley MS 119 D4
Hatteras NC 115 F3
Hattiesburg MS 126 C4
Hatton ND 19 E3
Haubstadt IN 99 D4
Haughton LA 125 D2
Hauppauge NY 149 D3
Hauser ID 14 B3
Hauula HI 152 A2
Havana FL 137 E2
Havana IL 88 A4
Havelock NC 115 D4
Haven KS 43 E4
Haverhill FL 143 F1
Haverhill MA 95 E1
Haverhill NH 81 E3
Haverstraw NY 148 B2
Havertown PA 248 B3
Haviland KS 43 D4
Havre MT 16 B2
Havre de Grace MD 145 D1
Hawaiian Gardens CA 228 E4
Hawaiian Ocean View HI 153 E4
Hawaiian Paradise Park HI 153 F3
Hawaii Co. HI 153 E2
Hawarden IA 35 F1
Hawesville KY 99 E4
Hawi HI 153 E2
Hawkins TX 124 B2
Hawkins Co. TN 111 D3
Hawkinsville GA 129 E3
Hawley MN 19 F4
Hawley PA 93 F2
Hawley TX 58 C2
Hawleyville CT 148 C1
Haw River NC 112 C4
Hawthorn PA 92 B3
Hawthorne CA 228 C3
Hawthorne FL 138 C3
Hawthorne NV 37 E3
Hawthorne NJ 148 B3
Hawthorne NY 148 B3
Hawthorn Woods IL 203 B1
Haxtun CO 34 A4
Hayden AL 119 F4
Hayden AZ 55 D2
Hayden CO 32 C4
Hayden ID 14 B3
Hayden Lake ID 14 B3
Haydenville MA 150 A1
Hayes LA 133 E2
Hayes Ctr. NE 34 B4
Hayes Co. NE 34 B4
Hayesville NC 121 D2
Hayesville OR 20 B2
Hayfield MN 73 D2
Hayfork CA 28 B4
Haymarket VA 144 A3
Haynesville LA 125 D1
Haynesville VA 103 E4
Hayneville AL 128 A3
Hays KS 43 D2
Hays MT 16 C2
Hays NC 112 A3
Hays Co. TX 61 D2
Hay Sprs. NE 34 A1
Haysville KS 43 E4
Hayti MO 108 B3
Hayti SD 27 F3
Hayti Hts. MO 108 B3
Hayward CA 36 B4
Hayward WI 67 F2
Haywood Co. NC 111 D4
Haywood Co. TN 108 C4
Hazard KY 111 D2
Hazardville CT 150 A2
Hazel KY 109 D3
Hazel Crest IL 203 E6
Hazel Green AL 119 F2
Hazel Green WI 74 A4
Hazel Park MI 210 C2
Hazelton ID 31 D1
Hazelton ND 18 C4
Hazelwood MO 256 B1
Hazen AR 117 F2
Hazen ND 18 B3
Hazlehurst GA 129 F3
Hazlehurst MS 126 B3
Hazleton IA 73 E4
Hazleton PA 93 E3
Hazlettville DE 145 E2
Headland AL 128 B4
Head of the Harbor NY 149 D3
Healdsburg CA 36 B3
Healdton OK 51 E4
Healy AK 154 C2
Heard Co. GA 128 B1
Hearne TX 61 F1
Heart Butte MT 15 E2
Heath OH 101 D1
Heathcote NJ 147 D1
Heath Sprs. SC 122 B2
Heathsville VA 103 F4
Heavener OK 116 B2
Hebbronville TX 63 E2
Hebbville MD 193 A2
Heber AZ 47 E4
Heber CA 53 F4
Heber City UT 31 F4
Heber Sprs. AR 117 E1
Hebron CT 149 E1
Hebron IL 74 C4
Hebron IN 89 E2
Hebron KY 100 B2
Hebron MD 103 F3
Hebron NE 43 E1
Hebron ND 18 B4
Hebron OH 101 D1
Hebron Estates KY 100 A4
Hecla SD 27 E1
Hector AR 117 D1
Hector MN 66 B4
Hedrick IA 87 E2
Hedwig Vil. TX 220 B2
Heeia HI 152 A3
Heflin AL 120 A4
Heidelberg MS 127 D3
Heidelberg PA 250 A3
Heilwood PA 92 B3
Helena AL 127 F1
Helena AR 118 A2
Helena GA 129 E3
Helena MS 195 C1
Helena MT 15 E4
Helena OK 51 D1
Helenwood TN 110 B3
Hellertown PA 146 C1
Helmetta NJ 147 E1
Helotes TX 61 D2
Helper UT 39 F1
Hemet CA 53 D3
Hemingford NE 34 A2
Hemingway SC 122 C4
Hemlock MI 76 B2
Hemphill TX 124 C4
Hemphill Co. TX 50 C2
Hempstead NY 148 C4
Hempstead TX 61 F2
Hempstead Co. AR 116 C4
Henagar AL 120 A2
Henderson KY 109 E1
Henderson LA 133 F2
Henderson MN 66 C4
Henderson NE 35 E4
Henderson NV 46 B2
Henderson NC 113 D3
Henderson TN 119 D1
Henderson TX 124 B3
Henderson Co. IL 87 F3
Henderson Co. KY 109 E1
Henderson Co. NC 121 E1
Henderson Co. TN 109 D4
Henderson Co. TX 124 A2
Hendersonville NC 121 E1
Hendersonville TN 109 F3
Hendricks MN 27 F3
Hendricks Co. IN 99 F1
Hendron KY 108 C2
Hendry Co. FL 143 D1
Henefer UT 31 F3
Henlopen Acres DE 145 F4
Hennepin IL 88 B2
Hennepin Co. MN 66 C4
Hennessey OK 51 E2
Henniker NH 81 F4
Henning MN 64 A4
Henning TN 108 B4
Henrico Co. VA 113 E1
Henrietta NY 78 C3
Henrietta TX 59 D1
Henry IL 88 B3
Henry SD 27 E2
Henry TN 109 D3
Henry Co. AL 128 B4
Henry Co. GA 129 D1
Henry Co. IL 88 A2
Henry Co. IN 100 A1
Henry Co. IA 87 F3
Henry Co. KY 100 A3
Henry Co. MO 96 C4
Henry Co. OH 90 B2
Henry Co. TN 109 D3
Henry Co. VA 112 B2
Henryetta OK 51 F3
Henryville IN 100 A3
Hephzibah GA 129 F1
Heppner OR 21 E2
Herculaneum MO 98 A4
Hercules CA 259 C1
Hereford PA 146 B1
Hereford TX 50 A4
Herington KS 43 F3

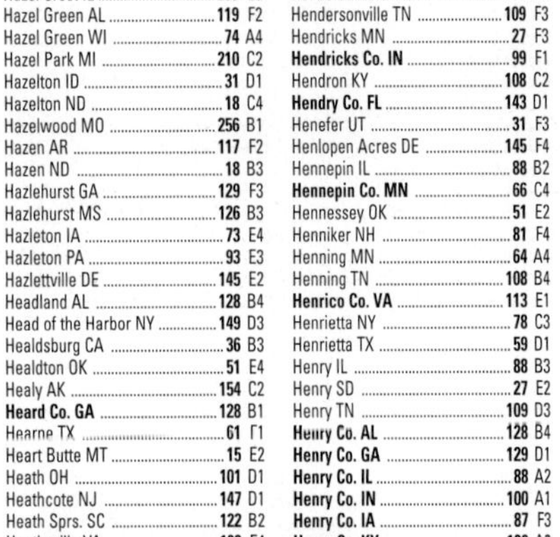
Helena MT
Helena
Helena Regional Airport (HLN)
County Fairgrounds
Carroll College
Civic Center
Cath. of St. Helena
Montana Hist. Society Mus.
State Capitol
0 0.5 1 mi
0 0.5 1 1.5 km

Entries in **bold black** indicate counties or parishes.
Entries in **bold color** indicate cities with detailed inset maps.

Herkimer NY 79 F3
Herkimer Co. NY 79 F2
Hermann MO 97 F3
Hermantown MN 64 C4
Herminie PA 92 A4
Hermiston OR 21 E1
Hermitage AR 117 E4
Hermitage MO 97 D4
Hermitage PA 91 F2
Hermon ME 83 D1
Hermosa CO 40 B4
Hermosa SD 26 A4
Hermosa Beach CA 228 C4
Hernandez NM 48 C2
Hernando FL 140 C1
Hernando MS 118 B2
Hickory MS 126 C2
Hickory NC 111 F4
Hickory Co. MO 97 D4
Hickory Flat MS 118 C2
Hickory Hills IL 203 D5
Hickory Withe TN 118 C1
Hicksville NY 148 C4
Hicksville OH 90 A2
Hico TX 59 E3
Hidalgo TX 63 E4
Hidalgo Co. NM 55 F4
Hidalgo Co. TX 63 E3
Hidden Hills CA 228 A2
Hiddenite NC 112 A4
Hideaway TX 124 A2
Higbee MO 97 E2
High Pt. FL 266 B2
High Pt. NC 112 B4
High Ridge MO 98 A3
High Rolls NM 56 C2
High Shoals NC 122 A1
Highspire PA 218 C2
High Sprs. FL 138 C3
Hightstown NJ 147 D2
Hightsville NC 275 A1
Highwood IL 203 D1
Hilbert WI 74 C1
Hilda SC 130 B1
Hildale UT 46 C1
Hiles WI 68 B2
Hillandale MD 270 E1
Hillburn NY 148 B2
Hillside NJ 148 A4
Hillside Lake NY 148 B1
Hillsville VA 112 A2
Hilltop MN 235 C1
Hillview KY 100 A4
Hilmar CA 36 C4
Hilo HI 153 F3
Hilshire Vil. TX 220 B2
Hilton NY 78 C3
Hilton Head Island SC 130 C3
Hinckley IL 88 C1
Hinckley MN 67 D2
Hinckley UT 39 D2
Hindman KY 111 D1
Hinds Co. MS 126 B3
Hines OR 21 E4
Hoke Co. NC 123 D2
Hokendauqua PA 189 A1
Hokes Bluff AL 120 A3
Holbrook AZ 47 F3
Holbrook MA 151 D2
Holbrook NY 149 D4
Holcomb KS 42 B3
Holcomb MO 108 B3
Holden MA 150 B1
Holden MO 96 C3
Holden UT 39 E2
Holden WV 111 E1
Holden Beach NC 123 E4
Holdenville OK 51 F3
Holdingford MN 66 B2
Holdrege NE 35 D4
Holgate OH 90 B2
Holiday FL 140 B2
Holiday Hills IL 203 A1
Holiday Lakes TX 132 A4
Holladay UT 257 B2
Holland AR 117 E1
Holland IN 99 E4
Holland MA 150 B2
Holland MI 75 E4
Holland NY 78 B4
Holland OH 90 C2
Holland TX 61 E1
Hollandale MS 126 A1
Holley FL 135 F2
Holley NY 78 B3
Holliday TX 59 D1
Hollidaysburg PA 92 C4
Hollins VA 112 B1
Hollis NH 95 D1
Hollis OK 50 C4
Hollis Ctr. ME 82 B3
Hollister CA 44 B2
Hollister MO 107 D3
Hollister NC 113 D3
Holliston MA 150 C2
Hollow Creek KY 230 E3
Hollow Rock TN 109 D4
Holly CO 42 A3
Holly MI 76 B4
Holly Grove AR 117 F2
Holly Hill FL 139 E4
Holly Hill SC 130 C1
Holly Park NJ 147 E3
Holly Pond AL 119 F3
Holly Ridge NC 115 C4
Holly Sprs. GA 120 C3
Holly Sprs. MS 118 C2
Holly Sprs. NC 112 C4
Hollyvilla KY 100 A4
Hollywood AL 120 A2
Hollywood FL 143 F2
Hollywood MD 103 E4
Hollywood SC 131 D2
Hollywood Park TX 61 D2
Holmdel NJ 147 E2
Holmen WI 73 F1
Holmes Beach FL 140 B3
Holmes Co. FL 136 C1
Holmes Co. MS 126 B1
Holmes Co. OH 91 D4
Holstein IA 72 A4
Holt AL 127 E1
Holt MI 76 A4
Holt Co. MO 86 A4
Holt Co. NE 35 D1
Holton KS 96 A2
Holts Summit MO 97 E3
Holtville CA 53 E4
Holualoa HI 153 E3
Holyoke CO 34 A4
Holyoke MA 150 A2
Holyrood KS 43 D3
Homecroft IN 99 F1
Homedale ID 22 A4
Home Gardens CA 229 H4
Homeland CA 229 K4
Homeland GA 139 D1
Homeland Park SC 121 E3
Homer AK 154 C3
Homer GA 121 D3
Homer IL 99 D1
Homer LA 125 D2
Homer MI 90 A1
Homer NE 35 F2
Homer NY 79 D4
Homer City PA 92 B4
Homer Glen IL 203 C6
Homerville GA 138 C1
Homestead FL 143 E3
Homestead PA 250 C2
Homestead Valley CA 259 A2
Hometown IL 203 D5
Hometown PA 93 E3
Hometown WV 101 E3
Homewood AL 119 F4
Hominy OK 51 F1
Homosassa FL 140 B1
Homosassa Sprs. FL 140 B1
Honaker VA 111 E2
Honalo HI 153 E3
Honaunau HI 153 E3
Hondo TX 60 C3
Honea Path SC 121 E3
Honeoye NY 78 C4
Honeoye Falls NY 78 C3
Honesdale PA 93 F2
Honey Brook PA 146 B2
Honey Grove TX 59 F1
Honeyville UT 31 E3
Honokaa HI 153 E2
Honokowai HI 153 D1
Honolulu HI 152 A3
Honolulu Co. HI 152 A3
Honomu HI 153 F3
Hood Co. TX 59 E3
Hood River OR 21 D1
Hood River Co. OR 20 C2
Hooker OK 50 B1
Hooker Co. NE 34 B2
Hooks TX 116 C4
Hooksett NH 81 F4
Hoonah AK 155 D4
Hooper NE 35 F3
Hooper UT 244 A2
Hooper Bay AK 154 B3
Hoopeston IL 89 D4
Hoople ND 19 E2
Hoosick Falls NY 94 B1
Hoover AL 127 F1
Hooverson Hts. WV 91 F4
Hooversville PA 92 B4
Hopatcong NJ 148 A3
Hope AR 117 D4
Hope IN 99 F2
Hope ND 19 F3
Hope RI 150 C3
Hopedale IL 88 B4
Hopedale MA 150 C2
Hopedale OH 91 F4
Hope Mills NC 123 D2
Hope Valley RI 150 C4
Hopewell NJ 147 D1
Hopewell TN 120 B1
Hopewell VA 113 E1
Hopewell Jct. NY 148 B1
Hopkins MI 75 F4
Hopkins MN 235 A3
Hopkins MO 86 B4
Hopkins Co. KY 109 E2
Hopkins Co. TX 124 A1
Hopkins Park IL 89 D3
Hopkinsville KY 109 E2
Hopkinton IA 73 F4
Hopkinton MA 150 C2
Hopkinton NH 81 F4
Hopwood PA 102 B1
Hoquiam WA 12 B4
Horace ND 19 E4
Horatio AR 116 C4
Horicon WI 74 C2

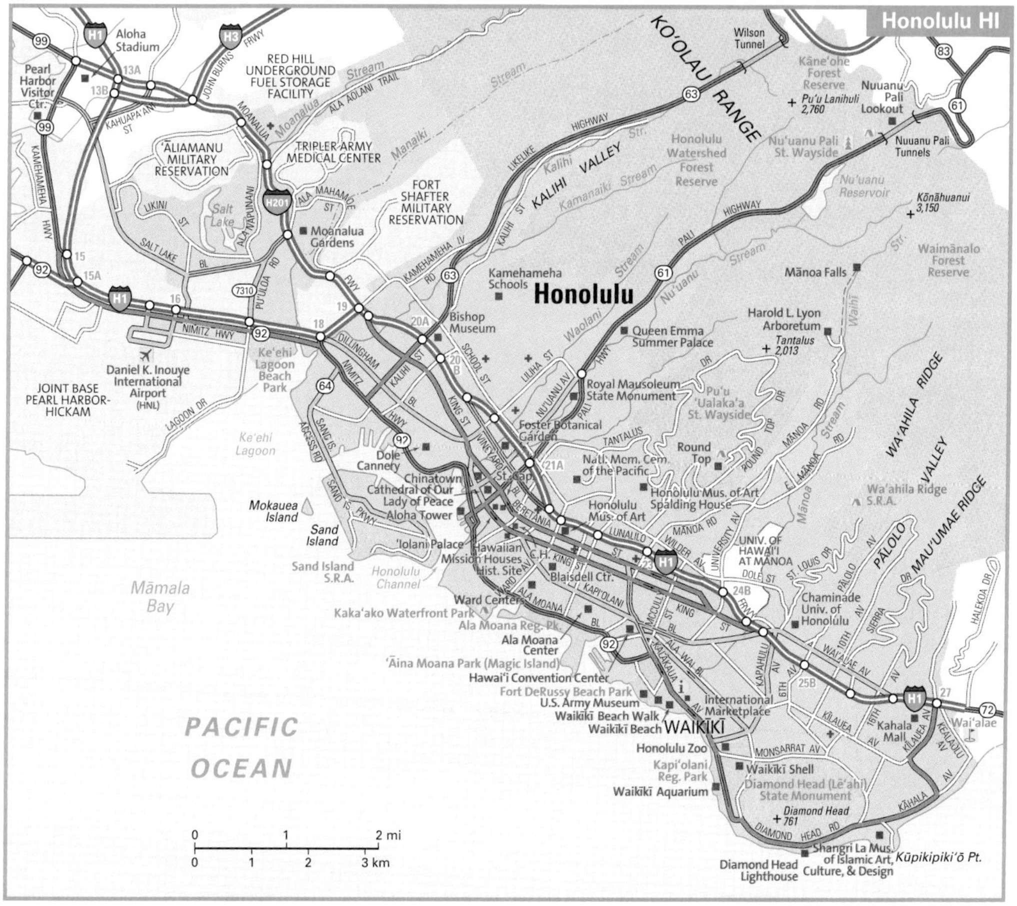

Hernando Beach FL 140 B1
Hernando Co. FL 140 B1
Herndon VA 144 A3
Heron Lake MN 72 A2
Herreid SD 26 C1
Herricks NY 241 G3
Herriman UT 31 E4
Herrin IL 108 C1
Herscher IL 89 D3
Hershey NE 34 B3
Hershey PA 93 E4
Hertford NC 113 F3
Hertford Co. NC 113 F3
Hesperia CA 53 D2
Hesperia MI 75 E2
Hessmer LA 133 F1
Hesston KS 43 E3
Hettinger ND 26 A1
Hettinger Co. ND 18 A4
Heuvelton NY 80 B2
Hewitt TX 59 E4
Hewitt WI 68 A4
Hewlett NY 241 G4
Hewlett Harbor NY 241 G5
Hewlett Neck NY 241 G5
Heyburn ID 31 D1
Heyworth IL 88 C4
Hialeah FL 143 E2
Hialeah Gardens FL 143 E2
Hiawassee GA 121 D2
Hiawatha IA 87 E1
Hiawatha KS 96 A1
Hibbing MN 64 B3
Hickman KY 108 C3
Hickman NE 35 F4
Hickman Co. KY 108 C3
Hickman Co. TN 109 E4
Higganum CT 149 E1
Higginsville MO 96 C2
High Bridge NJ 104 C1
Highgate Ctr. VT 81 D1
Highgrove CA 229 J3
Highland AR 107 F3
Highland CA 229 K2
Highland IL 98 B3
Highland IN 89 D2
Highland KS 96 A1
Highland MD 144 B2
Highland NY 94 B3
Highland UT 31 F4
Highland WI 74 A3
Highland Beach FL 143 F1
Highland City FL 140 C2
Highland Co. OH 100 C2
Highland Co. VA 102 B4
Highland Falls NY 148 B2
Highland Hts. KY 204 B3
Highland Hts. OH 204 G1
Highland Hills OH 204 G2
Highland Lakes NJ 148 A2
Highland Mills NY 148 B2
Highland Park IL 89 D1
Highland Park MI 210 C3
Highland Park NJ 147 E1
Highland Park PA 218 B2
Highland Park TX 207 D2
Highlands NJ 147 F1
Highlands NC 121 D2
Highlands TX 132 B3
Highlands Co. FL 141 D4
Highland Sprs. VA 254 C2
Highlands Ranch CO 209 C4
Highlandville MO 107 D2
Highmore SD 27 D3
Hill City KS 42 C2
Hill City MN 64 B4
Hill City SD 25 F4
Hill Country Vil. TX 257 E1
Hill Co. MT 16 A1
Hill Co. TX 59 E3
Hillcrest IL 88 B1
Hillcrest NY 148 B2
Hillcrest TX 132 B4
Hillcrest Hts. MD 144 B3
Hilliard FL 139 D1
Hilliard OH 101 D1
Hillman MI 70 C3
Hills IA 87 F2
Hills MN 27 F4
Hillsboro AL 119 E2
Hillsboro IL 98 B2
Hillsboro IN 89 E4
Hillsboro KS 43 E3
Hillsboro MO 98 A4
Hillsboro ND 19 E3
Hillsboro OH 100 C2
Hillsboro OR 20 B2
Hillsboro TX 59 E3
Hillsboro WI 74 A2
Hillsboro Beach FL 143 F1
Hillsborough CA 259 B4
Hillsborough NH 81 E4
Hillsborough NC 112 C4
Hillsborough Co. FL 140 C3
Hillsborough Co. NH 81 F4
Hillsdale IL 88 A2
Hillsdale MI 90 B1
Hillsdale MO 256 B2
Hillsdale NJ 148 B3
Hillsdale Co. MI 90 B1
Hillside IL 203 C4
Hinesburg VT 81 D2
Hinesville GA 130 B3
Hingham MA 151 D1
Hinsdale IL 203 C5
Hinsdale MA 94 C1
Hinsdale NH 94 C1
Hinsdale Co. CO 40 C4
Hinson FL 137 E2
Hinton IA 35 F1
Hinton OK 51 D3
Hinton WV 112 A1
Hiram GA 120 C4
Hiram OH 91 E2
Hitchcock TX 132 B4
Hitchcock Co. NE 34 B4
Hitchins KY 101 D4
Hobart IN 89 D2
Hobart OK 51 D3
Hobart WA 12 C3
Hobbs NM 57 F2
Hobe Sound FL 141 F4
Hoboken NJ 148 B4
Hobson MT 16 B4
Hockessin DE 146 B3
Hocking Co. OH 101 D1
Hockley Co. TX 58 A1
Hodge LA 125 E3
Hodgeman Co. KS 42 C3
Hodgenville KY 110 A1
Hodgkins IL 203 C5
Hoffman MN 66 A2
Hoffman NC 122 C2
Hoffman Estates IL 203 B3
Hogansville GA 128 C1
Hohenwald TN 119 E1
Hoisington KS 43 D3
Hokah MN 73 F2

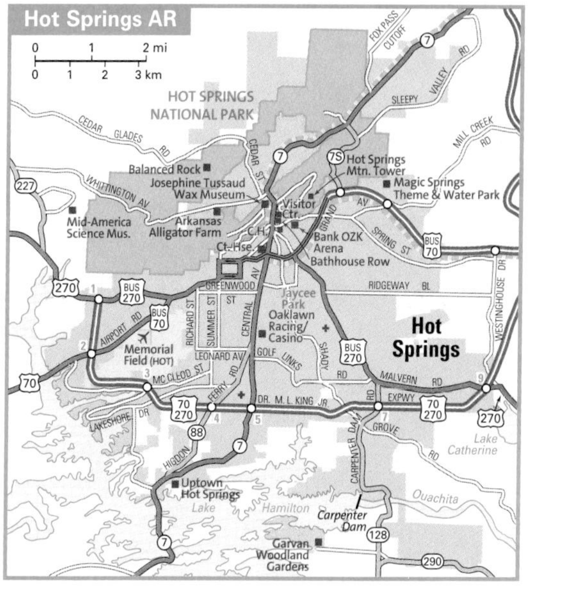

Figures after entries indicate page number and grid reference.

Aldine ... C1	Channelview ... D2	Fresno ... B4	Houston ... C2	Lynchburg ... D2	Pasadena ... D3	Spring Valley Village ... B2
Barrett ... D1	Cloverleaf ... D2	Friendswood ... D4	Humble ... C1	Magnolia Gardens ... D1	Pearland ... C4	Stafford ... B4
Beaumont Place ... D2	Crabb ... A4	Galena Park ... C3	Hunters Creek Vil. ... B2	Meadows Place ... A3	Piney Pt. Vil. ... B2	Sugar Land ... A3
Bellaire ... B3	Crosby ... D1	Hedwig Vil. ... B2	Jacinto City ... C2	Mission Bend ... A3	Satsuma ... A1	Webster ... D4
Booth ... A4	Cypress ... A1	Highlands ... D2	Jersey Vil. ... A1	Missouri City ... B4	Sheldon ... D2	W. University Place ... B3
Brookside Vil. ... C4	Deer Park ... D3	Hilshire Vil. ... B2	La Porte ... D3	Nassau Bay ... D4	S. Houston ... C3	
Bunker Hill Vil. ... B2	Four Corners ... A3	Houmont Park ... D2	League City ... D4	N. Houston ... B1	Southside Place ... B3	

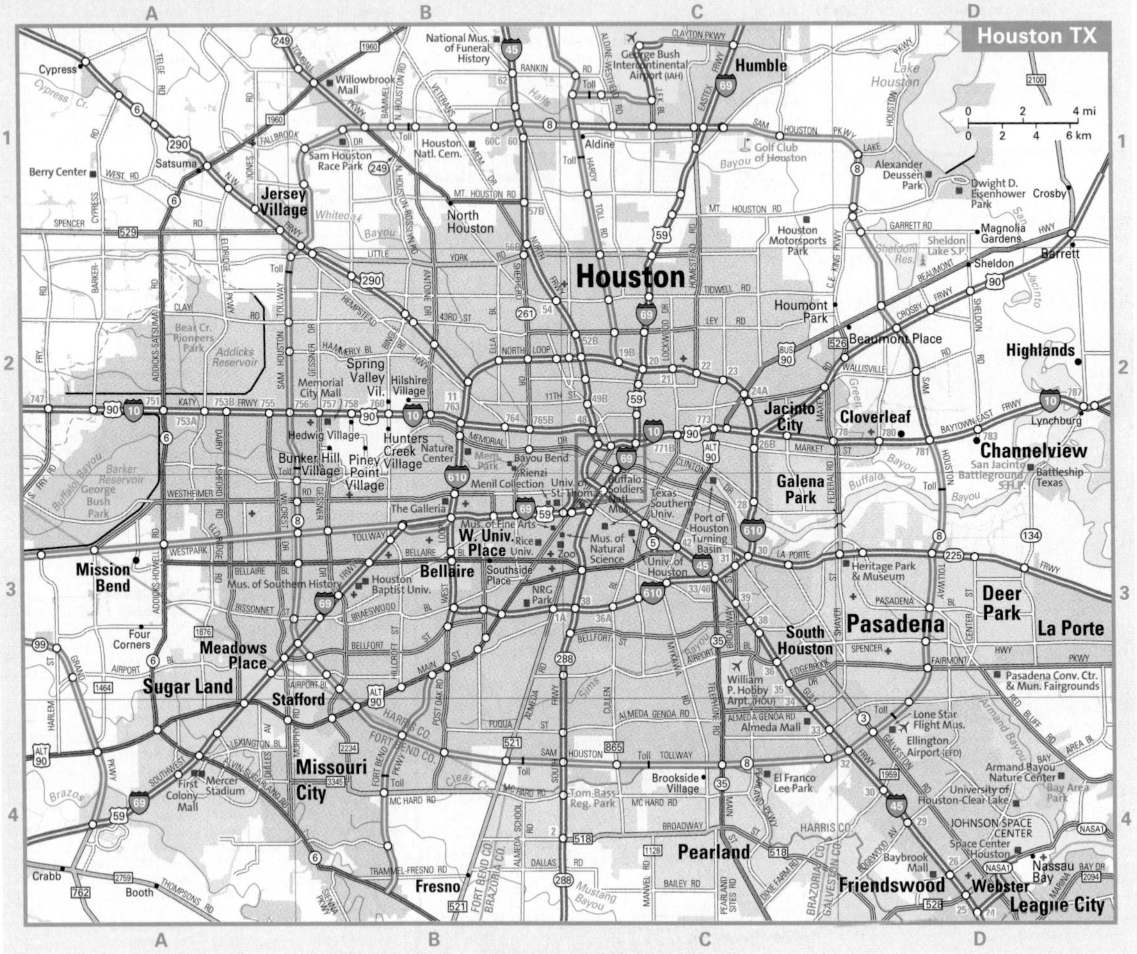

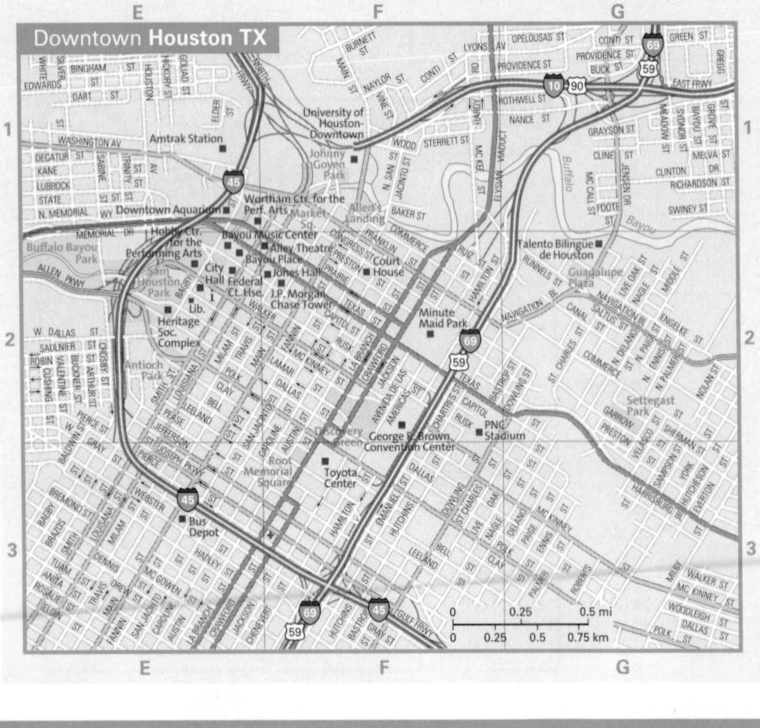

POINTS OF INTEREST

Allen's Landing ... F1
Alley Theatre ... F2
Amtrak Station ... E1
Bayou Music Center ... E2
Bayou Place ... E2
Bus Depot ... E3
City Hall ... E2
Court House ... F2
Downtown Aquarium ... E1
Federal Courthouse ... E2
George R. Brown Convention Center ... F2
Heritage Society Complex ... E2
Hobby Center for the Performing Arts ... E2
Jones Hall ... F2
J.P. Morgan Chase Tower ... F2
Library ... E2
Minute Maid Park ... F2
PNC Stadium ... F2
Talento Bilingüe de Houston ... G2
Toyota Center ... F3
Univ. of Houston-Downtown ... F1
Wortham Center for the Perf. Arts ... E1

Horizon City TX ... 56 C4
Hornbeak TN ... 108 C3
Hornbeck LA ... 125 D4
Hornell NY ... 78 C4
Hornersville MO ... 108 B4
Horn Lake MS ... 118 B2
Horry Co. SC ... 123 D3
Horse Cave KY ... 110 A2
Horseheads NY ... 93 D1
Horse Pasture VA ... 112 B3
Horseshoe Bay TX ... 61 D1
Horseshoe Bend AR ... 107 F3
Horseshoe Bend ID ... 22 B4
Horsham PA ... 146 C2
Horton KS ... 96 A1
Hortonville MA ... 151 D3
Hortonville WI ... 74 C1
Hoschton GA ... 121 D3
Hosmer SD ... 27 D1
Hospers IA ... 35 F1
Hotchkiss CO ... 40 B2
Hotchkissville CT ... 149 D1
Hotevilla-Bacavi AZ ... 47 E2
Hot Spr. Co. AR ... 117 D3
Hot Sprs. AR ... 117 D3
Hot Sprs. MT ... 14 C3
Hot Sprs. NC ... 111 D4
Hot Sprs. SD ... 25 F4
Hot Sprs. Co. WY ... 24 B4
Hot Sprs. Vil. AR ... 117 D2
Hot Sulphur Sprs. CO ... 41 D1
Houck AZ ... 48 A3
Houghton MI ... 65 F3
Houghton NY ... 78 B4
Houghton Co. MI ... 65 F4
Houghton Lake MI ... 76 A1
Houlton ME ... 85 E3
Houma LA ... 134 A3
Housatonic MA ... 94 B2
Houston AK ... 154 C3
Houston DE ... 145 E3
Houston MN ... 73 E2
Houston MS ... 118 C4
Houston MO ... 107 E1
Houston PA ... 92 A4
Houston TX ... 132 A3
Houston Acres KY ... 230 F2
Houston Co. AL ... 137 D1
Houston Co. GA ... 129 D2
Houston Co. MN ... 73 F2
Houston Co. TN ... 109 E3
Houston Co. TX ... 124 A4
Houtzdale PA ... 92 C3
Hoven SD ... 27 D2
Howard KS ... 43 F4
Howard PA ... 92 C3
Howard SD ... 27 E4
Howard WI ... 68 C4
Howard City MI ... 75 F2
Howard Co. AR ... 116 C3
Howard Co. IN ... 89 F4
Howard Co. IA ... 73 E3
Howard Co. MD ... 144 B2
Howard Co. MO ... 97 D2
Howard Co. NE ... 35 D3
Howard Co. TX ... 58 B3
Howard Lake MN ... 66 C3
Howards Grove WI ... 75 D2
Howe IN ... 90 A1
Howe OK ... 116 B2
Howe TX ... 59 F1
Howell MI ... 76 B4
Howell Co. MO ... 107 E3
Howells NE ... 35 F2
Howells NY ... 148 A1
Howey-in-the-Hills FL ... 140 C1
Howland ME ... 85 D4
Hoxie AR ... 108 A4
Hoxie KS ... 42 C2
Hoyt KS ... 96 A2
Hoyt Lakes MN ... 64 C3
Huachuca City AZ ... 55 D4
Hubbard IA ... 72 C4
Hubbard OH ... 276 C2
Hubbard OR ... 20 C2
Hubbard TX ... 59 F3
Hubbard Co. MN ... 64 A3
Hubbard Lake MI ... 71 D4
Hubbell MI ... 65 F3
Huber Hts. OH ... 100 C1
Huber Ridge OH ... 206 C1
Huddy KY ... 111 E1
Hudson CO ... 41 E1
Hudson FL ... 140 B2
Hudson IL ... 88 C3
Hudson IN ... 90 A2
Hudson IA ... 73 D4
Hudson MA ... 150 C1
Hudson MI ... 90 B1
Hudson NH ... 95 E1
Hudson NY ... 94 B2
Hudson NC ... 111 F4
Hudson OH ... 91 E2
Hudson SD ... 35 F1
Hudson TX ... 124 B4
Hudson WI ... 67 D4
Hudson WY ... 32 B1
Hudson Co. NJ ... 148 B4
Hudson Falls NY ... 81 D4
Hudsonville MI ... 75 F3
Hudspeth Co. TX ... 57 D4
Huerfano Co. CO ... 41 E4
Hueytown AL ... 119 F4
Huffs Church PA ... 146 B1
Hughes AR ... 118 A2
Hughes Co. OK ... 51 F3
Hughes Co. SD ... 26 C3
Hughes Sprs. TX ... 124 B1
Hughestown PA ... 261 C2
Hughesville MD ... 144 C4
Hughesville PA ... 93 E2
Hughson CA ... 36 C4
Hugo CO ... 41 F2
Hugo MN ... 67 D3
Hugo OK ... 116 A3
Hugoton KS ... 42 B4
Huguenot NY ... 148 A1
Huguley AL ... 128 B2
Hulbert OK ... 106 B4
Hulett WY ... 25 F3
Hull IA ... 35 F1
Hull MA ... 151 D1
Hulmeville PA ... 147 D2
Humansville MO ... 106 C1
Humarock MA ... 151 E2
Humble TX ... 132 B3
Humboldt IA ... 72 B4
Humboldt KS ... 106 A1
Humboldt NE ... 43 F1
Humboldt NV ... 29 F4
Humboldt SD ... 27 F4
Humboldt TN ... 108 C4
Humboldt Co. CA ... 28 A4
Humboldt Co. IA ... 72 B3
Humboldt Co. NV ... 29 F3
Humeston IA ... 86 C3
Hummelstown PA ... 93 E4
Humphrey AR ... 117 F3
Humphrey NE ... 35 E3
Humphreys Co. MS ... 126 B1
Humphreys Co. TN ... 109 E4
Hungerford TX ... 61 F3
Hungry Horse MT ... 15 D2
Hunt Co. TX ... 59 F2
Hunter ND ... 19 E3
Hunter TN ... 111 E3

Entries in **bold black** indicate counties or parishes.
Entries in **bold color** indicate cities with detailed inset maps.

Hunterdon Co. NJ 147 D1
Hunters Creek Vil. TX 220 B2
Hunters Pt. AZ 48 A3
Huntersville NC 122 A1
Huntertown IN 90 A2
Huntingburg IN 99 E4
Huntingdon PA 92 C4
Huntingdon TN 109 D4
Huntingdon Co. PA 92 C3
Huntington AR 116 C1
Huntington IN 89 F3
Huntington MA 94 C2
Huntington NY 148 C3
Huntington OR 22 A3
Huntington TX 124 B4
Huntington UT 39 F2
Huntington VA 270 C5
Huntington WV 101 D3
Huntington Bay NY 148 C3
Huntington Beach CA 52 C3
Huntington Co. IN 89 F3
Huntington Park CA 228 D3
Huntington Sta. NY 148 C3
Huntington Woods MI 210 B2
Huntingtown MD 144 C4
Hunting Valley OH 204 G2
Huntland TN 120 A2
Huntleigh MO 256 B2
Huntley IL 88 C1
Huntley MT 24 C1
Hunts Pt. WA 262 B3
Huntsville AL 119 F2
Huntsville AR 106 C4
Huntsville MO 97 E2
Huntsville TN 110 B3
Huntsville TX 132 A1
Huntsville UT 31 F3
Hurffville NJ 146 C4
Hurley MS 135 D1
Hurley NM 55 F2
Hurley NY 94 B2
Hurley SD 27 F4
Hurley WI 65 E4
Hurlock MD 145 E4
Huron CA 44 C3
Huron OH 91 D2
Huron SD 27 E3
Huron Co. MI 76 C2
Huron Co. OH 91 D3
Hurricane UT 39 D4
Hurricane WV 101 E3
Hurst IL 108 C1
Hurst TX 207 B2
Hurstbourne KY 230 F2
Hurstbourne Acres KY 230 F2
Hurt VA 112 C2
Hurtsboro AL 128 B3
Hustisford WI 74 C3
Hustonville KY 110 B1
Hutchins TX 207 E3
Hutchinson KS 43 E3
Hutchinson MN 66 C4
Hutchinson Co. SD 27 E4
Hutchinson Co. TX 50 B2
Hutsonville IL 99 D2
Huttig AR 125 E1
Hutto TX 61 E1
Huxley IA 86 C1
Hyannis MA 151 F3
Hyannis NE 34 B2
Hyannis Port MA 151 F4
Hyattsville MD 144 B3
Hyde PA 92 C3
Hyde Co. NC 113 F4
Hyde Co. SD 27 D3
Hyden KY 111 D2
Hyde Park NY 94 B3
Hyde Park UT 31 E2
Hyde Park VT 81 E2
Hydesville CA 28 A4
Hydetown PA 92 A2
Hydro OK 51 D3
Hymera IN 99 E2
Hyndman PA 102 C1
Hypoluxo FL 143 F1
Hyrum UT 31 E3
Hysham MT 25 D1

I

Iaeger WV 111 F1
Iberia MO 97 E4
Iberia Par. LA 133 F3
Iberville Par. LA 133 F2
Icard NC 111 F4
Ida MI 90 C1
Idabel OK 116 B4
Ida Co. IA 72 A4
Ida Grove IA 72 A4
Idaho City ID 22 B4
Idaho Co. ID 14 C4
Idaho Falls ID 23 F4
Idalou TX 58 A1
Ideal GA 129 D2
Ider AL 120 A2
Idyllwild CA 53 D3
Idylwood VA 270 B3
Ignacio CO 48 B1
Ilion NY 79 F3
Illiopolis IL 98 B1
Ilwaco WA 12 B4
Imboden AR 107 F3
Imlay NV 29 F4
Imlay City MI 76 C3
Immokalee FL 143 D1
Imperial CA 53 E4
Imperial MO 98 A4
Imperial NE 34 B4
Imperial PA 91 F4
Imperial Beach CA 53 D4
Imperial Co. CA 53 F4
Ina IL 98 C4
Incline Vil. NV 37 D2
Independence CA 45 E2
Independence IA 73 E4
Independence KS 106 A2
Independence KY 100 B3
Independence LA 134 B1
Independence MN 66 C4
Independence MO 96 B2
Independence OH 204 F3
Independence OR 20 B2
Independence VA 111 F3
Independence WI 73 E1
Independence Co. AR 107 F4
Independent Hill VA 144 A4
Indialantic FL 141 E2
Indiana PA 92 B3
Indiana Co. PA 92 B3
Indianapolis IN 99 F1
Indian Harbour Beach FL 141 E2
Indian Head MD 144 B4
Indian Head Park IL 203 C5
Indian Hills CO 209 A4
Indian Hills KY 230 E1
Indian Neck CT 149 D2
Indianola IA 86 C2
Indianola MS 118 A4
Indianola NE 34 C4
Indianola WA 262 A2
Indian Pt. MO 107 D3
Indian River MI 70 C3
Indian River Co. FL 141 E3
Indian River Estates FL 141 E3
Indian River Shores FL 141 E3
Indian Rocks Beach FL 140 B2
Indian Shores FL 266 A2
Indian Sprs. NV 46 A1
Indian Sprs. Vil. AL 127 F1
Indiantown FL 141 E4
Indian Trail NC 122 B2
Indian Wells CA 53 E3
Indio CA 53 E3
Indrio FL 141 E3
Industry CA 228 E3
Industry PA 91 F3
Inez KY 101 D4

Huntington WV

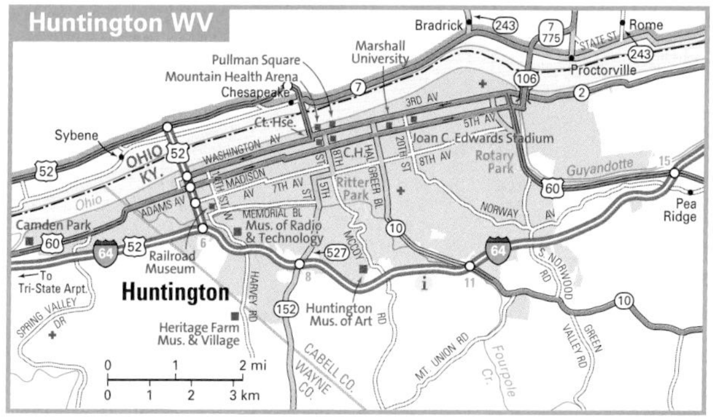

Huntsville AL

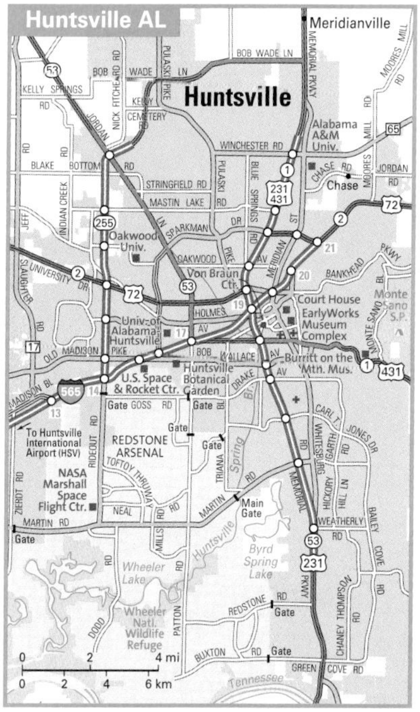

Idaho Falls ID

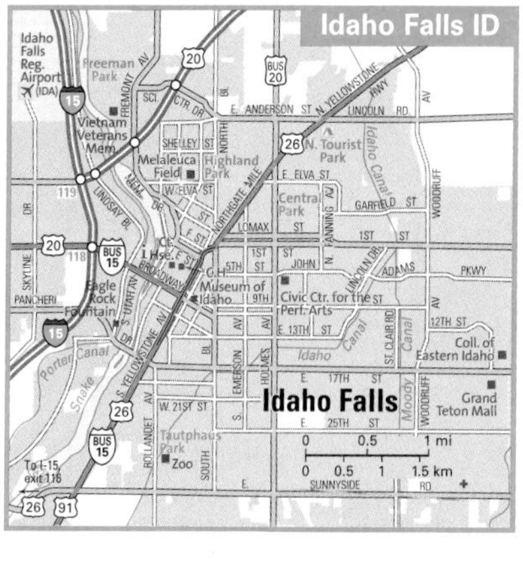

Indianapolis IN

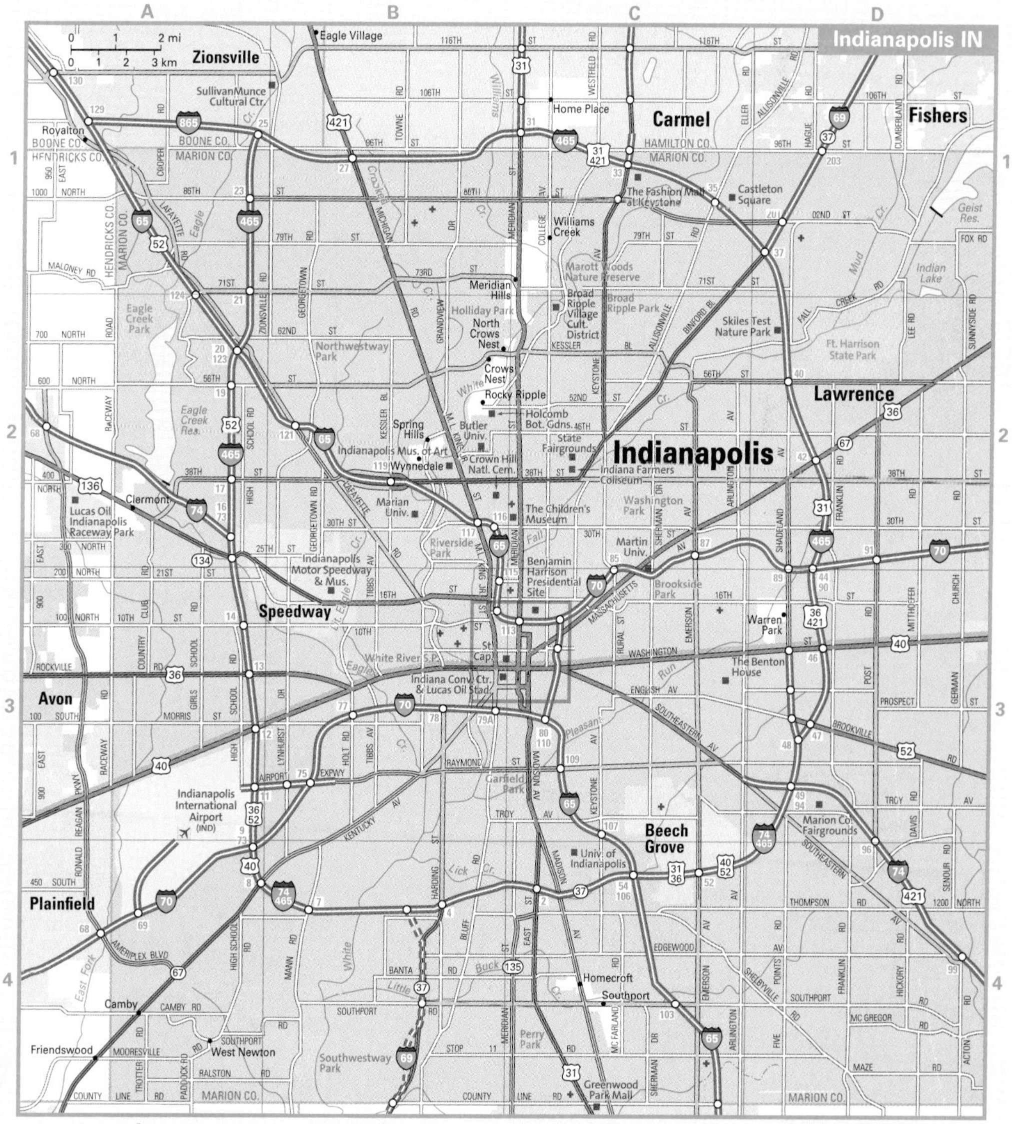

Avon A3
Beech Grove C3
Camby A4
Carmel C1
Clermont A2
Crows Nest B2
Eagle Vil. B1
Fishers D1
Friendswood A4
Homecroft C4
Home Place C1
Indianapolis C2
Lawrence D2
Meridian Hills C1
N. Crows Nest B2
Plainfield A4
Rocky Ripple B2
Royalton A1
Southport C4
Speedway B3
Spring Hills B2
Warren Park D3
W. Newton A4
Williams Creek C1
Wynnedale B2
Zionsville A1

Figures after entries indicate page number and grid reference.

POINTS OF INTEREST

American Legion National Headquarters. . A1
Artsgarden A2
Benjamin Harrison Presidential Site B1
Canal & State Park Cultural District A2
Circle Centre Mall A2
City Market B2
Eiteljorg Museum A2
Gainbridge Fieldhouse B2
Herron School of Art A2
Indiana Avenue Cultural District A1
Indiana Convention Center A2
Indianapolis Zoo A2
Indiana State Museum A2
Indiana Univ./Purdue Univ. Indianapolis . . A1
Indiana World War Memorial A1
James Whitcomb Riley Museum B1
Lucas Oil Stadium A2
Madame Walker Legacy Center A1
Massachusetts Avenue Cultural District . . B1
Morris-Butler House B1
NCAA Hall of Champions A2
Old National Centre B1
Scottish Rite Cathedral A1
Soldiers & Sailors Monument A2
State Capitol A2
Victory Field A2
White River State Park A2

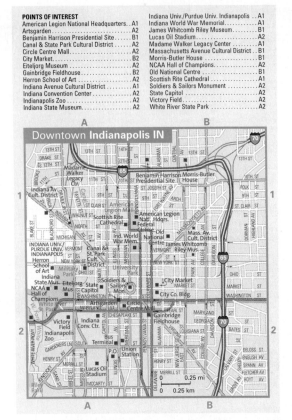

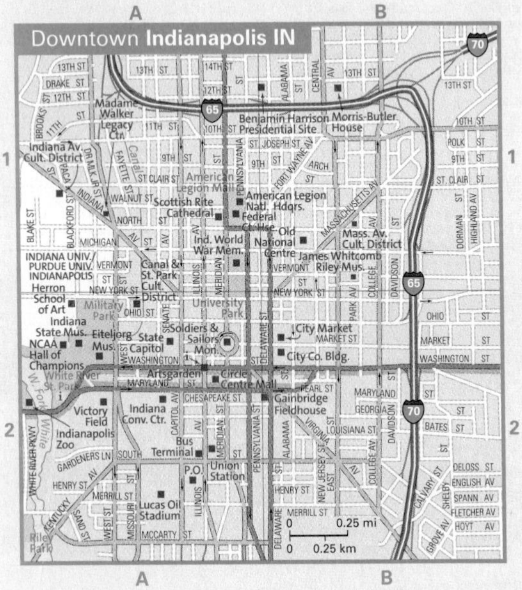
Downtown Indianapolis IN
A
B
1
2
70
65
Benjamin Harrison Presidential Site
Morris-Butler House
American Legion Natl. Hdqrs.
Scottish Rite Cathedral
Ind. World War Mem.
Old National Centre
James Whitcomb Riley Mus.
Mass. Av. Cult. District
Canal & St. Park Cult. District
City Market
City Co. Bldg.
Soldiers & Sailors Mon.
State Capitol
Eiteljorg Mus.
Artsgarden
Circle Centre Mall
Gainbridge Fieldhouse
Indiana Conv. Ctr.
Victory Field
Indianapolis Zoo
Union Station
Lucas Oil Stadium
0 0.25 mi
0 0.25 km

Inez TX 61 F3
Ingalls IN 99 F1
Ingham Co. MI 76 A4
Ingleside TX 63 F2
Ingleside on the Bay TX 63 F2
Inglewood CA 52 C2
Inglis FL 138 C4
Ingold NC 123 E2
Ingram PA 250 A2
Ingram TX 60 C2
Inkom ID 31 E1
Inkster MI 210 B4
Inman GA 128 C1
Inman KS 43 E3
Inman SC 121 F2
Inola OK 106 A4
Intercession City FL 141 D2
Interlachen FL 139 D3
Interlaken NJ 147 F2
Interlaken NY 79 D4
Interlochen MI 69 F4
International Falls MN 64 B2
Inver Grove Hts. MN 235 D4
Inverness CA 36 A3
Inverness FL 140 C1
Inverness IL 203 B2
Inverness MS 126 B1
Inwood FL 140 C2
Inwood IA 27 F4
Inwood NY 147 F1
Inwood WV 103 D2
Inyo Co. CA 37 F4
Inyokern CA 45 E4
Iola KS 96 A4
Iola WI 68 B4
Iona ID 23 E4
Ione CA 36 C3
Ione OR 21 E2
Ione WA 13 F1
Ionia MI 76 A3
Ionia Co. MI 75 F3
Iosco Co. MI 76 B1

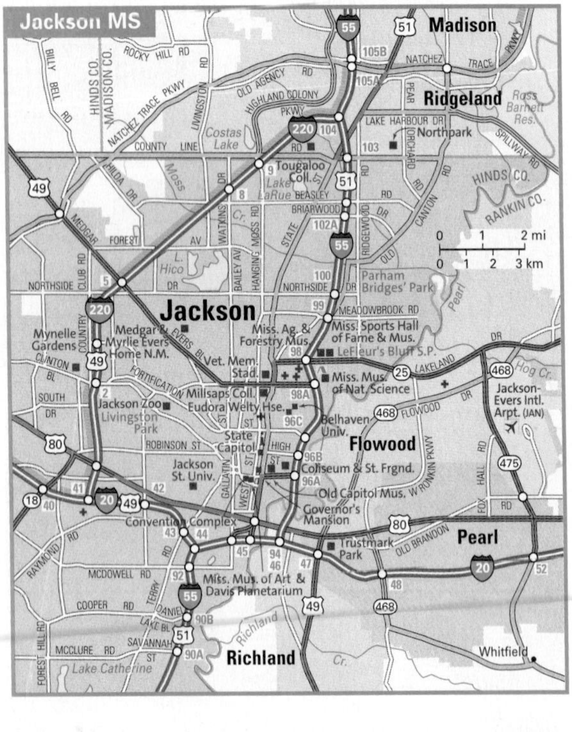
Jackson MS
Madison
Ridgeland
Jackson
Flowood
Pearl
Richland
Northpark
Tougaloo Coll.
Mynelle Gardens
Medgar & Myrlie Evers Home N.M.
Miss. Ag. & Forestry Mus.
Miss. Sports Hall of Fame & Mus.
LeFleur's Bluff S.P.
Millsaps Coll.
Eudora Welty Hse.
Jackson Zoo
Livingston Park
Miss. Mus. of Nat. Science
Belhaven Univ.
State Capitol
Jackson St. Univ.
Coliseum & St. Frgnd.
Old Capitol Mus.
Governor's Mansion
Convention Complex
Trustmark Park
Miss. Mus. of Art & Davis Planetarium
Jackson-Evers Intl. Arpt. (JAN)
Whitfield
Parham Bridges' Park
Costas Lake
Lake Hico
0 1 2 mi
0 1 2 3 km

Iota LA 133 E2
Iowa LA 133 D2
Iowa City IA 87 F2
Iowa Colony TX 132 A4
Iowa Co. IA 87 E2
Iowa Co. WI 74 A3
Iowa Falls IA 73 D4
Iowa Park TX 59 D1
Ipswich MA 151 F1
Ipswich SD 27 D2
Iraan TX 60 A1
Iredell Co. NC 112 A4
Irene SD 35 E1
Ireton IA 35 F1
Irion Co. TX 58 B4
Irmo SC 122 A3
Iron City TN 119 E2
Iron Co. MI 68 C1
Iron Co. MO 108 A1
Iron Co. UT 39 D4
Iron Co. WI 68 A1
Irondale AL 119 F4
Irondequoit NY 78 C3
Iron Gate VA 112 B1
Iron Mtn. MI 68 C2
Iron Mtn. Lake MO 108 A1
Iron Ridge WI 74 C2
Iron River MI 68 C2
Ironton MN 64 B4
Ironton MO 108 A1
Ironton OH 101 D3
Ironwood MI 65 E4
Iroquois SD 27 E3
Iroquois Co. IL 89 D3
Irrigon OR 21 E1
Irvine CA 52 C3
Irvine KY 110 C1
Irving IL 98 B2
Irving TX 59 F2
Irvington IL 98 C3
Irvington KY 99 F4
Irvington NE 245 A1
Irvington NJ 148 A4
Irvington NY 148 B3
Irvington VA 113 F1
Irvona PA 92 B3
Irwin PA 92 A4
Irwin SC 122 B2
Irwin Co. GA 129 E4
Irwindale CA 228 E2
Irwinton GA 129 E2
Isabel SD 26 B2
Isabella Co. MI 76 A2
Isanti MN 67 D3
Isanti Co. MN 67 D2
Iselin NJ 147 E1
Ishpeming MI 65 F4
Islamorada FL 143 E4
Island KY 109 E1
Island City OR 21 F2
Island Co. WA 12 C2
Island Falls ME 85 D3
Island Hts. NJ 147 E3
Island Lake IL 74 C4
Island Park ID 23 F3
Island Park NY 147 F1
Island Pond VT 81 E1
Isla Vista CA 52 A2
Isle MN 67 D2
Isle of Hope GA 130 C3
Isle of Palms SC 131 D2
Isle of Wight VA 113 F2
Isle of Wight Co. VA 113 F2
Isleta NM 48 C3
Isleton CA 36 C3
Islip NY 149 D4
Isola MS 126 B1
Issaquah WA 12 C3
Issaquena Co. MS 126 A2
Italy TX 59 F3
Itasca IL 203 B3
Itasca TX 59 E3
Itasca Co. MN 64 B3
Itawamba Co. MS 119 D3
Ithaca MI 76 A3
Ithaca NY 79 D4
Itta Bena MS 118 B4
Iuka IL 98 C3
Iuka MS 119 D2
Iva SC 121 E3
Ivanhoe CA 45 D3
Ivanhoe MN 27 F3
Ivanhoe VA 112 A2
Ivey GA 129 E1
Ivins UT 38 C4
Ixonia WI 74 C3
Izard Co. AR 107 F4

J

Jacinto City TX 220 C2
Jack Co. TX 59 D2
Jackman ME 84 B4
Jackman Sta. ME 84 B4
Jackpot NV 30 C2
Jacksboro TN 110 C3
Jacksboro TX 59 D2
Jackson AL 127 E4
Jackson CA 36 C3
Jackson GA 129 D1
Jackson KY 111 D1
Jackson LA 134 A1
Jackson MI 76 A4
Jackson MN 72 B2
Jackson MS 126 B2
Jackson MO 108 B1
Jackson NC 113 E3
Jackson OH 101 D2
Jackson SC 130 B1
Jackson TN 118 C1
Jackson WI 74 C3
Jackson WY 23 F4
Jackson Ctr. OH 90 B4
Jackson Co. AL 120 A2
Jackson Co. AR 118 A1
Jackson Co. CO 33 D4
Jackson Co. FL 137 D1
Jackson Co. GA 121 D3
Jackson Co. IL 98 B4
Jackson Co. IN 99 F3
Jackson Co. IA 87 F1
Jackson Co. KS 96 A2
Jackson Co. KY 110 C1
Jackson Co. MI 76 A4
Jackson Co. MN 72 B2
Jackson Co. MS 135 D2
Jackson Co. MO 96 C3
Jackson Co. NC 121 E1
Jackson Co. OH 101 D3
Jackson Co. OK 50 C4
Jackson Co. OR 28 B1
Jackson Co. SD 26 B4
Jackson Co. TN 110 A3
Jackson Co. TX 61 F3
Jackson Co. WV 101 E3
Jackson Co. WI 67 F4
Jackson Par. LA 125 E2
Jacksons Gap AL 128 B1
Jacksonville AL 120 A4
Jacksonville AR 117 E2
Jacksonville FL 139 D2
Jacksonville IL 98 A1
Jacksonville MD 144 C1
Jacksonville NC 115 D4
Jacksonville OR 28 B2
Jacksonville PA 92 B4
Jacksonville TX 124 A3
Jacksonville VT 94 C1
Jacksonville Beach FL 139 D2
Jacobstown NJ 147 D2
Jacobus PA 103 E1

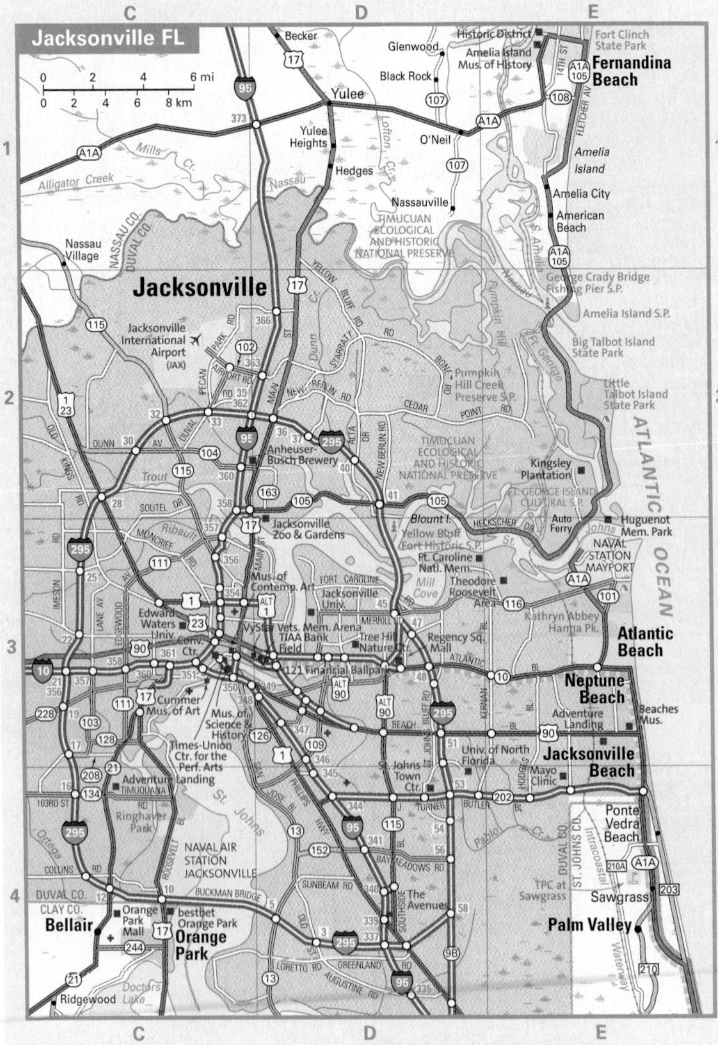
Jacksonville FL
C
D
E
1
2
3
4
0 2 4 6 mi
0 2 4 6 8 km
Becker
Glenwood
Historic District
Amelia Island Mus. of History
Fernandina Beach
Black Rock
Yulee
Yulee Heights
O'Neil
Hedges
Nassauville
Amelia Island
Amelia City
American Beach
Timucuan Ecological and Historic National Preserve
Nassau Village
Jacksonville
Jacksonville International Airport (JAX)
George Crady Bridge Fishing Pier S.P.
Amelia Island S.P.
Big Talbot Island State Park
Little Talbot Island State Park
Pumpkin Hill Creek Preserve S.P.
Kingsley Plantation
Anheuser-Busch Brewery
Jacksonville Zoo & Gardens
Huguenot Mem. Park
Naval Station Mayport
Atlantic Ocean
Mus. of Contemp. Art
Jacksonville Univ.
Ft. Caroline Natl. Mem.
Theodore Roosevelt Area
Kathryn Abbey Hanna Pk.
Atlantic Beach
Edward Waters Univ.
TIAA Bank Field
Tree Hill Nature Ctr.
Regency Sq. Mall
121 Financial Ballpark
Neptune Beach
Beaches Mus.
Adventure Landing
Cummer Mus. of Art
Mus. of Science & History
Times-Union Ctr. for the Perf. Arts
Univ. of North Florida
Jacksonville Beach
Mayo Clinic
St. Johns Town Ctr.
Ponte Vedra Beach
Naval Air Station Jacksonville
Ringhaver Park
The Avenues
TPC at Sawgrass
Sawgrass
Palm Valley
Bellair
Orange Park Mall
Orange Park
Ridgewood
Doctors Lake
St. Johns R.
Duval Co.
Clay Co.
Nassau Co.
St. Johns Co.

Amelia City E1
American Beach E1
Atlantic Beach E3
Becker D1
Bellair C4
Black Rock D1
Fernandina Beach . . E1
Glenwood D1
Hedges D1
Jacksonville D2
Jacksonville Beach . E3
Nassau Vil. C1
Nassauville D1
Neptune Beach E3
O'Neil D1
Orange Park C4
Palm Valley E4
Ponte Vedra Beach . E4
Ridgewood C4
Sawgrass E4
Yulee D1
Yulee Hts. D1

Entries in **bold black** indicate counties or parishes.
Entries in **bold color** indicate cities with detailed inset maps.

Jaffrey NH 95 D1
Jal NM 57 F3
Jamaica Beach TX 132 B4
Jamesburg NJ 147 E2
James City NC 115 D3
James City Co. VA 113 F1
Jamesport MO 96 C1
Jamesport NY 149 E3
Jamestown CA 37 D3
Jamestown IN 99 E1
Jamestown KS 43 E1
Jamestown KY 110 B2
Jamestown MI 75 F3
Jamestown NY 92 B1
Jamestown NC 112 B4
Jamestown ND 19 D4
Jamestown OH 100 C1
Jamestown PA 91 F2
Jamestown RI 150 C4
Jamestown TN 110 B3
James Town WY 32 A3
Jamesville NC 113 F4
Jamul CA 53 D4
Jane Lew WV 102 A2
Janesville CA 29 D4
Janesville IA 73 D4
Janesville MN 72 C1
Janesville WI 74 B4
Jarales NM 48 C4
Jarratt VA 113 E2
Jarrell TX 61 E1
Jarrettsville MD 144 C1
Jasmine Estates FL 140 B2
Jasonville IN 99 E2
Jasper AL 119 E4
Jasper AR 107 D4
Jasper FL 138 B2
Jasper GA 120 C3
Jasper IN 99 E4
Jasper MN 27 F4
Jasper MO 106 C1
Jasper OR 20 B4
Jasper TN 120 A2
Jasper TX 132 C1
Jasper Co. GA 129 D1
Jasper Co. IL 99 D2
Jasper Co. IN 89 E3
Jasper Co. IA 87 D2
Jasper Co. MS 126 C3
Jasper Co. MO 106 C2
Jasper Co. SC 130 C3
Jasper Co. TX 132 C1
Jay FL 135 F1
Jay ME 82 B2
Jay OK 106 B3
Jay Co. IN 90 A4
Jayton TX 58 B2
Jeanerette LA 133 F3
Jean Lafitte LA 134 B3
Jeannette PA 92 A4
Jeddito AZ 47 F2
Jeff Davis Co. GA 129 F3
Jeff Davis Co. TX 62 B2
Jefferson GA 121 D3
Jefferson IA 86 B1
Jefferson LA 239 B1
Jefferson MA 150 B1
Jefferson NC 111 F3
Jefferson OH 91 F1
Jefferson OR 20 B3
Jefferson PA 103 E1
Jefferson SC 122 B2
Jefferson SD 35 F1
Jefferson TX 124 C2
Jefferson WI 74 B3
Jefferson City MO 97 E3
Jefferson City MT 15 E4
Jefferson City TN 111 D4
Jefferson Co. AL 119 F4
Jefferson Co. AR 117 F3
Jefferson Co. CO 41 E1
Jefferson Co. FL 137 E2
Jefferson Co. GA 129 F1
Jefferson Co. ID 23 E4
Jefferson Co. IL 98 C4
Jefferson Co. IN 100 A3
Jefferson Co. IA 87 E3
Jefferson Co. KS 96 A2
Jefferson Co. KY 100 A4
Jefferson Co. MS 126 A3
Jefferson Co. MO 98 A4
Jefferson Co. MT 23 E1
Jefferson Co. NE 35 F4
Jefferson Co. NY 79 E2
Jefferson Co. OH 91 F4
Jefferson Co. OK 59 E1
Jefferson Co. OR 20 C3
Jefferson Co. PA 92 B2
Jefferson Co. TN 111 D4
Jefferson Co. TX 132 C3
Jefferson Co. WA 12 B3
Jefferson Co. WV 103 D2
Jefferson Co. WI 74 C3
Jefferson Davis Co. MS 126 B4
Jefferson Davis Par. LA 133 E2
Jefferson Hts. NY 94 B2
Jefferson Hills PA 92 A4
Jefferson Par. LA 134 B3
Jeffersontown KY 100 A4
Jefferson Valley NY 148 B2
Jeffersonville GA 129 E2
Jeffersonville IN 100 A4
Jeffersonville KY 100 C4
Jeffersonville OH 100 C1
Jeffersonville PA 248 A1
Jeffersonville VT 81 D1
Jellico TN 110 C3
Jemez Pueblo NM 48 C3
Jemez Sprs. NM 48 C2
Jemison AL 127 F1
Jena LA 125 E4
Jenison MI 75 F3
Jenkins KY 111 E2
Jenkins Co. GA 129 F2
Jenkintown PA 146 C2
Jenks OK 51 F2
Jennerstown PA 92 B4
Jennings FL 137 F2
Jennings LA 133 E2
Jennings MO 256 B1
Jennings Co. IN 100 A3
Jenny Lind AR 116 C1
Jensen Beach FL 141 E4
Jerauld Co. SD 27 D3
Jericho NY 148 C4
Jericho VT 81 D2
Jermyn PA 93 F2
Jerome AZ 47 D4
Jerome ID 30 C1
Jerome PA 92 B4
Jerome Co. ID 31 D1
Jersey City NJ 148 B4
Jersey Co. IL 98 A2
Jersey Shore PA 93 D2
Jersey Vil. TX 132 A3
Jerseyville IL 98 A2
Jerseyville NJ 147 E2
Jerusalem RI 150 C4
Jessamine Co. KY 100 B4
Jessup MD 144 C2
Jessup PA 93 F2
Jesup GA 130 A4
Jesup IA 73 D4
Jetmore KS 42 C3
Jewell IA 72 C4
Jewell KS 43 E1
Jewell Co. KS 43 E1
Jewett OH 91 F4
Jewett TX 59 F4
Jewett City (Griswold) CT 149 F1
Jim Hogg Co. TX 63 E3
Jim Thorpe PA 93 F3
Jim Wells Co. TX 63 E2
Joanna SC 121 F3
Joaquin TX 124 C3
Jo Daviess Co. IL 74 A4
John Day OR 21 F3
Johns Island SC 131 D2
Johnson AR 106 C4
Johnson VT 81 E2
Johnsonburg PA 92 B2
Johnson City KS 42 B4
Johnson City NY 93 E1
Johnson City OR 251 D3
Johnson City TN 111 E3
Johnson City TX 61 D1
Johnson Co. AR 117 D1
Johnson Co. GA 129 F2
Johnson Co. IL 108 C1
Johnson Co. IN 99 F2
Johnson Co. IA 87 F2
Johnson Co. KS 96 B3
Johnson Co. KY 111 D1
Johnson Co. MO 96 C3
Johnson Co. NE 35 F4
Johnson Co. TN 111 F3
Johnson Co. TX 59 E3
Johnson Co. WY 25 D4
Johnson Creek WI 74 C3
Johnsonville SC 122 C4
Johnston IA 86 C2
Johnston SC 121 F4
Johnston City IL 108 C1
Johnston Co. NC 113 D4
Johnston Co. OK 51 F4
Johnstown CO 33 E4
Johnstown NY 79 F3
Johnstown OH 91 D4
Johnstown PA 92 B4
Joiner AR 118 B1
Joliet IL 89 D2
Joliet MT 24 B2
Jollyville TX 61 E1
Jones OK 51 E3
Jonesboro AR 108 A4
Jonesboro GA 120 C4
Jonesboro IL 108 C1
Jonesboro IN 89 F4
Jonesboro LA 125 E3
Jonesborough TN 111 E3
Jonesburg MO 97 F3
Jones Co. GA 129 D1
Jones Co. IA 87 F1
Jones Co. MS 126 C4
Jones Co. NC 115 D3
Jones Co. SD 26 C4
Jones Co. TX 58 C2
Jones Creek TX 132 A4
Jonesport ME 83 E2
Jonestown MS 118 A3
Jonestown PA 93 E4
Jonestown TX 61 E1
Jonesville LA 125 F4
Jonesville MI 90 B1
Jonesville NC 112 A3
Jonesville SC 121 F2
Jonesville VT 81 D2
Jonesville VA 111 D3
Joplin MO 106 B2
Joplin MT 15 F2
Joppatowne MD 145 D1
Jordan MN 66 C4
Jordan MT 17 D3
Jordan NY 79 D3
Joseph OR 22 A2
Joseph City AZ 47 F3
Josephine TX 59 F2
Josephine Co. OR 28 B2
Joshua TX 59 E3
Joshua Tree CA 53 E2
Jourdanton TX 61 D3
Juab Co. UT 39 D1
Judith Basin Co. MT 16 A3
Judsonia AR 117 F1
Julesburg CO 34 A3
Juliaetta ID 14 B4
Julian CA 53 D4
Julian NC 112 B4
Jumpertown MS 119 D2
Junction TX 60 C1
Junction UT 39 E3
Junction City AR 125 E1
Junction City KS 43 F2
Junction City KY 110 B1
Junction City LA 125 E1
Junction City OH 101 E1
Junction City OR 20 B3
Juneau AK 155 E4
Juneau WI 74 C2
Juneau Co. WI 74 A1
Juniata NE 35 D4
Juniata Co. PA 93 D3
Junior WV 102 A2
Juno Beach FL 141 F4
Jupiter FL 141 F4
Jupiter Island FL 141 F4
Jurupa Valley CA 229 H3
Justice IL 203 D5
Justin TX 59 E2
Justus PA 261 E1

K

Kaaawa HI 152 A2
Kaanapali HI 153 D1
Kadoka SD 26 B4
Kahaluu HI 152 A3
Kahoka MO 87 E4
Kahuku HI 152 A2
Kahului HI 153 D1
Kaibab AZ 47 D1
Kaibito AZ 47 E1
Kailua HI 152 B3
Kailua-Kona HI 153 E3
Kake AK 155 F4
Kalaheo HI 152 B1
Kalama WA 20 C1
Kalamazoo MI 75 F4
Kalamazoo Co. MI 75 F4
Kalaoa HI 153 E3
Kalaupapa HI 152 C3
Kalawao Co. HI 152 C3
Kaleva MI 75 F1
Kalida OH 90 B3
Kalihiwai HI 152 B1
Kalispell MT 15 D2
Kalkaska MI 69 F4
Kalkaska Co. MI 70 B4
Kalona IA 87 E2
Kamas UT 31 F4
Kamiah ID 22 B1
Kanab UT 47 D1
Kanabec Co. MN 67 D2
Kanarraville UT 39 D4
Kanawha IA 72 C3
Kanawha WV 101 F2
Kanawha Co. WV 101 F4
Kandiyohi MN 66 B3
Kandiyohi Co. MN 66 B3
Kane PA 92 B2
Kane Co. IL 88 C1
Kane Co. UT 39 E4
Kaneohe HI 152 A3
Kankakee IL 89 D3
Kankakee Co. IL 89 D2
Kannapolis NC 122 B1
Kanopolis KS 43 E2
Kanosh UT 39 D2
Kansas IL 99 D1
Kansas OK 106 B3
Kansas City KS 96 B2
Kansas City MO 96 B2
Kapaa HI 152 B1
Kapaau HI 153 E2
Kaplan LA 133 E3
Karlstad MN 19 F2
Karnak IL 108 C2
Karnes City TX 61 E3
Karnes Co. TX 61 E3
Karns TN 110 C4
Kasigluk AK 154 B3
Kasota MN 72 C1
Kasson IN 99 D4
Kasson MN 73 D1
Kathleen FL 140 C2
Kathleen GA 129 D2
Katonah NY 148 C2
Katy TX 132 A3
Kauai Co. HI 152 B1
Kaufman TX 59 F2
Kaufman Co. TX 59 F3
Kaukauna WI 74 C1
Kaumakani HI 152 B1
Kaunakakai HI 152 C3
Kawkawlin MI 76 B2
Kaycee WY 25 D4
Kay Co. OK 51 E1
Kayenta AZ 47 F1
Kaysville UT 31 E3
Keaau HI 153 F3
Kealakekua HI 153 E3
Keams Canyon AZ 47 F2
Keansburg NJ 147 E1
Kearney MO 96 B2
Kearney NE 35 D4
Kearney Co. NE 35 D4
Kearneysville WV 103 D2
Kearns UT 257 A2
Kearny AZ 55 D2
Kearny NJ 148 B4
Kearny Co. KS 42 B3
Keauhou HI 153 E3
Keavy KY 110 C2
Kechi KS 43 E4
Keedysville MD 144 A1
Keegan ME 85 E1
Keego Harbor MI 210 A1
Keene NH 95 D1
Keene TX 59 E3
Keener NC 123 E2
Keenesburg CO 41 E1
Keeseville NY 81 D2
Keewatin MN 64 B3
Keiser AR 108 B4
Keith Co. NE 34 B3
Keithsburg IL 87 F3
Keizer OR 20 B2
Kekaha HI 152 B1
Keller TX 59 E2
Kellogg ID 14 B3
Kellogg IA 87 D1
Kellyville OK 51 F2
Kelseyville CA 36 B2
Kelso MO 108 B2
Kelso WA 20 B1
Kemah TX 132 B3
Kemblesville PA 146 B4
Kemmerer WY 31 F2
Kemp TX 59 F3
Kemper Co. MS 127 D2
Kempner TX 59 E4
Kenai AK 154 C3
Kenansville NC 123 E2
Kenbridge VA 113 D2
Kendall FL 143 E2
Kendall NY 78 B3
Kendall Co. IL 88 C2
Kendall Co. TX 61 D2
Kendall Park NJ 147 D1
Kendallville IN 90 A2
Kendrick FL 138 C4
Kendrick ID 14 B4
Kenedy TX 61 E3
Kenedy Co. TX 63 F3
Kenefick TX 132 B2
Kenesaw NE 35 D4
Kenilworth IL 203 D2
Kenilworth NJ 240 A4
Kenilworth PA 146 B2
Kenly NC 123 E1
Kenmare ND 18 B1
Kenmore NY 78 A3
Kenmore WA 262 B2
Kennebec SD 26 C4
Kennebec Co. ME 82 B2
Kennebunk ME 82 B4
Kennebunkport ME 82 B4
Kennedale TX 207 B3
Kennedy AL 119 D4
Kenner LA 134 B3
Kennesaw GA 120 C3
Kenneth City FL 266 A3
Kennett MO 108 B3
Kennett Square PA 146 B3
Kennewick WA 21 E1
Keno OR 28 C2
Kenosha WI 75 D4
Kenosha Co. WI 74 C4
Kenova WV 101 D4
Kensett AR 117 F1
Kensington CA 259 C2
Kensington CT 149 E1
Kensington KS 43 D1
Kensington MD 270 C1
Kensington NY 241 G2
Kensington Park FL 266 C5
Kent CT 94 B3
Kent OH 91 E3
Kent WA 12 C3
Kent City MI 75 F3
Kent Co. DE 145 E3
Kent Co. MD 145 D2
Kent Co. MI 75 F3
Kent Co. RI 150 C3
Kent Co. TX 58 B2
Kentfield CA 259 A1
Kentland IN 89 D3
Kenton DE 145 E2
Kenton KY 100 B3
Kenton OH 90 C3
Kenton TN 108 C3
Kenton Co. KY 100 B2
Kentwood LA 134 B1
Kentwood MI 75 F3
Kenvil NJ 148 A3
Kenwood MD 193 D2
Kenwood OH 204 C2
Kenwood Beach MD 144 C4
Kenyon MN 73 D1
Keokuk IA 87 F4
Keokuk Co. IA 87 E2
Keosauqua IA 87 E3
Keota IA 87 E2
Keota OK 116 B1
Kerens TX 59 F3
Kerhonkson NY 94 A3
Kerkhoven MN 66 B3
Kerman CA 44 C3
Kermit TX 57 F3
Kern Co. CA 45 D4
Kernersville NC 112 B4
Kernville CA 45 E4
Kerr Co. TX 60 C2
Kerrville TX 60 C2
Kersey CO 33 E4
Kershaw SC 122 B2
Kershaw Co. SC 122 B3
Keshena WI 68 C4
Ketchikan AK 155 E4
Ketchum ID 22 C4
Kettering OH 100 B1
Kettle Falls WA 13 F1
Kettleman City CA 44 C3
Kevil KY 108 C2
Kewanee IL 88 A2
Kewanna IN 89 E3
Kewaskum WI 74 C2
Kewaunee WI 75 D1
Kewaunee Co. WI 69 D4
Keweenaw Co. MI 65 F3
Keya Paha Co. NE 35 D1
Key Biscayne FL 143 F2
Key Colony Beach FL 143 D4
Keyes CA 36 C4
Key Largo FL 143 E3
Keyport NJ 147 E1
Keys OK 106 B4
Keyser WV 102 C2
Keystone CO 41 D1
Keystone IA 87 E1
Keystone SD 25 F4
Keystone WV 111 F1
Keystone Hts. FL 139 D3
Keysville VA 113 D2
Keytesville MO 97 D2
Key West FL 142 C4
Kezar Falls ME 82 A3
Kiamesha Lake NY 148 A1
Kiawah Island SC 131 D2
Kibler AR 116 C1
Kidder Co. ND 18 C4
Kiefer OK 51 F2

Jefferson City MO
Jefferson City
Jefferson City Mem. Airport (JEF)
State Capitol & State Mus.
Jefferson Landing State Hist. Site
Cole Co. Hist. Mus.
Runge Cons. Nature Center
Veterinary Museum
Memorial Park
Washington Park
Sunset Lake
Hough Park
Lincoln Univ.
Natl. Cemetery
Ellis-Porter/ Riverside Park
Miller Perf. Arts Ctr.
Missouri
CALLAWAY CO.
COLE CO.
KATY TRAIL S.P.
0 0.5 1 mi
0 0.5 1 km

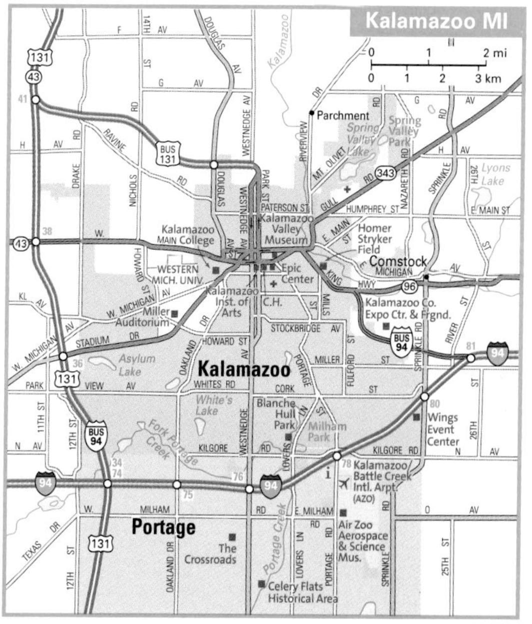
Kalamazoo MI
Kalamazoo
Portage
Comstock
Parchment
Kalamazoo Valley Museum
Kalamazoo College
Western Mich. Univ.
Kalamazoo Inst. of Arts
Epic Center
Miller Auditorium
Homer Stryker Field
Kalamazoo Co. Expo Ctr. & Frgnd.
Wings Event Center
Kalamazoo/Battle Creek Intl. Arpt. (AZO)
Air Zoo Aerospace & Science Mus.
The Crossroads
Celery Flats Historical Area
Spring Valley Park
Asylum Lake
Milham Park
Blanche Hull Park
0 1 2 mi
0 1 2 3 km

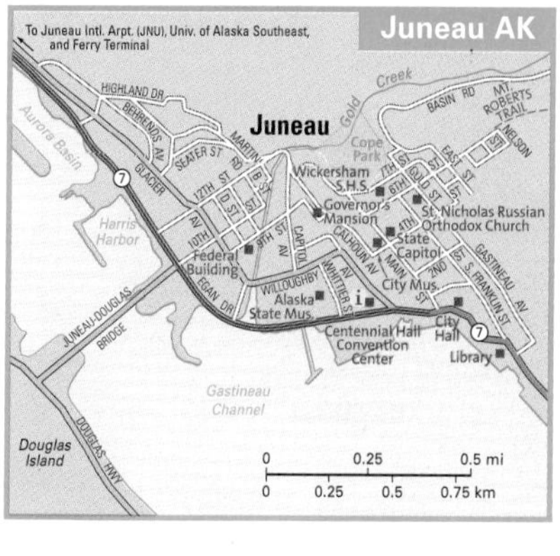
Juneau AK
To Juneau Intl. Arpt. (JNU), Univ. of Alaska Southeast, and Ferry Terminal
Juneau
Wickersham S.H.S.
Governor's Mansion
St. Nicholas Russian Orthodox Church
State Capitol
City Mus.
Alaska State Mus.
Centennial Hall Convention Center
City Hall
Library
Federal Building
Harris Harbor
Aurora Basin
Gastineau Channel
Douglas Island
0 0.25 0.5 mi
0 0.25 0.5 0.75 km

Figures after entries indicate page number and grid reference.

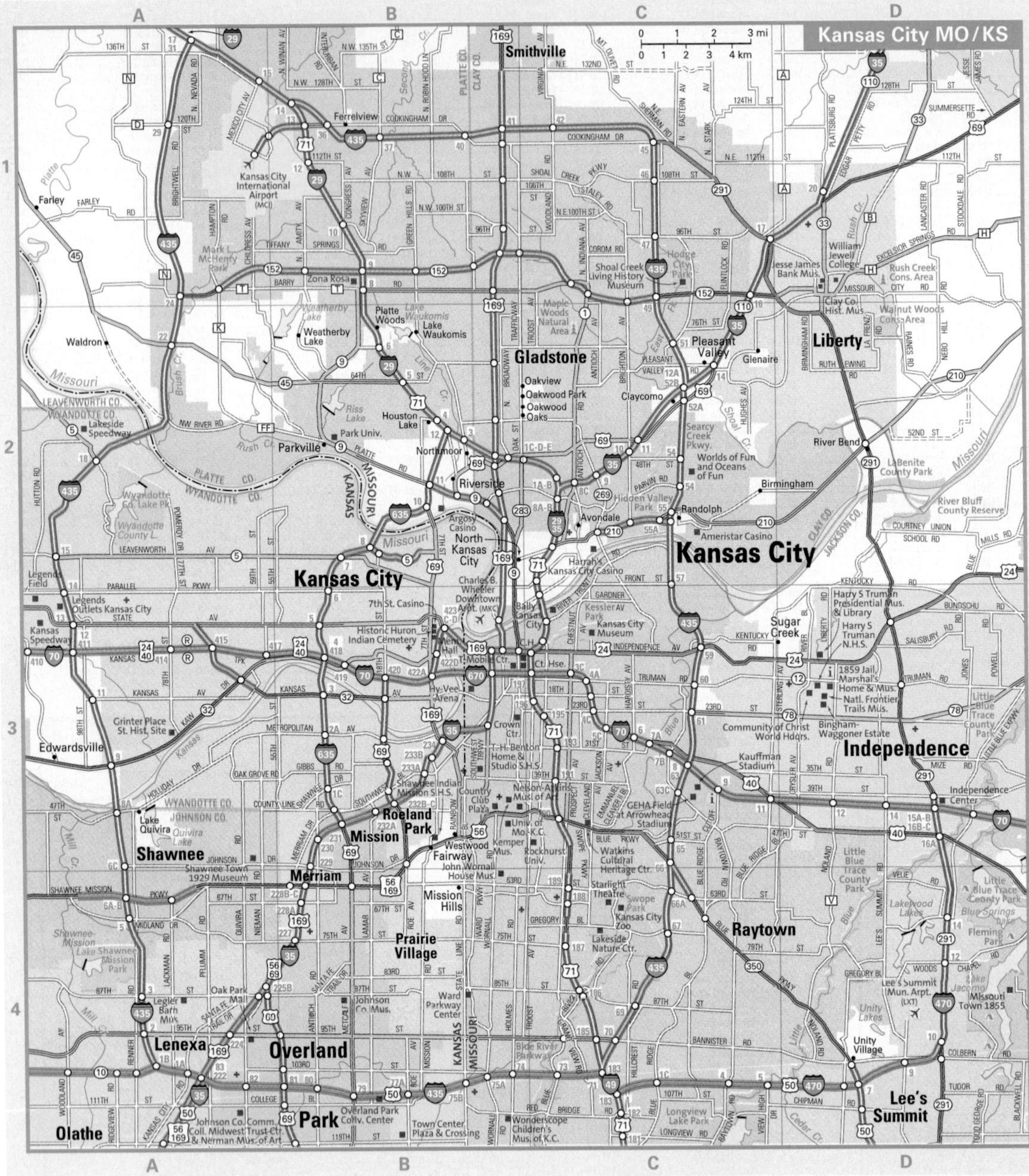
Kansas City MO / KS
A
B
C
D
1
2
3
4
Smithville
Ferrelview
Kansas City International Airport (MCI)
Farley
Waldron
Platte Woods
Lake Waukomis
Weatherby Lake
Gladstone
Oakview
Oakwood Park
Oakwood
Oaks
Houston Lake
Northmoor
Parkville
Riverside
Claycomo
Pleasant Valley
Glenaire
Liberty
River Bend
Birmingham
Avondale
Randolph
North Kansas City
Kansas City
Sugar Creek
Independence
Edwardsville
Lake Quivira
Shawnee
Roeland Park
Mission
Merriam
Fairway
Mission Hills
Prairie Village
Raytown
Lenexa
Overland Park
Olathe
Unity Village
Lee's Summit
Missouri
Kansas

Avondale C2
Birmingham C2
Claycomo C2
Countryside B4
Edwardsville. A3
Fairway B3
Farley. A1
Ferrelview. B1
Gladstone C2
Glenaire C2
Houston Lake. B2
Independence D3
Kansas City, KS B2
Kansas City, MO C2
Lake Quivira. A3
Lake Waukomis. B2
Lees Summit D4
Lenexa. A4
Liberty. D2
Merriam B4
Mission B3
Mission Hills B4
N. Kansas City. B2
Northmoor B2
Oaks. C2
Oakview C2
Oakwood. C2
Oakwood Park. C2
Olathe A4
Overland Park B4
Parkville B2
Platte Woods. B2
Pleasant Valley C2
Prairie Vil.. . . . . B4
Randolph. C2
Raytown C4
River Bend D2
Riverside. B2
Roeland Park. B3
Shawnee. A3
Smithville C1
Sugar Creek D3
Unity Vil.. . . . . D4
Waldron A2
Weatherby Lake B2
Westwood B3

Kiel WI **74** C2
Kiester MN **72** C2
Kihei HI **153** D1
Kilauea HI **152** B1
Kilbourne LA **125** F1
Kildeer IL **203** B2
Kilgore TX **124** B2
Killbuck OH **91** E4
Killdeer ND **18** A3
Kill Devil Hills NC **115** F2
Killeen TX **59** E4
Killen AL **119** E2
Killian LA **134** B2
Killona LA **239** A1
Kilmarnock VA **113** F1
Kilmichael MS **118** C4
Kiln MS **134** C2
Kimball MN **66** C3
Kimball NE **33** F3
Kimball SD **27** D4
Kimball TN **120** A2
Kimball WV **111** F1
Kimball Co. NE **33** F3
Kimberling City MO **107** D3
Kimberly AL **119** F4
Kimberly ID **30** C1
Kimberly WI **74** C1
Kimberton PA **146** B2
Kimble Co. TX **60** C1
Kincaid IL **98** B1
Kinde MI **76** C1
Kinder LA **133** E2
Kinderhook NY **94** B2
Kindred ND **19** E4
King NC **112** A3
King WI **74** B1
King and Queen Co. VA **113** F1
King and Queen C.H. VA **113** F1
King City CA **44** B3
King City MO **86** B4
King City OR **251** C3
King Co. TX **58** C1
King Co. WA **12** C3
King Cove AK **154** B4
Kingfield ME **82** B1
Kingfisher OK **51** E2
Kingfisher Co. OK **51** E2
King George VA **103** E4
King George Co. VA **103** E4
Kingman AZ **46** B3
Kingman IN **99** E1
Kingman KS **43** E4
Kingman Co. KS **43** E4
King of Prussia PA **146** C2
King Salmon AK **154** B3
Kings Beach CA **37** D2
Kingsburg CA **45** D3
Kingsbury TX **61** E2
Kingsbury Co. SD **27** E3
Kings Co. CA **44** C3
Kings Co. NY **147** F1
Kingsford MI **68** C2
Kingsford Hts. IN **89** E2
Kingsland AR **117** E4
Kingsland GA **139** D1
Kingsland TX **61** D1
Kingsley IA **35** F1
Kingsley MI **69** F4
Kings Mtn. NC **122** A1
Kings Park NY **149** D3
Kings Pt. NY **148** B4
Kingsport TN **111** E3
Kingston GA **120** B3
Kingston ID **14** B3
Kingston IL **88** C1
Kingston KY **110** C1
Kingston MA **151** E2
Kingston MI **76** C2
Kingston MO **96** C1
Kingston NH **95** E1
Kingston NJ **147** D1
Kingston NY **94** B2
Kingston OH **101** D2
Kingston OK **59** F1
Kingston PA **93** E2
Kingston RI **150** C4
Kingston TN **110** B4
Kingston WA **12** C3
Kingston Sprs. TN **109** E4
Kingstown MD **145** D2
Kingstown NC **121** F1
Kingstree SC **122** C4
Kingsville MD **193** E1
Kingsville TX **63** F2
King William VA **113** E1
King William Co. VA **113** E1

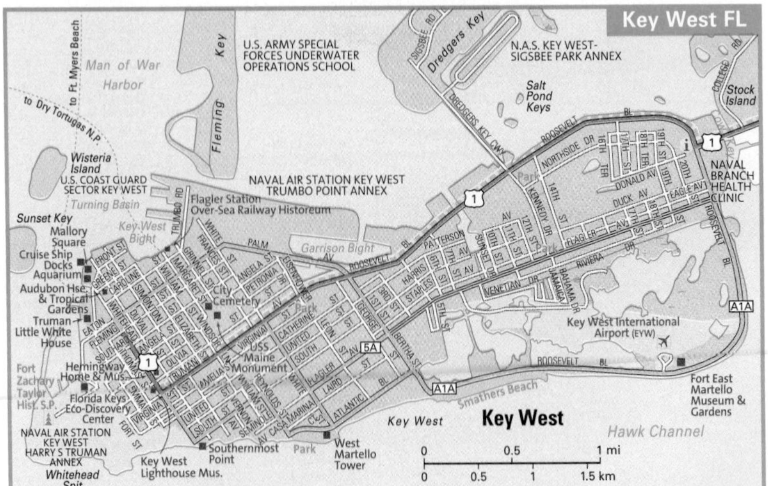
Key West FL
Man of War Harbor
Fleming Key
U.S. ARMY SPECIAL FORCES UNDERWATER OPERATIONS SCHOOL
N.A.S. KEY WEST-SIGSBEE PARK ANNEX
Salt Pond Keys
Stock Island
Wisteria Island
U.S. COAST GUARD SECTOR KEY WEST
NAVAL AIR STATION KEY WEST TRUMBO POINT ANNEX
Flagler Station Over-Sea Railway Historeum
Sunset Key
Mallory Square
Cruise Ship Docks
Aquarium
Audubon Hse. & Tropical Gardens
Truman Little White House
City Cemetery
Garrison Bight
NAVAL BRANCH HEALTH CLINIC
Key West International Airport (EYW)
Fort Zachary Taylor Hist. S.P.
Hemingway Home & Mus.
Florida Keys Eco-Discovery Center
USS Maine Monument
NAVAL AIR STATION KEY WEST HARRY S TRUMAN ANNEX
Whitehead Spit
Key West Lighthouse Mus.
Southernmost Point
West Martello Tower
Smathers Beach
Fort East Martello Museum & Gardens
Key West
Hawk Channel

Entries in **bold black** indicate counties or parishes.
Entries in **bold color** indicate cities with detailed inset maps.

Kingwood TX 132 B3
Kingwood WV 102 B2
Kinmundy IL 98 C3
Kinnelon NJ 148 A3
Kinney Co. TX 60 B3
Kinsey AL 128 B4
Kinsley KS 43 D4
Kinsman OH 91 F2
Kinston AL 128 A4
Kinston NC 115 C3
Kinzers PA 146 A3
Kiowa CO 41 E2
Kiowa KS 51 D1
Kiowa OK 116 A2
Kiowa Co. CO 42 A3
Kiowa Co. KS 43 D4
Kiowa Co. OK 51 D3
Kipnuk AK 154 B3
Kirby TX 61 D3
Kirbyville TX 132 C1
Kirkland IL 88 C1
Kirkland WA 12 C3
Kirklin IN 89 F4
Kirksville MO 87 D4
Kirkwood DE 145 E1
Kirkwood IL 87 F3
Kirkwood MO 98 A3
Kirtland NM 48 B1
Kirtland OH 91 E2
Kiryas Joel NY 148 B2
Kismet KS 42 B4
Kissimmee FL 141 D2
Kit Carson Co. CO 41 F1
Kitsap Co. WA 12 C3
Kittanning PA 92 A3
Kittery ME 82 B4
Kittery Pt. ME 82 B4
Kittitas WA 13 D4
Kittitas Co. WA 13 D3
Kittredge CO 209 A4
Kittson Co. MN 19 F1
Kitty Hawk NC 115 F2
Klamath CA 28 A3
Klamath Co. OR 28 C2
Klamath Falls OR 28 C2
Klawock AK 155 E4
Kleberg Co. TX 63 F2
Klemme IA 72 C3
Klickitat WA 21 D1
Klickitat Co. WA 21 D1
Knightdale NC 113 D4
Knights FL 266 D1
Knightsen CA 36 C3
Knights Landing CA 36 B2
Knightstown IN 100 A1
Knightsville IN 99 E1
Knippa TX 60 C3
Knob Noster MO 96 C3
Knollcrest CT 148 C1
Knollwood CT 149 E2
Knott Co. KY 111 D1
Knox IN 89 E2
Knox PA 92 A2
Knox City TX 58 C1
Knox Co. IL 88 A3
Knox Co. IN 99 E3
Knox Co. KY 110 C2
Knox Co. ME 82 C2
Knox Co. MO 87 E4
Knox Co. NE 35 E1
Knox Co. OH 91 D4
Knox Co. TN 110 C4
Knox Co. TX 58 C1
Knoxville AR 117 D1
Knoxville GA 129 D2
Knoxville IL 88 A3
Knoxville IA 87 D2
Knoxville PA 93 D1
Knoxville TN 110 C4
Kodiak AK 154 C4
Kohler WI 75 D2
Kokomo IN 89 F4
Kolin LA 125 E4
Koloa HI 152 B1
Komatke AZ 54 C2
Konawa OK 51 F3
Koochiching Co. MN 64 B2
Koontz Lake IN 89 E2
Kooskia ID 22 B1
Kootenai ID 14 B2
Kootenai Co. ID 14 B3
Koppel PA 91 F3
Kopperston WV 111 F1
Kosciusko MS 126 C1
Kosciusko Co. IN 89 F2
Kossuth Co. IA 72 C3
Kotlik AK 154 B2
Kotzebue AK 154 B1
Kountze TX 132 C2
Kouts IN 89 E2
Kreamer PA 93 D3
Krebs OK 116 A2
Kremmling CO 41 D1
Kress TX 50 A4
Krotz Sprs. LA 133 F2
Krum TX 59 E2
Kualapuu HI 152 C3
Kulm ND 27 D1
Kulpmont PA 93 E3
Kulpsville PA 146 C2
Kuna ID 22 B4
Kure Beach NC 123 E3
Kurtistown HI 153 F3
Kuttawa KY 109 D2
Kutztown PA 146 B1
Kwethluk AK 154 B3
Kykotsmovi Vil. AZ 47 E2
Kyle SD 26 B4
Kyle TX 61 E2

L

Labadieville LA 134 A3
La Barge WY 32 A2
LaBelle FL 141 D4
La Belle MO 87 E4
Labette Co. KS 106 A2
La Blanca TX 63 E4
La Cañada Flintridge CA 228 D1
Lac du Flambeau WI 68 A2
La Center KY 108 C2
La Center WA 20 C1
Lacey WA 12 C4
Laceys Spr. AL 119 F2
La Cienega NM 48 C3
Lackawanna NY 78 B3
Lackawanna Co. PA 93 F2
Laclede Co. MO 107 D1
Lacombe LA 134 C2
Lacon IL 88 B3
Lacona NY 79 E2
Laconia NH 81 F3
La Conner WA 12 C2
Lacoochee FL 140 C1
LaCoste TX 61 D3
Lac qui Parle Co. MN 27 F2
La Crescent MN 73 F2
La Crescenta CA 228 D1
La Croft OH 91 F3
La Crosse IN 89 E2
La Crosse KS 43 D3
La Crosse VA 113 D3
La Crosse WI 73 F2
La Crosse Co. WI 73 F2
La Cygne KS 96 B4
Ladd IL 88 B2
Laddonia MO 97 F2
Ladera Hts. CA 228 C3
Ladoga IN 99 E1
Ladonia AL 128 C2
Ladonia TX 59 F1
Ladson SC 131 D1
Ladue MO 256 B2
Lady Lake FL 140 C1
Ladysmith VA 103 D4
Ladysmith WI 67 F3
La Farge WI 73 F2
La Fargeville NY 79 E1
Lafayette AL 128 B1
Lafayette CA 259 D2
Lafayette CO 41 E1
LaFayette GA 120 B2
Lafayette IN 89 E4
Lafayette LA 133 F2
Lafayette MN 72 B1
Lafayette NJ 148 A3
Lafayette OR 20 B2
Lafayette TN 110 A3
Lafayette Co. AR 125 D1
Lafayette Co. FL 137 F3
Lafayette Co. MS 118 C3
Lafayette Co. MO 96 C2
Lafayette Co. WI 74 A4
Lafayette Par. LA 133 F2
La Feria TX 63 F4
Lafitte LA 134 B3
Laflin PA 261 B2
LaFollette TN 110 C3
La Fontaine IN 89 F3
Lafourche Par. LA 134 B4
Lago Vista TX 61 E1
La Grande OR 21 F2
LaGrange GA 128 C1
La Grange IL 203 C5
Lagrange IN 90 A2
La Grange KY 100 A3
La Grange MO 97 F1
La Grange NC 123 E1
LaGrange OH 91 D2
La Grange TX 61 F2
La Grange WY 33 F3
LaGrange Co. IN 90 A2
La Grange Park IL 203 C4
Lagrangeville NY 148 B1
La Grulla TX 63 E4
Laguna NM 48 B3
Laguna Beach CA 52 C3
Laguna Beach FL 136 C2
Laguna Hts. TX 63 F4
Laguna Hills CA 229 G5
Laguna Niguel CA 229 G6
Laguna Vista TX 63 F4
Laguna Woods CA 229 G5
Lagunitas CA 36 B3
La Habra CA 228 E3
La Habra Hts. CA 228 E3
Lahaina HI 153 D1
La Harpe IL 87 F3
La Harpe KS 96 A4
Lahoma OK 51 E2
Laie HI 152 A2
Laingsburg MI 76 A3
La Jara CO 41 D4
La Joya TX 63 E4
La Junta CO 41 F3
Lake MS 126 C2
Lake Alfred FL 140 C2
Lake Aluma OK 224 E2
Lake Andes SD 35 D1
Lake Ariel PA 93 F2
Lake Arrowhead CA 53 D2
Lake Arthur LA 133 E2
Lake Arthur NM 57 E2
Lake Barcroft VA 270 B4
Lake Barrington IL 203 B1
Lake Benton MN 27 F3
Lake Bluff IL 75 D4
Lake Butler FL 138 C3
Lake Carmel NY 148 C1
Lake Charles LA 133 D2
Lake City AR 108 A4
Lake City CO 40 C3
Lake City FL 138 C2
Lake City GA 190 D5
Lake City IA 72 B4
Lake City MI 75 F1

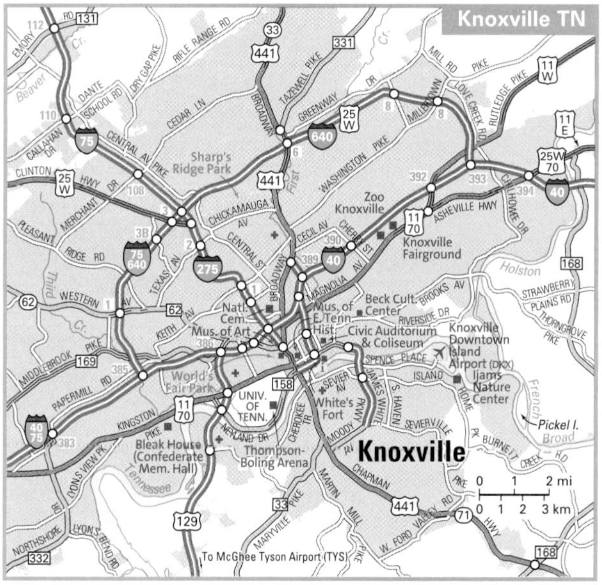
Knoxville TN
Knoxville

Bird in Hand C2
E. Petersburg A1
Lancaster B2
Landisville A1
Leacock C1
Leola C1
Millersville A2
Mountville A2
Neffsville B1
Rohrerstown A2
Salunga A1
Smoketown C2

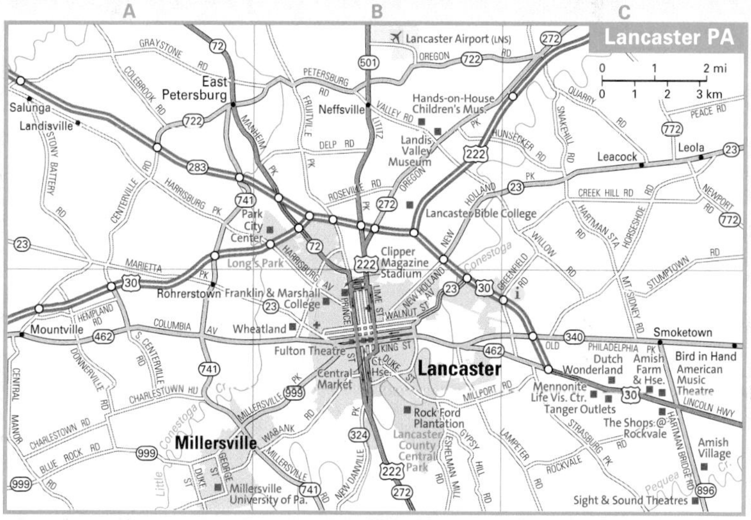
Lancaster PA
Lancaster
Millersville

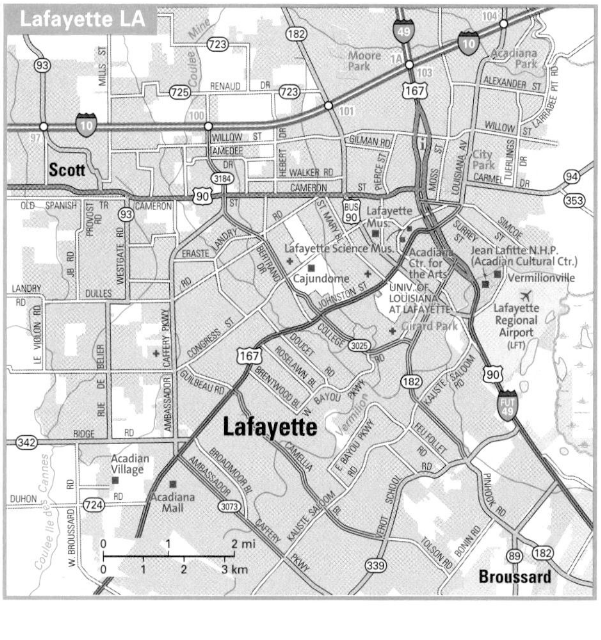
Lafayette LA
Lafayette
Scott
Broussard

Lansing MI
Lansing
East Lansing

Lake City MN 73 E1
Lake City PA 91 F1
Lake City SC 122 C4
Lake City TX 61 E4
Lake Clarke Shores FL 143 F1
Lake Co. CA 36 B2
Lake Co. CO 41 D2
Lake Co. FL 141 D1
Lake Co. IL 74 C4
Lake Co. IN 89 D2
Lake Co. MI 75 F1
Lake Co. MN 65 D3
Lake Co. MT 15 D3
Lake Co. OH 91 E1
Lake Co. OR 21 D4
Lake Co. SD 27 F3
Lake Co. TN 108 B3
Lake Crystal MN 72 C1
Lake Dallas TX 59 F2
Lake Delton WI 74 A2
Lake Elmo MN 235 E2
Lake Elsinore CA 53 D3
Lake Erie Beach NY 78 A4
Lakefield MN 72 A2
Lake Forest CA 229 G5
Lake Forest IL 75 D4
Lake Forest Park WA 262 B2
Lake Geneva WI 74 C4
Lake George NY 80 C4
Lake Grove NY 149 D3
Lake Hamilton AR 117 D3
Lake Hamilton FL 141 D2
Lake Havasu City AZ 46 B4
Lakehead CA 28 C4
Lake Helen FL 139 E4
Lakehills TX 61 D2

Figures after entries indicate page number and grid reference.

Lakehurst NJ 147 E3
Lake in the Hills IL 203 A2
Lake Isabella CA 45 E4
Lake Isabella MI 76 A2
Lake Jackson TX 132 A4
Lake Junaluska NC 121 E1
Lakeland FL 140 C2
Lakeland GA 137 F1
Lakeland MN 67 D4
Lakeland NY 265 A1
Lakeland TN 118 B1
Lakeland Vil. CA 229 J5
Lake Linden MI 65 F3
Lake Lotawana MO 96 C3
Lake Lure NC 121 F1
Lake Luzerne NY 80 C4
Lake Mary FL 141 D1
Lake Michigan Beach MI 89 E1
Lake Mills IA 72 C2
Lake Mills WI 74 B3
Lake Mohawk NJ 148 A3
Lake Mohegan NY 148 B2
Lakemont PA 92 C4
Lake Montezuma AZ 47 D4
Lakemoor IL 203 A1
Lakemore OH 188 B2
Lake Nebagamon WI 64 C4
Lake Norden SD 27 F3
Lake Odessa MI 75 F3
Lake of the Woods IL 88 C4
Lake of the Woods Co. MN 64 A1
Lake Orion MI 76 C4
Lake Oswego OR 20 C2
Lake Ozark MO 97 D4
Lake Panasoffkee FL 140 C1
Lake Park FL 141 F4
Lake Park GA 137 F1
Lake Park IA 72 A2
Lake Park MN 19 F4
Lake Peekskill NY 148 B2
Lake Placid FL 141 D3
Lake Placid NY 80 C2
Lake Pleasant NY 79 F2
Lake Pocotopaug CT 149 E1
Lakeport CA 36 A2
Lakeport MI 76 C3
Lakeport TX 124 B2
Lake Preston SD 27 E3
Lake Providence LA 126 A2
Lake Quivira KS 224 A3
Lake Ridge VA 144 A4
Lake St. Croix Beach MN 67 D4
Lake St. Louis MO 98 A3
Lakeshire MO 256 B3
Lake Shore MD 144 C2
Lake Shore MN 64 A4
Lakeside CA 53 D4
Lakeside CT 149 D1
Lakeside MT 15 D2
Lakeside OR 20 A4
Lakeside VA 113 E1
Lakeside City TX 59 D1
Lakeside Park KY 204 A3
Lakesite TN 120 B1
Lakes of the Four Seasons IN 89 D2
Lake Sta. IN 89 D2
Lake Stevens WA 12 C2
Lake Success NY 241 G3
Lake Summerset IL 74 B4
Lake Tanglewood TX 50 A3
Lake Tapawingo MO 96 C2
Laketon IN 89 F3
Lake View AL 127 F1
Lakeview AR 107 E3
Lake View AR 118 A3
Lakeview CA 229 K4
Lake View IA 72 B4
Lakeview MI 75 F2
Lake View NY 78 A4
Lakeview NY 241 G4
Lakeview OH 90 B4
Lakeview OR 29 D2
Lake View SC 122 C3
Lake Villa IL 74 C4
Lake Vil. AR 125 F1
Lake Vil. IN 89 D3
Lakeville CT 94 B2
Lakeville IN 89 F2
Lakeville MA 151 D3
Lakeville MN 67 D4
Lake Waccamaw NC 123 D3
Lake Wales FL 141 D2
Lake Waukomis MO 224 B2
Lakeway TX 61 E1
Lake Winnebago MO 96 B3
Lakewood CA 228 D4
Lakewood CO 41 E1
Lakewood IL 88 C1
Lakewood NJ 147 E2
Lakewood NY 92 B1
Lakewood OH 91 E2
Lakewood TN 109 F3
Lakewood WA 12 C3
Lakewood Club MI 75 E2
Lakewood Park FL 141 E3
Lakewood Park ND 19 D2
Lake Worth TX 207 A2
Lake Worth Beach FL 143 F1
Lake Wylie SC 122 A1
Lake Zurich IL 89 D1
Lakin KS 42 B3
Lakota ND 19 D2
La Luz NM 56 C2
Lamar AR 117 D1
Lamar CO 42 A3
Lamar MO 106 C1
Lamar SC 122 B3
Lamar Co. AL 119 D4
Lamar Co. GA 129 D1
Lamar Co. MS 126 C4
Lamar Co. TX 116 A4
La Marque TX 132 B4
Lamb Co. TX 50 A4
Lambert MS 118 B3
Lamberton MN 72 A1
Lambertville MI 90 C1
Lambertville NJ 147 D2
Lame Deer MT 25 D1
La Mesa CA 53 D4
La Mesa NM 56 C3
Lamesa TX 58 A2
La Mirada CA 228 E3
La Moille IL 88 B2
Lamoille Co. VT 81 E1
Lamoni IA 86 C3
Lamont CA 45 D4
Lamont IA 73 E4
Lamont OK 51 E1
La Monte MO 97 D3
LaMoure ND 19 D4
LaMoure Co. ND 19 D4
Lampasas TX 59 D4
Lampasas Co. TX 59 D4
Lampeter PA 146 A3
Lanai City HI 152 C4
Lanare CA 44 C3
Lanark IL 88 B1
Lanark PA 146 C1
Lanark Vil. FL 137 D3
Lancaster CA 52 C2
Lancaster KY 110 B1
Lancaster MA 150 C1
Lancaster MO 87 D4
Lancaster NH 81 F2
Lancaster NY 78 B3
Lancaster OH 101 D1
Lancaster PA 146 A3
Lancaster SC 122 B2
Lancaster TX 59 F2
Lancaster VA 113 F1
Lancaster WI 73 F3
Lancaster Co. NE 35 F3
Lancaster Co. PA 146 A3
Lancaster Co. SC 122 B2
Lancaster Co. VA 113 F1
Lander WY 32 B1
Lander Co. NV 30 A4
Landfall MN 235 E3
Landis NC 122 B1
Landisville PA 225 A1
Land O' Lakes FL 140 B2
Landover MD 270 E3
Landover Hills MD 271 F2
Landrum SC 121 F1
Lane SC 122 C4
Lane Co. KS 42 C3
Lane Co. OR 20 C4
Lanesboro MN 73 E2
Lanesboro PA 93 F1
Lanesborough MA 94 C1
Lanesville CT 148 C1
Lanesville IN 99 F4
Lanett AL 120 D2
Langdon ND 19 D1
Langdon Place KY 230 F1
Langford SD 27 E1
Langhorne PA 147 D2
Langlade Co. WI 68 B3
Langley OK 106 B3
Langley VA 270 B2
Langley WA 12 C2

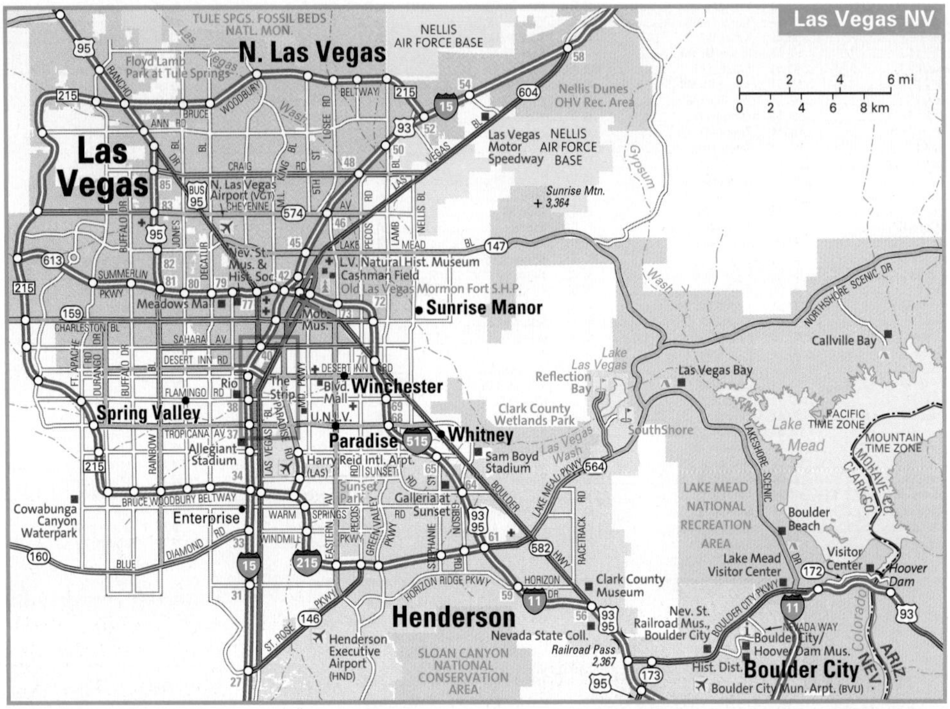
Las Vegas NV
N. Las Vegas
Las Vegas
NELLIS AIR FORCE BASE
TULE SPGS. FOSSIL BEDS NATL. MON.
Nellis Dunes OHV Rec. Area
Las Vegas Motor Speedway
Sunrise Mtn. 3,364
Sunrise Manor
Spring Valley
Winchester
Paradise
Whitney
Enterprise
Henderson
Boulder City
Lake Mead
LAKE MEAD NATIONAL RECREATION AREA
SLOAN CANYON NATIONAL CONSERVATION AREA
Harry Reid Intl. Arpt. (LAS)
Henderson Executive Airport (HND)
Allegiant Stadium
Hoover Dam
0 2 4 6 mi
0 2 4 6 8 km

Langley Park MD 270 D2
Langston OK 51 E2
Lanham MD 271 F2
Lanier Co. GA 137 F1
Lannon WI 234 A1
Lanoka Harbor NJ 147 E3
Lansdale PA 146 C2
Lansdowne MD 193 C3
Lansdowne PA 146 C3
L'Anse MI 65 F4
Lansford ND 18 B2
Lansford PA 93 E3
Lansing IA 73 F2
Lansing KS 96 B2
Lansing MI 76 A4
Lansing NY 79 D4
Lantana FL 143 F1
Laona WI 68 C3
La Palma CA 228 E4
La Paz IN 89 F2
La Paz Co. AZ 54 A1
Lapeer MI 76 C3
Lapeer Co. MI 76 C3
Lapel IN 89 F4
La Pine OR 21 D4
Laplace LA 134 B3
La Plata MD 144 B4
La Plata MO 97 E1
La Plata Co. CO 40 B4
Laporte CO 33 E4
La Porte IN 89 E2
Laporte PA 93 E2

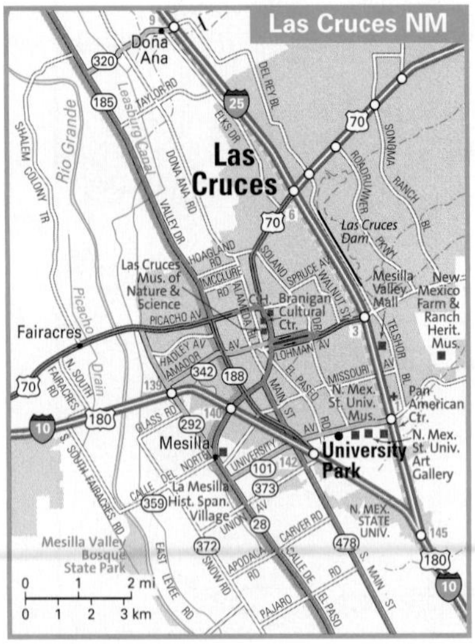
Las Cruces NM
Las Cruces
Doña Ana
Mesilla
University Park
Fairacres
Rio Grande
Las Cruces Dam
Mesilla Valley Mall
New Mexico Farm & Ranch Herit. Mus.
Branigan Cultural Ctr.
N. Mex. St. Univ. Mus.
Pan American Ctr.
N. MEX. STATE UNIV.
Mesilla Valley Bosque State Park
0 1 2 mi
0 1 2 3 km

La Porte TX 132 B3
La Porte City IA 73 E4
LaPorte Co. IN 89 E2
La Prairie MN 64 B3
La Pryor TX 60 C3
La Puente CA 228 E3
Lapwai ID 14 B4
La Quinta CA 53 E3
Laramie WY 33 E3
Laramie Co. WY 33 E3
Larchmont NY 241 F1
Larchwood IA 27 F4
Laredo TX 63 D2
Largo FL 140 B2
Largo MD 271 F3
Larimer Co. CO 33 E4
Larimore ND 19 E2
Larkspur CA 259 A1
Larksville PA 261 A1
Larned KS 43 D3
Larose LA 134 B3
La Rue OH 90 C4
Larue Co. KY 110 A1
La Sal UT 40 A3
La Salle CO 33 E4
LaSalle IL 88 B2
La Salle Co. IL 88 C2
La Salle Co. TX 60 C4
La Salle Par. LA 125 E3
Las Animas CO 41 F3
Las Animas Co. CO 41 F4
Lasara TX 63 E4
Las Cruces NM 56 C3
Las Lomas CA 236 E2
Lassen Co. CA 29 D4
Las Vegas NV 46 A2
Las Vegas NM 49 D3
Latah Co. ID 14 B4
Latham NY 188 E2
Lathrop CA 36 C4
Lathrop MO 96 B1
Lathrup Vil. MI 210 B2
Latimer IA 72 C4
Latimer MS 135 D2
Latimer Co. OK 116 B2
Laton CA 44 C3
Latrobe PA 92 A4
Latta OK 51 F4
Latta SC 122 C3
Lattingtown NY 148 C3
Lauderdale MN 235 C2
Lauderdale-by-the-Sea FL 233 C2
Lauderdale Co. AL 119 E2
Lauderdale Co. MS 127 D3
Lauderdale Co. TN 108 B4
Lauderdale Lakes FL 233 B2
Lauderhill FL 233 B2
Laughlin NV 46 B3
La Union NM 56 C3
Laura KY 111 E1
Laurel DE 145 E4
Laurel FL 140 B4
Laurel IN 100 A1
Laurel MD 144 B2
Laurel MS 126 C4
Laurel MT 24 B1
Laurel NE 35 F2
Laurel NY 149 E3
Laurel VA 113 E1
Laurel Bay SC 130 C2
Laurel Co. KY 110 C2
Laureldale NJ 147 D4
Laureldale PA 146 B1
Laurel Hill FL 136 B1
Laurel Hill NC 122 C2
Laurel Park NC 121 E1
Laurel Run PA 261 B2
Laurence Harbor NJ 147 E1
Laurens IA 72 B3
Laurens NY 79 F4
Laurens SC 121 F3
Laurens Co. GA 129 E3
Laurens Co. SC 121 F3
Laurinburg NC 122 C2
Laurium MI 65 F3
Lavaca AR 116 C1
Lavaca Co. TX 61 E3
Lava Hot Sprs. ID 31 E1
LaVale MD 102 C1
Lavalette WV 101 D4
Lavallette NJ 147 E3
La Vergne TN 109 F4
La Verkin UT 39 D4
La Verne CA 229 F2
Laverne OK 50 C1
La Vernia TX 61 D3
La Veta CO 41 E4
La Villa TX 63 E4
Lavina MT 24 B1
La Vista NE 35 F3
Lavonia GA 121 E3
Lawai HI 152 B1
Lawndale CA 228 C3
Lawndale NC 121 F1
Lawnside NJ 146 C3
Lawnton PA 218 C1
Lawrence IN 99 F1
Lawrence KS 96 A2
Lawrence MA 95 E1
Lawrence MI 89 F1
Lawrence NY 147 F1
Lawrenceburg IN 100 B2
Lawrenceburg KY 100 B4
Lawrenceburg TN 119 E1
Lawrence Co. AL 119 E3
Lawrence Co. AR 107 F4

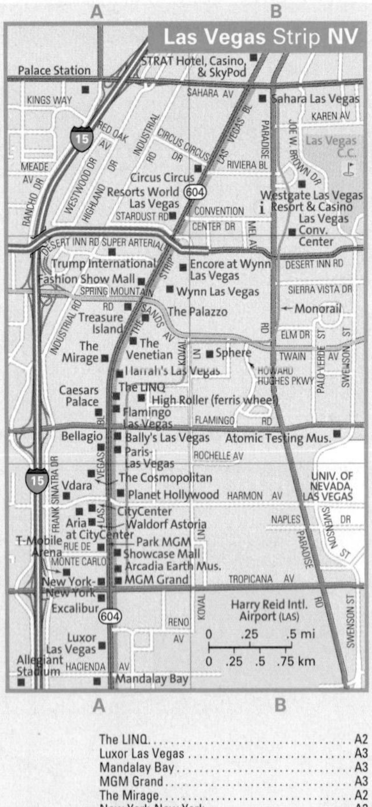
Las Vegas Strip NV
A
B
1
2
3
STRAT Hotel, Casino, & SkyPod
Palace Station
Sahara Las Vegas
Circus Circus
Resorts World Las Vegas
Westgate Las Vegas Resort & Casino
Las Vegas Conv. Center
Trump International
Fashion Show Mall
Encore at Wynn Las Vegas
Wynn Las Vegas
Treasure Island
The Palazzo
The Mirage
The Venetian
Sphere
Harrah's Las Vegas
Caesars Palace
The LINQ
High Roller (ferris wheel)
Flamingo Las Vegas
Bellagio
Bally's Las Vegas
Atomic Testing Mus.
Paris-Las Vegas
Vdara
The Cosmopolitan
Planet Hollywood
UNIV. OF NEVADA, LAS VEGAS
CityCenter
Aria at CityCenter
Waldorf Astoria
T-Mobile Arena
Park MGM
Showcase Mall
Arcadia Earth Mus.
New York-New York
MGM Grand
Excalibur
Harry Reid Intl. Airport (LAS)
Luxor Las Vegas
Allegiant Stadium
Mandalay Bay
0 .25 .5 mi
0 .25 .5 .75 km

POINTS OF INTEREST

Allegiant Stadium A3
Arcadia Earth Museum A3
Aria at CityCenter A3
Atomic Testing Museum B2
Bally's Las Vegas A2
Bellagio A2
Caesars Palace A2
Circus Circus B1
CityCenter A3
The Cosmopolitan A3
Encore at Wynn Las Vegas A2
Excalibur A3
Fashion Show Mall A2
Flamingo Las Vegas A2
Harrah's Las Vegas A2
Harry Reid Intl. Airport B3
High Roller (ferris wheel) A2
Las Vegas Convention Center B1
The LINQ A2
Luxor Las Vegas A3
Mandalay Bay A3
MGM Grand A3
The Mirage A2
New York-New York A3
Palace Station A1
The Palazzo A2
Paris-Las Vegas A2
Park MGM A3
Planet Hollywood A3
Resorts World Las Vegas A1
Sahara Las Vegas B1
Showcase Mall A3
STRAT Hotel, Casino, & SkyPod B1
T-Mobile Arena A3
Treasure Island A2
Trump International A2
Univ. of Nevada, Las Vegas B3
Vdara A3
The Venetian A2
Waldorf Astoria A3
Westgate Las Vegas Hotel & Casino B1
Wynn Las Vegas A2

Entries in **bold black** indicate counties or parishes.
Entries in **bold color** indicate cities with detailed inset maps.

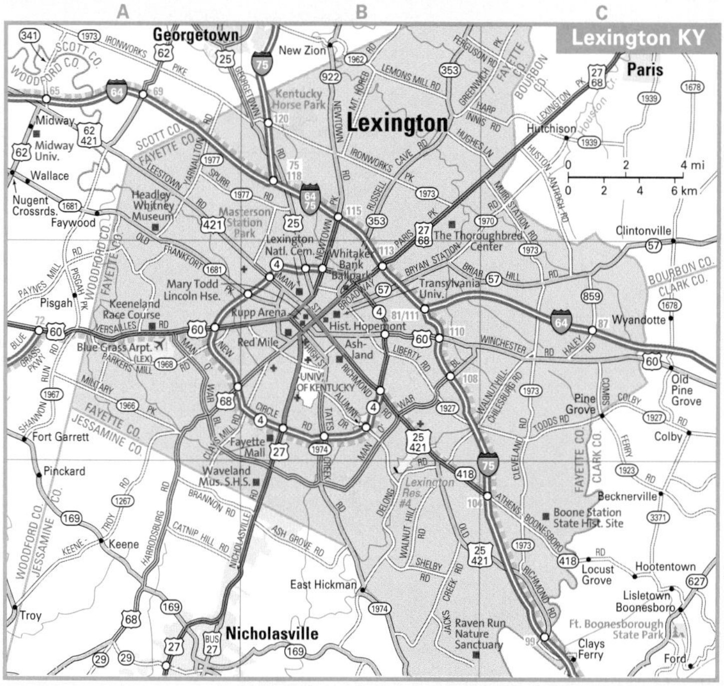

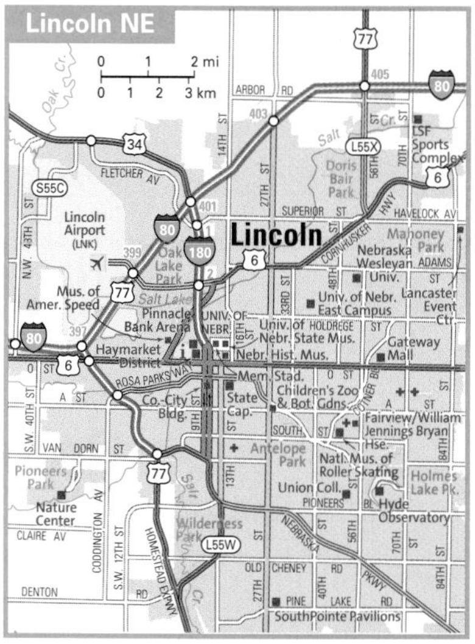

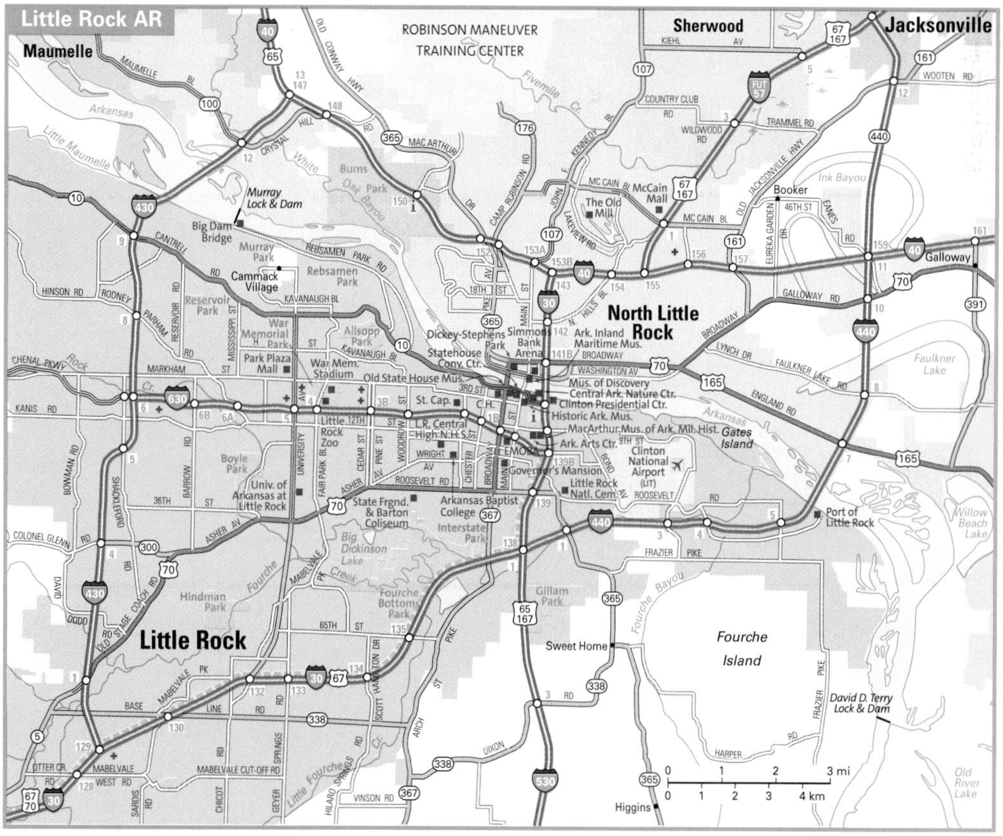

Figures after entries indicate page number and grid reference.

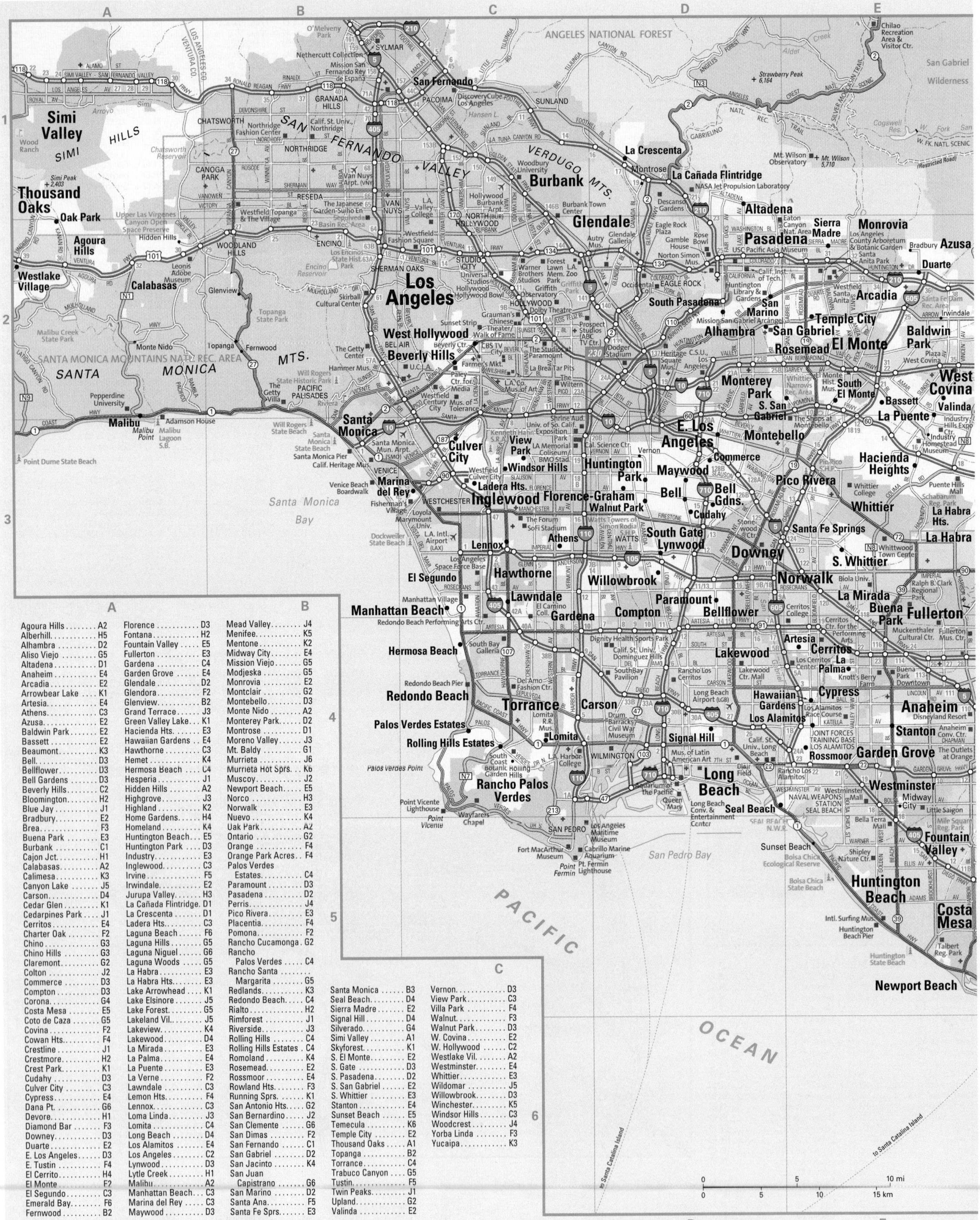
ANGELES NATIONAL FOREST
San Gabriel Wilderness
Simi Valley
Thousand Oaks
Oak Park
Agoura Hills
Westlake Village
Calabasas
Malibu
SANTA MONICA MTS.
SANTA MONICA MOUNTAINS NAT'L REC. AREA
CHATSWORTH
NORTHRIDGE
SAN FERNANDO VALLEY
San Fernando
SYLMAR
SUNLAND
La Crescenta
Montrose
La Cañada Flintridge
Burbank
VERDUGO MTS.
Glendale
Altadena
Pasadena
Sierra Madre
Monrovia
Azusa
Arcadia
Duarte
Los Angeles
West Hollywood
Beverly Hills
Santa Monica
Culver City
Marina del Rey
View Park
Windsor Hills
Ladera Hts.
Inglewood
Florence-Graham
Walnut Park
Huntington Park
Maywood
Bell
Bell Gdns.
Cudahy
Vernon
Commerce
E. Los Angeles
Montebello
Monterey Park
Alhambra
San Gabriel
Rosemead
Temple City
El Monte
South El Monte
Baldwin Park
West Covina
La Puente
Valinda
Hacienda Heights
Pico Rivera
Whittier
La Habra
La Habra Hts.
S. Whittier
Santa Fe Springs
Downey
South Gate
Lynwood
Athens
Lennox
El Segundo
Hawthorne
Lawndale
Manhattan Beach
Gardena
Compton
Willowbrook
Paramount
Bellflower
Norwalk
La Mirada
Buena Park
Fullerton
Cerritos
Artesia
Lakewood
La Palma
Hermosa Beach
Redondo Beach
Torrance
Carson
Lomita
Palos Verdes Estates
Rolling Hills Estates
Rancho Palos Verdes
Signal Hill
Long Beach
Seal Beach
Hawaiian Gardens
Los Alamitos
Cypress
Rossmoor
Anaheim
Stanton
Garden Grove
Westminster
Midway City
Fountain Valley
Huntington Beach
Costa Mesa
Newport Beach
Santa Monica Bay
San Pedro Bay
PACIFIC OCEAN
to Santa Catalina Island
0 5 10 mi
0 5 10 15 km

Agoura Hills A2
Alberhill H5
Alhambra D2
Aliso Viejo G5
Altadena D1
Anaheim E4
Arcadia E2
Arrowbear Lake K1
Artesia E4
Athens C3
Azusa E2
Baldwin Park E2
Bassett E2
Beaumont K3
Bell D3
Bellflower D3
Bell Gardens D3
Beverly Hills C2
Bloomington H2
Blue Jay J1
Bradbury E2
Brea F3
Buena Park E3
Burbank C1
Cajon Jct. H1
Calabasas A2
Calimesa K3
Canyon Lake J5
Carson D4
Cedar Glen K1
Cedarpines Park J1
Cerritos E4
Charter Oak F2
Chino G3
Chino Hills G3
Claremont G2
Colton J2
Commerce D3
Compton D3
Corona G4
Costa Mesa E5
Coto de Caza G5
Covina F2
Cowan Hts. F4
Crestline J1
Crestmore H2
Crest Park K1
Cudahy D3
Culver City C3
Cypress E4
Dana Pt. G6
Devore H1
Diamond Bar F3
Downey D3
Duarte E2
E. Los Angeles D3
E. Tustin F4
El Cerrito H4
El Monte E2
El Segundo C3
Emerald Bay F6
Fernwood B2
Florence D3
Fontana H2
Fountain Valley E5
Fullerton E3
Gardena C4
Garden Grove E4
Glendale D2
Glendora F2
Glenview B2
Grand Terrace J3
Green Valley Lake K1
Hacienda Hts. E3
Hawaiian Gardens E4
Hawthorne C3
Hemet K4
Hermosa Beach C4
Hesperia J1
Hidden Hills A2
Highgrove J3
Highland K2
Home Gardens H4
Homeland K4
Huntington Beach E5
Huntington Park D3
Industry E3
Inglewood C3
Irvine F5
Irwindale E2
Jurupa Valley H3
La Cañada Flintridge D1
La Crescenta D1
Ladera Hts. C3
Laguna Beach F6
Laguna Hills G5
Laguna Niguel G6
Laguna Woods G5
La Habra E3
La Habra Hts. E3
Lake Arrowhead K1
Lake Elsinore J5
Lake Forest G5
Lakeland Vil. J5
Lakeview K4
Lakewood D4
La Mirada E3
La Palma E4
La Puente E2
La Verne F2
Lawndale C4
Lemon Hts. F4
Lennox C3
Loma Linda J3
Lomita C4
Long Beach D4
Los Alamitos E4
Los Angeles C2
Lynwood D3
Lytle Creek H1
Malibu A2
Manhattan Beach C3
Marina del Rey C3
Maywood D3
Mead Valley J4
Menifee K5
Mentone K2
Midway City E4
Mission Viejo G5
Modjeska G5
Monrovia E2
Montclair G2
Montebello D3
Monte Nido A2
Monterey Park D2
Montrose D1
Moreno Valley J3
Mt. Baldy G1
Murrieta J6
Murrieta Hot Sprs. K6
Muscoy J2
Newport Beach E5
Norco H3
Norwalk E3
Nuevo K4
Oak Park A2
Ontario G2
Orange F4
Orange Park Acres F4
Palos Verdes Estates C4
Paramount D3
Pasadena D2
Perris J4
Pico Rivera E3
Placentia F4
Pomona F2
Rancho Cucamonga G2
Rancho Palos Verdes C4
Rancho Santa Margarita G5
Redlands K3
Redondo Beach C4
Rialto H2
Rimforest J1
Riverside J3
Rolling Hills C4
Rolling Hills Estates C4
Romoland K4
Rosemead E2
Rossmoor E4
Rowland Hts. F3
Running Sprs. K1
San Antonio Hts. G2
San Bernardino J2
San Clemente G6
San Dimas F2
San Fernando C1
San Gabriel D2
San Jacinto K4
San Juan Capistrano G6
San Marino D2
Santa Ana F5
Santa Fe Sprs. E3
Santa Monica B3
Seal Beach D4
Sierra Madre E2
Signal Hill D4
Silverado G4
Simi Valley A1
Skyforest K1
S. El Monte E2
S. Gate D3
S. Pasadena D2
S. San Gabriel E2
S. Whittier E3
Stanton E4
Sunset Beach E5
Temecula K6
Temple City E2
Thousand Oaks A1
Topanga B2
Torrance C4
Trabuco Canyon G5
Tustin F5
Twin Peaks J1
Upland G2
Valinda E2
Vernon D3
View Park C3
Villa Park F4
Walnut F3
Walnut Park D3
W. Covina E2
W. Hollywood C2
Westlake Vil. A2
Westminster E4
Whittier E3
Wildomar J5
Willowbrook D3
Winchester K5
Windsor Hills C3
Woodcrest J4
Yorba Linda F3
Yucaipa K3

Entries in **bold black** indicate counties or parishes.
Entries in **bold color** indicate cities with detailed inset maps.

Figures after entries indicate page number and grid reference.

POINTS OF INTEREST

Angels Flight . . . A1
Bradbury Building . . . A1
California Plaza . . . A1
Cathedral of Our Lady of the Angels . . A1
Chinese American Museum . . . B1
City Hall . . . B1
City Market . . . A2
Convention Center . . . A2
Court House . . . A1
Crypto.com Arena . . . A2
Dodger Stadium . . . B1
El Pueblo de Los Angeles Hist. Mon . . B1
Flower District . . . A2
GRAMMY Museum . . . A2
Institute of Contemporary Art . . . B2
Japanese American Natl. Museum . . B1
Jewelry District . . . A2
L.A. Center Studios . . . A1
L.A. Live . . . A2
Library . . . A1
Los Angeles State Historical Park . . . B1
Microsoft Theatre . . . A2
Mt. St. Mary's University . . . A2
Museum of Contemporary Art (MOCA) . . . A1
Museum of Neon Art . . . A2
Music Center . . . A1
Post Office . . . B1
The Geffen Contemporary at MOCA . . B1
Union Station . . . B1
Walt Disney Concert Hall . . . A1

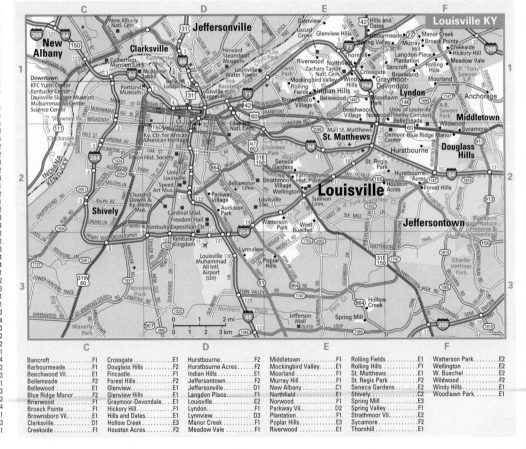

Downtown Los Angeles CA
A
B
1
2
DODGER STADIUM
ANGELINO HEIGHTS
Echo Park
CHINATOWN
Elysian Park
Los Angeles State Hist. Park
TEMPLE BEAUDRY
CROWN HILL
WESTLAKE
MacArthur Park
Cathedral of Our Lady of the Angels
Olvera Street
Chinese American Mus.
Union Station
CIVIC CENTER
Walt Disney Concert Hall
Music Ctr.
BUNKER HILL
City Hall
Mus. of Contemporary Art
L.A. Center Studios
Good Samaritan Hospital
PIH Health
California Plaza
Angel's Flight
Bradbury Bldg.
Japanese American Natl. Mus.
LITTLE TOKYO
The Geffen Contemporary at MOCA
HISTORIC CORE
TOY DISTRICT
ARTS DISTRICT
Library
Pershing Square
L.A. LIVE
Microsoft Theatre
GRAMMY Mus.
Mus. of Neon Art
Crypto.com Arena
Convention Center
PICO-UNION
Flower District
Jewelry District
WHOLESALE DISTRICT
SOUTH PARK
City Market
FASHION DISTRICT
PRODUCE DISTRICT
Inst. of Contemporary Art
BOYLE HEIGHTS
LAC+USC Med. Ctr.
Prospect Park
Hollenbeck Park
White Mem. Med. Ctr.
SOUTHEAST LOS ANGELES
Mt. St. Mary's Univ.
0 0.25 0.5mi
0 0.25 0.5 0.75 km

Lexington SC . . . 122 A3
Lexington TN . . . 109 D4
Lexington TX . . . 61 E1
Lexington VA . . . 112 C1
Lexington Co. SC . . . 122 A4
Lexington Park MD . . . 103 F4
Libby MT . . . 14 C2
Liberal KS . . . 50 B1
Liberal MO . . . 106 B1
Liberty IL . . . 97 F1
Liberty IN . . . 100 B1
Liberty KY . . . 110 B1
Liberty ME . . . 82 C2
Liberty MS . . . 134 A1
Liberty MO . . . 96 B2
Liberty NY . . . 94 A3
Liberty NC . . . 112 B4
Liberty PA . . . 250 C3
Liberty SC . . . 121 E2
Liberty TN . . . 110 A4
Liberty TX . . . 132 B3
Liberty Ctr. OH . . . 90 B2
Liberty City TX . . . 124 B2
Liberty Corner NJ . . . 147 D1
Liberty Co. FL . . . 137 D2
Liberty Co. GA . . . 130 B3
Liberty Co. MT . . . 15 F1
Liberty Co. TX . . . 132 B2
Liberty Hill TX . . . 61 E1
Liberty Lake WA . . . 14 B3
Libertyville IL . . . 74 C4
Licking MO . . . 107 E1
Licking Co. OH . . . 91 D4
Lidgerwood ND . . . 27 E1
Lido Beach NY . . . 147 F1
Lighthouse Pt. FL . . . 143 F1
Ligonier IN . . . 89 F2
Ligonier PA . . . 92 B4
Lihue HI . . . 152 B1
Lilbourn MO . . . 108 B3
Lilburn GA . . . 120 C4
Lillington NC . . . 123 D1
Lilly PA . . . 92 B4
Lily KY . . . 110 C2
Lilydale MN . . . 235 D3
Lily Lake IL . . . 88 C1
Lima MT . . . 23 E3
Lima NY . . . 78 C3
Lima OH . . . 90 B3
Lima PA . . . 248 A4
Lime Lake NY . . . 78 B4
Limeport PA . . . 146 C1
Limerick ME . . . 82 A3
Limerick PA . . . 146 B2
Lime Sprs. IA . . . 73 E2
Limestone ME . . . 85 E1
Limestone Co. AL . . . 119 F2
Limestone Co. TX . . . 59 F4
Limon CO . . . 41 F2
Lincoln AL . . . 120 A4
Lincoln AR . . . 106 B4
Lincoln CA . . . 36 C2
Lincoln DE . . . 145 F3
Lincoln ID . . . 23 E4
Lincoln IL . . . 88 B4
Lincoln KS . . . 43 E2
Lincoln ME . . . 85 D4
Lincoln MA . . . 197 A1
Lincoln MO . . . 97 D4
Lincoln MT . . . 15 E4
Lincoln NE . . . 35 F4
Lincoln NH . . . 81 F3
Lincoln ND . . . 18 C4
Lincoln Beach OR . . . 20 B2
Lincoln City OR . . . 20 B2
Lincoln Co. AR . . . 117 F3
Lincoln Co. CO . . . 41 F2
Lincoln Co. GA . . . 121 E4
Lincoln Co. ID . . . 31 D1
Lincoln Co. KS . . . 43 E2
Lincoln Co. KY . . . 110 B1
Lincoln Co. ME . . . 82 C2
Lincoln Co. MN . . . 27 F3
Lincoln Co. MS . . . 126 B4
Lincoln Co. MO . . . 97 F2
Lincoln Co. MT . . . 14 C2
Lincoln Co. NE . . . 34 C3
Lincoln Co. NV . . . 38 B4
Lincoln Co. NM . . . 49 D4
Lincoln Co. NC . . . 122 A1
Lincoln Co. OK . . . 51 F2
Lincoln Co. OR . . . 20 B3
Lincoln Co. SD . . . 35 F1
Lincoln Co. TN . . . 119 F1
Lincoln Co. WA . . . 13 F3
Lincoln Co. WV . . . 101 E4
Lincoln Co. WI . . . 68 A3
Lincoln Co. WY . . . 32 A2
Lincolndale NY . . . 148 C2
Lincoln Hts. OH . . . 204 B1
Lincolnia VA . . . 270 B4
Lincoln Par. LA . . . 125 E2
Lincoln Park CO . . . 41 E3
Lincoln Park MI . . . 90 C1
Lincoln Park NJ . . . 148 A3
Lincolnshire IL . . . 203 C2
Lincolnton GA . . . 121 E4
Lincolnton NC . . . 122 A1
Lincoln Vil. OH . . . 206 A3
Lincolnville SC . . . 131 D1
Lincolnville Ctr. ME . . . 82 C2
Lincolnwood IL . . . 203 D3
Lincroft NJ . . . 147 E2
Lind WA . . . 13 F4
Linda CA . . . 36 C2
Lindale GA . . . 120 B3
Lindale TX . . . 124 A2
Lindcove CA . . . 45 D3
Linden AL . . . 127 E2
Linden CA . . . 36 C3
Linden IN . . . 89 E4
Linden MI . . . 76 B3
Linden NJ . . . 147 E1
Linden TN . . . 119 E1
Linden TX . . . 124 C1
Linden WI . . . 74 A3
Lindenhurst IL . . . 74 C4
Lindenhurst NY . . . 148 C4
Lindenwold NJ . . . 146 C3
Lindon UT . . . 31 F4
Lindsay CA . . . 45 D3
Lindsay OK . . . 51 E4
Lindsay TX . . . 59 E1
Lindsborg KS . . . 43 E3
Lindstrom MN . . . 67 D3
Linesville PA . . . 91 F2
Lineville AL . . . 128 B1
Lingle WY . . . 33 F2
Linglestown PA . . . 93 D4
Linn KS . . . 43 F1
Linn MO . . . 97 C3
Linn TX . . . 63 E3
Linn Co. IA . . . 87 E1
Linn Co. KS . . . 96 B4
Linn Co. MO . . . 97 D1
Linn Co. OR . . . 20 C3
Linneus MO . . . 97 D1
Linn Valley KS . . . 96 B4
Lino Lakes MN . . . 235 D7
Linthicum MD . . . 193 C4
Linton IN . . . 99 E2
Linton ND . . . 26 C1
Linwood IN . . . 89 F4
Linwood KS . . . 96 B2
Linwood MI . . . 76 B2
Linwood NJ . . . 147 F4
Lionville PA . . . 146 B3
Lipscomb AL . . . 195 D2
Lipscomb TX . . . 50 C2
Lipscomb Co. TX . . . 50 C2
Lisbon IA . . . 87 F1
Lisbon ME . . . 82 B3
Lisbon NH . . . 81 E2
Lisbon ND . . . 19 E4
Lisbon OH . . . 91 F3
Lisbon Falls ME . . . 82 B3
Lisle IL . . . 203 B5
Lisman AL . . . 127 D3
Litchfield CT . . . 94 C3
Litchfield IL . . . 98 B2
Litchfield ME . . . 82 B2
Litchfield MI . . . 90 A1
Litchfield MN . . . 66 B3
Litchfield Co. CT . . . 94 B3
Litchfield Park AZ . . . 249 A2
Lithia Sprs. GA . . . 120 C4
Lithonia GA . . . 120 C4
Lithopolis OH . . . 101 D1
Lititz PA . . . 146 A2
Little Canada MN . . . 235 D2
Little Chute WI . . . 74 C1
Little Compton RI . . . 151 D4
Little Creek DE . . . 145 E2
Little Cypress TX . . . 132 C2
Little Eagle SD . . . 26 C1
Little Elm TX . . . 59 F2
Little Falls MN . . . 66 C2
Little Falls NJ . . . 148 A3
Little Falls NY . . . 79 F3
Little Ferry NJ . . . 240 C2
Littlefield TX . . . 58 A1
Little Flock AR . . . 106 C3
Littlefork MN . . . 64 B2
Little Heaven DE . . . 145 E3
Little River KS . . . 43 E3
Little River SC . . . 123 D4
Little River-Academy TX . . . 61 E1
Little River Co. AR . . . 116 C4
Little Rock AR . . . 117 E2
Littlerock CA . . . 52 C2
Little Silver NJ . . . 147 E2
Littlestown PA . . . 103 E1
Littleton CO . . . 41 E1
Littleton NH . . . 81 F2
Littleton NC . . . 113 D3
Little Valley NY . . . 92 B1
Littleville AL . . . 119 E2
Live Oak CA . . . 36 C2
Live Oak CA . . . 236 D1
Live Oak FL . . . 138 B2
Live Oak TX . . . 61 D2
Live Oak Co. TX . . . 61 D4
Livermore CA . . . 36 B4
Livermore KY . . . 109 E1
Livermore Falls ME . . . 82 B2
Liverpool NY . . . 265 A1
Liverpool PA . . . 93 D4
Livingston AL . . . 127 D2
Livingston CA . . . 36 C4
Livingston IL . . . 98 B2
Livingston LA . . . 134 A2
Livingston MT . . . 23 F1
Livingston NJ . . . 148 A4
Livingston TN . . . 110 A3
Livingston TX . . . 132 B1
Livingston WI . . . 74 A3
Livingston Co. IL . . . 88 C3
Livingston Co. KY . . . 109 D2
Livingston Co. MI . . . 76 B4
Livingston Co. MO . . . 96 C1
Livingston Co. NY . . . 78 C4
Livingston Manor NY . . . 94 A2
Livingston Par. LA . . . 134 B2
Livonia LA . . . 133 F2
Livonia MI . . . 76 B4
Livonia NY . . . 78 C3
Llangollen Estates DE . . . 145 E1
Llano TX . . . 61 D1
Llano Co. TX . . . 61 D1
Lloyd Harbor NY . . . 148 C3
Loa UT . . . 39 E3
Loami IL . . . 98 B1
Lobelville TN . . . 109 D4
Lochbuie CO . . . 209 D1
Lochearn MD . . . 144 C2
Loch Lynn Hts. MD . . . 102 B2
Loch Sheldrake NY . . . 94 A3
Lockeford CA . . . 36 C3
Lockesburg AR . . . 116 C4
Lockhart AL . . . 136 B1
Lockhart FL . . . 246 B1
Lockhart TX . . . 61 E2
Lock Haven PA . . . 93 D3
Lockland OH . . . 204 B1
Lockney TX . . . 50 B4
Lockport IL . . . 89 D2
Lockport LA . . . 134 B3
Lockport NY . . . 78 B3
Lockwood MO . . . 106 C1
Locust NC . . . 122 B1
Locust Fork AL . . . 119 F4
Locust Grove GA . . . 129 D1
Locust Grove OK . . . 106 B3
Locust Valley NY . . . 148 C3
Lodge Grass MT . . . 24 C2
Lodge Pole MT . . . 16 C2
Lodi CA . . . 36 C3
Lodi NJ . . . 240 C1
Lodi OH . . . 91 D3
Lodi WI . . . 74 B3
Logan IA . . . 86 A2
Logan KS . . . 42 C1
Logan NM . . . 49 F3
Logan OH . . . 101 D1
Logan UT . . . 31 E2
Logan WV . . . 101 E4
Logan Co. AR . . . 116 C1
Logan Co. CO . . . 34 A4
Logan Co. IL . . . 98 B1
Logan Co. KS . . . 42 B2
Logan Co. KY . . . 109 F2

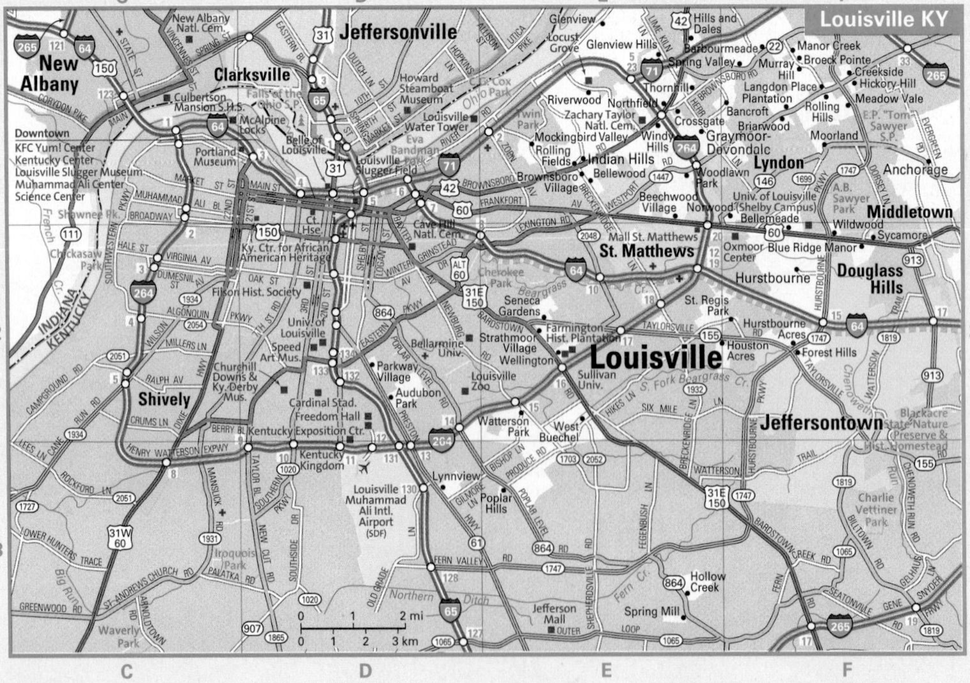
Louisville KY
C
D
E
F
1
2
3
New Albany
Clarksville
Jeffersonville
Downtown
KFC Yum! Center
Kentucky Center
Louisville Slugger Museum
Muhammad Ali Center
Science Center
Portland Museum
Culbertson Mansion S.H.S.
McAlpine Locks
Belle of Louisville
Howard Steamboat Museum
Louisville Water Tower
Glenview
Locust Grove
Glenview Hills
Hills and Dales
Barbourmeade
Spring Valley
Murray Hill
Manor Creek
Broeck Pointe
Creekside
Hickory Hill
Meadow Vale
Thornhill
Langdon Place
Plantation
Bancroft
Rolling Hills
Briarwood
Moorland
Riverwood
Northfield
Zachary Taylor Natl. Cem.
Mockingbird Valley
Rolling Fields
Windy Hills
Crossgate
Graymoor-Devondale
Indian Hills
Bellewood
Brownsboro Village
Woodlawn Park
Lyndon
Anchorage
Beechwood Village
Norwood
Univ. of Louisville (Shelby Campus)
Bellemeade
Wildwood
Middletown
Sycamore
Cave Hill Natl. Cem.
Mall St. Matthews
St. Matthews
Oxmoor Center
Blue Ridge Manor
Hurstbourne
Douglass Hills
Shawnee Pk.
Chickasaw Park
Ky. Ctr. for African American Heritage
Filson Hist. Society
Cherokee Park
Seneca Gardens
St. Regis Park
Hurstbourne Acres
Forest Hills
Farmington Hist. Plantation
Strathmoor Village
Wellington
Bellarmine Univ.
Louisville
Houston Acres
Univ. of Louisville
Speed Art Mus.
Parkway Village
Churchill Downs & Ky. Derby Mus.
Audubon Park
Louisville Zoo
Sullivan Univ.
Shively
Cardinal Stad.
Freedom Hall
Kentucky Exposition Ctr.
Kentucky Kingdom
Watterson Park
West Buechel
Jeffersontown
Blackacre State Nature Preserve & Hist. Homestead
Louisville Muhammad Ali Intl. Airport (SDF)
Lynnview
Poplar Hills
Charlie Vettiner Park
Iroquois Park
Hollow Creek
Spring Mill
Jefferson Mall
Waverly Park
INDIANA
KENTUCKY
0 1 2 mi
0 1 2 3 km

Bancroft . . . F1
Barbourmeade . . . F1
Beechwood Vil. . . . E1
Bellemeade . . . F2
Bellewood . . . E1
Blue Ridge Manor . . . F2
Briarwood . . . F1
Broeck Pointe . . . F1
Brownsboro Vil. . . . E1
Clarksville . . . D1
Creekside . . . F1
Crossgate . . . E1
Douglass Hills . . . F2
Fincastle . . . F1
Forest Hills . . . F2
Glenview . . . E1
Glenview Hills . . . E1
Graymoor-Devondale . . . E1
Hickory Hill . . . F1
Hills and Dales . . . E1
Hollow Creek . . . E3
Houston Acres . . . F2
Hurstbourne . . . F2
Hurstbourne Acres . . . F2
Indian Hills . . . E1
Jeffersontown . . . F2
Jeffersonville . . . D1
Langdon Place . . . F1
Louisville . . . E2
Lyndon . . . F1
Lynnview . . . D3
Manor Creek . . . F1
Meadow Vale . . . F1
Middletown . . . F1
Mockingbird Valley . . . E1
Moorland . . . F1
Murray Hill . . . F1
New Albany . . . C1
Northfield . . . E1
Norwood . . . F1
Parkway Vil. . . . D2
Plantation . . . F1
Poplar Hills . . . E3
Riverwood . . . E1
Rolling Fields . . . E1
Rolling Hills . . . F1
St. Matthews . . . E1
St. Regis Park . . . F2
Seneca Gardens . . . E2
Shively . . . C2
Spring Mill . . . E3
Spring Valley . . . F1
Strathmoor Vil. . . . E2
Sycamore . . . F2
Thornhill . . . E1
Watterson Park . . . E2
Wellington . . . E2
W. Buechel . . . E2
Wildwood . . . F2
Windy Hills . . . E1
Woodlawn Park . . . E1

Entries in **bold black** indicate counties or parishes.
Entries in **bold color** indicate cities with detailed inset maps.

Logan Co. NE 34 C3
Logan Co. ND 18 C4
Logan Co. OH 90 B4
Logan Co. OK 51 E2
Logan Co. WV 101 E4
Logandale NV 46 B1
Logansport IN 89 E3
Logansport LA 124 C3
Loganville GA 121 D4
Loganville PA 103 E1
Log Cabin TX 59 F3
Log Lane Vil. CO 33 F4
Loleta CA 28 A4
Lolita TX 61 F3
Lolo MT 15 D4
Loma Linda CA 229 J3
Long Beach MD 103 E3
Long Beach MS 135 D2
Long Beach NY 147 F1
Long Beach WA 12 B4
Longboat Key FL 140 B3
Long Branch NJ 147 F2
Long Co. GA 130 B3
Long Creek IL 98 C1
Long Green MD 144 C1
Long Grove IL 203 C2
Long Grove IA 88 A1
Long Lake MN 66 C4
Longmeadow MA 150 A2
Longmont CO 41 E1
Long Pond MA 151 E3
Longport NJ 147 F4
Loretto TN 119 E2
Loris SC 123 D3
Lorton VA 144 B4
Los Alamitos CA 228 E4
Los Alamos CA 52 A1
Los Alamos NM 48 C2
Los Alamos Co. NM 48 C2
Los Altos CA 36 B4
Los Altos Hills CA 259 C6
Los Angeles CA 52 C2
Los Angeles Co. CA 52 C2
Los Banos CA 44 B2
Los Chavez NM 48 C4
Los Fresnos TX 63 F4
Los Gatos CA 36 B4
Los Indios TX 63 F4

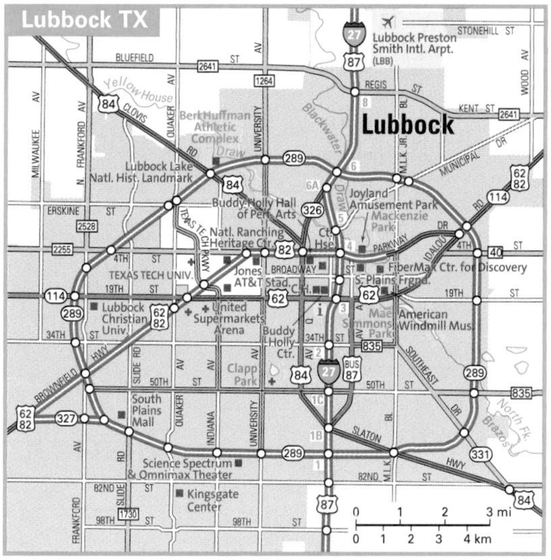

Loma Linda MO 106 B2
Loma Rica CA 36 C2
Lombard IL 203 B4
Lometa TX 59 D4
Lomira WI 74 C2
Lomita CA 228 C4
Lompoc CA 52 A2
Lonaconing MD 102 C1
London AR 117 D1
London KY 110 C2
London OH 100 C1
Londonderry NH 95 E1
Londonderry VT 81 D4
Londontowne MD 144 C3
Lone Grove OK 51 E4
Lone Jack MO 96 C3
Lone Oak KY 108 C2
Lone Oak TX 59 F2
Lone Pine CA 45 E3
Lone Rock WI 74 A3
Lone Star LA 239 A2
Lone Star TX 124 B1
Lone Tree CO 209 C4
Lone Tree IA 87 F2
Lone Wolf OK 51 D3
Long Beach CA 52 C3
Long Beach IN 89 E1
Long Prairie MN 66 B2
Longton KS 43 F4
Long Valley NJ 94 A4
Long View NC 111 F4
Longview TX 124 B2
Longview WA 20 B1
Longwood FL 141 D1
Lonoke AR 117 F2
Lonoke Co. AR 117 F2
Lonsdale MN 67 D4
Loogootee IN 99 E3
Lookout Mtn. GA 120 B2
Lookout Mtn. TN 120 B2
Loomis CA 36 C2
Loomis NE 35 D4
Lorain OH 91 D2
Lorain Co. OH 91 D2
Loraine TX 58 B3
Lorane PA 146 B2
Lordsburg NM 55 F3
Lordstown OH 91 F2
Loreauville LA 133 F3
Lorena TX 59 E4
Lorenzo TX 58 A1
Loretto KY 110 A1
Loretto MN 66 C3
Loretto PA 92 B4
Los Lunas NM 48 C4
Los Molinos CA 36 B1
Los Olivos CA 52 A2
Los Osos CA 44 B4
Los Padillas NM 48 C3
Los Ranchos de Albuquerque NM 48 C3
Lost Creek WV 102 A2
Lost Hills CA 44 C4
Lost Nation IA 87 F1
Lott TX 59 F4
Loudon TN 110 C4
Loudon Co. TN 110 C4
Loudonville NY 94 B1
Loudonville OH 91 D3
Loudoun Co. VA 144 A2
Loughman FL 141 D2
Louisa KY 101 D4
Louisa VA 103 D4
Louisa Co. IA 87 F2
Louisa Co. VA 103 D4
Louisburg KS 96 B3
Louisburg NC 113 D4
Louise TX 61 F3
Louisiana MO 97 F2
Louisville AL 128 B3
Louisville CO 41 E1

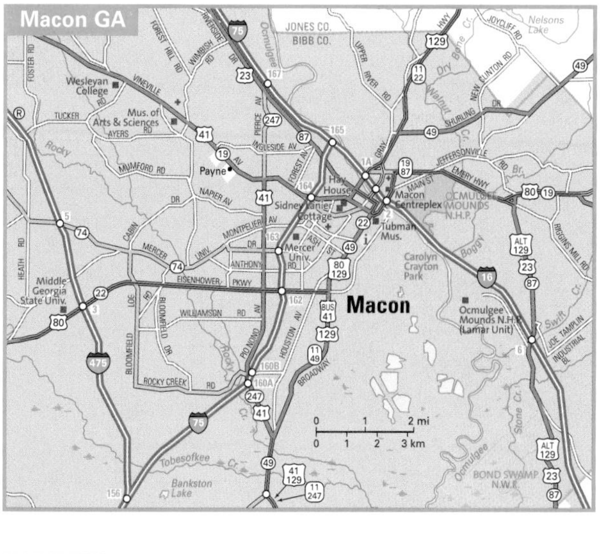

Louisville GA 129 F1
Louisville IL 98 C3
Louisville KY 100 A4
Louisville MS 126 C1
Louisville NE 35 F3
Louisville OH 91 E3
Louisville TN 110 C4
Loup City NE 35 D3
Loup Co. NE 35 D2
Love Co. OK 59 E1
Lovelady TX 132 A1
Loveland CO 33 E4
Loveland OH 100 B2
Loveland Park OH 204 C1
Lovell WY 24 C2
Lovelock NV 29 F4
Loves Park IL 74 B4
Lovettsville VA 144 A2
Loveville MD 103 E4
Lovilia IA 87 D3
Loving NM 57 E3
Loving Co. TX 57 E3
Lovingston VA 112 C1
Lovington IL 98 C1
Lovington NM 57 F2
Lowden IA 87 F1
Lowell AR 106 C3
Lowell IN 89 D2
Lowell MA 95 E1
Lowell MI 75 F3
Lowell NC 122 A1
Lowell OH 101 F1
Lowell OR 20 C4
Lowellville OH 91 F3
Lower Brule SD 27 D3
Lower Lake CA 36 B2
Lowesville NC 122 A1
Low Moor VA 112 B1
Lowndes Co. AL 127 F3
Lowndes Co. GA 137 F1
Lowndes Co. MS 127 D1
Lowry City MO 96 C4
Lowville NY 79 E2
Loxley AL 135 E2
Loyal WI 68 A4
Loyalhanna PA 92 B4
Loyall KY 111 D2
Loyalton CA 37 D1
Lubbock TX 58 A1
Lubbock Co. TX 58 A1
Lubec ME 83 F1
Lubeck WV 101 E2
Lucama NC 113 D4
Lucas KS 43 D2
Lucas OH 91 D3
Lucas TX 59 F2
Lucas Co. IA 87 D3
Lucas Co. OH 90 C2
Lucasville OH 101 D3
Luce Co. MI 69 F1
Lucedale MS 135 D1
Lucerne CA 36 B2
Lucerne WY 24 C4
Lucernemines PA 92 B4
Luck WI 67 E3
Luckey OH 90 C2
Ludington MI 75 E1
Ludingtonville NY 148 C1
Ludlow KY 204 A3
Ludlow MA 150 A2
Ludlow VT 81 E4
Ludowici GA 130 B4
Lufkin TX 124 B4
Lugoff SC 122 B3
Lukachukai AZ 48 A1
Lula GA 121 D3
Luling LA 239 A2
Luling TX 61 E2
Lumber City GA 129 F3
Lumberport WV 102 A2
Lumberton MS 134 C1
Lumberton NJ 147 D3
Lumberton NC 123 D2
Lumberton TX 132 C2
Lumpkin GA 128 C3
Lumpkin Co. GA 120 C2
Luna Co. NM 56 A3
Luna Pier MI 90 C1
Lunenburg MA 95 D1
Lunenburg VT 81 F2
Lunenburg VA 113 D2
Lunenburg Co. VA 113 D2
Lupton AZ 48 A3
Luray VA 102 C3
Lusby MD 103 F3
Lusk WY 33 E1
Lutcher LA 134 B3
Luther OK 51 E2
Luthersville GA 128 C1
Luttrell TN 110 C3
Lutz FL 140 B2
Luverne AL 128 A4
Luverne MN 27 F4
Luxemburg WI 69 D4
Luxora AR 108 B4
Luzerne PA 261 B1
Luzerne Co. PA 93 E3
Lycoming Co. PA 93 D2
Lydia LA 133 F3
Lydick IN 89 E2
Lyerly GA 120 B3
Lyford TX 63 F4
Lykens PA 93 E4
Lyle MN 73 D2
Lyle WA 21 D1
Lyman NE 33 F2
Lyman SC 121 F2
Lyman WA 12 C2
Lyman WY 32 A3
Lyman Co. SD 26 C4
Lynbrook NY 147 F1
Lynch KY 111 D2
Lynchburg MS 118 B2
Lynchburg OH 100 C2
Lynchburg SC 122 B3
Lynchburg TN 119 F1
Lynchburg VA 112 C1
Lynch Hts. DE 145 F3
Lynch Sta. VA 112 C2
Lyndell PA 146 B3
Lynden WA 12 C1
Lyndhurst NJ 240 C2
Lyndhurst OH 204 G2
Lyndhurst VA 102 C4
Lyndon KS 96 A3
Lyndon KY 230 F1
Lyndon NY 265 B2
Lyndon VT 81 E2
Lyndon Ctr. VT 81 E2
Lyndonville NY 78 B3
Lyndonville VT 81 E2
Lyndora PA 92 A3
Lynn AL 119 E3
Lynn IN 90 A4
Lynn MA 151 D1
Lynn Co. TX 58 A2
Lynn Haven FL 136 C2
Lynnview KY 230 D3
Lynnville IN 99 E4
Lynnwood WA 12 C3
Lynwood CA 228 D3
Lyon MS 118 A3
Lyon Co. IA 27 F4
Lyon Co. KS 43 F3
Lyon Co. KY 109 D2
Lyon Co. MN 72 A1
Lyon Co. NV 37 E2
Lyons CO 33 E4
Lyons GA 129 F3
Lyons IL 203 D5
Lyons IN 99 E2
Lyons KS 43 E3
Lyons MI 76 A3
Lyons NE 35 F2
Lyons NY 79 D3
Lyons OH 90 B2
Lyons OR 20 C3
Lyons Falls NY 79 E2
Lyons Plain CT 148 C2
Lytle TX 61 D3

M

Mabank TX 59 F3
Mabel MN 73 E2
Maben MS 118 C4
Mableton GA 120 C4
Mabscott WV 111 F1
Mabton WA 21 E1
Macclenny FL 138 C2
Macedon NY 78 C3
Macedonia OH 91 E2
Machesney Park IL 74 B4
Machias ME 83 E1
Machias NY 78 B4
Mack OH 204 A2
Mackay ID 23 D4
Mackinac Co. MI 70 B2
Mackinac Island MI 70 C2
Mackinaw IL 88 B4
Mackinaw City MI 70 C2
Macksville KS 43 D3
Macomb IL 88 A4
Macomb Co. MI 76 C4
Macon AR 117 E2
Macon GA 129 D2
Macon IL 98 C1
Macon MS 127 D1
Macon MO 97 E1
Macon Co. AL 128 B3
Macon Co. GA 129 D2
Macon Co. IL 98 C1
Macon Co. MO 97 D1
Macon Co. NC 121 D1
Macon Co. TN 110 A3
Macoupin Co. IL 98 B2
Macungie PA 146 B1
Macy NE 35 F2
Madawaska ME 85 D1
Maddock ND 19 D2

Fitchburg A2
Madison A1
Maple Bluff B1
McFarland B2
Middleton A1
Monona B2
Shorewood Hills A2
Sun Prairie B1
Waunakee A1

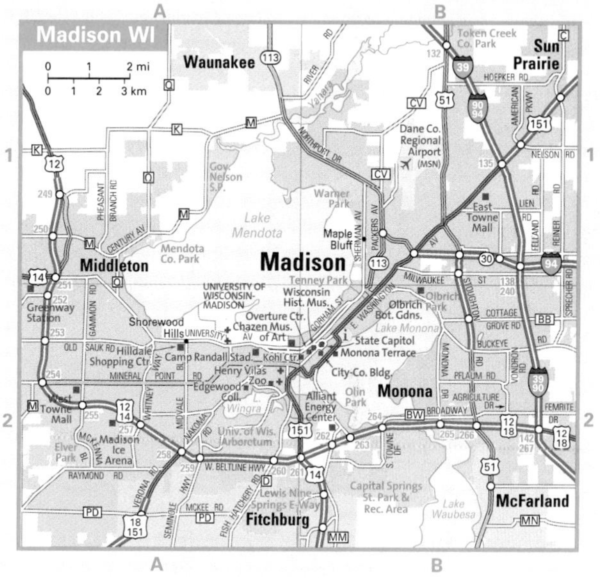

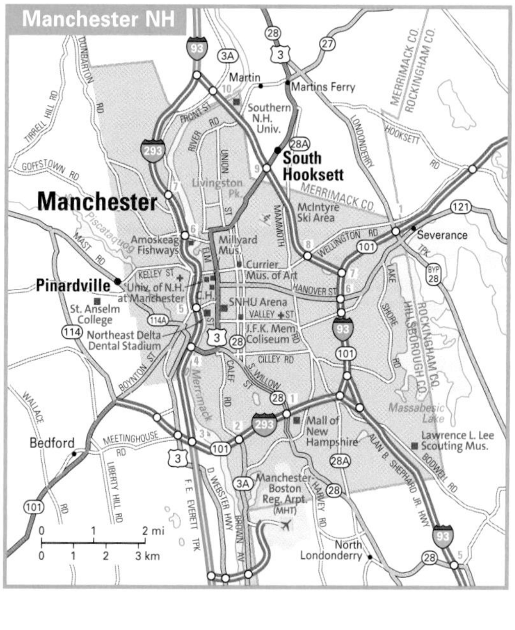

Madeira OH 204 C2
Madeira Beach FL 140 B3
Madelia MN 72 B1
Madera CA 44 C2
Madera Co. CA 44 C2
Madill OK 51 F4
Madison AL 119 F2
Madison AR 118 A2
Madison CT 149 E2
Madison FL 137 F2
Madison GA 121 D4
Madison IL 98 A3
Madison IN 100 A3
Madison KS 43 F3
Madison ME 82 B1
Madison MN 27 F2
Madison MS 126 B2
Madison MO 97 E2
Madison NE 35 E2
Madison NJ 148 A4
Madison NC 112 B3
Madison OH 91 F1
Madison SD 27 F3
Madison VA 102 C4
Madison WV 101 E4
Madison WI 74 B3
Madison Co. AL 119 F2
Madison Co. AR 106 C4
Madison Co. FL 137 F2
Madison Co. GA 121 E3
Madison Co. ID 23 F4
Madison Co. IL 98 B3
Madison Co. IN 89 F4
Madison Co. IA 86 C2
Madison Co. KY 110 C1
Madison Co. MS 126 B2
Madison Co. MO 108 A1
Madison Co. MT 23 E2
Madison Co. NE 35 E2
Madison Co. NY 79 E4
Madison Co. NC 111 E4
Madison Co. OH 100 C1
Madison Co. TN 108 C4
Madison Co. TX 61 F1
Madison Co. VA 102 C3
Madison Hts. MI 210 C2
Madison Hts. VA 112 C1
Madison Lake MN 72 C1
Madison Par. LA 126 A3
Madisonville KY 109 E1
Madisonville LA 134 B2
Madisonville TN 120 C1
Madisonville TX 61 F1
Madras OR 21 D3
Madrid IA 86 C1
Madrid NY 80 B1
Maeser UT 32 A4
Magalia CA 36 C1
Magazine AR 116 C1
Magdalena NM 48 B4
Magee MS 126 C3
Maggie Valley NC 121 E1
Magna UT 257 A2
Magnolia AR 125 D1
Magnolia DE 145 E2
Magnolia MS 134 B1
Magnolia NJ 248 D4
Magnolia NC 123 E2
Magnolia OH 91 E3
Magnolia TX 132 A2
Magoffin Co. KY 111 D1
Mahanoy City PA 93 E3
Mahaska Co. IA 87 D2
Mahnomen MN 19 F3
Mahnomen Co. MN 19 F3
Mahomet IL 88 C4
Mahoning Co. OH 91 F3
Mahopac NY 148 C2
Mahtomedi MN 235 E1
Mahwah NJ 148 B3
Maiden NC 122 A1
Maili HI 152 A3
Maine NY 93 E1
Maineville OH 100 B2
Maitland FL 141 D1
Maize KS 43 E4
Majestic KY 111 E1
Major Co. OK 51 D2
Makaha HI 152 A3
Makakilo City HI 152 A3
Makawao HI 153 D1
Makena HI 153 D1
Malabar FL 141 E2
Malad City ID 31 E2
Malaga CA 44 C3
Malaga NJ 145 F1
Malakoff TX 59 F3
Malcolm NE 35 F4
Malden MA 151 D1
Malden MO 108 B3
Malden WV 200 B2
Malheur Co. OR 22 A4
Malibu CA 52 B2
Malin OR 29 D2
Mallory WV 111 F1
Malone FL 137 D1
Malone NY 80 C1
Malone WA 12 B4
Malta ID 31 D2
Malta IL 88 C1
Malta MT 16 C2
Malta NY 94 B1
Malta OH 101 E1
Maltby WA 262 B2
Malvern AL 136 C1
Malvern AR 117 D3
Malvern IA 86 A3
Malvern OH 91 E3
Malvern PA 146 B3
Malverne NY 241 G4
Mamaroneck NY 148 C3
Mammoth AZ 55 D2
Mammoth Hot Sprs. WY 23 F2
Mammoth Lakes CA 37 E4
Mammoth Spr. AR 107 F3
Mamou LA 133 E2
Man WV 111 F1
Manahawkin NJ 147 E4
Manasquan NJ 147 E2
Manassa CO 41 D4
Manassas VA 144 A4
Manassas Park VA 144 A3
Manatee Co. FL 140 C3
Manawa WI 74 B1
Mancelona MI 70 B4
Manchaca TX 61 E2
Manchaug MA 150 C2
Manchester CT 150 A3
Manchester GA 128 C2
Manchester IA 73 F4
Manchester KY 110 C2
Manchester ME 82 B2
Manchester MD 103 E1
Manchester MI 90 B1
Manchester MO 256 A3
Manchester NH 81 F4
Manchester NY 78 C3
Manchester OH 100 C3
Manchester PA 93 E4
Manchester TN 120 A1
Manchester VT 81 D4
Manchester WA 262 A3
Manchester-by-the-Sea MA 151 F1
Manchester Ctr. VT 81 D4
Mancos CO 40 B4
Mandan ND 18 C4
Mandaree ND 18 A3
Manderson SD 26 A4
Mandeville AR 116 C4
Mandeville LA 134 B2
Mangham LA 125 F2
Mango FL 266 C2
Mangonia Park FL 141 F4
Mangum OK 50 C3
Manhasset NY 148 C4
Manhasset Hills NY 241 G3
Manhattan IL 89 D2
Manhattan KS 43 F2
Manhattan MT 23 F1
Manhattan Beach CA 228 C3
Manheim PA 93 E4
Manila AR 108 B4
Manila UT 32 A3
Manilla IA 86 A1
Manistee MI 75 E1
Manistee Co. MI 70 A4
Manistique MI 69 E2
Manito IL 88 B4
Manitou Beach MI 90 B1
Manitou Sprs. CO 41 E2
Manitowoc WI 75 D1
Manitowoc Co. WI 75 D1
Mankato KS 43 E1
Mankato MN 72 C1
Manlius NY 79 E3
Manly IA 73 D3
Mannford OK 51 F2
Manning IA 86 B1
Manning ND 18 A3
Manning SC 122 B4
Mannington WV 102 A1
Mannsville OK 51 F4
Manokotak AK 154 B3
Manomet MA 151 E3
Manor PA 92 A4
Manor TX 61 E1
Manorhaven NY 241 G2
Manorville NY 149 D3
Mansfield AR 116 C2
Mansfield IL 88 C4
Mansfield LA 124 C3
Mansfield MA 151 D2
Mansfield MO 107 E2
Mansfield OH 91 D3
Mansfield PA 93 D1
Mansfield TX 59 E3
Mansfield Ctr. CT 150 B3
Mansfield Four Corners CT 150 B3
Manson IA 72 B4
Manson WA 13 E2
Mansura LA 133 F1
Mantachie MS 119 D3
Manteca CA 36 C4
Manteno IL 89 D2
Manteo NC 115 F2
Manti UT 39 E2
Manton MI 75 F1
Mantorville MN 73 D1
Mantua OH 91 E2
Mantua UT 31 E3
Mantua VA 270 A4
Manvel ND 19 E2
Manvel TX 132 A4
Manville NJ 147 D1
Manville RI 150 C2
Many LA 125 D4
Many Farms AZ 47 F2
Manzanita OR 20 B1
Manzanola CO 41 F3
Maple Bluff WI 74 B3
Maple Grove MN 67 D3
Maple Hts. OH 91 E2
Maple Hill KS 43 F2
Maple Lake MN 66 C3
Maple Park IL 88 C1
Maple Plain MN 66 C4
Maple Rapids MI 76 A3
Maple Shade NJ 146 C3
Maplesville AL 127 F2

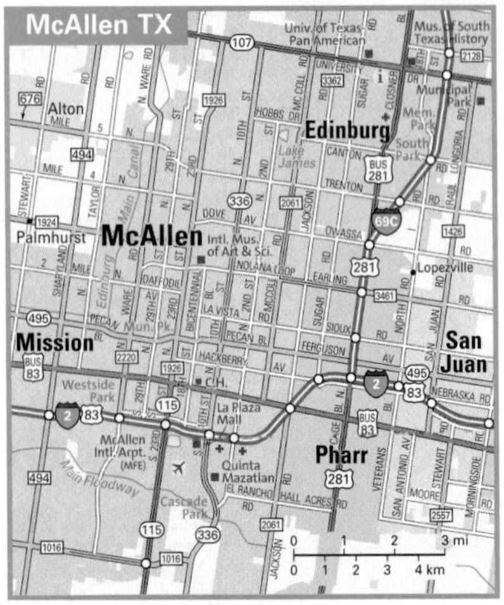
McAllen TX
McAllen
Edinburg
Mission
San Juan
Pharr
Alton
Palmhurst
Lopezville
McAllen Intl. Arpt. (MFE)

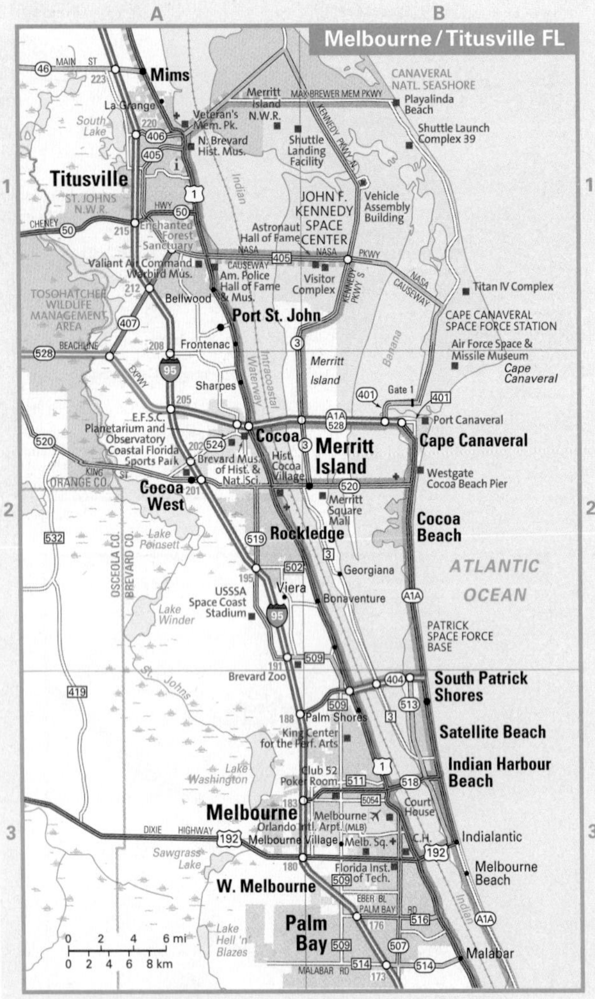
Melbourne / Titusville FL
Titusville
Mims
Port St. John
Cocoa
Merritt Island
Cape Canaveral
Cocoa West
Cocoa Beach
Rockledge
Viera
South Patrick Shores
Satellite Beach
Indian Harbour Beach
Melbourne
W. Melbourne
Palm Bay
Indialantic
Melbourne Beach
Malabar
ATLANTIC OCEAN
JOHN F. KENNEDY SPACE CENTER
CAPE CANAVERAL SPACE FORCE STATION
PATRICK SPACE FORCE BASE

Bellwood A1
Bonaventure B2
Cape Canaveral B2
Cocoa A2
Cocoa Beach B2
Cocoa West A2
Frontenac A1
Georgiana B2
Indialantic B3
Indian Harbour Beach B3
La Grange A1
Malabar B3
Melbourne A3
Melbourne Beach B3
Melbourne Vil. B3
Merritt Island B2
Mims A1
Palm Bay B3
Palm Shores B3
Pineda B3
Port St. John A1
Rockledge A2
Satellite Beach B3
Sharpes A2
S. Patrick Shores B3
Titusville A1
Viera A2
W. Melbourne B3

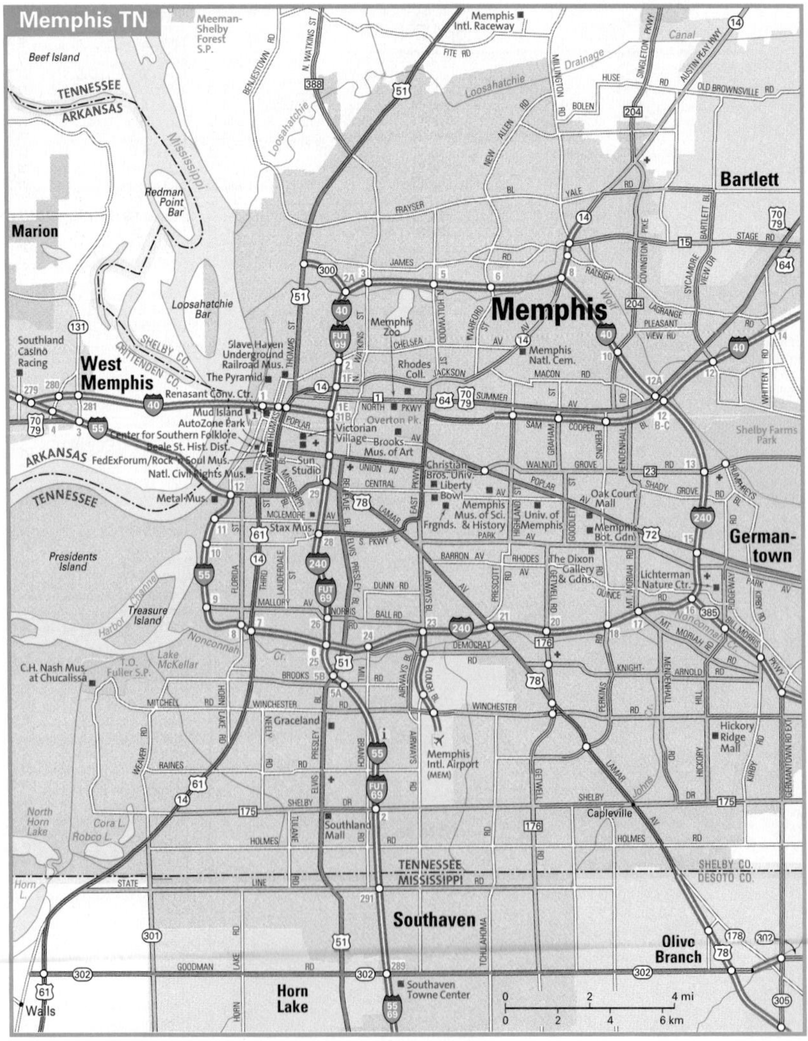
Memphis TN
Memphis
West Memphis
Bartlett
Germantown
Marion
Southaven
Horn Lake
Olive Branch
Walls
TENNESSEE
ARKANSAS
MISSISSIPPI
Memphis Intl. Airport (MEM)

Entries in **bold black** indicate counties or parishes.
Entries in **bold color** indicate cities with detailed inset maps.

Mapleton IA 86 A1
Mapleton ME 85 D2
Mapleton MN 72 C1
Mapleton ND 19 E4
Mapleton UT 39 E1
Maple Valley WA 12 C3
Maplewood MN 235 D2
Maplewood MO 256 B2
Maplewood NJ 240 A3
Mappsville VA 114 C2
Maquoketa IA 88 A1
Marana AZ 55 D3
Marathon FL 143 D4
Marathon NY 79 E4
Marathon City WI 68 A4
Marathon Co. WI 68 A4
Marble MN 64 B3
Marble Cliff OH 206 A2
Marble Falls TX 61 D1
Marblehead MA 151 D1
Marblehead OH 91 D2
Marble Hill MO 108 B1
Marbleton WY 32 A1
Marbury MD 144 B4
Marceline MO 97 D1
Marcellus MI 89 F1
Marcellus NY 79 D3
Marco Island FL 142 C2
Marcus IA 72 A3
Marcus Hook PA 146 C3
Marengo IL 88 C1
Marengo IN 99 F4
Marengo IA 87 E1
Marengo Co. AL 127 E3
Marfa TX 62 B3
Margaret AL 119 F4
Margaretville NY 94 A2
Margate FL 143 E1
Margate City NJ 147 F4
Marianna AR 118 A2
Marianna FL 137 D1
Marianna PA 102 A1
Maricopa AZ 54 C2
Maricopa CA 52 B1
Maricopa Co. AZ 54 B1
Mariemont OH 204 C2
Maries Co. MO 97 E4
Marietta GA 120 C4
Marietta OH 101 F2
Marietta OK 59 E1
Marietta PA 93 E4
Marietta SC 121 E2
Marietta WA 12 C1
Marina CA 44 B3
Marina del Rey CA 228 C3
Marin Co. CA 36 B3
Marine IL 98 B3
Marine City MI 76 C4
Marine on St. Croix MN 67 D3
Marinette WI 69 D3
Marinette Co. WI 68 C3
Maringouin LA 133 F2
Marinwood CA 259 A1
Marion AL 127 F2
Marion AR 118 B1
Marion CT 149 D1
Marion IL 108 C1
Marion IN 89 F4
Marion IA 87 E1
Marion KS 43 F3
Marion KY 109 D1
Marion LA 125 E1
Marion MD 103 F4
Marion MA 151 E3
Marion MI 75 F1
Marion MS 127 D2
Marion NY 78 C3
Marion NC 111 E4
Marion OH 90 C4
Marion PA 103 D1
Marion SC 122 C3
Marion SD 27 F4
Marion VA 111 F2
Marion WI 68 B4
Marion Co. AL 119 E3
Marion Co. AR 107 E3
Marion Co. FL 139 D4
Marion Co. GA 128 C3
Marion Co. IL 98 C3
Marion Co. IN 99 F1
Marion Co. IA 87 D2
Marion Co. KS 43 F3
Marion Co. KY 110 B1
Marion Co. MS 126 C4
Marion Co. MO 97 F1
Marion Co. OH 90 C3
Marion Co. OR 20 C2
Marion Co. SC 122 C3
Marion Co. TN 120 A1
Marion Co. TX 124 C2
Marion Co. WV 102 A1
Marion Hts. PA 93 E3
Marionville MO 106 C2
Mariposa CA 37 D4
Mariposa Co. CA 37 D4
Marissa IL 98 B4
Marked Tree AR 118 B1
Markesan WI 74 B2
Markham IL 203 D6
Markham TX 61 F3
Markle IN 90 A3
Markleeville CA 37 D2
Marks MS 118 B3
Marksville LA 133 F1
Marlboro NJ 147 E2
Marlboro NY 148 B1
Marlboro Co. SC 122 C3
Marlborough CT 149 E1
Marlborough MA 150 C1
Marlborough MO 256 B3
Marlborough NH 95 D1
Marlette MI 76 C3
Marley MD 144 C2
Marlin TX 59 F4
Marlinton WV 102 A4
Marlow OK 51 E4
Marlowe WV 103 D1
Marlow Hts. MD 270 E4
Marlton MD 144 C3
Marlton NJ 147 D3
Mar-Mac NC 123 E1
Marmaduke AR 108 A3
Marmet WV 101 F4
Marmora NJ 147 F4
Maroa IL 98 C1
Marquette KS 43 E3
Marquette MI 69 D1
Marquette Co. MI 65 F4
Marquette Co. WI 74 B2
Marrero LA 134 B3
Mars PA 92 A3
Marseilles IL 88 C2
Marshall AR 107 E4
Marshall IL 99 D2
Marshall MI 76 A4
Marshall MN 72 A1
Marshall MO 97 D2
Marshall NC 111 E4
Marshall TX 124 C2
Marshall VA 103 D3
Marshall WI 74 B3
Marshallberg NC 115 E4
Marshall Co. AL 119 F3
Marshall Co. IL 88 B3
Marshall Co. IN 89 F2
Marshall Co. IA 87 D1
Marshall Co. KS 43 F1
Marshall Co. KY 109 D2
Marshall Co. MN 19 F2
Marshall Co. MS 118 C2
Marshall Co. OK 51 F4
Marshall Co. SD 27 E1
Marshall Co. TN 119 F1
Marshall Co. WV 102 A1
Marshallton DE 146 B4
Marshallton PA 146 B3
Marshalltown IA 87 D1
Marshallville GA 129 D2
Marshallville OH 91 E3
Marshfield MA 151 E2
Marshfield MO 107 D1
Marshfield VT 81 E2
Marshfield WI 68 A4
Marshfield Hills MA 151 E2
Mars Hill ME 85 E2
Mars Hill NC 111 E4
Marshville NC 122 B2
Marsing ID 22 A4
Marston MO 108 B3
Marstons Mills MA 151 E3
Mart TX 59 F4
Martha Lake WA 262 B2
Marthasville MO 97 F3
Martin KY 111 E1
Martin LA 125 D3
Martin SD 34 B1
Martin TN 108 C3
Martin City MT 15 D2
Martin Co. FL 141 E4
Martin Co. IN 99 E3
Martin Co. KY 111 E1
Martin Co. MN 72 B2
Martin Co. NC 113 F4
Martin Co. TX 58 A3
Martindale TX 61 E2
Martinez CA 36 B3
Martins Additions MD 270 C2
Martinsburg PA 92 C4
Martinsburg WV 103 D2
Martins Creek PA 93 F3
Martins Ferry OH 91 F4
Martinsville IL 99 D2
Martinsville IN 99 F2
Martinsville NJ 147 D1
Martinsville VA 112 B3
Marty SD 35 D1
Marvell AR 118 A2
Marvin NC 122 A2
Mary Esther FL 136 B2
Maryland City MD 193 A5
Maryland Hts. MO 256 A1
Marysvale UT 39 E3
Marysville CA 36 C2
Marysville KS 43 F1
Marysville MI 76 C3
Marysville OH 90 C4
Marysville PA 93 D4
Marysville WA 12 C2
Maryville IL 256 D1
Maryville MO 86 B4
Maryville TN 110 C4
Marywood MD 145 D1
Masaryktown FL 140 B1

Miami / Fort Lauderdale FL
Boca Raton
Deerfield Beach
Coconut Creek
Parkland
Coral Springs
Margate
Pompano Beach
North Lauderdale
Tamarac
Lauderhill
Lauderdale Lakes
Oakland Park
Wilton Manors
Sunrise
Plantation
Fort Lauderdale
Weston
Davie
Southwest Ranches
Cooper City
Dania Beach
Hollywood
Pembroke Pines
West Park
Hallandale Beach
Miramar
Pembroke Park
Aventura
Miami Gardens
Ojus
Sunny Isles Beach
North Miami Beach
Palm Springs North
Miami Lakes
Opa-Locka
North Miami
Hialeah Gardens
Hialeah
Bal Harbour
Bay Harbor Islands
Surfside
Miami Shores
Miami
Miami Springs
Doral
Miami Beach
Sweetwater
Westchester
West Miami
Westwood Lakes
South Miami
Kendale Lakes
Coral Gables
Key Biscayne
Kendall
Pinecrest
Richmond Hts.
Palmetto Bay
S. Miami Hts.
Cutler Bay
Goulds
ATLANTIC OCEAN
BISCAYNE NATIONAL PARK
PALM BEACH CO.
BROWARD CO.
MIAMI-DADE CO.
0 2 4 6 mi
0 3 6 9 km

Aventura B3
Bal Harbour B3
Bay Harbor Islands C4
Biscayne Park B4
Boca Raton C1
Coconut Creek B1
Cooper City A3
Coral Gables B5
Coral Sprs. A1
Cutler Bay A5
Dania Beach B3
Davie A2
Deerfield Beach C1
El Portal B4
Ft. Lauderdale C2
Golden Beach C3
Goulds A5
Hallandale Beach C3
Hialeah A4
Hialeah Gardens A4
Hillsboro Beach C1
Indian Creek B3
Kendale Lakes A5
Kendall A5
Key Biscayne B5
Lauderdale-by-the-Sea C2
Lauderdale Lakes B2
Lauderhill B2
Lazy Lake B2
Lighthouse Pt. C1
Margate B1
Medley A4
Miami B4
Miami Beach C4
Miami Gardens B3
Miami Lakes A3
Miami Shores B4
Miami Sprs. A4
Miramar A3
N. Bay Vil. B4
N. Lauderdale B2
N. Miami C3
N. Miami Beach B3
Oakland Park B2
Opa-Locka B3
Ojus B3
Palmetto Bay A5
Palm Springs North A3
Parkland B1
Pembroke Park B3
Pembroke Pines A3
Perrine A5
Pinecrest A5
Plantation B2
Pompano Beach C1
Richmond Hts. A5
Rockdale A5
S. Miami A5
S. Miami Hts. A5
Southwest Ranches A3
Sunny Isles Beach C3
Sunrise B2
Surfside C4
Sweetwater A4
Tamarac A2
Virginia Gardens A4
W. Miami A4
Westchester A4
Weston A2
West Park B3
Westwood Lakes A4
Wilton Manors C2

Downtown Miami FL
OVERTOWN
DOWNTOWN
FINANCIAL DISTRICT
ARSHT CENTER
Knight Concert Hall
Frost Mus. of Sci.
Miami Children's Mus.
Kaseya Center
Freedom Tower
Bayside Marketplace
Klipsch Amphitheater at Bayfront Park
Bayfront Park
HistoryMiami
Olympia Theater
Flagler Palm Cottage
James L. Knight Center
Brickell Key
Jungle Island
Watson Island
San Marco Island
Miami Seaplane Base
PortMiami
Dodge I.
Biscayne I.
0 0.25 0.5 mi
0 0.25 0.5 0.75 km

POINTS OF INTEREST

Bayside Marketplace E2
Flagler Palm Cottage D2
Freedom Tower D1
Frost Museum of Science E1
HistoryMiami D2
James L. Knight Center D2
Jungle Island E1
Klipsch Amphitheater at Bayfront Park E2
Knight Concert Hall E1
Miami Children's Museum E1
Miami-Dade Arena E1
Miami Seaplane Base E1
Olympia Theater D2
PortMiami E2
Sanford & Dolores Ziff Ballet Opera House D1

Figures after entries indicate page number and grid reference.

Mascot TN 110 C4
Mascotte FL 140 C1
Mascoutah IL 98 B3
Mashpee MA 151 E3
Mason MI 76 A4
Mason NV 37 E2
Mason NH 95 D1
Mason OH 100 B2
Mason TN 118 C1
Mason TX 60 C1
Mason WV 101 E2
Masonboro NC 123 E3
Mason City IL 88 B4
Mason City IA 73 D3
Mason Co. IL 88 A4
Mason Co. KY 100 C3
Mason Co. MI 75 E1
Mason Co. TX 60 C1
Mason Co. WA 12 B3
Mason Co. WV 101 E3
Masontown PA 102 B1
Masontown WV 102 B1
Masonville KY 109 E1
Masonville NJ 147 D3
Massac Co. IL 108 C2
Massapequa NY 148 C4
Massapequa Park NY 148 C4
Massena NY 80 B1
Massillon OH 91 E3
Mastic NY 149 D4
Mastic Beach NY 149 D4
Masury OH 91 F2
Matador TX 58 B1
Matagorda Co. TX 132 A4
Matamoras PA 94 A3
Matawan NJ 147 E1
Matewan WV 111 E1
Matherville IL 88 A2
Mathews LA 134 B3
Mathews VA 113 F1
Mathews Co. VA 113 F1
Mathis TX 61 E4
Mathiston MS 118 C4
Matlacha FL 142 C1
Mattapoisett MA 151 E3
Mattawa WA 13 E4
Mattawamkeag ME 85 D4
Mattawan MI 89 F1
Mattawoman MD 144 B4
Matteson IL 89 D2
Matthews IN 89 F4
Matthews MO 108 B2
Matthews NC 122 B1
Mattituck NY 149 E3
Mattoon IL 98 C2
Mattydale NY 79 D3
Matunuck RI 150 C4
Maud OH 100 B2
Maud OK 51 F3
Maud TX 124 C1
Maugansville MD 103 D1
Maui Co. HI 153 D1
Mauldin SC 121 F2
Maumee OH 90 C2
Maumelle AR 117 E2
Maunawili HI 152 B3
Maupin OR 21 D2
Maurertown VA 102 C3
Maurice LA 133 F2
Mauriceville TX 132 C2
Maury City TN 108 C4
Maury Co. TN 109 E4
Mauston WI 74 A2
Maverick Co. TX 60 B3
Mavisdale VA 111 E2
Max ND 18 B3
Max Meadows VA 112 A2
Maxton NC 122 C2
Maxwell CA 36 B2
Maxwell IA 86 C1
Maxwell NM 49 E1
Maybee MI 90 C1
Maybeury WV 111 F1
Maybrook NY 148 B1
Mayer AZ 47 D4
Mayer MN 66 C4
Mayersville MS 126 A1
Mayes Co. OK 106 A3
Mayesville SC 122 B3
Mayfield KY 108 C3
Mayfield NY 80 C4
Mayfield OH 204 G1
Mayfield PA 93 F2
Mayfield UT 39 E2
Mayfield Hts. OH 91 E2
Mayflower AR 117 E2
Maynard IA 73 E4
Maynard MA 150 C1
Maynardville TN 110 C3
Mayo FL 137 F3
Mayo MD 144 C3
Mayo SC 121 F1
Mayodan NC 112 B3
Maypearl TX 59 F3
Mays Chapel MD 193 C1
Mays Landing NJ 105 D3
Maysville GA 121 D3
Maysville KY 100 C3
Maysville MO 96 B1
Maysville NC 115 D4
Maysville OK 51 E4
Maytown AL 195 D1
Mayville MI 76 C3
Mayville NY 78 A4
Mayville ND 19 E3
Mayville WI 74 C2
Maywood CA 228 D3
Maywood IL 203 C4
Maywood NJ 240 C1
Maywood NY 188 D2
Maywood Park OR 251 D2
Mazeppa MN 73 D1
Mazomanie WI 74 A3
Mazon IL 88 C2
McAdoo PA 93 E3
McAfee NJ 148 A2
McAlester OK 116 A2
McAlisterville PA 93 D3
McAllen TX 63 E4
McArthur OH 101 D2
McBain MI 75 F1
McBee SC 122 B3
McCall ID 22 B2
McCamey TX 58 A4
McCammon ID 31 E1
McCandless PA 92 A4
McCaysville GA 120 C2
McClain Co. OK 51 E3
McCleary WA 12 B4
McClellandville DE 146 B4
McClellanville SC 131 E1
McCloud CA 28 C3
McClure OH 90 B2
McClure PA 93 D3
McClusky ND 18 C3
McColl SC 122 C2
McComb MS 126 B4
McComb OH 90 B3
McCone Co. MT 17 E3
McConnellsburg PA 103 D1
McConnelsville OH 101 E1
McCook NE 42 C1
McCook Co. SD 27 E4
McCordsville IN 99 F1
McCormack Corners NY 188 C2
McCormick SC 121 F4
McCormick Co. SC 121 F4
McCracken Co. KY 108 C2
McCreary Co. KY 110 C2
McCrory AR 117 F1
McCulloch Co. TX 58 C4
McCune KS 106 B1
McCurtain OK 116 B1
McCurtain Co. OK 116 B3
McDermitt NV 30 A2
McDonald OH 276 B2
McDonald PA 92 A4
McDonald Co. MO 106 C3
McDonough GA 120 C4
McDonough Co. IL 87 F3
McDowell Co. NC 111 E4
McDowell Co. WV 111 F1
McDuffie Co. GA 129 F1
McEwen TN 109 E4
McFarland CA 45 D4
McFarland WI 74 B3
McGaheysville VA 102 C4
McGehee AR 117 F4
McGill NV 38 B2
McGrath AK 154 C2
McGraw NY 79 E4
McGregor IA 73 F3
McGregor TX 59 E4
McHenry IL 74 C4
McHenry KY 109 E1
McHenry Co. IL 74 C4
McHenry Co. ND 18 C2
McIntosh FL 138 C4
McIntosh MN 19 F3
McIntosh SD 26 B1
McIntosh Co. GA 130 B4
McIntosh Co. ND 27 D1
McIntosh Co. OK 116 A1
McIntyre GA 129 E2
McKean Co. PA 92 B1
McKee KY 110 C1
McKee City NJ 147 F4
McKeesport PA 92 A4
McKees Rocks PA 250 B1
McKenna WA 12 C4
McKenney VA 113 E2
McKenzie AL 127 F4
McKenzie TN 109 D4
McKenzie Co. ND 17 F2
McKinley Co. NM 48 A2
McKinleyville CA 28 A4
McKinney TX 59 F2
McKownville NY 188 D3
McLain MS 135 D1
McLaughlin SD 26 C1
McLean IL 88 B4
McLean TX 50 B3
McLean VA 144 B3
McLean Co. IL 88 C4
McLean Co. KY 109 E1
McLean Co. ND 18 B3
McLeansboro IL 98 C4
McLennan Co. TX 59 F4
McLeod Co. MN 66 C4
McLoud OK 51 E3
McLouth KS 96 A2
McMechen WV 101 F1
McMinn Co. TN 120 C1
McMinnville OR 20 B2
McMinnville TN 110 A4
McMullen Co. TX 61 D4
McMurray PA 92 A4
McNairy Co. TN 119 D1
McNary AZ 47 F4
McNeil AR 125 D1
McPherson KS 43 E3
McPherson Co. KS 43 E3
McPherson Co. NE 34 B3
McPherson Co. SD 27 D1
McQueeney TX 61 D2
McRae AR 117 F1
McRae GA 129 E3
McRoberts KY 111 E2
McSherrystown PA 103 E1
McVeigh KY 111 E1
McVille ND 19 E3
Mead CO 33 E4
Mead NE 35 F3
Mead WA 14 A3
Meade KS 42 C4
Meade Co. KS 42 C4
Meade Co. KY 99 F4
Meade Co. SD 26 A3
Meadow TX 58 A1
Meadowlakes TX 61 D1
Meadows Place TX 132 A3
Meadow Vale KY 230 F1
Meadow Valley CA 36 C1
Meadowview VA 111 F2
Meadville MS 126 A4
Meadville PA 92 A2
Meagher Co. MT 15 F4
Mebane NC 112 C4
Mecca CA 53 E3
Mechanic Falls ME 82 B2
Mechanicsburg OH 90 C4
Mechanicsburg PA 93 D4
Mechanicsville IA 87 F1
Mechanicsville MD 103 E3
Mechanicsville VA 113 E1
Mechanicville NY 94 B1
Mecklenburg Co. NC 122 B1
Mecklenburg Co. VA 113 D2
Mecosta Co. MI 75 F2
Medanales NM 48 C2
Medaryville IN 89 E3
Medfield MA 151 D2
Medford MA 151 D1
Medford MN 73 D1
Medford NJ 147 D3
Medford NY 149 D4
Medford OK 51 E1
Medford OR 28 B2
Medford WI 68 A3
Medford Lakes NJ 147 D3
Media PA 146 C3
Mediapolis IA 87 F3
Medical Lake WA 13 F3
Medicine Bow WY 33 D2
Medicine Lake MT 17 F2
Medicine Lodge KS 43 D4
Medina MN 66 C3
Medina NY 78 B3
Medina ND 19 D4
Medina OH 91 E3
Medina TN 108 C4
Medina WA 262 B3
Medina Co. OH 91 E3
Medina Co. TX 60 C3
Medinah IL 203 B3
Medley FL 233 A4
Medora IN 99 F3
Medora ND 18 A4
Medulla FL 140 C2
Medway ME 85 D4
Medway MA 150 C2
Meeker CO 40 B1
Meeker OK 51 F3
Meeker Co. MN 66 B3
Meenon WI 67 E2
Meeteetse WY 24 B3

Bayside D1	Elm Grove B2	Hales Corners B3	Pewaukee (city) A2	Sussex A1	Whitefish Bay D1
Brookfield B2	Fox Pt. D1	Lannon A1	Pewaukee (village) A2	Waukesha A2	
Brown Deer C1	Glendale C1	Menomonee Falls B1	River Hills D1	Wauwatosa C2	
Butler B1	Greendale C3	Milwaukee C2	St. Francis D3	W. Allis C3	
Cudahy D3	Greenfield C3	New Berlin B3	Shorewood D2	W. Milwaukee C3	

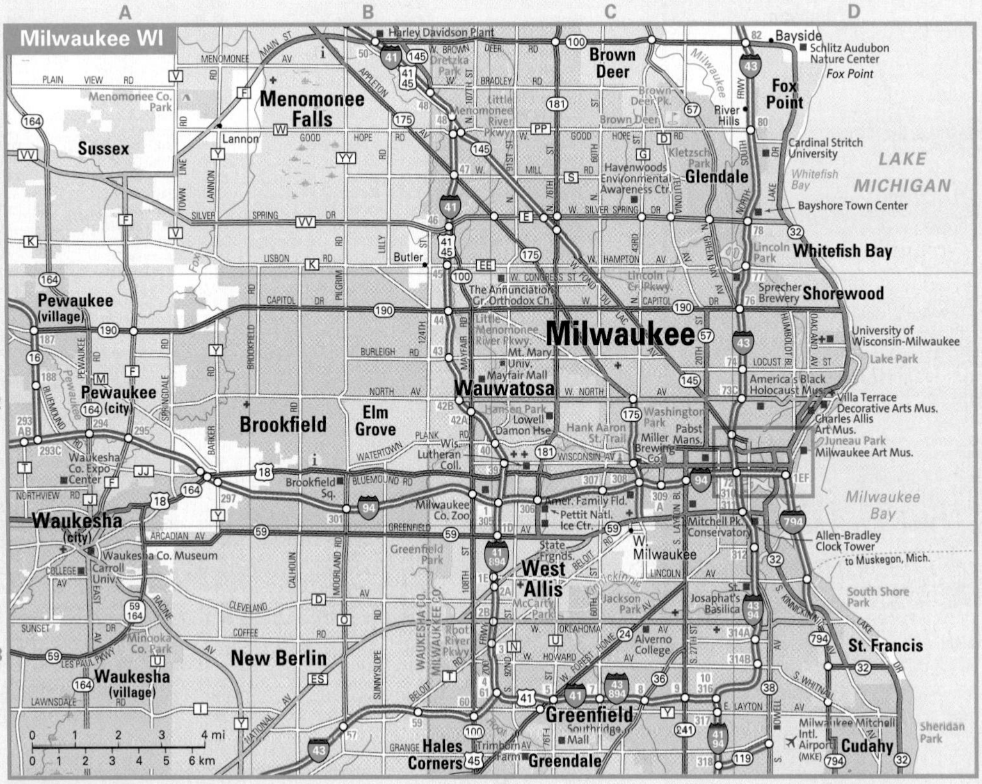

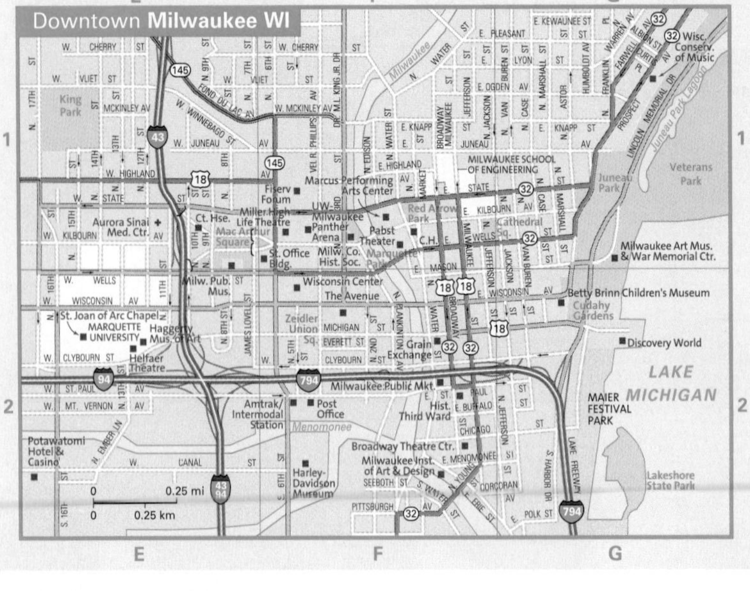

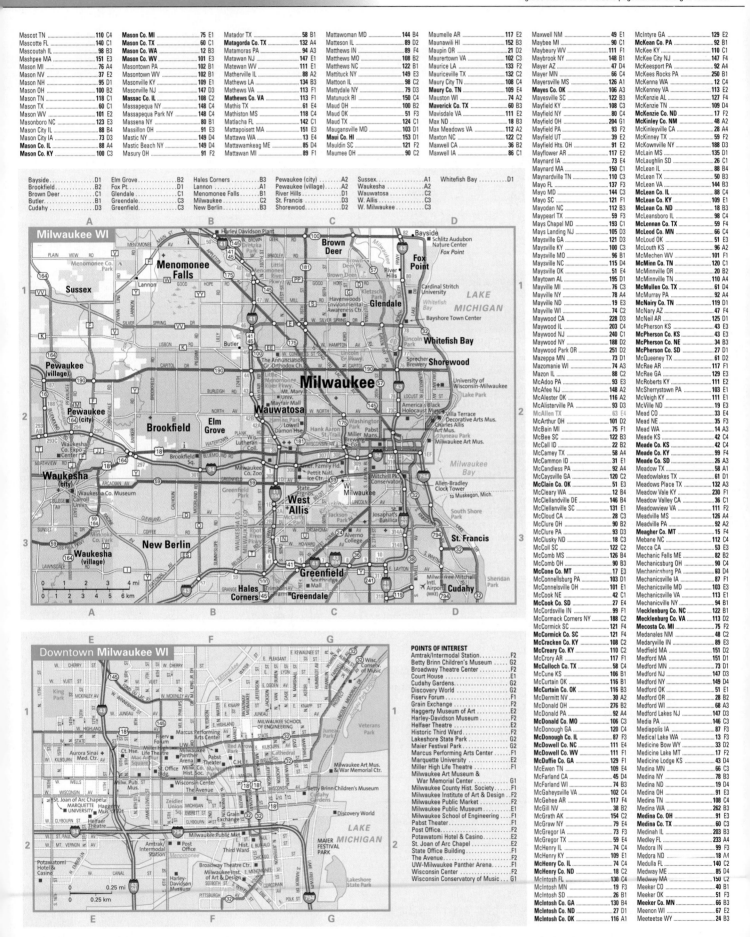

POINTS OF INTEREST

Amtrak/Intermodal Station F2
Betty Brinn Children's Museum G2
Broadway Theatre Center F2
Court House E1
Cudahy Gardens G2
Discovery World G2
Fiserv Forum F1
Grain Exchange F2
Haggerty Museum of Art E2
Harley-Davidson Museum E2
Helfaer Theatre E2
Historic Third Ward F2
Lakeshore State Park G2
Maier Festival Park G2
Marcus Performing Arts Center F1
Marquette University E2
Miller High Life Theatre F1
Milwaukee Art Museum & War Memorial Center G1
Milwaukee County Hist. Society F1
Milwaukee Institute of Art & Design F2
Milwaukee Public Market F2
Milwaukee Public Museum E1
Milwaukee School of Engineering F1
Pabst Theater F1
Post Office F2
Potawatomi Hotel & Casino E2
St. Joan of Arc Chapel E2
State Office Building F1
The Avenue F2
UW-Milwaukee Panther Arena F1
Wisconsin Center F2
Wisconsin Conservatory of Music G1

Entries in **bold black** indicate counties or parishes.
Entries in **bold color** indicate cities with detailed inset maps.

Meggett SC 131 D2
Mehlville MO 98 A3
Meigs GA 137 E1
Meigs Co. OH 101 E2
Meigs Co. TN 110 B4
Meiners Oaks CA 52 B2
Melba ID 22 B4
Melbourne AR 107 E4
Melbourne FL 141 E2
Melbourne IA 87 D1
Melbourne KY 204 C3
Melbourne Beach FL 141 E2
Melbourne Vil. FL 141 E2
Melcher-Dallas IA 87 D2
Melfa VA 114 C3
Melissa TX 59 F2
Mellen WI 65 D4
Mellette SD 27 E2
Mellette Co. SD 26 C4
Melrose MN 66 B2
Melrose NM 49 F4
Melrose NY 94 B1
Melrose WI 73 F1
Melrose Park IL 203 C4
Melrose Park NY 79 D3
Melvern KS 96 A3
Melville LA 133 F1
Melvindale MI 210 B4
Memphis FL 140 B3
Memphis MI 76 C3
Memphis MO 87 E4
Memphis TN 118 B1
Memphis TX 50 B4
Memphis Jct. KY 109 F2
Mena AR 116 C2
Menahga MN 64 A4
Menan ID 23 E4
Menands NY 188 E3
Menard TX 60 C1
Menard Co. IL 88 B4
Menard Co. TX 60 C1
Menasha WI 74 C1
Mendenhall MS 126 B3
Mendenhall PA 146 B3
Mendham NJ 148 A4
Mendocino CA 36 A2
Mendocino Co. CA 36 A1
Mendon IL 87 F4
Mendon MA 150 C2
Mendon MI 89 F1
Mendon OH 90 B3
Mendon UT 31 E3
Mendota CA 44 C3
Mendota IL 88 B2
Mendota Hts. MN 235 D3
Menifee CA 53 D3
Menifee Co. KY 100 C4
Menlo GA 120 B3
Menlo Park CA 259 C5
Menno SD 27 E4
Menominee MI 69 D3
Menominee Co. MI 69 D3
Menominee Co. WI 68 C3
Menomonee Falls WI 74 C3
Menomonie WI 67 E4
Mentone AL 120 B2
Mentone CA 53 D2
Mentone IN 89 F2
Mentone TX 57 E4
Mentor OH 91 E2
Mentor TN 110 C4
Mentor-on-the-Lake OH 91 E1
Mequon WI 74 C3
Meraux LA 134 C3
Merced CA 37 D4
Merced Co. CA 44 C2
Mercedes TX 63 E4
Mercer PA 91 F2
Mercer Co. IL 87 F2
Mercer Co. KY 110 B1
Mercer Co. MO 86 C4
Mercer Co. NJ 147 D2
Mercer Co. ND 18 B3
Mercer Co. OH 90 A4
Mercer Co. PA 91 F2
Mercer Co. WV 112 A1
Mercer Island WA 262 B3
Mercersburg PA 103 D1
Mercerville NJ 147 D2
Merchantville NJ 248 D3
Meredith NH 81 F3
Meredosia IL 98 A1
Meriden CT 149 D1
Meriden KS 96 A2
Meridian ID 22 B4
Meridian MS 127 D2
Meridian PA 92 A3
Meridian TX 59 E3
Meridian Hills IN 99 F1
Meridianville AL 119 F2
Merigold MS 118 A4
Meriwether Co. GA 128 C1
Merkel TX 58 C3
Merlin OR 28 B1
Mermentau LA 133 E2
Merriam KS 224 B4
Merriam Woods MO 107 D3
Merrick NY 148 C4
Merrick Co. NE 35 E3
Merrifield VA 270 A3
Merrill IA 35 F1
Merrill MI 76 A2
Merrill OR 28 C2
Merrill WI 68 B3
Merrillan WI 73 F1
Merrillville IN 89 D2
Merrimac MA 151 F1
Merrimack NH 95 D1
Merrimack Co. NH 81 F4
Merrionette Park IL 203 D6
Merritt Island FL 141 E2
Mer Rouge LA 125 F2
Merrow CT 150 A3
Merryville LA 133 D1
Merton WI 74 C3
Mertzon TX 58 B4
Mertztown PA 146 B1
Mesa AZ 54 C1
Mesa WA 13 E4
Mesa Co. CO 40 B2
Mescalero NM 56 C2
Mesilla NM 56 C3
Mesita NM 48 B3
Mesquite NV 46 B1
Mesquite NM 56 C3
Mesquite TX 59 F2
Metairie LA 134 B3
Metamora IL 88 B3
Metamora MI 76 C3
Metamora OH 90 B2
Metcalfe MS 118 A4
Metcalfe Co. KY 110 A2
Methuen MA 95 E1
Metlakatla AK 155 E4
Metolius OR 21 D3
Metropolis IL 108 C2
Metter GA 129 F2
Metuchen NJ 147 E1
Metzger OR 251 C2
Mexia TX 59 F4
Mexico IN 89 F3
Mexico ME 82 B2
Mexico MO 97 E2
Mexico NY 79 D2
Mexico Beach FL 136 C3
Meyersdale PA 102 C1
Meyers Lake OH 199 B2
Miami AZ 55 D1
Miami FL 143 F2
Miami OK 106 B2
Miami TX 50 B2

Apple Valley C4
Arden Hills C1
Bald Eagle E1
Birchwood Vil. E1
Blaine C1
Bloomington B4
Brooklyn Ctr. B1
Brooklyn Park B1
Burnsville B4
Circle Pines C1
Columbia Hts. C2
Coon Rapids B1
Cottage Grove E4
Crystal B2
Deephaven A3
Dellwood E1
Eagan D4
Eden Prairie A4
Edina B3
Falcon Hts. C2
Fridley C1
Gem Lake D1
Golden Valley B2
Grant E1
Hilltop C1
Hopkins A3
Hugo E1
Inver Grove Hts. D4
Lake Elmo E2
Landfall E3
Lauderdale C2
Lexington C1
Lilydale D3
Lino Lakes D1
Little Canada D2
Mahtomedi E1
Maple Grove A1
Maplewood D2
Medicine Lake A2
Mendota C3
Mendota Hts. D3
Minneapolis B3
Minnetonka A3
Mounds View C1
New Brighton C1
New Hope B2
Newport D3
Nininger E4
N. Oaks D1
N. St. Paul D2
Oakdale E2
Osseo A1
Pine Sprs. E2
Plymouth A2
Richfield B3
Robbinsdale B2
Rosemount D4
Roseville C2
St. Anthony C2
St. Louis Park B2
St. Paul D2
St. Paul Park E4
Savage B4
Shakopee A4
Shoreview C1
S. St. Paul D3
Spring Lake Park C1
Sunfish Lake D3
Vadnais Hts. D1
Wayzata A2
W. St. Paul D3
White Bear Lake D1
Willernie E1
Withrow E1
Woodbury E3
Woodland A3

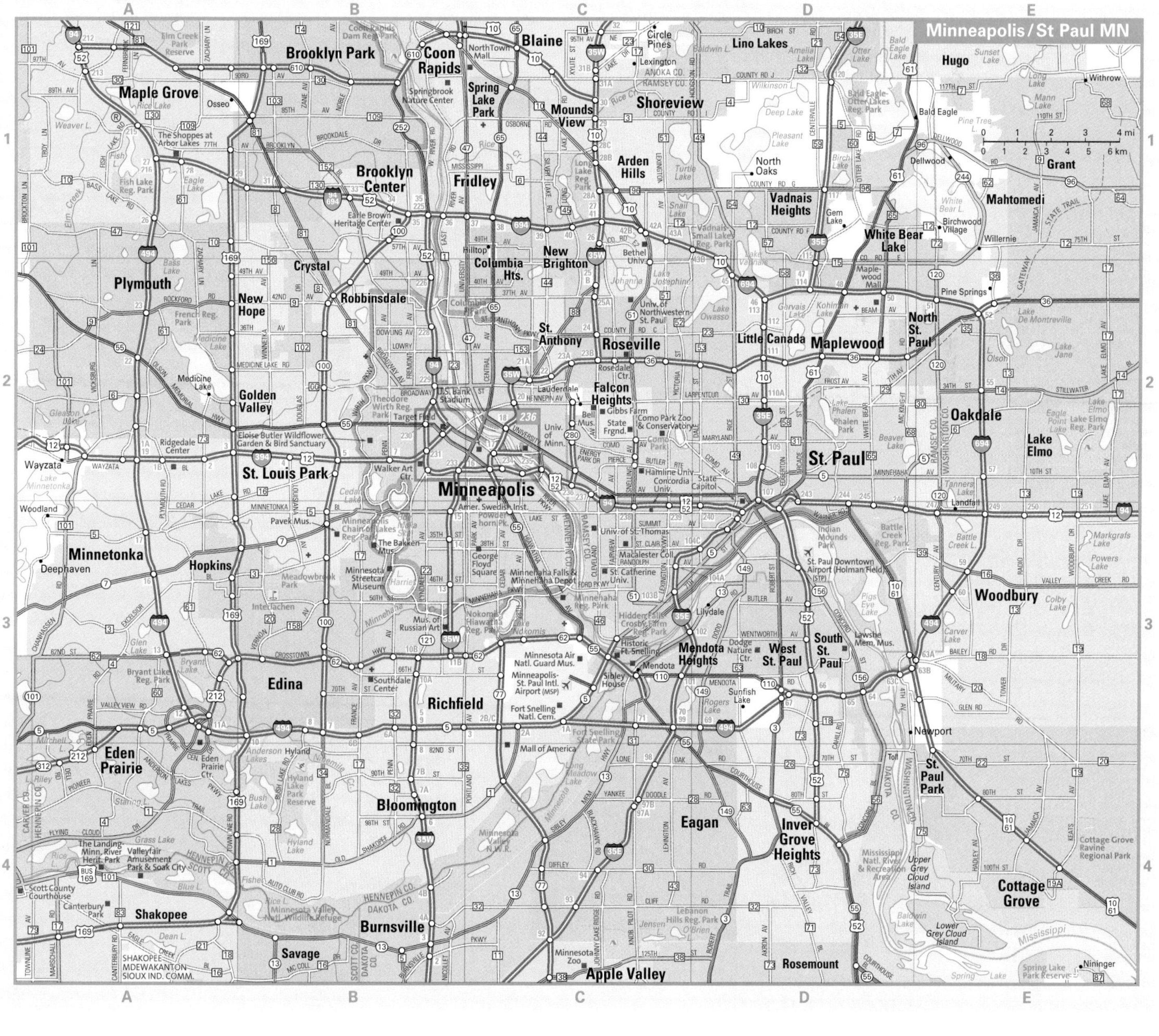

Minneapolis / St Paul MN
A
B
C
D
E
1
2
3
4
Blaine
Lino Lakes
Brooklyn Park
Coon Rapids
Hugo
Maple Grove
Osseo
Spring Lake Park
Mounds View
Shoreview
Circle Pines
Lexington
Bald Eagle
Withrow
Grant
Dellwood
Mahtomedi
Willernie
Birchwood Village
Brooklyn Center
Fridley
Arden Hills
North Oaks
Vadnais Heights
Gem Lake
White Bear Lake
New Brighton
Columbia Hts.
Hilltop
Crystal
Plymouth
New Hope
Robbinsdale
St. Anthony
Roseville
Little Canada
Maplewood
North St. Paul
Pine Springs
Golden Valley
Lauderdale
Falcon Heights
Oakdale
Lake Elmo
Wayzata
St. Louis Park
Minneapolis
St. Paul
Landfall
Woodland
Minnetonka
Deephaven
Hopkins
Woodbury
Edina
Richfield
Mendota Heights
West St. Paul
South St. Paul
Lilydale
Mendota
Sunfish Lake
Newport
Eden Prairie
Bloomington
Eagan
Inver Grove Heights
St. Paul Park
Cottage Grove
Shakopee
Savage
Burnsville
Apple Valley
Rosemount
Nininger
Mississippi
Minnesota Valley Natl. Wildlife Refuge
Mall of America
Minneapolis-St. Paul Intl. Airport (MSP)
0 1 2 3 4 mi
0 1 2 3 4 5 6 km

Figures after entries indicate page number and grid reference.

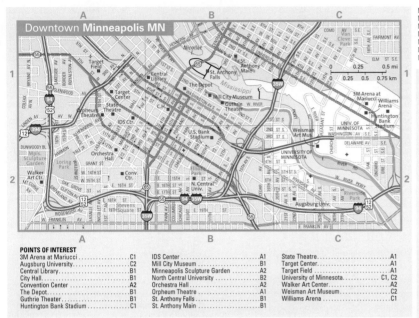

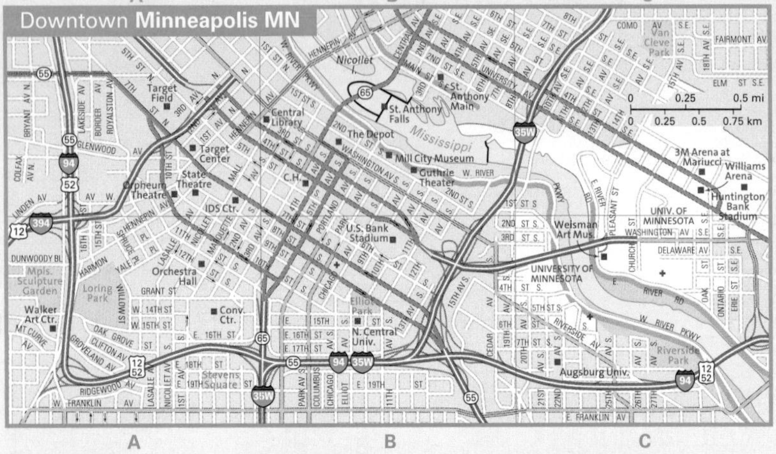
Downtown Minneapolis MN
Mississippi
Target Field
Central Library
The Depot
Mill City Museum
Guthrie Theater
St. Anthony Falls
St. Anthony Main
Target Center
State Theatre
Orpheum Theatre
IDS Ctr.
U.S. Bank Stadium
Weisman Art Mus.
UNIV. OF MINNESOTA
3M Arena at Mariucci
Williams Arena
Huntington Bank Stadium
Orchestra Hall
Conv. Ctr.
Mpls. Sculpture Garden
Loring Park
Walker Art Ctr.
N. Central Univ.
Elliot Park
Augsburg Univ.
Riverside Park
Stevens Square

POINTS OF INTEREST

3M Arena at Mariucci C1
Augsburg University....................C2
Central Library..........................B1
City Hall..................................B1
Convention Center A2
The Depot..................................B1
Guthrie Theater..........................B1
Huntington Bank Stadium C1
IDS Center A1
Mill City Museum B1
Minneapolis Sculpture Garden A2
North Central University B2
Orchestra Hall A2
Orpheum Theatre A1
St. Anthony Falls B1
St. Anthony Main B1
State Theatre...............................A1
Target Center...............................A1
Target Field A1
University of Minnesota............. C1, C2
Walker Art Center..........................A2
Weisman Art Museum....................C2
Williams Arena C1

Miami Beach FL 143 F2
Miami Co. IN 89 F3
Miami Co. KS 96 B3
Miami Co. OH 90 B4
Miami-Dade Co. FL 143 E2
Miami Gardens FL 143 E2
Miami Lakes FL 233 A3
Miamisburg OH 100 B1
Miami Shores FL 143 F2
Miami Sprs. FL 143 E2
Micanopy FL 138 C4
Micaville NC 111 E4
Micco FL 141 E2
Michie TN 119 D2
Michigan ND 19 E2
Michigan Ctr. MI 90 B1
Michigan City IN 89 E1
Middleboro MA 151 D3
Middlebourne WV 101 F2
Middleburg FL 139 D3
Middleburg PA 93 D3
Middleburg VA 144 A3
Middleburgh NY 79 F4
Middleburg Hts. OH 204 E3
Middlebury CT 149 D1
Middlebury IN 89 F2
Middlebury VT 81 D3
Middle Falls NY 81 D4
Middlefield CT 149 E1
Middlefield OH 91 F2
Middle Haddam CT 149 E1
Middle Island NY 149 D3
Middle Pt. OH 90 B3
Middleport NY 78 B3
Middleport OH 101 E2
Middle River MD 144 C2
Middlesboro KY 110 C3
Middlesex NJ 147 D1
Middlesex NC 113 D4
Middlesex Co. CT 149 E1
Middlesex Co. MA 151 D1
Middlesex Co. NJ 147 E2
Middlesex Co. VA 113 F1
Middleton ID 22 B4
Middleton MA 151 F1
Middleton TN 118 C2
Middleton WI 74 B3
Middletown CA 36 B2
Middletown CT 149 E1
Middletown DE 145 E1
Middletown IN 89 F4
Middletown IA 87 F3
Middletown KY 100 A4
Middletown MD 144 A1
Middletown NY 148 A1
Middletown OH 100 B1
Middletown PA 93 E4
Middletown PA 189 B1
Middletown RI 151 D4
Middletown VA 102 C2
Middle Valley TN 120 B1
Middleville MI 75 F4
Middleville NY 79 F3
Midfield AL 119 F4
Midland MI 76 B2
Midland NC 122 B1
Midland PA 91 F3
Midland TX 58 A3
Midland WA 262 A5
Midland City AL 128 B4
Midland Co. MI 76 A2
Midland Co. TX 58 A3
Midlothian IL 203 D6
Midlothian TX 59 F3
Midlothian VA 113 E1
Midtown TN 110 B4
Midvale UT 257 B3
Midway AL 128 B3
Midway DE 145 F4
Midway FL 137 E2
Midway GA 130 B3
Midway KY 100 B4
Midway LA 125 E4
Midway NM 57 E2
Midway NC 112 B4
Midway PA 91 F4
Midway TN 111 D4
Midway UT 31 F4
Midwest WY 25 D4
Midwest City OK 51 E3
Mifflin PA 93 D4
Mifflinburg PA 93 D3
Mifflin Co. PA 93 D3
Mifflintown PA 93 D4
Mifflinville PA 93 E3
Milaca MN 66 C2
Milam TX 124 C4
Milam Co. TX 61 F1
Milan GA 129 E3
Milan IL 88 A2
Milan IN 100 A2
Milan MI 90 C1
Milan MO 87 D4
Milan NM 48 B3
Milan OH 91 D2
Milan TN 108 C4
Milbank SD 27 F2
Milbridge ME 83 E2
Miles TX 58 C4
Milesburg PA 92 C3
Miles City MT 17 E4
Milford CT 149 D2
Milford DE 145 F3
Milford IL 89 D3
Milford IN 89 F2
Milford IA 72 A3
Milford KS 43 F2
Milford ME 83 D1
Milford MD 193 B2
Milford MA 150 C2

Missoula MT
Missoula
Rocky Mtn. Elk Foundation Visitor Center
Missoula Montana Arpt. (MSO)
Aerial Fire Depot & Smokejumper Center
Missoula Art Mus.
Mt. Jumbo 4,546
Ogren Park at Allegiance Field
Mont. Natural History Ctr.
Carousel
Ct. Hse.
UNIVERSITY OF MONTANA
Mt. Sentinel 5,158
Historical Mus. at Fort Missoula
Mem. Rose Gdn.
Missoula Co. Fairgrounds
Southgate Mall
Fort Missoula Hist. District
McCauley Butte 3,464
LOLO NATIONAL FOREST
LOLO NATL. FOR.
Pattee Creek
Bitterroot

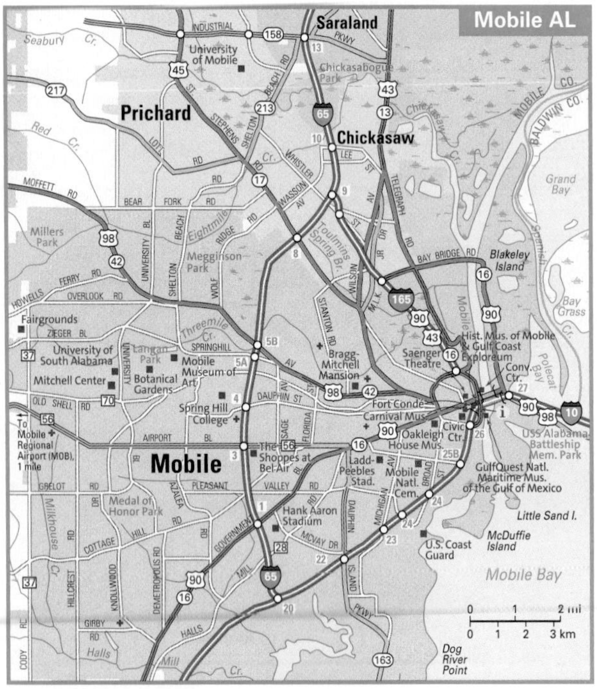
Mobile AL
Saraland
University of Mobile
Chickasabogue Park
Prichard
Chickasaw
Blakeley Island
Millers Park
Meggison Park
Fairgrounds
University of South Alabama
Langan Park
Mobile Museum of Art
Mobile Botanical Gardens
Mitchell Center
Bragg-Mitchell Mansion
Spring Hill College
Saenger Theatre
Hist. Mus. of Mobile
Gulf Coast Exploreum
Conv. Ctr.
Fort Condé
Carnival Mus.
Civic Ctr.
Oakleigh House Mus.
USS Alabama Battleship Mem. Park
GulfQuest Natl. Maritime Mus. of the Gulf of Mexico
Mobile
The Shoppes at Bel Air
Ladd-Peebles Stad.
Mobile Natl. Cem.
Medal of Honor Park
Hank Aaron Stadium
U.S. Coast Guard
Little Sand I.
McDuffie Island
Mobile Bay
Grand Bay
Dog River Point
To Mobile Regional Airport (MOB), 1 mile

Aptos.............. D1
Aromas E2
Ben Lomond........ D1
Bolsa Knolls.........E2
Capitola............ D1
Carmel-by-the-Sea .. D3
Carmel Highlands ... D3
Carmel Valley........E3
Castroville...........E2
Corralitos E1
Del Rey Oaks E3
Elkhorn E2
Felton............... D1
Freedom E1
Gabilan Acres E2
Gilroy.................E1
La Selva Beach..... D1
Las Lomas E2
Live Oak D1
Marina................E2
Monterey D3
Moss Landing E2
Mt. Hermon D1
Opal Cliffs.......... D1
Pacific Grove....... D3
Pajaro E1
Paradise Park D1
Pebble Beach D3
Prunedale.............E2
Rio del Mar......... D1
Salinas E3
Sand City E3
Santa Cruz D1
Scotts Valley D1
Seaside...............E3
Soquel............... D1
Spreckels E3
Twin Lakes......... D1
Watsonville E1
Zayante............. D1

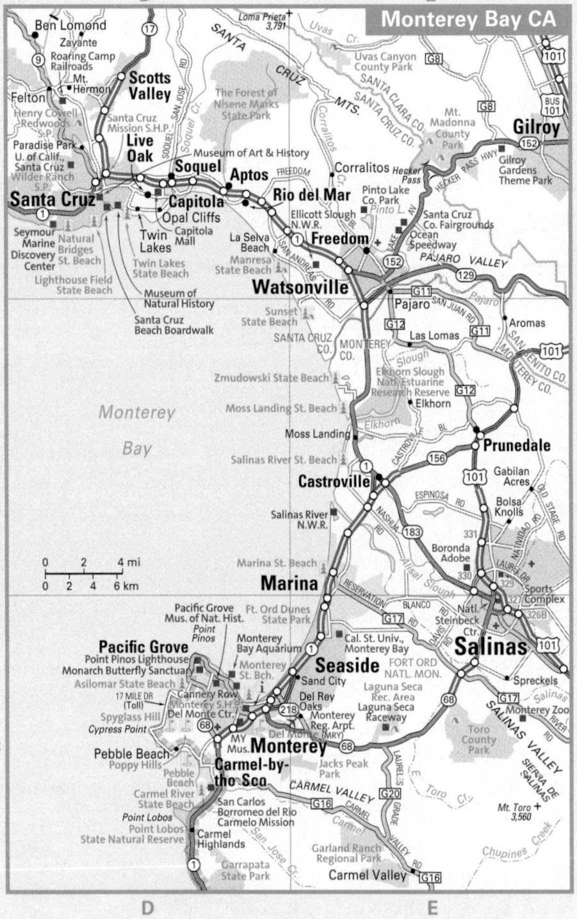
Monterey Bay CA
Ben Lomond
Zayante
Roaring Camp Railroads
Mt. Hermon
Felton
Scotts Valley
Loma Prieta 3,791
Uvas Canyon County Park
The Forest of Nisene Marks State Park
Gilroy
Live Oak
Soquel
Aptos
Santa Cruz
Capitola
Rio del Mar
Corralitos
Freedom
Watsonville
Pajaro
Aromas
Las Lomas
Elkhorn
Moss Landing
Prunedale
Castroville
Marina
Monterey Bay
Pacific Grove
Seaside
Sand City
Del Rey Oaks
Monterey
Carmel-by-the-Sea
Pebble Beach
Carmel Highlands
Carmel Valley
Salinas
Spreckels
Monterey Bay Aquarium
Mt. Toro 3,560

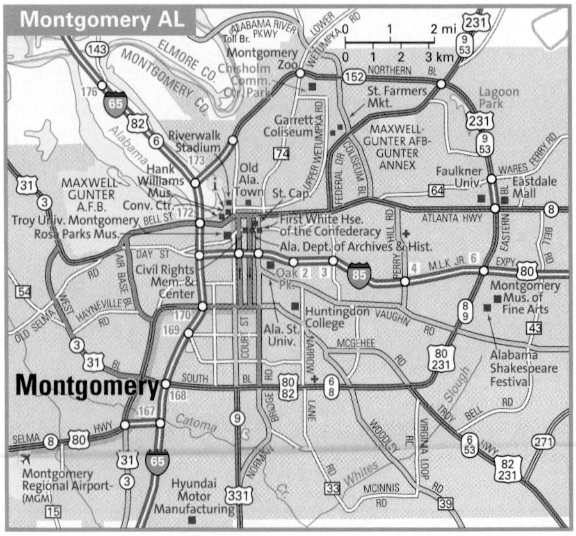
Montgomery AL
Montgomery Zoo
Chisholm Comm. Ctr. Park
St. Farmers Mkt.
Lagoon Park
Garrett Coliseum
MAXWELL-GUNTER AFB-GUNTER ANNEX
Riverwalk Stadium
Hank Williams Mus.
Old Ala. Town
St. Cap.
MAXWELL-GUNTER A.F.B.
Conv. Ctr.
Faulkner Univ.
Eastdale Mall
Troy Univ. Montgomery
Rosa Parks Mus.
First White Hse. of the Confederacy
Ala. Dept. of Archives & Hist.
Civil Rights Mem. & Center
Oak Pk.
Huntingdon College
Ala. St. Univ.
Montgomery Mus. of Fine Arts
Alabama Shakespeare Festival
Montgomery
Montgomery Regional Airport (MGM)
Hyundai Motor Manufacturing

Entries in **bold black** indicate counties or parishes.
Entries in bold color indicate cities with detailed inset maps.

Milford MI 76 B4
Milford NE 35 F4
Milford NH 95 D1
Milford NJ 146 C1
Milford NY 79 F4
Milford OH 100 B2
Milford PA 94 A3
Milford TX 59 F3
Milford UT 39 D3
Milford Ctr. OH 90 C4
Milford Square PA 146 C1
Mililani Town HI 152 A3
Millard Co. UT 39 D2
Millbourne PA 248 B3
Millbrae CA 259 B4
Millbrook AL 128 A2
Millbrook NY 94 B3
Millburn NJ 240 A3
Millbury MA 150 C2
Millbury OH 90 C2
Mill City NV 29 F4
Mill City OR 20 C3
Mill Creek WA 12 C3
Mill Creek WV 102 A3
Milledgeville GA 129 E1
Milledgeville IL 88 B1
Mille Lacs Co. MN 66 C2
Millen GA 129 F2
Miller MO 106 C2
Miller SD 27 D3
Miller Co. AR 124 C1
Miller Co. GA 128 C4
Miller Co. MO 97 E4
Miller Place NY 149 D3
Millersburg IN 89 F2
Millersburg KY 100 B4
Millersburg OH 91 E4
Millersburg OR 20 B3
Millersburg PA 93 D4
Millers Creek NC 111 F3
Millers Falls MA 94 C1
Millersport OH 101 D1
Millerstown PA 93 D4
Millersville PA 146 A3
Millersville TN 109 F3
Millerton NY 94 B2
Mill Hall PA 93 D3
Milliken CO 33 E4
Millington MI 76 B3
Millington NJ 148 A4
Millington TN 118 B1
Millinocket ME 85 D4
Millis MA 150 C2
Mill Neck NY 148 C3
Millport AL 119 D4
Millry AL 127 D4
Mills WY 33 D1
Millsboro DE 145 F4
Mills Co. IA 86 A3
Mills Co. TX 59 D4
Millstadt IL 98 A3
Millstone KY 111 E2
Milltown IN 99 F4
Milltown NJ 147 E1
Milltown WI 67 E3
Millvale PA 250 B1
Mill Valley CA 36 B4
Millville CA 28 C4
Millville DE 145 F4
Millville NJ 145 F1
Millville OH 100 B2
Millville PA 93 E3
Millville UT 31 E3
Millwood NY 148 B2
Millwood WA 14 A3
Milner GA 129 D1
Milnor ND 27 E1
Milo IA 86 C2
Milo ME 84 C4
Milpitas CA 36 B4
Milroy IN 100 A2
Milroy PA 93 D3
Milton DE 145 F3
Milton FL 135 F1
Milton IN 100 A1
Milton IA 87 E3
Milton KY 100 A3
Milton MA 151 D1
Milton NH 81 F4
Milton NY 148 B1
Milton PA 93 D3
Milton VT 81 D1
Milton WA 262 B5
Milton WV 101 E3
Milton WI 74 B4
Milton-Freewater OR 21 F1
Miltonvale KS 43 E2
Milwaukee WI 74 C3
Milwaukee Co. WI 75 D3
Milwaukie OR 251 D2
Mimosa Park LA 239 A2
Mims FL 141 E1
Mina NV 37 F3
Minatare NE 33 F2
Minco OK 51 E3
Minden IA 86 A2
Minden LA 125 D2
Minden NE 35 D4
Minden NV 37 D2
Mineola NY 148 C4
Mineola TX 124 A2
Miner MO 108 B2
Mineral VA 103 D4
Mineral City OH 91 E4
Mineral Co. CO 40 C4
Mineral Co. MT 14 C3
Mineral Co. NV 37 E3
Mineral Co. WV 102 C2
Mineral Pt. WI 74 A3
Mineral Ridge OH 276 B2
Mineral Sprs. AR 116 C4
Mineral Sprs. NC 122 B2
Mineral Wells TX 59 E2
Mineral Wells WV 101 E2
Miner Co. SD 27 E3
Minersville PA 93 E3
Minersville UT 39 D3
Minerva OH 91 F3
Minerva Park OH 206 B1
Minetto NY 79 D2
Mineville NY 81 D2
Mingo Co. WV 101 E4
Mingo Jct. OH 91 F4
Minidoka Co. ID 31 D1
Minier IL 88 B4
Minneapolis KS 43 E2
Minneapolis MN 67 D4
Minnehaha Co. SD 27 F4
Minneola FL 140 C1
Minneola KS 42 C4
Minneota MN 27 F3
Minnesota Lake MN 72 C2
Minnetonka MN 235 A3
Minnewaukan ND 19 D2
Minoa NY 79 E3
Minocqua WI 68 B2
Minong WI 67 E2
Minonk IL 88 B3
Minooka IL 88 C2
Minor Hill TN 119 E2
Minot ME 82 B3
Minot MA 151 E2
Minot ND 18 B2
Minster OH 90 B4
Mint Hill NC 122 B1
Minto ND 19 E2
Minturn CO 41 D1
Mio MI 70 C4
Miramar FL 143 E2
Miramar Beach FL 136 B2
Misenheimer NC 122 B1
Mishawaka IN 89 F2
Mishicot WI 75 D1
Missaukee Co. MI 75 F1
Mission KS 224 B3
Mission OR 21 F1
Mission SD 26 C4
Mission TX 63 E4
Mission Bend TX 220 A3
Mission Hills KS 224 B4
Mission Viejo CA 52 C3
Mississippi Co. AR 108 B4
Mississippi Co. MO 108 C2
Mississippi State MS 119 D4
Missoula MT 15 D4
Missoula Co. MT 15 D4
Missouri City TX 132 A3
Missouri Valley IA 86 A2
Mitchell IN 99 F3
Mitchell NE 33 F2
Mitchell SD 27 E4
Mitchell Co. GA 137 E1
Mitchell Co. IA 73 D2
Mitchell Co. KS 43 E2
Mitchell Co. NC 111 E4
Mitchell Co. TX 58 B3
Mitchellville AR 117 F4
Mitchellville IA 87 D2
Mi-Wuk Vil. CA 37 D3
Moab UT 40 A2
Moapa NV 46 B1
Moberly MO 97 E2
Mobile AL 135 E1
Mobile Co. AL 135 E1
Mobridge SD 26 C2
Mocksville NC 112 A4
Moclips WA 12 B3
Modena NY 148 B1
Modena PA 146 B3
Modesto CA 36 C4
Modoc Co. CA 29 D3
Moenkopi AZ 47 E2
Moffat Co. CO 32 B4
Mogadore OH 188 B2
Mohall ND 18 B1
Mohave Co. AZ 46 B3
Mohave Valley AZ 46 B3
Mohawk MI 65 F3
Mohawk NY 79 F3
Mohegan CT 149 F1
Mohnton PA 146 A2
Mohrsville PA 146 A1
Mojave CA 52 C1
Mokelumne Hill CA 36 C3
Mokuleia HI 152 A2
Molalla OR 20 C2
Molena GA 128 C1
Moline IL 88 A2
Moline KS 43 F4
Moline Acres MO 256 C1
Molino FL 135 F1
Momence IL 89 D2
Mona UT 39 E1
Monaca PA 91 F3
Monahans TX 57 F4
Monarch Mill SC 121 F2
Moncks Corner SC 131 D1
Mondovi WI 67 E4
Monee IL 89 D2
Monessen PA 92 A4
Monett MO 106 C2
Monette AR 108 A4
Monfort Hts. OH 204 A2
Moniteau Co. MO 97 D3
Monmouth IL 88 A3
Monmouth ME 82 B2
Monmouth OR 20 B2
Monmouth Beach NJ 147 F2
Monmouth Co. NJ 147 E2
Monmouth Jct. NJ 147 D1
Mono Co. CA 37 E4
Monon IN 89 E3
Monona IA 73 F3
Monona WI 74 B3
Monona Co. IA 86 A1
Monongah WV 102 A2
Monongahela PA 92 A4
Monongalia Co. WV 102 A1
Monponsett MA 151 E2
Monroe CT 149 D2
Monroe GA 121 D4
Monroe IN 90 A3
Monroe IA 87 D2
Monroe LA 125 E2
Monroe MI 90 C1
Monroe NY 148 B2
Monroe NC 122 B2
Monroe OH 100 B2
Monroe OR 20 B3
Monroe UT 39 E3
Monroe VA 112 C1
Monroe WA 12 C3
Monroe WI 74 B4
Monroe City IN 99 E3
Monroe City MO 97 E1
Monroe Co. AL 127 F4
Monroe Co. AR 118 A2
Monroe Co. FL 143 D3
Monroe Co. GA 129 D1
Monroe Co. IL 98 A4
Monroe Co. IN 99 F2
Monroe Co. IA 87 D3
Monroe Co. KY 110 A2
Monroe Co. MI 90 C1
Monroe Co. MS 119 D4
Monroe Co. MO 97 E2
Monroe Co. NY 78 C3
Monroe Co. OH 101 F1
Monroe Co. PA 93 F3
Monroe Co. TN 120 C1
Monroe Co. WV 112 A1
Monroe Co. WI 73 F1
Monroeville AL 127 F4
Monroeville IN 90 A3
Monroeville OH 91 D2
Monroeville PA 92 A4
Monrovia CA 228 E2
Monrovia IN 99 F1
Monsey NY 148 B2
Monson MA 150 A2
Montague CA 28 C3
Montague MA 94 C1
Montague MI 75 E2
Montague TX 59 E1
Montague Co. TX 59 E1
Mont Alto PA 103 D1
Montana City MT 15 E4
Montara CA 259 A4
Montauk NY 149 F3
Mont Belvieu TX 132 B3
Montcalm WV 111 F1
Montcalm Co. MI 75 F2
Montclair CA 229 G2
Montclair NJ 148 A3
Mont Clare PA 146 B2
Monteagle TN 120 A1
Monte Alto TX 63 E4
Montebello CA 228 D3
Montecito CA 52 B2
Montegut LA 134 B4
Montello WI 74 B2
Monterey CA 44 B3
Monterey TN 110 B4
Monterey VA 102 B3
Monterey Co. CA 44 B3
Monterey Park CA 228 D2
Monte Rio CA 36 A3
Montesano WA 12 B4
Montevallo AL 127 F1
Montevideo MN 66 A4
Monte Vista CO 41 D4
Montezuma GA 129 D3

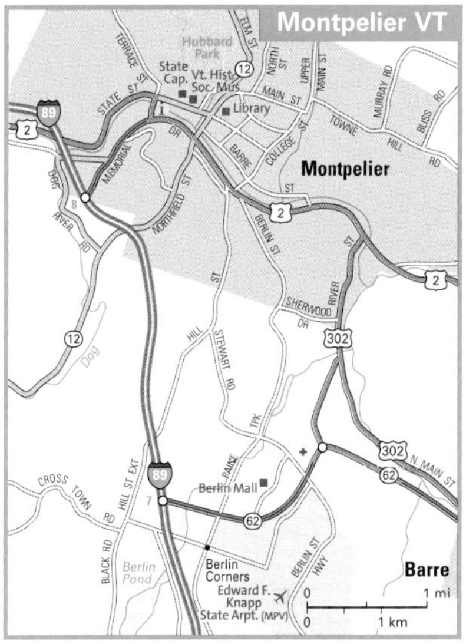
Montpelier VT
Montpelier
Barre
Berlin Mall
Berlin Corners
Edward F. Knapp State Arpt. (MPV)
Library
Hubbard Park
0 1 mi
0 1 km

Myrtle Beach SC
North Myrtle Beach
Myrtle Beach
Atlantic Beach
Cherry Grove Beach
Brooksville
Wampee
Nixonville
Conway
Forestbrook
Socastee
Surfside Beach
ATLANTIC OCEAN
Alabama Theatre
Barefoot Landing
Briarcliffe Acres
Myrtle Beach Mall
Tanger Outlet Ctr.
The Carolina Opry & Pirates Voyage
Broadway at the Beach
Ripley's Aquarium
Myrtle Waves Water Park
Conv. Ctr.
Family Kingdom
Myrtle Beach Intl. Arpt. (MYR)
Art Mus.
The Market Common
Springmaid Beach
Coastal Grand Mall
Tanger Outlet Ctr.
0 2 4 mi
0 2 4 6 km

Atlantic Beach. . . B1
Briarcliffe Acres . B2
Brooksville A1
Cherry Grove Beach B1
Conway. A3
Forestbrook A3
Myrtle Beach. B2
Nixonville A2
N. Myrtle Beach . B1
Socastee. A3
Springmaid Beach B3
Surfside Beach . . . B3
Wampee A1

Nashville TN
Nashville
Hendersonville
Brentwood
Forest Hills
Oak Hill
Berry Hill
Belle Meade
Lakewood
Old Hickory Lake
Nashville Intl. Airport (BNA)
Grand Ole Opry
Opry Mills
Nissan Stadium
Tenn. Perf. Arts Ctr.
Vanderbilt Univ.
Fisk U.
Meharry Med. Coll.
Tennessee State Univ.
Belmont Mansion
Belmont Univ.
Lipscomb Univ.
Trevecca Nazarene Univ.
Nashville Zoo at Grassmere
Travellers Rest Plantation & Museum
Cheekwood Estate & Gardens
Radnor Lake State Park
Ellington Agricultural Center
Tanger Outlets
Andrew Jackson's Hermitage
Convention Center Area
Bridgestone Arena
Country Music Hall of Fame & Mus.
Frist Art Museum
Hatch Show Print
Music City Center
Musicians Hall of Fame & Mus.
Ryman Auditorium
Schermerhorn Symphony Center
0 1 2 mi
0 1 2 3 km

Figures after entries indicate page number and grid reference.

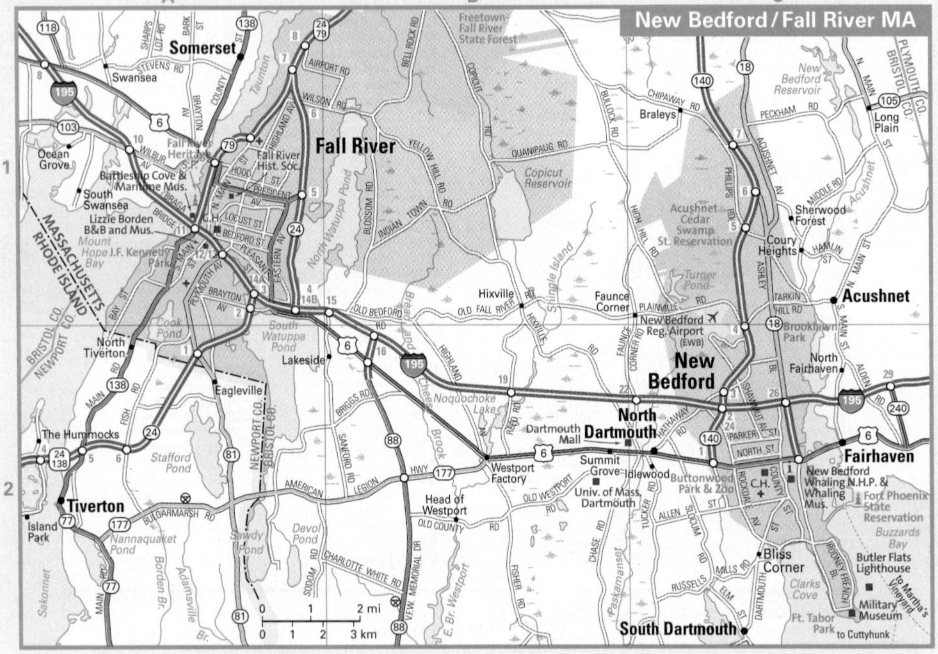

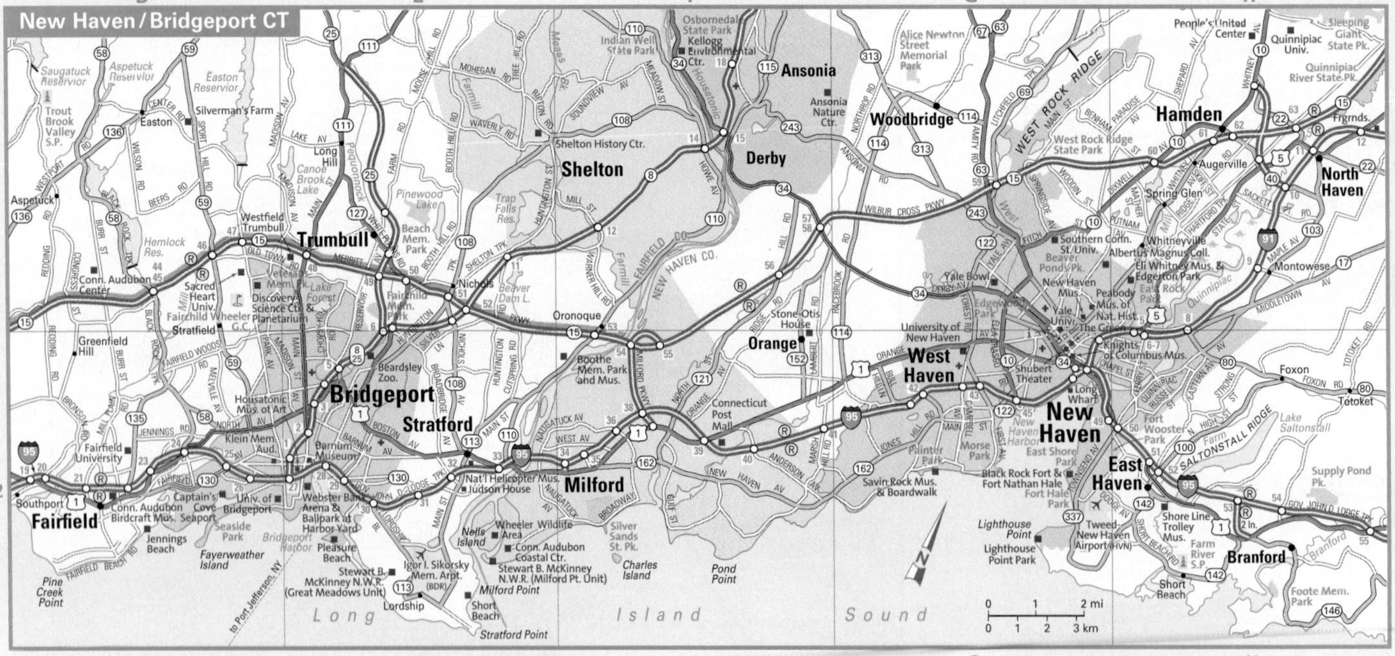

Entries in **bold black** indicate counties or parishes.
Entries in **bold color** indicate cities with detailed inset maps.

Ama B2
Arabi C1
Avondale B2
Belle Chasse C2
Boutte A2
Braithwaite D2
Bridge City B2
Caernarvon D2
Chalmette C2
Dalcour C2
Des Allemands A2
Destrehan A2
English Turn C2
Estelle C2
Frenier A1
Gretna C2
Hahnville A1
Harahan B2
Harvey C2
Jefferson B1
Kenilworth D2
Kenner B1
Killona A1
Laplace A1
Lone Star A2
Lucy A1
Luling A2
Marrero C2
Meraux D2
Metairie C1
Mimosa Park A2
Montz A1
New Orleans D1
New Sarpy A1
Norco A1
Oakville C2
Paradis A2
Poydras D2
River Ridge B1
St. Bernard D2
St. Rose B1
Scarsdale C2
Taft A1
Terrytown C2
Toca D2
Verret D2
Violet D2
Waggaman B2
Westwego B2

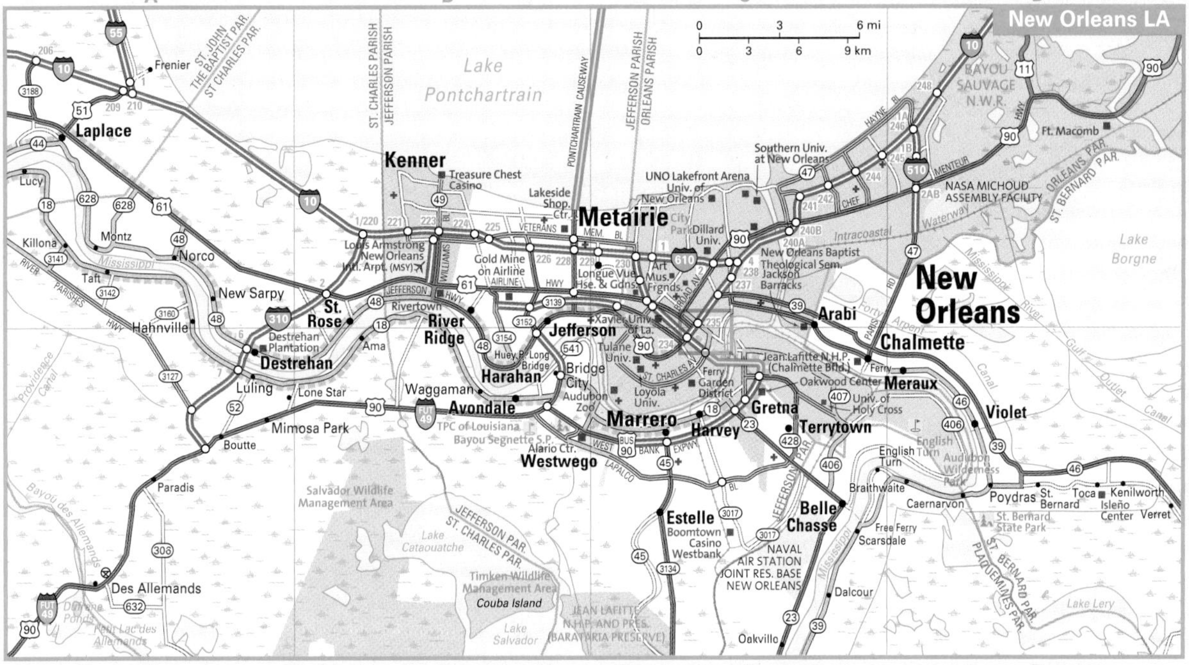

POINTS OF INTEREST

Audubon Aquarium of the Americas	F2
The Cabildo	F1
Ceasars Superdome	E2
Confederate Memorial Hall Museum	F2
Contemporary Arts Center	F2
Creole Queen	F2
Ernest N. Morial Convention Center	F2
French Quarter (Vieux Carré)	F1
Harrah's Casino	F2
Jackson Square	F1
Jean Lafitte Natl. Hist. Park (Visitor Center)	F1
M. Jackson Theatre for the Performing Arts	F1
National World War II Museum	F2
New Orleans Jazz Museum	F1
New Orleans Jazz N.H.P. Visitor Center	F1
Ogden Museum	F2
One Canal Place	F2
Orpheum Theatre	F1
Pontalba Buildings	F1
The Presbytère	F1
Public Library	E2
Saenger Theatre	F1
St. Charles Avenue Streetcar	F2
St. Louis Cathedral	F1
Smoothie King Center	E2
Woldenberg Riverfront Park	F2

Morrisville NY 79 E3
Morrisville NC 112 C4
Morrisville PA 102 A1
Morrisville PA 147 D2
Morrisville VT 81 E2
Morrisville VA 144 A4
Morro Bay CA 44 B4
Morrow GA 120 C4
Morrow OH 100 C2
Morrow Co. OH 91 D4
Morrow Co. OR 21 E2
Morse LA 133 E2
Morton IL 88 B3
Morton MS 126 C2
Morton PA 248 B4
Morton TX 57 F1
Morton WA 12 C4
Morton Co. KS 42 A4
Morton Co. ND 18 B4
Morton Grove IL 203 D3
Mortons Gap KY 109 E2
Morven GA 137 F1
Morven NC 122 B2
Moscow ID 14 B4
Moscow ME 82 B1
Moscow PA 93 F2
Moscow TN 118 C2
Moscow Mills MO 97 F2
Moses Lake WA 13 E3
Mosheim TN 111 D3
Mosier OR 21 D1
Mosinee WI 68 B4
Mosquero NM 49 E2
Moss Beach CA 259 A5
Moss Bluff LA 133 D2
Mosses AL 127 F3
Moss Pt. MS 135 D2
Mossville IL 88 B3
Mossyrock WA 12 C4
Motley MN 64 A4
Motley Co. TX 50 B4
Mott ND 18 A4
Moulton AL 119 E3
Moulton IA 87 D3
Moulton TX 61 E2
Moultrie GA 137 E1
Moultrie Co. IL 98 C1
Mound MN 66 C4
Mound Bayou MS 118 A4
Mound City IL 108 C2
Mound City KS 96 B4
Mound City MO 86 A4
Mound City SD 26 C1
Moundridge KS 43 E3
Mounds IL 108 C2
Mounds OK 51 F2
Mounds View MN 235 C1
Moundsville WV 101 F1
Mound Valley KS 106 A2
Moundville AL 127 E1
Mt. Aetna MD 144 A1
Mountainair NM 48 C4
Mountainaire AZ 47 E3
Mtn. Brook AL 119 F4
Mountainburg AR 116 C1
Mtn. City GA 121 D2
Mtn. City TN 111 F3
Mtn. City TX 61 E2
Mtn. Grove MO 107 E2
Mtn. Home AR 107 E3
Mtn. Home ID 30 B1
Mtn. Home NC 121 E1
Mountainhome PA 93 F2
Mtn. Iron MN 64 C3
Mtn. Lake MN 72 B1
Mtn. Lake Park MD 102 B2
Mtn. Lakes NJ 148 A3
Mtn. Pine AR 117 D2
Mtn. Ranch CA 36 C3
Mountainside NJ 148 A4
Mtn. Top PA 93 E2
Mtn. View AR 107 E4
Mtn. View CA 259 D5
Mtn. View CO 209 B3
Mtn. View HI 153 F3
Mtn. View MO 107 F2
Mtn. View OK 51 D3
Mtn. View WY 32 A3
Mtn. Vil. AK 154 B2
Mtn. Vil. CO 40 B3
Mt. Airy GA 121 D3
Mt. Airy MD 144 B1
Mt. Airy NC 112 A3
Mt. Angel OR 20 C2
Mt. Arlington NJ 148 A3
Mt. Ayr IA 86 C3
Mt. Bethel NJ 147 D1
Mt. Calvary WI 74 C2
Mt. Carmel IL 99 D3
Mt. Carmel OH 204 C2
Mt. Carmel PA 93 E3
Mt. Carmel TN 111 E3
Mt. Carroll IL 88 A1
Mt. Clemens MI 76 C4
Mt. Cobb PA 93 F2
Mt. Crested Butte CO 40 C2
Mt. Dora FL 141 D1
Mt. Enterprise TX 124 B3
Mt. Ephraim NJ 248 C4
Mt. Freedom NJ 148 A3
Mt. Gay WV 101 E4
Mt. Gilead NC 122 B1
Mt. Gilead OH 91 D4
Mt. Healthy OH 204 A1
Mt. Holly NJ 147 D3
Mt. Holly NC 122 A1
Mt. Holly Sprs. PA 93 D4
Mt. Hope KS 43 E4
Mt. Hope WV 101 F4
Mt. Horeb WI 74 A3
Mt. Ida AR 116 C2
Mt. Ivy NY 148 B2
Mt. Jackson VA 102 C3
Mt. Jewett PA 92 B1
Mt. Joy PA 93 E4
Mt. Juliet TN 109 F3
Mt. Kisco NY 148 C2
Mountlake Terrace WA 262 B2
Mt. Lebanon PA 92 A4
Mt. Morris IL 88 B1
Mt. Morris MI 76 B3
Mt. Morris NY 78 C4
Mt. Nebo PA 146 A3
Mt. Olive AL 119 F4
Mt. Olive IL 98 B2
Mt. Olive MS 126 C3
Mt. Olive NC 123 E1
Mt. Oliver PA 250 B2
Mt. Olivet KY 100 C3
Mt. Orab OH 100 C2
Mt. Pleasant AR 107 F4
Mt. Pleasant IA 87 F3
Mt. Pleasant MI 76 A2
Mt. Pleasant NC 122 B1
Mt. Pleasant PA 92 A4
Mt. Pleasant SC 131 D2
Mt. Pleasant TN 119 E1
Mt. Pleasant TX 124 B1
Mt. Pleasant UT 39 E1
Mt. Pleasant WI 75 D4
Mt. Plymouth FL 141 D1
Mt. Pocono PA 93 F3
Mt. Prospect IL 203 C3
Mt. Pulaski IL 98 B1
Mountrail Co. ND 18 A2
Mt. Rainier MD 270 E2
Mt. Royal NJ 146 C3
Mt. Savage MD 102 C1
Mt. Shasta CA 28 C3
Mt. Sidney VA 102 C4
Mt. Sinai NY 149 D3
Mt. Sterling IL 98 A1
Mt. Sterling KY 100 C4
Mt. Sterling OH 101 D1
Mt. Union PA 92 C4
Mt. Vernon AL 135 E1
Mt. Vernon GA 129 F3
Mt. Vernon IL 98 C4
Mt. Vernon IN 99 D4
Mt. Vernon IA 87 F1
Mt. Vernon KY 110 C1
Mt. Vernon MD 103 F4
Mt. Vernon MO 106 C2
Mt. Vernon NY 78 A4
Mt. Vernon NY 148 B3
Mt. Vernon OH 91 D4
Mt. Vernon OR 21 E3
Mt. Vernon SD 27 E4
Mt. Vernon TX 124 B1
Mt. Vernon VA 144 B4
Mt. Vernon WA 12 C2
Mt. Victory OH 90 C4
Mt. View RI 150 C4
Mountville PA 103 E1
Mt. Washington KY 100 A4
Mt. Wolf PA 93 E4
Mt. Zion GA 120 B4
Mt. Zion IL 98 C1
Moville IA 35 F1
Moweaqua IL 98 C1
Mower Co. MN 73 D2
Moxee WA 13 D4
Moyie Sprs. ID 14 B1
Mud Lake ID 23 E4
Muenster TX 59 E1
Muhlenberg Co. KY 109 E2
Muir MI 76 A3
Muir PA 93 E4
Mukilteo WA 12 C2
Mukwonago WI 74 C3
Mulberry AR 116 C1
Mulberry FL 140 C2
Mulberry IN 89 E4
Mulberry KS 106 B1
Mulberry NC 111 F3
Mulberry OH 100 B2
Mulberry Grove IL 98 B3
Muldraugh KY 99 F4
Muldrow OK 116 B1

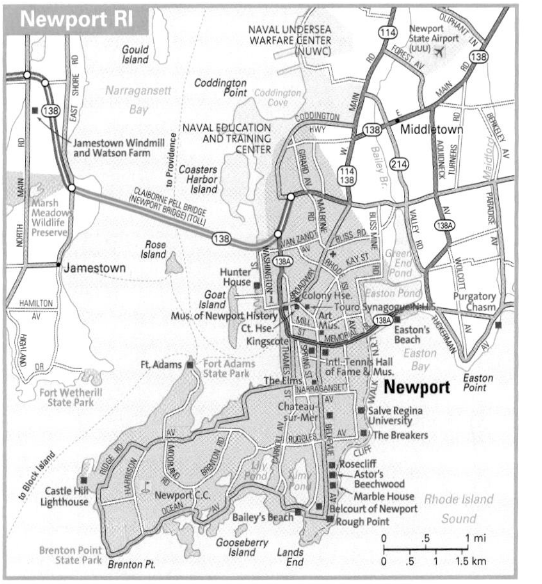

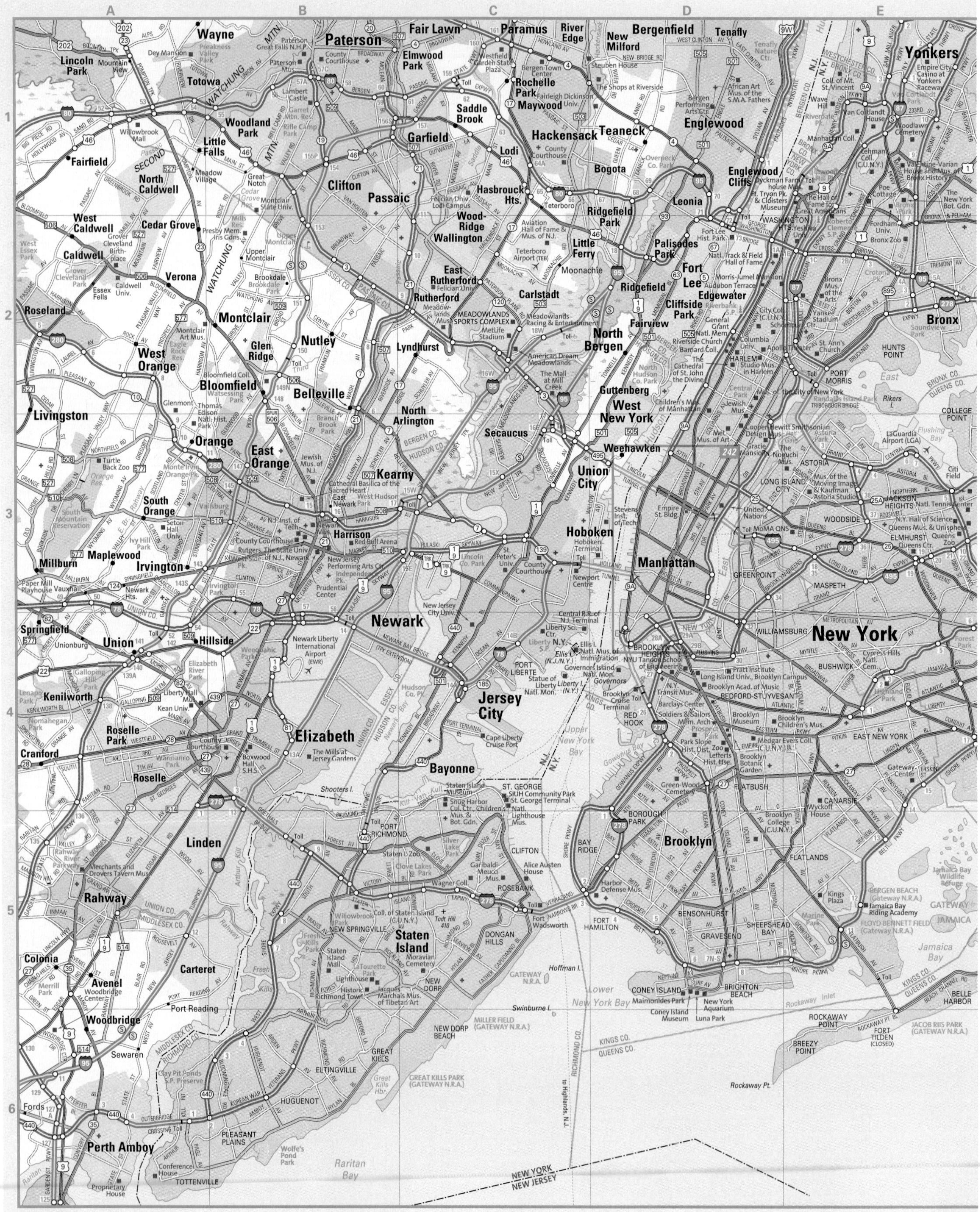

Wayne
Paterson
Fair Lawn
Paramus
River Edge
New Milford
Bergenfield
Tenafly
Yonkers
Lincoln Park
Totowa
Elmwood Park
Rochelle Park
Maywood
Saddle Brook
Woodland Park
Little Falls
Garfield
Hackensack
Teaneck
Englewood
Fairfield
North Caldwell
Clifton
Passaic
Lodi
Bogota
Englewood Cliffs
Hasbrouck Hts.
Leonia
West Caldwell
Cedar Grove
Wood-Ridge
Wallington
Ridgefield Park
Caldwell
Little Ferry
Palisades Park
Verona
East Rutherford
Moonachie
Fort Lee
Carlstadt
Ridgefield
Edgewater
Rutherford
Cliffside Park
Roseland
Montclair
Fairview
Nutley
Lyndhurst
North Bergen
Glen Ridge
West Orange
Bloomfield
Belleville
Guttenberg
West New York
Livingston
North Arlington
Secaucus
Weehawken
Orange
East Orange
Kearny
Union City
South Orange
Harrison
Hoboken
Millburn
Maplewood
Irvington
Manhattan
Newark
New York
Springfield
Union
Hillside
Kenilworth
Jersey City
Roselle Park
Elizabeth
Cranford
Bayonne
Roselle
Linden
Brooklyn
Rahway
Staten Island
Colonia
Carteret
Avenel
Woodbridge
Port Reading
Sewaren
Fords
Perth Amboy
Bronx
New York Bay
Raritan Bay
NEW YORK
NEW JERSEY
A
B
C
D
E
1
2
3
4
5
6

Entries in **bold black** indicate counties or parishes.
Entries in **bold color** indicate cities with detailed inset maps.

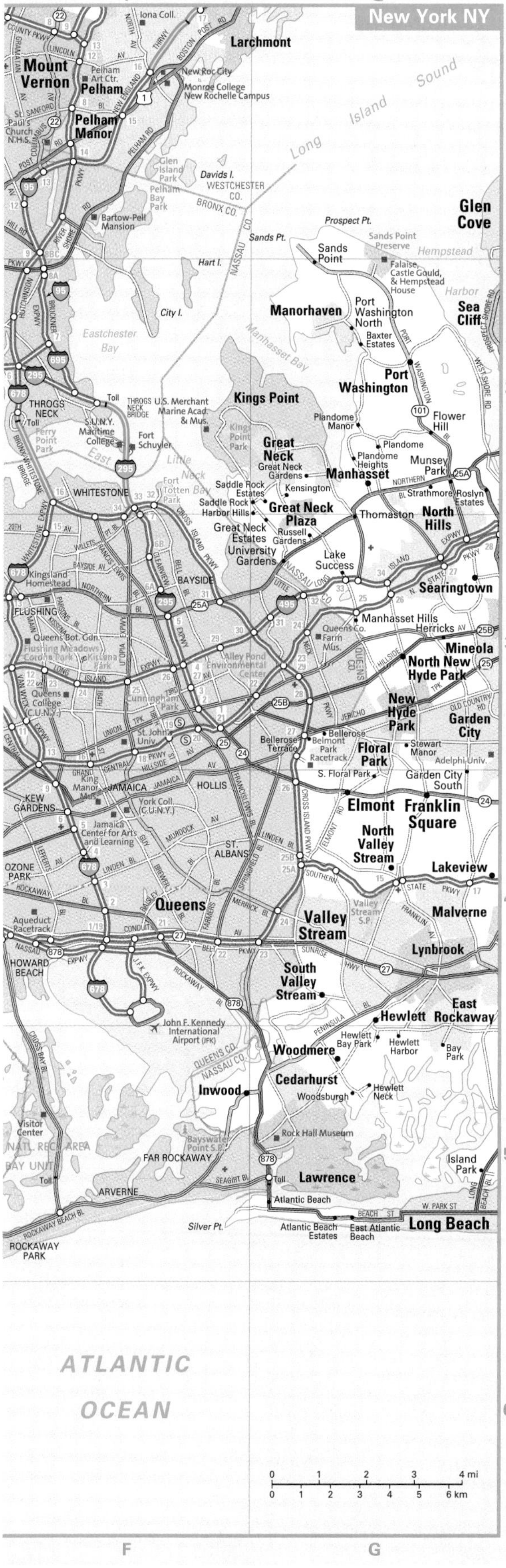
New York NY
Larchmont
Mount Vernon
Pelham
Pelham Manor
Long Island Sound
Glen Cove
Sea Cliff
Manorhaven
Port Washington
Kings Point
Great Neck
Manhasset
Great Neck Plaza
North Hills
Searingtown
Mineola
North New Hyde Park
New Hyde Park
Garden City
Floral Park
Elmont
Franklin Square
North Valley Stream
Lakeview
Malverne
Queens
Valley Stream
Lynbrook
South Valley Stream
East Rockaway
Hewlett
Woodmere
Cedarhurst
Inwood
Lawrence
Long Beach
ATLANTIC OCEAN
0 1 2 3 4 mi
0 1 2 3 4 5 6 km

Atlantic Beach G5
Atlantic Beach Estates . . G5
Avenel A5
Baxter Estates G2
Bayonne C4
Bay Park G5
Bellerose G3
Bellerose Terrace G3
Belleville B2
Bergenfield D1
Bloomfield B2
Bogota D1
Brookdale B2
Caldwell A2
Carlstadt C2
Carteret A5
Cedar Grove A2
Cedarhurst G5
Cliffside Park D2
Clifton B1
Colonia A5
Cranford A4
E. Atlantic Beach G5
E. Newark B3
E. Orange B3
E. Rockaway G4
E. Rutherford C2
Edgewater D2
Elizabeth B4
Elmont G4
Elmwood Park C1
Englewood D1
Englewood Cliffs D1
Essex Fells A2
Fairfield A1
Fair Lawn C1
Fairview D2
Floral Park G3
Flower Hill G2
Fords A6
Ft. Lee D2
Franklin Square G4
Garden City G3
Garden City South G4
Garfield C1
Glen Cove G1
Glen Ridge B2
Great Neck G2
Great Neck Estates G3
Great Neck Gardens G2
Great Neck Plaza G2
Great Notch B1
Guttenberg D2
Hackensack C1
Harbor Hills G2
Harrison B3
Hasbrouck Hts. C1
Herricks G3
Hewlett G4
Hewlett Bay Park G5
Hewlett Harbor G5
Hewlett Neck G5
Hillside A4
Hoboken C3
Inwood F5
Irvington A3
Island Park G5
Jersey City C4
Kearny B3
Kenilworth A4
Kensington G2
Kings Pt. G2
Lake Success G3
Lakeview G4
Larchmont F1
Lawrence G5
Leonia D1
Lincoln Park A1
Linden A5
Little Falls A1
Little Ferry C2
Livingston A2
Lodi C1
Long Beach G5
Lynbrook G4
Lyndhurst C2
Malverne G4
Manhasset G2
Manhasset Hills G3
Manorhaven G2
Maplewood A3
Maywood C1
Meadow Vil. A1
Millburn A3
Mineola G3
Montclair B2
Moonachie C2
Mtn. View A1
Mt. Vernon F1
Munsey Park G2
Newark B4
Newark Hts. A3
New Hyde Park G3
New Milford D1
New York E4
N. Arlington C2
N. Bergen D2
N. Caldwell A1
N. Hills G3
N. New Hyde Park G3
N. Valley Stream G4
Nutley B2
Orange A3
Palisades Park D2
Paramus C1
Passaic B1
Paterson B1
Pelham F1
Pelham Manor F1
Perth Amboy A6
Plandome G2
Plandome Hts. G2
Plandome Manor G2
Port Reading A5
Port Washington G2
Port Washington North . . G2
Rahway A5
Ridgefield D2
Ridgefield Park D1
River Edge C1
Rochelle Park C1
Roseland A2
Roselle A4
Roselle Park A4
Roslyn Estates G2
Russell Gardens G3
Rutherford C2
Saddle Brook C1
Saddle Rock G2
Saddle Rock Estates G2
Sands Pt. G2
Sea Cliff G2
Searingtown G3
Secaucus C3
Sewaren A6
S. Floral Park G4
S. Orange A3
S. Valley Stream G4
Springfield A4
Stewart Manor G3
Strathmore G2
Teaneck D1
Tenafly D1
Teterboro C1
Thomaston G3
Totowa A1
Union A4
Unionburg A4
Union City C3
University Gardens G3
Upper Montclair B2
Valley Stream G4
Vauxhall A3
Verona A2
Wallington C2
Wayne A1
Weehawken D3
W. Caldwell A2
W. New York D2
W. Orange A2
Woodbridge A6
Woodland Park B1
Woodmere G5
Wood-Ridge C2
Woodsburgh G5
Yonkers E1

Muleshoe TX 49 F4
Mulga AL 195 D1
Mullan ID 14 C3
Mullen NE 34 B2
Mullens WV 111 F1
Mullica Hill NJ 146 C4
Mulliken MI 76 A4
Mullins SC 122 C3
Multnomah Co. OR 20 C2
Mulvane KS 43 E4
Muncie IN 90 A4
Muncy PA 93 D2
Munday TX 58 C1
Mundelein Il 74 C4
Munds Park AZ 47 E3
Munford AL 120 A4
Munford TN 118 B1
Munfordville KY 110 A2
Munhall PA 250 C3
Munich ND 19 D1
Munising MI 69 E1
Munroe Falls OH 188 B1
Munsey Park NY 241 G2
Munsons Corners NY 79 D4
Munster IN 89 D2
Murchison TX 124 A3
Murdo SD 26 C4
Murfreesboro AR 116 C3
Murfreesboro NC 113 E3
Murfreesboro TN 109 F4
Murphy ID 30 B1
Murphy MO 98 A3
Murphy NC 120 C2
Murphy TX 207 E1
Murphys CA 37 D3
Murphysboro IL 108 C1
Murray IA 86 C3
Murray KY 109 D3
Murray NE 86 A3
Murray UT 31 E4
Murray Co. GA 120 C2
Murray Co. MN 72 A1
Murray Co. OK 51 F4
Murray Hill KY 230 F1
Murrayville IL 98 A1
Murrells Inlet SC 123 D4
Murrieta CA 53 D3
Murrieta Hot Sprs. CA 229 K6
Murrysville PA 92 A4
Muscatine IA 87 F2
Muscatine Co. IA 87 F2
Muscle Shoals AL 119 E2
Muscoda WI 74 A3
Muscogee Co. GA 128 C2
Muscoy CA 229 J2
Muskego WI 74 C3
Muskegon MI 75 E3
Muskegon Co. MI 75 F3
Muskegon Hts. MI 75 E3
Muskingum Co. OH 91 E4
Muskogee OK 106 A4
Muskogee Co. OK 106 A4
Musselshell Co. MT 16 C4
Mustang OK 51 E3
Mustang Ridge TX 61 E2
Muttontown NY 148 C3
Myers Corner NY 148 B1
Myerstown PA 146 A1
Myersville MD 144 A1
Myricks MA 151 D3
Myrtle MS 118 C2
Myrtle Beach SC 123 D4
Myrtle Creek OR 28 B1
Myrtle Grove FL 135 F2
Myrtle Grove NC 123 E3
Myrtle Pt. OR 28 A1
Mystic CT 149 F2
Mystic IA 87 D3
Mystic Island NJ 147 E4
Myton UT 32 A4

N

Naalehu HI 153 E4
Naches WA 13 D4
Naco AZ 55 E4
Nacogdoches TX 124 B4
Nacogdoches Co. TX 124 B4
Nageezi NM 48 B2
Nags Head NC 115 F2
Nahant MA 151 D1
Nahunta GA 129 F4
Nain VA 102 C2
Naknek AK 154 B3
Nambe NM 49 D2
Nameloc Hts. MA 151 E3
Nampa ID 22 B4
Nanakuli HI 152 A3
Nance Co. NE 35 E3
Nanticoke PA 93 E2
Nantucket MA 151 F4
Nantucket Co. MA 151 F4
Nanty Glo PA 92 B4
Nanuet NY 148 B3
Napa CA 36 B3
Napa Co. CA 36 B2
Napanoch NY 94 A3
Napaskiak AK 154 B3
Napavine WA 12 B4
Naperville IL 88 C1
Naples FL 142 C2
Naples NY 78 C4
Naples TX 124 B1
Naples UT 32 A4
Naples Manor FL 142 C2
Naples Park FL 142 C1
Napoleon MI 90 B1
Napoleon ND 18 C4
Napoleon OH 90 B2
Napoleonville LA 134 A3
Nappanee IN 89 F2
Naranja FL 143 E3
Narberth PA 248 B3
Narragansett Pier RI 150 C4
Narrows VA 112 A1
Naschitti NM 48 A2
Nash TX 116 C4
Nash Co. NC 113 D4
Nashotah WI 74 C3
Nashua IA 73 D3
Nashua MT 17 D2
Nashua NH 95 D1
Nashville AR 116 C4
Nashville GA 129 E4
Nashville IL 98 B4
Nashville IN 99 F2
Nashville MI 76 A4
Nashville NC 113 D4
Nashville TN 109 F4
Nashwauk MN 64 B3
Nassau DE 145 F4
Nassau NY 94 B1
Nassau Bay TX 132 B3
Nassau Co. FL 139 D2
Nassau Co. NY 148 C4
Nassau Vil. FL 222 C1
Nassawadox VA 114 B3
Natalbany LA 134 B2
Natalia TX 61 D3
Natchez LA 125 D4
Natchez MS 125 F4
Natchitoches LA 125 D3
Natchitoches Par. LA 125 D4
Natick MA 150 C1
National City CA 258 B2
National Park NJ 146 C3
Natrona Co. WY 33 D1
Natrona Hts. PA 92 A3
Naturita CO 40 B3
Naugatuck CT 149 D1
Nauvoo IL 87 F4
Navajo NM 48 A2
Navajo Co. AZ 47 F3
Navarre OH 91 E3
Navarro Co. TX 59 F3
Navasota TX 61 F1
Navesink NJ 147 F1
Naylor MO 108 A3
Naytahwaush MN 19 F3
Nazareth KY 100 A4
Nazareth PA 93 F3
Nazlini AZ 47 F2
Neah Bay WA 12 A2
Neapolis OH 90 B2
Nebraska City NE 86 A3
Necedah WI 74 A1
Neche ND 19 E1
Nederland CO 41 D1
Nederland TX 132 C3
Nedrow NY 79 D3
Needham MA 151 D1
Needles CA 46 B4
Needville TX 132 A4
Neelyville MO 108 A3
Neenah WI 74 C1
Neffs OH 101 F1
Negaunee MI 65 F4
Neillsville WI 68 A4
Nekoosa WI 74 A1
Neligh NE 35 E2
Nelliston NY 79 F3
Nelson GA 120 C3
Nelson NE 35 E4
Nelson Co. KY 100 A4
Nelson Co. ND 19 E2
Nelson Co. VA 112 C1
Nelsonville NY 148 B1
Nelsonville OH 101 E2
Nemacolin PA 102 A1
Nemaha Co. KS 96 A1
Nemaha Co. NE 86 A4
Nenana AK 154 C2
Neodesha KS 106 A1
Neoga IL 98 C2
Neola IA 86 A2
Neola UT 32 A4
Neopit WI 68 C4
Neosho MO 106 B2
Neosho WI 74 C3
Neosho Co. KS 106 A1
Neotsu OR 20 B2
Nephi UT 39 E1
Neptune NJ 147 F2
Neptune Beach FL 139 D2
Neptune City NJ 147 F2
Nesbit MS 118 B2
Nesconset NY 149 D3
Nescopeck PA 93 E3
Neshoba Co. MS 126 C2
Nesquehoning PA 93 F3
Ness City KS 42 C3
Ness Co. KS 42 C3
Netarts OR 20 B2
Netcong NJ 94 A4
Nettleton MS 119 D3
Nevada IA 86 C1
Nevada MO 106 C1
Nevada OH 90 C3
Nevada City CA 36 C2
Nevada Co. AR 117 D4
Nevada Co. CA 36 C2
New Albany IN 99 F4
New Albany MS 118 C3
New Albin IA 73 F2
New Alexandria PA 92 A4
Newark AR 107 F4
Newark CA 259 D5
Newark DE 146 B4
Newark IL 88 C2
Newark NJ 148 B4
Newark NY 78 C3
Newark OH 91 D4
Newark TX 59 E2
Newark Valley NY 93 E1
New Athens IL 98 B4
New Auburn MN 66 C4
New Auburn WI 67 F3
New Augusta MS 126 C4
Newaygo MI 75 F2
Newaygo Co. MI 75 F2
New Baden IL 98 B3
New Baltimore MI 76 C4
New Baltimore NY 94 B1
New Baltimore VA 144 A3
New Beaver PA 91 F3
New Bedford MA 151 D4
Newberg OR 20 B2
New Berlin IL 98 B1
New Berlin NY 79 E4
New Berlin PA 93 D3
New Berlin WI 74 C3
New Bern NC 115 D3
Newbern TN 108 C4
Newberry FL 138 C3
Newberry MI 69 F1
Newberry SC 121 F3
Newberry Co. SC 121 F3
New Bethlehem PA 92 B3
New Bloomfield MO 97 E3
New Bloomfield PA 93 D4
Newborn GA 121 D4
New Boston IL 87 F2
New Boston NH 81 F4
New Boston OH 101 D3
New Boston TX 116 B4
New Braunfels TX 61 D2
New Bremen OH 90 B4
New Brighton MN 235 C1
New Brighton PA 91 F3
New Britain CT 149 E1
New Britain PA 146 C2
New Brockton AL 128 A4
New Brunswick NJ 147 E1
New Buffalo MI 89 E1
Newburg WV 102 B2
Newburg WI 74 C2
Newburgh IN 99 E4
Newburgh NY 148 B1
Newburgh Hts. OH 204 F2
Newbury VT 81 E2
Newburyport MA 151 F1
New Canaan CT 148 C2
New Carlisle IN 89 E1
New Carlisle OH 100 C1
New Carrollton MD 144 B3
New Castle CO 40 C1
New Castle DE 146 B4
New Castle IN 100 A1
New Castle KY 100 A3
Newcastle ME 82 C3
Newcastle OK 51 E3
New Castle PA 91 F3
Newcastle TX 59 D2
New Castle VA 112 B1
Newcastle WA 262 B3
Newcastle WY 25 F4
New Castle Co. DE 145 E1
New Chapel Hill TX 124 B3
New City NY 148 B2

Figures after entries indicate page number and grid reference.

Newcomb MD 145 D4
Newcomb NM 48 A2
Newcomerstown OH 91 E4
New Concord OH 101 E1
New Cordell OK 51 D3
New Cumberland PA 218 B2
New Cumberland WV 91 F4
Newdale ID 23 F4
New Deal TX 58 A1
New Durham NH 81 F4
New Eagle PA 92 A4
New Effington SD 27 F1
New Egypt NJ 147 D3
Newell IA 72 B4
Newell SD 25 F3
Newell WV 91 F3
New Ellenton SC 121 F4
Newellton LA 126 A3
New England ND 18 A4
New Era MI 75 E2
New Fairfield CT 148 C1
New Fairview TX 59 E2
Newfane NY 78 B3
Newfane VT 81 E4
Newfield NJ 145 F1
Newfield NY 79 D4
Newfields NH 82 A4
New Florence MO 97 F3
New Florence PA 92 B4
New Franklin MO 97 D2
New Franklin OH 91 E3
New Freedom PA 103 E1
New Glarus WI 74 B3
New Gloucester ME 82 B3
New Gretna NJ 147 E4
Newhall IA 87 E1
New Hamburg NY 148 B1
New Hampton IA 73 E3
New Hampton NY 148 A1
New Hanover PA 146 B2
New Hanover Co. NC 123 E3
New Harmony IN 99 D4
New Hartford CT 94 C2
New Hartford IA 73 D4
New Haven CT 149 D2
New Haven IN 90 A3
New Haven KY 110 A1
New Haven MI 76 C4
New Haven MO 97 F3
New Haven WV 101 E2
New Haven Co. CT 149 D1
New Hebron MS 126 B4
New Hempstead NY 148 B2
New Holland OH 101 D1
New Holland PA 146 A2
New Holstein WI 74 C1
New Hope AL 119 F2
New Hope GA 120 B4
New Hope MN 235 B2
New Hope MS 119 D4
New Hope NC 123 E1
New Hope PA 147 D2
New Hope TN 120 A2
New Hope VA 102 C4
New Houlka MS 118 C3
New Hyde Park NY 241 G3
New Iberia LA 133 F3
Newington CT 149 E1
New Ipswich NH 95 D1
New Jerusalem PA 146 B1
New Johnsonville TN 109 D4
New Kensington PA 92 A4
New Kent VA 113 F1
New Kent Co. VA 113 F1
Newkirk OK 51 E1
New Knoxville OH 90 B4
Newland NC 111 F4
New Lebanon OH 100 B1
New Leipzig ND 18 B4
New Lenox IL 89 D2
New Lexington OH 101 E1
New Lisbon WI 74 A2
New Llano LA 133 D1
New London CT 149 F2
New London IA 87 F3
New London MN 66 B3
New London MO 97 F1
New London NH 81 E4
New London OH 91 D3
New London PA 146 B3
New London TX 124 B3
New London WI 74 C1

POINTS OF INTEREST

601 Lexington Avenue D2
African Burial Ground Natl. Mon. B5
Algonquin Hotel C2
Alvin Alley American Dance Th. .C1
American Folk Art Museum C1
American Radiation Building C2
Americas Society D1
Appellate Division of the Supreme Court of New York C3
Arcadia Earth Museum B4
Battery Park A6
Bernard M. Baruch College of the City University of N.Y. C3
Brookfield Place A5
Carnegie Hall C1
Castle Clinton Natl. Monument A6
Central Park D1
Central Park Zoo D1
Chanin Building D2
Chrysler Building D2
City Hall B5
Comcast Building C2
ConEdison Building C4
The Cooper Union C4
Criminal Courts Building B5
Cunard Building A6
Daily News Building D2
David Geffen Hall C1
David H. Koch Theatre C1
Empire State Building C3
Fashion Institute of Technology & Museum B3
Federal Hall National Memorial A6
Federal Reserve Bank A6
Flatiron Building C3
Fordham University C1
Foundation Building C4
Fraunces Tavern A6
French Building C2
The Frick Collection D1
Fuller Building D1
General Assembly Building D2
General Electric Building D2
Grace Church C4
Grand Central Terminal D2
High Line Park B2
Hotel Chelsea B3
Hunter College (C.U.N.Y.) D1
Intrepid Sea, Air & Space Mus. B1
Irish Hunger Memorial A5
Italian American Museum B5
Jackie Robinson Museum A5
Jacob Javits Convention Center .B2
Japan Society D2
Jazz at Lincoln Center Frederick P. Rose Hall C1
Jefferson Market Library B4
John Jay College (C.U.N.Y.) C1
Lever House D2
Lincoln Center C1
Lower East Side Tenement Mus. Natl. Hist. Site C5
Lyceum Theatre C2
Macdougal Alley B4
Macy's C2
Madame Tussauds-New York C2
Madison Square Garden B2
Manhattan Cruise Terminal B1
Meatpacking District A3
Merchant's House Museum B4
Met Life Building D2
Metropolitan Opera House C1
Mmuseumm B5
Morgan Library & Museum C2
Municipal Building B5
Museum at Eldridge Street B5
Museum of American Finance A6
Museum of Arts & Design C1
Museum of Broadway C2
Museum of Chinese in America B5
Museum of Jewish Heritage A6
Museum of Modern Art D2
Museum of Sex C3
National Museum of the American Indian A6
Natl. Sept. 11 Mem. & Mus. A6
New Mus. of Contemporary Art B5
New York City Fire Museum A4
New York Co. Supreme Court B5
New York Edition Hotel C3
New York Life Insurance Company Building C3
New York Mercantile Exchange .A5
The New York Public Library C2
New York Stock Exchange A6
New York Univ. B4
Nyack College A6
Old New York Co. Court House B5
One World Trade Ctr. (Freedom Tower) A5
Pace Univ. N.Y.C. Campus B5
Paley Center for Media D2
Paramount Building C2
Pennsylvania Station B2
Pier 17 Pavilion B6
Plaza Hotel D1
Port Authority Bus Terminal B2
Public Theater B4
Radio City Music Hall C2
Rockefeller Center C2
Roosevelt Island Aerial Tram D2
Rubin Museum of Art B3
St. Patrick's Cathedral D2
St. Paul's Chapel A6
Salmagundi Club B4
Seagram Building D2
Seaport Museum B6
Secretariat Building D2
Sheridan Square B4
Skyscraper Museum A6
Society of Illustrators D1
South Street Seaport B6
Staten Island Ferry Terminal A6
Stonewall National Monument B4
The Oculus A5
Theodore Roosevelt Birthplace Natl. Hist. Site C3
Times Square C2
Tisch Childrens Zoo D1
Trinity Church A6
Trump Tower D1
Ukrainian Museum C4
United Nations D2
U.S. Court House B5
Villard Houses D2
Waldorf-Astoria D2
Washington Arch B4
Washington Square B4
Whitney Mus. of American Art A3
Wollman Rink D1
Woolworth Building A5
World Trade Center A5

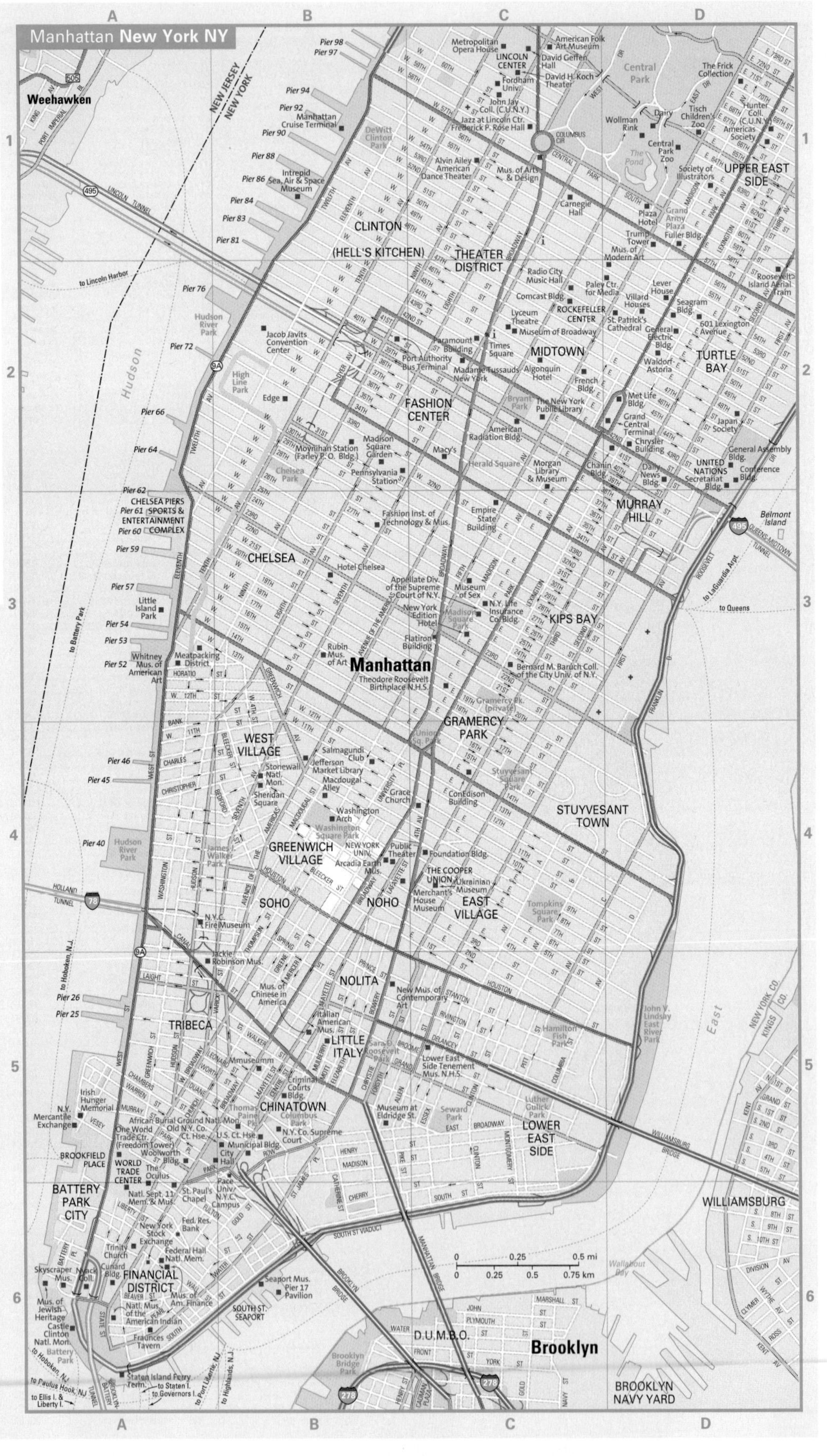

Manhattan New York NY
A
B
C
D
1
2
3
4
5
6
Weehawken
NEW JERSEY
NEW YORK
LINCOLN TUNNEL
to Lincoln Harbor
Hudson
Central Park
UPPER EAST SIDE
CLINTON
(HELL'S KITCHEN)
THEATER DISTRICT
MIDTOWN
TURTLE BAY
FASHION CENTER
MURRAY HILL
CHELSEA
KIPS BAY
Manhattan
GRAMERCY PARK
WEST VILLAGE
STUYVESANT TOWN
GREENWICH VILLAGE
SOHO
NOHO
EAST VILLAGE
NOLITA
TRIBECA
LITTLE ITALY
CHINATOWN
LOWER EAST SIDE
BATTERY PARK CITY
FINANCIAL DISTRICT
WILLIAMSBURG
Belmont Island
to LaGuardia Arpt.
to Queens
East
D.U.M.B.O.
Brooklyn
BROOKLYN NAVY YARD
HOLLAND TUNNEL
to Hoboken, N.J.
to Battery Park
to Staten I.
to Governors I.
to Ellis I. & Liberty I.
to Paulus Hook, NJ
0 0.25 0.5 mi
0 0.25 0.5 0.75 km

Entries in **bold black** indicate counties or parishes.
Entries in **bold color** indicate cities with detailed inset maps.

New London Co. CT 150 B4
New Lothrop MI 76 B3
New Madison OH 100 B1
New Madrid MO 108 B3
New Madrid Co. MO 108 B3
Newman CA 36 C4
Newman IL 99 D1
Newman Grove NE 35 E2
Newmanstown PA 146 A2
New Market AL 119 F2
New Market IN 99 E1
Newmarket NH 82 A4
New Market TN 111 D4
New Market VA 102 C3
New Martinsville WV 101 F1
New Matamoras OH 101 F1
New Meadows ID 22 B2
New Miami OH 100 B2
New Middletown OH 91 F3
New Milford CT 148 C1
New Milford NJ 240 D1
New Milford NY 148 A2
New Milford PA 93 F1
New Millford IL 88 B1
Newnan GA 128 C1
New Orleans LA 134 B3
New Oxford PA 103 E1
New Palestine IN 99 F1
New Paltz NY 94 B3
New Paris IN 89 F2
New Paris OH 100 B1
New Pekin IN 99 F3
New Philadelphia OH 91 E4
New Philadelphia PA 93 E3
New Plymouth ID 22 A4
Newport AR 117 F1
Newport DE 146 B4
Newport IN 99 E1
Newport KY 100 B2
Newport ME 82 C1
Newport MN 235 D3
Newport NH 81 E4
Newport NY 79 F3
Newport NC 115 D4
Newport OH 101 F2
Newport OR 20 B3
Newport PA 93 D4
Newport RI 151 D4
Newport TN 111 D4
Newport VT 81 E1
Newport WA 14 B2
Newport Beach CA 52 C3
Newport Ctr. VT 81 E1
Newport Co. RI 151 D4
Newport News VA 113 F2
New Port Richey FL 140 B2
New Prague MN 66 C4
New Preston CT 148 C1
New Providence NJ 148 A4
New Richland MN 72 C2
New Richmond OH 100 B3
New Richmond WI 67 E3
New River AZ 54 C1
New Roads LA 133 F1
New Rochelle NY 148 B3
New Rockford ND 19 D3
New Salem ND 18 B4
New Salem PA 102 B1
New Salem PA 275 E2
New Sarpy LA 239 A1
New Sharon IA 87 D2
New Site AL 128 B1
New Smyrna Beach FL 139 E4
New Stanton PA 92 A4
New Straitsville OH 101 E1
New Strawn KS 96 A4
New Stuyahok AK 154 B3
New Summerfield TX 124 B3
New Tazewell TN 111 D3
Newton AL 128 B4
Newton GA 128 C4
Newton IL 99 D2
Newton IA 87 D2
Newton KS 43 E3
Newton MA 151 D1
Newton MS 126 C2
Newton NH 95 E1
Newton NJ 94 A4
Newton NC 111 F4
Newton TX 132 C1
Newton UT 31 E2
Newton Co. AR 107 D4
Newton Co. GA 121 D4
Newton Co. IN 89 D3
Newton Co. MS 126 C2
Newton Co. MO 106 C2
Newton Co. TX 133 D1
Newton Falls OH 91 F2
Newton Grove NC 123 D1
Newtonville NJ 147 D4
Newtonville NY 188 E2
Newtown CT 148 C1
New Town ND 18 A2
Newtown OH 204 C2
Newtown PA 147 D2
New Ulm MN 72 B1
New Underwood SD 26 A3
New Vernon NJ 148 A4
New Vienna OH 100 C2
Newville AL 128 B4
Newville PA 93 D4
New Washington IN 100 A3
New Washington OH 91 D3
New Washoe City NV 37 D2
New Waterford OH 91 F3
New Waverly TX 132 A2
New Whiteland IN 99 F1
New Wilmington PA 91 F3
New Windsor IL 88 A2
New Windsor MD 144 B1
New Windsor NY 148 B1
New York NY 148 B4
New York Co. NY 148 B4
New York Mills MN 64 A4
Nezperce ID 22 B1
Nez Perce Co. ID 22 B1
Niagara WI 68 C2
Niagara Co. NY 78 B3
Niagara Falls NY 78 A3
Niantic CT 149 F2
Niantic IL 98 C1
Nibley UT 31 E3
Nice CA 36 B2
Niceville FL 136 B2
Nicholas Co. KY 100 C4
Nicholas Co. WV 101 F4
Nicholasville KY 100 B4
Nicholls GA 129 F4
Nichols NY 93 E1
Nichols Hills OK 244 D2
Nicholson GA 121 D3
Nicholson MS 134 C2
Nicholson PA 93 F2
Nickelsville VA 111 E2
Nickerson KS 43 E3
Nickerson NE 35 F3
Nicksville AZ 55 E4
Nicollet MN 72 C1
Nicollet Co. MN 72 B1
Nicoma Park OK 244 F2
Niederwald TX 61 E2
Nikiski AK 154 C3
Niland CA 53 E3
Niles IL 203 D3
Niles MI 89 F1
Niles OH 91 F2
Ninety Six SC 121 F3
Ninnekah OK 51 E3
Niobrara Co. WY 33 E1
Niota TN 120 C1
Nipomo CA 52 A1
Niskayuna NY 188 D2
Nisland SD 25 F3
Nissequogue NY 149 D3
Nisswa MN 64 A4
Nitro WV 101 E3
Niwot CO 41 E1
Nixa MO 107 D2
Nixon NV 37 D1
Nixon TX 61 E3
Noank CT 149 F2
Noatak AK 154 B1
Noble IL 99 D3
Noble OK 51 E3
Nobleboro ME 82 C3
Noble Co. IN 89 F2
Noble Co. OH 101 F1
Noble Co. OK 51 E2
Nobles Co. MN 72 A2
Noblesville IN 89 F4
Nocatee FL 140 C4
Nocona TX 59 E1
Nodaway Co. MO 86 B4
Noel MO 106 B3
Nogales AZ 55 D4
Nokesville VA 144 A4
Nokomis FL 140 B4
Nokomis IL 98 B2
Nolan Co. TX 58 B3
Nolanville TX 59 E4
Nolensville TN 109 F4
Nome AK 154 B2
Nome TX 132 C3
Nooksack WA 12 C1
Noonday TX 124 A3
Noorvik AK 154 B2
Nora Sprs. IA 73 D3
Norborne MO 96 C2
Norco CA 53 D2
Norco LA 134 B3
Norcross GA 120 C4
Norfolk CT 94 C2
Norfolk MA 151 D2
Norfolk NE 35 E2
Norfolk NY 80 B1
Norfolk VA 113 F2
Norfolk Co. MA 151 D2
Norfork AR 107 E3
Norlina NC 113 D3
Normal IL 88 C4
Norman AR 116 C3
Norman OK 51 E3
Norman Co. MN 19 F3
Normandy MO 256 B2
Normandy Park WA 262 B4
Normangee TX 59 F4
Norman Park GA 129 D4
Normans MD 145 D3
Norphlet AR 125 E1
Norridge IL 203 D3
Norridgewock ME 82 C1
Norris SC 121 E2
Norris TN 110 C4
Norris City IL 99 D4
Norristown PA 146 C2
North SC 122 A4
N. Acton MA 150 C1
N. Adams MA 94 C1
N. Adams MI 90 B1
N. Albany OR 20 B3
N. Amherst MA 150 A1
Northampton MA 150 A1
Northampton PA 93 F3
Northampton Co. NC 113 E3
Northampton Co. PA 93 F3
Northampton Co. VA 114 B3
N. Anson ME 82 B1
N. Apollo PA 92 A4

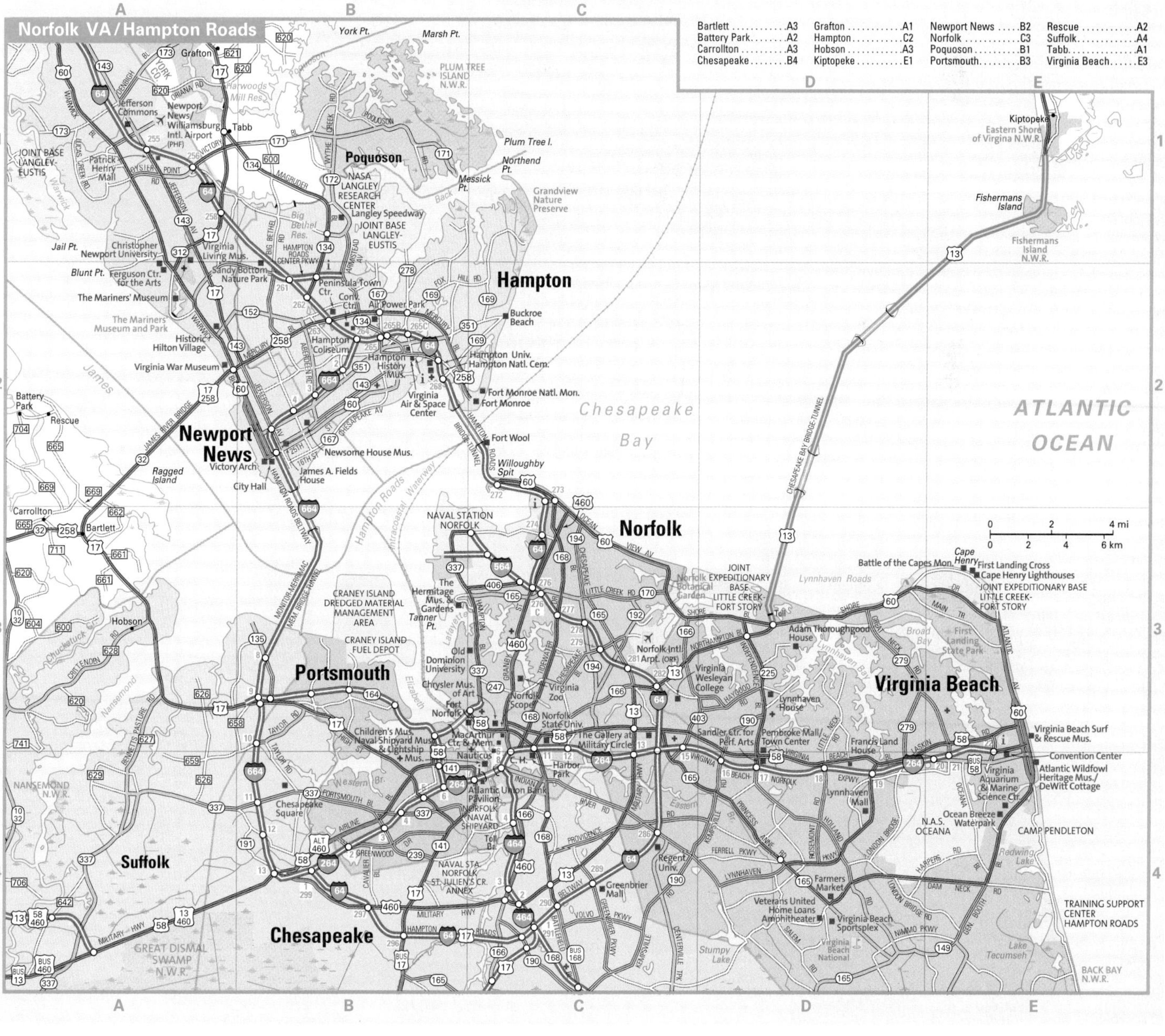
Norfolk VA/Hampton Roads
Bartlett A3
Battery Park........A2
Carrollton A3
Chesapeake........B4
Grafton A1
Hampton...........C2
Hobson A3
Kiptopeke E1
Newport News B2
Norfolk C3
Poquoson B1
Portsmouth.........B3
Rescue A2
Suffolk.............A4
Tabb...............A1
Virginia Beach......E3
Poquoson
Hampton
Newport News
Norfolk
Portsmouth
Virginia Beach
Suffolk
Chesapeake
Chesapeake Bay
ATLANTIC OCEAN
Kiptopeke
Fishermans Island
0 2 4 mi
0 2 4 6 km

Figures after entries indicate page number and grid reference.

N. Arlington NJ ... 240 C2
N. Atlanta GA ... 190 E2
N. Attleboro MA ... 150 C2
N. Augusta SC ... 121 F4
N. Aurora IL ... 88 C1
N. Baltimore OH ... 90 C2
N. Barrington IL ... 203 B2
N. Bay Vil. FL ... 233 B4
N. Beach MD ... 144 C4
N. Beach Haven NJ ... 147 E4
N. Bellport NY ... 149 D4
N. Bend NE ... 35 F3
N. Bend OR ... 20 A4
N. Bend WA ... 12 C3
N. Bennington VT ... 94 C1
N. Bergen NJ ... 240 D2
N. Berwick ME ... 82 B4
N. Bonneville WA ... 20 C1
Northborough MA ... 150 C1
N. Boston NY ... 78 B4
N. Braddock PA ... 250 C2
N. Branch MI ... 76 C3
N. Branch MN ... 67 D3
N. Branch NJ ... 147 D1
N. Branford CT ... 149 E2
N. Brentwood MD ... 270 E2
Northbridge MA ... 150 C2
Northbrook IL ... 89 D1
Northbrook OH ... 204 A1
N. Brookfield MA ... 150 B1
N. Brunswick NJ ... 147 E1
N. Caldwell NJ ... 240 A1
N. Canton OH ... 91 E3
N. Cape May NJ ... 104 C4
N. Carrollton MS ... 118 B4
N. Carver MA ... 151 E3
N. Catasauqua PA ... 189 A1
N. Charleston SC ... 131 D2
N. Chevy Chase MD ... 270 C1
N. Chicago IL ... 75 D4
N. Chili NY ... 78 C3
N. Clarendon VT ... 81 D3
N. Cohasset MA ... 151 E1
N. College Hill OH ... 204 A2
N. Collins NY ... 78 A4
N. Conway NH ... 81 F3
N. Corbin KY ... 110 C2
N. Courtland AL ... 119 E2
N. Crossett AR ... 125 F1
Northdale FL ... 266 C1
N. Dartmouth MA ... 238 C2
N. Decatur GA ... 190 E3
N. Dighton MA ... 151 D3
N. Druid Hills GA ... 190 E3
North East MD ... 145 D1
N. East PA ... 92 A1
N. Eastham MA ... 151 F3
Northeast Harbor ME ... 83 D2
N. Easton MA ... 151 D2
N. Edwards CA ... 52 C1
N. English IA ... 87 E2
N. Enid OK ... 51 E1
Northern Cambria PA ... 92 B3
N. Fairfield OH ... 91 D3
N. Fair Oaks CA ... 259 C5
N. Falmouth MA ... 151 E4
N. Ferrisburg VT ... 81 D2
Northfield CT ... 149 D1
Northfield IL ... 203 D2
Northfield KY ... 230 E1
Northfield MA ... 94 C1
Northfield MN ... 73 D1
Northfield NH ... 81 F4
Northfield NJ ... 147 F4
Northfield OH ... 204 G3
Northfield VT ... 81 E2
Northfield Falls VT ... 81 E2
N. Fond du Lac WI ... 74 C2
Northford CT ... 149 D2
Northfork WV ... 111 F1
N. Fork Vil. OH ... 101 D2
N. Ft. Myers FL ... 142 C1
N. Freedom WI ... 74 A2
Northglenn CO ... 209 C2
N. Grafton MA ... 150 C2
N. Grosvenor Dale CT ... 150 B2
N. Hartland VT ... 81 E3
N. Hartsville SC ... 122 B3
N. Hatfield MA ... 150 A1
N. Haven CT ... 149 D2
N. Haven NY ... 149 E3
N. Haverhill NH ... 81 E2
N. Oxford MA ... 150 B2
N. Palm Beach FL ... 141 F4
N. Pembroke MA ... 151 E2
N. Perry OH ... 91 E1
N. Swansea MA ... 151 D3
N. Syracuse NY ... 79 D3
N. Terre Haute IN ... 99 E1
N. Tonawanda NY ... 78 A3

Arcadia ... F1
Bethany ... D2
Blanchard ... D4
Choctaw ... F2
Del City ... E2
Edmond ... E1
Forest Park ... E2
Jones ... F1
Lake Aluma ... E2
Midwest City ... F2
Moore ... E3
Mustang ... C3
Newcastle ... D4
Nichols Hills ... D2
Nicoma Park ... F2
Norman ... E4
Oklahoma City ... C3
Piedmont ... C1
Richland ... C1
Smith Vil. ... E2
Spencer ... E2
The Village ... D1
Tuttle ... C3
Valley Brook ... E3
Warr Acres ... D2
Woodlawn Park ... D2
Yukon ... C2

Oklahoma City OK
Edmond
Piedmont
Yukon
The Village
Nichols Hills
Warr Acres
Bethany
Spencer
Midwest City
Choctaw
Del City
Oklahoma City
Mustang
Moore
Tuttle
Newcastle
Norman
Blanchard
Arcadia
Jones

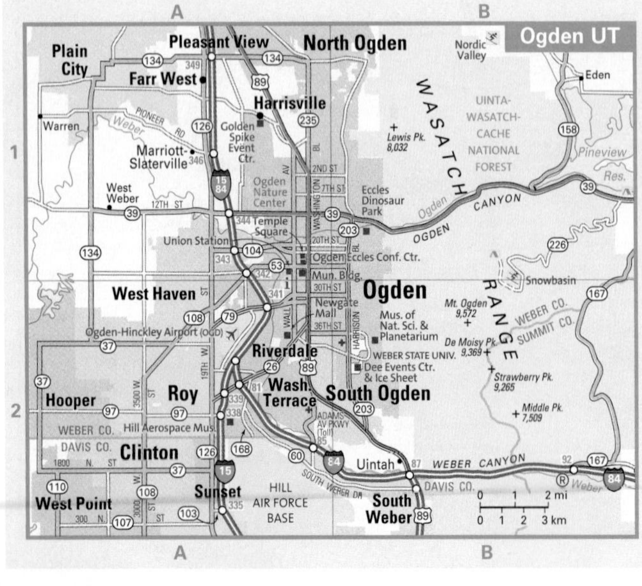
Ogden UT
Plain City
Pleasant View
North Ogden
Farr West
Harrisville
Ogden
West Haven
Riverdale
Roy
South Ogden
Hooper
Clinton
Sunset
West Point
South Weber
WASATCH RANGE

Clinton ... A2
Eden ... B1
Farr West ... A1
Harrisville ... A1
Hooper ... A2
Marriot-Slaterville ... A1
N. Ogden ... B1
Ogden ... B2
Plain City ... A1
Pleasant View ... A1
Riverdale ... A2
Roy ... A2
S. Ogden ... B2
S. Weber ... B2
Sunset ... A2
Uintah ... B2
Warren ... A1
Washington Terrace ... A2
W. Haven ... A1
W. Point ... A2
W. Weber ... A1

N. Hero VT ... 81 D1
N. Hickory NC ... 111 F4
N. Highlands CA ... 36 C3
N. Hills NY ... 241 G3
N. Hodge LA ... 125 E3
N. Hornell NY ... 78 C4
N. Houston TX ... 132 A3
N. Hudson WI ... 67 D4
N. Industry OH ... 91 E3
N. Judson IN ... 89 E2
N. Kansas City MO ... 224 B2
N. Kingsville OH ... 91 F1
Northlake IL ... 203 C4
N. Las Vegas NV ... 46 B2
N. Lauderdale FL ... 233 B2
N. Lewisburg OH ... 90 C4
N. Liberty IN ... 89 E2
N. Liberty IA ... 87 E1
N. Little Rock AR ... 117 E2
N. Logan UT ... 31 E2
N. Manchester IN ... 89 F3
N. Mankato MN ... 72 C1
N. Miami FL ... 143 F2
N. Miami OK ... 106 B2
N. Miami Beach FL ... 143 F2
N. Middleboro MA ... 151 D3
N. Middletown KY ... 100 C4
N. Muskegon MI ... 75 E3
N. Myrtle Beach SC ... 123 D4
N. Naples FL ... 142 C1
N. New Hyde Park NY ... 241 G3
N. Newton KS ... 43 E3
N. Oaks MN ... 235 D1
N. Ogden UT ... 31 E3
N. Olmsted OH ... 91 E2
N. Plainfield NJ ... 147 E1
N. Plains OR ... 20 B1
N. Platte NE ... 34 C3
N. Plymouth MA ... 151 E2
N. Pole AK ... 154 C2
Northport AL ... 127 E1
N. Port FL ... 140 C4
Northport MI ... 69 F3
Northport NY ... 148 C3
N. Powder OR ... 21 F2
N. Prairie WI ... 74 C3
N. Providence RI ... 150 C3
N. Randall OH ... 204 G2
N. Redington Beach FL ... 266 A3
N. Richland Hills TX ... 207 B2
Northridge OH ... 208 D1
Northridge OH ... 100 C1
N. Ridgeville OH ... 91 D2
N. River Shores FL ... 141 E4
N. Riverside IL ... 203 D4
N. Rose NY ... 79 D3
N. Royalton OH ... 91 E2
N. St. Paul MN ... 235 D2
N. Salem IN ... 99 E1
N. Salem NY ... 148 C2
N. Salt Lake UT ... 31 E4
N. Scituate MA ... 151 E2
N. Scituate RI ... 150 C3
N. Sea NY ... 149 E3
N. Shore LA ... 134 C2
N. Sioux City SD ... 35 F1
N. Somers CT ... 150 A2
N. Springfield VT ... 81 E4
N. Springfield VA ... 270 A5
N. Stonington CT ... 149 F1
N. Topsail Beach NC ... 115 D4
N. Troy VT ... 81 E1
N. Truro MA ... 151 F2
N. Tunica MS ... 118 B2
N. Turner ME ... 82 B2
Northumberland PA ... 93 D3
Northumberland Co. PA ... 93 E3
Northumberland Co. VA ... 103 F4
N. Uxbridge MA ... 150 C2
N. Valley Stream NY ... 241 G4
N. Vassalboro ME ... 82 C2
N. Vernon IN ... 100 A2
Northville MA ... 151 D2
Northville MI ... 210 A2
Northville NY ... 80 C4
Northville NY ... 149 E3
N. Wales PA ... 146 C2
N. Walpole NH ... 81 E4
N. Webster IN ... 89 F2
Northwest NC ... 123 E3
N. Westchester CT ... 149 E1
N. Wildwood NJ ... 104 C4
N. Wilkesboro NC ... 111 F4
N. Windham ME ... 82 B3
Northwood IA ... 73 D2
Northwood NH ... 81 F4
Northwood ND ... 19 E3
Northwood OH ... 90 C2
Northwoods MO ... 256 B2
N. Woodstock NH ... 81 F3
Northwye MO ... 97 E4
N. York PA ... 275 E1
Norton KS ... 42 C1
Norton MA ... 151 D2
Norton OH ... 91 E3

Entries in **bold black** indicate counties or parishes.
Entries in bold color indicate cities with detailed inset maps.

Norton VA 111 E2
Norton Co. KS 42 C1
Norton Shores MI 75 E3
Nortonville KS 96 A2
Nortonville KY 109 E2
Norwalk CA 52 C3
Norwalk CT 148 C2
Norwalk IA 86 C2
Norwalk OH 91 D2
Norwalk WI 73 F2
Norway IA 87 E1
Norway ME 82 B2
Norway MI 69 D2
Norwell MA 151 E2
Norwich CT 149 F1
Norwich KS 43 E4
Norwich NY 79 E4
Norwich VT 81 E3
Norwood CO 40 B3
Norwood KY 230 F1
Norwood MA 151 D2
Norwood MO 107 E2
Norwood NY 80 B1
Norwood NC 122 B1
Norwood OH 100 B2
Norwood PA 248 B4
Norwood Young America MN 66 C4
Notasulga AL 128 B2
Nottingham NH 81 F4
Nottoway VA 113 D2
Nottoway Co. VA 113 D2
Notus ID 22 B4
Novato CA 36 B3
Novi MI 76 B4
Novinger MO 87 D4
Nowata OK 106 A3
Nowata Co. OK 106 A2
Noxapater MS 126 C1
Noxon MT 14 C2
Noxubee Co. MS 127 D1
Noyack NY 149 E3
Nuangola PA 93 E3
Nuckolls Co. NE 35 E4
Nucla CO 40 B3
Nueces Co. TX 63 F2
Nuevo CA 53 D3
Nuiqsut AK 154 C1
Nunda NY 78 B4
Nunn CO 33 E4
Nutley NJ 148 B3
Nutter Fort WV 102 A2
Nyack NY 148 B3
Nye Co. NV 37 F3
Nyssa OR 22 A4

O

Oacoma SD 27 D4
Oak Bluffs MA 151 E4
Oakboro NC 122 B1
Oak Brook IL 203 C4
Oakbrook Terrace IL 203 C4
Oak City UT 39 D2
Oak Creek CO 32 C4
Oak Creek WI 74 C3
Oakdale CA 36 C4
Oakdale CT 149 F1
Oakdale KY 109 D2
Oakdale LA 133 E1
Oakdale MA 150 C1
Oakdale MN 235 E2
Oakdale NY 149 D4
Oakdale PA 92 A4
Oakes ND 27 E1
Oakesdale WA 14 A3
Oakfield ME 85 D3
Oakfield NY 78 B3
Oakfield WI 74 C2
Oak Forest IL 89 D2
Oak Grove AL 128 A1
Oak Grove IL 88 A2
Oak Grove KY 109 E3
Oak Grove LA 125 F1
Oak Grove MI 70 C4
Oak Grove MN 67 D3
Oak Grove MS 126 C4
Oak Grove OR 251 D3
Oak Grove SC 122 A3
Oak Grove TN 111 E3
Oak Grove Hts. AR 108 A4
Oak Grove Village MO 96 C2
Oak Harbor OH 90 C2
Oak Harbor WA 12 C2
Oak Hill FL 141 E1
Oak Hill OH 101 D3
Oak Hill WV 101 F4
Oak Hills IL 256 D2
Oakhurst CA 37 D4
Oakhurst NJ 147 F2
Oakhurst OK 51 F2
Oak Island NC 123 E4
Oakland CA 36 B4
Oakland FL 141 D1
Oakland IL 99 D1
Oakland IA 86 A2
Oakland ME 82 C2
Oakland MD 102 B2
Oakland MD 144 B1
Oakland MS 118 B3
Oakland MO 256 B3
Oakland NE 35 F2
Oakland NJ 148 A3
Oakland OK 51 F4
Oakland OR 20 B4
Oakland PA 93 F1
Oakland TN 118 C1
Oakland City IN 99 E4
Oakland Co. MI 76 B4
Oakland Park FL 143 F1
Oak Lawn IL 89 D1
Oakley ID 31 D2
Oakley KS 42 B2
Oakley UT 31 F4
Oaklyn NJ 248 D4
Oakman AL 119 E4
Oakmont PA 92 A4
Oak Orchard DE 145 F4
Oak Park CA 228 A2
Oak Park IL 89 D1
Oak Park MI 76 C4
Oak Park Hts. MN 67 D3
Oak Ridge NJ 148 A3
Oak Ridge NC 112 B4
Oakridge OR 20 C4
Oak Ridge TN 110 C4
Oak Ridge North TX 132 A2
Oak Shade NJ 147 D3
Oakton VA 144 A3
Oaktown IN 99 E3
Oak Trail Shores TX 59 E3
Oak View CA 52 B2
Oakville CT 149 D1
Oakville MO 98 A3
Oakville WA 12 B4
Oakwood GA 121 D3
Oakwood IL 89 D4
Oakwood OH 90 B3
Oakwood OH 204 G3
Oakwood OH 208 E2
Oakwood Beach NJ 145 E1
Oakwood Hills IL 203 A1
Oasis NV 30 C3
Oberlin KS 42 C1
Oberlin LA 133 E2
Oberlin OH 91 D2
Oberlin PA 218 C2
Obetz OH 206 B3
Obion TN 108 C3
Obion Co. TN 108 C3
Oblong IL 99 D2
O'Brien Co. IA 72 A3
Ocala FL 138 C4
Occidental CA 36 A3
Occoquan VA 144 B4
Oceana WV 111 F1
Oceana Co. MI 75 E2
Ocean Bluff MA 151 E2
Ocean Breeze Park FL 141 E4
Ocean City FL 136 B2
Ocean City MD 114 C1
Ocean City NJ 147 F4
Ocean Co. NJ 147 E3
Ocean Gate NJ 147 E3
Ocean Grove MA 151 D3
Ocean Grove NJ 147 F2
Oceano CA 52 A1
Ocean Park WA 12 B4
Ocean Pines MD 114 C1
Oceanport NJ 147 F2
Ocean Reef Club FL 143 E3
Ocean Ridge FL 143 F1
Ocean Shores WA 12 B4
Oceanside CA 53 D3
Oceanside NY 147 F1
Oceanside OR 20 B2
Ocean Sprs. MS 135 D2
Ocean View DE 145 F4
Ochelata OK 51 F1
Ocheyedan IA 72 A2
Ochiltree Co. TX 50 B2
Ochlocknee GA 137 E1
Ocilla GA 129 E4
Ocoee FL 141 D1
Oconee Co. GA 121 D4
Oconee Co. SC 121 E2
Oconomowoc WI 74 C3
Oconto WI 69 D4
Oconto Co. WI 68 C4
Oconto Falls WI 68 C4
Ocracoke NC 115 E3
Odebolt IA 72 A4
Odell IL 88 C3
Odell OR 20 C1
Odem TX 61 E4
Odenton MD 144 C2
Odenville AL 119 F4
Odessa DE 145 E1
Odessa FL 140 B2
Odessa MO 96 C2
Odessa NY 79 D4
Odessa TX 58 A3
Odessa WA 13 F3
Odin IL 98 C3
Odon IN 99 E3
O'Donnell TX 58 A2
Oelwein IA 73 E4
O'Fallon IL 98 B3
O'Fallon MO 98 A3
Ogallala NE 34 B3
Ogden IL 89 D4
Ogden IA 86 C1
Ogden KS 43 F2
Ogden NC 123 E3
Ogden UT 31 E3
Ogden Dunes IN 89 E2
Ogdensburg NJ 148 A3
Ogdensburg NY 80 B1
Ogemaw Co. MI 76 B1
Oglala SD 34 A1
Oglala Lakota Co. SD 26 A4
Ogle Co. IL 88 B1
Oglesby IL 88 B2
Oglethorpe GA 129 D3
Oglethorpe Co. GA 121 E4
Ogunquit ME 82 B4
Ohatchee AL 120 A4
Ohio City OH 90 B3
Ohio Co. IN 100 A2
Ohio Co. KY 109 F1
Ohio Co. WV 91 F4
Ohioville PA 91 F3
Oil City LA 124 C2
Oil City PA 92 A2
Oildale CA 45 D4
Oilton OK 51 F2
Ojai CA 52 B2
Okaloosa Co. FL 136 B2
Okanogan WA 13 E2
Okanogan Co. WA 13 E1
Okarche OK 51 E2
Okauchee WI 74 C3
Okawville IL 98 B3
Okay OK 106 A4
Okeechobee FL 141 E4
Okeechobee Co. FL 141 E3
Okeene OK 51 D2
Okemah OK 51 F3
Okemos MI 76 A4
Okfuskee Co. OK 51 F3
Oklahoma City OK 51 E3
Oklahoma Co. OK 51 E2
Okmulgee OK 51 F2
Okmulgee Co. OK 51 F2
Okoboji IA 72 A2
Okolona MS 119 D3
Oktibbeha Co. MS 118 C4
Ola AR 117 D2
Olanta SC 122 C4
Olathe CO 40 B3
Olathe KS 96 B3
Olcott NY 78 B3
Old Bennington VT 94 C1
Old Bridge NJ 147 E1
Oldenburg IN 100 A2
Old Field NY 149 D3
Old Forge NY 79 F2
Old Forge PA 93 F2
Old Fort NC 111 E4
Oldham SD 27 E3
Oldham Co. KY 100 A4
Oldham Co. TX 49 F3
Old Lyme CT 149 E2
Old Mystic CT 149 F2
Old Orchard Beach ME 82 B4
Old River-Winfree TX 132 B3
Old Saybrook CT 149 E2
Oldsmar FL 140 B2
Oldtown ID 14 B2
Old Town ME 83 D1
Old Zionsville PA 146 B1
Olean NY 92 C1
Oley PA 146 B1
Olin IA 87 F1
Olive Branch MS 118 B2
Olive Hill KY 101 D4
Olivehurst CA 36 C2
Oliver PA 102 B1
Oliver Co. ND 18 B4
Oliver Sprs. TN 110 C4
Olivet MI 76 A4
Olivet NJ 145 F1
Olivet SD 35 E1
Olivette MO 256 B2
Olivia MN 66 B4
Olla LA 125 E3
Olmos Park TX 257 E2
Olmsted Co. MN 73 E1
Olmsted Falls OH 204 D3
Olney IL 99 D3
Olney MD 144 B2
Olney TX 59 D1
Olney Sprs. CO 41 F3
Olpe KS 43 F3
Olton TX 50 A4
Olustee OK 50 C4
Olympia WA 12 B4
Olympian Vil. MO 98 A4
Olyphant PA 261 E2
Omaha NE 86 A2
Omaha TX 124 B1
Omak WA 13 E2
Omao HI 152 B1
Omega GA 129 D4
Omro WI 74 C1
Onaga KS 43 F1
Onalaska TX 132 B1
Onalaska WI 73 F2
Onamia MN 66 C2
Onancock VA 114 C3
Onarga IL 89 D3
Onawa IA 35 F2
Onaway ID 14 B4
Onaway MI 70 C3
Oneco FL 140 B3
Oneida IL 88 A3
Oneida NY 79 E3
Oneida TN 110 B3
Oneida WI 68 C4
Oneida Co. ID 31 E2
Oneida Co. NY 79 E2
Oneida Co. WI 68 B2
O'Neill NE 35 D2
Onekama MI 75 E1
Oneonta AL 119 F4
Oneonta NY 79 F4
Onida SD 26 C3
Onley VA 114 C3
Onondaga Co. NY 79 E3
Onset MA 151 E3
Onslow Co. NC 115 D4
Onsted MI 90 B1
Ontario CA 52 C2
Ontario OH 91 D3
Ontario OR 22 A4
Ontario Co. NY 78 C4
Ontonagon MI 65 E4
Ontonagon Co. MI 65 E4
Onyx CA 45 E4
Oolitic IN 99 F3
Oologah OK 106 A3
Ooltewah TN 120 B2
Oostburg WI 75 D2
Opal Cliffs CA 236 D1
Opa-Locka FL 143 E2
Opelika AL 128 B2
Opelousas LA 133 F2
Opp AL 128 A4
Oppelo AR 117 E1
Oquawka IL 87 F3
Oracle AZ 55 D2
Oracle Jct. AZ 55 D3
Oradell NJ 148 B3
Oran MO 108 B2
Orange CA 52 C3
Orange CT 149 D2
Orange MA 95 D1
Orange NJ 240 A3
Orange OH 204 G2
Orange TX 132 C2
Orange VA 103 D4
Orange Beach AL 135 F2
Orangeburg NY 148 B3
Orangeburg SC 122 A4
Orangeburg Co. SC 122 A4
Orange City FL 141 D1
Orange City IA 35 F1
Orange Co. CA 52 C3
Orange Co. FL 141 D1
Orange Co. IN 99 F3
Orange Co. NY 148 A2
Orange Co. NC 112 C4
Orange Co. TX 132 C2
Orange Co. VT 81 E3
Orange Co. VA 103 D4
Orange Cove CA 45 D3
Orange Grove TX 61 E4
Orange Lake FL 138 C4
Orange Lake NY 148 B1
Orange Park FL 139 D2
Orangeville IL 74 B4
Orangeville UT 39 F2
Orbisonia PA 92 C4
Orchard Beach MD 193 D5
Orchard City CO 40 B2
Orchard Lake MI 210 A1
Orchard Mesa CO 40 B2
Orchard Park NY 78 B4
Orchards WA 20 C1
Orcutt CA 52 A1
Ord NE 35 D3
Orderville UT 39 D4
Ordway CO 41 F3
Oreana IL 98 C1
Ore City TX 124 B2
Orefield PA 146 B1
Oregon IL 88 B1
Oregon MO 96 B1
Oregon OH 90 C2
Oregon WI 74 B3
Oregon City OR 20 C2
Oregon Co. MO 107 F3
Oreland PA 248 C1
Orem UT 31 F4
Orfordville WI 74 B4
Orient NY 149 F2
Oriental NC 115 E3
Orient Park FL 266 C2
Orinda CA 259 C2
Orion IL 88 A2
Oriskany NY 79 E3
Oriskany Falls NY 79 E3
Orland CA 36 B1
Orland ME 83 D2
Orland Hills IL 203 C6
Orlando FL 141 D1
Orland Park IL 89 D2
Orleans IN 99 F3
Orleans IA 72 B2
Orleans MA 151 F3
Orleans NE 43 D1
Orleans VT 81 E1
Orleans Co. NY 78 B3
Orleans Co. VT 81 E1
Orleans Par. LA 134 B2
Orlinda TN 109 F3
Orlovista FL 246 B2
Ormond Beach FL 139 E4
Ormond-by-the-Sea FL 139 E4
Orofino ID 14 B4
Orono ME 83 D1
Orono MN 66 C4
Oronoco MN 73 D1
Oronogo MO 106 B2
Orosi CA 45 D3
Oro Valley AZ 55 D3
Oroville CA 36 C1
Oroville WA 13 E1
Orrick MO 96 C2
Orrington ME 83 D1
Orrs Island ME 82 B3
Orrville OH 91 E3
Orting WA 12 C3
Ortonville MI 76 B3
Ortonville MN 27 F2
Orwell OH 91 F2
Orwigsburg PA 146 A1
Osage IA 73 D3
Osage WY 25 F4
Osage Beach MO 97 D4
Osage City KS 96 A3
Osage Co. KS 96 A3
Osage Co. MO 97 F4
Osage Co. OK 51 F1
Osakis MN 66 B2
Osawatomie KS 96 B3
Osborne KS 43 D2
Osborne Co. KS 43 D2
Osburn ID 14 B3
Oscawana Corners NY 148 B2
Osceola AR 108 B4
Osceola IN 89 F2
Osceola IA 86 C3
Osceola MO 96 C4
Osceola NE 35 E3
Osceola WI 67 D3
Osceola Co. FL 141 D2
Osceola Co. IA 72 A2
Osceola Co. MI 75 F1
Osceola Mills PA 92 C3
Oscoda MI 76 C1
Oscoda Co. MI 70 C4
Osgood IN 100 A2
Oshkosh NE 34 A3
Oshkosh WI 74 C1
Oskaloosa IA 87 D2
Oskaloosa KS 96 A2
Oslo FL 141 F3
Osmond NE 35 E2
Osprey FL 140 B4
Osseo MN 235 A1
Osseo WI 67 F4
Ossian IN 90 A3
Ossian IA 73 E3
Ossineke MI 71 D4
Ossining NY 148 B2
Ossipee NH 81 F3
Ossipee NC 112 B4
Osterville MA 151 E4
Oswego IL 88 C2
Oswego KS 106 B2
Oswego NY 79 D2
Oswego Co. NY 79 E2
Osyka MS 134 B1
Otego NY 79 F4
Otero Co. CO 41 F4

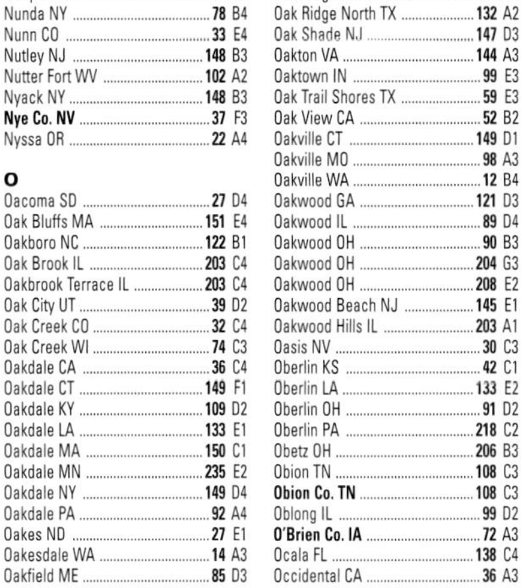

Bellevue B3
Boys Town A2
Briggs B1
Carter Lake B2
Council Bluffs C3
Crescent C1
Irvington A1
La Vista A3
Omaha B2
Papillion A3
Ralston A3

Figures after entries indicate page number and grid reference.

Otero Co. NM 57 D3
Othello WA 13 E4
Otho IA 72 C4
Otis CO 41 F1
Otisville MI 76 B3
Otisville NY 148 A1
Otoe Co. NE 35 F4
Otsego MI 75 F4
Otsego MN 66 C3
Otsego Co. MI 70 C3
Otsego Co. NY 79 F4
Ottawa IL 88 C2
Ottawa KS 96 A3
Ottawa OH 90 B3
Ottawa Co. KS 43 E2
Ottawa Co. MI 75 E3
Ottawa Co. OH 90 C2
Ottawa Co. OK 106 B2
Ottawa Hills OH 267 A1
Otterbein IN 89 E4
Otter Tail Co. MN 19 F4
Ottoville OH 90 B3
Ottumwa IA 87 E3
Otway NC 115 E4
Ouachita Co. AR 117 D4
Ouachita Par. LA 125 E2
Ouray CO 40 C3
Ouray Co. CO 40 B3
Outagamie Co. WI 74 C1
Overall TN 109 F4
Overbrook KS 96 A3
Overgaard AZ 47 F4
Overland MO 256 B2
Overland Park KS 96 B3
Overlea MD 144 C2
Overton NE 35 D4
Overton NV 46 B1
Overton TX 124 B3
Overton Co. TN 110 B3
Ovid CO 34 A3
Ovid MI 76 A3
Ovid NY 79 D4
Oviedo FL 141 D1
Ovilla TX 59 F3
Owasso OK 106 A3
Owatonna MN 73 D1
Owego NY 93 E1
Owen WI 68 A4
Owen Co. IN 99 E2
Owen Co. KY 100 B3
Owens VA 103 E4
Owensboro KY 109 E1
Owens Cross Roads AL 119 F2
Owensville IN 99 D4
Owensville MO 97 F4
Owensville OH 100 B2
Owenton KY 100 B3
Owings MD 144 C4
Owings Mills MD 144 C1
Owingsville KY 100 C4
Owosso MI 76 B3
Owsley Co. KY 110 C1
Owyhee NV 30 B2
Owyhee Co. ID 22 A4
Oxbow ND 19 F4
Oxford AL 120 A4
Oxford AR 107 E3
Oxford CT 149 D1
Oxford GA 121 D4
Oxford IN 89 D4
Oxford IA 87 E1
Oxford KS 43 E4
Oxford ME 82 B2
Oxford MD 145 D4
Oxford MA 150 B2
Oxford MI 76 C3
Oxford MS 118 C3
Oxford NE 35 D4
Oxford NJ 93 F3
Oxford NY 79 E4
Oxford NC 113 D3
Oxford OH 100 B1
Oxford PA 146 A3
Oxford WI 74 B2
Oxford Co. ME 82 A2
Oxford Jct. IA 87 F1
Oxnard CA 52 B2
Oxon Hill MD 144 B3
Oyster Bay NY 148 C3
Oyster Bay Cove NY 148 C3
Oyster Creek TX 132 A4
Ozark AL 128 B4
Ozark AR 116 C1
Ozark MO 107 D2
Ozark Co. MO 107 E3
Ozaukee Co. WI 75 D2
Ozawkie KS 96 A2
Ozona TX 60 B1

P

Paauilo HI 153 F2
Pablo MT 15 D3
Pace FL 135 F2
Pacheco CA 259 D1
Pacific MO 98 A3
Pacific WA 262 B5
Pacifica CA 36 B4
Pacific City OR 20 B2
Pacific Co. WA 12 B4
Pacific Grove CA 44 B3
Pacific Jct. IA 86 A3
Pacolet SC 121 F2
Paddock Lake WI 74 C4
Paden OK 51 F3
Paden City WV 101 F1
Paducah KY 108 C2
Paducah TX 58 C1
Page AZ 47 E1
Page Co. IA 86 B3
Page Co. VA 102 C3
Pagedale MO 256 B2
Pageland SC 122 B2
Pagosa Sprs. CO 40 C4
Paguate NM 48 B3
Pahala HI 153 E4
Pahoa HI 153 F3
Pahokee FL 141 E4
Pahrump NV 46 A2
Paia HI 153 D1
Paincourtville LA 134 A3
Painesville OH 91 E1
Painted Post NY 93 D1
Paint Rock TX 58 C4
Paintsville KY 111 D1
Paisley FL 139 D4
Pajaro CA 236 E1
Pala CA 53 D3
Palacios TX 61 F3
Palatine IL 89 D1
Palatine Bridge NY 79 F3
Palatka FL 139 D3
Palenville NY 94 B2
Palermo CA 36 C2
Palermo NJ 147 F4
Palestine AR 118 A2
Palestine IL 99 D2
Palestine TX 124 A3
Palisade CO 40 B2
Palisades Park NJ 148 B3
Palm Bay FL 141 E2
Palm Beach FL 143 F1
Palm Beach Co. FL 141 E4
Palm Beach Gardens FL 141 F4
Palm Beach Shores FL 141 F4
Palm City FL 141 E4
Palm Coast FL 139 E3
Palmdale CA 52 C2
Palm Desert CA 53 E3
Palmer AK 154 C3
Palmer MA 150 A2
Palmer NE 35 E3
Palmer TN 120 B1
Palmer TX 59 F3
Palmer Lake CO 41 E2
Palmer Park MD 271 F3
Palmerton PA 93 F3
Palmetto FL 140 B3
Palmetto GA 120 C4
Palmetto Bay FL 143 E3
Palm Harbor FL 140 B2
Palm River FL 266 C2
Palm Shores FL 141 E2
Palm Sprs. CA 53 D3
Palm Sprs. FL 143 F1
Palm Valley FL 139 D2
Palmview TX 63 E4
Palmyra IL 98 B2
Palmyra IN 99 F3
Palmyra MO 97 F1
Palmyra NE 35 F4
Palmyra NJ 146 C3
Palmyra NY 78 C3
Palmyra PA 93 E4
Palmyra VA 102 C4
Palmyra WI 74 C3

Altamonte Sprs. C1
Apopka A1
Azalea Park D2
Bay Hill B3
Belle Isle C3
Bertha D1
Buena Ventura Lakes C5
Casselberry C1
Celebration A5
Clarcona B1
Conway C3
Doctor Phillips B3
Eatonville C1
Edgewood C3
Fairview Shores C1
Fairvilla C2
Fern Park C1
Flamingo C4
Forest City B1
Goldenrod D1
Gotha A2
Jamestown D1
Kissimmee B5
Lake Buena Vista B4
Lake Cain Hills B3
Lockhart B1
Maitland C1
Morningside Park C3
Narcoossee D5
Ocoee A2
Orlando C2
Orlovista B2
Piedmont B1
Pine Castle C3
Pine Hills B2
Sky Lake C3
Slavia D1
S. Apopka B1
Taft C4
Tangelo Park B3
Union Park D2
Vineland B4
Williamsburg B4
Windermere A3
Winter Garden A2
Winter Park C1
Winter Sprs. D1

Entries in **bold black** indicate counties or parishes.
Entries in bold color indicate cities with detailed inset maps.

Palo IA 87 E1
Palo Alto CA 36 B4
Palo Alto Co. IA 72 B3
Palo Cedro CA 28 C4
Palo Pinto TX 59 D2
Palo Pinto Co. TX 59 D2
Palos Hts. IL 203 D6
Palos Hills IL 203 D5
Palos Park IL 203 D6
Palos Verdes Estates CA 228 C4
Palouse WA 14 B4
Pamlico Co. NC 115 E3
Pampa TX 50 B3
Pamplico SC 122 C3
Pana IL 98 C2
Panaca NV 38 C4
Panacea FL 137 E3
Panama OK 116 B1
Panama City FL 136 C2
Panama City Beach FL 136 C2
Pandora OH 90 B3
Pangburn AR 117 F1
Panguitch UT 39 D4
Panhandle TX 50 B3
Panola Co. MS 118 B3
Panola Co. TX 124 C3
Panora IA 86 B2
Panorama Vil. TX 132 A2
Pantano AZ 55 D3
Pantego TX 207 B3
Panthersville GA 190 E4
Paola KS 96 B3
Paoli IN 99 F3
Paoli OK 51 E4
Paoli PA 146 B3
Paonia CO 40 C2
Papaikou HI 153 F3
Papillion NE 35 F3
Parachute CO 40 B1
Paradis LA 239 A2
Paradise CA 36 C1
Paradise PA 146 A3
Paradise UT 31 E3
Paradise Hills NM 48 C3
Paradise Valley AZ 249 C2
Paragon IN 99 F2
Paragonah UT 39 D4
Paragould AR 108 A4
Paramount CA 228 D3
Paramus NJ 148 B3
Pardeeville WI 74 B2
Paris AR 116 C1
Paris ID 31 F2
Paris IL 99 D1
Paris KY 100 B4
Paris ME 82 B2
Paris MO 97 E2
Paris TN 109 D3
Paris TX 116 A4
Parish NY 79 D2
Parishville NY 80 B1
Park City KS 43 E4
Park City KY 110 A2
Park City MT 24 B1
Park City UT 31 F4
Park Co. CO 41 D2
Park Co. MT 23 F2
Park Co. WY 24 B3
Parke Co. IN 99 E1
Parker AZ 46 B4
Parker CO 41 E1
Parker FL 136 C2
Parker ID 23 E4
Parker PA 92 A3
Parker SD 27 F4
Parker City IN 90 A4
Parker Co. TX 59 E2
Parkersburg IA 73 D4
Parkersburg WV 101 E2
Parkers Prairie MN 66 B1
Parkertown NJ 147 E4
Parkesburg PA 146 A3
Park Falls WI 68 A2
Park Hill OK 106 B4
Park Hills KY 204 B3
Park Hills MO 98 A4
Parkin AR 118 A1
Parkland FL 143 E1
Parkland WA 12 C3
Park Lane CT 148 C1
Park Rapids MN 64 A4
Park Ridge IL 203 C3
Park Ridge NJ 148 B3
Park River ND 19 E2
Parks AZ 47 D3
Parks LA 133 F2
Parkside PA 248 A4
Parksley VA 114 C2
Parkston SD 27 E4
Park View IA 88 A1
Parkville MD 144 C1
Parkville MO 224 B2
Parkway Vil. KY 230 D2
Parlier CA 45 D3
Parma ID 22 A4
Parma MI 76 A4
Parma MO 108 B3
Parma OH 91 E2
Parma Hts. OH 204 E3
Parmelee SD 26 C4
Parmer Co. TX 49 F4
Parowan UT 39 D4
Parrish AL 119 E4
Parshall ND 18 B2
Parsons KS 106 A1
Parsons TN 109 D4
Parsons WV 102 B2
Pasadena CA 52 C2
Pasadena MD 193 D5
Pasadena TX 132 B3
Pascagoula MS 135 D2
Pasco WA 21 E1
Pascoag RI 150 C2
Pasco Co. FL 140 B2
Paso Robles CA 44 C4
Pasquotank Co. NC 115 E1
Passaic NJ 148 B3
Passaic Co. NJ 148 A3
Pass Christian MS 134 C2
Patagonia AZ 55 D4
Pataskala OH 101 D1
Patchogue NY 149 D4
Pateros WA 13 E2
Paterson NJ 148 B3
Patoka IL 98 C3
Patoka IN 99 D3
Patrick Co. VA 112 B3
Patrick Sprs. VA 112 B3
Patten ME 85 D3
Pattenburg NJ 146 C1
Patterson AR 117 F1
Patterson CA 36 C4
Patterson GA 129 F4
Patterson LA 134 A3
Patterson NY 148 C1
Patterson Gardens MI 90 C1
Patterson Sprs. NC 122 A1
Patton PA 92 B3
Patton Vil. TX 132 B2
Paul ID 31 D1
Paulden AZ 47 D3
Paulding MS 126 C3
Paulding OH 90 B3
Paulding Co. GA 120 B4
Paulding Co. OH 90 B3
Paullina IA 72 A3
Paulsboro NJ 146 C3

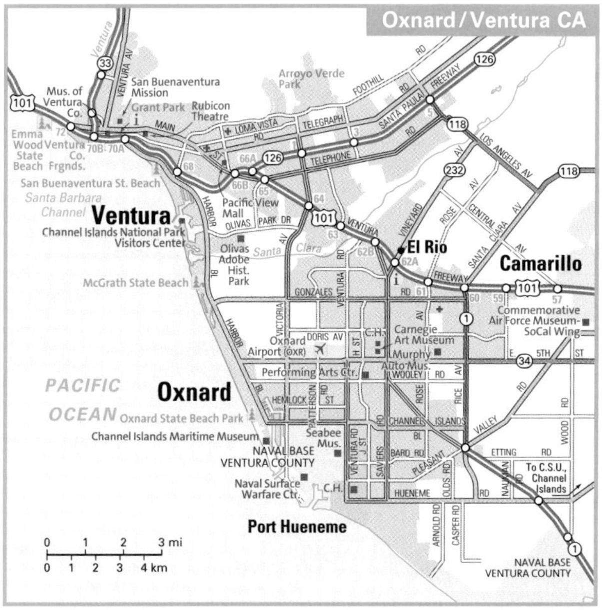

Bellview A1
Brent B1
Brownsville B2
Ensley A1
Ferry Pass B1
Goulding B1
Gulf Breeze B2
Myrtle Grove A2
Pensacola B1
Pleasant Grove A2
Warrington A2
W. Pensacola A1

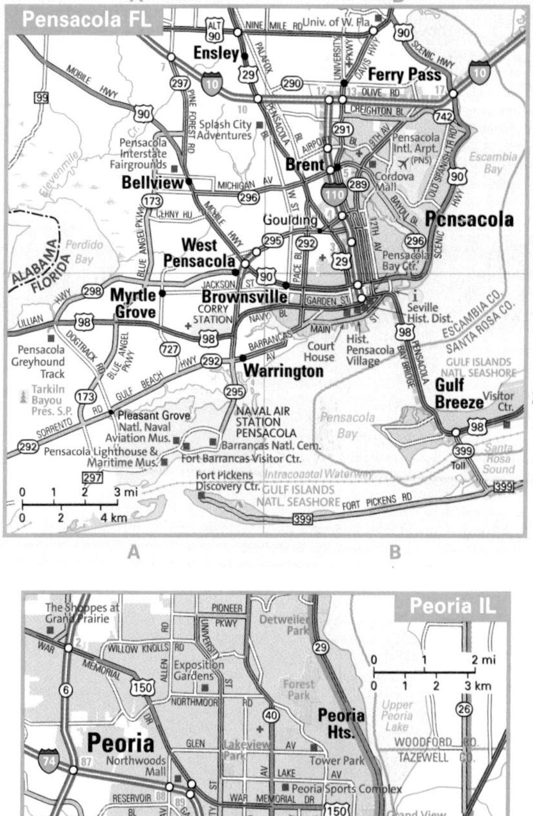

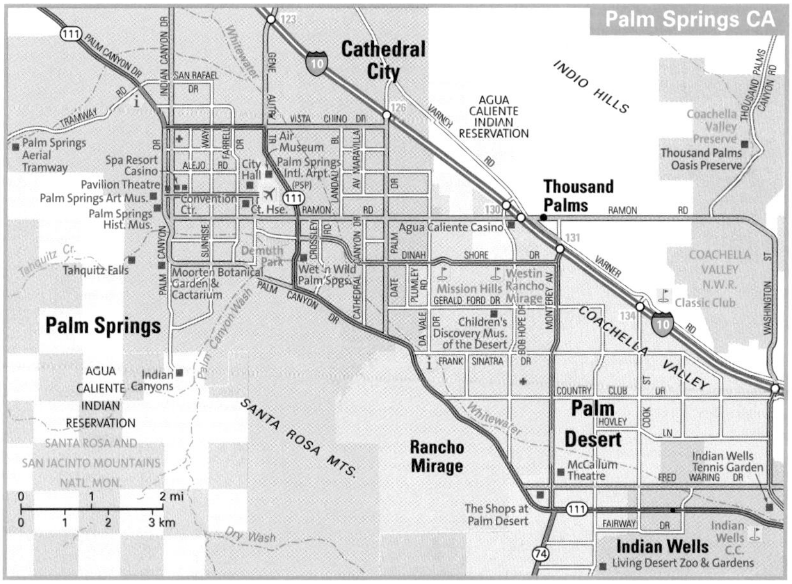

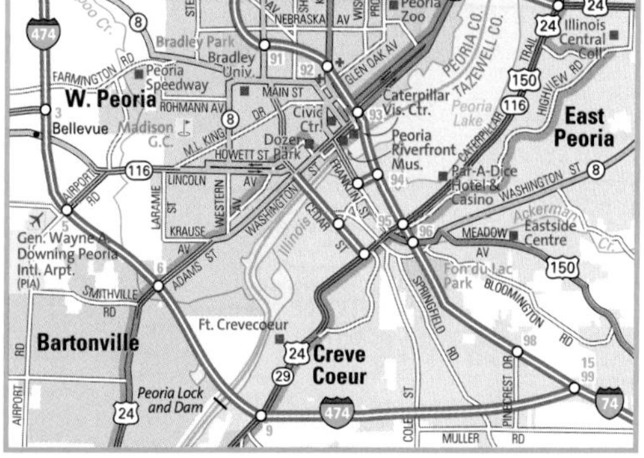

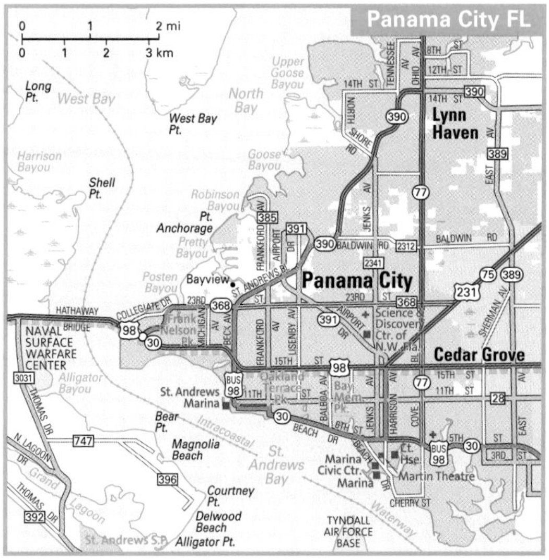

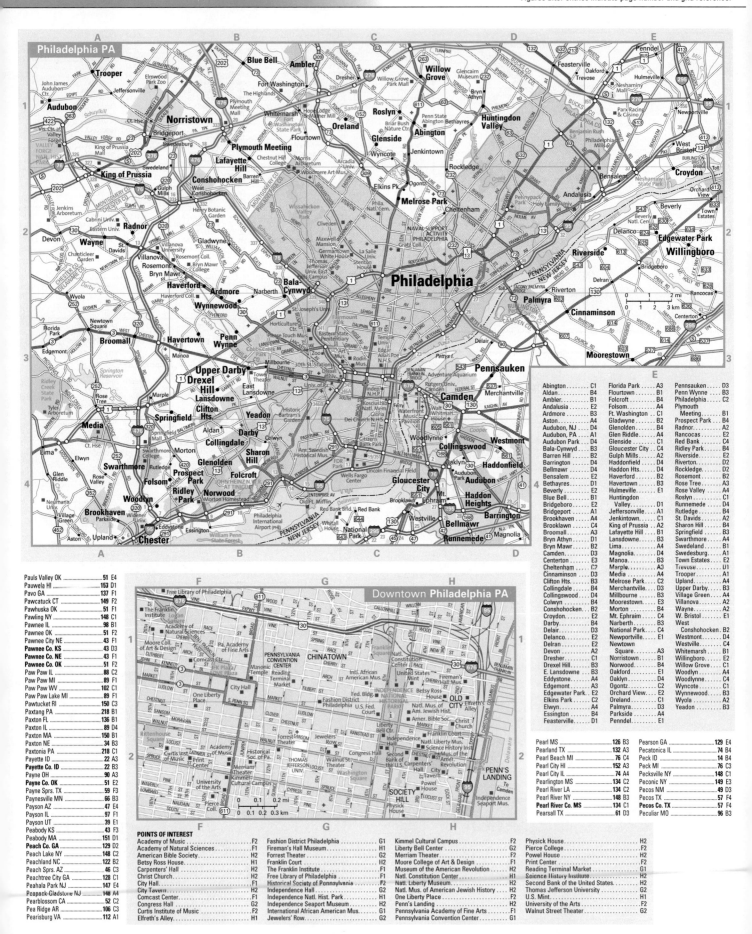

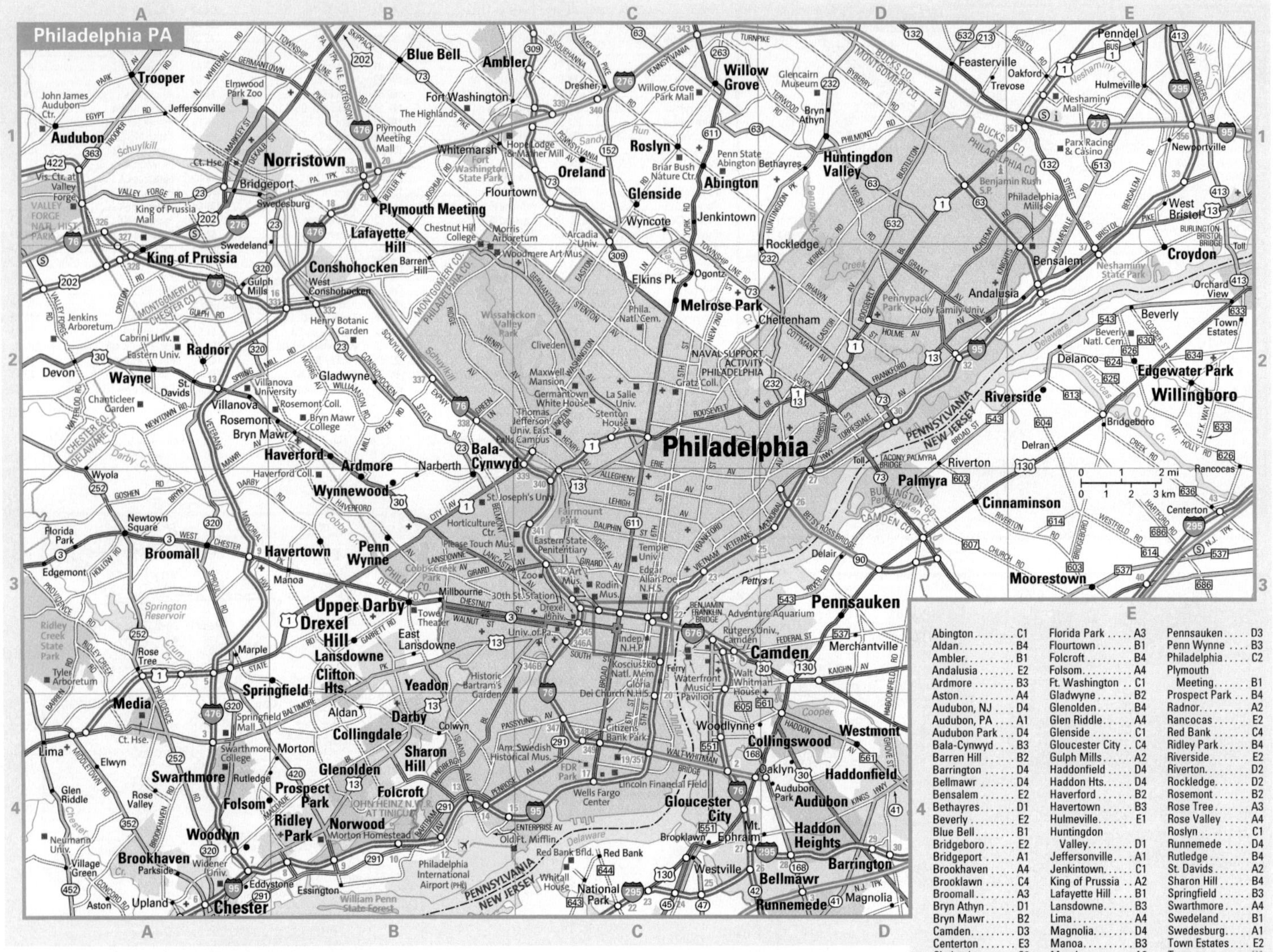
Philadelphia PA
Philadelphia
Camden
Norristown
Chester

Abington C1
Aldan B4
Ambler B1
Andalusia E2
Ardmore B3
Aston A4
Audubon, NJ D4
Audubon, PA A1
Audubon Park D4
Bala-Cynwyd B3
Barren Hill B2
Barrington D4
Bellmawr D4
Bensalem E2
Bethayres D1
Beverly E2
Blue Bell B1
Bridgeboro E2
Bridgeport A1
Brookhaven A4
Brooklawn C4
Broomall A3
Bryn Athyn D1
Bryn Mawr B2
Camden D3
Centerton E3
Cheltenham C2
Cinnaminson D3
Clifton Hts. B3
Collingdale B4
Collingswood D4
Colwyn B4
Conshohocken B2
Croydon E2
Darby B4
Delair D3
Delanco E2
Delran E2
Devon A2
Dresher C1
Drexel Hill B3
E. Lansdowne B3
Eddystone A4
Edgemont A3
Edgewater Park E2
Elkins Park C2
Elwyn A4
Essington B4
Feasterville D1
Florida Park A3
Flourtown B1
Folcroft B4
Folsom A4
Ft. Washington C1
Gladwyne B2
Glenolden B4
Glen Riddle A4
Glenside C1
Gloucester City C4
Gulph Mills A2
Haddonfield D4
Haddon Hts. D4
Haverford B2
Havertown B3
Hulmeville E1
Huntingdon Valley D1
Jeffersonville A1
Jenkintown C1
King of Prussia A2
Lafayette Hill B1
Lansdowne B3
Lima A4
Magnolia D4
Manoa B3
Marple A3
Media A4
Melrose Park C2
Merchantville D3
Millbourne B3
Moorestown E3
Morton B4
Mt. Ephraim C4
Narberth B3
National Park C4
Newportville E1
Newtown Square A3
Norristown B1
Norwood B4
Oakford E1
Oaklyn D4
Ogontz C2
Orchard View E2
Oreland C1
Palmyra D3
Parkside A4
Penndel E1
Pennsauken D3
Penn Wynne B3
Philadelphia C2
Plymouth Meeting B1
Prospect Park B4
Radnor A2
Rancocas E2
Red Bank C4
Ridley Park B4
Riverside E2
Riverton D2
Rockledge D2
Rosemont B2
Rose Tree A3
Rose Valley A4
Roslyn C1
Runnemede D4
Rutledge B4
St. Davids A2
Sharon Hill B4
Springfield B3
Swarthmore A4
Swedeland B1
Swedesburg A1
Town Estates E2
Trevose D1
Trooper A1
Upland A4
Upper Darby B3
Village Green A4
Villanova A2
Wayne A2
W. Bristol E1
West Conshohocken B2
Westmont D4
Westville C4
Whitemarsh B1
Willingboro E2
Willow Grove C1
Woodlyn A4
Woodlynne C4
Wyncote C1
Wynnewood B3
Wyola A2
Yeadon B3

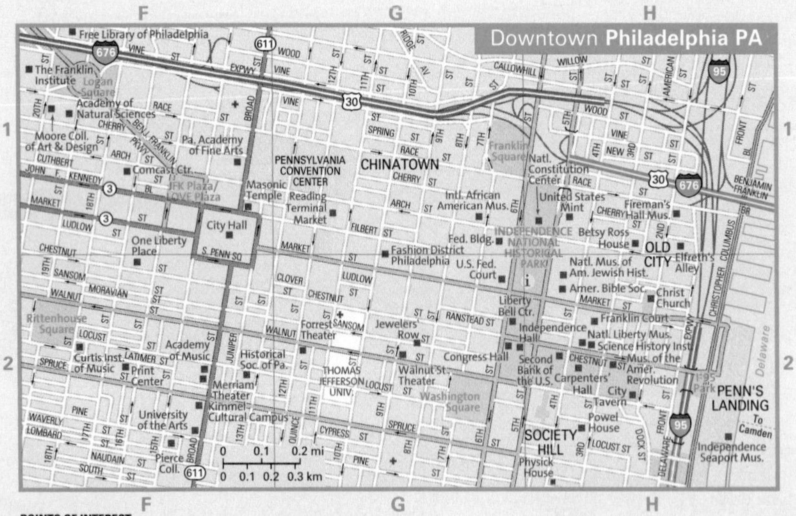
Downtown Philadelphia PA
CHINATOWN
OLD CITY
SOCIETY HILL
PENN'S LANDING

POINTS OF INTEREST

Academy of Music F2
Academy of Natural Sciences F1
American Bible Society H2
Betsy Ross House H1
Carpenters' Hall H2
Christ Church H2
City Hall F1
City Tavern H2
Comcast Center F1
Congress Hall G2
Curtis Institute of Music F2
Elfreth's Alley H1
Fashion District Philadelphia G1
Fireman's Hall Museum H1
Forrest Theater G2
Franklin Court H2
The Franklin Institute F1
Free Library of Philadelphia F1
Historical Society of Pennsylvania F2
Independence Hall G2
Independence Natl. Hist. Park H1
Independence Seaport Museum H2
International African American Mus. G1
Jewelers' Row G2
Kimmel Cultural Campus F2
Liberty Bell Center G2
Merriam Theater F2
Moore College of Art & Design F1
Museum of the American Revolution H2
Natl. Constitution Center H1
Natl. Liberty Museum H2
Natl. Mus. of American Jewish History H2
One Liberty Place F2
Penn's Landing H2
Pennsylvania Academy of Fine Arts F1
Pennsylvania Convention Center G1
Physick House H2
Pierce College F2
Powel House H2
Print Center F2
Reading Terminal Market G1
Science History Institute H2
Second Bank of the United States H2
Thomas Jefferson University G2
U.S. Mint H1
University of the Arts F2
Walnut Street Theater G2

Pauls Valley OK 51 E4
Pauwela HI 153 D1
Pavo GA 137 F1
Pawcatuck CT 149 F2
Pawhuska OK 51 F1
Pawling NY 148 C1
Pawnee IL 98 B1
Pawnee OK 51 F2
Pawnee City NE 43 F1
Pawnee Co. KS 43 D3
Pawnee Co. NE 43 F1
Pawnee Co. OK 51 F2
Paw Paw IL 88 C2
Paw Paw MI 89 F1
Paw Paw WV 102 C1
Paw Paw Lake MI 89 F1
Pawtucket RI 150 C3
Paxtang PA 218 B1
Paxton FL 136 B1
Paxton IL 89 D4
Paxton MA 150 B1
Paxton NE 34 B3
Paxtonia PA 218 C1
Payette ID 22 A3
Payette Co. ID 22 B3
Payne OH 90 A3
Payne Co. OK 51 E2
Payne Sprs. TX 59 F3
Paynesville MN 66 B3
Payson AZ 47 E4
Payson IL 97 F1
Payson UT 39 E1
Peabody KS 43 F3
Peabody MA 151 D1
Peach Co. GA 129 D2
Peach Lake NY 148 C2
Peachland NC 122 B2
Peach Sprs. AZ 46 C3
Peachtree City GA 128 C1
Peahala Park NJ 147 E4
Peapack-Gladstone NJ 148 A4
Pearblossom CA 52 C2
Pea Ridge AR 106 C3
Pearisburg VA 112 A1
Pearl MS 126 B3
Pearland TX 132 A3
Pearl Beach MI 76 C4
Pearl City HI 152 A3
Pearl City IL 74 A4
Pearlington MS 134 C2
Pearl River LA 134 C2
Pearl River NY 148 B3
Pearl River Co. MS 134 C1
Pearsall TX 61 D3
Pearson GA 129 E4
Pecatonica IL 74 B4
Peck ID 14 B4
Peck MI 76 C3
Pecksville NY 148 C1
Peconic NY 149 E3
Pecos NM 49 D3
Pecos TX 57 F4
Pecos Co. TX 57 F4
Peculiar MO 96 B3

Entries in **bold black** indicate counties or parishes.
Entries in **bold color** indicate cities with detailed inset maps.

Peebles OH 100 C3
Peekskill NY 148 B2
Pe Ell WA 12 B4
Peeples Valley AZ 47 D4
Peever SD 27 F2
Pegram TN 109 E4
Pekin IL 88 B4
Pelahatchie MS 126 B2
Peletier NC 115 D4
Pelham AL 127 F1
Pelham GA 137 E1
Pelham NH 95 E1
Pelham NY 148 B3
Pelham Manor NY 148 B3
Pelican Rapids MN 19 F4
Pelion SC 122 A4
Pella IA 87 D2
Pell City AL 120 A4
Pellston MI 70 C3
Pemberton NJ 147 D3
Pemberville OH 90 C2
Pembina ND 19 E1
Pembina Co. ND 19 E1
Pembroke GA 130 B3
Pembroke KY 109 E2
Pembroke ME 83 E1
Pembroke MA 151 E2
Pembroke NC 122 C2
Pembroke VA 112 A1
Pembroke Park FL 233 B3
Pembroke Pines FL 143 E2
Pemiscot Co. MO 108 B4
Pena Blanca NM 48 C3
Pen Argyl PA 93 F3
Peñasco NM 49 D2
Penbrook PA 218 B1
Pender NE 35 F2
Pender Co. NC 115 C4
Pendleton IN 99 F1
Pendleton MO 97 F3
Pendleton OR 21 F1
Pendleton SC 121 E2
Pendleton Co. KY 100 B3
Pendleton Co. WV 102 B3
Pend Oreille Co. WA 14 B2
Penhook VA 112 B2
Peninsula OH 91 E2
Penitas TX 63 E4
Penndel PA 147 D2
Penney Farms FL 139 D3
Penn Hills PA 92 A4
Pennington NJ 147 D2
Pennington Co. MN 19 F2
Pennington Co. SD 26 A4
Pennington Gap VA 111 D2
Pennock MN 66 B3
Pennsauken NJ 146 C3
Pennsboro WV 101 F2
Pennsburg PA 146 B1
Pennsbury Vil. PA 250 A2
Penns Creek PA 93 D3
Penns Grove NJ 146 B4
Pennsville NJ 145 E1
Pennville IN 90 A4
Penn Wynne PA 248 B3
Penn Yan NY 78 C4
Penobscot Co. ME 83 D1
Penrose CO 41 E3
Pensacola FL 135 F2
Pensacola Beach FL 135 F2
Pentwater MI 75 E2
Peoria AZ 54 C1
Peoria IL 88 B3
Peoria Co. IL 88 B3
Peoria Hts. IL 88 B3
Peosta IA 73 F4
Peotone IL 89 D2
Pepeekeo HI 153 F3
Pepin WI 73 E1
Pepin Co. WI 67 E4
Pepperell MA 95 D1
Pepper Pike OH 204 G2
Pequannock NJ 148 A3
Pequot Lakes MN 64 A4
Peralta NM 48 C4
Percy IL 98 B4
Perham MN 19 F4
Peridot AZ 55 D2
Perkasie PA 146 C1
Perkins OK 51 F2
Perkins Corner CT 150 B3
Perkins Co. NE 34 B4
Perkins Co. SD 26 B2
Perkinston MS 135 D1
Perkiomenville PA 146 B2
Perquimans Co. NC 113 F4
Perris CA 53 D3
Perry FL 137 F2
Perry GA 129 D2
Perry IA 86 C1
Perry KS 96 A2
Perry LA 133 F3
Perry MI 76 B3
Perry MO 97 F2
Perry NY 78 B4
Perry OH 91 E1
Perry OK 51 E2
Perry UT 31 E3
Perry Co. AL 127 F2
Perry Co. AR 117 D2
Perry Co. IL 98 B4
Perry Co. IN 99 E4
Perry Co. KY 111 D2

Avondale	A2	Gilbert	D3	Litchfield Park	A2	Phoenix	B1	Sun City	A1	Youngtown	A1
Chandler	C3	Glendale	A2	Maricopa Vil.	A3	Queen Creek	D3	Sun City West	A1		
El Mirage	A1	Goodyear	A2	Mesa	D2	Rio Verde	D1	Surprise	A1		
Ft. McDowell	D1	Guadalupe	C3	Paradise Valley	C2	Santa Cruz	B3	Tempe	C3		
Fountain Hills	D1	Komatke	B3	Peoria	A1	Scottsdale	C1	Tolleson	A2		

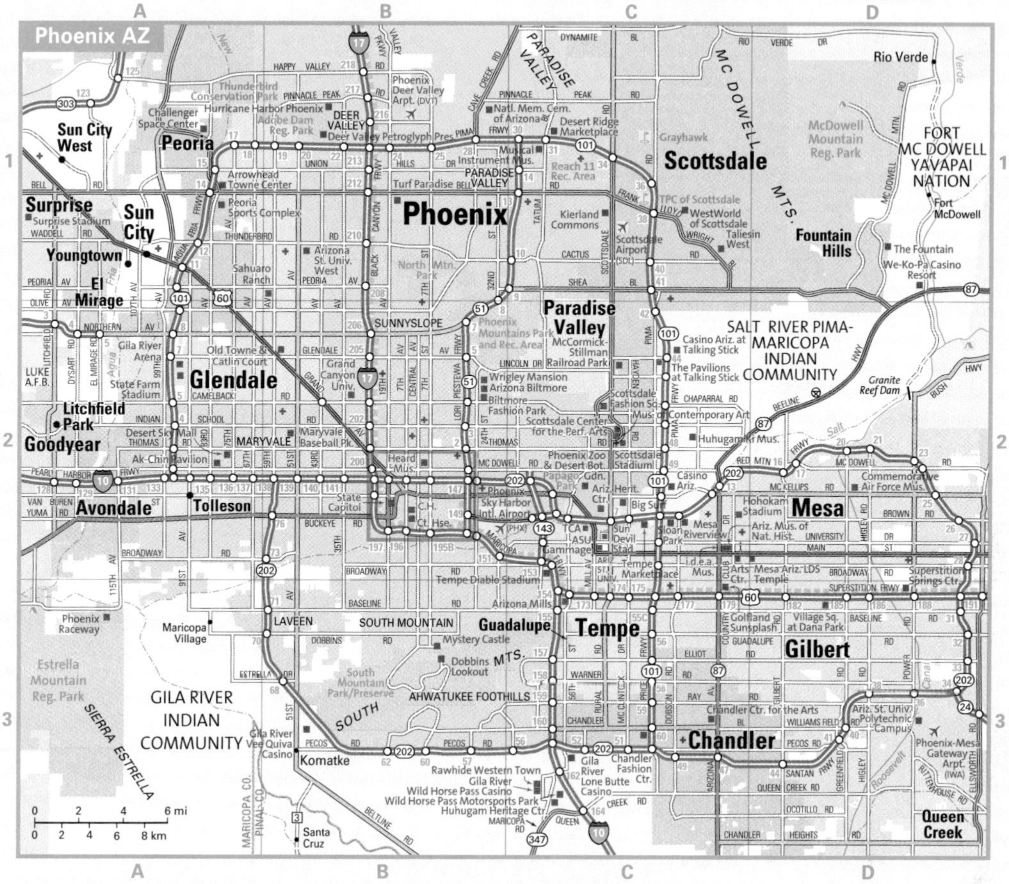

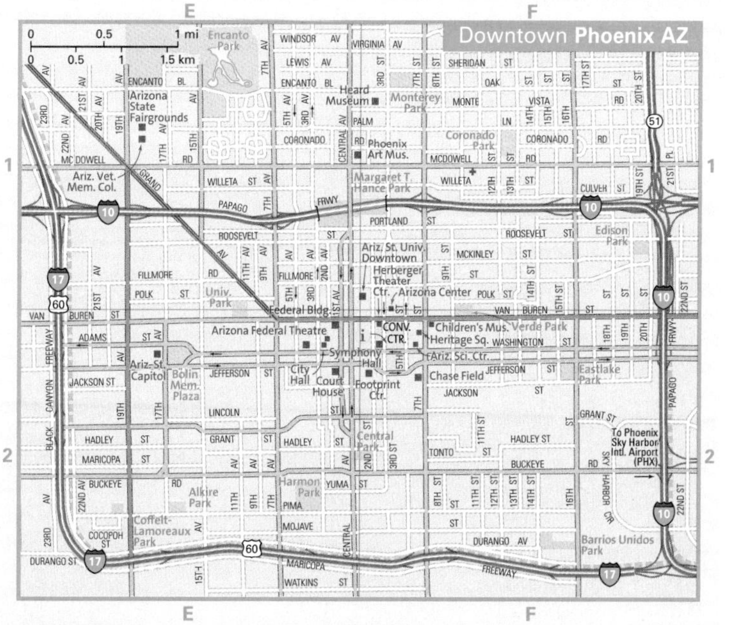

POINTS OF INTEREST

Arizona Center	F1	City Hall	E2
Arizona Federal Theatre	E2	Convention Center	F2
Arizona Science Center	F2	Footprint Center	F2
Arizona State Capitol	E2	Heard Museum	F1
Arizona State Fairgrounds	E1	Herberger Theater Center	F2
Arizona State University Downtown	F1	Heritage Square	F2
Arizona Veterans Memorial Coliseum	E1	Orpheum Theatre	E2
Chase Field	F2	Phoenix Art Museum	E1
Children's Museum	F2	Symphony Hall	F2

Perry Co. MS 135 D1
Perry Co. MO 108 B1
Perry Co. OH 101 E1
Perry Co. PA 93 D4
Perry Co. TN 119 E1
Perry Hall MD 144 C1
Perry Hts. OH 91 E3
Perryman MD 145 D1
Perryopolis PA 92 A4
Perrysburg OH 90 C2
Perrysville IN 89 D4
Perrysville OH 91 D3
Perryton TX 50 B2
Perryville AR 117 D2
Perryville KY 110 B1
Perryville MD 145 D1
Perryville MO 108 B1
Pershing Co. NV 29 F4
Person Co. NC 112 C3
Perth Amboy NJ 147 E1
Peru IL 88 B2
Peru IN 89 F3
Peru NE 86 A4
Peru NY 81 D2
Peshastin WA 13 D3
Peshtigo WI 69 D3

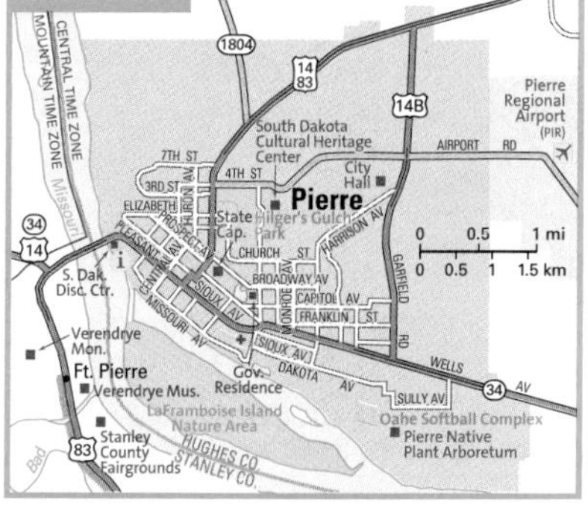

Petal MS 126 C4
Petaluma CA 36 B3
Peterborough NH 95 D1
Petersburg AK 155 E4
Petersburg IL 98 B1
Petersburg IN 99 E3
Petersburg KY 100 B2
Petersburg MI 90 C1
Petersburg NJ 148 A3
Petersburg PA 93 C4
Petersburg TN 119 F1
Petersburg TX 58 A1
Petersburg VA 113 E2
Petersburg WV 102 B2
Peterstown WV 112 A1
Petersville AL 119 E2
Petoskey MI 70 B3
Petroleum Co. MT 16 C3
Petrolia TX 59 D1
Petros TN 110 C4
Pettis Co. MO 97 D3
Pettit OK 106 B4
Pettus TX 61 E4
Pevely MO 98 A4
Pewamo MI 76 A3
Pewaukee (city) WI 234 A2
Pewaukee (village) WI 234 A2
Pewee Valley KY 100 A4
Pflugerville TX 61 E1
Pharr TX 63 E4
Phelan CA 53 D2
Phelps KY 111 E1
Phelps NY 78 C3
Phelps Co. MO 97 F4
Phelps Co. NE 35 D4
Phenix City AL 128 C2
Philadelphia MS 126 C2
Philadelphia NY 79 E1
Philadelphia PA 146 C3
Philadelphia TN 110 C4
Philadelphia Co. PA 146 C3
Phil Campbell AL 119 E3
Philip SD 26 B3
Philippi WV 102 A2
Philipsburg MT 15 D4
Philipsburg PA 92 C3
Phillips ME 82 B1
Phillips WI 68 A2
Phillipsburg KS 43 D1
Phillipsburg NJ 93 F3
Phillipsburg OH 100 B1
Phillips Co. AR 118 A3
Phillips Co. CO 34 A4
Phillips Co. KS 43 D1
Phillips Co. MT 16 C2
Philmont NY 94 B2
Philo IL 99 D1
Philo OH 101 E1
Philomath OR 20 B3
Philpot KY 109 E1
Phoenix AZ 54 C1
Phoenix IL 203 E6
Phoenix NY 79 D3
Phoenix OR 28 B2
Phoenixville PA 146 B2
Pia Oik AZ 54 B3
Piatt Co. IL 98 C1
Picacho AZ 54 C2
Picayune MS 134 C2
Picher OK 106 B2
Pickaway Co. OH 101 D1
Pickens MS 126 B1
Pickens SC 121 E2
Pickens Co. AL 119 D4
Pickens Co. GA 120 C3
Pickens Co. SC 121 E2
Pickensville AL 127 D1
Pickerington OH 101 D1
Pickett Co. TN 110 B3
Pico Rivera CA 228 E3
Picture Rocks PA 93 E2
Piedmont AL 120 A4
Piedmont CA 259 C2
Piedmont MO 108 A2
Piedmont OK 51 E2
Piedmont SC 121 E2
Piedmont SD 25 F3
Piedmont WV 102 B2
Pierce CO 33 E4

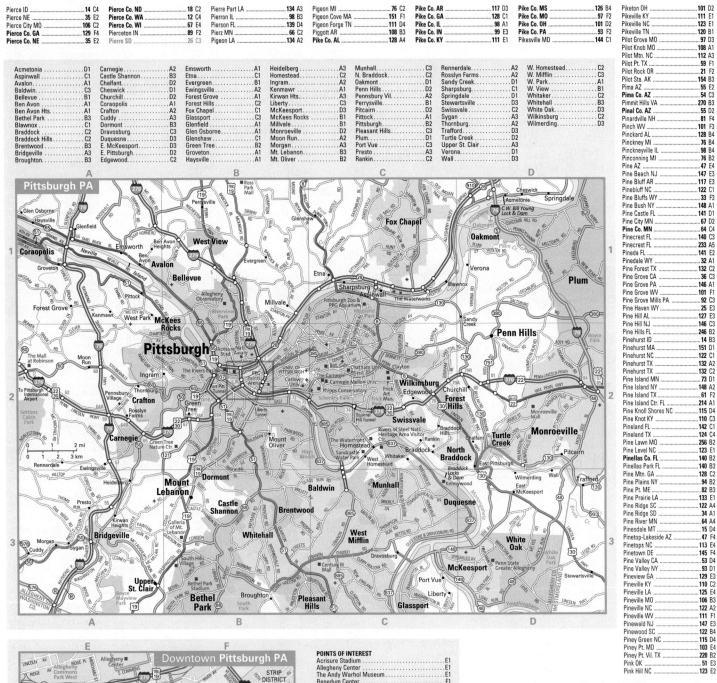

Figures after entries indicate page number and grid reference.

Pierce ID 14 C4
Pierce NE 35 E2
Pierce City MO 106 C2
Pierce Co. GA 129 F4
Pierce Co. NE 35 E2
Pierce Co. ND 18 C2
Pierce Co. WA 12 C4
Pierce Co. WI 67 E4
Pierceton IN 89 F2
Pierre SD 26 C3
Pierre Part LA 134 A3
Pierron IL 98 B3
Pierson FL 139 D4
Pierz MN 66 C2
Pigeon LA 134 A2
Pigeon MI 76 C2
Pigeon Cove MA 151 F1
Pigeon Forge TN 111 D4
Piggott AR 108 B3
Pike Co. AL 128 A4
Pike Co. AR 117 D3
Pike Co. GA 128 C1
Pike Co. IL 98 A1
Pike Co. IN 99 E3
Pike Co. KY 111 E1
Pike Co. MS 126 B4
Pike Co. MO 97 F2
Pike Co. OH 101 D2
Pike Co. PA 93 F2
Pikesville MD 144 C1
Piketon OH 101 D2
Pikeville KY 111 E1
Pikeville NC 123 E1
Pikeville TN 120 B1
Pilot Grove MO 97 D3
Pilot Knob MO 108 A1
Pilot Mtn. NC 112 A3
Pilot Pt. TX 59 F1
Pilot Rock OR 21 F2
Pilot Sta. AK 154 B3
Pima AZ 55 E2
Pima Co. AZ 54 C3
Pimmit Hills VA 270 B3
Pinal Co. AZ 55 D2
Pinardville NH 81 F4
Pinch WV 101 F3
Pinckard AL 128 B4
Pinckney MI 76 B4
Pinckneyville IL 98 B4
Pinconning MI 76 B2
Pine AZ 47 E4
Pine Beach NJ 147 E3
Pine Bluff AR 117 E3
Pinebluff NC 122 C1
Pine Bluffs WY 33 F3
Pine Bush NY 148 A1
Pine Castle FL 141 D1
Pine City MN 67 D2
Pine Co. MN 64 C4
Pinecrest FL 140 C3
Pinecrest FL 233 A5
Pineda FL 141 E2
Pinedale WY 32 A1
Pine Forest TX 132 C2
Pine Grove CA 36 C3
Pine Grove PA 146 A1
Pine Grove WV 101 F1
Pine Grove Mills PA 92 C3
Pine Haven WY 25 E3
Pine Hill AL 127 E3
Pine Hill NJ 146 C3
Pine Hills FL 246 B2
Pinehurst ID 14 B3
Pinehurst MA 151 D1
Pinehurst NC 122 C1
Pinehurst TX 132 A2
Pinehurst TX 132 C2
Pine Island MN 73 D1
Pine Island NY 148 A2
Pine Island TX 61 F2
Pine Island Ctr. FL 214 A1
Pine Knoll Shores NC 115 D4
Pine Knot KY 110 C3
Pineland FL 142 C1
Pineland TX 124 C4
Pine Lawn MO 256 B2
Pine Level NC 123 E1
Pinellas Co. FL 140 B2
Pinellas Park FL 140 B3
Pine Mtn. GA 128 C2
Pine Plains NY 94 B2
Pine Pt. ME 82 B3
Pine Prairie LA 133 E1
Pine Ridge SC 122 A4
Pine Ridge SD 34 A1
Pine River MN 64 A4
Pinesdale MT 15 D4
Pinetop-Lakeside AZ 47 F4
Pinetops NC 113 E4
Pinetown DE 145 F4
Pine Valley CA 53 D4
Pine Valley NY 93 D1
Pineview GA 129 E3
Pineville KY 110 C2
Pineville LA 125 E4
Pineville MO 106 B3
Pineville NC 122 A2
Pineville WV 111 F1
Pinewald NJ 147 E3
Pinewood SC 122 B4
Piney Green NC 115 D4
Piney Pt. MD 103 E4
Piney Pt. Vil. TX 220 B2
Pink OK 51 E3
Pink Hill NC 123 E2

Acmetonia D1
Aspinwall C1
Avalon A1
Baldwin C3
Bellevue B1
Ben Avon A1
Ben Avon Hts. A1
Bethel Park B3
Blawnox C1
Braddock C2
Braddock Hills C2
Brentwood B3
Bridgeville A3
Broughton B3
Carnegie A2
Castle Shannon B3
Chalfant D2
Cheswick D1
Churchill D2
Coraopolis A1
Crafton A2
Cuddy A3
Dormont B3
Dravosburg C3
Duquesne D3
E. McKeesport D3
E. Pittsburgh D2
Edgewood C2
Emsworth A1
Etna C1
Evergreen B1
Ewingsville A2
Forest Grove A1
Forest Hills C2
Fox Chapel C1
Glassport C3
Glenfield A1
Glen Osborne A1
Glenshaw C1
Green Tree B2
Groveton A1
Haysville A1
Heidelberg A3
Homestead C2
Ingram A2
Kenmawr A1
Kirwan Hts. A3
Liberty C3
McKeesport D3
McKees Rocks B1
Millvale B1
Monroeville D2
Moon Run A2
Morgan A3
Mt. Lebanon B3
Mt. Oliver B2
Munhall C3
N. Braddock C2
Oakmont D1
Penn Hills D2
Pennsbury Vil. A2
Perrysville B1
Pitcairn D2
Pittock A1
Pittsburgh B2
Pleasant Hills C3
Plum D1
Port Vue C3
Presto A3
Rankin C2
Rennerdale A2
Rosslyn Farms A2
Sandy Creek D1
Sharpsburg C1
Springdale D1
Stewartsville D3
Swissvale C2
Sygan A3
Thornburg A2
Trafford D3
Turtle Creek D2
Upper St. Clair A3
Verona D1
Wall D3
W. Homestead C2
W. Mifflin C3
W. Park A1
W. View B1
Whitaker C2
Whitehall B3
White Oak D3
Wilkinsburg C2
Wilmerding D3

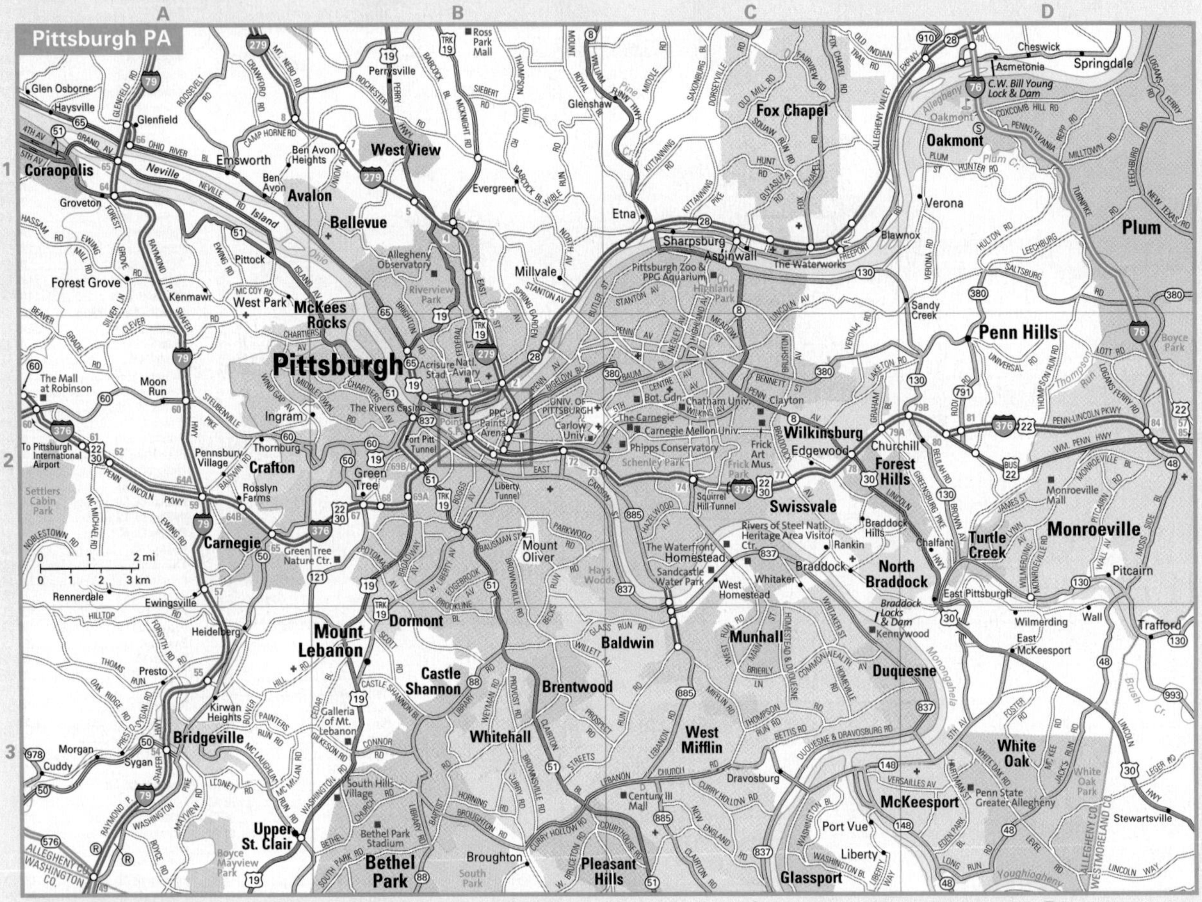

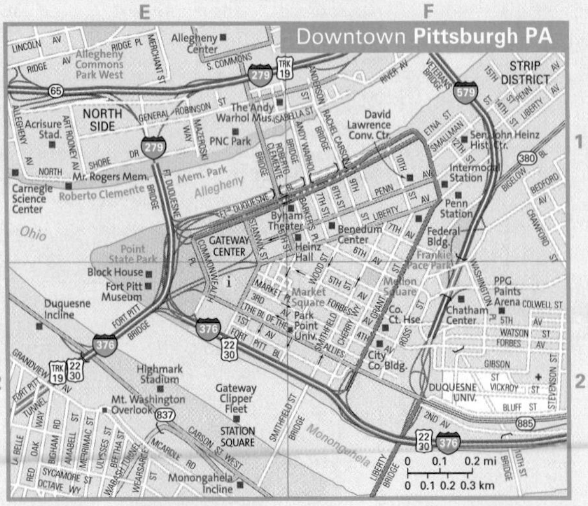

POINTS OF INTEREST

Acrisure Stadium E1
Allegheny Center E1
The Andy Warhol Museum E1
Benedum Center F1
Block House E2
Byham Theater F1
Carnegie Science Center E1
Chatham Center F2
City County Building F2
County Court House F2
David Lawrence Convention Center F1
Duquesne Incline E2
Duquesne University F2
Federal Building F1
Fort Pitt Museum E2
Gateway Center E1
Gateway Clipper Fleet E2
Heinz Hall F1
Highmark Stadium E2
Intermodal Station F1
Monongahela Incline E2
Mr. Rogers Memorial E1
Mt. Washington Overlook E2
Penn Station F1
PNC Park E1
Point Park University F2
Point State Park E1
PPG Paints Arena F2
Senator John Heinz Hist. Center F1
Station Square E2

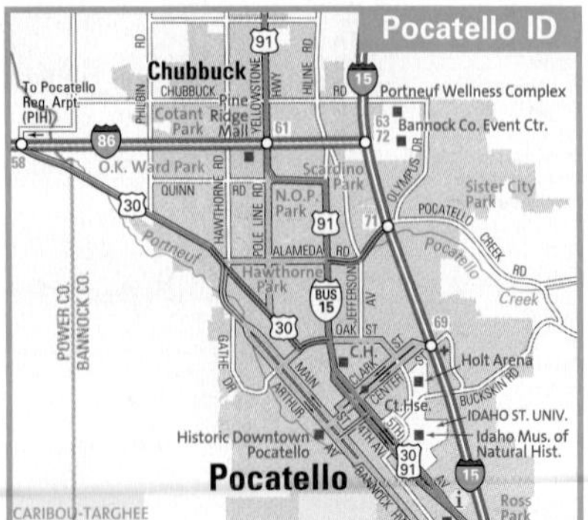

Entries in **bold black** indicate counties or parishes.
Entries in **bold color** indicate cities with detailed inset maps.

Pinnacle NC 112 A3
Pinole CA 259 C1
Pinon AZ 47 F2
Pinson AL 119 F4
Pioche NV 38 C3
Pioneer OH 90 B2
Pioneer Vil. KY 100 A4
Piper City IL 88 C3
Piperton TN 118 B2
Pipestone MN 27 F3
Pipestone Co. MN 27 F3
Piqua OH 90 B4
Pirtleville AZ 55 E4
Piru CA 52 B2
Piscataquis Co. ME 84 C3
Pisgah AL 120 A2
Pisgah Forest NC 121 E1
Pisinemo AZ 54 C3
Pismo Beach CA 52 A1
Pitcairn PA 250 D2
Pitkin Co. CO 40 C2
Pitman NJ 146 C4
Pitt Co. NC 113 E4
Pittman Ctr. TN 111 D4
Pittsboro IN 99 F1
Pittsboro MS 118 C4
Pittsboro NC 112 C4
Pittsburg CA 36 B3
Pittsburg IL 108 C1
Pittsburg KS 106 B1
Pittsburg TX 124 B1
Pittsburg Co. OK 116 A2
Pittsburgh PA 92 A4
Pittsfield IL 98 A1
Pittsfield ME 82 C1
Pittsfield MA 94 C1
Pittsfield NH 81 F4
Pittsford NY 78 C3
Pittsford VT 81 D3
Pittston ME 82 C2
Pittston PA 93 F2
Pittstown NJ 94 B1
Pittsville MD 114 C1
Pittsville WI 74 A1
Pittsylvania Co. VA 112 C2
Piute Co. UT 39 E3
Pixley CA 45 D4
Placentia CA 229 F4
Placer Co. CA 36 C2
Placerville CA 36 C2
Placid Lakes FL 141 D4
Placitas NM 48 C3
Plain WI 74 A3
Plain City OH 90 C4
Plain City UT 31 E3
Plain Dealing LA 124 C1
Plainfield CT 149 F1
Plainfield IL 88 C2
Plainfield IN 99 F1
Plainfield NH 81 E3
Plainfield NJ 147 E1
Plainfield VT 81 E2
Plainfield WI 74 B1
Plains GA 128 C3
Plains KS 42 C4
Plains MT 14 C3
Plains PA 261 B2
Plains TX 57 F2
Plainsboro NJ 147 D2
Plainview AR 117 D2
Plainview MN 73 E1
Plainview NE 35 E2
Plainview NY 148 C4
Plainview TN 110 C4
Plainview TX 50 A4
Plainville CT 149 D1
Plainville IN 99 E3
Plainville KS 43 D2
Plainville MA 150 C2
Plainwell MI 75 F4
Plaistow NH 95 E1
Planada CA 37 D4
Plandome NY 148 C4
Plandome Hts. NY 241 G2
Plandome Manor NY 241 G2
Plankinton SD 27 E4
Plano IL 88 C2
Plano TX 59 F2
Plantation FL 143 E2
Plantation KY 230 F1
Plant City FL 140 C2
Plantersville MS 119 D3
Plantsville CT 149 D1
Plaquemine LA 134 A2
Plaquemines Par. LA 134 C4
Platte SD 27 D4
Platte City MO 96 B2
Platte Co. MO 96 B2
Platte Co. NE 35 E3
Platte Co. WY 33 E2
Plattekill NY 148 B1
Platteville CO 33 E4
Platteville WI 74 A4
Plattsburg MO 96 B1
Plattsburgh NY 81 D1
Plattsmouth NE 86 A3
Pleak TX 132 A4
Pleasantdale NY 94 B1
Pleasant Gap PA 92 C3
Pleasant Garden NC 112 B4
Pleasant Grove AL 119 F4
Pleasant Grove OH 101 E1
Pleasant Grove UT 31 F4
Pleasant Groves AL 120 A2
Pleasant Hill CA 259 D2
Pleasant Hill IL 97 F2
Pleasant Hill IA 86 C2
Pleasant Hill LA 125 D3
Pleasant Hill MO 96 C3
Pleasant Hill OH 90 B4
Pleasant Hill TN 110 B4
Pleasant Hills MD 144 C1
Pleasant Hills PA 250 C3
Pleasant Hope MO 107 D1
Pleasant Lake IN 90 A2
Pleasant Lake MA 151 F3
Pleasant Lake MI 76 A4
Pleasant Mills NJ 147 D4
Pleasanton CA 36 B4
Pleasanton KS 96 B4
Pleasanton TX 61 D3
Pleasant Plains IL 98 B1
Pleasant Plains NJ 147 E3
Pleasant Pt. ME 83 F1
Pleasant Prairie WI 74 C4
Pleasant Ridge MI 210 C2
Pleasant Run OH 204 A1
Pleasants Co. WV 101 F2
Pleasant Valley MO 96 B2
Pleasant Valley NY 94 B3
Pleasant Valley PA 146 C1
Pleasant Valley WV 102 A2
Pleasant View IN 99 F1
Pleasant View TN 109 E3
Pleasant View UT 31 E3
Pleasantville IA 87 D2
Pleasantville NJ 147 F4
Pleasantville NY 148 B2
Pleasantville OH 101 D1
Pleasantville PA 92 A2
Pleasure Beach CT 149 F2
Pleasureville KY 100 A4
Pleasureville PA 275 F1
Plentywood MT 17 F1
Plover WI 74 B1
Pluckemin NJ 147 D1
Plum PA 92 A4
Plumas Co. CA 36 C1
Plum City WI 67 E4
Plumerville AR 117 E1
Plum Grove TX 132 B2
Plummer ID 14 B3
Plum Pt. RI 150 C4
Plum Sprs. KY 109 F2
Plymouth CA 36 C3
Plymouth DE 145 E3
Plymouth IN 89 F2
Plymouth MA 151 E2
Plymouth MI 76 B4
Plymouth MN 67 D4
Plymouth NE 35 F4
Plymouth NH 81 F3
Plymouth NC 113 F4
Plymouth OH 91 D3
Plymouth PA 261 A1
Plymouth UT 31 E2
Plymouth WI 74 C2
Plymouth Co. IA 35 F1
Plymouth Co. MA 151 E3
Plymouth Meeting PA 248 B1
Plympton MA 151 E2
Poca WV 101 E3
Pocahontas AR 108 A3
Pocahontas IL 98 B3
Pocahontas IA 72 B4
Pocahontas VA 111 F1
Pocahontas Co. IA 72 B4
Pocahontas Co. WV 102 A4
Pocasset MA 151 E3
Pocatello ID 31 E1
Pocola OK 116 B1
Pocomoke City MD 114 C2
Pocono Pines PA 93 F3
Poestenkill NY 94 B1
Poinciana FL 141 D2
Poinsett Co. AR 118 A1
Point TX 124 A1
Pt. Arena CA 36 A2
Pt. Blank TX 132 B1
Pt. Clear AL 135 E2
Pt. Comfort TX 61 F4
Pointe a la Hache LA 134 C3
Pointe Coupee Par. LA 133 F2
Pt. Hope AK 154 B1
Pt. Judith RI 150 C4
Pt. Marion PA 102 B1
Pt. of Rocks MD 144 A2
Pt. Pleasant NJ 147 E2
Pt. Pleasant WV 101 E3
Pt. Pleasant Beach NJ 147 E2
Pt. Reyes Sta. CA 36 B3
Poipu HI 152 B1
Pojoaque NM 49 D2
Polacca AZ 47 F2
Poland OH 276 C3
Polk PA 92 A2
Polk City FL 140 C2

Cape Cottage B2
Cape Elizabeth B2
Cumberland Foreside B1
Eight Corners A2
Falmouth B1
Falmouth Foreside B1
Portland B2
S. Portland A2
Westbrook A1
W. Falmouth A1

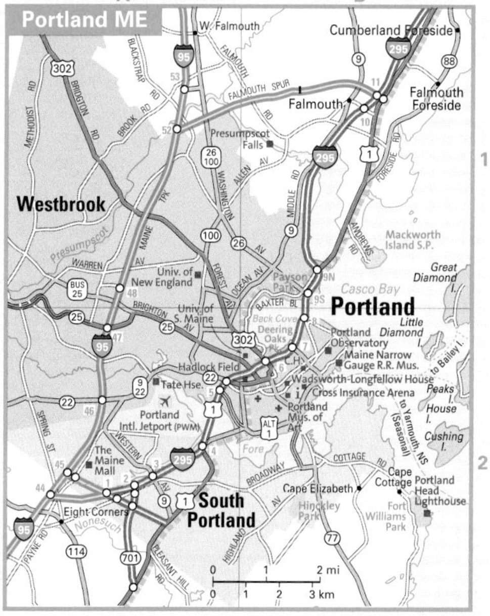

Beaverton C2
Carver D3
Cedar Hills C2
Clackamas D3
Durham C3
Garden Home C2
Gladstone D3
Gresham D2
Happy Valley D3
Johnson City D3
King City C3
Lake Oswego C3
Maywood Park D2
Metzger C2
Milwaukie D2
Oak Grove D3
Oregon City D3
Portland D2
Raleigh Hills C2
Rivergrove C3
Tigard C3
Tualatin C3
Vancouver D1
W. Linn D3
W. Slope C2

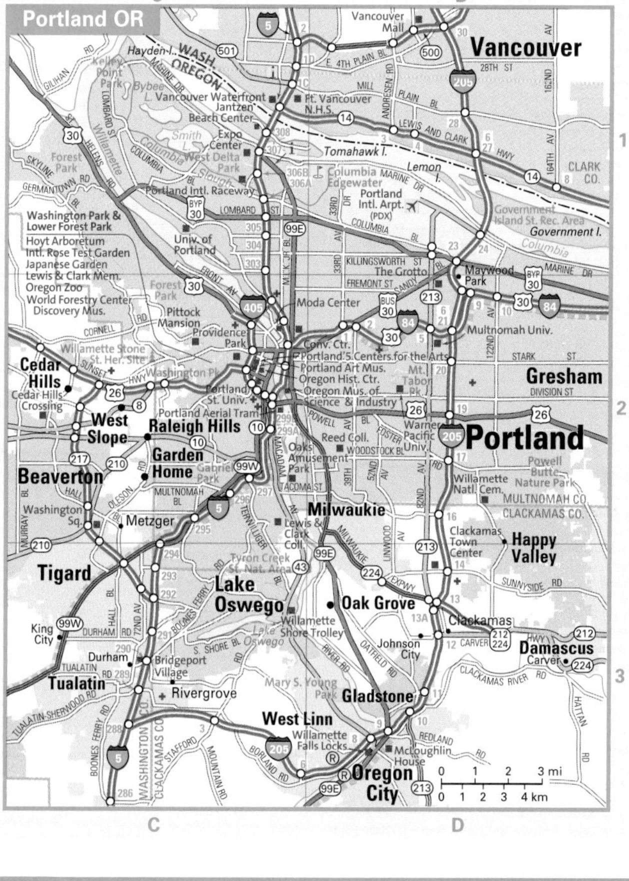

Abbott Run F1
Albion E1
Arctic E3
Ashton E1
Attleboro F1
Barrington F3
Berkeley E1
Central Falls F1
Centredale E2
Cranston E3
E. Providence F2
Esmond E1
Georgiaville E1
Hughesdale E2
Johnston E2
Lime Rock E1
Lonsdale F1
N. Providence E2
Pawtucket F2
Phenix E3
Providence E2
Quidnick E3
Quinnville E1
Riverside F3
Rumford F2
Saylesville F1
Seekonk F2
Stillwater E1
Thornton E2
Valley Falls F1
Warwick F3
W. Barrington F3
W. Warwick E3

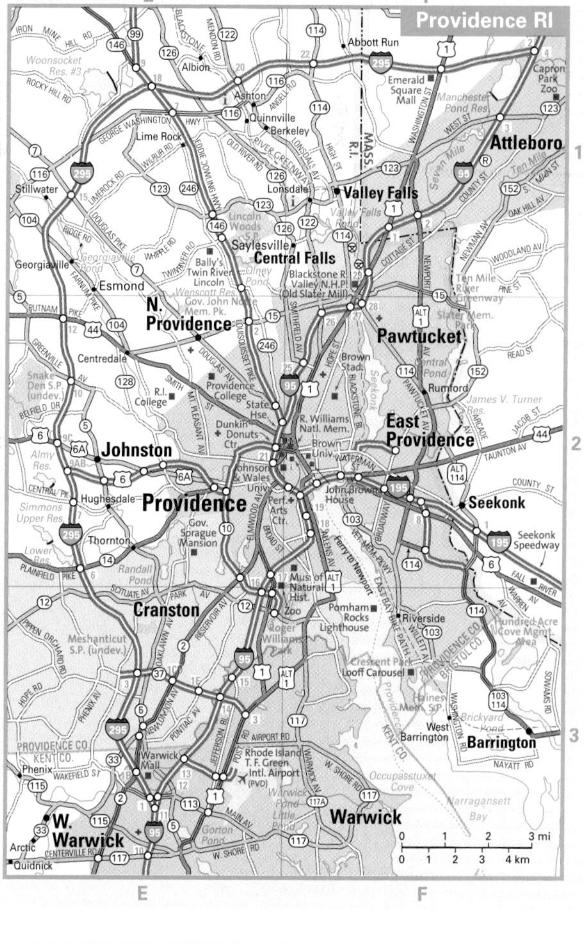

Figures after entries indicate page number and grid reference.

Polk City IA 86 C1
Polk Co. AR 116 C3
Polk Co. FL 140 C3
Polk Co. GA 120 B4
Polk Co. IA 86 C1
Polk Co. MN 19 F2
Polk Co. MO 107 D1
Polk Co. NE 35 E3
Polk Co. NC 121 F1
Polk Co. OR 20 B2
Polk Co. TN 120 C1
Polk Co. TX 132 B1
Polk Co. WI 67 E3
Polkton NC 122 B2
Polkville NC 121 F1
Pollock SD 26 C1
Pollock Pines CA 36 C2
Polo IL 88 B1
Polo MO 96 C1
Polson MT 15 D3
Pomeroy IA 72 B4
Pomeroy OH 101 E2
Pomeroy WA 13 F4
Pomona CA 52 C2
Pomona KS 96 A3
Pomona NJ 105 D3
Pomona NY 148 B2
Pomona Park FL 139 D4
Pomonkey MD 144 B4
Pompano Beach FL 143 F1
Pompton Lakes NJ 148 A3
Pompton Plains NJ 148 A3
Ponca NE 35 F1
Ponca City OK 51 E1
Ponce de Leon FL 136 C1
Ponce Inlet FL 139 E4
Poncha Sprs. CO 41 D3
Ponchatoula LA 134 B2
Pond Creek OK 51 E1
Pondera Co. MT 15 E2
Ponderay ID 14 B2
Ponderosa NM 48 C2
Ponemah MN 64 A2
Ponte Vedra Beach FL 139 D2
Pontiac IL 88 C3
Pontiac MI 76 C4
Pontoon Beach IL 256 D1
Pontotoc MS 118 C3
Pontotoc Co. MS 118 C3
Pontotoc Co. OK 51 F4
Pooler GA 130 B3
Poolesville MD 144 A2
Pope Co. AR 117 D1
Pope Co. IL 109 D1
Pope Co. MN 66 A3
Poplar CA 45 D3
Poplar MT 17 E2
Poplar WI 64 C4
Poplar Bluff MO 108 A2
Poplar Grove IL 74 B4
Poplar Hills KY 230 E3
Poplarville MS 134 C1
Poquetanuck CT 149 F1
Poquonock CT 150 A3
Poquonock Bridge CT 149 F2
Poquoson VA 113 F2
Poquott NY 149 D3
Porcupine SD 26 B4
Portage IN 89 E2
Portage MI 89 F1
Portage PA 92 B4
Portage WI 74 B2
Portage Co. OH 91 E3
Portage Co. WI 74 B1
Portage Lakes OH 188 A2
Portageville MO 108 B3
Portal GA 129 F2
Portales NM 49 F4
Port Allegany PA 92 C1
Port Allen LA 134 A2
Port Angeles WA 12 B2
Port Aransas TX 63 F2
Port Arthur TX 132 C3
Port Austin MI 76 C1
Port Barre LA 133 F2
Port Barrington IL 203 A1
Port Byron IL 88 A2
Port Byron NY 79 D3
Port Carbon PA 93 E3
Port Charlotte FL 140 C4
Port Chester NY 148 C3
Port Clinton OH 90 C2
Port Deposit MD 145 D1
Port Edwards WI 74 A1
Porter IN 89 E2
Porter OK 106 A4
Porter WA 12 B4
Porter Corners NY 80 C4
Porter Co. IN 89 E2
Porterdale GA 121 D4
Porter Hts. TX 132 A2
Porterville CA 45 D3
Port Ewen NY 94 B2
Port Gibson MS 126 A3
Port Hadlock WA 12 C2
Port Henry NY 81 D3
Port Hueneme CA 52 B2
Port Huron MI 77 D3
Portia AR 107 F4
Port Isabel TX 63 F4
Port Jefferson NY 149 D3
Port Jefferson Sta. NY 149 D3
Port Jervis NY 148 A2
Port La Belle FL 141 D4
Portland AR 125 F1
Portland CT 149 E1
Portland IN 90 A4
Portland ME 82 B3
Portland MI 76 A3
Portland ND 19 E3
Portland OR 20 C2
Portland PA 93 F3
Portland TN 109 F3
Portland TX 63 F2
Port Lavaca TX 61 F4
Port Leyden NY 79 E2
Port Ludlow WA 12 C2
Port Matilda PA 92 C3
Port Monmouth NJ 147 E1
Port Neches TX 132 C3
Port Norris NJ 145 F2
Portola CA 37 D1
Portola Valley CA 259 C6
Port Orange FL 139 E4
Port Orchard WA 12 C3
Port Orford OR 28 A1
Port Reading NJ 240 A5
Port Republic NJ 147 E4
Port Richey FL 140 B2
Port Royal PA 93 D4
Port Royal SC 130 C2
Port St. Joe FL 137 D3
Port St. John FL 141 E1
Port St. Lucie FL 141 E4
Port Salerno FL 141 E4
Port Sanilac MI 76 C2
Portsmouth NH 82 A4
Portsmouth OH 101 D3
Portsmouth RI 151 D4
Portsmouth VA 113 F2
Port Sulphur LA 134 C4
Port Townsend WA 12 C2
Portville NY 92 C1
Port Vincent LA 134 A2
Port Vue PA 250 C3
Port Washington NY 148 C3
Port Washington WI 75 D2
Port Washington North NY 241 G2
Port Wentworth GA 130 B3
Porum OK 116 A1
Posen IL 203 D6
Posey Co. IN 99 D4
Poseyville IN 99 D4
Post TX 58 B2
Post Falls ID 14 B3
Poston AZ 53 F2
Postville IA 73 E3
Poteau OK 116 B2
Poteet TX 61 D3
Poth TX 61 D3
Potlatch ID 14 B4
Potomac IL 89 D4
Potomac MD 144 B3
Potomac Hts. MD 144 B4
Potosi MO 98 A4
Potosi TX 58 C3
Potosi WI 73 F4
Potsdam NY 80 B1
Pottawatomie Co. KS 43 F2
Pottawatomie Co. OK 51 F3
Pottawattamie Co. IA 86 A2
Potter Co. PA 92 C2
Potter Co. SD 27 D2
Potter Co. TX 50 A3
Pottersville NY 80 C3
Potter Valley CA 36 A2
Potterville MI 76 A4
Pottsboro TX 59 F1
Potts Camp MS 118 C2
Pottstown PA 146 B2
Pottsville AR 117 D1
Pottsville PA 93 E3
Potwin KS 43 F3
Poughkeepsie NY 148 B1
Poughquag NY 148 C1
Poulan GA 129 D4
Poulsbo WA 12 C3
Poultney VT 81 D4
Pound VA 111 E2
Pound Ridge NY 148 C2
Poway CA 53 D4
Powderly KY 109 E2
Powder River Co. MT 25 E2
Powder Sprs. GA 120 C4
Powell AL 120 A2
Powell OH 90 C4
Powell TN 110 C4
Powell WY 24 B3
Powell Co. KY 100 C4
Powell Co. MT 15 D3
Powells Crossroads TN 120 B1
Powellton WV 101 F4
Power Co. ID 31 E1
Powers OR 28 A1
Powers Lake ND 18 A2
Powers Lake WI 74 C4
Poweshiek Co. IA 87 D1
Powhatan VA 113 D1
Powhatan Co. VA 113 E1
Powhatan Pt. OH 101 F1
Pownal VT 94 C1
Poydras LA 134 C3
Poynette WI 74 B2
Prague OK 51 F3
Prairie City IA 87 D2
Prairie City OR 21 F3
Prairie Co. AR 117 F2
Prairie Co. MT 17 E4
Prairie Creek AR 106 C3
Prairie du Chien WI 73 F3
Prairie du Rocher IL 98 A4
Prairie du Sac WI 74 A3
Prairie Grove AR 106 C4
Prairie Grove IL 203 A1
Prairie View TX 61 F2
Prairie Vil. KS 224 B4
Prairieville LA 134 A2
Pratt KS 43 D4
Pratt WV 101 F4
Pratt Co. KS 43 D4
Prattsburgh NY 78 C4
Prattville AL 128 A2
Preble Co. OH 100 B1
Premont TX 63 E2
Prentice WI 68 A3
Prentiss MS 126 B4
Prentiss Co. MS 119 D2
Prescott AZ 47 D4
Prescott AR 117 D4
Prescott WI 67 D4
Prescott Valley AZ 47 D4
Presho SD 26 C4
Presidential Lakes Estates NJ 147 D3
Presidio TX 62 B4
Presidio Co. TX 62 B3
Presque Isle ME 85 D2
Presque Isle Co. MI 70 C3
Preston GA 128 C3
Preston ID 31 E2
Preston IA 88 A1
Preston MD 145 E4
Preston MN 73 E2
Preston Co. WV 102 B2
Prestonsburg KY 111 E1
Pretty Prairie KS 43 E4
Price UT 39 F1
Price Co. WI 68 A2
Priceville AL 119 F3
Prichard AL 135 E1
Priest River ID 14 B2
Primghar IA 72 A3
Prince Edward Co. VA 113 D2
Prince Frederick MD 144 C4
Prince George VA 113 E2
Prince George Co. VA 113 E2
Prince George's Co. MD 144 C3
Princes Lakes IN 99 F2
Princess Anne MD 103 F4
Princeton FL 143 E3
Princeton IL 88 B2
Princeton IN 99 D4
Princeton IA 88 A2
Princeton KY 109 D2
Princeton MN 66 C3
Princeton MO 86 C4
Princeton NJ 147 D2
Princeton NC 123 E1
Princeton TX 59 F2
Princeton WV 111 F1
Princeton WI 74 B2
Princeton Jct. NJ 147 D2
Princeville HI 152 B1
Princeville IL 88 B3
Princeville NC 113 E4
Prince William Co. VA 144 A4
Prineville OR 21 D3
Pringle PA 261 B1
Prior Lake MN 67 D4
Proctor MN 64 C4
Proctor VT 81 D3
Proctorville OH 101 E3
Progreso TX 63 E4
Progress PA 218 B1
Progress Vil. FL 266 C2
Prophetstown IL 88 A2
Prospect CT 149 D1
Prospect KY 100 A4
Prospect OH 90 C4
Prospect PA 92 A3
Prospect Hts. IL 203 C2
Prospect Park PA 248 B4
Prosper TX 59 F2
Prosperity SC 122 A3
Prosser WA 21 E1
Protection KS 43 D4
Provencal LA 125 D4
Providence FL 140 C2
Providence KY 109 D1
Providence RI 150 C3
Providence UT 31 E3
Providence Co. RI 150 C3
Provincetown MA 151 F2
Provo UT 31 F4
Prowers Co. CO 42 A3
Prudenville MI 76 A1
Prue OK 51 F2
Prunedale CA 44 B2
Pruntytown WV 102 A2
Pryor MT 24 C2
Pryor OK 106 A3
Pueblo CO 41 E3
Pueblo Co. CO 41 E3
Pueblo Pintado NM 48 B2
Pueblo West CO 41 E3
Puhi HI 152 B1
Pukalani HI 153 D1
Pukwana SD 27 D4
Pulaski NY 79 D2
Pulaski TN 119 F1
Pulaski VA 112 A2
Pulaski WI 68 C4
Pulaski Co. AR 117 E2
Pulaski Co. GA 129 E3
Pulaski Co. IL 108 C2
Pulaski Co. IN 89 E3
Pulaski Co. KY 110 B2
Pulaski Co. MO 97 E4
Pulaski Co. VA 112 A2
Pullman MI 75 E4
Pullman WA 14 B4
Pumphrey MD 193 C4
Pumpkin Ctr. CA 45 D4
Pumpkin Ctr. NC 115 D4
Punaluu HI 152 A2
Punta Gorda FL 140 C4
Punta Rassa FL 142 C1
Punxsutawney PA 92 B3
Pupukea HI 152 A2
Purcell OK 51 E3
Purcellville VA 144 A2
Purdy MO 106 C2
Purdys NY 148 C2
Purvis MS 134 C1
Puryear TN 109 D3
Pushmataha Co. OK 116 A3
Putnam CT 150 B3
Putnam Co. FL 139 D3
Putnam Co. GA 129 E1
Putnam Co. IL 88 B2
Putnam Co. IN 99 E1
Putnam Co. MO 87 D4
Putnam Co. NY 148 B2
Putnam Co. OH 90 B3
Putnam Co. TN 110 A3
Putnam Co. WV 101 E3
Putnam Lake NY 148 C1
Putney GA 129 D4
Putney KY 111 D2
Putney VT 81 E4
Puxico MO 108 B2
Puyallup WA 12 C3
Pyatt AR 107 D3

Q
Quaker City OH 101 F1
Quaker Hill CT 149 F2
Quakertown PA 146 C1
Quanah TX 50 C4
Quantico VA 144 A4
Quapaw OK 106 B2
Quarryville CT 150 A3
Quarryville PA 146 A3
Quartz Hill CA 52 C2
Quartzsite AZ 54 A1
Quasqueton IA 73 E4
Quay Co. NM 49 F3
Quechee VT 81 E3
Queen Anne's Co. MD 145 D3
Queen City MO 87 D4
Queen City TX 124 C1
Queen Creek AZ 54 C2
Queens Co. NY 148 B4
Queenstown MD 145 D3
Quenemo KS 96 A3
Questa NM 49 D1
Quidnessett RI 150 C4
Quidnick RI 150 C3
Quilcene WA 12 C3
Quimby IA 72 A4
Quinby SC 122 C3
Quince Orchard MD 144 B2
Quincy CA 36 C1
Quincy FL 137 D2
Quincy IL 97 F1
Quincy MA 151 D1
Quincy MI 90 A1
Quincy OH 90 B4
Quincy PA 103 D1
Quincy WA 13 E3
Quinebaug CT 150 B2
Quinhagak AK 154 B3
Quinlan TX 59 F2
Quinnesec MI 68 C2
Quinter KS 42 C2
Quinton OK 116 A1
Quinwood WV 102 A4
Quitman AR 117 E1
Quitman GA 137 F1
Quitman MS 127 D3
Quitman TX 124 A2
Quitman Co. GA 128 C3

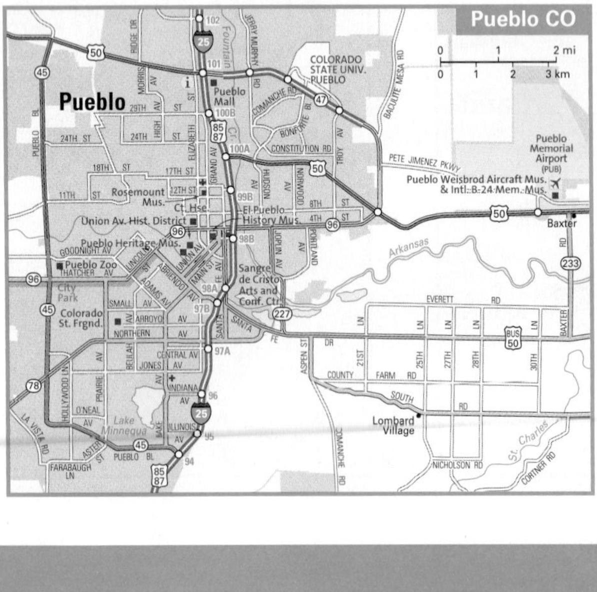

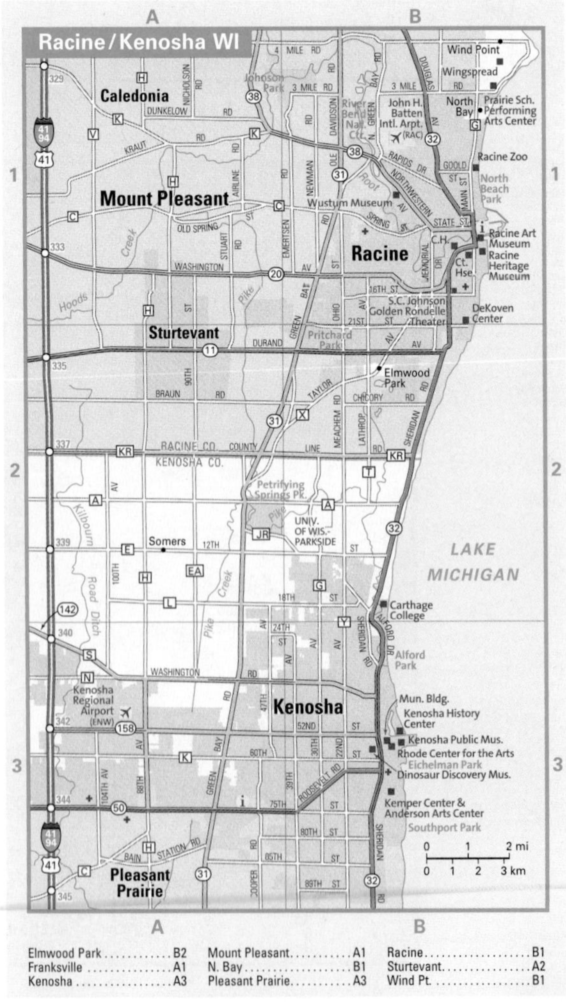

Elmwood Park B2
Franksville A1
Kenosha A3
Mount Pleasant A1
N. Bay B1
Pleasant Prairie A3
Racine B1
Sturtevant A2
Wind Pt. B1

Entries in **bold black** indicate counties or parishes.
Entries in bold color indicate cities with detailed inset maps.

Quitman Co. MS 118 B3
Quogue NY 149 E3

R

Rabun Co. GA 121 D2
Raceland KY 101 D3
Raceland LA 134 B3
Racine MN 73 D2
Racine OH 101 E2
Racine WV 101 E4
Racine WI 75 D4
Racine Co. WI 74 C4
Radcliff KY 99 F4
Radcliffe IA 72 C4
Radford VA 112 A2
Radium Sprs. NM 56 B3
Rancho Cordova CA 36 C3
Rancho Cucamonga CA 229 G2
Rancho Mirage CA 53 E3
Rancho Palos Verdes CA 228 C4
Rancho Santa Fe CA 53 D4
Rancho Santa Margarita CA 229 G5
Ranchos de Taos NM 49 D2
Rancocas NJ 147 D3
Rand WV 101 F4
Randall MN 66 B2
Randall Co. TX 50 A3
Randallstown MD 144 C1
Randle Cliff Beach MD 144 C4
Randleman NC 112 B4
Randlett OK 51 D4
Randolph ME 82 C2
Rapides Par. LA 125 E4
Rapids NY 78 B3
Rapids City IL 208 C1
Rappahannock Co. VA 103 D3
Raritan NJ 147 D1
Rathdrum ID 14 B3
Ratliff FL 139 D2
Raton NM 49 E1
Raubsville PA 146 C1
Ravalli Co. MT 23 D1
Raven VA 111 F2
Ravena NY 94 B1
Ravenden AR 107 F3
Ravenel SC 131 D2
Ravenna KY 110 C1
Ravenna MI 75 F3
Ravenna NE 35 D3
Ravenna OH 91 E3
Ravensdale WA 12 C3
Ravenswood WV 101 E3
Ravia OK 51 F4
Ravine PA 93 E4
Rawlings MD 102 C1
Rawlins WY 32 C2
Rawlins Co. KS 42 B1
Rawson OH 90 B3
Ray ND 18 A2
Ray City GA 137 F1
Ray Co. MO 96 C2
Raymond IL 98 B2
Raymond ME 82 B3
Raymond MN 66 B4
Raymond MS 126 B3
Raymond NH 81 F4
Raymond WA 12 B4
Raymondville TX 63 F4
Raymore MO 96 B3
Rayne LA 133 E2
Raynham MA 151 D2
Raynham Ctr. MA 151 D3
Raytown MO 96 B2
Rayville LA 125 F2
Readfield ME 82 B2
Reading MA 151 D1
Reading MI 90 A1
Reading OH 204 B1
Reading PA 146 A2
Readington NJ 147 D1
Readlyn IA 73 E4
Readsboro VT 94 C1
Reagan Co. TX 58 A4
Real Co. TX 60 C2
Reamstown PA 146 A2
Reardan WA 13 F3
Reaville NJ 147 D1
Rector AR 108 A3
Red Bank NJ 147 E2
Red Bank SC 122 A4
Red Bank TN 120 B1
Red Bay AL 119 D3
Red Bluff CA 36 B1
Red Boiling Sprs. TN 110 A3
Red Bud IL 98 B4
Redby MN 64 A2
Red Cloud NE 43 D1
Red Creek NY 79 D3
Reddick FL 138 C4
Redding CA 28 C4
Redding CT 148 C2
Redding Ridge CT 148 C2
Red Feather Lakes CO 33 E4
Redfield AR 117 E3
Redfield IA 86 C2
Redfield SD 27 D2
Redford MI 210 B3
Redford NY 80 C2
Redgranite WI 74 B1
Red Hill PA 146 B1
Red Hill SC 123 D4
Red Hook NY 94 B2
Redington Beach FL 140 B3
Redington Shores FL 266 A2
Red Jacket WV 111 E1
Redkey IN 90 A4
Red Lake MN 64 A2
Red Lake Co. MN 19 F2
Red Lake Falls MN 19 F2
Redland MD 144 B2
Redlands CA 53 D2
Red Level AL 128 A4
Red Lick TX 116 C4
Red Lion PA 103 E1
Red Lodge MT 24 B2
Red Mesa AZ 47 F1
Redmond OR 21 D3
Redmond UT 39 E2
Redmond WA 12 C3
Red Oak IA 86 A3
Red Oak NC 113 D4
Red Oak OK 116 B2
Red Oak TX 59 F3
Red Oaks Mill NY 148 B1
Redondo Beach CA 228 C4
Red River NM 49 D1
Red River Co. TX 116 B4
Red River Par. LA 125 D3
Red Sprs. NC 122 C2
Redwater MS 126 C2
Redwater TX 124 C1
Redway CA 36 A1
Red Willow Co. NE 42 C1
Red Wing MN 67 E4
Redwood NY 79 E1
Redwood City CA 36 B4
Redwood Co. MN 66 B4
Redwood Estates CA 36 B4
Redwood Falls MN 66 B4
Redwood Valley CA 36 A2
Reece City AL 120 A3
Reed City MI 75 F2
Reed Creek GA 121 E3
Reedley CA 45 D3
Reedsburg WI 74 A2
Reedsport OR 20 A4
Reedsville PA 93 D3
Reedsville WV 102 B1
Reedsville WI 74 C1
Reedville VA 103 F4
Reelsboro NC 115 D3
Reese MI 76 B2
Reeseville WI 74 B3
Reeves Co. TX 57 E4
Reeves Crossing DE 145 E3
Reform AL 127 E1
Refton PA 146 A3
Refugio TX 61 E4
Refugio Co. TX 61 E4
Regent ND 18 A4
Rehobeth AL 136 C1
Rehoboth MA 151 D3
Rehoboth NM 48 A3
Rehoboth Beach DE 145 F4
Reidland KY 109 D2
Reidsville GA 129 F3
Reidsville NC 112 B3
Reidville SC 121 F2
Reinbeck IA 73 D4
Reisterstown MD 144 C1
Reliance SD 27 D4
Reliance WY 32 B3
Remerton GA 137 F1
Remington IN 89 E3
Remington VA 103 D3
Remsen IA 35 F1
Remsen NY 79 F3
Remsenburg NY 149 E4
Reno NV 37 D1
Reno TX 59 E2
Reno TX 116 A4
Reno Co. KS 43 E4
Renova MS 118 A4
Renovo PA 92 C2
Rensselaer IN 89 E3
Rensselaer NY 94 B1
Rensselaer Co. NY 94 B1
Renton WA 12 C3
Renville MN 66 B4
Renville Co. MN 66 B4
Renville Co. ND 18 B1
Republic MI 65 F4
Republic MO 107 D2
Republic OH 90 C3
Republic PA 102 B1
Republic WA 13 F1
Republic Co. KS 43 E1
Resaca GA 120 B2
Reserve LA 134 B3

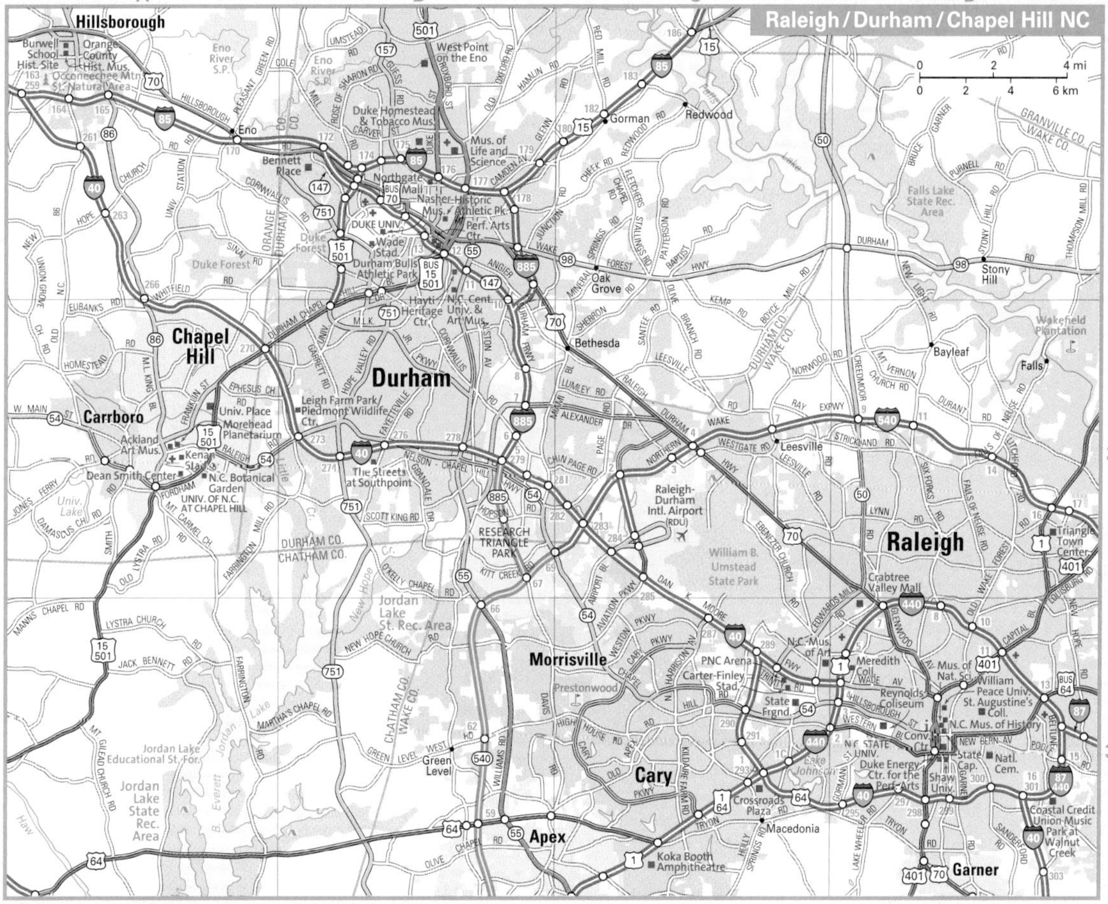
Raleigh / Durham / Chapel Hill NC
Hillsborough
Chapel Hill
Carrboro
Durham
Raleigh
Morrisville
Cary
Apex
Garner
Bethesda
Bayleaf
Leesville
Gorman
Redwood
Oak Grove
Stony Hill
Falls
Eno
Macedonia
Green Level
Raleigh-Durham Intl. Airport (RDU)
Research Triangle Park
William B. Umstead State Park
Jordan Lake St. Rec. Area
Jordan Lake State Rec. Area
Falls Lake State Rec. Area
Eno River S.P.
Duke Forest
DUKE UNIV.
UNIV. OF N.C. AT CHAPEL HILL
N.C. STATE UNIV.
Crabtree Valley Mall
PNC Arena
Carter-Finley Stad.
State Frgnd.
Koka Booth Amphitheatre
Coastal Credit Union Music Park at Walnut Creek
Triangle Town Center
Wakefield Plantation
DURHAM CO.
CHATHAM CO.
WAKE CO.
GRANVILLE CO.
0 2 4 mi
0 2 4 6 km

Apex B3
Bayleaf D2
Bethesda C2
Carrboro A2
Cary C3
Chapel Hill A2
Durham B2
Eno A1
Falls D2
Garner D3
Gorman C1
Green Level B3
Hillsborough A1
Leesville C2
Macedonia C3
Morrisville C3
Oak Grove C1
Raleigh D2
Redwood C1
Stony Hill D1

Radnor PA 248 A2
Raeford NC 122 C2
Ragland AL 120 A4
Rahway NJ 147 E1
Rainbow City AL 120 A4
Rainelle WV 101 F4
Rainier OR 20 B1
Rainier WA 12 C4
Rains SC 122 C3
Rains Co. TX 124 A1
Rainsville AL 120 A3
Raleigh MS 126 C3
Raleigh NC 113 D4
Raleigh Co. WV 101 F4
Raleigh Hills OR 251 C2
Ralls TX 58 B1
Ralls Co. MO 97 F2
Ralston NE 245 A3
Ralston WY 24 B3
Ramah NM 48 A3
Ramona CA 53 D4
Ramona OK 51 F1
Ramsay MI 65 E4
Ramseur NC 112 B4
Ramsey IL 98 C2
Ramsey MN 67 D3
Ramsey NJ 148 B3
Ramsey Co. MN 67 D3
Ramsey Co. ND 19 D2
Ranburne AL 120 B4
Ranchester WY 25 D2
Randolph MA 151 D2
Randolph NE 35 E2
Randolph NY 92 B1
Randolph UT 31 F3
Randolph VT 81 E3
Randolph WI 74 B2
Randolph Ctr. VT 81 E3
Randolph Co. AL 128 B1
Randolph Co. AR 107 F3
Randolph Co. GA 128 C4
Randolph Co. IL 98 B4
Randolph Co. IN 90 A4
Randolph Co. MO 97 E2
Randolph Co. NC 112 B4
Randolph Co. WV 102 B3
Randolph Hills MD 270 C1
Random Lake WI 74 C2
Rangeley ME 82 B1
Rangely CO 40 B1
Ranger TX 59 D3
Rankin IL 89 D4
Rankin PA 250 C2
Rankin TX 58 A4
Rankin Co. MS 126 B2
Ranlo NC 122 A1
Ransom Canyon TX 58 A1
Ransom Co. ND 19 E4
Ransomville NY 78 A3
Ranson WV 103 D2
Rantoul IL 88 C4
Rapid City SD 26 A3

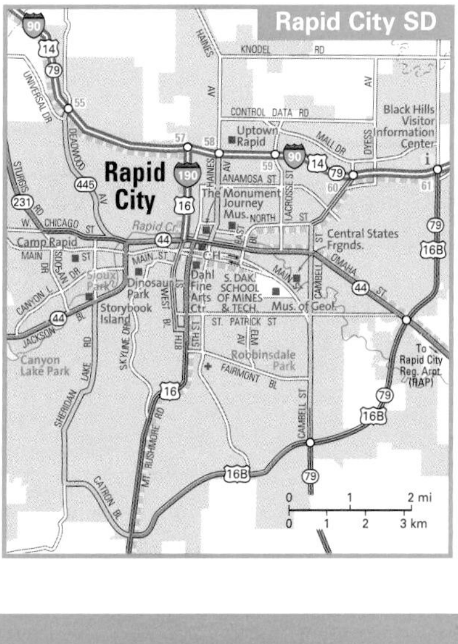
Rapid City SD
Rapid City
Uptown Rapid
Black Hills Visitor Information Center
The Monument
Journey Mus.
Central States Frgnds.
S. DAK. SCHOOL OF MINES & TECH.
Mus. of Geol.
Dahl Fine Arts Ctr.
Dinosaur Park
Storybook Island
Canyon Lake Park
Camp Rapid
Robbinsdale Park
To Rapid City Reg. Arpt. (RAP)
0 1 2 mi
0 1 2 3 km

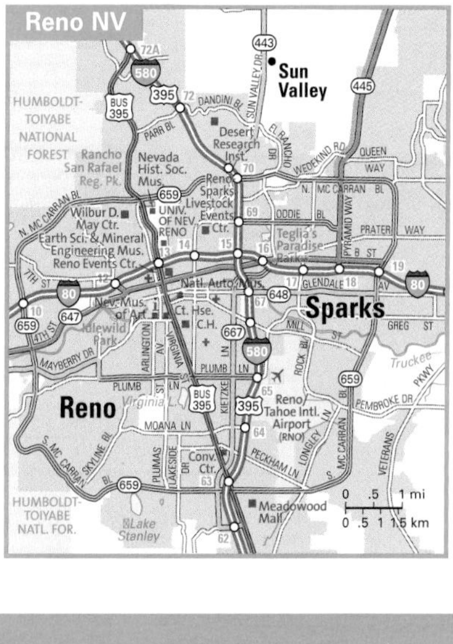
Reno NV
Sun Valley
Sparks
Reno
HUMBOLDT-TOIYABE NATIONAL FOREST
Rancho San Rafael Reg. Pk.
Nevada Hist. Soc. Mus.
Desert Research Inst.
Wilbur D. May Ctr.
UNIV. OF NEV. RENO
Reno Sparks Livestock Events Ctr.
Earth Sci. & Mineral Engineering Mus.
Reno Events Ctr.
Nev. Mus. of Art
Natl. Auto. Mus.
Teglia's Paradise Park
Idlewild Park
Reno Tahoe Intl. Airport (RNO)
Meadowood Mall
Conv. Ctr.
HUMBOLDT-TOIYABE NATL. FOR.
Virginia Lake
Lake Stanley
0 .5 1 mi
0 .5 1 1.5 km

Figures after entries indicate page number and grid reference.

Atlee B1
Bellwood B3
Bensley B3
Bon Air A2
Borkeys Store C1
Centralia B3
Chamberlayne Farms B1
Chester B3
Chesterfield B3
E. Highland Park B1
Fair Oaks C2
Glen Allen B1
Greendale B1
Highland Sprs. C2
Hunton B1
Lakeside B1
Laurel B1
Mechanicsville C1
Midlothian A2
Newmans C1
Old Cold Harbor C1
Pearsons Corner C1
Richmond B2
Rivermont C3
Sandston C2
Seven Pines C2
Short Pump A1
Studley C1
Varina C2

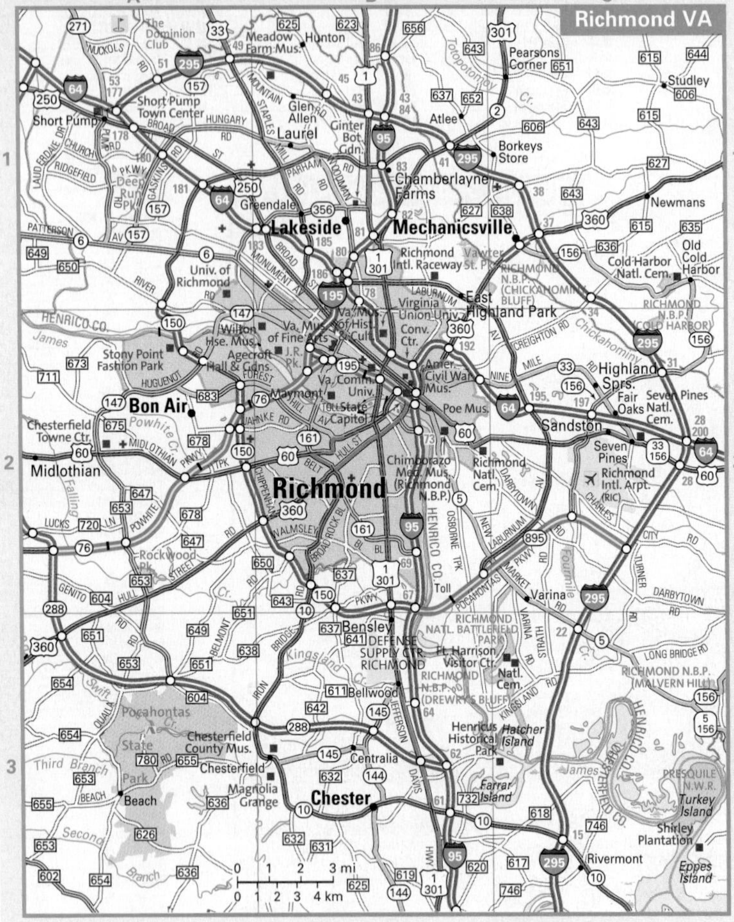
Richmond VA
A
B
C
1
2
3
Short Pump
Glen Allen
Laurel
Lakeside
Mechanicsville
Chamberlayne Farms
Richmond
Bon Air
Midlothian
Chester
Sandston
Highland Sprs.
Varina
Centralia
Bellwood
Rivermont
0 1 2 3 mi
0 1 2 3 4 km

Reserve NM 55 F1
Reston VA 144 A3
Revere MA 151 D1
Rexburg ID 23 E4
Reyno AR 108 A3
Reynolds GA 129 D2
Reynolds IN 89 E3
Reynolds ND 19 E3
Reynoldsburg OH 101 D1
Reynolds Co. MO 107 F1
Reynoldsville PA 92 B3
Rhea Co. TN 110 B4
Rhinebeck NY 94 B2
Rhinelander WI 68 B2
Rhome TX 59 E2
Rialto CA 53 D2
Rib Lake WI 68 A3
Rice MN 66 C2
Rice TX 59 F3
Riceboro GA 130 B4
Rice City RI 150 C3
Rice Co. KS 43 E3
Rice Co. MN 72 C1
Rice Lake WI 67 E3
Riceville IA 73 D3
Riceville TN 120 C1
Richardson TX 207 E1
Richardson Co. NE 86 A4
Richardton ND 18 A4
Richboro PA 146 C2
Rich Co. UT 31 F3
Rich Creek VA 112 A1
Richey MT 17 E3
Richfield ID 31 D1
Richfield MN 235 B3
Richfield NC 122 B1
Richfield OH 91 E2
Richfield UT 39 E2
Richfield Sprs. NY 79 F3
Richford VT 81 E1
Richgrove CA 45 D4
Rich Hill MO 96 B4
Richland GA 128 C3
Richland IA 87 E2
Richland MI 75 F4
Richland MS 126 B3
Richland MO 97 E4
Richland NJ 147 D4
Richland PA 146 A2
Richland WA 13 E4
Richland Ctr. WI 74 A3
Richland Co. IL 99 D3
Richland Co. MT 17 F2
Richland Co. ND 19 E4
Richland Co. OH 91 D3
Richland Co. SC 122 B3
Richland Co. WI 74 A2
Richland Hills TX 207 B2
Richland Par. LA 125 F3
Richlands NC 115 D4
Richlands VA 111 F2
Richlandtown PA 146 C1
Richmond CA 36 B3
Richmond IL 74 C4
Richmond IN 100 B1
Richmond KS 96 A3
Richmond KY 110 C1
Richmond LA 126 A2
Richmond ME 82 C3
Richmond MI 76 C4
Richmond MN 66 B3
Richmond MO 96 C2
Richmond TX 132 A3
Richmond UT 31 E2
Richmond VT 81 D2
Richmond VA 113 E1
Richmond Co. GA 130 A1
Richmond Co. NY 147 E1
Richmond Co. NC 122 C2
Richmond Co. VA 103 E4
Richmond Hts. FL 143 E2
Richmond Hts. MO 256 B2
Richmond Hts. OH 204 G1
Richmond Hill GA 130 B3
Richmondville NY 79 F4
Rich Square NC 113 E3
Richton MS 127 D4
Richwood LA 125 E2
Richwood OH 90 C4
Richwood TX 132 A4
Richwood WV 102 A4
Riddle OR 28 B1
Ridge NY 149 D3
Ridgebury CT 148 C2
Ridgebury NY 148 A2
Ridgecrest CA 45 E4
Ridgecrest LA 125 F4
Ridge Farm IL 99 D1
Ridgefield CT 148 C2
Ridgefield NJ 240 D2
Ridgefield WA 20 C1
Ridgefield Park NJ 240 D1
Ridgeland MS 126 B2
Ridgeland SC 130 C2
Ridgely MD 145 E3
Ridgely TN 108 B3
Ridge Manor FL 140 C1
Ridge Spr. SC 121 F4
Ridgetop TN 109 F3
Ridgeville IN 90 A4
Ridgeville SC 130 C1
Ridgeway MO 86 C4
Ridgeway VA 112 B3
Ridgeway WV 103 D2
Ridgeway WI 74 A3
Ridgewood NJ 148 B3
Ridgway CO 40 B3
Ridgway IL 109 D1
Ridgway PA 92 B2
Ridley Park PA 248 B4
Riegelsville PA 146 C1
Riesel TX 59 F4
Rifle CO 40 B1
Rigby ID 23 E4
Riggins ID 22 B2
Riley KS 43 F2
Riley Co. KS 43 F2
Rillito AZ 55 D3
Rimersburg PA 92 A3
Rincon GA 130 B3
Rindge NH 95 D1
Rineyville KY 110 A1
Ringgold GA 120 B2
Ringgold LA 125 D2
Ringgold Co. IA 86 B3
Ringling OK 51 E4
Ringoes NJ 147 D1
Ringtown PA 93 E3
Ringwood NJ 148 A2
Rio FL 141 E4
Rio WI 74 B2
Rio Arriba Co. NM 48 C1
Rio Blanco Co. CO 40 B1
Rio Bravo TX 63 D2
Rio Dell CA 28 A4
Rio del Mar CA 236 D1
Rio Grande NJ 104 C4
Rio Grande OH 101 E3
Rio Grande City TX 63 E4
Rio Grande Co. CO 41 D4
Rio Hondo TX 63 F4
Rio Linda CA 255 B1
Rio Rancho NM 48 C3
Rio Rico AZ 55 D4
Rio Verde AZ 54 C1
Rio Vista CA 36 B3
Rio Vista TX 59 E3
Ripley CA 53 F3
Ripley MS 118 C2
Ripley NY 78 A4
Ripley OH 100 C3
Ripley OK 51 F2
Ripley TN 108 B4
Ripley WV 101 E3
Ripley Co. IN 100 A2
Ripley Co. MO 108 A3
Ripon CA 36 C4
Ripon WI 74 B2
Ririe ID 23 E4
Rising Star TX 59 D3
Rising Sun DE 145 E2
Rising Sun IN 100 B2
Rising Sun MD 146 A4
Risingsun OH 90 C2
Rison AR 117 E4
Ritchie Co. WV 101 F2
Rittman OH 91 E3
Ritzville WA 13 F3
Riverbank CA 36 C4
River Bend NC 115 D3
River Bluff KY 100 A4
Riverdale CA 44 C3
Riverdale GA 120 C4
Riverdale IL 203 E6
Riverdale IA 208 B1
Riverdale ND 18 B3
Riverdale UT 244 A2
Riverdale Park MD 270 E2
River Edge NJ 240 C1
River Falls AL 128 A4
River Falls WI 67 D4
River Forest IL 203 D4
River Grove IL 203 D4
Rivergrove OR 251 C3
Riverhead NY 149 E3
River Hills WI 234 D1
River Oaks TX 207 A2
River Ridge LA 239 B1
River Rouge MI 210 C4
Riverside AL 120 A4
Riverside CA 53 D2
Riverside IL 203 D4
Riverside IA 87 F2
Riverside MO 224 B2

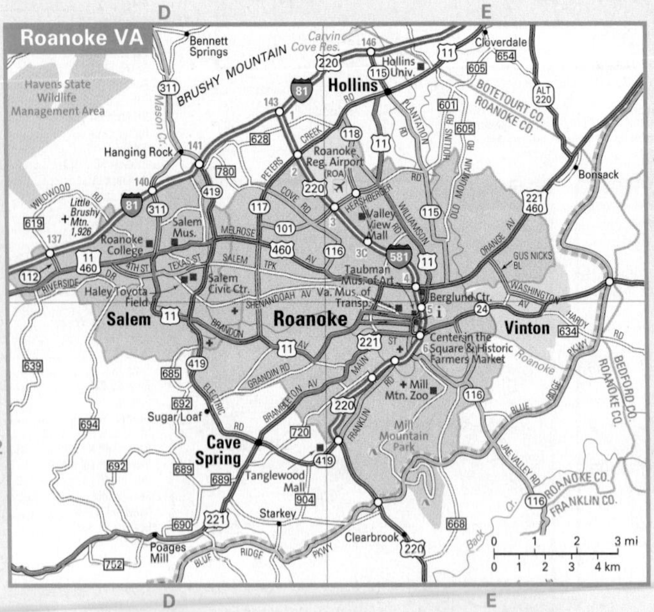
Roanoke VA
D
E
1
2
Hollins
Salem
Roanoke
Vinton
Cave Spring
0 1 2 3 mi
0 1 2 3 4 km

Bennett Sprs. D1
Bonsack E1
Cave Spr. D2
Clearbrook E2
Cloverdale E1
Hanging Rock D1
Hollins E1
Poages Mill D2
Roanoke D2
Salem D2
Starkey D2
Sugar Loaf D2
Vinton E2

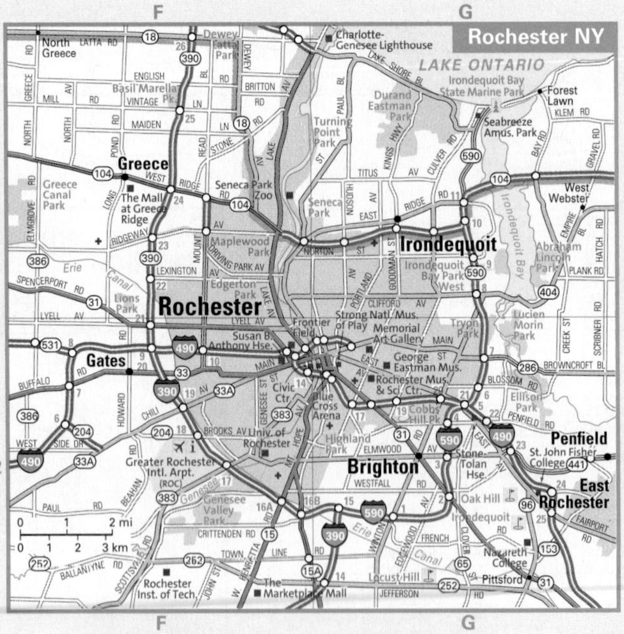
Rochester NY
F
G
1
2
LAKE ONTARIO
Greece
Irondequoit
Rochester
Gates
Brighton
Penfield
East Rochester
0 1 2 mi
0 1 2 3 km

Brighton G2
E. Rochester G2
Forest Lawn G1
Gates F2
Greece F1
Irondequoit G1
N. Greece F1
Penfield G2
Pittsford G2
Rochester F1

Entries in **bold black** indicate counties or parishes.
Entries in **bold color** indicate cities with detailed inset maps.

Riverside NJ 147 D3
Riverside NY 149 E3
Riverside OH 100 C1
Riverside PA 93 E3
Riverside Co. CA 53 E3
Riverton IL 98 B1
Riverton KS 106 B2
Riverton NJ 146 C3
Riverton UT 31 E4
Riverton WY 32 B1
Riverview FL 140 C2
Riverview MO 256 C1
Riverwood KY 230 E1
Riverwoods IL 203 C2
Rives Jct. MI 76 A4
Rivesville WV 102 A1
Riviera Beach FL 141 F4
Riviera Beach MD 144 C2
Roachdale IN 99 E1
Roaming Shores OH 91 F2
Roane Co. TN 110 B4
Roane Co. WV 101 F3
Roan Mtn. TN 111 E3
Roanoke AL 128 B1
Roanoke IL 88 B3
Roanoke IN 90 A3
Roanoke TX 207 B1
Roanoke VA 112 B2
Roanoke Co. VA 112 B1
Roanoke Rapids NC 113 E3
Roaring Spr. PA 92 C4
Robards KY 109 E1
Robbins IL 203 D6
Robbins NC 122 C1
Robbinsdale MN 235 B2
Robbinsville NJ 147 D2
Robbinsville NC 121 D1
Robersonville NC 113 E4
Roberta GA 129 D2
Robert Lee TX 58 B3
Roberts ID 23 E4
Roberts WI 67 E4
Roberts Co. SD 27 F1
Roberts Co. TX 50 B2
Robertsdale AL 135 E2
Robertson Co. KY 100 C3
Robertson Co. TN 109 F3
Robertson Co. TX 61 F1
Robertsville NJ 147 E2
Robeson Co. NC 123 D2
Robesonia PA 146 A2
Robins IA 87 E1
Robinson IL 99 D2
Robinson TX 59 E4
Robstown TX 63 F2
Roby TX 58 B2
Rochdale MA 150 B2
Rochelle GA 129 E3
Rochelle IL 88 B1
Rochelle Park NJ 240 C1
Rochester IL 98 B1
Rochester IN 89 F3
Rochester MN 73 D1
Rochester NH 81 F4
Rochester NY 78 C3
Rochester PA 91 F3
Rochester VT 81 D3
Rochester WA 12 B4
Rochester WI 74 C4
Rochester Hills MI 76 C4
Rock MA 151 D3
Rockaway NJ 148 A3
Rockaway Beach MO 107 D3
Rockaway Beach OR 20 B1
Rockbridge Co. VA 102 B4
Rockcastle Co. KY 110 C2
Rock Co. MN 27 F4
Rock Co. NE 35 D2
Rock Co. WI 74 B4
Rock Creek MN 67 D2
Rock Creek OH 91 F2
Rockdale MD 144 C2
Rockdale TX 61 E1
Rockdale Co. GA 120 C4
Rockfall CT 149 E1
Rock Falls IL 88 B1
Rockford AL 128 A1
Rockford IL 74 B4
Rockford IA 73 D3
Rockford MI 75 F3
Rockford MN 66 C3
Rockford OH 90 A3
Rockford TN 110 C4
Rockford WA 14 B3
Rock Hall MD 145 D2
Rock Hill MO 256 B2
Rock Hill NY 148 A1
Rock Hill SC 122 A2
Rockingham NC 122 C2
Rockingham Co. NH 81 F4
Rockingham Co. NC 112 B3
Rockingham Co. VA 102 C3
Rock Island IL 88 A2
Rock Island OK 116 B1
Rock Island WA 13 E3
Rock Island Co. IL 88 A2
Rockland ID 31 E1
Rockland ME 82 C2
Rockland MA 151 D2
Rockland WI 73 F1
Rockland Co. NY 148 B2
Rockledge AL 120 A3
Rockledge FL 141 E2
Rockledge PA 248 D2
Rocklin CA 36 C2
Rockmart GA 120 B3
Rock Mills AL 128 B1
Rock Pt. AZ 47 F1
Rockport AR 117 D3
Rockport IN 99 E4
Rockport KY 109 E1
Rockport ME 82 C2
Rockport MA 151 F1
Rock Port MO 86 A4
Rockport TX 61 E4
Rock Rapids IA 27 F4
Rock River WY 33 D2
Rocksprings TX 60 B2
Rock Sprs. WY 32 B3
Rockton IL 74 B4
Rockvale CO 41 E3
Rock Valley IA 35 F1
Rockville CT 150 A3
Rockville IN 99 E1
Rockville MD 144 B2
Rockville MN 66 C3
Rockville RI 150 C4
Rockwall TX 59 F2
Rockwall Co. TX 59 F2
Rockwell AR 117 D3
Rockwell IA 73 D3
Rockwell NC 122 B1
Rockwell City IA 72 B4
Rockwood MI 90 C1
Rockwood PA 102 B1
Rockwood TN 110 B4
Rocky Ford CO 41 F3
Rocky Hill CT 149 E1
Rocky Hill NJ 147 D1
Rocky Mount NC 113 E4
Rocky Mount VA 112 B2
Rocky Pt. NY 149 D3
Rocky Ridge UT 39 E1
Rocky Ripple IN 221 B2
Rocky River OH 204 E2
Rocky Top TN 110 C3
Rodeo CA 259 C1
Roebuck SC 121 F2
Roeland Park KS 224 B3
Roessleville NY 188 D2
Roff OK 51 F4
Roger Mills Co. OK 50 C2
Rogers AR 106 C3
Rogers MN 66 C3
Rogers TX 61 E1
Rogers City MI 71 D3
Rogers Co. OK 106 A3
Rogersville AL 119 E2
Rogersville MO 107 D2
Rogersville TN 111 D3
Rogue River OR 28 B2
Rohnert Park CA 36 B3
Roland IA 86 C1
Roland OK 116 B1
Rolesville NC 113 D4
Rolette ND 18 C1
Rolette Co. ND 18 C1
Rolfe IA 72 B3
Rolla KS 50 B1
Rolla MO 97 F4
Rolla ND 18 C1
Rolling Fields KY 230 E1
Rolling Fork MS 126 A1
Rolling Hills CA 228 C4
Rolling Hills KY 230 F1
Rolling Hills WY 33 D1
Rolling Hills Estates CA 228 C4
Rolling Meadows IL 203 B3
Rolling Prairie IN 89 E2
Rollingstone MN 73 E1
Rollinsford NH 82 A4
Roma TX 63 D4
Romancoke MD 145 D3
Roman Forest TX 132 B2
Rome GA 120 B3
Rome IL 88 B3
Rome NY 79 E3
Rome City IN 90 A2
Romeo CO 41 D4
Romeo MI 76 C4
Romeoville IL 89 D2
Romney WV 102 C2
Romoland CA 229 K4
Romulus MI 90 C1
Ronan MT 15 D3
Ronceverte WV 112 A1
Ronkonkoma NY 149 D3
Roodhouse IL 98 A2
Rooks Co. KS 43 D2
Roosevelt NJ 147 E2
Roosevelt UT 32 A4
Roosevelt Co. MT 17 E2
Roosevelt Co. NM 49 F4
Roosevelt Park MI 75 E3
Roper NC 113 F4
Ropesville TX 58 A1
Rosalia WA 14 A3
Rosamond CA 52 C1
Rosaryville MD 144 C4
Rosburg WA 12 B4
Roscoe IL 74 B4
Roscoe NY 94 A2
Roscoe SD 27 D2
Roscoe TX 58 B3
Roscommon MI 70 C4
Roscommon Co. MI 76 A1
Roseau MN 19 F1
Roseau Co. MN 19 F1
Roseboro NC 123 D2
Rose Bud AR 117 E1
Rosebud SD 34 C1
Rosebud TX 59 F4
Rosebud Co. MT 17 D4
Roseburg OR 28 B1
Rose City MI 76 B1
Rose City TX 132 C2
Rosedale IN 99 E1
Rosedale LA 133 F2
Rosedale MD 144 C2
Rosedale MS 118 A4
Rosedale Beach DE 145 F4
Rose Haven MD 144 C4
Rose Hill KS 43 F4
Rose Hill NC 123 E2
Rose Hill VA 111 D3
Rose Hill VA 270 C5
Roseland FL 141 E3
Roseland LA 134 B1
Roseland NJ 240 A2
Roselawn IN 89 D3
Roselle IL 203 B3
Roselle NJ 147 E1
Roselle Park NJ 147 E1
Rose Lodge OR 20 B2
Rosemead CA 228 E2
Rosemont CA 255 C3
Rosemont IL 203 C3
Rosemount MN 235 D4
Rosemount OH 101 D3
Rosenberg TX 132 A3
Rosendale NY 94 B3
Rosendale WI 74 C2
Rosenhayn NJ 145 F1
Rosepine LA 133 D1
Roseto PA 93 F3
Rose Valley PA 248 A4
Roseville CA 36 C2
Roseville IL 88 A3
Roseville MI 210 D2
Roseville MN 235 C2
Roseville OH 101 E1
Roseville Park DE 146 B4
Rosholt SD 27 F1
Rosiclare IL 109 D1
Roslyn PA 248 C1
Roslyn SD 27 E2
Roslyn WA 13 D3
Roslyn Estates NY 241 G2
Rosman NC 121 E1
Ross CA 259 A1
Ross OH 100 B2
Ross Co. OH 101 D2
Rossford OH 267 B2
Rossiter PA 92 B3
Rossmoor CA 228 E4
Rossmoor NJ 147 E2
Rossville GA 120 B2
Rossville IL 89 D4
Rossville IN 89 E4
Rossville KS 43 F2
Rossville MD 193 E2
Roswell GA 120 C3
Roswell NM 57 E1
Rotan TX 58 B2
Rothsay MN 19 F4
Rothschild WI 68 B4
Rothsville PA 146 A2
Rotonda FL 140 C4
Rotterdam NY 94 B1
Rotterdam Jct. NY 94 B1
Rougemont NC 112 C3
Rough Rock AZ 47 F1
Round Hill VA 103 D2
Round Lake NY 94 B1
Round Mtn. NV 37 F2
Round Pond ME 82 C3
Round Rock AZ 47 F1
Round Rock TX 61 E1
Roundup MT 16 C4
Rouses Pt. NY 81 D1
Routt Co. CO 32 C4
Rouzerville PA 103 D1
Rowan Co. KY 100 C4
Rowan Co. NC 112 A4
Rowland NC 122 C3
Rowland Hts. CA 229 F3
Rowlesburg WV 102 B2
Rowlett TX 207 E1
Rowley MA 151 F1
Roxana DE 145 F4
Roxboro NC 112 C3
Roxie MS 126 A4
Roxton TX 116 A4
Roy NM 49 E2
Roy UT 31 E3
Royal Ctr. IN 89 E3
Royal City WA 13 E4
Royal Oak MD 145 D4
Royal Oak MI 76 C4
Royal Palm Beach FL 143 E1
Royal Pines NC 121 E1
Royalton IL 98 C4
Royalton MN 66 C2
Royersford PA 146 B2
Royse City TX 59 F2
Royston GA 121 E3
Rubonia FL 266 B4
Ruch OR 28 B2
Rudyard MT 15 F2
Rugby ND 18 C2
Ruidoso NM 57 D2
Ruidoso Downs NM 57 D2
Rule TX 58 C2
Ruleville MS 118 A4
Rumford ME 82 B2
Rumson NJ 147 F2
Runaway Bay TX 59 E2
Runge TX 61 E3
Runnels Co. TX 58 C3
Runnemede NJ 146 C3
Running Sprs. CA 229 K1
Rupert ID 31 D1
Rupert WV 102 A4
Rural Hall NC 112 B3
Rural Retreat VA 111 F2
Rural Valley PA 92 B3
Rush City MN 67 D2
Rush Co. IN 100 A1
Rush Co. KS 43 D3
Rushford MN 73 E2
Rushford Vil. MN 73 E2
Rushmere VA 113 F2
Rush Sprs. OK 51 E4
Rush Valley UT 31 E4
Rushville IL 88 A4
Rushville IN 100 A1
Rushville NE 34 A1
Rushville NY 78 C4
Rusk TX 124 B3
Rusk Co. TX 124 B3
Rusk Co. WI 67 F3
Ruskin FL 140 B3
Russell IA 87 D3
Russell KS 43 D2
Russell KY 101 D3
Russell MA 94 C2
Russell PA 92 B1
Russell Co. AL 128 C3
Russell Co. KS 43 D2
Russell Co. KY 110 B2
Russell Co. VA 111 F2
Russell Gardens NY 241 G3
Russells Pt. OH 90 B4
Russell Sprs. KY 110 B2
Russellville AL 119 E3
Russellville AR 117 D1

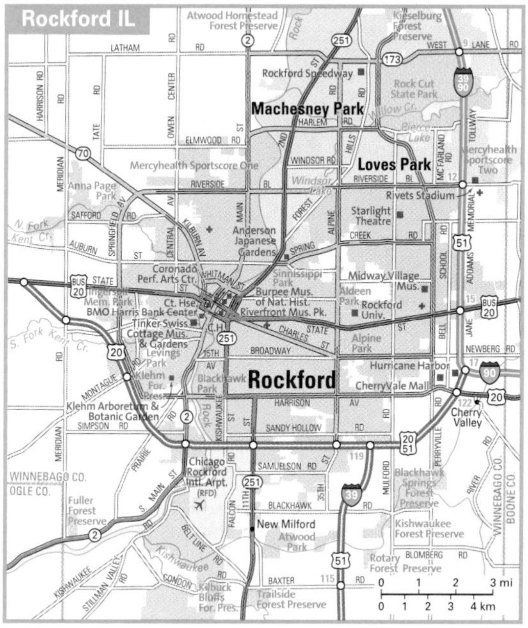

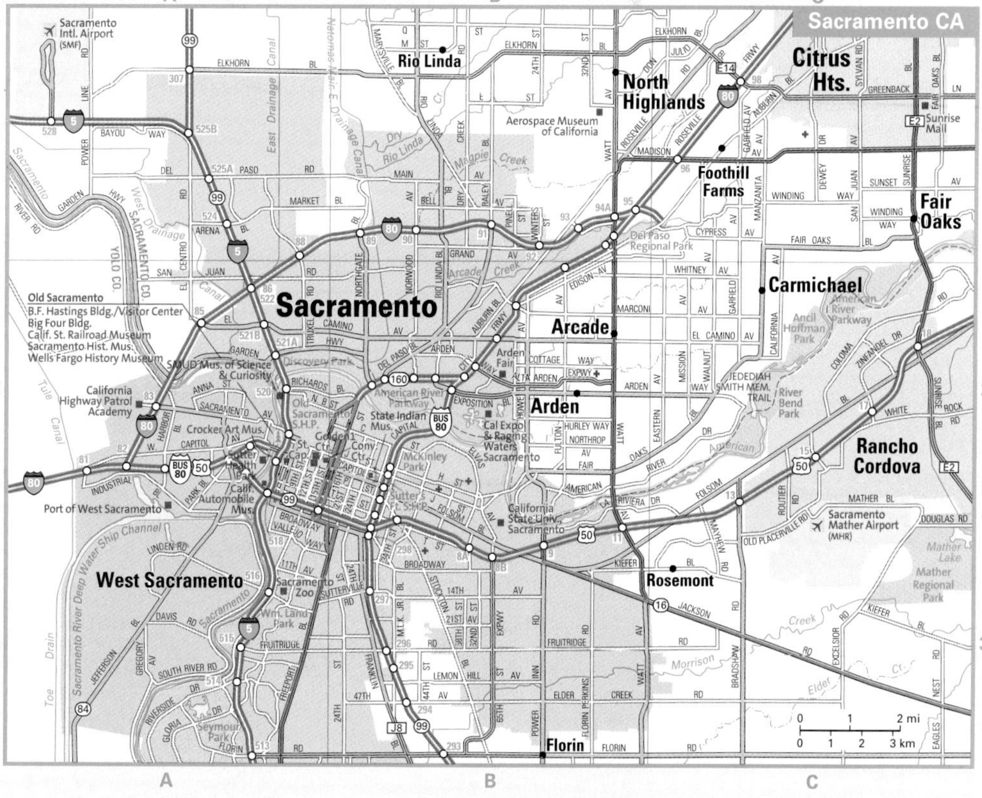

Arcade B2
Arden B2
Carmichael C2
Citrus Hts. C1
Fair Oaks C1
Florin B3
Foothill Farms C1
N. Highlands B1
Rancho Cordova C2
Rio Linda B1
Rosemont C3
Sacramento A2
W. Sacramento A3

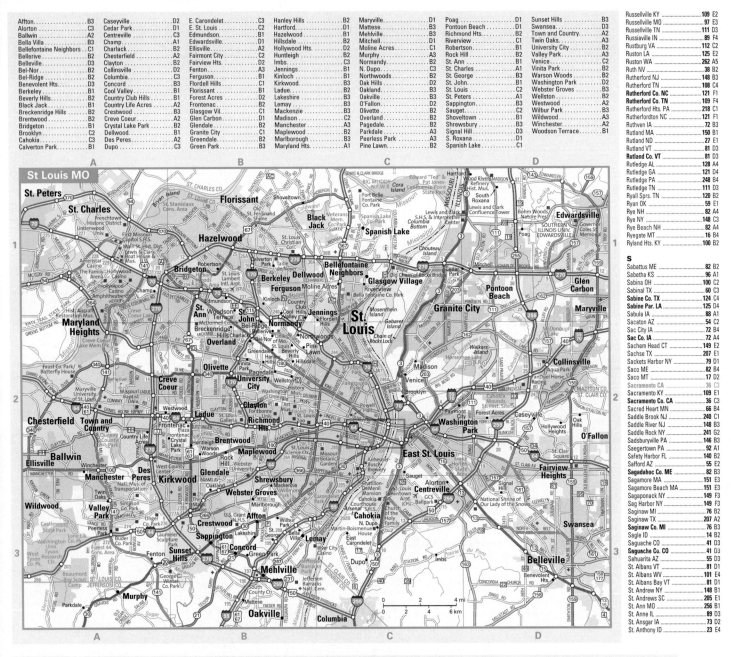

Figures after entries indicate page number and grid reference.

Affton B3
Alorton C3
Ballwin A2
Bella Villa B3
Bellefontaine Neighbors . . C1
Bellerive B2
Belleville D3
Bel-Nor B2
Bel-Ridge B2
Benevolent Hts. D3
Berkeley B1
Beverly Hills B2
Black Jack B1
Breckenridge Hills B2
Brentwood B2
Bridgeton B1
Brooklyn C2
Cahokia C3
Calverton Park B1
Caseyville D2
Cedar Park D1
Centreville C3
Champ A1
Charlack B2
Chesterfield A2
Clayton B2
Collinsville D2
Columbia C3
Concord B3
Cool Valley B1
Country Club Hills B1
Country Life Acres A2
Crestwood B3
Creve Coeur A2
Crystal Lake Park B2
Dellwood B1
Des Peres A2
Dupo C3
E. Carondelet C3
E. St. Louis C2
Edmundson B1
Edwardsville D1
Ellisville A2
Fairmont City C2
Fairview Hts. D2
Fenton A3
Ferguson B1
Flordell Hills C1
Florissant B1
Forest Acres D2
Frontenac B2
Glasgow Vil. C1
Glen Carbon D1
Glendale B2
Granite City C1
Greendale B2
Green Park B3
Hanley Hills B2
Hartford D1
Hazelwood B1
Hillsdale B2
Hollywood Hts. D2
Huntleigh B2
Imbs C3
Jennings B1
Kinloch B1
Kirkwood B3
Ladue B2
Lakeshire B3
Lemay B3
Mackenzie B3
Madison C2
Manchester A3
Maplewood B2
Marlborough B3
Maryland Hts. A1
Maryville D1
Mattese B3
Mehlville B3
Mitchell D1
Moline Acres C1
Murphy A3
Normandy B2
N. Dupo C3
Northwoods B2
Oak Hills D2
Oakland B3
Oakville B3
O'Fallon D2
Olivette B2
Overland B2
Pagedale B2
Parkdale A3
Peerless Park A3
Pine Lawn B2
Poag D1
Pontoon Beach D1
Richmond Hts. B2
Riverview C1
Robertson B1
Rock Hill B2
St. Ann B1
St. Charles A1
St. George B3
St. John B1
St. Louis C2
St. Peters A1
Sappington B3
Sauget C2
Shoveltown B1
Shrewsbury B3
Signal Hill D3
S. Roxana D1
Spanish Lake C1
Sunset Hills B3
Swansea D3
Town and Country A2
Twin Oaks A3
University City B2
Valley Park A3
Venice C2
Vinita Park B2
Warson Woods B2
Washington Park D2
Webster Groves B3
Wellston B2
Westwood A2
Wilbur Park B3
Wildwood A3
Winchester A2
Woodson Terrace B1

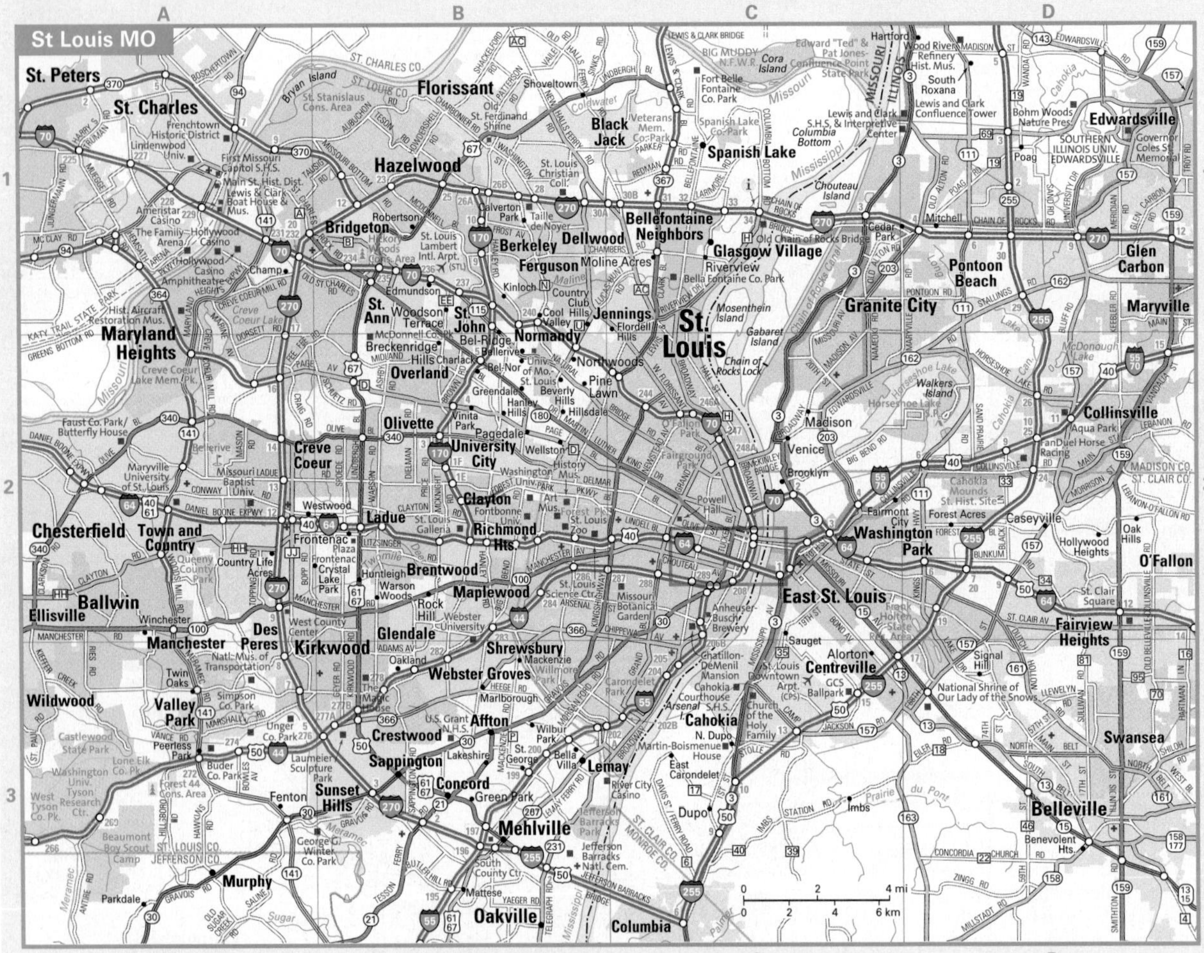
St Louis MO
St. Peters
St. Charles
Florissant
Hazelwood
Black Jack
Spanish Lake
Bridgeton
Bellefontaine Neighbors
Berkeley
Ferguson
Glasgow Village
Edwardsville
Glen Carbon
Pontoon Beach
Granite City
Maryville
Maryland Heights
St. Ann
Jennings
St. Louis
Overland
Collinsville
Madison
Venice
Creve Coeur
Olivette
University City
Clayton
Chesterfield
Town and Country
Ladue
Richmond Hts.
Washington Park
Brentwood
Maplewood
Ballwin
Ellisville
East St. Louis
Fairview Heights
O'Fallon
Manchester
Des Peres
Kirkwood
Glendale
Shrewsbury
Webster Groves
Centreville
Wildwood
Valley Park
Affton
Crestwood
Cahokia
Sappington
Lemay
Swansea
Concord
Sunset Hills
Fenton
Mehlville
Belleville
Murphy
Oakville
Columbia
Dupo

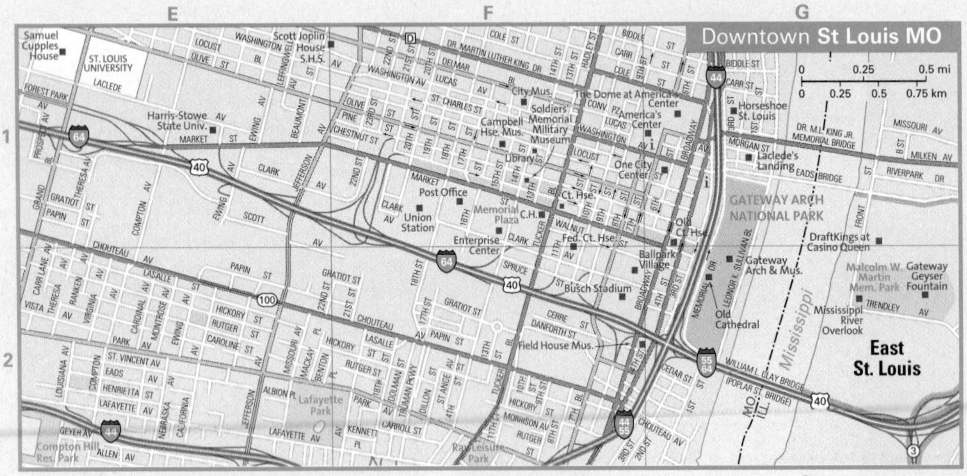
Downtown St Louis MO
Gateway Arch National Park
Mississippi
East St. Louis

POINTS OF INTEREST

America's Center G1
Ballpark Village F2
Busch Stadium F2
Campbell House Museum F1
City Hall F1
City Museum F1
Court House F1
DraftKings at Casino Queen G1
Enterprise Center F1
Federal Court House F1
Field House Museum F2
Gateway Arch & Museum G2
Gateway Arch National Park G1
Gateway Geyser Fountain G2
Harris-Stowe State University E1
Horseshoe St. Louis G1
Laclede's Landing G1
Library F1
Mississippi River Overlook G2
Old Cathedral G2
Old Court House G1
One City Center G1
Post Office F1
St. Louis University E1
Samuel Cupples House E1
Scott Joplin House State Hist. Site E1
Soldiers' Memorial Military Museum F1
The Dome at America's Center G1
Union Station F1

Russellville KY 109 E2
Russellville MO 97 E3
Russellville TN 111 D3
Russiaville IN 89 F4
Rustburg VA 112 C2
Ruston LA 125 E2
Ruston WA 262 A5
Ruth NV 38 B2
Rutherford NJ 148 B3
Rutherford TN 108 C4
Rutherford Co. NC 121 F1
Rutherford Co. TN 109 F4
Rutherford Hts. PA 218 C1
Rutherfordton NC 121 F1
Ruthven IA 72 B3
Rutland MA 150 B1
Rutland ND 27 E1
Rutland VT 81 D3
Rutland Co. VT 81 D3
Rutledge AL 128 A4
Rutledge GA 121 D4
Rutledge PA 248 B4
Rutledge TN 111 D3
Ryall Sprs. TN 120 B2
Ryan OK 59 E1
Rye NH 82 A4
Rye NY 148 C3
Rye Beach NH 82 A4
Ryegate MT 16 B4
Ryland Hts. KY 100 B2

S

Sabattus ME 82 B2
Sabetha KS 96 A1
Sabina OH 100 C2
Sabinal TX 60 C3
Sabine Co. TX 124 C4
Sabine Par. LA 125 D4
Sabula IA 88 A1
Sacaton AZ 54 C2
Sac City IA 72 B4
Sac Co. IA 72 A4
Sachem Head CT 149 E2
Sachse TX 207 E1
Sackets Harbor NY 79 D1
Saco ME 82 B4
Saco MT 17 D2
Sacramento CA 36 C3
Sacramento KY 109 E1
Sacramento Co. CA 36 C3
Sacred Heart MN 66 B4
Saddle Brook NJ 240 C1
Saddle River NJ 148 B3
Saddle Rock NY 241 G2
Sadsburyville PA 146 B3
Saegertown PA 92 A1
Safety Harbor FL 140 B2
Safford AZ 55 E2
Sagadahoc Co. ME 82 B3
Sagamore MA 151 E3
Sagamore Beach MA 151 E3
Sagaponack NY 149 F3
Sag Harbor NY 149 F3
Saginaw MI 76 B2
Saginaw TX 207 A2
Saginaw Co. MI 76 B3
Sagle ID 14 B2
Saguache CO 41 D3
Saguache Co. CO 41 D3
Sahuarita AZ 55 D3
St. Albans VT 81 D1
St. Albans WV 101 E4
St. Albans Bay VT 81 D1
St. Andrew NY 148 B1
St. Andrews SC 205 E1
St. Ann MO 256 B1
St. Anne IL 89 D3
St. Ansgar IA 73 D2
St. Anthony ID 23 E4

Entries in **bold black** indicate counties or parishes.
Entries in bold color indicate cities with detailed inset maps.

St. Anthony MN 235 C2
St. Augusta MN 66 C3
St. Augustine FL 139 D3
St. Augustine Beach FL 139 E3
St. Augustine Shores FL 139 D3
St. Bernard LA 134 C3
St. Bernard OH 204 B2
St. Bernard Par. LA 134 C3
St. Bonifacius MN 66 C4
St. Charles IL 88 C1
St. Charles IA 86 C2
St. Charles MD 144 B4
St. Charles MI 76 B3
St. Charles MN 73 E1
St. Charles MO 98 A3
St. Charles Co. MO 98 A3
St. Charles Par. LA 134 B3
St. Clair MI 76 C3
St. Clair MN 72 C1
St. Clair MO 97 F4
St. Clair PA 93 E3
St. Clair Co. AL 120 A4
St. Clair Co. IL 98 B4
St. Clair Co. MI 76 C3
St. Clair Co. MO 96 C4
St. Clair Shores MI 76 C4
St. Clairsville OH 91 F4
St. Cloud FL 141 D2
St. Cloud MN 66 C3
St. Croix Co. WI 67 E3
St. Croix Falls WI 67 D3
St. David AZ 55 E3
St. David IL 88 A4
St. Edward NE 35 E3

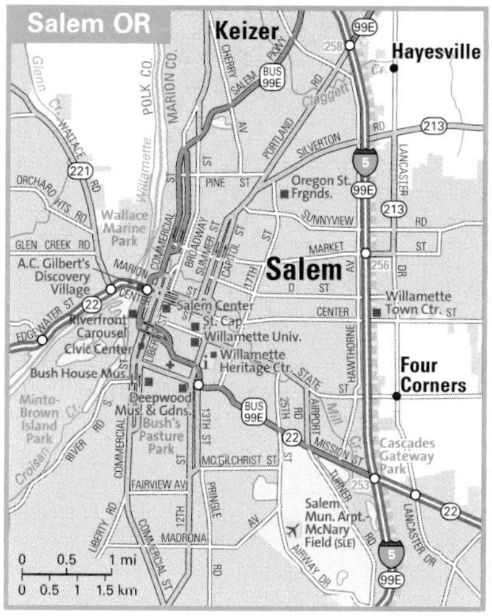
Salem OR
Keizer
Hayesville
Salem
Oregon St. Frgnds.
A.C. Gilbert's Discovery Village
Riverfront Carousel
Civic Center
Willamette Univ.
Willamette Heritage Ctr.
Willamette Town Ctr.
Bush House Mus.
Deepwood Mus. & Gdns.
Bush's Pasture Park
Minto-Brown Island Park
Four Corners
Cascades Gateway Park
Salem Mun. Arpt.-McNary Field (SLE)
0 0.5 1 mi
0 0.5 1 1.5 km

Alamo Hts. E2
Balcones Hts. E2
Bracken F1
Buena Vista E3
Castle Hills E2
China Grove F3
Cibolo F1
Converse F2
Garden Ridge F1
Grey Forest D1
Helotes D1
Hill Country Vil. E1
Hollywood Park E1
Kirby F2
Leon Valley D2
Live Oak F2
Macdona D3
Olmos Park E2
San Antonio F3
Sayers F3
Schertz F1
Selma F1
Shavano Park E1
Southton E3
Terrell Hills E2
Universal City F1
Von Ormy D3
Windcrest F2

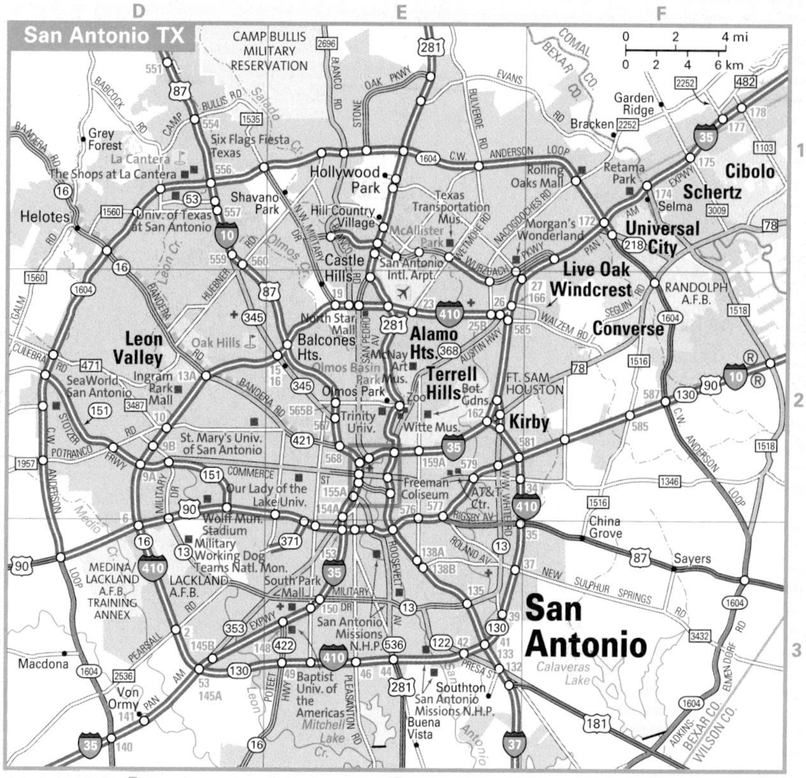
San Antonio TX
CAMP BULLIS MILITARY RESERVATION
Grey Forest
Helotes
Six Flags Fiesta Texas
The Shops at La Cantera
Univ. of Texas at San Antonio
Shavano Park
Hollywood Park
Hill Country Village
Castle Hills
Texas Transportation Mus.
San Antonio Intl. Arpt.
Leon Valley
Balcones Hts.
Alamo Hts.
Terrell Hills
Kirby
Live Oak
Windcrest
Universal City
Schertz
Cibolo
Selma
Converse
Garden Ridge
Bracken
SeaWorld San Antonio
St. Mary's Univ. of San Antonio
Our Lady of the Lake Univ.
Trinity Univ.
Witte Mus.
FT. SAM HOUSTON
Freeman Coliseum
AT&T Ctr.
RANDOLPH A.F.B.
China Grove
Sayers
LACKLAND A.F.B.
MEDINA/LACKLAND A.F.B. TRAINING ANNEX
South Park Mall
San Antonio Missions N.H.P.
Macdona
Von Ormy
Southton
Buena Vista
San Antonio
Calaveras Lake
0 2 4 mi
0 2 4 6 km

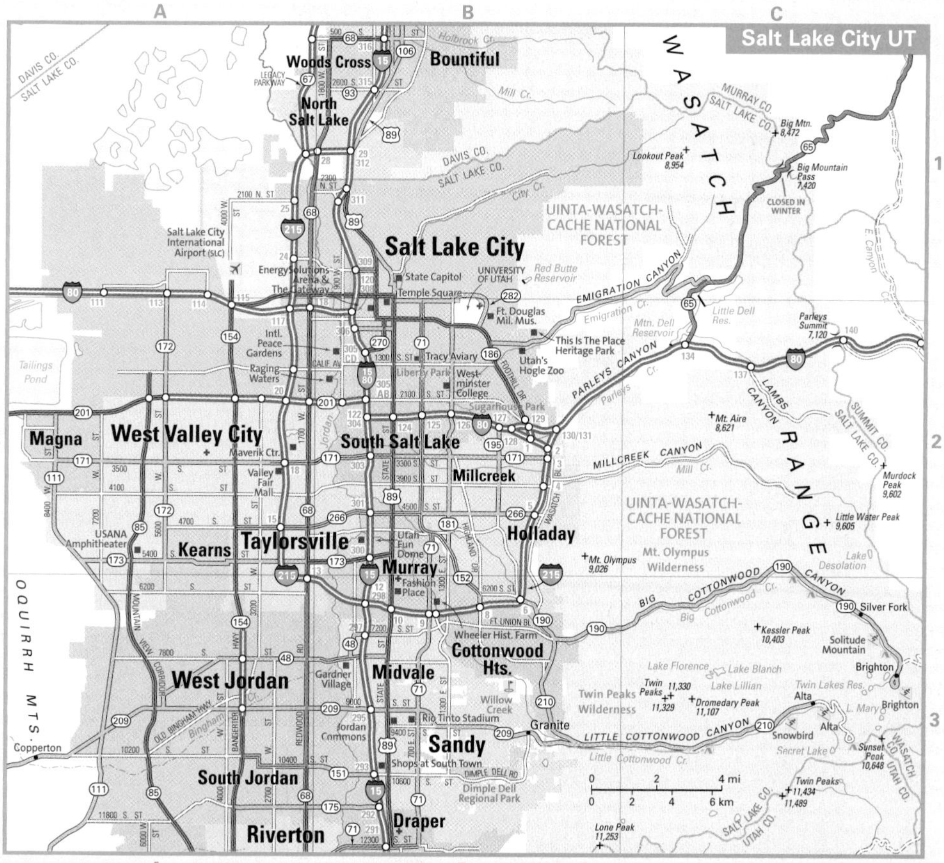
Salt Lake City UT
Woods Cross
Bountiful
North Salt Lake
Salt Lake City International Airport (SLC)
Salt Lake City
State Capitol
Temple Square
UNIVERSITY OF UTAH
Magna
West Valley City
South Salt Lake
Millcreek
Kearns
Taylorsville
Murray
Holladay
West Jordan
Midvale
Cottonwood Hts.
Sandy
South Jordan
Riverton
Draper
Copperton
OQUIRRH MTS.
WASATCH RANGE
UINTA-WASATCH-CACHE NATIONAL FOREST
Alta
Brighton
Silver Fork
Granite
0 2 4 mi
0 2 4 6 km

Alta C3
Bountiful B1
Brighton C3
Copperton A3
Cottonwood Hts. B3
Draper B3
E. Millcreek B2
Granite B3
Holladay B2
Kearns A2
Magna A2
Midvale B3
Millcreek B2
Murray B2
N. Salt Lake B1
Riverton A3
Salt Lake City B1
Sandy B3
Silver Fork C3
S. Jordan A3
S. Salt Lake B2
Taylorsville A2
W. Jordan A3
W. Valley City A2
Woods Cross B1

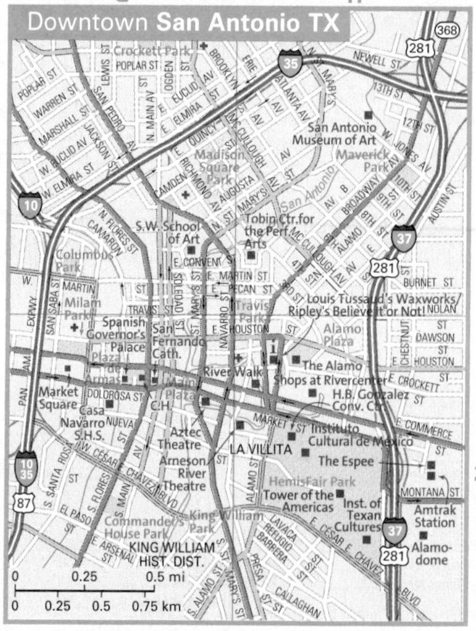
Downtown San Antonio TX
San Antonio Museum of Art
Tobin Ctr. for the Perf. Arts
S.W. School of Art
Spanish Governor's Palace
San Fernando Cath.
Market Square
Casa Navarro S.H.S.
River Walk
The Alamo
Shops at Rivercenter
H.B. Gonzalez Conv. Ctr.
Instituto Cultural de México
The Espee
Tower of the Americas
Inst. of Texan Cultures
Amtrak Station
Alamodome
LA VILLITA
KING WILLIAM HIST. DIST.
0 0.25 0.5 mi
0 0.25 0.5 0.75 km

POINTS OF INTEREST

The Alamo H2
Alamodome H2
Amtrak Station H2
Arneson River Theater H2
Aztec Theatre G2
Casa Navarro State Historic Site G2
H.B. Gonzalez Convention Center H2
HemisFair Park H2
Institute of Texan Cultures H2
Instituto Cultural de México H2
Louis Tussaud's Waxworks/ Ripley's Believe It or Not! H2
Market Square G2
River Walk H2
San Antonio Museum of Art H1
San Fernando Cathedral G2
Shops at Rivercenter H2
Spanish Governor's Palace G2
Southwest School of Art G1
The Espee H2
Tobin Center for the Performing Arts H1
Tower of the Americas H2

Figures after entries indicate page number and grid reference.

Bonita C2
Chula Vista B3
Coronado A2
El Cajon C1
Imperial Beach B3
Lakeside C1
La Mesa C2
Lemon Grove C2
National City B2
San Diego C2
Santee C1
Spring Valley C2
Sunnyside C2
Tijuana, MX C3

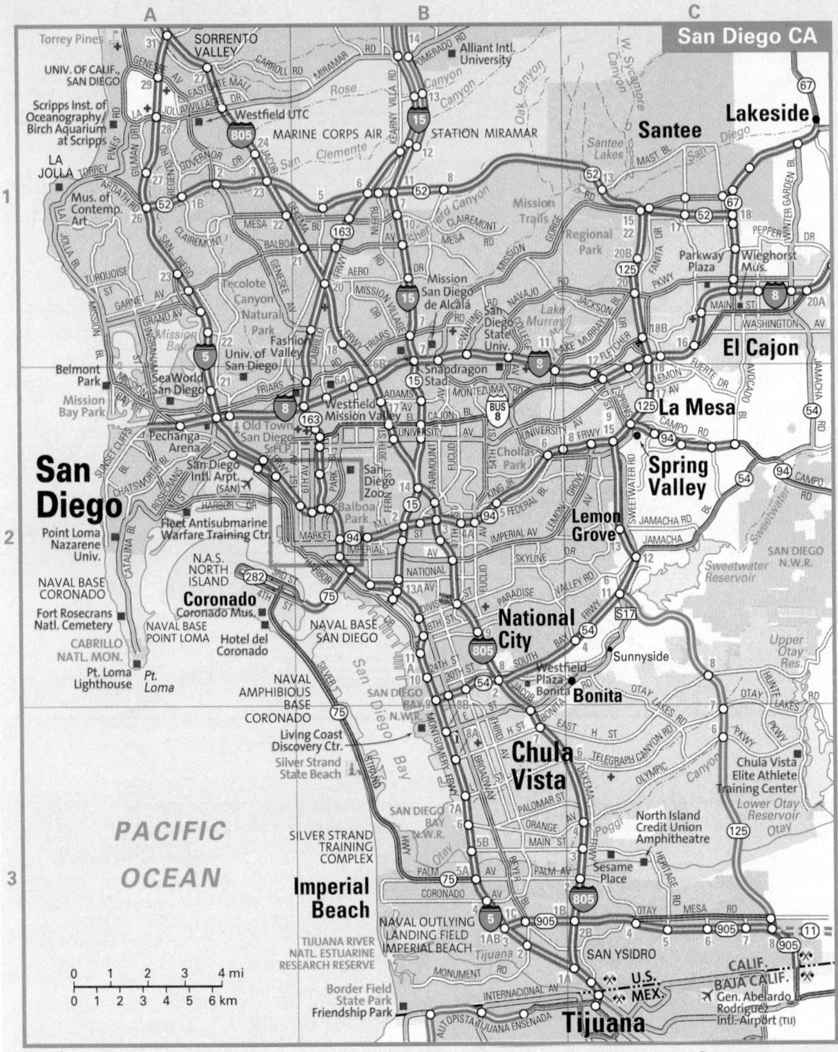
San Diego CA
Lakeside
Santee
El Cajon
La Mesa
Spring Valley
Lemon Grove
San Diego
Coronado
National City
Bonita
Sunnyside
Chula Vista
Imperial Beach
Tijuana
PACIFIC OCEAN
MARINE CORPS AIR STATION MIRAMAR
SAN YSIDRO
U.S.
MEX.
CALIF.
BAJA CALIF.

POINTS OF INTEREST

Automotive Museum E1
Balboa Park E1
Balboa Stadium E1
Casa del Prado E1
Civic Center D2
Comic-Con Museum E1
Copley Symphony Hall E2
County Court House D2
Cruise Ship Terminal D2
Fleet Science Center E1
Gaslamp Mus. at the Davis-Horton House E2
House of Hospitality E1
Maritime Museum D2
Museum of Contemporary Art, San Diego D2
Museum of Us E1
The New Children's Museum D2
The Old Globe Theatre E1
Petco Park E2
San Diego Air & Space Museum E1
San Diego Convention Center D2
San Diego International Airport D1
San Diego Museum of Art E1
San Diego Natural History Museum E1
San Diego Zoo E1
Santa Fe Depot D2
Seaport Village D2
Spanish Village Art Center E1
Spreckels Organ Pavilion E1
Spreckels Theatre D2
Starlight Bowl E1
Timken Museum of Art E1
U.S. Court House D2
USS Midway Museum D2
Veterans Museum & Memorial Center E1
Waterfront Park D1

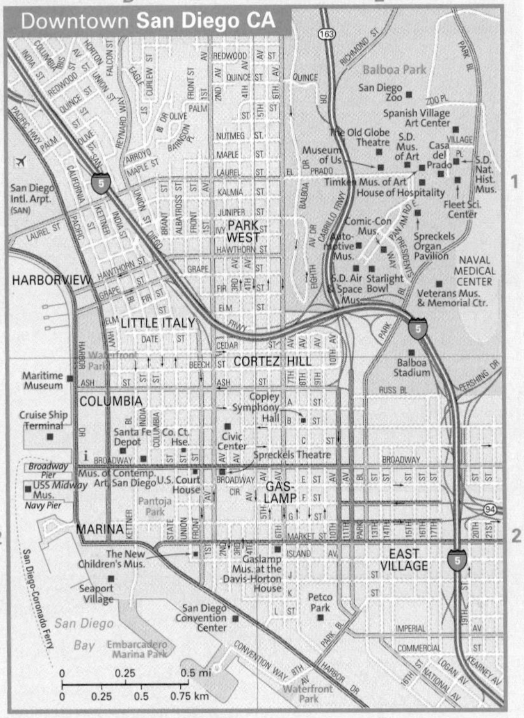
Downtown San Diego CA
Balboa Park
San Diego Zoo
LITTLE ITALY
CORTEZ HILL
COLUMBIA
HARBORVIEW
PARK WEST
MARINA
GASLAMP
EAST VILLAGE
San Diego Bay

Ste. Genevieve MO 98 B4
Ste. Genevieve Co. MO 98 A4
St. Elmo IL 98 C2
St. Francis KS 42 B1
St. Francis MN 67 D3
St. Francis SD 34 C1
St. Francis WI 234 D3
St. Francis Co. AR 118 A2
St. Francisville IL 99 D3
St. Francisville LA 134 A1
St. Francois Co. MO 98 A4
St. Gabriel LA 134 A2
St. George KS 43 F2
St. George ME 82 C3
St. George MO 256 B3
St. George SC 130 C1
St. George UT 46 C1
St. Hedwig TX 61 D3
St. Helen MI 76 A1
St. Helena CA 36 B3
St. Helena Par. LA 134 A1
St. Helens OR 20 C1
St. Henry OH 90 A4
St. Ignace MI 70 C2
St. Ignatius MT 15 D3
St. Jacob IL 98 B3
St. James MD 144 A1
St. James MN 72 B1
St. James MO 97 F4
St. James NY 149 D3
St. James NC 123 E4
St. James City FL 142 C1
St. James Par. LA 134 A3
St. Jo TX 59 E1
St. John IN 89 D2
St. John KS 43 D3
St. John MO 256 B1
St. John ND 18 C1
St. John WA 13 F3
St. Johns AZ 48 A4
St. Johns MI 76 A3
St. Johnsbury VT 81 E2
St. Johnsbury Ctr. VT 81 E2
St. Johns Co. FL 139 D3
St. Johnsville NY 79 F3
St. John the Baptist Par. LA 134 B2
St. Joseph IL 89 D4
St. Joseph LA 126 A3
St. Joseph MI 89 E1
St. Joseph MN 66 C3
St. Joseph MO 96 B1
St. Joseph TN 119 E2
St. Joseph Co. IN 89 F2
St. Joseph Co. MI 89 F1
St. Landry Par. LA 133 F1
St. Lawrence PA 146 B2
St. Lawrence SD 27 D3
St. Lawrence Co. NY 79 F1
St. Leo FL 140 C2
St. Libory IL 98 B4
St. Louis MI 76 A2
St. Louis MO 98 A3
St. Louis Co. MN 64 C3
St. Louis Co. MO 98 A3
St. Louis Park MN 235 B2
St. Lucie FL 141 E3
St. Lucie Co. FL 141 E3
St. Maries ID 14 B3
St. Martin Par. LA 133 F2
St. Martins MO 97 E3
St. Martinville LA 133 F2
St. Mary Par. LA 134 A3
St. Mary's AK 154 B2
St. Marys GA 139 D1
St. Marys KS 43 F2
St. Marys OH 90 B4
St. Marys PA 92 B2
St. Marys WV 101 F2
St. Mary's City MD 103 F4
St. Mary's Co. MD 103 E3
St. Matthews KY 230 E1
St. Matthews SC 122 B4
St. Meinrad IN 99 E4
St. Michael MN 66 C3
St. Michaels AZ 48 A2
St. Michaels MD 145 D3
St. Nazianz WI 74 C1
St. Paris OH 90 B4
St. Paul AK 154 A3
St. Paul IN 100 A2
St. Paul KS 106 B1
St. Paul MN 67 D4
St. Paul MO 98 A3
St. Paul NE 35 D3
St. Paul OR 20 B2
St. Paul TX 59 F2
St. Paul TX 61 E4
St. Paul VA 111 E2
St. Paul Park MN 235 E4
St. Pauls NC 123 D2
St. Pete Beach FL 140 B3
St. Peter MN 72 C1
St. Peters MO 98 A3
St. Petersburg FL 140 B3
St. Regis MT 14 C3
St. Regis Falls NY 80 C1
St. Regis Park KY 230 F2
St. Robert MO 107 E1
St. Rose LA 134 B3
St. Simons Island GA 139 D1
St. Stephen MN 66 C2
St. Stephen SC 131 D1
St. Stephens NC 111 F4
St. Tammany Par. LA 134 B2
St. Thomas ND 19 E2
Saks AL 120 A4
Salado TX 61 E1
Salamanca NY 92 B1
Sale Creek TN 120 B1
Salem AR 107 F3
Salem AR 117 E2
Salem IL 98 C3
Salem IN 99 F3
Salem KY 109 D2
Salem MA 151 D1
Salem MO 107 F1
Salem NH 95 E1
Salem NJ 145 E1
Salem NM 56 B2
Salem NY 81 D4
Salem NC 111 F4
Salem OH 91 F3
Salem OR 20 B2
Salem SD 27 E4
Salem UT 39 E1
Salem VA 112 B2
Salem WV 102 A2
Salem Co. NJ 145 F1
Salem Lakes WI 74 C4
Salesville AR 107 E3
Salida CA 36 C4
Salida CO 41 D3
Salina KS 43 E2
Salina OK 106 B3
Salina UT 39 E2
Salinas CA 44 B3
Saline MI 90 B1
Saline Co. AR 117 D2
Saline Co. IL 98 C4
Saline Co. KS 43 E2
Saline Co. MO 97 D2
Saline Co. NE 35 E4
Salineville OH 91 F3
Salisbury CT 94 B2
Salisbury MD 114 C1
Salisbury MA 151 F1
Salisbury MO 97 D2
Salisbury NC 112 A4
Salisbury PA 102 B1
Salisbury Beach MA 151 F1
Salix PA 92 B4
Sallisaw OK 116 B1
Salmon ID 23 D2
Salome AZ 54 A1
Salsbury Cove ME 83 D2
Saltillo MS 119 D3
Salt Lake City UT 31 E4
Salt Lake Co. UT 31 E4
Salt Lick KY 100 C4
Salton City CA 53 E3
Saltsburg PA 92 A4
Salt Sprs. FL 139 D4
Saltville VA 111 F2
Saluda NC 121 E1
Saluda SC 121 F3
Saluda VA 113 F1
Saluda Co. SC 121 F3
Salunga PA 225 A1
Salyersville KY 111 D1
Sammamish WA 12 C3
Samoset FL 266 B4
Sampit SC 131 E1
Sampson Co. NC 123 D1
Samson AL 136 C1
Samsula FL 139 E4
San Andreas CA 36 C3
San Angelo TX 58 B4
San Anselmo CA 259 A1
San Antonio FL 140 C2
San Antonio TX 61 D3
San Antonio Hts. CA 229 G2
San Ardo CA 44 B3
Sanatoga PA 146 B2
Sanatorium MS 126 B3
San Augustine TX 124 C4
San Augustine Co. TX 124 C4

SAN FRANCISCO BAY MAP INDEX

Alameda C3
Alamo D2
Albany C2
Antioch E1
Ashland D3
Atherton C5
Bay Pt. D1
Belmont C5
Belvedere B2
Benicia C1
Berkeley C2
Brisbane B3
Broadmoor B3
Burlingame B4
Campbell E6
Canyon C2
Castro Valley D3
Clayton E2
Clyde D1
Colma B3
Concord D1
Corte Madera A2
Crockett C1
Cupertino D6
Daly City B3
Danville D2
Diablo D2
Dublin E3
E. Palo Alto C5
El Cerrito B2
El Granada B5
El Sobrante C1
Emeryville C2
Fairfax A1
Foster City C4
Fremont D5
Greenbrae A2
Half Moon Bay B5
Hayward D4
Hercules C1
Hillsborough B4
Homestead Valley A2
Ignacio A1
Kensington C2
Kentfield A2
Ladera C5
Lafayette D2
La Honda C6
Larkspur A2
Livermore E3
Los Altos D6
Los Altos Hills C6
Marinwood A1
Martinez D1
Menlo Park C5
Millbrae B4
Mill Valley A2
Milpitas E5
Montara A4
Moraga D2
Moss Beach A5
Mtn. View D5
Muir Beach A2
Newark D5
N. Fair Oaks C5
N. Richmond B2
Novato A1
Oakland C3
Orinda C2
Pacheco D1
Pacifica A4
Palo Alto D5
Pescadero B6
Piedmont C2
Pinole C1
Pittsburg E1
Pleasant Hill D2
Pleasanton E4
Port Costa C1
Portola Valley C6
Redwood City C5
Richmond B2
Rodeo C1
Ross A1
San Anselmo A1
San Bruno B4
San Carlos C5
San Francisco A3
San Gregorio B6
San Jose E6
San Leandro C3
San Lorenzo D4
San Mateo B4
San Pablo B1
San Quentin A2
San Rafael B1
San Ramon D3
Santa Clara D6
Santa Venetia A1
Saratoga D6
Sausalito B2
S. San Francisco B4
Stinson Beach A2
Sunnyvale D6
Sunol E4
Tamalpais Valley A2
Tara Hills B1
Tiburon B2
Union City D4
Vallejo C1
Vine Hill D1
Walnut Creek D2
Woodacre A1
Woodside C5

Entries in **bold black** indicate counties or parishes.
Entries in **bold color** indicate cities with detailed inset maps.

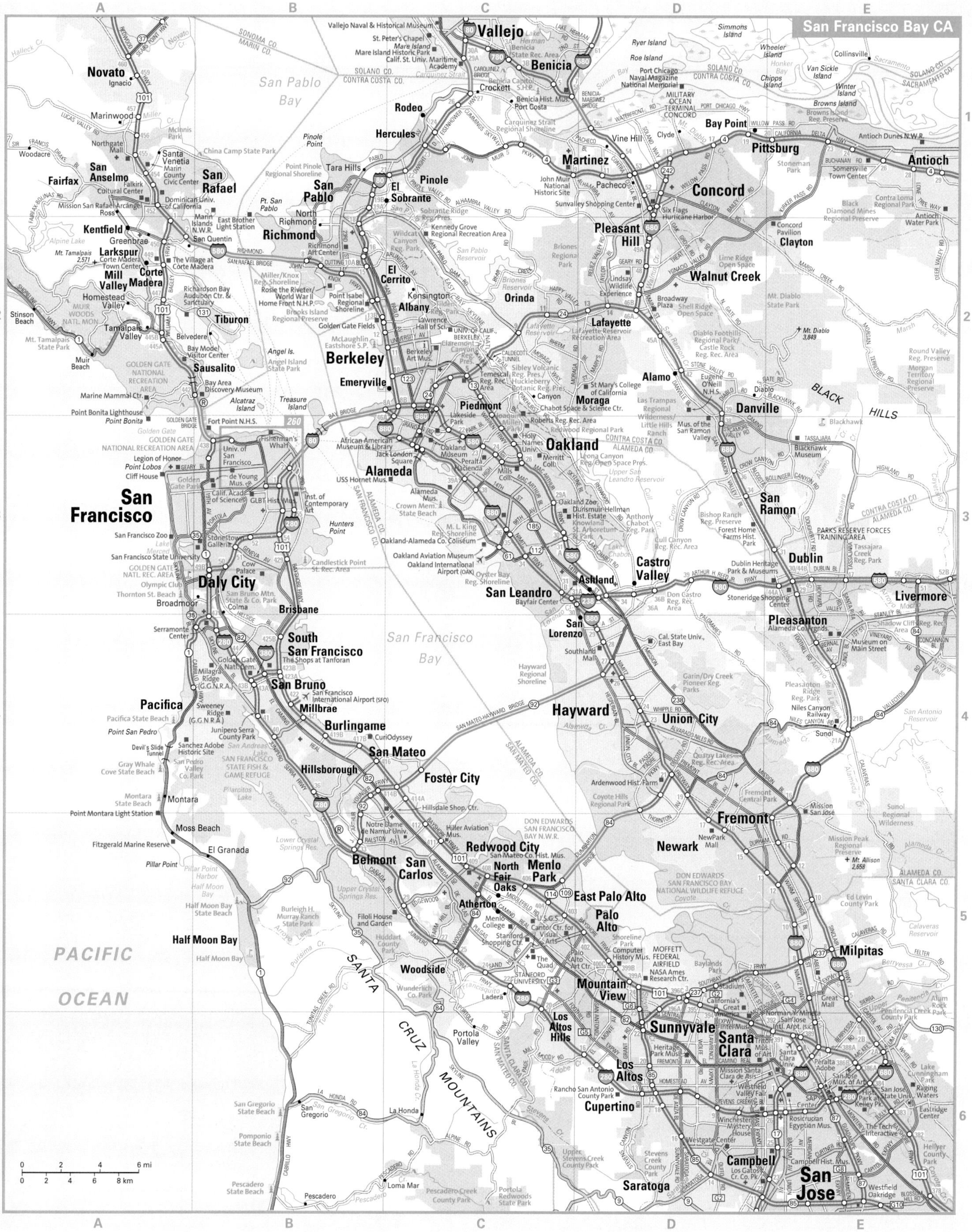

Figures after entries indicate page number and grid reference.

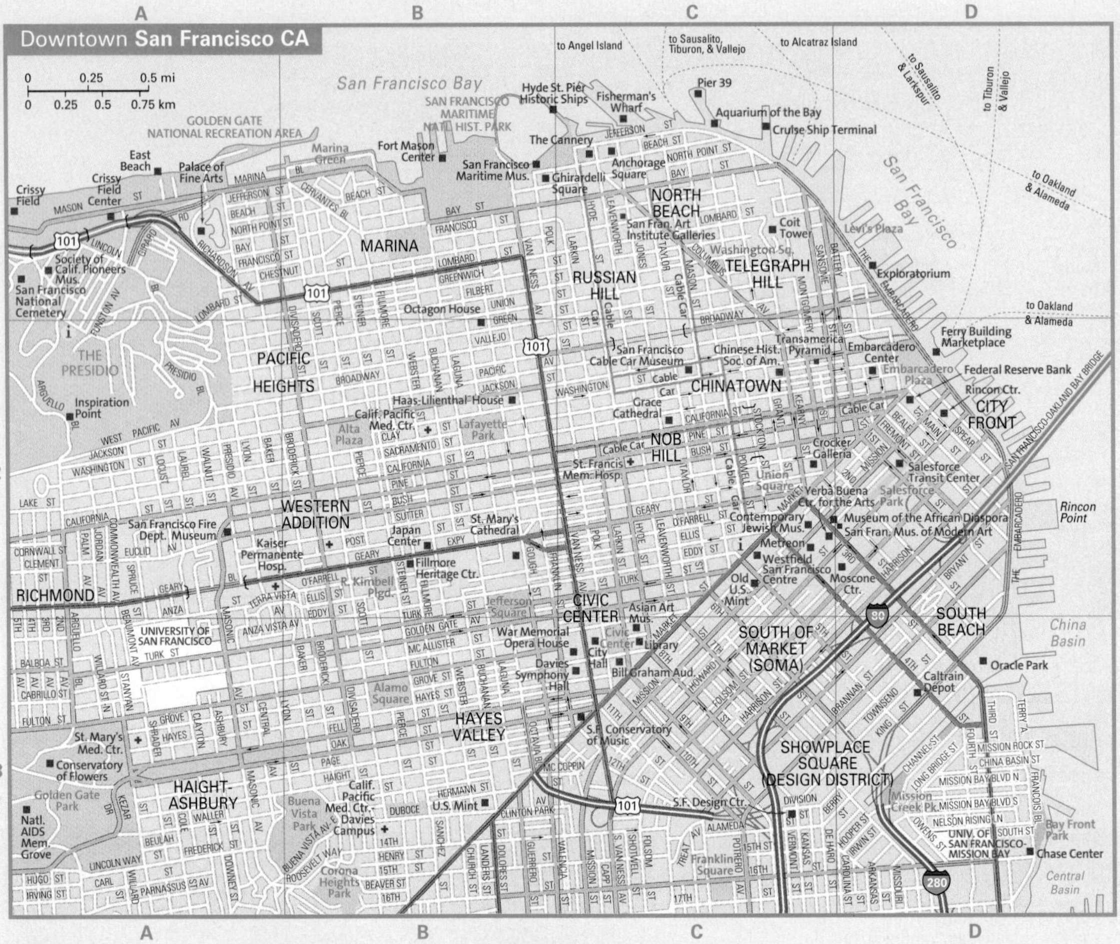

POINTS OF INTEREST
Anchorage Square C1
Aquarium of the Bay. C1
Asian Art Museum C3
Bill Graham Auditorium C3
Caltrain Depot D3
The Cannery. C1
Chase Center. D3
Chinese Historical Society of America. C2
City Hall. C3
Coit Tower C1
Conservatory of Flowers A3
Contemporary Jewish Mus. C2
Crissy Field. A1
Crissy Field Center A1
Crocker Galleria C2
Cruise Ship Terminal C1
Davies Symphony Hall C3
East Beach. A1
Embarcadero Center D2
Exploratorium. D1
Federal Reserve Bank D2
Fillmore Heritage Center B2
Ferry Building Marketplace D2
Fisherman's Wharf C1
Fort Mason Center B1
Ghirardelli Square. B1
Golden Gate Natl. Rec. Area. . . . A1
Golden Gate Park A3
Grace Cathedral C2
Haas-Lilienthal House B2
Hyde Street Pier Historic Ships . C1
Inspiration Point A2
Japan Center. B2
Levi's Plaza D1
Library. C3
Metreon C2
Moscone Center D2
Museum of the African Diaspora. D2
National AIDS Memorial Grove . A3
Octagon House B2
Old U.S. Mint C2
Oracle Park D3
Palace of Fine Arts. A1
Pier 39. . . . . C1
The Presidio. A2
Rincon Center D2
St. Mary's Cathedral. B2
San Francisco Art Institute Galleries. C1
San Francisco Cable Car Mus. . . C2
San Francisco Cons. of Music . . . C3
San Francisco Design Center. . . C3
San Francisco Fire Dept. Mus. . . A2
San Francisco Maritime Mus. . . . B1
San Francisco Maritime Natl. Hist. Park B1
San Francisco Museum of Modern Art D2
San Francisco Natl. Cemetery . . A1
Soc. of Calif. Pioneers Mus. A1
Transamerica Pyramid. C2
Transbay Transit Center D2
U.S. Mint. B3
Univ. of San Francisco. A3
Univ. of San Francisco-Mission Bay. D3
Walt Disney Family Mus. A1
War Memorial Opera House. . . . C3
Westfield San Francisco Centre. C2
Yerba Buena Center for the Arts C2

San Benito TX 63 F4
San Benito Co. CA 44 B3
San Bernardino CA 53 D2
San Bernardino Co. CA 45 F4
Sanborn IA 72 A3
Sanborn Co. SD 27 E3
Sanbornville NH 81 F3
San Bruno CA 36 B4
San Carlos AZ 55 D2
San Carlos CA 259 C5
San Carlos Park FL 142 C1
San Clemente CA 52 C3
Sanders Co. MT 14 C3
Sanderson TX 62 C3
Sandersville GA 129 E1
Sandersville MS 126 C3
Sand Hills MA 151 E2
Sandia Park NM 48 C3
San Diego CA 53 D4
San Diego TX 63 E2
San Diego Co. CA 53 E4
San Dimas CA 229 F2
Sand Lake MI 75 F3
Sandoval IL 98 C3
Sandoval Co. NM 48 C2
Sandown NH 95 E1
Sand Pt. AK 154 B4
Sandpoint ID 14 B2
Sand Ridge NY 79 D3
Sand Rock AL 120 A3
Sands Pt. NY 241 G2
Sand Sprs. OK 51 F2
Sand Sprs. TX 58 B3
Sandston VA 113 E1
Sandstone MN 67 D2
Sandusky MI 76 C2
Sandusky OH 91 D2
Sandusky Co. OH 90 C2
Sandwich IL 88 C2
Sandwich MA 151 E3
Sandy OR 20 C2
Sandy PA 92 B3
Sandy UT 31 E4
Sandy Creek NY 79 E2
Sandy Hook KY 101 D4
Sandy Lake PA 92 A2
Sandy Sprs. GA 120 C4
Sandy Sprs. SC 121 E2
Sandy Valley NV 46 A2
Sandyville MD 144 B1
San Elizario TX 56 C4
San Felipe TX 61 F2
San Felipe Pueblo NM 48 C3
San Fernando CA 52 C2
Sanford CO 41 D4
Sanford FL 141 D1
Sanford ME 82 A4
Sanford MI 76 A2
Sanford NC 122 C1
San Francisco CA 36 B4
San Francisco Co. CA 36 B4
San Gabriel CA 228 D2
Sangamon Co. IL 98 B1
Sanger CA 45 D3
Sanger TX 59 E1
Sangerville ME 82 C1
Sanibel FL 142 C1

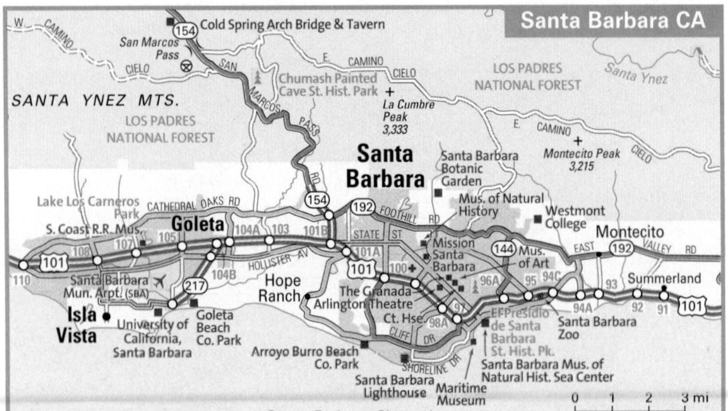

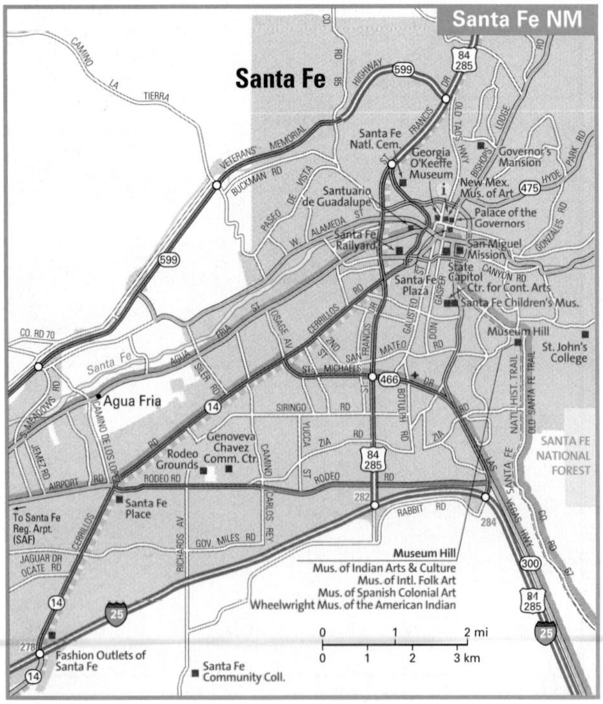

Entries in **bold black** indicate counties or parishes.
Entries in **bold color** indicate cities with detailed inset maps.

Sanilac Co. MI 76 C2
San Jacinto CA 53 D3
San Jacinto Co. TX 132 B1
San Joaquin CA 44 C3
San Joaquin Co. CA 36 C3
San Jon NM 49 F3
San Jose CA 36 B4
San Jose IL 88 B4
San Juan Bautista CA 44 B2
San Juan Capistrano CA 52 C3
San Juan Co. CO 40 C4
San Juan Co. NM 48 B1
San Juan Co. UT 39 F4
San Juan Co. WA 12 C2
Sankertown PA 92 B4
San Leandro CA 36 B4
San Lorenzo CA 259 D4
San Lucas CA 44 B3
San Luis AZ 53 F4
San Luis CO 41 D4
San Luis Obispo CA 44 C4
San Luis Obispo Co. CA 44 C4
San Manuel AZ 55 D2
San Marcos CA 53 D4
San Marcos TX 61 E2
San Marino CA 228 D2
San Martin CA 44 B2
San Mateo CA 36 B4
San Mateo FL 139 D3
San Mateo Co. CA 36 B4
San Miguel CA 44 C4
San Miguel NM 56 C3
San Miguel Co. CO 40 B3
San Miguel Co. NM 49 E3
Sanostee NM 48 A1
San Pablo CA 259 B1
San Patricio Co. TX 61 E4
San Perlita TX 63 F3
Sanpete Co. UT 39 E2
San Rafael CA 36 B3
San Ramon CA 36 B4
San Remo NY 149 D3
San Saba TX 59 D4
San Saba Co. TX 59 D4
Sansom Park TX 207 A2
Sans Souci SC 217 A2
Santa Ana CA 52 C3
Santa Ana Pueblo NM 48 C3
Santa Anna TX 58 C4
Santa Barbara CA 52 B2
Santa Barbara Co. CA 52 B1
Santa Clara CA 259 D6
Santa Clara NM 55 F2
Santa Clara OR 20 B3
Santa Clara UT 46 C1
Santa Clara Co. CA 36 C4
Santa Clarita CA 52 C2
Santa Claus IN 99 E4
Santa Cruz CA 44 A2
Santa Cruz NM 49 D2
Santa Cruz Co. AZ 55 D4
Santa Cruz Co. CA 44 A2
Santa Fe NM 49 D2
Santa Fe TX 132 B4
Santa Fe Co. NM 49 D3
Santa Fe Sprs. CA 228 E3
Santa Margarita CA 44 C4
Santa Maria CA 52 A1
Santa Maria TX 63 F4
Santa Monica CA 52 C2
Santa Nella CA 44 B2
Santa Paula CA 52 B2
Santaquin UT 39 E1
Santa Rosa AZ 54 C3
Santa Rosa CA 36 B3
Santa Rosa NM 49 E3
Santa Rosa TX 63 F4
Santa Rosa Co. FL 135 F1
Santa Teresa NM 56 C3
Santa Venetia CA 259 A1
Santa Ynez CA 52 A2
Santee CA 53 D4
Santee SC 122 B4
Santo Domingo Pueblo NM 48 C3
San Ysidro NM 48 C3
Sappington MO 256 B3
Sapulpa OK 51 F2
Saraland AL 135 E1
Saranac MI 75 F3
Saranac Lake NY 80 C2
Sarasota FL 140 B3
Sarasota Co. FL 140 C4
Saratoga CA 36 B4
Saratoga WY 33 D3
Saratoga Co. NY 80 C4
Saratoga Sprs. NY 80 C4
Sarcoxie MO 106 C2
Sardinia OH 100 C2
Sardis GA 130 B1
Sardis MS 118 B3
Sardis TN 119 D1
Sardis City AL 120 A3
Sarepta LA 125 D1
Sargent GA 120 B4
Sargent NE 35 D3
Sargent Co. ND 27 E1
Sarita TX 63 F3
Sarpy Co. NE 35 F3
Sartell MN 66 C2
Satanta KS 42 B4
Satellite Beach FL 141 E2
Satsop WA 12 B4
Satsuma AL 135 E1
Satsuma FL 139 D3
Satus WA 21 E1
Saucier MS 135 D2
Saugatuck MI 75 E4
Saugerties NY 94 B2
Saugus MA 151 D1
Sauk Centre MN 66 B2
Sauk City WI 74 A3
Sauk Co. WI 74 A3
Sauk Rapids MN 66 C2
Saukville WI 74 C2
Sault Ste. Marie MI 70 C1
Saunders Co. NE 35 F3
Saunderstown RI 150 C4
Sauquoit NY 79 E3
Sausalito CA 259 B2
Savage MD 144 C2
Savage MN 67 D4
Savanna IL 88 A1
Savanna OK 116 A2
Savannah GA 130 B3
Savannah MO 96 B1
Savannah TN 119 D1
Savona NY 78 C4
Savoonga AK 154 A2
Savoy IL 88 C4
Savoy TX 59 F1
Sawgrass FL 222 E4
Sawmill AZ 48 A2
Sawmills NC 111 F4
Sawyer ND 18 B2
Sawyer Co. WI 67 F2
Saxapahaw NC 112 C4
Saxis VA 103 F4
Saxon SC 217 C1
Saxonburg PA 92 A3
Saxton PA 92 C4
Saxtons River VT 81 E4
Saybrook IL 88 C4
Saybrook OH 91 F1
Saybrook Manor CT 149 E2
Saylorsburg PA 93 F3
Saylorville IA 86 C2
Sayre OK 50 C3
Sayre PA 93 E1
Sayreville NJ 147 E1
Sayville NY 149 D4
Scammon KS 106 B2
Scammon Bay AK 154 B2
Scandia KS 43 E1
Scanlon MN 64 C4
Scappoose OR 20 B1
Scarborough ME 82 B3
Scarbro WV 101 F4
Scarsdale NY 148 B3
Schaefferstown PA 146 A2
Schaghticoke NY 94 B1
Schaller IA 72 A4
Schaumburg IL 203 B3
Schenectady NY 94 B1
Schenectady Co. NY 94 B1
Schererville IN 89 D2
Schertz TX 257 F1
Schiller Park IL 203 C3
Schleicher Co. TX 60 B1
Schleswig IA 86 A1
Schley Co. GA 128 C3
Schnecksville PA 146 B1
Schofield WI 68 B4
Schoharie NY 94 A1
Schoharie Co. NY 79 F4
Schoolcraft MI 89 F1
Schoolcraft Co. MI 69 E1
Schram City IL 98 B2
Schriever LA 134 A3
Schroon Lake NY 80 C3
Schulenburg TX 61 F2
Schulter OK 51 F3
Schurz NV 37 E2
Schuyler NE 35 F3
Schuyler Co. IL 88 A4
Schuyler Co. MO 87 E4
Schuyler Co. NY 79 D4
Schuyler Falls NY 81 D1
Schuylerville NY 81 D4
Schuylkill Co. PA 146 A1
Schuylkill Haven PA 146 A1
Schwenksville PA 146 B2
Science Hill KY 110 B2
Scio OH 91 F4
Scio OR 20 B3
Scioto Co. OH 101 D3
Scipio UT 39 E2
Scituate MA 151 E2
Scobey MT 17 E1
Scooba MS 127 D2
Scotch Plains NJ 148 A4
Scotchtown NY 148 A1
Scotia CA 28 A4
Scotia NY 94 B1
Scotland MA 151 D2
Scotland PA 103 D1
Scotland SD 35 E1
Scotland Co. MO 87 E4
Scotland Co. NC 122 C2
Scotland Neck NC 113 E4
Scott LA 133 F2
Scott City KS 42 B3
Scott City MO 108 B2
Scott Co. AR 116 C2
Scott Co. IL 98 A1
Scott Co. IN 100 A3
Scott Co. IA 88 A2
Scott Co. KS 42 B3
Scott Co. KY 100 B4
Scott Co. MN 66 C4
Scott Co. MS 126 C2
Scott Co. MO 108 B2
Scott Co. TN 110 C3
Scott Co. VA 111 E2
Scottdale GA 190 E3
Scottdale PA 92 A4
Scott Depot WV 101 E3
Scottsbluff NE 33 F2
Scotts Bluff Co. NE 33 F2
Scottsboro AL 120 A2
Scottsburg IN 100 A3
Scottsdale AZ 54 C1
Scotts Hill TN 119 D1
Scotts Mills OR 20 C2
Scottsmoor FL 141 E1
Scotts Valley CA 44 A2
Scottsville KY 109 F2
Scottsville NY 78 C3
Scottsville VA 113 D1
Scottville MI 75 E1
Scranton IA 86 B1
Scranton KS 96 A3
Scranton ND 26 A1
Scranton PA 93 F2
Scranton SC 122 C4
Scraper OK 106 B4
Screven GA 129 F4
Screven Co. GA 130 B2
Scribner NE 35 F3
Scurry Co. TX 58 B2
Seaboard NC 113 E3
Sea Breeze NC 123 E3
Sea Bright NJ 147 F2
Seabrook MD 271 F2
Seabrook NH 95 E1
Seabrook NJ 145 F1
Seabrook TX 132 B3
Seabrook Island SC 131 D2
Sea Cliff NY 148 C3
Seadrift TX 61 F4
Seaford DE 145 E4

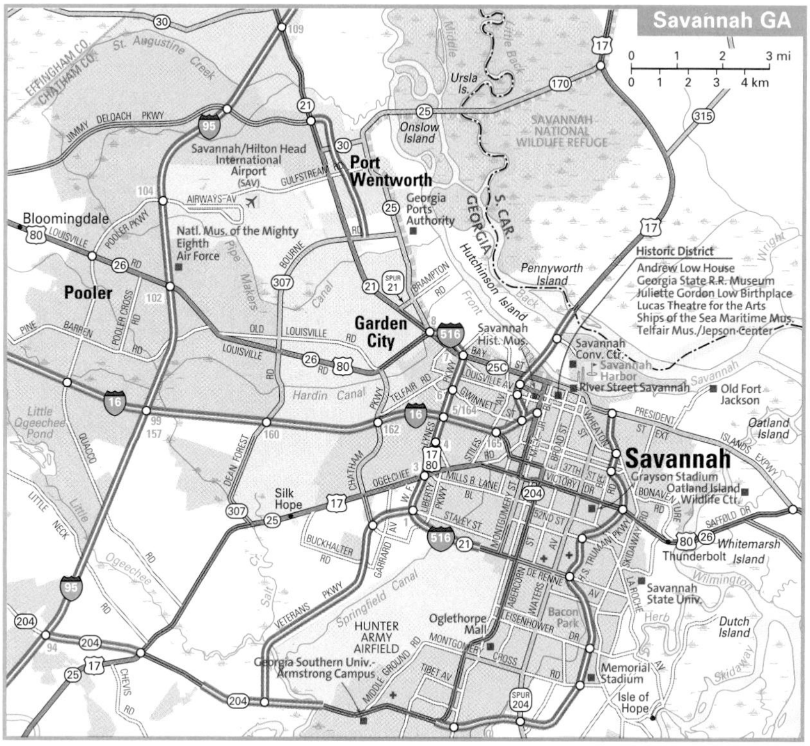
Savannah GA
Savannah
Pooler
Bloomingdale
Port Wentworth
Garden City
Savannah/Hilton Head International Airport (SAV)
Georgia Ports Authority
Natl. Mus. of the Mighty Eighth Air Force
Historic District
Andrew Low House
Georgia State R.R. Museum
Juliette Gordon Low Birthplace
Lucas Theatre for the Arts
Ships of the Sea Maritime Mus.
Telfair Mus./Jepson Center
Savannah Hist. Mus.
Savannah Conv. Ctr.
River Street Savannah
Old Fort Jackson
Oatland Island
Grayson Stadium
Oatland Island Wildlife Ctr.
Whitemarsh Island
Thunderbolt
Savannah State Univ.
Oglethorpe Mall
Hunter Army Airfield
Georgia Southern Univ.-Armstrong Campus
Memorial Stadium
Isle of Hope
Dutch Island
Silk Hope
Savannah National Wildlife Refuge
Onslow Island
Pennyworth Island
Hutchinson Island
Little Ogeechee Pond
0 1 2 3 mi
0 1 2 3 4 km

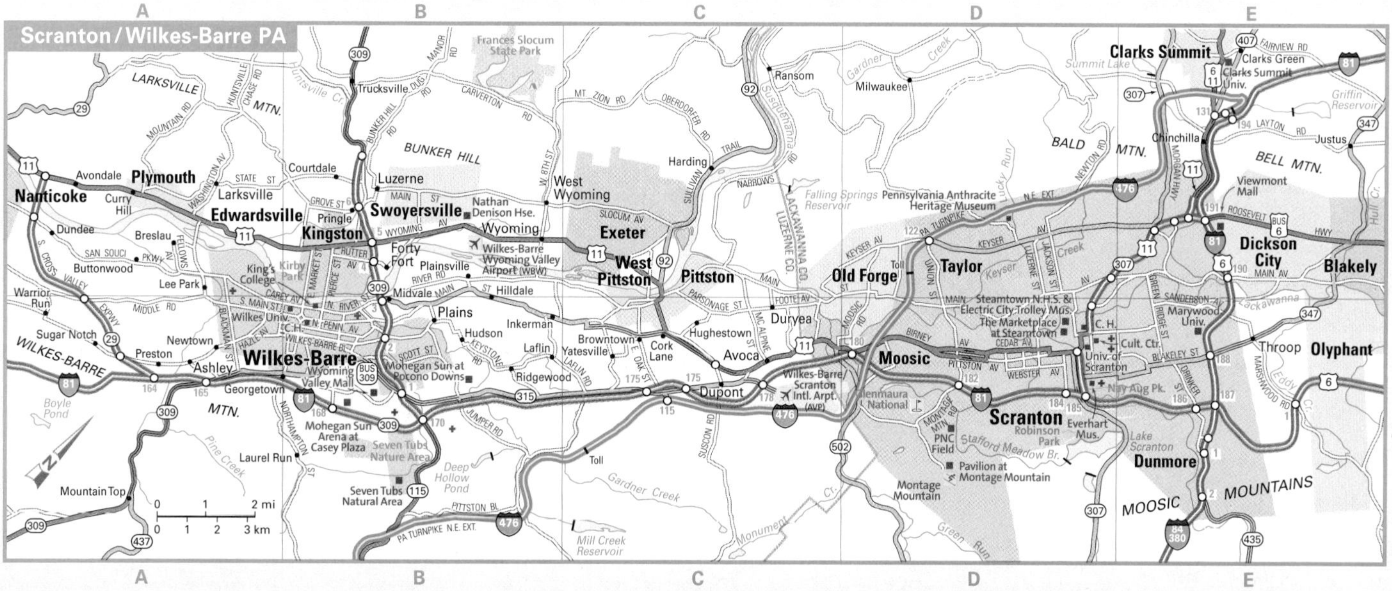
Scranton / Wilkes-Barre PA
Scranton
Wilkes-Barre
Clarks Summit
Clarks Green
Dickson City
Blakely
Olyphant
Throop
Dunmore
Taylor
Old Forge
Moosic
Pittston
West Pittston
Exeter
West Wyoming
Wyoming
Swoyersville
Kingston
Edwardsville
Plymouth
Nanticoke
Larksville
Luzerne
Forty Fort
Courtdale
Avoca
Dupont
Duryea
Hughestown
Laflin
Yatesville
Plains
Hudson
Georgetown
Ashley
Sugar Notch
Preston
Laurel Run
Mountain Top
Wilkes-Barre/Scranton Intl. Arpt. (AVP)
Wilkes-Barre Wyoming Valley Airport (WBW)
Mohegan Sun Arena at Casey Plaza
Mohegan Sun at Pocono Downs
Steamtown N.H.S. & Electric City Trolley Mus.
Pennsylvania Anthracite Heritage Museum
Montage Mountain
Seven Tubs Natural Area
Frances Slocum State Park
0 1 2 mi
0 1 2 3 km

Ashley A2
Avoca C2
Avondale A1
Blakely E1
Breslau A1
Browntown C2
Buttonwood A1
Chinchilla E1
Clarks Green E1
Clarks Summit E1
Cork Lane C2
Courtdale B1
Curry Hill A1
Dickson City E1
Dundee A1
Dunmore E2
Dupont C2
Duryea C2
Edwardsville A1
Exeter C1
Forty Fort B1
Georgetown A2
Harding C1
Hilldale B1
Hudson B2
Hughestown C2
Inkerman B2
Justus E1
Kingston B1
Laflin B2
Larksville A1
Laurel Run B2
Lee Park A1
Luzerne B1
Midvale B1
Milwaukee D1
Moosic D2
Mtn. Top A2
Nanticoke A1
Newtown A2
Old Forge D1
Olyphant E2
Pittston C1
Plains B2
Plainsville B1
Plymouth A1
Preston A2
Pringle B1
Ransom C1
Ridgewood B2
Scranton D2
Sugar Notch A2
Swoyersville B1
Taylor D1
Throop E2
Trucksville B1
Warrior Run A2
W. Pittston C1
W. Wyoming B1
Wilkes-Barre B2
Wyoming B1
Yatesville C2

Figures after entries indicate page number and grid reference.

Seaford VA 113 F2
Seagate NC 123 E3
Sea Girt NJ 147 F2
Seagoville TX 59 F2
Seagraves TX 57 F2
Sea Isle City NJ 105 D4
Seal Beach CA 228 D4
Sealy TX 61 F2
Seaman OH 100 C3
Sea Ranch Lakes FL 233 C2
Searchlight NV 46 B3
Searcy AR 117 F1
Searcy Co. AR 107 E4
Searingtown NY 241 G3
Searsport ME 83 D2
Seaside CA 44 B3
Seaside OR 20 B1
Seaside Hts. NJ 147 E3
Seaside Park NJ 147 E3
SeaTac WA 12 C3
Seat Pleasant MD 271 F3
Seattle WA 12 C3
Sebago Lake ME 82 B3
Sebastian FL 141 E3
Sebastian TX 63 F4
Sebastian Co. AR 116 C1
Sebastopol CA 36 B3
Sebeka MN 64 A4
Sebewaing MI 76 B2
Sebree KY 109 E1
Sebring FL 141 D3
Sebring OH 91 F3
Secaucus NJ 240 C3
Second Mesa AZ 47 F2
Secretary MD 145 D4
Section AL 120 A2
Security CO 41 E2
Sedalia MO 97 D3
Sedalia NC 112 B4
Sedan KS 43 F4
Sedgefield NC 112 B4
Sedgwick KS 43 E3
Sedgwick Co. CO 34 A4
Sedgwick Co. KS 43 E4
Sedley VA 113 F2
Sedona AZ 47 D3
Sedro-Woolley WA 12 C2
Seeley CA 53 E4
Seeley Lake MT 15 D3
Seelyville IN 99 E2
Seffner FL 266 D2
Seguin TX 61 E2
Seiling OK 51 D2
Seisholtzville PA 146 B1
Selah WA 13 D4
Selawik AK 154 B2
Selby SD 26 C2
Selbyville DE 114 C1
Selden NY 149 D3
Selfridge ND 26 C1
Seligman AZ 46 C3
Seligman MO 106 C3
Selinsgrove PA 93 D3
Selkirk NY 94 B1
Sellersburg IN 100 A3
Sellersville PA 146 C2
Sells AZ 54 C3
Selma AL 127 F2
Selma CA 45 D3
Selma IN 90 A4
Selma NC 123 E1
Selma TX 257 F1
Selma VA 112 B1
Selmer TN 119 D1
Selmont AL 127 F2
Seminole FL 140 B2
Seminole OK 51 F3
Seminole TX 57 F2
Seminole Co. FL 141 D1
Seminole Co. GA 137 D1
Seminole Co. OK 51 F3
Senath MO 108 B4
Senatobia MS 118 B2
Seneca IL 88 C2
Seneca KS 43 F1
Seneca MO 106 B2
Seneca PA 92 A2
Seneca SC 121 E2
Seneca Co. NY 79 D4
Seneca Co. OH 90 C3
Seneca Falls NY 79 D3
Seneca Gardens KY 230 E2
Senoia GA 128 C1
Sentinel OK 51 D3
Sequatchie Co. TN 120 B1
Sequim WA 12 B2
Sequoyah Co. OK 116 B1
Sergeant Bluff IA 35 F2
Sergeantsville NJ 147 D1
Sesser IL 98 C4
Setauket NY 149 D3
Seth Ward TX 50 A4
Seven Corners VA 270 B4
Seven Fields PA 92 A3
Seven Hills OH 204 F3
Seven Lakes NC 122 C1
Seven Mile OH 100 B2
Seven Pts. TX 59 F3
Severance CO 33 E4
Severn MD 144 C2
Severna Park MD 144 C2

Alderwood Manor B2
Algona B5
Arletta A5
Auburn B4
Bainbridge Island A3
Bay View A1
Beaux Arts B3
Bellevue B3
Bethel A4
Bonney Lake B5
Bothell B2
Bremerton A3
Brier B2
Brownsville A3
Burien B4
Burley A4
Burton A4
Cathcart B2
Clinton B1
Clyde Hill B3
Colby A3
Covington B4
Des Moines B4
Dockton A4
Edgewood B5
Edmonds B2
Ellisport A4
Everett B1
Federal Way B4
Fife B5
Fircrest A5
Fox Island A5
Freeland A1
Gig Harbor A4
Glendale B1
Hansville A1
Hunts Pt. B3
Indianola A2
Kenmore B2
Kent B4
Keyport A2
Kingston A2
Kirkland B2
Lake Forest Park B2
Lake Stevens B1
Lakewood A5
Langley A1
Lofall A2
Lynnwood B2
Maltby B2
Manchester A3
Martha Lake B2
Marysville B1
Maxwelton A1
McMillan B5
Medina B3
Mercer Island B3
Midland A5
Mill Creek B2
Milton B5
Mountlake Terrace B2
Mukilteo B1
Newcastle B3
Normandy Park B4
Olalla A4
Pacific B5
Parkland A5
Portage A4
Port Gamble A2
Port Orchard A3
Poulsbo A2
Purdy A4
Puyallup B5
Redmond B3
Redondo B4
Renton B4
Retsil A3
Rollingbay A3
Rosedale A4
Ruston A5
SeaTac B4
Seattle B2
Shine A2
Shoreline B2
Skyway B4
Snohomish B1
S. Colby A3
S. Hill B5
S. Prairie B5
Southworth A3
Steilacoom A5
Summit B5
Sumner B5
Suquamish A2
Tacoma A5
Tahlequah A4
Tracyton A3
Tukwila B4
Tulalip B1
University Place A5
Vashon A4
Vashon Hts. A3
Wauna A4
White Ctr. B4
Wollochet A5
Woodinville B2
Woodway A2
Yarrow Pt. B3

Seattle / Tacoma WA
A
B
1
2
3
4
5
Marysville
Lake Stevens
Everett
Snohomish
Mukilteo
Lynnwood
Edmonds
Mill Creek
Martha Lake
Mountlake Terrace
Bothell
Kenmore
Woodinville
Shoreline
Seattle
Kirkland
Redmond
Bellevue
Mercer Island
Newcastle
Renton
White Center
Burien
Tukwila
SeaTac
Normandy Park
Kent
Des Moines
Covington
Federal Way
Auburn
Tacoma
Pacific
Milton
Fircrest
University Place
Edgewood
Sumner
Steilacoom
Midland
Summit
Puyallup
Bonney Lake
Lakewood
Parkland
South Hill
Poulsbo
Bainbridge Island
Bremerton
Port Orchard
Gig Harbor
Puget Sound
Elliott Bay
0 2 4 mi
0 2 4 6 km

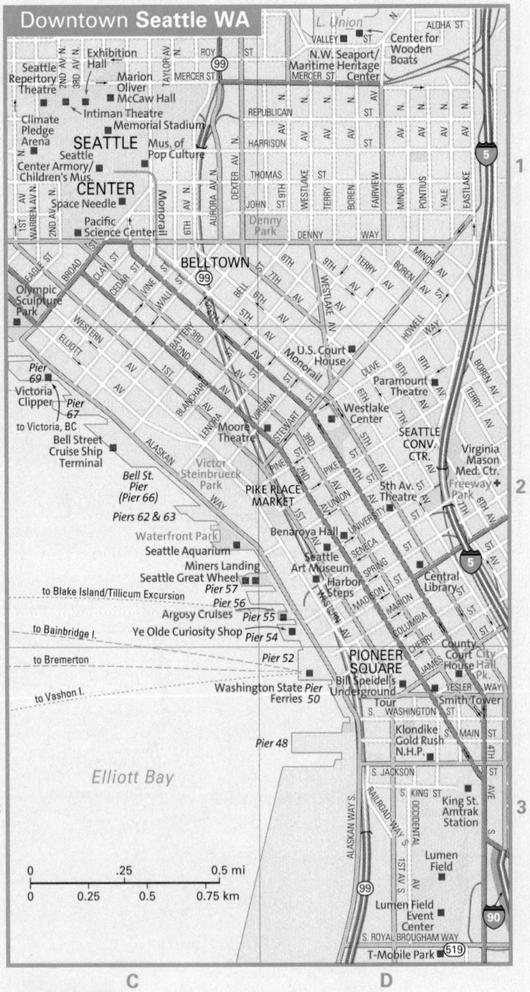
Downtown Seattle WA
C
D
1
2
3
SEATTLE CENTER
Space Needle
Pacific Science Center
BELLTOWN
PIKE PLACE MARKET
PIONEER SQUARE
Elliott Bay
Seattle Aquarium
Seattle Great Wheel
Olympic Sculpture Park
Washington State Ferries
Smith Tower
King St. Amtrak Station
Lumen Field
T-Mobile Park
0 .25 0.5 mi
0 0.25 0.5 0.75 km

POINTS OF INTEREST

5th Avenue Theatre D2
Argosy Cruises D2
Bell Street Cruise Ship Terminal C2
Benaroya Hall D2
Bill Speidel's Underground Tour D3
Center for Wooden Boats D1
Central Library D2
Climate Pledge Arena C1
Exhibition Hall C1
Harbor Steps D2
King Street Amtrak Station D3
Klondike Gold Rush Natl. Hist. Park D3
Lumen Field D3
Lumen Field Events Center D3
Marion Oliver McCaw Hall C1
Memorial Stadium C1
Miners Landing C2
Monorail C1, D2
Moore Theatre D2
Museum of Pop Culture C1
Northwest Seaport/ Maritime Heritage Center D1
Olympic Sculpture Park C1
Pacific Science Center C1
Paramount Theatre D2
Pike Place Market D2
The Seattle Aquarium C2
Seattle Art Museum D2
Seattle Center C1
Seattle Center Armory/Childrens Museum C1
Seattle Convention Center D2
Seattle Great Wheel C2
Seattle Repertory Theatre C1
Smith Tower D3
Space Needle C1
T-Mobile Park D3
Victoria Clipper C2
Washington State Ferries D3
Westlake Center D2
Ye Old Curiosity Shop D2

Entries in **bold black** indicate counties or parishes.
Entries in **bold color** indicate cities with detailed inset maps.

Sevier Co. AR 116 C3
Sevier Co. TN 111 D4
Sevier Co. UT 39 E2
Sevierville TN 111 D4
Seville OH 91 E3
Sewanee TN 120 A1
Seward AK 154 C3
Seward NE 35 F4
Seward Co. KS 42 B4
Seward Co. NE 35 E4
Sewaren NJ 240 A6
Sewell NJ 146 C4
Sewickley PA 92 A4
Seymour CT 149 D2
Seymour IN 99 F2
Seymour IA 87 D3
Seymour MO 107 D2
Seymour TN 110 C4
Seymour TX 58 C1
Seymour WI 68 C4
Seymourville LA 134 A2
Shabbona IL 88 C1
Shackelford Co. TX 58 C2
Shadeland IN 89 E4
Shady Cove OR 28 B1
Shady Pt. OK 116 B1
Shady Rest CT 148 C1
Shady Side MD 144 C3
Shadyside OH 101 F1
Shady Spr. WV 111 F1
Shafter CA 45 D4
Shaker Hts. OH 91 E2
Shakopee MN 66 C4
Shalimar FL 136 B2
Shallotte NC 123 D4
Shallowater TX 58 A1
Shamokin PA 93 E3
Shamokin Dam PA 93 D3
Shamrock TX 50 C3
Shandon CA 44 C4
Shannock RI 150 C4
Shannon GA 120 B3
Shannon IL 88 B1
Shannon MS 119 D3
Shannon Co. MO 107 F2
Shannon Hills AR 117 E2
Shannontown SC 122 B4
Sharkey Co. MS 126 A2
Sharon CT 94 B2
Sharon MA 151 D2
Sharon PA 91 F2
Sharon SC 122 A2
Sharon TN 108 C3
Sharon WI 74 C4
Sharon Hill PA 248 B4
Sharon Sprs. KS 42 B2
Sharon Sprs. NY 79 F4
Sharonville OH 100 B2
Sharp Co. AR 107 F4
Sharpes FL 141 E1
Sharpsburg MD 144 A1
Sharpsburg NC 113 E4
Sharpsburg PA 250 C1
Sharpsville IN 89 F4
Sharpsville PA 91 F2
Sharptown MD 145 E4
Shasta Co. CA 28 C3
Shasta Lake CA 28 C4
Shattuck OK 50 C2
Shavano Park TX 257 E1
Shaver Lake CA 45 D2
Shaw MS 118 A4
Shawanee TN 111 D3
Shawano WI 68 C4
Shawano Co. WI 68 C4
Shawnee KS 96 B2
Shawnee OH 101 E1
Shawnee OK 51 F3
Shawnee Co. KS 96 A2
Shawneetown IL 109 D1
Shawsville VA 112 B2
Sheboygan WI 75 D2
Sheboygan Co. WI 74 C2
Sheboygan Falls WI 75 D2
Sheep Sprs. NM 48 A2
Sheffield AL 119 E2
Sheffield IL 88 B2
Sheffield IA 73 D3
Sheffield MA 94 B2
Sheffield PA 92 B2
Sheffield Lake OH 91 D2
Shelbiana KY 111 E1
Shelbina MO 97 E1
Shelburn IN 99 E2
Shelburne VT 81 D2
Shelburne Falls MA 94 C1
Shelby IA 86 A2
Shelby MI 75 E2
Shelby MS 118 A4
Shelby MT 15 E2
Shelby NE 35 E3
Shelby NC 121 F1
Shelby OH 91 D3
Shelby Co. AL 127 F1
Shelby Co. IL 98 C2
Shelby Co. IN 99 F1
Shelby Co. IA 86 A1
Shelby Co. KY 100 A4
Shelby Co. MO 97 E1
Shelby Co. OH 90 B4
Shelby Co. TN 118 B1
Shelby Co. TX 124 C3
Shelbyville IL 98 C2
Shelbyville IN 99 F1
Shelbyville KY 100 A4
Shelbyville MO 97 E1
Shelbyville TN 119 F1
Sheldon IL 89 D3
Sheldon IA 35 F1
Sheldon MO 106 C1
Sheldon TX 220 D2
Shelley ID 23 E4
Shell Knob MO 106 C3
Shell Lake WI 67 E2
Shellman GA 128 C4
Shell Pt. SC 130 C2
Shell Rock IA 73 D4
Shellsburg IA 87 E1
Shelly PA 146 C1
Shelter Island NY 149 E3
Shelter Island Hts. NY 149 E3
Shelton CT 149 D2
Shelton NE 35 D4
Shelton WA 12 B3
Shenandoah IA 86 A3
Shenandoah PA 93 E3
Shenandoah TX 132 A2
Shenandoah VA 102 C3
Shenandoah Co. VA 102 C3
Shepherd MI 76 A2
Shepherd TX 132 B2
Shepherdstown WV 103 D2
Shepherdsville KY 100 A4
Sherando VA 102 C4
Sherborn MA 150 C1
Sherburn MN 72 B2
Sherburne NY 79 E4
Sherburne Co. MN 66 C3
Sheridan AR 117 E3
Sheridan CA 36 C2
Sheridan CO 209 B4
Sheridan IL 88 C2
Sheridan IN 89 F4
Sheridan MI 76 A3
Sheridan MT 23 E2
Sheridan OR 20 B2
Sheridan WY 25 D3
Sheridan Co. KS 42 C1
Sheridan Co. MT 17 E1
Sheridan Co. NE 34 A2
Sheridan Co. ND 18 C3
Sheridan Co. WY 25 D2
Sherman IL 98 B1
Sherman MS 118 C3
Sherman NY 92 A1
Sherman TX 59 F1
Sherman Co. KS 42 B2
Sherman Co. NE 35 D3
Sherman Co. OR 21 D2
Sherman Co. TX 50 A2
Sherrard IL 88 A2
Sherrill NY 79 E3
Sherrills Ford NC 112 A4
Sherwood ND 18 B1
Sherwood OH 90 B2
Sherwood OR 20 B2
Sherwood WI 74 C1
Sherwood Manor CT 150 A2
Sheyenne ND 19 D3
Shiawassee Co. MI 76 B4
Shickshinny PA 93 E3
Shidler OK 51 F1
Shields MI 76 B2
Shillington PA 146 A2
Shiloh NJ 145 F1
Shiloh OH 91 D3
Shiloh OH 208 D1
Shiloh PA 275 E1
Shiner TX 61 E3
Shinglehouse PA 92 C1
Shingle Sprs. CA 36 C3
Shingletown CA 28 C4
Shinnecock Hills NY 149 E3
Shinnston WV 102 A2
Shiocton WI 74 C1
Ship Bottom NJ 147 E4
Shipman IL 98 B2
Shippensburg PA 103 D1
Shiprock NM 48 A1
Shipshewana IN 89 F2
Shiremanstown PA 218 A2
Shirley IN 100 A1
Shirley MA 95 D1
Shirley NY 149 D4
Shishmaref AK 154 B2
Shively KY 99 F4
Shoals IN 99 E3
Shoemakersville PA 146 A1
Shokan NY 94 A2
Shongopovi AZ 47 E2
Shonto AZ 47 E1
Shore Acres NJ 147 E3
Shoreacres TX 132 B3
Shoreham MI 89 E1
Shoreham Beach MD 144 C3
Shoreline WA 12 C3
Shoreview MN 235 C1
Shorewood IL 88 C2
Shorewood MN 66 C4
Shorewood WI 234 D2
Shorewood Hills WI 231 A2
Short Beach CT 149 D2
Shortsville NY 78 C3
Shoshone ID 30 C1
Shoshone Co. ID 14 B3
Shoshoni WY 32 C1
Show Low AZ 47 F4
Shreve OH 91 D3
Shreveport LA 124 C2
Shrewsbury MA 150 C1
Shrewsbury MO 256 B3
Shrewsbury NJ 147 E2
Shrewsbury PA 103 E1
Shrub Oak NY 148 B2
Shubuta MS 127 D3
Shullsburg WI 74 A4
Shuqualak MS 127 D1
Sibley IA 72 A2
Sibley LA 125 D2
Sibley Co. MN 66 C4
Sicily Island LA 125 F3
Sicklerville NJ 147 D4
Sidell IL 99 D1
Sidman PA 92 B4
Sidney IL 99 D1
Sidney IA 86 A3
Sidney MT 17 F3
Sidney NE 34 A3
Sidney NY 79 E4
Sidney OH 90 B4
Sidon MS 126 B1
Sierra Blanca TX 57 D4
Sierra Co. CA 37 D1
Sierra Co. NM 56 B2
Sierra Madre CA 228 E2
Sierra Vista AZ 55 E4
Siesta Key FL 140 B4
Signal Hill CA 228 D4
Signal Mtn. TN 120 B1
Sigourney IA 87 E2
Sigurd UT 39 E2
Sikeston MO 108 B2
Silas AL 127 D3
Siler City NC 112 C4
Siletz OR 20 B3
Silica OH 90 C2
Siloam Sprs. AR 106 B3
Silsbee TX 132 C2
Silt CO 40 C1
Silters NY 94 B1
Silver Bay MN 65 D3
Silver Bow Co. MT 23 E1
Silver City NM 55 F2
Silver City NC 122 C2
Silver Cliff CO 41 D3
Silver Creek MO 106 B2
Silver Creek NE 35 E3
Silver Creek NY 78 A4
Silverdale PA 146 C2
Silverdale WA 12 C3
Silver Grove KY 100 B2
Silverhill AL 135 E2
Silver Hill MD 270 E4
Silver Lake IN 89 F3
Silver Lake KS 96 A2
Silver Lake MA 151 E2
Silver Lake MN 66 C4
Silver Lake NC 123 E3
Silver Lake OH 188 B1
Silver Ridge NJ 147 E3
Silver Spr. MD 144 B3
Silver Sprs. FL 139 D4
Silver Sprs. NV 37 E2
Silver Sprs. NY 78 B4
Silver Sprs. Shores FL 139 D4
Silverthorne CO 41 D1
Silverton CO 40 C4
Silverton NJ 147 E3
Silverton OH 204 B2
Silverton OR 20 C2
Silverton TX 50 B4
Silvis IL 208 C2
Simi Valley CA 52 B2
Simla CO 41 F2
Simmesport LA 133 F1
Simms MT 15 E3
Simonton TX 61 F2
Simpson LA 125 D4
Simpson Co. KY 109 F2
Simpson Co. MS 126 B3
Simpsonville KY 100 A4
Simpsonville MD 144 B2
Simpsonville SC 121 F2
Simsboro LA 125 E2
Simsbury CT 94 C3
Sinclair WY 32 C2
Sinclairville NY 78 A4
Sinking Spr. PA 146 A2
Sinton TX 61 E4
Sioux Ctr. IA 35 F1
Sioux City IA 35 F1
Sioux Co. IA 35 F1
Sioux Co. NE 33 F1
Sioux Co. ND 26 B1
Sioux Falls SD 27 F4
Sioux Rapids IA 72 A3
Sippewisset MA 151 E4
Sipsey AL 119 F4
Siren WI 67 E2
Siskiyou Co. CA 28 C3
Sisseton SD 27 F1
Sissonville WV 101 E3
Sister Bay WI 69 D3
Sister Lakes MI 89 F1
Sisters OR 21 D3
Sistersville WV 101 F1
Sitka AK 155 D4
Six Mile SC 121 E2
Skagit Co. WA 12 C2
Skagway AK 155 D3
Skamania Co. WA 12 C4
Skaneateles NY 79 D3
Skellytown TX 50 B3
Skiatook OK 51 F1
Skidaway Island GA 130 C3
Skidmore TX 61 E4
Skidway Lake MI 76 B1
Skippack PA 146 C2
Skokie IL 89 D1
Skowhegan ME 82 C1
Sky Lake FL 246 C3
Skyline AL 120 A2
Skyway WA 262 B4
Slater IA 86 C1
Slater MO 97 D2
Slater SC 121 E2
Slatersville RI 150 C2
Slatington PA 93 F3
Slaton TX 58 A1
Slaughter LA 134 A1
Slaughter Beach DE 145 F3
Slaughterville OK 51 E3
Slayton MN 72 A1
Sledge MS 118 B3
Sleepy Eye MN 72 B1
Sleepy Hollow IL 203 A2
Sleepy Hollow NY 148 B3
Slidell LA 134 C2
Sligo PA 92 A3
Slinger WI 74 C3
Slingerlands NY 188 D3
Slippery Rock PA 92 A3
Sloan IA 35 F2
Sloan NY 198 C3
Sloatsburg NY 148 B2
Slocomb AL 136 C1

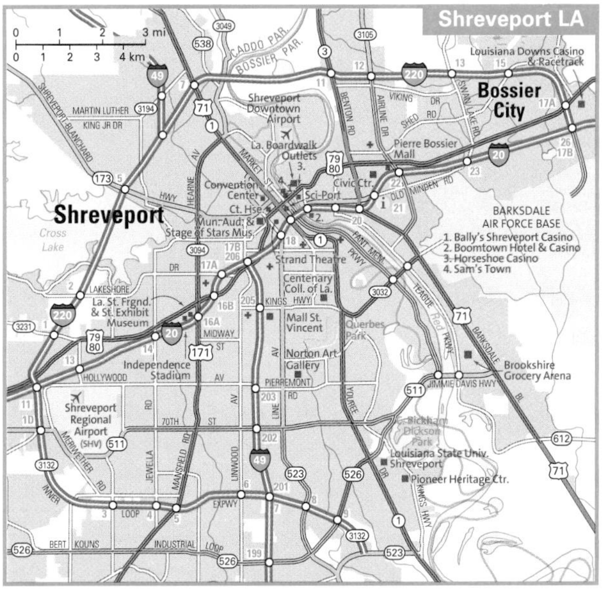

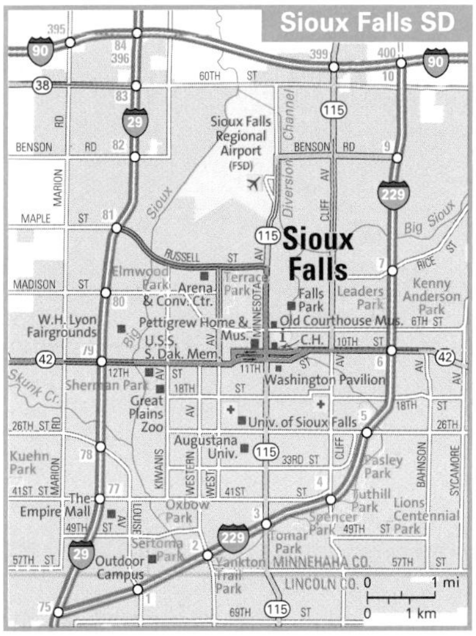

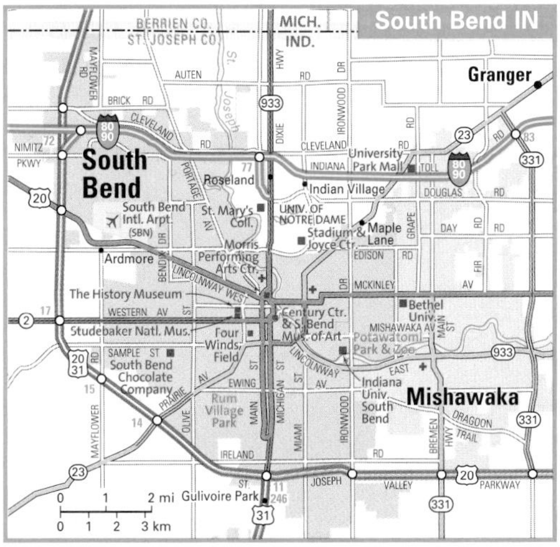

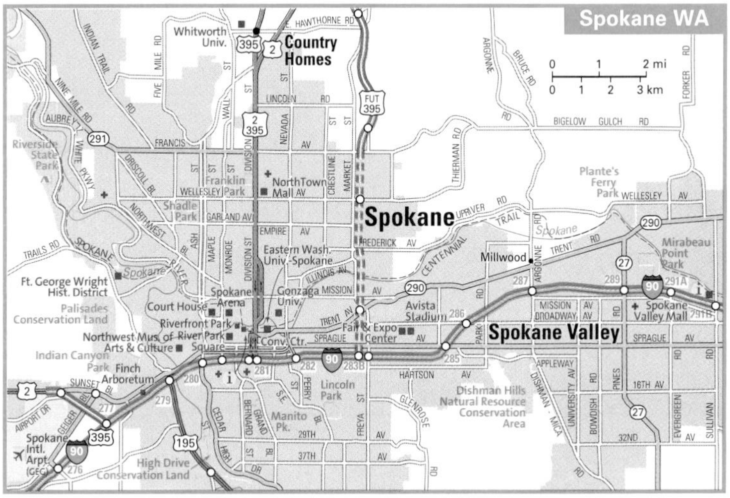

Figures after entries indicate page number and grid reference.

Slocum RI 150 C4
Slope Co. ND 18 A4
Smackover AR 125 E1
Smallwood MD 144 B1
Smallwood NY 94 A3
Smelterville ID 14 B3
Smethport PA 92 C1
Smith Ctr. KS 43 D1
Smith Co. KS 43 D1
Smith Co. MS 126 C3
Smith Co. TN 110 A3
Smith Co. TX 124 B2
Smithers WV 101 F4
Smithfield NC 123 E1
Smithfield OH 91 F4
Smithfield PA 102 B1
Smithfield UT 31 E2
Smithfield VA 113 F2
Smithland KY 109 D2
Smith River CA 28 A2
Smithsburg MD 144 A1
Smiths Grove KY 109 F2
Smiths Sta. AL 128 C2
Smithton IL 98 B3
Smithton MO 97 D3
Smithtown NY 149 D3
Smith Valley NV 37 D2
Smithville GA 129 D3
Smithville IN 99 F2
Smithville MS 119 D3
Smithville MO 96 B2
Smithville NJ 147 E4
Smithville OH 91 E3
Smithville PA 146 A3
Smithville TN 110 A4
Smithville TX 61 E2
Smyrna DE 145 E2
Smyrna GA 120 C4
Smyrna TN 109 F4
Smyth Co. VA 111 F2
Snead AL 119 F3
Sneads FL 137 D1
Sneads Ferry NC 115 D4
Sneedville TN 111 D3
Snellville GA 120 C4
Snohomish WA 12 C2
Snohomish Co. WA 12 C2
Snook TX 61 F1
Snoqualmie WA 12 C3
Snowflake AZ 47 F4
Snow Hill MD 114 C2
Snow Hill NC 115 C3
Snowmass Vil. CO 40 C2
Snow Shoe PA 92 C3
Snyder OK 51 D4
Snyder TX 58 B2
Snyder Co. PA 93 D3
Soap Lake WA 13 E3
Socastee SC 123 D4
Social Circle GA 121 D4
Society Hill SC 122 C3
Socorro NM 56 B1
Socorro TX 56 C4
Socorro Co. NM 48 C4
Soda Sprs. ID 31 F1
Sodaville OR 20 B3
Soddy-Daisy TN 120 B1
Sodus NY 78 C3
Sodus Pt. NY 79 D3
Solana FL 140 C4
Solana Beach CA 53 D4
Solano Co. CA 36 B3
Soldiers Grove WI 73 F2
Soldotna AK 154 C3
Soledad CA 44 B3
Solomon AZ 55 E2
Solomon KS 43 E2
Solomons MD 103 F4
Solon IA 87 F1
Solon OH 91 E2
Solon Sprs. WI 64 C4
Solvang CA 52 A2
Solvay NY 265 A2
Solway TN 110 C4
Somerdale NJ 146 C3
Somers CT 150 A2
Somers MT 15 D2
Somers NY 148 C2
Somers WI 74 C4
Somerset KY 110 B2
Somerset MD 270 C2
Somerset MA 151 D3
Somerset NJ 147 E1
Somerset OH 101 E1
Somerset PA 102 B1
Somerset TX 61 D3
Somerset WI 67 D3
Somerset Co. ME 82 B1
Somerset Co. MD 103 F4
Somerset Co. NJ 147 D1
Somerset Co. PA 92 B4
Somers Pt. NJ 147 F4
Somersworth NH 82 A4
Somerton AZ 53 F4
Somervell Co. TX 59 E3
Somerville MA 151 D1
Somerville NJ 147 D1
Somerville TN 118 C1
Somerville TX 61 F1
Somis CA 52 B2
Somonauk IL 88 C2
Sonoita AZ 55 D4
Sonoma CA 36 B3
Sonoma Co. CA 36 A2
Sonora CA 37 D3
Sonora KY 110 A1
Sonora TX 60 B1
Sopchoppy FL 137 E3
Soperton GA 129 F2
Sophia WV 111 F1
Soquel CA 236 D1
Sorento IL 98 B2
Sorrento LA 134 A2
Souderton PA 146 C2
Soulsbyville CA 37 D3
Sound Beach NY 149 D3
Sound View CT 149 F2
Sour Lake TX 132 C2
S. Acton MA 150 C1
S. Amboy NJ 147 E1
S. Amherst MA 150 A1
S. Amherst OH 91 D2
Southampton NY 149 E3
Southampton PA 146 C2
Southampton Co. VA 113 E3
S. Apopka FL 246 B1
Southaven MS 118 B2
S. Barrington IL 203 B2
S. Bay FL 143 E1
S. Belmar NJ 147 F2
S. Beloit IL 74 B4
S. Bend IN 89 F2
S. Bend WA 12 B4
S. Berlin MA 150 C1
S. Berwick ME 82 A4
S. Bethany DE 145 F4
S. Bloomfield OH 101 D1
Southborough MA 150 C1
S. Boston VA 112 C3
S. Bound Brook NJ 147 D1
Southbridge MA 150 B2
S. Bridgewater MA 151 D2
S. Burlington VT 81 D2
Southbury CT 149 D1
S. Cairo NY 94 B2
S. Carthage TN 110 A3
S. Casco ME 82 B3
S. Charleston OH 100 C1
S. Charleston WV 101 E4
S. Chatham MA 151 F3
S. China ME 82 C2
S. Cle Elum WA 13 D3
S. Coatesville PA 146 B3
S. Coffeyville OK 106 A2
S. Congaree SC 122 A4
S. Connellsville PA 102 B1
S. Corning NY 93 D1
S. Dartmouth MA 151 D4
S. Dayton NY 78 A4
S. Daytona FL 139 E4
S. Deerfield MA 150 A1
S. Dennis MA 151 F3
S. Dos Palos CA 44 C2
S. Dover NY 148 C1
S. Duxbury MA 151 E2
S. Easton MA 151 D2
S. Elgin IL 88 C1
S. Eliot ME 82 A4
S. El Monte CA 228 E2
Southern Pines NC 122 C1
Southern Shores NC 115 F2
S. Euclid OH 204 G1
S. Fallsburg NY 94 A3
Southfield MI 76 C4
S. Floral Park NY 241 G4
S. Fork CO 40 C4
S. Fork PA 92 B4
S. Fulton TN 108 C3
S. Gastonia NC 122 A1
S. Gate CA 228 D3
Southgate KY 204 B3
S. Gate MD 193 C5
S. Glastonbury CT 149 E1
S. Glens Falls NY 81 D4
S. Greensburg PA 92 A4
S. Hadley MA 150 A1
S. Hadley Falls MA 150 A2
S. Haven KS 51 E1
S. Haven MI 75 E4
S. Heart ND 18 A4
S. Hill NY 79 D4
S. Hill VA 113 D3
S. Hill WA 262 B5
S. Holland IL 203 E6
S. Hooksett NH 81 F4
S. Houston TX 220 C3
S. Hutchinson KS 43 E3
Southington CT 149 D1
S. Jacksonville IL 98 A1
S. Jamesport NY 149 E3
S. Jordan UT 31 E4
S. Killingly CT 150 B3
Southlake TX 207 B1
S. Lake Tahoe CA 37 D2
S. Lancaster MA 150 C1
S. Lebanon ME 81 F4
S. Lebanon OH 100 B2
S. Lockport NY 78 B3
S. Lyon MI 76 B4
Southmayd TX 59 F1
S. Miami FL 143 E2
S. Miami Hts. FL 233 A5
S. Middleboro MA 151 E3
S. Mills NC 113 F3
S. Milwaukee WI 75 D3
S. Monroe MI 90 C1
Southmont NC 112 B4
S. Naknek AK 154 B3
S. Ogden UT 244 A2
Southold NY 149 E3
S. Orange NJ 240 A3
S. Orleans MA 151 F3
S. Padre Island TX 63 F4
S. Palm Beach FL 143 F1
S. Paris ME 82 B2
S. Pasadena CA 228 D2
S. Pasadena FL 140 B3

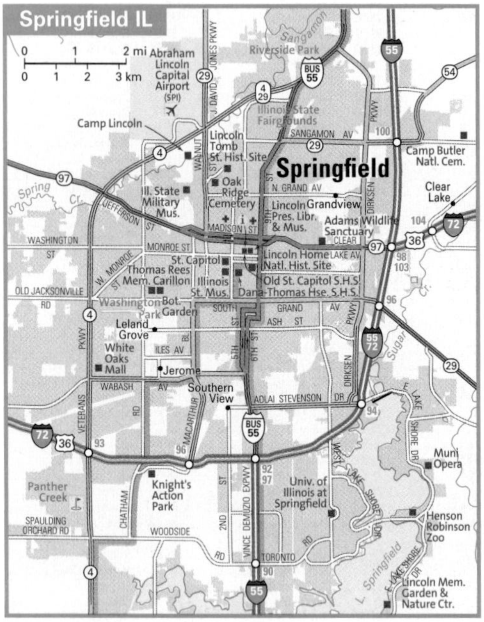

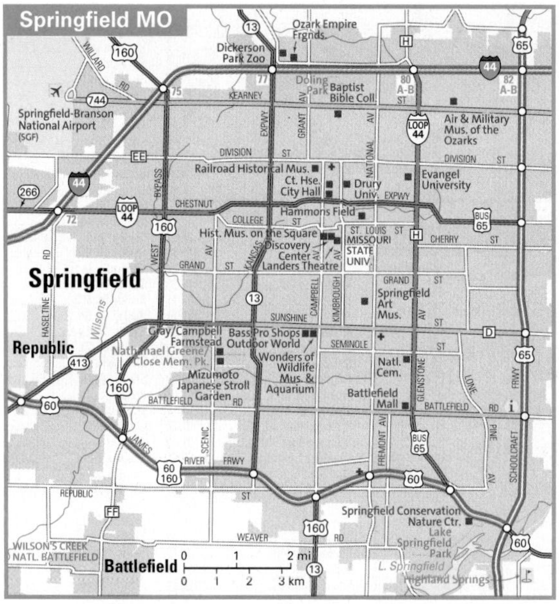

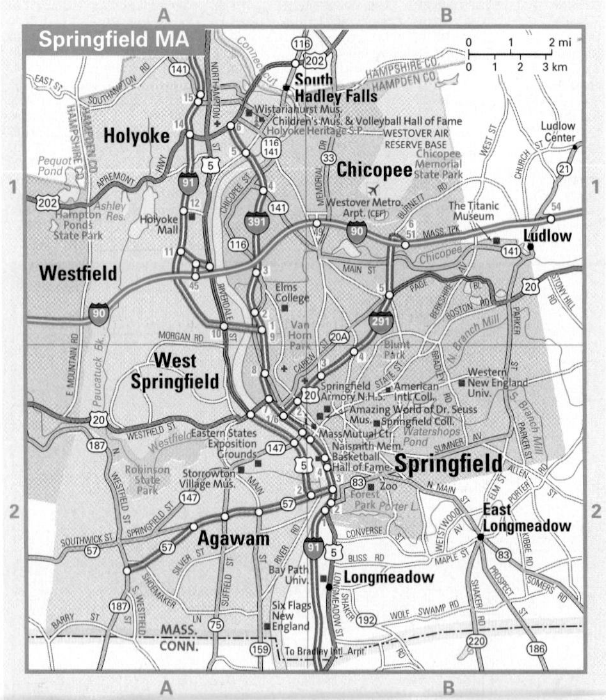

Agawam A2	Holyoke A1	Ludlow Ctr. B1	Westfield A1
Chicopee B1	Longmeadow B2	S. Hadley Falls A1	W. Springfield A2
E. Longmeadow B2	Ludlow B1	Springfield B2	

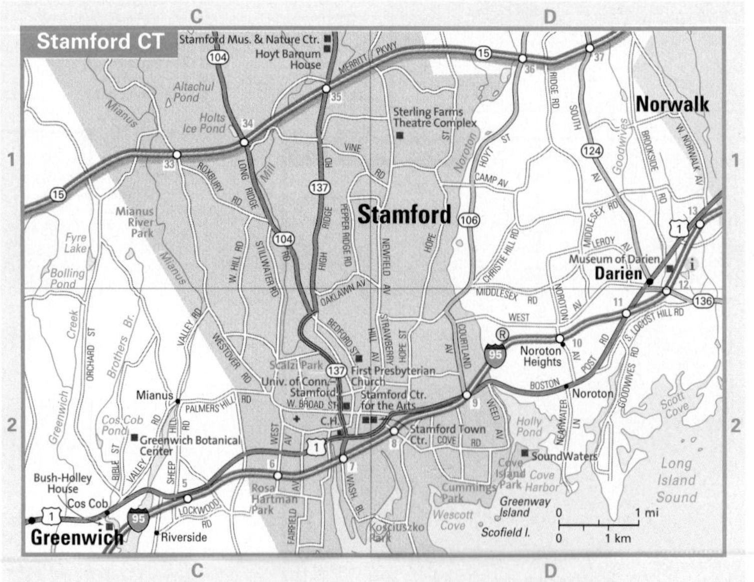

Cos Cob. C2	Greenwich C2	Noroton. D2	Norwalk D1	Stamford. D1
Darien D1	Mianus C2	Noroton Hts.. . . . . D2	Riverside. C2	

Entries in **bold black** indicate counties or parishes.
Entries in bold color indicate cities with detailed inset maps.

S. Patrick Shores FL 141 E2
S. Pekin IL 88 B4
S. Pittsburg TN 120 A2
S. Plainfield NJ 147 E1
S. Point OH 101 D3
Southport FL 136 C2
Southport IN 99 F1
Southport NY 93 D1
Southport NC 123 E4
S. Portland ME 82 B3
S. Pottstown PA 146 B2
S. Range MI 65 F3
S. River NJ 147 E1
S. Rockwood MI 90 C1
S. Roxana IL 256 D1
S. Royalton VT 81 E3
S. Russell OH 91 E2
S. St. Paul MN 235 D3
S. Salt Lake UT 257 B2
S. Sanford ME 82 B2
S. San Francisco CA 259 B4
S. San Gabriel CA 228 E2
S. Shaftsbury VT 94 C1
S. Shore KY 101 D3
S. Shore SD 27 F2
Southside AL 120 A4
Southside Place TX 220 B3
S. Sioux City NE 35 F2
S. Toms River NJ 147 E3
S. Torrington WY 33 F2
S. Tucson AZ 55 D3
S. Valley Stream NY 241 G4
S. Venice FL 140 B4
S. Wallins KY 111 D2
S. Walpole MA 151 D2
S. Waverly PA 93 E1
S. Weber UT 244 B2
S. Webster OH 101 D3
S. Weldon NC 113 E3
Southwest City MO 106 B3
Southwest Harbor ME 83 D2
S. Westport MA 151 D4
S. Weymouth MA 151 D2
S. Whitley IN 89 F3
S. Whittier CA 228 E3
Southwick MA 150 A2
S. Williamson KY 111 E1
S. Williamsport PA 93 D2
S. Willington CT 150 A3
S. Wilmington IL 88 C2
S. Windham CT 149 F1
S. Windham ME 82 B3
S. Windsor CT 150 A3
Southwood Acres CT 150 A2
S. Woodstock CT 150 B3
S. Yarmouth MA 151 F3
S. Zanesville OH 101 E1
Spalding NE 35 E3
Spalding Co. GA 128 C1
Spanaway WA 12 C3
Spanish Fork UT 39 E1
Spanish Fort AL 135 E1
Spanish Lake MO 256 C1
Sparkman AR 117 D4
Sparks GA 137 F1
Sparks MD 144 C1
Sparks NV 37 D1
Sparrow Bush NY 94 A3
Sparta GA 129 E1
Sparta IL 98 B4
Sparta MI 75 F3
Sparta MO 107 D2
Sparta NJ 148 A3
Sparta NC 112 A3
Sparta TN 110 A4
Sparta WI 73 F1
Spartanburg SC 121 F2
Spartanburg Co. SC 121 F2
Spavinaw OK 106 B3
Spearfish SD 25 F3
Spearman TX 50 B2
Spearville KS 42 C4
Speedway IN 99 F1
Speigner AL 128 A2
Spencer IN 99 E2
Spencer IA 72 A3
Spencer MA 150 B1
Spencer NE 35 D1
Spencer NY 93 E1
Spencer NC 112 A4
Spencer OH 91 D3
Spencer OK 51 E3
Spencer TN 110 A4
Spencer WV 101 F3
Spencer WI 68 A4
Spencer Co. IN 99 E4
Spencer Co. KY 100 A4
Spencerport NY 78 C3
Spencerville OH 90 B3
Speonk NY 149 E3
Sperry OK 51 F2
Spiceland IN 100 A1
Spicer MN 66 B3
Spindale NC 121 F1
Spink Co. SD 27 E2
Spinnerstown PA 146 C1
Spirit Lake ID 14 B2
Spirit Lake IA 72 B2
Spiro OK 116 B1
Splendora TX 132 B2
Spofford NH 94 C1
Spokane WA 14 A3
Spokane Co. WA 14 B2
Spokane Valley WA 14 B3
Spooner WI 67 E2
Spotswood NJ 147 E1
Spotsylvania VA 103 D4
Spotsylvania Co. VA 103 D4
Spottsville KY 99 E4
Spout Sprs. NC 123 D1
Sprague WA 13 F3
Spreckels CA 236 E3
Spring TX 132 A2
Spring Arbor MI 90 B1
Springboro OH 100 B1
Spring City PA 146 B2
Spring City TN 110 B4
Spring City UT 39 E1
Spring Creek NV 30 B4
Springdale AR 106 C4
Springdale OH 204 B1
Springdale PA 250 D1
Springdale SC 205 E2
Springdale UT 39 D4
Springer NM 49 E2
Springer OK 51 E4
Springerville AZ 48 A4
Springfield CO 42 A4
Springfield FL 136 C2
Springfield GA 130 B2
Springfield IL 98 B1
Springfield KY 110 B1
Springfield LA 134 B2
Springfield MA 150 A2
Springfield MI 75 F4
Springfield MN 72 B1
Springfield MO 107 D2
Springfield NE 35 F3
Springfield NJ 148 A4
Springfield OH 100 C1
Springfield OR 20 B4
Springfield PA 146 C3
Springfield SC 122 A4
Springfield SD 35 E1
Springfield TN 109 F3
Springfield VT 81 E4
Springfield VA 144 B3
Spring Garden Estates MD 144 A1
Spring Glen UT 39 F1
Spring Green WI 74 A3
Spring Grove IL 74 C4
Spring Grove MN 73 E2
Spring Grove PA 103 E1
Spring Hill FL 140 B1
Spring Hill KS 96 B3
Springhill LA 125 D1
Spring Hill TN 109 E4
Spring Hope NC 113 D4
Spring Lake MI 75 E3
Spring Lake NJ 147 F2
Spring Lake NC 123 D1
Spring Lake Hts. NJ 147 E2
Spring Lake Park MN 235 C1
Spring Mill KY 230 E3
Springport MI 76 A4
Springs NY 149 F3
Springtown TX 59 E2
Springvale ME 82 A4
Spring Valley CA 53 D4
Spring Valley IL 88 B2
Spring Valley KY 230 F1
Spring Valley MN 73 D2
Spring Valley NY 148 B2
Spring Valley WI 67 E4
Spring Valley Vil. TX 220 B2
Springview NE 34 C1
Springville AL 119 F4
Springville CA 45 D3
Springville IA 87 F1
Springville NJ 147 D3
Springville NY 78 B4
Springville UT 39 E1
Springwater NY 78 C4
Spruce Pine NC 111 E4
Spry PA 275 F2
Spur TX 58 B1
Squaw Valley CA 45 D3
Staatsburg NY 94 B3
Stacy MN 67 D3
Stafford CT 150 B2
Stafford KS 43 D3
Stafford TX 132 A3
Stafford VA 103 D3
Stafford Co. KS 43 D3
Stafford Co. VA 144 A4
Stafford Sprs. CT 150 A2
Stallings NC 122 B1
Stamford CT 148 C3
Stamford NY 79 F4
Stamford TX 58 C2
Stamping Ground KY 100 B4
Stamps AR 125 D1
Stanardsville VA 102 C4
Stanberry MO 86 B4
Standing Pine MS 126 C2
Standish ME 82 B3
Standish MI 76 B1
Stanfield AZ 54 C2
Stanfield NC 122 B1
Stanfield OR 21 E1
Stanford IL 88 B4
Stanford KY 110 B1
Stanford MT 16 B3
Stanhope NJ 94 A4
Stanislaus Co. CA 36 C4
Stanley KY 109 E1
Stanley NC 122 A1
Stanley ND 18 A2
Stanley VA 102 C3
Stanley WI 67 F4
Stanley Co. SD 26 C3
Stanleytown VA 112 B2
Stanly Co. NC 122 B1
Stannards NY 92 C1
Stanton CA 228 E4
Stanton DE 146 B4
Stanton IA 86 B3
Stanton KY 110 C1
Stanton MI 76 A3
Stanton NE 35 E2
Stanton ND 18 B3
Stanton TN 118 C1
Stanton TX 58 A3
Stanton Co. KS 42 B4
Stanton Co. NE 35 E2
Stantonsburg NC 123 E1
Stanwood IA 87 F1
Stanwood WA 12 C2
Staples MN 64 A4
Stapleton NE 34 C3
Star ID 22 B4
Star NC 122 C1
Starbuck MN 66 A2
Star City AR 117 F4
Star City WV 102 A1
Star Cross NJ 145 F1
Stark Co. IL 88 B3
Stark Co. ND 18 A4
Stark Co. OH 91 E3
Starke FL 138 C3
Starke Co. IN 89 E2
Starkey VA 254 D2
Starks LA 133 D2
Starkville MS 118 C4
Star Lake NY 79 F1
Star Prairie WI 67 E3
Starr Co. TX 63 E3
Startex SC 217 C1
Startup WA 12 C2
Star Valley AZ 47 E4
Stateburg SC 122 B4
State Ctr. IA 87 D1
State College PA 92 C3
State Line MS 127 D4
Stateline NV 37 D2
State Line PA 103 D1
Statenville GA 137 F1
State Road NC 112 A3
Statesboro GA 130 B2
Statesville NC 112 A4
Statham GA 121 D4
Staunton IL 98 B2
Staunton IN 99 E2
Staunton VA 102 B4
Stayton OR 20 C3
Steamboat AZ 47 F2
Steamboat NV 37 D2
Steamboat Sprs. CO 33 D4
Stearns KY 110 B3
Stearns Co. MN 66 B3
Stebbins AK 154 B2
Stedman NC 123 D2
Steele AL 120 A4
Steele MO 108 B4
Steele ND 18 C4
Steele Co. MN 73 D1
Steele Co. ND 19 E3
Steeleville IL 98 B4
Steelton PA 218 B2
Steelville MO 97 F4
Steilacoom WA 12 C3
Steinhatchee FL 137 F3
Stephen MN 19 E2
Stephens AR 125 D1
Stephens City VA 102 C2
Stephens Co. GA 121 D2
Stephens Co. OK 51 E4
Stephens Co. TX 59 D2
Stephenson MI 69 D3
Stephenson VA 103 D2
Stephenson Co. IL 74 B4
Stephenville TX 59 D3
Sterling CO 34 A4
Sterling CT 150 B3
Sterling IL 88 B1
Sterling KS 43 E3
Sterling MA 150 C1
Sterling MI 76 B1
Sterling NE 35 F4
Sterling OK 51 E4
Sterling VA 144 A3
Sterling City TX 58 B3
Sterling Co. TX 58 B4
Sterling Forest NY 148 A2
Sterling Hts. MI 76 C4
Sterlington LA 125 E2
Stetsonville WI 68 A3
Steuben Co. IN 90 A2
Steuben Co. NY 78 C4
Steubenville KY 110 B2
Steubenville OH 91 F4
Stevens Co. KS 42 B4
Stevens Co. MN 27 F2
Stevens Co. WA 13 F2
Stevens Creek VA 112 A2
Stevenson AL 120 A2
Stevenson CT 149 D2
Stevenson WA 20 C1
Stevens Pt. WI 68 B4
Stevensville MD 145 D3
Stevensville MI 89 E1
Stevensville MT 15 D4
Stewardson IL 98 C2
Stewart MN 66 B4
Stewart Co. GA 128 C3
Stewart Co. TN 109 D3
Stewart Manor NY 241 G3
Stewartstown PA 103 E1
Stewartsville MO 96 B1
Stewartville MN 73 D2
Stickney IL 203 D5
Stickney SD 27 E4
Stigler OK 116 B1
Stillman Valley IL 88 B1
Stillmore GA 129 F2
Stillwater ME 83 D1
Stillwater MN 67 D3
Stillwater NY 94 B1
Stillwater OK 51 F2
Stillwater Co. MT 24 B1
Stilwell KS 96 B3
Stilwell OK 106 B4
Stimson Crossing WA 12 C2
Stinnett TX 50 B2
Stinson Beach CA 259 A2
Stites ID 22 B1
Stockbridge GA 120 C4
Stockbridge MA 94 B2
Stockbridge MI 76 B4
Stockbridge WI 74 C1
Stockdale TX 61 E3
Stock Island FL 142 C4
Stockton CA 36 C3
Stockton IL 74 A4
Stockton KS 43 D2
Stockton MN 73 E1
Stockton MO 106 C1

Bayberry A1	Franklin Park B1	Lyndon B2	Solvay A2
Collamer B1	Galeville A1	Mattydale B1	Split Rock A2
DeWitt B2	Jamesville B2	Nedrow A2	Syracuse A2
E. Syracuse B2	Lakeland A1	N. Syracuse B1	Taunton A2
Fairmount A2	Liverpool A1	Onondaga Hill A2	Westvale A2

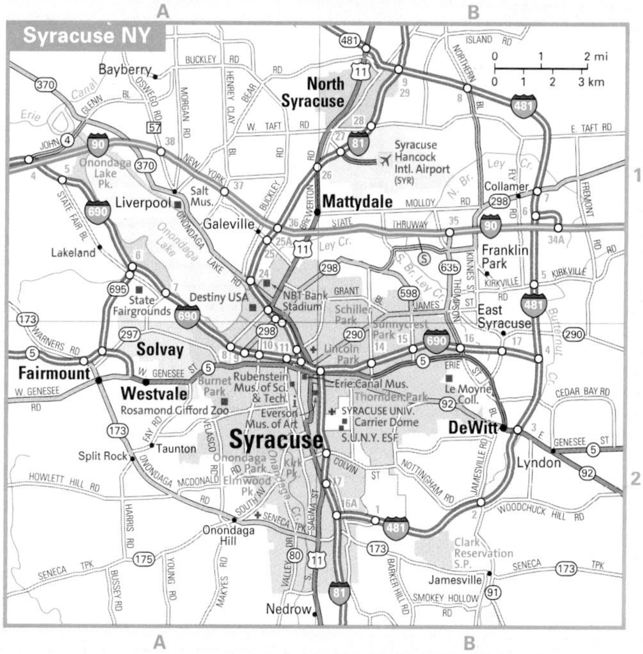

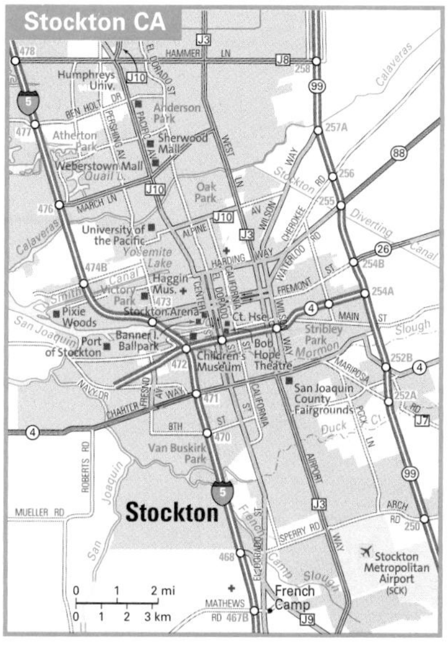

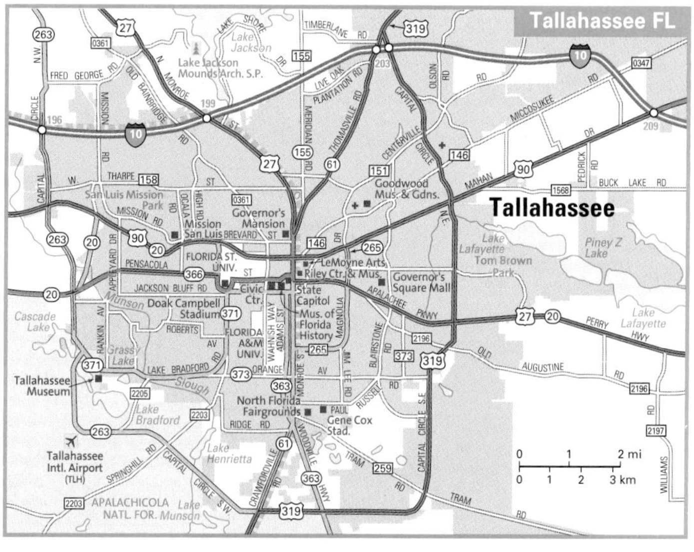

Figures after entries indicate page number and grid reference.

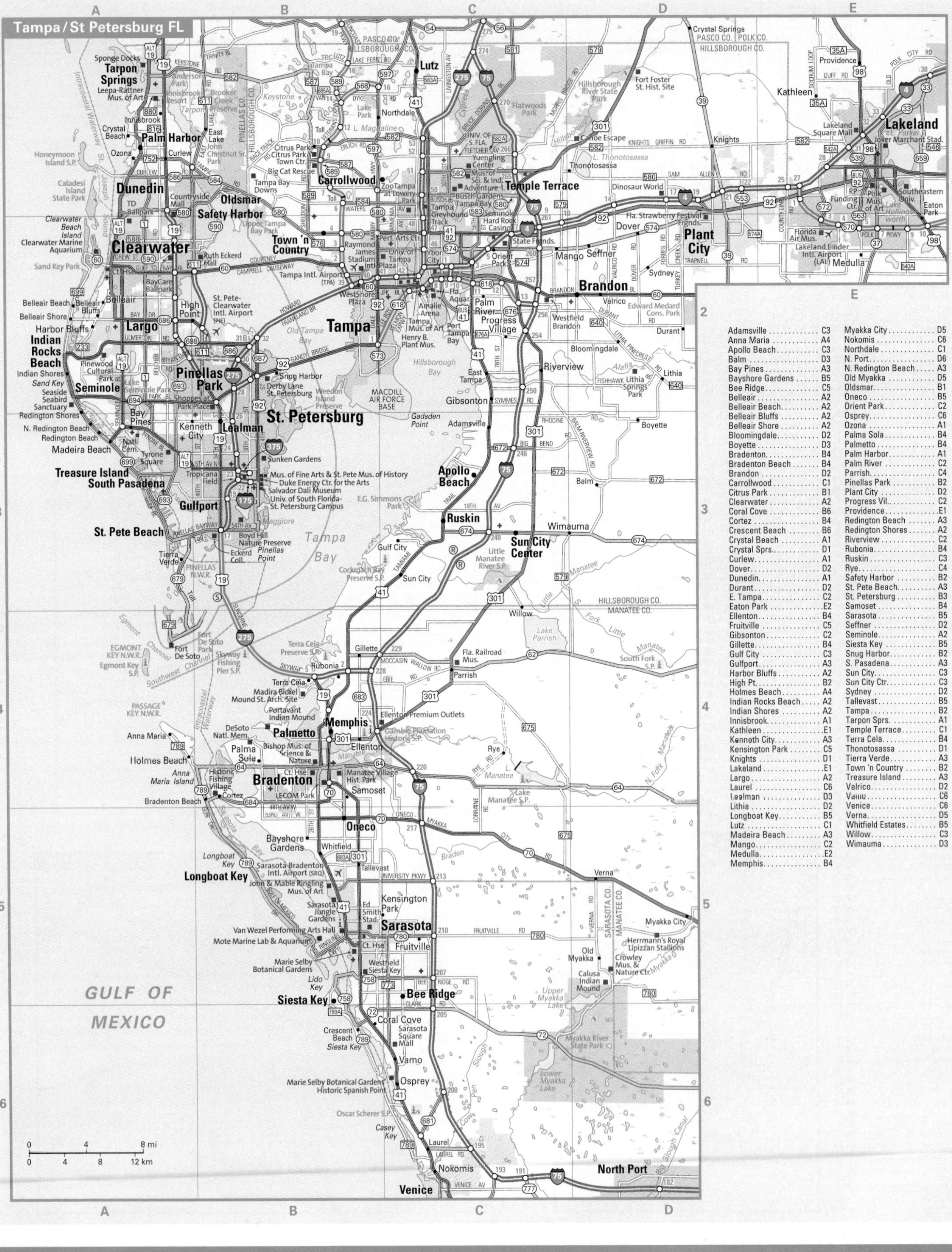
Tampa / St Petersburg FL
Tarpon Springs
Palm Harbor
Dunedin
Oldsmar
Safety Harbor
Clearwater
Largo
Indian Rocks Beach
Seminole
Pinellas Park
St. Petersburg
Gulfport
St. Pete Beach
Treasure Island
South Pasadena
Lutz
Carrollwood
Temple Terrace
Town 'n Country
Tampa
Brandon
Plant City
Lakeland
Apollo Beach
Ruskin
Sun City Center
Memphis
Palmetto
Bradenton
Oneco
Longboat Key
Sarasota
Siesta Key
Bee Ridge
Venice
North Port
Tampa Bay
GULF OF MEXICO
0 4 8 mi
0 4 8 12 km

Adamsville C3
Anna Maria A4
Apollo Beach C3
Balm D3
Bay Pines A3
Bayshore Gardens B5
Bee Ridge C5
Belleair A2
Belleair Beach A2
Belleair Bluffs A2
Belleair Shore A2
Bloomingdale D2
Boyette D3
Bradenton B4
Bradenton Beach B4
Brandon D2
Carrollwood C1
Citrus Park B1
Clearwater A2
Coral Cove B6
Cortez B4
Crescent Beach B6
Crystal Beach A1
Crystal Sprs. D1
Curlew A1
Dover D2
Dunedin A1
Durant D2
E. Tampa C2
Eaton Park E2
Ellenton B4
Fruitville C5
Gibsonton C2
Gillette B4
Gulf City C3
Gulfport A3
Harbor Bluffs A2
High Pt. B2
Holmes Beach A4
Indian Rocks Beach A2
Indian Shores A2
Innisbrook A1
Kathleen E1
Kenneth City A3
Kensington Park C5
Knights D1
Lakeland E1
Largo A2
Laurel C6
Lealman D3
Lithia D2
Longboat Key B5
Lutz C1
Madeira Beach A3
Mango C2
Medulla E2
Memphis B4
Myakka City D5
Nokomis C6
Northdale C1
N. Port D6
N. Redington Beach A3
Old Myakka D5
Oldsmar B1
Oneco B5
Orient Park C2
Osprey C6
Ozona A1
Palma Sola B4
Palmetto B4
Palm Harbor A1
Palm River C2
Parrish C4
Pinellas Park B2
Plant City D2
Progress Vil. C2
Providence E1
Redington Beach A3
Redington Shores A2
Riverview C2
Rubonia B4
Ruskin C3
Rye C4
Safety Harbor B2
St. Pete Beach A3
St. Petersburg B3
Samoset B4
Sarasota B5
Seffner D2
Seminole A2
Siesta Key B5
Snug Harbor B2
S. Pasadena A3
Sun City C3
Sun City Ctr. C3
Sydney D2
Tallevast B5
Tampa B2
Tarpon Sprs. A1
Temple Terrace C1
Terra Ceia B4
Thonotosassa D1
Tierra Verde A3
Town 'n Country B2
Treasure Island A3
Valrico D2
Vamo C6
Venice C6
Verna D5
Whitfield Estates B5
Willow C3
Wimauma D3

Entries in **bold black** indicate counties or parishes.
Entries in **bold color** indicate cities with detailed inset maps.

Stockton NJ 146 C1
Stockton UT 31 E4
Stockton Sprs. ME 83 D2
Stockville NE 34 C4
Stoddard WI 73 F2
Stoddard Co. MO 108 B2
Stokes Co. NC 112 B3
Stokesdale NC 112 B3
Stoneboro PA 92 A2
Stone Co. AR 107 E4
Stone Co. MS 135 D1
Stone Co. MO 107 D3
Stonega VA 111 D2
Stoneham MA 151 D1
Stone Harbor NJ 104 C4
Stone Mtn. GA 120 C4
Stone Park IL 203 C4
Stone Ridge NY 94 B3
Stoneville NC 112 B3
Stonewall LA 124 C3
Stonewall MS 127 D3
Stonewall OK 51 F4
Stonewall Co. TX 58 B2
Stonewood WV 102 A2
Stoney Creek Mills PA 146 B2
Stonington CT 149 F2
Stonington IL 98 C1
Stonington ME 83 D2
Stony Brook NY 149 D3
Stony Creek CT 149 E2
Stony Pt. NY 148 B2
Stony Pt. NC 112 A4
Storey Co. NV 37 D2
Storm Lake IA 72 A4
Stormstown PA 92 C3
Storrs CT 150 B3
Story WY 25 D3
Story City IA 86 C1
Story Co. IA 86 C1
Stottville NY 94 B2
Stoughton MA 151 D2
Stoughton WI 74 B3
Stoutsville OH 101 D1
Stover MO 97 D3
Stow OH 91 E2
Stowe PA 146 B2
Stowe VT 81 E2
Stowell TX 132 C3
Strafford MO 107 D2
Strafford Co. NH 81 F4
Straitsville CT 149 D1
Strasburg CO 41 E1
Strasburg IL 98 C2
Strasburg ND 26 C1
Strasburg OH 91 E4
Strasburg PA 146 A3
Strasburg VA 102 C2
Stratford CA 44 C3
Stratford CT 149 D2
Stratford IA 72 C4
Stratford NJ 146 C3
Stratford OK 51 F4
Stratford TX 50 A2
Stratford WI 68 A4
Stratham NH 82 A4
Strathmoor Vil. KY 230 E2
Strathmore CA 45 D3
Strathmore NJ 147 E1
Stratmoor Hills CO 205 D2
Stratton CO 42 A2
Stratton ME 82 B1
Stratton NE 42 B1
Strawberry AZ 47 E4
Strawberry Pt. IA 73 E4
Strawn TX 59 D3
Streamwood IL 203 B3
Streator IL 88 C3
Streetsboro OH 91 E2
Stroh IN 90 A2
Stromsburg NE 35 E3
Strong AR 125 E1
Strong ME 82 B1
Strong City KS 43 F3
Stronghurst IL 87 F3
Strongsville OH 91 E2
Stroud OK 51 F2
Stroudsburg PA 93 F3
Strum WI 67 F4
Struthers OH 91 F3
Stryker OH 90 B2
Stuart FL 141 E4
Stuart IA 86 B2
Stuart NE 35 D1
Stuart VA 112 B3
Stuarts Draft VA 102 C4
Sturbridge MA 150 B2
Sturgeon MO 97 E2
Sturgeon Bay WI 69 D4
Sturgis KY 109 D1
Sturgis MI 90 A1
Sturgis SD 25 F3
Sturtevant WI 74 C4
Stutsman Co. ND 19 D3
Stuttgart AR 117 F3
Suamico WI 68 C4
Subiaco AR 116 C1
Sublette KS 42 B4
Sublette Co. WY 32 A1
Sublimity OR 20 C2
Succasunna NJ 148 A3
Sudan TX 57 F1
Sudbury MA 150 C1
Suffern NY 148 B2
Suffield CT 150 A2
Suffolk VA 113 F3
Suffolk Co. MA 151 D1
Suffolk Co. NY 149 D3
Sugar City ID 23 E4
Sugar Creek MO 224 D3
Sugarcreek OH 91 E4
Sugarcreek PA 92 A2
Sugar Grove IL 88 C1
Sugar Grove PA 92 B1
Sugar Grove VA 111 F2
Sugar Hill GA 120 C3
Sugar Land TX 132 A3
Sugarland Run VA 144 A3
Sugar Loaf NY 148 A2
Sugar Notch PA 261 A2
Suisun City CA 36 B3
Suitland MD 144 B3
Sulligent AL 119 D4
Sullivan IL 98 C1
Sullivan IN 99 E2
Sullivan MO 97 F4
Sullivan WI 74 C3
Sullivan City TX 63 E4
Sullivan Co. IN 99 E2
Sullivan Co. MO 87 D4
Sullivan Co. NH 81 E4
Sullivan Co. NY 94 A2
Sullivan Co. PA 93 E2
Sullivan Co. TN 111 E3
Sullivan's Island SC 131 D2
Sully IA 87 D2
Sully Co. SD 26 C3
Sulphur LA 133 D2
Sulphur OK 51 F4
Sulphur Rock AR 107 F4
Sulphur Sprs. AR 106 B3
Sulphur Sprs. TX 124 A1
Sultan WA 12 C3
Sumas WA 12 C1
Sumiton AL 119 F4
Summerdale AL 135 E2
Summerfield NC 112 B3
Summerland Key FL 143 D4
Summers Co. WV 112 A1
Summerside OH 204 C2
Summersville MO 107 F2
Summersville WV 101 F4
Summerton SC 122 B4
Summertown TN 119 E1
Summerville GA 120 B3
Summerville SC 131 D1
Summit AR 107 E3
Summit IL 203 D5
Summit KY 101 D3
Summit MS 126 B4
Summit NJ 148 A4
Summit SD 27 F2
Summit WA 262 B5
Summit Co. CO 41 D1
Summit Co. OH 91 E3
Summit Co. UT 31 F4
Summitville IN 89 F4
Sumner IL 99 D3
Sumner IA 73 E3
Sumner MS 118 B3
Sumner WA 12 C3
Sumner Co. KS 51 E1
Sumner Co. TN 109 F3
Sumrall MS 126 C4
Sumter SC 122 B4
Sumter Co. AL 127 E2
Sumter Co. FL 140 C1
Sumter Co. GA 129 D3
Sumter Co. SC 122 B4
Sun LA 134 C1
Sunapee NH 81 E4
Sunbright TN 110 B3
Sunburst MT 15 E1
Sunbury OH 91 D4
Sunbury PA 93 D3
Sun City AZ 54 C1
Sun City Ctr. FL 140 C3
Sun City West AZ 249 A1
Suncook NH 81 F4
Sundance WY 25 F3
Sunderland MD 144 C4
Sunderland MA 150 A1
Sundown TX 57 F2
Sunfield MI 76 A4
Sunfish Lake MN 235 D3
Sunflower MS 118 A4
Sunflower Co. MS 118 A4
Sun Lakes AZ 54 C2
Sunland Park NM 56 C4
Sunman IN 100 A2
Sunnybrook MD 144 C1
Sunny Isles Beach FL 233 C3
Sunnyside UT 39 F1
Sunnyside WA 13 E4
Sunnyvale CA 36 B4
Sunol CA 259 E4
Sun Prairie WI 74 B3
Sunray TX 50 A2
Sunrise FL 143 E1
Sunrise Beach Vil. TX 61 D1
Sunset LA 133 F2
Sunset UT 244 A2
Sunset Beach NC 123 D4
Sunset Hills MO 256 B3
Sun Valley ID 22 C4
Superior AZ 55 D2
Superior CO 209 B1
Superior MT 14 C3
Superior NE 43 E1
Superior WI 64 C4
Superior WY 32 B2
Supreme LA 134 A3
Suquamish WA 262 A2
Surf City NJ 147 E4
Surf City NC 123 E3
Surfside FL 233 C4
Surfside Beach SC 123 D4
Surfside Beach TX 133 E4
Surgoinsville TN 111 D3
Suring WI 68 C4
Surprise AZ 54 C1
Surrey ND 18 B2
Surry VA 113 F2
Surry Co. NC 112 A3
Surry Co. VA 113 F2
Susan VA 113 F1
Susan Moore AL 119 F3
Susanville CA 29 D4
Susquehanna PA 93 F1
Susquehanna Co. PA 93 E2
Sussex NJ 148 A2
Sussex VA 113 E2
Sussex WI 74 C3
Sussex Co. DE 145 F4
Sussex Co. NJ 148 A2
Sussex Co. VA 113 E2
Sutcliffe NV 37 D1
Sutherland IA 72 A3
Sutherland NE 34 B3
Sutherlin OR 20 B4
Sutter CA 36 B2
Sutter Co. CA 36 B2
Sutter Creek CA 36 C3
Sutton AK 154 C3
Sutton MA 150 C2
Sutton NE 35 E4
Sutton WV 101 F3
Sutton Co. TX 60 B1
Suttons Bay MI 69 F4
Suwanee GA 120 C3
Suwannee Co. FL 138 B2
Swain Co. NC 121 D1
Swainsboro GA 129 F2
Swampscott MA 151 D1
Swannanoa NC 121 E1
Swann Keys DE 145 F4
Swanquarter NC 115 E3
Swansboro NC 115 D4
Swansea IL 98 B3
Swansea SC 122 A4
Swanton OH 90 B2
Swanton VT 81 D1
Swan Valley ID 23 F4
Swarthmore PA 146 C3
Swartz LA 125 F2
Swartz Creek MI 76 B3
Swayzee IN 89 F4
Swea City IA 72 B2
Swedesboro NJ 146 C4
Sweeny TX 132 A4
Sweet Briar VA 112 C1
Sweet Grass Co. MT 24 A1
Sweet Home OR 20 C3
Sweetser IN 89 F3
Sweet Sprs. MO 97 D3
Sweetwater FL 143 E2
Sweetwater TN 120 C1
Sweetwater TX 58 B3
Sweetwater Co. WY 32 B2
Swepsonville NC 112 C4
Swift Co. MN 66 A3
Swifton AR 107 F4
Swifts Beach MA 151 E3
Swift Trail Jct. AZ 55 E2
Swiftwater PA 93 F3
Swink CO 41 F3
Swisher IA 87 E1
Swisher Co. TX 50 A4
Swissvale PA 250 C2
Switzer WV 101 E4
Switzerland Co. IN 100 B3
Swoyersville PA 93 E2
Sycamore GA 129 D4
Sycamore IL 88 C1
Sycamore OH 90 C3
Sycaway NY 188 E2
Sykesville MD 144 B1
Sykesville PA 92 B3
Sylacauga AL 128 A1
Sylva NC 121 D1
Sylvan Beach NY 79 E3
Sylvania AL 120 A2
Sylvania GA 130 B2
Sylvania OH 90 C2
Sylvan Lake MI 210 B1
Sylvan Lake NY 148 C1
Sylvan Shores FL 141 D3
Sylvan Sprs. AL 195 D2
Sylvester GA 129 D4
Symsonia KY 109 D2
Syosset NY 148 C3
Syracuse IN 89 F2
Syracuse KS 42 B3
Syracuse NE 35 F4
Syracuse NY 79 D3
Syracuse OH 101 E2
Syracuse UT 31 E3

T

Tabor IA 86 A3
Tabor SD 35 E1
Tabor City NC 123 D3
Tacna AZ 54 A2
Tacoma WA 12 C3
Taft CA 52 B1
Taft FL 246 C4
Taft TX 61 E4
Tahlequah OK 106 B4
Tahoe City CA 37 D2
Tahoka TX 58 A2
Taholah WA 12 A3
Takoma Park MD 270 D2
Talbot Co. GA 128 C2
Talbot Co. MD 145 D3
Talbott TN 111 D4
Talbotton GA 128 C2
Talco TX 124 B1
Talcottville CT 150 A3
Talent OR 28 B2
Taliaferro Co. GA 121 E4
Talihina OK 116 B2
Talkeetna AK 154 C3
Talladega AL 120 A4
Talladega Co. AL 128 A1
Tallahassee FL 137 E2
Tallahatchie Co. MS 118 B4
Tallapoosa GA 120 B4
Tallapoosa Co. AL 128 B1
Tallassee AL 128 A2
Tallevast FL 266 B5
Talleyville DE 146 B3
Tallmadge OH 91 E3
Tallula IL 98 B1
Tallulah LA 126 A2
Talmage CA 36 A2
Talmo GA 121 D3
Taloga OK 51 D2
Talty TX 59 F2
Tama IA 87 D1
Tama Co. IA 87 D1
Tamalpais Valley CA 259 A2
Tamaqua PA 93 E3
Tamarac FL 143 E1
Tamaroa IL 98 B4
Tamms IL 108 C2
Tampa FL 140 B2
Tampico IL 88 B2
Taney Co. MO 107 D3
Taneytown MD 103 E1
Tangelo Park FL 246 B3
Tangent OR 20 B3
Tangier VA 114 B2
Tangipahoa LA 134 B1
Tangipahoa Par. LA 134 B1
Tanner AL 119 F2
Tannersville PA 93 F3
Tanque Verde AZ 55 D3
Tantallon MD 144 B4
Taos MO 97 E3
Taos NM 49 D1
Taos Co. NM 49 D1
Tappahannock VA 103 E4
Tappan NY 148 B3
Tappen ND 18 C4
Tara Hills CA 259 B1
Tarboro NC 113 E4
Tarentum PA 92 A3
Tariffville CT 150 A3
Tarkiln RI 150 C2
Tarkio MO 86 A4
Tarpon Sprs. FL 140 B2
Tarrant AL 119 F4
Tarrant Co. TX 59 E2
Tarrytown NY 148 B3
Tasso TN 120 B1
Tatamy PA 93 F3
Tate Co. MS 118 B2
Tattnall Co. GA 129 F3
Tatum NM 57 F2
Tatum TX 124 B2
Taunton MA 151 D3
Tavares FL 140 C1
Tavernier FL 143 E4
Tawas City MI 76 B1
Taylor AL 136 C1
Taylor AZ 47 F4
Taylor AR 125 D1
Taylor MI 90 C1
Taylor NE 35 D2
Taylor PA 261 D1
Taylor TX 61 E1
Taylor Co. FL 137 F3
Taylor Co. GA 129 D2
Taylor Co. IA 86 B3
Taylor Co. KY 110 B1
Taylor Co. TX 58 C3
Taylor Co. WV 102 A2
Taylor Co. WI 67 F3
Taylor Creek FL 141 E4
Taylor Lake Vil. TX 132 B3
Taylor Mill KY 204 B3
Taylors SC 121 F2
Taylors Falls MN 67 D3
Taylor Sprs. IL 98 B2
Taylorsville IN 99 F2
Taylorsville KY 100 A4
Taylorsville MD 144 B1
Taylorsville MS 126 C3
Taylorsville NC 111 F4
Taylorsville UT 257 A2
Taylortown NJ 148 A3
Taylortown NC 122 C1
Taylorville IL 98 B1
Tazewell TN 111 D3
Tazewell VA 111 F2
Tazewell Co. IL 88 B4
Tazewell Co. VA 111 F2
Tchula MS 126 B1
Tea SD 27 F4
Teague TX 59 F4
Teaneck NJ 148 B3
Teaticket MA 151 E4
Teays Val. WV 101 E3
Tecumseh MI 90 B1
Tecumseh NE 35 F4
Tecumseh OK 51 F3
Teec Nos Pos AZ 48 A1
Tega Cay SC 122 A2
Tehachapi CA 52 C1
Tehama CA 36 B1
Tehama Co. CA 36 B1
Tekamah NE 35 F2
Tekoa WA 14 B3
Tekonsha MI 90 A1
Telfair Co. GA 129 E3
Telford PA 146 C2
Tell City IN 99 E4
Teller Co. CO 41 E2
Tellico Plains TN 120 C1
Telluride CO 40 B3
Temecula CA 53 D3
Tempe AZ 54 C1
Temperance MI 90 C1
Temple GA 120 B4
Temple OK 51 E4
Temple PA 146 B1
Temple TX 59 E4
Temple City CA 228 E2
Temple Hills MD 270 E5
Temple Terrace FL 140 C2
Templeton CA 44 C4
Templeton MA 95 D1
Tenafly NJ 148 B3
Tenaha TX 124 C3
Tenants Harbor ME 82 C3
Tenino WA 12 C4
Tennent NJ 147 E2
Tennessee Ridge TN 109 D3
Tennille GA 129 E1
Tensas Par. LA 125 F3
Ten Sleep WY 24 C3
Tequesta FL 141 F4
Terra Alta WV 102 B2
Terra Bella CA 45 D4
Terrace Hts. WA 13 D4
Terrace Park OH 204 C2
Terrebonne OR 21 D3
Terrebonne Par. LA 134 A4
Terre Haute IN 99 E2
Terre Hill PA 146 A2
Terrell TX 59 F2
Terrell Co. GA 128 C4
Terrell Co. TX 60 A2
Terrell Hills TX 257 E2
Terry MS 126 B3
Terry MT 17 E4
Terry Co. TX 57 F2
Terrytown LA 134 B3
Terrytown NE 33 F2
Terryville CT 149 D1
Terryville NY 149 D3
Tesuque NM 49 D2
Teton ID 23 F4
Teton Co. ID 23 F4
Teton Co. MT 15 E3
Teton Co. WY 24 A3
Tetonia ID 23 F4
Teutopolis IL 98 C2
Tewksbury MA 95 E1
Texarkana AR 116 C4
Texarkana TX 116 C4

Harbor View B1
Holland A2
Lime City B2
Maumee A2
Moline B2
Northwood B2
Oregon B1
Ottawa Hills A1
Perrysburg A2
Rossford B2
Stony Ridge B2
Sylvania A1
Toledo A1
Walbridge B2

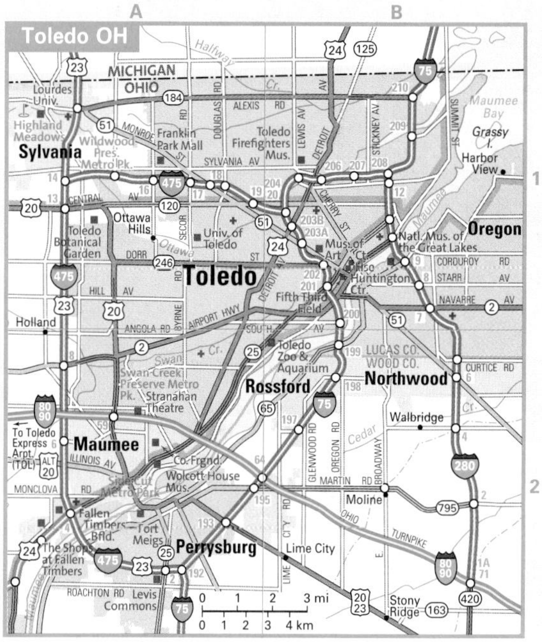

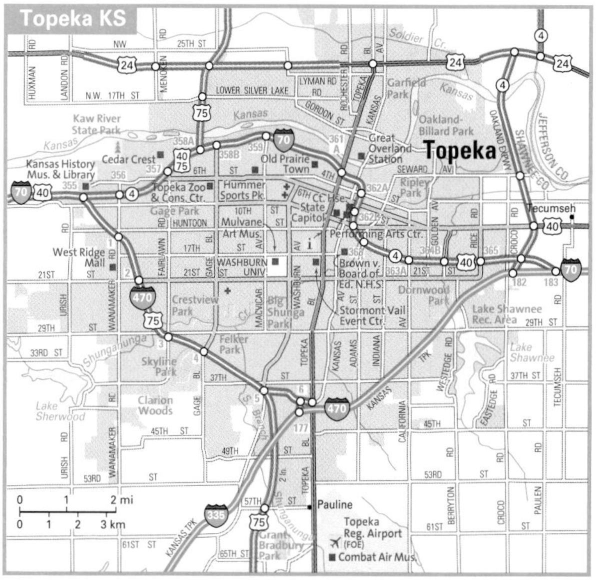

Figures after entries indicate page number and grid reference.

Texas MA 150 B2
Texas City TX 132 B4
Texas Co. MO 107 E1
Texas Co. OK 50 A1
Texhoma OK 50 A1
Texico NM 49 F4
Thatcher AZ 55 E2
Thaxton MS 118 C3
Thayer IL 98 B1
Thayer KS 106 A1
Thayer MO 107 F3
Thayer Co. NE 35 E4
Thayne WY 31 F1
The Colony TX 59 F2
The Dalles OR 21 D2
Thedford NE 34 C2
The Hills TX 61 E1
Theodore AL 135 E2
The Pinery CO 41 E1
The Plains OH 101 E2
Theresa NY 79 E1
Theresa WI 74 C2
Thermal CA 53 E3
Thermalito CA 36 C1
Thermopolis WY 24 C4
The Village OK 51 E3
The Vil. of Indian Hill OH 204 C2
The Villages FL 140 C1
The Woodlands TX 132 A2
Thibodaux LA 134 A3
Thief River Falls MN 19 F2
Thiells NY 148 B2
Thiensville WI 74 C3
Thomas OK 51 D2
Thomas WV 102 B2
Thomasboro IL 88 C4
Thomas Co. GA 137 E1
Thomas Co. KS 42 B2
Thomas Co. NE 34 C2
Thomaston CT 149 D1
Thomaston GA 128 C1
Thomaston ME 82 C3
Thomaston NY 241 G3
Thomasville AL 127 E3
Thomasville GA 137 E1
Thomasville NC 112 B4
Thompson IA 72 C2
Thompson ND 19 E3
Thompson Falls MT 14 C3
Thompson's Sta. TN 109 F4
Thompsontown PA 93 D4
Thompsonville CT 150 A2
Thompsonville IL 98 C4
Thompsonville MI 69 F4
Thomson GA 121 E4
Thomson IL 88 A1
Thonotosassa FL 140 C2
Thoreau NM 48 B3
Thorndale PA 146 B3
Thorndale TX 61 E1
Thorne Bay AK 155 E4
Thornton AR 117 E4
Thornton CA 36 C3
Thornton CO 41 E1
Thornton TX 59 F4
Thorntown IN 89 E4
Thornville OH 101 D1
Thornwood NY 148 B2
Thorofare NJ 146 C3
Thorp WI 67 F4
Thorsby AL 127 F1
Thousand Oaks CA 52 B2
Thousand Palms CA 53 E3
Thrall TX 61 E1
Three Bridges NJ 147 D1
Three Forks MT 23 F1
Three Oaks MI 89 E1
Three Pts. AZ 55 D3
Three Rivers CA 45 D3
Three Rivers MA 150 A2
Three Rivers MI 89 F1
Three Rivers TX 61 D4
Three Way TN 108 C4
Throckmorton TX 59 D2
Throckmorton Co. TX 59 D2
Throop PA 261 E2
Thurmont MD 144 A1
Thurston OH 101 D1
Thurston Co. NE 35 F2
Thurston Co. WA 12 C4
Tiana NY 149 E3
Tiburon CA 259 B2
Tice FL 142 C1
Tickfaw LA 134 B2
Ticonderoga NY 81 D3
Tidioute PA 92 B2
Tierra Amarilla NM 48 C1
Tierra Verde FL 266 A3
Tieton WA 13 D4
Tiffin IA 87 E1
Tiffin OH 90 C3
Tift Co. GA 129 E4
Tifton GA 129 E4
Tigard OR 20 C2
Tigerton WI 68 B4
Tignall GA 121 E4
Tijeras NM 48 C3
Tiki Island TX 132 B4
Tilden IL 98 B4
Tilden NE 35 E2
Tilden TX 61 D4
Tilghman MD 145 D4
Tillamook OR 20 B2
Tillamook Co. OR 20 B1
Tillman Co. OK 51 D4
Tillmans Corner AL 135 E2
Tillson NY 94 B3
Tilton IL 89 D4
Tilton NH 81 F4
Tiltonsville OH 91 F4
Timber Lake SD 26 C2
Timberlake VA 112 C1
Timberon NM 57 D2
Timberville VA 102 C3
Timmonsville SC 122 C3
Timpson TX 124 C3
Tinley Park IL 89 D2
Tinton Falls NJ 147 E2
Tioga LA 125 E4
Tioga ND 18 A2
Tioga PA 93 D1
Tioga TX 59 F1
Tioga Co. NY 93 E1
Tioga Co. PA 93 D1
Tionesta PA 92 A2
Tippah Co. MS 118 C2
Tipp City OH 100 B1
Tippecanoe Co. IN 89 E4
Tipton CA 45 D3
Tipton IN 89 F4
Tipton IA 87 F1
Tipton MO 97 D3
Tipton OK 51 D4
Tipton PA 92 C3
Tipton Co. IN 89 F4
Tipton Co. TN 118 B1
Tiptonville TN 108 B3
Tishomingo OK 51 F4
Tishomingo Co. MS 119 D2
Tiskilwa IL 88 B2
Titonka IA 72 C3
Titus Co. TX 124 B1
Titusville FL 141 E1
Titusville NJ 147 D2
Titusville PA 92 A2
Tiverton RI 151 D4
Tivoli NY 94 B2
Toano VA 113 F1
Toast NC 112 A3
Tobaccoville NC 112 A3
Toccoa GA 121 D2
Todd Co. KY 109 E2
Todd Co. MN 66 B1
Todd Co. SD 34 C1
Togiak AK 154 B3
Tohatchi NM 48 A2
Tok AK 155 D2
Toksook Bay AK 154 B3
Toledo IL 99 D2
Toledo IA 87 D1
Toledo OH 90 C2
Toledo OR 20 B3
Toledo WA 12 C4
Tolland CT 150 A3
Tolland Co. CT 149 E1
Tolles CT 149 D1
Tolleson AZ 249 A2
Tolono IL 99 D1
Toluca IL 88 B3
Tomah WI 74 A1
Tomahawk WI 68 B3
Tomball TX 132 A2
Tom Bean TX 59 F1
Tombstone AZ 55 E4
Tome NM 48 C4
Tom Green Co. TX 58 C4
Tomkins Cove NY 148 B2
Tompkins Co. NY 79 D4
Tompkinsville KY 110 A3
Toms River NJ 147 E3
Tonalea AZ 47 E2
Tonasket WA 13 E1
Tonawanda NY 78 A3
Tonganoxie KS 96 B2
Tonica IL 88 B2
Tonkawa OK 51 E1
Tonopah NV 37 F3
Tontitown AR 106 C4
Tooele UT 31 E4
Tooele Co. UT 31 D4
Tool TX 59 F3
Toole Co. MT 15 F1
Toombs Co. GA 129 F3
Toomsboro GA 129 E2
Topeka IN 89 F2
Topeka KS 96 A2
Toppenish WA 13 D4
Topsfield MA 151 F1
Topsham ME 82 B3
Topton PA 146 B1
Toquerville UT 39 D4
Tornillo TX 56 C4
Toronto OH 91 F4
Toronto SD 27 F3
Torrance CA 52 C3
Torrance Co. NM 49 D4
Torreon NM 48 B2
Torrington CT 94 C3
Torrington WY 33 F2
Totowa NJ 240 A1
Toughkenamon PA 146 B3
Toulon IL 88 B3
Towaco NJ 148 A3
Towanda KS 43 F4
Towanda PA 93 E1
Towaoc CO 40 B4
Tower MN 64 C3
Tower City ND 19 E4
Tower City PA 93 E4
Tower Hill IL 98 C2
Tower Lakes IL 203 B1
Town and Country MO 256 A2
Town Creek AL 119 E2
Towner ND 18 C2
Towner Co. ND 19 D1
Town Line NY 78 B3
Town 'n Country FL 266 B2
Town of Pines IN 89 E2
Towns Co. GA 121 D2
Townsend DE 145 E1
Townsend MA 95 D1
Townsend MT 15 F4
Towson MD 144 C1
Tracy CA 36 C4
Tracy MN 72 A1
Tracy City TN 120 A1
Tracyton WA 262 A3
Traer IA 87 E1
Trafalgar IN 99 F2
Trafford AL 119 F4
Trafford PA 250 D3
Trail Creek IN 89 E2
Traill Co. ND 19 E3
Trainer PA 146 C3
Tramway NC 122 C1
Tranquillity CA 44 C3
Transylvania Co. NC 121 E1
Trappe MD 145 D4
Trappe PA 146 B2
Trapper Creek AK 154 C3
Traskwood AR 117 E3
Travelers Rest SC 121 E2
Traver CA 45 D3
Traverse City MI 69 F4
Traverse Co. MN 27 F1
Travis Co. TX 61 E1
Treasure Co. MT 17 D4
Treasure Island FL 140 B3
Trego Co. KS 42 C2
Tremont IL 88 B4
Tremont PA 146 A1
Tremonton UT 31 E3
Trempealeau WI 73 F1
Trempealeau Co. WI 67 F4
Trent SD 27 F4
Trenton FL 138 C3
Trenton GA 120 B2
Trenton IL 98 B3
Trenton KY 109 E3
Trenton MI 90 C1
Trenton MO 86 C4
Trenton NE 42 B1
Trenton NJ 147 D2
Trenton NC 115 D3
Trenton OH 100 B2
Trenton TN 108 C4
Trenton TX 59 F1
Trenton UT 31 E2
Trent Woods NC 115 D3
Treutlen Co. GA 129 F2
Trevorton PA 93 E3
Trevose PA 146 C2
Trexlertown PA 146 B1
Treynor IA 86 A2
Trezevant TN 108 C4
Triadelphia WV 91 F4
Triana AL 119 F2
Triangle VA 144 A4
Tribes Hill NY 94 A1
Tribune KS 42 B3
Tri-City OR 28 B1
Trigg Co. KY 109 D3
Tri-Lakes IN 90 A2
Trilby FL 140 C1
Trimble CO 40 B4
Trimble TN 108 C3
Trimble Co. KY 100 A3
Trimont MN 72 B2
Trinidad CO 41 E4
Trinidad TX 59 F3
Trinity AL 119 F2
Trinity NC 112 B4
Trinity TX 132 A1
Trinity Co. CA 28 B4
Trinity Co. TX 132 B1
Trion GA 120 B2
Tripoli IA 73 E4
Tripp SD 35 E1
Tripp Co. SD 26 C4
Triumph LA 134 C4
Trona CA 45 E4
Trooper PA 146 C2
Trophy Club TX 207 B1
Tropic UT 39 E4
Trotwood OH 100 B1
Troup TX 124 B3
Troup Co. GA 128 C1
Trousdale Co. TN 109 F3
Trout Creek MT 14 C3
Troutdale OR 20 C2
Troutdale VA 111 F3
Trout Lake WA 21 D1
Troutman NC 112 A4
Trout Valley IL 203 A1
Troutville VA 112 B1
Trowbridge Park MI 69 D1
Troy AL 128 A3
Troy ID 14 B4
Troy IL 98 B3
Troy KS 96 B1
Troy MI 76 C4
Troy MO 97 F2
Troy MT 14 C2
Troy NH 95 D1
Troy NY 94 B1
Troy NC 122 C1
Troy OH 100 B1
Troy PA 93 D1
Troy TN 108 C3
Troy TX 59 E4
Troy VT 81 E1
Truckee CA 37 D2
Truman MN 72 B2
Trumann AR 108 A4
Trumansburg NY 79 D4
Trumbauersville PA 146 C1
Trumbull CT 149 D2
Trumbull Co. OH 91 F2
Trussville AL 119 F4
Truth or Consequences NM 56 B2
Tryon NE 34 B3
Tryon NC 121 F1

Bakersville	B1	Fallsington	A2	Mercerville	B1	Trenton	B2
Ewing	A1	Lawrenceville	B1	Morrisville	A2	W. Trenton	A1
Ewingville	A1	Lewisville	B1	Slackwood	B1	White Horse	B2

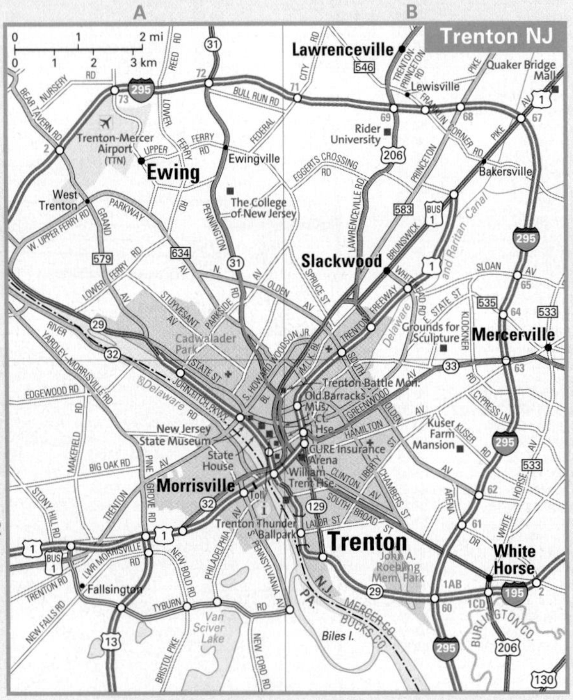

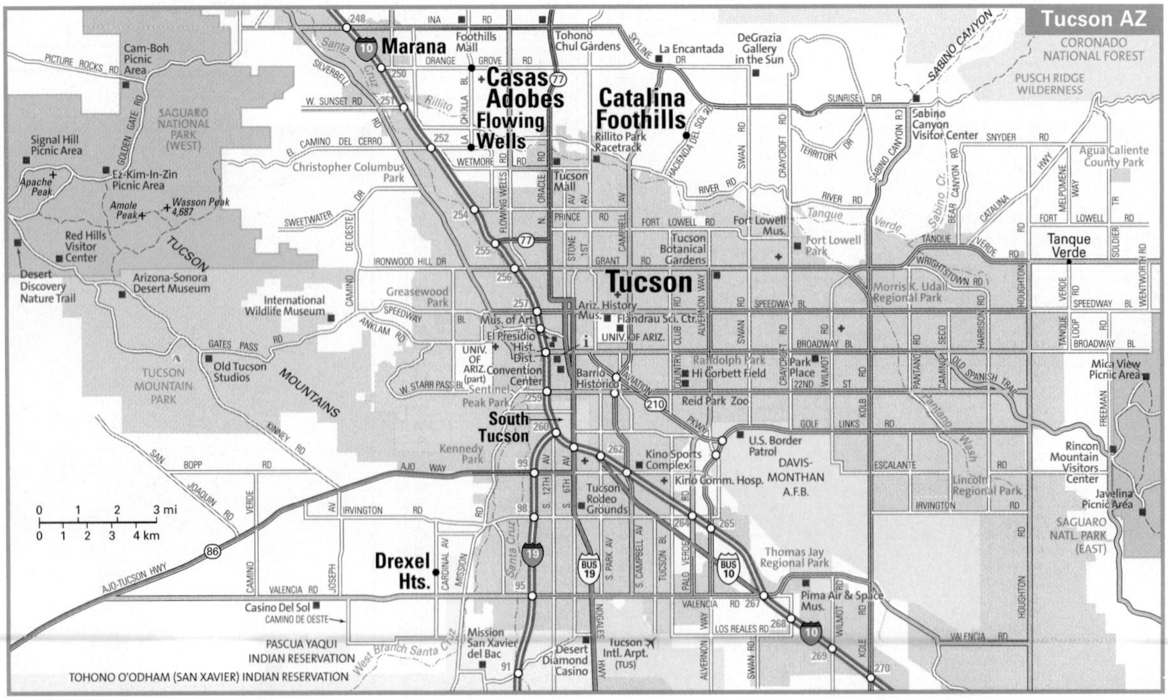

Entries in **bold black** indicate counties or parishes.
Entries in **bold color** indicate cities with detailed inset maps.

Tryon OK 51 F2
Tsaile AZ 48 A2
Tualatin OR 20 C2
Tubac AZ 55 D4
Tuba City AZ 47 E2
Tuckahoe NY 149 E3
Tucker MS 126 C2
Tucker Co. WV 102 B2
Tuckerman AR 107 F4
Tuckerton NJ 147 E4
Tucson AZ 55 D3
Tucumcari NM 49 F3
Tukwila WA 262 B4
Tulalip WA 262 B1
Tulare CA 45 D3
Tulare SD 27 E3
Tulare Co. CA 45 D3
Tularosa NM 56 C2
Tulelake CA 29 D2
Tulia TX 50 A4
Tullahoma TN 120 A1
Tullos LA 125 E3
Tully NY 79 E4
Tullytown PA 147 D2
Tulsa OK 51 F2
Tuscarora PA 93 E3
Tuscola IL 99 D1
Tuscola TX 58 C3
Tuscola Co. MI 76 C2
Tusculum TN 111 E4
Tuscumbia AL 119 E2
Tuscumbia MO 97 E4
Tuskegee AL 128 B2
Tustin CA 229 F5
Tuttle OK 51 E3
Tutwiler MS 118 A3
Tuxedo Park NY 148 B2
Twain Harte CA 37 D3
Twentynine Palms CA 46 A4
Twiggs Co. GA 129 E2
Twin Bridges MT 23 E2
Twin City GA 129 F2
Twin Falls ID 30 C1
Twin Falls Co. ID 30 C2
Twin Lake MI 75 E2
Twin Lakes CA 236 D1
Twin Lakes GA 137 F1
Twin Lakes NM 48 A2
Twin Lakes WI 74 C4
Twin Rivers NJ 147 E2
Uledi PA 102 B1
Ulen MN 19 F3
Ullin IL 108 C2
Ulm MT 15 F3
Ulster Co. NY 148 A1
Ulysses KS 42 B4
Ulysses PA 92 C1
Umatilla FL 141 D1
Umatilla OR 21 E1
Umatilla Co. OR 21 E2
Unadilla GA 129 D3
Unadilla NY 79 E4
Unalakleet AK 154 B2
Unalaska AK 154 A4
Uncasville CT 149 F1
Underhill VT 81 D2
Underwood IA 86 A2
Underwood ND 18 B3
Unicoi TN 111 E4
Unicoi Co. TN 111 E4
Union IL 88 C1
Union KY 100 B3
Union ME 82 C2
Union MS 126 C2
Union MO 97 F3
Union Co. TN 110 C3
Union Gap WA 13 D4
Union Grove WI 74 C4
Union Hall VA 112 B2
Union Lake MI 210 A1
Union Par. LA 125 E1
Union Park FL 246 D2
Union Pt. GA 121 E4
Union Sprs. AL 128 B3
Union Sprs. NY 79 D3
Uniontown AL 127 E2
Uniontown KY 109 D1
Uniontown OH 91 E3
Uniontown PA 102 B1
Unionville CT 94 C3
Unionville GA 129 E4
Unionville MI 76 B2
Unionville MO 87 D4
Unionville NV 29 F4
Unionville NY 148 A2
Unionville NC 122 B1
Unionville PA 146 B3
Unity ME 82 C2
Universal City TX 61 D2
University City MO 256 B2
Utah Co. UT 39 E1
Utica IN 100 A4
Utica MI 210 C1
Utica MS 126 A3
Utica NE 35 E4
Utica NY 79 E3
Utica OH 91 D4
Utica SC 121 E2
Uvalda GA 129 F3
Uvalde TX 60 C3
Uvalde Co. TX 60 C3
Uxbridge MA 150 C2

V

Vacaville CA 36 B3
Vader WA 12 B4
Vadito NM 49 D2
Vadnais Hts. MN 235 D1
Vado NM 56 C3
Vaiden MS 126 C1
Vail AZ 55 D3
Vail CO 41 D1
Vails Gate NY 148 B1
Valatie NY 94 B2
Valders WI 74 C1
Valdese NC 111 F4
Valdez AK 154 C3
Valdosta GA 137 F1
Vale OR 22 A4
Valencia NM 48 C4
Valencia Co. NM 48 C4
Valentine NE 34 C1
Valhalla NY 148 B3
Valier IL 98 C4
Valier MT 15 E2
Valinda CA 228 E2
Vallejo CA 36 B3
Vallersville MA 151 E3
Valley AL 128 B2
Valley NE 35 F3
Valley Brook OK 244 E3
Valley Ctr. CA 53 D3
Valley Ctr. KS 43 E4
Valley City ND 19 E4
Valley Cottage NY 148 B2
Valley Co. ID 22 C2
Valley Co. MT 17 D2
Valley Co. NE 35 D3
Valley Falls KS 96 A2
Valley Falls RI 150 C3
Valley Farms AZ 54 C2
Valley Forge PA 146 B2
Valley Grove WV 91 F4
Valley Head AL 120 A2
Valley Mills TX 59 E4
Valley Park MO 256 A3
Valley Sprs. CA 36 C3
Valley Sprs. SD 27 F4
Valley Stream NY 148 C4
Valley View OH 204 F3
Valleyview OH 206 A2
Valley View PA 93 E3
Valley View TX 59 E1
Valliant OK 116 B3
Valmeyer IL 98 A4
Valparaiso FL 136 B2
Valparaiso IN 89 E2
Valparaiso NE 35 F3
Valrico FL 266 D2
Val Verde CA 52 C2
Val Verde Co. TX 60 B2
Vamo FL 140 B4
Van TX 124 A2
Van Alstyne TX 59 F1
Van Buren AR 116 C1
Van Buren IN 89 F3
Van Buren ME 85 E1
Van Buren MO 107 F2
Van Buren Co. AR 117 E1
Van Buren Co. IA 87 E3
Van Buren Co. MI 75 F4
Van Buren Co. TN 110 A4
Vance AL 127 F1
Vanceboro NC 115 D3
Vanceburg KY 100 C3
Vance Co. NC 113 D3
Vancleave MS 135 D2
Vancouver WA 20 C1
Vandalia IL 98 C3
Vandalia MO 97 F2
Vandalia OH 100 B1
Vandenberg Vil. CA 52 A1
Vander NC 123 D2
Vanderbilt MI 70 C3
Vanderburgh Co. IN 99 D4
Vandercook Lake MI 90 B1
Vandergrift PA 92 A4
Vandling PA 93 F2
Van Etten NY 93 E1
Vanhiseville NJ 147 E2
Van Horn TX 57 D4
Van Horne IA 87 E1
Van Lear KY 111 E1
Vanlue OH 90 C3
Van Meter IA 86 C2
Vansant VA 111 E2
Van Vleck TX 132 A4
Van Wert OH 90 B3
Van Wert Co. OH 90 B3
Van Zandt Co. TX 124 A2
Vardaman MS 118 C4
Varnamtown NC 123 E4
Varnell GA 120 B2
Varnville SC 130 B2
Vashon WA 262 A4
Vashon Hts. WA 262 A3
Vass NC 122 C1
Vassalboro ME 82 C2
Vassar MI 76 B3
Vaughn MT 15 F3
Vaughn NM 49 D4
Veazie ME 83 D1
Veblen SD 27 E1
Veedersburg IN 89 D4
Vega TX 50 A3
Velma OK 51 E4
Velva ND 18 B2
Venango Co. PA 92 A2
Veneta OR 20 B3
Venice FL 140 B4
Venice IL 256 C2
Venice LA 134 C4
Venice Gardens FL 140 C4
Ventnor City NJ 147 F4
Ventura CA 52 B2
Ventura IA 72 C3
Ventura Co. CA 52 B2
Venus TX 59 E3
Verden OK 51 E3
Verdi NV 37 D1
Verdigre NE 35 E1
Vergennes VT 81 D2
Vermilion OH 91 D2
Vermilion Co. IL 89 D4
Vermilion Par. LA 133 E3
Vermillion SD 35 F1
Vermillion Co. IN 99 E1
Vermont IL 88 A4
Vermontville MI 76 A4
Vernal UT 32 A4
Verndale MN 64 A4
Vernon AL 119 D4
Vernon CT 150 A3
Vernon FL 136 C2
Vernon IN 100 A2
Vernon MI 76 B3
Vernon NY 79 E3
Vernon TX 51 D4
Vernon VT 94 C1
Vernon Co. MO 96 C4
Vernon Co. WI 73 F2
Vernon Hills IL 203 C1
Vernonia OR 20 B1
Vernon Par. LA 125 D4
Vernon Valley NJ 148 A2
Vero Beach FL 141 E3
Verona MS 119 D3
Verona MO 106 C2
Verona NJ 148 A3
Verona NC 115 D4

Bixby C3
Bowden A3
Broken Arrow C3
Catoosa C1
Jenks B3
Oakhurst A3
Sand Sprs. A2
Sapulpa A3
Tiger C1
Tulsa B2

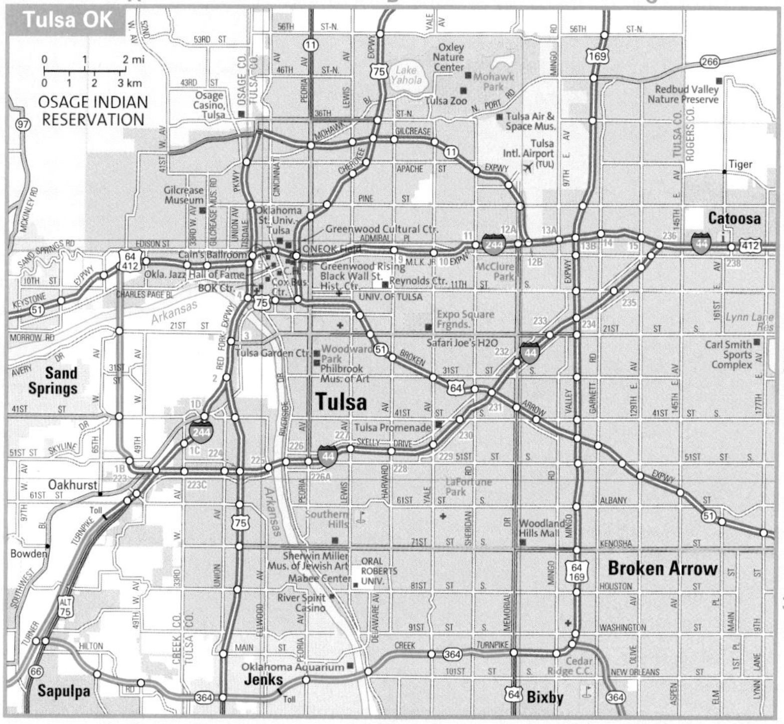
Tulsa OK
A
B
C
1
2
3
0 1 2 mi
0 1 2 3 km
OSAGE INDIAN RESERVATION
Oxley Nature Center
Mohawk Park
Lake Yahola
Tulsa Zoo
Redbud Valley Nature Preserve
Tulsa Air & Space Mus.
Tulsa Intl. Airport (TUL)
Gilcrease Museum
Oklahoma St. Univ. Tulsa
Greenwood Cultural Ctr.
Cain's Ballroom
ONEOK Field
Greenwood Rising Black Wall St. Hist. Ctr.
Okla. Jazz Hall of Fame
BOK Ctr.
Reynolds Ctr.
UNIV. OF TULSA
McClure Park
Expo Square Frgnds.
Safari Joe's H2O
Woodward Park
Philbrook Mus. of Art
Tulsa Garden Ctr.
Carl Smith Sports Complex
Tulsa
Tulsa Promenade
LaFortune Park
Southern Hills
Woodland Hills Mall
Sherwin Miller Mus. of Jewish Art
Mabee Center
ORAL ROBERTS UNIV.
River Spirit Casino
Oklahoma Aquarium
Jenks
Bixby
Broken Arrow
Catoosa
Tiger
Sand Springs
Oakhurst
Bowden
Sapulpa
Cedar Ridge C.C.
Lynn Lane Res.

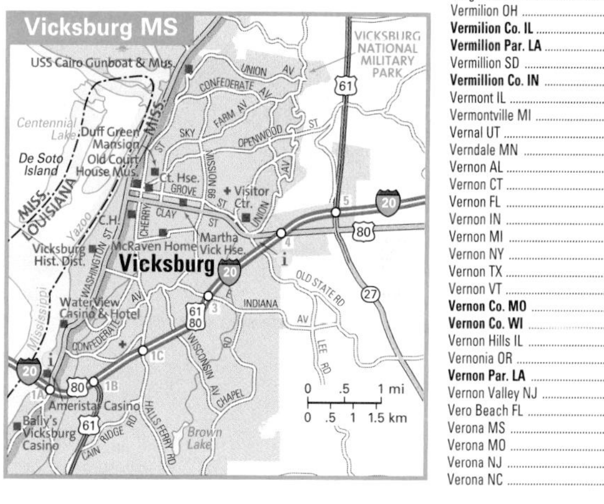
Vicksburg MS
USS Cairo Gunboat & Mus.
VICKSBURG NATIONAL MILITARY PARK
Centennial Lake
Duff Green Mansion
Old Court House Mus.
De Soto Island
Ct. Hse.
Visitor Ctr.
Martha Vick Hse.
McKaven Home
Vicksburg Hist. Dist.
Vicksburg
Waterview Casino & Hotel
Ameristar Casino
Bally's Vicksburg Casino
Brown Lake
MISS.
LOUISIANA
0 .5 1 mi
0 .5 1 1.5 km

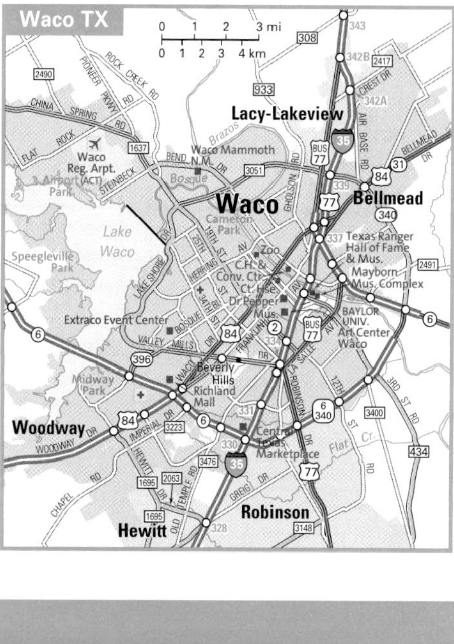
Waco TX
0 1 2 3 mi
0 1 2 3 4 km
Lacy-Lakeview
Waco Reg. Arpt. (ACT)
Airport Park
Waco Mammoth N.M.
Bosque
Waco
Bellmead
Lake Waco
Cameron Park
Zoo
Speegleville Park
Texas Ranger Hall of Fame & Mus.
Mayborn Mus. Complex
Dr Pepper Mus.
Extraco Event Center
BAYLOR UNIV.
Art Center Waco
Beverly Hills
Richland Mall
Midway Park
Woodway
Central Texas Marketplace
Robinson
Hewitt

Tulsa Co. OK 106 A4
Tuluksak AK 154 B3
Tumacacori AZ 55 D4
Tunica MS 118 B2
Tunica Co. MS 118 B2
Tunkhannock PA 93 E2
Tunnel Hill GA 120 B2
Tuolumne CA 37 D3
Tuolumne Co. CA 37 D3
Tupelo MS 119 D3
Tupper Lake NY 79 F1
Turbeville SC 122 B4
Turbotville PA 93 D3
Turley NM 48 B1
Turley OK 51 F2
Turlock CA 36 C4
Turner ME 82 B2
Turner OR 20 B2
Turner Co. GA 129 D4
Turner Co. SD 27 F4
Turners Falls MA 94 C1
Turnersville NJ 146 C4
Turon KS 43 D4
Turpin Hills OH 204 C3
Turrell AR 118 B1
Turtle Creek PA 250 D2
Turtle Lake ND 18 C3
Turtle Lake WI 67 E3
Tusayan AZ 47 D2
Tuscaloosa AL 127 E1
Tuscaloosa Co. AL 119 E4
Tuscarawas OH 91 E4
Tuscarawas Co. OH 91 E4
Twinsburg OH 91 E2
Twin Valley MN 19 F3
Twisp WA 13 E2
Two Harbors MN 64 C4
Two Rivers WI 75 D1
Tybee Island GA 130 C3
Tye TX 58 C3
Tyler MN 27 F3
Tyler TX 124 A2
Tyler Co. TX 132 C1
Tyler Co. WV 101 F2
Tylersport PA 146 C2
Tylertown MS 134 B1
Tyndall SD 35 E1
Tyrone GA 120 C4
Tyrone NM 55 F2
Tyrone OK 50 B1
Tyrone PA 92 C3
Tyronza AR 118 B1
Tyrrell Co. NC 113 F4
Tysons VA 270 A3
Ty Ty GA 129 D4

U

Ubly MI 76 C2
Ucon ID 23 E4
Udall KS 43 F4
Uhrichsville OH 91 E4
Uinta Co. WY 31 F3
Uintah UT 244 B2
Uintah Co. UT 32 A4
Ukiah CA 36 A2
Ulah NC 122 C1
Union NH 81 F4
Union NJ 148 A4
Union OH 100 B1
Union OR 21 F2
Union SC 121 F2
Union WV 112 A1
Union Beach NJ 147 E1
Union Bridge MD 144 B1
Union City CA 259 D4
Union City GA 120 C4
Union City IN 90 A4
Union City MI 90 A1
Union City NJ 148 B4
Union City OH 90 A4
Union City OK 51 E3
Union City PA 92 A1
Union City TN 108 C3
Union Co. AR 125 E1
Union Co. FL 138 C3
Union Co. GA 120 C2
Union Co. IL 108 C1
Union Co. IN 100 B1
Union Co. IA 86 B3
Union Co. KY 109 D1
Union Co. MS 118 C3
Union Co. NJ 147 E1
Union Co. NM 49 F1
Union Co. NC 122 B2
Union Co. OH 90 C4
Union Co. OR 21 F2
Union Co. PA 93 D3
Union Co. SC 121 F2
Union Co. SD 35 F1
University Gardens NY 241 G3
University Hts. OH 204 G2
University Park IA 87 D2
University Park MD 270 E2
University Park NM 56 C3
University Park TX 207 D2
University Place WA 12 C3
Upland CA 229 G2
Upland IN 89 F4
Upland PA 248 A4
Upper Arlington OH 101 D1
Upper Darby PA 248 B3
Upper Lake CA 36 A2
Upper Marlboro MD 144 C3
Upper Saddle River NJ 148 B3
Upper Sandusky OH 90 C3
Upshur Co. TX 124 B2
Upshur Co. WV 102 A3
Upson Co. GA 129 D2
Upton KY 110 A1
Upton MA 150 C2
Upton WY 25 F3
Upton Co. TX 58 A4
Urania LA 125 E3
Urbana IL 88 C4
Urbana IA 87 E1
Urbana OH 90 B4
Urbancrest OH 206 A3
Urbandale IA 86 C2
Urbanna VA 113 F1
Urich MO 96 C3
Ursa IL 87 F4
Usquepaug RI 150 C4

Figures after entries indicate page number and grid reference.

Adelphi .E1
Alexandria C5
Annandale B4
Arlington C3
Bailey's Crossroads B4
Ballston C3
Barcroft C4
Belle Haven C5
Belle View C5
Beltsville .E1
Berwyn Hts. .E2
Bethesda C2
Bladensburg .E3
Bren Mar Park B5
Brentwood .E2
Broyhill Park B4
Cabin John B2
Calverton .E1
Camp Sprs. .E5
Canterbury Woods A4
Capitol Hts. .E3
Cherrydale C3
Chesterbrook B3
Cheverly .E3
Chevy Chase C2
Chevy Chase View C1
Chillum D2
Clarendon C3
College Park .E1
Colmar Manor .E3
Coral Hills .E4
Cottage City .E3
Crystal City C4
District Hts. .F4
Dodge Park .F3
Dunn Loring A3
E. Falls Church B3
Edmonston .E2
Fairfax A4
Fairmount Hts. .E3
Falls Church B3
Forest Hts. D5
Forestville .F4
Ft. Foote Vil. D5
Franconia B5
Garrett Park C1
Glassmanor D5
Glenarden .F3
Glendale A2
Glen Echo B2
Glen Echo Hts. C2
Greenbelt .F1
Groveton C5
Hillandale .E1
Hillcrest Hts. .E4
Huntington C5
Hyattsville .E2
Idylwood B3
Kensington C1
Kentland .F3
Kings Park A5
Knollwood .E1
Lake Barcroft B4
Landover .E3
Landover Hills .F2
Langley B2
Langley Park D2
Lanham .F2
Largo .F3
Lewisdale .E2
Lincolnia B4
Luxmanor C1
Mantua A4
Marlow Hts. .E4
Martins Additions C2
McLean B2
Merrifield A3
Morningside .F4
Mt. Rainier .E2
New Carrollton .F2
N. Brentwood .E2
N. Chevy Chase C1
N. Springfield A5
Oaklawn .E5
Oakview .E1
Oxon Hill D5
Palmer Park .F3
Pimmit Hills B3
Potomac A1
Randolph Hills C1
Ravensworth A5
Ritchie .F4
Riverdale Hts. .E2
Riverdale Park .E2
Rosedale Estates .E5
Rose Hill C5
Rosslyn C3
Seabrook .F2
Seat Pleasant .F3
Seven Corners B4
Shirlington C4
Silver Hill .E4
Silver Spr. D2
Somerset C2
Springfield B5
Spring Hill A2
Suitland .E4
Takoma Park D2
Temple Hills .E5
Tysons A3
University Park .E2
Vienna A3
Virginia Hills C5
Walker Mill .F4
Washington D3
Westover B3
W. Springfield A5
Wheaton D1
White Oak D1
Woodyard .F5

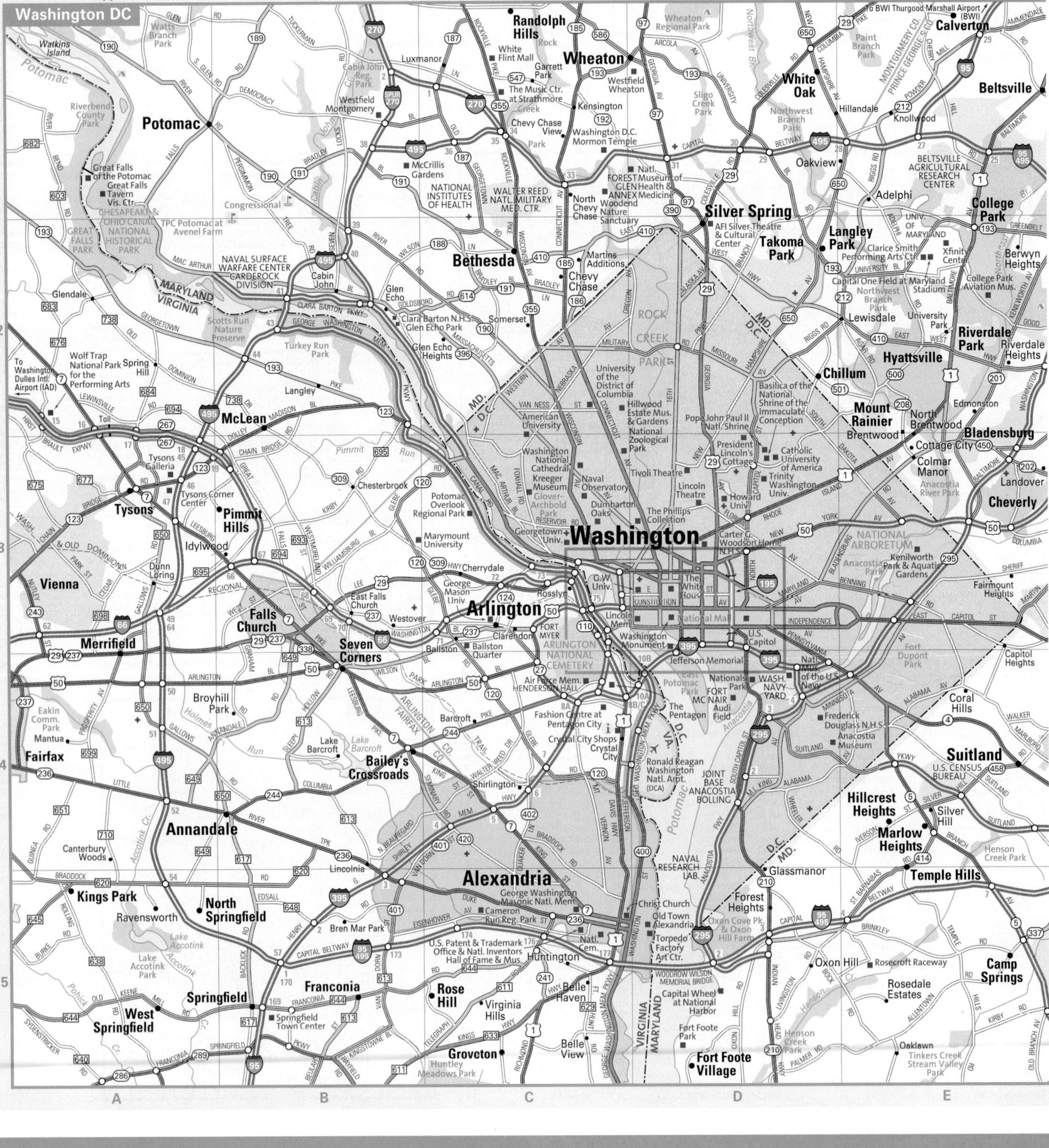

Washington DC
A
B
C
D
E
1
2
3
4
5
Potomac
Randolph Hills
Wheaton
White Oak
Calverton
Beltsville
Bethesda
Chevy Chase
Silver Spring
Takoma Park
Langley Park
College Park
Riverdale Park
Hyattsville
Chillum
Mount Rainier
Bladensburg
Cheverly
McLean
Tysons
Pimmit Hills
Vienna
Merrifield
Falls Church
Seven Corners
Arlington
Washington
Fairfax
Annandale
Bailey's Crossroads
Alexandria
Kings Park
North Springfield
Springfield
West Springfield
Franconia
Rose Hill
Groveton
Fort Foote Village
Oxon Hill
Camp Springs
Temple Hills
Marlow Heights
Hillcrest Heights
Suitland
Silver Hill
MARYLAND
VIRGINIA
To BWI Thurgood Marshall Airport (BWI)
To Washington Dulles Intl. Airport (IAD)

Entries in **bold black** indicate counties or parishes.
Entries in **bold color** indicate cities with detailed inset maps.

Verona PA 250 D1
Verona VA 102 C4
Verona WI 74 B3
Verplanck NY 148 B2
Versailles CT 149 F1
Versailles IN 100 A2
Versailles KY 100 B4
Versailles MO 97 D3
Versailles OH 90 B4
Vesper WI 68 A4
Vestal NY 93 E1
Vestal Ctr. NY 93 E1
Vestavia Hills AL 119 F4
Vevay IN 100 A3
Vian OK 116 B1
Viborg SD 35 F1
Viburnum MO 107 F1
Vici OK 51 D2
Vicksburg MI 89 F1
Vicksburg MS 126 A2
Victor CO 41 E2
Victor ID 23 F4
Victor IA 87 E1
Victor MT 15 D4
Victor NY 78 C3
Victoria KS 43 D2
Victoria MN 66 C4
Victoria TX 61 F3
Victoria VA 113 D2
Victoria Co. TX 61 F3
Victorville CA 53 D2
Victory Gardens NJ 148 A3
Vidalia GA 129 F3
Vidalia LA 125 F4
Vidor TX 132 C2
Vienna GA 129 D3
Vienna IL 108 C1
Vienna LA 125 E2
Vienna MO 97 E4
Vienna VA 144 B3
Vienna WV 101 E2
View Park CA 228 C3
Vigo Co. IN 99 E2
Vilano Beach FL 139 E3
Vilas Co. WI 68 B2
Village Green NY 79 D3
Village Green PA 248 A4
Villages of Oriole FL 143 F1
Villa Grove IL 99 D1
Villa Hills KY 204 A3
Villa Park CA 229 F4
Villa Park IL 203 C4
Villa Rica GA 120 B4
Villa Ridge MO 98 A3
Villas NJ 104 C4
Ville Platte LA 133 E1
Villisca IA 86 B3
Vilonia AR 117 E1
Vimy Ridge AR 117 E2
Vinalhaven ME 83 D3
Vincennes IN 99 D3
Vincent AL 128 A1
Vincent CA 52 C2
Vincentown NJ 147 D3
Vinco PA 92 B4
Vine Grove KY 110 A1
Vine Hill CA 259 D1
Vineland MN 66 C1
Vineland NJ 145 F1
Vinemont AL 119 F3
Vineyard Haven MA 151 E4
Vinings GA 190 C2
Vinita OK 106 B3
Vinita Park MO 256 B2
Vinton CA 37 D1
Vinton IA 87 E1
Vinton LA 133 D2
Vinton TX 56 C3
Vinton VA 112 B2
Vinton Co. OH 101 E2
Viola DE 145 E3
Viola IL 88 A2
Viola WI 73 F2
Violet LA 134 C3
Virden IL 98 B2
Virgin UT 39 D4
Virginia IL 98 A1
Virginia MN 64 C3
Virginia Beach VA 114 B4
Virginia City MT 23 E2
Virginia City NV 37 D2
Virginia Gardens FL 233 A4
Viroqua WI 73 F2
Visalia CA 45 D3
Vista CA 53 D3
Vivian LA 124 C1
Volcano HI 153 F4
Volga SD 27 F3
Volin SD 35 E1
Voluntown CT 149 F1
Volusia Co. FL 139 E4
Vonore TN 120 C1
Voorheesville NY 94 B1

W

Wabash IN 89 F3
Wabasha MN 73 E1
Wabasha Co. MN 73 E1
Wabash Co. IL 99 D3
Wabash Co. IN 89 F3
Wabasso FL 141 E3
Wabasso MN 72 A1
Wabaunsee Co. KS 43 F2
Waco TX 59 E4
Waconia MN 66 C4
Waddington NY 80 B1
Wade MS 135 D2
Wade NC 123 D1
Wadena MN 64 A4
Wadena Co. MN 64 A4
Wadesboro NC 122 B2
Wading River NY 149 D3
Wadley AL 128 B1
Wadley GA 129 F1
Wadsworth NV 37 D1
Wadsworth OH 91 E3
Waelder TX 61 E2
Wagener SC 122 A4
Waggaman LA 239 B2
Wagner SD 35 E1
Wagoner OK 106 A4
Wagoner Co. OK 106 A4
Wagon Mound NM 49 E2
Wagontown PA 146 B3
Wagram NC 122 C2
Wahiawa HI 152 A2
Wahkiakum Co. WA 12 B4
Wahoo NE 35 F3
Wahpeton ND 27 F1
Waialua HI 152 A2
Waianae HI 152 A3
Waiehu HI 153 D1
Waihee HI 153 D1
Waikane HI 152 A2
Waikapu HI 153 D1
Waikoloa Vil. HI 153 E3
Wailua HI 152 B1
Wailuku HI 153 D1
Waimalu HI 152 A3
Waimanalo HI 152 B3
Waimanalo Beach HI 152 B3
Waimea HI 152 B1
Waimea (Kamuela) HI 153 E2
Wainscott NY 149 F3
Wainwright AK 154 C1
Waipahu HI 152 A3
Waipio Acres HI 152 A3
Waite Park MN 66 C3
Waitsburg WA 13 F4
Waitsfield VT 81 D2
Wakarusa IN 89 F2
Wakeby MA 151 E3
Wake Co. NC 113 D4
WaKeeney KS 42 C2
Wakefield KS 43 F2
Wakefield MA 151 D1
Wakefield MI 65 E4
Wakefield NE 35 F2
Wakefield RI 150 C4
Wakefield VA 113 F2
Wake Forest NC 113 D4
Wakeman OH 91 D2
Wake Vil. TX 124 C1
Wakonda SD 35 F1
Wakulla Co. FL 137 E2
Walbridge OH 267 B2
Walcott IA 87 F2
Walden CO 33 D4
Walden NY 148 B1
Walden TN 120 B1
Waldo AR 125 D1
Waldo FL 138 C3
Waldoboro ME 82 C2
Waldo Co. ME 82 C2
Waldorf MD 144 B4
Waldport OR 20 B3
Waldron AR 116 C2
Waldron IN 100 A2
Waldron MI 90 B1
Wales MA 150 B2
Wales WI 74 C3
Waleska GA 120 C3
Walford IA 87 E1
Walhalla ND 19 E1
Walhalla SC 121 E2
Walker IA 73 E4
Walker LA 134 A2
Walker MI 75 F3
Walker MN 64 A3
Walker Co. AL 119 E4
Walker Co. GA 120 B2
Walker Co. TX 132 A1
Walker Mill MD 271 F4
Walkersville MD 144 A1
Walkerton IN 89 E2
Walkertown NC 112 B4
Walker Valley NY 148 A1
Walkerville MT 23 E1
Wall PA 250 D3
Wall SD 26 B3
Wallace ID 14 B3
Wallace NC 123 E2
Wallace VA 111 E3
Wallace Co. KS 42 B2
Walla Walla WA 21 F1
Walla Walla Co. WA 21 F1
Wallburg MI 112 B4
Walled Lake MI 210 A2
Waller TX 61 F2
Waller Co. TX 132 A3
Wallingford CT 149 D1
Wallingford VT 81 D4
Wallington NJ 148 B3
Wallis TX 61 F2
Wallkill NY 148 B1
Wall Lake IA 72 B4
Wallowa OR 22 A1
Wallowa Co. OR 22 A1
Walnut CA 229 F3
Walnut IL 88 B2
Walnut IA 86 A2
Walnut MS 118 C2
Walnut Cove NC 112 B3
Walnut Creek CA 36 B4
Walnut Creek NC 123 E1
Walnut Grove AL 120 A3
Walnut Grove CA 36 C3
Walnut Grove GA 121 D4
Walnut Grove MN 72 A1
Walnut Grove MS 126 C2
Walnut Grove MO 106 C1
Walnut Grove TN 109 F3
Walnut Hill TN 111 E3
Walnut Park CA 228 D3
Walnutport PA 93 F3
Walnut Ridge AR 108 A4
Walnut Sprs. TX 59 E3
Walpole MA 151 D2
Walpole NH 81 E4
Walsenburg CO 41 E4
Walsh CO 42 A4
Walsh Co. ND 19 E2
Walterboro SC 130 C1
Walterhill TN 109 F4
Walters OK 51 D4
Walthall MS 118 C4
Walthall Co. MS 134 B1
Waltham MA 151 D1
Walthill NE 35 F2
Walthourville GA 130 B3
Walton IN 89 F3
Walton KY 100 B3
Walton NY 93 F1
Walton Co. FL 136 B2
Walton Co. GA 121 D4
Walton Hills OH 204 G3
Walworth WI 74 C4
Walworth Co. SD 26 C2
Walworth Co. WI 74 C4
Wamac IL 98 C3
Wamego KS 43 F2
Wampsville NY 79 E3
Wamsutter WY 32 C3
Wanakah NY 78 A4
Wanamassa NJ 147 E2
Wanamingo MN 73 D1
Wanaque NJ 148 A3
Wanatah IN 89 E2
Wanblee SD 26 B4
Wanchese NC 115 F2
Wapakoneta OH 90 B4
Wapanucka OK 51 F4
Wapato WA 13 D4
Wapella IL 88 C4
Wapello IA 87 F2
Wapello Co. IA 87 D3
Waples TX 59 E3
Wappingers Falls NY 148 B1
War WV 111 F1
Ward AR 117 F2
Ward Co. ND 18 B2
Ward Co. TX 57 F4
Warden WA 13 E4
Wardner ID 14 B3
Wardsville MO 97 E3
Ware MA 150 B1
Ware Co. GA 129 F4
Wareham MA 151 E3
Ware Shoals SC 121 F3
Waretown NJ 147 E3
Warm Beach WA 12 C2
Warm Sprs. GA 128 C1
Warm Sprs. OR 21 D3
Warm Sprs. VA 102 B4
Warner NH 81 F4
Warner OK 116 A1
Warner SD 27 D2
Warner Robins GA 129 D2
Warr Acres OK 244 D2
Warren AR 117 E4
Warren IL 74 A4
Warren IN 90 A3
Warren ME 82 C2
Warren MA 150 B2
Warren MI 76 C4
Warren MN 19 F2
Warren OH 91 F2
Warren PA 92 B1
Warren RI 151 D3
Warren Co. GA 129 F1
Warren Co. IL 88 A3
Warren Co. IN 89 D4
Warren Co. IA 86 C2
Warren Co. KY 109 F2
Warren Co. MS 126 A2
Warren Co. MO 97 F3
Warren Co. NJ 93 F3
Warren Co. NY 80 C3
Warren Co. NC 113 D3
Warren Co. OH 100 C2
Warren Co. PA 92 B1
Warren Co. TN 110 A4
Warren Co. VA 103 D2
Warren Glen NJ 146 C1
Warren Park IN 99 F1
Warrensburg IL 98 C1
Warrensburg MO 96 C3
Warrensburg NY 80 C4
Warrensville PA 93 D2
Warrensville Hts. OH 204 G2
Warrenton GA 129 F1
Warrenton MO 97 F3
Warrenton NC 113 D3
Warrenton OR 20 B1
Warrenton VA 103 D3
Warrenville IL 203 A4
Warrick Co. IN 99 E4
Warrington FL 135 F2
Warrington PA 146 C2
Warrior AL 119 F4
Warrior Run PA 261 A2
Warroad MN 64 A1
Warsaw IL 87 F4
Warsaw IN 89 F2
Warsaw KY 100 B3
Warsaw MN 72 C1
Warsaw MO 97 D4
Warsaw NY 78 B4
Warsaw NC 123 E2
Warsaw OH 91 D4
Warsaw VA 103 E4
Warson Woods MO 256 B2
Wartburg TN 110 B4
Wartrace TN 120 A1
Warwick NY 148 A2
Warwick RI 150 C3
Wasatch Co. UT 31 F4
Wasco CA 45 D4
Wasco OR 21 D1
Wasco Co. OR 21 D2
Waseca MN 72 C1
Waseca Co. MN 72 C1
Washakie Co. WY 24 C4
Washburn IL 88 B3
Washburn IA 73 E4
Washburn ME 85 D2
Washburn ND 18 B3
Washburn WI 65 D4
Washburn Co. WI 67 E2
Washington CT 148 C1
Washington DC 144 B3
Washington GA 121 E4
Washington IL 88 B3
Washington IN 99 E3
Washington IA 87 E2
Washington KS 43 F1
Washington LA 133 F2
Washington MO 97 F3
Washington NJ 93 F3
Washington NC 115 D3
Washington OK 51 E3
Washington PA 91 F4
Washington UT 46 C1
Washington VT 81 E2
Washington VA 103 D3
Washington WV 101 E2
Washington Co. AL 127 E4
Washington Co. AR 106 B4
Washington Co. CO 34 A4
Washington Co. FL 136 C2
Washington Co. GA 129 E1
Washington Co. ID 22 A3
Washington Co. IL 98 B4
Washington Co. IN 99 F3
Washington Co. IA 87 E2
Washington Co. KS 43 E1
Washington Co. KY 110 B1
Washington Co. ME 83 E1
Washington Co. MD 103 D1
Washington Co. MN 67 D3
Washington Co. MS 126 A1
Washington Co. MO 97 F4
Washington Co. NE 35 F3
Washington Co. NY 81 D4
Washington Co. NC 113 F4
Washington Co. OH 101 E2
Washington Co. OK 106 A2
Washington Co. OR 20 B2
Washington Co. PA 92 A4
Washington Co. RI 150 C4
Washington Co. TN 111 E3
Washington Co. TX 61 F2
Washington Co. UT 38 C4
Washington Co. VT 81 E2
Washington Co. VA 111 F3
Washington Co. WI 74 C2
Washington C.H. OH 100 C1
Washington Crossing NJ 147 D2
Washington Crossing PA 147 D2
Washington Hts. NY 148 A1
Washington Par. LA 134 B1
Washington Park IL 256 D2
Washington Terrace UT 244 A2
Washingtonville NY 148 B1
Washingtonville OH 91 F3
Washita Co. OK 51 D3
Washoe Co. NV 29 E4
Washougal WA 20 C2
Washtenaw Co. MI 90 B1
Wasilla AK 154 C3
Waskom TX 124 C2
Wataga IL 88 A3
Watauga TN 111 E3
Watauga TX 207 B2
Watauga Co. NC 111 F3
Watchung NJ 147 E1
Waterboro ME 82 B3
Waterbury CT 149 D1
Waterbury VT 81 D2
Waterbury Ctr. VT 81 E2
Waterford CA 36 C4
Waterford CT 149 F2
Waterford MI 76 B4
Waterford NY 188 E1
Waterford PA 92 A1
Waterford WI 74 C4
Waterford Works NJ 147 D4
Waterloo IL 98 A4
Waterloo IN 90 A2
Waterloo IA 73 E4
Waterloo MD 144 C2
Waterloo NE 35 F3
Waterloo NY 79 D3
Waterloo WI 74 B3
Waterman IL 88 C1
Water Mill NY 149 E3
Waterproof LA 125 F3
Watertown CT 149 D1
Watertown FL 138 C2
Watertown MA 151 D1
Watertown MN 66 C4
Watertown NY 79 E1
Watertown SD 27 F2
Watertown TN 109 F4
Watertown WI 74 C3
Water Valley MS 118 B3
Waterville KS 43 F1
Waterville ME 82 C2
Waterville MN 72 C1
Waterville NY 79 E3
Waterville OH 90 C2
Waterville WA 13 E3
Watervliet MI 89 F1
Watervliet NY 188 E2
Watford City ND 18 A3
Wathena KS 96 B1
Watkins MN 66 C3
Watkins Glen NY 79 D4
Watkinsville GA 121 D4
Watonga OK 51 D2
Watonwan Co. MN 72 B1
Watseka IL 89 D3
Watson IL 98 C2
Watson LA 134 A2
Watsontown PA 93 D3
Watsonville CA 44 B2
Watterson Park KY 230 E2
Waubay SD 27 E2
Wauchula FL 140 C3
Wauconda IL 203 B1
Waukee IA 86 C2
Waukegan IL 75 D4
Waukesha WI 74 C3
Waukesha Co. WI 74 C3
Waukomis OK 51 E2
Waukon IA 73 E3
Waunakee WI 74 B3
Wauneta NE 34 B4
Waupaca WI 74 B1
Waupaca Co. WI 68 B4
Waupun WI 74 C2
Wauregan CT 150 B3
Waurika OK 51 E4
Wausa NE 35 E1
Wausau WI 68 B4
Wausaukee WI 68 C3
Wauseon OH 90 B2
Waushara Co. WI 74 B1
Wautoma WI 74 B1
Wauwatosa WI 234 C2
Wauzeka WI 73 F3
Waveland MS 134 C2
Waverly FL 141 D2
Waverly IL 98 B1
Waverly IA 73 D4
Waverly KS 96 A3
Waverly MN 66 C3
Waverly MO 96 C2
Waverly NE 35 F4
Waverly NY 93 E1
Waverly OH 101 D2
Waverly TN 109 D4
Waverly VA 113 E2
Waverly Hall GA 128 C2
Waxahachie TX 59 F3
Waxhaw NC 122 B2
Waycross GA 129 F4
Wayland IA 87 E2
Wayland MA 150 C1
Wayland MI 75 F4
Wayland NY 78 C4
Waymart PA 93 F2
Wayne IL 203 A4
Wayne MI 210 A4
Wayne NE 35 F2
Wayne NJ 148 A3
Wayne OH 90 C2
Wayne OK 51 E3
Wayne PA 146 C3
Wayne WV 101 D4
Wayne City IL 98 C4
Wayne Co. GA 130 A4
Wayne Co. IL 98 C3
Wayne Co. IN 100 A1
Wayne Co. IA 87 D3
Wayne Co. KY 110 B3
Wayne Co. MI 76 B4
Wayne Co. MS 127 D4
Wayne Co. MO 108 A2
Wayne Co. NE 35 F2
Wayne Co. NY 79 D3
Wayne Co. NC 123 E1
Wayne Co. OH 91 E3
Wayne Co. PA 93 F1
Wayne Co. TN 119 E1
Wayne Co. UT 39 F3
Wayne Co. WV 101 E4
Wayne Lakes OH 100 B1
Waynesboro GA 129 F1
Waynesboro MS 127 D4
Waynesboro PA 103 D1
Waynesboro TN 119 E1
Waynesboro VA 102 C4
Waynesburg OH 91 E3
Waynesburg PA 102 A1
Waynesfield OH 90 B4
Waynesville MO 107 E1
Waynesville NC 121 E1
Waynesville OH 100 C1
Waynetown IN 89 E4
Waynoka OK 51 D1
Wayzata MN 235 A2
Weakley Co. TN 108 C3
Weare NH 81 F4
Weatherby Lake MO 224 B2
Weatherford OK 51 D3
Weatherford TX 59 E2
Weatherly PA 93 F3
Weaubleau MO 96 C4
Weaver AL 120 A4
Weaverville CA 28 B4
Weaverville NC 111 E4
Webb AL 128 B4
Webb MS 118 B4
Webb City MO 106 B2

F
Howard University Beltsville Campus
Technology Univ.
BELTSVILLE
AGRICULTURAL
RESEARCH
CENTER
Greenbelt
Greenbelt Museum
NASA Goddard Space Flight Center
GREENBELT PARK
New Carrollton
Seabrook
Lanham
Landover Hills
Dodge Park
Glenarden
Kentland
Palmer Park
FedExField
Seat Pleasant
Largo
Walker Mill
Walker Mill Reg. Park
Ritchie
District Heights
Forestville
Morningside
JOINT BASE ANDREWS
Woodyard
1
2
3
4
5
0 1 2 mi
0 1 2 3 km
F

Figures after entries indicate page number and grid reference.

Webb Co. TX 60 C4
Webbers Falls OK 116 B1
Webberville MI 76 B4
Weber City VA 111 E3
Weber Co. UT 31 F3
Webster FL 140 C1
Webster MD 145 D1
Webster MA 150 B2
Webster NY 78 C3
Webster NC 121 D1
Webster SD 27 E2
Webster TX 132 B3
Webster WI 67 E2
Webster City IA 72 C4
Webster Co. GA 128 C3
Webster Co. IA 72 B4
Webster Co. KY 109 E1
Webster Co. MS 118 C4
Webster Co. MO 107 D2
Webster Co. NE 35 E4
Webster Co. WV 102 A3
Webster Groves MO 256 B3
Webster Par. LA 125 D2
Webster Sprs. WV 102 A3
Weddington NC 122 B2
Wedowee AL 128 B1
Weed CA 28 C3
Weedsport NY 79 D3
Weehawken NJ 148 B4
Weeki Wachee Gardens FL 140 B1
Weeping Water NE 35 F4
Weidman MI 76 A2
Weigelstown PA 103 E1
Weimar CA 36 C2
Weimar TX 61 F2
Weiner AR 108 A4
Weippe ID 14 B4
Weir KS 106 B2
Weir MS 126 C1
Weir TX 61 E1
Weirsdale FL 139 D4
Weirton WV 91 F4
Weiser ID 22 A3
Welaka FL 139 D4
Welby CO 209 C2
Welch OK 106 B2
Welch WV 111 F1
Welcome LA 134 A3
Welcome MN 72 B2
Welcome NC 112 B4
Welcome SC 217 A2
Weld Co. CO 33 F4
Weldon CA 45 E4
Weldon NC 113 E3
Weldon Spr. MO 98 A3
Weleetka OK 51 F3
Wellesley MA 151 D1
Wellfleet MA 151 F2
Wellford SC 217 C1
Welling OK 106 B4
Wellington CO 33 E4
Wellington FL 143 E1
Wellington KS 43 E4
Wellington KY 230 E2
Wellington MO 96 C2
Wellington OH 91 D2
Wellington TX 50 C4
Wellington UT 39 F1
Wellman IA 87 E2
Wells ME 82 B4
Wells MN 72 C2
Wells NV 30 C3
Wells TX 124 B4
Wells VT 81 D4
Wellsboro IN 89 E2
Wellsboro PA 93 D1
Wellsburg IA 73 D4
Wellsburg NY 93 D1
Wellsburg WV 91 F4
Wells Co. IN 90 A3
Wells Co. ND 18 C3
Wells River VT 81 E2
Wellston MO 256 B2
Wellston OH 101 D2
Wellston OK 51 F2
Wellsville KS 96 B3
Wellsville MO 97 F2
Wellsville NY 92 C1
Wellsville OH 91 F3
Wellsville UT 31 E3
Wellton AZ 54 A2
Welsh LA 133 E2
Wenatchee WA 13 D3
Wendell ID 30 C1
Wendell NC 113 D4
Wenden AZ 54 B1
Wendover UT 31 D4
Wenham MA 151 F1
Wenona IL 88 B3
Wenonah NJ 146 C3
Wentworth NC 112 B3
Wentzville MO 98 A3
Wernersville PA 146 A2
Weslaco TX 63 E4
Wesley Chapel FL 140 C2
Wesley Chapel NC 122 B2
Wesley Hills NY 148 B2
Wesleyville PA 92 A1
Wessington SD 27 D3
Wessington Sprs. SD 27 D3
Wesson MS 126 B4
West TX 59 E3
W. Alexandria OH 100 B1
W. Allis WI 74 C3
W. Alton MO 98 A3
W. Babylon NY 148 C4
W. Baden Sprs. IN 99 F3
W. Baraboo WI 74 A2
W. Barnstable MA 151 E3
W. Barrington RI 150 C3
W. Baton Rouge Par. LA 134 A2
W. Bend IA 72 B3
W. Bend WI 74 C2
W. Berlin NJ 147 D3
W. Blocton AL 127 F1
Westborough MA 150 C1

POINTS OF INTEREST

Arena Stage E4
Arlington Natl. Cemetery A4
Art Museum of the Americas C2
Arts & Industries Building E3
Belmont-Paul Women's Equality National Monument C2
Blair House C2
Bureau of Engraving & Printing D3
Capital One Arena E2
Cathedral of St. Matthew the Apostle C1
Daughters of the American Revolution Constitution Hall C2
Decatur House C1
Dept. of Agriculture D3
Dept. of Commerce D2
Dept. of Education E3
Dept. of Energy E3
Dept. of Housing and Urban Development E3
Dept. of Justice E2
Dept. of Labor F2
Dept. of State C2
Dept. of the Interior C2
Dept. of the Treasury D2
Dept. of Transportation G4
Dept. of Veterans Affairs D1
District of Columbia Court House E2
District of Columbia War Memorial C3
Donald W. Reynolds Center for American Art & Portraiture E2
Dwight D. Eisenhower Memorial E3
The Ellipse D2
Environmental Protection Agency D2
Fish Wharf D4
Folger Shakespeare Library G3
Ford's Theatre Natl. Hist. Site E2
Franklin Delano Roosevelt Memorial C3
Friendship Archway E1
Gallaudet Univ. G1
George Mason Memorial C4
Georgetown Park A1
Georgetown Univ. Law Center F2
George Washington Univ. C2
Government Publishing Office F1
Hirshhorn Mus. & Sculpture Garden E3
Ice Skating Rink E2
Internal Revenue Service E2
International Spy Museum E3
James Madison Building G3
J. Edgar Hoover FBI Building E2
John Adams Building G3
John Ericsson Memorial B3
John F. Kennedy Center for the Performing Arts B2
John F. Kennedy Gravesite A4
Judiciary Square E2
Korean War Veterans Memorial C3
Lafayette Square D1
Lansburgh Theatre E2
L'Enfant Plaza E3
Library of Congress G3
Lincoln Memorial B3
Lyndon B. Johnson Memorial Grove B4
Marine Corps War Memorial (Iwo Jima Memorial) A3
Martin Luther King, Jr. Mem. Library E2
Martin Luther King, Jr. Natl. Memorial C3
Military Women's Memorial A4
Museum of the Bible E3
NASA E4
Natl. Air & Space Museum E3
Natl. Acad. of Sciences, Engineering, & Medicine E2
The Natl. Archives E2
Natl. Building Museum E2
Natl. Gallery of Art East Building E3
Natl. Gallery of Art E3
Natl. Geographic Museum D1
National Mall E3
Natl. Mus. of African Art E3
Natl. Mus. of African Amerian Hist. & Culture D3
Natl. Mus. of American Hist. D2
Natl. Mus. of Asian Art D3
Natl. Mus. of Natural Hist. E2
Natl. Mus. of the American Indian E3
Natl. Mus. of Women in the Arts D1
Natl. Postal Museum F2
Natl. Theatre D2
Natl. WWI Memorial D2
Natl. WWII Memorial C3
Navy-Merchant Marine Memorial C4
The Netherlands Carillon A3
Octagon Museum C2
Old Stone House B1
Organization of American States C2
Reflecting Pool C3
Renwick Gallery C2
Ronald Reagan Building and Intl. Trade Center D2
Sackler Gallery E3
Seabee Memorial A3
Sidney Harman Hall E2
Signers of the Declaration of Independence Memorial C3
Smithsonian Institution Building (The Castle) E3
The Supreme Court G3
Taft Memorial Carillon F2
Theodore Roosevelt Memorial A2
Thomas Jefferson Building G3
Thomas Jefferson Memorial D4
Union Station F2
United Spanish War Veterans Memorial A3
U.S. Botanic Garden F3
U.S. Capitol F3
U.S. Capitol Visitor Center F3
U.S. Claims Court D1
U.S. District Court House E2
U.S. Grant Memorial F3
U.S. Holocaust Memorial Museum D3
U.S. Navy Memorial & Naval Heritage Center E2
U.S. Postal Service Headquarters E3
Vietnam Veterans Memorial C2
Vietnam Women's Memorial C3
Warner Theatre D2
Washington Convention Center E1
The Washington Design Center D1
Washington Harbour A1
Washington Monument D3
Washington Post D1
The White House D2
White House Visitor Center D2
Zero Milestone D2

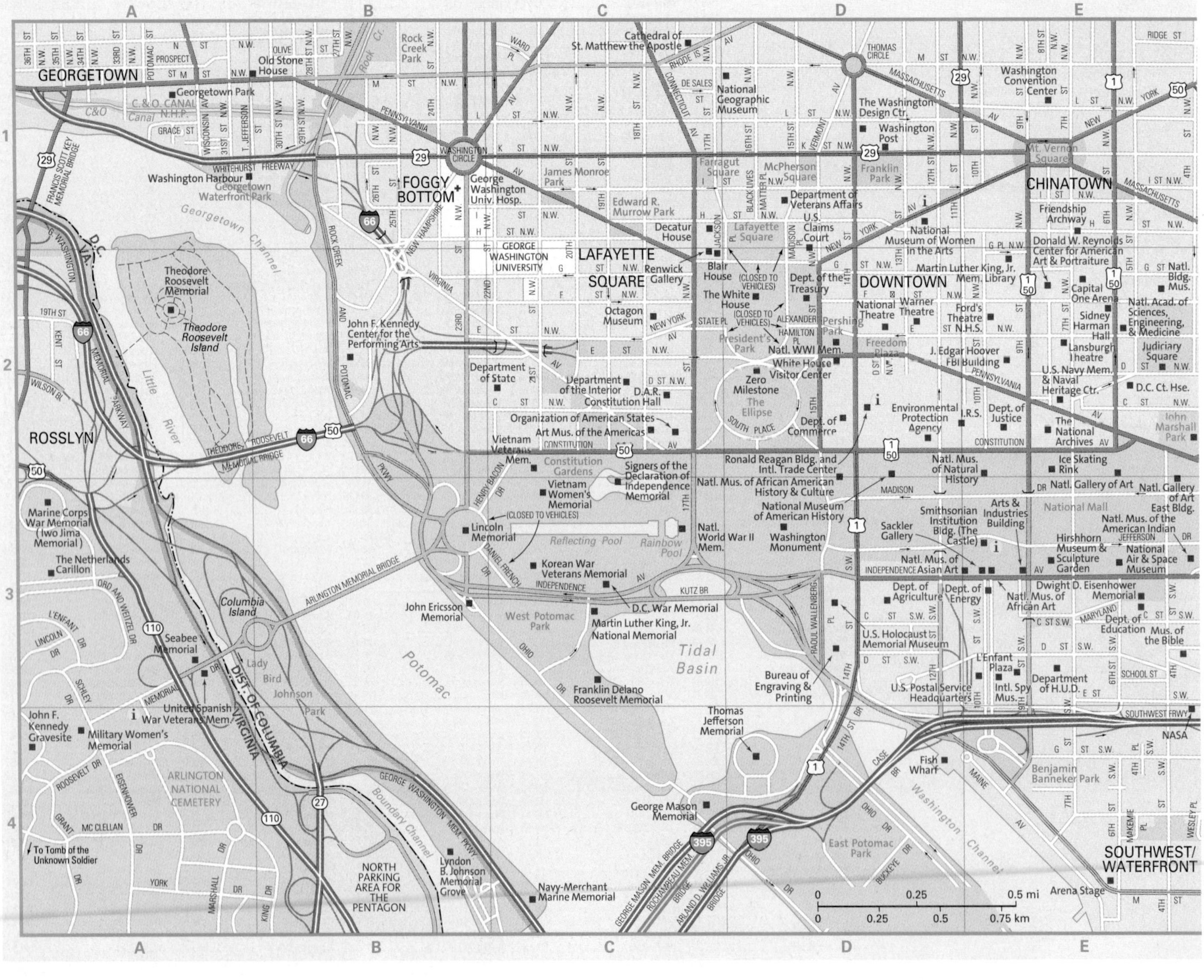
GEORGETOWN
FOGGY BOTTOM
LAFAYETTE SQUARE
DOWNTOWN
CHINATOWN
ROSSLYN
SOUTHWEST/ WATERFRONT
Theodore Roosevelt Island
Columbia Island
Potomac
Tidal Basin
Washington Channel
Little River
ARLINGTON NATIONAL CEMETERY
NORTH PARKING AREA FOR THE PENTAGON
Reflecting Pool
National Mall
The White House
The Ellipse
Washington Monument
Lincoln Memorial
Thomas Jefferson Memorial
West Potomac Park
East Potomac Park
D.C.
VA.
DIST. OF COLUMBIA
VIRGINIA
0 0.25 0.5 mi
0 0.25 0.5 0.75 km

Entries in **bold black** indicate counties or parishes.
Entries in **bold color** indicate cities with detailed inset maps.

W. Bountiful UT 31 E4
W. Bowdoin ME 82 B3
W. Boylston MA 150 C1
W. Branch IA 87 F2
W. Branch MI 76 B1
W. Bridgewater MA 151 D2
Westbrook CT 149 E2
Westbrook ME 82 B3
Westbrook MN 72 A1
W. Brookfield MA 150 B1
W. Buechel KY 230 E2
W. Burke VT 81 E1
W. Burlington IA 87 F3
Westbury NY 148 C4
W. Buxton ME 82 B3
Westby WI 73 F2
W. Caldwell NJ 240 A2
W. Carroll Par. LA 125 F2
W. Carrollton OH 100 B1
W. Carthage NY 79 E1
Westchester IL 203 C4
W. Chester PA 146 B3
Westchester Co. NY 148 B2
W. Chicago IL 203 A4
West City IL 98 C4
Westcliffe CO 41 D3
W. College Corner IN 100 B1
W. Columbia SC 205 E2
W. Columbia TX 132 A4
W. Concord MA 150 C1
W. Concord MN 73 D1
W. Conshohocken PA 248 B2
W. Covina CA 228 E2
W. Creek NJ 147 E4
W. Crossett AR 125 F1
W. Dennis MA 151 F3
W. Des Moines IA 86 C2
W. Dummerston VT 94 C1
W. Dundee IL 88 C1
W. Elmira NY 93 D1
W. End AL 120 A4
W. Enfield ME 85 D4
Westerly RI 150 B4
Western Grove AR 107 D4
Westernport MD 102 B2
Western Sprs. IL 203 C5
Westerville OH 90 C4
W. Fairlee VT 81 E3
W. Fairview PA 218 A1
W. Falmouth ME 251 A1
W. Falmouth MA 151 E4
W. Fargo ND 19 E4
W. Feliciana Par. LA 133 F1
Westfield IL 99 D2
Westfield IN 89 F4
Westfield MA 150 A2
Westfield NJ 147 E1
Westfield NY 78 A4
Westfield PA 93 D1
Westfield TX 132 A3
Westfield WI 74 B2
Westfield Ctr. OH 91 E3
W. Fork AR 106 C4
W. Frankfort IL 98 C4
W. Freehold NJ 147 E2
W. Friendship MD 144 B2
W. Gate of Lomond VA 144 A3
W. Glacier MT 15 D2
W. Glens Falls NY 80 C4
W. Grove PA 146 B3
W. Hamlin WV 101 E4
Westhampton NY 149 E3
Westhampton Beach NY 149 E4
W. Hartford CT 150 A3
W. Hartford VT 81 E3
W. Haven CT 149 D2
W. Haven UT 244 A1
W. Hazleton PA 93 E3
W. Helena AR 118 A2
W. Hollywood CA 228 C2
W. Homestead PA 250 C2
Westhope ND 18 B1
W. Hurley NY 94 B2
W. Islip NY 148 C4
W. Jefferson NC 111 F3
W. Jefferson OH 101 D1
W. Jordan UT 31 E4
W. Kennebunk ME 82 B4
W. Kingston RI 150 C4
W. Kittanning PA 92 A3
W. Lafayette IN 89 E4
W. Lafayette OH 91 E4
Westlake LA 133 D2
Westlake OH 91 E2
W. Lake Hills TX 61 E1
Westlake Vil. CA 52 B2
Westland MI 76 B4
W. Lebanon IN 89 D4
W. Leechburg PA 92 A3
Westley CA 36 C4
W. Liberty IA 87 F2
W. Liberty KY 101 D4
W. Liberty OH 90 B4
W. Liberty WV 91 F4
W. Linn OR 20 C2
W. Logan WV 101 E4
W. Long Branch NJ 147 F2
W. Mahopac NY 148 B2
W. Mansfield OH 90 C4
W. Mayfield PA 91 F3
W. Medway MA 150 C2
W. Melbourne FL 141 E2
W. Memphis AR 118 B1
Westmere NY 94 B1
W. Miami FL 143 E2
W. Middlesex PA 91 F2
W. Mifflin PA 250 C3
W. Milford NJ 148 A2
W. Milford WV 102 A2
W. Milton OH 100 B1
W. Milwaukee WI 234 C3
Westminster CA 228 E4
Westminster CO 41 E1
Westminster MD 144 B1
Westminster MA 95 D1
Westminster SC 121 E2
Westminster VT 81 E4
W. Monroe LA 125 E2
Westmont IL 203 C5
Westmont PA 92 B4
Westmoreland KS 43 F2
Westmoreland TN 109 F3
Westmoreland Co. PA 92 B4
Westmoreland Co. VA 103 E4
Westmorland CA 53 E4
W. Mystic CT 149 F2
W. Newton PA 92 A4
W. New York NJ 148 B4
W. Odessa TX 57 F3
W. Okoboji IA 72 A3
Weston CT 148 C2
Weston FL 143 E2
Weston ID 31 E2
Weston MO 96 B2
Weston NE 35 F3
Weston OH 90 B2
Weston OR 21 F1
Weston TX 59 F1
Weston WV 102 A2
Weston WI 68 B4
Weston Co. WY 25 F4
Weston Lakes TX 132 A3
Weston Mills NY 92 C1
W. Orange NJ 148 A4
W. Orange TX 132 C3
W. Ossipee NH 81 F3
Westover TN 118 C1
Westover Hills TX 207 A2
W. Palm Beach FL 143 F1
W. Paris ME 82 B2
W. Pelham MA 150 A1
W. Pelzer SC 121 E2
W. Pensacola FL 135 F2
W. Peoria IL 88 B3
Westphalia MI 76 A3
W. Pittston PA 261 C1
W. Plains MO 107 E3
W. Point CA 36 C3
W. Point GA 128 B1
Westpoint IN 89 E4
W. Point IA 87 F3
W. Point KY 99 F4
W. Point MS 119 D4
W. Point NE 35 F2
W. Point UT 31 E3
W. Point VA 113 F1
Westport CT 148 C2
Westport IN 100 A2
Westport KY 100 A3
Westport NY 81 D2
Westport OR 20 B1
Westport WA 12 B4
W. Portsmouth OH 101 D3
W. Redding CT 148 C2
W. Richland WA 13 E4
W. Rockport ME 82 C2
W. Rutland VT 81 D3
W. Sacramento CA 36 C3
W. St. Paul MN 235 D3
W. Salem IL 99 D3
W. Salem OH 91 D3
W. Salem WI 73 F2
W. Sand Lake NY 94 B1
W. Sayville NY 149 D4
W. Selmont AL 127 F2
W. Seneca NY 78 B3
W. Siloam Sprs. OK 106 B4
W. Slope OR 251 C2
W. Springfield MA 150 A2
W. Springfield VA 270 A5
W. Sterling MA 150 B1
W. Stockbridge MA 94 B2
W. Suffield CT 150 A2
W. Swanzey NH 95 D1
W. Tawakoni TX 59 F2
W. Terre Haute IN 99 E2
W. Topsham VT 81 E2
Westtown NY 148 A2
W. Townshend VT 81 E4
W. Union IA 73 E3
W. Union OH 100 C3
W. Union WV 101 F2
W. Unity OH 90 B2
W. University Place TX 132 A3
W. Upton MA 150 C2
Westvale NY 265 A2
W. Valley City UT 31 E4
W. View PA 250 B1
Westville IL 99 D1
Westville IN 89 E2
Westville NJ 248 C4
Westville OK 106 B4
W. Wareham MA 151 E3
W. Warren MA 150 B2
W. Warwick RI 150 C3
Westway TX 56 C3
Westwego LA 134 B3
W. Wendover NV 31 D4
W. Willington CT 150 A3
W. Winfield NY 79 F3
Westwood CA 29 D4
Westwood KS 224 B3
Westwood KY 101 D3
Westwood MA 151 D2
Westwood NJ 148 B3
Westwood Lakes FL 143 E2
Westworth Vil. TX 207 A2
W. Wyoming PA 261 B1
W. Yarmouth MA 151 F3
W. Yellowstone MT 23 F3
W. York PA 275 C1
Wethersfield CT 150 A3
Wetmore KS 96 A1
Wetumka OK 51 F3
Wetumpka AL 128 A2
Wetzel Co. WV 102 A1
Wewahitchka FL 137 D2
Wewoka OK 51 F3
Wexford Co. MI 69 F4
Weyauwega WI 74 B1
Weyers Cave VA 102 C4
Weymouth MA 151 D2
Wharton NJ 148 A3
Wharton OH 90 C3
Wharton TX 61 F3
Wharton Co. TX 61 F3
What Cheer IA 87 E2
Whatcom Co. WA 12 C1
Whately MA 150 A1
Wheatfield IN 89 E2
Wheatland CA 36 C2
Wheatland IN 99 E3
Wheatland IA 87 F1
Wheatland WY 33 E2
Wheatland Co. MT 16 B4
Wheatley AR 118 A2
Wheaton IL 89 D1
Wheaton MD 144 B3
Wheaton MN 27 F1
Wheaton MO 106 C2
Wheat Ridge CO 209 B3
Wheeler MS 119 D2

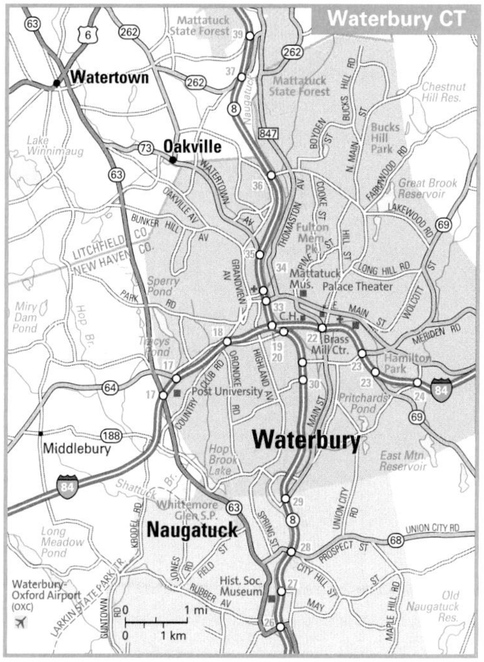
Waterbury CT
Watertown
Oakville
Waterbury
Naugatuck
Middlebury
Mattatuck State Forest
Post University
Hist. Soc. Museum
Mattatuck Mus.
Palace Theater
Brass Mill Ctr.
Hamilton Park
Whittemore Glen S.P.
Waterbury-Oxford Airport (OXC)
Fulton Mem. Pk.
Great Brook Reservoir
Chestnut Hill Res.
Bucks Hill Park
East Mtn. Reservoir
Old Naugatuck Res.
Lake Winnemaug
Sperry Pond
Pritchards Pond
Long Meadow Pond
Hop Brook Lake
0 1 mi
0 1 km

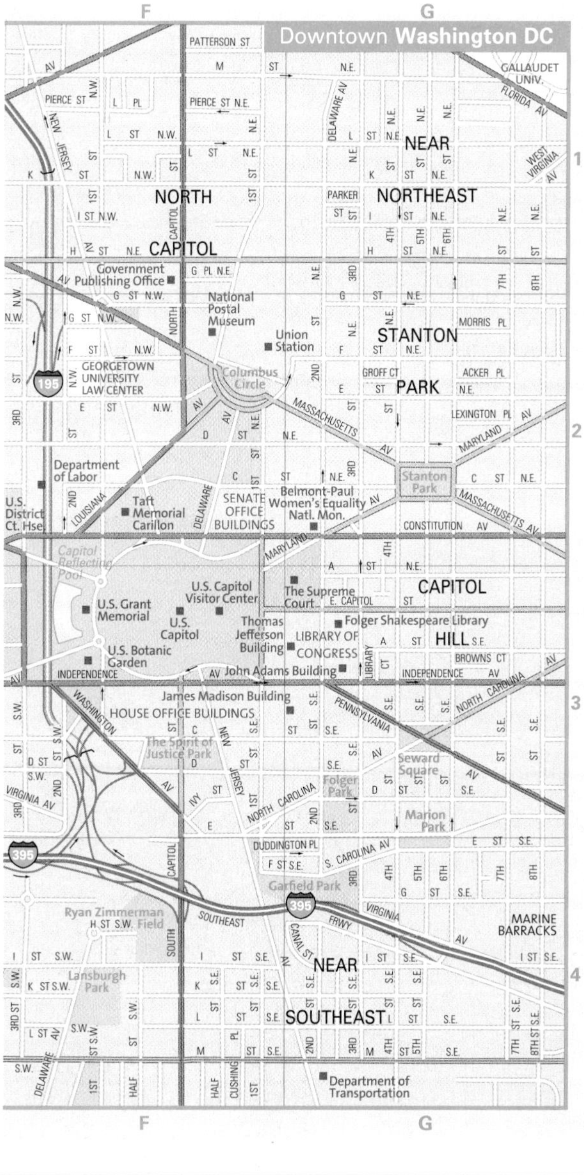
Downtown Washington DC
NORTH CAPITOL
NEAR NORTHEAST
STANTON PARK
CAPITOL HILL
NEAR SOUTHEAST
Government Publishing Office
National Postal Museum
Union Station
Georgetown University Law Center
Columbus Circle
Department of Labor
U.S. District Ct. Hse
Taft Memorial Carillon
Senate Office Buildings
Belmont-Paul Women's Equality Natl. Mon.
Stanton Park
Capitol Reflecting Pool
U.S. Grant Memorial
U.S. Capitol Visitor Center
U.S. Capitol
The Supreme Court
Folger Shakespeare Library
Thomas Jefferson Building
Library of Congress
John Adams Building
U.S. Botanic Garden
James Madison Building
House Office Buildings
The Spirit of Justice Park
Seward Square
Folger Park
Marion Park
Garfield Park
Ryan Zimmerman Field
Lansburgh Park
Marine Barracks
Department of Transportation
Gallaudet Univ.

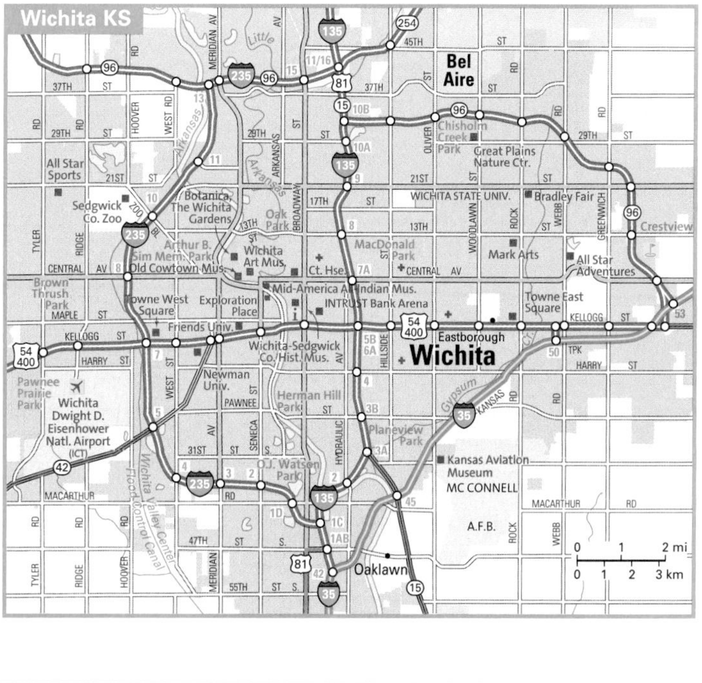
Wichita KS
Wichita
Bel Aire
Eastborough
Oaklawn
Crestview
Wichita State Univ.
Bradley Fair
Chisholm Creek Park
Great Plains Nature Ctr.
All Star Sports
Sedgwick Co. Zoo
Botanica, The Wichita Gardens
Oak Park
Arthur B. Sim Mem. Park
Old Cowtown Mus.
Wichita Art Mus.
Ct. Hse.
MacDonald Park
Mark Arts
All Star Adventures
Brown Thrush Park
Towne West Square
Exploration Place
Mid-America All-Indian Mus.
INTRUST Bank Arena
Towne East Square
Friends Univ.
Wichita-Sedgwick Co. Hist. Mus.
Newman Univ.
Herman Hill Park
Pawnee Prairie Park
Wichita Dwight D. Eisenhower Natl. Airport (ICT)
Planeview Park
O.J. Watson Park
Kansas Aviation Museum
MC CONNELL A.F.B.
Wichita Valley Center Flood Control Canal
0 1 2 mi
0 1 2 3 km

Figures after entries indicate page number and grid reference.

Wheeler OR 20 B1
Wheeler TX 50 C3
Wheeler Co. GA 129 E3
Wheeler Co. NE 35 D2
Wheeler Co. OR 21 E3
Wheeler Co. TX 50 C3
Wheelersburg OH 101 D3
Wheeling IL 89 D1
Wheeling WV 91 F4
Wheelwright KY 111 E1
Wheelwright MA 150 B1
Whigham GA 137 E1
Whippany NJ 148 A3
Whispering Pines NC 122 C1
White Pine TN 111 D4
White Pine Co. NV 38 B1
White Plains KY 109 E2
White Plains MD 144 B4
White Plains NY 148 B3
White Plains NC 112 A3
Whiteriver AZ 55 E1
White River SD 26 C4
White River Jct. VT 81 E3
White Rock NM 48 C2
Whiterocks UT 32 A4
White Salmon WA 21 D1
Whitesboro NY 79 E3
Whitesboro TX 59 F1
Wilber NE 35 F4
Wilberforce OH 100 C1
Wilbraham MA 150 A2
Wilbur WA 13 F3
Wilbur Park MO 256 B3
Wilburton OK 116 A2
Wilcox NE 35 D4
Wilcox PA 92 B2
Wilcox Co. AL 127 F3
Wilcox Co. GA 129 E3
Wilder ID 22 A4
Wilder KY 204 B3
Wilder VT 81 E3
Wilderness VA 103 D4
Williamston SC 121 E2
Williamstown KY 100 B3
Williamstown MA 94 C1
Williamstown NJ 146 C4
Williamstown NY 79 E2
Williamstown PA 93 E4
Williamstown VT 81 E2
Williamstown WV 101 F2
Williamsville DE 114 C1
Williamsville IL 98 B1
Williamsville MS 126 C1
Williamsville NY 198 C2
Willimantic CT 150 B3
Willingboro NJ 147 D3
Wilson Co. NC 113 E4
Wilson Co. TN 109 F3
Wilson Co. TX 61 E3
Wilson's Mills NC 123 D1
Wilsonville AL 128 A1
Wilsonville IL 98 B2
Wilsonville OR 20 C2
Wilton AL 127 F1
Wilton AR 116 C4
Wilton CA 36 C3
Wilton CT 148 C2
Wilton IA 87 F2
Wilton ME 82 B2
Wilton NH 95 D1
Wilton NY 80 C4
Wilton ND 18 C3
Wilton WI 73 F2
Wilton Manors FL 233 C2
Wimauma FL 140 C3
Wimberley TX 61 D2
Wimbledon ND 19 D3
Winamac IN 89 E3
Winchendon MA 95 D1
Winchester CA 53 D3
Winchester ID 22 B1
Winchester IL 98 A1
Winchester IN 90 A4
Winchester KS 96 A2
Winchester KY 100 B4
Winchester MA 151 D1
Winchester MO 256 A2
Winchester NH 94 C1
Winchester OH 100 C3
Winchester OK 51 F2
Winchester TN 120 A1
Winchester VA 103 D2
Winchester Bay OR 20 A4
Windber PA 92 B4
Windcrest TX 61 D2
Winder GA 121 D3
Windermere FL 141 D1
Windfall IN 89 F4
Wind Gap PA 93 F3
Windham CT 149 F1
Windham NH 95 E1
Windham OH 91 F2
Windham Co. CT 150 B3
Windham Co. VT 81 E4
Wind Lake WI 74 C3
Windom MN 72 B2
Window Rock AZ 48 A2
Wind Pt. WI 75 D4
Windsor CA 36 B3
Windsor CO 33 E4
Windsor CT 150 A3
Windsor IL 98 C2
Windsor MO 96 C3
Windsor NY 93 F1
Windsor NC 113 F4
Windsor PA 103 E1
Windsor VT 81 E4
Windsor VA 113 F2
Windsor WI 74 B3
Windsor Co. VT 81 E3
Windsor Hts. WV 91 F4
Windsor Hills CA 228 C3
Windsor Locks CT 150 A2
Windthorst TX 59 D1
Windy Hills KY 230 E1
Winfall NC 113 F3
Winfield AL 119 E4
Winfield IL 203 B4
Winfield IN 89 D2
Winfield IA 87 F3
Winfield KS 43 F4
Winfield MO 98 A2
Winfield TN 110 C3
Winfield TX 124 B1
Winfield WV 101 E3
Wingate NC 122 B2
Wingdale NY 148 C1
Wingo KY 108 C3
Winifred MT 16 B3
Wink TX 57 F4
Winkelman AZ 55 D2
Winkler Co. TX 57 F3
Winlock WA 12 B4
Winnebago IL 74 B4
Winnebago MN 72 C2
Winnebago NE 35 F2
Winnebago Co. IL 74 B4
Winnebago Co. IA 72 C2
Winnebago Co. WI 74 C1
Winneconne WI 74 C1
Winnecunnet MA 151 D2
Winnemucca NV 30 A3
Winner SD 26 C4
Winneshiek Co. IA 73 E3
Winnetka IL 203 D2
Winnett MT 16 C4
Winnfield LA 125 E3
Winnie TX 132 C3
Winnisquam NH 81 F4
Winn Par. LA 125 E3
Winnsboro LA 125 F3
Winnsboro SC 122 A3
Winnsboro TX 124 A1
Winnsboro Mills SC 122 A3
Winona MN 73 E1
Winona MS 118 B4
Winona MO 107 F2
Winona OH 91 F3
Winona TX 124 B2
Winona Co. MN 73 E1
Winona Lake IN 89 F2
Winooski VT 81 D2
Winside NE 35 E2
Winslow AZ 47 E3

Five Forks A1
Gloucester Pt. C2
Hayes C1
Lackey C2
Newport News C2
Scotland A2
Wicomico C1
Williamsburg A1
Yorktown C2

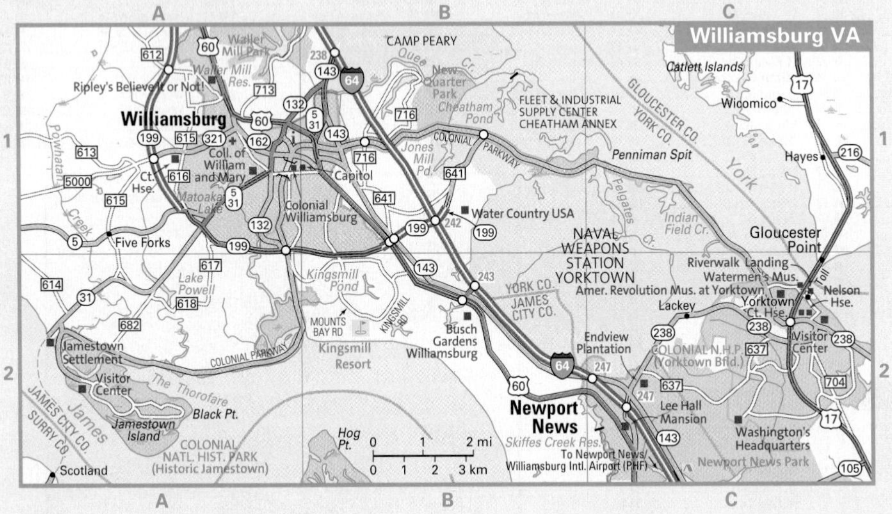
Williamsburg VA
A
B
C
1
2
CAMP PEARY
Catlett Islands
Wicomico
FLEET & INDUSTRIAL SUPPLY CENTER CHEATHAM ANNEX
Cheatham Pond
Ripley's Believe It or Not!
Waller Mill Park
Waller Mill Res.
Williamsburg
Coll. of William and Mary
Capitol
Ct. Hse.
Colonial Williamsburg
Matoaka Lake
Jones Mill Pd.
COLONIAL PARKWAY
Penniman Spit
Hayes
York
Water Country USA
NAVAL WEAPONS STATION YORKTOWN
Gloucester Point
Five Forks
Lake Powell
Kingsmill Pond
Kingsmill Resort
Riverwalk Landing
Watermen's Mus.
Amer. Revolution Mus. at Yorktown
Yorktown
Nelson Hse.
Lackey
Busch Gardens Williamsburg
Jamestown Settlement
Visitor Center
Endview Plantation
COLONIAL N.H.P. (Yorktown Bfld.)
The Thorofare
James
Black Pt.
Jamestown Island
COLONIAL NATL. HIST. PARK (Historic Jamestown)
Scotland
Hog Pt.
Newport News
Lee Hall Mansion
Washington's Headquarters
Skiffes Creek Res.
To Newport News/ Williamsburg Intl. Airport (PHF)
Newport News Park
0 1 2 mi
0 1 2 3 km

Whitaker PA 250 C2
Whitakers NC 113 E4
White GA 120 C3
White SD 27 F3
White Bear Lake MN 235 D1
White Bird ID 22 B1
White Bluff TN 109 E4
White Castle LA 134 A2
White Ctr. WA 262 B4
White City FL 141 E3
White City KS 43 F2
White City OR 28 B2
White Cloud MI 75 F2
White Co. AR 117 F1
White Co. GA 121 D2
White Co. IL 99 D4
White Co. IN 89 E3
White Co. TN 110 A4
White Deer TX 50 B3
White Earth MN 19 F3
Whiteface TX 57 F1
Whitefield NH 81 F2
Whitefish MT 15 D2
Whitefish Bay WI 234 D1
Whiteford MD 146 A4
White Hall AL 127 F2
White Hall AR 117 E3
White Hall IL 98 A2
Whitehall MI 75 E2
Whitehall MT 23 E1
Whitehall NY 81 D3
Whitehall OH 206 C2
Whitehall PA 146 B1
Whitehall PA 250 B3
Whitehall VA 102 C4
White Hall VA 103 D2
White Hall WV 102 A2
Whitehall WI 73 F1
White Haven PA 93 F3
White Horse NJ 147 D2
White Horse PA 146 A3
White Horse Beach MA 151 E3
Whitehouse OH 90 B2
White House TN 109 F3
Whitehouse TX 124 B3
White House Sta. NJ 147 D1
White Island Shores MA 151 E3
White Lake NY 94 A3
White Lake NC 123 D2
White Lake SD 27 D4
Whiteland IN 99 F1
Whitelaw WI 75 D1
White Marsh MD 193 E2
White Marsh VA 113 F1
White Oak MD 270 D1
White Oak OH 204 A2
White Oak PA 92 A4
White Oak TX 124 B2
White Pigeon MI 89 F1
White Pine MI 65 E4
Whitesburg GA 120 B4
Whitesburg KY 111 D2
White Settlement TX 207 A2
White Shield ND 18 B3
Whiteside Co. IL 88 A1
White Sprs. FL 138 C2
White Stone VA 113 F1
White Sulphur Sprs. MT 15 F4
White Sulphur Sprs. WV 112 B1
Whitesville KY 109 F1
Whitesville NY 92 C1
Whitesville WV 101 F4
White Swan WA 13 D4
Whiteville NC 123 D3
Whiteville TN 118 C1
Whitewater KS 43 E3
Whitewater WI 74 C3
Whitewood SD 25 F3
Whitewright TX 59 F1
Whitfield FL 140 B3
Whitfield Co. GA 120 B2
Whiting IN 89 D2
Whiting IA 35 F2
Whiting NJ 147 E3
Whiting WI 68 B4
Whitinsville MA 150 C2
Whitley City KY 110 C3
Whitley Co. IN 89 F3
Whitley Co. KY 110 C2
Whitman MA 151 D2
Whitman Co. WA 14 A4
Whitmire SC 121 F3
Whitmore Lake MI 76 B4
Whitmore Vil. HI 152 A2
Whitney TX 59 E3
Whitney Pt. NY 79 E4
Whitsett NC 112 B4
Whittemore IA 72 B3
Whittemore MI 76 B1
Whittier CA 52 C2
Whitwell TN 120 B1
Why AZ 54 B3
Wibaux MT 17 F4
Wibaux Co. MT 17 F4
Wichita KS 43 E4
Wichita Co. KS 42 B3
Wichita Co. TX 59 D1
Wichita Falls TX 59 D1
Wickenburg AZ 54 B1
Wickes AR 116 C3
Wickett TX 57 F4
Wickford RI 150 C4
Wickliffe KY 108 C2
Wickliffe OH 91 E2
Wicomico Church VA 113 F1
Wicomico Co. MD 114 C1
Widefield CO 205 D2
Wiggins CO 33 F4
Wiggins MS 135 D1
Wilbarger Co. TX 58 C1
Wildomar CA 53 D3
Wild Rose WI 74 B1
Wildwood FL 140 C1
Wildwood MO 98 A3
Wildwood NJ 104 C4
Wildwood TX 132 C2
Wildwood Crest NJ 104 C4
Wiley CO 42 A3
Wilhoit AZ 47 D4
Wilkes-Barre PA 93 E2
Wilkesboro NC 111 F4
Wilkes Co. GA 121 E4
Wilkes Co. NC 112 A3
Wilkeson WA 12 C3
Wilkin Co. MN 19 F4
Wilkinsburg PA 250 C2
Wilkinson Co. GA 129 E2
Wilkinson Co. MS 125 F4
Willacoochee GA 129 E4
Willacy Co. TX 63 F3
Willamina OR 20 B2
Willard MO 107 D2
Willard NM 49 D4
Willard OH 91 D3
Willard UT 31 E3
Willards MD 114 C1
Will Co. IL 89 D2
Willcox AZ 55 E3
Willernie MN 235 E1
Williams AZ 47 D3
Williams CA 36 B2
Williams IA 72 C4
Williams OR 28 B2
Williams Bay WI 74 C4
Williamsburg CO 41 E3
Williamsburg FL 246 B4
Williamsburg IA 87 E2
Williamsburg KS 96 A3
Williamsburg KY 110 C3
Williamsburg MA 150 A1
Williamsburg NM 56 B2
Williamsburg OH 100 C2
Williamsburg PA 92 C4
Williamsburg VA 113 F2
Williamsburg Co. SC 122 C4
Williams Co. ND 17 F2
Williams Co. OH 90 A2
Williams Creek IN 221 C1
Williamsfield IL 88 A3
Williamson NY 78 C3
Williamson WV 111 E1
Williamson Co. IL 108 C1
Williamson Co. TN 109 F4
Williamson Co. TX 61 E1
Williamsport IN 89 D4
Williamsport MD 103 D1
Williamsport OH 101 D1
Williamsport PA 93 D2
Williamston MI 76 A4
Williamston NC 113 E4
Willis TX 132 A2
Willisburg KY 110 B1
Williston FL 138 C4
Williston MD 145 E3
Williston ND 17 F2
Williston OH 90 C2
Williston SC 130 B1
Williston TN 118 C1
Williston VT 81 D2
Willisville IL 98 B4
Willis Wharf VA 114 B3
Willits CA 36 A2
Willmar MN 66 B3
Willoughby OH 91 E2
Willoughby Hills OH 204 G1
Willow AK 154 C3
Willowbrook CA 228 D3
Willowbrook IL 203 C5
Willow City ND 18 C2
Willow Creek CA 28 B4
Willow Creek MT 23 E1
Willow Grove PA 146 C2
Willowick OH 91 E2
Willow Lake SD 27 E3
Willow Park TX 59 E2
Willows CA 36 B1
Willows MD 144 C4
Willow Sprs. IL 203 C5
Willow Sprs. MO 107 E2
Willow Street PA 146 A3
Willsboro NY 81 D2
Willshire OH 90 A3
Wills Pt. TX 59 F2
Willwood WY 24 B3
Wilmar AR 117 F4
Wilmer AL 135 E1
Wilmer TX 207 E3
Wilmerding PA 250 D3
Wilmette IL 89 D1
Wilmington DE 146 B4
Wilmington IL 88 C2
Wilmington NC 123 E3
Wilmington OH 100 C2
Wilmington VT 94 C1
Wilmington Island GA 130 C3
Wilmington Manor DE 274 D3
Wilmore KY 100 B4
Wilmot AR 125 F1
Wilmot SD 27 F2
Wilsall MT 23 F1
Wilson AR 118 B1
Wilson KS 43 D2
Wilson LA 134 A1
Wilson NY 78 B3
Wilson NC 113 D4
Wilson OK 51 E4
Wilson PA 93 F3
Wilson TX 58 A2
Wilson WY 23 F4
Wilson Co. KS 106 A1

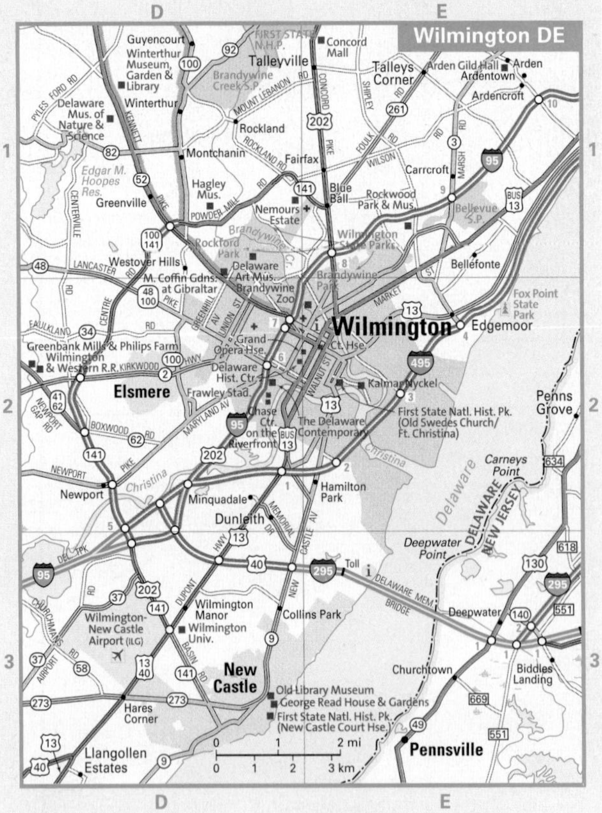
Wilmington DE
D
E
1
2
3
Guyencourt
Winterthur Museum, Garden & Library
Winterthur
FIRST STATE N.H.P.
Talleyville
Concord Mall
Talleys Corner
Arden Gild Hall
Arden
Ardentown
Ardencroft
Delaware Mus. of Nature & Science
Brandywine Creek S.P.
Rockland
Montchanin
Fairfax
Carrcroft
Hagley Mus.
Edgar M. Hoopes Res.
Greenville
Blue Ball
Rockwood Park & Mus.
Nemours Estate
Bellevue S.P.
Rockford Park
Wilmington State Parks
Westover Hills
Delaware Art Mus.
Brandywine Zoo
Bellefonte
M. Coffin Gdns. at Gibraltar
Fox Point State Park
Greenbank Mill & Philips Farm
Wilmington & Western R.R.
Grand Opera Hse.
Wilmington
Edgemoor
Ct. Hse.
Elsmere
Delaware Hist. Ctr.
Frawley Stad.
Kalmar Nyckel
Chase Ctr. on the Riverfront
The Delaware Contemporary
First State Natl. Hist. Pk. (Old Swedes Church/ Ft. Christina)
Penns Grove
Christina
Newport
Minquadale
Hamilton Park
Carneys Point
Dunleith
Delaware
DELAWARE
NEW JERSEY
Deepwater Point
DELAWARE MEM. BRIDGE
Deepwater
Wilmington Manor
Wilmington-New Castle Airport (ILG)
Wilmington Univ.
Collins Park
New Castle
Churchtown
Biddles Landing
Old Library Museum
George Read House & Gardens
First State Natl. Hist. Pk. (New Castle Court Hse.)
Hares Corner
Llangollen Estates
Pennsville
0 1 2 mi
0 1 2 3 km

Arden E1
Ardencroft E1
Ardentown E1
Bellefonte E1
Biddles Landing E3
Blue Ball E1
Carrcroft E1
Churchtown E3
Collins Park D3
Deepwater E3
Dunleith D2
Edgemoor E2
Elsmere D2
Fairfax E1
Greenville D1
Guyencourt D1
Hamilton Park E2
Hares Corner D3
Llangollen Estates D3
Minquadale D2
Montchanin D1
New Castle D3
Newport D2
Penns Grove E2
Pennsville E3
Rockland D1
Talleys Corner E1
Talleyville E1
Westover Hills D1
Wilmington E2
Wilmington Manor D3
Winterthur D1

Entries in **bold black** indicate counties or parishes.
Entries in **bold color** indicate cities with detailed inset maps.

Winslow AR 106 C4
Winslow IN 99 E4
Winslow ME 82 C2
Winslow NJ 147 D4
Winsted CT 94 C2
Winsted MN 66 C4
Winston OR 28 B1
Winston Co. AL 119 E3
Winston Co. MS 127 D1
Winston-Salem NC 112 B4
Winstonville MS 118 A4
Winter Beach FL 141 E3
Winter Garden FL 141 D1
Winter Harbor ME 83 D2
Winterhaven CA 53 F4
Winter Haven FL 140 C2
Winter Park CO 41 D1
Winter Park FL 141 D1
Winterport ME 83 D2
Winters CA 36 B3
Winters TX 58 C3
Winterset IA 86 C2
Winter Sprs. FL 141 D1
Winterstown PA 103 E1
Wintersville OH 91 F4
Winterville GA 121 D4
Winterville NC 115 D3
Winthrop CT 149 E2
Winthrop IA 73 E4
Winthrop ME 82 B2
Winthrop MA 151 D1
Winthrop MN 66 C4
Winthrop NY 80 B1
Winthrop Harbor IL 75 D4
Winton CA 36 C4
Winton NC 113 F3
Wirt Co. WV 101 F2
Wiscasset ME 82 C3
Wisconsin Dells WI 74 A2
Wisconsin Rapids WI 74 A1
Wisdom MT 23 D1
Wise VA 111 E2
Wise Co. TX 59 E2
Wise Co. VA 111 E2
Wishek ND 27 D1
Wisner LA 125 F3
Wisner NE 35 F2
Wister OK 116 B2
Withamsville OH 204 C3
Withee WI 68 A4
Witherbee NY 81 D2
Witt IL 98 B2
Witt TN 111 D4
Wittenberg WI 68 B4
Wittmann AZ 54 B1
Wixom MI 76 B4
Woburn MA 151 D1
Wofford KY 110 C2
Wofford Hts. CA 45 E4
Wolcott CT 149 D1
Wolcott IN 89 E3
Wolcott NY 79 D3
Wolcottville IN 90 A2
Wolfdale PA 91 F4
Wolfeboro NH 81 F3
Wolfeboro Falls NH 81 F3
Wolfe City TX 59 F1
Wolfe Co. KY 111 D1
Wolfforth TX 58 A1
Wolf Lake MI 75 E3
Wolf Pt. MT 17 E2
Wolsey SD 27 E3
Wolverine Lake MI 210 A1
Womelsdorf PA 146 A2
Wonewoc WI 74 A2
Wonnie KY 111 D1
Woodacre CA 259 A1
Woodbine GA 139 D1
Woodbine IA 86 A1
Woodbine KY 110 C2
Woodbine MD 144 B2
Woodbine NJ 104 C4
Woodbourne NY 94 A3
Woodbourne OH 208 E2
Woodbranch TX 132 B2
Woodbridge CT 149 D2
Woodbridge NJ 147 E1
Woodbridge VA 144 B4
Woodburn IN 90 A3
Woodburn KY 109 F2
Woodburn OR 20 B2
Woodbury CT 149 D1
Woodbury GA 128 C1
Woodbury MN 67 D4
Woodbury NJ 146 C3
Woodbury TN 110 A4
Woodbury VT 81 E2
Woodbury Co. IA 35 F2
Woodbury Hts. NJ 146 C3
Wood Co. OH 90 C2
Wood Co. TX 124 A2
Wood Co. WV 101 E2
Wood Co. WI 68 A4
Woodcreek TX 61 D2
Woodcrest CA 229 J4
Wood Dale IL 203 C3
Woodfield MD 144 B2
Woodfin NC 111 E4
Woodford Co. IL 88 B3
Woodford Co. KY 100 B4
Woodhaven MI 90 C1
Wood Heights MO 96 C2
Woodhull IL 88 A2
Woodhull NY 93 D1
Woodinville NY 148 C1
Woodinville WA 12 C3
Woodlake CA 45 D3
Wood Lake MN 66 A4
Woodland CA 36 B3
Woodland GA 128 C2
Woodland MI 76 A4
Woodland MN 235 A3
Woodland NC 113 E3
Woodland WA 20 C1
Woodland (Baileyville) ME 83 E1
Woodland Beach MI 90 C1
Woodland Hills UT 39 E1
Woodland Park CO 41 E2
Woodland Park NJ 240 B1
Woodlawn IL 98 C4
Woodlawn KY 204 B3
Woodlawn MD 145 D1
Woodlawn MD 193 B2
Woodlawn OH 204 B1
Woodlawn VA 112 A3
Woodlawn Park KY 230 E1
Woodlyn PA 248 A4
Woodlynne NJ 248 C4
Woodmere NY 241 G5
Woodmere OH 204 G2
Woodmont CT 149 D2
Woodmore MD 144 C3
Woodport NJ 148 A3
Woodridge IL 203 B5
Wood-Ridge NJ 240 C2
Woodridge NY 94 A3
Wood River IL 98 A3
Wood River NE 35 D4
Woodruff SC 121 F2
Woodruff WI 68 B2
Woodruff Co. AR 117 F1
Woodsboro MD 144 A1
Woodsboro TX 61 E4
Woodsburgh NY 241 G5
Woods Co. OK 51 D1
Woods Cross UT 257 B1
Woodsfield OH 101 F1
Woods Hole MA 151 E4
Woodside CA 259 C5
Woodside DE 145 E2
Woodside MT 15 D4
Woods Landing WY 33 D3
Woodson AR 117 E3
Woodson IL 98 A1
Woodson Co. KS 96 A4
Woodson Terrace MO 256 B1
Woodstock AL 127 F1
Woodstock GA 120 C3
Woodstock IL 74 C4
Woodstock NY 94 B2
Woodstock VT 81 E3
Woodstock VA 102 C3
Woodstock Valley CT 150 B2
Woodstown NJ 145 F1
Woodsville NH 81 E2
Woodville AL 120 A2
Woodville CA 45 D3
Woodville FL 137 E2
Woodville GA 121 E4
Woodville MA 150 C2
Woodville MS 134 A1
Woodville OH 90 C2
Woodville TX 132 C1
Woodville WI 67 E4
Woodward IA 86 C1
Woodward OK 50 C1
Woodward Co. OK 51 D2
Woodway TX 59 E4
Woodway WA 262 A2
Woodworth LA 133 E1
Woody Creek CO 40 C2
Woonsocket RI 150 C2
Woonsocket SD 27 E3
Wooster AR 117 E1
Wooster OH 91 E3
Worcester MA 150 C1
Worcester NY 79 F4
Worcester VT 81 E2
Worcester Co. MD 114 C2
Worcester Co. MA 150 B1
Worden IL 98 B3
Worden MT 24 C1
Workmans Corners DE 145 F4
Worland WY 24 C4
Worley ID 14 B3
Wormleysburg PA 218 B2
Worth IL 203 D6
Wortham TX 59 F3
Worth Co. GA 129 D4
Worth Co. IA 73 D2
Worth Co. MO 86 B4
Worthing SD 27 F4
Worthington IN 99 E2
Worthington IA 73 F4
Worthington KY 101 D3
Worthington MN 72 A2
Worthington OH 90 C4
Worthington PA 92 A3
Wounded Knee SD 34 A1
Wrangell AK 155 E4
Wray CO 42 A1
Wrens GA 129 F1
Wrentham MA 151 D2
Wright FL 136 B2
Wright WY 25 E4
Wright City MO 97 F3
Wright City OK 116 B3
Wright Co. IA 72 C4
Wright Co. MN 66 C3
Wright Co. MO 107 E2
Wrightsboro NC 123 E3
Wrightstown NJ 147 D3
Wrightstown PA 147 D2
Wrightstown WI 74 C1
Wrightsville AR 117 E2
Wrightsville GA 129 E2
Wrightsville PA 103 E1
Wrightsville Beach NC 123 E3
Wrightwood CA 52 C2
Wrigley TN 109 E4
Wurtland KY 101 D3
Wurtsboro NY 148 A1
Wyalusing PA 93 E2
Wyandot Co. OH 90 C3
Wyandotte MI 90 C1
Wyandotte OK 106 B2
Wyandotte Co. KS 96 B2
Wyanet IL 88 B2
Wyckoff NJ 148 B3
Wycombe PA 146 C2
Wykoff MN 73 E2
Wylie TX 59 F2
Wymore NE 43 F1
Wynantskill NY 188 E2
Wyncote PA 248 C1
Wyndmere ND 27 F1
Wynne AR 118 A1
Wynnewood OK 51 E4
Wynona OK 51 F1
Wyocena WI 74 B2
Wyodak WY 25 E3
Wyola MT 24 C2
Wyoming DE 145 E2
Wyoming IL 88 B3
Wyoming IA 87 F1
Wyoming MI 75 F3
Wyoming MN 67 D3
Wyoming NY 78 B3
Wyoming OH 204 B1
Wyoming PA 261 B1
Wyoming RI 150 C4
Wyoming Co. NY 78 B4
Wyoming Co. PA 93 E2
Wyoming Co. WV 111 F1
Wyomissing PA 146 A2
Wythe Co. VA 112 A2

Auburn C2
Bramanville D2
Chaffinville C1
Cherry Valley C2
Dorothy Pond D2
E. Millbury D2
Edgemere D2
Leicester C2
Millbury D2
Morningdale D1
Pondville C2
Rochdale C2
Stoneville C2
Worcester C1

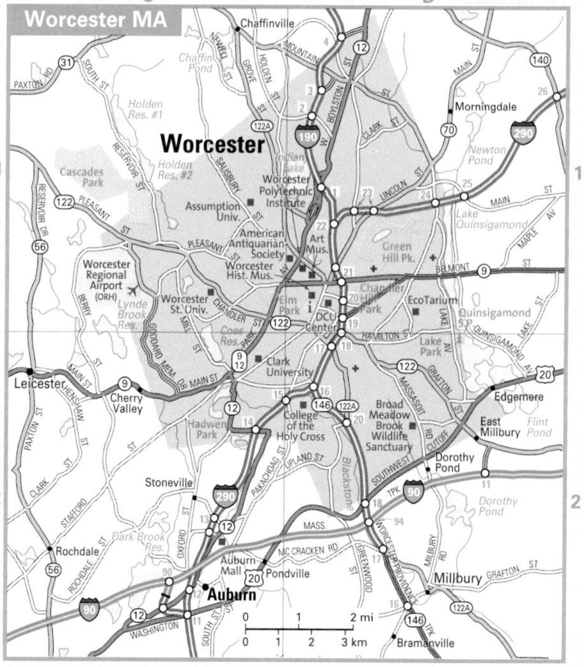

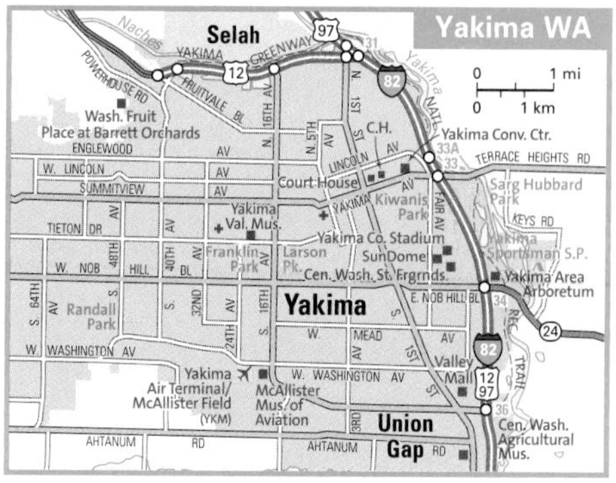

Belville A1	Masonboro B2	Seagate B2	Wrightsboro A1
Hightsville A1	Ogden B1	Wilmington A2	Wrightsville Beach B2

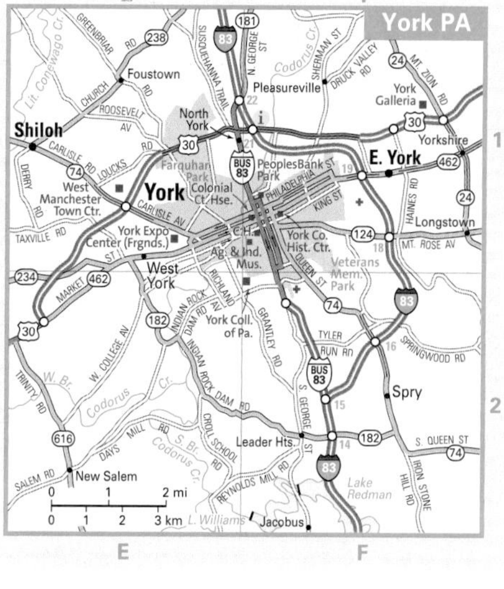

E. York F1
Foustown E1
Jacobus F2
Leader Hts. F2
Longstown F1
New Salem E2
N. York E1
Pleasureville F1
Shiloh E1
Spry F2
W. York E1
York E1
Yorkshire F1

Figures after entries indicate page number and grid reference.

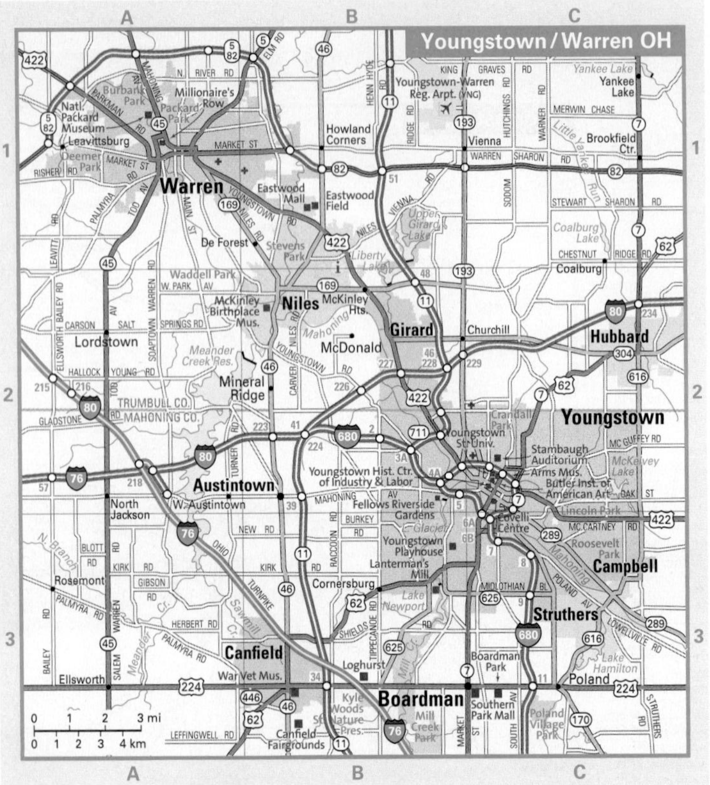
Youngstown / Warren OH
Warren
Niles
Girard
Hubbard
Youngstown
Austintown
Campbell
Struthers
Canfield
Boardman
Lordstown
McDonald
Mineral Ridge
Cornersburg
Poland
Howland Corners
Vienna
Brookfield Ctr.
Yankee Lake
Leavittsburg
Churchill
Coalburg
North Jackson
W. Austintown
Rosemont
Ellsworth
0 1 2 3 mi
0 1 2 3 4 km

Austintown.............. B2
Boardman.............. B3
Brookfield.............. C1
Campbell.............. C3
Canfield.............. B3
Churchill.............. C2
Coalburg.............. C1
Cornersburg.............. B3
De Forest.............. B1
Ellsworth.............. A3
Girard.............. B2
Howland Corners.............. B1
Hubbard.............. C2
Leavittsburg.............. A1
Lordstown.............. A2
McDonald.............. B2
McKinley Hts.............. B2
Mineral Ridge.............. B2
Niles.............. B2
N. Jackson.............. A2
Poland.............. C3
Rosemont.............. A3
Struthers.............. C3
Vienna.............. C1
Warren.............. A1
W. Austintown.............. A2
Yankee Lake.............. C1
Youngstown.............. C2

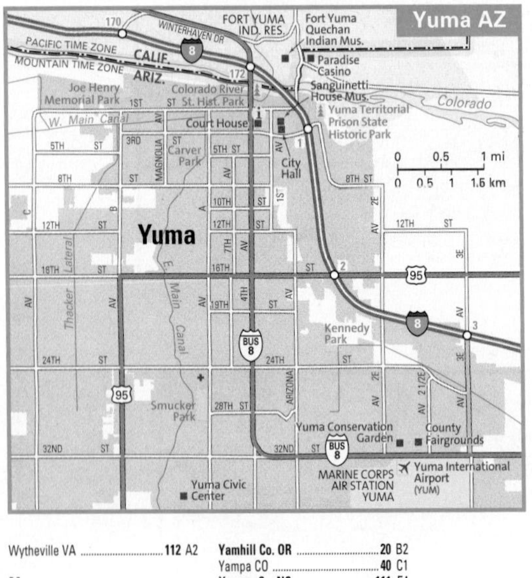
Yuma AZ
Yuma
FORT YUMA IND. RES.
Fort Yuma Quechan Indian Mus.
Paradise Casino
CALIF.
ARIZ.
PACIFIC TIME ZONE
MOUNTAIN TIME ZONE
Colorado
Court House
City Hall
Kennedy Park
Smucker Park
Yuma Civic Center
MARINE CORPS AIR STATION YUMA
Yuma International Airport (YUM)
0 0.5 1 mi
0 0.5 1 1.5 km

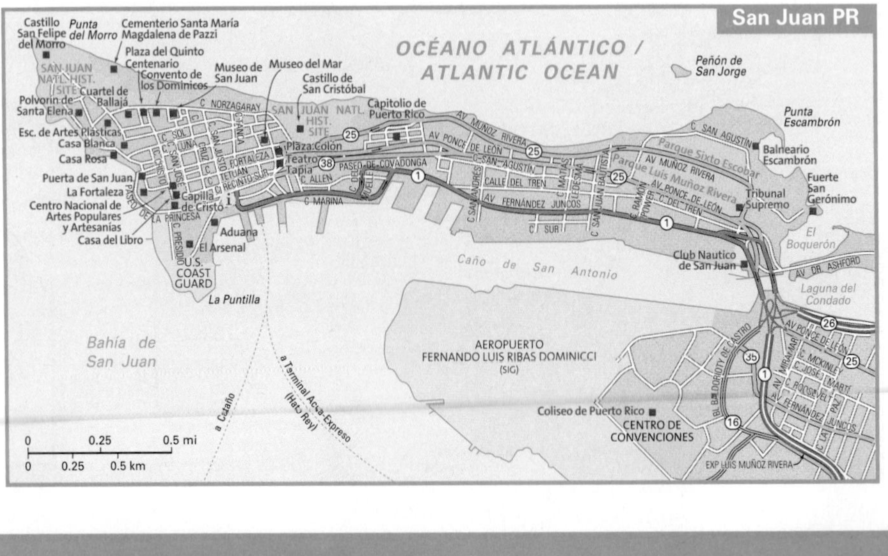
San Juan PR
OCÉANO ATLÁNTICO / ATLANTIC OCEAN
Bahía de San Juan
Caño de San Antonio
Castillo San Felipe del Morro
Punta del Morro
Cementerio Santa María Magdalena de Pazzi
Plaza del Quinto Centenario
Museo de San Juan
Museo del Mar
Castillo de San Cristóbal
Capitolio de Puerto Rico
Peñón de San Jorge
Punta Escambrón
Balneario Escambrón
Fuerte San Gerónimo
El Boquerón
Laguna del Condado
Club Nautico de San Juan
AEROPUERTO FERNANDO LUIS RIBAS DOMINICCI (SIG)
Coliseo de Puerto Rico
CENTRO DE CONVENCIONES
La Puntilla
U.S. COAST GUARD
El Arsenal
Aduana
Casa del Libro
La Fortaleza
Puerta de San Juan
Casa Rosa
Casa Blanca
Teatro Tapia
Plaza Colón
0 0.25 0.5 mi
0 0.25 0.5 km

Wytheville VA 112 A2

X

Xenia IL 98 C3
Xenia OH 100 C1

Y

Yachats OR 20 B3
Yacolt WA 20 C1
Yadkin Co. NC 112 A3
Yadkinville NC 112 A4
Yah-ta-hey NM 48 A2
Yakima WA 13 D4
Yakima Co. WA 13 D4
Yakutat AK 155 D3
Yalaha FL 140 C1
Yale MI 76 C3
Yale OK 51 F2
Yalesville CT 149 D1
Yalobusha Co. MS 118 B3
Yamhill OR 20 B2
Yamhill Co. OR 20 B2
Yampa CO 40 C1
Yancey Co. NC 111 E4
Yanceyville NC 112 C3
Yankeetown FL 138 C4
Yankton SD 35 E1
Yankton Co. SD 35 E1
Yaphank NY 149 D3
Yardley PA 147 D2
Yardville NJ 147 D2
Yarmouth ME 82 B3
Yarmouth MA 151 F3
Yarmouth Port MA 151 F3
Yarnell AZ 47 D4
Yarrow Pt. WA 262 B3
Yates Ctr. KS 96 A4
Yates City IL 88 A3
Yates Co. NY 78 C4
Yatesville GA 129 D1
Yatesville PA 261 C2
Yavapai Co. AZ 47 D4
Yazoo City MS 126 B2
Yazoo Co. MS 126 B2
Yeadon PA 146 C3
Yeagertown PA 93 D3
Yell Co. AR 117 D2
Yellow House PA 146 B2
Yellow Medicine Co. MN 66 A4
Yellow Sprs. MD 144 A1
Yellow Sprs. OH 100 C1
Yellowstone Co. MT 24 C1
Yellville AR 107 E3
Yelm WA 12 C4
Yemassee SC 130 C2
Yerington NV 37 E2
Yerkes KY 111 D2
Yermo CA 53 D1
Yoakum TX 61 E3
Yoakum Co. TX 57 F2
Yoder WY 33 F2
Yoe PA 103 E1
Yolo CA 36 B2
Yolo Co. CA 36 B2
Yoncalla OR 20 B4
Yonkers NY 148 B3
Yorba Linda CA 229 F3
York AL 127 D2
York NE 35 E4
York NY 78 C3
York PA 103 E1
York SC 122 A2
York Beach ME 82 B4
York Co. ME 82 B4
York Co. NE 35 E4
York Co. PA 103 E1
York Co. SC 122 A2
York Co. VA 113 F2
York Harbor ME 82 B4
York Haven PA 93 E4
Yorkshire NY 78 B4
Yorkshire VA 144 A3
York Sprs. PA 103 E1
Yorktown IN 89 F4
Yorktown NY 148 B2
Yorktown TX 61 E3
Yorktown VA 113 F2
Yorktown Hts. NY 148 B2
York Vil. ME 82 B4
Yorkville IL 88 C2
Yorkville OH 91 F4
Young AZ 47 E4
Young Co. TX 59 D2
Young Harris GA 121 D2
Youngstown NY 78 A3
Youngstown OH 91 F3
Youngstown PA 92 B4
Youngsville LA 133 F2
Youngsville NC 113 D4
Youngsville PA 92 B1
Youngtown AZ 249 A1
Youngwood PA 92 A4
Yountville CA 36 B3
Ypsilanti MI 90 C1
Yreka CA 28 C2
Yuba City CA 36 C2
Yuba Co. CA 36 C2
Yucaipa CA 53 D2
Yucca Valley CA 53 E2
Yukon OK 51 E3
Yulee FL 139 D2
Yuma AZ 53 F4
Yuma CO 42 A1
Yuma Co. AZ 54 A2
Yuma Co. CO 34 A4
Yutan NE 35 F3

Z

Zacata VA 103 E4
Zachary LA 134 A1
Zanesville IN 90 A3
Zanesville OH 101 E1
Zap ND 18 B3
Zapata TX 63 D3
Zapata Co. TX 63 D3
Zavala Co. TX 60 C3
Zavalla TX 132 C1
Zearing IA 87 D1
Zeb OK 106 B4
Zebulon GA 128 C1
Zebulon KY 111 E1
Zebulon NC 113 D4
Zeeland MI 75 F3
Zeigler IL 98 C4
Zelienople PA 92 A3
Zephyr Cove NV 37 D2
Zephyrhills FL 140 C2
Zia Pueblo NM 48 C3
Ziebach Co. SD 26 B2
Zillah WA 13 E4
Zimmerman MN 66 C3
Zion IL 75 D4
Zion KY 109 E1
Zion PA 92 C3
Zion Crossroads VA 102 C4
Zionsville IN 99 F1
Zolfo Sprs. FL 140 C3
Zumbrota MN 73 D1
Zuni Pueblo NM 48 A3
Zwolle LA 125 D4

PUERTO RICO

Aceitunas PR 187 D1
Adjuntas PR 187 D1
Aguada PR 187 D1
Aguadilla PR 187 D1
Aguas Buenas PR 187 E1
Aguilita PR 187 E1
Aibonito PR 187 E1
Añasco PR 187 D1
Arecibo PR 187 E1
Arroyo PR 187 E1
Bajadero PR 187 E1
Barceloneta PR 187 E1
Barranquitas PR 187 E1
Bayamón PR 187 E1
Betances PR 187 D1
Boquerón PR 187 D1
Cabo Rojo PR 187 D1
Caguas PR 187 E1
Camuy PR 187 D1
Canóvanas PR 187 F1
Carolina PR 187 F1
Cataño PR 187 E1
Cayey PR 187 E1
Cayuco PR 187 D1
Ceiba PR 187 F1
Ceiba PR 187 E1
Ciales PR 187 E1
Cidra PR 187 E1
Coamo PR 187 E1
Coco PR 187 E1
Comerío PR 187 E1
Comunas PR 187 F1
Coquí PR 187 E1
Corazón PR 187 E1
Corozal PR 187 E1
Coto Norte PR 187 E1
Daguao PR 187 F1
Dorado PR 187 E1
Duque PR 187 F1
El Mangó PR 187 F1
Esperanza PR 187 F1
Fajardo PR 187 F1
Florida PR 187 E1
Guánica PR 187 D1
Guayabal PR 187 E1
Guayama PR 187 E1
Guayanilla PR 187 D1
Guaynabo PR 187 E1
Gurabo PR 187 F1
Hatillo PR 187 D1
Hormigueros PR 187 D1
Humacao PR 187 F1
Isabela PR 187 D1
Jagual PR 187 E1
Jayuya PR 187 E1
Jobos PR 187 E1
Juana Diaz PR 187 E1
Juncos PR 187 F1
La Parguera PR 187 D1
La Plena PR 187 E1
Lajas PR 187 D1
Lares PR 187 D1
Las Marías PR 187 D1
Las Marías PR 187 D1
Las Piedras PR 187 F1
Levittown PR 187 E1
Loíza PR 187 F1
Los Llanos PR 187 E1
Luquillo PR 187 F1
Manatí PR 187 E1
Maricao PR 187 D1
Maunabo PR 187 F1
Mayagüez PR 187 D1
Moca PR 187 D1
Mora PR 187 D1
Morovis PR 187 E1
Naguabo PR 187 F1
Naranjito PR 187 E1
Orocovis PR 187 E1
Palmarejo PR 187 D1
Palomas PR 187 D1
Patillas PR 187 E1
Peñuelas PR 187 D1
Playita PR 187 F1
Pole Ojea PR 187 D1
Ponce PR 187 E1
Potala Pastillo PR 187 E1
Puerto Real PR 187 D1
Punta Santiago PR 187 F1
Quebrada PR 187 D1
Quebradillas PR 187 D1
Rafael Capó PR 187 D1
Rincón PR 187 D1
Río Grande PR 187 F1
Sabana Eneas PR 187 D1
Sabana Grande PR 187 D1
Sabana Hoyos PR 187 E1
Salinas PR 187 E1
San Antonio PR 187 E1
San Antonio PR 187 D1
San Germán PR 187 D1
San Isidro PR 187 F1
San Juan PR 187 E1
San Lorenzo PR 187 F1
San Sebastián PR 187 D1
Santa Isabel PR 187 E1
Santo Domingo PR 187 D1
Tallaboa PR 187 D1
Toa Alta PR 187 E1
Trujillo Alto PR 187 E1
Utuado PR 187 E1
Vázquez PR 187 E1
Vega Alta PR 187 E1
Vega Baja PR 187 E1
Vieques PR 187 F1
Villalba PR 187 E1
Yabucoa PR 187 F1
Yauco PR 187 D1
Yaurel PR 187 E1

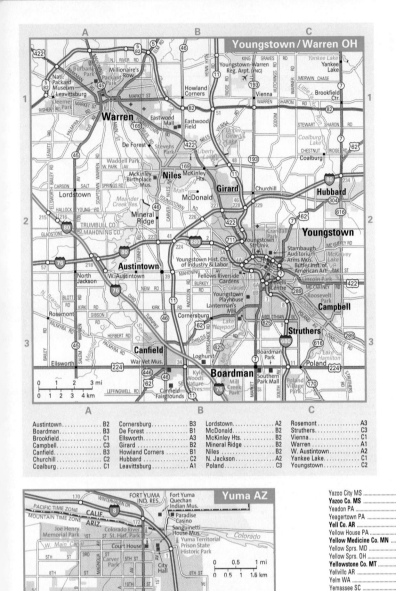

Entries in **bold color** indicate cities with detailed inset maps.

CANADA

Abbotsford BC 163 D3
Aberdeen SK 165 F1
Acton ON 172 C2
Acton Vale QC 175 D3
Adstock QC 175 E2
Airdrie AB 164 C2
Air Ronge SK 160 B3
Ajax ON 173 D2
Aklavik NT 155 D1
Alban ON 170 C3
Albanel QC 176 B3
Alberta Beach AB 158 C4
Alberton PE 179 E3
Aldergrove BC 163 D3
Alexandria ON 174 B3
Alfred ON 174 B3
Alix AB 164 C2
Allan SK 165 F2
Alliston ON 172 C1
Alma QC 176 C3
Almonte ON 174 A3
Altona MB 167 E4
Amherst NS 180 C1
Amherstburg ON 172 A4
Amos QC 171 E1
Amqui QC 178 B1
Ange-Gardien QC 175 D3
Angus ON 172 C1
Annapolis Royal NS 180 B3
Antigonish NS 181 E1
Arborg MB 167 E3
Arcola SK 166 C4
Armagh QC 175 F1
Armstrong BC 164 A3
Arnold's Cove NL 183 E4
Arnprior ON 174 A3
Arthur ON 172 C2
Ascot Corner QC 175 E3
Ashcroft BC 163 E1
Asquith SK 165 F2
Assiniboia SK 166 A4
Athabasca AB 159 D3
Athens ON 174 A4
Atholville NB 178 C2
Atikokan ON 168 C4
Aurora ON 173 D2
Austin QC 175 D3
Avondale NL 183 E4
Ayer's Cliff QC 175 D3
Aylesford NS 180 C2
Aylmer ON 172 C3
Aylmer QC 174 B3
Ayr ON 172 C3
Baddeck NS 181 F1
Badger NL 183 D3
Baie-Comeau QC 177 D2
Baie-du-Febvre QC 175 D2
Baie-Ste-Anne NB 179 D3
Baie-St-Paul QC 176 C4
Baie Verte NL 183 D2
Balcarres SK 166 B3
Balgonie SK 166 B3
Balmoral NB 178 C2
Bancroft ON 171 E4
Banff AB 164 B3
Barraute QC 171 E2
Barrhead AB 158 C3
Barrie ON 173 D1
Barry's Bay ON 171 E4
Bas-Caraquet NB 179 D2
Bashaw AB 164 C1
Bassano AB 165 D3
Bathurst NB 179 D2
Battleford SK 159 F4
Bay Bulls NL 183 F4
Bayfield ON 172 B2
Bay Roberts NL 183 E4
Beachburg ON 174 A3
Beamsville ON 173 D3
Beauceville QC 175 E2
Beauharnois QC 174 C3
Beaumont AB 159 D4
Beaumont QC 175 E1
Beaupré QC 175 E1
Beausejour MB 167 F3
Beauval SK 159 F2
Beaverlodge AB 157 F1
Beaverton ON 173 D1
Bécancour QC 175 D2
Bedford NS 181 D3
Bedford QC 175 D4
Beechville NS 181 D3
Beeton ON 173 D2
Behchokò NT 155 F2
Beiseker AB 164 C2
Bella Bella BC 156 C4
Belledune NB 178 C2
Bellefeuille QC 174 C3
Belleville ON 173 E1
Belmont ON 172 B3
Beloeil QC 175 D3
Benito MB 166 C2
Bentley AB 164 C2
Beresford NB 179 D2
Berthierville QC 175 D2
Bertrand NB 179 D2
Berwick NS 180 C2
Betsiamites QC 178 A1
Bible Hill NS 181 D2
Bienfait SK 166 C4
Biggar SK 165 F2
Big River SK 159 F3
Binscarth MB 166 C3
Birch Hills SK 160 B4
Birchy Bay NL 183 E2
Birtle MB 167 D3
Bishop's Falls NL 183 D3
Black Diamond AB 164 C3
Blackfalds AB 164 C2
Black Lake QC 175 E2
Blacks Hbr. NB 180 A2
Blackville NB 178 C4
Blaine Lake SK 160 B4
Blainville QC 174 C3
Blairmore AB 164 C4
Blanc-Sablon QC 183 D1
Blenheim ON 172 B4
Blind Bay BC 163 F1
Blind River ON 170 B3
Blue Mts. ON 172 C1
Bluewater ON 172 B2
Blyth ON 172 B2
Bobcaygeon ON 173 E1
Bois-Blanc NB 179 D2
Boischatel QC 175 E1
Boissevain MB 167 D4
Bolton ON 173 D2
Bon Accord AB 159 D4
Bonaventure QC 179 D2
Bonavista NL 183 E3
Bonnyville AB 159 E3
Borden-Carleton PE 179 E4
Bothwell ON 172 B3
Botwood NL 183 D2
Bouctouche NB 179 D4
Bourget ON 174 B3
Bowden AB 164 C2
Bowen Island BC 163 D3
Bow Island AB 165 D4
Bowmanville ON 173 D2
Bowser BC 162 C3
Bowsman MB 166 C2
Boyle AB 159 D3
Bracebridge ON 171 D4
Bradford ON 173 D2
Bradford-W. Gwillimbury ON 173 D1
Bragg Creek AB 164 C3
Brampton ON 173 D2
Brandon MB 167 D4
Brant ON 172 C3
Brantford ON 172 C3
Brantville NB 179 D3
Bridgenorth ON 173 E1
Bridgetown NS 180 B3
Bridgewater NS 180 C3
Brigham QC 175 D3
Brighton ON 173 E2
Brigus NL 183 E4
Bristol NB 178 B4
Broadview SK 166 C3
Brochet MB 161 D1
Brockville ON 174 B4
Bromont QC 175 D3
Bromptonville QC 175 E3
Brooklin ON 173 D2
Brooklyn NS 180 C4
Brooks AB 165 D3
Brookside NS 181 D3
Brownsburg-Chatham QC 174 C3
Bruderheim AB 159 D4
Bruno SK 166 B2
Brussels ON 172 B2
Buchans NL 183 D3
Buckingham QC 174 B3
Buffalo Creek BC 157 F4
Buffalo Lake AB 157 F1
Buffalo Narrows SK 159 F2
Burford ON 172 C3
Burgeo NL 182 C4
Burin NL 183 E4
Burk's Falls ON 171 D4
Burlington ON 173 D3
Burnaby BC 163 D3
Burns Lake BC 157 D2
Burnt Islands NL 182 C4
Bury QC 175 E3
Cabano QC 178 A2
Cache Creek BC 163 E1
Caledon ON 172 C2
Caledon East ON 172 C2
Caledonia ON 172 C3
Caledon Vil. ON 172 C2
Calgary AB 164 C3
Calmar AB 159 D4
Cambridge NS 180 C2
Cambridge ON 172 C3
Cambridge-Narrows NB 180 B1
Campbellford ON 173 E1
Campbell River BC 162 B2
Campbellton NB 178 C2
Camperville MB 167 D2
Camrose AB 159 D4
Canal Flats BC 164 B3
Candle Lake SK 160 B4
Canmore AB 164 B3
Canning NS 180 C2
Cannington ON 173 D1
Canora SK 166 C2
Canso NS 181 F2
Cantley QC 174 B3
Cap-aux-Meules QC 179 F3
Cap-Chat QC 178 C1
Cap-de-la-Madeleine QC 175 D2
Cape Breton Reg. Mun. NS 181 F1
Cape St. George NL 182 C3
Caplan QC 179 D2
Cap-Pele NB 179 E4
Capreol ON 170 C3
Cap-St-Ignace QC 175 F1
Cap-Santé QC 175 E1
Caraquet NB 179 D2
Carberry MB 167 D4
Carbonear NL 183 E4
Cardigan PE 179 F4
Cardinal ON 174 B4
Cardston AB 164 C4
Carleton Place ON 174 A3
Carleton St Omer QC 178 C2
Carlisle ON 172 C2
Carlyle SK 166 C4
Carmacks YT 155 D3
Carman MB 167 E4
Carmanville NL 183 E2
Carnduff SK 166 C4
Caronport SK 166 A3
Carrot River SK 160 C4
Carseland AB 164 C3
Carstairs AB 164 C2
Cartwright MB 167 D4
Cartwright NL 183 F1
Casselman ON 174 B3
Cassidy BC 162 C3
Castlegar BC 164 A4
Castor AB 165 D2
Catalina NL 183 E3
Causapscal QC 178 B1
Cavendish PE 179 E4
Cawston BC 163 F3
Cayuga ON 172 C3
Cedar BC 162 C3
Central Saanich BC 163 D4
Centreville NS 180 C2
Centreville-Wareham-Trinity NL 183 E3
Chalk River ON 171 E3
Chambly QC 175 D3
Chambord QC 176 B3
Champlain QC 175 D2
Chandler QC 179 D1
Channel-Port aux-Basques NL 182 C4
Chapais QC 176 A2
Chapleau ON 170 B2
Charlesbourg QC 175 E1
Charlie Lake BC 158 A2
Charlo NB 178 C2
Charlottetown PE 179 E4
Charny QC 175 E1
Chase BC 163 F1
Châteauguay QC 174 C3
Château-Richer QC 175 E1
Chatham ON 172 B4
Chatham-Kent ON 172 A4
Chemainus BC 162 C3
Chertsey QC 174 C2
Chesley ON 172 B1
Chester NS 180 C3
Chestermere AB 164 C3
Chesterville ON 174 B4
Chéticamp NS 181 E3
Chetwynd BC 157 E1
Chibougamau QC 176 A2
Chicoutimi QC 176 C3
Chilliwack BC 163 E3
Chipman NB 178 C4
Christina Lake BC 164 A4
Churchbridge SK 166 C3
Chute-aux-Outardes QC 177 D2
Clair NB 178 A3
Clairmont AB 157 F1
Clarence-Rockland ON 174 B3
Clarenville NL 183 E3
Claresholm AB 164 C4
Clarington ON 173 D2
Clarke's Beach NL 183 E4
Clark's Hbr. NS 180 B4
Clermont QC 176 C4
Clinton ON 172 B2
Clyde River PE 179 E4
Coaldale AB 165 D4
Coalhurst AB 165 D4
Coaticook QC 175 E4
Cobalt ON 171 D2

Calgary AB

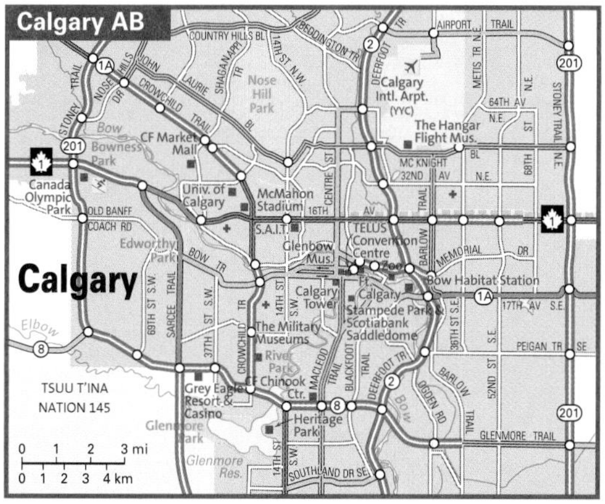

Edmonton AB

Fredericton NB

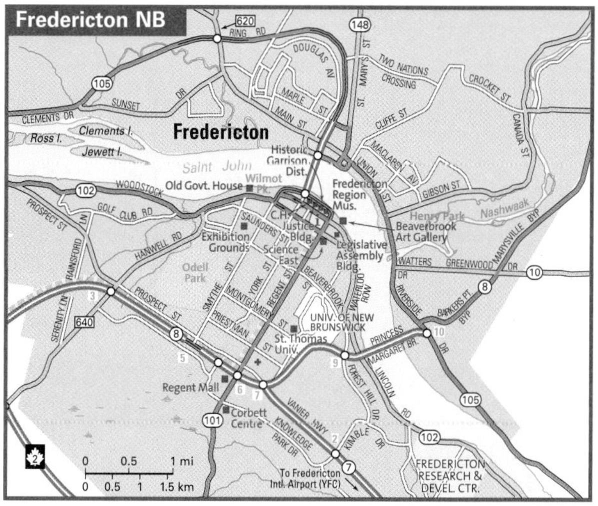

Charlottetown PE

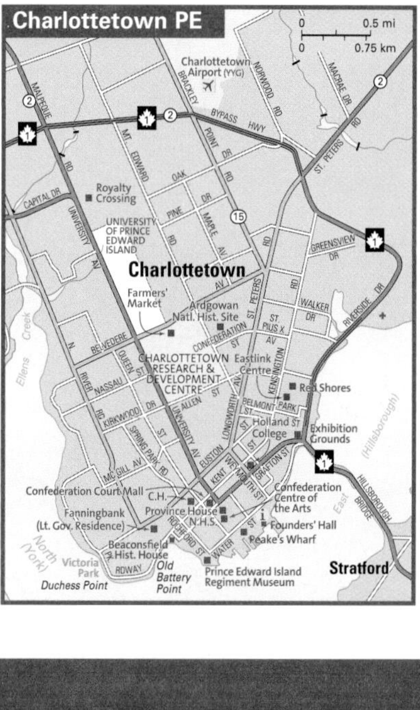

Halifax NS

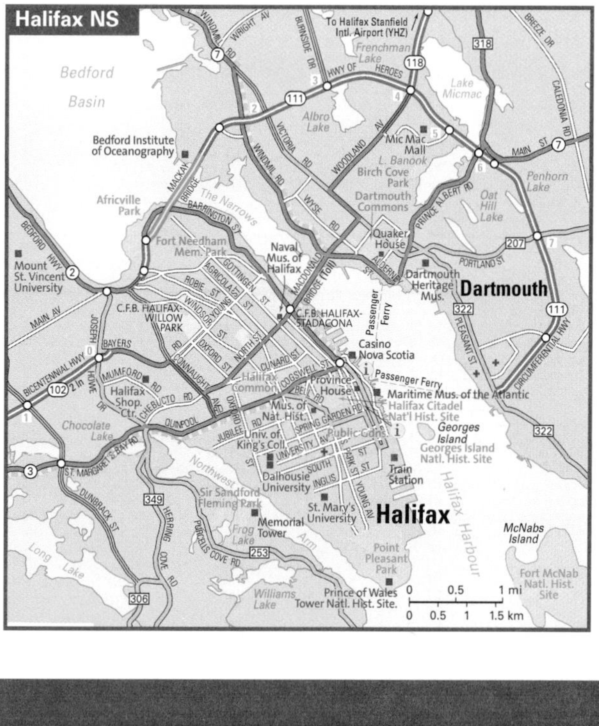

Figures after entries indicate page number and grid reference.

Cobble Hill BC 163 D4
Cobourg ON 173 E2
Cocagne NB 179 D4
Cochrane AB 164 C3
Cochrane ON 170 C1
Colborne ON 173 E2
Colchester ON 172 A4
Coldbrook NS 180 C2
Cold Lake AB 159 E3
Coldstream BC 164 A3
Coleraine QC 175 E2
Collingwood ON 172 C1
Comox BC 162 C2
Compton QC 175 E3
Conception Bay South NL 183 F4
Conception Hbr. NL 183 E4
Constance Bay ON 174 A3
Contrecoeur QC 175 D3
Cookshire QC 175 E3
Cookstown ON 173 D1
Coombs BC 162 C3
Coquitlam BC 163 D3
Cormack NL 182 C2
Cormorant MB 161 D3
Corner Brook NL 182 C3
Cornwall ON 174 B4
Cornwall PE 179 E4
Coronach SK 166 A4
Coronation AB 165 D2
Coteau-du-Lac QC 174 C3
Côte-Nord-du-Golfe-du-St-Laurent QC 182 B1
Courtenay BC 162 C2
Cowansville QC 175 D3
Cowichan Bay BC 163 D4
Cox's Cove NL 182 C2
Crabtree QC 174 C2
Cranbrook BC 164 B4
Crane River MB 167 D2
Creemore ON 172 C1
Creighton SK 161 D3
Creston BC 164 B4
Crossfield AB 164 C2
Cross Lake MB 161 E3
Crowsnest Pass AB 164 C4
Crystal Beach ON 173 D3
Crystal City MB 167 D4
Cudworth SK 165 F1
Cumberland BC 162 C3
Cumberland House SK 160 C4
Cupar SK 166 B3
Cupids NL 183 E4
Cut Knife SK 159 F4
Dalhousie NB 178 C2
Dalmeny SK 165 F2
Danville QC 175 D3
Dartmouth NS 181 D3
Dauphin MB 167 D3
Davidson SK 165 F2
Dawson YT 155 D2
Dawson Creek BC 157 F1
Daysland AB 159 D4
Deep River ON 171 E3
Deer Lake NL 182 C2
Dégelis QC 178 A2
Delburne AB 164 C2
Déléage QC 174 B2
Delhi ON 172 C3
Déline NT 155 E2
Delisle QC 176 C3
Delisle SK 165 F2
Deloraine MB 167 D4
Delson QC 174 C3
Delta BC 163 D3
Denare Beach SK 161 D3
Denman Island BC 162 C3
Deschaillons-sur-St-Laurent QC 175 D2
Deschambault Lake SK 160 C3
Deseronto ON 173 F1
Des Ruisseaux QC 174 B2
Devon AB 159 D4
Didsbury AB 164 C2
Dieppe NB 179 D4
Digby NS 180 B3
Disraeli QC 175 E2
Doaktown NB 178 C4
Dolbeau-Mistassini QC 176 B3
Dominion NS 181 F1
Donnacona QC 175 E2
Dorchester NB 180 C1
Dover NL 183 E3
Drayton ON 172 C2
Drayton Valley AB 158 C4
Dresden ON 172 B4
Drumheller AB 165 D2
Drummond NB 178 B3
Drummondville QC 175 D3
Dryden ON 168 C3
Duchess AB 165 E3
Duck Bay MB 167 D2
Duck Lake SK 160 B4
Dudswell QC 175 E3
Duncan BC 162 C4
Dundalk ON 172 C1
Dundee NB 178 C2
Dundurn SK 165 F2
Dunham QC 175 D4
Dunnottar MB 167 E3
Dunnville ON 173 D3
Durham ON 172 C1
Dutton ON 172 B3
E. Angus QC 175 E3
E. Broughton QC 175 E2
Eastend SK 165 E4
E. Gwillimbury ON 173 D1
Eckville AB 164 C2
Edmonton AB 159 D4
Edmundston NB 178 B3
Edson AB 158 C4
Eel River Crossing NB 178 C2
Eganville ON 174 A3
Elkford BC 164 C4
Elkhorn MB 166 C4
Elk Pt. AB 159 E4
Elliot Lake ON 170 C3
Elmira ON 172 C2
Elmsdale NS 181 D2
Elmvale ON 172 C1
Elrose SK 165 F2
Embree NL 183 E2
Embrun ON 174 B3
Emerson MB 167 E4
Enderby BC 164 A3
Enfield NS 181 D2
Englee NL 183 D1
Englehart ON 171 D2
Entwistle AB 158 C4
Erickson MB 167 D3
Erin ON 172 C2
Errington BC 162 C3
Eskasoni NS 181 F1
Espanola ON 170 C3
Essex ON 172 A4
Esterhazy SK 166 C3
Estevan SK 166 C4
Eston SK 165 E3
Ethelbert MB 167 D2
Evansburg AB 158 C4
Everett ON 172 C1
Exeter ON 172 B3
Fairisle NB 179 D3
Fairview AB 158 B2
Falher AB 158 B2
Falkland BC 163 F1
Fall River NS 181 D3
Fanny Bay BC 162 C3
Farnham QC 175 D3
Faro YT 155 E3
Fatima QC 179 F3
Fenelon Falls ON 173 D1
Fergus ON 172 C2
Ferme-Neuve QC 174 B1
Fermont QC 183 E1
Fernie BC 164 C4
Ferryland NL 183 F4
Flatrock NL 183 F4
Flin Flon MB 161 D3
Florence NS 180 C2
Florenceville NB 178 B4
Foam Lake SK 166 B2
Fogo NL 183 E2
Forest ON 172 B3
Forestburg AB 165 D1
Forestville QC 178 A1
Ft. Chipewyan AB 155 F2
Fort-Coulonge QC 174 A3
Ft. Erie ON 173 D3
Ft. Frances ON 168 B4
Ft. Good Hope NT 155 E2
Ft. Liard NT 155 E3
Ft. Macleod AB 164 C4
Ft. McMurray AB 159 E1
Ft. McPherson NT 155 D1
Ft. Nelson BC 155 F3
Ft. Providence NT 155 F2
Ft. Qu'Appelle SK 166 B3
Ft. Resolution NT 155 F2
Ft. St. James BC 157 D2
Ft. St. John BC 158 A2
Ft. Saskatchewan AB 159 D4
Ft. Simpson NT 155 F2
Ft. Smith NT 155 F2
Fortune NL 183 D4
Ft. Vermilion AB 155 F3
Fox Creek AB 158 B3
Frampton QC 175 E2
Frankford ON 173 E1
Franklin QC 174 C4
Fraser Lake BC 157 D2
Fredericton NB 180 A1
Fredericton Jct. NB 180 A1
Frelighsburg QC 175 D4
French Creek BC 162 C3
French River ON 171 D3
Frontenac QC 175 E3
Fruitvale BC 164 A4
Gabriola Island BC 162 C3
Gagetown NB 180 B1
Gambo NL 183 E3
Gananoque ON 173 F1
Gander NL 183 E3
Garnish NL 183 D4
Gaspé QC 179 D1
Gatineau QC 174 B3
Genelle BC 164 A4
Gentilly QC 175 D2
Georgetown ON 172 C2
Georgetown PE 179 F4
Georgina ON 173 D1
Geraldton ON 169 E3
Gibbons AB 159 D4
Gibsons BC 163 D3
Gift Lake AB 158 C2
Gilbert Plains MB 167 D3
Gillam MB 161 F3
Gimli MB 167 E3
Girardville QC 176 B3
Glace Bay NS 181 F4
Gladstone MB 167 D3
Glenboro MB 167 D4
Glencoe ON 172 B3
Glenwood NL 183 E3
Glovertown NL 183 E3
Goderich ON 172 B2
Golden BC 164 B2
Gold River BC 162 B2
Gold River NS 180 C3
Gore Bay ON 170 C4
Granby QC 175 D3
Grand Bank NL 183 D4
Grand Bay-Westfield NB 180 B2
Grand Bend ON 172 B3
Grand Ctr. AB 159 E3
Grande-Anse NB 179 D2
Grande Cache AB 157 F2
Grande-Digue NB 179 D4
Grande Prairie AB 157 F1
Grande-Rivière QC 179 D1
Grande-Vallée QC 179 D1
Grand Falls (Grand-Sault) NB 178 B3
Grand Falls-Windsor NL 183 D3
Grand Forks BC 164 A4
Grand Manan NB 180 A3
Grand-Mère QC 175 D2
Grand Rapids MB 161 F4
Grand-Remous QC 174 B2
Grand Valley ON 172 C2
Grandview MB 167 D3
Gravelbourg SK 165 F3
Gravenhurst ON 171 D4
Greater Napanee ON 173 F1
Greater Sudbury ON 170 C3
Greenstone ON 169 E3
Greenwood BC 164 A4
Greenwood NS 180 C2
Grenfell SK 166 C3
Grenville-sur-la-Rouge QC 174 C3
Gretna MB 167 E4
Grimsby ON 173 D3
Grimshaw AB 158 B2
Grindrod BC 164 A3
Guelph ON 172 C2
Gull Lake SK 165 E3
Guysborough NS 181 E2
Hagersville ON 172 C3
Hague SK 165 F1
Haileybury ON 171 D2
Haines Jct. YT 155 D3
Haldimand ON 173 D3
Halifax NS 181 D3
Halton Hills ON 172 C2
Hamilton ON 172 C3
Hamiota MB 167 D3
Hammonds Plains Road NS 181 D3
Hampton NB 180 B2
Hanna AB 165 D2
Hanover ON 172 C1
Hantsport NS 180 C2
Happy Valley-Goose Bay NL 183 F1
Harbour Breton NL 183 D4
Harbour Grace NL 183 E4
Hardisty AB 165 D1
Hardwicke NB 179 D3
Hare Bay NL 183 E3
Harrison Hot Sprs. BC 163 E3
Harriston ON 172 C2
Harrow ON 172 A4
Hartland NB 178 B4
Hartney MB 167 D4
Hastings ON 173 E1
Haute-Aboujagane NB 179 E4
Havelock ON 173 E1
Havre-aux-Maisons QC 179 F3
Havre Boucher NS 181 E1
Havre-St-Pierre QC 177 F1
Hawkesbury ON 174 B3
Hay River NT 155 F2
Hearst ON 170 B1
Heart's Delight-Islington NL 183 E4
Hebbville NS 180 C3
Hébertville QC 176 C3
Henryville QC 175 D4
Hensall ON 172 B2
Herbert SK 165 F3
Hermitage NL 183 D4
Hérouxville QC 175 D1
Herring Cove NS 181 D3
Highlands BC 163 D4
High Level AB 155 F3
High Prairie AB 158 C2
High River AB 164 C3
Hillsborough NB 180 C1
Hillsburgh ON 172 C2
Hinton AB 158 B4
Holyrood NL 183 E4
Hope BC 163 F3
Hornby Island BC 162 C3
Hornepayne ON 169 F3
Houston BC 156 C2
Hudson QC 174 C3
Hudson Bay SK 160 C4
Hudson's Hope BC 158 A2
Hull QC 174 B3
Humber Arm South NL 182 C3
Humboldt SK 166 B2
Hunter River PE 179 E4
Huntingdon QC 174 C4
Huntsville ON 171 D4
Huron East ON 172 B2
Iberville QC 175 D3
Île-à-la-Crosse SK 159 F2
Indian Head SK 166 B3
Ingersoll ON 172 C3
Inkerman NB 179 D2
Innisfail AB 164 C2
Innisfil ON 173 D1
Inuvik NT 155 D1
Invermere BC 164 B3
Inverness NS 181 E1
Iqaluit NU 7
Irishtown-Summerside NL 182 C3
Iroquois ON 174 B4
Iroquois Falls ON 170 C1
Irricana AB 164 C2
Isle-aux Morts NL 182 C4
Ituna SK 166 B3
Jarvis ON 172 C3
Jasper AB 158 B4
Joe Batt's Arm-Barr'd Islands-Shoal Bay NL 183 E2
Joliette QC 174 C2
Jonquière QC 176 C3
Kaleden BC 163 F3
Kamloops BC 163 F1
Kamsack SK 166 C2
Kanata ON 174 A3
Kapuskasing ON 170 C1
Kars ON 174 B3
Kaslo BC 164 B4
Kawartha Lakes ON 173 D1
Kedgwick NB 178 B2
Kelowna BC 163 F2
Kelvington SK 166 B2
Kemptville ON 174 B4
Kenora ON 167 F4
Kensington PE 179 E4
Kent BC 163 E3
Kentville NS 180 C2
Keremeos BC 163 F3
Kerrobert SK 165 E2
Keswick ON 173 D1
Keswick Ridge NB 180 A1
Kikino AB 159 D3
Killam AB 165 D1
Killarney MB 167 D4
Kimberley BC 164 B4
Kincardine ON 172 B1
Kindersley SK 165 E2
Kingsey Falls QC 175 D3
King's Pt. NL 183 D2
Kingston NS 180 C2
Kingston ON 173 F1
Kingsville ON 172 A4
Kinistino SK 160 B4
Kipling SK 166 C3
Kippens NL 182 C3
Kirkland Lake ON 171 D2
Kitchener ON 172 C2
Kitimat BC 156 B2
Kitscoty AB 159 E4
Kugluktuk NU 155 F1
La Baie QC 176 C3
Labelle QC 174 B2
Labrador City NL 183 E1
Labrecque QC 176 C3
Lac-au-Saumon QC 178 B1
Lac-aux-Sables QC 175 D1
Lac-Beauport QC 175 E1
Lac-Bouchette QC 176 B3
Lac-Brome QC 175 D3
Lac-Drolet QC 175 E3
Lac du Bonnet MB 167 F3
Lac-Etchemin QC 175 F2
Lachine QC 174 C3
Lachute QC 174 C3
Lac La Biche AB 159 D3
Lac-Mégantic QC 175 E3
Lacolle QC 174 C4
Lacombe AB 164 C2
La Conception QC 174 B2
La Crête AB 155 F3
Lac-Supérieur QC 174 C2
Ladysmith BC 162 C3
La Guadeloupe QC 175 E2
Lake Country BC 163 F2
Lake Cowichan BC 162 C4
Lake Echo NS 181 D3
Lakefield ON 173 E1
Lake Louise AB 164 B2
Lakeshore ON 172 A4
La Loche SK 159 E1
La Malbaie QC 176 C4
Lambton QC 175 E3
Lambton Shores ON 172 B3
Lamèque NB 179 D2
La Minerve QC 174 B2
Lamont AB 159 D4
Lampman SK 166 C4
Lanark ON 174 A4
Landrienne QC 171 E1
Langdon AB 164 C3
L'Ange-Gardien QC 175 E1
Langenburg SK 166 C3
Langford BC 163 D4
Langham SK 165 F1
Langley BC 163 D3
Lanigan SK 166 B2
L'Annonciation QC 174 B2
Lanoraie QC 175 D2
L'Anse-St-Jean QC 176 C3
Lantz NS 181 D2
Lantzville BC 162 C3
La Pêche QC 174 A3
La Plaine QC 174 C3
La Pocatière QC 175 F1
Lappe ON 169 D4
La Prairie QC 174 C3
Lark Hbr. NL 182 C2
La Ronge SK 160 B3
LaSalle ON 172 A4
La Sarre QC 171 D1
L'Ascension-de-Notre-Seigneur QC 176 C3
La Scie NL 183 D2
Lashburn SK 159 E4
L'Assomption QC 174 C3
Laterrière QC 176 C3
La Tuque QC 175 D1
Laurentian Hills ON 171 E4
Laurier-Station QC 175 E2
Laurierville QC 175 E2
Laval QC 174 C3
Lavaltrie QC 175 D3
L'Avenir QC 175 D3
Lawn NL 183 D4
Lawrencetown NS 180 C2
Leader SK 165 E3
Leaf Rapids MB 161 D2
Leamington ON 172 A4
Lebel-sur-Quévillon QC 171 E1
Le Bic QC 178 A1
Leduc AB 159 D4
Legal AB 159 D4
Le Goulet NB 179 D2
Lennoxville QC 175 E3
L'Épiphanie QC 174 C3
Léry QC 174 C3
Les Coteaux QC 174 C3
Les Éboulements QC 176 C4
Les Escoumins QC 178 A1
Les Méchins QC 178 C1
L'Étang-du-Nord QC 179 F3
Lethbridge AB 165 D4
Lévis QC 175 E1
Lewisporte NL 183 E2
Lillooet BC 163 E1
Lincoln NB 180 A1
Lincoln ON 173 D3
Lindsay ON 173 D1
Lions Bay BC 163 D3
L'Islet QC 175 F1
L'Isle-Verte QC 178 A2
Listowel ON 172 C2
Little Current ON 170 C4
Lively ON 170 C3
Liverpool NS 180 C4
Lloydminster AB 159 E4
Lloydminster SK 159 E4
Lockeport NS 180 C4
Logan Lake BC 163 E1
London ON 172 B3
Longlac ON 169 E3

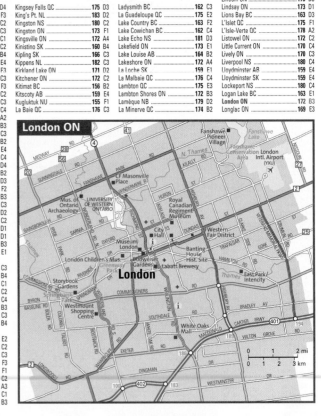

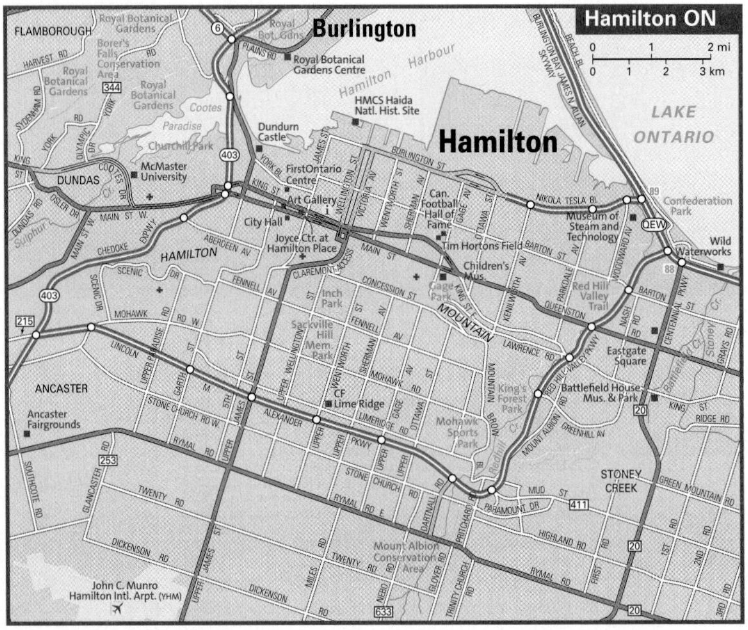
Hamilton ON
Burlington
Hamilton
FLAMBOROUGH
Royal Botanical Gardens
Royal Botanical Gardens Centre
Hamilton Harbour
HMCS Haida Natl. Hist. Site
LAKE ONTARIO
Dundurn Castle
McMaster University
DUNDAS
FirstOntario Centre
Art Gallery
City Hall
Can. Football Hall of Fame
Museum of Steam and Technology
Confederation Park
Wild Waterworks
Tim Hortons Field
Joyce Ctr. at Hamilton Place
Children's Mus.
Red Hill Valley Trail
Eastgate Square
Battlefield House Mus. & Park
King's Forest Park
Mohawk Sports Park
CF Lime Ridge
Sackville Hill Mem. Park
Inch Park
Gage Park
ANCASTER
Ancaster Fairgrounds
STONEY CREEK
Mount Albion Conservation Area
John C. Munro Hamilton Intl. Arpt. (YHM)
0 1 2 mi
0 1 2 3 km

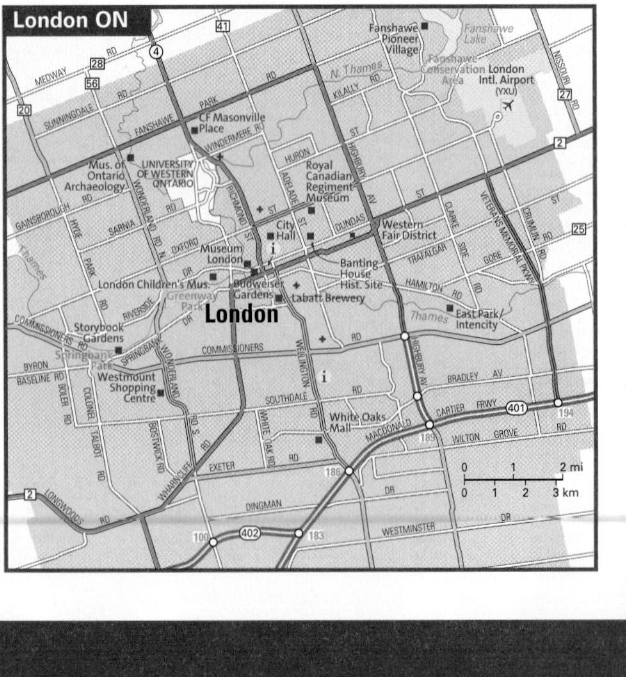
London ON
London
Fanshawe Pioneer Village
Fanshawe Conservation Area
Fanshawe Lake
London Intl. Airport (YXU)
CF Masonville Place
Mus. of Ontario Archaeology
UNIVERSITY OF WESTERN ONTARIO
Royal Canadian Regiment Museum
City Hall
Western Fair District
Museum London
Banting House Hist. Site
London Children's Mus.
Budweiser Gardens
Labatt Brewery
Greenway Park
East Park/ Intencity
Storybook Gardens
Springbank Park
Westmount Shopping Centre
White Oaks Mall
Thames
N. Thames
0 1 2 mi
0 1 2 3 km

Entries in **bold color** indicate cities with detailed inset maps.

Montréal QC

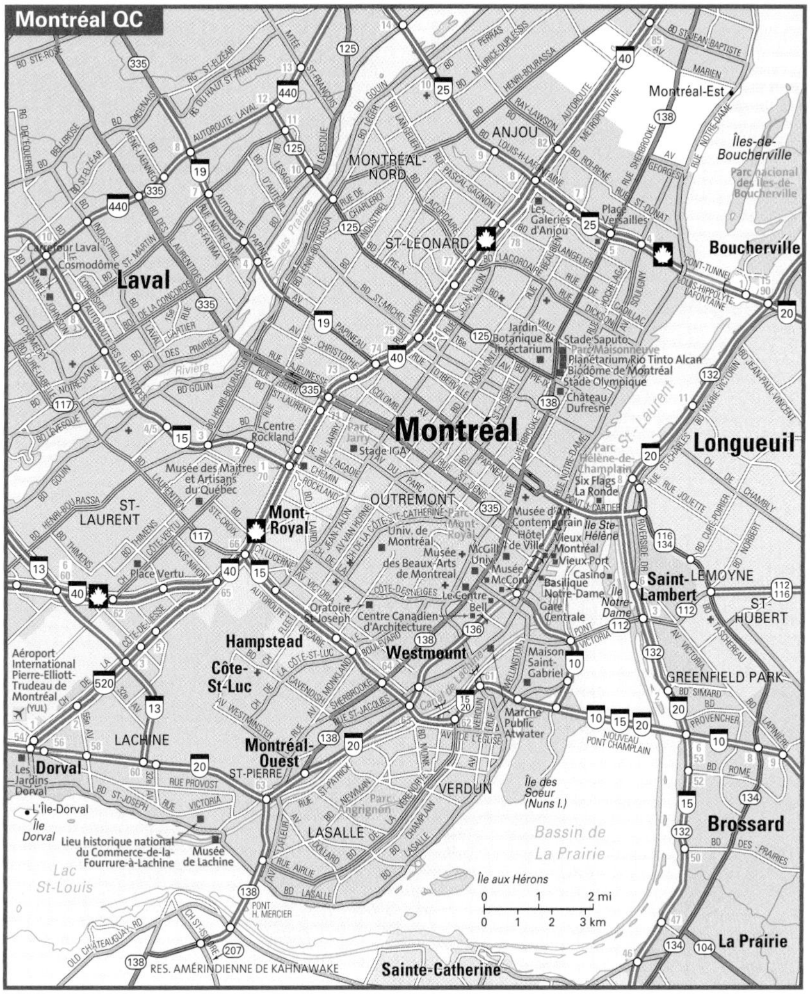

Longue-Rive QC 178 A1
Longueuil QC 174 C3
Loretteville QC 175 E1
L'Orignal ON 174 B3
Lorrainville QC 171 D2
Louisbourg NS 181 F4
Louiseville QC 175 D2
Lourdes NL 182 C3
Lucan ON 172 B3
Lucknow ON 172 B2
Lumby BC 164 A3
Lumsden NL 183 E2
Lumsden SK 166 B3
Lunenburg NS 180 C3
Luseland SK 165 E2
Lynn Lake MB 161 D1
Lyster QC 175 E2
Macamic QC 171 D1
MacGregor MB 167 E4
Mackenzie BC 157 E1
Macklin SK 165 E2
Madoc ON 173 E1
Magog QC 175 D3
Magrath AB 165 D4
Mahone Bay NS 180 C3
Maidstone SK 159 F4
Maisonnette NB 179 D2
Malartic QC 171 E2
Manawan QC 174 C1
Manigotagan MB 167 F3
Manitou MB 167 E4
Manitouwadge ON 169 F3
Maniwaki QC 174 A2
Manning AB 158 B1
Mannville AB 159 E4
Maple Creek SK 165 E4
Maple Ridge BC 163 D3
Marathon ON 169 E4
Maria QC 178 C2
Marieville QC 175 D3
Markdale ON 172 C1
Markham ON 173 D2
Markstay-Warren ON 171 D3
Marmora ON 173 E1
Marshall SK 159 E4
Martensville SK 165 F2
Marystown NL 183 E4
Mascouche QC 174 C3
Mashteuiatsh QC 176 B3
Maskinongé QC 175 D2
Masset BC 156 A2
Masson-Angers QC 174 B3
Matagami QC 171 E1
Matane QC 178 B1
Mattawa ON 171 D3
Maxville ON 174 B3
Mayerthorpe AB 158 C4
Mayo YT 155 D2
McAdam NB 180 A1
McBride BC 157 F3
McCreary MB 167 D3
McLennan AB 158 B2
McWatters QC 171 D2
Meadow Lake SK 159 F3
Meadows NL 182 C3
Meaford ON 172 C1
Medicine Hat AB 165 D4
Melfort SK 160 B4
Melita MB 167 D4
Melocheville QC 174 C3
Melville SK 166 C3
Memramcook NB 180 C1
Mercier QC 174 C3
Merrickville-Wolford ON 174 B4
Merritt BC 163 E2
Merville BC 162 C2
Messines QC 174 A2
Métabetchouan-Lac-à-la-Croix QC 176 C3
Metcalfe ON 174 B3
Metchosin BC 163 D4
Middleton NS 180 C2
Midland ON 172 C1
Mildmay ON 172 B2
Milestone SK 166 B4
Milk River AB 165 D4
Mill Bay BC 163 D4
Millbrook ON 173 E1
Mille-Isles QC 174 C3
Millet AB 159 D4
Milltown-Head of Bay d'Espoir NL 183 D3
Milton NS 180 C4
Milton ON 172 C2
Milverton ON 172 C2
Minitonas MB 167 D2
Minnedosa MB 167 D3
Minto NB 178 C4
Minto ON 172 C2
Mirabel QC 174 C3
Miracle Beach BC 162 B2
Miramichi NB 179 D3
Mira Road NS 181 F1
Miscou Ctr. NB 179 D2
Miscouche PE 179 E4
Mission BC 163 D3
Mississauga ON 173 D2
Mississippi Mills ON 174 A3
Mistissini QC 176 B1
Mitchell ON 172 B2
Moncton NB 179 D4
Mono ON 172 C2
Montague PE 179 F4
Mont-Carmel QC 176 C4
Mont-Joli QC 178 B1
Mont-Laurier QC 174 B2
Montmagny QC 175 F1
Montréal QC 174 C3
Montrose BC 164 A4
Moose Jaw SK 166 B3
Moose Lake MB 161 D4
Moosomin SK 166 C3
Morden MB 167 E4
Morin-Heights QC 174 C3
Morinville AB 159 D4
Morris MB 167 E4
Morrisburg ON 174 B4
Mt. Albert ON 173 D1
Mt. Brydges ON 172 B3
Mt. Forest ON 172 C2
Mt. Moriah NL 182 C3
Mt. Pearl NL 183 F4
Mt. Uniacke NS 181 D2
Mulgrave NS 181 E1
Mundare AB 159 D4
Munster ON 174 A3
Murdochville QC 179 D1
Murray Hbr. PE 179 F4
Murray River PE 179 F4
Musgrave Hbr. NL 183 E2
Musgravetown NL 183 E3
Nackawic NB 180 A1
Naicam SK 166 B2
Nakusp BC 164 A3
Nanaimo BC 162 C3
Nanoose Bay BC 162 C3
Nantes QC 175 E3
Nanton AB 164 C3
Napanee ON 173 F1
Napierville QC 174 C3
Naramata BC 163 F2
Nauwigewauk NB 180 B2
Neepawa MB 167 D3
Neguac NB 179 D3
Nelson BC 164 B4
Neuville QC 175 E1
New Aiyansh BC 156 B1
New Carlisle QC 179 D2
New Glasgow NS 181 D2
New Hamburg ON 172 C3
New Hazelton BC 156 C1
New Liskeard ON 171 D2
Newmarket ON 173 D2
New Maryland NB 180 A1
Newport QC 179 D2
New Richmond QC 178 C2
New Tecumseth ON 173 D2
New Victoria NS 181 F1
New Waterford NS 181 F1
New-Wes-Valley NL 183 E2
Niagara Falls ON 173 D3
Niagara-on-the-Lake ON 173 D3
Nicholas Denys NB 178 C2
Nicolet QC 175 D2
Nigadoo NB 179 D2
Nipawin SK 160 C4
Nipigon ON 169 E3
Niverville MB 167 E4
Nobleton ON 173 D2
Nominingue QC 174 B2
Norfolk ON 172 C3
Normandin QC 176 B3
Norman's Cove-Long Cove NL 183 E4
Norman Wells NT 155 E2
Norris Arm NL 183 D3
Norris Pt. NL 182 C2
N. Battleford SK 159 F4
N. Bay ON 171 D3
N. Cowichan BC 162 C4
Northeastern Manitoulin and the Islands ON 170 C4
N. Perth ON 172 C2
N. Rustico PE 179 E4
N. Saanich BC 163 D4
N. Sydney NS 181 F1
N. Tetagouche NB 178 C2
N. Vancouver BC 163 D3
Norton NB 180 B1
Norway House MB 161 E4
Norwich ON 172 C3
Norwood ON 173 E1
Notre Dame de Lourdes MB 167 E4
Notre-Dame-des-Érables NB 179 D2
Notre-Dame-des-Pins QC 175 E2
Notre-Dame-du-Bon-Conseil QC 175 D2
Notre-Dame-du-Lac QC 178 A2
Notre-Dame-du-Laus QC 174 B2
Notre-Dame-du-Mont-Carmel QC 175 D2
Notre-Dame-du-Nord QC 171 D2
Notre-Dame-du-Portage QC 178 A2
Nouvelle QC 178 C2
Noyan QC 175 D4
Oak Bay BC 163 D4
Oak Lake MB 167 D4
Oakville ON 173 D2
Oka QC 174 C3
Okanagan Falls BC 163 F3
Okotoks AB 164 C3
Old Perlican NL 183 E3
Olds AB 164 C2
O'Leary PE 179 E4
Oliver BC 163 F3
Omemee ON 173 E1
Onaping ON 170 C3
108 Mile Ranch BC 157 F4
150 Mile House BC 157 E4
100 Mile House BC 157 F4
Onoway AB 159 D4
Orangeville ON 172 C2
Orillia ON 173 D1
Ormstown QC 174 C4
Oromocto NB 180 B1
Orono ON 173 D2
Osgoode ON 174 B3
Oshawa ON 173 D2
Osler SK 165 F1
Osoyoos BC 163 F3
Ottawa ON 174 B3
Outlook SK 165 F2
Owen Sound ON 172 C1
Oxbow SK 166 C4
Oxford NS 181 D1
Oyen AB 165 E2
Pabos QC 179 D1
Pabos Mills QC 179 D2
Paisley ON 172 B1
Palmarolle QC 171 D1
Palmerston ON 172 C2
Papineauville QC 174 B3
Paquetville NB 179 D2
Paradise NL 183 F4
Paris ON 172 C3
Parkhill ON 172 B3
Parksville BC 162 C3
Parrsboro NS 180 C2
Parry Sound ON 171 D4
Pasadena NL 182 C3
Paspébiac QC 179 D2
Peace River AB 158 B2
Peachland BC 163 F2
Pelham ON 173 D3
Pelican Narrows SK 160 C3
Pelly Crossing YT 155 D3
Pemberton BC 163 D2
Pembroke ON 174 A3
Penetanguishene ON 172 C1
Penhold AB 164 C2
Pense SK 166 B3
Penticton BC 163 F3
Percé QC 179 E1
Perth ON 174 A4
Perth-Andover NB 178 B4
Petawawa ON 171 E4
Peterborough ON 173 E1
Peterview NL 183 D2
Petitcodiac NB 180 C1
Petit-Matane QC 178 B1
Petit-Rocher NB 179 D2
Petrolia ON 172 B3
Pickering ON 173 D2
Picton ON 173 F2
Pictou NS 181 D1
Picture Butte AB 165 D4
Pilot Butte SK 166 B3
Pilot Mound MB 167 D4
Pinawa MB 167 F3
Pincher Creek AB 164 C4
Pinehouse SK 159 F2
Pintendre QC 175 E1
Pitt Meadows BC 163 D3
Placentia NL 183 E4
Plantagenet ON 174 B3
Plaster Rock NB 178 B3
Plessisville QC 175 E2
Plum Coulee MB 167 E4
Plympton-Wyoming ON 172 B3
Pohénégamook QC 178 A3
Pointe-à-la-Croix QC 178 C2
Pointe-au-Père QC 178 B1
Pointe-aux-Outardes QC 178 B1
Pointe-Calumet QC 174 C3
Pointe-du-Lac QC 175 D2
Pt. Edward ON 172 A3
Pointe-Lebel QC 177 D2
Pointe-Sapin NB 179 D3
Pointe-Verte NB 178 C2
Pt. Leamington NL 183 D2
Ponoka AB 164 C1
Ponteix SK 165 F4
Pontiac QC 174 A3
Pont-Lafrance NB 179 D3
Pont-Landry NB 179 D2
Pont-Rouge QC 175 E1
Porcupine ON 170 C1
Porcupine Plain SK 166 C1
Portage la Prairie MB 167 E4
Port Alberni BC 162 C3
Port Alice BC 162 A1
Port au Choix NL 182 C1
Port au Port East NL 182 C3
Port-Cartier QC 177 E2
Port Colborne ON 173 D3
Port Coquitlam BC 163 D3
Port-Daniel-Gascons QC 179 D2
Port Dover ON 172 C3
Port Edward BC 156 B2
Port Elgin ON 172 B1
Port Hardy BC 162 A1
Port Hawkesbury NS 181 E1
Port Hope ON 173 E2
Port McNeill BC 162 A1
Portneuf QC 175 E1
Port Perry ON 173 D2
Port Saunders NL 183 D1
Port Stanley ON 172 B3
Pouce Coupe BC 157 F1
Pouch Cove NL 183 F4
Powassan ON 171 D3
Powell River BC 162 C2
Powerview MB 167 F3
Pré-d'en-Haut NB 180 C1

Ottawa ON

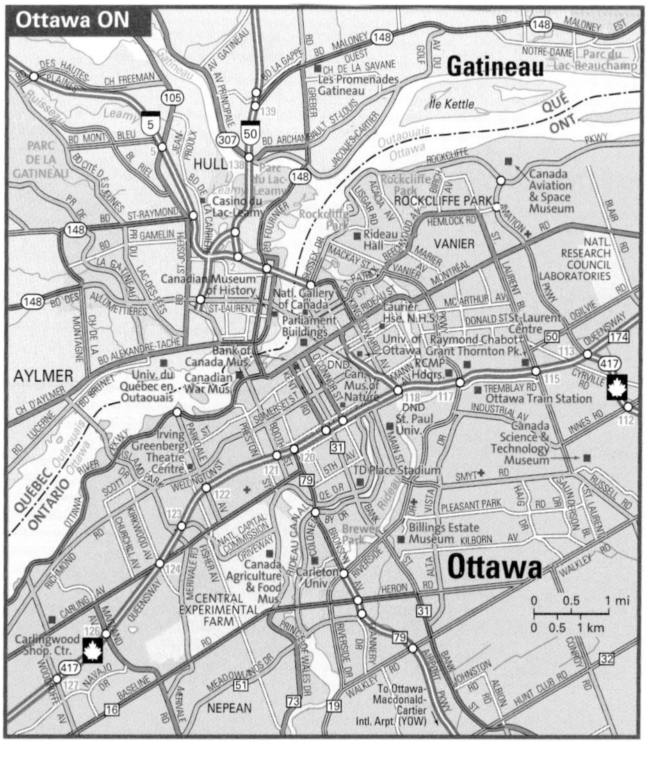

Figures after entries indicate page number and grid reference.

Preeceville SK 166 C2
Prescott ON 174 B4
Prévost QC 174 C3
Price QC 178 B1
Prince Albert SK 160 B4
Prince Edward ON 173 F2
Prince George BC 157 E2
Prince Rupert BC 156 B2
Princeton BC 163 F3
Princeville QC 175 E2
Provost AB 165 E2
Pugwash NS 181 D1
Qualicum Beach BC 162 C3
Qu'Appelle SK 166 B3
Regina SK 166 B3
Regina Beach SK 166 B3
Renfrew ON 174 A3
Renous NB 178 C3
Repentigny QC 174 C3
Reserve Mines NS 181 F1
Revelstoke BC 164 A3
Rexton NB 179 D4
Richelieu QC 175 D3
Richibucto NB 179 D4
Richmond BC 163 D3
Richmond ON 174 B3
Richmond QC 175 D3
Richmond Hill ON 173 D2
Roberval QC 176 B3
Roblin MB 166 C3
Robson BC 164 A4
Rocanville SK 166 C3
Rock Forest QC 175 E3
Rockland ON 174 B3
Rockwood ON 172 C2
Rocky Hbr. NL 182 C3
Rocky Mtn. House AB 164 C2
Roddickton NL 183 D1
Rodney ON 172 B4
Rogersville NB 179 D4
Rose Blanche-
Harbour Le Cou NL 182 C4
Rosetown SK 165 F2
Rossburn MB 167 D3
Rossland BC 164 A4
Ross River YT 155 E3
Rosthern SK 165 F1
Rothesay NB 180 B2
Rouyn-Noranda QC 171 D2
Roxboro QC 174 C3
Roxton Falls QC 175 D3
Roxton Pond QC 175 D3
Royston BC 162 C2
Rusagonis NB 180 A1
Russell MB 166 C3
Russell ON 174 B3
Saanich BC 163 D4
Sackville NB 180 C1
Sacré-Coeur QC 178 A2
St. Adolphe MB 167 E4
St-Agapit QC 175 E2
St-Aimé-des-Lacs QC 176 C4
St-Alban QC 175 D1
St. Alban's NL 183 D4
St. Albert AB 159 D4
St-Albert QC 175 D2
St-Alexandre QC 175 D3
St-Alexandre-
de-Kamouraska QC 178 A2
St-Alexis-des-Monts QC 175 D2
St-Alphonse-Rodriguez QC 174 C2
St-Ambroise QC 176 C3
St-André-Avellin QC 174 B3
St-André-d'Argenteuil QC 174 C3
St. Andrews NB 180 A2
St-Anselme QC 175 E2
St. Anthony NL 183 D1
St-Antoine NB 179 D4
St-Antoine QC 174 C3
St-Antoine-de-Tilly QC 175 E2
St-Antonin QC 178 A2
St-Apollinaire QC 175 E2
St-Armand QC 175 D4
St-Arsène QC 178 A2
St-Arthur NB 178 C2
St-Aubert QC 175 F1
St-Augustin-de-Desmaures QC 175 E1
St-Basile QC 175 E1
St-Benoît-Labre QC 175 E2
St-Bernard QC 175 E2
St. Bernard's-
Jacques Fontaine NL 183 E4
St-Boniface QC 175 D2
St-Brieux SK 166 B1
St-Bruno QC 176 C3
St-Bruno-de-Guigues QC 171 D2
St-Calixte QC 174 C2
St-Canut QC 174 C3
St-Casimir QC 175 D2
St. Catharines ON 173 D3
St-David-de-Falardeau QC 176 C3
St-Denis-sur-Richelieu QC 175 D3
St-Dominique QC 175 D3
St-Donat QC 174 C2
Ste-Adèle QC 174 C2
Ste-Agathe-de-Lotbinière QC 175 E2
Ste-Agathe-des-Monts QC 174 C2
Ste-Angèle-de-Mérici QC 178 B1
Ste. Anne MB 167 E4
Ste-Anne-de-Beaupré QC 175 E1
Ste-Anne de Kent NB 179 D4
Ste-Anne-de-la-Pérade QC 175 D2
Ste-Anne-de-Madawaska NB 178 B3
Ste-Anne-des-Monts QC 178 C1
Ste-Anne-des-Plaines QC 174 C3
Ste-Barbe QC 174 C3
Ste-Béatrix QC 174 C2
Ste-Blandine QC 178 B1
Ste-Brigide-d'Iberville QC 175 D3
Ste-Catherine-de-Hatley QC 175 D3
Ste-Catherine-de-la-
Jacques-Cartier QC 175 E1

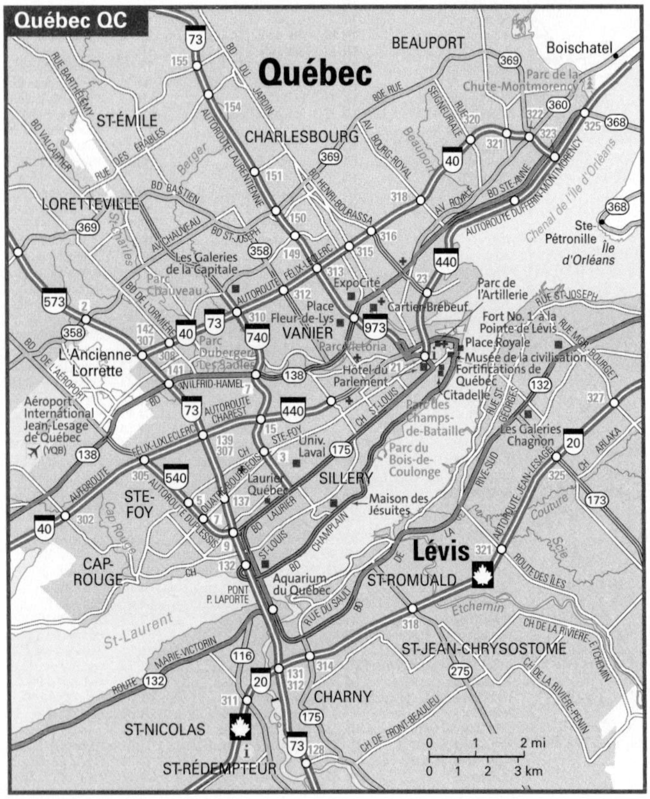

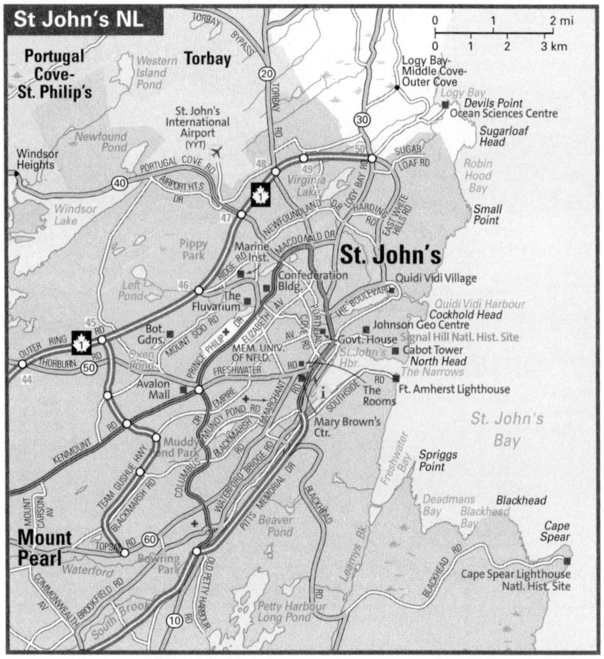

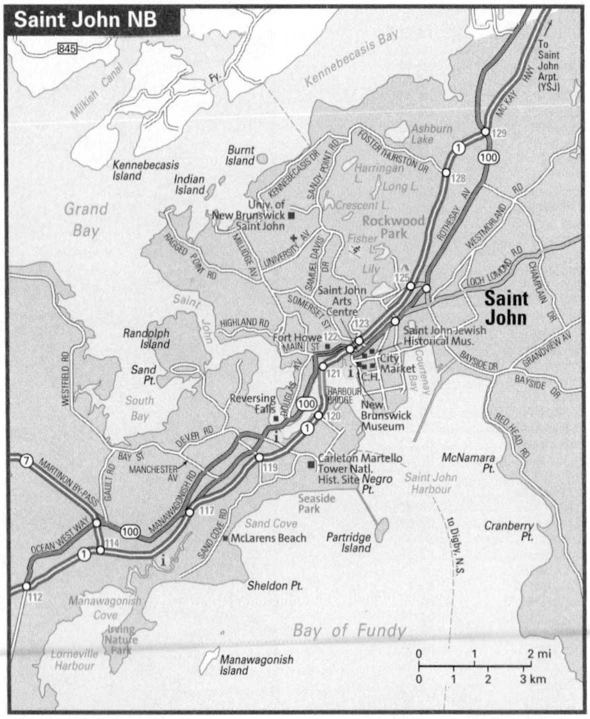

Québec QC 175 E1
Queens Reg. Mun. NS 180 C4
Quesnel BC 157 E3
Quinte West ON 173 E1
Quispamsis NB 180 B2
Racine QC 175 D3
Radium Hot Springs BC 164 B3
Radville SK 166 B4
Rainbow Lake AB 155 F3
Rainy River ON 167 F4
Ramea NL 182 C4
Rapid City MB 167 D3
Rawdon QC 174 C2
Raymond AB 165 D4
Raymore SK 166 B2
Redcliff AB 165 D3
Red Deer AB 164 C2
Red Lake ON 168 B2
Redvers SK 166 C4
Redwater AB 159 D4
Ridgetown ON 172 B4
Rigaud QC 174 C3
Rimbey AB 164 C1
Rimouski QC 178 A1
Rimouski-Est QC 178 A1
Ripon QC 174 B3
River Hebert NS 180 C1
Rivers MB 167 D4
Riverton MB 167 E3
Riverview NB 179 D4
Rivière-au-Renard QC 179 D1
Rivière-Beaudette QC 174 C3
Rivière-Bleue QC 178 A3
Rivière-du Loup QC 178 A2
Rivière-Ouelle QC 176 C4
Rivière-Verte NB 178 B3
Robert's Arm NL 183 D2
Roberts Creek BC 163 D3
Robertsonville QC 175 E2
Robertville NB 178 C2
St-Césaire QC 175 D3
St-Charles NB 179 D4
St. Charles ON 171 D3
St-Charles-Borromée QC 174 C2
St-Charles-de-Bellechasse QC 175 E1
St-Charles-de-Mandeville QC 174 C2
St-Charles-sur-Richelieu QC 175 D3
St-Chrysostome QC 174 C4
St. Claude MB 167 E4
St-Claude QC 175 E3
St-Clet QC 174 C3
St-Côme QC 174 C2
St-Côme-Linière QC 175 F2
St-Constant QC 174 C3
St-Cyprien QC 178 A2
St-Cyrille-de-Wendover QC 175 D2
St-Damase QC 175 D3
St-Damien QC 174 C2
St-Damien-de-Buckland QC 175 E2
Ste-Cécile NB 179 D2
Ste-Claire QC 175 E2
Ste-Clotilde-de-
Châteauguay QC 174 C3
Ste-Clotilde-de-Horton QC 175 D2
Ste-Croix QC 175 E2
St-Édouard QC 174 C3
St-Élisabeth QC 174 C2
Ste-Émélie-de-l'Énergie QC 174 C2
Ste-Félicité QC 178 B1
Ste-Fuy QC 175 E1
Ste-Hélène-de-Bagot QC 175 D3
Ste-Hénédine QC 175 E2
Ste-Jeanne-d'Arc QC 176 B3
Ste-Julie QC 174 C3
Ste-Justine QC 175 F2
Ste-Luce QC 178 B1
St-Elzéar QC 175 E2
Ste-Madeleine QC 175 D3

Entries in **bold color** indicate cities with detailed inset maps.

Ste-Marcelline de-Kildare QC ... 174 C2
Ste-Marguerite-Estérel QC ... 174 C2
Ste-Marie QC ... 175 E2
Ste-Marie-St-Raphaël NB ... 179 D2
Ste-Marthe-du-Cap QC ... 175 D2
Ste-Martine QC ... 174 C3
Ste-Mélanie QC ... 174 C2
Ste-Perpétue QC ... 175 F1
St-Éphrem-de-Beauce QC ... 175 E2
Ste-Rosalie QC ... 175 D3
Ste. Rose du Lac MB ... 167 D3
Ste-Sophie QC ... 174 C3
St-Esprit QC ... 174 C3
Ste-Thècle QC ... 175 D1
Ste-Thérèse QC ... 174 C3
Ste-Thérèse-de-Gaspé QC ... 179 D1
St-Étienne-de-Lauzon QC ... 175 E2
St-Eugène QC ... 175 D3
St-Eustache QC ... 174 C3
Ste-Véronique QC ... 174 B2
St-Fabien QC ... 178 A1
St-Faustin-Lac-Carré QC ... 174 C2
St-Félicien QC ... 176 B3
St-Félix-de-Kingsey QC ... 175 D3
St-Félix-de-Valois QC ... 174 C2
St-Ferdinand QC ... 175 E2
St-Ferréol-les-Neiges QC ... 175 E1
St-Flavien QC ... 175 E2
St-François-de-la-Rivière-du-Sud QC ... 175 E1
St-François-du-Lac QC ... 175 D2
St-Frédéric QC ... 175 E2
St-Fulgence QC ... 176 C3
St-Gabriel QC ... 174 C2
St-Gabriel-de-Rimouski QC ... 178 B1
St-Gédéon QC ... 176 C3
St-Gédéon-de-Beauce QC ... 175 F3
St. George NB ... 180 A2
St. George ON ... 172 C3
St. George's NL ... 182 C3
St-Georges QC ... 175 F2
St-Georges QC ... 175 D2
St-Georges-de-Cacouna QC ... 178 A2
St-Germain-de-Grantham QC ... 175 D3
St-Gervais QC ... 175 E1
St-Gilles QC ... 175 E2
St-Grégoire QC ... 175 D2
St-Guillaume QC ... 175 D3
St-Henri QC ... 175 E1
St-Hilarion QC ... 176 C4
St-Honoré QC ... 176 C3
St-Honoré-de-Shenley QC ... 175 E2
St-Hubert QC ... 174 C3
St-Hubert-de-Rivière-du-Loup QC ... 178 A2
St-Hugues QC ... 175 D3
St-Hyacinthe QC ... 175 D3
St-Ignace NB ... 179 D4
St-Ignace-de-Loyola QC ... 175 D2
St-Irénée NB ... 179 D3
St-Isidore NB ... 179 D3
St-Isidore QC ... 175 E2
St. Jacobs ON ... 172 C2
St-Jacques QC ... 174 C2
St. Jacques-Coomb's Cove NL ... 183 D4
St-Jean-de-Dieu QC ... 178 A2
St-Jean-de-Matha QC ... 174 C2
St-Jean-Port-Joli QC ... 175 F1
St-Jean-sur-Richelieu QC ... 175 D3
St-Jérôme QC ... 174 C3
Saint John NB ... 180 B2
St. John's NL ... 183 F4
St-Joseph-de-Beauce QC ... 175 E2
St-Jovite QC ... 174 C2
St-Jude QC ... 175 D3
St-Laurent QC ... 175 E1
St. Lawrence NL ... 183 D4
St-Lazare MB ... 166 C3
St-Lazare-de-Bellechasse QC ... 175 E1
St-Léolin NB ... 179 D2
St. Leonard NB ... 178 B3
St-Léonard-d'Aston QC ... 175 D2
St-Léon-de-Standon QC ... 175 F2
St-Léon-le-Grand QC ... 178 B1
St-Liboire QC ... 175 D3
St-Lin-Laurentides QC ... 174 C3
St-Louis-de-France QC ... 175 D2
St-Louis-de-Kent NB ... 179 D4
St-Ludger QC ... 175 E3
St. Lunaire-Griquet NL ... 183 D1
St-Malachie QC ... 175 E2
St-Marc-des-Carrières QC ... 175 D1
St-Marc-sur-Richelieu QC ... 175 D3
St-Martin QC ... 175 F2
St. Marys ON ... 172 B3
St-Mathieu-du-Parc QC ... 175 D2
St-Maxime-du-Mont-Louis QC ... 179 D1
St-Michel-de-Bellechasse QC ... 175 E1
St-Michel-des-Saints QC ... 174 C1
St-Narcisse QC ... 175 D2
St-Nazaire QC ... 176 C3
St-Nicéphore QC ... 175 D3
St-Nicolas QC ... 175 E1
St-Ours QC ... 175 D3
St-Pacôme QC ... 175 F1
St-Pamphile QC ... 175 F1
St-Pascal QC ... 178 A2
St-Patrice-de-Beaurivage QC ... 175 E2
St. Paul AB ... 159 E4
St-Paulin QC ... 175 D2
St-Pie QC ... 175 D3
St-Pierre-Jolys MB ... 167 E4
St-Pierre-les-Becquets QC ... 175 D2
St-Placide QC ... 174 C3
St-Polycarpe QC ... 174 C3
St-Prime QC ... 176 B3
St-Prosper QC ... 175 F2
St-Quentin NB ... 178 B3
St-Raphaël QC ... 175 E1
St-Raymond QC ... 175 E1
St-Rémi QC ... 174 C3
St-Roch-de-Richelieu QC ... 175 D3
St-Sauveur NB ... 179 D3

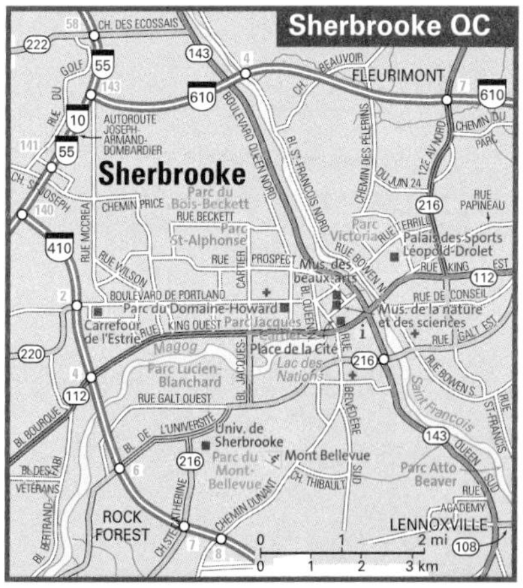

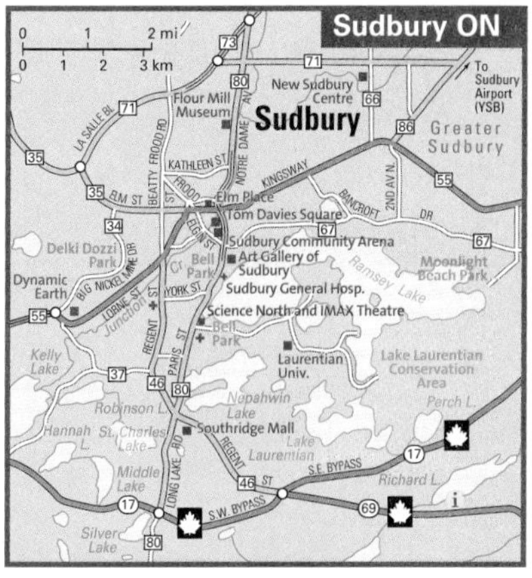

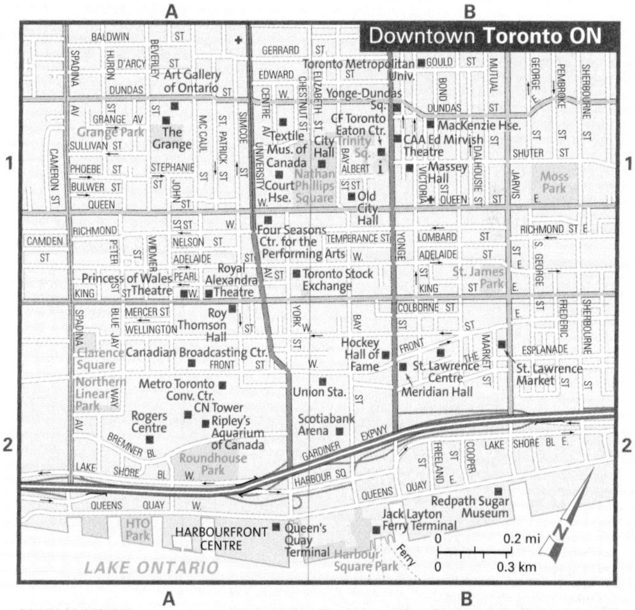

POINTS OF INTEREST

Art Gallery of Ontario ... A1
Canadian Broadcasting Center ... A2
CF Toronto Eaton Centre ... B1
CN Tower ... A2
CAA Ed Mirvish Theatre ... B1
Four Seasons Centre for the Performing Arts ... A1
The Grange ... A1
Harbourfront Centre ... A2
Hockey Hall of Fame ... B2
Jack Layton Ferry Terminal ... B2
MacKenzie House ... B1
Massey Hall ... B1
Meridian Hall ... B2
Metro Toronto Convention Ctr. ... A2
Old City Hall ... B1
Princess of Wales Theatre ... A1
Queen's Quay Terminal ... A2
Redpath Sugar Museum ... B2
Ripley's Aquarium of Canada ... A2
Rogers Centre ... A2
Royal Alexandra Theatre ... A1
Roy Thomson Hall ... A2
Saint Lawrence Centre ... B2
Saint Lawrence Market ... B2
Scotiabank Arena ... B2
Textile Museum of Canada ... A1
Toronto Metropolitan Univ. ... B1
Toronto Stock Exchange ... A1
Union Station ... B2
Yonge-Dundas Square ... B1

St-Sauveur-des-Monts QC ... 174 C3
St-Siméon QC ... 179 D2
St-Simon NB ... 179 D2
St-Stanislas QC ... 175 D2
St. Stephen NB ... 180 A2
St-Théodore-d'Acton QC ... 175 D3
St. Thomas ON ... 172 B3
St-Timothée QC ... 174 C3
St-Tite QC ... 175 D1
St-Tite-des-Caps QC ... 175 E1
St-Ubalde QC ... 175 D1
St-Ulric QC ... 178 B1
St-Urbain QC ... 176 C4
St-Valère QC ... 175 D2
St-Victor QC ... 175 E2
St. Walburg SK ... 159 F4
St-Wenceslas QC ... 175 D2
St-Zacharie QC ... 175 F2
St-Zénon QC ... 174 C2
St-Zotique QC ... 174 C3
Salaberry-de-Valleyfield QC ... 174 C3
Salisbury NB ... 180 C1
Salmo BC ... 164 B4
Salmon Arm BC ... 163 F1
Salmon Cove NL ... 183 F4
Salmon River NS ... 180 B4
Sandy Bay SK ... 160 C2
Saratoga Beach BC ... 162 B2
Sarnia ON ... 172 A3
Saskatoon SK ... 165 F2
Saugeen Shores ON ... 172 B1
Sault Ste. Marie ON ... 170 B3
Sayabec QC ... 178 B1
Schomberg ON ... 173 D2
Scott QC ... 175 E2
Scoudouc NB ... 179 D4
Seaforth ON ... 172 B2
Sechelt BC ... 162 C3
Sedgewick AB ... 165 D1
Selkirk MB ... 167 E3
Senneterre QC ... 171 E2
Sept-Îles QC ... 177 E2
Sexsmith AB ... 157 F1
Shannon QC ... 175 E1
Shaunavon SK ... 165 F4
Shawinigan QC ... 175 D2
Shawinigan-Sud QC ... 175 D2
Shawville QC ... 174 A3
Shediac NB ... 179 D4
Shediac Bridge NB ... 179 D4
Shediac Cape NB ... 179 D4
Shelburne NS ... 180 B4
Shelburne ON ... 172 C2
Shellbrook SK ... 160 B4
Sherbrooke QC ... 175 E3
Sherwood Park AB ... 164 C1

Figures after entries indicate page number and grid reference.

Shippagan NB 179 D2
Shoal Lake MB 167 D3
Shubenacadie NS 181 D2
Sicamous BC 164 A3
Sidney BC 163 D4
Silver Creek BC 163 F1
Simcoe ON 172 C3
Sioux Lookout ON 168 C2
Slave Lake AB 158 C3
Smithers BC 156 C2
Smiths Falls ON 174 A4
Smithville ON 173 D3
Smoky Lake AB 159 D3
Smooth Rock Falls ON 170 C1
Snow Lake MB 161 D3
Somerset MB 167 E4
Sooke BC 162 C4
Sorel-Tracy QC 175 D2
Sorrento BC 163 F1
Souris MB 167 D4
Souris PE 179 F4
Southampton ON 172 B1
S. Bruce Peninsula ON 172 B1
Southey SK 166 B3
S. Huron ON 172 B3
S. Indian Lake MB 161 E1
S. River ON 171 D4
Spallumcheen BC 164 A3
Spaniard's Bay NL 183 E4
Sparwood BC 164 C4
Spirit River AB 157 F1
Spiritwood SK 159 F4
Springdale NL 183 D2
Springhill NS 180 C1
Springside SK 166 C2
Sproat Lake BC 162 C3
Spruce Grove AB 159 D4
Squamish BC 163 D2
Stanstead QC 175 D4
Stayner ON 172 C1
Steinbach MB 167 E4
Stellarton NS 181 D2
Stephenville NL 182 C3
Stephenville Crossing NL 182 C3
Stettler AB 165 D2
Stewiacke NS 181 D2
Stirling AB 165 D4
Stirling ON 173 E1
Stoke QC 175 E3
Stonewall MB 167 E3
Stoney Pt. ON 172 A4
Stony Mtn. MB 167 E3
Stony Plain AB 159 D4
Stouffville ON 173 D2
Stoughton SK 166 C4
Strasbourg SK 166 B3
Stratford ON 172 C2
Strathmore AB 164 C3
Strathroy ON 172 B3
Sturgeon Falls ON 171 D3
Sturgis SK 166 C2
Sudbury ON 170 C3
Summerford NL 183 E2
Summerland BC 163 F2
Summerside PE 179 E4
Sundre AB 164 C2
Sundridge ON 171 D4
Sunny Corner NB 178 C3
Surrey BC 163 D3
Sussex NB 180 B1
Sussex Corner NB 180 B1
Sutton ON 173 D1
Sutton QC 175 D4
Swan Hills AB 158 C3
Swan River MB 166 C2
Swift Current SK 165 F3
Sydney NS 181 F1
Sydney Mines NS 181 F1
Sydney River NS 181 F1
Sylvan Lake AB 164 C2
Taber AB 165 D4
Tabusintac NB 179 D3
Tappen BC 163 F1
Tara ON 172 B1
Tatamagouche NS 181 D1
Tavistock ON 172 C3
Taylor BC 158 A2
Tecumseh ON 172 A4
Teeswater ON 172 B2
Telkwa BC 156 C2
Temagami ON 171 D3
Témiscaming QC 171 D3
Terrace BC 156 C2
Terrace Bay ON 169 E4
Terrebonne QC 174 C3
Teulon MB 167 E3
Thamesford ON 172 C3
Thamesville ON 172 B4
The Pas MB 161 D4
Thessalon ON 170 B3
Thetford Mines QC 175 E2
Thompson MB 161 E2
Thornbury ON 172 C1
Thorold ON 173 D3
Thorsby AB 159 D4
Three Hills AB 164 C2
Thunder Bay ON 169 D4
Thurso QC 174 B3
Tide Head NB 178 C2
Tignish PE 179 E3
Tilbury ON 172 A4
Tillsonburg ON 172 C3
Timberlea NS 181 D3
Timmins ON 170 C1
Tisdale SK 160 C4
Tofield AB 159 D4
Tofino BC 162 B3
Torbay NL 183 F4
Toronto ON 173 D2
Tottenham ON 173 D2
Tracadie-Sheila NB 179 D3
Trail BC 164 A4
Treherne MB 167 E4
Trent Hills ON 173 E1
Trenton NS 181 D2
Trenton ON 173 E2
Trepassey NL 183 E4
Tring-Jonction QC 175 E2
Triton NL 183 D2
Trochu AB 164 C2
Trois-Pistoles QC 178 A2
Trois-Rivières QC 175 D2
Truro NS 181 D2
Tuktoyaktuk NT 155 D1
Tumbler Ridge BC 157 F1
Turner Valley AB 164 C3
Tweed ON 173 E1
Twillingate NL 183 E2
Two Hills AB 159 E4
Ucluelet BC 162 B3
Union Bay BC 162 C3
Unity SK 165 E2
Upton QC 175 D3
Uxbridge ON 173 D2
Val-Comeau NB 179 D3
Valcourt QC 175 D3
Val-David QC 174 C2
Val-des-Monts QC 174 B3
Val-des-Sources QC 175 E3
Val-d'Or QC 171 E2
Valemount BC 157 F3
Val-Joli QC 175 E3
Vallée-Jonction QC 175 E2
Valleyview AB 158 B3
Val-Morin QC 174 C2
Val-Senneville QC 171 E2
Vancouver BC 163 D3
Vanderhoof BC 157 D2
Vankleek Hill ON 174 B3
Varennes QC 174 C3
Vaudreuil-Dorion QC 174 C3
Vauxhall AB 165 D4
Vegreville AB 159 D4
Venise-en-Québec QC 175 D4
Verchères QC 174 C3
Verdun QC 174 C3
Vermilion AB 159 E4
Vernon BC 164 A3
Victoria BC 163 D4
Victoria NL 183 E4
Victoriaville QC 175 E2
Viking AB 159 E4
Ville-Marie QC 171 D2
Virden MB 167 D4
Vulcan AB 164 C3
Wabana NL 183 F4
Wabasca AB 159 D2
Wabowden MB 161 E3
Wabush NL 183 E1
Wadena SK 166 B2
Wainwright AB 159 E4
Wakaw SK 165 F1
Waldheim SK 165 F1
Walkerton ON 172 B1
Wallaceburg ON 172 A3
Warfield BC 164 A4
Warman SK 165 F2
Warwick QC 175 E2
Wasaga Beach ON 172 C1
Waterford ON 172 C3
Waterloo ON 172 C2
Waterloo QC 175 D3
Waterville NS 180 C2
Waterville QC 175 E3
Watford ON 172 B3
Watrous SK 166 B2
Watson Lake YT 155 E3
Waverley NS 181 D3
Wawa ON 169 F4
Wawanesa MB 167 D4
Wawota SK 166 C4
Wedgeport NS 180 B4
Weedon QC 175 E3
Welland ON 173 D3
Wellesley ON 172 C2
Wellington ON 173 E2
Wellington PE 179 E4
Wembley AB 157 F1
Wentworth-Nord QC 174 C3
Westbank BC 163 F2
Western Shore NS 180 C3
Westlock AB 159 D3
W. Lorne ON 172 B4
W. Nipissing ON 171 D3
W. Vancouver BC 163 D3
Westville NS 181 D2
Wetaskiwin AB 159 D4
Weyburn SK 166 B4
Wheatley ON 172 A4
Whistler BC 163 D2
Whitbourne NL 183 E4
Whitby ON 173 D2
Whitchurch-Stouffville ON 173 D2
White City SK 166 B3
Whitecourt AB 158 C3
Whitehorse YT 155 D3
White Rock BC 163 D3
Whitewood SK 166 C3
Wiarton ON 172 B1
Wickham QC 175 D3
Wikwemikong ON 170 C4
Wilkie SK 165 E2
Williams Lake BC 157 E4
Winchester ON 174 B4
Windermere BC 164 B3
Windsor NS 180 C2
Windsor ON 172 A4
Windsor QC 175 E3
Wingham ON 172 B2
Winkler MB 167 E4
Winnipeg MB 167 E4
Winnipeg Beach MB 167 E3
Winnipegosis MB 167 D2
Witless Bay NL 183 F4
Wolfville NS 180 C2
Wolseley SK 166 C3
Wood Buffalo AB 159 E1
Woodstock NB 178 B4
Woodstock ON 172 C3
Woodville ON 173 D1
Wotton QC 175 E3
Wright QC 174 A2
Wynyard SK 166 B2
Wyoming ON 172 B3
Yamachiche QC 175 D2
Yarmouth NS 180 B4
Yellowknife NT 155 F2
Yorkton SK 166 C3
Youbou BC 162 C3

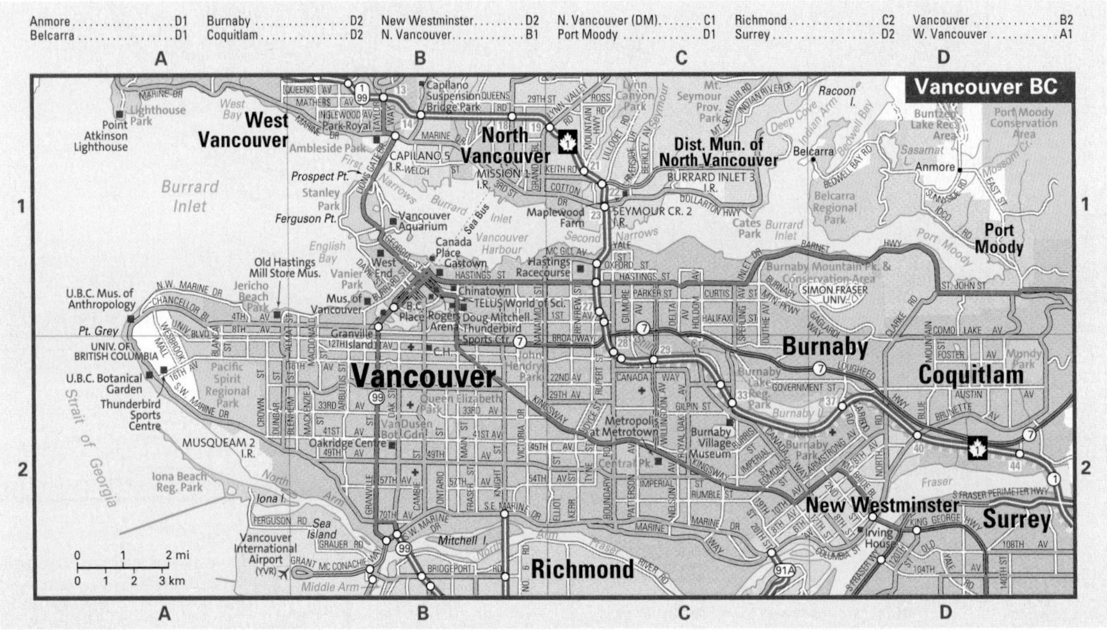
Anmore D1
Belcarra D1
Burnaby D2
Coquitlam D2
New Westminster D2
N. Vancouver B1
N. Vancouver (DM) C1
Port Moody D1
Richmond C2
Surrey D2
Vancouver B2
W. Vancouver A1
Vancouver BC
West Vancouver
North Vancouver
Dist. Mun. of North Vancouver
Burrard Inlet
Vancouver
Burnaby
Coquitlam
Port Moody
New Westminster
Surrey
Richmond
Strait of Georgia
0 1 2 mi
0 1 2 3 km

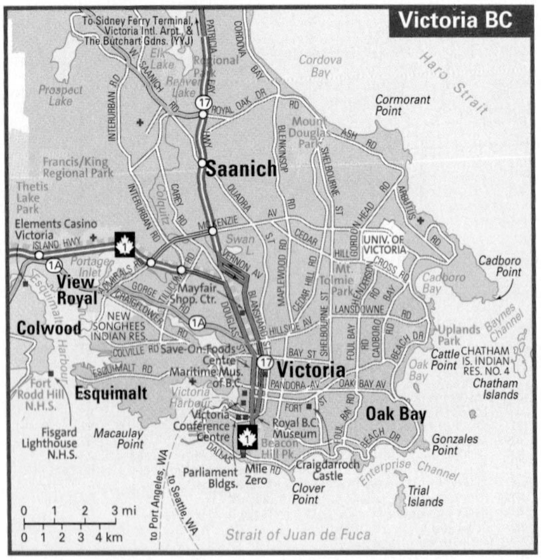
Victoria BC
Saanich
View Royal
Colwood
Esquimalt
Victoria
Oak Bay
Strait of Juan de Fuca
Haro Strait
0 1 2 3 mi
0 1 2 3 4 km

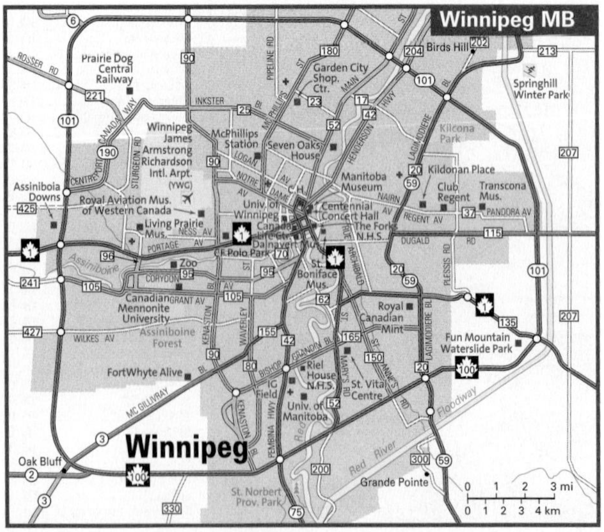
Winnipeg MB
Winnipeg
Birds Hill
Oak Bluff
Grande Pointe
0 1 2 3 mi
0 1 2 3 4 km

Entries in **bold color** indicate cities with detailed inset maps.

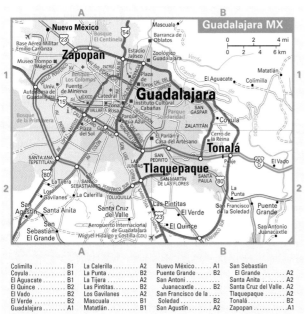

MEXICO

Acámbaro 186 B3
Acaponeta 186 A2
Acapulco 186 B4
Acayucan 187 D3
Actopan 186 C2
Agua Dulce 187 D3
Agua Prieta 184 C1
Aguascalientes 186 B2
Ajalpan 186 C3
Álamo 186 C2
Allende 185 E2
Altamira 186 C2
Alvarado 187 D3
Apan 186 C3
Apatzingán 186 B3
Apizaco 186 C3
Apodaca 185 E3
Arcelia 186 B3
Arriaga 187 D4
Atlixco 186 C3
Atoyac de Álvarez 186 B4
Autlán de Navarro 186 A2
Berriozábal 187 D4
Caborca 184 B1
Cabo San Lucas 184 C4
Calvillo 186 B2
Campeche 187 E2
Cananea 184 C1
Cancún 187 F2
Cárdenas 187 D3
Castaños 185 E3
Catemaco 187 D3
Celaya 186 B2
Cerro Azul 186 C2
Champotón 187 E3
Chapala 186 A2
Chetumal 187 F3
Chiapa 187 E4
Chihuahua 185 D2
Chilpancingo 186 C4
Cholula 186 C3
Cintalapa 187 D4
Cd. Acuña 185 E2
Cd. Altamirano 186 B3
Cd. Camargo 185 D3
Cd. Constitución 184 B4
Cd. del Carmen 187 E3
Cd. Guzmán 186 A3
Cd. Hidalgo 186 B3
Cd. Ixtepec 187 D4
Cd. Juárez 185 D1
Cd. Lerdo 185 D4
Cd. Madero 186 C2
Cd. Mante 186 C1
Cd. Mendoza 186 C3
Cd. Miguel Alemán 185 F3
Cd. Obregón 184 C3
Cd. Valles 186 C2
Cd. Victoria 185 F4
Coatepec 186 C3
Coatzacoalcos 187 D3
Colima 186 A3
Comalcalco 187 D3
Comitán de Domínguez 187 E4
Comonfort 186 B2
Córdoba 186 C3
Cosamaloapan 187 D3
Cosoleacaque 187 D3
Costa Rica 184 C4
Cozumel 187 F2
Cuauhtémoc 184 C2
Cuautla 186 C3
Cuernavaca 186 C3
Culiacán 184 C4
Delicias 185 D2
Dolores Hidalgo 186 B2
Durango 185 D4
Ébano 186 C2
Emiliano Zapata 187 E3
Empalme 184 B2
Ensenada 184 A1
Escárcega 187 E3
Escuinapa de Hidalgo 186 A1
Felipe Carrillo Puerto 187 F3
Francisco I. Madero 185 E3
Fresnillo 185 E4
Frontera 185 E3
Frontera 187 E3
Garza García 185 E3
Gómez Palacio 185 D3
Guadalajara 186 A2
Guadalupe 185 E3
Guadalupe 186 B1
Guamúchil 184 C4
Guanajuato 186 B2
Guasave 184 C3
Guaymas 184 B2
Hermosillo 184 B2
Hidalgo del Parral 185 D3
Huajuapan de León 186 C3
Huatabampo 184 C3
Huatusco 186 C3
Huauchinango 186 C2
Huejutla de Reyes 186 C2
Huetamo de Núñez 186 B3
Huimanguillo 187 D3
Huixtla 187 E4
Hunucmá 187 E2
Iguala 186 C3
Irapuato 186 B2
Ixmiquilpan 186 C2
Ixtlán del Río 186 A2
Izucar de Matamoros 186 C3
Jacona 186 B3
Jalostotitlán 186 B2
Jáltipan de Morelos 187 D3
Jérez de García Salinas 186 A1
Jiménez 185 D3
Jiutepec 186 C3
Juchitán de Zaragoza 187 D4
Kanasín 187 F2
La Barca 186 B2
Lagos de Moreno 186 B2
La Paz 184 B4
La Piedad de Cabadas 186 B2
Las Choapas 187 D3
Lázaro Cárdenas 186 B3
León 186 B2
Linares 185 F4
Loma Bonita 187 D3
Loreto 186 B2
Los Mochis 184 C3
Los Reyes de Salgado 186 B3
Macuspana 187 E3
Magdalena de Kino 184 B1
Manzanillo 186 A3
Martínez de la Torre 186 C2
Matamoros 185 E4
Matamoros 185 F3
Matehuala 185 E4
Matías Romero 187 D4
Mazatlán 185 D4
Melchor Múzquiz 185 E3
Meoqui 185 D2
Mérida 187 F2

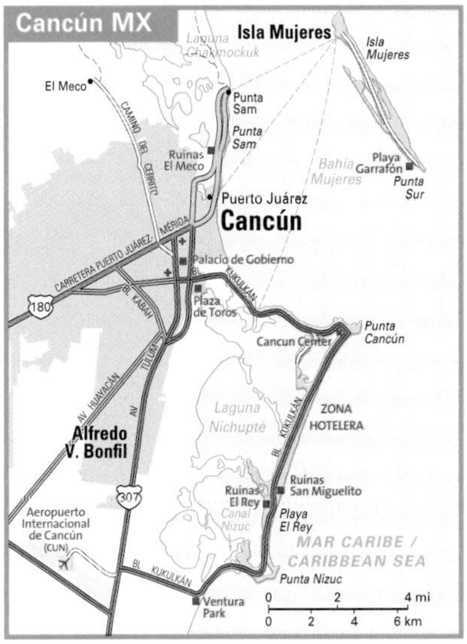
Cancún MX
Isla Mujeres
Isla Mujeres
Laguna Chacmochuk
El Meco
Punta Sam
Punta Sam
Ruinas El Meco
Bahía Mujeres
Playa Garrafón
Punta Sur
Puerto Juárez
Cancún
Palacio de Gobierno
Plaza de Toros
Punta Cancún
Cancun Center
Laguna Nichupté
ZONA HOTELERA
Alfredo V. Bonfil
Ruinas San Miguelito
Ruinas El Rey
Canal Nizuc
Playa El Rey
Aeropuerto Internacional de Cancún (CUN)
MAR CARIBE / CARIBBEAN SEA
Punta Nizuc
Ventura Park
0 2 4 mi
0 2 4 6 km

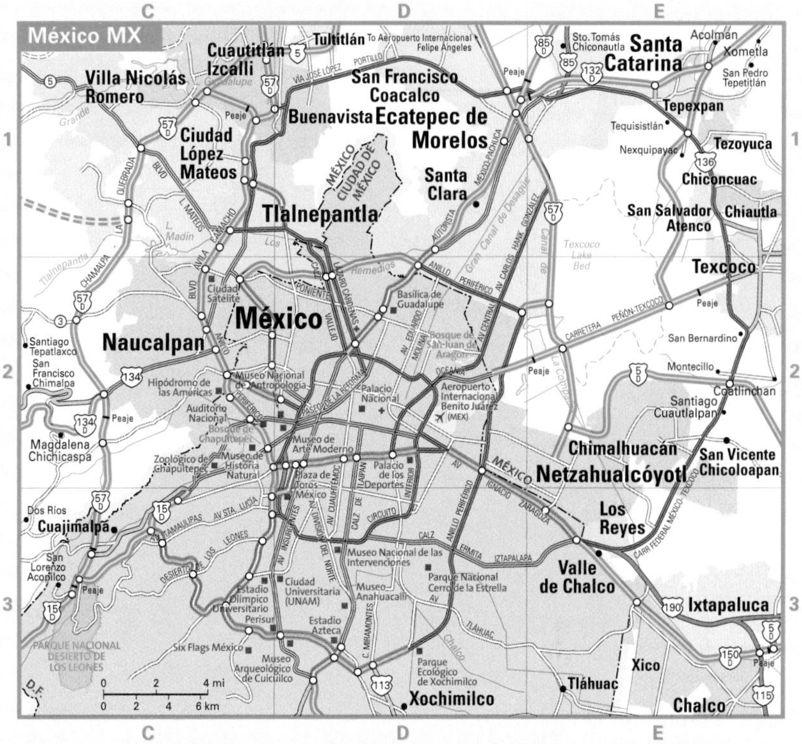
México MX
C D E
Tultitlán
Cuautitlán Izcalli
Villa Nicolás Romero
San Francisco Coacalco
Buenavista
Ecatepec de Morelos
Sto. Tomás Chiconautla
Santa Catarina
Acolman
Xometla
San Pedro Tepetitlán
Tepexpan
Tequisistlán
Nexquipayac
Tezoyuca
Chiconcuac
Ciudad López Mateos
Santa Clara
Tlalnepantla
San Salvador Atenco
Chiautla
Texcoco
Texcoco Lake Bed
Ciudad Satélite
Basílica de Guadalupe
México
Naucalpan
Santiago Tepatlaxco
San Francisco Chimalpa
San Bernardino
Montecillo
Coatlinchan
Santiago Cuautlalpan
Hipódromo de las Américas
Museo Nacional de Antropología
Palacio Nacional
Aeropuerto Internacional Benito Juárez (MEX)
Auditorio Nacional
Bosque de Chapultepec
Magdalena Chichicaspa
Museo de Arte Moderno
Zoológico de Chapultepec
Museo de Historia Natural
Plaza de Toros
Palacio de los Deportes
Chimalhuacán
San Vicente Chicoloapan
Netzahualcóyotl
Dos Ríos
Cuajimalpa
Los Reyes
San Lorenzo Acopilco
Museo Nacional de las Intervenciones
Parque Nacional Cerro de la Estrella
Valle de Chalco
Estadio Olímpico Universitario
Ciudad Universitaria (UNAM)
Museo Anahuacalli
Perisur
Estadio Azteca
Ixtapaluca
PARQUE NACIONAL DESIERTO DE LOS LEONES
Six Flags México
Museo Arqueológico de Cuicuilco
Parque Ecológico de Xochimilco
Xico
Tláhuac
Xochimilco
Chalco
0 2 4 mi
0 2 4 6 km

Acolman E1
Buenavista D1
Chalco E3
Chiautla E1
Chiconcuac E1
Chimalhuacán E2
Ciudad López Mateos C1
Coatlinchan E2
Cuajimalpa C3
Cuautitlán Izcalli C1
Dos Ríos C3
Ecatepec de Morelos D1
Ixtapaluca E3
Los Reyes E3
México D2
Magdalena Chichicaspa C2
Montecillo E2
Naucalpan C2
Netzahualcóyotl E2
Nexquipayac E1
San Bernardino E2
San Francisco Chimalpa C2
San Francisco Coacalco D1
San Lorenzo Acopilco C3
San Pedro Tepetitlán E1
San Salvador Atenco E1
San Vicente Chicoloapan E2
Santa Catarina E1
Santa Clara D1
Santo Tomás Chiconautla E1
Santiago Cuautlalpan E2
Santiago Tepatlaxco C2
Tepexpan E1
Tequisistlán E1
Texcoco E2
Tezoyuca E1
Tláhuac E3
Tlalnepantla C1
Tultitlán D1
Valle de Chalco E3
Villa Nicolás Romero C1
Xico E3
Xochimilco D3
Xometla E1

Mexicali 184 A1
México 186 C3
Minatitlán 187 D3
Misantla 186 C3
Monclova 185 E3
Montemorelos 185 F4
Monterrey 185 E3
Morelia 186 B3
Moroleón 186 B2
Naranjos 186 C2
Navojoa 184 C3
Navolato 184 C4
Netzahualcóyotl 186 C3
Nogales 184 B1
Nueva Italia de Ruiz 186 B3
Nueva Rosita 185 E3
Nuevo Casas Grandes 184 C2
Nuevo Laredo 185 F3
Oaxaca 186 C4
Ocotlán 186 A2
Ocozocoautla 187 D4
Orizaba 186 C3
Pachuca 186 C2
Pánuco 186 C2
Papantla 186 C2
Paraíso 187 D3
Parras de la Fuente 185 E4
Pátzcuaro 186 B3
Perote 186 C3
Petatlán 186 B4
Piedras Negras 185 E2
Playa del Carmen 187 F2
Poza Rica 186 C2
Progreso 187 E2
Puebla 186 C3
Puerto Peñasco 184 B1
Puerto Vallarta 186 A2
Puruándiro 186 B2
Querétaro 186 B2
Reynosa 185 F3
Rincón de Romos 186 B2
Río Bravo 185 F3
Río Grande 185 E4
Río Verde 186 B2
Sabinas Hidalgo 185 E3
Sahuayo 186 B2
Salamanca 186 B2
Salina Cruz 187 D4
Saltillo 185 E4
Salvatierra 186 B2
San Andrés Tuxtla 187 D3
San Buenaventura 185 E3
San Cristóbal de las Casas 187 E4
San Felipe 186 B2
San Fernando 185 F4
San Francisco del Rincón 186 B2
San José del Cabo 184 C4
San Juan de los Lagos 186 B2
San Juan del Río 186 B2
San Luis de la Paz 186 B2
San Luis Potosí 186 B2
San Luis Río Colorado 184 A1
San Miguel de Allende 186 B2
San Nicolás de los Garza 185 E3
San Pedro de las Colonias 185 E3
Santa Catarina 185 E3
Santiago 185 E4
Santiago Papasquiaro 185 D4
Sayula 186 A3
Silao 186 B2
Sombrerete 185 D4
Tacámbaro de Codallos 186 B3
Tala 186 A2
Tamazunchale 186 C2
Tampico 186 C2
Tantoyuca 186 C2
Tapachula 187 E4
Taxco 186 B3
Teapa 187 E3
Tecamachalco 186 C3
Tecate 184 A1
Tecomán 186 A3
Tehuacán 186 C3
Tehuantepec 187 D4
Tejupilco de Hidalgo 186 B3
Teloloapan 186 B3
Tenancingo 186 B3
Tenosique 187 E3
Teocaltiche 186 B2
Tepatitlán 186 B2
Tepeji de Ocampo 186 C3
Tepic 186 A2
Tequila 186 A2
Tequisquiapan 186 B2
Tequixquiac 186 C3
Teziutlán 186 C3
Ticul 187 F2
Tierra Blanca 187 D3
Tijuana 184 A1
Tizayuca 186 C3
Tizimín 187 F2
Tlapa de Comonfort 186 C3
Tlapacoyan 186 C3
Tlaxcala 186 C3
Toluca 186 B3
Tonalá 186 A2
Tonalá 187 D4
Torreón 185 D3
Tres Valles 187 D3
Tulancingo 186 C2
Tuxpam 186 C2
Tuxpan 186 A2
Tuxpan 186 A3
Tuxtepec 187 D3
Tuxtla Gutiérrez 187 E4
Umán 187 E2
Uruapan 186 B3
Valladolid 187 F2
Valle de Santiago 186 B2
Valle Hermoso 185 F3
Veracruz 187 D3
Víctor Rosales 186 B1
Villa Flores 187 D4
Villahermosa 187 E3
Xalapa 186 C3
Xicotepec de Juárez 186 C2
Zacapu 186 B3
Zacatecas 186 B1
Zacatlán 186 C2
Zamora de Hidalgo 186 B3
Zapopan 186 A2
Zapotiltic 186 A3
Zihuatanejo 186 B3
Zitácuaro 186 B3
Zumpango 186 C3
Zumpango del Río 186 B3

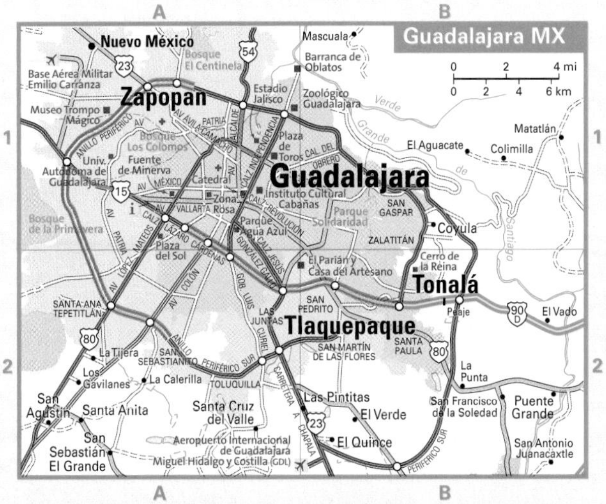
Guadalajara MX
A B
Nuevo México
Mascuala
Bosque El Centinela
Barranca de Oblatos
Base Aérea Militar Emilio Carranza
Zapopan
Estadio Jalisco
Zoológico Guadalajara
Museo Trompo Mágico
Matatlán
Bosque Los Colomos
El Aguacate
Colimilla
Univ. Autónoma de Guadalajara
Fuente de Minerva
Catedral
Guadalajara
Instituto Cultural Cabañas
Parque Solidaridad
Bosque de la Primavera
Plaza del Sol
Plaza del Sol
Coyula
El Parián y Casa del Artesano
Cerro de la Reina
Tonalá
Santa Ana Tepetitlán
Tlaquepaque
El Vado
La Tijera
San Sebastianito
San Martín de las Flores
Santa Paula
Los Gavilanes
La Calerilla
La Punta
Las Pintitas
San Agustín
Santa Anita
Santa Cruz del Valle
El Verde
San Francisco de la Soledad
Puente Grande
San Sebastián El Grande
Aeropuerto Internacional de Guadalajara Miguel Hidalgo y Costilla (GDL)
El Quince
San Antonio Juanacaxtle
0 2 4 mi
0 2 4 6 km

Colimilla B1
Coyula B1
El Aguacate B1
El Quince B2
El Vado B2
El Verde B2
Guadalajara A1
La Calerilla A2
La Punta B2
La Tijera A2
Las Pintitas B2
Los Gavilanes A2
Mascuala B1
Matatlán B1
Nuevo México A1
Puente Grande B2
San Antoni Juanacaxtle B2
San Francisco de la Soledad B2
San Agustín A2
San Sebastián El Grande A2
Santa Anita A2
Santa Cruz del Valle A2
Tlaquepaque A2
Tonalá B2
Zapopan A1

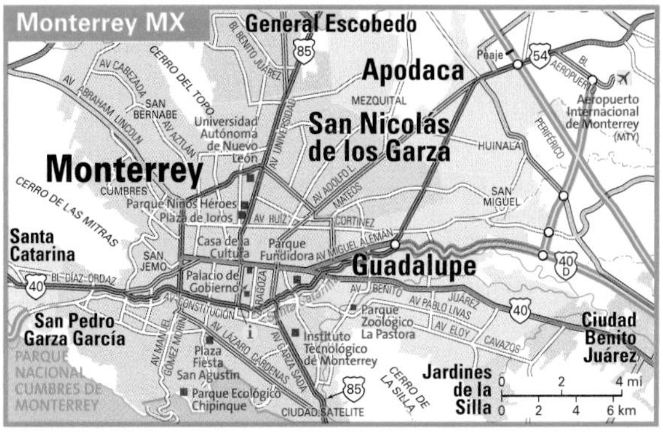
Monterrey MX
General Escobedo
Apodaca
Aeropuerto Internacional de Monterrey (MTY)
Universidad Autónoma de Nuevo León
San Nicolás de los Garza
Monterrey
Parque Niños Héroes
Plaza de Toros
Santa Catarina
Casa de la Cultura
Parque Fundidora
Guadalupe
Palacio de Gobierno
Parque Zoológico La Pastora
San Pedro Garza García
Plaza Fiesta San Agustín
Instituto Tecnológico de Monterrey
Ciudad Benito Juárez
PARQUE NACIONAL CUMBRES DE MONTERREY
Parque Ecológico Chipinque
Jardines de la Silla
0 2 4 mi
0 2 4 6 km

Miles

	Albuquerque, NM	Amarillo, TX	Anchorage, AK	Atlanta, GA	Baltimore, MD	Billings, MT	Birmingham, AL	Bismarck, ND	Boise, ID	Boston, MA	Buffalo, NY	Calgary, AB	Charleston, SC	Charleston, WV	Charlotte, NC	Cheyenne, WY	Chicago, IL	Cincinnati, OH	Cleveland, OH	Columbus, OH	Dallas, TX	Denver, CO	Des Moines, IA	Detroit, MI	El Paso, TX	Halifax, NS	Houston, TX	Indianapolis, IN	Jackson, MS	Jacksonville, FL	Kansas City, MO	Las Vegas, NV	Little Rock, AR	Los Angeles, CA	Louisville, KY
Albany, NY	2095	1811	4421	1010	333	2083	1093	1675	2526	172	292	2512	913	634	771	1789	832	730	484	621	1680	1833	1155	571	2326	877	1768	795	1331	1094	1282	2586	1354	2859	832
Albuquerque, NM		286	3563	1490	1902	991	1274	1333	966	2240	1808	1498	1793	1568	1649	538	1352	1409	1619	1476	754	438	1091	1608	263	2945	994	1298	1157	1837	894	578	900	806	1320
Amarillo, TX			3734	1206	1618	988	991	1398	1266	1957	1524	1669	1510	1285	1365	534	1069	1126	1335	1192	470	434	808	1324	438	2662	711	1014	874	1517	610	864	617	1092	1036
Anchorage, AK				4304	4297	2601	4253	2724	2745	4592	4133	2065	4495	4093	4348	3056	3584	3890	3935	3946	4087	3300	3421	3872	4002	4821	4328	3771	4294	4652	3547	3356	3929	3403	3886
Atlanta, GA					679	1889	150	1559	2218	1100	910	2395	317	503	238	1482	717	476	726	577	792	1403	967	735	1437	1805	800	531	386	344	801	2067	528	2237	419
Baltimore, MD						1959	795	1551	2401	422	370	2388	583	352	441	1665	708	521	377	420	1399	1690	1031	532	2045	1128	1470	600	1032	763	1087	2445	1072	2705	602
Billings, MT							1839	413	626	2254	1796	536	2157	1755	2012	455	1246	1552	1597	1608	1433	554	1007	1534	1255	2806	1673	1432	1836	2237	1088	965	1530	1239	1547
Birmingham, AL								1509	2170	1215	909	2346	466	578	389	1434	667	475	725	576	647	1356	919	734	1292	1921	678	481	241	494	753	1852	381	2092	369
Bismarck, ND									1039	1846	1388	794	1749	1347	1604	594	838	1144	1189	1200	1342	693	675	1126	1597	2398	1582	1024	1548	1906	801	1378	1183	1702	1139
Boise, ID										2697	2239	735	2520	2182	2375	737	1708	1969	2040	2036	1711	833	1369	1977	1206	3249	1952	1852	2115	2566	1376	760	1808	1033	1933
Boston, MA											462	2683	1003	741	861	1961	1003	862	654	760	1819	2004	1326	741	2465	714	1890	940	1453	1184	1427	2757	1493	3046	964
Buffalo, NY												2224	899	431	695	1502	545	442	197	333	1393	1546	868	277	2039	1167	1513	508	1134	1080	995	2299	1066	2572	545
Calgary, AB													2586	2184	2441	991	1675	1981	2026	2037	2114	1234	1512	1963	1936	2912	2355	1862	2385	2743	1638	1291	2020	1565	1977
Charleston, SC														468	204	1783	907	622	724	637	1109	1705	1204	879	1754	1708	1110	721	703	238	1102	2371	900	2554	610
Charleston, WV															265	1445	506	209	255	168	1072	1367	802	410	1718	1446	1192	320	816	649	764	2122	745	2374	251
Charlotte, NC																1637	761	476	520	433	1031	1559	1057	675	1677	1566	1041	575	625	385	956	2225	754	2453	464
Cheyenne, WY																	972	1233	1304	1300	979	100	633	1241	801	2513	1220	1115	1382	1829	640	843	1076	1116	1197
Chicago, IL																		302	346	359	936	1015	337	283	1543	1555	1108	184	750	1065	532	1768	662	2042	299
Cincinnati, OH																			253	105	958	1200	599	261	1605	1567	1079	116	700	803	597	1955	632	2215	106
Cleveland, OH																				144	1208	1347	669	171	1854	1359	1328	319	950	904	806	2100	882	2374	356
Columbus, OH																					1059	1266	665	192	1706	1465	1179	176	801	818	663	2021	733	2281	207
Dallas, TX																						887	752	1218	647	2524	241	913	406	1049	554	1331	327	1446	852
Denver, CO																							676	1284	701	2556	1127	1088	1290	1751	603	756	984	1029	1118
Des Moines, IA																								606	1283	1878	992	481	931	1315	194	1429	567	1703	595
Detroit, MI																									1799	1278	1338	318	960	1060	795	2037	891	2310	366
El Paso, TX																										3171	758	1489	1051	1642	1085	717	974	801	1499
Halifax, NS																											2595	1646	2158	1889	2133	3309	2198	3583	1669
Houston, TX																												839	445	884	795	1474	447	1558	972
Indianapolis, IN																													675	879	485	1843	587	2104	112
Jackson, MS																														598	747	1735	269	1851	594
Jacksonville, FL																															1148	2415	873	2441	766
Kansas City, MO																																1358	382	1632	516
Las Vegas, NV																																	1478	274	1874
Little Rock, AR																																		1706	526
Los Angeles, CA																																			2126

Kilometers

	Albany, NY	Albuquerque, NM	Amarillo, TX	Anchorage, AK	Atlanta, GA	Baltimore, MD	Billings, MT	Birmingham, AL	Bismarck, ND	Boise, ID	Boston, MA	Buffalo, NY	Calgary, AB	Charleston, SC	Charleston, WV	Charlotte, NC	Cheyenne, WY	Chicago, IL	Cincinnati, OH	Cleveland, OH	Columbus, OH	Dallas, TX	Denver, CO	Des Moines, IA	Detroit, MI	El Paso, TX	Halifax, NS	Houston, TX	Indianapolis, IN	Jackson, MS	Jacksonville, FL	Kansas City, MO	Las Vegas, NV	Little Rock, AR	Los Angeles, CA	Louisville, KY
Albuquerque, NM	3371																																			
Amarillo, TX	2914	460																																		
Anchorage, AK	7113	5733	6008																																	
Atlanta, GA	1625	2397	1940	6925																																
Baltimore, MD	536	3060	2603	6914	1093																															
Billings, MT	3352	1595	1590	4185	3039	3152																														
Birmingham, AL	1759	2050	1595	6843	241	1279	2959																													
Bismarck, ND	2695	2145	2249	4383	2508	2496	665	2428																												
Boise, ID	4064	1554	2037	4417	3569	3863	1007	3492	1672																											
Boston, MA	277	3604	3149	7389	1770	679	3627	1955	2970	4339																										
Buffalo, NY	470	2909	2452	6650	1464	595	2890	1463	2233	3603	743																									
Calgary, AB	4042	2410	2685	3323	3854	3842	862	3775	1278	1183	4317	3578																								
Charleston, SC	1469	2885	2430	7232	510	938	3471	750	2814	4055	1614	1446	4161																							
Charleston, WV	1020	2523	2068	6586	809	566	2824	930	2167	3511	1192	693	3514	753																						
Charlotte, NC	1241	2653	2196	6996	383	710	3237	626	2581	3821	1385	1118	3928	328	426																					
Cheyenne, WY	2879	866	859	4917	2385	2679	732	2307	956	1186	3155	2417	1595	2869	2325	2634																				
Chicago, IL	1339	2175	1720	5767	1154	1139	2005	1073	1348	2748	1614	864	2695	1459	814	1224	1564																			
Cincinnati, OH	1175	2267	1812	6259	766	838	2497	764	1841	3168	1387	711	3187	1001	336	766	1984	486																		
Cleveland, OH	779	2605	2148	6331	1168	607	2570	1167	1913	3282	1052	317	3260	1165	410	837	2098	557	407																	
Columbus, OH	999	2375	1918	6349	928	676	2587	927	1931	3276	1223	536	3278	1025	270	697	2092	578	169	232																
Dallas, TX	2703	1213	756	6576	1274	2251	2306	1041	2159	2753	2927	2241	3401	1784	1725	1659	1575	1506	1541	1944	1704															
Denver, CO	2949	705	698	5310	2257	2719	891	2182	1115	1340	3224	2488	1986	2743	2200	2508	161	1633	1931	2167	2037	1427														
Des Moines, IA	1858	1755	1300	5504	1556	1659	1620	1479	1086	2203	2134	1397	2433	1937	1290	1701	1018	542	964	1076	1070	1210	1088													
Detroit, MI	919	2587	2130	6230	1183	856	2468	1181	1812	3181	1192	446	3158	1414	660	1086	1997	455	420	275	309	1960	2066	975												
El Paso, TX	3743	423	705	6439	2312	3290	2019	2079	2570	1940	3966	3281	3115	2822	2764	2698	1289	2483	2582	2983	2745	1041	1128	2064	2895											
Halifax, NS	1411	4739	4283	7757	2904	1815	4515	3091	3858	5228	1149	1878	4685	2748	2327	2520	4043	2502	2521	2187	2357	4061	4113	3022	2056	5102										
Houston, TX	2845	1599	1144	6964	1287	2365	2692	1091	2545	3141	3041	2434	3789	1786	1918	1675	1963	1783	1736	2137	1897	388	1813	1596	2153	1220	4175									
Indianapolis, IN	1279	2088	1632	6068	854	965	2304	774	1648	2980	1512	817	2996	1160	515	925	1794	296	187	513	283	1469	1751	774	512	2396	2648	1350								
Jackson, MS	2142	1862	1406	6909	621	1660	2954	388	2491	3403	2338	1825	3837	1131	1313	1006	2224	1207	1126	1529	1289	653	2076	1498	1545	1691	3472	716	1086							
Jacksonville, FL	1760	2956	2441	7485	553	1228	3599	795	3067	4129	1905	1738	4413	383	1044	619	2943	1714	1292	1455	1316	1688	2817	2116	1706	2642	3039	1422	1414	962						
Kansas City, MO	2063	1438	981	5707	1289	1749	1751	1212	1289	2214	2296	1601	2636	1773	1229	1538	1030	856	961	1297	1067	891	970	312	1279	1746	3432	1279	780	1202	1847					
Las Vegas, NV	4161	930	1390	5400	3326	3934	1553	2980	2217	1223	4436	3699	2077	3815	3414	3580	1356	2845	3146	3379	3252	2142	1216	2299	3278	1154	5324	2372	2965	2792	3886	2185				
Little Rock, AR	2179	1448	993	6322	850	1725	2462	613	1903	2909	2402	1715	3250	1448	1199	1213	1731	1065	1017	1419	1179	526	1583	912	1434	1567	3537	719	944	433	1405	615	2378			
Los Angeles, CA	4600	1297	1757	5475	3599	4352	1994	3366	2739	1662	4901	4138	2518	4109	3820	3947	1796	3286	3564	3820	3670	2327	1656	2740	3717	1289	5765	2507	3385	2978	3928	2626	441	2745		
Louisville, KY	1339	2124	1667	6253	674	969	2489	594	1833	3110	1551	877	3181	981	404	747	1926	481	171	573	333	1371	1799	957	589	2412	2685	1564	180	956	1232	830	3015	846	3421	
Memphis, TN	1953	1662	1207	6570	626	1501	2615	388	2151	3144	2177	1492	3498	1223	975	988	1958	867	793	1194	956	750	1796	1158	1210	1789	3311	943	747	339	1179	862	2592	225	2959	621
México, MX	4520	2352	2051	8061	2821	3899	3641	2624	3952	3985	4574	4058	4737	3319	3541	3208	2911	3421	3360	3760	3522	1815	2750	3002	3776	1926	5709	1535	3287	2249	2956	2684	2846	2344	2981	3187
Miami, FL	2315	3467	2951	7997	1064	1784	4109	1307	3578	4639	2460	2293	4925	938	1599	1175	3455	2224	1836	2011	1871	2200	3329	2626	2254	3152	3595	1932	1924	1472	555	2359	4397	1915	4439	1744
Milwaukee, WI	1495	2294	1837	5651	1308	1295	1891	1228	1234	2813	1770	1033	2579	1614	967	1379	1628	143	640	713	730	1625	1697	608	611	2602	2658	1920	449	1344	1866	922	2909	1202	3350	634
Minneapolis, MN	2003	2154	1697	5110	1817	1804	1350	1736	693	2357	2280	1541	2039	2122	1477	1887	1418	658	1149	1223	1241	1607	1487	396	1121	2462	3168	1995	959	1852	2376	710	2698	1310	3139	1144
Mobile, AL	2162	2162	1780	7258	534	1630	3249	415	2840	3704	2306	1874	4187	1033	1347	920	2526	1485	1176	1578	1339	1028	2378	1794	1595	1981	1981	761	1186	301	660	1496	3092	735	3268	1006
Montréal, QC	370	3495	3038	6607	1997	907	3368	2074	2711	4079	504	639	3535	1842	1323	1614	2895	1353	1311	946	1167	2851	2965	1874	907	3802	1150	3044	1403	2436	2132	2187	4177	2327	4616	1480
Nashville, TN	1614	2008	1553	6534	389	1152	2652	312	2116	3179	1828	1152	3463	874	636	639	1995	763	452	854	615	1096	1870	1167	870	2137	2962	1289	462	681	948	899	2938	571	3305	282
New Orleans, LA	2317	2053	1598	7207	761	1837	3146	565	2790	3595	2515	2018	4135	1260	1490	1147	2417	1504	1319	1722	1482	845	2267	1797	1736	1799	3649	579	1329	298	895	1500	2983	732	3084	1149
New York, NY	243	3242	2785	7062	1398	309	3297	1585	2640	4008	346	644	3990	1244	829	1015	2824	1282	1023	750	861	2557	2895	1804	1001	3596	1480	2671	1150	1968	1533	1934	4106	2031	4537	1189
Oklahoma City, OK	2492	879	422	6245	1519	2179	1974	1173	1828	2423	2726	2031	3070	2008	1644	1773	1244	1298	1389	1726	1496	336	1096	879	1709	1186	3862	722	1210	985	2077	560	1809	571	2175	1245
Omaha, NE	2079	1566	1168	5409	1591	1879	1455	1514	991	1986	2354	1617	2338	2076	1532	1841	800	763	1184	1297	1290	1076	870	219	1195	1989	3242	1464	994	1504	2150	302	2082	917	2521	1133
Orlando, FL	1987	3112	2595	7641	708	1455	3754	951	3223	4283	2130	1905	4570	610	1271	845	3099	1868	1480	1681	1541	1844	2972	2270	1899	2796	3266	1577	1569	1117	227	2003	4042	1559	4084	1389
Ottawa, ON	486	3392	2936	6455	1866	842	3265	1971	2608	3977	665	536	3384	1780	1221	1483	2793	1252	1208	845	1064	2748	2862	1772	805	3701	1324	2941	1302	2333	2069	2085	4074	2224	4515	1377
Philadelphia, PA	359	3144	2689	7010	1258	167	3249	1443	2592	3961	516	666	3939	1102	730	874	2776	1236	927	703	763	2415	2806	1755	953	3455	1651	2529	1054	1826	1393	1836	4023	1891	4441	1091
Phoenix, AZ	4121	750	1212	5776	3006	3807	1929	2772	2674	1598	4354	3659	2454	3514	3274	3390	1615	2927	3018	3355	3125	1733	1455	2507	3337	695	5490	1911	2838	2385	3334	2188	459	2200	594	2874
Pittsburgh, PA	780	2687	2230	6526	1088	396	2766	1228	2109	3477	953	349	3455	1033	349	705	2293	751	470	219	306	2005	2349	1273	470	3046	2087	2198	595	1590	1323	1379	3564	1480	3984	634
Portland, ME	434	3762	3305	7546	1926	837	3784	2113	3128	4497	172	901	4475	1772	1350	1543	3313	1772	1545	1208	1381	3084	3382	2291	1348	4124	872	3199	1670	2494	2061	2454	4594	2558	5059	1709
Portland, OR	4753	2245	2727	3902	4259	4553	1430	4182	2093	695	5030	4291	1371	4743	4199	4508	1876	3438	3858	3973	3965	3443	2029	2893	3870	2843	5918	3831	3669	4093	4817	2904	1911	3599	1562	3800
Québec, QC	582	3734	3279	6846	2209	1120	3607	2314	2951	4320	624	879	3775	2055	1564	1826	3136	1595	1564	1187	1406	3091	3205	2114	1147	4043	940	3284	1644	2676	2344	2428	4417	2566	4858	1720
Raleigh, NC	1028	2867	2412	7157	637	497	3395	880	2739	4014	1173	1033	4085	449	504	254	2829	1385	840	914	776	1913	2703	1862	1165	2951	2307	1928	1028	1260	740	1733	3797	1430	4164	907
Rapid City, SD	2816	1353	1347	4795	2431	2616	610	2354	515	1496	3091	2354	1472	2935	2288	2700	491	1469	1961	2034	2051	1733	650	1012	1932	1778	3979	2121	1772	2346	2991	1142	1665	1759	2106	1955
Reno, NV	4420	1641	2101	4843	3926	4220	1545	3849	2208	692	4697	3958	2069	4410	3866	4175	1543	3105	3525	3640	3632	3110	1696	2560	3537	2116	5585	3334	3335	3760	4484	2571	711	3266	835	3467
Richmond, VA	776	3018	2563	7065	848	245	3303	1091	2647	4016	920	780	3994	689	518	465	2832	1290	853	758	832	2106	2716	1812	1009	3146	2055	2140	1031	1471	980	1746	3932	1582	4315	920
St. Louis, MO	1667	1691	1234	6113	883	1353	2158	806	1694	2619	1900	1205	3041	1368	824	1133	1435	473	563	901	671	1022	1376	702	883	1998	3036	1389	385	813	1442	405	2590	669	2986	425
Salt Lake City, UT	3578	1004	1551	4729	3083	3379	882	3006	1545	550	3854	3115	1406	3569	3025	3334	702	2262	2682	2796	2790	2269	854	1717	2695	1390	4742	2655	2492	2917	3643	1728	671	2425	1112	2624
San Antonio, TX	3142	1316	825	6833	1609	2689	2414	1413	2573	2833	3366	2679	3511	2108	2162	1997	1683	2043	1981	2383	2143	436	1522	1623	2397	895	4500	322	1908	1036	1744	1307	2047	965	2182	1810
San Diego, CA	4697	1327	1788	5673	3485	4383	2095	3252	2840	1763	4932	4235	2619	3995	3850	3870	1897	3387	3595	3921	3701	2212	1757	2841	3818	1175	5866	2393	3414	2864	3813	2727	542	2740	200	3450
San Francisco, CA	4769	1788	2248	4940	4212	4570	1892	3977	2814	1039	5044	4307	2409	4721	4216	4439	1892	3453	3873	3987	3981	2940	2045	2907	3886	1900	5932	3118	3685	3591	4541	2919	925	3237	619	3817
Seattle, WA	4664	2354	2837	3623	4352	4465	1313	4275	1977	805	4940	4203	1093	4784	4137	4549	1986	3318	3810	3883	3900	3553	2138	2932	3781	3128	5828	3940	3619	4203	4911	3012	2021	3709	1847	3804
Tampa, FL	2076	3136	2619	7664	732	1545	3778	975	3247	4307	2220	2053	4592	698	1360	935	3123	1892	1504	1772	1667	1868	2996	2294	1921	2821	3355	1601	1593	1141	315	2026	4064	1583	4108	1413
Toronto, ON	644	2962	2505	6595	1541	909	2835	1541	2179	3546	917	171	3524	1619	864	1290	2362	821	779	488	708	2319	2433	1342	375	3269	1681	2512	870	1903	1910	1654	3644	1794	4084	948
Vancouver, BC	4878	2570	3052	3430	4566	4679	1527	4491	2191	1018	5155	4417	899	4998	4352	4763	2201	3533	4024	4098	4116	3768	2354	3147	3995	3358	6043	4156	3834	4418	5126	3229	2237	3924	2077	4018
Washington, DC	594	3051	2594	6903	1023	61	3142	1220	2486	3854	737	618	3831	867	557	639	2669	1128	832	595	669	2191	2713	1649	846	3231	1873	2306	959	1603	1158	1743	3928	1667	4348	959
Wichita, KS	2367	1138	681	5921	1591	2053	1717	1348	1503	2166	2600	1905	2814	2077	1533	1842	986	1171	1263	1601	1371	591	838	628	1583	1445	3736	978	1084	1241	2151	309	2053	747	2434	1134
Winnipeg, MB	2730	2507	2285	4385	2542	2531	1324	2463	668	2336	3006	2269	1313	2850	2203	2615	1821	1384	1876	1948	1966	2193	1892	1121	1847	3010	3361	2581	1685	2526	3102	1324	3012	1939	3453	1870

Milles

	Memphis, TN	México, MX	Miami, FL	Milwaukee, WI	Minneapolis, MN	Mobile, AL	Montréal, QC	Nashville, TN	New Orleans, LA	New York, NY	Oklahoma City, OK	Omaha, NE	Orlando, FL	Ottawa, ON	Philadelphia, PA	Phoenix, AZ	Pittsburgh, PA	Portland, ME	Portland, OR	Québec, QC	Raleigh, NC	Rapid City, SD	Reno, NV	Richmond, VA	St. Louis, MO	Salt Lake City, UT	San Antonio, TX	San Diego, CA	San Francisco, CA	Seattle, WA	Tampa, FL	Toronto, ON	Vancouver, BC	Washington, DC	Wichita, KS	Winnipeg, MB
Albany, NY	1214	2809	1439	929	1245	1344	230	1003	1440	151	1549	1292	1235	302	223	2561	485	270	2954	362	639	1750	2747	482	1036	2224	1953	2919	2964	2899	1290	400	3032	369	1471	1697
Albuquerque, NM	1033	1462	2155	1426	1339	1344	2172	1248	1276	2015	546	973	1934	2108	1954	466	1670	2338	1395	2321	1782	841	1020	1876	1051	624	818	825	1111	1463	1949	1841	1597	1896	707	1608
Amarillo, TX	750	1275	1834	1142	1055	1106	1888	965	993	1731	262	726	1613	1825	1671	753	1386	2054	1695	2038	1499	837	1306	1593	767	964	513	1111	1397	1763	1628	1557	1897	1612	423	1420
Anchorage, AK	4083	5010	4970	3512	3176	4511	4106	4061	4479	4389	3881	3362	4749	4012	4357	3590	4056	4690	2425	4255	4448	2980	3010	4391	3799	2939	4247	3526	3070	2252	4763	4099	2132	4290	3680	2725
Atlanta, GA	389	1753	661	813	1129	332	1241	242	473	869	944	989	440	1160	782	1868	676	1197	2647	1373	396	1511	2440	527	549	1916	1000	2166	2618	2705	455	958	2838	636	989	1580
Baltimore, MD	933	2423	1109	805	1121	1013	564	716	1142	192	1354	1168	904	523	104	2366	246	520	2830	696	309	1626	2623	152	841	2100	1671	2724	2840	2775	960	565	2908	38	1276	1573
Billings, MT	1625	2263	2554	1175	839	2019	2093	1648	1955	2049	1227	904	2333	2029	2019	1199	1719	2352	889	2242	2110	379	960	2053	1341	548	1500	1302	1176	816	2348	1762	949	1953	1067	823
Birmingham, AL	241	1631	812	763	1079	258	1289	194	351	985	729	941	591	1225	897	1723	763	1313	2599	1438	547	1463	2392	678	501	1868	878	2021	2472	2657	606	958	2791	758	838	1531
Bismarck, ND	1337	2456	2224	767	431	1765	1685	1315	1734	1641	1136	616	2003	1621	1611	1662	1311	1944	1301	1834	1702	320	1372	1645	1053	960	1599	1765	1749	1229	2018	1354	1362	1545	934	415
Boise, ID	1954	2477	2883	1748	1465	2302	2535	1976	2234	2491	1506	1234	2662	2472	2462	993	2161	2795	432	2685	2495	930	430	2496	1628	342	1761	1096	646	500	2677	2204	633	2395	1346	1452
Boston, MA	1353	2843	1529	1100	1417	1433	313	1136	1563	215	1694	1463	1324	413	321	2706	592	107	3126	388	729	1921	2919	572	1181	2395	2092	3065	3135	3070	1380	570	3204	458	1616	1868
Buffalo, NY	927	2522	1425	642	958	1165	397	716	1254	400	1262	1005	1221	333	414	2274	217	560	2667	546	642	1463	2460	485	749	1936	1665	2632	2677	2612	1276	106	2745	384	1184	1410
Calgary, AB	2174	2944	3061	1603	1267	2602	2197	2152	2570	2480	1908	1453	2840	2103	2448	1525	2147	2781	852	2346	2539	915	1286	2482	1890	874	2182	1628	1497	679	2854	2190	559	2381	1749	816
Charleston, SC	760	2063	583	1003	1319	642	1145	543	783	773	1248	1290	379	1106	685	2184	642	1101	2948	1277	279	1824	2741	428	850	2218	1310	2483	2934	2973	434	1006	3106	539	1291	1771
Charleston, WV	606	2201	994	601	918	837	822	395	926	515	1022	952	790	759	454	2035	217	839	2610	972	313	1422	2403	322	512	1880	1344	2393	2620	2571	845	537	2705	346	953	1369
Charlotte, NC	614	1994	730	857	1173	572	1003	397	713	631	1102	1144	525	922	543	2107	438	959	2802	1135	158	1678	2595	289	704	2072	1241	2405	2759	2827	581	802	2960	397	1145	1625
Cheyenne, WY	1217	1809	2147	1012	881	1570	1799	1240	1502	1755	773	497	1926	1736	1725	1004	1425	2059	1166	1949	1758	305	959	1760	892	436	1046	1179	1176	1234	1941	1468	1368	1659	613	1132
Chicago, IL	539	2126	1382	89	409	923	841	474	935	797	807	474	1161	778	768	1819	467	1101	2137	991	861	913	1930	802	294	1406	1270	2105	2146	2062	1176	510	2196	701	728	860
Cincinnati, OH	493	2088	1141	398	714	731	815	281	820	636	863	736	920	751	576	1876	292	960	2398	972	522	1219	2191	530	350	1667	1231	2234	2407	2368	935	484	2501	517	785	1166
Cleveland, OH	742	2337	1250	443	760	981	588	531	1070	466	1073	806	1045	525	437	2085	136	751	2469	738	568	1264	2262	471	560	1738	1481	2437	2478	2413	1101	303	2547	370	995	1211
Columbus, OH	594	2189	1163	454	771	832	725	382	921	535	930	802	958	661	474	1942	190	858	2464	874	482	1275	2257	517	417	1734	1332	2300	2474	2424	1036	440	2558	416	852	1222
Dallas, TX	466	1128	1367	1010	999	639	1772	681	525	1589	209	669	1146	1708	1501	1077	1246	1917	2140	1921	1189	1077	1933	1309	635	1410	271	1375	1827	2208	1161	1441	2342	1362	367	1363
Denver, CO	1116	1709	2069	1055	924	1478	1843	1162	1409	1799	681	541	1847	1779	1744	904	1460	2102	1261	1992	1680	404	1054	1688	855	531	946	1092	1271	1329	1862	1512	1463	1686	521	1176
Des Moines, IA	720	1866	1632	378	246	1115	1165	725	1117	1121	546	136	1411	1101	1091	1558	791	1424	1798	1314	1157	629	1591	1126	436	1067	1009	1766	1807	1822	1426	834	1956	1025	390	697
Detroit, MI	752	2347	1401	380	697	991	564	541	1079	622	1062	743	1180	500	592	2074	292	838	2405	713	724	1201	2198	627	549	1675	1490	2373	2415	2350	1194	233	2483	526	984	1148
El Paso, TX	1112	1197	1959	1617	1530	1231	2363	1328	1118	2235	737	1236	1738	2300	2147	432	1893	2563	1767	2513	1834	1105	1315	1955	1242	864	556	730	1181	1944	1753	2032	2087	2008	898	1871
Halifax, NS	2058	3548	2234	1652	1969	1231	715	1841	2268	920	2400	2015	2030	823	1026	3412	1297	542	3678	584	1434	2473	3471	1277	1887	2947	2797	3646	3687	3622	2085	1045	3756	1164	2322	2089
Houston, TX	586	954	1201	1193	1240	473	1892	801	360	1660	449	910	980	1828	1572	1188	1366	1988	2381	2041	1198	1318	2072	1330	863	1650	200	1487	1938	2449	995	1561	2583	1433	608	1604
Indianapolis, IN	464	2043	1196	279	596	737	872	287	826	715	752	618	975	809	655	1764	370	1038	2280	1022	639	1101	2073	641	239	1549	1186	2122	2290	2249	990	541	2383	596	674	1047
Jackson, MS	211	1398	915	835	1151	187	1514	423	185	1223	612	935	694	1450	1135	1482	988	1550	2544	1663	783	1458	2337	914	505	1813	644	1780	2232	2612	709	1183	2746	996	771	1570
Jacksonville, FL	733	1837	345	1160	1477	410	1325	589	556	953	1291	1336	141	1286	866	2072	822	1281	2994	1457	460	1859	2787	609	896	2264	1084	2370	2822	3052	196	1187	3186	720	1337	1928
Kansas City, MO	536	1668	1466	573	441	930	1359	559	932	1202	348	188	1245	1296	1141	1360	857	1525	1805	1509	1077	710	1598	1085	252	1074	812	1695	1814	1872	1259	1028	2007	1083	192	823
Las Vegas, NV	1611	1760	2733	1808	1677	1922	2596	1826	1854	2552	1124	1294	2512	2532	2500	285	2215	2855	1188	2745	2360	1035	442	2444	1610	417	1272	337	575	1256	2526	2265	1390	2441	1276	1872
Little Rock, AR	140	1457	1190	747	814	457	1446	355	455	1262	355	570	969	1382	1175	1367	920	1590	2237	1595	889	1093	2030	983	416	1507	600	1703	2012	2305	984	1115	2439	1036	464	1205
Los Angeles, CA	1839	1853	2759	2082	1951	2031	2869	2054	1917	2820	1352	1567	2538	2806	2760	369	2476	3144	971	3019	2588	1309	519	2682	1856	691	1356	124	385	1148	2553	2538	1291	2702	1513	2148
Louisville, KY	386	1981	1084	394	711	625	920	175	714	739	774	704	863	856	678	1786	394	1062	2362	1069	564	1215	2155	572	264	1631	1125	2144	2372	2364	878	589	2497	596	705	1162
Memphis, TN		1595	1051	624	940	395	1306	215	396	1123	487	724	830	1243	1035	1500	780	1451	2382	1456	749	1247	2175	843	294	1652	739	1841	2144	2440	846	975	2574	896	597	1359
México, MX			2154	2200	2113	1426	2900	1810	1313	2619	1323	1783	1933	2838	2525	1484	2375	2941	2819	3051	2151	2365	2367	2283	1825	2135	853	1683	2233	2996	1948	2570	3139	2386	1481	2477
Miami, FL				1478	1794	727	1671	907	874	1299	1609	1654	232	1631	1211	2390	1167	1627	3312	1803	805	2176	3105	954	1214	2581	1401	2688	3140	3370	274	1532	3504	1065	1655	2246
Milwaukee, WI					337	1019	939	569	1020	894	880	514	1257	875	865	1892	564	1198	2063	1088	956	842	1970	899	367	1446	1343	2145	2186	1991	1272	607	2124	799	769	789
Minneapolis, MN						1335	1255	886	1337	1211	793	383	1573	1192	1181	1805	881	1515	1727	1405	1273	606	1839	1216	621	1315	1257	2014	2055	1654	1588	924	1788	1115	637	452
Mobile, AL							1575	450	146	1203	799	1119	506	1481	1115	1662	1019	1531	2731	1707	730	1641	2545	861	688	2000	673	1960	2411	2799	521	1214	2933	970	958	1787
Montréal, QC								1094	1632	383	1625	1300	1466	121	454	2637	607	282	2963	155	871	1758	2756	714	1112	2232	2043	2931	2972	2907	1522	330	3041	600	1547	1374
Nashville, TN									539	906	703	747	686	1031	818	1715	569	1234	2405	1244	532	1269	2198	626	307	1675	954	2056	2360	2463	701	764	2597	679	748	1337
New Orleans, LA										1332	731	1121	653	1570	1245	1548	1108	1660	2663	1783	871	1643	2431	1002	690	1932	560	1846	2298	2731	668	1302	2865	1106	890	1755
New York, NY											1469	1258	1094	439	91	2481	367	313	2920	515	499	1716	2713	342	956	2189	1861	2839	2929	2864	1150	507	2998	228	1391	1665
Oklahoma City, OK												463	1388	1563	1408	1012	1124	1792	1934	1776	1237	871	1727	1331	505	1204	466	1370	1657	2002	1403	1295	2136	1350	161	1158
Omaha, NE													1433	1238	1228	1440	928	1561	1662	1451	1265	525	1455	1263	440	932	927	1630	1672	1719	1448	971	1853	1162	307	638
Orlando, FL														1427	1006	2169	963	1422	3091	1598	601	1955	2884	750	993	2360	1180	2467	2918	3149	82	1327	3283	860	1434	2025
Ottawa, ON															451	2575	545	382	2921	257	831	1696	2694	675	1050	2170	1981	2869	2910	2845	1483	268	2978	562	1485	1280
Philadelphia, PA																2420	306	419	2890	586	411	1686	2683	254	895	2160	1774	2779	2900	2835	1062	522	2968	140	1330	1633
Phoenix, AZ																	2136	2804	1335	2788	2249	1308	883	2343	1517	651	987	358	750	1513	2184	2307	1655	2362	1173	2075
Pittsburgh, PA																		690	2590	758	497	1386	2383	341	611	1859	1519	2494	2599	2534	1019	321	2668	240	1046	1332
Portland, ME																			3223	264	827	2019	3016	670	1279	2493	2189	3162	3233	3168	1478	668	3301	556	1714	1966
Portland, OR																				3114	2923	1268	578	2925	2057	771	2322	1093	638	170	3106	2633	313	2824	1775	1463
Québec, QC																					1003	1908	2905	846	1261	2381	2193	3080	3122	3057	1654	479	3190	732	1696	1523
Raleigh, NC																						1777	2716	157	825	2193	1398	2563	2894	2926	656	820	3065	265	1266	1724
Rapid City, SD																							1151	1720	963	628	1335	1372	1368	1195	1970	1429	1328	1620	712	792
Reno, NV																								2718	1850	524	1870	642	217	755	2899	2426	898	2617	1568	1867
Richmond, VA																									834	2194	1530	2684	2934	2869	805	660	3003	108	1274	1667
St. Louis, MO																										1326	968	1875	2066	2125	1008	782	2259	837	441	1075
Salt Lake City, UT																											1419	754	740	839	2375	1902	973	2094	1044	1455
San Antonio, TX																												1285	1737	2275	1195	1714	2410	1635	624	1621
San Diego, CA																													508	1271	2481	2601	1414	2720	1531	2209
San Francisco, CA																														816	2933	2643	958	2834	1784	2193
Seattle, WA																															3164	2577	140	2769	1843	1390
Tampa, FL																																1383	3297	916	1448	2039
Toronto, ON																																	2711	563	1217	1375
Vancouver, BC																																		2902	1977	1375
Washington, DC																																			1272	1566
Wichita, KS																																				956

Kilomètres

	Memphis, TN	México, MX	Miami, FL	Milwaukee, WI	Minneapolis, MN	Mobile, AL	Montréal, QC	Nashville, TN	New Orleans, LA	New York, NY	Oklahoma City, OK	Omaha, NE	Orlando, FL	Ottawa, ON	Philadelphia, PA	Phoenix, AZ	Pittsburgh, PA	Portland, ME	Portland, OR	Québec, QC	Raleigh, NC	Rapid City, SD	Reno, NV	Richmond, VA	St. Louis, MO	Salt Lake City, UT	San Antonio, TX	San Diego, CA	San Francisco, CA	Seattle, WA	Tampa, FL	Toronto, ON	Vancouver, BC	Washington, DC	Wichita, KS
México, MX	2566																																		
Miami, FL	1691	3466																																	
Milwaukee, WI	1004	3540	2378																																
Minneapolis, MN	1512	3400	2887	542																															
Mobile, AL	636	2294	1170	1640	2148																														
Montréal, QC	2101	4666	2689	1511	2019	2534																													
Nashville, TN	346	2912	1459	916	1426	724	1760																												
New Orleans, LA	637	2113	1406	1641	2151	235	2626	867																											
New York, NY	1807	4214	2090	1438	1948	1936	616	1458	2143																										
Oklahoma City, OK	784	2129	2589	1416	1276	1286	2615	1131	1176	2364																									
Omaha, NE	1165	2869	2661	827	616	1800	2092	1202	1804	2024	745																								
Orlando, FL	1335	3110	373	2023	2531	814	2359	1104	1051	1760	2233	2306																							
Ottawa, ON	2000	4566	2624	1408	1918	2383	194	1659	2526	706	2515	1992	2296																						
Philadelphia, PA	1665	4063	1948	1392	1900	1794	730	1316	2003	146	2265	1976	1619	726																					
Phoenix, AZ	2414	2388	3846	3044	2904	2674	4243	2759	2491	3992	1628	2317	3490	4143	3894																				
Pittsburgh, PA	1255	3821	1878	907	1418	1640	977	916	1783	591	1809	1493	1549	877	492	3437																			
Portland, ME	2335	4732	2618	1928	2438	2463	454	1986	2671	504	2883	2512	2288	615	674	4512	1110																		
Portland, OR	3833	4536	5329	3319	2779	4394	4767	3870	4285	4698	3112	2674	4973	4668	4650	2148	4167	5186																	
Québec, QC	2343	4909	2901	1751	2261	2747	249	2002	2869	829	2858	2335	2571	414	943	4486	1220	425	5010																
Raleigh, NC	1205	3461	1295	1538	2048	1175	1401	856	1401	803	1990	2035	967	1337	661	3619	800	1331	4703	1614															
Rapid City, SD	2006	3805	3501	1355	975	2640	2829	2042	2644	2761	1401	845	3146	2729	2713	2105	2230	3249	2040	3070	2859														
Reno, NV	3500	3809	4996	3170	2959	4095	4434	3537	3911	4365	2779	2341	4640	4317	4325	1421	3834	4853	930	4674	4370	1852													
Richmond, VA	1356	3673	1535	1446	1957	1385	1149	1007	1612	550	2142	2032	1207	1086	409	3770	549	1078	4706	1361	253	2767	4373												
St. Louis, MO	473	2936	1953	591	999	1107	1789	494	1110	1538	813	708	1598	1689	1440	2441	983	2058	3310	2029	1327	1549	2977	1342											
Salt Lake City, UT	2658	3435	4153	2327	2116	3218	3591	2695	3109	3522	1937	1500	3797	3492	3475	1047	2991	4011	1241	3831	3529	1010	843	3530	2134										
San Antonio, TX	1189	1372	2254	2161	2023	1083	3287	1535	901	2994	750	1492	1899	3187	2854	1588	2444	3522	3736	3529	2249	2148	3009	2462	1558	2283									
San Diego, CA	2962	2708	4325	3451	3241	3154	4716	3308	2970	4568	2204	2623	3969	4616	4471	576	4013	5088	1759	4956	4124	2208	1033	4319	3017	1213	2068								
San Francisco, CA	3450	3593	5052	3517	3306	3879	4782	3797	3697	4713	2266	2690	4695	4682	4666	1207	4182	5202	1027	5023	4656	2201	349	4721	3324	1191	2795	817							
Seattle, WA	3926	4821	5422	3204	2661	4504	4677	3963	4394	4608	3221	2766	5067	4578	4562	2434	4077	5097	274	4919	4708	1923	1215	4616	3419	1350	3660	2045	1313						
Tampa, FL	1360	3134	441	2047	2555	838	2449	1128	1075	1850	2257	2330	132	2386	1709	3514	1640	2378	4998	2661	1056	3170	4664	1295	1622	3821	1923	3992	4719	5091					
Toronto, ON	1569	4135	2465	977	1487	1953	531	1229	2095	816	2084	1562	2135	431	840	3712	516	1075	4236	771	1319	2299	3903	1062	1258	3060	2758	4185	4253	4146	2225				
Vancouver, BC	4142	5051	5638	3418	2877	4719	4893	4179	4610	4824	3437	2981	5282	4792	4776	2663	4293	5311	504	5133	4924	2137	1445	4832	3635	1566	3878	2275	1541	225	5305	4362			
Washington, DC	1442	3839	1714	1286	1794	1561	965	1093	1780	367	2172	1870	1384	904	225	3800	386	895	4544	1178	426	2607	4211	174	1347	3369	2631	4376	4560	4455	1474	906	4669		
Wichita, KS	961	2383	2663	1237	1025	1541	2489	1204	1432	2238	259	494	2307	2389	2140	1887	1683	2758	2856	2729	2037	1146	2523	2050	710	1680	1004	2463	2870	2965	2330	1958	3181	2047	
Winnipeg, MB	2187	3985	3614	1270	727	2875	2211	2151	2824	2679	1863	1027	3258	2060	2627	3339	2143	3163	2354	2451	2774	1274	3004	2682	1730	2341	2608	3554	3529	2237	3281	2212	2212	2520	1538

Distances and Driving Times across North America

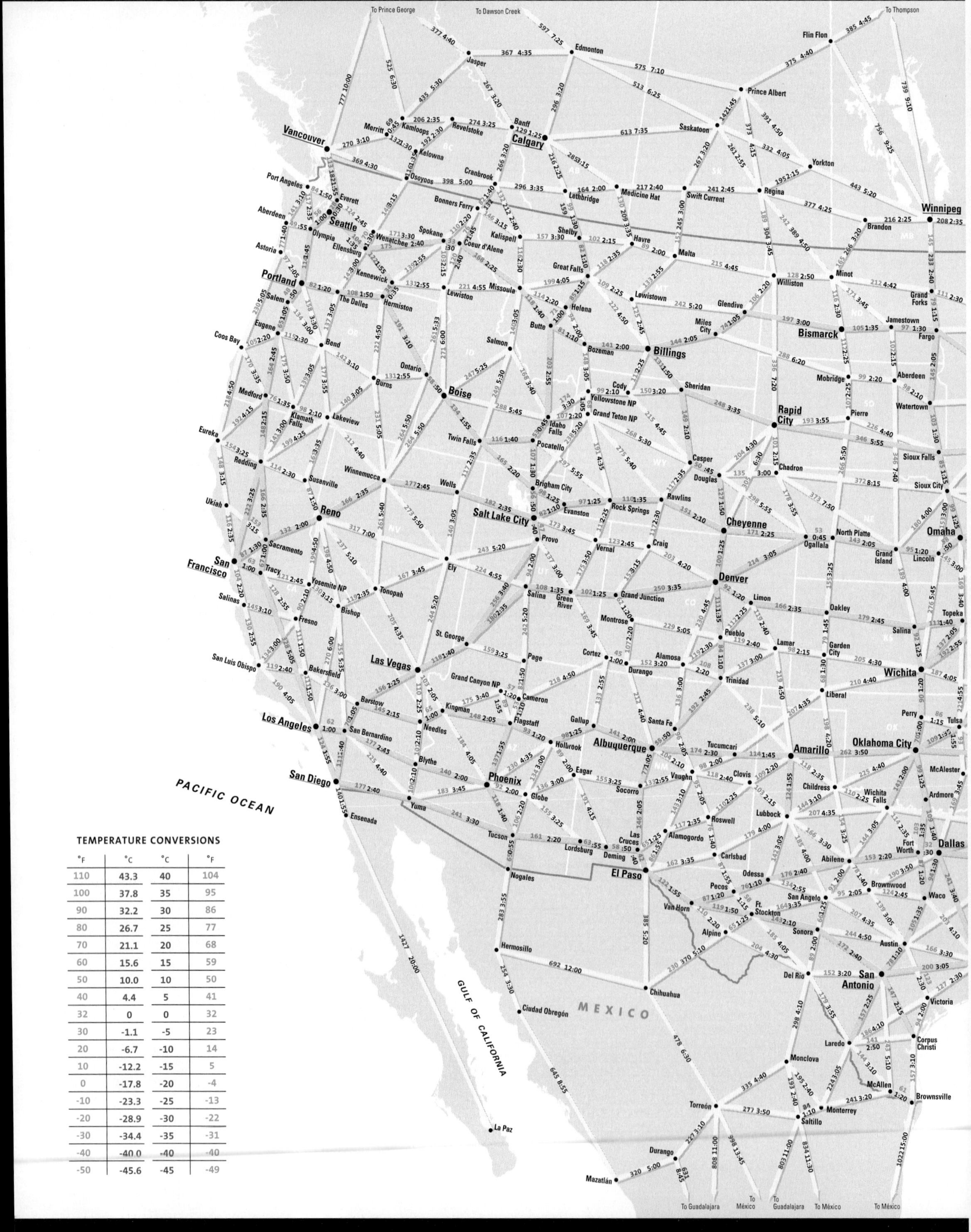

TEMPERATURE CONVERSIONS

°F	°C	°C	°F
110	43.3	40	104
100	37.8	35	95
90	32.2	30	86
80	26.7	25	77
70	21.1	20	68
60	15.6	15	59
50	10.0	10	50
40	4.4	5	41
32	0	0	32
30	-1.1	-5	23
20	-6.7	-10	14
10	-12.2	-15	5
0	-17.8	-20	-4
-10	-23.3	-25	-13
-20	-28.9	-30	-22
-30	-34.4	-35	-31
-40	-40.0	-40	-40
-50	-45.6	-45	-49

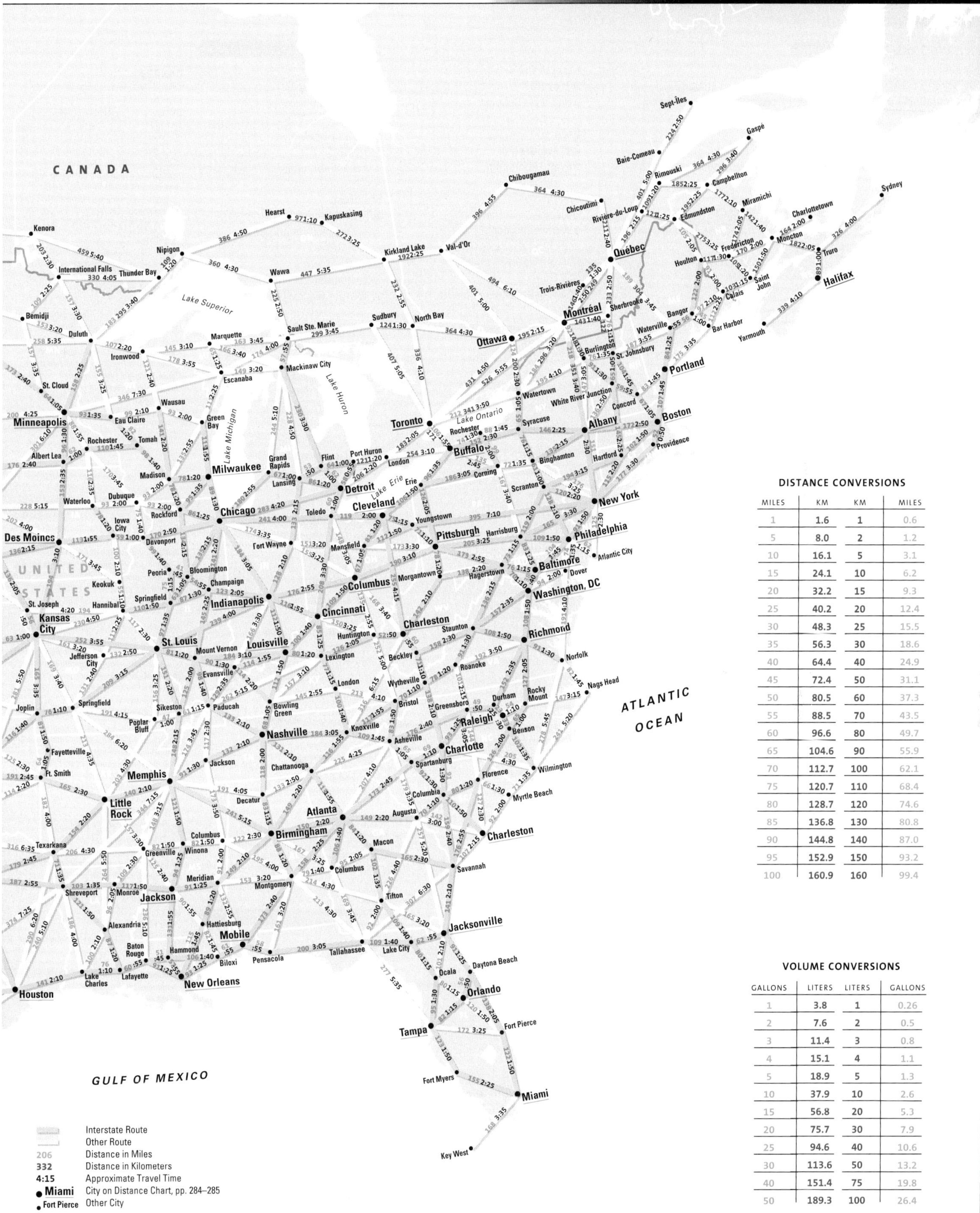

Distances and driving times may vary depending on actual route traveled and driving conditions.

DISTANCE CONVERSIONS

MILES	KM	KM	MILES
1	1.6	1	0.6
5	8.0	2	1.2
10	16.1	5	3.1
15	24.1	10	6.2
20	32.2	15	9.3
25	40.2	20	12.4
30	48.3	25	15.5
35	56.3	30	18.6
40	64.4	40	24.9
45	72.4	50	31.1
50	80.5	60	37.3
55	88.5	70	43.5
60	96.6	80	49.7
65	104.6	90	55.9
70	112.7	100	62.1
75	120.7	110	68.4
80	128.7	120	74.6
85	136.8	130	80.8
90	144.8	140	87.0
95	152.9	150	93.2
100	160.9	160	99.4

VOLUME CONVERSIONS

GALLONS	LITERS	LITERS	GALLONS
1	3.8	1	0.26
2	7.6	2	0.5
3	11.4	3	0.8
4	15.1	4	1.1
5	18.9	5	1.3
10	37.9	10	2.6
15	56.8	20	5.3
20	75.7	30	7.9
25	94.6	40	10.6
30	113.6	50	13.2
40	151.4	75	19.8
50	189.3	100	26.4

TOURISM INFORMATION

UNITED STATES

Alabama
@TweetHomeAla
www.alabama.travel

Alaska
@TravelAlaska
www.travelalaska.com

Arizona
@ArizonaTourism
www.visitarizona.com

Arkansas
@artourism
www.arkansas.com

California
@VisitCA
www.visitcalifornia.com

Colorado
@Colorado
www.colorado.com

Connecticut
@CTvisit
www.ctvisit.com

Delaware
@DelawareTourism
www.visitdelaware.com

District of Columbia
@washingtondc
washington.org

Florida
@VisitFlorida
www.visitflorida.com

Georgia
@ExploreGeorgia
www.exploregeorgia.org

Hawai'i
@gohawaii
www.gohawaii.com

Idaho
@visitidaho
visitidaho.org

Illinois
@enjoyillinois
www.enjoyillinois.com

Indiana
@visitindiana
visitindiana.com

Iowa
@Travel_Iowa
www.traveliowa.com

Kansas
@TravelKS
www.travelks.com

Kentucky
@KentuckyTourism
www.kentuckytourism.com

Louisiana
@LouisianaTravel
www.louisianatravel.com

Maine
@visitmaine
visitmaine.com

Maryland
@TravelMD
www.visitmaryland.org

Massachusetts
@VisitMA
visitma.com

Michigan
@PureMichigan
www.michigan.org

Minnesota
@ExploreMinn
www.exploreminnesota.com

Mississippi
@visitms
visitmississippi.org

Missouri
@VisitMO
www.visitmo.com

Montana
@visitmontana
www.visitmt.com

Nebraska
@NebraskaTourism
visitnebraska.com

Nevada
@TravelNevada
travelnevada.com

New Hampshire
@VisitNH
www.visitnh.gov

New Jersey
@VisitNewJersey
www.visitnj.org

New Mexico
@NewMexico
www.newmexico.org

New York
@I_LOVE_NY
www.iloveny.com

North Carolina
@VisitNC
www.visitnc.com

North Dakota
@NorthDakota
www.ndtourism.com

Ohio
@OhioFindItHere
ohio.org

Oklahoma
@TravelOK
www.travelok.com

Oregon
@TravelOregon
traveloregon.com

Pennsylvania
@visitPA
www.visitpa.com

Rhode Island
@RITourism
www.visitrhodeisland.com

South Carolina
@Discover_SC
www.discoversouthcarolina.com

South Dakota
@southdakota
www.travelsouthdakota.com

Tennessee
@TNVacation
www.tnvacation.com

Texas
@TravelTexas
www.traveltexas.com

Utah
@VisitUtah
www.visitutah.com

Vermont
@VermontTourism
www.vermontvacation.com

Virginia
@VisitVirginia
www.virginia.org

Washington
@TheStateOfWa
www.stateofwatourism.com

West Virginia
@WVtourism
wvtourism.com

Wisconsin
@TravelWI
www.travelwisconsin.com

Wyoming
@visitwyoming
www.travelwyoming.com

Puerto Rico
@discover_PR
www.discoverpuertorico.com

CANADA

Alberta
@TravelAlberta
www.travelalberta.com

British Columbia
@HelloBC
www.hellobc.com

Manitoba
@TravelManitoba
www.travelmanitoba.com

New Brunswick
@DestinationNB
www.tourismnewbrunswick.ca

Newfoundland & Labrador
www.newfoundlandlabrador.com

Northwest Territories
@spectacularNWT
spectacularnwt.com

Nova Scotia
@VisitNovaScotia
www.novascotia.com

Nunavut
@TravelNunavut
www.travelnunavut.ca

Ontario
@OntarioTravel
www.destinationontario.com

Prince Edward Island
@tourismpei
www.tourismpei.com

Québec
@TourismeQuebec
www.bonjourquebec.com

Saskatchewan
@Saskatchewan
www.tourismsaskatchewan.com

Yukon
@TravelYukon
www.travelyukon.com

MEXICO

@VisitMex
www.visitmexico.com

BORDER CROSSING INFORMATION

TRAVEL ADVISORY

All U.S. citizens are now required to present a passport, passport card, or WHTI (Western Hemisphere Travel Initiative)-compliant document when entering the United States by air, sea or land. U.S. citizens traveling directly to or from Puerto Rico and the U.S. Virgin Islands are not required to have a passport. For more detailed information and updated schedules, please see http://travel.state.gov.

CANADA

Canadian law requires that all persons entering Canada carry both proof of citizenship and proof of identity. A valid U.S. passport, passport card or other WHTI-compliant document satisfies these requirements for U.S. citizens. U.S. citizens entering Canada from a third country must have a valid U.S. passport. A visa is not required for U.S. citizens to visit Canada for up to 180 days.

U.S. driver's licenses are valid in Canada. Drivers should be prepared to present proof of their vehicle's registration, ownership, and insurance.

UNITED STATES (FROM CANADA)

Canadian citizens are required to present valid WHTI-compliant documents when entering the United States by land or water. These documents include a passport or an Enhanced Driver's Licence/Enhanced Identification Card. Canadian citizens traveling by air to, through or from the United States must present a valid passport (see Travel Advisory). Visas are not required for customary tourist travel.

Canadian driver's licenses are valid in the U.S. for one year. Drivers should be prepared to present proof of their vehicle's registration, ownership, and insurance.

MEXICO

All persons entering Mexico need either a valid passport or their original birth certificate along with a valid photo ID such as a drivers license (U.S. citizens should bear in mind the requirements set by the U.S. government for re-entry to the U.S.). Visas are not required for stays of up to 180 days. Naturalized citizens and alien permanent residents should carry the appropriate official documentation. Individuals under the age of 18 traveling alone, with one parent, or with other adults must carry notarized parental/legal guardian authorization. All U.S. citizens visiting for up to 180 days must also procure a tourist card, obtainable from Mexican consulates, tourism offices, border crossing points, and airlines serving Mexico. However, tourist cards are not needed for visits shorter than 72 hours to areas within the Border Zone (extending approximately 25 km into Mexico)

U.S. driver's licenses are valid in Mexico. Visitors who wish to drive beyond the Baja California Peninsula or the Border Zone must obtain a temporary import permit for their vehicles. To acquire a permit, one must submit evidence of citizenship and of the vehicle's title and registration, as well as a valid driver's license. A processing fee must be paid. Permits are available at any Mexican Army Bank (Banjercito) located at border crossings or selected Mexican consulates. Mexican law also requires the posting of a refundable bond, via credit card or cash, at the Banjercito to guarantee the departure of the vehicle. Do not deal with any individual operating outside of official channels.

All visitors driving in Mexico should be aware that U.S. auto insurance policies are not valid and that buying short-term tourist insurance is mandatory. Many U.S. insurance companies sell Mexican auto insurance. American Automobile Association (for members only) and Sanborn's Mexico Insurance (800.638.9423) are popular companies with offices at most U.S. border crossings.

IMPORTANT WEB SITES

U.S. State Department, www.travel.state.gov
U.S. Customs and Border Protection, www.cbp.gov
Canada Border Services Agency, www.cbsa-asfc.gc.ca
Citizenship and Immigration Canada, www.cic.gc.ca
Mexican Ministry of Foreign Affairs, www.gob.mx/sre
Mexican National Institute of Migration, www.gob.mx/inm

COMMON ABBREVIATIONS

Arch.	Archaeological	**N.H.S.**	National Historic Site
Bfld.	Battlefield	**N.H.P.**	National Historical Park
Cons.	Conservation	**N.M.P.**	National Military Park
Ent.	Entrance	**N.R.A.**	National Recreation Area
Hist.	Historic(al)	**Pk. Hqtrs.**	Park Headquarters
Mem.	Memorial	**Pres.**	Preserve
Mon.	Monument	**Prov.**	Provincial
Mtn.	Mountain	**Rec.**	Recreation(al)
Mts.	Mountains	**Res.**	Reservation–Reserve
Mus.	Museum	**S.H.S.**	State Historic Site
Natl.	National	**S.P.**	State Park
Nat.	Natural	**Sta.**	Station
		Vis. Ctr.	Visitor Center

ALABAMA	PAGE	GRID	LATITUDE LONGITUDE
National Park & Rec. Areas			
Freedom Riders Natl. Mon.	120	A4	33.635108 -85.908448
Horseshoe Bend N.M.P.-Vis. Ctr.	128	B1	32.977130 -85.739600
Russell Cave Natl. Mon.-Main Road	120	A2	34.980220 -85.809650
Russell Cave Natl. Mon.-Vis. Ctr.	120	A2	34.980400 -85.809800
Tuskegee Airmen N.H.S.	128	B2	32.424942 -85.691052
Tuskegee Airmen N.H.S.-Pk. Hqtrs.	128	B2	32.428600 -85.708500
Tuskegee Institute N.H.S.	128	B2	32.428751 -85.704120
Tuskegee Institute N.H.S.-Pk. Hqtrs.	128	B2	32.428600 -85.708500
State Park & Rec. Areas			
Bladon Springs S.P.	127	E4	31.730920 -88.195580
Blue Springs S.P.	128	B4	31.661990 -85.508150
Bucks Pocket S.P.	120	A3	34.469560 -86.049080
Cathedral Caverns S.P.	120	A2	34.572299 -86.221499
Cheaha S.P.	120	A4	33.474490 -85.807260
Chewacla S.P.	128	B2	32.554520 -85.481920
Desoto S.P.	120	A3	34.495460 -85.618860
Frank Jackson S.P.	128	A4	31.291400 -86.255900
Gulf S.P.	135	F2	30.270490 -87.582130
Joe Wheeler S.P.	119	E2	34.793020 -87.379950
Lake Guntersville S.P.	120	A3	34.367530 -86.222850
Lake Jackson RV Park at Florala	136	B1	30.998590 -86.329980
Lake Lurleen S.P.	127	E1	33.295880 -87.676870
Lakepoint S.P.	128	C3	31.990320 -85.114970
Meaher S.P.	135	E1	30.669720 -87.936030
Monte Sano S.P.	119	F2	34.745220 -86.511650
Oak Mtn. S.P.	127	F1	33.324710 -86.758740
Paul M. Grist S.P.	127	F2	32.595380 -86.996080
Rickwood Caverns S.P.	119	F4	33.876870 -86.867230
Roland Cooper S.P.	127	F3	32.055350 -87.245330
Wind Creek S.P.	128	A1	32.856820 -85.946540

ALASKA	PAGE	GRID	LATITUDE LONGITUDE
National Park & Rec. Areas			
Admiralty Island Natl. Mon.	155	E4	57.618060 -134.161110
Aleutian WWII Natl. Hist. Area	154	A4	53.888889 -166.527222
Aniakchak Natl. Mon. & Pres.	154	B4	56.833333 -158.250556
Bering Land Bridge Natl. Pres.	154	B2	65.595320 -164.301800
Cape Krusenstern Natl. Mon.	154	B1	67.471630 -163.312300
Denali Natl. Park & Pres.-Denali Vis. Ctr.	154	C2	63.737000 -148.895000
Denali Natl. Park & Pres.-Eielson Vis. Ctr.	154	C2	63.440900 -150.239000
Gates of the Arctic Natl. Park & Pres.- Anaktuvuk Pass Ranger Sta.	154	C1	68.139900 -151.735400
Gates of the Arctic Natl. Park & Pres.- Arctic Interagency Vis. Ctr.	154	C1	67.253700 -150.187000
Gates of the Arctic Natl. Park & Pres.- Bettles Ranger Sta.	154	C1	66.912500 -151.667100
Gates of the Arctic Natl. Park & Pres.- Coldfoot Ranger Sta.	154	C1	67.253700 -150.187000
Glacier Bay Natl. Park & Pres.- Glacier Bay Lodge & Vis. Ctr.	155	D3	58.454900 -135.882600
Katmai Natl. Park & Pres.	154	C3	58.667030 -156.524600
Kenai Fjords Natl. Park-Vis. Ctr.	154	C3	60.105300 -149.435000
Klondike Gold Rush N.H.P.	155	D3	60.113550 -149.441342
Kobuk Valley Natl. Park	154	B1	67.073230 -159.839500
Lake Clark Natl. Park & Pres.	154	C3	60.471450 -154.576390
Misty Fiords Natl. Mon.	155	E4	55.472600 -130.429700
Noatak Natl. Pres.	154	C1	67.320740 -162.646370
White Mts. N.R.A.	154	C2	65.524300 -147.156400
Wrangell-Saint Elias Natl. Park & Pres.- Kennecott Vis. Ctr.	155	D3	61.485600 -142.881100
Wrangell-Saint Elias Natl. Park & Pres.- Wrangell-Saint Elias Vis. Ctr.	155	D3	61.964300 -145.317900
Yukon-Charley Rivers Natl. Pres.	155	D2	65.341680 -143.120650
State Park & Rec. Areas			
Afognak Island S.P.	154	C4	58.227100 -152.067300
Chilkat S.P.	155	D3	59.211111 -135.398056
Chugach S.P.	154	C3	61.037440 -149.780830
Denali S.P.	154	C3	62.734600 -150.199600
Point Bridget S.P.	155	E3	58.671225 -134.958801
Shuyak Island S.P.	154	C4	58.533100 -152.486100
Wood-Tikchik S.P.	154	B3	59.909600 -158.672000

ARIZONA	PAGE	GRID	LATITUDE LONGITUDE
National Park & Rec. Areas			
Agua Fria Natl. Mon.	47	D4	34.276490 -112.114350
Canyon de Chelly Natl. Mon.-Vis. Ctr.	48	A2	36.153200 -109.539000
Casa Grande Ruins Natl. Mon.-Ent. Sta.	54	C2	32.994700 -111.537000
Chiricahua Natl. Mon.-Main Road	55	E3	32.009250 -109.382230
Chiricahua Natl. Mon.-Ent. Sta.	55	E3	32.007500 -109.388900
Coronado Natl. Mem.-Vis. Ctr.	55	E4	31.346300 -110.254000
Fort Bowie N.H.S.-Vis. Ctr.	55	E3	32.146600 -109.435000
Glen Canyon N.R.A.-Ent. Sta.	47	E1	36.943300 -111.493600
Grand Canyon Natl. Park-East Ent.	47	D2	36.038800 -111.828000
Grand Canyon Natl. Park-North Ent.	47	D2	36.334900 -112.116000
Grand Canyon Natl. Park-South Ent.	47	D2	36.000100 -112.121600
Grand Canyon-Parashant Natl. Mon.	46	C2	36.452170 -113.724367
Ironwood Forest Natl. Mon.	54	C3	32.478380 -111.530220
Lake Mead N.R.A.-Boulder City Ent.	46	C2	36.020800 -114.796000
Lake Mead N.R.A.-Henderson Ent.	46	C2	36.105400 -114.901200
Lake Mead N.R.A.-Las Vegas–Rt 147 Ent.	46	C2	36.161000 -114.905100
Lake Mead N.R.A.-South Ent.	46	C2	35.225600 -114.551000
Montezuma Castle Natl. Mon.-Vis. Ctr.	47	D4	34.611600 -111.839000
Navajo Natl. Mon.-Betatakin Ruin	47	E1	36.683500 -110.541470
Navajo Natl. Mon.- Inscription House Ruin-Closed To Public	47	E1	36.661250 -110.775940
Navajo Natl. Mon.-Keet Seel Ruin	47	E1	36.683500 -110.541470
Navajo Natl. Mon.-Vis. Ctr.	47	E1	36.678200 -110.541000
Organ Pipe Cactus Natl. Mon.-Vis. Ctr.	54	B3	31.954800 -112.801000
Petrified Forest Natl. Park-North Ent.	47	F3	35.069600 -109.778000
Petrified Forest Natl. Park-South Ent.	47	F3	34.799600 -109.885000
Pipe Spring Natl. Mon.-Vis. Ctr.	47	D1	36.862500 -112.737000
Saguaro Natl. Park-East	55	D3	32.178430 -110.737990
Saguaro Natl. Park-Vis. Ctr.	55	D3	32.180200 -110.736000
Saguaro Natl. Park-West	55	D3	32.251660 -111.191660
Sonoran Desert Natl. Mon.	54	C2	33.001730 -112.421220
Sunset Crater Volcano Natl. Mon.-Vis. Ctr.	47	E3	35.368800 -111.543000
Tonto Natl. Mon.-Vis. Ctr.	55	D1	33.645200 -111.113000
Tumacácori N.H.P.-Vis. Ctr.	55	D4	31.567800 -111.051000
Tuzigoot Natl. Mon.-Pk. Hqtrs.	47	D4	34.561000 -111.853000
Vermilion Cliffs Natl. Mon.	47	D1	36.806389 -111.741111
Walnut Canyon Natl. Mon.- Walnut Canyon Vis. Ctr.	47	E3	35.171700 -111.509000
Wupatki Natl. Mon.-Vis. Ctr.	47	E3	35.520300 -111.372000
State Park & Rec. Areas			
Alamo Lake S.P.	46	C4	34.234270 -113.553220
Buckskin Mtn. S.P.	46	B4	34.255000 -114.134070
Catalina S.P.	55	D3	32.416760 -110.937500
Cattail Cove S.P.	46	B4	34.355075 -114.165877
Dead Horse Ranch S.P.	47	D4	34.748490 -112.022930
Homolovi S.P.	47	E3	35.023940 -110.630120
Kartchner Caverns S.P.	55	D3	31.840770 -110.342710
Lake Havasu S.P.	46	B4	34.473970 -114.345850
Lost Dutchman S.P.	54	C1	33.464920 -111.481350
Lyman Lake S.P.	48	A4	34.362870 -109.375370
Oracle S.P.	55	D2	32.610239 -110.740619
Patagonia Lake S.P.	55	D4	31.488970 -110.853790
Picacho Peak S.P.	54	C2	32.646340 -111.398090
Red Rock S.P.	47	D4	34.818920 -111.836700
Roper Lake S.P.	55	E2	32.758710 -109.709520
San Rafael State Nat. Area	55	D4	31.454275 -110.632850
Slide Rock S.P.	47	D3	34.944340 111.752810
Tonto Nat. Bridge S.P.	47	E4	34.323400 -111.449460

ARKANSAS	PAGE	GRID	LATITUDE LONGITUDE
National Park & Rec. Areas			
Fort Smith N.H.S.-Main Road	116	B1	35.387480 -94.429660
Fort Smith N.H.S.-Vis. Ctr.	116	B1	35.385800 -94.429800
Hot Springs Natl. Park-Main Road	117	D2	34.511660 -93.053980
Hot Springs Natl. Park-Vis. Ctr.	117	D2	34.513800 -93.053400
Pea Ridge N.M.P.-Main Road	106	C3	36.442600 -94.025980
Pea Ridge N.M.P.-Vis. Ctr.	106	C3	36.443800 -94.025900
State Park & Rec. Areas			
Bull Shoals-White River S.P.	107	E3	36.365590 -92.557490
Conway Cemetery S.P.	124	C1	33.101909 -93.683161
Crater of Diamonds S.P.	116	C3	34.038610 -93.667630
Crowley's Ridge S.P.	108	A4	36.044840 -90.666770
Degray Lake Resort S.P.-North Ent.	117	D3	34.248870 -93.116880
Degray Lake Resort S.P.-South Ent.	117	D3	34.217390 -93.085820
Hampson Arch. Mus. S.P.	118	B1	35.568990 -90.041060
Historic Washington S.P.	116	C4	33.774005 -93.683235
Hobbs S.P.-Cons. Area	106	C3	36.244880 -93.972640
Jacksonport S.P.	107	F4	35.641440 -91.305350
Jenkins' Ferry Bfld. S.P.	117	E3	34.212070 -92.547490
Lake Charles S.P.	107	F4	36.066870 -91.132700
Lake Chicot S.P.	126	A1	33.373070 -91.194940
Lake Dardanelle S.P.	117	D1	35.251690 -93.213380
Lake Fort Smith S.P.	106	C4	35.654040 -94.150140
Lake Frierson S.P.	108	A4	35.988570 -90.717540
Lake Ouachita S.P.	117	D2	34.610990 -93.165520
Lake Poinsett S.P.	118	A1	35.535510 -90.688700
Louisiana Purchase S.P.	118	A2	35.150340 -90.734990
Lower White River Mus. S.P.	117	F2	34.977035 -91.495131
Mammoth Spring S.P.	107	F3	36.496010 -91.535960
Marks' Mills Battleground S.P.	117	E4	33.781085 -92.256427
Moro Bay S.P.	125	E1	33.298890 -92.348940
Mount Magazine S.P.	116	C1	35.149900 -93.563600
Mount Nebo S.P.	117	D1	35.224870 -93.229930
Ozark Folk Center S.P.	107	E4	35.883480 -92.116340
Parkin Arch. S.P.	118	A1	35.268607 -90.554809
Petit Jean S.P.	117	D1	35.128320 -92.898530
Poison Springs Battleground S.P.	117	D4	33.638340 -93.005250
Powhatan Hist. S.P.	107	F4	36.083234 -91.117858
Prairie Grove Bfld. S.P.	106	C4	35.983120 -94.305590
Toltec Mounds Arch. S.P.	117	E2	34.647370 -92.058510
Village Creek S.P.	118	A1	35.199650 -90.724540
White Oak Lake S.P.	117	D4	33.687490 -93.117240
Withrow Springs S.P.	106	C4	36.203800 -93.578200
Woolly Hollow S.P.	117	E1	35.286402 -92.285646

CALIFORNIA	PAGE	GRID	LATITUDE LONGITUDE
National Park & Rec. Areas			
Amboy Crater Natl. Nat. Landmark	53	E2	34.542196 -115.790920
Berryessa Snow Mountain Natl. Mon.	36	B2	38.902521 -123.411455
Carrizo Plain Natl. Mon.	52	B1	35.191000 -119.792000
Castle Mountains Natl. Mon.	53	F1	35.250563 -115.116773
Channel Islands Natl. Park	52	B2	34.248500 -119.267000
Death Valley Natl. Park- Furnace Creek Vis. Ctr.	45	F3	36.461800 -116.867000
Devils Postpile Natl. Mon.	37	E4	37.630330 -119.084300
Giant Sequoia Natl. Mon.-North Unit	45	D2	36.705501 -118.824821
Giant Sequoia Natl. Mon.-South Unit	45	E3	36.062389 -118.317784
Golden Gate N.R.A.-Marin Headlands	36	B4	37.830900 -122.525000
Golden Gate N.R.A.-Mott Vis. Ctr.	36	B4	37.799800 -122.460000
Joshua Tree Natl. Park-Indian Cove	53	E3	34.120000 -116.156000
Joshua Tree Natl. Park-North Ent.	53	E3	34.078300 -116.037000
Joshua Tree Natl. Park-West Ent.	53	E3	34.093600 -116.266000
Kings Canyon Natl. Park-East Ent.	45	D2	36.715870 -118.940420
Kings Canyon Natl. Park-West Ent.	45	D2	36.723720 -118.956490
Lassen Volcanic Natl. Park-Ent.	29	D4	40.537900 -121.571000
Lava Beds Natl. Mon.-Vis. Ctr.	29	D2	41.713900 -121.509000
Manzanar N.H.S.	45	E3	36.732260 -118.148500
Mojave Trails Natl. Mon.	53	E2	34.169528 -115.788162
Pinnacles Natl. Park-East Ent.	44	B3	36.483200 -121.162000
Pinnacles Natl. Park-West Ent.	44	B3	36.473300 -121.224400
Point Reyes Natl. Seashore- Bear Valley Vis. Ctr.	36	A3	38.043100 -122.799000
Point Reyes Natl. Seashore- Kenneth C. Patrick Vis. Ctr.	36	A3	38.027800 -122.961000
Point Reyes Natl. Seashore-Vis. Ctr.	36	A3	37.996500 -123.021000
Redwood Natl. Park-Kuchel Vis. Ctr.	28	A3	41.286800 -124.090900
Redwood Natl. Park-Prairie Creek Vis. Ctr.	28	A3	41.365300 -124.022000
Sand to Snow Natl. Mon.	53	D2	34.045197 -117.054096
San Gabriel Mountains Natl. Mon.	52	C2	34.286213 -117.884488
Santa Monica Mts. N.R.A.-Vis. Ctr.	52	B2	34.188600 -118.887000
Santa Rosa & San Jacinto Mts. Natl. Mon.	53	E3	33.755173 -116.729736
Sequoia Natl. Park-North Ent.	45	D3	36.647900 -118.826370
Sequoia Natl. Park-South Ent.	45	D3	36.487130 -118.836810
Shasta-Trinity N.R.A.	28	C4	40.633204 -122.601127
Trona Pinnacles Natl. Nature Landmark	45	F4	35.611944 -117.369444
Tule Lake Natl. Mon.	29	D2	41.969322 -121.567626
Whiskeytown-N.R.A.	28	C4	40.751500 -122.320580
Yosemite Natl. Park-Arch Rock Ent.	37	D3	37.687500 -119.730000
Yosemite Natl. Park-Big Oak Flat Ent.	37	D3	37.800800 -119.874000
Yosemite Natl. Park-South Ent.	37	D3	37.507000 -119.632000
Yosemite Natl. Park-Tioga Pass Ent.	37	D3	37.910700 -119.258000
State Park & Rec. Areas			
Ahjumawi Lava Springs S.P.	29	D3	41.107140 -121.468600
Anza-Borrego Desert S.P.	53	E4	33.256550 -116.399340
Big Basin Redwoods S.P.	44	A2	37.168380 -122.221530
Bothe-Napa Valley S.P.	36	B3	38.553410 -122.525640
Butano S.P.	44	A2	37.200660 -122.344140
Carlsbad State Beach	53	D3	33.147530 -117.345280
Castle Crags S.P.	28	C3	41.149280 -122.317480
China Camp S.P.	36	B3	38.003990 -122.466480
Clear Lake S.P.	36	B2	39.009780 -122.809400
Cuyamaca Rancho S.P.	53	D4	32.933790 -116.562560
Del Norte Coast Redwoods S.P.	28	A3	41.603280 -124.100130
Doheny State Beach	52	C3	33.463820 -117.688830
Donner Mem. S.P.	37	D2	39.323880 -120.228370
Ed Z'Berg Sugar Pine Point S.P.	37	D2	39.056290 -120.119200
Emerald Bay S.P.	37	D2	38.956710 -120.108850
Fremont Peak S.P.	44	B3	36.760340 -121.502670
Garrapata S.P.	44	B3	36.475310 -121.936280
Gaviota S.P.	52	A2	34.475250 -120.228590
Grizzly Creek Redwoods S.P.	28	B4	40.486630 -123.903520
Grover Hot Springs S.P.	37	D3	38.695230 -119.836760
Henry Cowell Redwoods S.P.	44	A2	37.044020 -122.070990
Henry W. Coe S.P.	44	B2	37.085600 -121.467340
Humboldt Lagoons S.P.	28	A3	41.284330 -124.089720
Humboldt Redwoods S.P.	28	A4	40.284740 -124.056950
Jedediah Smith Redwoods S.P.	28	A2	41.798190 -124.084030
Julia Pfeiffer Burns S.P.	44	B3	36.160700 -121.668210
Manchester S.P.	36	A2	38.980450 -123.703020
Marina State Beach	44	B3	36.683030 -121.809440
McGrath State Beach	52	B2	34.227270 -119.256460
Mendocino Headlands S.P.	36	A2	39.307570 -123.798910
Morro Bay S.P.	44	B4	35.354020 -120.843800
Morro Strand State Beach	44	B4	35.435390 -120.888060
Mount Diablo S.P.	36	B4	37.844210 -121.950200
Mount Tamalpais S.P.	36	B3	37.904290 -122.604040
Navarro River Redwoods S.P.	36	A2	39.175000 -123.676390
Pacheco S.P.	44	B2	37.055650 -121.016250

Palomar Mtn. S.P.	53	D3	33.325340 -116.893330
Patrick's Point S.P.	28	A3	41.135690 -124.150500
Pfeiffer Big Sur S.P.	44	B3	36.250930 -121.786550
Placerita Canyon S.P.	52	C2	34.377530 -118.470290
Plumas-Eureka S.P.	36	C1	39.758360 -120.695360
Point Dume State Beach	52	B2	34.003110 -118.807250
Point Sal State Beach	52	A1	34.897760 -120.642760
Prairie Creek Redwoods S.P.	28	A3	41.355490 -124.073670
Red Rock Canyon S.P.	52	C1	35.359734 -117.978351
Russian Gulch S.P.	36	A2	39.330990 -123.805050
Saddleback Butte S.P.	52	C2	34.689820 -117.824340
Samuel P. Taylor S.P.	36	B3	38.004660 -122.708400
San Gregorio State Beach	36	B4	37.321490 -122.401640
San Onofre State Beach	53	D3	33.383380 -117.580790
Sonoma Coast State Beach	36	A3	38.441060 -123.122970
Sunset State Beach	44	B2	36.897780 -121.835450
The Forest of Nisene Marks S.P.	44	B2	37.042024 -121.856231
Tolowa Dunes S.P.	28	A2	41.825800 -124.187500
Trinidad State Beach	28	A3	41.061090 -124.142290
Van Damme S.P.	36	A2	39.273990 -123.790490
Westport-Union Landing State Beach	36	A1	39.658350 -123.784930
Wilder Ranch S.P.	44	A2	36.962160 -122.080850
Zmudowski State Beach	44	B2	36.845580 -121.804300

COLORADO	PAGE	GRID	LATITUDE LONGITUDE
National Park & Rec. Areas			
Arapaho N.R.A.	41	D1	40.197870 -105.869440
Bent's Old Fort N.H.S.	41	F3	38.045980 -103.431440
Black Canyon-Gunnison Natl. Park-North Ent.	40	C3	38.586890 -107.695940
Black Canyon-Gunnison Natl. Park-South Ent.	40	C3	38.553980 -107.686390
Browns Canyon Natl. Mon.	41	D2	38.753093 -105.973528
Canyons of the Ancients Natl. Mon.	40	A4	37.587880 -108.916890
Colorado Natl. Mon.-Northwest Ent.	40	B2	39.117620 -108.730910
Colorado Natl. Mon.-Southeast Ent.	40	B2	39.032860 -108.631460
Colorado Natl. Mon.-South Ent.	40	B2	39.021100 -108.659540
Colorado Natl. Mon.-Southwest Ent.	40	B2	39.055070 -108.742500
Curecanti N.R.A.-East Ent.	40	C3	38.515010 -107.020560
Curecanti N.R.A.-North Ent.	40	C3	38.463380 -107.419580
Curecanti N.R.A.-South Ent.	40	C3	38.473160 -107.076450
Curecanti N.R.A.-West Ent.	40	C3	38.444680 -107.341980
Dinosaur Natl. Mon.-East Ent.	32	B4	40.443120 -108.517790
Dinosaur Natl. Mon.-South Ent.	32	B4	40.243920 -108.973750
Florissant Fossil Beds Natl. Mon.	41	E2	38.937440 -105.283400
Great Sand Dunes Natl. Park-Ent. Sta.	41	D4	37.725000 -105.519000
Hovenweep Natl. Mon.-Cutthroat	40	A4	37.413000 -108.720240
Hovenweep Natl. Mon.-Hackberry	40	A4	37.398890 -109.036680
Hovenweep Natl. Mon.-Holly	40	A4	37.398890 -109.036680
Hovenweep Natl. Mon.-Horseshoe	40	A4	37.464610 -108.974680
Mesa Verde Natl. Park-Ent. Sta.	40	B4	37.331100 -108.416000
Rocky Mtn. Natl. Park-Beaver Meadows Ent.	33	E4	40.367300 -105.578000
Rocky Mtn. Natl. Park-Fall River Ent.	33	E4	40.404000 -105.590000
Rocky Mtn. Natl. Park-Grand Lake Ent.	33	E4	40.267300 -105.833000
Rocky Mtn. Natl. Park-Wild Basin Ent.	33	E4	40.219000 -105.534000
Sand Creek Massacre N.H.S.	42	A3	38.541250 -102.505910
Yucca House Natl. Mon.	40	B4	37.251678 -108.684911
State Park & Rec. Areas			
Barr Lake S.P.	41	E1	39.938160 -104.733470
Boyd Lake S.P.	33	E4	40.428990 -105.045400
Castlewood Canyon S.P.	41	E2	39.325860 -104.737640
Crawford S.P.	40	C3	38.708000 -107.617550
Eleven Mile S.P.	41	D2	38.948570 -105.526450
Golden Gate Canyon S.P.	41	D1	39.875560 -105.453650
Harvey Gap S.P.	40	C1	39.606210 -107.659010
Highline Lake S.P.	40	B2	39.270910 -108.835930
Jackson Lake S.P.	33	F4	40.409110 -104.070130
James M. Robb-Colorado River S.P.-Corn Lake	40	B2	39.062709 -108.455110
James M. Robb-Colorado River S.P.-Island Acres	40	B2	39.165709 -108.300610
John Martin Reservoir S.P.	42	A3	38.065390 -102.927110
Lake Pueblo S.P.	41	E3	38.258130 -104.719160
Lathrop S.P.	41	E4	37.602830 -104.833740
Lory S.P.	33	E4	40.593143 -105.185413
Mancos S.P.	40	B4	37.399890 -108.266750
Mueller S.P.	41	E2	38.884940 -105.157710
Navajo S.P.	48	B1	37.067800 -107.407599
North Sterling S.P.	34	A4	40.787740 -103.264990
Paonia S.P.	40	C2	38.980440 -107.342900
Pearl Lake S.P.	33	D4	40.790160 -106.894610
Ridgway S.P.	40	B3	38.229710 -107.729410
Rifle Falls S.P.	40	B1	39.695290 -107.701090
Rifle Gap S.P.	40	B1	39.627460 -107.762520
Roxborough S.P.	41	E2	39.451300 -105.070200
San Luis S.W.A.	41	D4	37.663130 -105.734480
Spinney Mtn. S.P.	41	D2	39.014760 -105.625880
Stagecoach S.P.	33	D4	40.286100 -106.866920
Staunton S.P.	41	D1	39.509959 -105.394411
Steamboat Lake S.P.	32	C4	40.805240 -106.943600
Sweitzer Lake S.P.	40	B2	38.712050 -108.042640
Sylvan Lake S.P.	40	C1	39.516710 -106.753170
Trinidad Lake S.P.	49	E1	37.149700 -104.563650
Vega S.P.	40	B2	39.226890 -107.810250
Yampa River S.P.	32	C4	40.533190 -107.444483

CONNECTICUT	PAGE	GRID	LATITUDE LONGITUDE
National Park & Rec. Areas			
Weir Farm N.H.P.	148	C2	41.255890 -73.455980
State Park & Rec. Areas			
Bigelow Hollow S.P.	150	B2	41.991600 -72.134840
Bluff Point S.P.	149	F2	41.335800 -72.033520
Chatfield Hollow S.P.	150	A4	41.361400 -72.580190
Day Pond S.P.	150	A4	41.553432 -72.418419
Devil's Hopyard S.P.	150	A4	41.486529 -72.342462
Gay City S.P.	150	A3	41.716100 -72.434470
Gillette Castle S.P.	150	A4	41.430670 -72.427990
Hammonasset Beach S.P.	149	E2	41.273640 -72.562350
Haystack Mtn. S.P.	94	C2	42.002010 -73.209960
Hurd S.P.	150	A4	41.530650 -72.537650
John A. Minetto S.P.	94	C2	41.884020 -73.170280
Lake Waramaug S.P.	148	C1	41.706290 -73.382460
Mashamoquet Brook S.P.	150	B3	41.860320 -71.987230
Mount Riga S.P.	94	B2	42.028830 -73.428620
Putnam Mem. S.P.	148	C2	41.344200 -73.381500
Rocky Neck S.P.	149	F2	41.316920 -72.242690
Selden Neck S.P.	150	A4	41.287500 -72.331100
Silver Sands S.P.	149	D2	41.198410 -73.076180
Southford Falls S.P.	149	D1	41.455700 -73.166150
Squantz Pond S.P.	148	C1	41.508580 -73.471040
Stoddard Hill S.P.	150	B4	41.461900 -72.065500
Sunrise S.P.	149	E1	41.502642 -72.477201
Wadsworth Falls S.P.	150	A4	41.536080 -72.687380
West Rock Ridge S.P.	149	D2	41.347810 -72.968260

DELAWARE	PAGE	GRID	LATITUDE LONGITUDE
State Park & Rec. Areas			
Cape Henlopen S.P.	145	F3	38.782360 -75.103010
Delaware Seashore S.P.	145	F4	38.614420 -75.071540
Fenwick Island S.P.	145	F4	38.469740 -75.051550
Fort Delaware S.P.	145	E1	39.578700 -75.588320
Fort Dupont S.P.	145	E1	39.568930 -75.588590
Holts Landing S.P.	145	F4	38.584080 -75.128380
Killens Pond S.P.	145	E3	38.990320 -75.544920
Lums Pond S.P.	145	E1	39.570520 -75.733490
Trap Pond S.P.	145	E4	38.525860 -75.483170
White Clay Creek S.P.	146	B4	39.709810 -75.776560

FLORIDA	PAGE	GRID	LATITUDE LONGITUDE
National Park & Rec. Areas			
Biscayne Natl. Park-Dante Fascell Vis. Ctr.	143	F3	25.464400 -80.334900
Canaveral Natl. Seashore	141	E1	28.611410 -80.808390
Castillo de San Marcos Natl. Mon.	139	D3	29.897747 -81.311461
Dry Tortugas Natl. Park-Vis. Ctr.	142	B4	24.628500 -82.873400
Everglades Natl. Park-Ent.	143	E3	25.394400 -80.589300
Fort Matanzas Natl. Mon.	139	E3	29.715660 -81.234190
Gulf Islands Natl. Seashore	135	F2	30.362880 -87.139630
State Park & Rec. Areas			
Alafia River S.P.	140	C3	27.789920 -82.120830
Amelia Island S.P.	139	D2	30.543900 -81.449700
Anastasia S.P.	139	E3	29.874740 -81.285030
Anclote Key Pres. S.P.	140	B2	28.193070 -82.850660
Avalon S.P.	141	E3	27.542840 -80.318060
Bahia Honda S.P.	143	D4	24.659540 -81.277810
Bald Point S.P.	138	A3	29.902700 -84.408600
Big Lagoon S.P.	135	F2	30.322290 -87.401170
Big Shoals S.P.	138	C2	30.339115 -82.683182
Big Talbot Island S.P.	139	D2	30.460500 -81.421950
Blue Spring S.P.	141	D1	28.952270 -81.331300
Bulow Creek S.P.	139	E4	29.388000 -81.132399
Bulow Plantation Ruins Hist. S.P.	139	E4	29.433590 -81.144590
Caladesi Island S.P.	140	B2	28.059890 -82.813780
Cedar Key Mus. S.P.	138	B4	29.151172 -83.048299
Charlotte Harbor Pres. S.P.	140	C4	26.850691 -82.022026
Collier-Seminole S.P.	143	D2	25.991630 -81.591700
Crystal River Pres. S.P. & Arch. S.P.	140	B1	28.909530 -82.628680
Curry Hammock S.P.	143	E4	24.742640 -80.984793
Dade Bfld. Hist. S.P.	140	C1	28.654430 -82.124970
Deleon Springs S.P.	139	D4	29.131920 -81.360400
Delnor-Wiggins Pass S.P.	142	C1	26.272500 -81.826900
Dudley Farm Hist. S.P.	138	C3	29.649617 -82.630738
Eden Gardens S.P.	136	B2	30.361530 -86.125010
Egmont Key S.P.	140	B3	27.723490 -82.679390
Fakahatchee Strand Pres. S.P.	143	D2	25.961900 -81.364600
Faver-Dykes S.P.	139	E3	29.668050 -81.268030
Florida Caverns S.P.	137	D1	30.809160 -85.212270
Fort Clinch S.P.	139	D1	30.668010 -81.434300
Fort Cooper S.P.	140	C1	28.801300 -82.309200
Fort Pierce Inlet S.P.-East Ent.	141	E3	27.485160 -80.299430
Fort Pierce Inlet S.P.-West Ent.	141	E3	27.475930 -80.316980
Gasparilla Island S.P.	140	C4	26.718200 -82.261400
Grayton Beach S.P.	136	B2	30.328930 -86.155790
Henderson Beach S.P.	136	B2	30.387000 -86.447499
Highlands Hammock S.P.	141	D3	27.476554 -81.557148
Hontoon Island S.P.	141	D1	28.976680 -81.357690
Hugh Taylor Birch S.P.	143	F1	26.138220 -80.104450
Indian Key Hist. S.P.	143	E4	24.888056 -80.678056
John Gorrie Mus. S.P.	137	D3	29.725768 -84.983244
John Pennekamp Coral Reef S.P.	143	E3	25.127620 -80.409650
Jonathan Dickinson S.P.	141	F4	27.002920 -80.099980
Kissimmee Prairie Pres. S.P.	141	D3	27.538826 -81.022945
Lafayette Blue Springs S.P.	138	B2	30.115136 -83.229417
Lake Griffin S.P.	140	C1	28.857450 -81.902240
Lake Kissimmee S.P.	141	D2	27.971930 -81.380220
Lake Louisa S.P.	140	C1	28.460070 -81.751620
Lake Manatee S.P.	140	C3	27.475140 -82.336800
Little Talbot Island S.P.	139	D2	30.460500 -81.421950
Long Key S.P.	143	E4	24.821580 -80.819510
Lovers Key S.P.	142	C1	26.391000 -81.877800
Manatee Springs S.P.	138	B4	29.496230 -82.958630
Myakka River S.P.	140	C4	27.242670 -82.332240
Natural Bridge Bfld. Hist. S.P.	138	A2	30.284730 -84.152260
O'Leno S.P.	138	C3	29.809100 -82.550700
Olustee Bfld. Hist. S.P.	138	C2	30.214650 -82.428960
Oscar Scherer S.P.	140	B4	27.168840 -82.477360
Paynes Prairie Pres. S.P.	138	C3	29.520720 -82.300400
Perdido Key S.P.	135	F2	30.291480 -87.465360
Ponce De Leon Springs S.P.	136	C1	30.713260 -85.922490
Rainbow Springs S.P.	138	C4	29.103818 -82.438782
Ravine Gardens S.P.	139	D3	29.637490 -81.646830
River Rise Pres. S.P.	138	C3	29.859961 -82.605395
Saint Sebastian River Pres. S.P.	141	E3	27.815241 -80.513820
San Marcos de Apalache Hist. S.P.	138	A2	30.152890 -84.210030
Savannas Pres. S.P.	141	E3	27.245960 -80.250270
Sebastian Inlet S.P.	141	E2	27.870200 -80.453599
Silver River S.P.	139	D4	29.202550 -82.053610
Suwannee River S.P.	138	B2	30.389610 -83.157850
Three Rivers S.P.	137	D1	30.736800 -84.936500
Tomoka S.P.	139	E4	29.342210 -81.086200
Torreya S.P.	137	D2	30.553530 -84.946740
Troy Spring S.P.	138	B3	29.918000 -82.893300
Waccasassa Bay Pres. S.P.	138	B4	29.188100 -82.925500
Washington Oaks Gardens S.P.	139	E3	29.634670 -81.205500
Wekiwa Springs S.P.	141	D1	28.710490 -81.462810
Windley Key Fossil Reef Geological S.P.	143	E4	24.914100 -80.642800
Yulee Sugar Mill Ruins Hist. S.P.	140	B1	28.784730 -82.607370

GEORGIA	PAGE	GRID	LATITUDE LONGITUDE
National Park & Rec. Areas			
Chattahoochee River N.R.A.	120	C3	34.002910 -84.349180
Chickamauga & Chattanooga N.M.P.	120	B2	34.941430 -85.258790
Cumberland Island Natl. Seashore	139	D1	30.720300 -81.548760
Ed Jenkins N.R.A.	120	C2	34.682900 -84.198200
Fort Frederica Natl. Mon.	130	B4	31.219790 -81.386570
Fort Pulaski Natl. Mon.	130	C3	32.016520 -80.891680
Jimmy Carter N.H.P.	128	C3	32.034090 -84.401600
Kennesaw Mtn. Natl. Battlefied Park-Vis. Ctr.	120	C3	33.983000 -84.577900
Ocmulgee Mounds N.H.P.	129	D2	32.848560 -83.602140
State Park & Rec. Areas			
A.H. Stephens S.P.	121	E4	33.561998 -82.897677
Amicalola Falls S.P.	120	C2	34.558940 -84.248890
Black Rock Mtn. S.P.	121	D2	34.918150 -83.400310
Cloudland Canyon S.P.	120	B2	34.830430 -85.482040
Crooked River S.P.	139	D1	30.844840 -81.559350
Dames Ferry S.P	129	D1	33.043709 -83.758201
Don Carter S.P.	121	D3	34.387622 -83.746462
Elijah Clark S.P.	121	E4	33.854210 -82.391913
Florence Marina S.P.	128	C3	32.090988 -85.043263
Fort Mtn. S.P.	120	C2	34.763090 -84.689330
Fort Yargo S.P.	121	D4	33.984940 -83.733580
Franklin D. Roosevelt S.P.	128	C2	32.848670 -84.793230
General Coffee S.P.	129	E4	31.511490 -82.745360
George L. Smith S.P.	130	A2	32.570310 -82.103760
George T. Bagby S.P.	128	C4	31.739940 -85.074820
Georgia Veterans S.P.	129	D3	31.957951 -83.903787
Gordonia-Alatamaha S.P.	130	A3	32.081900 -82.123550
Hamburg S.P.	129	E1	33.208800 -82.774870
Hard Labor Creek S.P.	121	D4	33.677820 -83.593840
High Falls S.P.	129	D1	33.176590 -84.020280
Indian Springs S.P.	129	D1	33.247480 -83.921190
James H. "Sloppy" Floyd S.P.	120	B3	34.440260 -85.347580
Kolomoki Mounds S.P.	128	C4	31.468633 -84.948533
Laura S. Walker S.P.	138	C1	31.143130 -82.212920
Little Ocmulgee S.P.	129	E3	32.100590 -82.886360
Magnolia Springs S.P.	130	A1	32.875760 -81.962560
Mistletoe S.P.	121	E4	33.638770 -82.390540
Moccasin Creek S.P.	121	D2	34.845160 -83.589140
Panola Mtn. S.P.	120	C4	33.622042 -84.173078
Providence Canyon S.P.	128	C3	32.068270 -84.929150
Red Top Mtn. S.P.	120	C3	34.145950 -84.720190
Reed Bingham S.P.	137	F1	31.161310 -83.538880
Richard B. Russell S.P.	121	E3	34.166778 -82.745691
Seminole S.P.	137	D1	30.811420 -84.873570
Skidaway Island S.P.	130	C3	31.947720 -81.052550
Stephen C. Foster S.P.	138	C1	30.827020 -82.361310
Tallulah Gorge S.P.	121	D2	34.736350 -83.391950
Tugaloo S.P.	121	E3	34.501940 -83.082320

	Page	Grid	Latitude Longitude
Unicoi S.P.	121	D2	34.724620 -83.728170
Victoria Bryant S.P.	121	E3	34.299380 -83.158770
Vogel S.P.	121	D2	34.766190 -83.922000
Watson Mill Bridge S.P.	121	E3	34.041140 -83.126990

HAWAII

HAWAII	PAGE	GRID	LATITUDE LONGITUDE
National Park & Rec. Areas			
Haleakala Natl. Park-Main Road	153	D1	20.769130 -156.242850
Haleakala Natl. Park-Kipahulu Ent.	153	D1	20.662000 -156.045600
Haleakala Natl. Park-North Ent.	153	D1	20.769000 -156.243000
Hawaii Volcanoes Natl. Park-Ent.	153	F4	19.428700 -155.254500
Honouliuli N.H.S.	152	A3	21.354145 -158.090528
Kalaupapa N.H.P.	152	C3	21.174110 -157.002830
Pearl Harbor Natl. Mem.	152	A3	21.367603 -157.941052
State Park & Rec. Areas			
Ahupua'a 'O Kahana S.P.	152	A2	21.555210 -157.873260
Haena S.P.	152	B1	22.220930 -159.579600
Kaena Point S.P.	152	A2	21.551270 -158.244180
Kokee S.P.	152	B1	22.112580 -159.671050
Makena S.P.	153	D1	20.634030 -156.444180
Palaau S.P.	152	C3	21.174110 -157.002830
Polihale S.P.	152	B1	22.084480 -159.756700
Puaa Kaa State Wayside	153	D1	20.817560 -156.125800
Waianapanapa S.P.	153	E1	20.786230 -156.003010
Wailua River S.P.	152	B1	22.044180 -159.337250
Wailua Valley State Wayside	153	D1	20.840110 -156.139980
Wailuku River S.P.	153	F3	19.713340 -155.130490
Waimea Canyon S.P.	152	B1	22.031990 -159.671100

IDAHO

IDAHO	PAGE	GRID	LATITUDE LONGITUDE
National Park & Rec. Areas			
City of Rocks Natl. Res.	31	D2	42.078950 -113.677650
Craters of the Moon Natl. Mon. & Pres.	23	D4	43.462030 -113.559930
Hagerman Fossil Beds Natl. Mon.	30	C1	42.760980 -114.928220
Minidoka Natl. Hist. Site	31	D1	42.636944 -114.232222
Nez Perce N.H.P.-Clearwater Bfld.	22	B1	46.072600 -115.975400
Nez Perce N.H.P.-East Kamiah Site	22	B1	46.216600 -115.992400
Nez Perce N.H.P.-Vis. Ctr.	22	B1	46.446500 -116.817000
Nez Perce N.H.P.-White Bird Bfld.	22	B1	45.794400 -116.282000
Sawtooth N.R.A.	22	C3	44.211000 -114.946000
State Park & Rec. Areas			
Bear Lake S.P.	31	F2	42.026180 -111.257690
Bruneau Dunes S.P.	30	B1	42.910940 -115.713890
Castle Rocks S.P.	31	D2	42.135400 -113.670000
Dworshak S.P.	14	B4	46.577610 -116.327310
Eagle Island S.P.	22	B4	43.684510 -116.400300
Farragut S.P.	14	B2	47.952790 -116.602170
Harriman S.P.	23	F3	44.321000 -111.471200
Hells Gate S.P.	14	B4	46.380500 -117.044780
Henrys Lake S.P.	23	F3	44.620000 -111.373060
Heyburn S.P.	14	B3	47.353840 -116.748770
Lake Cascade S.P.	22	B3	44.520686 -116.046685
Lake Walcott S.P.	31	D1	42.674850 -113.482570
Land of the Yankee Fork S.P.	22	C3	44.475190 -114.208860
Lucky Peak S.P.	22	B4	43.530880 -116.055160
Massacre Rocks S.P.	31	D1	42.672200 -112.990800
McCroskey S.P.	14	B4	47.721080 -116.826310
Old Mission S.P.	14	B3	47.549420 -116.356940
Ponderosa S.P.	22	B2	44.926810 -116.083860
Priest Lake S.P.	14	B1	48.622082 -116.827798
Round Lake S.P.	14	B2	48.166110 -116.634230
Thousand Springs S.P.-Box Canyon	30	C1	42.709800 -114.791900
Thousand Springs S.P.-Malad Gorge	30	C1	42.864400 -114.854600
Thousand Springs S.P.-Niagara Springs	30	C1	42.662800 -114.672400
Three Island Crossing S.P.	30	C1	42.945280 -115.314850
Winchester Lake S.P.	22	B1	46.232280 -116.635570

ILLINOIS

ILLINOIS	PAGE	GRID	LATITUDE LONGITUDE
National Park & Rec. Areas			
Lincoln Home N.H.S.	98	B1	39.798120 -89.645150
Ronald Reagan Boyhood Home N.H.S.	88	B1	41.836700 -89.481100
State Park & Rec. Areas			
Apple River Canyon S.P.	74	A4	42.443990 -90.053280
Argyle Lake S.P.	87	F4	40.450680 -90.805080
Banner Marsh State Fish & Wildlife Area	88	B4	40.539600 -89.864500
Beall Woods S.P.	99	D4	38.351540 -87.836380
Beaver Dam S.P.	98	B2	39.214390 -89.959390
Big Bend State Fish & Wildlife Area	88	A2	41.634900 -90.044600
Buffalo Rock S.P.	88	C2	41.329720 -88.913090
Carlyle Lake State Fish & Wildlife Area	98	C3	38.768500 -89.193900
Castle Rock S.P.	88	B1	41.978230 -89.357040
Cave-In-Rock S.P.	109	D1	37.468010 -88.159950
Chain O'Lakes S.P.	74	C4	42.458390 -88.211950
Channahon S.P.	88	C2	41.415826 -88.223133
Coffeen Lake State Fish & Wildlife Area	98	B2	39.057000 -89.412400
Crawford County State Fish & Wildlife Area	99	D2	39.099800 -87.713100
Delabar S.P.	87	F3	40.957830 -90.939460
Des Plaines State Fish & Wildlife Area	88	C2	41.376600 -88.207400
Dixon Springs S.P.	108	C1	37.383600 -88.672830
Donnelley–Depue State Fish & Wildlife Area	88	B2	41.324000 -89.314100
Edward R. Madigan State Fish & Wildlife Area	88	B4	40.115280 -89.402240
Eldon Hazlet State Rec. Area	98	B3	38.667610 -89.327200
Ferne Clyffe S.P.	108	C1	37.532550 -88.966430
Fort Massac S.P.	108	C2	37.161720 -88.693850
Fox Ridge S.P.	99	D2	39.406020 -88.134810
Gebhard Woods S.P.	88	C2	41.357350 -88.440210
Giant City S.P.	108	C1	37.612250 -89.181790
Green River State Wildlife Area	88	B2	41.631600 -89.516500
Hamilton County State Fish & Wildlife Area	98	C4	38.065100 -88.404700
Hazel & Bill Rutherford Wildlife Prairie S.P.	88	B3	40.734180 -89.747270
Henderson County Cons. Area	87	F3	40.857505 -90.975005
Horseshoe Lake State Fish & Wildlife Area	108	C2	37.130465 -89.338505
Illini S.P.	88	C2	41.318770 -88.711070
Illinois Beach S.P.	75	D4	42.429920 -87.820150
Iroquois County State Wildlife Area	89	D3	40.994300 -87.598700
Jim Edgar Panther Creek State Fish & Wildlife Area	98	B1	40.011700 -90.177005
Johnson-Sauk Trail S.P.	88	A2	41.327510 -89.904850
Jubilee College S.P.	88	B3	40.844580 -89.827260
Kankakee River S.P.	89	D2	41.203400 -88.001880
Kaskaskia River State Fish & Wildlife Area	98	B4	38.229700 -89.879500
Kickapoo State Rec. Area	89	D4	40.138290 -87.737770
Lake Le Aqua-Na State Rec. Area	74	A4	42.422800 -89.823900
Lake Murphysboro S.P.	108	C1	37.771800 -89.382670
Lasalle Lake State Fish & Wildlife Area	88	C2	41.238400 -88.655500
Lincoln Trail S.P.	99	D2	39.346480 -87.696460
Lowden S.P.	88	B1	42.034860 -89.324950
Mackinaw River State Fish & Wildlife Area	88	B4	40.545801 -89.294301
Marshall State Fish & Wildlife Area	88	B3	41.007900 -89.410100
Matthiessen S.P.	88	C2	41.285010 -89.010050
Mautino State Fish & Wildlife Area	88	B2	41.323100 -89.718900
Middle Fork State Fish & Wildlife Area	89	D4	40.258300 -87.795900
Mississippi Palisades S.P.	88	A1	42.135820 -90.163300
Mississippi River State Fish & Wildlife Area	98	A2	38.991900 -90.542100
Morrison-Rockwood S.P.	88	A1	41.856350 -89.950120
Nauvoo S.P.	87	F4	40.543590 -91.386650
Newton Lake State Fish & Wildlife Area	99	D2	38.922400 -88.306700
Pere Marquette S.P.	98	A2	38.968110 -90.497430
Prophetstown S.P.	88	B2	41.672090 -89.920310
Pyramid State Rec. Area	98	B4	38.004110 -89.425680
Ray Norbut State Fish & Wildlife Area	98	A1	39.685000 -90.648500
Red Hills S.P.	99	D3	38.728850 -87.838660
Rend Lake State Fish & Wildlife Area	98	C4	38.043800 -88.988900
Rice Lake State Fish & Wildlife Area	88	A4	40.476785 -89.949205
Saline County State Fish & Wildlife Area	109	D1	37.691300 -88.379100
Sam Dale Lake State Fish & Wildlife Area	98	C3	38.536005 -88.565605
Sam Parr State Fish & Wildlife Area	99	D2	39.011022 -88.126955
Sanganois State Fish & Wildlife Area	88	A4	40.091605 -90.283205
Sangchris Lake State Rec. Area	98	B1	39.656830 -89.487940
Shabbona Lake S.P.	88	C1	41.732250 -88.864930
Shelbyville State Fish & Wildlife Area	98	C2	39.566300 -88.566200
Siloam Springs S.P.	97	F1	39.899340 -90.955050
Silver Springs State Fish & Wildlife Area.	88	C2	41.627500 -88.518550
Snakeden Hollow State Fish & Wildlife Area	88	A3	41.030200 -90.080100
South Shore S.P.	98	B3	38.610250 -89.314570
Starved Rock S.P.	88	C2	41.321750 -89.010850
Stephen A. Forbes State Rec. Area	98	C3	38.718140 -88.743250
Ten Mile Creek State Fish & Wildlife Area	98	C4	38.081200 -88.594200
Turkey Bluffs State Fish & Wildlife Area	98	B4	37.877200 -89.771100
Walnut Point S.P.	99	D1	39.705150 -88.030390
Wayne Fitzgerrell S.P.	98	C4	38.089250 -88.937010
Weinberg-King S.P.	87	F4	40.226830 -90.899700
Weldon Springs S.P.	88	C4	40.125080 -88.921400
White Pines Forest S.P.	88	B1	41.988730 -89.461590
Wolf Creek S.P.	98	C2	39.488310 -88.680370
Woodford State Fish & Wildlife Area	88	B3	40.878900 -89.444800

INDIANA

INDIANA	PAGE	GRID	LATITUDE LONGITUDE
National Park & Rec. Areas			
George Rodgers Clark N.H.P.	99	D3	38.677880 -87.535350
Indiana Dunes Natl. Park	89	D1	41.653160 -87.062630
Lincoln Boyhood Natl. Mem.	99	E4	38.116800 -86.997860
State Park & Rec. Areas			
Bass Lake State Beach	89	E2	41.220100 -86.580200
Brown County S.P.	99	F2	39.197170 -86.215830
Chain O' Lakes S.P.	90	A2	41.336000 -85.422950
Charlestown S.P.	100	A3	38.448300 -85.644700
Clifty Falls S.P.	100	A3	38.761220 -85.420720
Fort Harrison S.P.	99	F1	39.871921 -86.018859
Harmonie S.P.	99	D4	38.089210 -87.934080
Indiana Dunes S.P.	89	E2	41.651470 -87.062620
Lincoln S.P.	99	E4	38.118370 -86.980080
McCormick's Creek S.P.	99	E2	39.283340 -86.726680
O'Bannon Woods S.P.	99	F4	38.200600 -86.254678
Ouabache S.P.	90	A3	40.728090 -85.111060
Pokagon S.P.	90	A1	41.707960 -85.029320
Potato Creek S.P.	89	E2	41.534950 -86.360290
Prophetstown S.P.	89	E4	40.500211 -86.829548
Shades S.P.	99	E1	39.941630 -87.057670
Shakamak S.P.	99	E2	39.181800 -87.232200
Spring Mill S.P.	99	F3	38.723330 -86.418460
Summit Lake S.P.	100	A1	40.018680 -85.302720
Tippecanoe River S.P.	89	E3	41.117330 -86.602750
Turkey Run S.P.	99	E1	39.882010 -87.200550
Versailles S.P.	100	A2	39.063900 -85.205330
Whitewater Mem. S.P.	100	B1	39.611300 -84.942300

IOWA

IOWA	PAGE	GRID	LATITUDE LONGITUDE
National Park & Rec. Areas			
Effigy Mounds Natl. Mon.	73	F3	43.089310 -91.192350
Herbert Hoover N.H.S.	87	F1	41.671390 -91.346640
State Park & Rec. Areas			
Ambrose A. Call S.P.	72	B3	43.049650 -94.243430
Backbone S.P.	73	E4	42.600730 -91.532700
Beeds Lake S.P.	73	D4	42.767209 -93.241705
Bellevue S.P.	88	A1	42.247870 -90.416920
Big Creek S.P.	86	C1	41.767799 -93.777615
Black Hawk S.P.	72	B4	42.302700 -95.048680
Clear Lake S.P.	72	C3	43.110281 -93.394441
Cold Springs S.P.	86	B2	41.289540 -95.083810
Elk Rock S.P.	87	D2	41.400470 -93.063050
Fort Defiance S.P.	72	B2	43.393260 -94.851290
Geode S.P.	87	F3	40.832500 -91.385000
George Wyth Mem. S.P.	73	E4	42.536980 -92.394210
Green Valley S.P.	86	B3	41.114490 -94.377270
Gull Point S.P.	72	A3	43.486153 -96.536551
Honey Creek S.P.	87	D3	40.863940 -92.939050
Lacey Keosauqua S.P.	87	E3	40.839296 -92.222861
Lake Ahquabi S.P.	86	C2	41.286710 -93.572690
Lake Anita S.P.	86	B2	41.434150 -94.762470
Lake Keomah S.P.	87	D2	41.286570 -92.541660
Lake Macbride S.P.	87	F1	41.803090 -91.570950
Lake of Three Fires S.P.	86	B3	40.716391 -94.691671
Lake Wapello S.P.	87	D3	40.824890 -92.570530
Ledges S.P.	86	C1	41.998970 -93.896110
Maquoketa Caves S.P.	87	F1	42.119890 -90.770950
McIntosh Woods S.P.	72	C3	43.132580 -93.457580
Mini-Wakan S.P.	72	B2	43.498460 -95.102320
Nine Eagles S.P.	86	C3	40.591250 -93.765130
Palisades-Kepler S.P.	87	F1	41.916880 -91.497050
Pikes Peak S.P.	73	F3	43.028215 -91.329671
Pikes Point S.P.	72	A2	43.415320 -95.162860
Pilot Knob S.P.	72	C3	43.255470 -93.574840
Prairie Rose S.P.	86	A2	41.601590 -95.210660
Preparation Canyon S.P.	86	A1	41.901570 -95.911670
Rice Lake S.P.	72	C2	43.401350 -93.502490
Rock Creek S.P.	87	D1	41.760580 -92.835410
Springbrook S.P.	86	B1	41.776390 -94.459440
Stone S.P.	35	F1	42.555460 -96.476050
Trappers Bay S.P.	72	A2	43.453630 -95.335510
Twin Lakes S.P.	72	B4	42.480180 -94.629860
Viking Lake S.P.	86	B3	40.973170 -95.053710
Wapsipinicon S.P.	87	F1	42.204448 -91.396368
Waubonsie S.P.	86	A3	40.677770 -95.683680
Wildcat Den S.P.	87	F2	41.467700 -90.869330

KANSAS

KANSAS	PAGE	GRID	LATITUDE LONGITUDE
National Park & Rec. Areas			
Fort Larned N.H.S.	43	D3	38.188740 -99.220620
Fort Scott N.H.S.	106	B1	37.843350 -94.704840
Monument Rocks Natl. Landmark	42	B2	38.790569 -100.762366
Nicodemus N.H.S.	42	C2	39.390833 -99.617500
State Park & Rec. Areas			
Atchison State Fishing Lake	96	B1	39.639010 -95.171830
Black Kettle State Fishing Lake	43	E3	38.229240 -97.509390
Bourbon State Fishing Lake	106	B1	37.793450 -95.069690
Brown State Fishing Lake	96	A1	39.847030 -95.373860
Cedar Bluff S.P.	42	C2	38.798230 -99.715060
Chase State Fishing Lake	43	F3	38.368480 -96.588000
Cheney S.P.	43	E4	37.732700 -97.844350
Clark State Fishing Lake	42	C4	37.391670 -99.784720
Clinton S.P.	96	A3	38.941970 -95.353960
Cowley State Fishing Lake	51	F1	37.104040 -96.795000
Crawford S.P.	106	B1	37.634320 -94.809820
Cross Timbers S.P.	106	A1	37.774514 -95.943431
Douglas State Fishing Lake	96	B3	38.796030 -95.165150
Eisenhower S.P.	96	A3	38.535720 -95.744270
El Dorado S.P.	43	F4	37.861420 -96.749460
Elk City S.P.	106	A2	37.251130 -95.774090
Fallriver S.P.	43	F4	37.653550 -96.043600
Glen Elder S.P.	43	D1	39.512160 -98.339140
Hain State Fishing Lake	42	C4	37.854250 -99.858020
Hamilton State Fishing Lake	42	B3	38.039090 -101.816940
Hillsdale S.P.	96	B3	38.660700 -94.894000
Kanopolis S.P.	43	E3	38.600340 -97.979500
Kingman State Fishing Lake	43	E4	37.651390 -98.306940
Kiowa State Fishing Lake	43	D4	37.612570 -99.299000
Leavenworth State Fishing Lake	96	B2	39.126970 -95.141700
Logan State Fishing Lake	42	B2	38.940280 -101.236940
Lovewell S.P.	43	E1	39.903310 -98.043090
Lyon State Fishing Lake	43	F3	38.546520 -96.058050
McPherson State Fishing Lake	43	E3	38.478667 -97.468267
Meade S.P.	42	C4	37.172220 -100.450000
Miami State Fishing Lake	96	B3	38.422220 -94.785280
Milford S.P.	43	F2	39.104290 -96.895520
Mushroom Rock S.P.	43	E2	38.722222 -98.032222
Nebo State Fishing Lake	96	A2	39.447220 -95.595830

Neosho State Fishing Lake	106	B1	37.430570 -95.202550
Ottawa State Fishing Lake	43	E2	39.103040 -97.573060
Perry S.P.	96	A2	39.140210 -95.492480
Pomona S.P.	96	A3	38.652400 -95.600800
Pottawatomie State Fishing Lake No. 1	43	F1	39.470370 -96.407510
Pottawatomie State Fishing Lake No. 2	43	F2	39.228100 -96.533660
Prairie Dog S.P.	42	C1	39.811810 -99.963920
Prairie Spirit Trail S.P.	96	A4	38.280278 -95.242222
Rooks State Fishing Lake	43	D2	39.398290 -99.315020
Saline State Fishing Lake	43	E2	38.903159 -97.657510
Sand Hills S.P.	43	E3	38.116667 -97.833333
Scott S.P.	42	B2	38.684867 -100.922500
Shawnee State Fishing Lake	96	A2	39.206940 -95.804170
Tuttle Creek S.P.	43	F2	39.255560 -96.583330
Washington State Fishing Lake	43	E1	39.929780 -97.118830
Webster S.P.	43	D2	39.407840 -99.454550
Wilson State Fishing Lake	106	A1	38.910450 -98.497950
Wilson S.P.	43	D2	38.915000 -98.500000

KENTUCKY	PAGE	GRID	LATITUDE LONGITUDE
National Park & Rec. Areas			
Abraham Lincoln Birthplace N.H.P.	110	A1	37.532280 -85.733570
Camp Nelson Natl. Mon..	110	B1	37.761697 -84.779784
Land Between the Lakes N.R.A.	109	D2	36.776912 -88.059988
Mammoth Cave Natl. Park-Vis. Ctr.	109	F2	37.186800 -86.101300
Mill Springs Bfld. Natl. Mon.	110	B2	37.195931 -85.031625
State Park & Rec. Areas			
Barren River Lake State Resort Park	110	A2	36.853220 -86.053850
Blue Licks Bfld. State Resort Park	100	C3	38.434960 -83.991340
Buckhorn Lake State Resort Park	111	D1	37.312890 -83.423040
Carter Caves State Resort Park	101	D4	38.371470 -83.108510
Columbus-Belmont S.P.	108	C2	36.761990 -89.107000
Cumberland Falls State Resort Park	110	C2	36.834390 -84.350170
Fishtrap Lake S.P.	111	E1	37.432048 -82.417926
Fort Boonesborough S.P.	110	C1	37.899345 -84.270040
General Butler State Resort Park	100	A3	38.669950 -85.146050
Grayson Lake S.P.	101	D4	38.208630 -83.014910
Greenbo Lake State Resort Park	101	D3	38.479130 -82.867630
Green River Lake S.P.	110	A2	37.277440 -85.338730
Jenny Wiley State Resort Park	111	E1	37.697427 -82.726617
John James Audubon S.P.	99	D4	37.889250 -87.556510
Kentucky Dam Village State Resort Park	109	D2	36.996880 -88.285716
Kingdom Come S.P.	111	D2	36.981850 -82.982210
Lake Barkley State Resort Park	109	D2	36.809190 -87.928310
Lake Cumberland State Resort Park	110	B2	36.930320 -85.040960
Lake Malone S.P.	109	E2	37.076110 -87.038060
Levi Jackson Wilderness Road S.P.	110	C2	37.085250 -84.059250
Lincoln Homestead S.P.	110	B1	37.760080 -85.215930
My Old Kentucky Home S.P.	110	A1	37.808140 -85.458840
Natural Bridge State Resort Park	110	C1	37.777470 -83.676310
Nolin Lake S.P.	109	F1	37.297641 -86.212624
Old Fort Harrod S.P.	110	B1	37.762130 -84.845670
Pennyrile Forest State Resort Park	109	E2	37.057410 -87.649390
Pine Mtn. State Resort Park	110	C3	36.735270 -83.700790
Rough River Dam State Resort Park	109	F1	37.615410 -86.504410
Taylorsville Lake S.P.	100	A4	37.993990 -85.227813
Yatesville Lake S.P.	101	D4	38.093300 -82.617800

LOUISIANA	PAGE	GRID	LATITUDE LONGITUDE
National Park & Rec. Areas			
Cane River Creole N.H.P.	125	D4	31.739690 -93.083080
Jean Lafitte N.H.P. & Pres.-Chalmette Vis. Ctr.	134	A3	29.942100 -89.994400
Jean Lafitte N.H.P. & Pres.-French Quarter Vis. Ctr.	134	A3	29.954600 -90.065100
Jean Lafitte N.H.P.-Wetlands Acadian Cultural Center	134	A3	29.795969 -90.824480
Poverty Point Natl. Mon. & S.H.S.	125	F2	32.633370 -91.403880
State Park & Rec. Areas			
Bayou Segnette S.P.	134	B3	29.902720 -90.153800
Bogue Chitto S.P.	134	B1	30.774546 -90.168394
Chemin-A-Haut S.P.	125	F1	32.913460 -91.847550
Chicot S.P.	133	E1	30.829870 -92.276180
Cypremort Point S.P.	133	F3	29.731960 -91.840740
Fairview-Riverside S.P.	134	B2	30.408730 -90.140360
Fontainebleau S.P.	134	B2	30.345470 -90.022850
Grand Isle S.P.-Temp. Closed	134	B4	29.256640 -89.958480
Jimmie Davis S.P.	125	E3	32.265000 -92.540300
Lake Bistineau S.P.	125	D2	32.440250 -93.395910
Lake Bruin S.P.	126	A3	31.955370 -91.198080
Lake Claiborne S.P.	125	D2	32.713000 -92.923360
Lake D'Arbonne S.P.	125	E2	32.784850 -92.490310
Lake Fausse Pointe S.P.	133	F3	30.067820 -91.615790
North Toledo Bend S.P.	124	C4	31.558910 -93.732060
Palmetto Island S.P.	133	F3	29.862877 -92.144165
Poverty Point Reservoir S.P.	125	F2	32.540446 -91.421356
Saint Bernard S.P.	134	C3	29.864460 -89.899190
South Toledo Bend S.P.	125	D4	31.213889 -93.575000
Tickfaw S.P.	134	B2	30.382180 -90.631150

MAINE	PAGE	GRID	LATITUDE LONGITUDE
National Park & Rec. Areas			
Acadia Natl. Park-Park Loop Road	83	D2	44.338700 -68.183200
Acadia Natl. Park-Sieur de Monts Ent.	83	D2	44.360000 -68.205200
Acadia Natl. Park-Stanley Brook Ent.	83	D2	44.296300 -68.242000
Katahdin Woods & Waters Natl. Mon.	85	D3	45.883549 -68.737849
State Park & Rec. Areas			
Aroostook S.P.	85	E2	46.612720 -68.005840
Baxter S.P.	84	C3	45.950290 -69.049080
Camden Hills S.P.	82	C2	44.232050 -69.046530
Cobscook Bay S.P.	83	E1	44.855290 -67.171680
Damariscotta Lake S.P.	82	C2	44.200070 -69.452900
Ferry Beach S.P.	82	B4	43.482410 -70.391520
Lake Saint George S.P.	82	C2	44.398950 -69.345710
Lamoine S.P.	83	D2	44.456000 -68.298520
Mount Blue S.P.	82	B1	44.721780 -70.417080
Peaks-Kenny S.P.	84	C4	45.256680 -69.254600
Popham Beach S.P.	82	C3	43.738740 -69.795830
Rangeley Lake S.P.	82	B1	44.919550 -70.696950
Range Pond S.P.	82	B3	44.033540 -70.345080
Roque Bluffs S.P.	83	E2	44.614680 -67.479300
Saint Croix Island International Hist. Site	83	E1	45.128333 -67.133333
Sebago Lake S.P.	82	B3	43.916590 -70.570190
Shackford Head S.P.	83	F1	44.906191 -66.989979
Swan Lake S.P.	82	C2	44.568860 -68.981070
Vaughan Woods Mem. S.P.	82	A4	43.212680 -70.809320
Warren Island S.P.	82	C2	44.260445 -68.952255
Wolfes Neck Woods S.P.	82	B3	43.827190 -70.084460

MARYLAND	PAGE	GRID	LATITUDE LONGITUDE
National Park & Rec. Areas			
Assateague Island Natl. Seashore	114	C2	38.239580 -75.140410
Harriet Tubman Underground RR N.H.P.	103	F3	38.322307 -76.176243
Thomas Stone N.H.S.	144	B4	38.529700 -77.032370
State Park & Rec. Areas			
Assateague S.P.	114	C2	38.250170 -75.156270
Big Run S.P.	102	B1	39.545090 -79.137254
Catoctin Mtn. Park-Vis. Ctr.	144	A1	39.633100 -77.449700
Cunningham Falls S.P.	144	A1	39.625040 -77.458130
Deep Creek Lake S.P.	102	B1	39.512110 -79.300150
Elk Neck S.P.	145	D1	39.482890 -75.983630
Fort Frederick S.P.	103	D1	39.616050 -78.007060
Gambrill S.P.	144	A1	39.468330 -77.495730
Greenwell S.P.	103	E4	38.364930 -76.525260
Gunpowder Falls S.P.	144	C1	39.536710 -76.502800
Hart-Miller Island S.P.	144	C2	39.251219 -76.376903
Janes Island S.P.	103	F4	38.009810 -75.846380
Martinak S.P.	145	E3	38.862920 -75.837790
North Point S.P.	144	C2	39.221910 -76.431600
Patapsco Valley S.P.	144	B2	39.296580 -76.781500
Patuxent River S.P.	144	B2	39.280790 -77.129620
Pocomoke River S.P.	114	C2	38.135410 -75.494870
Point Lookout S.P.	103	F4	38.066190 -76.336550
Rocks S.P.	144	C1	39.630140 -76.418120
Rocky Gap S.P.	102	C1	39.698430 -78.651150
Rosaryville S.P.	144	C3	38.778450 -76.799260
Saint Clement's Island S.P.	103	E4	38.225200 -76.749690
Saint Mary's River S.P.	103	E4	38.262940 -76.525640
Sandy Point S.P.	144	C3	39.021750 -76.420280
Seneca Creek S.P.	144	A2	39.152200 -77.247710
Smallwood S.P.	144	B4	38.556509 -77.185257
South Mtn. S.P.	144	A1	39.540058 -77.607422
Susquehanna S.P.	145	D1	39.599840 -76.154590
Swallow Falls S.P.	102	B1	39.506550 -79.448750
Tuckahoe S.P.	145	D3	38.967120 -75.943410
Washington Mon. S.P.	144	A1	39.499810 -77.631890
Wye Oak S.P.	145	D3	38.939150 -76.080230

MASSACHUSETTS	PAGE	GRID	LATITUDE LONGITUDE
National Park & Rec. Areas			
Adams N.H.P.-Vis. Ctr.	151	D1	42.257000 -71.011200
Boston Harbor Island N.R.A.	151	D1	42.319705 -70.928555
Cape Cod Natl. Seashore	151	F2	41.835890 -69.973730
Lowell N.H.P.-Market Mills Vis. Ctr.	95	E1	42.644400 -71.312800
Minute Man N.H.P.-Minute Man Vis. Ctr.	151	D1	42.449000 -71.268700
Minute Man N.H.P.-North Bridge Vis. Ctr.	151	D1	42.470800 -71.352600
New Bedford Whaling N.H.P.	151	D4	41.635570 -70.924250
Salem Maritime N.H.S.	151	D1	42.521490 -70.886980
Saugus Iron Works N.H.S.	151	D1	42.468230 -71.009110
Waquoit Bay Natl. Estuarine Research Res.	151	E4	41.581300 -70.524800
State Park & Rec. Areas			
Ames Nowell S.P.	151	D2	42.113140 -70.975230
Ashland S.P.	150	C2	42.246380 -71.475560
Blackstone River & Canal Heritage S.P.	150	C2	42.099500 -71.618780
Borderland S.P.	151	D2	42.058560 -71.166330
Bradley Palmer S.P.	151	F1	42.652180 -70.911000
Callahan S.P.	150	C1	42.315140 -71.367710
Demarest Lloyd S.P.	151	D4	41.525790 -70.990530
Dighton Rock S.P.	151	D3	41.811230 -71.098440
Halibut Point S.P.	151	F1	42.686100 -70.631070
Hampton Ponds S.P.	150	A2	42.178350 -72.690030
Joseph Sylvia State Beach	151	E4	41.424140 -70.553870
Lake Wyola S.P.-Carroll Holmes Rec. Area	150	A1	42.500366 -72.430642
Moore S.P.	150	B1	42.312354 -71.954269
Mount Holyoke Range S.P.	150	A1	42.297270 -72.530890
Nickerson S.P.	151	F3	41.775550 -70.028290
Pilgrim Mem. (Plymouth Rock) S.P.	151	E2	41.958850 -70.662870
Red Bridge S.P.	150	A2	42.175500 -72.406600
Robinson S.P.	150	A2	42.081680 -72.658650
Rutland S.P.	150	B1	42.371470 -71.997680
Savoy Mtn. State Forest	94	C1	42.626540 -73.015580
Skinner S.P.	150	A1	42.304220 -72.598790
South Cape Beach S.P.	151	E4	41.554582 -70.508194
Wahconah Falls S.P.	94	C1	42.491430 -73.120790
Watson Pond S.P.	151	D2	41.956260 -71.116090
Wells S.P.	150	B2	42.142290 -72.042400
Whitehall S.P.	150	C2	42.227210 -71.584330
Wompatuck S.P.	151	D2	42.218770 -70.866600

MICHIGAN	PAGE	GRID	LATITUDE LONGITUDE
National Park & Rec. Areas			
Father Marquette Natl. Mem.	70	C2	45.853912 -84.728874
Grand Island N.R.A.	70	A1	46.500405 -86.657605
Isle Royale Natl. Park-Rock Harbor Vis. Ctr.	65	F2	48.145530 -88.482220
Isle Royale Natl. Park-Windigo Vis. Ctr.	65	F2	47.912700 -89.156990
Keweenaw N.H.P.	65	F3	47.242160 -88.448020
Pictured Rocks Natl. Lakeshore-East Ent.	70	A1	46.657450 -86.021160
Pictured Rocks Natl. Lakeshore-West Ent.	70	A1	46.474000 -86.553000
Sleeping Bear Dunes Natl. Lakeshore	70	A4	44.785210 -86.049690
State Park & Rec. Areas			
Albert E. Sleeper S.P.	76	C2	43.972880 -83.205530
Algonac S.P.	76	C4	42.654760 -82.514510
Aloha S.P.	70	C3	45.525850 -84.464390
Baraga S.P.	65	F4	46.762070 -88.499320
Bewabic S.P.	68	C2	46.094260 -88.422290
Brimley S.P.	70	C1	46.412970 -84.555040
Burt Lake S.P.	70	C3	45.401305 -84.619505
Cambridge Junction Hist. S.P.	90	B1	42.066990 -84.225550
Charles Mears S.P.	75	E2	43.781980 -86.439670
Cheboygan S.P.	70	C2	45.644860 -84.420440
Clear Lake S.P.	70	C3	45.127390 -84.173910
Coldwater Lake S.P.	90	A1	43.665975 -84.948703
Craig Lake S.P.	68	C1	46.538810 -88.127700
Duck Lake S.P.	75	E3	43.354880 -86.397560
F.J. Mclain S.P.	65	F3	47.239400 -88.587190
Fayette Hist. S.P.	70	A2	45.717200 -86.664000
Fisherman's Island S.P.	70	B3	45.307550 -85.301540
Fort Wilkins Hist. S.P.	65	F3	47.466780 -87.878240
Fred Meijer White Pine Trail S.P.	75	F2	44.222900 -85.426700
Grand Haven S.P.	75	E3	43.056100 -86.245990
Grand Mere S.P.	89	E1	41.995190 -86.538790
Harrisville S.P.	71	D4	44.649800 -83.293920
Hart-Montague Trail S.P.	75	E2	43.688800 -86.371900
Hartwick Pines S.P.	70	C4	44.744180 -84.648340
Holland S.P.	75	E4	42.780310 -86.201410
Indian Lake S.P.	70	A2	45.960420 -86.364400
Interlochen S.P.	70	B4	44.631370 -85.766630
J.W. Wells S.P.	69	D3	45.389070 -87.371360
Kal-Haven Trail S.P.	75	E4	42.324698 -85.667739
Keith J. Charters Traverse City S.P.	70	B4	44.748050 -85.553800
Lake Gogebic S.P.	68	B1	46.459950 -89.573110
Lakeport S.P.	76	C3	43.129120 -82.501820
Leelanau S.P.	70	B3	45.209320 -85.546220
Ludington S.P.	75	E1	44.031100 -86.505460
Mackinac Island S.P.	70	C2	45.849880 -84.617650
Mike Levine Lakelands Trail S.P.	76	B4	42.408249 -83.964043
Muskallonge Lake S.P.	70	B1	46.677100 -85.625210
Muskegon S.P.	75	E3	43.247900 -86.341480
Negwegon S.P.	71	D4	44.855020 -83.329240
Newaygo S.P.	75	F2	43.500600 -85.582260
North Higgins Lake S.P.	70	C4	44.515030 -84.753980
Onaway S.P.	70	C3	45.430530 -84.229020
Orchard Beach S.P.	75	E1	44.278860 -86.314480
Otsego Lake S.P.	70	C4	44.927770 -84.688980
P.H. Hoeft S.P.	70	C3	45.463700 -83.883560
P.J. Hoffmaster S.P.	75	E3	43.132870 -86.265460
Palms Book S.P.	70	A2	46.003280 -86.385130
Petoskey S.P.	70	B3	45.407950 -84.902160
Porcupine Mts. Wilderness S.P.	65	E4	46.816070 -89.621850
Port Crescent S.P.	76	C1	44.007570 -83.051290
Sanilac Petroglyphs Hist. S.P.	76	C2	43.649367 -83.018016
Saugatuck Dunes S.P.	75	E4	42.695990 -86.186840
Seven Lakes S.P.	76	B3	42.816750 -83.648120
Silver Lake S.P.	75	E2	43.663650 -86.492660
Sleepy Hollow S.P.	76	A3	42.925020 -84.408620
South Higgins Lake S.P.	76	A1	44.432818 -84.670299
Sterling S.P.	90	C1	41.921490 -83.342680
Straits S.P.	70	C2	45.858090 -84.720200
Tahquamenon Falls S.P.-East Ent.	70	B1	46.598030 -85.147890
Tahquamenon Falls S.P.-West Ent.	70	B1	46.564190 -85.292530
Tawas Point S.P.	76	B1	44.255820 -83.443050
Thompson's Harbor S.P.	71	D3	45.346705 -83.567431
Twin Lakes S.P.	65	E4	46.892210 -88.856560
Van Buren S.P.	75	E4	42.333830 -86.304830
Van Buren Trail S.P.	89	F1	42.211405 -86.171105
Van Riper S.P.	68	C1	46.525260 -87.991150
Walter J. Hayes S.P.	90	B1	42.072830 -84.137820
Warren Dunes S.P.	89	E1	41.900980 -86.595260
Warren Woods S.P.	89	E1	41.840680 -86.631290

Wetzel Rec. Area	76	C4	42.596720 -82.825140
Wilderness S.P.-East Ent.	70	B2	45.748160 -84.853500
Wilderness S.P.-West Ent.	70	B2	45.679360 -84.964170
William Mitchell S.P.	75	F1	44.236880 -85.453990
Wilson S.P.	76	A1	44.029620 -84.806070
Young S.P.	70	B3	45.235240 -85.041450

MINNESOTA

MINNESOTA	PAGE	GRID	LATITUDE LONGITUDE
National Park & Rec. Areas			
Grand Portage Natl. Mon.	65	E2	47.996274 -89.734256
Pipestone Natl. Mon.	27	F3	44.013150 -96.325360
Voyageurs Natl. Park-Ash River Vis. Ctr.	64	C2	48.435600 -92.850300
Voyageurs Natl. Park-Kabetogama Lake Vis. Ctr.	64	C2	48.446100 -93.030100
Voyageurs Natl. Park-Rainy Lake Vis. Ctr.	64	C2	48.584400 -93.161500
State Park & Rec. Areas			
Afton S.P.	67	D4	44.847930 -92.791020
Banning S.P.	67	D2	46.179730 -92.855170
Bear Head Lake S.P.	64	C3	47.792720 -92.083720
Beaver Creek Valley S.P.	73	E2	43.636790 -91.573190
Blue Mounds S.P.	27	F4	43.714340 -96.183100
Buffalo River S.P.	19	F4	46.866260 -96.469980
Camden S.P.	27	F3	44.362880 -95.917480
Caribou Falls State Wayside	65	D3	47.463890 -91.030660
Carley S.P.	73	E1	44.116790 -92.169320
Cascade River S.P.	65	D3	47.712950 -90.497930
Charles A. Lindbergh S.P.	66	C2	45.959410 -94.387640
Crow Wing S.P.	66	C1	46.272630 -94.316400
Father Hennepin S.P.	66	C1	46.144520 -93.484260
Flandrau S.P.	72	B1	44.294360 -94.482020
Flood Bay State Wayside	64	C4	47.038500 -91.642540
Forestville Mystery Cave S.P.	73	E2	43.637520 -92.220270
Fort Ridgely S.P.	72	B1	44.454810 -94.718310
Franz Jevne S.P.	64	B2	48.641140 -94.058260
Frontenac S.P.	67	E4	44.525200 -92.338730
George H. Crosby Manitou S.P.	65	D3	47.478990 -91.123070
Glacial Lakes S.P.	66	A3	45.540550 -95.529600
Glendalough S.P.	19	F4	46.313314 -95.679290
Gooseberry Falls S.P.	65	D3	47.145430 -91.462380
Grand Portage S.P.	65	E2	47.999150 -89.598690
Great River Bluffs S.P.	73	E1	43.939100 -91.430050
Hayes Lake S.P.	19	F1	48.641070 -95.570600
Hill Annex Mine S.P.	64	B3	47.327490 -93.277520
Inspiration Peak State Wayside	66	A1	46.136880 -95.578650
Interstate S.P.	67	D3	45.391631 -92.664111
Itasca S.P.	64	A3	47.194490 -95.166740
Jay Cooke S.P.	64	C4	46.658790 -92.349200
John A. Latsch S.P.	73	E1	44.164720 -91.823860
Joseph R. Brown State Wayside	66	B4	44.750328 -95.324425
Judge C.R. Magney S.P.	65	E3	47.818090 -90.051230
Kilen Woods S.P.	72	B2	43.732140 -95.072220
Kodonce River State Wayside	65	E3	47.793930 -90.154140
Lac Qui Parle S.P.	27	F2	45.024680 -95.896580
Lake Bemidji S.P.	64	A3	47.536890 -94.832320
Lake Bronson S.P.	19	F1	48.730940 -96.630720
Lake Carlos S.P.	66	B2	46.000540 -95.334430
Lake Louise S.P.	73	D2	43.532620 -92.509250
Lake Maria S.P.	66	C3	45.304810 -93.935570
Lake Shetek S.P.	72	A1	44.105740 -95.699730
Lake Vermilion-Soudan Underground Mine S.P.	64	C2	47.818130 -92.246090
Maplewood S.P.	19	F4	46.549910 -95.966720
McCarthy Beach S.P.	64	B3	47.674110 -93.027350
Mille Lacs Kathio S.P.	66	C2	46.160740 -93.758020
Minneopa S.P.	72	C1	44.162190 -94.110310
Minnesota Valley St. Rec. Area	66	C4	44.650309 -93.715927
Monson Lake S.P.	66	B3	45.321300 -95.270470
Moose Lake S.P.	64	C4	46.436360 -92.743090
Myre-Big Island S.P.	73	D2	43.623847 -93.289096
Nerstrand Big Woods S.P.	73	D1	44.327040 -93.111210
Old Mill S.P.	19	F2	48.369790 -96.569420
Ray Berglund State Wayside	65	D3	47.608200 -90.771930
Rice Lake S.P.	73	D1	44.095380 -93.063940
Saint Croix S.P.	67	D2	45.960615 -92.611630
Sakatah Lake S.P.	72	C1	44.218000 -93.509970
Sam Brown Mem. State Wayside	27	F1	45.596160 -96.841410
Savanna Portage S.P.	64	B4	46.819130 -93.176040
Scenic S.P.	64	B3	47.702450 -93.564710
Schoolcraft S.P.	64	B3	47.223040 -93.805320
Sibley S.P.	66	B3	45.318990 -95.011930
Split Rock Creek S.P.	27	F4	43.907240 -96.367970
Split Rock Lighthouse S.P.	65	D3	47.189800 -91.395010
Temperance River S.P.	65	D3	47.558780 -90.867930
Tettegouche S.P.	65	D3	47.337210 -91.200670
Upper Sioux Agency S.P.	66	B4	44.734540 -95.456460
Whitewater S.P.	73	E1	44.068880 -92.040100
Wild River S.P.	67	D3	45.524100 -92.754500
William O'Brien S.P.	67	D3	45.223900 -92.763500
Zippel Bay S.P.	64	A1	48.840630 -94.849950

MISSISSIPPI

MISSISSIPPI	PAGE	GRID	LATITUDE LONGITUDE
National Park & Rec. Areas			
Gulf Islands Natl. Seashore	135	D2	30.407200 -88.749220
Natchez N.H.P.-Vis. Reception Ctr.	125	F4	31.553900 -91.412400
State Park & Rec. Areas			
Bogue Homa State Fishing Lake	127	D4	31.703200 -89.026400
Calling Panther State Fishing Lake	126	B3	32.197100 -90.265100
Clarkco S.P.	127	D3	32.108500 -88.693970
Columbia State Fishing Lake	134	C1	31.183500 -89.738400
Florewood S.P.	118	B4	33.525120 -90.250362
George Payne Cossar S.P.	118	B3	34.122710 -89.882100
Golden Mem. S.P.	126	C2	32.568560 -89.407640
Great River Road S.P.	118	A4	33.851733 -91.027574
Hugh White S.P.	118	B4	33.796080 -89.743010
J.P. Coleman S.P.	119	D2	34.924254 -88.171706
Jeff Davis State Fishing Lake	126	B4	31.567700 -89.839800
John W. Kyle S.P.	118	B3	34.438060 -89.807500
Kemper County State Fishing Lake	127	D2	32.804167 -88.730556
Lake Lincoln S.P.	126	B4	31.684354 -90.337142
Legion S.P.	127	D1	33.148690 -89.042460
Leroy Percy S.P.	126	A1	33.160500 -90.938250
Mary Crawford State Fishing Lake	126	B4	31.574900 -90.154000
Monroe State Fishing Lake	119	D4	33.941500 -88.568700
Natchez S.P.	126	A4	31.589580 -91.220350
Neshoba County State Fishing Lake	126	C2	32.706200 -89.010500
Paul B. Johnson S.P.	134	C1	31.133800 -89.233910
Percy Quin S.P.	134	B1	31.189020 -90.510660
Perry State Fishing Lake	135	D1	31.132400 -88.899800
Prentiss Walker State Fishing Lake	126	C3	31.833200 -89.589500
Roosevelt S.P.	126	C2	32.321920 -89.664980
Simpson County State Fishing Lake	126	C3	31.913500 -89.794500
Tippah County State Fishing Lake	118	C2	34.794290 -88.950660
Tishomingo S.P.	119	D2	34.615670 -88.183390
Tom Bailey State Fishing Lake	127	D3	32.425030 -88.523069
Tombigbee S.P.	119	D3	34.231870 -88.628870
Trace S.P.	118	C3	34.260020 -88.886560
Wall Doxey S.P.	118	C2	34.660270 -89.459290
Walthall State Fishing Lake	134	B1	31.059184 -90.133939

MISSOURI

MISSOURI	PAGE	GRID	LATITUDE LONGITUDE
National Park & Rec. Areas			
George Washington Carver Natl. Mon.	106	C2	36.986160 -94.351890
Ozark Natl. Scenic Riverways	107	F2	37.281400 -91.408000
Ste. Genevieve Natl Hist. Park	98	A4	38.107373 -91.08916
State Park & Rec. Areas			
Bennett Spring S.P.	107	D1	37.725440 -92.856390
Big Lake S.P.	86	A4	40.092090 -95.347300
Big Oak Tree S.P.	108	C3	36.641990 -89.290180
Big Sugar Creek S.P.	106	C3	36.584106 -93.819122
Crowder S.P.	86	C4	40.082140 -93.669310
Cuivre River S.P.	97	F2	39.062380 -90.938640
Echo Bluff S.P.	107	F1	37.315893 -91.411322
Elephant Rocks S.P.	108	A1	37.652150 -90.690810
Finger Lakes S.P.	97	E2	39.075400 -92.314750
Graham Cave S.P.	97	F3	38.908850 -91.576090
Grand Gulf S.P.	107	F3	36.544100 -91.636370
Ha Ha Tonka S.P.	97	D4	37.975410 -92.762230
Harry S. Truman S.P.	97	D4	38.274650 -93.442390
Hawn S.P.	108	B1	37.833660 -90.241610
Johnson's Shut-Ins S.P.	108	A1	37.547920 -90.853020
Katy Trail S.P.	97	E3	38.975190 -92.750160
Knob Noster S.P.	96	C3	38.753020 -93.577440
Lake of the Ozarks S.P.	97	E4	38.133990 -92.564260
Lake Wappapello S.P.	108	C2	36.942210 -90.344400
Lewis & Clark S.P.	96	B1	39.538900 -95.052900
Long Branch S.P.	97	E1	39.767610 -92.526480
Mark Twain S.P.	97	E2	39.485270 -91.795340
Meramec S.P.	97	F4	38.215350 -91.123070
Montauk S.P.	107	F1	37.454710 -91.690970
Morris S.P.	108	B3	36.554166 -90.043220
Onondaga Cave S.P.	97	F4	38.064310 -91.230140
Pershing S.P.	97	D1	39.776270 -93.211130
Pomme de Terre S.P.	107	D1	37.874380 -93.318700
Roaring River S.P.	106	C3	36.590110 -93.834420
Robertsville S.P.	98	A3	38.429120 -90.818110
Saint Francois S.P.	98	A4	37.972900 -90.536210
Saint Joe S.P.	108	A1	37.824990 -90.537480
Sam A. Baker S.P.	108	A2	37.254530 -90.505080
Stockton S.P.	106	C1	37.622470 -93.753070
Table Rock S.P.	107	D3	36.583440 -93.309150
Taum Sauk Mtn. S.P.	108	A1	37.669500 -90.673400
Thousand Hills S.P.	87	D4	40.185160 -92.643070
Trail of Tears S.P.	108	B1	37.452880 -89.490760
Van Meter S.P.	97	D2	39.262590 -93.267210
Wakonda S.P.	97	F1	40.004250 -91.526060
Wallace S.P.	96	C1	39.660760 -94.213290
Washington S.P.	98	A4	38.085600 -90.685650
Watkins Mill S.P.	96	C2	39.383920 -94.265130
Weston Bend S.P.	96	B2	39.392960 -94.863430

MONTANA

MONTANA	PAGE	GRID	LATITUDE LONGITUDE
National Park & Rec. Areas			
Bighorn Canyon N.R.A.	24	C2	45.330090 -107.871650
Fort Benton Natl. Hist. Landmark	16	A2	47.823210 -110.661910
Glacier Natl. Park-Many Glacier Ent.	15	D1	48.827150 -113.551540
Glacier Natl. Park-St Mary Ent.	15	D1	48.747120 -113.439650
Glacier Natl. Park-Two Medicine Ent.	15	D1	48.494210 -113.262250
Glacier Natl. Park-West Ent.	15	D1	48.499890 -113.987190
Grant-Kohrs Ranch N.H.S.	15	E4	46.398900 -112.736680
Little Bighorn Bfld. Natl. Mon.	24	C1	45.570080 -107.434710
Natl. Bison Range	15	D3	47.371674 -114.262066
Rattlesnake N.R.A.	15	D4	47.040775 -113.933333
State Park & Rec. Areas			
Ackley Lake S.P.	16	B4	46.947220 -109.936110
Anaconda Smoke Stack S.P.	23	D1	46.111037 -112.969599
Bannack S.P.	23	D2	45.159170 -112.997780
Beaverhead Rock S.P.	23	E2	45.383330 -112.458330
Beavertail Hill S.P.	15	D4	46.721660 -113.576420
Big Arm S.P.	15	D3	47.815360 -114.307930
Black Sandy S.P.	15	E4	46.756940 -111.888890
Chief Plenty Coups S.P.	24	B2	45.429700 -108.532500
Clark's Lookout S.P.	23	E2	45.236110 -112.630560
Cooney S.P.	24	B2	45.435050 -109.225330
Council Grove S.P.	15	D4	46.912500 -114.150000
Finley Point S.P.	15	D3	47.763830 -114.078723
First Peoples Buffalo Jump S.P.	16	A3	47.494887 -111.525201
Fish Creek S.P.	14	C4	46.990214 -114.715914
Fort Owen S.P.	15	D4	46.519440 -114.095830
Frenchtown Pond S.P.	15	D3	47.039530 -114.259220
Granite Ghost Town S.P.	23	D1	46.319000 -113.257000
Greycliff Prairie Dog Town S.P.	24	B1	45.767600 -109.794180
Hell Creek S.P.	17	D3	47.620290 -106.884510
Lake Elmo S.P.	24	C1	45.845280 -108.481310
Lake Mary Ronan S.P.	15	D2	48.204020 -114.330340
Lewis & Clark Caverns S.P.	23	E1	45.821840 -111.848510
Logan S.P.	14	C2	48.204020 -114.330340
Lone Pine S.P.	15	D2	48.175580 -114.339560
Lost Creek S.P.	23	D1	46.203020 -112.993810
Madison Buffalo Jump S.P.	23	F1	45.665140 -111.062770
Makoshika S.P.	17	F4	47.090240 -104.709970
Medicine Rocks S.P.	25	F1	46.046460 -104.456740
Missouri Headwaters S.P.	23	F1	45.909129 -111.497411
Painted Rocks S.P.	22	C1	45.706650 -114.282530
Pictograph Cave S.P.	24	C1	45.737500 -108.430830
Pirogue Island S.P.	17	E4	46.440560 -105.816670
Placid Lake S.P.	15	D3	47.138040 -113.524960
Rosebud Bfld. S.P.	25	D2	45.208270 -106.944460
Salmon Lake S.P.	15	D4	47.042270 -113.390390
Sluice Boxes S.P.	16	A3	47.211400 -110.939660
Smith River S.P.	16	A4	46.721219 -111.173819
Spring Meadow Lake S.P.	15	E4	46.612220 -112.075000
Thompson Falls S.P.	14	C3	47.618060 -115.387500
Tongue River Reservoir S.P.	25	D2	45.093520 -106.804670
Tower Rock S.P.	15	E3	47.181000 -111.816000
Travelers' Rest S.P.	15	D4	46.751000 -114.089000
Wayfarers S.P.	15	D2	48.057400 -114.079550
West Shore S.P.	15	D2	47.948780 -114.189160
Whitefish Lake S.P.	15	D2	48.204020 -114.330340
Wild Horse Island S.P.	15	D3	47.844640 -114.279970
Yellow Bay S.P.	15	D2	47.874500 -114.027080

NEBRASKA

NEBRASKA	PAGE	GRID	LATITUDE LONGITUDE
National Park & Rec. Areas			
Agate Fossil Beds Natl. Mon.	33	F2	42.423860 -103.791120
Chimney Rock N.H.S.	33	F3	41.719650 -103.336070
Homestead N.H.P.	35	F4	40.296246 -96.858057
Pine Ridge N.R.A.	33	F1	42.625880 -103.205570
Scotts Bluff Natl. Mon.	33	F2	41.832380 -103.717550
State Park & Rec. Areas			
Chadron S.P.	34	A1	42.711540 -103.008500
Eugene T. Mahoney S.P.	35	F3	41.026387 -96.314180
Fort Robinson S.P.	33	F1	42.654050 -103.492100
Indian Cave S.P.	86	A4	40.263280 -95.586630
Platte River S.P.	35	F3	40.986840 -96.219290
Ponca S.P.	35	F1	42.600360 -96.714940
Smith Falls S.P.	34	C1	42.891670 -100.316670

NEVADA

NEVADA	PAGE	GRID	LATITUDE LONGITUDE
National Park & Rec. Areas			
Basin & Range Natl. Mon.	38	B3	37.931620 -115.350935
Devils Hole (Death Valley Natl. Park)	45	F3	36.423889 -116.305833
Gold Butte Natl. Mon.	46	B1	36.390553 -114.170000
Great Basin Natl. Park-Vis. Ctr.	38	C2	39.005600 -114.220000
Lake Mead N.R.A.-North Ent.	46	B2	36.161180 -114.905200
Lake Mead N.R.A.-South Ent.	46	B2	36.021230 -114.796340
Lake Mead N.R.A.-West Ent.	46	B2	36.105980 -114.900940
Spring Mts. N.R.A.	46	A1	36.245200 -115.233910
Tule Springs Fossil Beds Natl. Mon.	46	A1	36.324457 -115.293643
State Park & Rec. Areas			
Berlin-Ichthyosaur S.H.P.	37	F2	38.880300 -117.607930
Big Bend of the Colorado State Rec. Area	53	F1	35.116730 -114.640820
Cathedral Gorge S.P.	38	C4	37.820280 -114.407890
Dayton S.P.-North Ent.	37	D2	39.253540 -119.587190
Echo Canyon S.P.	38	C4	38.195000 -114.512900
Kershaw-Ryan S.P.	38	C4	37.586380 -114.533260
Lake Tahoe-Nevada S.P.	37	D2	39.213670 -119.928300
Spring Mtn. Ranch S.P.	46	A2	36.073830 -115.443710
Spring Valley S.P.	38	C3	38.003920 -114.207570

Valley of Fire S.P.	46	B1	36.429710 -114.513590
Wild Horse State Rec. Area	30	B3	41.670739 -115.799805

NEW HAMPSHIRE	PAGE	GRID	LATITUDE LONGITUDE
National Park & Rec. Areas			
Saint-Gaudens N.H.P.	81	E4	43.501570 -72.362510
State Park & Rec. Areas			
Bear Brook S.P.	81	F4	43.133800 -71.366040
Cardigan Mountain S.P.	81	E3	43.647990 -71.949570
Crawford Notch S.P.	81	F2	44.181760 -71.398780
Echo Lake S.P.	81	F3	44.067430 -71.166000
Forest Lake S.P.	81	F2	44.354490 -71.673180
Hampton Beach S.P.	95	E1	42.898333 -70.812778
Kingston S.P.	95	E1	42.929020 -71.054680
Lake Tarleton S.P.	81	E3	43.975833 -71.963333
Miller S.P.	95	D1	42.861630 -71.878750
Monadnock S.P.	95	D1	42.845440 -72.086590
Mount Sunapee S.P.	81	E4	43.332120 -72.079800
Pawtuckaway S.P.	81	F4	43.082150 -71.152130
Pillsbury S.P.	81	E4	43.236860 -72.122830
Pisgah S.P.	94	C1	42.810310 -72.408340
Umbagog Lake S.P.	81	F1	44.712990 -71.072700
Wellington S.P.	81	F3	43.641280 -71.782980
Wentworth S.P.	81	F3	43.603056 -71.136389
White Lake S.P.	81	F3	43.830880 -71.218220
Winslow S.P.	81	E4	43.391730 -71.869540

NEW JERSEY	PAGE	GRID	LATITUDE LONGITUDE
National Park & Rec. Areas			
Delaware Water Gap N.R.A.	94	A4	40.970390 -75.128100
Gateway N.R.A.	147	F1	40.396420 -73.981160
Morristown N.H.P.	148	A4	40.744670 -74.565290
Thomas Edison N.H.P.	148	A4	40.787188 -74.256497
State Park & Rec. Areas			
Allaire S.P.	147	E2	40.153470 -74.111390
Allamuchy Mtn. S.P.	104	C1	40.921244 -74.782222
Barnegat Lighthouse S.P.	147	E4	39.762750 -74.107950
Cape May Point S.P.	104	C4	38.932950 -74.961010
Corson's Inlet S.P.	105	D4	39.216340 -74.647070
Delaware & Raritan Canal S.P.	147	D1	40.473230 -74.571100
Double Trouble S.P.	147	E3	39.900550 -74.225120
Farny S.P.	148	A3	40.997170 -74.459060
Fortescue State Marina	145	F2	39.243178 -75.176636
Fort Mott S.P.	146	B4	39.612100 -75.543430
Hacklebarney S.P.	105	D1	40.751170 -74.736590
High Point S.P.	148	A2	41.304800 -74.669650
Hopatcong S.P.	148	A3	40.911780 -74.667000
Island Beach S.P.	147	E3	39.905240 -74.081510
Liberty S.P.	148	B4	40.697330 -74.063870
Long Pond Ironworks S.P.	148	A2	41.140986 -74.309228
Monmouth Bfld. S.P.	147	E2	40.269340 -74.302800
Parvin S.P.	146	C4	39.524490 -75.160460
Pigeon Swamp S.P.	147	E1	40.394420 -74.487150
Princeton Bfld. S.P.	147	D2	40.332490 -74.675650
Rancocas S.P.	147	D3	39.990420 -74.837480
Ringwood S.P.	148	A2	41.127600 -74.260130
Swartswood S.P.	94	A4	41.081680 -74.813620
Voorhees S.P.	104	C1	40.695060 -74.887030
Washington Crossing S.P.	147	D2	40.296920 -74.866420
Washington Rock S.P.	148	A4	40.613580 -74.472860
Wawayanda S.P.	148	A2	41.199240 -74.392440

NEW MEXICO	PAGE	GRID	LATITUDE LONGITUDE
National Park & Rec. Areas			
Aztec Ruins Natl. Mon.	48	B1	36.833920 -108.000570
Bandelier Natl. Mon.	48	C2	35.780130 -106.264830
Capulin Mtn. Natl. Mon.	49	E1	36.781990 -103.986110
Carlsbad Caverns Natl. Park-Vis. Ctr.	57	E3	32.175400 -104.444000
Chaco Culture N.H.P.	48	B2	36.016190 -107.924060
Datil Well N.R.A.	48	B4	34.154130 -107.852610
El Malpais Natl. Cons. Area	48	B4	35.059720 -107.876400
El Morro Natl. Mon.	48	B3	35.043480 -108.346250
Fort Union Natl. Mon.	49	D2	35.904230 -105.010740
Gila Cliff Dwellings Natl. Mon.	56	A2	33.229540 -108.264630
Kasha-Katuwe Tent Rocks Natl. Mon.	48	C2	35.663200 -106.410800
Manhattan Project N.H.P.	48	C2	35.882455 -106.304212
Pecos N.H.P.	49	D3	35.578750 -105.762400
Petroglyph Natl. Mon.	48	C3	35.139490 -106.709670
Rio Grande Del Norte Natl. Mon.	49	D1	36.640260 -105.877033
Salinas Pueblo Missions Natl. Mon.	48	C4	34.520370 -106.241250
Salinas Pueblo Missions Natl. Mon.-Gran Quivira	49	D4	34.260000 -106.091000
White Sands Natl. Park	56	C2	32.820130 -106.272980
State Park & Rec. Areas			
Bluewater Lake S.P.	48	B3	35.302730 -108.106930
Bottomless Lakes S.P.	57	E2	33.316630 -104.332880
Brantley Lake S.P.	57	E3	32.571390 -104.366210
Caballo Lake S.P.	56	B2	32.911370 -107.313580
Cerrillos Hills S.P.	49	D3	35.446413 -106.098498
Cimarron Canyon S.P.	49	D1	36.537600 -105.221130
City of Rocks S.P.	56	A2	32.594860 -107.973850
Clayton Lake S.P.	49	F1	36.573070 -103.300690
Conchas Lake S.P.	49	E3	35.394760 -104.181790
Coronado S.P.	48	C3	35.329130 -106.557870
Coyote Creek S.P.	49	D2	36.188020 -105.233260
Eagle Nest S.P.	49	D1	36.542100 -105.261300
Elephant Butte Res. S.P.-South Ent.	56	B1	33.176180 -107.207460
El Vado Lake S.P.	48	C1	36.593710 -106.735790
Fenton Lake S.P.	48	C2	35.887230 -106.723170
Heron Lake S.P.	48	C1	36.693840 -106.654230
Hyde Mem. S.P.	49	D2	35.737890 -105.836540
Leasburg Dam S.P.	56	B3	32.492680 -106.922380
Living Desert Zoo & Gardens S.P.	57	E3	32.449839 -104.286341
Manzano Mtn. S.P.	48	C4	34.603880 -106.360960
Morphy Lake S.P.	49	D2	35.968660 -105.366600
Navajo Lake S.P.	48	B1	36.831950 -107.586950
Oasis S.P.	49	F4	34.259740 -103.334280
Oliver Lee Mem. S.P.	56	C2	32.744640 -105.934520
Pancho Villa S.P.	56	B4	31.828050 -107.641200
Percha Dam S.P.	56	B2	32.873610 -107.308100
Rockhound S.P.	56	B3	32.185550 -107.613090
Santa Rosa Lake S.P.	49	E3	34.987930 -104.658750
Smokey Bear Hist. S.P.	57	D1	33.545620 -105.573170
Storrie Lake S.P.	49	D2	35.655720 -105.231840
Sugarite Canyon S.P.	49	E1	36.944191 -104.381651
Sumner Lake S.P.	49	E4	34.607520 -104.389050
Ute Lake S.P.	49	F3	35.340630 -103.442500
Villanueva S.P.	49	D3	35.259530 -105.368970

NEW YORK	PAGE	GRID	LATITUDE LONGITUDE
National Park & Rec. Areas			
Eleanor Roosevelt N.H.S.	94	B3	41.763170 -73.902960
Fire Island Natl. Seashore	149	D4	40.735320 -72.866620
Fort Stanwix Natl. Mon.	79	E3	43.211930 -75.454740
Gateway N.R.A.	148	B4	40.581100 -73.887790
Home of F.D.R. N.H.S.	94	B3	41.767038 -73.938193
Sagamore Hill N.H.S.	148	C3	40.882480 -73.505550
Saratoga N.H.P.	81	D4	43.002690 -73.612110
Statue of Liberty Natl. Mon.	148	B4	40.689547 -74.044029
Thomas Cole N.H.S.	94	B2	42.225900 -73.861600
Van Buren N.H.S.	94	B2	42.370610 -73.701010
Vanderbilt Mansion N.H.S.	94	B3	41.796482 -73.942359
Women's Rights N.H.P.	79	D3	42.910580 -76.800260
State Park & Rec. Areas			
Adirondack Park	80	C2	43.455590 -73.695930
Allegany S.P.	92	B1	42.106480 -78.765940
Battle Island S.P.	79	D3	43.362780 -76.442150
Bear Mtn. S.P.	148	B2	41.278350 -73.970290
Beaver Island S.P.	78	A3	42.968170 -78.969560
Bowman Lake S.P.	79	E4	42.516970 -75.670400
Buttermilk Falls S.P.	79	D4	42.347410 -76.489130
Caleb Smith S.P. Pres.	149	D3	40.854190 -73.221190
Canandaigua Lake State Marine Park	78	C3	42.875964 -77.275600
Captree S.P.	149	D4	40.636640 -73.263210
Catskill Park	94	A2	42.050290 -74.288840
Cedar Point S.P.	79	D1	44.200670 -76.191000
Chenango Valley S.P.	93	E1	42.215040 -75.818020
Chittenango Falls S.P.	79	E3	42.981520 -75.845030
Clarence Fahnestock S.P.	148	B1	41.423620 -73.799560
Cold Spring Harbor S.P.	148	C3	40.867450 -73.461900
Connetquot River S.P. Pres.	149	D4	40.748070 -73.153510
Cumberland Bay S.P.	81	D1	44.725090 -73.421450
Darien Lakes S.P.	78	B3	42.908460 -78.433300
Delta Lake S.P.	79	E3	43.290030 -75.414910
Evangola S.P.	78	A4	42.604460 -79.105610
Fair Haven Beach S.P.	79	D3	43.320570 -76.696210
Fort Niagara S.P.	78	A3	43.261790 -79.061460
Four Mile Creek S.P.	78	A3	43.272530 -78.996270
Franny Reese S.P.	148	B1	41.704118 -73.956553
Gilbert Lake S.P.	79	F4	42.572720 -75.128170
Golden Hill S.P.	78	B2	43.365250 -78.489310
Goosepond Mtn. S.P.	148	A2	41.354460 -74.254470
Gov. Alfred E. Smith/Sunken Meadow S.P.	149	D3	40.911970 -73.262940
Green Lakes S.P.	79	E3	43.060000 -75.969030
Hamlin Beach S.P.	78	C2	43.361130 -77.944460
Harriman S.P.	148	B2	41.293010 -74.026560
Heckscher S.P.	149	D4	40.712860 -73.168480
Highland Lakes S.P.	148	A1	41.489806 -74.325085
Hither Hills S.P.	149	F3	41.007700 -72.014500
Hudson Highlands S.P.	148	B2	41.428060 -73.966740
Hudson River Islands S.P.	94	B2	42.318574 -73.778343
James Baird S.P.	148	B1	41.689100 -73.799390
Jones Beach S.P.	148	C4	40.595000 -73.521070
Keewaydin S.P.	79	E1	44.322390 -75.925740
Keuka Lake S.P.	78	C4	42.594280 -77.130360
Lake Erie S.P.	78	A4	42.419070 -79.434430
Lakeside Beach S.P.	78	B2	43.367090 -78.236040
Lake Superior S.P.	94	A3	41.658590 -74.869280
Letchworth S.P.	78	B4	42.693530 -77.961210
Lodi Point S.P.	79	D4	42.619210 -76.863980
Long Point S.P.	79	D1	44.026130 -76.219650
Mark Twain S.P.	93	D1	42.205200 -76.823799
Mary Island S.P.	79	E1	44.350460 -75.930400
Max V. Shaul S.P.	79	F4	42.546790 -74.410370
Minnewaska S.P. Pres.	148	A1	41.745910 -74.268370
Montauk Point S.P.	149	F3	41.065020 -71.886700
Moreau Lake S.P.	80	C4	43.226370 -73.707710
Oquaga Creek S.P.	93	F1	42.172320 -75.442840
Orient Beach S.P.	149	F2	41.154580 -72.245600
Pixley Falls S.P.	79	E2	43.401100 -75.345960
Point Au Roche S.P.	81	D1	44.779990 -73.411090
Robert Moses S.P.	148	C4	40.624930 -73.261900
Saratoga Spa S.P.	80	C4	43.056950 -73.801490
Selkirk Shores S.P.	79	D2	43.544300 -76.191510
Seneca Lake S.P.	79	D3	42.873410 -76.960940
Southwick Beach S.P.	79	D2	43.767270 -76.196230
Sterling Forest S.P.	148	A2	41.220200 -74.187210
Storm King S.P.	148	B2	41.432560 -73.987020
Taconic S.P.	94	B2	42.007680 -73.508400
Tallman Mtn. S.P.	148	B3	41.037270 -73.915920
Verona Beach S.P.	79	E3	43.179070 -75.725090
Waterson Point S.P.	79	E1	44.339030 -76.010580
Watkins Glen S.P.	79	D4	42.375896 -76.871078
Wellesley Island S.P.	79	E1	44.315970 -76.019480
Whetstone Gulf S.P.	79	E2	43.702310 -75.459120
Wildwood S.P.	149	D3	40.954230 -72.788470
Wilson-Tuscarora S.P.	78	B3	43.307080 -78.854500

NORTH CAROLINA	PAGE	GRID	LATITUDE LONGITUDE
National Park & Rec. Areas			
Cape Hatteras Natl. Seashore	115	F3	35.766700 -75.526640
Cape Lookout Natl. Seashore	115	E4	34.886110 -76.331220
Carl Sandburg Home N.H.S.	121	E1	35.270000 -82.450000
Fort Raleigh N.H.S.	115	F2	35.932360 -75.708500
Great Smoky Mts. Natl. Park-Cades Cove Vis. Ctr.	121	D1	35.585300 -83.842900
Great Smoky Mts. Natl. Park-Oconaluftee Vis. Ctr.	121	D1	35.515300 -83.305300
Great Smoky Mts. Natl. Park-Sugarlands Vis. Ctr.	121	D1	35.685600 -83.536700
State Park & Rec. Areas			
Carolina Beach S.P.	123	E3	34.045240 -77.903430
Cliffs of the Neuse S.P.	123	E1	35.232900 -77.898390
Crowders Mtn. S.P.	122	A1	35.212350 -81.292920
Dismal Swamp S.P.	113	F3	36.517470 -76.360720
Fort Macon S.P.	115	E4	34.697750 -76.699580
Goose Creek S.P.	123	F1	35.483140 -76.902290
Gorges S.P.	121	E1	35.108400 -82.943900
Hammocks Beach S.P.	123	F2	34.671810 -77.138720
Hanging Rock S.P.	112	B3	36.413030 -80.253950
Haw River S.P.	112	B3	36.249719 -79.755971
Jockey's Ridge S.P.	115	F2	35.961820 -75.626970
Jones Lake S.P.	123	D2	34.698900 -78.624990
Lake James S.P.	111	F4	35.728064 -81.901980
Lake Norman S.P.	112	A4	35.665780 -80.938410
Lake Waccamaw S.P.	123	D3	34.272650 -78.466040
Lumber River S.P.	123	D3	34.390831 -79.004145
Medoc Mtn. S.P.	113	D3	36.280410 -77.877820
Merchants Millpond S.P.	113	F3	36.450601 -76.692978
Morrow Mtn. S.P.	122	B1	35.370390 -80.102410
Mount Mitchell S.P.	111	E4	35.814600 -82.146100
Pettigrew S.P.	113	F4	35.789580 -76.406980
Pilot Mtn. S.P.	112	A3	36.345530 -80.478390
Raven Rock S.P.	123	D1	35.461520 -78.912660
Singletary Lake S.P.	123	D2	34.581570 -78.452070
South Mts. S.P.	121	F1	35.601190 -81.626700
Stone Mtn. S.P.	112	A3	36.374390 -81.018010

NORTH DAKOTA	PAGE	GRID	LATITUDE LONGITUDE
National Park & Rec. Areas			
Fort Union N.H.S.	17	F2	48.002390 -104.04356
Knife River N.H.S.	18	B3	47.336680 -101.38745
Theodore Roosevelt Natl. Park-Elkhorn Site	17	F3	47.226950 -103.62231
Theodore Roosevelt Natl. Park-North Unit	18	A3	47.600300 -103.26100
Theodore Roosevelt Natl. Park-South Unit	18	A4	46.915500 -103.52700
State Park & Rec. Areas			
Beaver Lake S.P.	18	C4	46.401260 -99.61586
Cross Ranch S.P.	18	B3	47.213530 -101.00018
Doyle Mem. S.P.	27	D1	46.204880 -99.48215
Fort Abercrombie S.P.	19	F4	46.444530 -96.71880
Fort Lincoln S.P.	18	B4	46.769420 -100.84786
Fort Ransom S.P.	19	E4	46.544100 -97.92557
Fort Stevenson S.P.	18	B3	47.596890 -101.42053
Grahams Island S.P.	19	D2	48.052500 -99.06830
Icelandic S.P.	19	E1	48.772620 -97.73699
Lake Metigoshe S.P.	18	C1	48.980640 -100.32671
Lake Sakakawea S.P.	18	B3	47.511020 -101.44935
Lewis & Clark S.P.	18	A2	48.115350 -103.24149
Little Missouri Bay S.P.	18	A3	47.550030 -102.73824
Pembina S.P.	19	E1	48.964720 -97.24050
Turtle River S.P.	19	E2	47.931660 -97.50539
Whitestone Bfld. S.P.	27	D1	46.169190 -98.85733

OHIO	PAGE	GRID	LATITUDE LONGITUDE
National Park & Rec. Areas			
Charles Young Buffalo Soldiers Natl. Mon.	100	C1	39.689722,-83.89111
Cuyahoga Valley Natl. Park-Canal Vis. Ctr.	91	E2	41.372600 -81.61370

Cuyahoga Valley Natl. Park-Hunt Farm Vis. Info. Ctr.	91	E2	41.200900 -81.573100
Hopewell Culture N.H.P.	101	D2	39.298360 -82.917810
James A. Garfield N.H.S.	91	E2	41.663600 -81.351260
State Park & Rec. Areas			
A.W. Marion S.P.	101	D1	39.633730 -82.885720
Adams Lake S.P.	100	C3	38.812900 -83.519400
Alum Creek S.P.	90	C4	40.226870 -82.981320
Barkcamp S.P.	101	F1	40.047030 -81.031710
Beaver Creek S.P.	91	F3	40.726220 -80.613590
Blue Rock S.P.	101	E1	39.832780 -81.858370
Buck Creek S.P.	100	C1	39.946410 -83.729550
Buckeye Lake S.P.	101	D1	39.906540 -82.526270
Burr Oak S.P.	101	E1	39.527740 -82.023260
Caesar Creek S.P.	100	C1	39.515730 -84.041070
Catawba Island S.P.	91	D2	41.573530 -82.855780
Cowan Lake S.P.	100	C2	39.387600 -83.882970
Crane Creek S.P.	90	C2	41.603770 -83.192910
Deer Creek S.P.	101	D1	39.649260 -83.246340
Delaware S.P.	90	C4	40.377690 -83.071590
Dillon S.P.	101	E1	40.023600 -82.111910
East Fork S.P.	100	C2	39.002050 -84.151210
East Harbor S.P.	91	D2	41.540930 -82.820830
Findley S.P.	91	D3	41.122990 -82.219390
Forked Run S.P.	101	E2	39.085000 -81.770460
Geneva S.P.	91	F1	41.852760 -80.963280
Grand Lake Saint Marys S.P.	90	B4	40.549240 -84.436500
Guilford Lake S.P.	91	F3	40.796100 -80.893760
Harrison Lake S.P.	90	B2	41.637190 -84.361760
Headlands Beach S.P.	91	E1	41.752140 -81.294480
Hocking Hills S.P.	101	D2	39.494180 -82.611910
Hueston Woods S.P.	100	B1	39.573820 -84.715380
Independence Dam S.P.	90	B2	41.282470 -84.313500
Indian Lake S.P.	90	B4	40.510360 -83.842980
Jackson Lake S.P.	101	D3	38.902850 -82.596780
Jefferson Lake S.P.	91	F4	40.472050 -80.808930
John Bryan S.P.	100	C1	39.791020 -83.867790
Kelleys Island S.P.	91	D2	41.614080 -82.712110
Kiser Lake S.P.	90	B4	40.197650 -83.981740
Lake Alma S.P.	101	D2	39.153450 -82.516810
Lake Hope S.P.	101	E2	39.318500 -82.354920
Lake Logan S.P.	101	D1	39.536400 -82.460590
Lake Loramie S.P.	90	B4	40.359750 -84.359730
Lake White S.P.	101	D2	39.109160 -83.040330
Madison Lake S.P.	100	C1	39.866250 -83.374930
Malabar Farm S.P.	91	D3	40.649590 -82.398390
Mary Jane Thurston S.P.	90	B2	41.409630 -83.881320
Maumee Bay S.P.	90	C2	41.678020 -83.353360
Mohican S.P.	91	D4	40.609510 -82.257600
Mosquito Lake S.P.	91	F2	41.301940 -80.767990
Mount Gilead S.P.	91	D4	40.547820 -82.816770
Muskingum River S.P.	101	E1	40.044140 -81.978260
Nelson-Kennedy Ledges S.P.	91	F2	41.330090 -81.040190
Paint Creek S.P.	100	C2	39.228360 -83.374450
Pike Lake S.P.	101	D2	39.158270 -83.220950
Portage Lakes S.P.	91	E3	40.966260 -81.565190
Punderson S.P.	91	E2	41.461540 -81.219590
Pymatuning S.P.	91	F2	41.580110 -80.541530
Quail Hollow S.P.	91	E3	40.970200 -81.325100
Rocky Fork S.P.	100	C2	39.188310 -83.529730
Salt Fork S.P.	91	E4	40.081830 -81.460400
Scioto Trail S.P.	101	D2	39.223620 -82.931210
Shawnee S.P.	101	D3	38.747670 -83.211220
South Bass Island S.P.	91	D2	41.644690 -82.835950
Stonelick S.P.	100	C2	39.226160 -84.057210
Strouds Run S.P.	101	E2	39.334320 -82.017690
Sycamore S.P.	100	B1	39.803410 -84.373470
Tar Hollow S.P.	101	D2	39.353790 -82.780200
Tinkers Creek S.P.	91	E2	41.276180 -81.368910
Van Buren S.P.	90	C3	41.138290 -83.644940
West Branch S.P.	91	E3	41.133310 -81.189660
Wolf Run S.P.	101	F1	39.789770 -81.540180

OKLAHOMA	PAGE	GRID	LATITUDE LONGITUDE
National Park & Rec. Areas			
Chickasaw N.R.A.	51	F4	34.497390 -96.970110
Washita Battlefield N.H.S.	50	C3	35.621151 -99.709854
Winding Stair Mtn. N.R.A.	116	B2	34.749705 -94.793055
State Park & Rec. Areas			
Alabaster Caverns S.P.	51	D1	36.697490 -99.149430
Arrowhead at Lake Eufaula S.P.	116	A1	35.168240 -95.639970
Beaver Dunes Park	50	B1	36.841129 -100.514988
Beavers Bend S.P.	116	B3	34.131792 -94.701382
Bernice Area at Grand Lake S.P.	106	B3	36.626670 -94.901670
Black Mesa S.P.	49	F1	36.855620 -102.885680
Boiling Springs S.P.	51	D1	36.452950 -99.298900
Brushy Lake Park	116	B1	35.543680 -94.817676
Cherokee Landing S.P.	106	B4	35.758890 -94.908610
Cherokee Area at Grand Lake S.P.	106	B3	36.480280 -95.050560
Clayton Lake S.P.	116	A2	34.549420 -95.308330
Disney Area at Grand Lake S.P.	116	B3	36.480260 -95.009130
Dripping Springs Lake and Rec. Are	51	F3	35.611437 -96.068911
Fort Cobb S.P.	51	D3	35.203720 -98.464990
Foss S.P.	51	D3	35.578510 -99.186830
Gloss Mtn. S.P.	51	D2	36.367190 -98.576460
Great Plains S.P.	51	D4	34.730340 -98.985690
Great Salt Plains S.P.	51	E1	36.753170 -98.149930
Greenleaf S.P.	106	A4	35.623260 -95.180950
Honey Creek Area at Grand Lake S.P.	106	B3	36.574060 -94.784370
Hugo Lake S.P.	116	A3	34.016384 -95.375061
Keystone S.P.	51	F2	36.137440 -96.264340
Little Blue Area at Grand Lake S.P.	116	B3	36.464053 -95.002535
Lake Eufaula S.P.	116	A1	35.427900 -95.546100
Lake Murray S.P.	51	F4	34.154880 -97.120950
Lake Texoma S.P.	59	F1	33.997590 -96.651310
Lake Thunderbird S.P.	51	E3	35.232320 -97.247550
Lake Wister S.P.	116	B2	34.948700 -94.710400
Little Sahara S.P.	51	D1	36.532900 -98.890870
McGee Creek S.P.	116	A3	34.302927 -95.875467
Natural Falls S.P.	106	B4	36.151900 -94.673300
Okmulgee Lake Rec. Area	51	F2	35.621900 -96.067700
Osage Hills S.P.	51	F1	36.757360 -96.176220
Quartz Mountain S.P.	50	C3	34.955790 -99.275244
Raymond Gary S.P.	116	A3	33.997580 -95.253860
Robbers Cave S.P.	116	A2	34.564650 -95.290393
Roman Nose S.P.	51	D2	35.929213 -98.42995
Sequoyah Bay S.P.	106	A4	35.886000 -95.276000
Sequoyah S.P.	106	A4	35.932960 -95.230650
Spavinaw Area at Grand Lake S.P.	106	B3	36.385890 -95.053290
Talimena S.P.	116	B2	34.788290 -94.950690
Tenkiller S.P.	116	B1	35.598000 -95.031100
Twin Bridges Area at Grand Lake S.P.	106	B2	36.804320 -94.757920
Wha-Sha-She Park	51	F1	36.926000 -96.091000
Winding Stair Mtn. N.R.A.-Cedar Lake	116	B2	34.778566 -94.693

OREGON	PAGE	GRID	LATITUDE LONGITUDE
National Park & Rec. Areas			
Cascade-Siskiyou Natl. Mon.	28	C2	42.068300 -122.399940
Crater Lake Natl. Park-Annie Spring Ent. Sta.	28	C1	42.868700 -122.169000
Crater Lake Natl. Park-North Ent. Sta.	28	C1	43.086900 -122.116000
Hells Canyon N.R.A.-East Ent.	22	B1	45.500680 -116.806560
Hells Canyon N.R.A.-South Ent.	22	B1	44.903300 -116.957080
Hells Canyon N.R.A.-West Ent.	22	B1	45.176360 -117.040740
John Day Fossil Beds Natl. Mon.-Clarno Unit	21	D2	44.911250 -120.431780
John Day Fossil Beds Natl. Mon.-Painted Hills Unit	21	D3	44.661170 -120.254750
John Day Fossil Beds Natl. Mon.-Sheep Rock Unit	21	E3	44.555480 -119.645010
Lewis & Clark N.H.P.-Fort Clatsop	20	B1	46.138260 -123.876670
Lewis & Clark N.H.P.-Salt Works	20	B1	46.134551 -123.880420
Lewis & Clark N.H.P.-Sunset Beach	20	B1	46.099430 -123.936390
Newberry Natl. Volcanic Mon.	21	D4	43.716800 -121.376960
Oregon Caves Natl. Mon. & Pres.	28	B2	42.103910 -123.414300
Oregon Dunes N.R.A.-North Ent.	20	A4	43.885610 -124.120860
Oregon Dunes N.R.A.-South Ent.	20	A4	43.579470 -124.186490
State Park & Rec. Areas			
Ainsworth S.P.	20	C2	45.595720 -122.052980
Alfred A. Loeb S.P.	28	A2	42.113180 -124.188520
Beverly Beach S.P.	20	B3	44.726250 -124.057290
Bob Straub S.P.	20	B2	45.183160 -123.965116
Brian Booth S.P.	20	B3	44.518060 -124.075960
Bullards Beach S.P.	28	A1	43.150990 -124.395480
Cape Arago S.P.	20	A4	43.326140 -124.381770
Cape Blanco S.P.	28	A1	42.826660 -124.524640
Cape Lookout S.P.	20	B2	45.367667 -123.961127
Carl G. Washburne Mem. S.P.	20	A3	44.141990 -124.117490
Cascadia S.P.	20	C3	44.397100 -122.477480
Catherine Creek S.P.	22	A2	45.148890 -117.733990
Collier Mem. S.P.	28	C1	42.641810 -121.880630
Ecola S.P.	20	B1	45.916550 -123.967430
Elijah Bristow S.P.	20	C4	43.935470 -122.844270
Fort Columbia S.P.	20	B1	46.252580 -123.921500
Fort Stevens S.P.	20	B1	46.183200 -123.959940
Harris Beach S.P.	28	A2	42.067930 -124.305860
Hat Rock S.P.	21	E1	45.908260 -119.164510
Hilgard Junction S.P.	21	F2	45.342060 -118.236470
Humbug Mtn. S.P.	28	A1	42.686870 -124.445970
Illinois River Forks S.P.	28	B2	42.154870 -123.649870
Jessie M. Honeyman Mem. S.P.	20	A4	43.933440 -124.106440
L.L. Stub Stewart S.P.	20	B1	45.739050 -123.199461
Lake Owyhee S.P.	22	A4	43.638380 -117.229090
Lapine S.P.	21	D4	43.768452 -121.513399
Maryhill S.P.	21	D1	45.683060 -120.825830
Mayer S.P.	21	D1	45.682780 -121.301080
Milo Mciver S.P.	20	C2	45.306110 -122.372220
Molalla River S.P.	20	C2	45.294840 -122.696400
Nehalem Bay S.P.	20	B1	45.710000 -123.931470
Oswald West S.P.	20	B1	45.770000 -123.958610
Port Orford Heads S.P.	28	A1	42.739470 -124.509730
Prineville Reservoir S.P.	21	D3	44.144660 -120.737770
Rooster Rock S.P.	20	C2	45.546320 -122.236500
Shore Acres S.P.	20	A4	43.329940 -124.376510
Silver Falls S.P.	20	C2	44.853752 -122.662258
Smith Rock S.P.	21	D3	44.360540 -121.138400
South Beach S.P.	20	B3	44.598450 -124.059350
Starvation Creek S.P.	20	C1	45.688550 -121.690180
Sunset Bay S.P.	20	A4	43.339010 -124.353990
The Cove Palisades S.P.	21	D3	44.557460 -121.262110
Tumalo S.P.	21	D3	44.086760 -121.308730
Umpqua Lighthouse S.P.	20	A4	43.669610 -124.182830
Valley of the Rogue S.P.	28	B1	42.410770 -123.129310
Viento S.P.	20	C1	45.697240 -121.668310
Wallowa Lake S.P.	22	A2	45.280690 -117.208230
White River Falls S.P.	21	D2	45.166870 -121.087420
Willamette Mission S.P.	20	B2	45.080740 -123.031510
William M. Tugman S.P.	20	A4	43.623640 -124.181910

PENNSYLVANIA	PAGE	GRID	LATITUDE LONGITUDE
National Park & Rec. Areas			
Allegheny N.R.A	92	B1	41.943055 -78.867025
Allegheny Portage Railroad N.H.S.	92	B4	40.377020 -78.835870
Eisenhower N.H.S.	103	E1	39.818000 -77.232610
Flight 93 Natl. Mem.	92	B4	40.055200 -78.900900
Fort Necessity Natl. Bfld.	102	B1	39.816340 -79.584310
Friendship Hill N.H.S.	102	B1	39.777778 -79.929167
Gettysburg N.M.P.	103	E1	39.811600 -77.226100
Grey Towers N.H.S.	94	A3	41.325224 -74.871113
Hopewell Furnace N.H.S.	146	B2	40.206760 -75.773570
Johnstown Flood Natl. Mem.	92	B4	40.350710 -78.772480
Valley Forge N.H.P.	146	C2	40.102240 -75.422960
State Park & Rec. Areas			
Bald Eagle S.P.	92	C3	41.041960 -77.642780
Big Spring S.P.	92	C4	40.266850 -77.654410
Black Moshannon S.P.	92	C3	40.915190 -78.058570
Blue Knob S.P.	92	B4	40.265800 -78.584480
Buchanan's Birthplace S.P.	103	D1	39.872660 -77.953190
Caledonia S.P.	103	D1	39.905610 -77.478880
Chapman S.P.	92	B1	41.757850 -79.170350
Cherry Springs S.P.	92	C2	41.662778 -77.823056
Codorus S.P.	103	E1	39.783180 -76.908920
Colonel Denning S.P.	93	D4	40.281820 -77.416630
Colton Point S.P.	93	D2	41.711180 -77.465430
Cook Forest S.P.	92	B2	41.333790 -79.210440
Cowans Gap S.P.	103	D1	39.997980 -77.921530
Delaware Canal S.P	146	C1	40.545565 -75.087831
Elk S.P.	92	B2	41.606100 -78.564780
Erie Bluffs S.P.	91	F1	42.008333 -80.410833
Evansburg S.P.	146	C2	40.197510 -75.407080
Frances Slocum S.P.	93	E2	41.347380 -75.893760
French Creek S.P.	146	B2	40.236580 -75.795660
Gouldsboro S.P.	93	F2	41.232250 -75.495730
Greenwood Furnace S.P.	92	C3	40.649610 -77.756090
Hickory Run S.P.	93	F3	41.035170 -75.736220
Hills Creek S.P.	93	D1	41.805190 -77.187600
Hyner Run S.P.	92	C2	41.359150 -77.623850
Kettle Creek S.P.	92	C2	41.377120 -77.930130
Keystone S.P.	92	A4	40.374250 -79.377830
Lackawanna S.P.	93	F2	41.575030 -75.711520
Laurel Hill S.P.	102	B1	39.984470 -79.234840
Laurel Mtn. S.P.	92	B4	40.179670 -79.131530
Laurel Ridge S.P.	92	B4	39.958400 -79.360160
Lehigh Gorge S.P.	93	F3	40.971900 -75.761840
Leonard Harrison S.P.	93	D2	41.698420 -77.450810
Little Buffalo S.P.	93	D4	40.454420 -77.169170
Little Pine S.P.	93	D2	41.371240 -77.360310
Lyman Run S.P.	92	C1	41.723650 -77.768470
Marsh Creek S.P.	146	B3	40.069360 -75.717320
Maurice K. Goddard S.P.	92	A2	41.428380 -80.145140
McConnells Mill S.P.	92	A3	40.963530 -80.168810
Memorial Lake S.P.	93	E4	40.424760 -76.590540
Mont Alto S.P.	103	D1	39.839130 -77.540630
Moraine S.P.	92	A3	40.940280 -80.098520
Nescopeck S.P.	93	E3	41.067100 -75.925300
Nockamixon S.P.	146	C1	40.463630 -75.242010
Ohiopyle S.P.	102	B1	39.865030 -79.504310
Oil Creek S.P.-East Ent.	92	A2	41.512130 -79.661810
Ole Bull S.P.	92	C2	41.543590 -77.709430
Parker Dam S.P.	92	C2	41.205140 -78.504310
Penn-Roosevelt S.P.	92	C3	40.726389 -77.702500
Pine Grove Furnace S.P.	103	D1	40.032910 -77.305070
Poe Paddy S.P.	93	D3	40.834150 -77.417380
Presque Isle S.P.	92	A1	42.114200 -80.153590
Prince Gallitzin S.P.	92	B3	40.669760 -78.575650
Promised Land S.P.	93	F2	41.313560 -75.210370
Pymatuning S.P.	91	F2	41.605440 -80.387840
Raccoon Creek S.P.	91	F4	40.503160 -80.424460
Ralph Stover S.P.	146	C1	40.440420 -75.106050
Raymond B. Winter S.P.	93	D3	40.992340 -77.200450
Ricketts Glen S.P.	93	E2	41.336190 -76.300420
Ryerson Station S.P.	102	A1	39.892310 -80.450030
S.B. Elliott S.P.	92	C3	41.112740 -78.526100
Salt Springs S.P.	93	E1	41.911090 -75.868720
Samuel S. Lewis S.P.	103	E1	39.996500 -76.550410
Shawnee S.P.	102	C1	40.038060 -78.645850
Shikellamy S.P.	93	D3	40.879390 -76.802950
Sinnemahoning S.P.	92	C2	41.450650 -78.055090
Susquehannock S.P.	146	A3	39.805770 -76.283410

Swatara S.P.	93	E4	40.481480 -76.551350
Tobyhanna S.P.	93	F2	41.214130 -75.384030
Trough Creek S.P.	92	C4	40.311620 -78.131820
Tyler S.P.	146	C2	40.233330 -74.951170
Warriors Path S.P.	92	C4	40.193330 -78.249880
Washington Crossing Hist. Park	104	C2	40.312256 -74.859711
Whipple Dam S.P.	92	C3	40.682250 -77.868410
Worlds End S.P.	93	E2	41.471880 -76.587060
Yellow Creek S.P.	92	B4	40.575830 -79.004420

RHODE ISLAND

RHODE ISLAND	PAGE	GRID	LATITUDE LONGITUDE
State Park & Rec. Areas			
Beavertail S.P.	150	C4	41.457030 -71.396950
Brenton Point S.P.	150	C4	41.450430 -71.355870
Burlingame S.P.	150	C4	41.361610 -71.701370
Charlestown Breachway S.B.	150	C4	41.356053 -71.640494
Colt S.P.	151	D3	41.684590 -71.288860
East Matunuck State Beach	150	C4	41.378350 -71.525630
Fishermen's Mem. S.P.	150	C4	41.380630 -71.488000
Fort Adams S.P.	150	C4	41.469150 -71.339990
Goddard Mem. S.P.	150	C3	41.651030 -71.442040
Haines Mem. S.P.	150	C3	41.752960 -71.348600
Misquamicut State Beach	95	D4	41.324510 -71.800670
Pulaski S.P. & Rec. Area	150	C3	41.950000 -71.766670
Rocky Point S.P.	150	C3	41.691482 -71.363654
R.W. Wheeler State Beach	150	C4	41.372620 -71.495530
Scarborough State Beach	150	C4	41.389770 -71.474260

SOUTH CAROLINA

SOUTH CAROLINA	PAGE	GRID	LATITUDE LONGITUDE
National Park & Rec. Areas			
Charles Pinckney N.H.S.	131	D2	32.847150 -79.824090
Congaree Natl. Park	122	A4	33.836100 -80.827660
Kings Mtn. N.M.P.	122	A1	35.140120 -81.386890
Ninety Six N.H.S.	121	F3	34.162740 -82.010980
Reconstruction Era N.H.P.	130	C2	32.432790 -80.670458
State Park & Rec. Areas			
Andrew Jackson S.P.	122	B2	34.839560 -80.810110
Barnwell S.P.	130	B1	33.329250 -81.300400
Calhoun Falls S.P.	121	E3	34.106792 -82.604200
Cheraw S.P.	122	C2	34.642370 -79.927640
Devils Fork S.P.	121	E2	34.952527 -82.946085
Edisto Beach S.P.	130	C2	32.505410 -80.310310
Givhans Ferry S.P.	130	C1	33.031640 -80.382150
Goodale S.P.	122	B3	34.281580 -80.525150
Hickory Knob State Resort Park	121	E4	33.884250 -82.416010
Huntington Beach S.P.	123	D4	33.502650 -79.081200
Jones Gap S.P.	121	E1	35.126360 -82.558350
Kings Mtn. S.P.	122	A1	35.113030 -81.394040
Lake Warren S.P.	130	B2	32.844830 -81.165070
Little Pee Dee S.P.	122	C3	34.331020 -79.282170
Myrtle Beach S.P.	123	D4	33.649210 -78.938600
Oconee S.P.	121	E2	34.867297 -83.106098
Paris Mtn. S.P.	121	E2	34.924970 -82.365540
Poinsett S.P.	122	B4	33.804360 -80.544920
Santee S.P.	122	B4	33.500200 -80.489820
Table Rock S.P.	121	E2	35.022050 -82.710700

SOUTH DAKOTA

SOUTH DAKOTA	PAGE	GRID	LATITUDE LONGITUDE
National Park & Rec. Areas			
Badlands Natl. Park-Interior Ent.	26	B4	43.741900 -101.957000
Badlands Natl. Park-Northeast Ent.	26	B4	43.792400 -101.906000
Badlands Natl. Park-Pinnacles Ent.	26	B4	43.885500 -102.238000
Jewel Cave Natl. Mon.	25	F4	43.736500 -103.819940
Minuteman Missile N.H.S.	26	B4	43.833931 -101.899685
Mount Rushmore Natl. Mem.	26	A4	43.886730 -103.440610
Wind Cave Natl. Park-Vis. Ctr.	26	A4	43.556100 -103.478000
State Park & Rec. Areas			
Bear Butte S.P.	26	A3	44.460580 -103.433750
Custer S.P.	26	A4	43.770310 -103.440130
Fisher Grove S.P.	27	E2	44.883340 -98.356640
Hartford Beach S.P.	27	F2	45.398870 -96.665260
Lake Herman S.P.	27	F4	43.993120 -97.159790
Newton Hills S.P.	35	F1	43.218860 -96.569700
Oakwood Lakes S.P.	27	F3	44.454310 -96.989490
Palisades S.P.	27	F4	43.687970 -96.511470
Roy Lake S.P.	27	E1	45.703360 -97.419650
Sica Hollow S.P.	27	E1	45.740690 -97.229150
Union Grove S.P.	35	F1	42.922630 -96.785530

TENNESSEE

TENNESSEE	PAGE	GRID	LATITUDE LONGITUDE
National Park & Rec. Areas			
Andrew Johnson N.H.S.	111	D4	36.157710 -82.836880
Big South Fork Natl. River & Rec. Area	110	B3	36.475400 -84.752100
Manhattan Project N.H.P.	37	D2	35.928419 -85.350923
State Park & Rec. Areas			
Big Hill Pond S.P.	119	D1	35.078890 -88.718860
Big Ridge S.P.	110	C3	36.241600 -83.929280
Bledsoe Creek S.P.	109	F3	36.378050 -86.356660
Cedars of Lebanon S.P. & Forest	109	F4	36.093930 -86.335620
Chickasaw S.P.	119	D1	35.393241 -88.772298
Cove Lake S.P.	110	C3	36.305830 -84.210750
Cumberland Mtn. S.P.	110	B4	35.898460 -84.995130
David Crockett S.P.	119	E1	35.242690 -87.354850
Davy Crockett Birthplace S.P.	111	E3	36.221980 -82.662770
Edgar Evins S.P.	110	A4	36.086050 -85.812460
Fall Creek Falls S.P.	120	B1	35.622200 -85.208000
Frozen Head S.P.-North Ent.	110	B4	36.122550 -84.433320
Frozen Head S.P.-South Ent.	110	B4	36.102180 -84.446970
Harpeth River S.P.	109	E4	36.079240 -86.956920
Harrison Bay S.P.	120	B1	35.175850 -85.115350
Henry Horton S.P.	119	F1	35.596510 -86.698690
Hiwassee–Ocoee Scenic Rivers S.P.	120	C1	35.224557 -84.504269
Indian Mtn. S.P.	110	C3	36.583050 -84.139900
Long Hunter S.P.	109	F4	36.094340 -86.557330
Meeman-Shelby Forest S.P.	118	B1	35.336800 -90.029010
Montgomery Bell S.P.	109	E4	36.106750 -87.268690
Mousetail Landing S.P.	109	D4	35.581900 -87.859100
Natchez Trace S.P.	109	D4	35.839580 -88.252820
Nathan Bedford Forrest S.P.	109	D4	36.087900 -87.979750
Norris Dam S.P.	110	C3	36.234560 -84.127020
Old Stone Fort State Arch. Park	120	A1	35.487270 -86.101330
Panther Creek S.P.	111	D3	36.212760 -83.412420
Paris Landing State Resort Park	109	D3	36.441760 -88.090180
Pickett S.P.	110	B3	36.537374 -84.802126
Pickwick Landing S.P.	119	D2	35.051790 -88.242650
Pinson Mounds State Arch. Park	119	D1	35.504130 -88.683020
Reelfoot Lake S.P.	108	B3	36.414410 -89.426880
Roan Mtn. S.P.	111	E4	36.161110 -82.097000
Rock Island S.P.	110	A4	35.810000 -85.641550
Standing Stone S.P.	110	A3	36.458910 -85.437690
T.O. Fuller S.P.	118	B2	35.057810 -90.113650
Tims Ford S.P.	120	A1	35.220999 -86.255889
Warriors Path S.P.	111	E5	36.504610 -82.481090

TEXAS

TEXAS	PAGE	GRID	LATITUDE LONGITUDE
National Park & Rec. Areas			
Alibates Flint Quarries Natl. Mon.	50	A3	35.571900 -101.633880
Amistad N.R.A.	60	B2	29.449920 -101.053170
Big Bend Natl. Park-North Ent.	62	C4	29.680900 -103.167000
Big Bend Natl. Park-West Ent.	62	C4	29.306600 -103.523000
Fort Davis N.H.S.	62	B2	30.604120 -103.886010
Guadalupe Mts. Natl. Park-Vis. Ctr.	57	D3	31.894300 -104.822000
Lyndon B. Johnson N.H.P.	61	D2	30.276020 -98.411990
Padre Island Natl. Seashore	63	F3	27.553470 -97.248370
Palo Alto Bfld. N.H.P.	63	F4	26.011630 -97.481570
State Park & Rec. Areas			
Abilene S.P.	58	C3	32.241360 -99.879230
Atlanta S.P.	124	C1	33.229500 -94.249300
Balmorhea S.P.	62	B2	30.946270 -103.784890
Bastrop S.P.	61	E2	30.098960 -97.229090
Bentsen-Rio Grande Valley S.P.	63	E4	26.182530 -98.382360
Big Bend Ranch S.P.	62	B4	29.265070 -103.791910
Big Spring S.P.	58	A3	32.229650 -101.483090
Blanco S.P.	61	D2	30.093240 -98.423420
Bonham S.P.	59	F1	33.543100 -96.149640
Brazos Bend S.P.	132	A4	29.371480 -95.631890
Buescher S.P.	61	E2	30.073570 -97.176140
Caddo Lake S.P.	124	C2	32.684230 -94.177070
Caprock Canyons S.P. & Trailway	50	B4	34.406440 -101.048830
Choke Canyon S.P.-Calliham Unit	61	D4	28.460970 -98.356380
Choke Canyon S.P.-South Shore Unit	61	D4	28.467610 -98.239550
Cleburne S.P.	59	E3	32.265180 -97.560680
Colorado Bend S.P.	61	D1	31.062510 -98.504250
Cooper Lake S.P.	124	A1	33.305282 -95.648346
Copper Breaks S.P.	50	C4	34.113660 -99.747800
Daingerfield S.P.	124	B1	33.028720 -94.714510
Davis Mts. S.P.	62	B2	30.599520 -103.929220
Dinosaur Valley S.P.	59	E3	32.250020 -97.814620
Eisenhower S.P.	59	F1	33.822670 -96.616120
Fairfield Lake S.P.	59	F3	31.765910 -96.076220
Falcon S.P.	63	D3	26.583500 -99.144790
Fort Boggy S.P.	124	A4	31.189627 -95.986069
Fort Griffin S.H.S.	58	C2	32.924690 -99.219370
Fort Parker S.P.	59	F4	31.592650 -96.524370
Fort Richardson S.P. & Hist. Site	59	D2	33.206060 -98.164810
Franklin Mts. S.P.	56	C3	31.912060 -106.517140
Galveston Island S.P.	132	B4	29.196240 -94.956210
Garner S.P.	60	C2	29.600900 -99.744220
Goliad S.P. & Hist. Site	61	E4	28.655190 -97.383580
Goose Island S.P.	61	F4	28.134060 -96.984350
Guadalupe River S.P.	61	D2	29.849890 -98.509590
Hueco Tanks S.P. & Hist. Site	56	C3	31.926453 -106.042437
Huntsville S.P.	132	A2	30.638130 -95.511370
Inks Lake S.P.	61	D1	30.738290 -98.366450
Kickapoo Cavern S.P.	60	B2	29.610016 -100.452465
Lake Arrowhead S.P.	59	D1	33.759300 -98.396610
Lake Bob Sandlin S.P.	124	B1	33.054090 -95.101250
Lake Brownwood S.P.	59	D3	31.857370 -99.021280
Lake Casa Blanca International S.P.	63	D2	27.536739 -99.432449
Lake Colorado City S.P.	58	B3	32.313460 -100.924800
Lake Corpus Christi S.P.	61	E4	28.060360 -97.867690
Lake Livingston S.P.	132	B1	30.671300 -95.008200
Lake Mineral Wells S.P. & Trailway	59	E2	32.814570 -98.042270
Lake Somerville S.P. & Trailway	61	F1	30.315760 -96.625080
Lake Tawakoni S.P.	59	F2	32.841610 -95.990710
Lake Whitney S.P.	59	E3	31.924780 -97.356280
Lockhart S.P.	61	E2	29.857610 -97.697400
Longhorn Cavern S.P.	61	D1	30.686610 -98.351380
Lyndon B. Johnson S.P. & Hist. Site-Ranch Unit	61	D2	30.235180 -98.629100
Martin Creek Lake S.P.	124	B3	32.283090 -94.583470
Martin Dies Junior S.P.	132	C1	30.848980 -94.164720
Meridian S.P.	59	E3	31.892440 -97.695670
Mission Tejas S.P.	124	A4	31.546110 -95.234720
Monahans Sandhills S.P.	57	F4	31.634940 -102.814850
Mother Neff S.P.	59	E4	31.319150 -97.474210
Mustang Island S.P.	63	F2	27.677020 -97.173730
Old Tunnel S.P.	61	D2	30.101079 -98.820704
Palmetto S.P.	61	E2	29.597280 -97.584640
Palo Duro Canyon S.P.	50	B3	34.985710 -101.703190
Pedernales Falls S.P.	61	D1	30.273110 -98.256830
Possum Kingdom S.P.	59	D2	32.878970 -98.561740
Purtis Creek S.P.	124	A2	32.373340 -95.974530
Ray Roberts Lake S.P.	59	F1	33.444050 -96.925860
Sabine Pass Battleground S.H.S.	132	C3	29.726520 -93.878280
San Angelo S.P.	58	B4	31.491919 -100.547148
Sea Rim S.P.	132	C3	29.677900 -94.039900
Seminole Canyon S.P. & Hist. Site	60	A2	29.709000 -101.298480
South Llano River S.P.	60	C1	30.445430 -99.804610
Stephen F. Austin S.P.	61	F2	29.812030 -96.108200
Tyler S.P.	124	A2	32.481750 -95.281760
Village Creek S.P.	132	C2	30.250499 -94.178700

UTAH

UTAH	PAGE	GRID	LATITUDE LONGITUDE
National Park & Rec. Areas			
Arches Natl. Park	40	A2	38.615570 -109.616920
Bears Ears Natl. Mon.	41	A3	37.703318 -109.919962
Bryce Canyon Natl. Park	39	E4	37.641700 -112.168000
Canyonlands Natl. Park-East Ent.	40	A3	38.168510 -109.750980
Canyonlands Natl. Park-Horseshoe Canyon Unit	39	F3	38.497740 -110.205960
Canyonlands Natl. Park-North Ent.	40	A3	38.490150 -109.807930
Canyonlands Natl. Park-West Ent.	40	A3	38.255440 -110.180050
Capitol Reef Natl. Park	39	E3	38.291020 -111.261410
Cedar Breaks Natl. Mon.-East Ent.	39	D4	37.655230 -112.811350
Cedar Breaks Natl. Mon.-North Ent.	39	D4	37.665730 -112.838130
Cedar Breaks Natl. Mon.-South Ent.	39	D4	37.598730 -112.850080
Glen Canyon N.R.A.	39	F4	38.255440 -110.180050
Golden Spike N.H.P.	31	E3	41.620482 -112.547471
Grand Staircase-Escalante Natl. Mon.	39	E4	37.420000 -111.550000
Natural Bridges Natl. Mon.	39	F4	37.608120 -109.966280
Rainbow Bridge Natl. Mon.	47	E1	37.110810 -110.406050
Zion Natl. Park-East Ent.	39	D4	37.235370 -112.864470
Zion Natl. Park-Main Ent.	39	D4	37.201970 -112.988380
State Park & Rec. Areas			
Anasazi S.P. Mus.	39	E3	37.922399 -111.425743
Antelope Island S.P.	31	E4	41.089290 -112.116490
Bear Lake (Rendezvous Beach) S.P.	31	F2	41.962200 -111.400320
Bear Lake S.P.	31	F2	41.965360 -111.399480
Camp Floyd S.P. Mus.	31	E4	40.258360 -112.097270
Coral Pink Sand Dunes S.P.	47	D1	37.036964 -112.731196
Dead Horse Point S.P.	40	A3	38.510220 -109.729460
Deer Creek S.P.	31	F4	40.452620 -111.477820
Edge of the Cedars S.P. Mus.	40	A4	37.629760 -109.491730
Escalante Petrified Forest S.P.	39	E4	37.783820 -111.630220
Fred Hayes S.P. at Starvation	32	A4	40.104100 -110.33090
Fremont Indian S.P. Mus.	39	D3	38.579537 -112.31477
Frontier Homestead S.P. Mus.	39	D4	37.688349 -113.06189
Goblin Valley S.P.	39	F3	38.580620 -110.71258
Goosenecks S.P.	40	A4	37.174730 -109.92695
Green River S.P.	39	F2	38.995500 -110.15691
Gunlock S.P.-North Ent.	38	C4	37.275970 -113.76878
Gunlock S.P.-South Ent.	38	C4	37.251490 -113.77282
Huntington S.P.	39	F2	39.315200 -110.97710
Hyrum Lake S.P.	31	E3	41.626220 -111.87217
Kodachrome Basin S.P.	39	E4	37.501670 -111.99361
Millsite S.P.	39	E2	39.099020 -111.18424
Otter Creek S.P.	39	E3	38.167430 -112.02157
Palisade S.P.	39	E2	39.195800 -111.69160
Piute S.P.	39	E3	38.322530 -112.20420
Quail Creek S.P.	39	D4	37.105000 -113.57660
Red Fleet S.P.	32	B4	40.553300 -109.51847
Rockport S.P.	31	F4	40.751890 -111.36741
Sand Hollow S.P.	46	C1	37.144830 -113.38213
Scofield S.P.	39	E1	39.708600 -110.92100
Snow Canyon S.P.-East Ent.	38	C4	37.212120 -113.63087
Snow Canyon S.P.-North Ent.	38	C4	37.256790 -113.63299
Snow Canyon S.P.-South Ent.	38	C4	37.183380 -113.64501
Steinaker S.P.-North Ent.	32	A4	40.534870 -109.52244
Steinaker S.P.-South Ent.	32	A4	40.504850 -109.52887
Territorial Statehouse S.P.	39	D2	38.985880 -112.35353
Wasatch Mtn. S.P.	31	F4	40.477770 -111.51999
Willard Bay S.P.-North Ent.	31	E3	41.418810 -112.05239
Willard Bay S.P.-South Ent.	31	E3	41.350610 -112.06906
Yuba S.P.	39	E2	39.381240 -112.02836

VERMONT

VERMONT	PAGE	GRID	LATITUDE LONGITUDE
National Park & Rec. Areas			
Marsh-Billings-Rockefeller N.H.P.	81	E3	43.635833 -72.538333
Moosalamoo Natl. Rec. Area	81	D3	43.879457 -73.098532
State Park & Rec. Areas			
Allis S.P.	81	E3	44.051150 -72.626440
Branbury S.P.	81	D3	43.904250 -73.065370
Burton Island S.P.	81	D1	44.779660 -73.180050
Camp Plymouth S.P.	81	E4	43.475810 -72.694987
D.A.R. S.P.	81	D3	44.058850 -73.409210
Emerald Lake S.P.	81	D4	43.283790 -73.002250
Half Moon S.P.	81	D3	43.699720 -73.223220
Kingsland Bay S.P.	81	D2	44.226230 -73.277660
Lake Saint Catherine S.P.	81	D4	43.483000 -73.202580
Little River S.P.	81	D2	44.388940 -72.768360
Molly Stark S.P.	94	C1	42.854920 -72.813790
North Hero S.P.	81	D1	44.908210 -73.235110
Ricker Pond S.P.	81	E2	44.251467 -72.247550
Stillwater S.P.	81	E2	44.280200 -72.275060
Townshend S.P.	81	E4	43.041920 -72.691600
Underhill S.P.	81	D2	44.528880 -72.843920
Woodford S.P.	94	C1	42.894450 -73.037790
Woods Island S.P.	81	D1	44.802500 -73.209283

VIRGINIA

VIRGINIA	PAGE	GRID	LATITUDE LONGITUDE
National Park & Rec. Areas			
Appomattox Court House N.H.P.	112	C1	37.377367 -78.795290
Booker T. Washington Natl. Mon.	112	B2	37.120500 -79.733340
Cedar Creek & Belle Grove N.H.P.	102	C2	39.023500 -78.289000
Colonial N.H.P.	114	A4	37.211390 -76.776730
Cumberland Gap N.H.P.-Vis. Ctr.	111	D3	36.602600 -83.695400
Fredericksburg & Spotsylvania Co. Bflds. Mem. N.M.P.	103	D4	38.254300 -77.451890
George Washington Birthplace Natl. Mon.	114	A2	38.192353 -76.927192
Manassas Natl. Bfld. Park	144	A3	38.806030 -77.572810
Mount Rogers N.R.A.	111	F2	36.811360 -81.420130
Shenandoah Natl. Park-Front Royal North Ent.	102	C3	38.903300 -78.192400
Shenandoah Natl. Park-Rockfish Gap South Ent	102	C3	38.033900 -78.858900
Shenandoah Natl. Park-Swift Run Gap Ent.	102	C3	38.359100 -78.546700
Shenandoah Natl. Park-Thornton Gap Ent.	102	C3	38.662300 -78.320600
State Park & Rec. Areas			
Bear Creek Lake S.P.	113	D1	37.532970 -78.274890
Belle Isle S.P.	114	B2	37.774526 -76.599222
Chippokes Plantation S.P.	114	A4	37.140400 -76.748590
Claytor Lake S.P.	112	A2	37.057620 -80.622140
Douthat S.P.	102	B4	37.914520 -79.796740
Fairy Stone S.P.	112	B2	36.791790 -80.117890
False Cape S.P.	115	F1	36.691370 -75.924410
First Landing S.P.	114	B4	36.915601 -76.057000
Grayson Highlands S.P.	111	F3	36.611920 -81.489900
Holliday Lake S.P.	113	D1	37.404610 -78.644920
Hungry Mother S.P.	111	F2	36.880860 -81.525750
James River S.P.	112	C1	37.540400 -78.839300
Kiptopeke S.P.	114	B4	37.169292 -75.982919
Lake Anna S.P.	103	D4	38.125850 -77.821690
Mason Neck S.P.	103	E3	38.640740 -77.194400
Natural Bridge S.P.	112	C1	37.633038 -79.543034
Natural Tunnel S.P.	111	E3	36.707520 -82.744090
New River Trail S.P.	112	A2	36.870180 -80.868550
Occoneechee S.P.	113	D3	36.633330 -78.525420
Pocahontas S.P.	113	E1	37.366240 -77.573870
Powhatan S.P.	113	D1	37.678066 -77.925997
Sailor's Creek Bfld. Hist. S.P.	113	D1	37.298470 -78.229470
Sky Meadows S.P.	103	D2	38.988703 -77.968913
Smith Mtn. Lake S.P.	112	B2	37.091110 -79.592110
Twin Lakes S.P.	113	D2	37.336900 -77.934100
Westmoreland S.P.	103	E4	38.158690 -76.870120
York River S.P.	113	F1	37.414190 -76.713650

WASHINGTON

WASHINGTON	PAGE	GRID	LATITUDE LONGITUDE
National Park & Rec. Areas			
Columbia River Gorge Natl. Scenic Area	21	D1	45.715322 -121.818667
Fort Vancouver N.H.S.	20	C1	45.626940 -122.656310
Hanford Reach Natl. Mon.	13	E4	46.483333 -119.533333
Lake Chelan N.R.A.	13	D2	48.309080 -120.657730
Lake Roosevelt N.R.A.	13	F2	47.972680 -118.970580
Lewis & Clark N.H.P.-Discovery Trail	12	B4	46.370033 -124.053503
Lewis & Clark N.H.P.-Dismal Nitch	20	B1	46.249033 -123.862903
Lewis & Clark N.H.P.-Sta. Camp	20	B1	46.263111 -123.932571
Manhattan Project N. H.P.	13	E4	46.316332 -119.301848
Mount Baker N.R.A.	12	C1	48.714167 -121.805900
Mount Rainier Natl. Park-Nisqually Ent.	12	C5	46.741400 -121.919040
Mount Rainier Natl. Park-Stevens Can. Ent.	12	C7	46.754730 -121.557010
Mount Rainier Natl. Park-White River Ent.	12	C8	46.902040 -121.554340
Mount Saint Helens Natl. Mon.	12	C4	46.277590 -122.218820
North Cascades Natl. Park-Golden West	13	D1	48.308200 -120.655000
North Cascades Natl. Park-Northern Cascades Vis. Ctr.	13	D1	48.666100 -121.264000
Olympic Natl. Park-Vis. Ctr.	12	B2	48.096700 -123.428000
Olympic Natl. Park-Vis. Ctr.-Hoh Rain Forest	12	B2	47.860700 -123.935000
Olympic Natl. Park-Vis. Ctr.-Hurricane Ridge	12	B2	47.969200 -123.498000
Ross Lake N.R.A.	13	D1	48.674250 -121.244730
San Juan Island N.H.P.	12	B2	48.534580 -123.016250
San Juan Islands Natl. Mon.	12	C2	48.531944,-123.029167
Whitman Mission N.H.S.	21	F1	46.040910 -118.468110
State Park & Rec. Areas			
Alta Lake S.P.	13	E2	48.031990 -119.934710
Anderson Lake S.P.	12	C2	48.014590 -122.810680
Belfair S.P.	12	C3	47.430630 -122.881400
Birch Bay S.P.	12	C1	48.903210 -122.757880
Bogachiel S.P.	12	A2	47.894790 -124.362820
Bridgeport S.P.	13	E2	48.012549 -119.618571
Brooks Mem. S.P.	21	D1	45.950590 -120.664200
Camano Island S.P.	12	C2	48.131680 -122.503240
Cape Disappointment S.P.	20	B1	46.294210 -124.053610
Columbia Hills S.P.	21	D1	45.643030 -121.106410
Crawford S.P.	14	A1	48.992070 -117.370370
Curlew Lake S.P.	13	F1	48.719280 -118.661740
Deception Pass S.P.	12	C2	48.390970 -122.646880
Dosewallips S.P.	12	C3	47.687570 -122.899860
Fields Spring S.P.	22	A1	46.087520 -117.173650
Flaming Geyser S.P.	12	C3	47.280230 -122.041870
Fort Casey S.P.	12	C2	48.159760 -122.672410
Fort Columbia S.P.	20	B1	46.256833 -123.923070
Fort Simcoe S.P.	13	D4	46.345340 -120.823460
Fort Townsend S.P.	12	C2	48.078260 -122.805690
Ginkgo Petrified Forest S.P.	13	E4	46.949010 -119.997490
Goldendale Observatory S.P.	21	D1	45.837090 -120.815890
Grayland Beach S.P.	12	B4	46.792382 -124.097802
Ike Kinswa S.P.	12	C4	46.555780 -122.536570
Jarrell Cove S.P.	12	B3	47.285940 -122.881080
Joseph Whidbey S.P.	12	C2	48.308370 -122.713170
Kitsap Mem. S.P.	12	C3	47.816580 -122.646840
Lake Chelan S.P.	13	D2	47.869430 -120.191110
Lake Easton S.P.	13	D3	47.249380 -121.190920
Lake Wenatchee S.P.	13	D3	47.816340 -120.729780
Larrabee S.P.	12	C2	48.650620 -122.489810
Lewis & Clark S.P.	12	C4	46.525850 -122.817910
Lewis & Clark Trail S.P.	13	F4	46.287600 -118.073340
Lincoln Rock S.P.	13	D3	47.535490 -120.282280
Millersylvania S.P.	12	B4	46.909610 -122.905950
Moran S.P.	12	C1	48.657700 -122.859630
Mount Spokane S.P.	14	B2	47.899290 -117.124350
Nolte S.P.	12	C3	47.267320 -121.943420
Ocean City S.P.	12	B4	47.038520 -124.158130
Pacific Beach S.P.	12	A3	47.205980 -124.202220
Pacific Pines S.P.	12	B4	46.507610 -124.049150
Palouse Falls S.P.	13	F4	46.664030 -118.228660
Peace Arch S.P.	12	C1	49.000980 -122.751580
Pearrygin Lake S.P.	13	E2	48.496720 -120.146950
Peshastin Pinnacles S.P.	13	D3	47.578810 -120.613860
Potholes S.P.	13	E4	46.970780 -119.351180
Potlatch S.P.	12	B3	47.363000 -123.158140
Rainbow Falls S.P.	12	B4	46.631010 -123.237350
Rockport S.P.	12	C2	48.487920 -121.601870
Sacajawea S.P.	21	F1	46.210140 -119.046050
Scenic Beach S.P.	12	C3	47.649250 -122.845470
Seaquest S.P.	12	C4	46.295880 -122.820860
Sequim Bay S.P.	12	B2	48.040750 -123.030920
Shine Tidelands S.P.	12	C2	47.867990 -122.638700
Steamboat Rock S.P.	13	E2	47.828650 -119.134340
Sun Lakes-Dry Falls S.P.	13	E3	47.596540 -119.387760
Triton Cove S.P.	12	B3	47.609112 -122.986526
Twenty-Five Mile Creek S.P.	13	D2	47.992520 -120.263610
Twin Harbors S.P.	12	B4	46.858850 -124.104210
Wallace Falls S.P.	12	C2	47.865610 -121.680050
Wanapum Rec Area	13	E4	46.924760 -119.991690
Westport Light S.P.	12	B4	46.891700 -124.111630

WEST VIRGINIA

WEST VIRGINIA	PAGE	GRID	LATITUDE LONGITUDE
National Park & Rec. Areas			
Bluestone Natl. Scenic River	112	A1	37.584300 -80.957900
Gauley River N.R.A.	101	F4	38.191800 -81.001920
Harpers Ferry N.H.P.	103	D2	39.318820 -77.759060
New River Gorge Natl. Park & Pres.	101	F4	37.875670 -81.077598
Spruce Knob Seneca Rocks N.R.A.	102	B3	38.681180 -79.544480
State Park & Rec. Areas			
Audra S.P.	102	A2	39.041110 -80.067500
Beartown S.P.	102	A4	38.051750 -80.275420
Blennerhassett Island Hist. S.P.	101	E2	39.273300 -81.644800
Bluestone S.P.	112	A1	37.623050 -80.934710
Cacapon Resort S.P.	102	C1	39.502980 -78.291330
Camp Creek S.P.	111	F1	37.508173 -81.132873
Carnifex Ferry Bfld. S.P.	101	F4	38.211290 -80.941850
Cass Scenic Railroad S.P.	102	A3	38.396520 -79.914280
Cedar Creek S.P.	101	F3	38.880780 -80.849420
Droop Mtn. Bfld. S.P.	102	A4	38.113200 -80.271670
Holly River S.P.	102	A3	38.653140 -80.382620
Little Beaver S.P.	112	A1	37.756570 -81.079780
Moncove Lake S.P.	112	B1	37.616950 -80.354730
Pinnacle Rock S.P.	111	F1	37.308190 -81.291430
Prickett's Fort S.P.	102	A1	39.514090 -80.099960
Tomlinson Run S.P.	91	F4	40.550660 -80.595950
Tygart Lake S.P.	102	A2	39.248160 -80.021060
Valley Falls S.P.	102	A2	39.392900 -80.070480
Watoga S.P.	102	A4	38.122510 -80.155660
Watters Smith Mem. S.P.	102	A2	39.174520 -80.414260

WISCONSIN

WISCONSIN	PAGE	GRID	LATITUDE LONGITUDE
National Park & Rec. Areas			
Apostle Islands Natl. Lakeshore	65	D4	46.812210 -90.820780
Saint Croix Natl. Scenic Riverway	67	E2	45.415700 -92.646270
State Park & Rec. Areas			
Amnicon Falls S.P.	64	C4	46.608210 -91.887850
Aztalan S.P.	74	B3	43.068310 -88.863750
Belmont Mound S.P.	74	A4	42.768611 -90.349444
Big Bay S.P.	65	D4	46.811030 -90.696960
Big Foot Beach S.P.	74	C4	42.567330 -88.436790
Blue Mound S.P.	74	A3	43.026990 -89.840740
Brunet Island S.P.	67	F3	45.176220 -91.161610
Buckhorn S.P.	74	A1	43.948280 -90.002130
Copper Culture S.P.	68	C4	44.887440 -87.897940
Copper Falls S.P.	65	D4	46.351710 -90.643670
Council Grounds S.P.	68	A3	45.184840 -89.734290
Devil's Lake S.P.	74	A2	43.429010 -89.734900
Governor Dodge S.P.	74	A3	43.019560 -90.141950
Governor Thompson S.P.	68	C3	45.326309 -88.219205
Harrington Beach S.P.	75	D2	43.499430 -87.811890
Hartman Creek S.P.	74	B1	44.318070 -89.194320
High Cliff S.P.	74	C1	44.166680 -88.291760
Interstate S.P.	67	D3	45.396410 -92.636580
Kinnickinnic S.P.	67	D4	44.837280 -92.733190
Kohler-Andrae S.P.	75	D2	43.672740 -87.719320
Lake Kegonsa S.P.	74	B3	42.978005 -89.230300
Lake Wissota S.P.	67	F4	44.980950 -91.313740
Merrick S.P.	73	E1	44.152740 -91.744120
Mill Bluff S.P.	74	A1	43.961610 -90.317980
Mirror Lake S.P.	74	A2	43.568770 -89.834930
Natural Bridge S.P.	74	A2	43.344930 -89.928290
Nelson Dewey S.P.	73	F4	42.743740 -91.037860
New Glarus Woods S.P.	74	B4	42.786830 -89.631980
Newport S.P.	69	D3	45.241470 -86.998830
Pattison S.P.	64	C4	46.535290 -92.121410
Peninsula S.P.	69	D3	45.133080 -87.213280
Perrot S.P.	73	F1	44.016350 -91.479670
Potawatomi S.P.	69	D4	44.849990 -87.407640
Rib Mtn. S.P.	68	B4	44.915800 -89.669360
Roche-A-Cri S.P.	74	A1	43.996120 -89.812370
Rock Island S.P.	69	E3	45.398990 -86.855970
Rocky Arbor S.P.	74	A2	43.647890 -89.808240
Straight Lake S.P.	67	E2	45.597399 -92.406609
Tower Hill S.P.	74	A3	43.147090 -90.043750
Whitefish Dunes S.P.	69	D4	44.928910 -87.182150
Wildcat Mtn. S.P.	74	A2	43.688870 -90.566800
Willow River S.P.	67	D3	45.017610 -92.672610
Wyalusing S.P.	73	F3	42.978770 -91.118560
Yellowstone Lake S.P.	74	A4	42.777360 -89.993540

WYOMING

WYOMING	PAGE	GRID	LATITUDE LONGITUDE
National Park & Rec. Areas			
Devils Tower Natl. Mon.	25	E3	44.586870 -104.706710
Flaming Gorge N.R.A.	32	A3	41.254860 -109.611400
Fort Laramie N.H.S.	33	E2	42.202530 -104.558590
Fossil Butte Natl. Mon.	31	F2	41.855370 -110.782340
Grand Teton Natl. Park-Granite Canyon Ent.	23	F4	43.597990 -110.801640
Grand Teton Natl. Park-Moose Ent.	23	F4	43.655860 -110.718350
Grand Teton Natl. Park-Moran Ent.	23	F4	43.843640 -110.511950
John D. Rockefeller Jr. Mem. Parkway	24	A3	44.108800 -110.685508
Medicine Wheel Natl. Hist. Landmark	24	C2	44.826200 -107.921717
Yellowstone Natl. Park-East Ent.	23	F3	44.489540 -110.001560
Yellowstone Natl. Park-North East Ent.	23	F3	45.006120 -109.991550
Yellowstone Natl. Park-North Ent.	23	F3	45.030110 -110.705460
Yellowstone Natl. Park-South Ent.	23	F3	44.134730 -110.666170
Yellowstone Natl. Park-West Ent.	23	F3	44.658720 -111.098970
State Park & Rec. Areas			
Bear River S.P.	31	F3	41.267257 -110.938030
Boysen S.P.	32	C1	43.270160 -108.115260
Buffalo Bill S.P.	24	B3	44.505020 -109.249540
Curt Gowdy S.P.	33	E3	41.175380 -105.243640
Edness K. Wilkins S.P.	33	D1	42.857220 -106.177370
Glendo S.P.	33	E1	42.476060 -104.998910
Guernsey S.P.	33	E2	42.287400 -104.763460
Hawk Springs S.R.A.	33	F2	41.712959 -104.199482
Hot Springs S.P.	24	C4	43.653980 -108.201790
Keyhole S.P.	25	E3	44.356490 -104.825810
Seminoe S.P.	33	D2	42.150350 -106.905870
Sinks Canyon S.P.	32	B1	42.752600 -108.804770

CANADA

ALBERTA

ALBERTA	PAGE	GRID	LATITUDE LONGITUDE
National Park & Rec. Areas			
Banff Natl. Park-Banff Vis. Ctr.	164	B2	51.177400 -115.570900
Banff Natl. Park-Lake Louise Vis. Ctr.	164	B2	51.425200 -116.178400
Banff Park Mus. N.H.S.	164	B3	51.174300 -115.571100
Bar U Ranch N.H.S.	164	C3	50.420300 -114.244400
Cave and Basin N.H.S.	164	B3	51.168300 -115.591400
Elk Island Natl. Park	159	D4	53.572500 -112.841900
Jasper Natl. Park-Icefield Center	164	A1	52.233500 -117.234800
Jasper Natl. Park-Jasper Information Center	164	A1	52.877300 -118.080900
Rocky Mtn. House N.H.S.	164	C2	52.377590 -114.931237
Waterton Lakes Natl. Park-Waterton Vis. Ctr.	164	C4	49.051400 -113.906300
Wood Buffalo Natl. Park-Fort Chipewyan Vis. Ctr.	155	F2	48.714100 -111.154300
Provincial Park & Rec. Areas			
Aspen Beach Prov. Park	164	C2	52.454530 -113.975750
Beauvais Lake Prov. Park	164	C4	49.409500 -114.117000
Big Hill Springs Prov. Park	164	C3	51.251670 -114.386940
Big Knife Prov. Park	165	D2	52.489720 -112.210560
Birch Mts. Wildland Prov. Park	159	D1	57.509400 -112.957000
Bluerock Wildland Prov. Park	164	C3	50.642300 -114.654000
Bob Creek Wildland Prov. Park	164	C4	49.973700 -114.286000
Bow Valley Prov. Park	164	C3	51.040400 -115.077000
Bow Valley Wildland Prov. Park	164	B3	51.032600 -115.259000
Brown-Lowery Prov. Park	164	C3	50.813900 -114.430600
Calling Lake Prov. Park	159	D3	55.179720 -113.272500
Caribou Mts. Wildland Prov. Park	155	F3	59.205600 -114.897000
Carson-Pegasus Prov. Park	158	C3	54.295800 -115.645000
Castle Wildland Prov. Park	164	C4	49.306456 -114.299287
Chain Lakes Prov. Park	164	C3	50.200000 -114.183330
Chinchaga Wildland Prov. Park	158	B1	57.163400 -119.582000
Cold Lake Prov. Park	159	E3	54.602400 -110.072000
Cold Lake Prov. Park-North Shore	159	E3	54.644800 -110.103600
Crimson Lake Prov. Park	164	C2	52.466900 -115.048000
Cross Lake Prov. Park	159	D3	54.649300 -113.791000
Crow Lake Prov. Park	159	D2	55.800456 -112.152014
Dillberry Lake Prov. Park	165	E1	52.570200 -110.030000
Dinosaur Prov. Park	165	D3	50.770100 -111.480000
Don Getty Wildland Prov. Park	164	B2	50.893000 -114.993000
Dry Island Buffalo Jump Prov. Park	164	C2	51.929500 -112.975000
Dunvegan Prov. Park	158	B2	55.923600 -118.594400
Dunvegan West Wildland Prov. Park	158	B2	56.088900 -119.297000
Elbow Sheep Wildland Prov. Park	164	C3	50.703500 -114.939000
Fort Assiniboine Sandhills Wildland Prov. Park	158	C3	54.387100 -114.608000
Garner Lake Prov. Park	159	D3	54.183420 -111.741000
Gipsy Lake Wildland Prov. Park	159	E2	56.493500 -110.386000
Gooseberry Lake Prov. Park	165	D2	52.116940 -110.759170
Grand Rapids Wildland Prov. Park	159	D1	56.484200 -112.343000
Greene Valley Prov. Park	158	B2	56.140900 -117.242000
Gregoire Lake Prov. Park	159	E1	56.485000 -111.182780
Grizzly Ridge Wildland Prov. Park	158	C3	55.137700 -115.049000
Hay-Zama Lakes Wildland Prov. Park	155	F3	58.774100 -119.016000
Hilliard's Bay Prov. Park	158	C2	55.502900 -116.001000
Hubert Lake Wildland Prov. Park	158	C3	54.554100 -114.244000
Kakwa Wildland Prov. Park	158	A3	54.034600 -119.810000
Kinbrook Island Prov. Park	165	D3	50.437180 -111.910595
La Biche River Wildland Prov. Park	159	D3	54.987000 -112.626000
Lakeland Prov. Park	159	E3	54.759300 -111.557000
Lakeland Prov. Rec. Area	159	E3	54.721800 -111.398000
Lesser Slave Lake Prov. Park	158	C2	55.448000 -114.817000
Lesser Slave Lake Wildland Prov. Park	158	C2	55.497700 -115.567000
Little Bow Prov. Park	164	C3	50.227930 -112.926590
Little Fish Lake Prov. Park	165	D2	51.374246 -112.200944
Long Lake Prov. Park	159	D3	54.439986 -112.763465
Marguerite River Wildland Prov. Park	159	E1	57.638400 -110.266000
Midland Prov. Park	165	D2	51.478295 -112.771085
Miquelon Lake Prov. Park	159	D4	53.246900 -112.874000
Moonshine Lake Prov. Park	158	B2	55.883800 -119.216000
Moose Lake Prov. Park	159	E3	54.272986 -110.931143
Notikewin Prov. Park	158	C1	57.218300 -117.148000
Obed Lake Prov. Park	158	B4	53.558200 -117.101000
O'Brien Prov. Park	158	B3	55.065242 -118.822285
Otter-Orloff Lakes Wildland Prov. Park	159	D2	55.364200 -113.551000
Park Lake Prov. Park	164	C4	49.806621 -112.924681
Peace River Wildland Prov. Park	158	B2	55.983200 -117.765000
Pembina River Prov. Park	158	C4	53.611859 -114.985313
Peter Lougheed Prov. Park	164	B3	50.684100 -115.184000
Pigeon Lake Prov. Park	164	C1	53.029547 -114.150507
Police Outpost Prov. Park	164	C4	49.004503 -113.464980
Queen Elizabeth Wildlands Prov. Park	158	B2	56.219120 -117.693540
Red Lodge Prov. Park	164	C2	51.947917 -114.243862
Rochon Sands Prov. Park	165	D2	52.461755 -112.892373
Rock Lake Solomon Creek Wildland Prov. Park	158	B4	53.413700 -118.118000
Saskatoon Island Prov. Park	158	B2	55.205201 -119.085401
Sheep River Prov. Park	164	C3	50.647300 -114.660000
Sir Winston Churchill Prov. Park	159	D3	54.832050 -111.976109
Spray Valley Prov. Park	164	B3	50.888700 -115.293000
Stony Mtn. Wildland Prov. Park	159	E2	56.211500 -111.244000
Sundance Prov. Park	158	B4	53.668700 -116.926000
Sylvan Lake Prov. Park	164	C2	52.315760 -114.092272
Thunder Lake Prov. Park	158	C3	54.131941 -114.725882
Tillebrook Prov. Park	165	D3	50.538593 -111.812268
Vermilion Prov. Park	159	E4	53.367679 -110.909771
Wabamun Lake Prov. Park	158	C4	53.565029 -114.441575
Whitehorse Wildland Prov. Park	164	B1	52.957900 -117.395000
Whitemud Falls Wildland Prov. Park	159	E1	56.703400 -110.084000
Whitney Lakes Prov. Park	159	E4	53.847100 -110.537000
William A. Switzer Prov. Park	158	B4	53.492000 -117.804000
Williamson Prov. Park	158	B3	55.081821 -117.560174
Willow Creek Prov. Park	164	C3	50.118067 -113.776021
Winagami Lake Prov. Park	158	C2	55.627500 -116.738000
Winagami Wildland Prov. Park	158	C2	55.611900 -116.635000
Woolford Prov. Park	164	C4	49.178498 -113.190438
Writing-On-Stone Prov. Park	165	D4	49.061400 -111.639000
Wyndham-Carseland Prov. Park	164	C3	50.827750 -113.436542
Young's Point Prov. Park	158	B3	55.148000 -117.572000

BRITISH COLUMBIA

BRITISH COLUMBIA	PAGE	GRID	LATITUDE LONGITUDE
National Park & Rec. Areas			
Chilkoot Trail N.H.S.	155	D3	59.756667 -134.960833
Fort Langley N.H.S.	163	D3	49.168056 -122.569167
Fort McLeod N.H.S.	157	E1	54.992384 -123.039629
Fort Saint James N.H.S.	157	D2	54.440278 -124.255556
Gitwangak Battle Hill N.H.S.	156	C1	55.119444 -128.018056
Glacier Natl. Park-Eastern Welcome Sta.	164	A2	51.511700 -117.442000
Glacier Natl. Park-Rogers Pass Discovery Center	164	A2	51.300600 -117.521500
Gulf Islands Natl. Park Res.	163	D4	48.769400 -123.210000
Gulf of Georgia Cannery N.H.S.	163	D3	49.124722 -123.199722
Gwaii Haanas Natl. Park Res. & Haida Heritage Site	156	A3	52.349722 -131.433056
Kootenay Natl. Park-Radium Hot Springs Vis. Ctr.	164	B3	50.619500 -116.069800
Kootenay Natl. Park-Vermilion Crossing Vis. Ctr.	164	B3	51.000000 -115.966000
Mount Revelstoke Natl. Park-Western Welcome Sta.	164	A2	51.042000 -117.983900
Pacific Rim Natl. Park Res.-Broken Group Islands	162	B3	48.891100 -125.300800
Pacific Rim Natl. Park Res.-Pacific Rim Vis. Ctr.	162	B3	48.992000 -125.587200
Pacific Rim Natl. Park Res.-West Coast Trail	162	C4	48.704800 -124.866100
Pacific Rim Natl. Park Res.-Wickaninnish Interpretive Center	162	B3	49.012700 -125.674200
Yoho Natl. Park-Field Vis. Ctr.	164	B2	51.397800 -116.492000
Provincial Park & Rec. Areas			
Akamina-Kishinena Prov. Park	164	C4	49.032700 -114.178000
Alexandra Bridge Prov. Park	163	E2	49.700000 -121.399722
Alice Lake Prov. Park	163	D2	49.783056 -123.116667
Allison Lake Prov. Park	163	F2	49.683056 -120.599722
Anstey Hunakwa Prov. Park	164	A2	51.140600 -118.924300
Arctic Pacific Lakes Prov. Park	157	E2	54.384400 -121.553000
Arrow Lakes Prov. Park	164	A3	49.883056 -118.065667
Arrowstone Prov. Park	163	E1	50.879900 -121.273000
Atlin Prov. Park	155	E3	59.165400 -133.914000
Babine Lake-Pendleton Bay Marine Prov. Park	157	D2	54.533000 -125.724800
Babine Lake-Smithers Landing Marine Prov. Park	156	C1	55.098400 -126.600000
Babine Mountains Prov. Park	156	C1	54.913100 -126.928000
Babine River Corridor Prov. Park	156	C1	55.577400 -127.032000
Bear Creek Prov. Park	163	F2	49.930556 -119.520556
Bearhole Lake Prov. Park	158	A3	55.043400 -120.568000
Beatton Prov. Park	158	A1	56.333056 -120.933056
Beaumont Prov. Park	157	D2	54.050000 -124.616667
Beaver Creek Prov. Park	164	A4	49.066667 -117.600000
Beaver Valley Prov. Park	157	E3	52.523583 -122.081938
Big Bar Lake Prov. Park	157	E4	51.316667 -121.816667
Big Bunsby Marine Prov. Park	162	A2	50.120800 -127.504200
Big Creek Prov. Park	157	E4	51.301500 -123.158000
Bijoux Falls Prov. Park	157	E1	55.300000 -122.666667
Birkenhead Lake Prov. Park	163	D1	50.577900 -122.737000
Bishop River Prov. Park	162	C1	50.912500 -124.038000
Blanket Creek Prov. Park	164	A3	50.833056 -118.083056
Bligh Island Marine Prov. Park	162	A2	49.633300 -126.553000
Bowron Lake Prov. Park	157	F3	53.174100 -121.012000
Boya Lake Prov. Park	155	E3	59.380500 -129.090000
Brandywine Falls Prov. Park	163	D2	50.033056 -123.116667
Bridal Veil Falls Prov. Park	163	E3	49.183056 -121.733056
Bridge Lake Prov. Park	157	F4	51.483056 -120.700000
Bromley Rock Prov. Park	163	F3	49.416667 -120.258056
Brooks Peninsula Prov. Park	162	A2	50.180300 -127.657000
Broughton Archipelago Marine Prov. Park	162	A1	50.687100 -126.663000
Bugaboo Prov. Park	164	B3	50.794700 -116.808000
Callaghan Lake Prov. Park	163	D2	50.206000 -123.189000
Bull Canyon Prov. Park	157	E4	52.091667 -123.374722
Canal Flats Prov. Park	164	B3	50.183056 -115.816667
Canim Beach Prov. Park	157	F4	51.816667 -120.872667
Cape Scott Prov. Park	162	A1	50.765900 -128.246000
Cariboo Mts. Prov. Park	157	F3	52.852600 -120.538000
Cariboo River Prov. Park	157	F3	52.873600 -121.222000
Carmanah Walbran Prov. Park	162	C4	48.654500 -124.628000
Carp Lake Prov. Park	157	E2	54.769400 -123.387000
Catala Island Marine Prov. Park	162	A2	49.835833 -127.054167
Cathedral Prov. Park	163	F3	49.069800 -120.174000
Champion Lakes Prov. Park	164	A4	49.184100 -117.624000
Charlie Lake Prov. Park	158	A1	56.316667 -120.999722
Chasm Prov. Park	157	F4	51.178900 -121.438000
Chilliwack Lake Prov. Park	163	E3	49.072200 -121.436000
Clayoquot Arm Prov. Park	162	B3	49.172800 -125.560000
Clayoquot Plateau Prov. Park	162	B3	49.225100 -125.428000
Clendinning Prov. Park	162	C1	50.429700 -123.733000
Codville Lagoon Marine Prov. Park	156	C4	52.060833 -127.855556
Conkle Lake Prov. Park	164	A4	49.166667 -119.100000
Coquihalla Canyon Prov. Park	163	E3	49.371944 -121.366667
Cormorant Channel Marine Prov. Park	162	A1	50.593500 -126.850900
Cowichan River Prov. Park	162	C4	48.780800 -123.920000
Crooked River Prov. Park	157	E2	54.466667 -122.666667
Crowsnest Prov. Park	164	C4	49.649722 -114.699722
Cummins Lakes Prov. Park	164	A2	52.104100 -118.066000
Cypress Prov. Park	163	D3	49.425800 -123.209000
Dahl Lake Prov. Park	157	E2	53.769900 -123.293000
Desolation Sound Marine Prov. Park	162	C2	50.101100 -124.710000
Diana Lake Prov. Park	156	B2	54.216667 -130.166667
Downing Prov. Park	163	E1	51.000000 -121.783056
Dry Gulch Prov. Park	164	B3	50.583056 -116.033056
Duffey Lake Prov. Park	163	D1	50.407500 -122.337000
Dune Za Keyih Prov. Park	155	E3	58.323000 -126.355000
Echo Lake Prov. Park	164	A3	50.199722 -118.700000
Edge Hills Prov. Park	163	E1	51.035900 -121.871000
Elk Falls Prov. Park	162	B2	50.041000 -125.324000
Elk Lakes Prov. Park	164	C3	50.480800 -115.088000
Ellison Prov. Park	164	A3	50.173333 -119.433056
Emory Creek Prov. Park	163	E3	49.516667 -121.416667
Eneas Lakes Prov. Park	163	F2	49.752400 -119.936000
Entiako Prov. Park	157	D3	53.221500 -125.443000
Epper Passage Prov. Park	162	B3	49.219167 -125.949722
Eskers Prov. Park	157	E2	54.081300 -123.205000
Ethel F. Wilson Mem. Prov. Park	157	D2	54.416667 -125.683056
Fillongley Prov. Park	162	C3	49.534100 -124.755200
Finger-Tatuk Prov. Park	157	D2	53.515600 -124.226000
Flat Lake Prov. Park	157	F4	51.499400 -121.52100…
Flores Island Prov. Park	162	B3	49.291000 -126.173000
Francois Lake Prov. Park	157	D2	53.966667 -125.166667
French Beach Prov. Park	162	C4	48.383056 -123.93305…
Garibaldi Prov. Park	163	D2	49.943200 -122.75100…
Gibson Marine Prov. Park	162	B3	49.266667 -126.066667
Gitnadoiks River Prov. Park	156	B2	54.161700 -129.16200…
Gladstone Prov. Park	164	A4	49.268900 -118.26900…
God's Pocket Marine Prov. Park	162	A1	50.837200 -127.56200…
Goldpan Prov. Park	163	E2	50.350000 -121.38305…
Gordon Bay Prov. Park	162	C4	48.833056 -124.19972…
Graham-Laurier Prov. Park	155	F4	56.594900 -123.46600…
Graystokes Prov. Park	164	A3	49.986200 -118.85000…
Green Inlet Marine Prov. Park	156	C3	52.918167 -128.48594…
Green Lake Prov. Park	157	F4	51.400000 -121.19972…
Hamber Prov. Park	164	A2	52.380300 -117.88200…
Harmony Islands Marine Prov. Park	162	C2	49.862222 -124.01222…
Ha'thayim Marine Prov. Park	162	C2	50.169400 -124.95500…
Heather-Dina Lakes Prov. Park	157	E1	55.508300 -123.28500…
Height of the Rockies Prov. Park	164	B3	50.488900 -115.22800…
Herald Prov. Park	164	A3	50.788056 -119.20100…
Hesquiat Lake Prov. Park	162	B3	49.500000 -126.38583…
Hitchie Creek Prov. Park	162	C4	48.795556 -124.73750…
Horne Lake Caves Prov. Park	162	C3	49.344167 -124.75555…
Horsefly Lake Prov. Park	157	F3	52.383056 -121.30000…
Inkaneep Prov. Park	163	F3	49.233056 -119.53305…
Inland Lake Prov. Park	162	C2	49.953800 -124.48100…
Itcha Ilgachuz Prov. Park	157	D3	52.711500 -124.97400…
Jackman Flats Prov. Park	164	A1	52.950000 -119.41666…
Jedediah Island Marine Prov. Park	162	C3	49.500000 -124.19972…
Jewel Lake Prov. Park	164	A4	49.183056 -118.59972…
Jimsmith Lake Prov. Park	164	B4	49.483056 -115.83305…
Joffre Lakes Prov. Park	163	D2	50.344100 -122.47700…
Johnstone Creek Prov. Park	164	A4	49.050000 -119.04972…
Juan De Fuca Prov. Park	162	C4	48.489800 -124.29000…
Junction Sheep Range Prov. Park	157	E4	51.801000 -122.43500…
Juniper Beach Prov. Park	163	E1	50.785833 -121.08305…
Kakwa Prov. Park & Protected Area	158	A3	54.057200 -120.29600…
Kekuli Bay Prov. Park	164	A3	50.183056 -119.34027…
Kentucky-Alleyne Prov. Park	163	F2	49.916667 -120.56666…
Kianuko Prov. Park	164	B4	49.421600 -116.45600…
Kikomun Creek Prov. Park	164	B4	49.233056 -115.25000…
Kilby Prov. Park	163	E3	49.237500 -121.96083…
Kinaskan Lake Prov. Park	155	E4	57.496100 -130.23400…
Kiskatinaw Prov. Park	158	A2	55.950000 -120.56666…
Kleanza Creek Prov. Park	156	C2	54.599722 -128.39972…
Klewnuggit Inlet Marine Prov. Park	156	B2	53.688500 -129.69700…
Kluskoil Lake Prov. Park	157	D3	53.202900 -123.89200…
Kokanee Creek Prov. Park	164	B4	49.605722 -117.13305…
Kokanee Glacier Prov. Park	164	B4	49.781800 -117.13600…
Kootenay Lake Prov. Park	164	B3	50.085000 -116.93118…

Kwadacha Wilderness Prov. Park	155	E3	57.820400 -125.058000
Lac Le Jeune Prov. Park	163	F1	50.483056 -120.483056
Lakelse Lake Prov. Park	156	C2	54.398900 -128.533000
Lawn Point Prov. Park	162	A1	50.333056 -127.966667
Lockhart Beach Prov. Park	164	B4	49.516667 -116.783056
Lockhart Creek Prov. Park	164	B4	49.497300 -116.705000
Loveland Bay Prov. Park	162	B2	50.049722 -125.450000
Lowe Inlet Marine Prov. Park	156	B2	53.555556 -129.580278
MacMillan Prov. Park	162	C3	49.283056 -124.666667
Main Lake Prov. Park	162	B2	50.210000 -125.215000
Mansons Landing Prov. Park	162	C2	50.121500 -124.928300
Maquinna Marine Prov. Park	162	B3	49.390500 -126.342000
Marble River Prov. Park	162	A1	50.544300 -127.526000
Martha Creek Prov. Park	164	A3	51.141667 -118.198122
McConnell Lake Prov. Park	163	F1	50.521944 -120.456667
McDonald Creek Prov. Park	164	A3	50.131056 -117.813667
Mehatl Creek Prov. Park	163	E2	50.036100 -122.054000
Moberly Lake Prov. Park	158	A2	55.800000 -121.700000
Momich Lakes Prov. Park	164	A2	51.327200 -119.353000
Monck Prov. Park	163	F2	50.178667 -120.533056
Moose Valley Prov. Park	157	E4	51.649800 -121.648000
Morton Lake Prov. Park	162	B2	50.116667 -125.483056
Mount Assiniboine Prov. Park	164	B3	50.937400 -115.761000
Mount Blanchet Prov. Park	157	D1	55.275500 -125.863000
Mount Fernie Prov. Park	164	C4	49.483056 -115.099722
Mount Pope Prov. Park	157	D2	54.490700 -124.331000
Mount Robson Prov. Park	164	A1	52.927000 -118.831000
Mount Seymour Prov. Park	163	D3	49.392400 -122.926000
Mount Terry Fox Prov. Park	164	A1	52.940800 -119.254000
Moyie Lake Prov. Park	164	B4	49.373333 -115.837222
Myra-Bellevue Prov. Park	164	A4	49.752100 -119.374000
Nahatlatch Prov. Park	163	E2	49.980200 -121.780000
Naikoon Prov. Park	156	A2	53.863400 -131.889000
Nairn Falls Prov. Park	163	D2	50.283056 -122.833056
Nancy Greene Prov. Park	164	A4	49.250000 -117.933056
Nickel Plate Prov. Park	163	F3	49.399722 -119.949722
Nicolum River Prov. Park	163	E3	49.366667 -121.341667
Nimpkish Lake Prov. Park	162	A2	50.337700 -127.005000
Niskonlith Lake Prov. Park	163	F1	50.795556 -119.777778
Norbury Lake Prov. Park	164	B4	49.533056 -115.483056
Nuchatlitz Prov. Park	162	A2	49.015700 126.981000
Octopus Island Marine Prov. Park	162	B2	50.278400 -125.242100
Okanagan Lake Prov. Park	163	F2	49.683056 -119.719867
Okanagan Mtn. Prov. Park	163	F2	49.724600 -119.629000
Okeover Arm Prov. Park	162	C2	49.999722 -124.726667
One Island Lake Prov. Park	158	A2	55.300000 -120.266667
Paarens Beach Prov. Park	157	D2	54.416667 -124.399722
Paul Lake Prov. Park	163	F1	50.741667 -120.120556
Pinecone Burke Prov. Park	163	D3	49.526200 -122.721000
Porpoise Bay Prov. Park	162	C3	49.516667 -123.749722
Porteau Cove Prov. Park	163	D3	49.549722 -123.233056
Premier Lake Prov. Park	164	B4	49.900000 -115.650000
Princess Louisa Marine Prov. Park	162	C2	50.203722 -123.766667
Ptarmigan Creek Prov. Park	157	F2	53.487600 -120.880000
Puntchesakut Lake Prov. Park	157	E3	52.983056 -122.933056
Purden Lake Prov. Park	157	E2	53.928000 -121.912000
Quatsino Prov. Park	162	A1	50.491667 -127.816667
Rearguard Falls Prov. Park	157	F3	52.973333 -119.366667
Redfern-Keily Prov. Park	155	F3	57.405600 -123.878000
Roberts Creek Prov. Park	162	C3	49.433056 -123.666667
Rolley Lake Prov. Park	163	D3	49.250000 -122.400000
Rosebery Prov. Park	164	B3	50.033056 -117.400000
Rubyrock Lake Prov. Park	157	D2	54.677100 -125.348000
Ruckle Prov. Park	163	D4	48.766667 -123.383056
Rugged Point Marine Prov. Park	162	A2	49.963889 -127.238889
Saint Mary's Alpine Prov. Park	164	B4	49.877000 -116.348000
Sandy Island Marine Prov. Park	162	C3	49.616667 -124.849722
Schoen Lake Prov. Park	162	B2	50.176500 -126.245000
Schoolhouse Lake Prov. Park	157	F4	51.883600 -120.993000
Seeley Lake Prov. Park	156	C1	55.199722 -127.683056
Seven Sisters Prov. Park	156	C1	54.946900 -128.150000
Silver Beach Prov. Park	164	A2	51.240278 -118.955556
Silver Lake Prov. Park	163	E3	49.316667 -121.399722
Silver Star Prov. Park	164	A3	50.376900 -119.082000
Simson Prov. Park	162	C3	49.479700 -123.962900
Skihist Prov. Park	163	E2	50.249722 -121.500000
Skookumchuck Narrows Prov. Park	162	C2	49.744700 -123.915500
Smelt Bay Prov. Park	162	C2	50.033056 -124.983056
Sowchea Bay Prov. Park	157	D2	54.419167 -124.448333
Sproat Lake Prov. Park	162	C3	49.300000 -124.916667
Squitty Bay Prov. Park	162	C3	49.454167 -124.166667
Stagleap Prov. Park	164	B4	49.058700 -117.048000
Steelhead Prov. Park	163	E1	50.752778 -120.868056
Stemwinder Prov. Park	163	F3	49.366667 -120.133056
Stone Mtn. Prov. Park	155	E3	58.588600 -124.757000
Strathcona Prov. Park	162	B2	49.629300 -125.710000
Stuart Lake Marine Prov. Park	157	D2	54.650000 -125.000000
Sugarbowl Prov. Park	157	E2	53.801200 -121.589000
Sukunka Falls Prov. Park	157	E1	55.316667 -121.700000
Sulphur Passage Prov. Park	162	B3	49.412000 -126.094000
Summit Lake Prov. Park	164	A3	50.150000 -117.666667
Surge Narrows Prov. Park	162	B2	50.233056 -125.149722
Sutherland River Prov. Park	157	D2	54.338300 -124.818000
Sydney Inlet Prov. Park	162	B3	49.480000 -126.283000
Syringa Prov. Park	164	A4	49.378000 -117.906000
Tahsish-Kwois Prov. Park	162	A2	50.189100 -127.161000
Tatlatui Prov. Park	155	E4	56.996200 -127.386000
Tatshenshini-Alsek Prov. Park	155	D3	59.595900 -137.443000
Taylor Arm Prov. Park	162	B3	49.283056 -125.049722
Ten Mile Lake Prov. Park	157	E3	53.066667 -122.450000
Thurston Bay Marine Prov. Park	162	B2	50.383056 -125.316667
Ts'il-os Prov. Park	157	D4	51.191700 -123.971000
Tudyah Lake Prov. Park	157	E1	55.066667 -123.033056
Tunkwa Prov. Park	163	E1	50.615200 -120.887000
Tyhee Lake Prov. Park	156	C2	54.700000 -127.033056
Union Passage Marine Prov. Park	156	B3	53.410900 -129.436000
Upper Adams River Prov. Park	164	A2	51.682700 -119.228000
Valhalla Prov. Park	164	A4	49.873700 -117.567000
Vargas Island Prov. Park	162	B3	49.174000 -126.031000
Vaseux Lake Prov. Park	164	A4	49.268200 -119.474000
Walsh Cove Prov. Park	162	C2	50.268056 -124.800000
Wasa Lake Prov. Park	164	B4	49.793056 -115.738056
West Arm Prov. Park	164	B4	49.507000 -117.118000
West Lake Prov. Park	157	E2	53.733056 -122.866667
Whiskers Point Prov. Park	157	E1	54.900000 -122.933056
White Pelican Prov. Park	157	E3	52.284000 -123.031000
Whiteswan Lake Prov. Park	164	B3	50.145300 -115.487000
Woss Lake Prov. Park	162	A2	50.060400 -126.626000
Yahk Provincial Park	164	B4	49.083056 -116.083056
Yard Creek Prov. Park	164	A3	50.899722 -118.799722

MANITOBA	PAGE	GRID	LATITUDE LONGITUDE
National Park & Rec. Areas			
Lower Fort Garry N.H.S.	167	E3	50.136850 -96.940569
Riding Mtn. Natl. Park-Deep Lake Ranger Sta.	167	D3	50.860300 -100.836600
Riding Mtn. Natl. Park-Lake Audy Ranger Sta.	167	D3	50.712900 -100.230600
Riding Mtn. Natl. Park-McKinnon Creek Ranger Sta.	167	D3	50.787100 -99.579500
Riding Mtn. Natl. Park-Moon Lake Ranger Sta.	167	D3	50.995900 -100.067200
Riding Mtn. Natl. Park-South Lake Ranger Sta.	167	D3	50.655200 -100.061600
Riding Mtn. Natl. Park-Sugarloaf Ranger Sta.	167	D3	50.985300 -100.742100
Riding Mtn. Natl. Park-Whirlpool Ranger Sta.	167	D3	50.683300 -99.553500
Provincial Park & Rec. Areas			
Asessippi Prov. Park	166	C3	50.966400 -101.379700
Atikaki Prov. Wilderness Park	167	F2	51.532200 -95.547000
Bakers Narrows Prov. Park	161	D3	54.671100 -101.675000
Beaudry Prov. Park	167	E4	49.853900 -97.473300
Bell Lake Prov. Park	166	C1	52.541700 -101.241400
Birds Hill Prov. Park	167	E3	50.028800 -96.893200
Camp Morton Prov. Park	167	E3	50.710000 -96.990300
Clearwater Lake Prov. Park	161	D3	54.096200 -101.162000
Criddle–Vane Homestead Prov. Park	167	D4	49.707600 -99.596600
Duck Mtn. Prov. Park	167	D2	51.715600 -101.112000
Elk Island Prov. Park	167	E3	50.758300 -96.536500
Grand Beach Prov. Park	167	E3	50.567900 -96.554900
Grass River Prov. Park	161	D3	54.655500 -101.092000
Hecla–Grindstone Prov. Park	167	E2	51.198300 -96.660200
Hnausa Beach Prov. Park	167	E3	50.900300 -96.992200
Kettle Stones Prov. Park	167	D2	52.359200 -100.595300
Lake Saint George Prov. Park	167	E2	51.719703 -97.406772
Lundar Beach Prov. Park	167	E3	50.724000 -98.273000
Manipogo Prov. Park	167	D2	51.517000 -99.550000
Nopiming Prov. Park	167	F3	50.662500 -95.305600
North Steeprock Lake Prov. Park	166	C1	52.611800 -101.380000
Paint Lake Prov. Park	161	E2	55.492100 -98.018000
Patricia Beach Prov. Park	167	E3	50.467300 -96.575300
Pembina Valley Prov. Park	167	E4	49.038500 -98.296400
Pinawa Dam Prov. Park	167	F3	50.145200 -95.945700
Rainbow Beach Prov. Park	167	D3	51.099400 -99.718400
Saint Ambroise Beach Prov. Park	167	E3	50.275500 -98.074300
Saint Malo Prov. Park	167	E4	49.321400 -96.930490
South Atikaki Prov. Park	167	F3	51.041400 -95.417600
Spruce Woods Prov. Park	167	D4	49.703100 -99.141900
Stephenfield Prov. Park	167	E4	49.523400 -98.300500
Turtle Mtn. Prov. Park	167	D4	49.041500 -100.216000
Watchorn Prov. Park	167	E2	51.293100 -98.598500
Whitefish Lake Prov. Park	166	C2	52.333900 -101.587100
Whiteshell Prov. Park	167	F3	50.140900 -95.584400
William Lake Prov. Park	167	D4	49.055000 -100.038800
Winnipeg Beach Prov. Park	167	E3	50.512300 -96.967000

NEW BRUNSWICK	PAGE	GRID	LATITUDE LONGITUDE
National Park & Rec. Areas			
Beaubears Island N.H.S.	179	D3	46.972778 -65.569444
Fort Beauséjour N.H.S.	180	C1	45.865278 -64.290278
Fort Gaspareaux N.H.S.	180	C1	46.040833 -64.072778
Fundy Natl. Park-Vis. Ctr.	180	C1	45.659500 -65.132600
Kouchibouguac Natl. Park-Vis. Ctr.	179	D3	46.773200 -65.004900
Monument Lefebvre N.H.S.	180	C1	45.979167 -64.567222
Roosevelt Campobello International Park	180	A2	44.849722 -66.949722
Saint Andrews Blockhouse N.H.S.	180	A2	45.076389 -67.063889
Saint Croix Island International Hist. Site	180	A2	45.127778 -67.133333
Provincial Park & Rec. Areas			
De la République Prov. Park	178	B3	47.442778 -68.395556
Herring Cove Prov. Park	180	A2	44.866667 -66.933056
Mactaquac Prov. Park	180	A1	45.959025 -66.892556
Mount Carleton Prov. Park	178	C3	47.392300 -66.835500
Murray Beach Prov. Park	180	C1	46.016667 -63.983056
New River Beach Prov. Park	180	A2	45.133056 -66.533056
Parlee Beach Prov. Park	180	C1	46.233056 -64.499722
Sugarloaf Prov. Park	178	C2	47.974000 -66.671900
The Anchorage Prov. Park	180	A3	44.649722 -66.800000

NEWFOUNDLAND & LABRADOR	PAGE	GRID	LATITUDE LONGITUDE
National Park & Rec. Areas			
Castle Hill N.H.S.	183	E4	47.251389 -53.971111
Gros Morne Natl. Park-Vis. Ctr.	182	C2	49.571500 -57.877900
Hawthorne Cottage N.H.S.	183	E4	47.543333 -53.210833
L'Anse aux Meadows N.H.S.	183	F1	51.595000 -55.532778
Port au Choix N.H.S.	182	C1	50.712222 -57.375278
Red Bay N.H.S.	183	F1	51.733056 -56.415556
Ryan Premises N.H.S.	183	E3	48.648056 -53.112500
Terra Nova Natl. Park-Information Center	183	E3	48.394900 -54.204000
Terra Nova Natl. Park-Saltons Vis. Ctr.	183	E3	48.580600 -53.958900
Provincial Park & Rec. Areas			
Barachois Pond Prov. Park	182	C3	48.477100 -58.256600
Blow Me Down Prov. Park	182	C2	49.090833 -58.364444
Butter Pot Prov. Park	183	F4	47.390900 -53.071300
Chance Cove Prov. Park	183	F4	46.776900 -53.045400
Codroy Valley Prov. Park	182	C4	47.833333 -59.337778
Deadman's Bay Prov. Park	183	E2	49.331389 -53.692500
Dildo Run Prov. Park	183	E2	49.535556 -54.721667
Dungeon Prov. Park	183	E3	48.666667 -53.083611
Frenchman's Cove Prov. Park	183	D4	47.209444 -55.401667
Gooseberry Cove Prov. Park	183	E4	47.068056 -54.087778
J.T. Cheeseman Prov. Park	182	C4	47.631111 -59.249444
La Manche Prov. Park	183	F4	47.175200 -52.901200
Lockston Path Prov. Park	183	E3	48.437778 -53.379722
Notre Dame Prov. Park	183	E2	49.115833 -55.086389
Pinware River Prov. Park	183	F1	51.631667 -56.704167
Sandbanks Prov. Park	182	C4	47.607222 -57.646944
Sir Richard Squires Mem. Prov. Park	183	D2	49.354000 -57.213400
The Arches Prov. Park	182	C2	50.113333 -57.663056

NORTHWEST TERRITORIES	PAGE	GRID	LATITUDE LONGITUDE
National Park & Rec. Areas			
Nááts'ihch'oh Natl. Park Res.	155	E2	62.617399 -128.787113
Nahanni Natl. Park Res.	155	E3	61.083333 -123.600000
Tuktut Nogait Natl. Park	155	E1	69.283333 -123.016667

NOVA SCOTIA	PAGE	GRID	LATITUDE LONGITUDE
National Park & Rec. Areas			
Alexander Graham Bell N.H.S.	181	F1	46.102778 -60.745556
Cape Breton Highlands Natl. Park-East Ent.	182	B4	46.642800 -60.404200
Cape Breton Highlands Natl. Park-West Ent.	182	B4	46.647300 -60.950200
Fort Anne N.H.S.	180	B3	44.741667 -65.519167
Fort Edward N.H.S.	180	C2	44.995556 -64.135278
Fortress of Louisbourg N.H.S.	181	F1	45.900300 -59.995100
Grand-Pré N.H.S.	180	C2	45.108889 -64.311944
Grassy Island N.H.S.	181	F2	45.336667 -60.973611
Kejimkujik Natl. Park (Seaside Adjunct)	180	C4	43.865800 -64.836900
Kejimkujik Natl. Park and N.H.S.	180	B3	44.336700 -65.268200
Marconi N.H.S.	181	F4	46.211111 -59.952778
Port-Royal N.H.S.	180	B3	44.712500 -65.610556
Saint Peters Canal N.H.S.	181	F1	45.655556 -60.870556
York Redoubt N.H.S.	181	D3	44.596583 -63.552439
Provincial Park & Rec. Areas			
Amherst Shore Prov. Park	180	C1	45.961181 -63.879025
Battery Prov. Park	181	F1	45.657022 -60.866764
Beaver Mtn. Prov. Park	181	E2	45.567556 -62.153683
Blomidon Prov. Park	180	C2	45.255869 -64.352056
Boylston Prov. Park	181	E2	45.426839 -61.510603
Cape Chignecto Prov. Park	180	C2	45.375800 -64.891300
Caribou–Munroes Island Prov. Park	181	D1	45.721800 -62.656914
Ellenwood Lake Prov. Park	180	B4	43.929481 -66.005700
Five Islands Prov. Park	180	C2	45.407781 -64.021500
Graves Island Prov. Park	180	C3	44.565550 -64.218642
Laurie Prov. Park	181	D2	44.878175 -63.602194
Martinique Beach Prov. Park	181	D3	44.689911 -63.147567
Mira River Prov. Park	181	F1	46.026006 -60.037433
Porters Prov. Park	181	D3	44.691106 -63.308892
Rissers Beach Prov. Park	180	C3	44.232397 -64.423919
Salsman Prov. Park	181	E2	45.236856 -61.767150
Salt Springs Prov. Park	181	D2	45.545280 -62.878890
Shubenacadie Prov. Wildlife Park	181	D2	45.087222 -63.387500
Smileys Prov. Park	180	C2	45.013925 -63.961247
The Islands Prov. Park	180	B4	43.765503 -65.340347
Thomas Raddall Prov. Park	180	C4	43.844783 -64.919694
Valleyview Prov. Park	180	B2	44.875200 -65.316064
Wentworth Prov. Park	181	D2	45.627222 -63.567222
Whycocomagh Prov. Park	181	F1	45.968094 -61.109908

ONTARIO	PAGE	GRID	LATITUDE LONGITUDE
National Park & Rec. Areas			
Battle of the Windmill N.H.S.	174	B4	44.722778 -75.486944
Bell Homestead N.H.P.	172	C3	43.107946 -80.273060
Bellevue House N.H.S.	173	F1	44.220556 -76.506667
Bruce Peninsula Natl. Park	170	C4	45.189100 -81.485500
Fathom Five Natl. Marine Park	170	C4	45.304800 -81.727600
Fort George N.H.S.	173	D3	43.252778 -79.051111
Fort Henry N.H.S.	173	F1	44.230833 -76.459444
Fort Malden N.H.S.	172	A4	42.108056 -83.113889
Fort Mississauga N.H.S.	173	D3	43.260833 -79.076667
Fort Saint Joseph N.H.S.	170	B3	46.063889 -83.944167
Fort Wellington N.H.S.	174	B4	44.713889 -75.510833
Georgian Bay Islands Natl. Park-Welcome Center	171	D4	44.803900 -79.720400
Glengarry Cairn N.H.S.	174	C3	45.121667 -74.490278
Merrickville Blockhouse N.H.S.	174	B4	44.916667 -75.837500
Peterborough Lift Lock N.H.S.	173	E1	44.308056 -78.300556
Point Clark Lighthouse N.H.S.	172	B2	44.073056 -81.756667
Point Pelee Natl. Park-Park Ent. Kiosk	172	A4	41.987700 -82.549900
Point Pelee Natl. Park-Vis. Ctr.	172	A4	41.931700 -82.513500
Pukaskwa Natl. Park-Information Center	170	A2	48.700400 -86.197200
Queenston Heights N.H.S.	173	D3	43.158056 -79.052778
Sault Ste. Marie Canal N.H.S.	170	B3	46.511667 -84.355556
Sir John Johnson House N.H.S.	174	C4	45.144444 -74.580000
Southwold Earthworks N.H.S.	172	B3	42.677778 -81.351389
Thousand Islands Natl. Park-Vis. Ctr.	174	A4	44.452300 -75.860300
Trent-Severn Waterway N.H.S.	173	E1	44.137500 -77.559100
Woodside N.H.S.	172	C2	43.466667 -80.499722
Provincial Park & Rec. Areas			
Abitibi-De-Troyes Prov. Park	171	D1	48.786500 -80.066300
Albany River Prov. Park	169	E1	51.358200 -88.134000
Algonquin Prov. Park	171	E4	45.605300 -78.323900
Arrowhead Prov. Park	171	D4	45.391700 -79.197200
Awenda Prov. Park	172	C1	44.854400 -79.989800
Balsam Lake Prov. Park	173	D1	44.642000 -78.864000
Bass Lake Prov. Park	173	D1	44.602000 -79.475000
Batchawana Prov. Park	170	B3	46.941900 -84.587010
Blue Lake Prov. Park	168	B3	49.904200 -93.525600
Bon Echo Prov. Park	171	E4	44.905600 -77.246600
Bonnechere Prov. Park	171	E4	45.658400 -77.570800
Bonnechere River Prov. Park	171	E4	45.674400 -77.661500
Brightsand River Prov. Park	169	D3	49.936700 -90.265400
Bronte Creek Prov. Park	173	D2	43.410490 -79.767830
Caliper Lake Prov. Park	168	B3	49.061670 -93.912780
Carson Lake Prov. Park	171	E4	45.502780 -77.746390
Chapleau-Nemegosenda River Prov. Park	170	B2	48.262300 -83.035300
Charleston Lake Prov. Park	174	A4	44.515400 -76.013600
Chutes Prov. Park	170	C3	46.219510 -82.071480
Craigleith Prov. Park	172	C1	44.535000 -80.367000
Darlington Prov. Park	173	D2	43.875480 -78.778300
Devil's Glen Prov. Park	172	C1	44.361000 -80.207800
Driftwood Prov. Park	171	E3	46.179000 -77.843000
Earl Rowe Prov. Park	172	C1	44.150000 -79.898000
Emily Prov. Park	173	D1	44.340530 -78.532860
Esker Lakes Prov. Park	171	D2	48.290100 -79.906100
Fairbank Prov. Park	170	C3	46.468070 -81.440410
Ferris Prov. Park	173	E1	44.293000 -77.788000
Finlayson Point Prov. Park	171	D3	47.055000 -79.797000
Fitzroy Prov. Park	174	A3	45.482680 -76.209400
French River Prov. Park	171	D3	46.000600 -80.620900
Frontenac Prov. Park	174	A4	44.540500 -76.512700
Fushimi Lake Prov. Park	169	F3	49.824800 -83.913800
Greenwater Prov. Park	170	C1	49.215900 -81.291000
Grundy Lake Prov. Park	171	D4	45.939800 -80.530400
Halfway Lake Prov. Park	170	C3	46.905700 -81.650500
Inverhuron Prov. Park	172	B1	44.298000 -81.580000
Ivanhoe Lake Prov. Park	170	C2	47.957600 -82.742600
John E. Pearce Prov. Park	172	B4	42.617000 -81.444000
Kakabeka Falls Prov. Park	169	D4	48.403290 -89.624130
Kap-Kig-Iwan Prov. Park	171	D2	47.789960 -79.884990
Kettle Lakes Prov. Park	170	C1	48.569400 -80.865400
Killarney Prov. Park	170	C3	46.099400 -81.386900
Killbear Prov. Park	171	D4	45.346200 -80.191200
Kopka River Prov. Park	169	D2	50.006300 -89.493000
Lady Evelyn-Smoothwater Prov. Park	171	D2	47.368500 -80.489300
Lake of the Woods Prov. Park	168	B3	49.221200 -94.606000
Lake on the Mtn. Prov. Park	173	F1	44.039940 -77.056080
Lake Saint Peter Prov. Park	171	E4	45.322000 -78.024000
Lake Superior Prov. Park	170	A2	47.595200 -84.756500
Larder River Prov. Park	171	D2	47.936300 -79.642800
La Verendrye Prov. Park	169	D4	48.138300 -90.431300
Little Abitibi Prov. Park	170	C1	49.637900 -80.922900
Little Current River Prov. Park	169	E2	50.724100 -86.211000
Long Point Prov. Park	172	C4	42.565000 -80.306000
Lower Madawaska River Prov. Park	171	E4	45.236200 -77.289300
MacGregor Point Prov. Park	172	B1	44.403700 -81.465600
Macleod Prov. Park	169	E3	49.676190 -86.931000
Makobe-Grays River Prov. Park	171	D2	47.617200 -80.376300
Mara Prov. Park	173	D1	44.589000 -79.349000
Mark S. Burnham Prov. Park	173	E1	44.299900 -78.257000
Marten River Prov. Park	171	D3	46.729000 -79.807000
Mattawa River Prov. Park	171	D3	46.315000 -79.108400
McRae Point Prov. Park	173	D1	44.569000 -79.320000
Mikisew Prov. Park	171	D4	45.820000 -79.512000
Missinaibi River Prov. Park	170	B1	49.101400 -83.234700
Mississagi Prov. Park	170	C3	46.596500 -82.682500
Mississagi River Prov. Park	170	C3	47.012600 -82.632700
Murphys Point Prov. Park	174	A4	44.774300 -76.240700
Nagagamisis Prov. Park	169	F3	49.475700 -84.771000
Neys Prov. Park	169	E4	48.750500 -86.591900
North Beach Prov. Park	173	E2	43.951050 -77.522660
Oastler Lake Prov. Park	171	D4	45.309000 -79.964800
Obabika River Prov. Park	171	D3	47.221200 -80.262600
Obatanga Prov. Park	170	A2	48.323000 -85.093700
Ojibway Prov. Park	168	C3	49.990900 -92.144400
Opeongo River Prov. Park	171	E4	45.576256 -77.887363
Otoskwin-Attawapiskat River Prov. Park	169	D1	52.235700 -87.491300
Ottawa River Prov. Park	174	A3	45.741700 -76.779800
Ouimet Canyon Prov. Park	169	D4	48.773350 -88.667400
Oxtongue River-Ragged Falls Prov. Park	171	D4	45.366900 -78.914100
Pakwash Prov. Park	168	B2	50.749800 -93.551400
Pancake Bay Prov. Park	170	B3	46.967200 -84.661100
Petroglyphs Prov. Park	173	E1	44.618300 -78.041700
Pigeon River Prov. Park	169	D4	48.025041 -89.572294
Pinery Prov. Park	172	B3	43.257200 -81.834000
Pipestone River Prov. Park	169	D1	52.244300 -90.313500
Point Farms Prov. Park	172	B2	43.804000 -81.700000
Port Bruce Prov. Park	172	B3	42.664000 -81.027000
Port Burwell Prov. Park	172	C3	42.646000 -80.816000
Potholes Prov. Park	170	B2	47.958700 -84.294020
Presqu'Ile Prov. Park	173	E2	44.007000 -77.735000
Quetico Prov. Park	168	C4	48.404500 -91.498700
Rainbow Falls Prov. Park	169	E4	48.830090 -87.389580
Renè Brunelle Prov. Park	170	C1	49.453700 -82.147900
Restoule Prov. Park	171	D3	46.080400 -79.839800
Rideau River Prov. Park	174	B4	45.060000 -75.672000
Rock Point Prov. Park	173	D3	42.854000 -79.552000
Rondeau Prov. Park	172	B4	42.278200 -81.865100
Rushing River Prov. Park	168	B3	49.681850 -94.234890
Samuel de Champlain Prov. Park	171	D3	46.301900 -78.864100
Sandbanks Prov. Park	173	F2	43.910200 -77.267200
Sandbar Lake Prov. Park	168	C3	49.491000 -91.555700
Sauble Falls Prov. Park	172	B1	44.673170 -81.257350
Selkirk Prov. Park	172	C3	42.824000 -79.961000
Sharbot Lake Prov. Park	174	A4	44.775500 -76.724600
Sibbald Point Prov. Park	173	D1	44.322160 -79.325570
Silent Lake Prov. Park	171	E4	44.907500 -78.047200
Silver Lake Prov. Park	174	A4	44.829770 -76.574680
Sioux Narrows Prov. Park	168	B3	49.429570 -94.037260
Six Mile Lake Prov. Park	171	D4	44.819500 -79.733500
Sleeping Giant Prov. Park	169	D4	48.419300 -88.795500
Solace Prov. Park	170	C3	47.189200 -80.683500
Springwater Prov. Park	173	D1	44.443500 -79.748500
Steel River Prov. Park	169	E3	49.161900 -86.812600
Sturgeon Bay Prov. Park	171	D4	45.623400 -80.414100
Sturgeon River Prov. Park	170	C3	46.949800 -80.523900
The Massasauga Prov. Park	171	D4	45.203400 80.044300
The Shoals Prov. Park	170	B2	47.884800 -83.808000
Turkey Point Prov. Park	172	C3	42.694000 -80.333150
Turtle River-White Otter Lake Prov. Park	168	C3	49.129700 -92.042300
Upper Madawaska River Prov. Park	171	F4	45.513700 -78.078700
Wabakimi Prov. Park	169	D2	50.719100 -89.448500
Wakami Lake Prov. Park	170	C2	47.489700 -82.842000
Wasaga Beach Prov. Park	172	C1	44.494000 -80.027100
Wheatley Prov. Park	172	A4	42.098000 -82.448800
White Lake Prov. Park	170	A1	48.603500 -85.880900
Windy Lake Prov. Park	170	C3	46.619820 -81.455980
Woodland Caribou Prov. Park	168	B2	51.096900 -94.744900

PRINCE EDWARD ISLAND	PAGE	GRID	LATITUDE LONGITUDE
National Park & Rec. Areas			
Port-la-Joye–Fort Amherst N.H.S.	179	E4	46.195278 -63.133611
Prince Edward Island Natl. Park-Brackley Vis. Ctr.	179	E4	46.406200 -63.196600
Prince Edward Island Natl. Park-Cavendish Vis. Ctr.	179	E4	46.492300 -63.379700
Provincial Park & Rec. Areas			
Brudenell River Prov. Park	179	F4	46.209583 -62.588556
Buffaloland Prov. Park	179	F4	46.092500 -62.617778
Cabot Beach Prov. Park	179	E4	46.557250 -63.704250
Cedar Dunes Prov. Park	177	F4	46.622222 -64.381944
Chelton Beach Prov. Park	179	E4	46.303944 -63.747167
Green Park Prov. Park	177	F4	46.590972 -63.890333
Jacques Cartier Prov. Park	177	F4	46.851222 -64.013000
Kings Castle Prov. Park	179	F4	46.019167 -62.567389
Linkletter Prov. Park	179	E4	46.402694 -63.850361
Lord Selkirk Prov. Park	179	F4	46.091889 -62.906000
Mill River Prov. Park	177	F4	46.749722 -64.166667
Northumberland Prov. Park	179	F4	45.966667 -62.716667
Panmure Island Prov. Park	179	F4	46.133056 -62.466667
Red Point Prov. Park	179	F4	46.366667 -62.133056
Wood Islands Prov. Park	181	D1	45.949722 -62.749722

QUÉBEC	PAGE	GRID	LATITUDE LONGITUDE
National Park & Rec. Areas			
Lieu Historique Natl. du Fort-Lennox	175	D4	45.120556 -73.268056
Lieu Historique Natl. du Fort-Témiscamingue	171	D2	47.295000 -79.456667
Parc Natl. de Forillon	179	D1	48.854300 -64.396300
Parc Natl. de la Mauricie-East Ent.	175	D1	46.752600 -72.792600
Parc Natl. de la Mauricie-South Ent.	175	D1	46.650000 -72.969200
Parc Natl. d'Opémican	171	D3	46.884041 -79.096604
Réserve de Parc Natl. de l'Archipel-de-Mingan	177	F1	50.237100 -63.606900
Provincial Park & Rec. Areas			
Parc d'Aiguebelle	171	D1	48.510300 -78.745800
Parc d'Anticosti	182	A2	49.463200 -62.819000
Parc de Frontenac	175	E3	45.848600 -71.184600
Parc de la Gaspésie	178	C1	48.941500 -66.214400
Parc de la Gatineau	174	A3	45.566667 -75.949722
Parc de la Jacques-Cartier	175	E1	47.317300 -71.347000
Parc de la Pointe-Taillon	176	C3	48.717300 -71.993600
Parc de la Yamaska	175	D3	45.429400 -72.601800
Parc de l'Île-Bonaventure-et-du-Rocher-Percé	179	E1	48.496389 -64.161944
Parc de Miguasha	178	C2	48.110556 -66.369444
Parc de Plaisance	174	B3	45.597900 -75.123600
Parc de Récréation du Mont-Orford	175	D3	45.344700 -72.212900
Parc des Grands-Jardins	176	C4	47.681300 -70.836900
Parc des Hautes-Gorges-de-la-Rivière-Malbaie	176	C3	47.918700 -70.498700
Parc des Monts-Valin	176	C3	48.598600 -70.825300
Parc du Bic	178	A1	48.355300 -68.797600
Parc du Mont-Mégantic	175	E3	45.450700 -71.167300
Parc du Mont-Saint-Bruno	175	D3	45.555278 -73.309722
Parc du Mont-Tremblant	174	C2	46.443000 -74.344600
Parc du Saguenay	176	C3	48.289900 -70.243400
Parc Marin du Saguenay-Saint-Laurent	178	A2	48.133056 -69.733056
Parc Régional du Massif du Sud	175	F2	46.581389 -70.467778

SASKATCHEWAN	PAGE	GRID	LATITUDE LONGITUDE
National Park & Rec. Areas			
Batoche N.H.S.	165	F1	52.752800 -106.116700
Battle of Fish Creek N.H.S.	165	F1	52.550000 -106.180300
Fort Battleford N.H.S.	165	E1	52.713800 -108.259600
Fort Espèrance N.H.S.	166	C3	50.451400 -101.712800
Fort Livingstone N.H.S.	166	C2	51.903880 -101.960620
Fort Pelly N.H.S.	166	C2	51.795900 -101.951800
Fort Walsh N.H.S.	165	E4	49.559100 -109.901700
Grasslands Natl. Park-East Block Vis. Ctr.	166	A4	49.370800 -106.384800
Grasslands Natl. Park-West Block Vis. Reception Ctr.	166	A4	49.203800 -107.732700
Prince Albert Natl. Park-Waskesiu Vis. Ctr.	160	B3	53.922500 -106.081800
Provincial Park & Rec. Areas			
Blackstrap Prov. Park	166	A2	51.755600 -106.458300
Buffalo Pound Prov. Park	166	B3	50.576200 -105.361000
Candle Lake Prov. Park	160	B4	53.845000 -105.252000
Cannington Manor Prov. Hist. Park	166	C4	49.712900 -102.027300
Clearwater River Prov. Park	159	E1	56.929300 -109.043000
Crooked Lake Prov. Park	166	C3	50.592200 -102.741400
Cumberland House Prov. Hist. Park	160	C4	53.948000 -102.421400
Cypress Hills Interprovincial Park	165	E4	49.632400 -109.809000
Danielson Prov. Park	166	A2	51.252200 -106.866000
Douglas Prov. Park	166	A3	51.025300 -106.480000
Echo Valley Prov. Park	166	B3	50.808500 -103.891900
Fort Carlton Prov. Park	166	A1	52.867100 -106.542700
Fort Pitt Prov. Park	165	E1	53.577000 -109.806300
Good Spirit Lake Prov. Park	166	C2	51.543500 -102.707000
Greenwater Lake Prov. Park	166	C1	52.532000 -103.448000
Katepwa Point Prov. Park	166	B3	50.693165 -103.62602[illegible]
Lac La Ronge Prov. Park	160	C3	55.249200 -104.769000
Last Mtn. House Prov. Park	166	B3	50.722800 -104.823300
Makwa Lake Prov. Park	159	E3	54.016800 -109.234000
Meadow Lake Prov. Park	159	E3	54.501400 -109.07600[illegible]
Moose Mtn. Prov. Park	166	C4	49.821300 -102.424000
Narrow Hills Prov. Park	160	C3	54.091300 -104.64300[illegible]
Pike Lake Prov. Park	166	A2	51.893200 -106.81900[illegible]
Rowan's Ravine Prov. Park	166	B3	50.995600 -105.179700
Saint Victor Prov. Park	166	A4	49.395300 -105.87320[illegible]
Saskatchewan Landing Prov. Park	165	F3	50.664600 -107.99700[illegible]
Steele Narrows Prov. Park	159	E3	54.025900 -109.318400
The Battlefords Prov. Park	165	E1	53.132500 -108.38130[illegible]
Touchwood Hills Prov. Park	166	B2	51.306400 -104.01410[illegible]
Wildcat Hill Prov. Park	166	C1	53.273946 -102.49282[illegible]
Wood Mtn. Post Prov. Hist. Park	166	A4	49.320833 -106.37916[illegible]

YUKON	PAGE	GRID	LATITUDE LONGITUDE
National Park & Rec. Areas			
Dawson Hist. Complex N.H.S.	155	D2	64.050000 -139.43333[illegible]
Ivvavik Natl. Park	155	D1	69.519722 -139.52500[illegible]
Kluane Natl. Park and Res.-North Vis. Ctr.	155	D3	60.991800 -138.52080[illegible]
Kluane Natl. Park and Res.-South Vis. Ctr.	155	D3	60.752900 -137.51010[illegible]
Vuntut Natl. Park	155	D1	68.306944 -140.04750[illegible]
Provincial Park & Rec. Areas			
Herschel Island-Qikiqtaruk Territorial Park	155	D1	69.592100 -139.09240[illegible]

Continued from page 11

SOUTHEAST

Blue Ridge Parkway★★
574 miles/924 kilometers
Maps 102, 112, 111, 90, 121

From **Front Royal**, take US-340 S to begin **Skyline Drive★★**, the best-known feature of **Shenandoah NP★★**. The drive follows former Indian trails along the **Blue Ridge Parkway★★**. **Marys Rock Tunnel to Rockfish Entrance Station★★** passes the oldest rock in the park and **Big Meadows★**. The Drive ends at **Rockfish Gap** at I-64, but continue S on the Parkway. From Terrapin Hill Overlook, detour 16mi W on Rte. 130 to see **Natural Bridge★★**. Enter NC at **Cumberland Knob**, then pass **Blowing Rock★**, **Grandfather Mountain★★** and **Linville Falls★★**. Detour 4.8mi to **Mount Mitchell SP★** to drive to the top of the tallest mountain (6,684ft) E of the Mississippi. At mile 382, the **Folk Art Center** stocks high-quality regional crafts. Popular **Biltmore Estate★★** in **Asheville★** (North Exit of US-25, then 4mi N) includes formal **gardens★★**. The rugged stretch from **French Broad River to Cherokee** courses 17 tunnels within two national forests. **Looking Glass Rock★★** is breathtaking. The Parkway ends at **Cherokee**, gateway to **Great Smoky Mountains NP★★★** and home of Cherokee tribe members.

Skyline Drive, Shenandoah NP, Blue Ridge Parkway
© zrfphoto/Getty Images Plus

Central Kentucky★★
379 miles/610 kilometers
Maps 230, 100, 214, 227, 110

From **Louisville★★**, home of the **Kentucky Derby★★★**, take I-64 E to **Frankfort**, the state capital. Continue E to **Lexington★★**, heart of **Bluegrass Country★★** with its rolling meadows and white-fenced horse farms. Stop at the **Kentucky Horse Park★★★** (4089 Iron Works Pkwy.) for the daily **Parade of Breeds**. Then head S on I-75 through Richmond to the craft center/college town of **Berea**. Return to Lexington and follow the Blue Grass Parkway SW to Exit 25. There, US-150 W leads to Bardstown, site of **My Old Kentucky Home SP★**, immortalized by Stephen Foster in what is now the state song. Drive S from Bardstown on US-31E past **Abraham Lincoln Birthplace NHS★**. Turn right onto Rte. 70 to Cave City, then take US-31W to Park City, gateway to **Mammoth Cave NP★★★**, which features the world's longest cave system. Return to Louisville via I-65 to end the tour.

Florida's Northeast Coast★★
174 miles/280 kilometers
Maps 222, 139, 141, 232

From **Jacksonville★**, drive E on Rte. 10 to **Atlantic Beach**, the most affluent of Jacksonville's beach towns. Head S on Rte. A1A through residential **Neptune Beach**, **Jacksonville Beach** and upscale **Ponte Vedra Beach** to reach **St. Augustine★★★**, the oldest city in the US and former capital of Spanish Florida. Farther S, car-racing mecca **Daytona Beach** is known for its **international speedway**. Take US-92 across the Intracoastal Waterway to US-1, heading S to **Titusville**. Take Rte. 402 across the Indian River to **Merritt Island NWR★★** to begin **Black Point Wildlife Drive★**. Return to **Titusville** and follow Rte. 405 to **Kennedy Space Center★★★**, one of Florida's top attractions, to end the tour.

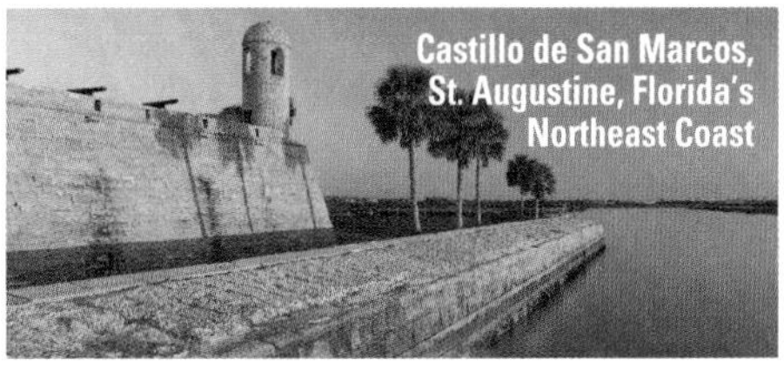
Castillo de San Marcos, St. Augustine, Florida's Northeast Coast
© S. Greg Panosian/Getty Images Plus

Florida Keys★★
168 miles/270 kilometers
Maps 143, 142

*Note: Green **mile-marker** (MM) posts, sometimes difficult to see, line US-1 (Overseas Hwy.), showing distances from Key West (MM 0). Much of the route is two-lane, and traffic can be heavy from December to April and on weekends. Allow 3hrs for the drive. Crossing 43 bridges and causeways (only one over land), the highway offers fine views of the Atlantic Ocean (E) and Florida Bay (W).*

Drive S from **Miami★★★** on US-1. Near **Key Largo★**, **John Pennekamp Coral Reef SP★★** habors tropical fish, coral and fine snorkeling waters. To the SW, **Islamorada** is known for **charter fishing**. At **Marathon** (MM 50), **Sombrero Beach** is a good swimming spot, but **Bahia Honda SP★★** (MM 36.8) is considered the best **beach★★** in the Keys. Pass **National Key Deer Refuge★** (MM 30.5), haven to the 2ft-tall deer unique to the lower Keys. End at **Key West★★★**, joining others at **Mallory Square Dock** to view the **sunset★★**.

Bahia Honda SP, Florida Keys
© fotoVoyager/Getty Images Plus

The Ozarks★
343 miles/552 kilometers
Maps 227, 117, 219, 107, 106

From the state capital of **Little Rock**, take I-30 SW to Exit 111, then US-70 W to Hot Springs. Drive N on Rte. 7/Central Ave. to **Hot Springs NP★★** to enjoy the therapeutic waters. Travel N on Rte. 7 across the Arkansas River to Russellville.

Continue on **Scenic Highway 7★** N through **Ozark National Forest** and across the **Buffalo National River** to Harrison. Take US-62/65 NW to Bear Creek Springs, continuing W on US-62 through **Eureka Springs★**, with its historic district, to **Pea Ridge NMP★**, a Civil War site. Return E on US-62 to the junction of Rte. 21 at Berryville. Travel N on Rte. 21 to Blue Eye, taking Rte. 86 E to US-65, which leads N to the entertainment hub of **Branson**, Missouri, to end the tour.

River Road Plantations★★
200 miles/323 kilometers
Maps 239, 134, 194

From **New Orleans★★★**, take US-90 W to Rte. 48 along the Mississippi River to Destrehan. **Destrehan★★** is considered the oldest plantation house in the Mississippi Valley. Continue NW on Rte. 48 to US-61 to Laplace to connect to Rte. 44. Head N past **San Francisco Plantation★**, built in 1856. At Burnside, take Rte. 75 N to St. Gabriel. En route, watch for **Houmas House★** (40136 Hwy. 942). Take Rte. 30 to **Baton Rouge★**, the state capital. Then drive S along the **West Bank★★** on Rte. 1 to White Castle, site of **Nottoway★**, the largest plantation home in the South. Continue to Donaldsonville, then turn onto Rte. 18. Travel E to Gretna, passing **Oak Alley★★** (no. 3645) and **Laura Plantation★★** (no. 2247) along the way. From Gretna, take US-90 to New Orleans, where the tour ends.

CANADA

Gaspésie, Québec★★★
933 kilometers/578 miles (loop)
Map 178, 179

Leave **Sainte-Flavie** via Rte. 132 NE, stopping to visit **Reford Gardens★★★** en route to **Matane**. After Cap-Chat, take Rte. 299 S to **Gaspésie Park★** for expansive **views★★**.

Percé Rock, Québec
© Elenathewise/Getty Images Plus

Back on Rte. 132, follow the **Scenic Route from La Martre to Rivière-au-Renard★★**. Continue to **Cap-des-Rosiers**, entrance to majestic **Forillon NP★★**. Follow Rte. 132 along the coast through **Gaspé★**, the administrative center of the peninsula, to **Percé★★★**, a coastal village known for **Percé Rock★★**, a mammoth offshore rock wall. Drive SW on Rt. 132 through **Paspébiac** to **Carleton**, which offers a **panorama★★** from the summit of **Mont Saint-Joseph**. Farther SW, detour 6km/4mi S to see an array of fossils at **Parc de Miguasha★**. Back on Rte. 132, travel W to **Matapédia**, then follow Rte. 132 N, passing **Causapscal**—a departure point for salmon fishing expeditions—to end the tour at Sainte-Flavie.

North Shore Lake Superior★★

275 kilometers/171 miles Map 169

From the port city of **Thunder Bay★★**—and nearby **Old Fort William★★**—drive the Trans-Canada Hwy. (Rte. 11/17) E to Rte. 587. Detour to **Sleeping Giant PP★**, which offers fine **views★** of the lake. Back along the Trans-Canada Hwy., **Amethyst Mine** (take E. Loon Rd.) is a rock hound's delight (fee). Farther NE, located 12km/8mi off the highway, **Ouimet Canyon★★** is a startling environment for the area. Just after the highway's Red Rock turnoff, watch for **Red Rock Cuesta**, a natural formation 210m/690ft high. Cross the Nipigon River and continue along **Nipigon Bay★★**, enjoying **views★★** of the rocky, conifer-covered islands. The **view★★** of **Kama Bay** through **Kama Rock Cut** is striking. Continue to **Schreiber** to end the tour.

Nova Scotia's Cabot Trail★★

338 kilometers/210 miles Map 181

From **Baddeck★**, follow Hwy. 105 S to the junction with **Cabot Trail** to **North East Margaree★** in salmon-fishing country. Take this road NW to Margaree Harbour, then N to **Chéticamp**, an enclave of Acadian culture. Heading inland, the route enters **Cape Breton Highlands NP★★**, combining seashore and mountains. At Cape North, detour N around Aspy Bay to **Bay St. Lawrence★★**. Then head W to tiny **Capstick** for shoreline **views★**. Return S to Cape North, then drive E to South Harbour. Take the coast road, traveling S through the fishing villages of **New Haven** and **Neils Harbour★**. Rejoin Cabot Trail S, passing the resort area of the **Ingonishs**. Take the right fork after Indian Brook to reach St. Ann's, home of **Gaelic College★**, specializing in bagpipe and Highland dance classes. Rejoin Hwy. 105 to return to Baddeck.

Cabot Trail, Cape Breton Highlands NP
©Birdimages/Getty Images Plus

Canadian Rockies★★★

467 kilometers/290 miles Map 164

Note: Some roads in Yoho NP are closed to cars mid-Oct to June due to snow, but are open for skiing.

Leave Banff★★ by Hwy. 1, traveling W. After 5.5km/3.5mi, take **Bow Valley Parkway★** (Hwy. 1A) NW within **Banff NP★★★**. At Lake Louise Village, detour W to find **Lake Louise★★★**. Back on Hwy. 1, head N to the junction of Hwy. 93, turn W and follow Hwy. 1 past Kicking Horse Pass into **Yoho NP★★**. Continue through Field, and turn right onto the road N to **Emerald Lake★★★**. Return to the junction of Rte. 93 and Hwy. 1, heading N on Rte. 93 along the Icefields **Parkway★★★**. Pass **Crowfoot Glacier★★** and **Bow Lake★★** on the left. **Peyto Lake★★★** is reached by spur road. After **Parker Ridge★★**, massive **Athabasca Glacier★★★** looms on the left. Continue to **Jasper★** and **Jasper NP★★★**. From Jasper, turn left onto Hwy. 16 and head into **Mount Robson PP★★**, home to **Mount Robson★★★** (3,954m/12,972ft.). End the tour at Tête Jaune Cache.

Moraine Lake, Banff NP, Canadian Rockies
© YinYang/Getty Images Plus

Vancouver Island★★★

337 kilometers/209 miles

Maps 282, 163, 162

To enjoy a scenic drive that begins 11mi N of **Victoria★★★**, take Douglas St. N from Victoria to the Trans-Canada Highway (Hwy. 1) and follow **Malahat Drive★** (between Goldstream PP and Mill Bay Rd.) for 12mi. Continue N on Hwy. 1 past Duncan, **Chemainus★** —known for its murals—and Nanaimo to

Tofino harbor, Vancouver Island
© rgbspace/Getty Images Plus

Parksville. Take winding Rte. 4 W (Pacific Rim Hwy.) passing **Englishman River Falls PP★** and **Cameron Lake**. Just beyond the lake, **Cathedral Grove★★** holds 800-year-old Douglas firs. The road descends to **Port Alberni**, departure point for cruises on Barkley Sound, and follows Sproat Lake before climbing Klitsa Mountain. The route leads to the Pacific along the Kennedy River. At the coast, turn left and drive SE to Ucluelet. Then head N to enter **Pacific Rim NPR★★★**. Continue to road's end at **Tofino★** to end the tour.

Yukon Circuit★★

1,485 kilometers/921 miles Map 155

Note: Top of the World Highway is closed mid-Oct to mid-May due to snow.

From **Whitehorse★**, capital of Yukon Territory, drive N on the **Klondike Hwy.** (Rte. 2), crossing the Yukon River at **Carmacks**. After 196km/122mi, small islands divide the river into fast-flowing channels at **Five Finger Rapids★**. From Stewart Crossing, continue NW on Rte. 2 to **Dawson★★**, a historic frontier town. Ferry across the river and drive the **Top of the World Hwy.★★** (Rte. 9), with its **views★★★**, to the Alaska border. Rte. 9 joins Rte. 5, passing tiny **Chicken**, Alaska. At Tetlin Junction, head SE on Rte. 2, paralleling **Tetlin NWR**. Enter Canada and follow the **Alaska Highway★★** (Rte. 1) SE along **Kluane Lake★★** to **Haines Junction**, gateway to **Kluane NPR★★**, home of **Mount Logan**, Canada's highest peak (5,959m/19,550ft). Continue E to Rte. 2 to return to Whitehorse.

Kluane NPR, Yukon Circuit

MICHELIN

viamichelin.com

Notes

Notes

Édition 22.1 - 2024 – Éditeur : MICHELIN Éditions
Société par actions simplifiée au capital de 487 500 EUR
57 rue Gaston Tessier – 75019 Paris (France)
R.C.S. Paris 882 639 354 - DL : AVRIL 2024

Printed by Transcontinental - Beauceville (Quebec) G5X 3P3 - April 2024 - Printed in Canada

MICHELIN